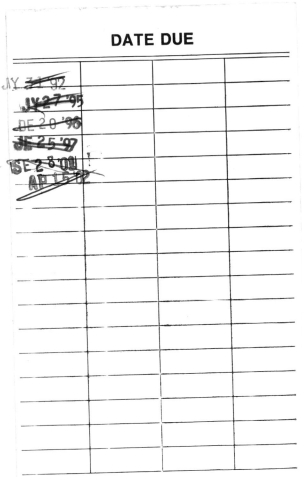

DATE DUE

JY 31 92			
JY 27 95			
DE 20 96			
JE 25 97			
SE 2 8 00			
AP 15 02			

DEMCO 38-296

INDIA

Fodor's 26th TWENTY-SIXTH EDITION

INDIA

FODOR'S TRAVEL PUBLICATIONS, INC.
New York & London

Fodor's India

Editor: Andrew E. Beresky
Area Editor: Kathleen Cox
Contributing Editors: Trevor Fishlock, Karl Samson, Lisa Samson, Amit Shah
Drawings: Lorraine Calaora
Maps: C. W. Bacon
Cover Photograph: Kugler/FPG International

Cover Design: Vignelli Associates

Special Sales

Fodor's Travel Publications are available at special discounts for bulk purchases (100 copies or more) for sales promotions or premiums. Special editions, including personalized covers, excerpts of existing guides, and corporate imprints, can be created in large quantities for special needs. For more information, write to Special Marketing, Fodor's Travel Publications, 201 East 50th Street, New York, NY 10022. Inquiries from the United Kingdom should be sent to Fodor's Travel Publications, 20 Vauxhall Bridge Rd., London, England SW1V 2SA.

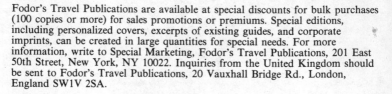
iv

CONTENTS

CONTENTS

SOUTHERN REGION

EASTERN REGION

NEPAL

SUPPLEMENTS

FOREWORD

The subcontinent of India offers the tourist a million miles of scenic natural wonders: some of the world's highest mountains; awesome rivers and valleys; deserts, jungles, and wildlife. Everything seems to be on an epic scale. Five thousand years of continuous civilization have left a legacy of aesthetic grandeur in architecture, literature, music, and art. India's strongest attraction for the visitor is in its interplay of contrasts. Nowhere do the past and present coexist in more colorful abandonment.

This edition includes Nepal, fabled for its mountain adventures, as well as its spectacular Kathmandu Valley.

We wish to express our gratitude to the various offices of the Government of India Tourist Office in India for their invaluable assistance in the preparation of this guidebook, especially to B. K. Goswami, Director General of Tourism and Additional Secretary. Our thanks also to Gour Kanjilal, Director of Hospitality; Kanta Thakur, Regional Director–North; and O. Terang, Regional Director–East and Northeast; and to the following officials for their assistance on the state and city level: Karma Gyatso Khangsarpa and Aungi and Choki Namgyal, Sikkim; A. Didar Singh, Meghalaya; Anil Baruah and Leena Barua, Assam; Dev Mehta and Minal Talim, Maharastra; Ajay Mittal and B. K. Chaunhan, Himachal Pradesh; M. P. Rajan, Madhya Pradesh; Shantanu Consul, Karnataka; J. Sanyal and Purbani Mitra, West Bengal; M. P. Shukla, Bihar; V.A.P. Mahajan, Goa; Jaya Kumar, Kerala; and S. M. Gani, Orissa.

We would also like to thank the Government of India Tourist Office officials in New York and Air India and Indian Airlines officials in New York and throughout India.

While every care has been taken to ensure the accuracy of the information contained in this guide, the passage of time will always bring change and, consequently, the publisher cannot accept responsibility for errors that may occur.

All prices and opening times quoted here are based on information supplied to us at press time. Hours and admission fees may change, however, and the prudent traveler will avoid inconvenience by calling ahead when possible.

Fodor's wants to hear about your travel experiences, both pleasant and unpleasant. When a hotel or restaurant fails to live up to its billing, let us know and we will investigate the complaint and revise our entries where the facts warrant it. Send your letters to the editors of Fodor's Travel Publications, 201 E. 50th Street, New York, NY 10022.

INTRODUCTION

by
TREVOR FISHLOCK

Journalist, author, and broadcaster, Trevor Fishlock in 1987 won the International Reporter of the Year prize in the British Press Awards. Five years earlier, while a staff correspondent in Delhi for The Times of London, *he won the David Holden Award for outstanding foreign reporting from India. He is now chief roving correspondent for* The Daily Telegraph, London. *He visits India frequently and has had stints in Australia and the Soviet Union. His most recent books are* India File *and* The State of America.

India will change you. It is not possible to be unmoved by it. For old hands already in its thrall and for new explorers about to set off, there is nothing quite so stimulating or sharpening as the prospect of India's immense drama. All journeys to this vast and varied land are adventures. The very name of it stirs the imagination and holds out the promise of astonishments, great spectacles, and sudden challenges to preconceptions. It is neither bland nor always comfortable. It is not for everybody. Many of its sights, flavors, and evident contradictions are strong and sometimes provocative. There are subtleties and baffling complexities and opaquenesses not easily penetrated. But India pays large and enduring dividends to travelers who come with open minds, particularly those who take things in their stride and keep in their minds Rudyard Kipling's admonition, "A fool lies here who tried to hustle the East."

Nearly 2,000 years ago, the Greek geographer Strabo struck a cautious note when he wrote, "We must hear accounts of India with indulgence

1

for not only is it very far away, but even those who have seen it saw only some parts of it."

Modern transport has shrunk the distances, but Strabo's observation still has some validity. India's great size and variety mean that even today, most travelers may see only a small area of it. And it really is large. Walled off in the north by the massive bulwarks of the Himalayas, the source of the great rivers Indus and Ganges, India unrolls for more than 2,000 miles—over deserts and jungles, rain forests and well-tilled fields, and plains so vast they make your eyes ache—to the hot southern tip of Cape Comorin. It also spreads for 2,000 miles from the edges of Burma and China to a remote area of mudflats near the mouth of the Indus, the river, now mostly in Pakistan, from which India derives its name.

The peoples who came in waves through the mountain passes to conquer and to settle have created an amazingly complex society in a single country the size of Europe. India embraces great religions. Hinduism, which has its roots in the country's earliest history and remains one of the unifying elements, is the dominant faith. But Islam and Sikhism have helped to shape the country and are significant forces, part of India's fabric. The modern republic acknowledges 15 official languages, but there are hundreds of minor tongues. Among the 23 states and eight territories there are fierce regional loyalties. But in spite of the disparities, strains, and rivalries, the great bulk of Indians are loyal to the idea of India.

One of the keys to understanding today's India is to recognize that it is a country that exists in several centuries at once. India is, in part, a sophisticated and modern society, an industrial leader. It is also the home of primitive tribes, of millions of wretchedly poor people who live seemingly without hope. Between ancient and modern, rich and poor, lives a remarkable spectrum of humanity. The paradoxes of modern India can be seen in the existence of two important research centers: one for space, the other devoted to building a better bullock cart.

Cultures Meshed by Caste

The wonderful tapestry of cultures, languages, religions, diets, and costumes form a heterogeneity linked by the mesh of the caste system. This system has evolved over thousands of years, under racial, social, and religious pressures, as a way of ordering a huge mass of people in a large land area.

Caste provides people with an identity—the knowledge of where they stand in society and how they should live. It can provide security, govern a person's eating customs and other rituals, and determine the choice of a husband or wife (there is a widespread insistence on marriage within one's caste). India has more than 3,000 of these social divisions, from Brahmans to the untouchables.

Caste is so powerful a part of Indian life that it long ago penetrated the Moslem, Sikh, and Christian communities that are meant to be outside it. It is undoubtedly a force for stability in Indian life, strong and conservative, and possibly a defense against revolution. But it is one of the paradoxes of India in that it is also a cause of dissension and deadly rivalry. Caste prejudice, the labyrinth of petty apartheids, is one of the unpleasant facts of Indian life. The struggle of the lower castes and the untouchables to find justice and a decent life is enduring. Caste plays a significant part in the politics of the modern democracy because it is part of the very fiber of India, woven into Hindu ideas of life, rebirth, and predestination.

India is an ancient land, its roots going back 5,000 years. It is fabulous, intricate, and teeming. When, in 1947, the British bid farewell to the jewel in the crown of their empire, India had 350 million people. Now it has 850 million and is growing by more than a million a month. The government is trying to put the brakes on this phenomenal growth with a birth-control program. But nothing will stop India, the second most populous country on earth, from growing to a billion and beyond. It is expected to outstrip China as the world's giant early in the next century. Today, one person in every six in the world is an Indian.

Recent Impressive Advances

The pressures of population create enormous problems for the country's leaders. It is not just a matter of food. In a society whose expectations are constantly raised, there is an ever-increasing demand for better education, health care, jobs, housing, and transport, and these demands are translated into political pressures.

India can point with pride to advances made in recent years. Improvements in public health and disease control have obviously been a big factor in the growth of the population. The years of appalling food shortages and the burden of having to import grain belong to the past. India has learned how to feed its swelling millions through its agricultural revolution, the investment in healthier and stronger crops and improved irrigation. People are manifestly better clothed, fed, educated, and housed. Huge sections of Indian society are moving up and the nation can feel justifiably proud of what has been achieved. But there is also a darker side. It is impossible to ignore the evidence of poverty and the fact that there are millions in want.

Indians take pride in their country's place as the largest democratic society on earth. In the postcolonial, post-World War II era, many newly independent countries pledged their devotion to the democratic ideal, only to retreat to old ways as traditions and enmities in their societies reemerged and took over. In India, the democratic ideal may be battered in practice, but it endures. It is a fact of modern history that sets India apart, and Indians are deeply conscious of it. In such a large and complex society, it is not an easy road. But it can also be argued that in such a society, it is the only practical road.

India is by far the giant of south Asia, its population, economy, and military strength dwarfing the surrounding countries of Pakistan, Nepal, Bangladesh, and Sri Lanka. Its population is three and a half times greater than the total of the populations of all its neighbors, and its land mass is three times larger than all the others combined.

The political shape of the subcontinent in modern times was changed first by partition in 1947, when the two wings of Pakistan were carved out to create a Moslem homeland, and then by the war of 1971 in which East Pakistan broke away to become Bangladesh. The most important political matter in subcontinental relations is the enduring tension between India and Pakistan. This tension, whose roots are deep in historical rivalries and suspicions, is compounded by mutual mistrust and by the quarrel over the possession of Kashmir, the cause of two of the three wars the countries have fought since partition.

Diversity of People

It is hard to generalize about India and its people. One always runs into the exceptions and contradictions, for the diversity is astonishing. The people of Kashmir, Assam, and Nagaland are different from those of Kerala, Punjab, and Maharashtra. Languages, customs, traditions, histories, diets, and clothing are different, just as, in Europe, Norwegians are different from Spaniards. One has to keep in mind the sheer vastness of India.

Which brings us back to what the wise old geographer Strabo said about seeing only part of India. You can see some of the country by making the great triangular trip of Delhi-Agra-Jaipur. It is a familiar route for travelers and is not to be despised simply because it is well worn. Delhi is more than the capital. It is a repository of history and has been rebuilt several times. The Taj Mahal really is a marvel, well worth the trip, and Jaipur is a particular splendor. If you travel by road around these places, and pause often, you can see and learn much. But travelers do themselves and India an injustice if they do not get out of their comfortable hotels and walk in the streets and lanes and meet the people around them. They sell themselves short if they travel only on the jets of Indian Airlines and shut themselves away in luxurious lobbies and expensive restaurants.

Glamour and wealth are as much a part of the real India as anything else, even if the very rich are only a small minority. And in the smart hotels of great cities like Delhi, Bombay, Calcutta, and Madras, you can see the gatherings of tycoons, film producers, and other entrepreneurs and get a feeling of India's strong business tradition.

You can also see beautiful women, expensively dressed in saris or the long shirt and trousers favored by Punjabis, their bangles gently tinkling. In Bombay, particularly, you might think that these women are stars or starlets, part of the largest movie industry in the world. And you will probably be right.

Bustling City Life

Study the rush hour in any city for a while and you will get a good idea of India at work. One of the striking developments of recent times is the way cities and towns have swelled to create a large and important commercial and industrial population, a burgeoning middle class. The buses are crammed with office workers. Squadrons of bicycles weave to and fro. Young managers perch on motor scooters, often with a wife and children on board. Cars are expensive, but there are plenty of them, ranging from the veteran Ambassador—the great car of India based on a British 1950s design—to the newer Japanese models. And all the vehicles compete for road space with pony carts, rickshaws, camels, and elephants. The noise is tremendous.

The great majority of Indians, however, live in rural areas. Nearly 75 percent of the people depend on farming. They live in 576,000 villages, some large and prosperous, some little more than poor hamlets. In many respects, the routines of their lives have changed little over the centuries. When you go to a village, you might imagine that here is the simplest of existences, but village life is a complex pattern of hard work, family problems, disputes, caste consciousness and rivalries, and religious rituals.

The rhythms of crop growing and the weather are central concerns. But the overriding concern is the monsoon—the wind that brings the annual rains—which plays a part in the politics of the country. Politicians and economists, as well as the millions who live off the land, wait anxiously and hopefully as the monsoon moves northward. Radio and newspaper reports are followed with keen interest. Everyone prays for a good monsoon. The air grows hot and the sky turns dark. Then the monsoon breaks with lightning and thunder. People dance in the heavy rain and give thanks. But, from time to time, the rains are scanty and the harvests are poor.

Farming Prospers in the North

The most prosperous farming region is Punjab, home of the "green revolution," which enabled India to feed itself. Punjabis are big, outgoing people, energetic and business minded. They have made Punjab the most prosperous state in the country. They are great farmers and took readily to mechanization, modern fertilizers, and new varieties of crops, the bases of the green revolution. Punjabis have spread throughout the north. Delhi has a strong Punjabi presence, and Punjabis are a major force in the film business in Bombay, India's Hollywood.

Punjab is also the home state of the Sikhs, perhaps the most distinctive Indians, who form over half the state's population. Sikhs are only about 2 percent of the Indian population, but their contribution to national life is in much larger proportion. They have a strong military tradition and retain an important presence in the army, navy, and air force. They are also big in medicine, engineering, and trucking. Sikhs are adherents of a religion founded in the sixteenth century, as an offshoot of Hinduism, and codified by 10 *gurus,* or teachers. To keep their unshorn hair tidy, Sikhs tuck it into a turban, their distinctive headgear (although other Indians also wear turbans).

The complex politics of the Sikhs and the fundamentalists' belief that their religion is in danger of being swallowed up by Hinduism are reasons for the troubles in Punjab. Hindus and Sikh Punjabis have traditionally lived in harmony, often worshiping in each other's temples. It was once common for one son in a Hindu family in Punjab to be raised as a Sikh. Sikh extremists, however, have been trying to drive a wedge between the two communities.

You will see a different style of turban in Rajasthan, the home of the Rajput people. The turbans here are big, bright edifices made out of 40 feet of muslin.

Bengalis are also distinctive. Their chief city is Calcutta, vigorous and teeming, with a strong cultural tradition. Bengalis are great debaters, poets, artists, and writers, and their politics are lively and contentious. Many Bengalis have names ending in *ji,* or *jee,* as in Chatterji.

Clothing, of course, is governed by the climate. Warm woolen jackets and shawls are worn in the north and cool sarongs are worn in the south. Although many men wear Western-style clothing (trousers and shirts or suits), most women wear the traditional sari or shirt and trousers, the trousers being baggy or narrow. The sari endures because it is graceful, cool, modest, and available in a vast array of patterns and colors.

Many men in the north favor the cool *kurta*—a long shirt and loose trousers, usually white. Also popular is the *dhoti,* the comfortable garment that is often worn loose and baggy or as a loincloth. Many Bengalis like wearing the dhoti, and you'll often see it worn in the countryside.

Land of Many Languages

The languages of India form part of its complexity. By and large, the country's political and regional boundaries are drawn on linguistic lines. With 15 major languages and hundreds of minor ones, as well as dialects, every state in the union is multilingual.

Each main language has an ancient literature and is spoken by millions of people. There is no majority language. Even Hindi, the main official language and the fifth major language of the world after Chinese, English, Russian, and Spanish, is not spoken by a majority. Only English is known throughout India, and only about three people in every hundred speak it. But this Anglophone minority has the greatest influence on running the country. They are the administrators, judges, industrialists, businessmen, leading politicians, and educators.

The languages of India are great unifiers within their home regions; but there are places where language is a sensitive—and political—issue.

Legacy of the Raj

The English language is one of the chief legacies of the British raj, and spoken English in India often has a distinctive and musical lilt. Many Indian words have entered English as part of the cross-fertilization: *bungalow, chintz, pajama,* and *calico* are familiar ones.

English was only one important legacy. A system of justice and the democratic ideal were others. And Indians from north to south love another legacy, the game of cricket. They are as devoted to it as any Englishman—more so, some would say. Listen to Indians discussing cricket, in any language, and you will hear something of the international cricket language: "sticky wicket," "keep a straight bat," and "well played, sir!" Test matches attract huge crowds, and employers complain about people taking the day off to attend. As you travel about, you can see even the poorest boys playing cricket in the dust or on a patch of grass, with makeshift bats and other gear, and dreaming of being cricket stars. The top players are national heroes. Cricket is one of the things that Pakistan and India have in common. When the two countries play each other, the crowds forget other rivalries and concentrate on sporting ones. When there was tension on the shared frontier in 1987, a cricket match defused it.

The British left little or no residue of bitterness when they quit India in 1947. The relations between the two countries have usually been cordial and remain special. Many Indians suffered during the years of the struggle for independence; Nehru and Gandhi were only two of the many thousands who were imprisoned for their activities against the British. But once independence was achieved, there was no attempt to erase the evidence of British management. Nehru, for example, always had a good relationship with the British, and many Indians look back with affection on their years in British schools and universities. India has done what it has usually done throughout history. It absorbed what the British had to offer and took it in its stride.

Traditional Values vs. Modern Cities

India respects its past and reveres old values and rituals, no more so than in the countryside. If you bear in mind that most of the people derive their living from the land, the social and family structures in the villages form a massive bedrock of stability. People live together in a joint family, an efficient way of sharing resources, work, and problems. Major decisions, such as a woman's wish to be sterilized in the birth-control program, may involve the whole family. For decisions affecting the whole community, villagers turn to the *panchayat,* the elected village council. This practice supervises development projects and lobbies the authorities for improvements like wells, irrigation pumps, and health facilities.

Although the countryside in many parts of India has a timeless appearance, with plodding oxen drawing carts and women balancing water jars on their heads, time does not stand still. Agricultural production has been modernized in many areas, new power stations drive irrigation pumps, most villages have electricity, and many villages now own a community television set. In some areas, you will be impressed by the sheer number of shiny new tractors. But bear in mind that these improvements and changes are based on centuries of tradition, of caste divisions and the close loyalties of the joint family—a strict social pecking order.

In the country in particular, you can plainly see that customs, religion, and economic demands put a heavy emphasis on the male. Men rule the roost. Couples fervently desire sons, and girls are often regarded as a burden. The birth of a son is always a matter of celebration; the birth of a girl is usually not. In general, boys in rural India get better treatment, food, education, and medical care. The life expectancy of women in the countryside is shorter than that of men.

It is a different story in the towns and cities whose populations are growing rapidly. It is difficult to keep caste barriers in crowded buses, trains, offices, factories, and restaurants. The rise of urban India has eroded caste differences. The extended family, with parents and sons and daughters-in-law all living together, is still important in the cities, as is the tradition of arranged marriages, with parents finding brides for their sons through personal contacts and newspaper advertisements. However, many young middle-class are opting for Western-style courtship and marriage.

It is in urban India that women are at their most emancipated and can compete as equals with men. Women are steadily advancing in medicine, education, law, science, civil service, commerce, and politics. And instead of being kept apart, many men and women in the cities get to know each other socially and professionally in universities and other places of work. The growth of the middle class in the cities is bringing about great changes in Indian life.

The cities are the dynamos, and people stream in from the countryside in search of the better life and more money. The result is that the cities have become overcrowded, and, in some places like Bombay and Calcutta, overcrowding creates a permanent and desperate crisis. In Bombay, for example, about half the city's 10 million people live in slums. Indeed, some of these shanty settlements are almost towns in their own right: the largest has a population of more than half a million. But people continue to pour in because they believe they will earn more than they can in the fields at home. And they are right. Even a lowly job in Bombay pays more than a laboring job in the country, enough to enable a man to send money back home. So many people, rich and poor, want to be in Bombay that property prices have soared to astonishing levels. Bombay's best areas have become as expensive as New York and Tokyo.

Since the early 1970s, the cities of India have grown by 40 percent and 12 cities now have populations of more than a million. Nearly a quarter of the Indians are town or city dwellers, and the migration into cities—with all the problems it creates—is one of the significant forces that is changing Indian life. It is shaping new attitudes and breaking ancient molds.

FACTS AT YOUR FINGERTIPS

THE LAND. Though you may think of India as a place that's hot and tropical, all of it is in the northern hemisphere. India's territory makes it the seventh largest country in the world, with a land frontier of 15,260 kilometers (9,425 miles), a total land area of about 3,287,000 square kilometers (1,261,000 square miles), and a coastline of 6,100 kilometers (3,535 miles)—approximately the cross-country distance of the United States. In the north, the Himalayas separate India from China. Situated between the two countries is Nepal; to its east is Bhutan, which is still closely connected to India by special treaty. All three countries lie along the chain of the Himalayas, and still more mountains separate India from Burma on India's eastern border. Also in the east lies Bangladesh, wedged between the Indian states of Assam and West Bengal. In the northwest, Pakistan and a small hook of Afghanistan border India and separate it from the USSR.

Stretching southward, the country crosses the Tropic of Cancer, then tapers off into a peninsula with the Arabian Sea to the west and the Bay of Bengal to the east. Just off the eastern tip of the subcontinent lies Sri Lanka (formerly Ceylon), separated from the mainland by a sliver of water, the Palk Straits. Sri Lanka, just 50 kilometers (31 miles) away, is an independent nation, whereas islands much farther away from India, such as the Lakshadweep Islands in the Arabian Sea and the distant Andaman and Nicobar Islands in the Bay of Bengal, are part of the Indian Union.

The mainland itself is a geographer's and geologist's paradise. The Himalayan range (*hima* = snow; *laya* = abode) is dramatically high, the altitude of the Indo-Gangetic plain varies little from sea to sea, and the southern peninsula is a high plateau with coastal strips. The Himalayan mountains are three parallel ranges with wide plateaus and valleys that are fertile and spectacular. The mountain wall, which is 2,419 kilometers (1,500 miles) long with a depth of 241 to 323 kilometers (150 to 200 miles), boasts one of the world's highest altitudes. Until recently, Mount Everest, at 8,874 meters (29,108 feet), was undisputedly the highest peak in the world, but astronomers making calculations via satellite measurements in early 1987 claimed that K-2 in Pakistan is taller. The dispute was resolved later in 1987 when an Italian expedition confirmed that Everest is still tops—256 meters (840 feet) higher than K-2.

The Garo, Khasi, and Naga hills in the northeast are dwarfs in comparison to their Himalayan neighbors. They run east-west to join the north-south Lushai and Arakan Hills that separate India from Burma.

The unvarying Indo-Gangetic Plain is the home of probably more people per square mile than any other spot on earth. The basins of the Indus, the Ganges, and the Brahmaputra make the land rich and fertile. Between India's capital of Delhi and the Bay of Bengal, nearly 1,613 kilometers (1,000 miles), the elevation of the Gangetic plain drops only 213 meters (700 feet). The peninsular plateau is marked off from this plain by mountain and hill ranges, among them the Aravali and the Vindhya ranges. The Eastern Ghats move down the peninsula and follow its shape, marking off a broad coastal strip between it and the Bay of Bengal, while on the opposite side of the peninsula, the Western Ghats define a narrower coast off the Arabian Sea. The two ranges meet near the southern tip of India in the Nilgiri Hills.

Geologically, the country has this three-part division: The Himalayas are formed by layers of marine deposits and were once covered by the sea, the soil of the Indo-Gangetic plain comes from river deposits, and the rocks of the southern peninsula are among the oldest in the world. The Himalayan rivers are snow fed and flow continuously, often causing great floods during the monsoons; the Deccan rivers are rain fed and fluctuate greatly in volume; and the coastal rivers are short and drain little territory.

The Ganges is the mother of India's rivers, the bedrock of mythology and veneration. Its basin drains about a quarter of the country's entire area. The second-largest basin is that of the Godavari, which claims about 10 percent of the total land mass.

The most important rivers are the Brahmaputra in the east, the Indus in the west, and the Krishna in the south.

Basic Statistics for India

Land area: 1,261,000 square miles (3,287,000 square km)
Population: 1988 (est.) 850 million
Population, average annual growth: 2.1 percent
Population, literate adults: 37 percent as per 1981 census; unofficially 40 percent
Average life expectancy: 56 years
Average per capita income (1988 estimate): $270 (in U.S. dollars)
Population of 18–25 year olds: 80 million
Agriculture as a percentage of the gross national product (GNP): 41.9 percent (73 percent of the work force)
Industry as a percentage of the GNP: 22 percent
Religions (percentage of population):

Hindu	83.3
Muslim	11.0
Christian	2.6
Sikh	1.9
Buddhist	0.9
Other	0.3

Languages: Hindi is the official language, but English is spoken widely. Twenty-two states also use regional languages for administrative and educational purposes

WHAT IT WILL COST. With a favorable exchange rate continuing to stretch the dollar's value, India remains a bargain destination and a shopper's dream. Though rises in fuel costs are pushing up the fares for air and rail travel as well as for taxis, inland travel expenses are still low compared with other destinations. The cost of renting a car with driver, a good way to travel within each state, remains about Rs. 3–4 per kilometer, with a halt (stopover) charge of Rs. 50 per night.

Good accommodations in Western-style hotels with air-conditioned rooms and deluxe hotel services can be expensive in the major cities of Bombay, Calcutta, Delhi, and Madras; but, throughout the country, fine hotels exist that will satisfy every budget. Dining is also economical, especially if you eat outside the hotels. Unless you order a feast, you'll find it hard to spend more than $10 per person for a hearty meal.

Visitors should also plan on paying an airport departure tax when they leave India. If you're heading for a neighboring country such as Nepal, the tax is Rs. 150; for all other international destinations the tax is Rs. 300.

CURRENCY. The units of Indian currency are the rupee and paisa (a hundred paise equal one rupee). Paper money comes in the following rupee denominations: 1, 2, 5, 10, 20, 50, and 100. Coins are in denominations of 5, 10, 20, 25, and 50 paise; and 1, 2, and 5 rupees. At press time, the rate of exchange was about U.S.$1 = Rs. 17; £1 = Rs. 26.

India and Nepal have strict rules against bringing in their country's currency. International airports in each country have currency exchange booths that are always open for arriving or departing flights. When you change your money, remember to get a certain amount in small denominations. Also reject torn bills. Many merchants, hotels, and restaurants won't accept worn or tattered bills and it's a hassle to go to the *one* bank where you can get them exchanged.

Cash, bank notes, and traveler's checks up to U.S. $1,000 or equivalent don't have to be declared at the time of entry. Visitors in possession of more than that amount are required to fill out a Currency Declaration Form on arrival. This form allows you to exchange your unused currency (providing you've held onto your encashment slips), and lets you leave the country with your unchanged money. You receive an encashment slip every time you change money or checks. If you want to pay a hotel bill in rupees, you must have this slip. Foreigners and Indian residents abroad must also pay internal air travel expenses in foreign currency.

Traveler's Checks. American Express and Thomas Cook traveler's checks are the international drafts of choice. Buy a fair percentage of them in small denominations for those times when you need instant cash and the banks are closed. Along with your traveler's checks, bring a list of foreign offices where you can get refunds if they're lost or stolen. And remember, though most hotels will gladly exchange your checks, they usually give a lower rate than banks and exchange houses. You may also be tempted to change money on the black market, which gives a better rate of exchange but is illegal.

Getting Money from Home. Currently, the only reasonable way to get money from home is to cash a personal check with an American Express card or, if you're a highly placed executive, with the Thomas Cook Carte d'Or at these companies' respective offices.

CREDIT CARDS. In India and Nepal, Western-style hotels, restaurants, and fancier shops usually accept the following credit cards: American Express, Diners Club, MasterCard, and Visa. Throughout the book we use the following abbreviations: AE, DC, MC, V.

Planning Your Trip

Note: Because of continuing tensions and disturbances in Assam, Jammu, and Kashmir, the U.S. State Department at press time advises deferring travel to these states. Travelers to other parts of Northern and Eastern India, especially Punjab, Uttar Pradesh, Rajasthan, and northern Madhya Pradesh, should exercise caution. Special permits (see "Restricted Area Permit" below) are required for many areas. Since sporadic incidents of violence due to political unrest can occur at any time throughout India, it is suggested that you call the U.S. State Department (202–647–5225) for its latest recorded travel advisory. Be prepared for a lengthy message, especially if your phone is not a touch-tone type. While in India, you are urged to contact the American Embassy in New Delhi or the American Consulates General in Bombay, Calcutta, and Madras for the latest information on the security situation in the area you are visiting or plan to visit.

India is one country where you should plan your trip in advance. It is too vast and complex a land to start organizing your itinerary after you arrive. Unless you are traveling on a package tour, with a fixed itinerary and schedule, read every possible brochure first and then settle on priorities.

Most first-time visitors to India try to pack in too many objectives. Distances are huge, traveling tiring, and sightseeing exhausting. Wise travelers plan a couple of days' complete relaxation, in a beach resort or hill station, for every 7–10 days of touring, to digest all the wonders they have seen and to catch up on rest and laundry before the next phase of the trip.

The *Government of India Tourist Office* is one of the best of the national tourism-promotion organizations. Here, you will get informative leaflets covering the diverse attractions and regions of India. We hope you will find most of the planning information you need in this book, but public libraries will provide more in-depth information about social or political aspects. State-run tourist offices vary in reliability and information; some are informative about local events and some offer reasonably priced tour packages.

Major Government of India Tourist Offices are located at the following addresses:

USA: 30 Rockefeller Plaza, Room 15, North Mezzanine, New York, NY 10020, tel. 212–586–4901; 3550 Wilshire Blvd., Los Angeles, CA 90010, tel. 213–380–8855; 230 North Michigan Ave., Chicago, IL 60601, tel. 312–236–6899.

UK: 7 Cork St., London W1X 2AB, tel. 071–437–3677 or 78.

CANADA: 60 Bloor St. West, Suite 1003, Toronto, Ontario M4W3B8, tel. 416–962–3787 or 88.

AUSTRALIA: Carlton Center, 55 Elizabeth St., Sydney, NSW 2000, tel. 02–232–1600.

There are also overseas offices in Bangkok, Dubai, Frankfurt, Geneva, Kuwait, Milan, Paris, Singapore, Stockholm, Tokyo, and Vienna. Visitors will find Government of India Tourist Offices in all the major towns of India; these offices will be even more helpful than the overseas branches because they have more detailed information pertaining to their own areas.

The services of Indian Airlines, the major domestic carrier, have improved greatly in recent years. Bookings can be made through Air-India offices abroad, since Indian Airlines does not have overseas facilities. It is critical that you reconfirm all airline flights, domestic or international, throughout your stay in India. Train reservations and ticket purchases usually have to be made on the spot in each major city. Special lines for tourists are set up at major airports and railroad terminals. Indian railways are in the process of computerizing reservations, cancellations, and the like. Delhi is already on-line, and Calcutta and Bombay will be on-line by mid-1988.

The growth of major hotel chains in recent years has made advance booking much simpler, and accommodations for a complete tour itinerary can now be reserved through just one or two central reservations systems. Details of the major chains are given in the *Hotels* section of this chapter.

City sightseeing, car hire, and guide services can be easily arranged on arrival at each destination, either through hotel travel desks, the local Government of India Tourist Office, or the state tourist organization. The excursions and tours detailed in this section can also be arranged easily, but one should make airline reservations well in advance, especially during peak travel times.

The wise traveler to India builds in several reserve days in case of unexpected delays or the impulse to see more of a particular place. We would most strongly advise that you do not try to work within a tight itinerary. Take it easy and, if you cannot see all of India in one trip (an impossibility!), come back again, just as many do, to this fascinating land.

This book will help you to decide what you want to see in India. Study our maps of the tourist highlights, consult the list of itineraries appearing later in this chapter while building up your own itinerary, and then try to reconcile the itinerary you plan with the time at your disposal. Remember that airline schedules change slightly according to season, so be sure to check them.

TRAVEL DOCUMENTS. Travelers to India require a passport and a visa. **Americans** applying for a new U.S. passport must appear in person; renewals can be obtained in person or by mail (*see* below). First-time applicants should apply well in advance of their departure at a U.S. passport agency in Boston, Chicago, Honolulu, Houston, Los Angeles, Miami, New Orleans, New York, Philadelphia, San Francisco, Seattle, Stamford (CT), Washington DC, or at their local county courthouse or certain post offices. Necessary documents include a completed passport application (Form DSP-11); proof of citizenship (birth certificate with raised seal or naturalization papers); proof of identity (driver's license, employee ID card, or any document with your photograph and signature); two recent, identical, two-inch-square photographs (black-and-white or color); $42 application fee for a 10-year passport (those under 18 pay $27 for a five-year passport). Passports are mailed to you in about 10 working days.

To renew your passport by mail, you'll need completed Form DSP-82; two recent, identical passport photographs; and a check or money order for $35.

British Citizens. Applications are available from travel agencies or a main post office. Send the completed form to your nearest regional passport office (locations include London, Liverpool, Newport, Peterborough, Glasgow, and Belfast). The application must be countersigned by your bank manager or by a solicitor, barrister, doctor, clergyman, or justice of the peace who knows you personally. In addition, you'll need two photographs and the £15 fee.

Canadian Citizens. Canadians can apply in person at regional passport offices in Edmonton, Halifax, Montreal, Toronto, Fredericton, Hamilton, London, Ottawa, Hull, Quebec, St. John's, Saskatoon, North York, Victoria, Windsor, Vancouver, or Winnipeg. You can also send a completed application (available at any post office or passport office) to the Bureau of Passports, Complexe Guy Favreau, 200 Dorchester West, Montreal, Quebec, H2Z 1X4. Include $25, two photographs, a guarantor, and proof of Canadian citizenship. Passports are valid for five years and are non-renewable.

VISAS

Citizens of all countries must have a valid tourist visa obtained from Indian consulates or high commissions (*see* list below). To get a visa, you need a valid passport and a passport photo. The visa cost for Americans and Canadians is $15; for Britons, £24. The visa is good for four months, with a four-month extension possible. You must arrive in India within six months of the date your visa is issued. Individuals who need to extend their visas should visit the Foreigners' Regional Registration Office at New Delhi or Calcutta or any of the offices of the Superintendent of Police in the various district headquarters. If you appear in person at an Indian consulate or high commission, your initial visa is usually granted within 48 hours. If you apply through the mail, allow a month and include a self-addressed and stamped envelope.

U. S. Citizens can apply to the following offices of the Consulate General of India: 3 E. 64th St., New York, NY 10021, tel. 212–879–7800; 150 North Michigan Ave., Chicago, IL 60601, tel. 312–781–6280; 540 Arguello Blvd., San Francisco, CA 94118, tel. 415–668–0662. You can also apply to the Embassy of India, 2107 Massachusetts Ave., Washington, DC 20008, tel. 202–939–7000.

British Citizens can apply to the India High Commission, India House, Aldwych, London WC2B 4NA; tel. 071–836–8484.

Canadians can apply to the Indian High Commission at 10 Springfield Rd., Ottawa, Quebec K1M 109, tel. 613–744–3751; or to the Consulates General at 2 Bloor St., Suite 500, West Cumberland, Toronto, Ontario M4W 3E2, tel. 416–960–0751; or 325 Howe St., Vancouver, British Columbia V6C 1Z7; tel. 604–662–8811.

RESTRICTED AREA PERMIT

A Restricted Area Permit is obligatory for Assam, Meghalaya, and Sikkim. You also need the permit to visit the Andaman Islands (a 15-day permit is available on arrival at Port Blair) and Lakshadweep Island (also easily obtained through the one resort open to foreigners). A permit is also necessary to travel by train or car to northern West Bengal. If you fly into Bagdogra Airport to visit Darjeeling or Kalimpong in northern West Bengal, the permit is not necessary.

Obtain a copy of the Restricted Area Permit from any consular office abroad. With Sikkim, where permission for a 15-day visit is now easy to procure, send the permit application to the Sikkim office or any Indian mission. With Meghalaya, tight restrictions were relaxed at press time. Seven-day permits for parties of four or more travelers are now granted through these same Indian government offices. Currently, individual travelers were advised to send their permit to the Resident Commissioner at Meghalaya House, 10 Aurangzeb Rd., New Delhi, who will help expedite the process. Check with the Government of India Tourist Office for the latest details.

With Assam and train and car trips to northern West Bengal, don't use the consular offices or missions to get permission, as many travel agents or even the Government of India Tourist Office will suggest. Send the permit application to the Ministry of Home Affairs, Government of India, Lok Nayak Bhavan, Khan Market, New Delhi, India. Other offices are more likely to say "no" than go through the paperwork to make your trip happen.

For all permits, you must be specific about your trip plans and provide a precise list of destinations within the state. For acceptable destinations, see the permit guidelines in each destination chapter. Also note the time restrictions and figure them into your itinerary. With Sikkim, you can also procure a permit from the following offices: the Sikkim Tourist Office in New Delhi; the Foreign Regional Registration offices in Delhi, Bombay, and Calcutta; and the Immigration Offices at airports in Delhi, Bombay, Calcutta, and Madras. With Meghalaya, you can also procure a permit from the Foreign Regional Registration offices.

With all destinations, except Sikkim and group permits into Meghalaya, allow three months for clearance. When you get your permit, make two copies and keep them with you when you travel. Travelers have recounted terrible stories in which they've either lost their only copy due to carelessness or had it inexplicably taken from them by the police at a checkpoint—which meant they couldn't proceed on their trip. The permit must be shown at various checkposts and to every hotel manager when you check in (or you won't be given a room).

Travelers can also visit most of these restricted areas as part of a tour group listed under each destination chapter and below under *Tour Operators*. Under these circumstances, the tour operator will help you secure the necessary permits.

TOUR OPERATORS. The following companies offer excellent tours to India and Nepal. A few also offer some outdoor adventures. Many companies offer a two-tiered price structure, one with or without airfare from the West. If you choose a package based exclusively on land costs, you can arrive or depart according to your own schedule. With all recommended companies you can join a fixed departure tour, or you can ask for a more expensive custom-designed trip. Those travelers who don't like group travel should consider a mini-tour that lasts for a week or less. This is one way to get into destinations that have group travel restrictions. Finally, ask tour operators about expenses covered in the tour cost, such as supplementary insurance coverage. If your trip involves physical exertion, ask about the degree of difficulty and prior experience required.

General-Interest Tours. U.S. and Canada. *Abercrombie & Kent International* (1420 Kensington Rd., Oak Park, IL 60521, tel. 312–954–2944 or 800–323–7308) is the granddaddy in the travel business offering excellent cultural tours.

Distant Horizons (679 Tremont St., Boston, MA 02118, tel. 617–267–5343 or 800–333–1240) offers excellent cultural tours with Asian authorities as your guides.

Indoculture Tours (Suite 272, 5601 W. Slauson Ave., Culver City, CA 90230, tel. 213–649–0424 or 800–234–4085) sponsors theme-oriented tours based around festivals, visits to monasteries, and excellent pilgrimages.

Journeyworld International (410 E. 51st St., New York, NY 10022, tel. 212–752–8308 or 800–635–3900) sponsors high-quality cultural "theme" tours.

Lindblad Travel (Box 912, Westport, CT 06881, tel. 203–226–8531 or 800–243–5657) offers classy general tours and wildlife safaris.

Mercury Travels (300 E. 42nd St., New York, NY 10017, tel. 212–661–0380 or 800–223–1474) offers excellent cultural "theme" tours, and some outdoor adventure trips including skiing, rafting, and camel safaris.

Odyssey Tours (1821 Wilshire Blvd., Santa Monica, CA 90403, tel. 213–453–1042 or 800–654–7975) offers numerous cultural "theme" tours, including homestays, festivals, pilgrimages, and study tours focusing on traditional medicine.

Our Personal Guest (150 W. 55th St., Apt. 2B, New York, NY 10019, tel. 212–581–7329) creates personalized luxury trips to India around your special interests.

Salen Lindblad (133 E. 55th St., New York, NY 10019, tel. 212–751–2300 or 800–223–5688) sponsors tours around India in a private Dornier Aircraft.

Tours of Distinction (141 E. 44th St., New York, NY 10017, tel. 212–661–4680 or 800–888–8634) offers quality excursions, including a comprehensive wildlife tour.

Trade Wings (Suite 805, 25 W. 43rd St., New York, NY, 10036, tel. 212–354–8328) sponsors excellent cultural "theme" tours, including a tour of tribal areas, and outdoor adventures—elephant and camel safaris, fishing, bird-watching, and golfing.

Wilderness Travel (801 Allston Way, Berkeley, CA 94710, tel 415–548–0420 or 800–247–6700) offers over a dozen adventure trips to India and Nepal each year, including river rafting, Himalayan trekking, and jungle safaris.

Britain. *Abercrombie & Kent* (Sloane Square House, Holbein Pl., London SW1W 8NS, tel. 071–730–9600) is the British-based office of this excellent company mentioned above.

India. *Travel Corporation of India, Pvt. Ltd.* (Chander Mukhi, Nariman Point, Bombay, tel. 2021881; and Hotel Metro, First Floor, N-49 Connaught Place, New Delhi, tel. 3315181), India's largest travel agency, offers excellent general- and special-interest tours—cultural and adventure. They have branches in major Indian cities.

Special-Interest Tours. U.S. and Canada. *Above the Clouds Trekking* (Box 398, Worcester, MA 01602, tel. 617–799–4499 or 800–233–4499) sponsors vehicular tours and treks (including family treks), biking trips, photo workshops, health-related treks offering university credits, and an international mountaineering camp.

Adventures on Skis (815 North Rd., Rte. 202, Westfield, MA 01085, tel. 413–568–2855 or 800–628–9655) sponsors heliskiing trips in the Indian Himalayas.

Archaeological Tours (Suite 1202, 30 E. 42nd St., New York, NY 10017, tel. 212–986–3054) sponsors excellent scholar-led tours.

InnerAsia Expeditions (2627 Lombard St., San Francisco, CA 94123, tel. 415–922–0448 or 800–551–1769) offers vehicular tours and treks (many with a cultural emphasis), rafting trips and safaris, and mountain climbing.

Journeys (4011 Jackson Rd., Ann Arbor, MI 48103, tel. 313–665–4407 or 800–255–8735) promotes active participation in foreign cultures. You plant trees, pick up garbage, go on a medical trek to a poor village in Nepal, or help restore a monastery in Ladakh. The company also offers theme-oriented treks and rafting and jungle safaris.

King Bird Tours (Box 196, Planetarium Station, New York, NY 10024, 212–866–7923) sponsors in-depth bird-watching tours.

Lute Jerstad Adventures (Box 19537, Portland, OR 97219, tel. 503–244–6075), a small concern run by a Himalayan scholar, offers rafting and jungle safaris, treks, and excellent culture and nature tours, including a snow leopard nature camp in Ladakh and a trip through South India.

Mountain Travel (6420 Fairmount Ave., El Cerrito, CA 94530, tel. 415–525–7710 or 800–227–2384), a pioneer in outdoor adventure, offers rugged vehicular trips; treks, mountain climbing, rafting, and boating adventures; and camel, elephant, and jungle safaris.

Nature Expeditions International (474 Willamette St., Box 11496, Eugene, OR 97440, tel. 503–484–6529) sponsors nature and culture tours led by anthropologists and biologists.

Overseas Adventure Travel (349 Broadway, Cambridge, MA 02139, tel. 617–876–0533 or 800–221–0814) offers vehicular tours and treks, rafting, and jungle safaris. A percentage of the trekking fee is donated to the protection of the trails.

Photo Adventure Tours (2035 Park St., Atlantic Beach, NY 11509, tel. 516–371–0067) sponsors photography-oriented tours in India.

Questers: Worldwide Nature Tours (257 Park Ave. South, New York, NY 10010, tel. 212–673–3120) offers naturalists' tours.

Tiger Tops International (2627 Lombard St., San Francisco, CA 94123, tel. 415–346–3402) has pioneered many of the best treks and mountain expeditions in Nepal. The company also offers treks in India, wildlife safaris in their idyllic game-park retreats, and rafting.

Wilderness Travel (801 Allston Way, Berkeley, CA 94710, tel. 415–548–0420 or 800–247–6700) offers trekking, rafting, mountain biking, jungle safaris, camel safaris, and mountain climbing.

Britain. *ExplorAsia* (13 Chapter St., London SWIP 4NY, tel. 071–630–7102) serves as a liaison for Tiger Tops and its subsidiaries—arranging treks, rafting, or safaris to the Tiger Tops Wildlife Resorts.

Karakoram Experience (Trekkers Lodge, 32 Lake Rd., Keswick, Cumbria 12 5DQ, tel. 081–687–73966) offers excellent treks and mountaineering.

India. *Arventures Adventure Holidays* (Post Bag No. 7, Dehradun 248001, Uttar Pradesh, tel. 29172) creates every conceivable fixed or customized outdoor experience in the Himalayas: treks by elephant, bike, horse, jeep; wildlife safaris; and water-trips by *shikara* (Kashmiri gondola). It creates "theme" treks that focus on nature, photography, village life, or religion.

Empl Tours (108 Vishal Phawan, 95 Nehru Place, New Delhi 110019, tel. 6428310) is an excellent outfit that creates customized "adventure" trips throughout India. They offer hang gliding in Karnataka; numerous wildlife safaris, including elephant trips in Uttar Pradesh and camel trips in Rajasthan; treks in southern villages and the Himalayas; exotic boat cruises on the Ganges River in Uttar Pradesh, the Brahmaputra in Assam, and the Chambal in Rajasthan; catamaran trips in West Bengal; and biking in Kerala and Karnataka.

Exotic Journeys (26 Sector 2 Market, R. K. Puram, New Delhi 110022, tel. 670221) offers elephant safaris in northern India; safaris in Gujarat's Rann of Kutch desert; biking in Rajasthan; bird-watching in the Himalayas; trekking in Tamil Nadu's Nilgiris Hills; plus photo safaris, educational tours, village stays, and a novel program called "Travel As You Like" where they supply a jeep, driver, and guide and create a trip through an Indian state or states, which can involve camping (equipment provided) or luxury hotel, palace, or inn stays.

Himalayan River Runners (188-A Jor Bagh, New Delhi 110003, tel. 615736) is India's best rafting company, pioneering the latest runs in the Indian Himalayas with excellent personal attention and equipment. Fixed departures and customized trips are available.

Potala Tours and Travels (16 Jor Bagh, Lodi Road, New Delhi 110003, tel. 616813), an undertaking of the Tibetan Administration set up by the government-in-exile in Dharamsala, organizes group tours to Buddhist places in Nepal and India.

Special Tours for Special Needs. *Evergreen Travel Service* (19505L 44th Ave. W., Lynnwood, WA 98036, tel. 206–776–1184 or 800–435–2288) creates customized skiing and rafting trips and generalized tours for the handicapped traveler. Trekking is currently under study. No matter how severe your handicap, this well-run organization will find the way for you to enjoy India and Nepal.

U.S. AGENTS WHO PROMOTE TRAVEL TO INDIA AND NEPAL

American Express, 3 World Financial Center, American Express Tower-Lobby Level, New York, NY 10285-0230; tel. 212–640–5130.

Cox & Kings Ltd., 511 Lexington Ave., Suite 335, New York, NY 10017; tel. 212–935–3935 or 800–999–1758.

General Tours, 770 Broadway, New York, NY 10003; tel. 212–598–1800 or 800–221–2216.

International Travel House, 148 E. 48th St., New York, NY 10017; tel. 212–593–1277 or 212–838–1811.

Journeyworld International, 410 E. 51st St., New York, NY 10022; tel. 212–752–8308 or 800–635–3900.

Mercury Travels, 300 E. 42nd St., New York, NY 10017; tel. 212–661–0380 or 800–223–1474.

Nouvelles Frontières, 12 E. 33rd St., New York, NY 10036; tel. 212–779 0600 or 800–366–6387.

Sita World Travel (Indrama), Suite 1708, 501 Fifth Ave., New York, NY 10017; tel. 212–972–5500.

Tours of Distinction, 141 E. 44th St., New York, NY 10017; tel. 212–661–4680 or 800–888–8634.

Trade Wings, Suite 805, 25 W. 43rd St., New York, NY 10036; tel. 212–354–8328.

BRITAIN

American Express, 6 Haymarket, London SW1Y 4BS; tel. 071–930–4411.

Cox & Kings, St. James Court, Buckingham Gate, London SW1E 6AS; tel. 071–931–9106 or 071–834–7446.

Indtravels, Brite House, 74 Willesden Lane, London NW6 7TA; tel. 071–625–55900.

Sita World Travel, Naresh Sarvaria, Chesham House, 136 Regent St., London W1R SFA; tel. 071–437–6900.

Swan Hellenic Tours Ltd., 77 New Oxford St., London WC1A 1PP. tel. 071–831–1616.

Thomas Cook, 45 Berkeley St., Piccadilly, London W1A 1EB; tel. 071–499–4000.

TOURING ITINERARIES. In planning tours of India one should either select one city as a base, radiating out to other places of interest, or make up an itinerary that includes major attractions between key cities. This plan is particularly valid for brief visits of up to a week, such as might be undertaken by a business or transit traveler. The following tours will need Indian Airlines and Vayudoot timetables for detailed planning, but flight frequencies are convenient, mostly daily, between adjacent points.

One-Week Tours (based on major cities):

Out of Bombay (West India): Bombay city sightseeing plus boat ride to Elephanta Caves (Sept.–May only) or Khaneri Caves. Fly to Aurangabad, visiting Ajanta and Ellora caves by car or bus. Fly to Jaipur, returning to Bombay, or return directly to Bombay and fly to Goa to relax at the seaside. Alternative destinations to the south are Cochin or Trivandrum, for the Kovalum Beach resort and the Periyar Game Sanctuary.

Out of Delhi (Northwest India): Old and New Delhi sightseeing excursions include an evening Sound and Light Show at the Red Fort. Trips out of Delhi include Agra, with the magnificent Taj Mahal and the haunting beauty of Fatehpur Sikri; Khajaraho, its temples covered lavishly with erotic sculpture; Varanasi, the holiest Hindu pilgrimage site and perhaps the world's oldest living city; Leh, capital of Ladakh, with its Buddhist monasteries (*gompas*) and stark mountainous setting; and Jaipur or Udaipur in Rajasthan, with their Rajput palaces.

Out of Calcutta (East India): City sightseeing. After the stimulus of this great city, trips to the mountains or beaches are reviving; Darjeeling, a cool Himalayan hill station; mountainous Sikkim with its spectacular scenery and intriguing Buddhist culture; and the Andaman Islands, a developing beach resort with excellent coral reefs. Bhubaneswar, south of Calcutta, offers a rich opportunity to study the architecture of Hindu temples, and driving to the nearby cities of Puri and Konarak, one passes through rich farmlands (the beaches between Puri and Konarak are beautiful). Pilgrimage spots in Bihar, such as Bodhgaya, can be reached most easily from Calcutta. Assam's wildlife sanctuaries, Kaziranga and Manas, and Orissa's, Simlipal, are special-interest spots. *For Darjeeling, Sikkim, and Assam, one needs special permits.*

Out of Madras (Southeast Madras): Local sightseeing in Madras and in the temple towns of Kanchipuram and Mahabalipuram, both easily reached by road. Mahabalipuram has a delightful beach resort. Farther south by road are the ex-French city of Pondicherry and Chidambaram, with its fine temples. There are many easy excursions by air from Madras: flying to Coimbatore, one connects by bus or car to the "Queen of Hill Stations," Ootacamund; via Trivandrum one can reach Kovaluam, a beach resort, and the Periyar game reserve; Tiruchirapalli and Madurai, can be seen for their temples and other interesting sights; from Bangalore one can drive to Mysore; the Andaman Islands are a few hours away; and Hyderabad is also reached easily from Madras. Colombo, Sri Lanka, can be reached by air from Madras, Madurai, or Trivandrum, with international connections to Singapore and Bangkok.

"Connecting" One-Week Tours

Delhi-Calcutta (or reverse): A convenient air service provides "bus stop" service between major attractions across North India, from Delhi to Calcutta. Included could be Agra, to see the Taj Mahal, with a car ride to Fatehpur Sikri, or by air to Jaipur, Khajuraho, and Varanasi. From Varanasi, one could fly to Calcutta directly or via Kathmandu in Nepal or take a train to Patna with an onward domestic flight to Calcutta.

Bombay-Madras (southern circle tour): Out of Bombay, one has a number of choices: Goa with its beach resorts, Cochin, or Trivandrum. By road, one can reach Kavalam Beach Resort, Periyar Game Sanctuary, or Cape Comorin in the extreme south. Other trips include Bombay-Bangalore-Bombay-Hyderabad-Madras. From Trivandrum, one can fly to Madras or Colombo, Sri Lanka.

15-Day Tour of India. Two days in Delhi and New Delhi seeing sights. Sound and Light Show at Red Fort one evening. Proceeding from Delhi, spend two more days visiting Agra and Fatehpur Sikri. One day each in Jaipur, Khajuraho, Varanasi. Spend the next seven days visiting pretty Himachal Pradesh or northern Uttar Pradesh; Calcutta and Darjeeling or the Andaman Islands; Calcutta and Bhubaneswar, Puri, Konarak, and Chilka Lake; Madras, Mahabalipuram, Bangalore, and Mysore; Bombay, Ajanta and Ellora Caves, Sanchi.

21-Day Air Tour (with side trips) could include Bombay, the Ajanta and Ellora Caves outside Hurangabad, Jaipur, Udaipur, Delhi, Agra, Khajuraho, Varanasi and Sarnath, Kathmandu, Calcutta, Darjeeling or the Andaman Islands, Madras, Madurai, Cochin, and Bangalore.

30-Day All-India Air Tour could bring you to the following places, but at least one day of complete rest a week is strongly recommended:

Day:	Place:	Program:
1	Bombay	City sightseeing and, between mid-September and mid-May, excursion to Elephanta Caves.
2	Bombay	Fly in the morning to Aurangabad (30 min.). During the day, visit Ellora by bus or car and take a city tour.
3	Aurangabad	Visit Ajanta by bus or car; return to Aurangabad for overnight stay.
4	Udaipur	Fly in the morning to Bombay. Change flights. Leave by air for Udaipur (45 min.).
5	Udaipur	City sightseeing and excursions by car to Sas Bahu Temples, Nathdwara, or Eklingji.
6	Jaipur	Fly to Jaipur (35 min.).
7	Jaipur-Delhi	City sightseeing and visit Amber. Fly in the evening to Delhi (35 min.).
8 and 9	Delhi	Sightseeing of Old and New Delhi. Evening, attend "Son et Lumière" show at the Red Fort (except in monsoon).
10	Shimla	City sightseeing while staying at a perfect inn.
11	Shimla	Fly to Kullu and visit Manikaran or Naggar—Himalayan villages where you can spend the night.
12	Kullu-Delhi	Return to Delhi.
13	Agra	Fly in the morning to Agra (35 min.). City sightseeing, and visit Fatehpur Sikri. See Taj, by moonlight if possible.
14	Khajuraho	Fly in the morning to Khajuraho (45 min.). Visit temples.
15	Varanasi (Benares)	Fly in the morning to Varanasi (50 min.). City sightseeing and visit Sarnath.
16	Varanasi-Kathmandu	Early morning boat ride on the Ganges. Fly to Kathmandu (Nepal) in the morning (55 min.). City sightseeing.
17	Kathmandu	Visit places of interest around Kathmandu.

Day:	Place:	Program:
18	Calcutta	Fly to Calcutta in the afternoon (1 hr.).
19	Calcutta-Bhubaneswar	Morning: City sightseeing. Fly in the afternoon to Bhubaneswar (1 hr.). Visit temples in Bhubaneswar.
20	Bhubaneswar	Excursion by car to Konarak and Puri. Have lunch or snacks at Toshali Sands.
21	Bhubaneswar	Fly in the afternoon to Hyderabad (1 hr.).
22	Hyderabad-Madras	City sightseeing. Fly late evening to Madras (1 hr.).
23 and 24	Madras	City sightseeing and excursion by car to Mahabalipuram, Pondicherry, and Kanchipuram.
25	Madurai	To Madurai. City sightseeing.
26	Trivandrum	Continue to Trivandrum. City sightseeing and relax at Kovalam Beach. (We suggest staying overnight at Kovalam.)
27	Cochin	Fly in the morning to Cochin (30 min.). City sightseeing and boat ride on backwaters.
28	Bangalore-Mysore	Fly in the morning to Bangalore (40 min.). Go by car to Mysore; en route visit Srirangapatnam and Somnathpur. City tour.
29	Mysore	Excursion by car to Halebid and Belur, via Sravanabelgola.
30	Bangalore-Bombay	Leave in the morning by car for Bangalore. Fly in the afternoon to Bombay (1 hr., 25 min.).

THE CLIMATE. India's climate can be described as monsoon-tropical, in spite of some local variations like the winter rains in the northwest. Keep in mind that India is a subcontinent and make allowances for that fact in the following broad classification of the seasons: the cool weather lasts from October to the end of February, and the really hot weather from the beginning of April to the beginning of June, at which point the monsoon (rainy) season sets in until the end of September. The clear cool weather arrives again and moves gradually eastward and southward. The monsoon deserves special emphasis. This seasonal trade wind blows across the Arabian Sea and reaches India with almost mathematical regularity in May and traverses the country in June and July. It brings with it rain-laden clouds that water practically every part of India to some degree and return to the Arabian Sea in September and October. In the far north, the Himalayas, Nepal, Sikkim, and Kashmir can be extremely cold during winter, when many mountain passes and valleys are closed because of deep snow. The temperatures in these mountainous areas also vary a great deal, depending on elevation; evenings are generally cool.

Temperature and Rainfall Chart (Averages)

		Calcutta	Darjeeling	Delhi	Madras	Srinagar
Jan.	*	81	46	70	84	39
	†	0.37	0.53	0.99	1.41	3
Feb.	*	84	48	75	88	46
	†	1.17	1.19	0.83	0.41	3
Mar.	*	93	57	88	91	55
	†	1.36	1.88	0.51	0.29	—
Apr.	*	97	63	97	95	66
	†	1.75	4.14	0.33	0.61	—
May	*	97	64	106	100	77
	†	5.49	9.63	0.52	1.03	2
June	*	91	64	102	100	84
	†	11.69	24.18	3.03	1.86	—
July	*	90	66	97	97	88
	†	12.81	32.92	7.03	3.60	2
Aug.	*	90	64	93	95	86
	†	12.92	26.56	7.23	4.58	2
Sept.	*	90	64	93	90	82
	†	9.95	18.90	4.84	4.68	1
Oct.	*	90	61	93	90	73
	†	4.48	5.41	0.40	12.04	1
Nov.	*	84	54	84	84	61
	†	0.81	0.81	0.10	13.96	1
Dec.	*	79	48	73	84	48
	†	0.18	0.27	0.43	5.45	1

*Average maximum temperature in Fahrenheit.
†Average rainfall in inches.

WHEN TO GO. The peak tourist season runs from mid-September through March, but consider India a year-round destination. Just pick your climatic preferences. You can also plan a vacation around a spectacular festival, such as Dussehra in Himachal Pradesh, Wangala in Meghalaya, Carnival in Goa, Puram in Kerala, or Pushkar Fair in Rajasthan. If outdoor adventure is your objective, the time that it's offered will determine when you make your trip. During the winter months, for example, you can enjoy good skiing in the Himalayas at such places as Auli in Uttar Pradesh. Springtime anywhere in the Himalayas is spectacular, as orchards and hillsides come into bloom. In these regions, travel is best from April through October, though Manali in Himachal Pradesh is usually crowded in July.

Since India is such a vast land, additional information on the best times to visit is included in each chapter.

WHAT TO PACK. Travelers should realize that what is appropriate in the West isn't necessarily appropriate in the East. Only children can get away with short shorts. Men should dress in comfortable jeans or long shorts. A T-shirt is not offensive, but the topless look should be left to the wandering *sadhu* (Hindu holy man). If it's warm, women should wear skirts or lightweight slacks. Women who reveal bare legs under a conservative pair of shorts remain a dubious curiosity to the people of the East. To enter a holy shrine, women must wear a skirt, dress, or neat pants. To go bra-less is mindless; and any woman dressed in a scooped or plunging neckline must be prepared to accept wandering eyes and unflattering remarks. Travel in a Moslem area of India calls for even more discretion. Women should consider wearing *shalwar kameez,* the local long blouse and loose trousers, which are inexpensive and very flattering. At the beaches, bathing suits should be conservative.

When you pack, remember to travel light and pay attention to the climate and pack accordingly. In India, delicate fabrics do not stand up well to laundering facilities except at deluxe hotels. Plain cottons or cotton/synthetic blends are the most practical and the coolest in summer. Synthetic materials that don't "breathe" should be avoided.

There is no difficulty in getting over-the-counter medicines in India, but if you take prescription drugs, bring along enough for your stay, and then some. Also bring the following necessities: sewing kit, fold-up umbrella if you're traveling during the monsoon, premoistened towelettes, high-power impact resistant flashlight, and spare batteries (unless they're a popular size). Women should bring sanitary napkins or tampons—Asian brands are substandard.

Carry your passport and your money (most of it should be in traveler's checks) on your person. Keep multiple records of your checks and put a copy in each bag. Leave behind all your unnecessary credit cards.

Use good-quality soft luggage or well-made duffles that are waterproof, and keep them locked. Airlines will not accept untagged luggage. Add your destination address, with dates of arrival and departure, to luggage tags in case your bags go astray. Also put identification inside and remove all old tags.

While porters are available throughout India, it's a good idea to carry two small bags, to distribute the weight, rather than one large one. Airlines allow two pieces of check-in luggage and one carry-on piece, per passenger. Each piece of check-in luggage cannot exceed 62 inches (length + width + height) or weigh more than 70 pounds. The carry-on luggage cannot exceed 45 inches (length + width + height) and must fit under the seat or in the overhead luggage compartment.

HEALTH INFORMATION. For entry into India, no vaccination certificate or inoculations are required. Though immigration officials don't normally ask to see an International Health Certificate, this is one destination where it's smart to have one: The certificate contains invaluable information in case you need medical attention. See your doctor about obtaining one.

Three months before departure, talk to your doctor about protection (highly recommended) against malaria, typhoid, cholera, tetanus, polio (a shot or booster), measles, mumps, rubella, and meningitis. To get the latest inoculation information and requirements, contact *U.S. Department of Health and Human Services,* Public Health Services, Centers for Disease Control, Center for Prevention Services, Division of Quarantine, Atlanta, GA; tel. 404–639–2572.

Medical Precautions. It is advisable to carry a few basic remedies with you in India. Stomach upsets may be due as much to the richness of Indian food as to the lack of hygiene. Ask your doctor to prescribe suitable pills for stomach upsets.

The sun can be very dangerous in India if you are not careful. Beware of overexposure while sightseeing or on the beach even on overcast days. Take a sunscreen and use it. A hat is also a worthwhile precaution.

Always carry a tube of antiseptic cream, with adhesive or lint bandages, and treat any minor scratches, cuts, or blisters at once. India is a dusty place and dust carries infection.

Some doctors recommend taking daily multivitamin tablets, especially those with B-complex, during a tropical tour, when you are using more-than-usual energy and your diet may be changed from its usual pattern.

Water is said to be safe in most big Indian cities, but we still recommend drinking bottled or boiled water. If in doubt, drink hot tea, refreshing as well as safe. Be cautious over Indian food at first, if you are not used to such spiciness. Eat only fruit that can be peeled (do it yourself) and beware of green salad. Be especially careful about eating from roadside stalls or vendors. Soft drinks in India are plentiful and good; drink them rather than water from street vendors.

Warning: Japanese encephalitis, a mosquito-borne disease, occurs in epidemics during the summer months in some rural sections of India, Nepal, and Sri Lanka. The risks to travelers to urban centers is low. However, precautions should be taken to guard against mosquito bites: sleep in screened quarters, wear protective clothing, and use insect repellents liberally. If you wish to inquire about a new investigational vaccine for Japanese encephalitis, contact the Division of Vector-Borne Viral Diseases in Fort Collins, CO (303–221–6429) or the American Embassies in India, Nepal, or Sri Lanka.

If you plan to travel over 3,048 meters (10,000 feet) above sea level, remember to acclimatize. High-altitude sickness, an adverse reaction to low oxygen pressure, can be deadly. If your urine turns bright yellow, you're not drinking enough water. Eat foods that are high in carbohydrates and cut back on salt. Stop and rest immediately if you develop any of the following symptoms: nausea, loss of appetite, extreme headache or lightheadedness, unsteady feet, sleeplessness. If resting doesn't help, head for lower ground.

For an up-to-date directory of U.S. doctors who specialize in tropical illnesses, contact Dr. Leonard Marcus at the *American Society of Tropical Medicine and Hygiene*, 148 Highland Ave., Newton, MA 02160. Include a 9-×12-inch stamped envelope with $1 in postage.

The *International Association for Medical Assistance to Travelers* (IAMAT) is a worldwide association offering a list of approved doctors. For their directory, contact IAMAT at 417 Center St., Lewiston, NY 14092; in Canada: 188 Nicklin Rd., Guelph, Ontario N1H 75L; in Europe: 57 Voirets, 1212 Grand-Lancy-Geneva, Switzerland.

For $4.95, the U.S. government offers an annual publication, *Health Information for International Travel.* Contact Superintendent of Documents, U.S. Government Printing Office, Washington, DC 20402, tel. 202–783–3238.

HINTS TO THE DISABLED. Most countries in Asia, including India, are not prepared for travelers who are disabled. There are no special boarding ramps in buses, trains, airplanes, on public sidewalks, or at museums or monuments. Disabled travelers must rely on careful preplanning and should have a companion to assist them. Wheelchair travelers should have a collapsible, easily folding, compact wheelchair with lightweight, sturdy wheels for city sidewalks. Also bring easily removable accessories since replacement will be difficult.

For more information, we advise that you contact the following organizations:

Society for the Advancement of Travel for the Handicapped (26 Court St., Brooklyn, NY 11242, tel. 718–858–5483) provides, free of charge, a list of travel agents who are experienced in handling itineraries for disabled travelers.

Information Center for Individuals with Disabilities (20 Park Plaza, Room 330, Boston, MA 02116, tel. 617–727–5540) also offers useful assistance and a list of travel agents that specialize in tours for the disabled.

Moss Rehabilitation Hospital Travel Information Service (12th St. and Taber Rd., Philadelphia, PA 19141, tel. 215–329–5715) provides information on tourist sights, transportation, and accommodations in destinations around the world.

Mobility International (Box 3551, Eugene, OR 97403, tel. 503–343–1284) has information on accommodations and organized study around the world.

The Itinerary (Box 1084, Bayonne, NJ 07002, tel. 201–858–3400) is a bimonthly travel magazine for the disabled.

INSURANCE. We suggest that you be fully covered with theft, loss, and especially, medical policies before your arrival in India. Review your existing health and home-owner policies; some health insurance plans cover health expenses incurred while traveling, some major medical plans cover emergency transportation, and some home-owner policies cover the theft of luggage.

Several companies offer coverage designed to supplement existing health insurance for travelers:

Carefree Travel Insurance (Box 310, 120 Mineola Blvd., Mineola, NY 11501, tel. 516–294–0220 or 800–645–2424) provides coverage for medical evacuation.

Health Care Abroad, International Underwriters Group (243 Church St. West, Vienna, VA 22180, tel. 703–281–9500 or 800–237–6615) offers comprehensive medical coverage, including emergency evacuation.

International SOS Insurance (Box 11568, Philadelphia, PA 19116, tel. 215–244–1500 or 800–523–8930) provides medical evacuation services.

Travel Guard International (1100 Centerpoint Dr., Stevens Point, WI 54481, tel. 715–345–0505 or 800–826–1300) offers medical insurance, with coverage for emergency evacuation.

British travelers may apply to *Europe Assistance* (252 High St., Croydon, Surrey CR0 1NF, tel. 081–680–1234), which insures against sickness and motoring mishaps.

If your baggage disappears, report it to the police immediately. Airlines and many insurance companies insist that notification be made within 24 hours. Lost luggage is usually covered as part of a comprehensive travel insurance package that includes personal accident, trip cancellation, and sometimes default and bankruptcy insurance.

Several companies offer comprehensive policies:

Access America Inc. (Box 807, New York, NY 10163, tel. 800–851–280) is a subsidiary of Blue Cross-Blue Shield.

Near, Inc. (1900 N. MacArthur Blvd., Suite 210, Oklahoma City, OK 73127, tel. 800–654–6700).

Travel Guard International (*see* above).

The Association of British Insurers (Aldermary House, Queen St., London EC4N 1TT, tel. 071–248–4477) offers British travelers comprehensive advice on vacation insurance.

Flight insurance is often included in the price of a ticket when paid for with American Express, Visa, and other major credit cards. It is usually included in combination with travel insurance packages available from most tour operators, travel agents, and insurance agents. Most policies, however, don't cover natural disasters, such as landslides or earthquakes.

TRAVEL TO INDIA

BY AIR. Nonstop service to Bombay and Delhi is available from Great Britain and Europe; from Asia and Australia, one can fly nonstop to these two cities and to Calcutta and Madras. U.S. travelers can either take a direct flight with a stop in England or Germany or take a connecting flight with two or more planes and two or more stops.

From North America. Flying time from New York is about 16 hours, not including stops. *Air India* (in the U.S., tel. 800–223–7776; in Montreal, 800–268–9582; in Vancouver, 800–663–3433; in Toronto, 416–865–1033) offers a direct flight from Chicago or New York with a stop at London. *Pan American* (tel. 800–221–1111) also has a direct flight from New York with a stop in Frankfurt. The following airlines offer connecting flights: *KLM,* tel. 212–759–3600; *Air France,* tel. 800–237–2747; *British Airways,* tel. 800–247–9297; *Lufthansa,* tel. 718–895–1277; *Pakistan Airlines,* tel. 212–370–9157 in New York, in Chicago 312–263–3082, in Los Angeles 213–559–6409, in Montreal 514–626–5250, in Toronto 416–591–5490; *Gulf Air,* tel. 800–772–4642; *Thai Airways,* tel. 800–426–5204; *Royal Jordanian,* tel. 800–223–0470; *Singapore Airlines,* tel. 800–742–3330; *Air New Zealand,* tel. 800–262–1234.

Fares. Major airlines offer a wide range of ticket prices. As a rule, the earlier you buy the ticket, the lower the price and the greater the cancellation penalty (up to 100 percent).

An APEX (advance purchase) ticket on a major airline can be a good value if you can work around the restrictions: The tickets must be bought in advance, they restrict your travel time, and they include penalties for travel changes.

Charter flights offer the lowest fares but have limited departures, poor on-time records, and strict cancellation policies. Check with a travel agency about the charter flight packager's reputation. One popular charter operator is *Council Charter,* a division of the Council on International Educational Exchange, 205 E. 42nd St., New York, NY 10017; tel. 212–661–1414.

Somewhat more expensive—but up to 50 percent less than APEX fares—are tickets purchased through consolidators that buy blocks of tickets on scheduled airlines and sell them at wholesale prices. You may lose all or most of your money if you change plans, but you will be on a scheduled flight with less risk of cancellation than a charter. Once you've made your reservation, call the airline to make sure you're confirmed. Two popular consolidators are *UniTravel,* tel. 800–325–2222, and *Access International,* 250 W. 57th St., New York, NY 10107, tel. 212–333–7280.

You can also join a travel club that offers its members special discounts, such as *Moments Notice,* 40 E. 49th St., New York, NY 10017; tel. 212–486–0503; *Discount Travel International,* 114 Forrest Ave., Narberth, PA 19072; tel. 215–668–2182; and *Worldwide Discount Travel Club,* 1647 Meridian Ave., Miami Beach, FL 33139; tel. 305–534–2082.

Student Travel. *Council Travel,* a CIEE subsidiary, is the foremost U.S. student travel agency, specializing in low-cost charters and serving as the exclusive U.S. agent for many student airfare bargains and student tours. CIEE's 80-page *Student Travel Catalog* and "Council Charter" brochure are available from any Council

Travel office in the United States (enclose $1 if ordering by mail). In addition to the CIEE headquarters in New York (address above), there are offices in Berkeley, La Jolla, Long Beach, Los Angeles, San Diego, and San Francisco, CA; Chicago, IL; Amherst, Boston, and Cambridge, MA; Portland, OR; Providence, RI; Austin and Dallas, TX; and Seattle, WA.

From Britain. Flying time from London to Delhi is about nine hours, not including stops. *British Airways* (tel. 081–759–5511), *Air India* (tel. 071–491–7979), *Pan American* (tel. 071–409–0688), and *Thai Airways* (tel. 071–499–9113) all have direct flights. *Lufthansa, Royal Jordanian, Gulf Air, Air France, KLM,* and *Emirates Airways* offer connecting flights.

Fares. There are no APEX fares between London and India, but there are some charters. Check with your travel agent. There are also some promotional excursion fares and beyond this, some undercutting by a few travel agents in conjunction with lesser-known airlines. We do not vouch for the legality of this practice, but we cannot ignore the fact that it occurs. A good place to look for budget fares is in the London weekly entertainment magazine, *Time Out,* and the national Sunday press.

OVERLAND. It is unfortunately not at present feasible to travel overland from Europe to India by successive local train and bus connections. We hope politics will allow one to undertake the journey again in the future. You will need time, patience, flexibility, and a certain amount of stamina, but this trip would be a memorable one.

CUSTOMS ON ARRIVAL. The foreigner who enters India for a period of up to six months as a tourist has a choice of two channels for customs clearance. The Green Channel is for passengers who don't have dutiable articles or unaccompanied baggage. The Red Channel is for passengers with dutiable articles, unaccompanied baggage, or high-value articles that must be entered on a Tourist Baggage Re-Export Form (TBRE). If you leave behind an item declared on the TBRE, you will have to pay duty on the missing item.

You can bring in the following duty-free articles: personal effects (clothes and jewelry), a camera with five rolls of film, binoculars, a portable musical instrument, a radio or portable tape recorder, a tent and camping equipment, sports equipment (fishing rod, a pair of skis, two tennis rackets), 200 cigarettes or 50 cigars, .95 liters of liquor, and gifts not exceeding a value of Rs. 500 (about $50). You may not bring in dangerous drugs, gold coins, gold and silver bullion and silver coins not in use, or live plants.

AIRPORT TOURIST OFFICES. All major Indian airports have a tourist office or desk, usually open until late at night, where useful general information may be obtained. Some also have a hotel accommodation booking service (no commission) for those without confirmed reservations.

AIRPORT-TO-TOWN TRANSPORTATION. Transportation is plentiful, but if you take a taxi or auto rickshaw to your hotel or to the center of the city, be sure that the meter is working or agree on a price beforehand. Fares will vary from Rs. 40 to Rs. 100, depending on where you are and how far you must travel. Buses, operated by ex-servicemen's organizations, are run from some airports into city centers or to major hotels. The schedule is usually well timed with arriving flights, though not always with departures, and tickets cost Rs. 20–Rs. 30. Pre-paid taxi counters are available at Bombay, Delhi, and Madras. You pay a rate in advance based on your destination and are assigned a taxi; the fixed price takes care of the problem of bargaining. In Calcutta, bargain hard or wait for a metered taxi.

Staying in India

HOTELS AND OTHER ACCOMMODATIONS. The greatest single advance made by the tourism industry of India in the past decade has been in providing new and renovated hotels. In the cities and the major tourist centers, including beach and hill resorts, these hotels are well up to international standards, yet the prices are lower (except for rooms in Bombay) than similar hotels elsewhere. The need for hotel rooms is great, since India's tourist traffic (foreign and domestic) is now close to two million visitors each year.

The following list describes the range of accommodations that are available within India. If you decide to book accommodations in advance, remember to check carefully for what is included in the quoted room price. Also follow this advice once you arrive in India. Ask, in particular, about service charges and state taxes, which are frequently revised and vary from place to place.

Western-style Hotels. These hotels, which are the most expensive and accept credit cards, are much like their American and European counterparts. While many of these hotels have little local ambience, the deluxe hotels often surpass the West in luxuries and round-the-clock service. They also offer a full array of services for the business traveler: Secretarial services; access to copiers, computers, fax machines, and conference rooms; and executive suites are among the available amenities. The following abbreviations for credit cards are used: AE, American Express; DC, Diners Club; MC, MasterCard; V, Visa.

Indian-style Hotels. An Indian-style hotel is less fancy, less costly, and often comes with a bathroom that has a shower instead of a shower/bathtub. Rooms have the basic necessities, including air-conditioning, but no opulent appointments. Very few Indian-style hotels accept credit cards; some take traveler's checks, all take rupees.

Inns and Lodges. The traveler with an old-fashioned notion of class and charm should stay in any of the recommended inns and lodges. Some are rustic properties tucked away in the mountains; others are in hill stations and are elegant down to the sterling silver tea service that appears with breakfast and afternoon tea. Pampering is part of the experience. The cost is a bargain and meals are usually included. Don't expect to pay by credit card or traveler's check; payment is usually in rupees. Make your reservation well in advance.

Houseboats. Unfortunately, these are exclusive to Kashmir, now a troubled state. If the tensions quiet down, don't miss this idyllic experience. For details, see under Lodging section in the Kashmir chapter, and reserve before you arrive.

Camping. Some areas, such as the beautiful Maharashtra coastline, have camping sites, set up with roomy safari-style tents, available at nominal cost. You can also rent equipment from private companies or some state tourist departments.

Government Lodging. The Government of India and individual state governments, the Public Works Department (PWD), and the Forestry Department provide inexpensive accommodations throughout India. Some government tourist bungalows are fine; others provide a dreary ambience. PWD and Forest Department Inspection bungalows are usually rustic—small lodges or cabins set in secluded areas. Circuit Houses, originally built by the British, are also occasionally available and some continue to evoke the spirit of the Raj. Staying in PWDs, Forest Department Inspection Bungalows, or Circuit Houses can be difficult; since the cost is nominal, priority is given to Indian government employees.

Ratings. The ratings in this guide are based on double occupancy, excluding taxes and service charges. At press time, the rate of exchange was Rs. 17 to U.S. $1; or Rs. 26 to the U.K. pound sterling. For all accommodations, we use the following price categories: *Deluxe* over Rs. 1,450; *Expensive*, Rs. 950–Rs. 1,450; *Moderate*, Rs. 500–Rs. 950; *Inexpensive*, under Rs. 500.

GROUP HOTELS

Booking hotels has been simplified because of the number of hotel chains that cover important cities and popular tourist destinations in India. Some of the major hotel groups are listed below.

ASHOK GROUP (INDIA TOURISM DEVELOPMENT CORPORATION).

ITDC covers most key tourist destinations with properties ranging from five-star luxury hotels, such as the Ashok in Delhi and an ex-maharajah's palace in Mysore, to simple and inexpensive lodges for travelers in places of pilgrimage, hill stations, and major archaeological sites. ITDC also operates a nationwide travel agency, restaurants, duty-free shops at airports, city sightseeing tours in many major tourism centers, and sound and light shows. The group's accommodation facilities include the following:

Cities. *Lakeview Ashok,* Bhopal; *Airport Ashok,* Calcutta; *Hotel Ashok,* Bangalore; *Ashok, Janpath, Lodhi, Qutab, Ranjit, Samrat, Kanishka,* and *Ashok Yatri Niwas* in Delhi; *Hotel Brahmaputra,* Guwahati; *Bhasker Palace Ashok,* Hyderabad; *Lalitha Mahal Palace,* Mysore; *Patiliputra Ashok,* Patna; *Executive Ashok,* Pune; *Ranchi Ashok,* Ranchi; *Pinewood Ashok,* Shillong.

Resorts and Tourist Centers. *Agra Ashok,* Agra; *Aurangabad Ashok,* Aurangabad; *Kalinga Ashok,* Bhubaneswar; *Bodhgaya Ashok,* Bodhgaya; *Ashok,* Hassan; *Jaipur Ashok,* Jaipur; *Jammu Ashok,* Jammu; *Khajuraho Ashok,* Khajuraho; *Kovalam Ashok Resort,* Kovalam; *Ashok,* Madurai; *Temple Bay Ashok Beach Resort,* Mahabalipuram; *Madurai Pondicherry Ashok Beach Resort,* Pondicherry; *Nilachal Ashok,* Puri; *Laxmi Vilas Palace Hotel,* Udaipur; *Varanasi Ashok,* Varanasi.

ITDC also operates forest and travelers' lodges in Bharatpur and Manali.

Reservations. In the U.S., contact *Ashok Hotels Central Reservations,* Golden Tulip World-Wide Hotels, 437 Madison Ave., New York, NY 10022; tel. 212–838–6554 or 800–333–1212. In England, tel. 081–847–3951. In India, contact ITDC, *Central Reservations Service,* Ashok Hotel, New Delhi; tel. 600121.

CENTAUR GROUP. A subsidiary of Air-India with four hotels.

Cities. *Centaur Hotel,* Bombay (airport); *Centaur Hotel,* Delhi (airport).

Resorts and Tourist Centers. *Centaur Hotel,* Juhu Beach, Bombay; *Centaur Lake View Hotel,* Srinagar.

Reservations. Information about reservations may be obtained from Air-India offices in India. In the United States, reservations may be made through Air-India for any of these hotels, provided one is traveling on Air-India.

CLARKS GROUP. One of the older chains of good-quality deluxe hotels, with more modest rates and located in major provincial tourism centers.

Resorts and Tourist Centers. *Clarks Chiraz,* Agra; *Clarks Amer,* Jaipur; *Clarks Avadh,* Lucknow; *Clarks Varanasi,* Varanasi.

Reservations. *U.P. Hotels Ltd.* 1101 Surya Kiran, 19, Kasturba Gandhi Marg, New Delhi 110 001; tel. 331–2367, telex. 031–2447 or, in Bombay, 103 Embassy Center, Nariman Point, Bombay 400 021; tel. 23–0030, telex. 011–2733.

OBEROI GROUP. This chain should take the credit for raising the standards of luxury-grade hotel accommodations in India. The rates are at the top of the scale, but their services and comprehensive range of facilities are excellent.

Cities. *Oberoi Towers* and *The Oberoi,* Bombay; *Oberoi Grand,* Calcutta; *The Oberoi,* New Delhi; *Oberoi Maidens,* Delhi. In Nepal, *Soaltee Oberoi,* Kathmandu.

Resorts and Tourist Centers. *Oberoi Bhubaneswar,* Bhubaneswar; *Oberoi Mount View,* Chandigarh; *Oberoi Mount Everest* (under renovation), Darjeeling; *Oberoi Bogmalo Beach,* Goa; *Oberoi Palm Beach,* Gopalpur-on-Sea; *Jass Oberoi,* Khajuraho; *Oberoio Shambha-La,* Ladakh; *Oberoi Cecil* and *Oberoi Clarkes,* Shimla; *Oberoi Palace,* Srinagar.

Reservations. In the U.S., contact *Oberoi,* tel. 800–223–1474 or 212–682–7655, or *Loews Representation International,* tel. 212–545–2222 or 800–223–0888. In Britain, contact *Oberoi,* tel. 071–439–0268 or *Morris Kevan International,* tel. 081–367–5175. In India, contact *Oberoi Central Reservations Service,* The Oberoi, New Delhi, tel. 363030.

TAJ GROUP. Superb luxury hotels and resorts in key tourist areas offer the finest-quality facilities and services. This chain has started to open less luxurious hotels, usually called "gateways," that offer very good service and lower priced rooms.

Cities. *Gateway Hotel* on Residency Road, *Taj Residency* and *Taj West End Hotel,* Bangalore; *Taj Mahal, Hotel President,* and *Taj Mahal Inter-Continental,* Bombay; *Taj Bengal,* Calcutta; *Gateway Hotel* on Banjara Hill, Hyderabad; *Taj Coromandel, Connemara,* and *The Fisherman's Cove,* Madras; and *Taj Palace Hotel* and *Taj Mahal Hotel,* New Delhi.

Resorts and Tourist Centers. *Taj View Hotel,* Agra; *Gateway Riverview Lodge,* Chiplun; *Malabar Hotel,* Cochin; *The Aguada Hermitage, Taj Holiday Village,* and the *Fort Aguada Beach Resort,* Goa; *Rambagh Palace, Jai Mahal Palace Hotel,* and *Raj Mahal,* Jaipur; *Hotel Chandela,* Khajuraho; *Taj Lucknow Hotel,* Lucknow; *Savoy Hotel,* Ooty; *Taj Sawai Madhopur Lodge,* Rajasthan; *Lake Palace,* Udaipur; and *Hotel Taj Ganges,* Varanasi.

Reservations. Contact the worldwide offices of *Utell International* or *Taj Hotels:* in the U.S., Utell tel. 800–448–8355 or Taj tel. 800–458–8825 or 212–972–6830; in Britain, Utell tel. 081–995–8211 or Taj tel. 0800–282699 or 071–828–5909; in Canada, Utell tel. 800–668–1513 or in Quebec 800–387–8842, or Taj tel. 212–972–6830 (collect). In India, use *Central Reservation Service,* Taj Mahal Inter-Continental, Bombay, tel. 2023366.

WELCOMGROUP. One of the newest hotel groups, less than 20 years old, its rates are at the top end of the scale, and the services are excellent.

Cities. *Windsor Manor,* Bangalore; *Vadodara,* Baroda; *SeaRock,* Bombay; *Chola Sheraton* and *Park Sheraton,* Madras; *Manjarun,* Mangalore; *Maurya Sheraton,* New Delhi; *Maurya Patna,* Patna; and *Everest Sheraton* in Kathmandu, Nepal. In the planning stages is a hotel in Calcutta, where Welcomgroup has its headquarters.

Resorts and Tourist Centers. *Mughal Sheraton,* Agra; *Bay Island,* Andaman Islands; *Rama International,* Aurangabad; *Nilambag Palace,* Bhavnagar; *Usha Kiran Palace,* Gwalior; *Mansingh,* Jaipur; *Umaid Bhawan Palace,* Jodhpur; *Royal Castle,* Khimsar; and *Nedous Hotel* and *Gurkha Houseboats,* Srinagar.

Reservations. Contact *Loews Representation International:* in the U.S. and Canada, tel. 800–223–0888 or 212–545–2222; in Britain, tel. 44–1–5411199 in London or 800–282811 outside London. In India, contact *Welcomgroup Maurya Sheraton,* New Delhi, tel. 3014127.

In addition to the major groups listed above, privately operated hotels may be booked direct, or reservations may be made through hotel counters in many of the major airports in India on arrival. During peak seasons, especially in Delhi, it is best to arrive with hotel reservations.

HILL AND BEACH RESORTS. India owes its hill stations to the British who found the summer heat of the plains unbearable and retreated to mountainous hideouts. The lower spurs of the Middle Himalayas, Kashmir, the Vindhyas in Central India, the Nilgiri Hills in the south, with their pleasant climate, sparkling streams and alpine forests, offered ample scope for the development of such resorts which they called "hill stations." It then became customary for central and provincial governments to shift their headquarters to these summer seats, islands of modern civilization. While these places have ceased to be administrative centers in summer, the practice of retreating to hill stations during the hot period—with some of India's best hotels, plenty of sports, and exquisite scenery—survived and has become increasingly fashionable.

From Calcutta, the most easily accessible hill stations are at 7,000 ft.-high Darjeeling, which has a good range of hotels, and Shillong, 2,000 ft. lower, with pine forests and a delightful countryside. From Delhi, the nearest hill station is at Mussoorie, a lively and cosmopolitan little town; not much farther is Shimla, once the summer capital of the British Raj and currently the capital of Himachal Pradesh. The nearest hill station to Bombay is Mahabaleshwar, which offers jungle scenery, a refreshing climate, boating, and fishing. In the South, there is Ootacamund, the "Queen of Hill Stations," located in the rolling Nilgiri Hills and surrounded by acres of forests and tea plantations.

Recently, India has established an international reputation for its beach resorts. India has always had beaches, in boundless variety, but modern and comfortable accommodations and other facilities were lacking. As part of its overall planning for the development of international tourism, India launched an intensive program to create fully integrated beach resorts, especially in the south. The results can now be seen in the shape of some of Asia's most delightfully escapist resorts.

The availability of good beach resorts has added an entirely new dimension to traveling through India. The visitor on an extensive tour itinerary can now spend a few days of total relaxation in comfortable hotels or beach cottages, with superb beaches and guaranteed tropical sunshine. The government's Ministry of Tourism has plans for the extensive development of water sports in Goa, Kovalam, Puri, the Andaman Islands, Srinagar, and Jaipur. Currently, you can go para-sailing and windsurfing at Goa.

At present, the most developed resorts can be found at the following places. On the former Portuguese colony of Goa, the most comfortable resorts are the Taj Group's Fort Aguada Beach, set amid the ruins of a 17th-century Portuguese fortress and their Taj Holiday village, and Oberoi's Bogmalo Beach. The beautiful Maharashtra coastline to Goa's north is now dotted with lovely inexpensive tented beach resorts, set up by the state's tourist corporation. Beaches, here, are palm-fringed, unspoiled, and nearly empty of tourists; but this will undoubtedly change. In southwest India, there is the Kovalam beach in the heart of Kerala. Unfortunately, these beaches have been invaded by drug-smoking hippies and topless women bathers which has created problems at Kovalam. South of Madras, there is Mahabalipuram, where lovely resorts overlook famous temple ruins. The Andaman Islands in the Bay of Bengal and Lakshadweep Islands in the Arabian Sea, though not enjoying the easy access that mainland beach resorts have, offer spectacular opportunities for seeing coral reefs.

For further details of hill and beach resorts and how to reach them, see the regional chapters for the areas concerned.

STUDENT LODGING. STILE (Students International Lodgings Exchange), a nonprofit organization, operates through some 2,000 universities and other institutions of higher learning to help students exchange their lodging during their travel to India and more than 50 other countries. The membership fee of $29 includes two directories from which students may choose their partners. For further details, write STILE, 210 Fifth Ave., New York, NY (no phone), or contact its headquarters at 9 Rue Charcot 92200 Neilly/Seine, Paris, France (tel. 33–1.47472888).

MEETING THE PEOPLE AT HOME. Although there are enough museums, scenery, historic sites, and artistic monuments in India to keep the average tourist on the run, many travelers want to penetrate the surface to learn what Indian people are like in their own homes. The government tourist bureaus and the ITDC offices in Delhi, Bombay, Madras, and Calcutta have lists of families who board international visitors as part of an organized Meet-The-People project.

ROUGHING IT. This means traveling overland or hitchhiking, moving about the country in the cheapest-class trains or on buses, or bicycling, carrying your luggage on your back and sleeping in youth hostels or pilgrim accommodations. A number of specialized student-travel guidebooks and a few general guidebooks are now available for this particular kind of travel. Those who tour this way should gather material from various sources—guidebooks, local tourist centers, and meetings with people who have gone on similar trips. A visit to a specialized travel bookstore is recommended before leaving the home country. For further material on youth hostels, write *American Youth Hostels,* Box 37613, Washington, DC 20013; or call your local chapter. In Canada, write *Youth Hostels Association,* 1600 James Naismith Dr., Gloucester, Ontario K1B 5N4. In England, write *Youth Hostels Association,* 14 Southampton St., London WC2E 7HA. In India, contact *Youth Hostels Association of India,* 5 Nyaya Marg, Chanakyapuri, New Delhi 110 021; *World University Service,* University of Delhi, Delhi 110 008. A free Youth Hostel directory listing 16 places in the four regions of India is available from the YHA. In addition to maintaining hostels throughout India, the YHA sponsors cultural programs and organizes treks.

DINING OUT. When you visit India, mealtime can mean a delectable adventure with cuisines encompassing all of Asia, the Middle East, and the West. Indian dishes, which vary from region to region, are elevated to high art. Meats, fish, vegetables, lentils, and grains proliferate in splendid combinations—subtle and enticing.

Just as the cuisines are numerous so are the ambiences in places where you can eat. Hotel restaurants with live music create an elegant tone. Local restaurants, always ethnic, offer great meals at bargain rates in a setting that makes you feel far from home. Street stalls, cooking up simple specialties, can satisfy an eating urge at almost no cost.

Most restaurants don't have a dress code; casual, neat attire is fine. Unless you arrive with a large party, reservations are rarely required. But it is advisable to reserve to avoid disappointments. In major cities, restaurants normally stay open until

11 P.M. or midnight. In other areas expect an earlier dinner unless you're staying in a Western-style hotel. Visitors should also be aware that some Indian states also observe a weekly meatless day, when no slaughtering is done and no red meat is sold or served in most restaurants.

Spirits and Beverages. Indian beer, which is good and plentiful, costs Rs. 40–Rs. 60 per bottle at hotel bars, Rs. 25 in shops. Imported beer is usually unavailable. Imported whiskey and gin are expensive, around Rs. 850 per liter bottle. Indian whiskey, vodka, gin, and rum are good and cost Rs. 80–Rs. 160 per bottle outside hotels. Prices vary from state to state. Sikkim makes good rum and brandies; Goa has tasty sweet wines and *feni* (a potent liquor made from cashew nuts).

Gujarat observes prohibition, but foreign travelers may apply to the Gujarat Tourism Development Corporation for a permit that allows them to buy liquor in the state. The Government of India Tourist Offices in the United States also issue a three-month liquor permit allowing you to carry liquor into the state. Elsewhere, most localities have six "dry" days per month: one day per week (often coinciding with the weekly meatless day), and the first and last days of the month (coinciding with pay days).

Indian coffee has a caramel tang and is inexpensive. Tea is excellent and inexpensive, although those who take it black or without sugar should indicate so, since it is frequently brewed Indian-style with milk and sugar. India has a tremendous variety of good soft drinks that cost Rs. 2, and recently some delicious bottled fruit juices, including a refreshing mango fruit drink, costing Rs. 2.

Ratings. Restaurants in this guidebook are classified by price categories. Prices are per person and include a first course, main course, and dessert, but exclude costs for liquor, taxes, and tips. At press time, the rate of exchange was Rs. 17 to U.S. $1; or Rs. 26 to the U.K. pound sterling. The price categories are: *Deluxe,* over Rs. 110; *Expensive,* Rs. 80–Rs. 110; *Moderate,* Rs. 40–Rs. 80; *Inexpensive,* under Rs. 40.

TOUR-GUIDE SERVICES. English-speaking guides may be arranged in advance by your travel agent or by the agent's correspondent in India, but it is easier to get suitable services locally through *Government of India Tourist Offices* or through regional state-level tourist offices. Guides who are fluent in French, Italian, German, Russian, and Japanese will cost more. The following is a sample of approximate rates for guides:

Local sightseeing	Half day	Full day
Group of four or fewer	Rs. 50	Rs. 75
Group of five to 15	Rs. 75	Rs. 100

Inquire at *Government of India Tourist Offices* about overnight, long-distance travel guides. Tipping and paying for meals is customary. The *Archaeological Survey of India* has authorized guides, wearing green identification badges, at many national monuments. This service is free and saves you the problem of having to determine the level of competence of the many "guides" who throng tourist sites.

FESTIVALS AND SEASONAL EVENTS. India, one of the world's great spiritual sanctuaries, holds religious celebrations year-round, along with numerous fairs, cultural festivals, and sporting events. Since the specific dates of many celebrations each year are determined by the lunar calendar, check with the Government of India Tourist Office or your travel agent for details. Also refer to the individual state chapters for additional festivals and seasonal events.

January. *Desert Fair.* Five days of traditional dances and music at Jaisalmer, in Rajasthan.

January. *Pongal Festival.* This harvest festival in Kerala shows off the culture of South India with music, dancing, and tasty regional food.

Jan. 26. *Republic Day.* A big parade in Delhi celebrates India's adoption of its Constitution.

Late January. *Vasanta Panchami.* This Hindu festival is devoted to Saraswati, Goddess of Wisdom and Learning. In Bengal, her images are carried in a procession to bathe in the rivers. Kite flying is also associated with this festival.

February. *Losar.* This festival, which celebrates the Buddhist New Year, is especially big in Sikkim, where costumed *lamas* (monks) perform dances.

February. *Konark Festival.* This festival, held near the famous Sun Temple, highlights Orissa's culture, especially the Odissi danceform.

February. *Tirumala Nayak.* The great southern temple city of Madurai holds a spectacular procession of floats in temple tanks, with music and dancing—extremely colorful.

February/March. *Maha Shivaratri.* This celebration, honoring the Hindu god Shiva, is held at all Shiva temples. It's especially interesting at Guwahati, Mandi, Baijnath, Khajuraho, Konarak, Chidambaram, and Varanasi.

February/March. *Holi.* On the first night of this festival of spring, Hindu devotees light a bonfire in which a demoness goes up in flames as people dance. On the second day, kids throw colored water on each other and you. Dress in dispensible clothes; you'll be a favorite target.

February/March. *Kumbh Mela.* Haridwar's Kumbh Mela in Uttar Pradesh, the largest fair in India, honors the city's special religious sanctity. The next scheduled Haridwar Kumbh Mela is 1998. Ardh Kumbh Mela is 1992.

March. *Carnival.* Goa's fabulous Mardi Gras features masked dancers, floats, and good eating.

March. *Festival of Dances.* India's best dancers perform regional dances at the Khajuraho Temples in Madhya Pradesh.

April. *Baisakhi.* All of India celebrates the Hindu solar New Year with ritual bathing and visits to temples. This day is also important to Sikhs who hold a spectacular festival in Amritsar.

Mid-April. *Rongali.* This week-long festival celebrates the advent of spring and the Assamese New Year, with traditional dancing and singing in ethnic costumes—a fabulous event.

April/May. *Meenakshi Kalyanam.* Goddess Meenakshi's wedding is celebrated for 10 days in Madurai, with a huge procession in which vast chariots carry temple images through the streets to musical accompaniment.

April/May. *Puram.* During Kerala's most spectacular temple festival, decorated elephants carry images of Shiva in a colorful procession followed by fireworks.

May. *Buddha Jayanti.* Buddhists celebrate the birthday of Sakyamuni (Historic Buddha), his enlightenment, and death with rituals and chantings at monasteries. Special celebrations are held at major centers of Buddhist pilgrimage, such as Sarnath near Varanasi and Bodhgaya in Bihar.

May. *Id-ul-Fitr.* This Moslem holiday signals the end of Ramadan, a month-long period of daytime fasting to commemorate the descent of the Quran from heaven. Alms are given to the poor, prayers are offered, and there is much feasting and rejoicing—big in Kashmir.

June. The *Hemis Festival* in Ladakh honors the birthday of Guru Padmasambhava with masked lamas and musicians performing ritual *chaams* (dances).

June/July. *Rath Yatra.* The most spectacular temple festival in Puri, Orissa honors Lord Krishna with a procession of huge chariots.

August. *Raksha Bandhan.* During this festival for brothers and sisters, girls tie decorative threads around a boy's wrist and receive a gift in return.

August 15. *Independence Day.* Special commemorative celebrations mark the country's independence from British rule in 1947.

August. *Bakrid* or *Id-ul-Zuha* celebrates the sacrifice of Harrat Ibrahim (who willingly killed his son at the behest of God) with animal sacrifices. This solemn festival concludes with a feast and joyous celebration—big in Kashmir.

August. *Janmashtami.* On Lord Krishna's birthday, people flock to temples to see dance dramas enacting scenes from his life.

August/September. *Ganesha Chaturthi.* This festival honors Ganesha, the popular elephant-headed god of good fortune. In Bombay, his image is carried in processions and immersed in the sea.

August/September. *Pang Lhabsol* offers thanks to Mount Kanchenjunga, Sikkim's guardian deity. Stately dances are performed in monasteries by costumed lamas.

September. *Muharram.* Shiite Moslems commemorate the martyrdom of Mohammed's grandson, Hussain, who died at the battle of Karbala, with all-night chanting and intense self-flagellation—big in Kashmir.

September. *Onam.* Kerela celebrates this harvest festival with feasting, dances, and boat races by "snake" boats with up to 100 paddlers.

September/**October.** *Dussehra* or *Durga Puja.* This 10-day festival honors the Hindu goddesses Durga, Lakshmi, and Saraswati and commemorates the victory of Rama, who represents the force of good, over the force of evil, represented by the demon Ravana. This is one of India's most colorful celebrations, with the classic Ramayana enacted throughout the country. In West Bengal, Calcutta turns into one giant festival. Dussehra in Kullu Valley is the most famous event in Himachal Pradesh; also big at the Kamayaka Temple in Assam.

October 2. *Gandhi Jayanti.* On Mahatma Gandhi's birthday, pilgrims from all over India pay respect at the Raj Ghat in Delhi, where Gandhi was cremated.

October/**November.** *Diwali.* This festival, also called the Festival of Lights, is the most important Hindu celebration in India. Diwali signals the New Year and celebrates the day the hero Rama ended a 14-year exile. Oil lamps flicker in most homes. Celebrations are also held in many temples dedicated to Lakshmi and Kali.

November. *Shillong Tourist Festival.* Meghalaya's celebration coincides with Ka Pamblang Nongkrem, a five-day knock-out Khasi ceremony with colorful tribal dances.

November. *Guru Purab.* This major Sikh festival marks the birthday of Guru Nanak, the founder of the religion—especially festive in Amritsar and Patna.

November. *Pushkar Fair.* In a small village near Ajmer, in Rajasthan, tribal folk assemble with their camels for one of the world's most spectacular fairs and a pilgrimage to a nearby lake.

November/December. *Wangala.* Also called the Hundred Drums Festival, this four-day tribal celebration in Meghalaya is important to the Garos, who dress in traditional costumes and dance for days to musical accompaniment—an amazing affair.

BUSINESS HOURS AND HOLIDAYS. India has numerous government holidays, when the commercial world shuts down, and Sunday is the weekly day off. On workdays, shops are open 10 A.M.–7 P.M. Small traders stay open longer. Office hours are usually 10 A.M.–1 P.M. and 2 P.M.–5 P.M. Monday–Friday; Saturdays 10 A.M.–noon. Banks are open 10 A.M.–2 P.M. Monday–Friday; Saturdays 10–noon. International airports, some domestic airports, and a couple of luxury hotels have 24-hour money changing facilities. They're noted in the appropriate chapter. Post offices are generally open 10 A.M.–4:30 P.M. Monday–Saturday. Most museums are closed on Mondays and Site Museums (set near archaeological monuments) are normally closed on Fridays. All museums close for government holidays.

Try to get your business done in offices and banks as early in the day as possible. The afternoon lunch hours can extend into the late afternoon, especially in government offices. Carry business cards. Indians are conscious of this protocol.

TIPPING. Most major hotels include a service charge of about 10 percent on your bill, but waiters, room service, housekeepers, porters, and doormen all expect to be tipped, as they do in the rest of the world. You won't go wrong if you tip Rs. 5 per night to your room waiter. Bellboys and bell captains should be paid Rs. 2 per bag. If you are staying in a private home, it is customary to tip the domestic workers. Taxi drivers do not expect tips unless they go through a great deal of trouble to get you to your destination. However, tip a hired driver Rs. 10 for a half day's trip and Rs. 20–Rs. 25 for a full day's trip. It is also customary to give a hired driver money for his meals if you are on a day trip.

There are no service charges at government-run houses, bungalows, or hostelries. Tip individuals according to the rates just cited. Railroad porters should be given Rs. 2 per bag. Set the rate before he picks up your bags. Unusually heavy luggage should be tipped at a higher rate. When you arrive at the airport in Delhi, Bombay, Calcutta, or Madras, you can get your own baggage cart and wheel your luggage. If you opt for a porter, bargain the price to Rs. 2 per bag.

MEASUREMENTS. India has fully adopted the metric system. In this book, we have given most distances in miles and have listed heights in feet, but you will often be faced with the kilometer, meter, and centimeter. The kilometer is 0.62 mile, and an easy rule of thumb is that 8 kilometers equal 5 miles. There are, of course,

1,000 meters in a kilometer, and 100 centimeters in a meter. A meter is just over 3 feet in length and a centimeter is about four-tenths ($\frac{4}{10}$) of an inch.

Temperature in India is now measured by the Centigrade system. Water boils at 100 degrees Centigrade, which is 212 degrees Fahrenheit. Water freezes at 0 degrees Centigrade and at 32 degrees Fahrenheit. To convert to Fahrenheit, multiply Centigrade by nine-fifths ($\frac{9}{5}$) and add 32. To convert to Centigrade, subtract 32 and multiply Fahrenheit by five-ninths ($\frac{5}{9}$). There are 2.2 pounds in every kilogram, but we doubt that you will be buying anything in terms of weight here.

When you hire a car and buy gasoline (petrol), you should remember that four liters are slightly over a U.S. gallon and just under a British imperial gallon.

Indians refer to large numbers with two words peculiar to the country. You will often read in English-language newspapers and magazines about a *crore* of rupees and a *lakh* of people. Crore is 10 million; lakh is 100,000.

ELECTRICITY. Electric voltage is 220 volts, 50 cycles. If you have appliances that adapt to this voltage, bring converters with two-pin round-headed plugs.

TIME ZONES. Indian Standard Time is 5½ hours ahead of Greenwich Mean Time and 9½ hours ahead of the U.S. Eastern Standard Time. Thus, noon in India is 2:30 A.M. in New York. Nepal has recently stopped adhering to the ancient sundial and is now 15 minutes ahead of Indian Standard Time.

POSTAGE AND MAIL. Domestic and international mail delivery is reliable in India. The cost of an airmail letter (weighing 10 grams) to England, Europe, Canada, and the United States is Rs. 6.50. Aerograms cost Rs. 5; airmail postcards, Rs. 4.50.

The easiest way to receive mail in India is through a local office of American Express. Mail is held for 30 days before it's returned to the sender. It can also be forwarded for a nominal fee. To get your mail you show your American Express card or American Express traveler's checks, plus one piece of identification, preferably a passport. It's a free service to American Express traveler's check or card holders.

If you need to send a package that has to get to Europe or North America in 1–3 days, you can use a courier service. Contact Express Couriers, with offices in London and New York. Domestic offices are in New Delhi (62 Janparth, tel. 3318071) and Bombay (15 Rex Chambers Walchand Hirachand Marg, Ballard Estate, tel. 268855). Also in New Delhi, contact DHL International (tel. 3318947).

METRIC CONVERSION

CONVERTING METRIC TO U.S. MEASUREMENTS

Multiply:	by:	to find:
Length		
millimeters (mm)	.039	inches (in.)
meters (m)	3.28	feet (ft.)
meters	1.09	yards (yd.)
kilometers (km)	.62	miles (mi.)
Area		
hectare (ha)	2.47	acres
Capacity		
liters (L)	1.06	quarts (qt.)
liters	.26	gallons (gal.)
liters	2.11	pints (pt.)
Weight		
gram (g)	.04	ounce (oz.)
kilogram (kg)	2.20	pounds (lb.)
metric ton (MT)	.98	tons (t.)

Multiply:	by:	to find:
Power		
kilowatt (kw)	1.34	horsepower (hp)
Temperature		
degrees Celsius	⅗ (then add 32)	degrees Fahrenheit

CONVERTING U.S. TO METRIC MEASUREMENTS

Multiply:	by:	to find:
Length		
inches (in.)	25.40	millimeters (mm)
feet (ft.)	.30	meters (m)
yards (yd.)	.91	meters
miles (mi.)	1.61	kilometers (km)
Area		
acres	.40	hectares (ha)
Capacity		
pints (pt.)	.47	liters (L)
quarts (qt.)	.95	liters
gallons (gal.)	3.79	liters
Weight		
ounces (oz.)	28.35	grams (g)
pounds (lb.)	.45	kilograms (kg)
tons (t.)	1.11	metric tons (MT)
Power		
horsepower (hp)	.75	kilowatts
Temperature		
degrees Fahrenheit	⅝ (after subtracting 32)	degrees Celsius

OVERSEAS TELEPHONES AND TELEX. Telex facilities and international calls may be subject to long delays. Go through your hotel switchboard. All major hotels have excellent telex and telegraph services. Insist on a copy after the dispatch. Main post offices have cable services. India is linked to the United Kingdom, Australia, France, Japan, Hong Kong, Singapore, and other parts of Southeast Asia and Europe with direct dial codes.

Domestic long-distance telephones are also subject to delays. Use hotel services or the public telephones at major post offices. Ask for Lightning Call (the fastest, top-priority service) or Demand Call (the second-fastest). The rates are appropriately higher.

A local phone call in India costs a rupee when made from a pay phone located in airports, post offices, or even on streets in cities. With pay phones, you dial the number, then drop in the money once the connection is made.

If you need telephone assistance dial tel. 199; for directory inquiries dial tel. 197.

LAUNDRY AND DRY CLEANING. In deluxe and expensive hotels in India, you can get your laundry or dry cleaning done usually within a day or even faster if you pay a nominal surcharge. Outside these places, or at some resort areas, you must wait two days to have it done. Laundry methods in Asia differ from those of local laundromats in the United States and the United Kingdom. Mark Twain meant it when he said that the Indian *dhobi* (washerman) breaks stones with people's shirts. Ordinary cottons and linens are safely turned over to the dhobi, and will cost a fraction of what you are accustomed to paying. Dry cleaning chemicals are generally harsh, so you should not entrust delicate fabrics to the ordinary establishment. At higher-priced hotels, you can expect the standards of both services to be up to those of North America or Europe.

No matter how you are traveling, deluxe or budget, it's a good idea to carry a small container of laundry detergent to wash out clothes. Except for the monsoon seasons, light cottons or cotton blends will dry in one's bathroom overnight.

MUSEUMS AND GALLERIES. India has superb museums, especially for history, archaeology, and art. In addition to the large-scale museums in most cities, you will find smaller ones close to most major archaeological sites that can give much greater meaning to the study of the ruins themselves.

Most museums, galleries, and historical sites have a modest entrance fee, usually 0.50 paise–Rs. 1, and charge extra for photography, when it is allowed (some require that you check your camera before entering and retrieve it at the end of your visit). Tourist information counters have local listings of museums and their hours. Temples that are open to non-Hindus usually do not charge admission, but donations are customary. They will charge for photography, whenever it's allowed (most will not allow you to photograph in the inner sanctum). Entrance fees are charged at forts and other monuments, ranging from 0.50 paise to Rs. 2. Many locations charge neither for entrance nor photography.

BEHAVIOR. Each country has its own rhythm and pace, and in India there are many "countries," almost separate cultures, mores, and ways of behaving. Some general rules are these: remove your shoes before entering shrines, temples, and holy places, even if they seem in ruins (in some places, such as the Taj Mahal, cloth overshoes are provided for a small charge); casual clothes should not include brief shorts or revealing tops; do not drink alcoholic beverages, such as beer, on temple grounds; be restrained while photographing holy places (much as you would be in a cathedral or a synagogue). Many inner sanctums of Hindu temples are off limits to non-Hindus, and some temples are entirely off limits. Most temples have signs in English telling you so or guards at the entrance. Many Hindu temples and *gurud-waras* (Sikh temples) do not allow any leather to be worn inside—shoes, belts, handbags, or camera cases. Remember to walk clockwise around Buddhist structures, both inside and out. When a woman enters a mosque, she should cover her head. In some shrines, the sexes are also separated. Look around before you sit, and let the situation govern what you do.

BEGGING. India has a large number of beggars, partly because many Indians give money to them for religious reasons and partly because begging can be profitable for the beggar. On the whole, begging is a racket, and the central government and local authorities are trying to wipe it out. For the traveler with a pocketful of just-converted currency, it's hard to resist a plea, especially from a child. But remember, charity that turns children into beggars, dependent on the beneficence of foreigners, is misdirected. Travelers are encouraged to contribute to a worthy Indian charity or to visit a local school or medical clinic and make a donation to a responsible adult.

Foreign visitors to Indian cities are often approached by "students" or supporters of political parties who offer little paper flags in exchange for a "contribution." These requests should be politely resisted. At temples, Brahmin priests might approach you to give a blessing that involves touching your forehead with sandalwood paste and vermillion; a few rupees donation to the temple is expected in exchange.

SPORTS AND OUTDOOR ADVENTURES. India provides ample facilities for sports. Popular spectator sports are cricket, soccer, field hockey, polo, and horse racing. If you want to be more energetic, golf is available in large towns and in the hill stations. The Royal Calcutta Golf Club is the oldest club outside the British Isles, and New Delhi's course is listed in the *World Atlas of Golf* as one of the most outstanding 100 courses in the world. Other good courses are in Ooty, Ranikhet, Dalhousie, Shillong, Bangalore, Gulmarg, and Ladakh.

You can swim everywhere—in seas, lakes, and hotel pools. Hotels and private clubs that offer temporary memberships have tennis, squash, and badminton courts. At seaside and lake-front resorts like the Andamans, Srinagar, Goa, Kovalam, and Mahabalipuram, sailing, rowing, canoeing, scuba diving, snorkeling, para-sailing, some windsurfing (especially in Sri Lanka), fishing, and waterskiing are available. See regional sections for specific information on how to obtain gear for these activities.

Winter sports are also popular in India. You can ski in Gulmarg, Manali, Kufri, and Auli. You can ice skate in Shimla. In much of the north, you can raft, trek, mountain climb, hang glide, horseback ride, fish for great trout, or bike. You can go on an elephant or camel safari. Whatever your interest, it's happening somewhere in India. Just refer to this category in each destination chapter; also check the listings in *Special-Interest Tours,* above.

The *Mountaineering Institutes* in India (Himachal Pradesh, Uttar Pradesh, and West Bengal) and Nepal also offer inexpensive summer trekking and mountaineering experiences that are open to foreign youngsters. For details, refer to each destination chapter. The *Youth Hostels Association* (5 Nyaya Marg, Chanakyapuri, New Delhi 110021), with branches throughout India, offers treks even for children as young as 12 years. Also contact the following organizations that provide information on sports: *Bangalore's Spark Club,* which includes people in their 60s; *Indian Mountaineering Foundation,* Benito Juarez Road, New Delhi 110021; the *Himalayan Club,* Box 1905, Bombay. Outdoor enthusiasts should also contact individual state tourist departments.

HINTS TO PHOTOGRAPHERS. Some people whom you want to photograph may demand money, so carry a pocketful of small coins if you feel you must pay. Most Indians are good natured about having their photographs taken and will say "thank you," but Moslems may object, especially where women are veiled. Be cautious about photography in tribal areas. Military installations, airports, bridges, railway stations, and trains are not supposed to be photographed for security reasons.

Color and black-and-white film is available in larger towns and cities, made locally or imported from eastern Europe or Japan. A roll of 35 mm, 36-exposure film will cost Rs. 50–Rs. 90.

Warning. Normally, five trips through modern airport scanners won't affect film; six or more trips, and the film could be damaged. In many airports you can avoid the scanner by showing your camera to the security-check officials. Some officials will demand that you disassemble your camera and remove the lens and all batteries. If you don't trust scanners, bring special lined film-protection bags. Dust is a problem throughout India; buy an inexpensive skylight filter to protect your lens and keep your camera under wraps when it's not in use.

WILDLIFE SANCTUARIES. India has 59 national parks and 254 sanctuaries, a striking number for its land mass and population. Before 1947, wildlife were not protected. Travelers on safaris indiscriminately hunted on trips sponsored by maharajahs and their English guests, decimating the rich splendor of wild animals from the Himalayas to the central grasslands, the sparsely forested south, and the marshes to the east.

The government has done much to develop sanctuaries and reserves in the face of the constant demands of the population for land and the needs of the rural people who live on the perimeters of these habitats. Poaching and illegal logging are severe problems. Currently, all the reserves are jammed into 4 percent of the country's geographic area.

In 1952, 13 species were on the endangered list; today, the list contains 70 species of mammals, 16 species of reptiles, and 36 species of birds. Among the endangered species are the snow leopard (fewer than 300 are left), male musk deer (widely hunted for a gland whose secretions are used in the manufacture of cosmetics in the West and elsewhere), desert fox, golden langur, bison, Himalayan ibex, sloth bear, lesser florican, and black-necked crane. The Asian lion has risen to only 200 in number after it dwindled to 50 in the 1920s. Tigers, the symbolic mascot of India, were killed so frequently that by 1970, there were only 1,500. Under the ambitious "Project Tiger," the government banned killing and set up nine reserves; the total number has risen dramatically to 1,800.

India's sanctuary program is caught between the economic problems of a developing country—the rural poor and their needs versus the need for habitats for wildlife. Much of India's wildlife is peculiar to the subcontinent, and you should avail yourself of every opportunity to visit some of the sanctuaries. Among India's unique animals are the swamp deer, the Asian lion, and the four-horned antelope. The spotted chital deer has its home in India, Pakistan, and Nepal, and the prehistoric-looking one-horned Indian rhinoceros is found only in India and Nepal. The Indian bison is not a bison at all but a gaur, a species of wild ox.

There are also excellent reserves in Nepal (see appropriate chapter). All states have booklets on their specific sanctuaries, and the Government of India Tourist Office publishes a number of brochures outlining all the reserves. We highly recommend a visit to this unique aspect of India's mosaic. See regional sections for complete listings of each sanctuary and provisions for accommodations and travel.

SHOPPING. India, which will please the bargain hunter, has an array of exotica well designed to embellish the collection of even the most discriminating souvenir hunter. Many of the items combine good design, marvelous color, and elegant usefulness—others may look perfect in a romantic "moonlight on the Ganges" type setting, but not quite so well on your hall table. We have no warnings to proffer; we just suggest that before you take a tumble for some irresistible object, picture it in its eventual setting—you will come away with the best India has to offer!

State-run emporiums sell good-quality, regional crafts at fixed prices. You will find these handloom-handcraft emporia in many large cities, including Bombay, Calcutta, Madras, and New Delhi. For "local color" and some bargaining, visit the bazaars where silversmiths, goldsmiths, gem-cutters, enamelers, and copper beaters work and sell in tiny shops.

Street peddlers usually ask about three times the price they hope to get. It is best to decide beforehand how much the coveted object is worth to you and to remember that the vendor has been at the game much longer than you have.

From Agra comes exquisite marble inlay work. Jewels are sliced petal thin and embedded in the marble with such precision that you cannot see the joints even with a magnifying glass. This craft goes back to the days of the Moguls. A set of dessert plates would be a memorable possession. Talking of plates, enamel *Nirmalware* looks like Rajput paintings and is handsome; the three-metal plates from Thanjavur depict scenes with an Oriental love of detail.

Genuine pieces of the Pallava, Chola, or even Vijayanagar period bronzes are usually not obtainable on the market. You will be lucky if you obtain a good imitation at a reasonable price. Genuine antiques need export permits, which are not likely to be granted for any but the most ordinary pieces.

You should take a look at India's hand-loomed rugs. It is India, not Iran, that has the world's largest rug industry—whose products are close in design to their Persian counterparts because they were introduced by the Moguls. Rather more than a simple souvenir, an Indian rug is an attractive investment. And in Delhi and many of the Himalayan towns, where there are groups of Tibetan refugees, you will find superb rugs and other craft objects in an entirely different and remarkably attractive artistic tradition.

To get back to the pocket-sized items, there are enchanting terra cotta or brightly painted wooden toys for children and for grown-ups with taste. For something less breakable, there is metalwork like the jet and silver *bidriware* and the wares of Moradabad which combine bright enamel and brass. You can also pick up attractive and simple souvenirs made of more unpretentious materials like pottery, hand-painted tiles, ceramics, and cane or bamboo ware.

If you want to brighten your wardrobe and express your personality, you might choose a pair of embroidered slippers or gilt sandals that would look spectacular in a Western boudoir or beach house. You will be dazzled when confronted with bags, belts, scarves, shawls (like the Kashmiri "Paisley" ones, recently put back into the high-fashion category), and all sorts of costume jewelry in precious metals, filigree, gems, jade, or ivory.

If you can resist buying a sari—or at least an embroidered silk stole—you will be one of the very few women of cast-iron willpower in the Western world. Indian textiles have a variety and beauty unmatched anywhere else—you can have the fiber, the color, and the texture you choose. The south specializes in heavy silks and brilliant contrasting colors. Uttar Pradesh is famed for its *chikan* embroidery on white voile and Varanasi for its brocades. Bengal offers off-white shot with gold, while the Deccan provides a choice of summer saris. The Chanderi cottons have tiny floral motifs in gold while their first cousins of Maheshwari prefer interesting variations in texture to a pattern. Either could make an unforgettable summer evening dress. True Oriental splendor is attained in the Jamdani muslins—as costly as they are beautiful, since eight men may spend all day weaving a single inch—and in the Baluchar saris of eastern India whose intricate designs are woven by a secret process handed down from generation to generation. Rajasthan introduces a bright and gay note in its saris made by the "tie and dye" method, which results in startling and successful patterns.

Indian women manage to wear their saris with spectacular grace—but, of course, they have been doing so for several millennia. If you feel bound to imitate them, then you will need a *choli* (blouse) and a long skirt petticoat, threaded through the top like men's pajamas, a draping lesson, and a good memory (or a notebook) to avoid tying yourself up in knots. So try draping your sari once, and if you feel utterly unself-conscious, wear it that way.

Particular handicraft emporiums, shopping streets, and bazaar areas are listed under each town heading in the regional sections of this guide, together with particular local specialties.

A word of warning: Be alert when shopping. Bargain hard and generally do not trust shopkeepers' descriptions of age or quality. Check goods after paying, and count your change. Do *not* let taxi drivers take you to their favorite shops—you will pay much more.

NIGHTLIFE. India's nightlife is tame in comparison to that of the Western capitals, Bangkok, and Hong Kong. Delhi, Bombay, Madras, and Calcutta all have a handful of discos and sedate dinner dances, and floor shows are usually featured in the major resort areas. Most Indians entertain at home. What the cities offer most at night are cultural shows of outstanding Indian music, dance dramas and recitals, folk theater, and regional-language theater. Philharmonic orchestras can be heard in Bombay. Zubin Mehta, a native son who won international renown as conductor of the New York Philharmonic Orchestra, recently brought down the house. See regional sections for detailed information such as *jatras* in Calcutta, *Kathakali* in Kerala, and *Ram-lila* in Delhi.

Traveling in India

BY AIR. Since India is more of a continent than a country, good internal air transportation has proved to be as vital to India's development as a nation as it is to you, the tourist. The state-owned *Indian Airlines* serves over 73 cities, and *Vayudoot,* a feeder airline with mostly 19-seat Dornier 228s, operates over 45 routes out of major and regional airports throughout India. Domestic flights usually operate on a daily basis, but in small, remote destinations the flights are less frequent, the aircraft smaller, and there are more delays or cancellations. For domestic flights on Indian Airlines or Vayudoot, get your tickets when you purchase your international ticket to the subcontinent. In the summer, some tickets are hard to get once you've arrived.

It is vital to reconfirm your flights individually, at least 72 hours before departure. If you wish to change your itinerary as you go along, you run the risk of failing to get a seat on the desired flight, since each journey can only be changed once you get to your next destination. Waiting lists are common, but the airlines have a high number of no-show passengers, so one often does get on at the last minute, especially on larger jet aircraft.

Check in no later than 90 minutes before domestic flights and two hours before international flights. Even on domestic flights there is advance seat selection and rigid check-in procedures. Expect tight security at all airports. Do not pack a pocketknife in your hand luggage. Even golf clubs are not allowed as hand luggage. Checked-in baggage also must be identified on the tarmac, next to the aircraft, before boarding. This careful security has led to a high safety rate on these airlines.

Also, plan on paying an airport tax of Rs. 300 for international flights and Rs. 150 for flights to neighboring countries. There is no airport tax on domestic services.

Fares. A sample of one-way fares: Delhi–Bombay, $115; Delhi–Calcutta, $132; Delhi–Madras, $162; Delhi–Srinagar, $77; Delhi–Agra, $23; Delhi–Jaipur, $28;

Calcutta–Madras, $137; Calcutta–Point Blair, Andaman Islands, $134; Calcutta–Bagdogra, Darjeeling, or Sikkim, $45; Bombay–Madras, $110; Bombay–Trivandrum, $124.

Special concessional fares are available on both carriers, such as "Discover India," which allows unlimited travel for 21 days within India for $375. Payment must be made in foreign currency. Other special fares promote regions of the country and offer a 50 percent concession. From November to April, Indian Airlines also offers a 30 percent discount on round-trips to Srinagar for groups of four or more persons staying 3–14 nights. A special fare ticket can be purchased (and reservations made) when you book your trip to India, or on arrival, but in the latter instance it must be bought in foreign currency.

Students aged 12 to 26, with valid student identity card, qualify for a 25 percent concession (payable in foreign currency) on Indian Airlines flights. A child under age two who sits on your lap pays 10 percent of the adult fare. Children aged 2 to 12 pay 50 percent. *The Travel Junction* is a handy monthly updated guide to all schedules and fares and provides airport information. It costs Rs. 15 at bookstores amd newspaper stands. Indian Airlines and Vayudoot offices in all sectors also have free information.

On arrival, you can expect to wait 15 to 20 minutes for your baggage. Use this time to visit the airport tourist desk, hotel accommodations desk, or attend to banking. Hang on to your baggage tags since you may need to show them before you will be permitted to leave the airport with your belongings. Although early morning mist can cause delays at certain times of the year, most flights depart more or less on schedule, even during the stormy monsoon. High-season "extra" flights are more frequently delayed, sometimes for hours.

If you take a coach from the city air terminal, it will usually be timed to arrive two hours before departure. In the larger centers, ex-servicemen's organizations run the town-to-airport transport service. Indian Airlines and local tourist offices do the job in smaller places, but there are seldom any buses for flights departing early in the morning. Coach fares usually range from Rs. 15 to Rs. 30, depending on the distance. Taxi fares should be based on the meter or set in advance. A of couple larger airports have a pre-paid taxi counter where you pay the fare beforehand and are assigned to a taxi. Taxi fares are usually two to three times the coach fare, and are a good value for two or more persons traveling together.

BY TRAIN. India's first passenger train ran in 1853, from Bombay to Thana—a distance of 21 miles. In the following year, the line from Calcutta (Howrah) to Raniganj was opened and, by 1880, all the major cities of India had been connected. The present railway system is the fourth largest in the world, having a route total of 37,700 miles. It is the second largest system in the world under one management, the USSR claiming first place. Every day, 10 million people in India travel by train. There are over 7,000 stations in the country.

Speeds are slow compared with Western countries, and the climate and distance are not generally conducive to rail travel for tourists or business travelers. It is also impossible to keep non-air-conditioned cars free of the all-pervading dust. Distances in India are such that air travel is much more sensible between the main cities. The distance between Bombay and Delhi is covered in 18–24 hours by train, but in two hours by air. For those with time and an interest in seeing India's countryside and the variety it embraces, however, train travel is the only way to go. Most of the fast trains stop about once an hour for about 10 minutes, giving travelers an opportunity to stretch their legs and observe the continually changing landscape and markings of Indian culture, such as the variations in dress.

India is a paradise for the railway enthusiast. There are still many steam locomotives to be seen, and while most of the fast trains are now electric or diesel hauled on the broad gauge, steam is still king on the narrow gauge. The mountain railways, the Shimla and Darjeeling lines in the Himalayas, the Matheran Hill Railway near Bombay—all narrow gauge—and the Nilgiri Railway meter gauge track in the south are well worth a visit.

Classes of Accommodation. There are five classes of passenger service on Indian trains—air-conditioned (AC) sleeper, first, AC two-tier sleeper, AC chair, and second. Air conditioning is found mainly on the top express services between major cities and provides decent facilities, cleanliness, and service. In this class, reasonable food and all bedding are supplied at no extra cost. First and AC two-tier sleeper classes are charged on the same fare basis. A number of special "superfast" trains between major cities entail a surcharge. Air-conditioned cars consist of two- and four-berth compartments, with transverse upper and lower berths opening off a corridor which has toilets, Western-style and Indian at each end. These coaches are usually vestibuled. They are well equipped and bedding, including towels and toilet paper, is provided without extra charge. An attendant is on duty in each car. The compartments are larger than those in Western countries and the standard of comfort compares favorably. First-class cars are similar in layout and have an attendant, but the standard of accommodation is comparable to the European "couchette"; some first-class cars, but by no means all, are vestibuled. Two-tier AC sleepers provide couchette-type berths in open saloons and second-class AC chair cars have reclining seats. In both first-class and second AC sleepers, the lower berth must be utilized to full seating capacity between 6 A.M. and 9 P.M.; thus a four-berth compartment will seat six by day. Bedding may be hired either on the train, in the case of certain important trains, or at the starting station, on payment of a small fee. Western travelers should provide their own toilet paper except in AC class. Ordinary second-class has hard seats and is usually very crowded. It is not recommended for Western travelers.

Train Services. All the major cities are linked by "Mail" trains which, except for the special expresses, are normally the fastest trains. Most have AC class accommodations and many, but not all, have dining cars. The most famous is *The Frontier Mail*—Bombay (Central) to Amritsar. *The Deccan Queen* is a luxury day train but is not air-conditioned—Bombay (Victoria Terminus) to Poona (Pune); this is a scenic route as the line rises about 1,000 feet in 16 miles, winding up the hillside, through 25 tunnels and over eight high viaducts. This line is electrified. In recent years a tourist train, *The Taj Express,* with first-class accommodation has been put on between New Delhi and Agra. It takes three hours to cover the 124 miles. A similar "tourist" express, The Pink City, also daily links Delhi and Jaipur.

There are also the special expresses, of which pride of place must be given to *The Rajdhani,* which carry only AC and second AC classes and two-tier passengers. These trains have cut the overall time from Bombay to Delhi by five hours and from Calcutta to Delhi by seven hours. They only run two days in each week.

One of the most fascinating rail travel experiences available in India, if not in the world, is the *Palace-on-Wheels,* which uses several historic, and extremely luxurious, private rail coaches of ex-maharajas for two to seven-day inclusive package tours from Delhi to major tourist destinations in Rajasthan. One travels and lives in this unique environment, with sightseeing side trips arranged in such places as Jaipur, Agra, Jaisalmer, Udaipur, and Jodhpur. For information and bookings, contact Central Reservations, Rajasthan Tourism, Chandralok Building, 36 Janpath, New Delhi 110 001. The fare is currently $940. You can also book your trip through your travel agent, but expect the fare to be higher.

COMPARATIVE DISTANCES AND TIMES

Broad Gauge

Bombay-Delhi 860 m (1,384 km)	
Rajdhani Express	18 hrs.
Frontier Mail	24 hrs.
Bombay-Calcutta, 1,223 m (1,968 km)	36 hrs.
Delhi-Calcutta 892 m (1,437 km)	
Rajdhani Express	17 hrs.
Mail	23 hrs.
Delhi-Madras 1,294 m (2,185 km)	40 hrs.
AC Express	30 hrs.
Calcutta-Madras 1,039 m (1,662 km)	25 hrs.

Meter Gauge

Delhi-Bikanir 289 m (463 km)	12 hrs.
Delhi-Jodhpur 388 m (625 km)	15½ hrs.
Delhi-Udaipur 466 m (750 km)	20 hrs.

Itineraries. Indian Tourist Offices abroad or the tourist guides at the offices of the Western and Central Railways at Bombay, the Eastern Railway at Calcutta, and the Northern at Delhi will assist in planning itineraries.

There are few day trips that can be taken owing to the distances involved, but a visit to Agra from Delhi can be made in a day by using *The Taj Express;* this allows nine hours for sightseeing. The scenic route to Poona (Pune) can also be enjoyed in a day by leaving Bombay at 7 A.M., arriving at Pune at 11:35 A.M. and returning at 3:25 P.M. reaching Bombay at 7:40 P.M. The Matheran Hill Railway is on this route and can be visited in the day. There is also a daily return train service from Delhi to Jaipur, which allows time for sightseeing by taxi or tour coach in the Pink City.

Timetables, Fares, and Reservations. A *Tourist Railway Timetable* can be obtained at the Government of India Tourist Offices abroad. It gives much useful information. For the railway enthusiast, the *All India Railway Timetable* is published by the Railway Board, but it is difficult to obtain outside India. Thomas Cook's superb *International Railway Timetable* also gives details of many Indian rail services. In India, railway station bookstores sell Eastern, Western, Northern, and Southern Zone timetables.

Fares, which are low by Western standards, are calculated on a kilometer basis, but become cheaper the greater the distance. When you travel first-class, however, the ticket cost will be close to the price of airfare.

Kilometers	AC Class	Sleepers	First Class	Second Class
200	Rs. 220	150	105	40
1,000	Rs. 800	475	400	120
1,500	Rs. 1,050	600	470	150
2,000	Rs. 1,300	750	600	180

The above fares apply to all trains, except the Rajdhani Expresses. The second-class fare shown is for mail or express trains; fares for passenger trains only are about $\frac{2}{3}$ of the mail or express fare.

Special fares apply for the Rajdhani Expresses, which include bedding, meals, and the reservation fee. They are

	AC sleeper	Two-tier	AC chair
Bombay–Delhi	Rs. 1,350	600	400
Calcutta–Delhi	Rs. 1,370	760	405

For a few fast trains, such as the Frontier Mail, Taj Express, Tamil Nadu Express, a "Rapide" supplement is charged, irrespective of the distance traveled.

AC class	Rs. 25
First class	Rs. 12
Second AC class	Rs. 12
Second class	Rs. 6

Prior reservations are essential for all Mail and Express trains. If you travel overnight, you must also reserve a sleeping berth or you could be put off the train. Fees are

AC class	Rs. 10
First class 1A two-tier sleeper	Rs. 4
Second AC chair class	Rs. 2
Second class	Rs. 2

Sample fares between major cities are

	Distances km	AC class	AC two-tier sleeper	First class
Delhi–Agra	199	Rs. 220	150	105
Delhi–Madras	2,194	Rs. 1,400	780	660

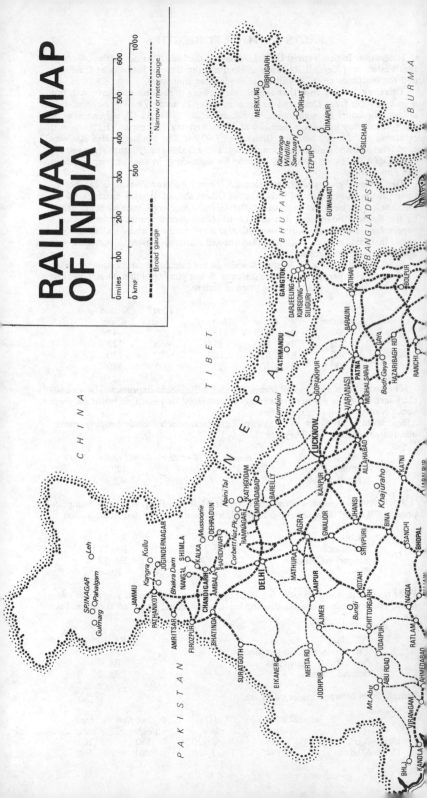

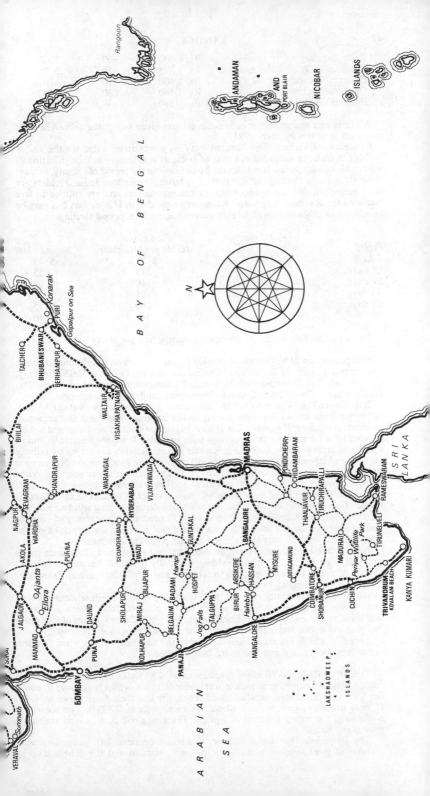

Delhi–Bombay	1,388	Rs. 1,000	600	500
Calcutta–Delhi	1,441	Rs. 1,025	610	510
Calcutta–Bombay	2,173	Rs. 1,400	790	670
Calcutta–Madras	1,663	Rs. 1,160	680	550
Bombay–Madras	1,279	Rs. 580	—	460

All fares and charges are approximate and are given as a guide only. Allow for projected increases by early 1991.

Concessional Tickets. The "Indrail Pass" is a wonderful value for the visitor wishing to make an extended rail tour of India. It is sold only to foreign nationals who reside outside India. It entitles the holder, within the period of validity, to travel by all trains, including the Rajdhani Expresses, throughout India. Holders are not charged the fast train supplement or reservation fees and are entitled to free meals on the Rajdhani Expresses. Rates are calculated in U.S. dollars but may be purchased in other approved foreign currencies, such as pound sterling.

Period	AC superior class	First class/ AC sleeper/AC chair	Second class
7 days.........	U.S. $180	$ 95	$ 45
15 days........	230	115	55
21 days........	280	140	65
30 days........	350	175	75
60 days........	520	260	115
90 days........	690	345	150

Fares for children under 12 are approximately half the above rates.

Indrail passes cannot be purchased outside India; they can be bought only through leading travel agents or the Railway Central Reservation Offices at Delhi, Bombay, Calcutta, Madras, Secunderabad, Hyderabad, Rameswaram, Bangalore, Vasco-Da-Gama, Jaipur, Trivandrum Central, Chandigarh, and Agra Cantonment.

Rail Travel Tips. Travel by rail in India is safe and comfortable, but can be confusing until one knows the ropes, owing to the booking procedures and crowded, confused conditions of stations. Local travel agents can obtain bookings and tickets on your behalf, but may have to borrow your passport. It is quite feasible to undertake these arrangements for oneself because special facilities are set up by railway authorities for foreign tourists in major rail centers. The local tourist office or your hotel will tell you which ticket office to go to for your particular journey. When booking, look for the "Tourist Information" section of the reservations office, where staff are usually helpful, if slow. They will issue a voucher, which one usually takes to the adjacent ticket purchase counter, where the actual booking will be made and the ticket paid for. Check which station you will need and allow plenty of time for finding your seat on the train—the sleeper and seat numbers are displayed on the platform and on each carriage, along with the passengers' names.

It is advisable to take overnight sleepers, AC or two-tier first class, since travel by night is cooler. In AC class, bedding is usually provided, but not in two-tier first class, unless one arranges this in advance and pays a little extra. Remember to reserve your sleeping berth.

At the departure station, get any help from the station superintendent. Passengers' names are posted on notice boards on the platform from which your train will leave, and on each carriage. Local people will generally be tolerant of foreigners jumping the queue for information, but not at ticket purchase windows.

Travel by rail is not recommended during the summer months when the heat is the most oppressive and trains are overcrowded.

THE HILL RAILWAYS are of special interest. The Kalka-Shimla Railway starts from Kalka and climbs to Shimla in just under 60 miles. Kalka is at 2,400 ft. above sea level and 5,200 ft. is reached in 23 miles; the line then drops down to 4,600 ft. only to climb again to reach Shimla at an altitude of 6,700 ft. The scenery is superb and the ruling gradient is 1 in 33. The gauge is 2 ft. 6 in. and trains are now diesel hauled.

The Darjeeling Himalayan Railway is a steam operated 2 ft. gauge line, with features of great interest, notably the reversing stations and the double loop by which the railway gains height. It climbs to 7,400 ft. at Ghoom, the highest altitude attained by any railway in the Indian subcontinent, before dropping down to 6,800 ft. at Darjeeling. The ruling gradient is 1 in 25 with some lengths of 1 in 22 and a short length of 1 in 20.

The Matheran Hill Railway near Bombay is a 2 ft. gauge line of only 12 miles, with gradients of 1 in 20. It is now diesel operated. Regrettably the Matheran Hill Railway can be visited only as a day excursion.

BY CAR. *Hertz* self-drive cars are now available for hire in India's major cities, including Bombay, Delhi, Hyderabad, and Madras. Potential drivers should remember, however, that cities are congested and that traffic in India moves on the left side of the road. Hiring a car with driver or a tourist taxi is a better alternative and is reasonably priced. Hire a car or tourist taxi only from a government-approved and licensed operator. For reliable companies, consult the listings in each chapter. You can also hire a car through your travel agent or the India Tourism Development Corporation (ITDC, Kanishka Shopping Plaza, Ashok Rd., New Delhi, 10001, India), which has the old-fashioned, yet delightful, Ambassadors up to the Mercedes. Write well in advance. Rates are about Rs. 4–Rs. 5 per kilometer, with an added Rs. 100 halt charge per night on the road.

Rules of the Road. Traffic keeps to the left and passes on the right, as in the British system. Subject to local regulations, tram cars can be passed on either side. There is no general speed limit for cars apart from the 30 MPH limit in the cities. In rural areas, slow-moving cyclists, bullock carts, and occasional camels or elephants share the road with daredevil long-distance trucks and buses. Speeds vary according to what you find yourself behind. The horn is used as a warning whenever one is passing. The constant horn-honking, particularly in the cities, greatly adds to the nerve-wracking experience of road travel. Remember that for Hindus, cows are considered sacred; for them or any other animals on the road, slow down and use your horn; bypassers will help to shoo them off the road. In a rural society, the loss or damage of any livestock can bring economic hardship.

Roads. Main trunk roads are generally good, but secondary roads may be bad, especially during monsoons and in the hot, dusty season. In addition to other drivers (of whatever transportation) and animals, one may encounter rural roads being used as an extension of farms, with food grains laid out to dry or sisal rope being strung out over the pavement.

The present national highway system includes roads whose total length is 31,000 km (approximately 20,000 miles).

Monsoons usually play havoc with roads and bridges, and it is advisable, before you set out for a long car trip, to consult one of the following automobile associations (AAs) that periodically issue regional motoring maps, excellent road information, and detailed charts:

A.A. of Eastern India, 13 Promothesh Barua Sarani, Calcutta 700 019

A.A. of South India, 38-A Mount Rd., Madras 600 006

A.A. of Upper India, Lilaram Building, 14–F, Connaught Pl., New Delhi 110 001

A.A. of Uttar Pradesh, 32–A, Mahatma Gandhi Marg, Allahabad

A.A. of Western India, L.N. Memorial Building, 76 Veer Nariman Rd., Bombay 400 020

Gasoline (Petrol) costs, at the time of writing, are about Rs. 7.60 per liter. The government controls the price, which changes every year during March when the central government releases the annual budget figures.

Driving License and Insurance. An International Driving License is recognized in India. In case of loss, one of the automobile associations will issue a replacement license on presentation of your national driving permit. Third-party insurance is compulsory and must be obtained locally; international motor insurance is not acceptable in India.

BY SHIP. There are a number of ways to travel by ship around the coasts of India. It is possible to sail from Madras or Calcutta to Port Blair in the Andaman Islands. Contact the *Shipping Corporation of India,* 13 Strand Rd., Calcutta 700 001; tel. 23–2354, telex: VMO495, cable: SHIPINDIA.

Regular, frequent sailings are available for the journey from Bombay to Goa between October and May. Rates vary from Rs. 300 for the "owner's cabin" to Rs.

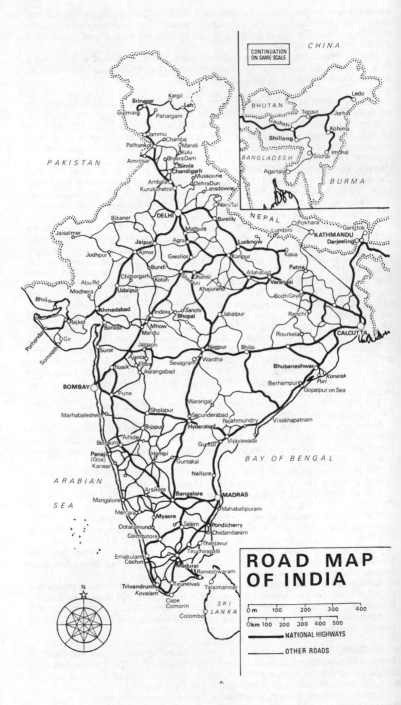

ROAD MAP
OF INDIA

0 m   100   200   300   400

0 km 100 200 300 400 500

——— NATIONAL HIGHWAYS

——— OTHER ROADS

48 for the lower deck class. For reservations to Goa (no round-trip fares), in Bombay, contact *Mogul Lines Ltd.,* 16 Bank St., Fort Bombay; tel. 25–6835, telex: 011–4049, cable: MOGHI. Boarding is at New Ferry Wharf, Mallet Bunder, Bombay. In Goa, contact *M/s V.S. Dempo and Co. Prt. Ltd.,* Campal, Panaji, Goa; tel. 3842, telex: 0194–217, cable: AIRTRADE. Boards at Passenger Jetty, Campel, Panaji.

At the time of writing, ferry service between Rameshwaram and Sri Lanka's southern port of Talaimannar is suspended. When operating, it sails three times a week except from the third week in September to the first week in January. The trip takes three hours. Inquire at the *Government of India Tourist Office* in Madras for current information on this service.

Cabins are available for the above journeys, but conditions are not that of a luxury cruise ship, and on some ships, you must provide your own food.

Departing from India

CUSTOMS. If you propose to take on your holiday any *foreign-made* articles, such as cameras, binoculars, expensive timepieces and the like, it is wise to put with your travel documents the receipt from the retailer or some other evidence that the item was bought in your home country. If you bought the article on a previous holiday abroad and have already paid duty on it, carry the receipt for this. Without such a receipt, customs officials may appraise the items at a higher value than their worth, and, should you lose them during your stay in India, you will have to pay duty on this higher rate when you leave.

Airport Tax. All travelers must pay on departure from the airport a tax of Rs. 150 for neighboring countries, such as Nepal or Pakistan, and Rs. 300 for all other international flights. No tax is levied for domestic flights.

Banking Facilities. Rupees are not allowed out of India. You must exchange them before you leave India. Banking facilities for changing rupees back into foreign currency are usually located in the same airport hall as the check-in counters. You have no access to these facilities once you pass through immigration.

The following articles, up to a value of Rs. 15,000 (about $882), can be exported without any formality: souvenirs, silks, woolens, artwork, precious stones, and jewelry up to a value of Rs. 10,000 (about $588), articles made of silver up to a value of Rs. 1,000 (about $58), gold jewelry up to a value of Rs. 2,000 (about $118). All animal products, souvenirs, and trophies are subject to the protected list under the Wildlife (Protection) Act, 1972. The export of skins made from protected wildlife species is not allowed, and India is becoming increasingly rigorous in its monitoring of such exports. Such items cannot be imported into many countries, including the United States. As a general rule, avoid any souvenir made of wild animal skins (except crocodile leather goods). Ivory, unless it can be proved to be old, is also not allowed into the United States, although it is widely available for purchase. Ivory poaching, especially in southern India, is reducing the size of elephant herds. The illegal ivory market is in souvenirs.

Export of Antiquities. Generally, items more than 100 years old cannot be exported without a permit from the director-general of the Archaeological Survey, Janpath, New Delhi; the director, Prince of Wales Museum, Port Bombay; or the superintendent, Archaeological Survey of India, Museums Branch, Indian Museum, Calcutta. Articles will be detained by Indian Customs if they are believed to be over 100 years old.

American residents may now bring home up to $400 worth of purchases duty free. Each member of the family is entitled to the same exemption, regardless of age, and exemptions can be pooled. For the next $1,000 worth of goods, a flat 10 percent rate is assessed; above $1,400, duties vary with the merchandise. Included for travelers 21 or older are one liter of alcohol, 100 cigars (non-Cuban), and 200 cigarettes. Only one bottle of perfume trademarked in the United States may be brought in. However, there is no duty on antiques or art over 100 years old.

Gifts that cost less than $50 may be mailed to friends or relatives at home, but not more than one per day or receipt to any one address. Mark the package "unsolicited gift—value less than $50." Those gifts must not include perfumes costing more than $5, tobacco, or liquor.

Note that the United States now has strict limitations on the import of any items made from protected animal species, including ivory and most animal furs.

British subjects may import duty-free 200 cigarettes or 100 cigarillos or 50 cigars or 250 grams of tobacco (note: if you live outside Europe, these allowances are doubled), plus one liter of alcoholic drinks over 22 percent volume or two liters of alcoholic drinks not over 22 percent volume or fortified or sparkling wine, plus two liters of still table wine, plus 50 grams of perfume, plus nine fluid ounces of toilet water, plus other goods to the value of £32.

In addition, no animals or pets of any kind may be brought into the United Kingdom. The penalties for doing so are severe and strictly enforced.

Canadian residents have a $300 exemption and may also bring in duty-free up to 50 cigars, 200 cigarettes, two pounds of tobacco, and 40 ounces of liquor, provided these are declared in writing to customs on arrival and accompany the traveler in hand or checked-through baggage. Personal gifts can be mailed as "Unsolicited Gift—Value under $40." Request the Canadian Customs brochure, *I Declare* for further details.

THE SHAPING OF
MODERN INDIA

A Look Backward and Forward

by
TREVOR FISHLOCK

Modern India is the new political and social ordering of one of the world's most ancient societies. Measured against the 5,000-year antiquity of Indian civilization, the four decades since independence in 1947 are but a brief time. And the British raj, which had considerable influence on the shaping of modern India, was a relatively short episode. India's history is a marvelous progression. It has been fashioned by the interaction of invaders, by the dynamics of Hinduism and Islam, by the monsoon, and by the impact of Europeans. It has also been conditioned by India's peninsular shape, which made it a net rather than a place of transit, and which has contributed to its unique development and character.

India's historical roots lie in the Indus civilization, known to archaeologists as the Harappa culture. This civilization grew out of earlier and more primitive developments and sprang up on the plain of the Indus River and in other parts of northern and western India. It flourished for about 1,000 years, until around 1550 B.C., but disappeared from historical view until archaeologists began to unearth its treasures in the 1920s. At that time, they found the remnants of the subcontinent's first major urban growth.

In the years of its greatest vigor, this civilization spread over an area of 500,000 square miles.

The chief seats of its power were Mohenjo Daro and Harappa, both in modern Pakistan. These were great cities, run by merchants and priests, and well planned. Their principal features were large raised citadels that were the focus of government and religion, streets laid out in grids, and an elaborate drainage system: the Harappans liked to keep clean, and many of the houses had bathrooms. There were planned residential sections and districts of nondescript brick houses for workers, foreshadowing the monotonous urban districts of so many modern cities. At harvest time, carts brought in grain for the cities' huge granaries. The Indus people were traders and, as far as we know, the world's first cultivators of cotton.

The Harappan script survives on some 2,000 seals that have yet to be deciphered. These seals have pictures of people and animals and may have been merchants' tokens, a form of currency. The archaeological excavations have revealed that Harappans liked making carvings of monkeys, squirrels, and cattle. They made little carts and bird-shaped whistles for their children. The bull played an important part in their religion. And in many houses, there was a statuette of a nude woman, wearing an ornate headdress, perhaps worshipped as the Mother Goddess—one of the elements of the Indus civilization that persists to this day in the Hindu religion.

Arrival of the Aryans

The decline and fall of the Harappan culture was caused by the arrival of the Aryans. This powerful race of hunters and herders lived originally in the vast sweep of steppeland that stretches from Poland into central Asia. In one of humankind's great migrations, they spread south, west, and east in the early part of the second millenium B.C. It was a movement spread over several centuries. As they traveled, the Aryans conquered local peoples, intermarried, and adapted their language to local ones. In Europe, they were the ancestors of Greeks, Celts, Teutons, and Latins.

As the Aryans advanced and settled in India, they gradually took to agriculture and became traders. Their society developed on distinct lines, with groupings of warriors, priests, craftsmen, and serfs—the seeds of a caste system that, vastly more complex and subtle, is the social framework of India. Sacrifice was the fundamental part of their religion, and the strongly patriarchal family was the basic unit of their society. Their language was Sanskrit, which is related to Latin and Greek, and their developing philosophical thought was expressed in the *Upanishads,* the mystical verses set down in their early writings, known as *Vedas.* One of the great documents of India is the *Rig Veda,* a collection of 1,028 hymns dedicated to the Aryan gods. It is the earliest of the Hindu scriptures and is in an ancient form of Sanskrit.

According to many authorities, some of the *Rig Veda* was written before 1000 B.C.; but in dealing with the early history of the Indo-Aryans, we need to remember that much of the evidence is sketchy and that dating can, for the most part, only be speculative. Through their language, the evolution of religious thought and rituals, their cultural institutions and caste, the Indo-Aryans started to create a way of life that was self-contained and that sustained them as they progressed across India and through the centuries. They developed a social matrix that has shaped India for 30 centuries, and, in many respects, persists today.

The Indo-Aryans pushed eastward across the Punjab, clearing the forests as they went. They spread eastward along the Ganges, which developed as a major route for expansion. Around the ninth and eighth centuries B.C., the Aryans began to migrate south into the Deccan. The great Hindu epic poem, the *Ramayana,* says Aryans conquered Sri Lanka during this period, but there is no evidence of it.

Network of Kingdoms

In any event, the Aryans were certainly on the move, penetrating all of northern India and bringing their ideas to the Dravidian people in the south. During the period from the seventh to the fifth century B.C., there emerged in the fertile Ganges plain a network of about 16 kingdoms and tribal republics with a coherent political and religious basis. Indeed, there was a common cultural pattern across all northern India. But there was always volatility.

Religion was in a state of flux, and many people wanted more than the ritualism of early Hinduism, with its sacrifices to Indra, the thunderbolt god; to Mitra, the sun; and to Agni, the god of fire. Out of a cauldron of religious speculation and assertion emerged a number of influential spiritual leaders. One of these was Mahavira, born about 540 B.C., who founded the Jain religion, which is today a significant minor faith with many adherents among India's traders. Another was Gautama Buddha, born in what is now Nepal, about 566 B.C. Buddha's teachings laid the foundations for one of the world's major faiths.

During the fifth century B.C., the disparate territories ruled by chiefs and kings were steadily reduced by conquest to four and, finally, to one great superpower kingdom: Magadha. The capital of Magadha was at Pataliputra, on the Ganges, where Patna now stands. It was a magnificent city, mostly made of timber, and was protected by wooden walls.

Meanwhile, the Indus valley had been brought under the control of the Persian empire. Given the name of India, it was ruled as a province. In the fourth century B.C., Alexander the Great conquered the Persians and marched to the Indus. Thus Europe met Asia. And what was important for India was that a young Indian prince, Chandragupta Maurya, who is said to have met Alexander near the Indus in 325 B.C., took advantage of the confusion caused by Alexander's conquest and the further confusion caused by the conqueror's departure. Chandragupta seized the throne in Magadha, proclaiming himself emperor. He seized territory east of the Indus and then progressed triumphantly southward to bring all central India under his rule. In 303 B.C., he beat Seleucus Nicator, Alexander's successor in the northwest, and annexed the immense Greek province that included much of what is now Afghanistan.

Mauryan Empire Founded

Chandragupta was the founder of the Mauryan empire. He lived in luxury in his grand wooden palace in Pataliputra and reigned for 24 years. But he was always in fear of assassination and, according to legend, he abdicated to become a Jain monk. His son, Bindusara, extended the empire, and Chandragupta's grandson, Ashoka, completed the process with a series of bloody conquests along the coast of the Bay of Bengal. Thus, for the first time, most of the subcontinent, from Kabul almost to the southern tip, came under a single political authority. India was then, much as it is today, a land of farming villages.

The empire lived for a century and a half. Its third leader, the emperor Asoka, is reckoned by Indians to have been their greatest ruler. Certainly, he ranks as one of the great kings of world history. After his early years of war and conquest, he became a Buddhist and adopted a humanitarian code for living and for government. In other words, he advocated the abandonment of warfare in favor of setting an example of moral leadership through a creed of peace and tolerance. He practiced the code of *ahimsa* (nonviolence to humans and animals), stopped animal sacrifice, and encouraged pilgrimages in place of hunting for sport. He was a far-sighted man, a ruler well ahead of his time, a reformer, a builder of roads, and a planter of trees. He was also a shrewd administrator. He set out his philosophy in edicts inscribed on stone pillars in many parts of the country. These edicts are the oldest inscriptions of any importance in India and remain Asoka's monuments. The emperor's symbol of four lions sitting together, a mark of his authority, is the symbol of modern India, the government's official crest. Another of his symbols, a chariot wheel, is incorporated in the country's green, white, and saffron tricolor.

The emperor died about 232 B.C., and the Mauryan empire steadily declined, its age of glory perishing with Asoka. New invaders entered northern India from Greece, Persia, and central Asia. New kingdoms sprang up in many parts of the country, and the Greek and Indian cultures and religions fertilized each other. Hinduism established itself in greater strength in the Ganges plain, and Sanskrit literature enjoyed a renaissance. Buddhism developed two distinct codes that still exist. The fundamentalist Hinayana Buddhism is strongest in Southeast Asia, Sri Lanka, and Burma. Mahayana Buddhism is dominant in Japan, China, and Tibet.

Trade Flourishes

During this period, there was a surge in trade between India and the Middle East, which increased as Greek power gave way to Roman expansion. India sent vast quantities of silk, spices, jewelry, indigo, and animals. The goods were sent through the port of Barbaricum, at the mouth of the Indus, and by camel caravan from Taxila, now in Pakistan.

Kingdoms and dynasties rose and fell. The Satavahanas who emerged in the Deccan plateau of central India became a formidable force and spread and conquered in the north. The lands of the south became divided between Cholas, Padyas, and Cheras. In the fourth century A.D., northern India gradually came under the authority of the imperial dynasty of the Guptas. The seat of power became, as it had been years before, Magadha and the city of Pataliputra, and the Gupta empire extended from the Punjab to Assam. It lasted into the sixth century.

The most outstanding of the Gupta monarchs was Samudra Gupta, who ruled from A.D. 335 to 375. Under his rule and that of his successors, particularly Chandragupta II, A.D. 375–415, India enjoyed another golden age. Trading with the Middle East and the Mediterranean flourished, and the empire was efficiently managed.

The next event of significance was the rise of Harsha, son of a Punjab king, who succeeded to the throne at age 16 in the early seventh century and ruled for 41 years. Harsha extended his rule over much of northern India and restored some of the lost splendor of the Guptas. He was the first Indian ruler to open diplomatic links with China, and we know much about the life at his court from the journals of the Chinese traveler Hsuan Tsang, which have survived intact.

King Harsha was a cultured man, a playwright among other things, and he loved the showy ceremony of his court. He was an indefatigable traveler through his vast domain. He was the last Hindu king to govern all of northern India. But he had no heirs, and the glitter faded. After his death, his empire collapsed and India became once more a confusion of warring states. During this period and the following centuries, Hinduism expanded vigorously. Buddhism and Hinduism were integrated in the eighth century under the influence of the teacher and philosopher Sankaracharya, from Kerala, but as Hinduism steadily gained ascendancy, Buddhism began to wane in India, the country of its birth.

Advance of Islam

The most significant, most far-reaching, event in the centuries after the fall of the Roman empire was the advance of Islam. The Prophet Mohammed was born in Mecca in A.D. 570 and, by the time of his death in 632, the faith he founded was strong and expanding. In the seventh century, Moslems conquered Afghanistan, Iran, and central Asia and under Mahmud of Ghazni thrust into India. In the eighth century, they took the province of Sind, which has remained Moslem ever since. In the tenth century, Punjab was conquered, and in the years that followed, the twilight of Hindu independence, Islamic invaders increasingly took control. Hindu India was weakened by disunity, by its patchwork of rival rulers, that made it vulnerable to invaders. Late in the twelfth century, Mohammed of Ghor and his general Qutbuddin Aibak, a freed slave, marched into the Hindu states. In a decisive battle at Tarain in 1191, the Hindus, under Prithvaraja—a Rajput hero sung about to this day—beat back the invaders. But in the following year, the Moslems returned with a larger force, beat the Hindu army, and killed Prithvaraja. The road to Delhi and all the riches of India were now open.

Within a decade, the Ganges plain was dominated by Islamic rulers, and in 1206, Qutbuddin became the first Sultan of Delhi. The Sultanate of Delhi imposed stability on much of northern India for several hundred years and, indeed, the Moslem hegemony was only ended by the conquests of the British in the 18th century. There is a historical thread extending from the founding of the Delhi Sultanate in 1206 to the Indian Mutiny in 1857.

Between the fourteenth and sixteenth centuries, Hinduism made the adjustments that enabled it to survive and to grow. There were important reforms in the religion, and many holy men denied any contradiction between Moslem and Hindu ideas of deity. But politically, India was a loose collection of kingdoms, both Hindu and Moslem, often at war with each other, so that the country lacked unity and was ripe for invasion. In 1523, Babur the Mogul, a descendant of the Mongol warlord Genghis Khan and of the conqueror Timur (Tamerlane), marched into the Punjab from Afghanistan. He defeated the Sultan of Delhi at Panipat, north of the city, in 1526, and proclaimed himself emperor of India. The age of the great Moguls had begun.

Rule of the Moguls

It was difficult at first for the conquerors to gain a secure footing because the warriors of northern India fought back fiercely. Indeed, the invaders were thrown out in 1539 by the brilliant leader Sher Shah. But they returned in massive force. Babur's young grandson, Akbar, headed the invasion and restored and consolidated the rule of the Moguls. He took full power at the early age of 18 and became one of the great figures of Indian, and world, history. He extended his power throughout northern India, including Bengal, Kashmir, Baluchistan, Afghanistan, and Gujarat. His fortress-palace at Agra and his now-deserted capital at Fatehpur Sikri are physical memorials to the power of this, the greatest of the Mogul emperors. But there was much else. Akbar was a masterful administrator. He was also a unifier. He sought peaceful coexistence with the Hindu majority. He was an enthusiastic patron of the arts, adored painting and architecture, and filled his court with artists and poets. The Mogul school of miniature painting blossomed. The wonderful city of Fatehpur Sikri was a blend of Islamic and Hindu architecture. Akbar's reign, from 1556 to 1605, was a classical age, a brilliant time.

Akbar sought to bring the Deccan kingdoms of central India under his rule, and this policy of expansion was continued by his successors, Jahangir and Shah Jahan (who built the Taj Mahal). And under Aurangzeb, Akbar's great-grandson, the Mogul empire reached its broadest extent. But Aurangzeb reversed the policy of tolerance toward his Hindu subjects. He reimposed the discriminatory taxes lifted by his great-grandfather and squeezed out the Hindus who held positions in his court and administration. Inevitably, the earlier mood of cooperation was replaced by bitterness. The court and government became weaker. Angry Rajputs, the proud warrior people of the northwest who had been important supporters of the Mogul emperors, revolted against Aurangzeb's discrimination. The Sikhs, whose religion had been founded in the early sixteenth century, one of the by-products of the meeting between Hinduism and Islam, also rose in rebellion. So did the Jat people of the north. The powerful Marathas, renowned as skilled and disciplined cavalrymen, also pitted themselves against the emperor. Their leader, Shivaji (1627–80), is revered today as a hero of Hindu resistance and revival. His son was captured, blinded, and killed by Aurangzeb.

War, intolerance, and the decaying of a once-magnificent administration began to put an end to the Mogul empire. Aurangzeb died in 1707, but his empire was already well past its zenith, and it was effectively finished within a few years. The Maratha troops pushed northward, occupied Gujarat and invaded Hindustan, reaching Lahore, Orissa, the Ganges plain, and much of central India. They took over a large part of the Mogul empire, having marched into Delhi in 1719. The emperor himself had to concede allegiance to a Maratha chief. With the close of the empire, there ended a marvelous time in the story of India. For the most part, the epoch of the great Moguls, 1560–1707, was one of creativity and economic expansion. The courts were dazzling in their luxury, and we only have to look at some of the buildings that remain—the Taj Mahal, the Red Fort in Delhi, Fatehpur Sikri, the mosques, the palaces, and the forts—to gain an idea of the power and the glory of it all.

In the years of the empire's decline, in the eighteenth century, a new force began to emerge in India: the Europeans. Merchant venturers from Portugal, France, Britain, Holland, and Denmark set up stations around the coasts and opened up trade to Europe.

European Influence

The story of Europe in India really began in 1498 with the arrival in Calicut, on the west coast, of the Portuguese navigator Vasco da Gama. The Portuguese established bases in other places, most importantly in Goa, their headquarters, and for 100 years had the India trade mostly to themselves. The Dutch, British, and French secured a hold in the seventeenth century. The English East India Company, which was to play such a large part in the development of commerce and political power in India, was granted its first charter by Queen Elizabeth I in 1600. Trade was carried on from coastal bases under concessions granted by local rulers or by the Mogul emperors.

The British acquired Bombay from the Portuguese and also built major bases in Madras and Bengal for the export of textiles, sugar, indigo, and the spices. In those early years, the authority of Indian rulers was strong enough to prevent Europeans from interfering politically in local affairs. But later, the rulers began to appreciate the military skills and equipment of Europeans and gradually began to court them for assistance in their own struggles.

Around the middle of the eighteenth century, when the power of the Moguls had waned, French and British trading companies began fighting along the Carnatic coast of the southeast. Their warfare was an offshoot of two European struggles, the War of the Austrian Succession (1740–48) and the Seven Years War (1756–63). The outstanding British figure of this time was Robert Clive, a former clerk in the East India Company, whose military brilliance effectively ended France's ventures in India. After 1763, the French were never a serious threat to British ambitions in the subcontinent. With the help of Indian leaders, Clive went on to defeat the Mogul emperor's army at Plassey, in Bengal, in 1757, and thus secured Orissa, Bihar, and Bengal, where the East India Company had a trading center in Calcutta since 1690.

British Power Asserted

As conqueror of Bengal, Clive was the original force behind British power in India. More battles against local rulers won more territory for the East India Company. And as the British newcomers pushed their way into the interior, local rulers threatened by the might of the Marathas put themselves under British protection. Thus, the flabby outposts of the Mogul empire came under British control. The East India Company (John Company, as it was known), became a power in the land.

In the early nineteenth century, consolidation of the gains was achieved by Richard Wellesley, the Duke of Wellington's brother. His forces broke the power of the Marathas in 1803 and the Mogul emperor in Delhi agreed to put himself under Wellesley's protection. Wellesley left India in 1805, satisfied that much of India lay under British rule. Sind was conquered in 1843, and the kingdom of Punjab, the homeland of the Sikhs, was annexed five years later; the Sikhs were the last, and probably the toughest, opponents. They later became firm allies of the British. But not all of India lay under direct British rule. Princes continued to govern in many parts, and the British could not have managed India without their cooperation. India, as a colony of Britain, became part of the global economy. It was the imperial pivot, the jewel in the crown of the empire.

In 1857 the Indian Mutiny shook Britain's composure and arrogance. Its causes were complex. In the background, there was the resentment of rulers who had lost power to the British and a natural dislike of a foreign ruler. Some deplored British interference with Hindu customs, like *suttee,* in which a widow immolated herself on her husband's funeral pyre. Some Indian historians see the mutiny as a war of independence or as an explosive reaction against change.

The trigger was the scandal of cartridges, greased with the fat of tabooed animals, the cow in the case of Hindus, the pig in the case of Moslems. These cartridges were issued to *sepoys,* the native soldiers. Enraged sepoys rose up at Meerut, east of Delhi, and there was bitter fighting. At one time, a large part of northern India was caught up in the revolt, which took the British 14 months to put down. They did so with rigor. The rebellion had the nominal leadership of the last of the Mogul emperors, Bahadur Shah, who hardly knew what was going on. The British exiled him to Rangoon. As a result of the mutiny, the power of the discredited East India Company came to an end, and India came under the direct rule of the British crown. In due course, Queen Victoria was proclaimed Empress of India.

Results of British Rule

This was the beginning of modern India. The British built an extensive network of railways and a postal and telegraph service. They undertook irrigation projects and other public works. They established an administration with a huge bureaucracy, trained Indians in British techniques, spread the English language and education, and set up a system of justice. The railways, of course, enabled the British to expand their commerce. The British Indian empire grew even larger with the annexation of Burma in the 1850s and 1880s.

But, at the time of its greatest strength, the seeds of its demise were firmly planted. British education for Indians had been encouraged since 1835, and some of the sons of rich men went to Britain for their education in the best schools and universities. These young people imbibed British ideas of the liberal tradition and of democracy. Naturally they were struck by the incongruity of India being a colony, contributing to British wealth. There was a surge of intellectual curiosity in India's past, sparked by European and Indian scholars, so that more Indians developed the pride that springs from a grasp of history. Meanwhile, the Indian middle class and a new breed of capitalists grew and expanded. Indian entrepreneurs developed mills and mines. This significant class of young intellectuals was trained, aware of their country's position, and increasingly frustrated.

New Nationalism Rises

The springboard for the new nationalism was the Indian National Congress, founded in 1885 by an Englishman, to be a focus for the ideas and aspirations of the educated class. At first, the Indian National Congress was a debating society, a safety valve for the steam of intellectuals. But it quickly became a significant movement that questioned the British presence in India. In 1905, there was the first large-scale demonstration calling for self-rule, sparked by the partition of Bengal along Hindu-Moslem lines. There were also terrorist incidents.

The pace quickened during World War I, in which many Indians fought and died for Britain. The disruption caused by the war and the growing revolutionary spirit among the people led to a more insistent demand for home rule. The government responded with a proclamation that responsible government was a long-term aim and with reforms setting up provincial councils. These reforms were not enough. Meanwhile, Indian Moslems were angered by the British treatment of the Turkish sultan (*khalifa*), their spiritual head, after World War I.

Gandhi and the People's Struggle

In answer to the disturbances, the government became more repressive. In 1919, hundreds of civilians were massacred in the walled garden of Jallianwallabagh, in Amritsar, on the orders of General Reginald Dyer. This massacre was the turning point, and nothing was ever the same after that. Far from showing strength, the British showed they had lost their authority. The outrage united Indians. In the aftermath, Mahatma Gandhi became a national figure, the leader of the independence movement. It was

Gandhi who transformed a mostly middle-class and intellectual movement into a people's struggle. He took it from the city into the villages, into the heart of India. His simplicity and charisma, his saintly quality, made him an adored leader.

Gandhi was one of those men who, in his youth, had gone to England to study. His devoted follower, Jawaharlal Nehru, who later became the first prime minister of independent India, was another. Gandhi's technique of opposition to the British was one he had used in South Africa in his struggle against race laws: *satyagraha,* or nonviolent mass demonstration and non-cooperation. There was also a boycott of British goods. Given the mood of the times, the British concessions to Indian demands looked stingy. The Indian National Congress was the unstoppable vehicle of the push for self-rule, a moral as well as a political force, and Gandhi was its president from 1924 to 1934. Radicals like Jawaharlal Nehru and Subhas Chandra Bose persuaded the congress to harden its attitude and demand complete independence.

There were countless demonstrations in the great civil disobedience campaign of 1930–34. Gandhi and tens of thousands of his supporters were arrested, and many freedom fighters were jailed. Gandhi went to London in 1931 for talks with the British, but these failed and Gandhi returned to the struggle. Confrontation was the order of the day.

For a time, there had been unity in the independence movement, with Hindus and Moslems working together. But the split that Gandhi feared began to show itself more clearly. Elections to provincial councils embittered relationships. Although a minority, Moslems formed the majority in some areas, and the Moslem League became increasingly strident in its assertion that Moslems would not accept domination by the Hindus. In Mohammed Ali Jinnah, they found a brilliant, steely, and single-minded leader.

India's entry into World War II was automatic. The lack of consultation infuriated many Indians. The Indian National Congress decided not to take part in the war effort. Meanwhile, the differences between Hindus and Moslems grew more raw. In 1940, the Moslem League called for the founding of a separate homeland: Pakistan. This idea was Gandhi's nightmare because he stood for a united India, as did a large number of his Moslem supporters. But Jinnah was immovable. At the end of the war, it was clear to the British that the game was up, that they would have to quit a country whose people would no longer consent to be governed by them. It was clear, too, that the Moslem leaders would stand for nothing less than partition.

In 1947, Lord Mountbatten was sent by the British Labour government to be the last viceroy, with orders to bring about a final settlement. It was he who cut the Gordian knot. He reconciled himself to the inevitability of partition, as the lesser of two evils. In the meantime, he persuaded some 500 princes who ruled about two-fifths of India to give allegiance to the new, democratic India, thus buttressing the country's political integrity.

Independence Arrives

On August 15, 1947, India and Pakistan became independent. In Delhi, the ancient capital built and rebuilt down the centuries on a great crossroads of the northern plains, Prime Minister Nehru addressed his countrymen: "Long years ago, we made a tryst with destiny, and now the time comes when we shall redeem our pledge, not wholly or in full measure, but very substantially. At the stroke of midnight, while the world sleeps, India will wake to life and freedom."

It was a time of celebration and the birth of hope. It was also a time of turbulence and terror. When the borders between India and Pakistan were drawn by a British civil servant, millions of Hindus and Moslems packed their bags and exchanged countries. It was one of the most astonishing migrations of history. Five million Sikhs and Hindus left Pakistan for India, and five million Moslems left India for Pakistan. It was a bitter exchange, with fighting and massacres. About 500,000 people were killed. At the same time, there was a quarrel over Kashmir. The Hindu maharajah of this key Moslem state vacillated over whether to join India or Pakistan. In the end, he opted for India, and there was fighting between the two new countries. Pakistan still claims Kashmir, and the dispute endures.

Mahatma Gandhi was still working for peace. On January 30, 1948, while he was in Delhi to use his influence to prevent attacks on Moslems, he was murdered by a Hindu fanatic, one of a group incensed by his conciliatory approach to Moslems. Nehru, to an extent, took on Gandhi's mantle. Nehru was a natural aristocrat, an energetic and magnetic man, with firm ideas about the way India should develop. India was fortunate to have had such a strong leader in the tumultuous years after independence.

India as a Republic

In 1950, India became a republic, a federal union of states with a strong center. Today, 23 states and eight union territories are administered from Delhi. The national parliament is set up along the lines of the British Parliament and is bicameral. The Lok Sabha (lower house or house of the people) has 544 members. The Rajya Sabha (upper house) has 250 members, most of whom are elected by the state legislatures, and 12 who are nominated by the president of India. As in Britain, the life of a parliament is five years, unless a general election is called beforehand. All Indian adults have the vote, and an election in the world's largest democracy is a truly amazing feat of organization.

In the new republic's first general election, in 1951, Nehru and the Congress party were given their mandate to solve the problems of low industrialization and low productivity. The swelling population wanted food, better education, and better health care. Nehru believed in a strong public sector, with power, steel, manufacturing, and transport having priority. He saw great industrial plants as the new temples. In 1951, he launched India on the first of a series of five-year plans.

Nehru's plans were grand and ambitious. The first plan aimed to free India from its burden of importing food and to establish a strong industrial base. Three excellent harvests followed, and optimism was in the air. At the same time, Nehru steered social legislation through Parliament. His reforms of Hindu law were not popular with some conservatives, but they provided important rights for women in regard to marriage and property. Nehru was a strong supporter of giving greater political and public power to women. He was also a leader of the drive to spread education, to build universities and technical colleges.

The five-year plans had mixed success. Poor harvests, the result of poor monsoons, damaged the second and third plans. India certainly made great progress, but Nehru's economic aims were undermined by a lack of capital, overconfidence, and insufficient realistic planning. Meanwhile, the public sector and a great bureaucracy simply grew more sprawling.

Foreign policy was Nehru's abiding interest and he set out, successfully, to increase India's international prestige. India was active in the United Nations and a founder in the 1950s of the Non-Aligned Movement. But it was in foreign policy that Nehru ran into damaging trouble. India and

China quarreled over disputed borders in the northeast and in the area where Kashmir meets China. In 1962, the quarrel caused fighting, and Chinese troops marched into the Indian northeast. They eventually pulled back, but India was humiliated. Nehru never recovered from the episode. Some say it hastened his death in 1964. He was 74 and had been prime minister for 17 years. He certainly had disappointments, and not all of his ambitious goals were reached. But his achievements were remarkable.

Rule Under Indira Gandhi

In 1965, India and Pakistan fought a second war, in Punjab and Kashmir, which was settled at a peace conference. The following year, Indira Gandhi, Nehru's daughter, became prime minister. The Congress party bosses thought she would be easy to manipulate, but they were wrong. She had learned politics at her father's side; indeed, she had been involved in politics and political argument since she was a small girl receiving the letters her father wrote her from jail. She herself had been imprisoned, like Nehru, for her part in the independence struggle. Far from being soft, she was tough. Henry Kissinger noted her "cold-blooded calculation of the elements of power."

Mrs. Gandhi gained her magical surname through her marriage to the journalist and member of parliament, Feroze Gandhi, by whom she had two sons, Rajiv and Sanjay. She became popular with ordinary people, traveling constantly through India and meeting villagers. Her popularity reached its apogee in 1971 through her policies with respect to the Bangladesh war of independence. India supported the guerrillas of East Pakistan, who were fighting to break away from West Pakistan and found a new country. The Indian army defeated Pakistani forces in 12 days, and Bangladesh was born. India earned praise for the way it coped with caring for 10 million refugees from the war zone. For Mrs. Gandhi, it was a triumphant time. Her election victory in 1971 was overwhelming.

But in the way of such things, the euphoria ended. The economy soured, harvests failed, food prices rose, India was squeezed by the oil crisis. People grew angry and reacted with demonstrations and strikes. In June 1975, Mrs. Gandhi declared a state of emergency, suspending basic rights and rounding up her opponents. The press was censored and strikes banned. Her blow was swift and stunning. The 19 months of the emergency were notable for the rise of Mrs. Gandhi's younger son and confidant, Sanjay. Always ambitious, ruthless and pushy, he was the enthusiastic mover behind a population-control campaign that left a legacy of fear with its stories of compulsory sterilizations.

In 1977, Mrs. Gandhi felt she could win an election and she restored the democratic process. The people decisively threw her out and installed the Janata coalition, headed by Morarji Desai. But the Janata squandered its opportunities. It was riven by factionalism and unable to pursue workable policies. Meanwhile, Mrs. Gandhi was fighting back and rebuilding her support. In 1980 she and the Congress party stormed back to power.

In the summer of that year the daredevil Sanjay was killed performing an aerobatic stunt in Delhi. Having lost her right-hand man, Mrs. Gandhi replaced him with Rajiv, then a self-effacing airline pilot with little interest in politics. At his mother's side he became an apprentice to power.

Sikh Terrorism

During the early 1980s, trouble festered in the Punjab. Sikh grievances against Hindus were compounded by rivalries among Sikh politicians and by the flaring of religious extremism under the turbulent leadership of Jarnail Singh Bhindranwale, whose headquarters were in the Golden Temple, the very heart of the Sikh faith, in Amritsar. Sikh terrorists tried to drive a wedge between Hindus and Sikhs with a campaign of massacre and murder.

In June 1984, with Punjab a powder keg, Mrs. Gandhi sent the army to root out Sikh extremists in their sacred temple. There was a fierce battle. Bhindranwale was one of many men killed. Punjab was put under martial law, and some Sikhs vowed vengeance for the attack on their most revered shrine. On October 31, 1984, her Sikh bodyguards murdered Mrs. Gandhi in her garden in Delhi, ending her 17 years of rule. Within hours of her death, Rajiv Gandhi was sworn in as prime minister.

He was 40 years old, a Nehru, a man of modern outlook, technology minded, who had grown up in independent India. In the general election in December 1984, he won a huge mandate. Indians looked on him as the symbol of their fresh start, and he plunged into a task he knew would be formidably difficult.

Rajiv Gandhi made a positive attempt to handle India's most serious problem—the growth of Sikh terrorism in the Punjab. Extremists, who aimed to make their Punjab homeland a separate Sikh state (to be known as Khalistan), stepped up a ruthless campaign of terrorism. In a state where Hindu and Sikh had traditionally enjoyed an amicable relationship, the extremists fueled hatred by indiscriminate shootings of Hindus and of Sikh moderates. Hindus demanded action. Gandhi's policy was tough police action coupled with a backing of the moderate leaders of the Sikh-led Punjab government. But the terrorism grew worse and Mr. Gandhi had to impose direct rule from Delhi.

Meanwhile, other problems grew. The new prime minister and his ruling Congress party were demoralized by corruption scandals—allegations that the party had profited from kickbacks in arms deals—and the press and the opposition were relentless in their criticism. There were also attacks on the prime minister's management style; Gandhi frequently changed his government team. On top of this, his party crashed to defeat after defeat in state elections. To some old Congress hands Mr. Gandhi looked a loser. The euphoria that had accompanied the new leader's arrival to power soon vanished. Concern about runaway population growth and the great drought of 1987 added to his difficulties.

In October 1989, Gandhi called for national elections. That December, his Congress Party was trounced in former state strongholds, falling short of the prerequisite majority needed to form a new government. Instead, his rival, Vishwanath Pratap (V.P.) Singh, leader of the Janata Party and formerly a member of Gandhi's own cabinet, pulled together various minority parties to create a majority coalition, called the National Front, and assumed the mantle of prime minister.

V.P. Singh's National Front Government and the country face serious challenges. In 1990, violence erupted in Kashmir. Moslem extremists resorted to terrorism to punctuate their demands to quit India and form their own Islamic state. The mood in the valley, which has been plagued by unemployment, political corruption, and a long-term sense of alienation from India, is unsettled at best. What started out as a movement of radicals seems to have captured the minds of a large number of Kashmiris in this once-peaceful vale. In the Punjab, Sikh unrest remains just as volatile.

This young country, declared a secular nation, seems cursed by an uncontrollable spread of religious fanaticism and minority unrest that defies easy solutions. Because of these problems, the V.P Singh government finally toppled in late 1990. A new minority government took power and it most likely will not succeed.

SUMMARY OF HISTORICAL AND ARTISTIC PERIODS

Note: In the following table, 1 describes the *Historical Period,* 2 the developments in *Art, Religion and Literature.*

Approximate Period:

3500–2500 B.C.	1.	Indus Valley (Sumerian) Civilization
	2.	(Harappa, Mohenjo-Daro)
2000–1500	2.	*Rig Veda* compiled
1500–1000	2.	Early *Upanishads;* development of caste system
1000–500	2.	Later *Upanishads, Ramayana, Mahabharata* and *Bhagavad Gita*
514–512	1.	Persian king Darius invades the Punjab
	2.	Gautama Buddha (563–483); Mahavira Jina (550–475); first Buddhist *jatakas;* emergence of Shaivism and Vishnuism
327–325	1.	Alexander the Great in India
320–184	1.	Mauryan Dynasty
	2.	Ashoka's column edicts; Sanchi Stupa; Buddhist Mission arrives in Ceylon
250 B.C.–A.D. 60	1.	Bactrian and Parthian (Indo-Greek) dynasties in the Punjab
250 B.C.–A.D. 250	1.	Andhra Dynasty in S.E. Deccan
	2.	Amaravati Stupa; first Buddhist caves (Bhaja)
184 B.C.–A.D. 70	1.	Sunga Period
	2.	Early Ajanta wall paintings; Buddh-Gaya shrine; Buddhist caves at Karla, Bedsa, Kanheri, etc.
A.D. 64–225	1.	Kushan Dynasty in N.W. India; South India Kingdoms of the Cholas (Madras region), Cheras (Malabar coast) and Pandyas (southern tip)
	2.	Gandhara (Helleno-Buddhist) art; Mathura school of art; Buddhism arrives in China; commerce with Rome (Malabar); Manu's religious laws; *Kama Sutra* written
320–475	1.	Gupta Dynasty
	2.	Early Gupta art (Sarnath, Gaya); Nalanda University; writers, musicians, scientists; Ajanta Cave frescos; Ellora Cave carvings
4th century	1.	Hun invasion
5th–10th century	1.	Pallava Dynasty in the South
	2.	Appearance of Dravidian architecture (Mahabalipuram)
6th–12th century	1.	Chalukya Dynasty in the Deccan
	2.	Temples at Aihole, Badami, Pattadkal; decline of Buddhism in India; disappearance of Jainism in the South
8th century	1.	Emergence of Rajputs; Sind invaded by Arabs
	2.	Hindu cave temples at Ellora and Elephanta
8th–12th century	1.	Pala Dynasty in Bengal
	2.	Bengal school of sculpture; Shankara, teacher of Advaita; Shaivism in Kashmir and the South
9th–end of 17th century	1.	Hindu medieval period
	2.	Chandella art at Khajuraho; Chalukya art in Gujarat; Kalinga art at Konarak; Nepal school of art; Sena art in Bengal; Chola art at Tanjore; Hoysala art at Belur, Halebid and Somnathpur; Pandya art at Madurai; Vijayanager art at Hampi
11th–15th century	2.	Hindu art penetrates Cambodia and Java
11th–14th century	1.	Moslems conquer Delhi, Khilji and other dynasties; Timur destroys Delhi

Approximate Period:

	2.	The Italian Marco Polo visits South India; Guru Nanak, first Sikh teacher; Ramanuja and Madhava, mystic philosophers

15th–16th century 1. Three Moslem Dynasties; Lodis in Delhi, Brahmanis in the Deccan, Adil Shahis at Bijapur. The Portuguese arrive in South India

2. Flowering of Hindu and Bengali literature

16th–17th century 1. Mogul Dynasty (Babur, Humayun, Akbar, Jahangir, Shah Jahan, Aurangzeb)

2. Reigns over North and Central India; Akbar brings Hindus and Moslems together, epoch finds expression in architecture and Mogul and Rajput miniature painting

17th century 1. Establishment in the South of British East India Company, followed by Dutch and French; emergence of two Indian military powers: Marathas under Shivaji and Sikhs in Punjab

18th century 1. See-saw wars all over India; British tighten their hold (Clive); Nadir Shah sacks Delhi

1857 1. First stirrings of Indian nationalism: Sepoy Rising

1858 1. British Crown takes over from East India Company

Second half of
   19th century 2. Hindu religious reform movements: Arya Samaj, Brahmo Samaj, Ramakrishna Mission

1885 1. Establishment of Indian National Congress

1913 1. Rabindranath Tagore wins Nobel Prize for literature

1915 1. Mahatma Gandhi returns from South Africa to lead struggle for emancipation and independence

2. Excavations culminate in Archaeological Survey of India; Bengal school of modern painting

1930 2. Chandrasekara Vekata Raman wins Nobel Prize for physics

1947 1. Independence and partition of subcontinent into India and Pakistan (predominantly Moslem)

Post-Independence Period:

1948   January, Assassination of Mahatma Gandhi
1950   January 26, India declared a Republic, with its own constitution
1951   First General Election. Nehru confirmed as Premier
1954   Repossession of Pondicherry, from the French
1961   Annexation of Goa, taken back from Portuguese
1962   November–December. War with China over northern border disputes
1964   Death of Jawaharlal Nehru
1965   War between India and Pakistan over Kashmir
1966   January. Mrs. Gandhi becomes Prime Minister
1971   Second major war with Pakistan. Bangladesh becomes separate state
1974   India explodes first nuclear device in Rajasthan desert
1975   June. Declaration of "State of Emergency" by Mrs. Gandhi
1977   March. General Election, Mrs. Gandhi out, Mararji Desai becomes Prime Minister
1980   January. Mrs. Gandhi returned to power
1981   June. India launches communications satellite
1984   Mrs. Gandhi assassinated. Rajiv Gandhi elected Prime Minister by largest post-independent majority
1984   Dec. 3. Methyl isocyanate gas escapes from tank owned by Union Carbide in Bhopal. Worst industrial accident in history of technology
1987   Peace accord signed by governments of India and Sri Lanka aimed at ending the communal conflict between the central government and the Tamil separatist fighters in the northern and eastern provinces of Sri Lanka.

Approximate Period:

1989   Vishwanath Pratap Singh elected Prime Minister in a coalition of minority parties called the National Front.

1990   Moslem extremists in Kashmir resort to terrorism in their demands to quit India and form their own Islamic state.

RELIGIONS BLEND
WITH CULTURE

by
TREVOR FISHLOCK

Religion is a dominant force in India and plays an integral part in everyday life. Its influence and symbolism are pervasive, and visitors will soon see that they have come to a deeply religious society.

On city pavements, devotees create small religious paintings out of chalk, colored powder, and petals. There are shrines in the streets, where people offer *puja,* or homage. The dashboards of taxis are decorated with pictures of gods. Many homes contain a niche to hold a sacred picture or idol. There is a large number of wandering religious men, or *sadhus,* dressed in saffron robes, their bodies smeared with ash, who carry their worldly possessions—a bowl, a staff, and a blanket—with them. Some are silent; some preach and sing religious songs.

The greatest inspiration for India's architecture has come from the various religions of the country. India has marvelous temples built by Hindus, Buddhists, and Jains. These temples are encrusted with carvings of gods, animals, plants, and religious motifs. There are wonderful temple complexes as well. The important Jain temple city of Shatrunjaya Hill, in Gujarat, contains 863 lavishly decorated temples.

There are innumerable religious festivals and rites, in addition to small celebrations, associated not only with gods and goddesses, but also with water, animals, the planets, the sun, and the moon. The visitor should try to be present at one of these occasions because they are a lavish spectacle.

Of the 850 million people who live in India today, roughly 82.7 percent are Hindu, 11.2 percent are Moslems, 2.6 percent are Christians, 1.9 percent Sikhs, .7 percent are Buddhist, .5 percent are Jains, and .3 percent are Zoroastrians.

Hinduism Allows Liberties

Hinduism is one of the world's most powerful religious and social forces. A Hindu's religion rules his or her whole life, from the ceremonies performed at birth to food, clothing, employment, marriage, and death. Hinduism provides a means of supporting and improving one's existence in the world, and the religious part of the system is no more important than the social. The whole provides a framework for dealing with all manner of superstitions and beliefs.

Hinduism is not dogmatic, and although there is a belief in the power of the the Supreme Being, it is not the central focus. Millions of gods are admitted to the Hindu pantheon, allowing great freedom of worship. Indeed, Hindus often have a businesslike arrangement with their gods. They offer sacrifices and gifts when prayers are answered, but shout abuse at them when things do not go according to plan.

For simplicity, Hindus have assigned the major attributes of the Deity to a trinity of principal gods: Brahma, the creator; Vishnu, the preserver; and Shiva, the destroyer. Brahma is often shown with four heads, each holding sway over a quarter of the universe. The four *Vedas* are believed to have emanated from his heads, and he is therefore the god of wisdom. His bride, Saraswati, is the goddess of learning. Vishnu is the highest of the gods, who periodically visits the world to destroy evil and preserve truth. His incarnations as Rama and Krishna have inspired great fervor among Hindus. Rama is the hero of the great epic, the *Ramayana,* which is staged annually all over India. Krishna is represented as a handsome youth, holding or playing a flute. The Krishna cult is Hinduism's expression of human love. Krishna has inspired much of India's art.

Shiva is the terrible god of destruction, and he controls war, pestilence, famine, and death as well as related calamities like floods and drought. His consort, Parvati, is benevolent and affectionate, but she can take on the form of Durga, goddess of battle. She can also become Kali, the black goddess who has conquered time.

Ganesh, the son of Shiva and Parvati, wears an elephant's head; he is the god of luck and success. Hanuman, the monkey who, according to the *Ramayana,* helped Rama construct a bridge between Ceylon and India, is worshiped as a god in some parts of India.

The Hindu code for living is based on *dharma,* doing one's duty, as dictated by conscience, custom, and social background. Dharma is linked to *karma,* the belief that present actions affect future existence. The soul is eternal and goes through a cycle of births, deaths, and rebirths. Hindus believe that present difficulties are caused by the sins committed in a former life. The future may be improved by a series of selfless actions. If one's motives are truly altruistic, they can lead to a state of *moksha,* or serene peace and liberation from the pain and problems of the world. Many techniques are prescribed for the attainment of moksha: pilgrimages, yoga, ascetic practices, and the following of a *guru,* or spiritual teacher.

The Western notion is that the most profound part of Hinduism is an esoteric religious experience. But Hindus say that this mysterious aspect, the harnessing of forces through meditation and yoga, is not the most important. Hinduism is realistic; it provides a way of living in the real world

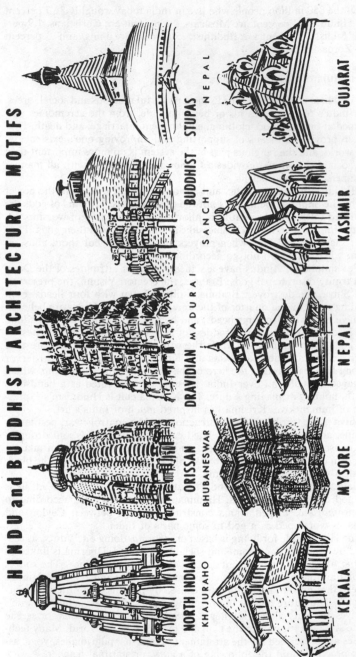

HINDU and BUDDHIST ARCHITECTURAL MOTIFS

STUPAS

NEPAL

GUJARAT

BUDDHIST

SANCHI

KASHMIR

DRAVIDIAN

MADURAI

NEPAL

ORISSAN

BHUBANESWAR

MYSORE

NORTH INDIAN

KHAJURAHO

KERALA

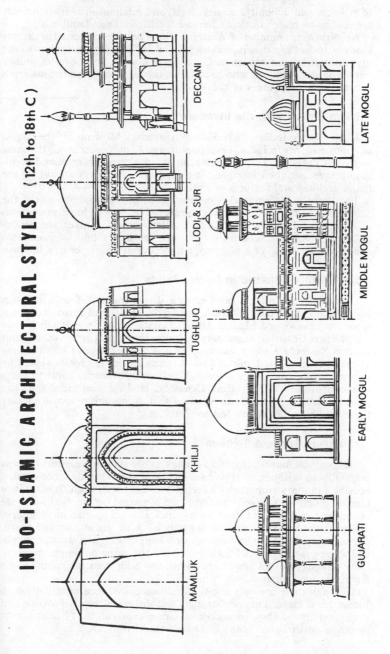

INDO-ISLAMIC ARCHITECTURAL STYLES (12th to 18th C)

MAMLUK KHILJI TUGHLUQ LODI & SUR DECCANI

GUJARATI EARLY MOGUL MIDDLE MOGUL LATE MOGUL

of sickness and difficulty, money, food, and relationships. Its adherents are told to be materialistic and create wealth for their families.

Nevertheless, a number of Westerners have become interested in various kinds of Indian mysticism, and they travel India seeking solutions to the mysteries of human existence. Gurus have made a great deal of money out of the more gullible, who go to India, they say, to escape the materialism and decaying values of the West.

Islam Enters with the Invaders

Islam came to India with the Moslem invaders. Moslems are the largest religious minority in India. Their population, 77 million, is about the same as that of Pakistan. They are the remnant of a once-powerful and dominant people, and their mosques, forts, and other buildings are among the major architectural features of India.

The Prophet Mohammed is believed to be the last and greatest of the prophets, and the Holy Koran is the sacred book. The basic injunctions of Islam are a belief in one true god, Allah, frequent prayer, the performance of charitable acts, fasting through the holy month of Ramadan, and the undertaking of a pilgrimage to Mecca at least once in a lifetime.

Christianity Ushered in by the Saints

Christianity in India, according to a strong tradition found in South India, is as old as Saint Thomas, one of the apostles of Jesus. The saint is said to have visited Madras. Others maintain that Saint Bartholomew was the first Christian missionary in India. However, the arrival of Saint Francis Xavier, a Jesuit missionary, in 1542, really began Christian missionary activity. The tomb of Saint Francis Xavier in Goa is visited by thousands of Catholics each year. Protestant missionaries came to India in the eighteenth century from Denmark, Holland, and Germany. The years of British rule in India ensured that Anglicanism spread. Today there are about 18 million Indian Christians.

Hinduism Sprouts Sikhism

Sikhism was founded by Guru Nanak in the sixteenth century. It was originally an offshoot of Hinduism—pacifist and rejecting caste—but it became a military community to resist Moslem persecution. It was Guru Gobind Singh who forged the Sikhs into a martial people. Sikhs are one of the most distinctive of India's minorities. Every Sikh man must observe and wear the five *kakkari* (visible symbols): *kesh,* uncut hair and beard; *kachh,* short boxer pants; *kara,* an iron bangle; *kanga,* a wooden comb; and *kirpan,* a dagger. All Sikh men have the surname Singh, meaning "lion" (though not all Singhs are Sikhs), and Sikh women have the name Kaur, meaning "lioness" or "princess."

Although there are only about 15 million Sikhs, their contribution to Indian life is large. They are strongly established in the civil service and the armed forces. They are successful farmers and run road haulage companies in north India. Many of Delhi's taxi drivers are Sikhs.

Ascetic Jains

Jainism is a severely ascetic religion, practiced by about 3.5 million people in India. Its followers maintain that right faith, right knowledge, and right conduct lead to salvation. Right conduct means the rejection of falsehood, theft, lust, greed, and violence. The highest virtue is the rejection of any action that could harm a living being. Some Jains, therefore, wear masks over their mouths to prevent them breathing in, and therefore killing, insects. Some devotees do not eat after dark in case insects get into their food and die. But Jains are also successful in commerce and are an important minority.

Zoroastrianism on Decline

Zoroastrianism is an ancient Persian religion founded by Zoroaster in the fifth century B.C. Its followers, about 90,000 people, are known as Parsis and live primarily in the Bombay region. Their holy book, the *Avesta,* describes the conflict between the Wise Lord, Ahura Mazda, and Ahriman, the Evil Force. Parsis are renowned for their ability to prosper, and India's most successful business family, the Tatas, are Parsis. But the Parsi community is dwindling, and there has been a decline in their interest in their own religion and traditions.

Four Truths of Buddhism

Buddhism was founded in India in the sixth century B.C. Siddhartha, who became known as Buddha, the Enlightened One, was born in the foothills of the Himalayas. It was prophesied that he would reject worldly pleasures and search for the way to true knowledge and happiness. He saw suffering around him and eventually began his search for enlightenment. After meditating under the Bodhi tree for several days, he became the Buddha and started preaching a new faith.

Buddhism is based on four truths: suffering is universal; it is caused and sustained by "birth sin," an accumulation of sins committed during previous existences; pain is ended only by nirvana, enlightenment; and the way to nirvana is the eightfold path—right faith, judgment, language, purpose, practice, memory, obedience, and meditation.

Buddha wandered from place to place preaching his gospel until his death in 487 B.C. He is usually shown sitting cross-legged on a lotus plinth. When his hands are raised in a graceful position, he is teaching; his hands are folded when he is meditating; and witnessing, his right arm is forward and his left hand is in his lap. There are about 5 million Buddhists in India.

Judaism was brought to India about 2,000 years ago by a group of Jewish refugees who landed on the west coast. Today small Jewish communities live in Bombay, Pune, Calcutta, Delhi, and Cochin, where they have built synagogues and prayer halls. They have assimilated into the mainstream of Indian life.

Merger of Cultures

The visitor to India cannot fail to be impressed by the individuality of its people, their character and culture. In the upheavals of its long history, India's traditions and mores have been continuously evolving. India has absorbed, adopted, and adapted outside cultures and influences, which have merged into Indian society, contributing to its Indianness. Religion and social life are closely interwoven, and religious symbolism can be seen in every aspect of the people's lifestyle, from great architecture, sculpture, and dance to the humblest Indian home where arts and crafts are used to great effect.

The people show a great flair for cultural expression, which illustrates the richness and variety of their cultural heritage. Tradition is evident, in spite of India's rapid modernization.

Since Independence, Indians have become increasingly keen to promote their sense of national identity, and there has been a revival of interest in Indian art, music, and dance. The successful Festival of India in 1985 was the most extensive series of cultural events ever to be staged in several cities in Britain, France, and the United States.

A brief survey of the main elements of Indian culture follows. Many specialist publications are available for those who want to gain greater knowledge of a particular aspect.

Architecture

Indians take great pride in their ancient civilization. Archaeological research has revealed that the roots of Indian life can be traced back almost 5,000 years to the settlements in the Indus valley. The Indus and Harappa civilization, with its great cities of Mohenjo-Daro and Harappa, lasted from the third to the middle of the second millenium B.C. *Mohenjo-Daro and Harappa* had two main intersecting streets, and houses constructed from sun-dried bricks and wood. The streets had drainage systems, and the houses had wells.

The Vedic Aryan and Buddhist period, from about 1400 B.C. to A.D. 300, saw the beginning of the fashioning of *stupas* (shrines) and pillars. The earliest Aryans were content with a simple wooden railing enclosing their idols, but later the style became far more elaborate. Caskets containing precious metals or bones, ashes, golden leaves engraved with prayers, beads, and coins were placed just below the summit of the stupa. On top, a square enclosed by a railing represented the heaven from where the gods governed the world.

The Hindu civilization, from about A.D. 400, saw stone coming into its own for whole buildings. The constructions are large, with thick walls, sturdy pillars, heavy lintels and ceiling slabs, corbeled arches and domes. Some of the carvings were erotic, symbolizing, in Hindu eyes, the sanctity of the creative force.

The Islamic Civilization, from the twelfth century, endowed India and Pakistan with some of their most beautiful buildings. The Moslems built mosques, forts, gardens, and tombs. The early Mogul emperors were cultivated men, patrons of art, architecture, and literature. Akbar encouraged artists and poets, and the deserted city of Fatehpur Sikri, an important tourist attraction, was his capital for 12 years. The mausoleum of Empress Mumtaz Mahal—the Taj Mahal—was built by Emperor Shah Jahan in memory of his wife who died in childbirth in 1630.

The Mogul style of architecture was regal and imperial, worthy of the wealthy, refined rulers. The most important buildings were constructed in white marble, sometimes encrusted with semiprecious stones, while others were built of red sandstone.

The European colonizers brought their architectural styles with them. The Portuguese built their towns on the west coast in late Renaissance and baroque styles, and the French introduced Louis XVI architecture in the eighteenth century.

The architecture of British India shows that there was constant experimentation with different building styles. One of the grandest edifices is the Victoria railway terminus in Bombay. It is an architectural sensation, the finest Victorian Gothic building in India. Bombay glories in other Gothic Revival buildings, while in Calcutta there are many decaying buildings in the English Classical style. On a smaller scale, vice-regal lodges, hotels, and churches abound, and an Englishman can usually find something architecturally familiar in an Indian city.

The grandly imperialistic city of New Delhi was designed by Sir Edwin Lutyens in the 1920s to make an emphatic statement about the grandeur of empire. It was the new capital of British India. Some of its landmarks are Rashtrapati Bhavan, the official residence of India's president, which was the former Vice-Regal Lodge; India Gate; Parliament House; and Connaught Circus.

Sculpture and Painting

The fact that India has an ancient tradition of sculpture has been known in the West since the thirteenth century, but no real understanding or appreciation of it existed until the nineteenth century. Before that, it was dismissed as the product of bizarre religions and of having no aesthetic value.

But the study of excavated Indian antiquities by the British and other Europeans slowly changed intellectual attitudes. As people began to understand Indian religions, they came to appreciate Indian sculpture.

The earliest examples of Indian sculpture date from the Harappan period. The objects are assured and mature. Artists depicted animals—the mythical unicorn, revered throughout ancient Asia, being one of the most popular. The elegant figure of a dancing girl from Mohenjo Daro is world famous.

After the founding of Buddhism in the sixth century B.C., much sculpture was Buddhist in feeling, and artists sought to express the eternal and infinite. The Buddha represented one of the highest aspirations of human thought and art.

During the reign of the emperor Ashoka (268–232 B.C.), about 84,000 stupas (the emperor converted to Buddhism) were erected. Ashoka ordered his philosophy and edicts to be carved on stone pillars throughout India. Sculpture of the time showed the glory of ancient India, covering every aspect of life.

The fourth century A.D. marked the rise of the classical phase of Indian sculpture. The centuries of the Gupta dynasty (320–600) produced sculptors who excelled not only in stone but also in metal casting by the technically advanced cire perdue process. Unfortunately, much of this sculpture was destroyed by Moslem invaders.

During the medieval period, different styles of sculpture evolved in different parts of India. The work is unrivaled for sheer exuberance, and its vibrancy leaves no aspect of life unexplored. Gods with attendant dancers festooned with jewelery were given the full baroque treatment. At Bhubaneswar, in Orissa, sculptors carved lithe figures representing traditional ideals and at Konarak, also in Orissa, a temple to Surya, the sun god, takes the form of a giant chariot, covered with erotic sculptures depicting a variety of sexual postures. Other temples were covered with figures of loving couples, heavenly beings, deities, and animals. They are all a lasting testament to the vigor of Indian sculptors.

Indian painting can be traced back to the beautiful work found in the Ajanta caves. About 200 B.C., artists were producing work of lyrical beauty, naturalism, and grace. This rhythmic line formed the basis of Indian painting through the ages. The Ajanta paintings had a wide influence on Indian art.

India is renowned for the scope of its large murals—and for its long tradition of painting in miniature. Walls of palaces and temples were decorated with scenes from Buddhist, Hindu, and Jain religious teachings. The majority of these murals have disappeared, but miniature paintings are more accessible. The earliest are the Buddhist religious texts painted on palm leaves.

Under the Moguls, miniature painting flourished. Akbar encouraged painting and installed more than 100 artists, mostly Hindus, at Fatehpur Sikri, to work under two Persian masters, Abdus Samad and Mir Sayyid Ali. The paintings reflected the exuberance of their patron.

Other schools of painting were developing in India at the same time. In Rajasthan, the miniatures showed happy people in bright clothing and had a wider appeal than the courtly scenes of the Moguls.

As the power of the British grew, Western ideas and values became popular among fashionable and wealthy Indians. So traditional painting became less appealing. Many Indian artists switched to painting the sort of subjects and scenes that the British liked—costume, occupations, festivals, flowers, birds, and animals.

Later, Indian artists, reacting against foreign domination, began a revival of interest in the traditional folk art of their ancestors. Nevertheless, the great figures in Indian art in this century belong to the international tradition, although their Indian roots can be seen. Some of the most original current work creates a dynamic synthesis between the Indian past and Western materials and techniques.

Music

The music of India is the result of a sophisticated and ancient tradition. Music and dance are all pervading, bringing vitality to festivals and ceremonies. The beginnings of Indian music can be traced to the Vedas, and music has developed definite laws of theory and practice. There are many legends—the notes of the scale and basic rhythms are said to have come from the Lord Himself.

Music developed as an adjunct to worship, and temples became the most important repositories of music and dance. It is the logical development of a long historical process that is a distinctive and integral part of Indian history and culture. Music should not be judged in Western terms; time and perseverance are needed to appreciate it.

Indian music is broadly divided into two forms—Carnatic in south India and Hindustani in the north—both having a common heritage and philosophy. North Indian music uses a wide range of beautiful instruments like the sitar and the flute. In the south, the forms of music are stricter, with little improvisation. In general, the composition of Indian music is lyrical and exciting and offers the Western ear a new dimension in musical appreciation.

There has been a growing interest lately in all kinds of Eastern music among the young in North America and Europe. Some of this interest is faddish, but there are musicians who are genuinely experimenting. Renowned masters like Yehudi Menuhin are working out ways of collaborating with Indian musicians, while Indian artists like Ravi Shankar tour the West with great success.

Dance

Indian dance has a rich and varied background. Folk dances derive from various sources, but the origin of all the classical systems is the temple, where they were conceived and attained their full stature. Dance formed an intrinsic part of worship. Indian dance demands a spirit of devotion and surrender because it is believed that a high spiritual experience can be gained from a sincere practice of the art.

Dancing is mentioned in the Vedas, and there are references to it in the great epics, the *Ramayana* and the *Mahabharata*. There are several well-defined dance forms, each from a different part of the country. The four main ones are Bharata Natyam in the south, particularly in Tamil Nadu; Kathakali in Kerala; Manipur in the northeast; and Kathak in the north.

Bharata Natyam is a dynamic, precise dance style. The dancer wears anklets of bells that emphasize the rhythm. In many south Indian temples, one can see Bharata Natyam dance poses in sculpture.

Kathakali is one of the most popular dance forms. It developed during the sixteenth and seventeenth centuries and was inspired by the heroic myths and legends of Hindu religious writings, with gods, warriors, demons, wise men and villains. Boys aged 12–20 are trained for six years in this dance form. Kathakali makeup is an elaborate process, the characters being classified into distinct types according to the color of their make-up and costumes. Performances are held all over Kerala in temple courtyards, clubs, and open spaces.

Manipur dances are vigorous when performed by men and lyrical when performed by young women. They revolve around episodes in the life of Vishnu. The women's costumes are picturesque and richly embroidered.

Kathak is exciting and entertaining—the most secular of all the dance forms. The footwork is complicated, and long strings of bells adorn the dancers' ankles.

There has recently been a revival of interest in Indian classical dance, and artists have traveled to the West. In spite of some experiments, dance remains close to its traditional form and does not portray contemporary themes.

Literature

The great tradition of Indian writing centers on the epic, romantic dramas and poems. The *Ramayana* and *Mahabharata*, like the great Homeric epics, take their place among the great literature of the world. They are available in English translation and help the reader to understand the rich traditional background that has inspired India's creative arts.

Poetry has grown and flourished, and the Bengali poet, Rabindranath Tagore, who won the Nobel Prize for Literature in 1913, is ranked among the great poets of the world. Sri Aurobindo, who was born in Calcutta in 1872, spent much of his youth in England, and English was his mother tongue. His poem, *Savitri*, is an epic. He founded the famous *ashram* (retreat) in Pondicherry.

British rule meant that English became the common language, and a number of Indian authors have written in English. However, over the past 50 years, several have developed a style and approach that is quintessentially Indian. R. K. Narayan, who began writing in 1930, delights his readers with scenes from Indian middle-class life. Raja Rao and Kamala Markandaya use social and political themes.

An excellent way to get the authentic feel of the country is to read the autobiographies of India's famous creative citizens. Mahatma Gandhi and Jawaharlal Nehru both wrote fascinating books. Ved Mehta, a regular contributor to *New Yorker* magazine, gives vivid accounts of his experiences during partition and as a student in the United States. V. S. Naipaul, who was born in Trinidad in 1932, analyzed the Indian scene brilliantly in such books as *India, A Wounded Civilization*. More recently, Salman Rushdie's *Midnight's Children*, which won the Booker prize, was hailed as a masterpiece. The work of Anita Desai also has received critical acclaim.

A number of English authors have written fascinating accounts of India as they experienced it. Rudyard Kipling was the first. E. M. Forster produced the classic, *A Passage to India,* and Paul Scott wrote the superb *Raj Quartet.*

The Mass Media

For most Indians, movies are an accessible form of entertainment. India's film industry, centered in Bombay, is the largest in the world, making about 700 features a year, most of them very long. The majority of the movies fulfill a need for escapism, romance, drama, and color. They follow a set formula: a love story, a battle between good and evil, a lot of action, a little comedy, and breaks in the action when the stars sing a song. Happy endings are almost compulsory. Social issues are explored, but the audience prefers the filmmaker not to dwell too long on them.

In addition, a number of high-quality films are being made by idealistic filmmakers like Satyajit Ray and Mrinal Sen. Their work is strong and original.

Radio and television are government controlled and the programs are, for the most part, dull and unimaginative. One listener threatened to put a bomb in his local radio station because the programs were so boring. Many other listeners sympathized with him!

The government says that radio and television should educate and enlighten and not be a forum for political controversy. Many of India's radio sets are communally owned and listened to by whole villages. All-India Radio broadcasts in many of India's languages and dialects. Television is slowly growing more important, and Indian-made soap operas are becoming popular. But those who can afford to do so buy video equipment and watch Western programs, pirated or otherwise.

Newspaper and book publishing are growing industries. The circulation of newspapers is about 40 million, the highest ever, and in some regions sales of the vernacular press are larger than that of the English-language newspapers. Indians feel proud that their country has a free press, although some, especially politicians, argue that India is "not ready" for it.

NORTHERN REGION

DELHI

India's Capital—Ancient and New

by
KATHLEEN COX

Kathleen Cox, author of Fodor's The Himalayan Countries, *is a contributing writer for* Indian Express, Lear's, Harper's Bazaar, Indrama, Travel and Leisure, *and* Vogue. *A former columnist for* The Village Voice *and* Playboy, *she is also the writer and co-producer of the documentary comedy,* Gizmo!

In the mid-1600s, when Bombay and Madras were trading posts and Calcutta a village of mud flats, Delhi flourished in a state of magnificent pomp and glory—the 450-year-old capital of a string of empires. First, it served the various Hindu and Moslem dynasties, then the powerful Moguls who ruled India until the 1800s when the British wheedled their way in. One after another, each new power created its own new Delhi, with each successive capital (there are eight) pushing the boundary farther north until the British came along. While building their predominantly residential district called Civil Lines on this northerly route, the British hit marshy flood-prone land that forced them to stop. Years later, they changed the course of development, building the bulk of their capital, the Imperial City, to the south.

Although the demands of the post-Independence population—over 6 million people now live in Delhi—have squeezed new neighborhoods into

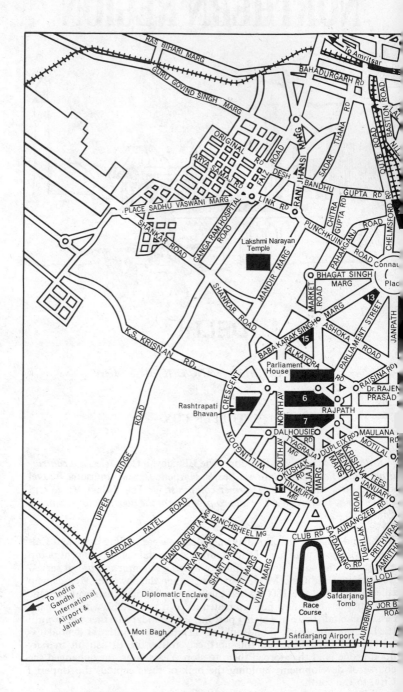

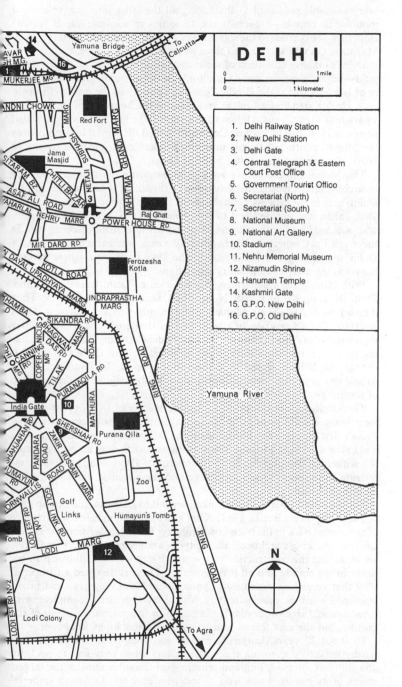

DELHI

0   1 mile

0   1 kilometer

1. Delhi Railway Station
2. New Delhi Station
3. Delhi Gate
4. Central Telegraph & Eastern Court Post Office
5. Government Tourist Office
6. Secretariat (North)
7. Secretariat (South)
8. National Museum
9. National Art Gallery
10. Stadium
11. Nehru Memorial Museum
12. Nizamudin Shrine
13. Hanuman Temple
14. Kashmiri Gate
15. G.P.O. New Delhi
16. G.P.O. Old Delhi

every available pocket of Delhi, fusing all the cities into one, celebrated monuments remain—especially the 18 tombs or mausoleums of various emperors—that attest to the significance of Delhi's political heritage. Even Mahatma Gandhi's *samadhi* (place of cremation) lies here.

Delhi's massive collection of monuments—there are more than a thousand—began in earnest when Qutub-ud-din Aibak, an Afghan and follower of Islam, defeated the Hindu Chauhan Dynasty in the late twelfth century. He declared himself sultan and founded the Sultanate of Delhi. After a parade of Turkish and Afghan rulers, Babur, the first great Mogul, seized power in 1526. But he loathed Delhi and moved his capital to Agra, where the Moguls continued to rule until Shaḥ Jahan controlled the empire in 1650. He switched the capital back to Delhi.

This Mogul emperor who possessed an exquisite artistic eye, especially in architecture, created the seventh city (much of it still stands in Old Delhi) and, in the process, brought about Delhi's glorious renaissance. But Shah Jahan was not destined to rule long. In 1658, his son, Aurangzeb, who was anxious for the throne, deposed his father, imprisoning him in the Agra Fort, where he died. After 20 years, Aurangzeb grew sick of Delhi, too, and moved his capital to the Deccan plateau, where he kept busy waging a series of military campaigns.

With Aurangzeb's departure, the fortunes of Delhi began to decline. First, the Emperor of Persia, Nadir Shah, sacked the city in 1739. Then Ahmad Shah Abdali, an Afghan, swept in and wreaked havoc in 1757. By 1803, Delhi's position of eminence was shattered; chaos ruled better than any leader. The British-owned East India Company, actively expanding its power over the subcontinent, grabbed hold of Delhi in 1803. Although the British agreed to protect and support the remnants of the Mogul dynasty, they were propping up a hollow regime—a frail vestige of former glory.

Then Delhi suffered through the Indian Mutiny of 1857 (a four-month-long savage battle pitting the British against their subjects, considered India's first struggle for Independence). The outcome essentially put an end to the age of the Moguls. The victorious British may have proclaimed the withering Bahadur Shah "the Emperor of Hindustan," but the conquering forces were clearly in charge and the so-called emperor died in exile in Burma.

For the next 54 years, Delhi ranked second to Calcutta, the British chosen seat of power. But in 1911, King George V announced the transfer of the capital back to the once-powerful city. With this decision, Sir Edwin Lutyens, the king's architect, and Lutyens's colleague, Sir Herbert Baker, set in motion the construction of the eighth city—New Delhi. A firm believer in the empire and all it represented, Lutyens designed an Imperial City that verged on grandiosity; palatial-sized buildings set amid broad tree-lined avenues punctuated by Mogul-style gardens, complete with fountains and shallow pools. He intended to use marble on many of the facades, but the cost forced him to use less-ostentatious sandstone.

In about 20 years, Lutyens's capital was completed. But the British hardly finished decorating the vast interiors when they had to pack up and ship out. In 1947, England relinquished the subcontinent, the largest chunk of its empire. India won its independence and Lutyens's Imperial City now served the proud leaders of a young democracy.

EXPLORING DELHI

To write about all Delhi's monuments would create a guide of stagger-
ing dimensions, so what follows is a selective list that gives a glimpse of
the best of Delhi down through the ages. We'll start with the earliest monuments, the most logical way to organize a tour. It's also a convenient
method, since the growth of Delhi's first seven cities represented a steady
march north.

Our tour begins in South Delhi at Qutab Minar, a 234-foot-high tower—
the seventh wonder of Hindustan and the tallest stone tower in India, with
376 steps leading to a great view of Delhi. Qutab Minar also happens to
be located near the site of the first city, created by the Rajput Prithviraj
Chauhan. This Tower of Victory, started by Qutub-ud-din Aibak in 1199
after his capture of Delhi, can be called a joint family project since Qutub-
ud-din only completed the first story. His son-in-law and successor, Iltut-
mish, added the top four stories. The combined effort led to a handsome
sandstone example of Indo-Islamic architecture with terra-cotta frills and
outbursts of balconies that mark each story. Unfortunately, after the tower
was damaged in the fourteenth century, Firoze Shah Tughlaq made re-
pairs that destroyed the originally harmonious lines. He added not only
height and marble to the two upper stories, but a heavy dose of incongruity. The lower sandstone sections are fluted, but his renovation adopted
a "round" motif. Instead of continuing vertical lines, he chose horizontal.
He also decided to change the degree of the taper. The decorative bands
of intricately carved inscription are Arabic quotations from the Quran.

At the foot of the Qutab Minar lies the Quwwat-ul-Islam Mosque, the
first Moslem building in Delhi and India. It was erected in the twelfth century after the Moslem defeat of the Hindu Chauhan dynasty. The Moslems
clearly relished their victory that introduced Islamic rule. As if to prove
their supremacy over the Hindus, they built their mosque on the site of
a Hindu temple and used materials, especially columns, from 27 other demolished Hindu shrines. Note the Hindu and Jain sculptures in various
parts of the mosque. Since the mosque was probably built by Hindu craftsmen, the presence of the large stone screen across the front of the prayer
hall may have been intended to block out the strong Hindu influence.

The mosque is also famous for a strange object, a fifth-century Iron Pillar, which originally stood before a temple of Vishnu and was possibly
brought here in the eleventh century. This solid shaft of iron, 24 feet high,
is inscribed with six lines of Sanskrit. No one knows why the pillar has
remained rust free for so many years. According to legend, if you stand
with your back to the pillar and can reach around and touch your fingers,
any wish you make will come true.

A hundred yards west of the Qutab Minar is another strange structure,
a tower 87 feet high. It was supposed to be twice the height of the Qutab
Minar, but its designer, Ala-ud-Din, died and no one bothered to complete
it. Northwest of the mosque is the tomb (now roofless) of Emperor Iltut-
mish. This is the oldest tomb of a Moslem ruler in Delhi.

The second Delhi capital, Siri, also created by Ala-ud-Din during his
short reign from 1296 to 1316, had a more dismal fate than his unfinished
tower. His seat of power, almost completely ravaged by the passage of
time, was also a coveted building site for Ghiyas-ud-din Tughlak who ultimately created the third Delhi capital, Tughlaqabad.

Tughlaqabad

Nine kilometers (five miles) east of the Qutab Minar, Tughlaqabad served as the hill fortress-palace-town of this first Tughlaq king, a soldier of fortune and the founder of the Tughlak dynasty (1320–1400). The extensive city, with its vast number of mosques, palaces, and residences set behind seven miles of heavy battlements and inwardly sloping walls, was built in a speedy two years that was nearly mirrored in its similarly quick demise. In five short years, Tughlaqabad turned into an Indian ghost town. One legend claims that a Sufi saint put a curse on the village. Another attributes the hasty decline to a guilty conscience. When the king returned victorious from battle, a newly erected pavilion, which just happened to be built by his own son, proved to be more perilous than any military campaign. It collapsed on top of Ghiyas-ud-din, putting an unexpected end to the celebration, not to mention his life. His son, Muhammad Shah, the successor, fled the royal headquarters.

Despite the disposable nature of Tughlaqabad, the actual ruins have managed to survive on an impressive scale. Stark walls stand out on the landscape, and the fortress remains still provide a sense of the city within the enclosure. You can imagine the lay of the streets and the series of structures and even see the large stone-lined reservoir that supplied the water to this capital and the remnants of an ingenious network of underground passages. Facing the ruins of the fort, its founder's tomb, a small, solid pentagonal mausoleum, has remained miraculously intact. The structure is made of red sandstone with a marble dome, the first of its kind in India. By a quirk of fate, this tomb also contains the remains of Muhammad-bin-Tughlaq, the patricidal son.

About three kilometers (two miles) south of Tughlaqabad on the road to Badarpur, you'll find Suraj Kund, a sacred tank that is the largest Hindu monument around Delhi, built in the eleventh century by a Rajput king. It is believed that a Sun temple, one of the few in India, once stood here, its steps leading down to the rock-cut pool that is shaped like an amphitheater.

Little remains of the fourth city, Jahanpanah, created by Muhammad-bin Tughlak and his successor, Firoze Shah Tughlaq, who decided in 1351 to shift the capital closer to the Yamuna River. With the move, the capital acquired a new name, Firozabad, in tribute to himself ("bad" means city).

Lodi Gardens

On your way to Lodi Gardens, visit Hauz Khas Village, a new attraction that celebrates Indian village life. Set behind walls, this artists' colony has excellent boutiques, cafés, and art galleries.

In the intervening years leading up to the creation of the sixth capital in the 1500s, Delhi went through a terrible phase. After Timur (Tamerlane) ransacked the city at the end of the fourteenth century, he ordered the massacre of the entire population—just retribution, he thought, for the murder of some of his soldiers. As if in subconscious response to this mournful period, the subsequent Lodi dynasty built no city, only mausoleums and tombs.

A visit to Lodi Gardens, which contains the fifteenth- and sixteenth-century tombs of the Lodi rulers, offers a peaceful stroll along winding walks that cut through landscaped lawns with flowers and trees. See, especially, the dignified tomb of Mohammad Shah, the third ruler of the Lodi Dynasty—a tomb that also houses the graves of various other members of the ruling family. The octagon rises up near the southern entrance. Also see the imposing octagonal tomb of Sikandar Lodi, set in the northwest corner. Delhi is a city of gardens, and Lodi Gardens is one of the finest.

The Mogul Monuments

Delhi's sixth capital rests on the site of the Purana Qila, an old fort near the Delhi Zoo. This area of Delhi was the scene of a fierce sixteenth-century power struggle between the Afghan Sher Shah and the Mogul Emperor Humayan. In the 1530s Humayun began to build his own capital, Dinpanah, on these grounds, but Sher Shah defeated him in 1540. After destroying the Moguls' fledgling city, Sher Shah constructed his own city, Shergarh, over the remains, only to have Humayun strike back 15 years later and seize control.

Unfortunately, once you enter the massive Bara Darwaza (western gate), only two buildings remain intact: the Kila Kana Masjid, Sher Shah's private mosque, an excellent example of Indo-Afghan architecture with lovely proportions; and a two-story octagonal red sandstone tower, the Sher Mandal, which ultimately became Humayun's library. This small building also served as Humayun's deathtrap a few years later. Hearing the call to prayer, Humayun started down the steep steps, slipped, and fell—so much for Humayun. This untimely accident leads us to a magnificent structure just south of the zoo: Humayun's tomb, built by his grieving widow, Hameda Begum, who is also buried inside.

Humayun's Tomb

This tomb, erected in the middle of the sixteenth century, marks the beginning of a new architectural era that culminated in the glorious Mogul masterpieces at Agra and Fatehpur Sikri. The Moguls, who brought to India their love of gardens, fountains, and water, produced sublime structures, such as this mausoleum, which combines severe symmetry with Oriental splendor.

Built in a style reminiscent of Persian architecture, the tomb stands on a raised platform set amid spacious gardens enclosed by walls, the first "tomb-in-a-garden" complex in India. The color effect of Humayun's Tomb—a soothing blend of red sandstone and white, black, and yellow marble—is stunning. The marble dome, a lovely departure from former heavy domes, is India's first example of the dome within a dome (the interior dome is set inside the soaring larger dome seen from the exterior), a style that is also used in the Taj Mahal.

Many other notable Moguls are buried here, including the builder and possibly Humayun's barber, who is supposedly entombed inside the blue domed, square structure. Finally, as you enter or leave, stand a moment in the gateway. Notice how the entire monument is framed in the arch; this, too, happens again at the Taj Mahal. And, as you contemplate the serene setting, consider that many of the dead buried inside were murdered princes, victims of foul play.

Shahjahanabad—Lal Qila (Red Fort)

After you pass through Delhi Gate, you soon see the silhouette of the massive outer walls of the Lal Qila (Red Fort) just ahead on the right. Lal Qila is the greatest wonder of all the cities of Delhi, even outdoing Lutyens's Imperial City. Here is Shah Jahan's symbol of Mogul power and elegance, built behind red sandstone walls that gave the fort its name.

It's easy to imagine imperial elephants swaying by with their *mahouts* (elephant drivers) or any conceivable vestige of Shah Jahan's pomp.

The formerly unobstructed view of the main entrance, called the Lahore Gate, flanked by semioctagonal towers and facing Chandni Chowk, is blocked by a barbican (a kind of gatehouse), which the paranoid Aurangzeb added for greater security—much to the grief of Shah Jahan, his father. From his prison, where he was held captive by his power-hungry offspring, Shah Jahan wrote, "You have made a bride of the palace and thrown a veil over her face."

Once you enter the main gate, continue along a vaulted arcade, Chhatta Chowk, originally the shopping district for the royal ladies and now a bazaar selling goods of significantly lower quality. The arcade leads to the Naubat Khana (Imperial Bandstand), the main gateway of the palace—a red sandstone structure, where music was played five times daily. Beyond this point, everyone but the emperor and princes had to proceed on foot, a rule that was observed until 1857. A spacious lawn, once a courtyard serving as the boundary where all but the nobility had to stop, leads to the great Diwan-i-Am, the Hall of Public Audience.

Now, you've entered the seventh city of Delhi, the Delhi of Shah Jahan. Marble dominates. Seen against a background of green grass and blue sky, the hall, raised on a platform and open on three sides, evokes a time of irretrievable glory—like the moment described by Bernier, a seventeenth-century French traveler, who was overwhelmed by the hall's magnificence. Here the emperor sat on a royal throne, set in a marble alcove in the center of the back wall—a throne studded with decorative panels that sparkled with countless inlaid precious stones. These panels, stolen by British soldiers after the Indian Mutiny of 1857, were restored 50 years later by Lord Curzon. It was here that the emperor listened to and judged the plight of subjects brought before him in full view of the throngs of people who watched from the courtyard below. The rest of the hall, Bernier explained, was reserved for rajahs and foreign envoys, all standing with "their eyes bent downwards and their hands crossed." High above them, under a pearl-fringed canopy resting on golden shafts in the royal recess, "glittered the dazzling figure of the Grand Mogul, a figure to strike terror, for a frown meant death." Facing the emperor's throne is the marble seat of the prime minister.

Behind the Diwan-i-Am stands a row of palaces that overlook the not-too-distant Yamuna River. To the extreme south is the Mumtaz Mahal—now the Red Fort Museum of Archaeology, with relics from the Mogul period and numerous paintings and drawings. The next palace is the Rang Mahal (the Painted Palace), which used to be richly decorated. The hall, which had a silver ceiling until the treasury ran too low, may have been a sitting room for the royal ladies. It contains a marble basin constructed into the center of the floor (the bottom is carved in the shape of a lotus), with a water channel—called the Canal of Paradise—running through this palace and many of the others.

The third palace is the Khas Mahal, the exclusive palace of the emperor, divided into three sections: the sitting room, the dream chamber (obviously for sleeping), and the prayer chamber, with lavishly decorated walls and painted ceilings still intact. The lovely marble screen contains the carved Scale of Justice—two swords and a scale that symbolize punishment and justice. From the attached octagonal tower, Muthamman Burj, the emperor, would appear before his subjects every morning. He also came here to watch elephant fights held in the fields.

The next palace is the famous Diwan-i-Khas (Hall of Private Audience), the most exclusive pavilion. Here Shah Jahan consulted with his ministers and held private meetings. He would sit on his famous solid-gold Peacock Throne, which was inlaid with hundreds of stones. Back then, its value was 12 million pounds sterling, or $19.8 million at today's rate of exchange. It was too precious, too beautiful! When Nadir Shah sacked Delhi in 1739, he hauled the throne to Persia. A Persian couplet written in gold above an arch sums up Shah Jahan's sentiments about his city: If there be a paradise on earth/It is this! It is this! It is this!

Finally, you reach the Royal Hammams, exquisite Mogul baths with inlaid marble floors. Imagine the self-indulgence as you wander through the three rooms. There's a fountain that supposedly had rose-scented water, and a state-of-the-art hot steam bath. No wonder Shah Jahan called his city paradise.

From here, a short path leads to the Moti Masjid (the Pearl Mosque), designed by Aurangzeb for his personal use and the use of the royal ladies. Once the ceiling was copper plated. The prayer hall is inlaid with *musalla* (prayer rugs) outlined in black marble. Though the mosque has the purity of white marble, some claim the excessively ornate style reflects the decadence that set in before the end of Shah Jahan's reign.

Jama Masjid

Looming majestically on a high platform across the street stands an exquisite statement in red sandstone and white marble: the Jama Masjid, India's largest mosque, completed in 1658 by Shah Jahan. Broad steps lead up to the double-story gateways and a magnificent courtyard (where thousands still gather to pray), which is enclosed by pillared corridors with domed pavilions in each corner. The best time to visit is Friday, the holy day; the exact hour is tricky. Check beforehand to be certain you'll be able to go inside. For a small fee, you can also climb to the top of a minaret (however, a woman must be escorted by a "responsible" male). From here, you have an extended view of Old Delhi.

The mosque, with its onion-shaped dome and tapering minarets, is characteristically Mogul. But Shah Jahan added an innovation. Note the novel stripes running up and down the well-proportioned marble domes. Just standing in the courtyard, you are engulfed in the quiet power of Islam; tranquility prevails, enhanced by the architecture. Each dome, portico, and minaret of this mosque is subordinated to the whole, producing an overal impression of harmony.

Inside the prayer hall (entered by the devout after a ritual washing in the big water basin—a symbolic purification), the pulpit is carved from a single slab of marble. In one corner of the hall is a room where Shah Jahan installed the footprints of Hazrat Muhammad, the Holy Prophet.

The northern gate of the mosque leads into Chandi Chowk, the former imperial avenue, down which Shah Jahan would ride at the head of a lavish cavalcade. Today, everything rushes indiscriminately into the congested avenue—bullock carts, wandering cows, limousines, taxis, private cars, dogs, auto rickshaws, bicycles, bicycle rickshaws, horse-drawn tongas, and crowds of pedestrians. It's a great place to explore (see the section on Delhi markets and bazaars).

As we move toward the twentieth century, two other monuments should be seen, built during the decline of the Mogul period.

Jantar Mantar and Safdarjang's Tomb

The first monument is on Parliament Street near Connaught Place (the center hub of New Delhi); the Jantar Mantar (observatory) built by Maharajah Jai Singh II of Jaipur in 1725. This astronomer-king, who left five similar structures in India, created precise masonry instruments that look like they stepped out of science fiction. The largest structure is a huge right-angle sundial, the Samrat Yantra (supreme instrument). Next, head south to the tomb of Safdarjang, one of the last prime ministers of the Moguls in Delhi. Erected in 1754 by Nawab Shuja-ud-Daula, the son of Mirza Shuja-ud-Daula, it is also the last Mogul mausoleum built in this city.

Now, leap to the twentieth century. . . .

The Imperial City and Modern Delhi

Start at the War Memorial Arch, better known as India Gate: a memorial to the Indian Army dead of the First World War, modeled along the lines of the Menin Gate in Belgium. The names of the dead, all 90,000, are inscribed on the arch. Majestic Raj Path—the broadest avenue of Delhi and the scene of the yearly parade on Republic Day (January 26)—heads west to the sight of the eighth and last capital of Delhi: Sir Edwin Lutyens's Imperial City. As you move up the avenue, you come first to the enormous Secretariat buildings that face one another on Raj Path. Identical in design, the two buildings have 1,000 rooms and miles of corridors. Directly behind the North Secretariat is the Sansad Bhavan (Parliament House), a huge circular building in red and gray sandstone with an open colonnade that extends around the circumference. Proceedings in the two houses of Parliament—Lok Sabha (House of the People) and the Rajya Sabha (Council of States)—are in Hindi, the national language, or English.

Continue up Raj Path to Rashtrapati Bhavan, the Presidential Palace. Though built in the twentieth century, its daunting proportions seem to come from an earlier and more lavish time. The Bhavan contains 340 rooms and its grounds cover 330 acres. The shape of the central brass dome, the main feature of the palace, copies a Buddhist *stupa* (shrine). A majestic courtyard bearing the Jaipur Column leads to the yawning Greek portico of the building. The overall effect is nearly overwhelming, with the building practically spilling over the small Raisini Hill.

A newer part of Delhi is the Diplomatic Enclave to the south, where a few excellent examples of modern architecture can be seen in the residences and office buildings of the diplomatic corps assigned to the Indian capital.

Our tour of Delhi concludes with a stop at a hospital across from the Red Fort. This is no ordinary hospital for humans; it is a bird hospital—the Charity Bird Hospital run by Jains for over 35 years. Vegetarian birds (and rabbits) are treated inside, and nonvegetarian birds are treated in the courtyard. Bathed, fed, and given vitamins, the healthy birds refuse to leave. That's how you can spot the building—flocks of birds fly happily over its roof. Visiting hours, unlike most hospitals, are liberal, and donations are welcome.

Delhi's Markets and Bazaars

If you were born to shop or if you just like to wander through markets and bazaars, Delhi will keep you happy for days. After a brief introduction to the Old Delhi markets, especially Chandni Chowk, you'll find a list of other shopping districts, some where you can barter or just gaze. For those who don't like to shop or for those who are stuck with a long list and too little time, the best bet is a single trip to the Central Cottage Industries

Emporium on Jan Path near Connaught Place. Here, you'll find all India's handicrafts under one gigantic roof. But no bartering; prices are fixed.

Old Delhi and Chandni Chowk

Chandni Chowk, that perpetually congested avenue heading west from the Red Fort, is the best way to get into Old Delhi, with its twisting lanes, small streets, and crowded bazaars. As in the days of the Moguls, astrologers set up their booths on the narrow pavement. Shoemakers squat outside and repair sandals, blithely ignoring the human swirl around them. If you peer through a portico, you may see men getting shaved, silver being weighed, plus every other conceivable form of intense commerce, while outside, a cow sits complacently in the street.

If you visit the old town on an auspicious day, you will meet wedding processions with bridegrooms dressed like princes—their turbans flashing with cut-glass jewels—astride jade-festooned horses. The groom is accompanied by relatives and friends and colorful brass bands who demonstrate the exuberance and the importance of this cavalcade. Often such processions take place at night, with portable chandeliers held high like torches.

Strange aromas fill the air, the pungent odor of Oriental spices and the unfortunate and overwhelming smell of garbage. Cattle stroll in the middle of the road, chewing some grocer's vegetables or abandoned refuse. Jewelry, delicate ivory carvings, and rich silks and brocades are exhibited in closely packed profusion. Medicine booths conceal doctors attending to a row of patients, who sit resignedly in open-air waiting rooms. Old Delhi is nothing if not superoriental—the glory and the guile, grandeur and grime, of the fascinating and slowly changing East. Chandni Chowk is a place to wander, to lose yourself, for you're never really lost.

Around Connaught Place

The sorrowfully neglected Connaught Circus, which encircles a park in the central hub of New Delhi, is another shopper's mecca, with fixed prices, for the most part. A little sprucing up of the dilapidated facades would improve the atmosphere, but once you step inside the fancier shops (like the Ivory Palace or Banaras Silk House), the former elegance takes over.

Built underneath a portion of the green park is Palika Bazaar, India's bad idea of a modern market. Entering this underground shopping arcade is like descending into the Times Square subway station—dreary, dirty, and crowded. But Palika Bazaar has a lot to offer. Check out the silver jewelry at the Jewel Mine in the central hall. For great *kurtas* (hand embroidery), visit Lal Behari Tandon, halfway around the same circle. Every item is in this bazaar, if you can tolerate hunting through dingy surroundings.

Also visit Shankar Market, northwest of the Block of the Outer Circle of Connaught Place. If you don't see signs for this market, ask. Here you can buy great fabrics, especially cottons—handblocked and superfine. Often the merchant doubles as a tailor.

Finally, browse along Jan Path. At the southern end, you'll find the Tibetan Market. Sometimes a careful search can turn up a Tibetan treasure. But basically, buy what you like; most of the "antiques" are brand-new. Besides, you can't take any article out of India if it's 100 years old.

PRACTICAL INFORMATION FOR DELHI

WHEN TO GO. Delhi is at its best between October and April, and the choice months are November–March. At this time, there's a minimum of rainfall, the countryside is green, the gardens in bloom, and the climate is agreeable. A coat is recommended for evening wear from mid-December to February. The big event of the year is the Republic Day Parade on January 26. Visitors are advised to make their hotel bookings for this date well in advance. October and November are good months for the festivals—*Dussehra* and *Diwali.*

HOW TO GET THERE. By Air. For information on flights from the United States or Britain to Delhi's Indira Gandhi International Airport, see *Facts at Your Fingertips. Indian Airlines* also has international flights between Delhi and the following neighboring countries: Kathmandu (Nepal), Kabul (Afghanistan), Lahore and Karachi (Pakistan). Indian Airlines also flies from the nearby National Airport (Air Bus terminal or Boeing terminal) to all important destinations in India. *Vayu-doot* feeder airline connects small cities in India, including hill stations like Kullu, Shimla, and Shillong. All terminals are about 15 km (9 mi.) from the center of New Delhi. Remember to confirm your ticket 72 hours before departure and arrive at the terminal an hour before flight time.

By Bus. Every day, deluxe buses from Haryana, Himachal Pradesh, Jammu and Kashmir, Uttar Pradesh, and Rajasthan—all with their videos blaring—come rolling into the *Inter State Bus Terminus* at Kashmiri Gate, 8 km (5 mi.) north of Connaught Place. For information and details, call the following numbers: Haryana, 2521262, open: 6 A.M.–noon and 1–9 P.M.; Himachal Pradesh, 2516725, open 7 A.M.–7 P.M.; Jammu and Kashmir, 3324422 or 343400, open 10 A.M.–5 P.M.; Rajasthan, 2522246, open 6 A.M.–10 P.M.; Uttar Pradesh, 2518709, open 6 A.M.–8 P.M. Deluxe buses to Jaipur (Rajasthan) also leave daily from Bikaner House, near India Gate.

By Train. Some of India's best trains roll through Delhi. The Delhi Railway Station is 7 km (4½ mi.) north of Connaught Place and the New Delhi Railway Station is directly north of Connaught Place. Most trains leave from the New Delhi Railway Station; but check before you set out. For tickets and information, contact the International Tourist Guide, New Delhi Railway Station, Platform No. 1 (open 10 A.M.–5 P.M., closed Sunday; tel. 3352164). Tickets must be paid in foreign currency, usually dollars or sterling. You can also purchase a ticket in rupees at the general counter at the same location (open daily, 9:30 A.M.–8 P.M.). Before you board any train, you must have a confirmed ticket, and if you travel at night, a reservation for a sleeper and a berth.

By Rented Car with Driver. Hire a car with driver from a recommended tour operator listed below. Expect fares to be about Rs. 4 per km, including a halt charge of Rs. 50–Rs. 100 per night. Delhi is 200 km (120 mi.) from Agra, 249 km (149 mi.) from Chandigarh, 261 km (162 mi.) from Jaipur, 586 km (363 mi.) from Jammu, 569 km (353 mi.) from Lucknow, 368 km (228 mi.) from Shimla, 765 km (474 mi.) from Varanasi. Although renting a car with a driver in Delhi costs slightly more than in most other areas in India (Rs. 2.50 per km), it's still an economical way of getting around if you've the money to spare and want to really see the area.

TOURIST INFORMATION. Lots of information is available in Delhi on everywhere in India and nearby countries for that matter. The Government of India Tourist Office is usually crowded, but the staff are helpful and have good current information. Some of the separate state offices are better than others, with Jammu and Kashmir and Kerala outshining the rest.

Government of India Tourist Office, main office: 88 Jan Path; tel. 3320005 or 3320008; open Mon.–Fri. 9 A.M.–6 P.M., Sat. 9 A.M.–1 P.M. They have an excellent map of Delhi plus information on most of India. The International Airport and railroad stations have counters that are open around the clock.

State Tourist Offices. Go to the Chandralok Building at 36 Jan Path, New Delhi, and you'll find the following offices: Rajasthan (tel. 3322332), Uttar Pradesh (tel.

3322251), Haryana (tel. 3324911) and Himachal Pradesh (tel. 3325320). At Kanishka Plaza, 19 Ashok Rd., you'll find Bihar (tel. 3324422), Punjab (tel. 3323055), Jammu and Kashmir (tel. 3324422), Kerala (tel. 3316541), and Madhya Pradesh (tel. 3321187). The Andhra Pradesh office is at Ashok Road (tel. 389182). Goa is at Goa Sadan, 18 Amrita Shergill Marg (tel. 692065). Offices for the other states are located at the State Emporia Complex on Baba Kharak Singh Marg: Assam (B–1; tel. 343961), Gujarat (A–6; tel. 343173), Karnataka (C–4; tel. 343862), Maharashtra (A–8; tel. 343773), Orissa (B–4; tel. 344580), Tamil Nadu (C–1; tel. 344651), and West Bengal (A–2; tel. 343775). Sikkim's office is located at New Sikkim House, 14 Panchsheel Marg, Chanakyapuri (tel. 3014901). The office for Andaman and Nicobar Islands is at F–105 Curzon Road Hostel, Kasturba Gandhi Marg (tel. 387015). In general, the state offices are open Monday–Friday, 10 A.M.–5 P.M., and most Saturday mornings.

FOREIGN CURRENCY EXCHANGE. Most of the Western-style hotels have money exchange counters that will cash your traveler's checks with twice the speed and half the hassle. *American Express* (at Wenger House, Connaught Place, tel. 344119) and Thomas Cook Pvt. Ltd. (Hotel Imperial, Jan Path, tel. 312468) will cash their own traveler's checks. At American Express, bring a book or lunch; the lines can get long. Open generally Monday–Friday 10 A.M.–5 P.M., Saturday mornings. You can also cash checks at the following banks: *Bank of America,* Hansalaya Bldg., Barakhamba Road 6; *Citibank,* Jeevan Bharti Bldg., 124 Connaught Circus; *Grindlays Bank,* H Block, Connaught Circus; *Reserve Bank of India,* 6 Parliament Street; *State Bank of India,* SBI New Bldg., Parliament Street. The *Central Bank of India* (Hotel Ashok, Chanakyapuri) is open 24 hours. Other banks are open Monday–Friday 10 A.M.–2 P.M., Saturdays till noon.

ACCOMMODATIONS. Delhi has luxurious Western-style hotels, moderately priced hotels, and even some lovely guest houses that are cozy and a real bargain. Book reservations early if you want to stay at a fancy Western-style hotel. Unless noted, all hotels accept credit cards and have these amenities: shops, swimming pool, TV, restaurants galore, travel agencies, secretarial services, baby-sitters, international communication set-ups, foreign-exchange counters. Bedrooms have low-key modern decor; all have well-appointed bathrooms. Prices are based on double occupancy and don't include taxes: *Deluxe,* over Rs. 1,450; *Expensive,* Rs. 950–Rs. 1,450; *Moderate,* Rs. 500–Rs. 950; *Inexpensive,* under Rs. 500.

Deluxe

Ashok Hotel. Chanakyapuri, New Delhi; tel. 600121. 10 km (6 mi.) from the airport. 576 rooms. Ashok's palatial red-and-white sandstone exterior befits India's first national hotel, still run by the government and popular with visiting VIPs. The rooms aren't exquisite, but they're spacious. Ashok also has a 24-hour bank. AE, DC, V.

Holiday Inn Crowne Plaza. Barakamba Ave., Connaught Pl., New Delhi; tel. 3320101 or 800–HOLIDAY in U.S. 24 km (15 mi.) from airport. 500 rooms. Delhi's newest luxury hotel has a high-tech, vaguely art-deco atrium lobby with a waterfall. It also features a no-smoking floor and wheel chair accommodations. AE, V.

Hyatt Regency. Bhikaiji Cama Pl., Ring Rd., New Delhi; tel. 609911 or 800–233–1234 in U.S. 8 km (5 mi.) from the airport. 535 rooms. Super posh, this hotel even has a micro-waterfall in the lobby. Make sure your room doesn't face the noisy parking lot or the shanty town out back. AE, MC, V.

Oberoi. Dr. Zakir Hussain Marg, New Delhi; tel. 363030 or 800–223–6800 in U.S. 20 km (12 mi.) from the airport. 288 rooms. A marble high rise with black-marble floors and bouquets of flowers in the lobby, the Oberoi is Delhi's most elegant hotel. Best rooms overlook the pool. AE, CB, DC.

Taj Mahal Hotel. 1 Mansingh Rd., New Delhi; tel. 3016162. 18 km (11 mi.) from the airport. 300 rooms. This white-marble hotel has an appealing fancy glitz. In the beamed ceiling lobby, reminiscent of Mexico, you might catch sight of a lavish wedding. You can also visit the resident astrologer. AE, DC, MC, V.

Taj Palace Inter-Continental. 2 Sardar Patel Marg, Diplomatic Enclave, New Delhi; tel. 3010404 or 800–33–AGAIN in U.S. 12 km (7 mi.) from the airport. 504 rooms. If the Taj Mahal Hotel is booked up, try its other hotel. Expect the same fine service, just less razzle-dazzle. AE, DC, MC, V.

Welcomgroup Maurya Sheraton. Diplomatic Enclave, New Delhi; tel. 3010101 or 800–325–3535 in U.S. 6 km (4 mi.) from the airport. 500 rooms. Another marble monolith, its good restaurants make this a popular choice. AE, DC, V.

Expensive

Claridges Hotel. 12 Aurangzeb Rd., New Delhi; tel. 3010211. 12 km (7 mi.) from the airport. 140 rooms. This is an old British staple—tidy, nearly stodgy in decor. The primary aim is pleasing the guest with great service. AE, DC, V.

Hotel Imperial. Janpath, New Delhi; tel. 3325332. 23 km (14 mi.) from the airport. 175 rooms. This British Raj hotel and Delhi landmark is ragged around the edges, but its location in the heart of New Delhi makes it popular. Good ambience for the non-flashy traveler. AE, DC, V.

Hotel Samrat. Chanakyapuri, New Delhi; tel. 603030. 10 km (6 mi.) from the airport. 272 rooms. This Ashok group hotel adjoins the Hotel Ashok. Less fancy, its rooms are spacious and attractive. Ask for a room overlooking the swimming pool. AE, MC, V.

Moderate

The Connaught Palace. 37 Shaheed Bhagat Singh Marg, New Delhi; tel. 344225. 23 km (14 mi.) from the airport. 78 rooms with bath. This new hotel doesn't have a swimming pool, but rooms are extremely clean with an attractive modern decor. Best views overlook the stadium. Good value and good service. AE, DC, V.

Hotel Hans Plaza. 15 Barakhamba Rd., New Delhi; tel. 3316861. 20 km (12 mi.) from the airport. 67 rooms. You won't find a swimming pool, but this newish Western-style hotel in the center of New Delhi has attractive, clean rooms. AE, MC, V.

Lodhi Hotel. Lala Lajpat Rai Marg, New Delhi; tel. 362422. 15 km (9 mi.) from the airport. This Ashok chain Western-style hotel is under renovation. At press time, spacious rooms were a bit dreary, but for the budget traveler who wants a swimming pool, it's here. Rooms are clean and simple. AE, DC, V.

Inexpensive

The following three guest houses in Sunder Nagar, 16 km (10 mi.) from the airport, are quiet havens with attractive lawns and clean air-conditioned rooms that add up to a terrific bargain. All rooms are quite pleasant, with modern decor, TV, and Western-style bathrooms. Unless noted, they lack a dining room, but offer multicuisine room service.

Jukaso Inn. 50 Sunder Nagar, New Delhi; tel. 692137. 5 rooms. This inn also has an interior courtyard with a cozy restaurant. AE.

Kailish Inn. 10 Sunder Nagar, New Delhi; tel. 617401. 16 rooms. This inn offers car-rental arrangements. AE, MC, V.

Maharani Guest House. 3 Sunder Nagar, New Delhi; tel. 693128. 25 rooms. AE, DC, MC, V.

Tourist Camp. J.L. Nehru Marg, Box 7110, New Delhi; tel. 272898. About 20 km (12 mi.) from the airport. Numerous huts. This popular facility has modest yet attractive huts laid out on a spacious lawn with gardens. Deluxe rooms are best, with attached bathrooms (showers); but all rooms are clean. Amenities include multicuisine restaurant, travel agency, foreign-exchange counter, doctor on call, laundry service. A 'great bargain. Rupees only.

YMCA Tourist Hostel. Jai Singh Rd.; Box 612, New Delhi; tel. 311915. 14 km (7 mi.) from the airport. 123 rooms. This hostel offers simple, clean rooms (some are air-conditioned). It also has a multicuisine restaurant. Rupees only.

DINING OUT. Delhi is cosmopolitan, with cosmopolitan tastes and international cuisines. Delhi dry days are strictly observed—no alcohol available on the first and seventh day of the month and national holidays. Recently, the law that restricted liquor to hotel restaurants was changed; however, private restaurant liquor permits will take time to procure, so don't expect a drink with your meal at most independent restaurants.

While we include only the best options, most accommodations listed above also have restaurants. Breakfast is usually served 8–10:30; lunch, 12:30–3; dinner, 8–11. The restaurants listed below are informal and unless noted are open for all three meals and don't require reservations. Price categories, based on one person eating a three-course meal, excluding taxes, tip, or beverage, are: *Deluxe,* over Rs. 120; *Expensive,* Rs. 80–Rs. 120; *Moderate,* Rs. 40–Rs. 80; *Inexpensive,* under Rs. 40. Unless noted, they all accept credit cards.

MULTICUISINE

Expensive–Deluxe

Cafe Prominade. Hyatt Regency, Bhikaiji Cama Pl., Ring Rd.; tel. 609911. This airy restaurant, spilling into a downstairs lobby, serves the best buffet in Delhi, with imported cheeses, cold cuts, a well-stocked salad bar, and tasty desserts. You can also order à la carte. At night, you often have to contend with a rock band. This café also has a monthly food-fest that highlights a foreign cuisine. Open 24 hours.

Moderate–Expensive

Pickwicks. Claridges Hotel, 12 Aurangzeb Rd.; tel. 3010211. Called a coffee shop, this cozy place has an upscale British ambience that includes a fireplace and wood paneling. You can enjoy Indian dishes, plus great sizzlers, pork chops, even omelets and spaghetti. Open 7 A.M.–midnight.

Moderate

The Host. F–28 Connaught Pl.; tel. 3316576. This handsome restaurant, with a subdued decor and a quiet ambience, serves tasty Chinese, Continental, and Indian cuisines. Open 10 A.M.–11:30 P.M. Rupees only.

Machan. Taj Mahal Hotel, 1 Mansingh Rd.; tel. 3016162. Any time of day or night, enjoy assorted international cuisines at Machan, done up in light and airy tropical colors with reminders of wildlife. "Machan" means wildlife look-out tower. After 3 P.M., it serves great pizza.

United Coffee House. E–15 Connaught Pl.; tel. 3322075. In this old Delhi restaurant with turn-of-the-century Regency decor, you can choose from very good Chinese, Continental, and Indian cuisines. Open 9:30 A.M.–midnight, closed Sun. Rupees only.

Inexpensive–Moderate

Nirula's. L-Block, Connaught Circus; tel. 3322419. Delhi's best fast-food eatery serves reliable Chinese, Indian, and Continental food (including pizza) in a decor that is heavy on coffee-shop plastic, but not offensive. Their ice-cream parlor is nearby and they have numerous branches in the city. Open 11 A.M.–10:30 P.M. Rupees only.

INDIAN

Expensive–Deluxe

Bukhara. Welcomgroup Maurya Sheraton, Diplomatic Enclave; tel. 3010101. This handsome copper- and wood-decorated restaurant emphasizes superb northwest frontier specialities: leg of lamb, tandooris, and kebabs. Dinner reservations advised. Open 8 A.M.–noon and 12:30 P.M.–2:30 A.M.

Dhaba. Claridges Hotel, 12 Aurangzeb Rd., New Delhi; tel. 3010211. Dhaba refers to a curbside truck that serves inexpensive meals. That's the motif in this popular restaurant, which offers extremely tasty dishes. Dinner reservations advised. Open noon–3 P.M. and 7:30–11:30 P.M.

Dum Pukht. Welcomgroup Maurya Sheraton, Diplomatic Enclave; tel. 3010101. Heavy brocade fans and Nawabi costumes adorn the walls here, where the menu is printed on silk and set in silver. The cuisine, *Dum Pukht* (aromatic Indian dishes cooked in sealed pots), originated with the Moslem nawab rulers. Splurge and have a sumptuous feast—*Dumpukht Asafjahi* or *Dumpukht Wajid Shahi*—meals named for two nawabs in Uttar Pradesh. Reservations advised. Open 12:30–3 P.M. and 8–12 P.M.

Frontier Room. Ashok Hotel, 50 B. Chanakyapuri; tel. 600121. This rustic-style restaurant gets high marks for its northwest frontier cuisine served in a subdued setting. Roving minstrels entertain at night. Try the kebabs. Dinner reservations advised. Open 1–2:45 P.M. and 8–11:45 P.M.

Haveli. Taj Mahal, 1 Mansingh Rd.; tel. 3016162. Enjoy classical Indian music and dances nightly in this cheery restaurant with lots of wood trim and Indian paintings on the walls. Dishes are tasty. Dinner reservations advised. Open 12:30–3 P.M. and 7:30–11:30 P.M.

Moderate

Gulati Restaurant. 6 Pandara Rd. Market; tel. 388839. You can hob-nob with politicos and eat good Mughlai servings and tasty *dahls* (lentil dishes) in this small crowded restaurant. Open noon–midnight, closed Mon. Rupees only.

Inexpensive–Moderate

Karim Hotel. Gali Kababian, Jama Masjid, Old Delhi; tel. 269880. This extremely simple restaurant is an Old Delhi institution that offers an ethnic ambience and terrific Mughlai cuisine. Open 10 A.M.–midnight. Rupees only.

Karim's Nemat Kada. 168/2 Jha House, Hazrat Nizamuddin West, near the police station; tel. 698300. This attractive restaurant in an Islamic neighborhood has a welcoming ambience and serves very good Mughlai dishes. Open noon–midnight. Rupees only.

Moti Mahal. Netaji Subhash Marg, Daryaganj, Old Delhi; tel. 220077. Popular with tourists, this open-air restaurant has lost some of its luster, but it still serves fabulous tandoori. With Indian entertainment at night, reservations are advised. Open noon–midnight; closed Tues. Rupees only.

Peshawari Restaurant. 3711 Netaji Subhash Marg, Daryaganj, Old Delhi; tel. 262168. This clean, upstairs restaurant, with an Indian coffee-shop decor, is extremely popular. Its butter chicken is sublime. Open noon–4 P.M. and 6–11:30 P.M. Rupees only.

Woodlands. Lodhi Hotel, Lala Lajput Rai Marg; tel. 362422. This restaurant has a south Indian decor with a clay wall covered with village hut designs and masks mounted on another wall. The lighting is subdued. The south Indian vegetarian cuisine is delicious. Go for the *thali* (assorted dishes) or the good *dosas* (Indian-style stuffed crêpe). Open for meals noon–3 P.M. and 7:30–10:30 P.M. Snacks available during non-meal hours. Rupees only.

Inexpensive

Kake da Hotel. 74 Outer Circle, Connaught Pl. (between L and M blocks); tel. 3316580. The best butter chicken in town is served here. Bring handiwipes or wear old clothes; napkins are scarce. Expect a crowd and a steal of a meal in ethnic surroundings. Open 11 A.M. until the chicken is gone, closed Sun. Rupees only.

CHINESE

Expensive–Deluxe

House of Ming. Taj Mahal Hotel, 1 Mansingh Rd.; tel. 3016162. With just a few Chinese decorations on the wall, this elegant restaurant serves wonderful Cantonese and Szechuan dishes. Dinner reservations advised. Open 12:30–3 P.M. and 7:30–midnight.

Taipan. Oberoi, Dr. Zakir Hussain Marg; tel. 363030. This elegant rooftop restaurant, with Chinese watercolors on the walls, handsome smoked-glass and brass lanterns, and polished teak lattice screens, serves excellent Szechuan cuisine. Try the spinach in hot sesame oil and chili sauce, the steamed chicken in lotus leaves, or tasty king prawns in garlic. Dinner reservations advised. Open 12:30–3 P.M. and 8–midnight. AE, DC, MC, V.

Tea House of the August Moon. Taj Palace, Sardar Patel Marg, Diplomatic Enclave; tel. 3010404. Dine in a "tea house" complete with goldfish pond, bridge, bamboo grove, and dragons on the wall that emit smoke at night. The chef serves good

Cantonese, Szechuan, and dim sum. Dinner reservations advised. Open 12:30–2:45 P.M. and 7:30–11:45 P.M.

Moderate

Berco's. E–8 Connaught Pl.; tel. 3323757. In this coffee shop–style restaurant, you get fast service but not fast-food fare. Choose from good spicy and non-spicy Chinese (also Japanese and Indian) dishes. There's always a crowd at 2 P.M. Open noon–11 P.M. Rupees only.

Chungwa. D–13, Defense Colony; tel. 625976. A small neighborhood restaurant, Chungwa has a quiet, informal decor and serves excellent Szechuan and Cantonese food, with especially good prawn and chicken dishes. Open noon–3 P.M. and 7:30–11:30 P.M. Rupees only.

JAPANESE

Expensive

Tokyo Restaurant. Ashok Hotel, Chanakyapuri, New Delhi; tel. 600412. Japanese paper lanterns hanging from the ceiling, delicate bamboo screens, and taped Japanese music get you into the mood for the Tokyo's good Japanese cuisine. Specialties include tempura, *kappa-maki* (cucumber sushi roll), *yakitori* (barbecued chicken), or *yaki-udon* (noodles with pork and vegetables). Open 12:30–3 P.M. and 7:30–11 P.M. Reservations advised.

CONTINENTAL

Expensive–Deluxe

Brasserie. Le Meridien Hotel, Windsor Pl., Janpath; tel. 383960. This spacious and attractive restaurant, off the hotel's lobby, is popular and serves numerous cuisines around the clock.

Casa Medici. Taj Mahal, 1 Mansingh Rd.; tel. 3016162. This elegant rooftop restaurant serves tasty Italian dishes. At lunch, enjoy a good buffet; at night, dance to a live band. Dinner reservations advised. Open 1–3 P.M. and 7–midnight.

Oriental Express. Taj Palace, 2 Sardar Patel Marg, Diplomatic Enclave; tel. 3010404. The decor here befits its name—styled like a fancy dining car on the *Orient Express*. You can choose from numerous Continental cuisines. Dinner reservations advised. Open noon–3 P.M. and 7:30–11:30 P.M.

Valentino's. Hyatt Regency, Bhikaiji Cama Pl., Ring Rd.; tel. 609911. In this elegant restaurant, with an art-deco decor, you can enjoy very good Italian cuisine. Dinner reservations advised. Open noon–2:30 P.M. and 7:30–11:30 P.M.

SWEETS AND TREATS. Don't be put off by the shabby appearance of the rooftop *Coffee House* on top of Mohan Singh Place Building on Baba Khara Singh Marg, across the street from the state emporia complex. This is a Delhi landmark and a favorite hangout that serves good snacks and, yes, great coffee. Open 8 A.M.–10 P.M.

Bengali Sweet Shop, tucked in the corner of South Extension I Market, off Ring Rd., sells fabulous sweets. Try their *kulfi* (Indian ice cream), *gulabs* (milk sweets), *samosa* (fried vegetable dumplings), *aloo chat* (spicy cold "potato salad"). Open 10 A.M.–10 P.M.

Sweets Corner at Sunder Nagar Market, a good shopping area near the Oberoi Hotel, also has a similar range of great snacks. Open 7 A.M.–7 P.M. daily.

HOW TO GET AROUND. From the Airports. It's approximately 18 km (11 mi.) to the center of New Delhi from either airport. Numerous hotels provide airport pick-up service. You can also take the airport bus (Rs. 10 from the national airport, Rs. 15 from the international airport) which runs frequently to major hotels and the center of town. Taxis are also available. Don't try to hail one yourself, but go to the Pre-paid Taxi counter; your destination determines the exact rate. Don't give the driver your payment slip until you arrive. If he demands more rupees, complain to the hotel doorman. A taxi from the airport to the center of New Delhi should cost about Rs. 90.

Once you're in Delhi, you've arrived in an enormous sprawl of a city, with numerous neighborhoods that have restaurants, monuments, and parks that appeal to tourists. There are a few good ways to get around the city.

By Taxi. Taxis are Rs. 3.30 for the first km, Rs. 2.40 per additional km.

By Auto Rickshaw. This is the best way to scoot around town. The driver can be surly, can claim that the meter is broken, and can rig the meter to go faster than the scooter. But still, they're the most fun and cheap. Auto rickshaws charge Rs. 2.50 for the first 1.6 km and Rs. 1.20 per additional km.

By Bus. Forget the bus, unless you're good at catching fast-moving vehicles and like top-heavy tilters.

By Bike Rickshaw. In Old Delhi if you're not up to walking, this is the best alternative. A real bargain. It should be cheaper than the auto rickshaw.

By Deisel Rickshaw (twice as big as an auto rickshaw). From behind Palika Bazaar, you'll find these oversized rickshaws that will take you to fixed points at set fees. Slow moving, although faster than a bus.

TOURS. Numerous companies offer the following fixed-departure tours by bus (guide included): half-day tour of Old Delhi, Rs. 40; half-day tour of New Delhi, Rs. 40; Delhi by Evening tour, including sound-and-light show at the Red Fort, Rs. 40; day tour to Agra, Rs. 165; two-day tour to Jaipur, Agra, and Fatehpur Sikri, and Bharatpur, Rs. 475; three-day Golden Triangle tour to Agra, Fatehpur Sikri, and Jaipur, Rs. 475; and a weekend tour to Haridwar and Rishikesh, Rs. 175.

Delhi Tourism Development Corporation (DTDC, Bombay Life Building, N-Block, Connaught Circus, tel. 3315322) offers the tours listed above by non-air-conditioned coach.

Ashok Travels and Tours (ITDC, L-Block, Connaught Pl., tel. 320005, with counters at all Ashok hotels) offers the same tours by air-conditioned buses at a slightly higher price.

The tour operators listed below can also arrange similar tours.

To hire your own guide in Delhi, contact the Government of India Tourist Office (see *Tourist Information* above).

TOUR OPERATORS. For all travel needs, including renting a car with driver, contact any of these reliable agencies: *American Express*, A-Block, Connaught Place, tel. 3324119; *Cox & Kings*, Indra Place, H-Block, Connaught Place, tel. 3320067; *Thomas Cook*, Yogeshwar Building, 4th Floor, M-2, Connaught Circus, tel. 3329408; *Mercury Travels*, Jeevan Tara Building, Parliament Street, tel. 321403; *Sita World Travel*, F-12, Connaught Place, tel. 3311133; *Travel House*, 14 A & B, Community Centre, Basant Lok, Vasant Vihar, tel. 603400; *Travel Corporation*, TCI, Hotel Metro, N-49, Connaught Circus, tel. 3315181. You can also arrange for a car or tours through Ashok Travels and Tours (address above). Most of these companies are open 10 A.M.–5 P.M., closed Sundays.

SEASONAL EVENTS. Lots of events happen regularly in Delhi. Just let a foreign dignitary arrive and advance preparations have truckloads of workers planting flowers, hanging posters, spiffying up the city. The specific dates for many events each year are determined by the lunar calendar; consult the Government of India Tourist Office for details.

January 26. *Republic Day Parade.* You need a ticket to see this event on Raj Path, and tickets go from the ordinary to the VVIP. Lots of military hoopla, floats from each state with great cultural highlights: dancers, musicians, planes flying overhead. **Cameras not allowed,** nor conspicuous handbags of any kind. The entire week is a celebration including festivals held in various auditoriums and hotels.

February 1–15. *Surajkund Crafts Mela.* In an ethnic village, set up at Hotel Raj Hans, 8 km (5 mi.) south of Delhi in neighboring Haryana, master craftsmen show how they create their terrific handicrafts, which you can also buy. Dancers, musicians, magicians, and village gymnasts perform. Lots of fun.

March. *Holi.* This festival marks the start of spring and marks you as the target for water bombs filled with red color (permanent or washable)—stay indoors or wear old clothes.

May (full moon). *Buddha Jayanti.* The birth, enlightenment, and death of the Buddha are celebrated with prayer meetings at Ladakh Buddha Vihara (Bela Road).

August. *Raksha Bandhan.* Once, according to Hindu mythology, Indra, the king of the heavens, warred with demons and his consort tied a silk amulet around his wrist to help him win back his kingdom. Now, sisters and brothers pledge their love to one another and the sister ties a silk string around the brother's wrist. That explains all the stalls you'll see selling glittery paper wrist bands.

Aug. 15. *Independence Day.* Lots of speeches, and that's about it.

October 2. *Gandhi Jayanti.* This day honors the birthday of Mahatma Gandhi, with special singing and ceremonies at the Raj Ghat.

October. *Dussehra.* This 10-day celebration with plays and music recitals of *Ramlila* recalls the mythological victory of Rama over evil. The most spectacular rendering is held at the Delhi Gate (performances for one month). On the 10th day, an elaborate procession heads to the Ram Lila grounds, where enormous effigies of the demon Ravana, his brother, and son (all stuffed with firecrackers) are exploded before a crowd of people.

October/November. *Diwali.* The Festival of Lights and start of the Hindu New Year is celebrated with thousands of candles lit at night on balconies of houses. The city crackles with the explosion of fireworks. Lots of fun.

HISTORIC SITES. Entrance to most temples and monuments is free or extremely inexpensive; where a donation is asked, a few rupees will suffice. Important sites are open daily sunrise to sunset, unless noted below.

Baha'i Temple of Worship. On Bahapur hill near Nehru Pl., it's open 9:30 A.M.–12:30 P.M.; 2–5 P.M. every day, except Mondays. On Saturdays, Sundays and public holidays, hours are extended until 7 P.M.

Firozabad. 3 km from Connaught Pl., near Delhi Gate. See the Kotla Firoze Shah (the remains of Firoze Shah Tughlaq's palace), with its third-century Ashoka pillar mounted on the top. Also see the partially ruined Jami Masjid—the largest mosque from the Tughlaq era and still a Moslem religious shrine.

Hazrat Nizamudin Aulia. 4.8 km from Connaught Pl., near Humayun's Tomb. Shrine of Sheikh Nizamuddin Chisti, fourth in the line of Chisti saints, and an important place of Moslem pilgrimage. Chisti died in 1325. Many other notables are buried nearby, including Jahanara, Shahjahan's daughter.

Humayun's Tomb. 4.8 km from Connaught Pl. in Nizamuddin. Built in the mid-sixteenth century by Haji Begum for her husband (she's also buried here), the tomb represents a new architectural era that culminated in Agra and Fatehpur Sikri. Definite Persian influences include the first "tomb-in-a-garden" complex in India.

Jama Masjid. In Old Delhi. Built of red sandstone and marble in 1658 by Shah Jahan. The largest mosque in India and the last building constructed by Shah Jahan. Some areas within the mosque are restricted to non-Moslems. Check with tourist department for the appropriate visiting hours, which vary.

Jantar Mantar (Observatory). 0.4 km from Connaught Pl. Scientific instruments built by the astronomer-king, Maharajah Jai Singh II of Jaipur in 1725. Accurate instruments that measure celestial movements act as a sundial.

Lakshmi Narayan Temple. 2 km from Connaught Pl. Built in 1938 by the industrialist Birla Mandir in the Orissan style. Contains the deities of Narayan, Lakshmi, Durga, and Shiva. Remove your shoes once you enter the courtyard.

Lal Qila (Red Fort). Across from Jama Masjid. The site of the seventh capital of Delhi begun by the Mogul Emperor Shah Jahan around 1638. Built of red sandstone (Lal Qila); inside are a series of beautiful buildings in red sandstone and marble. *Son et lumiere* show is held nightly: Nov.–Feb., 7:30–8:30; Feb.–May, 8:30–9:30; May–Sept., 9–10; and Sept.–Nov., 8:30–9:30. Call tel. 3274580 for details.

Lodi Tombs. 4.8 km from Connaught Pl. on Rodi Road. Fifteenth- and sixteenth-century tombs of the rulers of the Sayyid and Lodi Dynasties: Mohammad Shah and Sikander Lodi. Also some believe that within the Bara Gumbad Mosque lie the remains of the unknown architect.

Lutyen's Imperial City. Near Lodi Tombs. See particularly the Sandad Bhavan and the Rashtrapati Bhavan (Presidential Palace). To gain entry into the Rashtrapati, you need an entry pass from the Government of India Tourist Office.

Purana Qila. 3.2 km from Connaught Pl., off Mathura Rd. The ruins of this fifteenth-century fort constructed by the Afghan Sher Shah still have three imposing gateways. Inside is the octagonal red sandstone tower (Sher Manzil) that the Mogul Emperor Humayun used as his library, with the steep steps that became the instrument of his death—he slipped, fell, and died. Also see the Qila-i-Kuhna Masjid (Sher Shah's private mosque) built in Indo-Afghan style.

Qutab Minar. 14.4 km from Connaught Pl. in South Delhi. Construction of this 234-foot tower was begun in 1199 by Qutub-ud-din Aibak, was finished by his son-in-law, then redesigned in the fourteenth century by Firoze Shah Tughlaq. Also see the Quwwat-ul-Islam Mosque nearby, the first Moslem building in Delhi and India, erected in the twelfth century, with its Iron Pillar.

Raj Ghat. 4 km from Connaught Pl. on the banks of the Yamuna River. A square platform of polished black marble that marks the site where Mahatma Gandhi was cremated on Jan. 31, 1948.

Safdarjang's Tomb. 4.8 km from Connaught Pl. on Aurobindo Marg. The last Mogul mausoleum built in Delhi, constructed in 1754 by Nabob Shuja-ud-Daula for his father Mirsa Shuja-ud-Daula (Safdarjang).

Tughlaqabad. 5 km east of Qutab Minar. The ruins of Delhi's third capital begun in 1320 by Giyas-ud-din Tughlaq. Thirteen gates of the fortress still guard the remains and the landscape; you can see the tomb of the capital's founder.

MUSEUMS AND GALLERIES. Crafts Museum. Bhairon Rd.; tel. 3318287. Terrific examples of traditional Indian crafts—folk and tribal arts from all over India. The museum spreads over an eight-acre complex and includes a craft demonstration complex plus 15 structures that represent the village dwellings of various states in India. Inside these huts are the day-to-day cultural objects from the specific areas. The galleries are open daily 9:30 A.M.–5 P.M.; crafts demonstrations are held October to July, 9:30 A.M.–6 P.M.

National Gandhi Museum. Opposite Raj Ghat; tel. 3310168. A display of some of Gandhi's personal possessions, plus a library. Open 9:30 A.M.–5:30 P.M.; closed Mondays and holidays.

National Gallery of Modern Art. Sher Shah Rd., Jaipur House, former residential palace of the Jaipur maharajah; tel. 382835. Exhibits the work of modern Indian artists: paintings, graphics, and sculpture. Open 10 A.M.–5 P.M., closed Mondays.

National Museum. Jan Path; tel. 3019538. Wide-ranging collection of India's and Central Asia's artistic treasures, art and archaeology, anthropology, decorative art, calligraphy, and textiles. Among the Indian collections are 5,000-year-old relics of the Indus Valley civilization (Mohenjo-daro, Harappa, and so forth). Brahmanical, Jain, and Buddhist sculptures in stone, bronze, and terra cotta of the early and medieval periods of Indian history. Good miniatures of the Mogul, Rajput, Deccani, and Pahari schools, as well as earlier work. Among the old manuscripts, you can see the famous Gita Govinda and the profusely illustrated *Mahabharata;* the *Bhagavad Gita,* written and illuminated in golden ink; the miniature octagonal *Koran* and Mogul Emperor Babur's *Babarnama* in his handwriting. Temple hangings and brocaded saris, costumes from different parts of India, beautifully worked weapons, set with precious stones from the Mogul and earlier periods, ancient jewelry, and painted pottery are part of the collection. In addition, the Aurel Stein collection of antiquities he recovered during his explorations in Central Asia and the western borders of China includes mural paintings from Buddhist shrines (some of the few examples removed from that area), silk paintings, and sculpture. Open 10 A.M.– 5 P.M.; closed Mondays.

Nehru Memorial Museum. Teen Murti House on Teen Murti Marg; tel. 3015026. Official residence of Nehru, preserved as it was when he lived there—books, mementos, and pictures. 10 A.M.–5 P.M.; closed Mondays.

Rail Transport Museum. Shanti Path, Chanakyapuri; tel. 601816. A must for railway buffs. 26 vintage locomotives and numerous old carriages and saloon cars on 10 acres of track. A lot of fancy forms of transport that no longer race along the rails. Open 9:30 A.M.–5:30 P.M.; closed Mondays.

Red Fort Museum of Archaeology. Red Fort; tel. 273703. Small historical collection devoted to the Mogul period. Exhibits consist of old arms, dresses, paintings, documents, and seals. Open 9 A.M.–5 P.M.; closed Fridays.

Tibet House Museum. Institutional Area, Lodi Rd.; tel. 611515. Open 10 A.M.– 5 P.M.; closed Mondays.

PARKS, GARDENS, ZOOS. Delhi has numerous lovely parks and gardens in which you can sit and watch the passing sights after too much big-city running around. They're open every day between sunrise and sunset, except when noted. Here are some of the best:

Children's Park, near India Gate, has nice walkways and good play equipment for the kids.

Deer Park, in the Chinkara complex near Hauz Khas, features deer and peacocks. It is a pleasant place to stop after seeing Qutab Minar.

Mughal Gardens, located in the Rashtrapati Bhavan estate, is laid out along the lines of the Mughal Gardens. There are red stone paths, fountains, and a lovely rose garden. This garden is open to the public only during February when the flowers are in bloom. For permission to visit at that time, contact the Government of India Tourist Office.

Nehru Park, comprises 85 acres of walks and landscaping with rocks inscribed with remembered words of Jawaharlal Nehru. There are lots of birds and many lovely places just to sit.

Yamuna Waterfront, has Mogul-style gardens near the Raj Ghat, where Gandhi was cremated; the Shanti Vana, where Nehru was cremated; and the Vijay Ghat, where Prime Minister Shastri was cremated.

Delhi Zoo Not a great modern zoo with lots of freedom for the animals, but, set against the Purana Qila (old fort), you get some pleasure just in walking around. Open 8 A.M.–6:30 P.M. in summer, 9 A.M.–5 P.M. in winter.

PARTICIPANT SPORTS. Golf. Play golf against a backdrop of ancient monuments at *Delhi Golf Club,* Zakir Hussain Marg. Open 6 A.M.–3 P.M.; tel. 699239 for reservations and details.

Horseback Riding. *Delhi Riding Club,* Safdarjang Road. For details, tel. 3011891.

Swimming. All deluxe and expensive hotels have swimming pools. Check hotel listings. The Imperial Hotel (tel. 3325332) allows nonguests to use their pool for a small fee.

SPECTATOR SPORTS. Delhi is a **polo** town, and just by virtue of its existence as capital of India, you'll find a **cricket** match somewhere almost any time. For details about polo, call *Delhi Polo Club,* President's Estate, Rashtrapati Bhavan; tel. 3015604. For cricket matches, check the newspapers. Tickets may be hard to come by, however, for some games when the rivalry is intense.

THEATER, DANCE, MUSIC. For serious cultural events, Delhi is rich. Just open up the newspaper and find out what's happening where. Numerous auditoriums put on cultural events and many hotels have performers. Or just contact the Government of India Tourist Office to see what's doing. This is a great city to see good dance and theater and to hear some of India's finest musical performers.

RECOMMENDED READING. *Delhi Diary* (Rs. 3), a weekly small magazine available free in many hotels and at most newsstands, is excellent. It tells you what is happening; lists restaurants, hotels, shopping information; and has a handy, albeit limited, map in the back. It's small enough to fit in your pocket. If you're into shopping (and Delhi is a great shopping city), try to find a copy of *Explore and Shop in the Delhi Markets* by Colette Galas (Rs. 45). A little dated, but the best shops never die (at least rarely) and she knows her stuff. The book is also available in paperback. The best bookstores (in the Connaught place area): *Book Worm,* B–29 Connaught Pl.; *New Book Depot,* B–18 Connaught Pl.; *Oxford Book and Stationery Co.,* N Block, Connaught Pl., excellent for books on India—a serious place; *Piccadilly Book Stall,* Shop No. 64, Shankar Market, deceptive tiny-sized stall crammed with treasures, many out of print, on the occult, India, and neighboring countries. These bookstores are generally open 10 A.M.–6 P.M., closed Sundays.

SHOPPING. Delhi is the marketplace for all of India; shopping can be fun, and bargaining is the rule, except at fixed-price shops. Go for a 30–50 percent reduction from the first price they give you. Walk away. Let them chase after you. It's part of the game. Besides the *Central Cottage Industries Emporium,* on Janpath (open 10 A.M.–6 P.M.; closed on Sundays), which has every handicraft of India somewhere under its roof, also visit the *State Emporia,* a string of shops on Baba Kharak Singh

Marg. The state shops are also closed on Sundays and take a lunch break usually 1:30–2:30 P.M. The better shops on Connaught Place take a lunch break during that time and observe Sundays as a day of rest. Also visit the new boutiques in *Hauz Khas Village* (open 10:30 A.M.–6 P.M., closed Sundays). Central Cottage Industries Emporium, some of the State Emporia, and many fixed-price stores accept credit cards.

Another extremely good shopping area in Delhi is *Sunder Nagar Market* (closed Sundays), near Oberoi Inter-Continental. In particular, visit these shops:

The Studio (4 Sunder Nagar) sells excellent contemporary silver jewelry.

Ladakh Art Gallery (10 Sunder Nagar) has a great collection of old silver jewelry.

Padma Gems Jewellers (9-A Sunder Nagar) sells exquisite gold and silver jewelry, including semi-precious and precious stones.

Kumar Gallery (11 Sunder Nagar) specializes in original tribal statues, old dhurries and Tibetan carpets, miniatures, Tanjore and Mysore paintings, and temple art.

Also visit these other reputable stores in Delhi:

For silk: *Banaras House Limited*, N–13 Connaught Pl., and *Handloom House* (government run), 9–A Connaught Pl.; both shops close for lunch and close on Sundays.

For tailoring: Women, *Charisma*, 9–N Connaught Pl., inside a jewelry shop; an excellent seamstress and designer here works fast yet carefully. Men, *Style*, 13–E Connaught Pl., tailors suits and jackets.

For handmade shoes: Don't be lured by the shops on Connaught Pl.; Mr. Lee's your man to see—*K.K. See*, 30–B, Khan Market. He's reliable and honest; closed Sundays.

For the best *kurtas* and *chikan* work (hand embroidery): *Lal Behari Tandon*, 20 Palika Bazar (central hall); closed Sundays.

For interesting ready-made clothes, from antique saris to exquisite sequin work: *Once Upon a Time*, H5/6 Mehrauli Rd., opposite the Qutab Minar; closed Sundays.

NIGHTLIFE AND BARS. Delhi is a good place to see Indian classical dance or music. Regional dances are performed daily at *Parsi Anjuman Hall*, Bahadurshah Zafar Marg, Delhi Gate. Shows starts at 7 P.M. For details, call tel. 3275978 (after 5:30 P.M., call tel. 3317228). Also check with your hotel or the tourist office for other special performances. All the major hotels have bars; check listings under *Hotels*. The classiest of these are at the *Oberoi;* sedate and elegant. Most hotel bars are open from lunch through late at night.

96

and Moslem
killed.
The P
of Hin
Sikh
an
t

THE PUNJAB AND HARYANA

Sikhs, Hindus, and Mountain Shrines

by
KATHLEEN COX

Note: Because of sporadic incidents of political violence in the Punjab, the U.S. State Department advises Americans to exercise special caution in the state; especially avoid traveling by bus or train to or through the Punjab.

For centuries, the Punjab, the northwest border state of India, has been the scene of communal strife pitting Moslem against Hindu. In the mid-1500s, around the time of Babur, a new movement began that initially gave rise to the hope of a peaceful future. A Punjabi Hindu, Baba Nanak, began to preach a new gospel—a fusion of the best of Hinduism and Islam—a gospel that spurned the notion of castes and the worship of idols. Nanak developed a following, a title—Guru (*gu:* one who dispells darkness, by teaching enlightenment: *ru*)—and numerous disciples called Sikhs. By 1708, the Sikhs had their own city, Amritsar, with its beautiful Golden Temple, their headquarters.

Unfortunately, communalism flared up anew. As the relationship between Islam and Sikhism soured, the Sikhs turned militant. Communalism continued into the twentieth century, erupting finally into a wholesale slaughter of Hindus, Sikhs, and Moslems during the post-World War II partitioning. As Hindus and Sikhs tried to flee Moslem Pakistan for India

tried to flee India for Pakistan, an estimated 500,000 were

njab still suffers from religious intolerance. Only now, instead
u and Sikh against Moslem, the hostility rages between Hindu and
—with disastrous consequences. The Golden Temple was stormed
seriously damaged, Indira Gandhi was assassinated, and relations be-
ween Pakistan and India were strained (India considers Pakistan a training ground and refuge for Sikh terrorists). Fear grips the people who are
caught in the struggle of the Sikh extremists who want their people, a minority, to have their own Sikh state called Khalistan.

For all these reasons, travel to the Punjab is ill advised. For a vicarious
trip under these circumstances—or if differences between the groups are
settled—this can serve as your guide.

The Golden Temple of Amritsar

Amritsar was founded in 1579 by Ram Das, the fourth teacher (guru)
of the Sikh religion (the Sikhs have had 10 gurus), as a central place of
worship for the followers of his faith. He constructed a pool, the "Pool
of Nectar" (which is what Amritsar means) and planned the temple that
his son and successor expanded.

Known as the Golden Temple (Darbar Sahib), it is the glory of Amritsar
and nucleus of Sikh worship. The pool is surrounded by a pavement of
white marble, and the temple itself is reached by a marble causeway. Its
bronze plates, heavily covered with pure gold leaf, burn in the tropical
sun and flash their light in piercing gleams while their reflection in the
still waters leaps up at you. Over the whole there reigns a stillness, a power
of peace that seems to stem from that uplift that inhales the cosmic *prana*
(breath) of the universe. For the Sikhs still practice that consciously physical correspondence with the environment is the inner meaning of this word
and that which feeds the adept with the celestial food they believe can conquer doubt, disease, and even death. In the Sanctuary, under a canopy,
lies the *Granth Sahib,* the sacred book of the Sikhs, which is read out from
time to time by a priest, to the accompaniment of devotional music.

The buildings around the Sacred Tank shelter pilgrims who come to
worship from distant places. The Akal Takht (the Immortal Throne) is
the supreme seat of Sikh religious authority and contains several relics.
Incidentally, the only restriction imposed on those who visit these sacred
places is that they must remove their shoes. As is the way with mosques
and shrines, slippers are provided, but here no charge is made and no donation is accepted. The gardens that surround the Baba Atal Tower—
richly painted with frescoes depicting scenes from the life of Guru
Nanak—are of a strange and wistful beauty. The whole is impregnated
with an energy that typifies the soul of the Sikh.

Haryana

Haryana has a minimal share of attractions, but it has roadside tourist
conveniences (à la Howard Johnson motels) that put the state light years
ahead of the rest of the country.

Take the Grand Trunk Road from Delhi, the start of a journey north
to Chandigarh, the joint capital of the Punjab and Haryana. The first point
of interest is Panipat, a sprawling industrial city, with numerous architectural reminders of decisive battles that changed the fate of India. Just outside the city, you can see the Kabuli Bagh Mosque, built by Babur to commemorate his victory in 1526 over Ibrahim Lodi, king of Delhi—a victory

that gave birth to the Mogul Empire. You can also visit the tomb of the vanquished Lodi, who lost his life as well as his kingdom during the decisive battle.

The next attraction on the road is Kurukshetra, where the epic battle described in the *Mahabharata* was supposedly fought. Another legend claims that under an ancient spreading banyan tree, Krishna delivered his sermon of Bhagavad Gita. And, finally, a dip in Kurukshetra's sacred tank, especially during a solar eclipse, has an unbelievable redeeming effect, or so it is claimed.

Chandigarh, a few miles north, is either an urban planner's dream or a futuristic blight, depending on your point of view. An old city, it's not! In fact, if you've traveled through India for a few weeks before arriving here, Chandigarh is bound to astonish you. Where are the bullock carts, roadside stalls, and bustling produce markets? You might even think, Where is India? But it's right before your eyes. Chandigarh is always described as Le Corbusier's city (Le Corbusier contributed to the design of the United Nations), but Chandigarh is more accurately the creation of Nehru. At the time of partition, when the greater part of the Punjab, including its graceful capital Lahore, fell to Pakistan, a new capital had to be found—or created. A site was chosen under the Siwalki Hills, with two small rivers flowing on either side. This site was Chandigarh and, according to an enthusiastic Nehru, who was Prime Minister at the time, the new capital would be "a new town, symbolic of the freedom of India, unfettered by the traditions of the past."

The city is divided into 47 sectors. Each one is 800 by 2,200 meters—a self-contained unit for living with housing, marketing, schools, and banks. It's all there. Building height, population density, traffic flow—all have been considered. To some visitors, this may sound like a vision out of *Brave New World*, but Chandigarh must be viewed within the context of India. It is, and should be, a source of pride—living evidence that India doesn't see itself confined to confusion, poverty, crushing crowds, heart-wrenching contrasts, and improvised solutions that often characterize urban life in many of its great cities. In this sense, Chandigarh is as much a symbol as a specific place. And though it may not be everyone's dream to live life in a symbol, Chandigarh is well worth visiting and knowing.

A few of the specifics about Chandigarh: Get yourself a map from the tourist office. Sector One is the Capital Complex, featuring Secretariat, Assembly, High Court, and Open Hand Monument (which resembles Picasso's dove of peace). Because of political tensions, entry into the buildings is restricted. Sector 10 is the Museum and Art Gallery, with a good collection of contemporary Indian art. Sector 14 is the Punjab University campus. The Gandhi Bhawan here is perhaps the most elegant building in the city. Designed by Pierre Janerat, Le Corbusier's cousin, it is a gem of a building, small and shaped like an open lotus blossom. Sector 16 is the Zakir Rose Garden, supposedly the largest such garden in all Asia, extending over 30 acres with 1,500 varieties of roses.

Nek Chand's Rock Garden

It's ironic and wonderful that Chandigarh, the totally planned city, should have spawned this spectacular homage to imagination and intuitive construction—the Rock Garden located on the edge of Sector One. Some 30 years ago, Nek Chand (the name means benign moon) was a Public Works Department official whose job was to inspect roads and write maintenance reports. As he went about his work, he began collecting rocks, stones, and refuse that people dumped along the roadside. Soon, he began assembling his bits of junk—tiles, torn clothes, broken bangles, shards of glass, electric and plumbing fixtures—into a vision, his "kingdom of the gods and goddesses." Without the knowledge of any of Chandigarh's city planners, Nek Chand's Rock Garden took shape on the edge of the city. Chand had absolutely no artistic training when he embarked on his project, and, even today, he shrugs when the discussion turns to art. Yet, Nek Chand's talent was recognized early by the Indian government. Land was set aside for his project, and he was given several assistants to help bring his dream to life.

Visiting the Rock Garden today, you'll enter a low Alice-in-Wonderland entranceway ("it is good to bow down when you enter the kingdom of the gods and goddesses") and walk along a winding path through a series of environments. You'll see waterfalls, pools, imaginary forests, and miniature villages. You'll go up steps, around corners, and stoop under several more arches. Wherever you go, you'll be in the midst of hundreds of delightful figures—humans and animals—fashioned from recycled junk. Americans who are acquainted with the work of Red Grooms will have an idea of what to expect. But whereas Red Grooms is a sophisticated self-conscious artist using the idiom of naif art, Nek Chand is the real McCoy.

That the Rock Garden is in a state of perpetual expansion seems altogether appropriate. It's so filled with the energy of life that one feels good to know that the garden is alive and growing. Nek Chand has been honored throughout the world (including a Fantasy Garden in Washington D.C., which he supervised), but, in all likelihood, he'll be in the Rock Garden when you visit. His office is a cozy rock grotto that any Hobbit would gladly call home. You might think Nek Chand is a "simple" man, but once you've seen his elaborate fantasy kingdom, you realize that he's a man with a vision—and the skill and perseverance to execute it. He is a rare individual who gave Chandigarh a gift that neither Nehru nor Le Corbusier could provide—a spirit of gaiety, surprise, and love—a testament of faith in uniqueness and eccentricity of human beings. Nek Chand gave India's determinedly modern city a bit of personality.

PRACTICAL INFORMATION FOR
THE PUNJAB AND HARYANA

WHEN TO GO. October–March is the time to visit the Punjab and Haryana. They're both *very hot* in the summer.

HOW TO GET THERE. To travel through Haryana to Chandigarh, you can go by air, train, or car. Do not travel by bus or train. The frequent target of terrorists, they're extremely risky.

By Air. *Indian Airlines* and *Vayudoot* have numerous flights to Chandigarh from Delhi, Srinagar, Leh, Shimla, and Kullu.

By Car. Chandigarh is 248 km from Delhi by very good roads; 380 km from Jammu; and 119 km from Shimla.

TOURIST INFORMATION. Tourists are well advised to go to one of the following tourist departments on their arrival in Chandigarh to get a good map and up-to-date information.

Chandigarh Tourist Office (General Bus Stand, Sector 17; tel. 22548) has good information on Chandigarh.

Haryana Tourism (No. 17–18–19, Sector 17–B, Chandigarh, tel. 21955) also has good information on the entire state.

FOREIGN CURRENCY EXCHANGE. Most Western-style hotels have money-exchange counters as do branches of the *State Bank of India,* open Mon.–Fri. 10 A.M.–2 P.M., Sat. 10 till noon.

ACCOMMODATIONS. Chandigarh has adequate hotels; however, most have a dreary shopping mall setting, that is, they are large buildings that front an unattractive parking lot. The rest of Haryana is dotted with numerous roadside stops (named after birds) that offer the travelers rest and relaxation. These modern facilities, run by Haryana Tourism, are extremely good value. Expect a spacious, clean room with a contemporary decor, a multicuisine restaurant, and room service. The better-quality rooms have TV and air-conditioning. Additional amenities are noted in each listing. All places listed here are in the *Inexpensive* (under Rs. 500) price range.

CHANDIGARH

Hotel Chandigarh Mountview. Sector 10, Chandigarh, Punjab; tel. 21257. 33 rooms with bath. The best hotel in the city, this three-story Western-style hotel has an attractive lawn and spacious modern rooms. Amenities include air-conditioning, TV, room service, multicuisine restaurant/bar, foreign-exchange counter. AE, DC, MC, V.

Hotel President. Madhya Marg, Sector 26, Chandigarh, Punjab; tel. 40840. 20 rooms with bath. Don't let the dreary shopping-mall environment of this Western-style hotel faze you. Modern decor rooms here are spacious and clean. Air-conditioning, TV, room service, multicuisine restaurants, bar, health club, foreign-exchange and travel counters, secretarial service. AE, DC, MC, V.

Hotel Sunbeam. Udyog Path, Sector 22-B, Chandigarh, Punjab; tel. 41335. 57 rooms with bath. This Western-style hotel has a reasonably attractive lobby and air-conditioned rooms with a contemporary decor. TV, room service, multicuisine restaurants, bar. DC, MC.

All the following Haryana Tourism hotels are also *Inexpensive.*

AMBALA
55 km (34 mi.) from Chandigarh

Kingfisher. District Ambala, Haryana; tel. 58352. 12 rooms with attached bath. The Kingfisher has a health club, swimming pool, and bar. Rupees only.

BADKHAL LAKE
32 km (20 mi.) from Delhi

Badkhal Lake. Badkhal Village, District Faridabad, Haryana; tel. 26900. 29 rooms with bath and 8 camper huts with bath. This lake-side complex is 5 km (3 mi.) from the Delhi-Agra Highway, with a swimming pool, steam bath, massage, boating, and fishing. Rupees only.

HODAL
92 km (57 mi.) from Delhi

Dabchick. Hodal, District Faridabad, Haryana; tel. 91. 6 rooms with bath in a motel and 6 rooms in cottages. This complex on the Delhi-Agra Highway has a bar as well as camel, horse, and elephant rides, plus a snake charmer. Rupees only.

PINJORE
22 km (14 mi.) from Chandigarh

Yadavindra Gardens. District Ambala, Haryana; tel. 455. 18 rooms with bath. This complex, near the Mogul-designed Pinjore Gardens, is on National Highway

No. 22. It has a bar, shops, mini zoo, children's park, Japanese gardens, camel rides. Rupees only.

SULTANPUR
46 km (29 mi.) from Delhi

Sultanpur Bird Sanctuary. District Gurgaon, Haryana; tel. 42. Two rooms and eight huts with bath. This complex, near National Highway No. 8, has a bar and is ideal for bird-watching. Rupees only.

SURAJKUND
8 km (5 mi.) from South Delhi

Hotel Rajhans. District Faridabad, Haryana; tel. 6830766. About 80 rooms with bath. The Rajhans has an elaborate health club, along with swimming pool, golf course, tennis court, horseback riding, cycling, and a lake. Rupees only.

UCHANA
124 km (77 mi.) from Delhi

Karna Lake. District Karna, Haryana; tel. 4279. 19 rooms with bath. This complex on National Highway No. 1 has a bar and facilities for boating and fishing. Rupees only.

DINING OUT. Since most people pass through Haryana on their way to another destination, this state has wisely chosen to provide excellent eateries along the national highways that lead from Delhi to Agra, Jaipur, Chandigarh, and further north. These Indian-style "Howard Johnson's" are open until very late or 24 hours. The multicuisine food and service are good; prices, per person for a 3-course meal, excluding taxes, tip, or beverage, are *Moderate* (Rs. 40–Rs. 80) to *Inexpensive* (under Rs. 40). Payment is in rupees. In Chandigarh, the best meals (also moderately priced) are served in the hotels. Breakfast is usually served 8–10:30 A.M.; lunch, noon–3 P.M.; and dinner, 7:30–10 P.M.

SWEETS AND TREATS. In Chandigarh, stop at the **Indian Coffee House,** Sector 22, for good south Indian snacks and coffee. **Sindhi Sweets** (two shops in Sector 17) creates a vast array of desserts and milk drinks. Try Karachi halwa, made of *ghee* (clarified butter), nuts, and arrowroot. It has the color and consistency of apricot taffy—delicious! Or try *keser milk badam* (ice-cold milk laced with crushed cashews, pistachios, and seasonings).

HOW TO GET AROUND. From the Airport. Unmetered taxis charge about Rs. 70 between the Chandigarh airport and the city.
By Taxi. Unmetered taxis charge a flat fee (about Rs. 20) from one sector of the city to another.
By Auto Rickshaw. Auto rickshaws are metered. Fare: about Rs. 2.50 for the first 1.5 km and 30 paise for every part thereof, with a waiting charge of 10 paise for every eight minutes. Plus a 7 percent surcharge on the overall meter reading.
By Cycle Rickshaw. Cycle rickshaws will also pedal you around Chandigarh. Fares: negotiable, with a minimum sector-to-sector fare of Rs. 2.
By Bus. Due to the communal problems in Haryana and the Punjab, buses have become a dangerous way to travel.

TOURS. *Chandigarh Tourism* conducts tours in deluxe buses and eight-seater Matador vans in and around Chandigarh and Haryana. For details contact them at Hotel Chandigarh Mountview, Sector 10 (tel. 21257), or *Chandigarh Tourist Information Office,* General Bus Stand, Sector 17 (tel. 22548). The following tours are available at reasonable rates: Local sightseeing; Chatbir Zoo; Pinjore Gardens; Pinjore Gardens via Mansa Devi; Pinjore Gardens via Nada Sahib; Mansa Devi; Bhakra Dam, Nagal, Gobind Sagar Lake, Ropar Boat Club, and Anandpur Sahib shrine.

TOUR OPERATORS. For all travel needs, including a car with driver, use an agency recommended in the Delhi chapter above.

SEASONAL EVENTS. Feb. 1–15. *Surajkund Crafts Mela.* This two-week fair at an ethnic village at Surajkund, 8 km (5 mi.) from South Delhi, brings together some of India's finest artisans who sell their products and show you how they're created. You can also see dance and music performances. A wonderful event! February–March. *Rose Festival.* The Zakir Rose Garden in Chandigarh holds an annual two-day rose festival. Contact the tourist department for the exact date.

HISTORIC SITES. Important monuments and temples in Punjab and Haryana are generally open daily from sunrise to sunset. Entrance is usually free; where a donation is asked, a few rupees will suffice.

Chandigarh. *Darbar Sahib* (Golden Temple). Founded in 1579, this marble temple is the most important Sikh shrine in India. Remember to remove your shoes before entering.

Panipat. *Kabuli Bah Mosque.* Built by the Mogul Emperor Babur, this mosque commemorates a victory that launched the Mogul Era in the subcontinent.

Kurukshetra. At Jyotisar under a banyan tree, the Hindu god Krishna supposedly delivered the sermon of the Bhagavad Gita.

MUSEUM AND GALLERY. Chandigarh. *Government Museum and Art Gallery* (Sector 10, tel. 25568) has an excellent collection of contemporary paintings and sculpture, plus a good collection of old miniature paintings from the Kangra, Rajasthani, and Mogul schools. Open 10 A.M.–4:30 P.M., closed Mon. Nominal entrance fee.

PARKS AND GARDENS. *Leisure Valley* in Chandigarh is a 300-acre sprawl that runs through the length of the city and is filled with untouched greenery and gardens. The most famous is the Zakir Rose Garden, named after the late President Zakir Hussain. Located in Sector 16, the garden is the biggest in Asia, with 1,500 varieties planted over 30 acres. Rock Garden is the creation of Nek Chand, carved out of rocks and whatever refuse he found. The garden covers six acres and is still a work in progress. Entry fee: 50 paise. Summer: 9 A.M.–1 P.M.; 3–7 P.M. Winter: 9 A.M.–1 P.M.; 2–6 P.M.

The Pinjore (Yadavindra) Gardens are the former great Mogul gardens designed by Nawab Fidai Khan, the architect for Emperor Aurangzeb in the seventeenth century. Open every day. Motel accommodations are available.

ZOO. *Chattbir Zoo,* on the Chandigarh-Patiala Road, has Bengal tigers, Himalayan black bears, and birds galore. Open every day. Entry fee: Rs. 1.

SPORTS. Fishing on Sukhna Lake, Chandigarh. Rs. 3 per day. Contact Lake Club, Sector 1 (tel. 26661), for details. You can **golf** at Haryana Tourism's nine-hole course at Hotel Raj Hans, Surajkund, 8 km (5 mi.) south of Delhi. Call tel. 6830766 for details.

BARS. Most of the hotels have bars, but the *Suroor Bar* at the Hotel Pankaj, Sector 22, is probably the closest you'll come to visiting a downtown New York City bar. Everything is modern, minimal, and carefully lighted. Where else, but in Le Corbusier's city of tomorrow?

UTTAR PRADESH

Abode of the Gods

by
KATHLEEN COX

Although smaller in size than Britain, the state of Uttar Pradesh has 20 million more inhabitants. Before Independence, *Zamindars,* absentee landowners, lorded over the peasantry, usually exploiting them mercilessly. Former tenant-farmers are now small landholders, but they still have to cope with the lack of equipment, enormous families, and sometimes unsympathetic officials. They find solace in religion; two of the holiest rivers meet at Allahabad—the Yamuna (or Jumna) and the Ganges (or Ganga). At the *sangam*—their confluence—India's biggest religious bathing festival, the Magh Mela, is held each spring. Every twelfth year, on an auspicious date that is chosen by astrologers, millions converge on the riverbanks in Haridwar to join in the Kumbh Mela, an even more important ritual to the devout.

It was along the Ganges and Yamuna that the first Aryans made advances into India, calling their newly won territory Aryavarta ("Land of the Aryans"). It was the kings of this valley who fought in the Great Battle recorded in the *Mahabharata*. It was in the foothill area (in present-day Nepal) that Siddhartha Gautama, a prince of the Sakyamuni clan, was born, the man who became the Historic Buddha.

The Gangetic plain served as a pivot to the Mauryan Empire whose most outstanding figures were Chandragupta and Ashoka. Harsha of

Kanauj made himself master of northern India in the seventh century, and the region remained Hindu until Mahmud of Ghazni invaded and captured the imperial city in 1019. For at least 500 years, Moslem dynasties ruled over north India. Then, in the eighteenth century, when the Mogul Empire began its decline, the British East India Company—with Calcutta as its base—moved to expand its control, which finally led to the battle of Buxar (1764). The work of British conquest was now under way and a few months later when Robert Clive, founder of British India, returned to India, he reported: "It is scarcely a hyperbole to say that tomorrow the whole Mogul empire is in our power."

EXPLORING UTTAR PRADESH

Leaving Delhi, bypass Meerut, a small city known as the cradle of that memorable insurrection, the Indian Mutiny of 1857–58, commonly referred to as India's First War of Independence. The British governor-general's order of 1856 that all units were liable for overseas service upset the Indian troops, since, by Hindu religious law, those who leave their native land become outcasts. The Indians, especially the sepoy regiments, predominantly high-caste Rajputs, were offended by the British blunder and interpreted it as a deliberate act of religious intolerance.

Just a spark would trigger the move for sedition. This the British government provided the next year; it re-armed the troops with a new rifle that required a greased cartridge. The grease was rumored to be cow's fat, defiling the Hindu who touched it. The grease was also rumored to be pig's fat, which outraged Moslem soldiers. Insubordination burst into open rebellion at the Meerut garrison. The Indians shot their officers and then marched on Delhi to transfer their allegiance to the Mogul emperor's descendant, who still kept his court and imperial title. This revolt, which can be regarded as the initial stirring of a nationalist movement, lasted several months. Although it didn't spread beyond the confines of Northern India, it resulted in grim battles and the liquidation of the East India Company. The British Crown took over, but the mood was never again the same.

ALIGARH, KANAUJ, AND KANPUR

For centuries a Rajput fortress, Aligarh lost its independence to the Moguls at the beginning of the sixteenth century. Then, in the middle of the eighteenth century, Afghans, Jats, and Marathas fought over Aligarh. In 1803, during the Maratha occupation, the Aligarh fort was reputed to be impregnable. Finally, in the second Maratha War, Aligarh was captured by the British. The massive fort, heavily involved in these events, lies four kilometers (2½ miles) north of Aligarh.

Today a small town on the Ganges, Kanauj was for many centuries the Hindu capital of northern India—a city of wealth and beauty, of fine temples and shining palaces. Its prestige remained until the Moslem invasion of the eleventh century. Ransacked and ruined, Kanauj passed into oblivion. Little remains of its ancient glories, except the melancholy ruins of a few ramparts and temples.

Some 81 kilometers (50 miles) farther, is Kanpur—the Pittsburgh of India—one of India's great industrial cities, created by trade and manufacture. Tragic events took place here at the time of the 1857 Indian Muti-

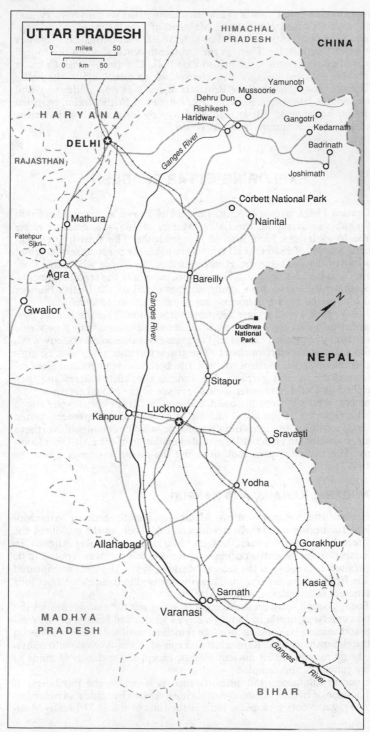

ny—the equally heroic exploits of Tantia Topi, the Indian fighter, and the defense of Wheeler's entrenchment, which ended in the massacre of British citizens.

LUCKNOW

Far less industrialized than neighboring Kanpur, Lucknow has a population of more than a million, including a good portion of Shiite and Sunni Moslems living among Hindu neighbors. Lucknow is the eighteenth-century capital of the Persian sheiks, called Nawab Wazirs, who originally arrived in Avadh (Lucknow and surrounding territory) during Emperor Akbar's reign in the 1500s. Over time, successive Mogul rulers, whose own fortunes were on the decline, granted the nawabs more and more power.

For a time, the nawab capital was in Faizabad, but around 1775, Asaf-ud Daula, the fourth nawab, shifted his seat of power to Lucknow. His charity and perhaps megalomania endowed Lucknow with some of the best of its architecturally rich and sometimes outlandish structures, which are located near the left bank of the River Gomti in the northern part of the capital. Asaf's munificence was real and ingenious.

Great Imambara

In 1784, after a year of life-threatening famine that affected everyone regardless of status, Asaf began the construction of the Great Imambara, his relief project. He divided the starving into two distinct work forces: the poor who built by day and the rich who destroyed by night. Obviously, this arrangement retarded forward momentum. But the nabob wanted to extend the time of employment to keep paying the poor. Besides, the poor outnumbered the formerly rich and the rich weren't such hot demolition experts.

The Imambara stands directly behind two elaborate gateways. The outer gate, where musicians used to play, is on the opposite side of the public road, which unfortunately cuts the original perspective; the inner gate is purely for symmetry. Once you enter the second gate, Asaf's mosque with its 152-foot minarets stands to the right, a row of cloisters that supposedly conceals a bottomless well is on the left.

The Imambara (tomb) is built with clay and brick—no cement or iron; and wood is used in the interior only for decoration. The walls are 16 feet thick but of hollow construction, and the roof is 10 feet thick. Throughout the structure, there are no supporting beams or pillars. An ingenious distribution of weight holds up the ceiling on each floor.

The ground floor is divided into three halls. To the extreme left is an octagonal chamber of Chinese design. Its Chinese saucer-shaped ceiling has a 216-foot dome that extends up to the third floor. The priest sat on his throne (the original, which was of gold and sandalwood, was stolen and replaced with silver) in this room and addressed his devotees. The middle chamber features a ceiling whose shape is an inverted boat. Measuring 162 feet long, 53 feet wide, and 50 feet high, this hall is the largest in the world. A gallery extends around the upper story from which the harem viewed the events below. The nawab and the Imambara's architect are buried in the center of the room. The numerous mirrors are collected from assorted nawab palaces. The chamber to the right is of Indian design.

As you leave the Imambara, notice on the left a small paper replica of a shrine (*tazia*), made and replaced annually for the woman who, reportedly on receiving the word from God, gave the land to the nawab who had been badgering her for years to sell it. She relented, but only on condition that he construct this tazia to her. No one knows her name or what happened to her. Originally, tazias were constructed of wax that mysteriously refused to melt after hours in the sun. Now only one man understands this delicate craft, but he, too, is awaiting the word of God before he reveals his secret.

From outside the Imambara, a set of stairs leads up to an extraordinary labyrinth called Bhul Bhulaiya, which came about as a result of the building design required to support the ceilings. Try to find your way around. Every 20 steps or so leads to an intersection with four choices, three of which lead nowhere (here's a secret: think right). Guides do a brisk "escort" business. From the rooftop there's a great view of Lucknow.

Chhota Imambara

The Chhota Imambara, or Hussainabad Imambara, was built in 1836 by the Muhammad Ali Shan, the eighth nawab, as his burial place. A fish as a weathervane, just inside the gate, may seem odd, but the fish is auspicious in Hindu and Moslem mythology; its presence is a good omen. The chain that leads to the statue of the woman, at the left of the entrance, is no act of whimsy either. It served then and now as a lightning rod to protect the statue and the building from storms.

The tiny mosque on the right was for women. The next building on the right as you walk along the channel that leads to the Chhota is a burial tomb for the nawab's daughter, Zinat Asuja, and is a miniature replica of the Taj Mahal. The building directly across from it, which holds her husband's remains, was originally planned for symmetry.

The Chhota, with its gilded dome and vast number of turrets and minarets, is almost baroque. Its handsome black and white facade is, in fact, a vast collection of verses from the Quran. Inside, you are confronted by a dazzling collection of mirrors, chandeliers, and lamps. The tall red and white lamp near the middle of the floor, with its 500 moving pieces, was purchased by the nawab in 1836. The center chandelier in the entry room has 1,000 moving pieces. Here, too, you'll see a vast collection of tazias. Also on the left-hand wall, as you face the entrance, you'll see an extremely old print in blue lettering on white; it contains the entire Quran.

Jama Masjid, Picture Gallery

To the west of the Chhota is the elegant Jama Masjid, started by Muhammad Ali Shah and completed after his death. This royal mosque of the nawabs, closed to non-Moslems, is a lovely long building crowded by three onion-shaped domes and flanked by two lofty minarets.

For a glimpse of the fancy men who ruled over Lucknow, visit the Picture Gallery (originally a building built by Muhammad Ali Shah), reflecting into a pool of water and surrounded by a grove. It's a portrait gallery that could be called the Nawab Hall of Fame.

The Residency

Toward the heart of Lucknow stands the Residency, the battle-scarred remains of Asaf-ud Daula's other elaborate architectural contribution. Originally conceived as a pleasure house with a network of underground chambers that provided relief from the summer heat, it was acquired by the British when they annexed the province and deposed and deported the last nawab, Wajid Ali Shah. That act sealed the fate of this building. During the 1857 Indian Mutiny, British inhabitants crowded into the elegant building, which then became the scene of some of the fiercest fighting. For 87 days, the British held out until Sir Colin Campbell broke through the Indian lines and relieved the half-starved defenders. Of the 3,000 troops and noncombatants who had refused to surrender, less than 1,000 staggered out. Although the marks of cannon shots gouge every remaining wall, the surrounding gardens and lawns are kept in order. Peace and goodwill prevail; unpleasant memories lie buried with the past.

Tombs

In the center of Lucknow are the perfectly proportioned tombs of Nawab Saddat Ali Khan and his beautiful wife, Khurshed Begum, built in the beginning of the nineteenth century. The Kaisar Bagh adjoining the tombs contains rows of apartments that housed the ladies of the royal harem. Near the river is Shahnajaf Imambara, which derives its name from Najaf, a city in Iraq. It is the early-nineteenth-century tomb of Nabob Ghazi-ud-din Haider and his wives, including Mubarak Mahal (a European). This building, constructed in 1814, was a stronghold for independence fighters in 1857. Like the Residency, what you see today—its low frontage and large flattened-out dome—diffuses an atmosphere of great turmoil.

La Martiniere

On the outskirts of the city, in a park close to a small lake, rises a rococo structure built in 1795, not by a nawab but by a Frenchman, Claude Martin, during the reign of Asaf-ud Daula. Nothing is missing in this compendium of styles; gargoyles rub shoulders with Corinthian columns and Roman arches are next to Oriental turrets. This fantastic hodgepodge was designed as a boys' school, with Kipling's protégé for *Kim* a student.

Chowk

Chowk is the bazaar in the old city of Lucknow, where the Moslem servants of the nawabs originally lived. Note the architectural detail of many of the buildings: stone lacework along the upper stories, later 1920s and '30s style facades that add up to a curious blend. Once you enter the main gate, you hit the bustle of the bazaar—rows and rows of silver and jewelry merchants, shops and stalls selling hand-embroidered *chikan* work. The former haunt of the nawab feudal aristocracy, ancestral dwellings abound, some still inhabited by old-time families. Here, gracious nawab manners still persist, and you sense that eighteenth-century charm when Lucknow was the center of culture and refinement.

ALLAHABAD

In ancient times Allahabad, which is at the confluence of the Ganges and Yamuna rivers, was known as Prayag. It was and still is an important place of Hindu pilgrimage. By the end of the twelfth century, Prayag fell under Moslem rule and in 1584 was given its new name.

The Patal Puri Temple lies underneath an enormous fort built by the Mogul Emperor Akbar. Descending a long sloping passage, you see a tree in the dim square-shaped hall. This tree, watered continuously by the priests, was mentioned by the Chinese traveler, Hsuan Tsang, in 640 and is known as Akshaya Batt, the Undying Banyan Tree. Another shrine of tremendous importance to the Hindus is Bharadwaja. Named after the great sage who occupied a hermitage on the high bank overlooking the place where the waters meet, it is mentioned in the *Ramayana*. Bharadwaja had 10,000 pupils and, as the head of a clan, he provided his students with free board and lodging. His *ashram* became a cross between a seat of learning and a welfare institution. Now, Allahabad University occupies this site.

Akbar's Fort and Mogul Monuments

Akbar's Fort is an impressive work of masonry. It houses an Ashoka Pillar, a single shaft of polished sandstone 35 feet high. Its capital disappeared during its 2,200 years of existence, but it still shows some of the edicts the emperor inscribed around its base—even though Jahangir's inscriptions of his family tree partially obliterated them. The mausoleum of Prince Khusrao, Emperor Jahangir's eldest son, is covered with paintings and a Persian verse that ends with a chronogram giving the Moslem year of 1031 (A.D. 1622) as the date of his death.

If you're in Allahabad during the Magh Mela, held each spring at the confluence of the two rivers, don't miss the ceremonies. Bundle-laden pilgrims in the thousands arrive each day, setting up tents and makeshift huts. Holy men lie on beds of nails or read out scriptures to worshipers before they take the ritual plunge. Rows of barbers shave the heads of pilgrims to comply with orthodox precepts that bald is the beatific best. Hindu women throw rose petals and marigolds into the holy river as offerings. Improvised stalls sell food, souvenirs, and images of deities. There are no bathing *ghats* (riverbank steps), and most pilgrims are rowed by innumerable boats into mid-river to perform their immersion.

Allahabad is famous for its literary traditions. The Sahitya Sammalan is a pioneer institution for the study of the Hindi language. Outside the city, the ancestral home of the late Jawaharlal Nehru, called Anand Bhavan (Place of Joy), is now a museum set up in his memory. Next to it stands Swaraj Bhavan (House of Freedom), which he donated to the nation in 1930 as a children's home.

FAIZABAD AND AJODHYA

On leaving Lucknow, go due east and you will arrive at Faizabad, capital of the nabobs of Avadh before they switched to Lucknow. Of its numerous monuments, the mausoleum of Behbu Begum is the finest in the region. Adjoining Faizabad is Ayodhya, principal city of the ancient Kingdom of Kosala. Revered by Hindus as the birthplace of Lord Rama, hero of the *Ramayana,* it is one of India's seven sacred places. The most important buildings are the Hanuman temple and Kanak Vhavan Temple, said to have been the palace of the God-King Rama. Siddhartha Gautama (Historic Buddha) supposedly traveled extensively in these parts, and Hsuan Tsang, that tireless seventh-century tourist, reported glowingly of the place.

SARNATH: CRADLE OF BUDDHIST FAITH

Sarnath, 11 kilometers (six miles) from Varanasi, is the center of the Buddhist world, just as Varanasi is the spiritual center for Hindus. At Sarnath, Siddhartha Gautama preached his first sermon more than 2,500 years ago. Here, he revealed the Eightfold Path that leads to the end of sorrow, the attainment of inner peace, enlightenment, and ultimate nirvana. Here, he established his doctrine of the Middle Way, the golden path between extremes of asceticism and self-indulgence.

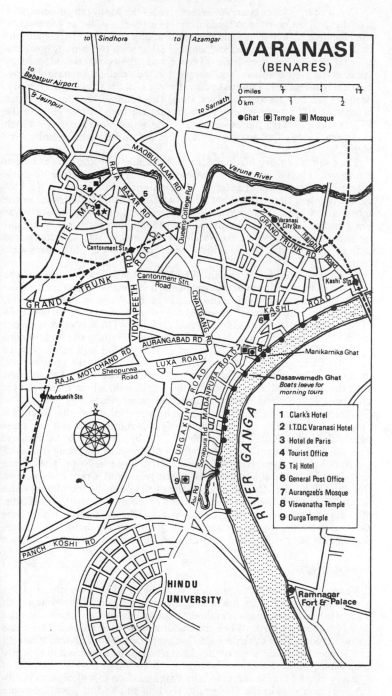

VARANASI
(BENARES)

0 miles ¼ ½ 1 1½
0 km 1 2

● Ghat ◉ Temple ■ Mosque

to Sindhora to Azamgar

to Babatpur Airport

to Jaunpur

to Sarnath

MAQBUL ALAM RD

RAJA BAZAR RD

Varuna River

Queens College Rd

THE MALL

Varanasi City Stn

GRAND TRUNK RD

Raighat Road

ROAD

Cantonment Stn.

Kashi Stn

VIDYAPEETH

GRAND TRUNK

Cantonment Stn. Road

KASHI ROAD

CHATGANG

AURANGABAD RD

LUXA ROAD

Manikarnika Ghat

RAJA MOTICHAND RD

Sheopurwa Road

MADANPURA ROAD

Dasaswamedh Ghat
Boats leave for morning tours

Manduadih Stn

N

DURGAKUND ROAD

Sonapura Rd

Asi Rd

RIVER GANGA

1 Clark's Hotel
2 I.T.D.C. Varanasi Hotel
3 Hotel de Paris
4 Tourist Office
5 Taj Hotel
6 General Post Office
7 Aurangzeb's Mosque
8 Viswanatha Temple
9 Durga Temple

PANCH KOSHI RD

HINDU UNIVERSITY

Ramnagar Fort & Palace

Two hundred years later, Ashoka arrived—the Mauryan emperor who was the greatest convert to Buddhism. He erected a pillar at Lumbini on the Nepalese border where the Historic Buddha was born. In Sarnath, he built several *stupas* (shrines) and another pillar with the famous lion capital that symbolizes the ideals of peace and righteousness—adopted by India as the State emblem. You can see it in the excellent Sarnath Archaeological Museum. Six hundred years after that, under the Gupta Dynasty, Sarnath reached its zenith. Back then, the Chinese traveler Fa Hsien claimed, 1,500 priests sat every day around the banyan tree close to the Vihara Temple. This tree is supposedly the actual Bo-Tree under which Gautama Siddhartha meditated for years before he realized Enlightenment.

The twelfth century marked Sarnath's decline, with the devout Queen Kumaradevi building a large monastery: the final tribute, before Varanasi rulers dismantled the stupas for building materials. In the sixteenth century, the Moslem Emperor Akbar built a brick tower on top of some of the most sacred remaining stupas to commemorate his father's visit some years earlier. The demise continued until 1836, when Sir Alexander Cunningham started extensive excavations. First, a stone slab was discovered with an inscription of the Buddhist creed; then numerous other relics were found.

Five great monuments remain: The Dhamekh Stupa (A.D. 500) is the largest survivor, with geometric ornaments on its walls. This stupa supposedly marks the location where the Buddha set the Wheel of Law in motion, although excavations have unearthed the remains of an even earlier stupa of Mauryan bricks of the Gupta period (200 B.C.). The second monument is the Dharamrajika Stupa, set up by Ashoka to contain the bodily relics of the Buddha. It's basically in ruins, thanks to the eighteenth-century king, Jagan Singh, who decided he had a better use for the construction materials. Also see the main shrine where Ashoka used to sit in meditation with the Ashoka pillar in front, and the Chankama, which marks the sacred promenade along which the gautama paced while preaching.

In recent years, Sarnath has undergone a revival. Near the Dhamekh Stupa and joining the old foundations of seven monasteries is a new temple, Mulagandha Kuti Vihara, built in 1931 by the Mahabodhi Society. The walls of the temple are decorated with frescoes depicting scenes of the Buddha's life, painted by a Japanese artist, Kosetsu Nosu. The temple also contains a fine collection of Buddhist relics and a rare collection of Buddhist literature. On the anniversary of the temple's foundation—the first full moon in November—an assembly of monks and lay devotees from all parts of Asia come together. Also visit the Chinese temple, which contains an attractive marble image of the great teacher. Before you leave, buy carrots (one rupee) and feed the deer in the nearby park.

VARANASI

Varanasi, or Kashi ("resplendent with divine light"), as it was called in the twelfth century B.C., has been the religious capital of the Hindu faith since recorded time and is a microcosm of Indian life. No one knows the date of Varanasi's birth. When the Buddha came here around 500 B.C., he encountered an ancient settlement. Contemporary with Babylon, Nineveh, and Thebes, Varanasi is one of the oldest cities in the world, a hub of firmly rooted traditions.

Every devout Hindu wants to visit Varanasi once in a lifetime to purify the body and soul in the Ganges, to shed all sin, and, if possible, to die here in old age and find release from the cycle of rebirth, which is the ultimate goal of the Hindus. This release means eternal unity with Brahma: "sinless, stirless rest, that change which never changes." Descending from the Himalayas on its long trek to the Bay of Bengal, each drop of the Ganga—as the Hindus call it—is august and propitious; the waters hold the powers of salvation, and the main sanctuary is Varanasi. Every year, the city welcomes millions of pilgrims, a lengthy trail many of them never retrace.

The old city of Varanasi (800,000 inhabitants) is a maze of small streets and alleyways, hiding in disorderly array no less than 2,000 temples and shrines. Domes, minarets, pinnacles and towers, and derelict eighteenth-century palaces dominate the sacred left bank of the river. The streets are noisy; color is rife. The air hangs heavy, as if in collaboration with the clang of temple gongs and bells. Some houses have simply decorated entrances; other buildings are ornate (notice the Indian-style gingerbread on balconies and verandahs). You'll see marriage processions and funeral processions and cows grabbing big flower necklaces destined for the gods, and you'll probably be hounded by phony guides and assertive hawkers.

For all its variety of sacred spots, Varanasi is really one big shrine dedicated to Shiva. Shaivism, the worship of Shiva, is one of the oldest forms of cult worship, and was practiced in the Indus Valley thousands of years ago. Legend recounts how the Ganges was created. The water goddess Ganga was ordered to redeem the souls of some humans of great merit. But the fall of such a quantity of water would cause great damage to the world, so Shiva caught the goddess in his hair and let her seep out slowly to wash the ashes of the worthy mortals, and their souls ascended to heaven.

Along the Ganges

Along a seven-kilometer (four-mile) stretch of the Ganges, you see steps called *ghats* that lead down from the steep city bank to the sacred river. These stone steps (there are about 70 sets of them) wed the great Hindu metropolis to the Ganges. The numerous *linga* (phallic-shaped stones) set on most terraces emphasize this religious connection.

The best time to visit the ghats is at early dawn, when residents of the city shake off sleep and proceed down to the river. A solemn multitude of people and even animals—thousands of spots of color, lit by the sun's first rays—all move in one direction, bent on immersion in the holy stream.

If you decide to hire a boat, which is not expensive, go to the Dasash-wamedh Ghat, the main ghat. As you slowly move along the river, you'll be drawn in by what you witness. Young men perform vigorous Hatha Yoga exercises; older men sit cross-legged in the lotus position, eyes closed in deep meditation. Brahmin priests sit under huge umbrellas offering prayers. Devotees drink from the polluted water. A carcass may even float by. Women glide in and out of saris with such perfect finesse that they reveal nothing and you don't think to avert your eyes. Others beat and swoosh linen against the stone, purifying the clothes they wear.

Thin blue smoke twists up to the sky from the burning ghat, the Mani-karnika, the chief cremation center of Varanasi (the other smaller cremation ghat is called Harish Chandra Ghat). Corpses wrapped in silk or linen—traditionally white for men and red for women—are carried on bamboo stretchers to the smoking pyres, where they are deposited and wait their turn: first an immersion into the Ganges, then, after a short wait, placement on the pyre for the ritual that precedes the cremation. These funeral ghats are not to be photographed; but you are allowed to watch.

Monuments Along the River

In the seventeenth century, the Mogul Emperor Aurangzeb pulled down the Vishwewara Temple and erected the Gyanvapi Mosque on its site. The foundation and rear of the mosque still reveal parts of the original temple. The tallest of its minarets, dominating the skyline of the holy city, collapsed during the great flood of 1948.

North of the Gyanvapi Mosque and also on the river is another of Aurangzeb's creations—the Alamgir Mosque—an odd blend of Hindu and Moslem design. Aurangzeb destroyed the seventeenth-century Beni Madhav ka Darera, which was dedicated to Vishnu, and replaced it with the mosque. The lower portions and wall are Hindu, the mosque is Islamic.

Ramnager Fort

Due south, on the opposite side of the Ganges, is the residential palace of the former maharajah of Varanasi. Called the Ramnager Fort, the Durbar Hall (Public Audience) and the Royal Museum have interesting collections that are open to the public. The palace was built to resist the floods of the monsoon, which play havoc with the city side of the river.

The Inner City

Start your tour of the old city with a visit to the Kashi Vishwanath Temple, dedicated to Shiva. The temple is located back from the Ganges in between the Dasashwanedh and Manikarnika ghats. Follow narrow streets crowded with animals, people, and little shops crammed with customers bargaining back and forth—often for the world-famous silver and gold brocades, for the appropriate wedding ornament, or even for a cremation cloth.

The most sacred shrine in all Varanasi, which is off limits to non-Hindus, is the Kashi Vishwanath. It is best seen from the top floor of the opposite house (pay a small fee to the owner). You'll see men and women making flower offerings to the lingam in the inner shrine. The present temple was built by Rani Ahalyabai of Indore in 1776 near the site of the original shrine destroyed by Aurangzeb. The spire is covered with gold plate, a gift from the Maharaja Ranjit Singh in 1835.

NORTHERN UTTAR PRADESH

Uttar Pradesh is a state of extremes—Mogul architecture at its best in Agra, Hindu reverence at Varanasi, and spectacular scenery and outdoor adventure in its northern expanse. Start your tour at Bareilly, 100 kilometers (62 miles) northwest of Lucknow, now an important rail and industrial center and formerly the chief city of the Rohillas, a marauding Afghan tribe that provoked a short but bloody war (1773–74) with the nawabs of Avadh and the British. The Khandan Mosque here has some Persian inscriptions that date back to the thirteenth century.

Thirty-three kilometers (20 miles) west, you'll find the ruins of the fortress city, Ahich Chatra, excavations of which have yielded sculptures, pottery, and Buddhist stupas ranging from the third century B.C. to A.D. 900. Not far from Ahich Chatra, you get your first glimpse of the distant Himalayas that divide India from Tibet and Nepal. Almost immediately, the road narrows and winds into the Himalayan Foothills, the favorite area of Mahatma Gandhi. Finally, you enter the Lake District of the Kumaon Hills and arrive at Nainital, 1,981 meters (6,500 feet) above sea level.

Nainital

Divided into Malli Tal and Talli Tal (upper and lower lake), Nainital is a base for forays into the Kumaon Hills, including a long climb to the top of Naina Peak, with its view of the Himalayas and Nainital. The name of this town—the summer capital of the state until 1947—comes from an old temple of Goddess Naina Devi that stands on the shore of the lake. Naina Devi is the presiding deity of the hill people who consider the lake sacred. Other nearby lakes are the Bhim Tal and Naukutchia Tal (the nine-cornered lake), only a short distance away.

Almora and Pindari Glacier

From Nainital, head north to Almora, surrounded by the Himalayas. Set on a hill where Vishnu supposedly stayed, Almora was founded in the sixteenth century as the chief city of the Chand rajahs who ruled in this area. The Gurkhas of Nepal also had a fling of power here, until the British seized control during the Gurkha War in 1815. Almora, compact and picturesque, is perched on a ridge with each surrounding hill topped by a temple. A small hill station with a distinct air of antiquity, it offers numerous walks leading to exquisite views.

To the west is another tiny hill station, Ranikhet (queen's field, for the queen who supposedly came and never left). A visit to the Pindari Glacier, due north, is a journey controlled by weather conditions and made by jeep or on foot; it's a journey that takes you through dramatic scenery and leads to the very shadow of the snow-covered Himalayas. You proceed stage by stage, with well-equipped bungalows at frequent intervals. At each level, the tree line thins until the pines cease, and you see the extensive glacier backed by mighty mountains.

Corbett National Park

India's oldest wildlife sanctuary (started in 1935), Corbett National Park is named after the fearless hunter and generous wildlife pioneer, Jim Corbett, author of *Man-Eaters of Kumaon.* Corbett grew up in these westernmost hills, and the local people, a number of whom he saved at the risk of his own life, held him in high esteem. But it wasn't until his death in Kenya in 1955 that India honored him by renaming the Hailey National Park for this well-liked man.

The park, with elephant grass, sal forests, and the Ramganga River covering its entire length, extends over an area of 520 square kilometers (125 square miles). From the back of an elephant, from inside a car, or from the height of a stationary watch tower, you may see elephants, tigers, leopards, black bear, wild boar, deer, snakes (including the python and king cobra), crocodiles, and birds and more birds. This is a *great* park, well worth a visit. The best time is from December to May; the park is closed during the monsoon (May to October).

HARIDWAR

Back in Ramnagar, travel northwest, hugging the edge of the mountains until you reach Haridwar, a sacred city of pilgrimage on the bank of the Ganges. Haridwar has the religious fervor of Varanasi, but its mood is joyous, not solemn. Here, King Bhagirath brought the Ganges down from heaven to provide a path of salvation for his ancestors. Here, the three supreme deities—Brahma, Vishnu, and Shiva—left their mark. In fact, a set of Vishnu's footprints is supposedly embedded in an upper portion of the wall of Haridwar's most important ghat, Har-ki-pauri. You see *swamis* (monks or teachers), *sadhus* (wandering holy men), devotees, over 150 *ashrams* (spiritual retreats), and *dharmshalas* (religious guest houses), temples, statues of deities, and numerous ghats set against the Ganges canal and river. The bustling scene serves as a constant reminder of Haridwar's importance in Hindu mythology. Religious strictures have also made Haridwar "dry" and strictly vegetarian, where even eggs are taboo.

One of the earliest names of this ancient city was Gangadwara, which means the Gate of the Ganges. A gate it is—sitting at the mouth of a gorge in the Shivalik mountains where the fast-moving Ganges rushes out, then slows dramatically as it enters the plains on its seaward course toward the Bay of Bengal. The devout believe that to bathe here once means salvation, and all along the banks, you see the faithful bathers congregating. At sunrise or at sunset, you must witness the celebration of *puja* (the offering of prayers to the Ganges) held at the Har-ki-pauri Ghat.

Moti Bazaar and Arti of the Ganges

The most festive puja is at evening and is called Arti of the Ganges. The event is heavily attended, so leave early and allow for at *least* an hour just to walk through the part of the city that hugs the Ganges canal and takes you to the Har-ki-pauri Ghat. Here, every ashram and dharmshala is bathed in a tropical hue often outlined in contrasting trim. There's a vague aura of old Miami Beach. Many of the buildings were built in the 1920s and '30s and are distinctly art deco.

Start your walk at the Lalto Rao Bridge by the Bhola Giri Temple and Ashram, done up in the shade of natural terra cotta with its dharmshala set off by light blue trim. Next, as you head northeast along Jodhamal Road, is the Chiniot Bhawan, a yellow temple with lacy stone trim. Step inside and see ornate marble gods and goddesses dressed in their festive clothes.

Move along Jodhamal to the Moti Bazaar—pleasantly congested and busy, yet not overwhelming. Ayurvedic medicine shops sell *jalzeera* (Indian spice powder for stomachaches); religious shops sell small polished stones (omens and lingams) and beads of coral or sandalwood for devotees to hold while saying mantras. Stalls sell fresh pickle chutneys, shawls, and saris.

At the end of the bazaar, the narrow street spills into a large square, where open-air stalls sell *dias*—leaves woven together like little boats and filled with fresh flowers and thimble-sized clay bowls and wicks. These beautiful vessels are set afloat on the Ganges during Arti. Men sell enormous balloons and boys sell wooden whistles and pipes. There's a carnival air. You've arrived at Har-ki-pauri Ghat surrounded by a complex of temples—mostly new except for the sixteenth-century Shri Ganga Mandir.

A short bridge leads to the Pant Dweep (tiny terraced island), the best vantage point. If you can, sit on the top ghat step. The preliminary show is as fascinating as Arti, with all India walking by: Rajasthanis in colorful turbans and wild mustaches, Sikhs, Nagas, sadhus, and swamis. People bathe, and many set off their dias in hasty anticipation.

A few minutes before Arti begins, temple bells ring and priests from surrounding temples descend the steps of the ghat—each carrying bells and a large brass lamp filled with oil. The priests ignite the lamps—the start of Arti. Flames rise up as they hold the vessels over the Ganges. Bells ring continuously. The priests swing the vessels up and down across the surface of the water. The fragrance of *dwoop* (incense) circulates. Chants, barely audible, silence the throngs. Burning dias flicker away on their downward journey along the swift moving Ganges. Within 15 minutes, Arti is over.

In Haridwar, the temples aren't old, but they're always festive, and some are erected on mythologically important sites. See the Daksh Mahadev Temple and Sati Jund in Kankhal, a part of Haridwar, with yellow stone lions at the entrance. Here, the father of Sati (Shiva's first wife) performed a sacrifice and neglected to invite Shiva. Sati was so insulted that she arrived uninvited and performed her own sacrifice—throwing herself into the fire at Yagva Kund now inside the Deksh Mahadev. A large statue of the devoted Nandi (Shiva's bull) stands outside. There are other temples in this complex. One contains a Shiva lingam surrounded by a copper cobra, with the water dripping down on the stone; another shows this goddess in all her manifestations. There is also a ghat for devotees to step down to the Ganges to bathe.

For a good view of Haridwar, visit the Mansa Devi Temple dedicated to the goddess Mansi, which stands on the top of one of the nearby Shivalik Hills. You can go by cable car or on foot.

Pawan Dham

Pawan may mean holy and *Dham* may mean house, but once you step inside the Pawan Dham Ashram, constructed in 1970 by Swami Vedanta Maharaj, you almost need sunglasses, and you can't help but smile. No wonder this swami had such a large following. The gigantic building is pure religious fun. Most walls are covered with elaborate mythological frescoes made of inlaid and painted glass. Ceilings dazzle with more colored glass. The few walls without a fresco have mirrors—perhaps so devotees see themselves as part of the Hindu pantheon. Step close to one of the numerous cubicles that contain gaily decorated marble gods and goddesses. Now look into the mirrored side walls inside the chamber. The statue appears in infinite reflection. The crowning *piéce de kitsch* is a large freestanding inlaid glass chariot drawn by horses, with Krishna and Arjun inside and Hanuman, the monkey god, riding on top of a stanchion. His weight kept the heavenly chariot earthbound.

RISHIKESH

Rishikesh, 24 kilometers (15 miles) north of Haridwar, is a busy, new city. It may be another city of religious significance tied to the Ganges and it may have important ashrams, but Rishikesh also pays homage to concrete and dust.

For hundreds of years, Rishikesh has been an important retreat for those on the spiritual path. There are over 100 ashrams here, including Maharishi Mahesh Yogi's Transcendental Meditation Center, which once hooked the Beatles; Swami Sivananda's Divine Life Society; and the Yoga Sadhan Ashram.

Triveni Ghat, with its sprawling terrace, is Rishikesh's main bathing ghat. Each evening, from 5 to 6 P.M., a local swami comes down to preach, his service followed by a small-scale Arti. The fish, considered sacred in this part of the river, seem to understand their peculiar status. Over the years, they've become so tame that they swarm to the surface to catch daily offerings.

Two mythological stories are connected to Rishikesh and commemorated by temples. Supposedly, Lakshman (a brother of Lord Rama) stood on one foot in the middle of the Ganges and meditated for 100 years as an act of penance for killing his guru—an unfortunate event that occured while he was attempting to help his brother, Rama. A suspension bridge, the Laxmanjhoola, crosses the Ganges where Lakshman evidently did his prolonged act of physical balance. The Bharat Temple is connected to Bharat, another brother of Rama, who also did penance in Rishikesh during the same period as did Lakshman and for the same approximate duration. Only he had committed no sin; his motivation was self-purification.

DEHRA DUN

Dehra Dun, 42 kilometers (26 miles) from Rishikesh, is the largest Uttar Pradesh city in the lower Himalayan foothills. It's an important government administration center, home of the super-exclusive Doon School (Rajiv Gandhi is one of its alumni), and the location of Asia's largest forest research institute, with museums open to the public. Dehra Dun's no great beauty of a city, thanks to unregulated limestone quarrying. But it's a good stopover for those heading north and it offers two nearby diversions to break up a long ride.

Visit the Tapkeshwar Cave Temple, set in the woods along a stream. To the sound of piped religious music, you descend a stone staircase with pesky monkeys lying in wait, pass under a natural rock ledge with mossy grass hanging down, and reach a series of caves. Inside are shrines with small statues of Nandi, Ganesh, Hanuman and, in the main cave, a Shiva lingam set on a copper base—all tended by a gregarious *pujari* (priest). If you have a translator, this is one time to believe the stories. The pujari will explain how the temple is at least 5,000 years old and he'll recount how the water that used to drip steadily from the roof of the cave onto the lingum has decreased over the years with each disaster: the two world wars; the Chinese invasion of Tibet; the deaths of Mahatma Gandhi, Nehru, and Indira Gandhi; and a famine. Now you're lucky if you see much more than a droplet or two.

You can also cool yourself at Sahastradhara, where sulphur springs tumbling down from the mountains form a natural pool in which people can bathe. It's open from sunrise to sunset. There's a limited-menu Indian cafe and a temple on the side of the hill that leads up to yet another cave with another Shiva lingam. This time, plenty of water drenches the sacred stone.

Mussoorie

Mussoorie, 2,005 meters (6,576 feet) above sea level, rises on a horseshoe-shaped foothill that overlooks the Ganges River, sluggishly moving through the plains on one side and the vibrant silhouette of the lower Himalayas on the other.

At first glance, Mussoorie looks like another former British hill station turned "honeymoon retreat," where the emphasis is on short walks and relaxation. You're bombarded with billboards that advertise hotels and see cars loaded with young couples. But then something happens. Tucked away here and there, some of that grand old elegance peeks out. Some of it is a bit musty around the edges and some of it even totters on old Victorian legs, but it's there and it's holding its own in a way that makes this particular hill station still special.

Stop at Hakmans Hotel and have a drink for old time's sake. As you sit and look around, it's as if time stood still—when the stiff upright British got up and left. Check the artwork on the walls and the old telephones. Walk through the former cabaret theater and linger a moment in the grand yet bizarre entrance to the hotel. For another trip into nostalgia—this one quite elegant—visit the chateaulike Hotel Savoy, a sprawl of Victorian charm sitting on a hill all its own.

While in old Mussoorie, walk west along Charleville Road to Happy Valley, a Tibetan township where Buddhist flags wave in the breeze and small restaurants entice you with good Tibetan cooking. At the other end of Mussoorie, you'll find bazaars. Stroll through the Mall to Kulri, set up for tourists, and the more interesting Landaur Bazaar. It's an ethnic market with a lengthy string of tiny shops built along a narrow winding ridge. Wherever you walk—along the Mall, up to Camel's Back Road, or Gun Hill—the views explain why British Captain Young decided that this particular ridge was an ideal retreat for his countrymen back in 1827.

Mussoorie is also a great base for day excursions. Visit Kempty Falls (15 km), a short drive to the north that ends at appealing falls that spill into a refreshing pool of water with an unassuming cafe set up alongside. Go east to Dhanolti (24 km) along a narrow road that climbs and winds, passing men leading pack horses that are laden with pails of collected milk. Occasionally, you will see tiny shrines mounted with flags erected along the road, terraced fields of wheat, small villages with simple stone or sod houses linked together, foot paths, and potato fields. This rugged terrain brings you to a tiny village set in a pine forest: Dhanolti. There's a new hotel under construction and an Uttar Pradesh Tourist Bungalow, which serves food and supplies an outdoor map that points the way to good walks.

Mussoorie is also the "gateway" to Yamnotri and Gangotri—two essential goals of pilgrimage that mark the source of the Yamuna and Ganges rivers. The shrines here draw thousands of devotees to this part of India, which also is scenically beautiful—reason enough to make the trip.

Yamnotri

Yamnotri is 140 kilometers (87 miles) almost due north of Mussoorie. The road, which takes you to Hanumanchatti within 13 kilometers (eight miles) of the temple, is Himalayan beautiful with the Yamuna River escorting you on the left. You pass through tiny villages like Barkot, encircled by pine forests, with stunning snow-clad peaks forming a picturesque backdrop. Walking sadhus share the road. Once the road ends and you start out for the temple, you come to Jankibaichatti, a good overnight halt, with rest houses and hot-water springs.

Yamnotri itself is huddled against the western bank of the snow-covered Banderpunch (20,720 feet above sea level). Here, an ancient Hindu sage is said to have built his hermitage and bathed daily in the Yamuna and Ganges. When old age prevented more treks to the Gangotri, a stream of the Ganges emerged from the Yamnotri rocks. Yamunaji Temple, dedicated to the goddess Yamuna, nearby hot springs gushing out of the mountain (the Surya Kund is considered the most sacred), and a rock (Divya Shila) are revered by Hindus, who flock here from May to November to offer prayers.

Gangotri

The Gangotri Temple, built in the eighteenth century and dedicated to the goddess Ganga, commemorates the source of the Ganges. Here, too, pilgrims flock during the season to pay respect to this shrine and their holiest river. The scenery on the way to Gangotri is magnificent, with canyons, cascades, and rushing rivulets at each turn of the way. At an elevation of 10,000 feet, Gangotri shows off its famous temple on the right bank of the river. On the opposite bank are a few huts, inhabited by sadhus who have settled here: some mere escapists from the turmoil of the world; others inflamed by zeal. You can also continue on from Gangotri, traveling by foot or pony, to the Gaumukh Glacier, a distance of about 20 kilometers (12 miles), where you can offer tribute to that exact starting point of the river.

Kedarnath and Badrinath

Hindu pilgrims also hope to visit two other important shrines in this northern area of Uttar Pradesh—Kedarnath and Badrinath, the assumed abodes of Shiva and Vishnu, set over 3,049 meters (10,000 feet) up in the mountains.

Instead of taking the direct route to Kedarnath, try to go via Deoprayag, a charming Indian village built into the slope of a hill at the confluence of the Bhagirathi and Alakandanda rivers. You can even spend a night in the minimal but clean tourist bungalow. Deoprayag (God's place) is the site of the ancient and recently renovated Raghunath Temple, which commemorates the spot where Rama supposedly came to meditate. It is also in Deoprayag that the merging rivers assume the known name River Ganges. The whitewashed old village, connected to the new part of town by a pedestrian-sized suspension bridge, is filled with local *pandits* (priests), who lead visiting Hindus in their prayers on the bathing ghat that provides access to the river. As you walk through the narrow lanes, there's an abundance of charm in the architecture and hillside setting and a prevailing sense of tranquility, with the dominant sound that of the river thrashing along on its course.

On leaving Deoprayag, you find that the road narrows and winds. Occasionally, you see distant pastoral hamlets in which life moves to a quiet rhythm. At Gaurikund, with hot water springs and a temple, the road ends. From here, you go by foot or pony (there are rest huts along the way) on a 15-kilometer (nine-mile) journey near glaciers and waterfalls. You clomp through rocky forests until just after you cross a narrow bridge above a village, where you see a simple gray stone temple standing on a raised platform guarding the dwellings in Kedarnath. The temple, snow-bound and closed from November to May, stands on the banks of the Mandakini. A statue of Nandi, Shiva's mount, is in the courtyard. Several holy bathing spots are around the temple, and inside the simple shrine are beautiful carvings of Shiva, Parvati, and the five *pandavas* (legendary rulers), who built this temple as atonement for the sins they committed during the Great Battle, recorded in the *Mahabharata*.

To get to Badrinath, return to Rudraprayag and take the road passing through the Alaknanda valley and the village of Karnaprayag, a busy meeting place for the surrounding hill people. Then, you enter the Pipalkoti Valley, with its important township, Joshimath, which is also the winter seat of the Badrinath shrine. Here, you come across the Buddhist Bhutias, an Indo-Mongoloid people whose life underwent severe change when trading with Tibet became impossible. Their greatest possession is the yak, their beast of burden that also provides milk, butter, and meat. To the east, the steep Nanda Devi Summit (25,650 feet) appears like a pyramid. Snow, blown by the winds, gives the impression of smoke blowing over gray rock; the locals call it the Nandi Devi, "kitchen of their deity."

In the winter, skiers can check out Joshimath's nearby Auli, India's newest ski resort—with some runs still under construction, including one 32 kilometers (20 miles) long that will make the trail one of the longest in the world.

The brightly painted Badrinath Temple, 52 kilometers (32 miles) north of Joshimath, is dedicated to Vishnu and also figures in Buddhist mythology. Hindus claim that a sage chastised Vishnu for indulging in earthly pleasure—allowing his consort, Lakshmi, to rub his feet. Vishnu fled to this valley and meditated in a posture associated with the Buddha, who also happens to be the ninth incarnation of this deity. Over time, Lakshmi found Vishnu and begged him to give up this un-Vishnu-like pose. He agreed, but only if Badrinath remained a valley of meditation.

Much of the Badrinath Temple has been enlarged; only the inner sanctum has escaped alteration. The main shrine has a *mandapa* (pavilion) and inner sanctum, with a black stone idol of Vishnu that sits under a gold canopy. The main temple is surrounded by shrines, dedicated to Lakshmi and Hanuman (the monkey god), and numerous sacred *kunds* (tanks). Try to attend an evening prayer service; it's a highly charged event.

PRACTICAL INFORMATION FOR
UTTAR PRADESH

WHEN TO GO. For the non-Himalayan areas (the plains region): This part of Uttar Pradesh has a variable climate. It can be very hot and dry in summer and fairly cool in winter. From November to February, the maximum temperature rarely exceeds 65°F in daytime; at night, it falls to 45°F. The main tourist season for the plains lasts from October to March. For the Himalayas: The best visiting seasons are from May to July and mid-September to early November. Temperatures are pleasant during the day and cool by night. The Valley of Flowers bursts into bloom in July and August, which is the time of the monsoon. Corbett National Park is open from mid-November to mid-June, with the best viewing time from March to June.

HOW TO GET THERE. By Air. *Indian Airlines* makes four weekly flights into Allahabad from Delhi and daily flights to Lucknow. The airline also makes occasional weekly flights to Lucknow from Patna (in Bihar), Calcutta, and Bombay. Indian Airlines makes daily flights to Varanasi from Agra, Delhi, Kathmandu, and Khajuraho. *Vayudoot* makes three weekly flights from Delhi to Pantnagar (near Nainital and Corbett) and three weekly flights to Varanasi from Agra, Delhi, and Khajuraho. Vayudoot also flies daily from Delhi to Dehra Dun.

By Bus. The *Uttar Pradesh State Road Transport Corporation* (UPSRTC) runs deluxe interstate buses from Delhi and other large northern cities, including Shimla and Chandigarh; it also provides excellent and frequent service between most areas in the state that are of interest to the tourist. For fares and details: In Delhi, call 2518709, 6 A.M.–8 P.M. at *Interstate Bus Terminus,* Kashmiri Gate. In Lucknow, call *Kaiserbagh Bus Station,* 42503. In Varanasi, call UPSTRC, 63233.

By Train. Uttar Pradesh is well covered with railroad tracks. You can get to most important cities (Lucknow, Allahabad, Dehra Dun, and Varanasi) from either Delhi or Calcutta. Keep in mind, however, that some of these journeys are overnight. When you reserve a sleeper (first- or second-class and air-conditioned), you must also reserve a berth, or you might just find yourself ejected from the train. For train information in Delhi, contact the *International Tourist Guide* at the New Delhi Railroad Station, tel. 3352164. In Calcutta, contact *Railway Tourist Guide,* 6 Fairlie Place, tel. 202789. In Lucknow, call *Northern Railway Enquiry,* 51234 or *North Eastern Railway Enquiry,* 51433. In Varanasi, call *Varanasi Cantonment Railway Station,* 43404.

By Rented Car with Driver. Delhi is 541 km from Lucknow, 756 km from Varanasi (Calcutta is 677 km from Varanasi). Heading toward the Himalayas, Delhi is 222 km from Haridwar, 322 km from Nainital, 255 km from Dehra Dun, and 270 km from Mussoorie. The cost of renting a car is approximately Rs. 5 per km, plus night-halt charges (never more than Rs. 50 per night).

TOURIST INFORMATION. Uttar Pradesh Tourist departments are extremely helpful, offering specific brochures and maps. (The only exception is in Varanasi, where the Government of India Tourist Department outshines.) Most offices are open 10 A.M.–5 P.M., closed Sunday and second Saturday of each month.

Allahabad. Uttar Pradesh Tourist Office, 35 Mahatma Gandhi Rd.; tel. 53883.

Dehra Dun. Regional Tourist Office, Hotel Drona, 45 Mahatma Gandhi Rd.; tel. 23217.

Haridwar. Regional Tourist Bureau, Lalta Rao Bridge, Station Rd.; tel. 19. Also, Information Counter, Railway Station; tel. 817.

Joshimath. (on the way to Badrinath and Kedarnath). Tourist Office; tel. 81.

Lucknow. Tourist Bureau, 10 Station Rd., tel. 246205; and Tourist Reception Center, Railway Station, Charbagh (no phone).

Mussoorie. Tourist Office, The Mall; tel. 2863.

Nainital. Tourist Bureau, The Mall; tel. 2337.

Pauri (Garhwal). Tourist Bureau, tel. 2241.

Rishikesh. Tourist Bureau, Yatayat Bus Station; tel. 209.

Srinagar (Garhwal). Tourist Bureau; tel. 10.

Uttarkashi. Tourist Bureau, near the bus station; tel. 190.

Varanasi. Government of India Tourist Office, 15-B, The Mall, Cantonment; tel. 43189. Government of India Tourist Information Counter, Babatpur Airport (open flight times only). Tourist Bureau, Parade Khothi; tel. 43486. Tourist Information Counter, Cantonment Railway Station (no phone).

For information about Corbett National Park, contact the Field Director, Project Tiger, Ramnagar, tel. 189; or the Chief Wildlife Warden, Lucknow, U.P., tel. 46140.

FOREIGN CURRENCY EXCHANGE. Most Western-style hotels have money-exchange counters. Otherwise, go to a branch of the *State Bank of India;* open Mon.–Fri. 10 A.M.–2 P.M., Sat. till noon.

ACCOMMODATIONS. Uttar Pradesh has some Western-style hotels in the major tourist areas (including Lucknow, Varanasi, and Mussoorie) and a few charming old-fashioned guest houses. For some areas of the state—Badrinath, Kedarnath, Gangotri, and Yamunotri—the choice is limited. Most accommodations in this area are listed below under "Tourist Rest Houses" and "Safari-Style Tents." Despite the lack of choice accommodations, don't avoid this part of Uttar Pradesh. Prices are based on double occupancy and don't include taxes: *Expensive,* over Rs. 950; *Moderate,* Rs. 500–Rs. 950; *Inexpensive,* under Rs. 500. Some Western-style hotels take major credit cards.

ALLAHABAD

Inexpensive

Hotel Allahabad Regency. 16 Tashkent, Allahabad; tel. 56043. 13 rooms with bath. The city's newest hotel has a pleasant garden and modern air-conditioned rooms with TV. Those rooms listed as "Deluxe" (still in the inexpensive price range) are best. Multicuisine restaurant, room service, swimming pool, car rental. Rupees only.

Hotel Presidency. 19-D, Sarojini Naidu Marg, Allahabad; tel. 4460. 10 air-conditioned rooms with bath. This small hotel has a nice ambience and good management. Rooms have Western-style decor. TV, room service, multicuisine restaurant, swimming pool, foreign-exchange counter, doctor. DC, V.

BADRINATH

Inexpensive

Hotel Devlok. Reservations: Manager, Hotel Devlok, Badrinath; tel. 12. 30 rooms with attached bathrooms. This government-run hotel, within walking distance of the famous temple, offers Western-style rooms, with clean, warm bed comforters. Best rooms are called "deluxe" and "executive." There is a lounge and a vegetarian restaurant. Rupees only.

CORBETT NATIONAL PARK

Moderate–Expensive

Camp Corbett. Kaladhungi; no phone. 30 cabins, numerous tents. In a forest an hour outside the actual park, this new, privately run "luxury camp" offers a choice of accommodations—"deluxe" cabins with thatched roof and modern attached bathroom, or a safari-style tent with shared bathroom. Included are a rustic-style rooftop multicuisine restaurant, fishing, jungle guides, natural swimming pools, bar. Rupees only.

Inexpensive

For all reservations in the park, contact: Field Director, Project Tiger, Ramnagar, tel. 189 or the Chief Wildlife Warden, Lucknow, tel. 46140.

Bijrani, Khinanauli, and Sarpduli Rest Houses. Each rest house has about four to six rooms, with simple bath. Set into the forest and not convenient to the complex's restaurant, all rooms are rustic, have no-frills kitchens, and are private. Bring a sleeping bag and provisions. Very inexpensive (under Rs. 100). Rupees only.

Dhikhala Forest Rest House Complex. This facility, inside the park, has simple clean rooms with bath. The old lodge has better ambience than the new lodge. You can also rent a cabin for more privacy or a tent (bring a sleeping bag). Multicuisine restaurant and a reception center. Rupees only.

DEHRA DUN

Moderate

Hotel Madhuban. 97 Rajpur Rd., Dehra Dun; tel. 24097. 42 rooms and cottages with bath. You can stay in the Western-style hotel with modern furnishings or in a cottage where the interiors are done up in different Indian state decors. Air-conditioning, TV, room service, multicuisine restaurant, bar, foreign-exchange counter, secretarial services, doctor. AE, DC, MC, V.

Hotel Nidhi. 74-C Rajpur Rd., Dehra Dun; tel. 24611. 24 rooms with bath. This newish, multistory hotel is attractive and modern. Rooms have a Western-style decor. Air-conditioning, TV, room service, multicuisine restaurant, doctor, foreign-exchange counter. AE, DC.

Inexpensive

Hotel Drona. 45 Gandhi Rd., Dehra Dun; tel. 24371. 78 rooms with bath. This Western-style hotel, run by the government, offers a variety of rooms. The best rooms are "deluxe," with air-conditioning and TV. Room service, multicuisine restaurant, tourist office, shops. Rupees only.

DHANOLTI

Inexpensive

Dhanolti Tourist Bungalow. Reservations: Manager of Tourist Complex, Dhanolti, tel. 2, or Tourist Department in Mussoorie, tel. 2863. 5 rooms with bath.

This rustic government-run bungalow has clean, spacious rooms with working fire-places. Bathrooms have Indian-style toilets; hot water is available by bucket. Simple meals are available at nominal cost. Rupees only.

HARIDWAR

Moderate

Hotel Surprise. Haridwar-Delhi Rd., Jwala Pur, Haridwar; tel. 1146 or 1148. 55 rooms with bath. This mini high rise has the upscale traveler in mind. The lobby is an overstatement in marble with an enormous chandelier; but rooms are pleasant-ly unpretentious. "Deluxe" rooms have TV and air-conditioning. It's 1½ km (1 mi.) from Haridwar to get beyond the vegetarian limits. Room service, multicuisine restaurants, foreign-exchange desk, travel agency, swimming pool, shopping arcade, doctor. AE, DC, MC, V.

Inexpensive

Haridwar Tourist Bungalow. Haridwar. Reservations: Manager, Uttar Pradesh State Tourism Development Corp., Haridwar; tel. 379. 22 rooms with bath. A government facility and currently under renovation, this bungalow is within walking distance of the center of Haridwar and faces the Ganga Canal. Rooms have minimal furnishings; ask for an air-cooled room. There is a vegetarian restaurant, with room service. Rupees only.

LUCKNOW

Moderate

Hotel Carlton. Shahnajaf Rd., Lucknow; tel. 44021. 66 air-conditioned rooms with bath and TV. This older, rambling British bungalow should be wonderful; it has character and lovely gardens. But the genteel air of the spacious bedrooms has been replaced by an air of neglect. Multicuisine restaurant, room service, bar, foreign-exchange counter, car-rental and secretarial services, doctor. Breakfast included. AE, DC.

Clarks Avadh. 8 Mahatma Gandhi Marg, Lucknow; tel. 40130. 98 rooms with bath. This Western-style "luxury" hotel has attractive air-conditioned rooms with a subdued contemporary decor. TV, room service, multicuisine restaurant, bar, travel agency, foreign-exchange counter, secretarial services, golfing arrangements. AE, DC, MC, V.

Inexpensive

Hotel Kohinoor. 6 Station Rd., Lucknow; tel. 35421. 52 rooms with bath. This simple Western-style hotel offers clean, attractive rooms with a modern decor. Air-conditioning, room service, multicuisine restaurant, travel counter, secretarial services, doctor. DC.

MUSSOORIE

Moderate–Expensive

Savoy. The Mall, Mussoorie; tel. 2510 or 2601. 121 rooms with bath. The château-style Savoy located on a hill overlooking the mountains opened in 1902 when no road led to Mussoorie. Queen Mary stayed in these grand rooms when she was the Princess of Wales; so did Nehru and the Dalai Lama. The Victorian mood is deliberate, the owner and his wife are refined, and the tarnished edges are part of the charm. Request a "deluxe" suite, if you can afford it ($90 with meals), or an upstairs double off the veranda. Restaurants, room service, beer garden, bar, laundry, travel counter, doctor, foreign-exchange counter, post office. Meals included. AE, DC, MC, V.

Moderate

Carlton's Hotel Plaisance. Happy Valley Rd., Mussoorie; tel. 2800. 10 rooms with bath. If cozy elegance appeals to you, stay in this small bungalow built by an English barrister in the early 1900s. The dining room and parlor have handsome antiques, hunting trophies, and family memorabilia. Bedrooms are modest, yet comfortable. Gracious hosts cater to your needs. No Himalayan views; you're nestled in an orchard. No bar. Discount mid-Nov.–Mar. Rupees only.

NAINITAL

Moderate

Hotel Arif Castles. Nainital; tel. 2231. 66 rooms with bath. Nainital's new fine hotel, just outside the downtown area, is Western-style and has spacious rooms with a modern decor. Included are air-conditioning, TV, room service, multicuisine restaurants, bar, health club, billiards, foreign-exchange and travel counter. Off-season discount: July 16–Sept. 15 and Nov. 1–Apr. 1. AE, DC, MC, V.

Shervani Hilltop Inn. Shervani Lodge, Mallital, Nainital; tel. 2128. 21 rooms with bath. This Western-style hotel lacks great character, but it does have good views and provides excellent service. Rooms have a contemporary decor. TV, room service, multicuisine restaurant, bar, foreign-exchange and travel counter, children's park, doctor. Breakfast and dinner included. July 1–Sept. 15 and Nov. 1–Apr. 30 rooms are discounted (inexpensive), with meals not included in rate. AE, DC, V.

Inexpensive

Swiss Hotel. Nainital; tel. 2603. 18 rooms with bath. A lovely chalet-style exterior, a pretty rose garden, and good views are offered at the Swiss. Rooms have a simple Western-style decor and fireplaces; some rooms have TV. Unfortunately, service can be indifferent; don't hesitate to complain. Room service, multicuisine restaurant, sailing and bird-watching arrangements, doctor. Rupees only.

RISHIKESH

Moderate

Hotel Ganga Kinare. 16 Virbadra Rd., Rishikesh; tel. 566. 34 rooms with bath. This new Western-style hotel on the Ganga River has a back lawn and terrace with steps that lead down to the water for a holy dip. The modern rooms are attractive, with air-conditioning and TV; best rooms have a river view and no view of dusty Rishikesh. Vegetarian restaurant, travel counter, picnic arrangements. Rupees only.

Hotel Natraj. Dehra Dun Rd., Rishikesh; tel. 1099. 75 rooms with bath. A three-story stucco-and-marble hotel, the Natraj's rooms have a quietly elegant, contemporary decor. Best rooms are on the upper floor. TV, air-conditioning, multicuisine vegetarian restaurants, health club, yoga, shopping arcade, swimming pool, free airport transfer, travel agency, foreign-exchange counter, secretarial services. AE, DC.

Inexpensive

Inderlok Hotel. Railway Rd., Rishikesh; tel. 555. 50 rooms with bath. In the heart of Rishikesh, this well-managed, modest Western-style hotel offers clean air-conditioned and fan-cooled rooms. Room service, multicuisine restaurant, tour and yoga instruction arrangements, terrace. DC.

Rishikesh Tourist Bungalow. Tourist Complex, Rishilok; Munikireti; tel. 373. 48 rooms with bath (Indian-style toilet). Located near interesting ashrams, this bungalow-style hotel, run by the government, has lovely grounds and offers spacious, clean rooms. Rooms are fan-cooled, and room service is provided. There is a multicuisine vegetarian restaurant. Rupees only.

VARANASI

Expensive

Hotel Clarks Varanasi. The Mall, Varanasi Cantonment, Varanasi; tel. 42401. 140 rooms with bath. A modern Western-style hotel, Clarks offers attractive air-conditioned rooms with a light, cheery decor and TV. Best rooms overlook the pool.

Room service, multicuisine restaurant, bar, foreign-exchange and travel counter, yoga center, and swimming pool. Indian classical dance and music performances are presented on request. AE, DC, MC, V.

Hotel Taj Ganges. Nadesar Palace Grounds, Varanasi; tel. 42481. 120 rooms with bath. This Western-style high rise has a handsome lobby and spacious modern rooms; but it lacks the expected Taj chain class. Best rooms have a view of the swimming pool. Air-conditioning, TV, room service, multicuisine restaurants, bar, foreign-exchange and travel counter, doctor, swimming pool, tennis court, secretarial service, shopping arcade. AE, DC, MC, V.

Moderate

Hotel de Paris. 15 The Mall, Varanasi Cantonment, Varanasi; tel. 43582. 50 rooms with bath. Set on pretty grounds, the handsome cream-and-pink exterior of this old bungalow evokes not Paris but the British Raj. Bedrooms are spacious and have a simple decor. Some rooms are air-conditioned. Room service, multicuisine restaurant, TV lounge, foreign-exchange and travel counter, classical Indian dance and music performances and astrologer on request, bank, shopping arcade. AE, DC, V.

Hotel Varanasi Ashok. The Mall, Varanasi; tel. 46020. 84 rooms with bath. This multistory Western-style hotel is set on landscaped grounds. Rooms have a contemporary decor and balconies, with the best rooms overlooking the Varuna River. Air-conditioning, TV, room service, multicuisine restaurants, bar, foreign-exchange and travel counter, swimming pool, secretarial services, shopping arcade. AE, DC, MC, V.

Inexpensive

Hotel Malti. Vidyapith Rd., Varanasi; tel. 56844. 42 rooms with bath. This new multistory Western-style hotel has a spacious lobby and pleasant modern-decor rooms. Best rooms are air-conditioned. TV, room service, multicuisine restaurant, travel counter. Rupees only.

Hotel Parvaaz. 56 Patel Nagar, Varanasi; tel. 43045. 33 rooms with bath. This small Western-style hotel has pleasant rooms with overhead fans. Room service, multicuisine restaurant, doctor, travel counter. Rupees only.

Hotel Pradeep. Jagatganj, Varanasi; tel. 66363. 20 rooms with bath. Another small hotel with clean rooms and overhead fans. There is room service as well as a multicuisine restaurant. Rupees only.

TOURIST REST HOUSES AND SAFARI-STYLE TENTS. In Uttar Pradesh the government has constructed simple, yet basically clean, tourist rest houses and a few safari-style tent facilities. They're very inexpensive (under Rs. 250 per room), accept only rupees, and should be reserved in advance. The Tourist Rest Houses usually offer a range of rooms. For an attached bathroom, request a "deluxe" or "executive" room with two twin beds or a family suite with four beds. Other options are "ordinary double" or a dormitory with a shared bath. Most bathrooms have an Indian-style toilet and simple shower, most often with hot water available by bucket. A *chawkidar* (caretaker) will fix you a simple meal (called catering) for a nominal fee. Bring a sleeping bag or a sleeping bag sheet, a towel, a bar of soap, and a roll of toilet paper.

Contact the Asst. General Manager (Tourism), Garhwal Mandal Vikas Nigam Ltd., Munikireti, Rishikesh (tel. 372 or 357), to reserve a room in the following Tourist Rest Houses: Bhojwasa (near the Gaumukh Glacier), Chopta, Gangotri, Hanumanchatti, Jankibaichatti, and Kedarnath.

GMVN also handles reservations for the Chandra Puri Tent Camp (north of Rudraprayag), which has delightful safari-style tents by a riverbank. To reserve a cottage at the Auli ski resort, contact GMVN, 74/1, Rajpur Rd., Dehra Dun, tel. 26817.

To reserve a room in the following Tourist Rest Houses, contact the manager in each individual facility:

Barkot Tourist Rest House. Barkot; tel. 36.

Deoprayag Tourist Rest House. Deoprayag; tel. 33.

Gaurikund Tourist Rest House. Gaurikund; tel. 2.

Guptakashi Tourist Rest House. Guptakashi; tel. 21.

Joshimath Tourist Rest House. Joshimath; tel. 81.
Rudraprayag Tourist Rest House. Rudraprayag; tel. 46.
Srinagar Tourist Rest House. Srinagar; tel. 99.
Uttarkashi Tourist Rest House. GMVN, Uttarkashi; tel. 36.

DINING OUT. Except for the big cities and Mussoorie, eating well can't be considered a major draw in Uttar Pradesh. Breakfast is usually served 8–10:30; lunch, noon–3; and dinner, 7:30–10. Payment is normally in rupees unless the restaurant is connected to a Western-style hotel. The restaurants listed below are informal and, unless noted, are open for all three meals and don't require reservations. Prices, based on one person eating a three-course meal, excluding taxes, tip, or beverage, are *Deluxe,* over Rs. 120; *Expensive,* Rs. 80–Rs. 120; *Moderate,* Rs. 40–Rs. 80; *Inexpensive,* under Rs. 40.

DEHRA DUN

Moderate

Vatika. Hotel Madhuban, 97 Rajpur Rd.; tel. 24094. This cheery restaurant, with lots of windows, serves Continental and Indian cuisines, including especially good Mughlai dishes. At night you're entertained by live Indian *ghazals* (musicians). Dinner reservations advised. Open 7 A.M.–midnight. AE, DC, MC, V.

HARIDWAR

All food in Haridwar is vegetarian. If you want meat or even eggs, try Hotel Surprise, outside Haridwar's city limits.

Expensive

Hotel Surprise. Haridwar-Delhi Rd., Jwala Pur; tel. 1146. The decor at the air-conditioned **Gazal** restaurant is Western and the food is non-vegetarian Continental or Chinese. You can also dine outside at **Barbeque for South Indian** for tandoori items or at the **Rooftop Restaurant** for grilled specialties, with good views in either place. Gazal is open 8–11 A.M., noon–3 P.M., and 7–midnight. Barbeque and Rooftop are open 6–10 P.M. AE, DC, MC, V.

Inexpensive–Moderate

Chotiwala Restaurant. Railway Station Rd.; tel. 242. Booths and tables are crowded into a narrow space here. While a radio plays Hindi music, diners eat ample portions, Indian fashion, with the right hand. Friendly ambience. Open 8 A.M.–10:30 P.M. Rupees only.

LUCKNOW

Expensive

Falaknuma Restaurant. Clarks Avadh, 8 Mahatma Gandhi Marg; tel. 40130. In this rooftop restaurant, be sure to ask for a table with a Gopti River view. The chef serves Continental, Chinese, and Indian cuisines, with especially good kebabs and *kadai se* (regional casserole dishes). Dinner reservations advised. Open 12:30–3:30 P.M. and 8–11:30 P.M. AE, DC, MC, V.

Moderate

Carlton Hotel Restaurant and Bar. Shahnajaf Rd., Lucknow; tel. 44021. A strange charm and a vaguely worn-out Raj ambience are evident here, with a marble floor and old animal trophies on the walls. A good Continental, Chinese, and Indian buffet (also à la carte) is featured. Open 8–10 A.M., 12:30–2:30 P.M. and 7:30–10:30 P.M. AE, DC.

Inexpensive

Royal Cafe. Capoor's Hotel. 52 Hazratganj; tel. 43958. This popular restaurant, with a neon 1930-ish decor, is cozy. Its extensive menu offers Continental, Chinese, and Indian meals, including Mughlai and South Indian dishes—Indian is best. Open 7 A.M.–10 P.M. Rupees only.

MUSSOORIE

Expensive–Deluxe

The Savoy. Tel. 2510 or 2601. Whether you eat inside in the large dining hall, in the lovely enclosed front terrace, or outside gazing at the mountains, the Savoy is definitely for epicureans. You might even get a bottle of good imported wine. Menu includes good Chinese, Continental, and Indian cuisines. Open 7:30–10 A.M., 12:30–2:45 P.M., 7:30–10 P.M. AE, DC, MC, V.

Expensive

Carlton's Hotel Plaisance. Happy Valley Rd.; tel. 2800. Meals are served in a family dining room or on the enclosed porch of this attractive inn. Tasty Indian and Continental cuisines. Reservations required. Open 1–2:30 P.M. and 8–10 P.M. Rupees only.

Moderate

Jungli Murgi Restaurant. Roselynn Estate Hotel, The Mall; tel. 2201. The decor here is "woodsy" informal and the menu offers good Indian and tandoori food. Open 9 A.M.–9 P.M. Rupees only.

RISHIKESH

Like the neighboring city of Haridwar, Rishikesh is devoutly "dry" and only strictly vegetarian foods—not even eggs—are served.

Moderate

Indrani Restaurant. Inderlok Hotel, Railway Rd.; tel. 555. This small hotel has a delightful, informal restaurant. You can choose between Continental and Indian cuisines. Open 8 A.M.–10 P.M. DC.

Kautilya. Hotel Natraj, Dehra Dun Rd.; tel. 1099. This upstairs restaurant has an elegant modern decor, with fine linen on the tables. The chef creates very good Indian, Chinese, and Continental vegetarian dishes. Try *natraj au gratin* (vegetables baked in a cream sauce). Dinner reservations are advised. AE, DC, V.

Inexpensive

Darpan Restaurant. Railway Rd.; no phone. This popular in-town restaurant is always crowded with patrons enjoying Indian and Chinese food. The chef also prepares a limited selection of reasonably good Continental dishes. Open 8 A.M.–9 P.M. Rupees only.

VARANASI

Expensive

Amrapali. Clarks Varanasi, The Mall; tel. 62021. The best food in town is served at this restaurant with subdued lighting and a vaguely Indian decor. Chinese, Continental, and Indian cuisines, including some tasty regional dishes, are available. Dinner reservations advised. Open 12:30–3 P.M. and 7:30–10:30 P.M. AE, DC, MC, V.

Moderate

Tulsi Restaurant. Lahurabir; no phone. A simple restaurant, Tulsi has an Indian coffee-shop decor. It's also normally crowded with patrons eating good Indian dishes. Open 8 A.M.–10 P.M. Rupees only.

Win-fa. Prakesh Cinema Building, Lahurabir; no phone. Don't be put off by the no-frills decor in this Chinese restaurant. It's popular and the food is tasty. Open 11 A.M.–10 P.M. Rupees only.

SWEETS AND TREATS. Lucknow. *Thandai ke Dookam,* a one-of-kind Lucknow institution, is nothing more than a stall opposite Gol Darwaza (the gate that leads into Chowk), not far from the Police Station. Try their famous *thandai,* a delicious concoction of milk, dry fruits, pistachios, and spices—an Indian milk shake—for about Rs. 5. Open 8 A.M. to late at night.

HOW TO GET AROUND. For some inexplicable reason, while Uttar Pradesh does very well at getting people from town to town by bus, train, and airplane, local transportation is sloppily controlled—or not controlled at all.

From the Airport. Allahabad. A taxi is your best bet; figure about Rs. 30 into the city. **Dehra Dun.** An airport bus (Rs. 18) meets each plane and goes to Dehra Dun, where you can get a taxi for Mussoorie for Rs. 100 (the trip takes about 3 hours). Taxis from the airport to **Mussoorie** cost Rs. 250, or to **Haridwar** or **Rishikesh** about Rs. 150–Rs. 200 (the trip takes about 90 minutes). **Lucknow.** A taxi is best; figure about Rs. 40 into the city. **Nainital** and **Corbett.** From the Pantnagar airport, a taxi will take you to Corbett in about two hours for Rs. 300–Rs. 400 and to Nainital in about 90 minutes for Rs. 200–Rs. 300. **Varanasi.** An airport bus will take you into town for about Rs. 25; a taxi will take you directly to your hotel for about Rs. 100–Rs. 125.

By Train. Numerous tracks connect the major cities in Uttar Pradesh: Allahabad, Lucknow, Haridwar, Varanasi.

By Bus. *Uttar Pradesh State Transport Road Corporation* has a network of buses running throughout the state. For routes and schedules, contact the tourist office in each city.

By Rented Car with Driver. This is the best way to tour this state, especially the Himalayan region. Rates are about Rs. 3–Rs. 4 per km, with a halt charge of Rs. 50–Rs. 100 per night. Hire a car from a recommended tour operator below or from GMVN (see *Tourist Information* above). It's best to book in advance.

By Taxi. Rates are about Rs. 3.30 for the first km, Rs. 2.40 per additional km. Bargain.

By Auto Rickshaw. This should be cheaper than a taxi. Beware of the drivers in Varanasi—they're often cheats. Be firm in setting the price.

By Bike Rickshaw. This is the best way to get around the congested cities. Figure about Rs. 20 per hour.

TOURS. Contact the local tourist offices about the following inexpensive bus tours:

Dehra Dun. Daily city tour, including Malsi Deer Park, Tapkeshwar Temple Cave, and Sahastradhara (sulphur spring). For further details, call 23217.

Haridwar. Local tours in Haridwar and Riskikesh, plus tours to Badrinath and Kedarnath, contact *Haridwar Tourist Bureau* for details (tel. 19), or *Garhwal Mandal Vikas Nigas Ltd.,* Muni-ki-reti in Rishikesh (tel. 372). The latter also conducts many tours to Kedarnath, Badrinath, Ganotri, Yamunotri, and Valley of Flowers.

Lucknow. Local sightseeing tours by *Uttar Pradesh State Tourism Development Corporation* (tel. 48849), plus longer tours to Dudhwa National Park.

Mussoorie. Kempty Falls tour (peaceful bathing spot) daily. Dhanolti, scenic pine forest with good views of the Himalayas, and Surkhanda Devi Temple, on a hill with more good views. Tel. 2863.

Nainital. Numerous tours run by *Kumaon Division Development Corporation;* tel. 2656. Local sightseeing, two-day tour to Corbett National Park, three-day tour to Badrinath.

Rishikesh. Four-day tour from Rishikesh to Badrinath; seven-day tour to Badrinath and Kedrinath; four-day tour to Yamunotri, Gangotri, Kedarnath, and Badrinath; seven-day tour to Yamunotri and Gangotri; seven-day tour to Valley of Flowers, Hemkund, and Badrinath.

Varanasi. *U.P.S. Road Transport Corporation* offers two deluxe coach tours: one of the Ganges, temples, and the university; the other to Sarnath and Ramnagar Fort. Call 63233 for fares and details.

TOUR GUIDES. In most important destinations, you can hire a good guide through the tourist department. For one to four people, rates are about Rs. 50 for four hours.

TOUR OPERATORS. In Uttar Pradesh, adventure travel is on the rise, with the variety of opportunities expanding each year. Here are a few reliable outfits that offer terrific trips (also see this category in *Facts at Your Fingertips*) and make all arrangements in advance:

Arventure Adventure Holidays. Box 7, Dehra Dun; tel. 29172. Arranges treks galore, mountaineering, wildlife safaris, and biking led by an experienced staff.

Himalayan River Runners. 188-A, Jor Bagh, New Delhi; tel. 615736. This is the best rafting company, offering good trips on all of Uttar Pradesh's white-water rivers.

GMVN. Trekking and Tour Executive, Mountaineering Division, Munkireti, Rishikesh; tel. 373. This government undertaking offers inexpensive treks and mountaineering, skiing packages, biking near Corbett, and fishing.

For all travel needs, contact these agencies:

GMVN. 74–1 Rajpur Rd., Dehra Dun; tel. 26817.

ITDC. Hotel Varanasi Ashoka, The Mall, Varanasi; tel. 46020.

Travel Corporation India. Clarks Hotel, Varanasi; tel. 65498.

SEASONAL EVENTS. Since the lunar calendar determines most dates, contact the Government of India Tourist Office for details.

February. *Lucknow Festival.* Classic Indian culture displayed on a grand scale for over a week: theater, music, and dance, including the *kathak,* one of India's four classical dance forms, which has its home in this region. From a temple dance, it developed under the patronage of Moslem rulers into a court dance with a different gesture code and foot technique. The knotted Hindu draperies are replaced by tight-fitting pajamas and loose tunics made of heavy brocades.

Mid-February. *Shiva Rati* at Dehra Dun. Shiva's birthday is celebrated with a fair at Tapkeswar Cave Temple.

Spring. *Magh Mela* held at the confluence of the Ganges and Yamuna, in Allahabad. An amazing spectacle of thousands of Hindu devotees undergoing a sacred immersion.

May. *Buddha Purnima,* Sarnath. Birthday of Gautama Siddhartha, the Historic Buddha. A large fair with a procession of his relics. Very big occasion.

May. Mahashivratri celebrates the opening of the *Kedarnath Temple;* Akhand Jyoti Darshan celebrates the opening of *Badrinath Temple;* Akshayata-Tritaya the opening of *Yamunotri* and *Gangotri* temples. Temple priests make offerings to temple idols. Big events.

June/August. *Id-ul-Fitr,* Lucknow. Moslem celebration marking the end of Ramadan (month of fasting). Religious; big splash of festivity.

July. *Rath Yatra.* Held at Ramnagar Fort, Varanasi. Festive celebration in honor of Lord Jagannath, the Lord of the Universe, attracts big crowds. Temple "chariot" procession with sacred deities in seats of honor.

September–October. *Dussehra,* Varanasi. Big Hindu festival commemorating the victory of Lord Rama over Ravana. Enactments of *Ramila* held all over the city. At Ramnagar, elephants are available for hire and on the tenth day, a large procession culminates with the burning of effigies and a big fireworks display. In Varanasi proper, deities are taken in procession to be immersed in the Ganges.

October. *Muharram,* Lucknow. Moslem commemoration of the martyrdom of the grandson of the Prophet Mohammed Imam Hussain. Procession of beautiful tazias and illumination of the two Imambaras.

Once every 12 years (next time, 1998) *Kumbh Mela* is observed in Haridwar. *Sadhus* (devotees) fill up the city to have a sacred dip in the Ganges. Fakirs and yogis practice their amazing acts. Very religious, very festive. India's biggest festival—possibly the biggest in Asia. Lasts for days, *Ardh Kumbh* is held every six years. (Next time, 1992.) Half as big as Kumbh Mela, but still amazing.

HISTORIC SITES. Entrance to most places is generally free; where a temple donation is asked, a few rupees will suffice. Historic sites are open daily sunrise to sunset, unless noted below.

AJODHYA

This is the principal city of the ancient kingdom of Kosala and the birthplace of Lord Rama, hero of the *Ramayana.* It is one of India's seven most sacred places.

See *Hamuman Temple* and *Kanak Vhavan Temple,* mentioned in writings that go back to the seventh century.

ALLAHABAD

Akbar's fort sits atop the *Patal Puri Temple* with a tree that is continuously watered by Hindu priests. The tree is called the Undying Banyan Tree (Akshaya Batt) and is mentioned in writings that go back to A.D. 640. Unfortunately, the rest of the fort is off limits.

BADRINATH

A colorfully decorated temple with stone carvings is believed to be Vishnu's former abode. In the inner sanctum is a black stone deity of Vishnu. The temple is closed during the winter months, usually late October until May. During the season, the inner sanctum is open 4:30 A.M.–1 P.M. and 3–9 P.M. Evening *arti* (prayer service) is 6–7.

DEHRA DUN

Tapkeshwar Caves (5½ km from Dehra Dun) are shrines, dedicated to Shiva, that are claimed to be 5,000 years old. In a delightful pastoral setting.

DEOPRAYAG

Ancient *Raghunath Temple,* dedicated to Vishnu, commemorates the spot where Rama (avatar of Vishnu) supposedly came to meditate. Very simple structure of granite, the temple was recently renovated.

FAIZABAD

In this ancient capital of the nabobs, there's a lovely *mausoleum* of Behbu Begum, one of the best in Uttar Pradesh.

GANGOTRI

The temple is closed during the winter months, usually late October until May. During the season, the inner sanctum is open 6 A.M.–noon and 2–9 P.M. Morning *arti* (service) begins at 6 and evening arti is at 6–7.

HARIDWAR

Har-ki-Pauri Ghat is where Vishnu left a set of his footprints—hard to see—but it *is* the most sacred ghat and backed by temples. See Arti at sunset, a beautiful prayer offering to the Ganges, which concludes with hundreds of little flower boats lit with candles set loose on the river. Visit the *Daksh Mahadev Temple,* dedicated to Shiva, and *Sati Kund* in Kankhal (part of Haridwar). Go up to the *Mansa Devi Temple,* dedicated to the goddess Mansi, an avatar of Durga, from which you get a good view of Haridwar. Also see three ashram on the northern edge of Haridwar: *Pawan Dham Ashram,* built in 1970, a sort of a Hindi psychedelic show—wonderful fun; *Parmarth Ashram,* more subdued; and *Sapt Rishi Ashram,* downright solemn in comparison.

KEDARNATH

In this supposed abode of Shiva is a simple gray temple on a raised platform set against the banks of the Mandakini, with a Nandi statue standing in the courtyard. A visit here represents an extremely important pilgrimage to be approached on foot or pony (15 km from the road). The temple is closed during the winter months, usually late October until May. During the season, the inner sanctum is open 4:30 A.M.–1 P.M. and 2–9 P.M. Morning arti begins at 6 and evening arti is at 6–7.

LUCKNOW

Great Imambara was built by Asaf-ud-Daula as his burial place in 1784 after a year-long famine. The project created "relief work" for the rich and poor—it contains neither cement, nor iron. There are three interior chambers in different styles (from left to right after you enter): Chinese, Persian, and Indian. Find your way through the Bhul-Bhulaiya maze upstairs. Open 6 A.M.–5 P.M.;

Rumi Darwaza, beyond the outer gate of Imambara, was built in 1784 by Asaf-ud-Daula as another relief project. It is a facsimile of a gate in Constantinople.

Chhota Imambara was built in 1836 by Muhammad Ali Shah as his burial place. A miniature replica of the Taj Mahal is on the right after you enter the gate that contains the tomb of his daughter, Zinat Asuja. In the Imambara is a dazzling display of chandeliers, lamps, and *tazias.* Open 6 A.M.–5 P.M.

Residency is the remains of Asaf-ud-Daula's pleasure house, which was taken over by the British and subsequently became the scene of fierce fighting during the 1857 Indian Mutiny. If you want to go into the hall, called the Model Room (Rs. 2), entrance time is 8 A.M.–5 P.M. No restrictions to visit the rest of the Residency.

Also in the center of town, see the tombs of *Nawab Ali Khan* and his wife, Khurshed Begum, constructed in the nineteenth century. Nearby are the *Kaisar Bagh,* rows of apartments that housed the ladies of the royal harem.

Shahnajaf Imambara is the tomb of Nawab Ghazi-ud-din Haiden and his wives. Built in 1814, it became a stronghold for Indians during the 1857 mutiny. Open 6 A.M.–5 P.M.

La Martiniere was built in a jumble of styles by Claude Martin in 1795. An architectural compendium dedicated to whimsy, it is now a school.

RISHIKESH

Important Hindu ashrams that can be visited here: *Swami Sivananda's Divine Life Society; Maharshi Mahesh Yogi's Transcendental Meditation Center;* and *Triveni Ghat,* the main sacred ghat and scene of a mini-arti performed each evening.

SARNATH

At this center of the Buddhist world, six km from Varanasi, Buddha preached his first sermon 2,500 years ago in which he revealed the Eightfold Path leading to enlightenment. Ashoka is responsible for the construction of many of the third-century stupas. Sarnath reached its zenith under the Gupta dynasty in the sixth century. It's a lovely, peaceful place with new Buddhist temples.

VARANASI

Dasashwamedh Ghat is the main ghat to visit here. *Manikarnika Ghat* and *Harish Chandra Ghat* are the cremation ghats. You can watch cremations at no cost, but photographs are forbidden.

Gyanapi Mosque is Aurangzeb's seventeenth-century creation erected on the site of the Vishwewara Temple, which he destroyed.

Alamgir Mosque. After Aurangzeb destroyed a temple—the Beni Madhav Ka Darera, which was dedicated to Vishnu—he put up this mosque with an odd fusion of the abhorred Hindu (lower portion) and Moslem (upper portion) designs.

Ramnagar Fort is the former residential palace of the ex-maharajah of Varanasi; approached by boat, most of it is now a museum.

INNER CITY OF VARANASI

Kashi Vishwanath Temple, dedicated to Shiva, is in between the Dasashwamedh and Manikarnika ghats. It is off limits to non-Hindus, but pay a small fee and see the interior from the house opposite. Watch morning or evening prayers—flower offerings given to the lingam. The temple was constructed in 1776, with its spire covered in gold plate—a gift from Maharajah Ranjit Singh in 1835.

Durga Temple, dedicated to Durga, consort of Shiva; this eighteenth-century construction is located due west of Asi Ghat. Shikara is formed on top of five lower spires—a convergence that is a visual symbol of the belief that all five elements of the world merge with the Supreme. Durga is also called the Monkey Temple; the pests are everywhere and they'll steal anything.

Bharat Mata Mandir, on Vidya Peeth Road, is a temple inaugurated by Mahatma Gandhi and dedicated to India. Inside is a large relief map of India carved of marble.

YAMUNOTRI

The temple is closed during the winter months, usually late October until May. During the season, the inner sanctum is open 6 A.M.–noon and 2–9 P.M. Evening arti is 6–7.

MUSEUMS AND GALLERIES. Museums are free or a nominal fee is requested. In Allahabad, *Allahabad Museum,* Alfred Park, has terra cottas, good Rajasthani miniatures, and modern paintings. Open generally 10 A.M.–6 P.M. Closed Wednesdays. *Anand Bhavan* (Place of Joy), is the former home of Jawaharlal Nehru and contains personal momentos of this freedom fighter/politician. Open mornings and afternoons. Closed Mondays.

In Lucknow, *Archaeological Museum,* Kaiserbagh, contains archaeological finds, with a heavy concentration from Uttar Pradesh. Open 10 A.M.–5 P.M.; Rs. 0.50. *Picture Gallery,* between the two Imambaras, was built by Nawab Mohammad Ali Shah. Kind of a *Who's Who* portrait gallery of the megalomanical *nabobs* (provincial governors). Open 8 A.M.–5 P.M.

State Museum, Banarsi Bagh, is a general all-around museum with paintings and artifacts. Open 10 A.M.–5 P.M., closed Mondays.

In Sarnath, *Archaeological Museum* contains great Buddhist treasures. Open 10 A.M.–5 P.M., closed Fridays.

In Varanasi, *Bharat Kala Bhavan* (Art Gallery) at Banaras Hindu University has a good collection of paintings and art objects. Closed Sundays and university holidays. Open 9:30 A.M.–4:30 P.M.; in summer, 8 A.M.–noon.

In Ramnagar, *Fort Museum* houses a fine collection of palanquins, furniture, arms, weapons, and costumes. Open 9 A.M.–noon; 2–5 P.M.

GARDENS AND ZOOS. Dehra Dun. *Forest Research Institute Botanical Garden* and *Malso Deer Park* are both open sunrise to sunset. Free.

Lucknow. *Zoological Garden of Lucknow* in the Banarasi Bagh, founded in 1921 as a memorial to a visit by the Prince of Wales, is open 5 A.M.–7 P.M.

Lucknow is a city of lovely gardens. See in particular *Sikandar Bagh* (open 6 A.M.–5 P.M.), former site of fierce fighting in 1857; gardens under the management of the National Botanical Research Institute; and the *Gautama Buddha Park,* a delightful park for children.

SPORTS AND OUTDOOR ADVENTURES. Uttar Pradesh is an adventure state. Boating, fishing, skiing, trekking or wonderful walks, and white-water rafting are all here to experience in beautiful surroundings. What follows is a partial list. Contact the Uttar Pradesh tourist departments for the current range of possibilities.

Boating. Mussoorie and Nainital. Sailing down to Ganges.

Bicycling. GMVN arranges a six–eight-day trip (including bike) for excursions Nov.–June near Corbett National Park. You pedal through sal and bamboo forests and see wild animals. Bring binoculars and your fishing rod. Make arrangements in advance; tel. 373.

Fishing. *Corbett National Park* (see under *Wildlife* section). *Dehra Dun.* For details and permit, contact Divisional Forest Officer (East), Dehra Dun, Uttar Pradesh. *Mussoorie.* For details and permits, contact Divisional Forest Officer, Yamuna Division, Mussoorie, Uttar Pradesh.

Rafting. You can raft one–three days (Oct.–mid-Dec. and Feb.–June) on the Ganga from Deoprayag to Rishikesh; take a six-day run (Nov.–mid-Dec. and Feb.–

Apr.) on the Alakananda from Rudraprayag to Rishikesh; or run the Bhagirathi from Tehri to Rishikesh, the greatest challenge (November–mid-December and February–April). Make arrangements in advance; tel. 373.

Skiing. Auli, near Joshimath, has a tow rope 3.8 km in length. This is a brand-new and developing resort. Garhwal Mandal Vikas Nigam, Ltd., runs ski courses from January to March for five, 10, and 15 days. They will supply the skiing equipment. For further details, reservations, and cost, contact Garhwal Mandal Vikas Nigam. This resort will be spectacular once it's in full operation. For now, just to ski it's an inexpensive treat.

Trekking. Here are some of the most popular possibilities in Uttar Pradesh:

Rudraprayag to Badrinath via Chamoh–Pipalkou–Gulabkoti–Joshimath (by bus). On foot: Joshimath–Pandukeshwar (13 km or 8 mi.)–Badrinath (18 km or 11 mi.). Elevation 1,829–5,564 meters (6,000–10,250 feet). At all these stages there is a Public Works Department (P.W.D.) Inspection Bungalow. Reservations authority: Executive Engineer, P.W.D. Pauri. A three–four day hike.

Rudraprayag to Kedarnath via Kakaragad (last bus stop)–Gupta Kashi (6 km or 4 mi.)–Phata (14 km or 9 mi.)–Gauri Kund (13 km or 8 mi.)–Kedarnath (11 km or 7 mi.). Elevation 914–3,567 meters (3,000–11,700 feet). Reservations authority for accommodations along this route: Secretary, District Board, and Executive Engineer, both at Pauri. A two-day hike. Hire porters at Rudraprayag.

Kedarnath to Chamoli via Gauri Kund–Phata–Nalapatan–Ukimath–Tungnath–Gopeshwar–Chamoli (total 80 km or 50 mi.). Elevation 914–3,567 meters (3,000–11,700 feet). P.W.D. Inspection Bungalow at all stages. Reservations authority: Executive Engineer, P.W.D., Pauri. Four days or less.

Almora to Pindari Glacier, by bus to Kapkot (where you must wait for ponies and porters)–Lharkhet (16 km or 10 mi.)–Dhakuri (9 km or 6 mi.)–Khati (9 km or 6 mi.)–Dwali (11 km or 7 mi.)–Phurkia (5 km or 3 mi.)–Pindari Glacier (5 km or 3 mi.). P.W.D. Bungalows at all stages. Reservations authority: P.W.D., Bageshwar. Bring a tent for camping at Martoli, near the glacier. Elevation 1,067–3,354 meters (3,500–11,000 feet). Sundardhhunga and Kaphini Glaciers can be visited en route.

A trip to Pindari Glacier is well within the capacity of any hiker, and the effort involved is amply rewarded by the views en route as well as the magnificence of the glacier itself. Six or seven days are required for this trek. The best time to visit is May 14–June 15, when the flowers are in bloom and the snow bridges have not melted away, or Sept. 15–early October, when the air is free from haze and the Trail Pass is still negotiable. The glacier is three miles from Phurkia, and the trek involves a climb of 762 meters (2,500 feet). An early start enables you to spend some time on the glacier and to take in its grandeur and beauty. The return journey can be shortened by halting only at Dwali, Dhakuri, and Kapkot.

Mussoorie to Chakrata via Saingi (14 km or 9 mi.)–Lakhwar (11 km or 7 mi.)–Nayhtat (9 km or 6 mi.)–Chorani (14 km or 9 mi.)–Chakrata (11 km or 7 mi.). Dak Bungalows at all stages. Reservations not necessary but accommodations are usually primitive.

Chakrata to Himachal Pradesh boundary (toward Shimla) via Desban (11 km or 7 mi.)–Mandali (19 km or 12 mi.)–Kalhyan–Tinuni (19 km or 12 mi.)–Arakot (14 km or 9 mi.). Elevation: 884–2,134 meters (2,900–7,000 feet). Forest Rest Houses at all stations. Reservations authority: District Forest Officer, Chakrata.

At press time, the *Nanda Devi Sanctuary* was closed for environmental preservation.

WILDLIFE SANCTUARIES. *Corbett National Park,* 320 km (199 mi.) from Delhi, is India's oldest sanctuary and one of its best. From the back of an elephant, inside a jeep, or waiting patiently in a *machan* (watch tower), you may see elephants, tigers, leopards, black bear, wild boar, deer (numerous species), snakes (including the python and king cobra), crocodiles, and birds. The park is open November–mid-June. The main entrance is at Dhikala, and you must arrive before dark. Admission is Rs. 35 for three days, each subsequent day costs less. Vehicle fee is Rs. 10. At Dhikala, you can also arrange for elephant or jeep rides and guides. Daylight photography only is allowed. Fishing is currently banned to increase the stocks.

During the park season, GMVN operates a three-day tour (Friday–Sunday) from New Delhi. For details, contact *Uttar Pradesh Government,* Chandralok Building, 36 Janpath, New Delhi; tel. 3322251.

SHOPPING. The main shopping areas are in the cities of Lucknow and Varanasi, two places where it's hard to say no. The main shopping bargains are, of course, the exquisite Varanasi silks, brocades, and saris. Lucknow's gold and silver and white embroidery (called chikan), table covers, and silverware, and Mirzapur's carpets. Brassware and lacquered toys complete the list. In the Himalayan area, look at handwoven products made of Garhwal wool: shawls, hats, and gloves. The main centers of shopping at Allahabad are the Civil Lines, Johnstonganj, and the Chowk. In Lucknow, fixed-price shopping is concentrated at Hazratganj. Aminabad (a market area) is the place to go for perfume essences (attars). The following three cities have great bazaars or *chowks:*

In Lucknow, *The Chowk* is great for browsing and getting a sense of lively Lucknow. Lots of special hand-embroidered chikan work. The best shops are *Lal Bihari Tandon,* Gota Bazar, Chowk, and *Delux Kurta Industry,* 11 Gota Bazar, Chowk, which has great *dhotis* (skirtlike garments) for babies and small children.

In Haridwar, *Moti Bazaar* is a delightful, manageable size, with medicine shops and religious stalls. Fun; mostly for browsing.

Varanasi has two good areas: *Chowk* and *Vishwanath Lane.* If you want to buy silk, play safe so you won't get stuck with shoddy goods. Get a list of approved shops from the Government of India Tourist Department. Good-quality silk costs money. If you get a steal, you're the one who's probably been robbed. The following are reputable good shops: *Brijraman Das & Sons,* K37/32, Golghar, *Vishwanath Lane, Mohanlal Gopal Das,* Chowk, *Oriental Emporium,* 10/252 Maqbool Alam Rd.

BARS AND NIGHTLIFE. Don't expect too much nightlife in Uttar Pradesh, but most of the hotels have bars where you can enjoy an afternoon cocktail or a pleasant evening. Bars generally are open 11 A.M.–3 P.M. and 6–11 P.M. or midnight. A selection includes the *Polo Bar* in the Hotel President, Dehra Dun, which is in a cozy downstairs room. Also in Dehra Dun, the subdued lighting in the *Madhushala,* Hotel Madhuban, gives the feeling of intimacy. In Lucknow, the new bar at the Taj will probably be best. To reminisce about the Raj era, have a drink in the Victorian barroom of *Hakman's Hotel* or try the comfortable cocktail lounge in the *Savoy,* which has a pleasant ambience. In Varanasi, the *Kambari* in Clarks Varanasi is an attractive and quiet place.

AGRA AND FATEHPUR SIKRI

The Road into the Past

by
KATHLEEN COX

As distances go, the trip from Delhi to Agra is not more than a stone's throw—200 kilometers (124 miles) by car from the capital of modern India to the former seat of the Mogul Empire. But few trips in India—or anywhere else in the world—offer such an extensive journey into history and ethereal historic beauty. This is the royal road of the Mogul emperors established in the sixteenth and seventeenth centuries, when their capital fluctuated between Delhi and Agra. Today, Delhi reigns over India, but Agra still reigns over that unforgettable past created by warriors as skilled in art and architecture as they were on the battlefield.

A trip to Agra should include Fatehpur Sikri, the abandoned capital of Akbar the Great, and extend farther south to Jhansi, home of Lakshmi Bai, India's Joan of Arc, and to Gwalior and Shivpuri, which are in neighboring Madhya Pradesh.

Vrindaban

When you enter Vrindaban, 131 kilometers (82 miles) south of Delhi, it's like entering holy ground. This is a city of 1,000 shrines, the biggest being Gobind Deo. Erected to Hindu glory, with the encouragement of the tolerant Mogul Akbar, the temple suffered a dismal reversal during the reign of one of Akbar's descendants. The continual glare of a giant oil lamp burning from an upper story so annoyed Aurangzeb that he over-reacted and lopped off the entire top half of the shrine. The site of a walled-in garden, Nikunja Ban, Vrindaban is also significant to the Hindu pilgrim. Here, Krishna, the most popular of the incarnations of Vishnu, the preserver, supposedly appeared before his worshipers. In fact, most every step you take in this city follows the path of this adored god, as does the road that takes you to Mathura, about 10 kilometers (six miles) south.

Mathura

Mathura, situated on the west bank of the Yamuna River, which flows from Delhi to Agra, is supposedly the birthplace of Krishna. Hindu pilgrims from the world over visit a shrine in a part of the city called Katra. Originally the site of a Hindu temple, it, too, was destroyed by the intolerant Aurangzeb, who built a mosque in its place. But the basement of the original Kesava Deo remains, as does a sign proclaiming that Krishna was born here.

The holiness of Mathura is all pervasive—drawing worshipers of Vishnu the way that Varanasi draws the adorers of Shiva, the destroyer. Even the Hare Krishnas are headquartered here. Just as the followers of Shiva flock to the Ganges, pilgrims to Mathura are drawn to the Yamuna—in particular to the Vishram Ghat. Here Krishna supposedly rested after killing the tyrant Kansa (in whose prison he is believed to have been born). Religious ceremonial acts on the Yamuna are less intense than those on the Ganges: at sunset, hundreds of flickering oil lamps are launched on the river. But rites are performed and they are worth seeing.

Mathura is one of the oldest cities of India, far older than Agra, with a history that goes back to before the Maurya Dynasty, which ruled India from 325 to 184 B.C. This explains why the government museum has such an accumulation of artistic wealth left behind by foreign conquerors, including the Parthians and the Greeks. This also explains the flowering of Mathura sculpture, which started in the first century A.D. and lasted for a startling 1,200 years, going into decline when sculptors gave up sacred Buddhist and Hindu subjects to turn their chisels to the frivolous figures of full-bosomed dancing girls. Unfortunately, much of the grandeur of Mathura suffered the wrath of its conquerors, and few Hindu monuments remain.

Sikandra: Akbar's Tomb

Ten kilometers (six miles) down the royal road, you come to the glorious introduction to Agra: Sikandra, named after Sultan Sikander Lodi of the dynasty conquered by the Moguls. Sikandra is the site of the tomb of Akbar, the great Mogul emperor (1542–1605) who planned its design and began its construction in 1602. The tomb was finally completed by his son Jahangir in 1613.

A model of symmetry, built out of red sandstone and marble, the mausoleum stands in the center of a huge garden. The entrance is through an imposing, two-story gateway, 75 feet high, with exquisite mosaic and inlay work, and is topped by four slim marble minarets that rise up from each corner.

The main tomb is a fusion of Hindu and Moslem styles, as if reflecting the religious tolerance of Akbar, who dreamed of peaceful coexistence between the two religions. Each floor of the five-story structure has a series of arcades, tapering to a marble cloister that seems to float on the top of the cloister beneath it.

A narrow passageway leads to the cryptlike grave, now dimly lit by a hanging lamp (the gift of Lord Curzon). A replica of the white marble cenotaph rests precisely above it on the upper floor so no one can ever walk on Akbar's resting place. This identical crypt is inscribed with the 99 names attributed to Allah, plus the phrase, "Allah-o-Akbar" (God is Great), at the head; and the phrase, "Jalla Jalalahu" (Great Is His Glory), at the foot.

AGRA

Akbar the Great made Agra great. The city's origins before the Mogul conquest are dim: The conquering Babur, Akbar's grandfather, practically founded the ultimately important Moslem center. And, by some strange process of mutation, the warlike Moguls—Babur was a descendant of the wicked Tamerlane of Central Asia—were transformed into the most civilized and refined rulers of their day, revering the arts and thirsting for learning with a tolerance seldom found in history. The pitifully short golden age of Agra came to an end with the seventeenth-century reign of Shah Jahan, but it had an unforgettable climax in the Taj Mahal.

Not much happened in Agra before the Moguls and not much has happened since. Sacked by the Jats and occupied by the Marathas, the city entered a peaceful slumber in 1803, when it fell into the hands of the British. Today, its population has reached 1.2 million, but it is still a small city by Indian standards. The surrounding countryside of sandy stretches somehow produces a rice crop, cultivated by patient and hard-working farmers.

To the lover of art and to the traveler seeking the wonders of the world, Agra is the goal of a pilgrimage to the creative best: the Agra Fort and the Taj Mahal.

The Fort and Its Palaces

At the Agra Fort, the story of that portion of the Mogul Empire extending from Akbar to his son Jahangir to Shah Jahan is recorded in stone: the rusty-red sandstone of forbidding walls raised by Akbar, the shimmering white marble of palaces built by Shah Jahan. The fort, which is open from sunrise to sunset, is an excellent introduction to Agra. It took centuries for the castles of Europe to evolve from stern medieval citadels to graceful Renaissance palaces. At Agra, this process of evolution took place within the span of these three generations.

No one would question the fort's indomitable appearance. It stands on the banks of the Yamuna, surrounded by a wall 70 feet high, which guards a 40-foot moat with another 70-foot wall behind it. These double walls, pierced with slits and loopholes, seem capable of barring anyone from an inner paradise whose towers can only be glimpsed from the outside. Luckily, this daunting mass can be penetrated for the price of admission at the Amar Singh Gate, where visitors usually enter the fort.

In all, the walls around the Agra Fort measure 1½ miles in circumference. The original military structure was begun by Akbar, who is believed to have demolished an ancient castle on the site. He completed the fort eight years later, then built the palace called the Jahangiri Mahal, the first of the many interior constructions—built with the simpler architecture and intricate decoration so typical of the Mogul era.

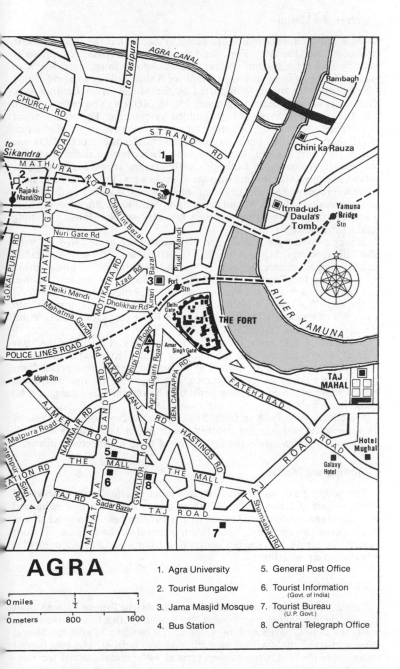

AGRA

0 miles | ½ | 1
0 meters | 800 | 1600

1. Agra University
2. Tourist Bungalow
3. Jama Masjid Mosque
4. Bus Station
5. General Post Office
6. Tourist Information (Govt. of India)
7. Tourist Bureau (U.P. Govt.)
8. Central Telegraph Office

Jahangiri Mahal

Once you enter the Amar Singh Gate, to the north is the biggest private residence inside the Agra Fort, the Jahangiri Mahal (palace), supposedly built by Akbar for his son (Akbar's Palace, closer to the entrance, is in ruins). Here, you see a striking example of Akbar's ability to blend Hindu architecture with the style imported by the Moguls from Central Asia. The palace is huge, measuring about 250 by 300 feet. You enter through a hall leading to a courtyard surrounded by columns. The central court of the palace is lined by two-story facades bearing remnants of the rich gilded decorations that once covered a great deal of the structure. On one side of the court is a hall known as Jodh Bai's dressing room (Jodh Bai was the Hindu mother of Jahangir), with a ceiling supported by serpents carved in stone. Also leading into the court is a hall known as Jodh Bai's reception room and a series of rooms, one of which is known as the library and is remarkable for its Mogul decoration. Most likely, these rooms were used both by Jahangir's mother and his empress, Nur Jahan (meaning light of the world).

Jahangir loved wine and the arts almost as much as he loved his wife. Nur Jahan attempted to convince him to settle down to the serious occupation of ruling an empire, but, finally, she had to do the job for him—sitting by his side in their palace in the Agra Fort, dispensing imperial justice. She was a strong-willed woman and made short shrift of anyone who stood in her way. One favorite method she employed was dropping rivals into a pit that conveniently led to the Yamuna River (the grim underground chambers near this pit are still intact).

Nur Jahan is also given credit for the discovery of distilling the attar of roses. After a quarrel with Jahangir, she went off to brood in the palace courtyard, where she noticed that, in the heat of the sun, rose petals floating in a pond oozed an oily substance. The fragrance was overwhelming. With a clever daub of this new perfume, she returned to Jahangir, who found her irresistible.

After Jahangir's death in 1628, Shah Jahan (whose mother was one of the other wives of Jahangir) assumed the throne and started his own collection of buildings inside the fort, some of them architectural pearls.

Shahjahani Mahal

The building known as Shahjahani Mahal is actually the remodeled northern part of Jahangiri Mahal; three rooms and a corridor enhanced by a tapering tower gallery topped with a pavilion bearing a spike. From this imperial vantage point, Shah Jahan watched elephant fights. In more tranquil moments, he received instruction from a Hindu holy man who was carried up in a litter.

Khas Mahal

Shah Jahan outdid himself in the Khas Mahal (the Private Palace), built in 1637: three pavilions overlooking the Yamuna with a fountain tank opposite the central pavilion. This white marble building follows the Mogul pattern in style: three arches on each side, five in front, and two turrets rising out of the roof. Once flowers created with precious stones were encrusted in its walls, but the jewels were looted in the eighteenth century. Of the other two pavilions, one is of white marble and is supposed to have been decorated with gold leaf, while the other is made of redstone. In one part of the Khas Mahal, a staircase leads down to the "air-conditioned" quarters of the palace, cool underground rooms that were probably inhabited during the scorching heat of summer.

Sheesh Mahal

On the northeastern end of the courtyard of the Khas Mahal stands the Sheesh Mahal (Palace of Mirrors), built in 1637. This building was the bath of the private palace and the dressing room of the harem, with each of the two chambers containing a bathing tank that was once fed by marble channels. In its glory, small mirrors that covered the ceilings and walls caught the sunlight and turned the interior of the Sheesh Mahal into a dazzling vision of brilliance. Cleanliness was evidently a greater concern to the Moguls than to their contemporary counterparts who lived in seventeenth-century castles and palaces in Europe (where fountains were only for show).

Anguri Bagh

A rectangle in front of the Khas Mahal bears the mysterious name of Anguri Bagh (Vineyard Garden), but no one has ever found any trace of the grapevines. This was apparently a Mogul garden, with fountains and flowerbeds on a marble-paved platform divided by stone partitions. Apartments that might have been used by members of the emperor's harem surround three sides of the garden. Below the terrace, a marble cistern leads to the platform.

Diwan-i-Am

To the people of the empire and to the European emissaries who came to see this powerful monarch, the most impressive part of the fort was the Diwan-i-Am (Hall of Public Audience), set within the large quadrangle. A huge low structure, it rests on a stage four feet high, with nine cusped Mogul arches held aloft by rows of slender supporting pillars. There is considerable disagreement about which of the three Mogul emperors—Akbar, Jahangir, or Shah Jahan—built this hall, but none at all about the creator of its throne room. Only Shah Jahan could have conceived this alcove with its inlaid mosaics, one of the marvels of Mogul art. Here, the emperor sat and dispensed justice to his subjects, rich and poor alike. Below the throne, his *wazir* (prime minister) sat on a small platform with a silver railing, where he received the petitioners as they came in.

The petitioner bowed three times before he reached the wazir, never daring to raise his eyes to the Grand Mogul, while a herald proclaimed that the poor mortal stood in the presence of the "Sun of the World." Bernier, a French traveler of the day, dared to lift his gaze on the ruler, however, and recorded what he saw: "The monarch, every day about noon, sits upon his throne with some of his sons at his right and left, while eunuchs, standing about the royal persons, flap away flies with peacock tails, agitate the air with large fans or wait with profound humility to perform the different services allotted to them."

Unlike the contemporaries of the Moguls, you get to wander freely through the palace that was once reserved for the private life of the emperor and his courts. For example, not far from the public audience hall lies what is believed to have been the Inner Mina Bazaar, where ladies of the court shopped for jewelry or silks. Sometimes, too, the Grand Mogul and his intimates played store—a game in which the wives of noblemen acted as vendors while the emperor amused himself by haggling. The exact location of this regal shopping center is unknown; it may have been in the Macchi Bhavan.

In the Macchi Bhavan (Palace of Fish), gaily colored fish danced through water channels for the amusement of the court. Evidently, this was one part of the fort in which the emperor and his harem could escape all the inhibitions of pomp and ceremony.

Diwan-i-Khas

Contrasted with the Hall of Public Audience is the Diwan-i-Khas, or Hall of Private Audience, built by Shah Jahan in 1636–37. Here, the emperor received foreign ambassadors or dignitaries of his kingdom. The Diwan-i-Khas, which is due east of the Diwan-i-Am, contains two halls connected by three arches. White marble covers their red sandstone walls and lavish carvings can still be seen at the base of the columns that support the arches. Outside this light structure is the famous throne terrace with its pair of black-and-white thrones. The black throne was carved from a single block of marble and stands on a marble platform overlooking the Yamuna. A low railing of white marble contrasts with the black throne. According to the inscriptions found on it, this seat of power was apparently made for Jahangir. The white throne, consisting of several blocks of marble, was installed for Shah Jahan, who is said to have relaxed here by fishing below the terrace or by watching the magnificent elephant fights staged in the fort.

Musamman Burj

Near the Diwan-i-Khas is the tall Musamman Burj, originally built by Shah Jahan for Mumtaz Mahal, his wife, who is buried in the Taj Mahal. It is an octagonal tower with a courtyard on the lower floor paved with octagonal marble slabs. Here, too, are those delicate lattices of marble, no doubt used as screens to enable the ladies of the court to look out on the fort without being seen. In the center of the tower is a beautifully carved fountain. But all this beauty turned into the setting for a tragedy: Shah Jahan died here in 1666, after seven years as a prisoner of his own son, Aurangzeb. Here, he breathed his last, looking out at the Taj Mahal. Only his devoted daughter, Jahanara, remained with him during his final days.

The Mussamman Burj is another of the exceptional monuments left by Shah Jahan. One writer compared it to "a fairy tower hanging over grim ramparts." Unfortunately, only the barest trace still exists of the decorative designs that once adorned this tower: plunderers removed all the precious stones in 1761.

Nagina Masjid

To the northeast of the Diwan-i-Khas, you'll find the white marble Nagina Masjid, a private mosque raised by Shah Jahan with typical cusped arches. Walled in on three sides, it has a marble courtyard for worshipers and three graceful domes. This mosque was probably used by the royal ladies or by those seeking audience with the emperor.

Moti Masjid

A short distance away stands the Moti Masjid, a pearl mosque built in white marble by Shah Jahan and considered ideal in its proportions. The beauty of the Moti Masjid hits you suddenly—it's not at all evident from the outside. But a marble courtyard with arcaded cloisters on three sides unfolds before your eyes (the fourth side on the west has a place for the leader of the worshipers). Marble screens conceal what may have been the section reserved for women. Seven archways support the roof of this mosque, which bears three handsome domes. Over the arches of the prayer chamber, a Persian inscription compares the mosque to a pearl and states that as ordered by Shah Jahan, it took seven years to build. Unfortunately, as of this writing, the Moti Masjid is temporarily closed for renovations.

Also of interest are the two main gates, the Amar Singh and Delhi Gates, a pavilion known as Salim's Fort near the entrance, and the intriguing Hauz-i-Jahangiri. The Hauz-i-Jahangiri is a bath carved out of a huge block of stone five feet high and 25 feet in circumference that, according to the inscription, connects it to Jahangir. There are many theories regarding its purpose: some insist that Akbar ordered it carved to celebrate Jahangir's birth; others say it was Jahangir's wedding present to Nur Jahan in 1611.

Finally, just who is Lieutenant Governor Colvin, whose tomb is in the fort? The unfortunate soldier died here during the Indian Mutiny of 1857, when the fort was under seige.

THE TAJ MAHAL—MONUMENT TO LOVE

To some, the Taj Mahal is overrated. To others, it's a sublime experience to be ranked with the Pyramids of Egypt, the Palace of Versailles, or the Parthenon of Athens as the esthetic epitome of a civilization. To still others, it simply represents the greatest love story ever told. This should make it clear that the Taj Mahal, despite the imposing dimensions of its architecture and all the good and bad literature it has inspired, is very much a matter of taste.

One other preliminary word: give the Taj Mahal a chance. It speaks a different language when seen by moonlight, through the shimmer of dawn, in the bright light of midday, and at sunset. Although a full moon brings out its distinct and heavenly beauty, it also brings out the crowds who destroy the serenity and stately aura. So, taking everything into consideration, probably the best time to see the Taj Mahal is in the early morning when it emerges from the night ahead of the sun whose first pale rays give a soft luster to the marble, which glistens in a coat of pink, blue, or even mauve. And the surroundings at this time of day are calm and peaceful—nothing upstages its grandeur.

You can't experience the Taj Mahal if you don't know its story. Nearly all the world's great monuments were the product of the religious fervor of a people or the vanity of a king. But the Taj Mahal is an exception; it was built as a monument to love.

Arjuman Banu, the niece of Jangir's queen, Nur Jahan, was the second wife of Emperor Shah Jahan, the artist among the Mogul builders. In 1612, at the age of 21, she married him and took on the names that have passed down through time: Mumtaz Mahal, the Exalted of the Palace, and Mumtazul-Zamani, the Distinguished of the Age. Numerous tales speak of her generosity and her wisdom, both as a household manager and as an adviser to her imperial husband, but even these qualities were overshadowed by the love that bound her to Shah Jahan. She bore him 14 children, and it was in childbirth that she died in 1630 at Burhanpur, where her husband was waging a military campaign.

When she died, Shah Jahan was grief stricken. His hair supposedly turned gray within a few months and it is said that he put aside his royal robes for simple white muslin clothes. A huge procession brought her body from Burhanpur, where it had been temporarily buried, to Agra six months after her death. Shah Jahan vowed to build her a memorial surpassing anything the world had ever seen in beauty and in wild extravagance. He brought in skilled craftsmen from Persia, Turkey, France, and Italy. He put a huge army of 20,000 laborers to work, building a whole new village (Taj Ganj, which still stands) to house them. The cost of reproducing the Taj Mahal today has been estimated at nearly $70 million, but who would try?

A Masterpiece in Marble

The Taj Mahal lies on the banks of the Yamuna River, where it can be seen, like a fantastic mirage, from the nearby Agra Fort. Construction began in 1632; although no one knows who drew up the actual plans, Shah Jahan's chief architect, Ustad Ahmad Lahori, was clearly involved. Some people accuse the Taj Mahal of architectural exaggeration and coldness (not so inappropriate for a mausoleum), but no one has ever denied its perfect proportions. This huge mass of white marble resting on red sandstone is a jewel, fashioned over 17 years. The work ended on the exact anniversary of the Mumtaz Mahal's death.

Glimpsed from the enormous main gateway inscribed with verses of the Quran (the entire Quran is said to be reproduced on its walls), the Taj Mahal reveals itself with the suddenness of a jewel box opened before your eyes. This gate leads you inside a walled garden—and there, the magic spell is cast. A rectangular pool (unfortunately with too-shallow water), bordered by cypresses, catches the shimmering image of the tomb.

In the Agra Fort, virile red sandstone and elegant white marble symbolize different periods of Mogul architecture in a juxtaposition wrought by time. But here, the two materials have been brought together with deliberate effect. The Taj Mahal is built on two bases, one of sandstone and, above it, a marble platform measuring 313 feet square and worked into a black-and-white chessboard design. A slender marble minaret stands on each corner of the platform; these towers blend so well into the general composition that it's hard to believe their 130-foot height. Each one is also purposely constructed at a slight tilt away from the tomb (in case of an earth tremor, they'd fall away from the beautiful building).

In the mausoleum itself, the easy curves of pointed Mogul arches on the facade set off the square corners of the building. The entrance to the tomb is an archway soaring more than 90 feet high and inscribed with more verses from the Quran. Mogul inlay work, used so lavishly throughout the Taj Mahal, is carefully worked into the entrance. Notice the tiny, intricate flowers—the detailed stonework on each petal and leaf. Shine a flashlight and see the delicate translucence of some of the stones. Feel the perfectly smooth surfaces. Step inside and succumb to the pull of another dimension that draws your gaze to the graceful curve of the dome, a marble sky that is actually a dome within a dome. The dome seen from the exterior is above the dome you now see inside.

The Royal Tombs

Directly under the dome lie the tombs of Mumtaz Mahal and Shah Jahan, but they aren't immediately visible. The Taj Mahal plays a tantalizing game of illusion, revealing its treasures one by one. Originally, the tombs were surrounded by a barrier of gold encrusted with precious stones, but this barrier was apparently removed by Shah Jahan's rupee-pinching son Aurangzeb, who replaced it with a marble screen that is the height of a man. Carved from a single block of stone, the screen is a latticework as intricate as lace.

The tomb of Mumtaz Mahal is in the center of the enclosure behind the screen: diminishing rectangles leading up to what looks like a coffin. In fact, both Mumtaz Mahal and Shah Jahan are buried in a crypt below these tombs in obedience to a tradition that no one should ever walk over their graves. Supposedly, Shah Jahan originally planned to build a black marble mausoleum for himself on the other side of the Yamuna, linking it by bridge to the Taj. But Aurangzeb had other ideas, which explains why the emperor is buried next to his wife. It was most likely done as another money-saving measure—an ironic postscript to the munificence of Shah Jahan.

The cenotaph of Mumtaz Mahal bears this Persian inscription: "The illustrious sepulcher of Arjuman Banu Begum, called Mumtaz Mahal. God is everlasting, God is sufficient. He knoweth what is concealed and what is manifest. He is merciful and compassionate. Nearer unto him are those who say: Our Lord is God."

The epitaph of the builder of the Taj Mahal reads: "The illustrious sepulcher of His Exalted Majesty Shah Jahan, the Valiant King, whose dwelling is in the starry Heaven. He traveled from this transient world to the World of Eternity on the twenty-eighth night of the month of Rajab in the year of 1076 of the Hegira [February 1, 1666]."

Inlay Work and Marble Screens

The inlay work of the Taj achieved unrivaled grace with the tomb of Mumtaz Mahal. Designs, executed in jasper, agate, lapis lazuli, carnelian, and bloodstone, are rendered with such skill that neither your sense of touch nor a magnifying glass can detect breaks between two stones. For example, one flower that measures only a square inch contains 60 different inlays. There is less unanimity over the tomb of Shah Jahan, which dwarfs that of Mumtaz Mahal and has been called pompous and out of proportion. But maybe it's fitting that he should lie for eternity next to his favorite wife, and the romantically inclined give Aurangzeb credit for bringing the two together.

More than just the tombs of these royal lovers is under the dome of the Taj Mahal. In each corner of the mausoleum, small domes rise over round chambers about 30 feet in diameter. Light from these rooms filters into the chamber through marble screens. The play of light within the entire Taj is fascinating. Precious stones inlaid in the tombs, in the screens surrounding them, and in the walls glow against the background of white marble.

So fantastic is the decoration of the Taj that it inspired the imagination of marauders who raided the mausoleum in 1764 and managed to stagger off with two silver doors that once served as an entrance. Thieves also made away with the gold sheets that formerly lined the burial vault below the tombs. But they never got around to plucking out the pietra dura inlay work—probably because they didn't believe it was real.

Outside the mausoleum stand a pair of red sandstone mosques, one on each end. Much simpler than the central building, they frame the Taj from the river.

It is easy to leave the Taj Mahal with a sense of disbelief. Somehow, the wealth of marble and precious stones (35 different varieties of carnelian can be counted in a single carnation leaf on the tomb of Mumtaz Mahal) seems disassociated from the airy dream you first envision from a distance. But then, outside the gateway to the garden, where fountains used to play, look again. The Taj is real—a vivid, real dream.

OTHER AGRA LANDMARKS

Agra offers several other landmarks that would probably be far better known if it weren't for the illustrious Taj Majal and the Agra Fort.

Another beautiful mausoleum, in a more subdued key than the Taj, is the tomb of Itmad-ud-Daula, father of Queen Nur Jahan and grandfather of Mumtaz Mahal. Though small, this monument (about five kilometers, or three miles, north of the Taj on the left bank of the Yamuna) is wonderfully proportioned; some call it more pleasing than the Taj. Through a gate near the river, you enter a garden with a two-storied tomb of white marble standing on a plinth of red sandstone. Almost the entire surface is covered in mosaics inlaid with semiprecious stones: geometrics, flowers, and typically Persian designs. Four small minarets rise up from the corners of the lower story. Within the sepulchral chamber, light penetrates through more screens of marble latticework. Actually, the tomb, a forerunner of the Taj, is the first Mogul building of all white marble, with designs even more delicate than those of the Taj Mahal.

The Chini-ka-Rauza, or China Tomb, lies half a mile north of the tomb of Itmad-ud-Daula. Its name apparently comes from the brilliant glazed tiles used in its mosaics. Afzal Khan, the prime minister of Shah Jahan and a Persian poet, and his wife are buried here. Not far from this tomb is the Rambagh (originally Arambagh, Garden of Leisure), designed by the Mogul Babur, according to one version of its origin. Babur's body was taken here before it was removed to Kabul. The Rambagh is supposed to be India's first Mogul garden.

Finally, mention should be made of the Jami Masjid, the huge congregational mosque of Agra built in 1648 by Shah Jahan's daughter, Jahanara.

Fatehpur Sikri, the Ghost City

Thirty-seven kilometers (24 miles) southwest of Agra lies an imperial capital frozen in time. When Elizabethan Englishmen came to Fatehpur Sikri in 1583 to meet the great emperor Akbar, they were amazed. Here was a city exceeding London both in population and in grandeur. They lost count of the rubies, the diamonds, and the plush silks. Today, Fatehpur Sikri is deserted, left in solitude to reminisce over its past.

The history of the city began when Akbar, desperate because he had no heir, decided to visit a Moslem holy man, Salim Chisti, who lived in a small village. Chisti blessed Akbar and, in turn, the emperor was blessed with a son, whom he named Salim in honor of the holy man. Salim later took the throne as Jahangir. The grateful Akbar decided to move his capital to the village, where he died in 1569.

Fatehpur Sikri lies on a rocky ridge about three kilometers (two miles) long and 1½ kilometers (one mile) wide. But this ridge was no problem

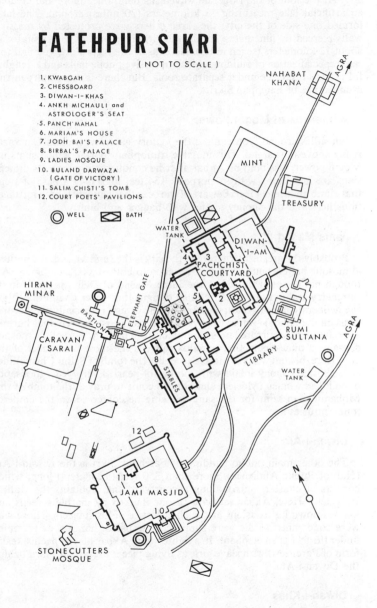

FATEHPUR SIKRI

(NOT TO SCALE)

1. KWABGAH
2. CHESSBOARD
3. DIWAN-I-KHAS
4. ANKH MICHAULI and
   ASTROLOGER'S SEAT
5. PANCH'MAHAL
6. MARIAM'S HOUSE
7. JODH BAI'S PALACE
8. BIRBAL'S PALACE
9. LADIES MOSQUE
10. BULAND DARWAZA
    (GATE OF VICTORY)
11. SALIM CHISTI'S TOMB
12. COURT POETS' PAVILIONS

◎ WELL   ◇ BATH

AGRA

NAHABAT
KHANA

MINT

TREASURY

WATER
TANK

DIWAN
-I-AM

PACHCHIST
COURTYARD

HIRAN
MINAR

ELEPHANT GATE

BASTION

CARAVAN
SARAI

STABLES

LADIES MOSQUE

RUMI
SULTANA

LIBRARY

WATER
TANK

AGRA

N

12

11

JAMI MASJID

10

STONECUTTERS
MOSQUE

to the Mogul emperor, who simply sliced off the top to find room for his city. At the foot of the ridge, he waved his hand once more and created an artificial lake measuring 33 kilometers (20 miles) around. The lake formed one side of the city; the three others were protected by massive walls pierced by nine gates. In all, the circumference of the capital was about 12 kilometers (seven miles). Here, as at the Agra Fort, you find the same specialization of buildings with impressive public halls and a delightful private residence under separate roofs. But there is more unity in the architecture of Fatehpur Sikri.

Momentos of Mogul Power

For miles around, you can see the victory gateway, Buland Darwaza, rising above the capital. This massive triumphant portal, which sums up Mogul power, was built by Akbar after he conquered Gujarat. Its dimensions are in keeping with its purpose: 134 feet high over a base of steps that climb another 34 feet. Beware of the bees that have their own fortifications here and the phoney guides who badger and bluff.

Jama Masjid

Probably the greatest structure in the city is the Jami Masjid, the imperial mosque built around 1575 and designed to hold 10,000 worshipers. Although not as sophisticated as the Jama Masjid of Delhi, it excels in its symmetry and in the geometric inlay designs that cover its interior. Note the deliberate use of Hindu elements in the design (especially the decorations on the pillars)—more examples of Akbar's wish for religious harmony so frequently mirrored in his architecture. The courtyard of the mosque contains a mausoleum that paradoxically, is the most living part of the city. Here, behind walls of marble lace, lies the tomb of Salim Chisti under an elaborate canopy inlaid with mother-of-pearl. Every year, thousands of childless women (Moslem and Hindu) come to pray at the tomb of this Mohammedan saint for the same blessing he conferred on the emperor four centuries ago.

Diwan-i-Am

The other main public building of Fatehpur Sikri is the Diwan-i-Am (Hall of Public Audience), more than 350 feet (92 meters) long, which consists of cloisters surrounding a courtyard that contains the Hall of Judgment. Here, Akbar sat on a throne flanked by marble screens and handed down his decisions as the chief justice of his subjects. Those who were condemned to die were supposedly impaled, hanged, or trampled under the feet of an elephant. In a lighter vein, Akbar played pachisi (early form of Parcheesi) with slave girls as living pieces in the courtyard behind the Diwan-i-Am.

Diwan-i-Khas

The Hall of Private Audience (Diwan-i-Khas) has an unimpressive exterior; but inside the hall, divided by galleries, stands a strange stone column blossoming into a flat-topped flower. Elaborate designs on the column sweep up to the top, which served as Akbar's throne, used when he was receiving ambassadors or nobles. Four stone bridges connect the top of the pillar to the surrounding galleries. The intent behind such a lofty seat is not clear, but apparently it enabled the emperor to receive visitors without having to mingle with them.

Though small in size and not much more than a summer house in appearance (it is open and covered with an umbrella), the Astrologer's seat near the Diwan-i-Khas was an important cog in the Mogul empire. Open-minded Akbar was so intrigued by the trust his Hindu subjects placed in astrologers that he, too, consulted an astrologer. The astrologer determined what color the emperor wore each day (Akbar's favorite colors were yellow, purple, and violet).

Ankh Michauli

Nearby is the Ankh Michauli (its name means blindman's bluff). Supposedly, Akbar loved playing this "grope-and-feel" game inside this building with the ladies of his harem. Fantasy and whimsy prevail in the decorative stone monsters who were supposed to frighten thieves away from the crown jewels believed to have been kept in secret niches carved into the walls.

Jodh Bai's Palace

A feminine touch exists in the Jodh Bai Palace, built for Akbar's Hindu wife. Moslem and Hindu architecture blend together once again: the sculpture found inside the rooms is Hindu while Mogul domes extend above the top of the palace. Living quarters and bathrooms were located around a large interior court. An upper-story room, walled in by a red sandstone screen, is called the "Palace of Winds," the coolest vantage point from which the ladies of the court could watch what was happening without being seen.

Joan of Arc—India-style

Fatehpur Sikri can be the end of your trip or the starting point for an excursion south to Jhansi. Here, the Rani of Jhansi, Lakshmi Bai, began her career as the Joan of Arc of India. The widow of the Rajah of Jhansi, she decided to succeed her husband as the head of his tiny state after he died in 1853, leaving no male heir. Unfortunately, the British had just proclaimed a new policy of taking over princely states whose rulers had left no son. They pensioned off the young widow rani, still in her twenties.

The rani joined the Indian Mutiny in 1857. In April 1858, a British general captured Jhansi, but the rani slipped through his lines. After a wild ride on horseback, she reached Kalpi and joined another rebel leader, but their troops were defeated on May 22. The rani and her followers moved into Gwalior Fort, which was immediately attacked by the British. On June 17, 1858, the rani rode out of the fort, holding the reins of her horse in her teeth, and took the offensive: wielding her sword with both hands. Dressed as a man like the Maid of Orleans, she was shot and sliced by a saber. She slumped to her death clutching her horse. Her room in the old fort of Jhansi is now a shrine of Indian independence.

The medieval city, Orchha, is about 12 kilometers (seven miles) south of Jhansi. Built by the Bundela Rajputs, it has a fortress with some exquisite palaces; most noteworthy is the seventeenth-century Jahangir Mahal, built by Bir Singh Ju Deo, friend of Prince Salim, the future Mogul Emperor Jahangir. Murals in the Lakshmi Temple are fine examples of Bundela art.

Deogarh and Shivpuri

Another different style of architecture is at Deogarh, 110 kilometers (66 miles) south of Jhansi and 13 kilometers (eight miles) east of the famed Dasavatara Temple. Built 1,500 years ago, this temple is a classic of Gupta art, with its tapering tower and its four portals standing majestically over stone steps. Otherwise, you might prefer to stick to the main road and head west from Jhansi to Shivpuri, 53 kilometers (32 miles) away, the one-time summer capital of the Majarajah of Gwalior. Here, the beauty is natural.

Shivpuri, on a cool, wooded plateau at an altitude of 1,400 feet, is on the edge of a national park where you may encounter tigers or other wild animals. About 22 kilometers (13 miles) before Shivpuri on the Jhansi road stands a ruined village, Surwaya, with an old Hindu monastery. But Shivpuri is far better known for relaxation than history. In the park, outside town, a silvery lake (Sakhya Sagar or Chandpatha), with 12 kilometers (seven miles) of shoreline, is inlaid in Mogul fashion against a green setting of wooded hills. From Shivpuri, a delightful road or a toylike railway leads to Gwalior; then it's almost a straight line back to Delhi.

PRACTICAL INFORMATION FOR AGRA

WHEN TO GO. The best time to visit is from mid-October to March. The mornings and evenings are cool, the days warm and sunny. From early March to the end of May, it's hot. Temperatures in the day can soar to over 100°F. Visitors are advised to sightsee in the early morning or late afternoon. Between mid-June and early July, the monsoon arrives, lasting until the end of September.

HOW TO GET THERE. By Air. *Indian Airlines* flies daily to Agra from Delhi, Khajuraho, and Varanasi. This airline also makes three weekly flights into Gwalior from Bhopal, Indore, and Bombay. *Vayudoot* also flies three times a week to Agra from Delhi, Khajuraho, and Varanasi.

By Bus. Both *India Tourism Development Corporation* (ITDC) and *Delhi Tourism Development Corporation* (DTDC) provide inexpensive bus tours from Delhi to Agra and Fatehpur Sikri. (*See* the Delhi chapter, above, for details.)

By Train. From Delhi, take the *Taj Express,* which runs daily, leaving in early morning and returning that evening (about a three-hour journey). Taj Express and numerous other trains continue from Agra to Gwalior (inquire at Agra Railway station, tel. 72515). Once you arrive at the train station in Agra, you can take a day tour to the Agra monuments and Fatehpur Sikri conducted by Uttar Pradesh State Road Transport Corp. (a deluxe bus with guide, fare: Rs. 55). Tour begins at 10:40 A.M. from the Agra Cant. Railway Station and returns in time for the Taj Express departure to Delhi.

From Jaipur, take the *Jaipur Agra Fort Express.* Inquire at the Jaipur Railway Station, tel. 72121.

By Car. Agra is 200 km from Delhi; 230 km from Jaipur; and 119 km from Gwalior. The roads are good from any direction. The round trip from Delhi to Agra (including Fatehpur Sikri) via hired car and driver is about Rs. 1,200.

TOURIST INFORMATION. In Agra, two good sources of information that offer different brochures are *Uttar Pradesh State Tourist Office,* 64 Taj Rd. (tel. 76516); and the *Government of India Tourist Office,* 191 The Mall (tel. 72377). The Government of India has the best map of Agra. It's wise to come armed with your own detailed information on the monuments if you want to get into the nitty-gritty of the architecture. Guides can be good, but their speil has a worn-out and overused superficial edge. The Uttar Pradesh State Tourist Office is open Monday–Saturday, 10 A.M.–5 P.M., closed Sunday and the second Saturday of each month. The Government of India Tourist Office is open Monday–Friday, 9 A.M.–5:30 P.M. and till 1 P.M. Saturday.

In **Jhansi,** *Tourist Bureau,* Prakash Hotel, Civil Lines, tel. 1267.

FOREIGN CURRENCY EXCHANGE. Most Western-style hotels have exchange counters. Otherwise, go to Agra's *State Bank of India* on Mahatma Gandhi Rd. or the *Canera Bank* at Sadar Bazaar. The banks are open Monday–Friday, 10 A.M.–2 P.M.; till noon Saturday.

ACCOMMODATIONS. The full range of accommodations is available in Agra, which is a convenient base for excursions to Fatehpur Sikri and Mathura. Room rates are based on double occupancy and don't include taxes: *Deluxe,* over Rs. 1,450; *Expensive,* Rs. 950–Rs. 1,450; *Moderate,* Rs. 500–Rs. 950; *Inexpensive,* under Rs. 500. During peak season (mid-October to March), book early at better hotels.

AGRA

Deluxe

Welcomgroup Mughal Sheraton. Taj Ganj, Agra; tel. 64701 or 800–325–3535 in U.S. 230 rooms with bath. Winner of the Aga Khan Award for excellence in architecture, this stunning hotel, done up in brick and marble, is the class act in Agra. Spacious rooms have a low-key modern decor, accentuated by soft-white walls and handsome dark-wood trim. Some rooms offer a view of the Taj. There are multicuisine restaurants, and room service, bar, TV, air-conditioning, foreign-exchange counter, travel agency, swimming pool, tennis courts, croquet, mini-golf course, health club, camel and elephant rides, astrologer, shops. AE, DC, MC, V.

Expensive

Hotel Agra Ashok. 6B, The Mall, Agra; tel. 76223. 80 rooms with bath. This attractive Western-style hotel is also inspired by Mogul architecture: lots of marble, lattice trim, and an interior water fountain. Spacious rooms have a modern decor, TV, and air-conditioning. Some rooms offer a view of the Taj. Amenities include coffee shop and multicuisine restaurant, bar, room service, foreign-exchange counter, travel agency, swimming pool, shops, baby-sitters, doctor, puppet show, palm reader. AE, DC, MC, V.

Hotel Clarks Shiraz. 54 Taj Rd., Agra; tel. 72421. 150 rooms with bath. A sprawling white high rise set on eight acres with extensive gardens, the Clarks Shiraz evokes the 1960s, not the age of the Moguls. Rooms have a subdued contemporary decor. Some rooms offer a view of the Taj. Multicuisine restaurants, bar, room service, TV, air-conditioning, foreign-exchange counter, travel agency, swimming pool, mini-golf course, badminton, shops, doctor, baby-sitters. AE, DC, MC, V.

Taj View. Fatehabad Rd., Agra; tel. 64171. 100 rooms with bath. The Taj View may lack architectural inspiration, but it offers good service and spacious modern air-conditioned rooms with TV. Multicuisine restaurants, bar, room service, foreign-exchange counter, car rental, doctor, baby-sitters, swimming pool, health club, shops, astrologer. AE, DC, MC, V.

Moderate

Hotel Mumtaz. Fatehabad Rd., Agra; tel. 64771. 100 rooms with bath. Under renovation at press time, this Western-style hotel has simply decorated, modern rooms with air-conditioning and TV. Multicuisine restaurant, bar, room service, foreign-exchange counter, travel agency, doctor, baby-sitters, shops, palm reader. AE, DC, MC, V.

Inexpensive

Mayur Tourist Complex. Fatehabad Rd., Agra; tel. 67302. 30 cottages with bath. Nestled around a landscaped lawn, this delightful enclave offers rooms in cottages done up in an ethnic decor. Air-conditioning on request, multicuisine restaurant, rooftop barbecue, room service, TV, children's playground, doctor. AE, DC, MC, V.

New Bakshi House. 5 Laxman Nagar, Agra; tel. 61292. Six rooms with bath. If you'd like to stay in a typical Indian middle-class neighborhood, this guest house is perfect. Each room is cozy and clean. In the restaurant you can choose between home-cooked Indian and Continental meals. Amenities include free pick-up and transfer service, doctor, and travel arrangements. Rupees only.

JHANSI

Inexpensive

Jhansi Hotel. Shastri Marg, Jhansi; tel. 1360. 25 rooms with bath. This simple Western-style hotel is the best option in Jhansi. Clean rooms have a modest contemporary decor. Some rooms are air-conditioned and have TV. Multicuisine restaurant, bar, room service, car rental, foreign-currency exchange, doctor. Rupees only.

DINING OUT. Maybe because of Agra's heavy tourist draw, food in this destination can be pricey by Indian standards. Many accommodations listed above have restaurants, some of which are included here. Breakfast is usually served 7–10; lunch, noon–3; dinner, 7:30–11. The restaurants listed below are informal and, unless noted, are open for all three meals and don't require reservations. Prices are based on a three-course dinner for one person, excluding beverage, tip, and taxes: *Deluxe,* over Rs. 120; *Expensive,* Rs. 80–Rs. 120; *Moderate,* Rs. 40–Rs. 80; *Inexpensive,* under Rs. 40.

AGRA

Deluxe

Bagh-e-Bahar. Mughal Sheraton, Taj Ganj; tel. 64701. This sumptuous garden restaurant serves good Continental cuisine and provides music to dance to at night. Open 7:30–11 P.M. Reservations advised. AE, DC, MC, V.

Expensive

Mahjong Room. Mughal Sheraton, Taj Ganj; tel. 64701. Enjoy excellent Chinese dishes in this darkly lit, intimate restaurant with an elegant Oriental decor. Open 12:30–3 P.M. and 7:30 P.M.–midnight. Dinner reservations advised. AE, DC, MC, V.

Mughal Room. Clarks Shiraz, 54 Taj Rd.; tel. 72421. This handsome rooftop restaurant is done up in pinks and reds, with a twinkling-star ceiling. At night enjoy live performances of Indian *ghazals* (musicians). You can choose from good Indian, Chinese, and Continental cuisines. Open 7:30–11:30 P.M. Reservations advised. AE, DC, MC, V.

Nauratna. Mughal Sheraton, Taj Ganj; tel. 64701. This intimate restaurant has an opulent Mogul decor, with lots of marble. During the evening, expect live performances of Indian ghazels. Open 12:30–3 P.M. and 7:30 P.M.–midnight. Dinner reservations advised. AE, DC, MC, V.

Moderate–Expensive

Sonam. 51 Taj Rd.; tel. 77039. Set in an old British bungalow, the Sonam has a weathered patina; there's linen on the tables, a gigantic chandelier, a working fireplace in winter and air-conditioning in summer. You can also eat at tables set up on the spacious lawn. The multicuisine food and ambience are reliably good. Try *murg samandar* (whole chicken for two cooked with cardamon) or *dum-e-ran* (leg of lamb curry). Open 6 A.M.–midnight. Rupees only.

Moderate

Sonar Restaurant. 25 Mall Rd., Phool Sayad Crossing; tel. 76144. This informal restaurant, crowded with tables, has a no-frills decor. Tables are also set up on its pleasant lawn. Chef serves good multicuisine meals, especially tasty chicken dishes. Open 6 A.M.–11 P.M. Rupees only.

SWEETS AND TREATS. For excellent Indian sweets and snacks, head for **Brijwasi**, D-2, Shopping Arcade, Sadar Bazar. The pastry shop is downstairs, while upstairs you can relax in a charming coffee shop with tile-and-mirror walls. It's very popular. Open 7:30 A.M.–10:30 P.M. Rupees only.

HOW TO GET AROUND. From the Airport. There's good passenger coach service to hotels from the airport (Rs. 15). Taxis run about Rs. 50 to most main hotels and Agra.

By Taxi. Rate: Rs. 2.50 per km. If the driver claims his meter is broken, set the rate before you depart.

By Auto Rickshaw. Cheaper than cabs (Rs. 2 per km), they're ideal in the traffic-jammed streets. You can also hire a rickshaw for a half-day (Rs. 75) or full-day (Rs. 150).

By Bike Rickshaw. This pleasant option, also good in Agra, should cost no more than Rs. 20 per hour.

By Rented Car and Driver. Good only if you want to travel beyond Agra and maintain your own schedule. Only hire a car with driver from a recommended tour operator listed below. A non-air-conditioned car for two hours or 20 km should cost about Rs. 60, the minimum charge; for eight hours or 100 km, about Rs. 300. For overnight excursions, there's an additional Rs. 50 halt charge.

JHANSI

By Tongas (horse drawn carriages). Cheap and about the only way to get around here other than walking.

TOURS. *Uttar Pradesh State Road Transport Corporation* (96 Gwalior Rd., tel. 72206; and Platform No. 1, near Enquiry Window, Agra Cant. Railway Station) offers a daily bus tour with guide of Fatehpur Sikri, Agra Fort, and Taj Mahal. Rs. 55 per person. Call for booking and further details.

Excellent guides are available from the *Take-A-Guide Office* (opposite Hotel Taj View, Fatehabad Rd.). For up to four persons, half-day charges are Rs. 60; full-day charges are Rs. 90. The office is open 9 A.M.–6 P.M. daily.

TOUR OPERATORS. For all travel needs, including a rented car with driver, contact the following agencies: *India Tourism Development Corporation,* ITDC, 6-B, The Mall, Agra, tel. 73271; *Travel House,* Mughal Sheraton, Taj Ganj, Agra, tel. 73271; *Sita World Travel,* A-2, Shopping Arcade, Sadar Bazar, Agra, tel. 64978; *Travel Corporation India,* TCI, Hotel Clarks Shiraz, 54 Taj Rd., Agra, tel. 72421. In the peak season, book a rented car with driver in advance.

SEASONAL EVENTS. The specific dates for many events are determined by the lunar calendar; consult the Government of India Tourist Office for details.

February/March. *Holi.* During this exuberant spring festival, the women of Barsana (near Mathura, the legendary home of Radha, Krishna's consort) challenge the men of nearby Nandgaon (Krishna's home) in numerous unusual battles that get fairly frisky.

August/September. *Ganmashtami.* Lord Krishna's birthday is celebrated with nightlong prayers and temple festivities in Agra and Mathura.

October/November. In Mathura, *Diwali* marks the start of the Hindu New Year, most festive of Indian festivals. Thousands of candles, and flickering lights illuminate the city, homes, and public buildings. A noisy, firecracker good time.

In Mathura, see a *puja* (prayer service) held every evening at the Vishram Ghat on the Ganges. A beautiful ceremony that ends with the release of flickering oil lamps into the holy river.

HISTORIC SITES. All historic monuments are open sunrise to sunset, except for the Taj Mahal, which is open sunrise to 7:30 P.M. Entrance fee is about Rs. 2, except on Friday when it is free. *Agra Fort.* Construction on the red-sandstone fort and white-marble palaces started with Akbar in 1565 and continued through the next two generations (Jahangir and Shah Jahan). Enter via the Amar Singh Gate, then follow the extensive description in this chapter under The Essay Section. If you hire a guide, make sure he's been approved by the government.

Chini-ka-Rauza (China Tomb) is a half mile north of Itmad-ud-Daulah. Constructed by Afzal Khan, the prime minister of Shah Jahan and a Persian poet, the building is sadly neglected.

Itmad-ud-Daulah. Built in 1622–1628 by the Empress Nur Jahan, the tomb of Nur Jahan's father is 5 km (3 mi.) north of the Taj on the left bank of the Yamuna. Her mother is also buried here. This is the first Mogul structure constructed entirely of marble.

Jami Masjid. The congregational mosque of Agra was built in 1648 by Shah Jahan's daughter, Jahanara.

Ram Bagh, near China Tomb. This is the earliest example of a Mogul garden, designed by the Emperor Babur in 1526. Unfortunately, it's not well maintained.

Akbar's Mausoleum is in Sikandra, 10 km from Agra. Designed and begun by the emperor in 1602 before his death, it was completed by his son Jahangir in 1613. Its graceful red sandstone and marble construction represents a fusion of Hindu and Moslem architecture.

Taj Mahal. This memorial tomb, created by Shah Jahan for his queen, Mumtaz, was started in 1632 and completed around 1653. Once you enter this architectural masterpiece of red sandstone and marble, follow the description in the chapter essay under *Taj Mahal: Monument to Love.*

Fatehpur Sikri. After a sixteenth-century mystic, Salim Chisti, blessed the Mogul Emperor Akbar with a much-wanted male heir, Akbar built his capital in the mystic's tiny community, 39 km (23 mi) west of Agra. He constructed his impressive city on a rocky eminence, enclosing three sides with walls, the fourth protected by a lake. The well-preserved royal edifices occupied a central position; lesser buildings were scattered around them, with the rest of the space taken up by the people's dwellings, now vanished.

MUSEUMS. *Taj Mahal Museum,* within the Taj Mahal, Agra, contains a collection of findings from the Mogul period and a history of the Taj. In Jhansi, the *Archaeological Museum,* Rani Mahal, is the former home of the heroine Rani Lakshmi Bai. Here you see a good collection of sculptures from the ninth to the twelfth centuries. Open 8 A.M.–5 P.M. Free. *Mathura Archaeological Museum,* Dampier Park, Mathura. One of India's best museums, it has a great collection of sculpture going back to the fifth century B.C., beautiful sculptures of the Mathura school that flourished in the region, and the art of the Kushan period (the most comprehensive collection in existence); plus good bronzes and terra cottas. Closed Monday and official holidays. Open July 1–April 15 (10:30 A.M.–4:30 P.M.); April 16–June 30 (7:30 A.M.–12:30 P.M.). Guides can be arranged at the museum for a nominal fee.

SHOPPING. In Agra, look for good bargains in hand-knotted carpets and *dhurries* (rugs), precious and semi-precious stones, inlaid marble work, and brass statues. Visit the following reliable shops:

Chirali, Fatehabad Rd. (near Hotel Amar), sells high-quality precious and semiprecious stones and beautiful *zari* (embroidery work). It also designs jewelry on order. Open 9:30 A.M.–7:30 P.M. AE, DC, MC, V.

Cottage Industry, 18 Munro Rd., sells good dhurries and carpets. Open 10 A.M.–7 P.M. AE, DC, MC, V.

Ganesha, also at 18 Munro Rd., has new and old curios in brass, copper, and bronze. Open 7 A.M.–9 P.M. AE, DC, MC, V.

Jewel Palace, Pertappura, is another high-quality shop selling precious and semiprecious stones. It also designs jewelry on order. Open 8 A.M.–8 P.M. AE, DC, MC, V.

Oswal Emporium, 30 Munro Rd., produces excellent marble inlaid items. Prices range from Rs. 125 to over a million. Open 9:30 A.M.–7 P.M. AE, DC, MC, V.

NIGHTLIFE AND BARS. In Agra, bars in all the better hotels usually serve until 11 P.M. Otherwise, nightlife is rather sedate in this area.

RAJASTHAN

Shrine to Chivalry

by
KATHLEEN COX

Desert with dunes, scrub, cactus, and rock, fertile green tracks, hills, ravines, enchanting lakes, and jungles—all exist in Rajasthan, the second largest state in India. Here, the Aravalli Mountain Range cuts the state into two distinct regions: northwestern and southwestern, with the western part (the Thar Desert) only sparcely populated.

Rajasthan is also rich in history, legend, and lore. Formerly called Rajputana ("Abode of Kings") the area was originally made up of at least 22 princely states, each ruled by a proud *Rajput* (prince). From the earliest centuries, the conflict for control over Northern India between the Hindu Rajput rulers, who were (and still are) great horsemen, and the powerful Moslems was passionately contested in a series of military campaigns and intrigues—some of them downright sneaky. One story has an eleventh-century Hindu guide, supposedly in league with an invading Moslem army, generously helping the soldiers get lost in the desert where they nearly died of thirst. Or consider the exploits of the seventeenth-century Mogul Emperor Akbar, whose "strategy" was the reverse of divide and conquer. To expand his empire, he took a Rajput princess of Jaipur as one of his wives (his son and successor Jahangir was the product of this union). And several of Akbar's most trusted generals were Rajputs who had previously fought against him. One of them, Man Singh, was even appointed governor of a great imperial province.

Whatever the outcome of a battle, the Rajputs were masterful warriors, who held onto an unwavering sense of honor and pride in a tradition that decreed, when the battle went against them, that they had to make the supreme sacrifice. Clothed in saffron robes of immolation, they went to battle and died. If the sign of defeat was displayed on the battlefield, the women in the fortress performed the rite of *sati,* the Hindu act of throwing oneself into a flaming pyre—far superior to the indignity of capture. The Rajputs, who claim direct lineage with Hindu divinities and the heroes of India's great epic poems (the *Ramayana* and the *Mahabharata*), are in a class by themselves in world history.

Even when these independent rulers were forced to merge after Independence, each one kept title to an impressive accumulation of palaces, private lands, jewels, and miscellaneous mind-boggling possessions and, of course, none gave any thought to compromising his princely lifestyle. To compensate each ruler for the loss of control over his state and subjects, the maharajah also received a "privy purse," which was paid out annually until 1973, when then-Prime Minister Indira Gandhi decided that the princes had been paid enough. Mrs. Gandhi also cut off many of the royal privileges.

Without the stipend, some of the maharajahs proved they were poor businessmen and nearly went broke (many had to sell their palaces and live off their horded wealth). The elimination of pomp and privileges reduced them all to a humbler status; some turned their exclusive estates into fancy hotels catering to the upper crust.

In spirit, however, Rajasthan is still the legendary land of the Rajput. Forts and palaces, lakes and gardens—all steeped in romance and chivalry—bear witness to a history of conquest and power. Here, the best martial qualities of a race are linked to the refinements of courtesy and an elegant culture. Nowhere else can you see people more intrinsically Indian and more true to their heritage than in Rajasthan.

EXPLORING RAJASTHAN

JAIPUR

Encircled on all but the southern side by the rugged Aravalli hills with numerous peaks crowned by imposing forts, Jaipur, the capital of Rajasthan, still looks cradled and well protected. Jaipur takes its name from Maharajah Jai Singh II, who, in the early 1700s, became king of Amber at the age of 13. Precocious and inquisitive, the young king soon proved to be so distinguished a scholar and diplomat, that Aurangzeb, the reigning Mogul emperor, called him Sawai (One-and-a-Quarter), his way of claiming the young boy's superiority over all his Rajput predecessors. History proved him right.

At that moment, the Mogul Empire was approaching dissolution. With the milder rule from Delhi, it no longer was necessary for the Rajputs to bury themselves in mountain fortresses. They could now come down to the fertile plains with impunity. So, not long after Jai Singh came to the throne, he realized the need to shift the capital from Amber, the ancient rock-bound stronghold of his ancestors, down to the new site in the adjoining valley.

In no time, Sawai Jai Singh could add architect and astronomer to his list of credentials. In 1727, he conceived and designed the bulk of his new

capital, with its exquisite buildings of rose-colored terra cotta described in historical writings as the "tone of the autumn sunset." Although the Sawai's city is dusty and is crammed with camels, horses, dogs, and people, and is reminiscent of a gold-rush frontier town in its heyday, it remains an astonishing model of city planning. Enclosed inside fortified walls 20 feet high and guarded by eight gates, every aspect—the streets, sidewalks, height of the buildings, number and division of blocks—was based on geometric harmony, sound environmental and climatic considerations, and the intended use of each zone within the city. No detail escaped the sawai's attention. With pink and orange the dominant colors, the effect is magic at dusk even if the city is not kept up as it was in his time.

City Palace

Enter the City Palace complex through the Sireh Deorhi Gate, the principal entrance on the east. This complex, with its numerous pavilions, courtyards, chambers, and palace, was begun by the sawai, with further additions made by later maharajahs. Once you're inside the outer courtyard, the building directly in front is the Mubarak Mahal (guest pavilion), built by Maharajah Madho Singh II fewer than 100 years ago. This marble and sandstone building, with its delicate marble lacework, surrounds the original guest pavilion built earlier by the sawai. It now houses the textile and costume museum, which displays a collection of brocades, silks, and handblocked traditional royal garments and robes, plus musical instruments (all donated by the royal family). Some of the exhibits go back to the seventeenth century. Also visit the armory in the northwest corner of the courtyard. You'll see one of India's best collections of arms and weapons, including an 11-pound sword belonging to the Rajput General of Akbar.

Proceed to the inner courtyard (through the gateway guarded by two stone elephants) and enter the art gallery housed in the Diwan-i-Am (Hall of Public Audience). The building, constructed by another descendant, Pratap Singh, in the late 1700s, is gorgeous—huge—with rows of massive gray marble columns, the second largest chandelier in India, and a magnificient painted ceiling (painted in the 1930s for the maharajah's second marriage). The art gallery contains an extensive collection of miniatures from the Mogul and various Rajput schools, rare manuscripts, and gigantic carpets form the 1600s that were originally on the floors of the Amber Palace.

In the center of the inner courtyard, you'll notice a pair of mammoth silver urns inside the Hall of Private Audience, a raised platform with beautiful marble pillars. This building was used for formal banquets and ceremonial occasions. When Maharajah Madho Singh II sailed to England to attend the coronation of King Edward VII, these solid silver urns carried water from the Ganges (the only water the devout Hindu would dare drink)—a seemingly inefficient yet ostentatious method of hauling water.

From the inner courtyard, enter the Zanana courtyard on the left. Here you'll see the famous Chandra Mahal, or Moon Palace, with its seven stories that tower above the other structures. Built by Sawai Singh II, the lovely cream-hued building is still the official residence of the present Maharajah "Bubbles," or, more formerly, Lieutenant Colonel Sawai Bhawani Singh, who lives in the upper stories. The ground floor is also exquisite, with sumptuous chandeliers, murals, and a quasi-three-dimensional painting of an old maharajah.

Adjoining the palaces are the Jai Niwas gardens (off limits to the paying public), which offer the romantic prospect of splashing fountains and ornamental water. A legend claims that the Rajah Jagat Singh, oppressed by the heat of the palace, frequently escaped into some shady corner of this greenery. From here, he supposedly amused himself by exchanging love letters with his *zenana* (harem)—the letters dutifully carried back and forth in the mouth of his favorite dog. A monument to this trusty hound stands in the garden—his reward for his services as "post dog."

Jantar Mantar

Not content with designing this famous palace, Jai Singh also supervised the design and construction of five remarkable observatories in northern India. The largest and best preserved—the Jantar Mantar—is in Jaipur near the entrance to the City Palace. Built of masonry, marble, and brass, it is equipped with gigantic, futuristic scientific instruments, called *yantras,* each one designed by the Sawai "Newton of the East," who was well aware of European developments in this field and wanted to create observatories that would outdo anything already in existence—an attitude befitting this maharajah.

Abstract and weirdly beautiful, each yantra is uncannily accurate in measuring various celestial data. Samrat Yantra, a 90-foot-high right-angle triangle, is a sundial that tells local time that is accurate to within a few seconds. The *dhruva,* a peculiar brass slab, determines the position of the North Star at night. Numerous other *yantras* determine celestial latitude and longitude, and serve as alternative sundials (some relating to the zodiac). Of course, Jai Singh provided himself with an observer's seat from which he supervised his scientific calculations.

Hava Mahal—"Palace of Winds"

Also worth a visit in the old city is the Hawal Mahal (Palace of Winds), a landmark built by Maharajah Sawai Pratap Singh in Jaipur in 1799. The Hawa Mahal is located on the bustling commercial thoroughfare called Siredeori Bazaar (directly after Johari Bazaar heading north). The curious five-story structure, which gets its name from the westerly winds that send cool breezes through the windows, is elaborate and fanciful. Constructed of pink sandstone, its delicate honeycomb design glows in the evening light. Every story has semioctagonal overhanging windows, each with a perforated screen, from which the ever-discreet women of the court could view the activities on the street below. The roof is curvilinear, with domes and finials, which adds to the general effect of lightness and delicacy.

Ram Niwas Garden and the Albert Hall Museum

Outside the walled city, relax in quiet at the Ram Niwas Garden, then see the strange Albert Hall Museum located in the beautiful grounds. The sandstone and marble building, constructed in the Indo-Saracenic style in the late 1800s, contains eclectic displays, not your ordinary run of paintings and sculpture. Many of the unexpected exhibits offer convenient cultural explanations for the curious foreigner. Look at the one devoted to *Mehendi,* the Indian art of decorating hands and feet with henna, and the one that identifies the folk instruments you may have heard and dances you may have seen in Rajasthan. Upstairs you'll find a table display of numerous clay models that demonstrate the vast range of yoga positions mastered by the physically agile yogi.

Amber Palace

For six centuries, the capital of Rajasthan and the nucleus of Rajput history, Amber is now little more than a deserted palace, surrounded by majestic ramparts. The construction, started by Maharajah Man Singh in the early 1700s and completed 100 years later, is a blend of Rajput and Mogul influences. The palace, which rises on the slopes of a steep hill behind the Maota Lake, retains an aura of great beauty. As soon as you enter the Valley of Flowers and pass through the pink gate, Amber Palace glows with variegated colors and nobility.

To get to the palace, you can either walk or arrive, pompously enough, on the back of a gaily caparisoned elephant. This archaic means of transportation explains the unusual height of the palace gateways. Inside the palace, the principal hall, known as the Hall of Victory, presents a galaxy of decorative art—panels of alabaster with fine inlay work of the tenderest hues, together with every kind of workmanship for which Jaipur is famous. And, typical of the Mogul period, the rooms are essentially small and intimate, while the successive courtyards and narrow passages are particularly Rajput.

Each room shows some vestige of its former glory, especially the Sheesh Mahal (Chamber of Mirrors). When you step inside, close the doors, strike a match, and watch the ceiling twinkle and glow. Numerous narrow flights of stairs lead up to the royal apartments that provide the best views of the valley, the lovely palace courtyards, the formal gardens abutting an octagon pool that edges the lake, and the ancient fortress (the Jaigash Fort) that stands guard from the crest of the hill above you. Vast and somber, its vaults still hide the treasures of Jaipur—or at least that's the rumor.

Alwar, Deeg, and Bharatpur

Continuing northeast, the next place of interest is Alwar, built into the jagged Aravalli Hills. Alwar, founded in 1771, is dominated by its medieval fort that crowns a conical rock. Once the capital of the princely state of the same name, Alwar contains a city palace (Vinai Vilas Mahal) that was constructed in the late 1800s. The palace is separated from the hill by the Sagar Tank (an artificial water tank). The upstairs is a museum devoted to manuscripts (over 7,000, the most notable being an illuminated copy of the Quran in Arabic with Persian translation in red lettering) and paintings, including a rare collection of Mogul and Rajasthani miniatures. An armory contains the personal weapons of Akbar, Jahangir, Shah Jahan, and Aurangzeb, with hilts of gold studded with jewels.

Also visit Gunijankhana, the feudal academy of arts, and see excellent examples of the Alwar School of painting. Unlike conventional Rajput paintings, the pictures here of dancing girls do not conceal the limbs and sensuousness of Rajput women. Also see the marble mausoleum of Bakhtawar Singh (1781–1815)—an excellent example of Indo-Islamic architecture—south of the Sagar Tank. Another spot to visit is the Purjan Vihar, a public park on the outskirts of town, with its renowned Summer House.

Siliserh Lake, about 13 kilometers (eight miles) from Alwar, is fringed by a dense forest and adorned with *chhatris* (domed cenotaphs). A magnificent former hunting lodge, built by a nineteenth-century maharajah for his queen, and now converted into a hotel, is nestled in the hills and overlooks the lovely lake. Travel another 29 kilometers (18 miles) to Sariska, a tiger reserve surrounded by the Aravallis. Here, too, you'll find a royal hunting lodge, the Sariska Palace (now a hotel), set on the edge of the sanctuary.

Continuing east from Alwar you reach Deeg, renowned for its massive fort and pleasure palaces (built by Badan Singh in the 1700s), surrounded by sumptuously laid-out gardens, tanks, and fountains, added by his son, Suraj Mal. Richly carved columns, cornices, and eaves are arranged with an exquisite sense of balance; kiosks are scattered about like sentinels, giving the palace an air of mystery and romance. The largest of the palaces, Gopal Bhavan, contains a curious marble swing. Originally the property of the Nawabs of Oudh, this eccentric plaything was carried off to Deeg by Maharajah Jawahar Singh. (Indeed, a good portion of the gorgeous inlaid marble you see here was stolen from Mogul palaces in Agra and Delhi.) Among the other buildings are the Suraj Bhavan, built of marble and ornamented with semiprecious inlaid stones; the Nand Bhavan, the big hall of audience; and the Macchi Bhavan, a decorative pavilion surrounded by fountains and ornamental ponds.

Bharatpur, capital of the former state of the same name and one of the chief cities of Rajasthan, is some 35 kilometers (22 miles) farther south. Founded by Suraj Mal, considered an outstanding military figure of the eighteenth century, Bharatpur is famous for its Lohagarh (Iron Fort), which successfully repulsed numerous Mogul and British attacks. No wonder—Suraj Mal's fortifications were an ingenious design: two massive mud ramparts, each encircled by a moat of formidable dimensions (over 150 feet wide and about 50 feet deep), which surrounded the central fortress built of solid masonry that had yet another ditch around it filled with water. Cannon balls stuck in the mud walls and caused no damage to the stone bastions of the inner fort. To get a better idea of the scale of the fortification, keep in mind this fact: The outer mud rampart, which is now demolished, had and 11-kilometer (seven-mile) circumference. The inner fortress, which was octagonal in shape, had two gates, both trophies of war captured from Delhi. The central and most important tower of the fort, set up in 1765, commemorated the successful assault on the Mogul capital. The museum contains sculptures and other testimonies to the art and culture of the region.

Shekhavati

From Bharatpur, head back to Jaipur, then travel northwest to Sikar, about 97 kilometers (60 miles) from Jaipur. From here, give yourself a day or two to take a picturesque excursion through an area called Shekhavati, named after the fifteenth-century King Shekha of Amarsar. First, head northeast to Nawalgarh, about 29 kilometers (18 miles) away—a beautiful village with hundreds of *havelis* (traditional Rajput homes with interior courtyards). Many of the older havelis have colorful frescoes covering the exterior and interior walls. You have now entered the land of the wealthy Marwaris, successful merchants on this formerly important and historic caravan route and great patrons. From the nineteenth-century houses that remain, the Marwaris were obviously devoted to the visual arts—recording contemporary world events and their passions on the walls of their homes. Go farther north to Dundlod village, with its lovely palace-hotel, and then on to Mandawa, with its giant medieval fort, and spend a night as the guest of the maharajah in his well-appointed seventeenth-century castle/hotel, with its stunning views. See more havelis and then continue in your leisurely pace to Fatehpur, a small city. All along the route you will pass through villages with color and fanciful art.

Bikaner

About 160 kilometers (100 miles) due west of Fatehpur is Bikaner. Founded at the close of the fifteenth century by Rao Bika, a descendant of Jodhai, the founder of Jodhpur, Bikaner stands aloof on high ground surrounded by walls and the Thar Desert. Visit the sixteenth-century Junagarh Fort built by Raja Raj Singh, an outstanding general of the Mogul Emperor Akbar. Within this massive edifice (located in the heart of the city), protected by a moat, are housed some of the rarest gems of Rajput architecture. Especially beautiful are the ancient palaces of sandstone and marble, including the Chandra Mahal (Moon Palace) and the Phool Mahal (Flower Palace), with lavish mirror work, carvings, and paintings. There are also temples, a mosque, and Har Mandir, a handsome chapel in which royal weddings and important births were celebrated. Also visit Durbar Hall, built in the Mogul style and lavishly decorated with paintings. Floral bouquets, set in red and gold borders, gilded leaf work, and vases are the leading motifs. Two or three stories high, with slender columns, cusped arches, and intricate screens, palaces rise on all sides. The zenana is separated by a broad court with paneled niches. Gilt reliefs, glass mosaics, and lacelike mirrors adorn graceful and intimate apartments.

Bikaner is also the home of the famous Camel Corps, still useful in desert warfare. Outside the city are other palaces and temples—imposing edifices of carved red sandstone. Jain temples and monasteries abound in this city and neighborhood. Most of them early sixteenth century, they are rich in carvings. Eight kilometers (five miles) away are the *chhatris,* cenotaphs of the rulers of Bikaner.

For a squeamish experience, visit the Karni Mata Temple in Deshnok, about 32 kilometers (20 miles) from Bikaner, on the road to Jodhpur. This temple devoted to Karni Mata, an incarnation of Durga, is also the home of hundreds of rats, which are considered sacred and roam freely inside the temple. It is said that if a rat touches you or, better still, jumps on you, you'll be blessed with a lifetime of good luck (not rabies).

Jaisalmer: Island in the Sand

Some 484 kilometers (300 miles) in a southwesterly direction is the ancient city of Jaisalmer, founded by Rawal Jaisal in 1156. Lying at the extreme edge of Rajasthan, Jaisalmer is a tiny jewel in the heart of the Thar, the great Indian desert. Once the capital of the Bhati Rajputs, the medieval city rises in a sea of sand on a low range of hills surrounded by a stone wall three miles around—a towering vision in delicate yellow hue—only infrequently broken by green oases.

Your first sighting of Jaisalmer sets off an ethereal vision, but one that is slightly seamy when you examine its past. Jaisalmer started out as an important caravan center—remnants of caravansaries still exist (some of them converted into hotels). Right through the eighteenth century, rulers amassed their wealth from taxes levied on those passing through. Jaisalmer was also a smuggler's paradise, with opium the long-time best-seller.

Two great gateways, from east to west, pierce the towered battlements of the twelfth-century citadel. Inside are numerous Jain and Hindu temples, palaces, and more charming havelis. It's a walker's utopia, with tiny lanes and visually rich rewards. Most of the buildings are exquisitely carved, especially the facades with elaborate workmanship, frequently filigreed like lace. Don't miss these gems: The seven-story palace built by

Maharawal (1763–1820)—a conglomeration of buildings crowned by a vast umbrella of metal, mounted on a stone shaft. Notice the historic spot, Satiyar-ka-Pagthiya, just before the palace entrance. Here, the royal ladies performed seti, the act of self-immolation when husbands were slain, at the fall of the fortress in 1294. Also, see the eight Jain temples and four Hindu temples built in the fifteenth and sixteenth centuries. The Jain temples, dedicated to Rikhabdevji and Sambhavnathji, are filled with thousands of deities and dancing figures in mythological settings. The Gyan Bhandar (Jain library), inside the Jain temple complex contains over 1,000 old manuscripts—some of them dating back to the twelfth century and written on palm leaf in black ink with painted wooden covers. The library also has a good collection of Jain, pre-Mogul, and Rajput paintings.

Outside the fortress, walk through the narrow lanes with more of the delicate, lacy architecture that shimmers in soft yellow. See the Patva Havelis—a string of five connected havelis built by the Patva brothers in the 1800s. Two of the five are now owned by the government and are open to the public. It's also possible to visit the interiors of the others (offer a small fee to the current residents). Next, visit the Nathamal Ki Haveli, flanked by stone elephants, built by two brothers. Instead of working in tandem, each brother concentrated exclusively on the left or right side. Although the result is harmonious, look carefully. You'll see subtle differences in the windows and carvings. Here, too, a courteous request may get you inside. The interior of Salim Singh's Havelis is in sad disrepair. Perhaps that's a fitting denouement. Salim Singh, financier for Jaisalmer, nearly bankrupted the state with his excessive extortion. He also went overboard when he committed a series of murders to avenge the murder of his father. The exterior six-story eighteenth-century haveli, however, is still lovely, with 38 balconies and elaborate carvings.

Jodhpur

Once the capital of the state of Marwar, Jodhpur, about 210 kilometers (130 miles) southeast of Jaisalmer, tumbles down a low sandstone hill on the edge of the Thar Desert. Today, remnants of an immense fortification wall, nine kilometers (six miles) in circumference, with eight gates facing various directions, guard the old city from the sand that surrounds Thar Desert and the new city growing around the base of the rocky eminence. At the summit soars the majestic Meherangarh Fort, built in 1459 by Rao Jodha when he shifted his capital from Mandore. Standing above a perpendicular cliff, the fort looks impregnable—an imposing landmark, especially at night when it is bathed in yellow light.

The walls of the fort enclose a variety of handsome, red sandstone buildings, palaces, barracks, temples, and havelis. The Victory Gate, leading up from the city to the fort, was erected by Maharajah Ajit Singh to commemorate his military successes over the Moguls at the beginning of the eighteenth century. Seven other gateways stand in honor of other victories—internecine—involving warfare between the various Rajput princes. On the walls of the final gate of entry are the palm marks of Rajput widows who immolated themselves on flaming pyres after their husbands were defeated in battle.

Delicately latticed windows and pierced screens worked in sandstone are the surprising motifs inside the rugged fort. The palaces—Moti Mahal, Phool Mahal, Sheesh Mahal, and the other apartments—are exquisitely decorated, with paintings still gracing some of the ceilings and walls. Outside the fort are more interesting old buildings and temples, such as the Jaswant Thada, a royal crematorium in marble, built in 1899 for Maharajah Jaswant Singh II. Also visit the Umaid Bhawan Palace, built from 1929 to 1942 by the Maharajah Umaid Singh. This sandstone palace has been partially converted into a deluxe hotel. The Umaid Bhawan also houses the Government Museum, with its fancy collection of royal finery, local arts and crafts, and miniature paintings. You might also catch a glimpse of the family of the current maharajah who live in their accustomed splendor in one extensive wing of the palace.

While in Jodhpur, also wander through the Girdikot and Sardar markets, crowded with fruit and vegetable stalls and tiny shops, and noisy with the day-to-day bustle of a typical Indian market. Don't be surprised if you see some of the local folk wearing those favored equestrian pants, jodhpurs; they originated here.

About eight kilometers (five miles) to the north are the Mandore Gardens, the site of the ancient capital of the State of Marwar. Here, surrounded by lovely gardens and mischievous monkeys, you'll find the *devals,* or cenotaphs, of the former royalty.

Mount Abu—Hill Station

Situated on lush, verdant hills about 1,219 meters (4,000 feet) above sea level, Mount Abu, with its famous Dilwara Jain temples, is a hill resort endowed with antiquity. To reach Mount Abu, a place of pilgrimage for Jains, take the road that heads almost due south from Jodhpur. Originally a center of the cult of Shiva, Mount Abu became the Jainist religious stronghold by the eleventh century. Abu (a shortened form of Arbuda) was known in Hindu legend as the son of the Himalayas. This son, supposedly a serpent, rescued Shiva's sacred bull Nandi when it fell into a chasm. Here, too, Vasishta, the great sage of the epic period, established his *ashram*—something between a hermitage and a seat of learning. The four fire-born Rajput clans claim they were created from his sacrificial fire.

High in the steep valleys between the rocky peaks are five Jain shrines. For ornamental skill in intricate stonework and as pieces of architectural virtuosity, the Vimal Vasashi and the Tejpal temples stand out in the history of stone carving. The Vimal Vasashi was built in 1031 and is dedicated to Adinath, the first Jain Tirthanka. Composed of pure white marble, its exterior is deceptively simple, giving no hint of the wealth of ornamentation and sculpture hidden inside.

A procession of marble elephants leads up from the pavilion to the domed porch. On the backs of the carved animals sit the founder, Vimala, and his family. The central courtyard is surrounded by a high wall enclosing some 50 cells, each one enshrining its saintly image. In the central shrine, laden with jewels, sits the figure of Adinath. The octagonal dome, decorated with finely carved human and animal shapes and processions, is supported by eight sculptured pillars. The ceiling is a mass of intricate fretted marble lacework.

The second temple of major importance was built 200 years later. Here, exuberance knows no bounds, reaching the zenith of Indian inventive genius in decorative art. The most striking feature is the pendant of the temple's dome. To stimulate their talent, the carvers were supposedly offered rewards in silver equal in weight to that of the marble filings. Not content with this, Tejpal, the lavish founder offered the weight in gold of any further filings that could be pared off after work was completed. Whatever the truth, there's no doubt that the proportion of perspiration to inspiration was clearly well balanced.

Ranakpur

About 160 kilometers (100 miles) northeast of Mount Abu is Ranakpur, a famous Jain temple, nestled in a lovely glen. As at Mount Abu, the shrine is dedicated to Adinath and dates from the beginning of the fifteenth century. Despite its current state of tranquility, *dacoits* (Indian bandits) formerly used the sacred shrine for their headquarters. They were finally ejected about 25 years ago, when the temple was cleaned up and restored to its impeccable condition.

Inside the temple are 29 halls supported by 200 different pillars, plus subsidiary shrines, in the shape of side-altars, that face all four directions. A wall, about 200 feet high, encircles the entire structure. Its inner face contains a quantity of elaborately sculptured cells, each adorned with a graceful spire. Embedded in this galaxy of spires rise the central shrines; 20 domes constitute the complex roofing of the pillared hall. Intricate carvings, friezes, and sculptured figures in close formation adorn the ceilings of all these structures. And, beneath the floor are hidden meditation chambers. In front of this temple are two more Jain shrines and a temple dedicated to the sun god (displaying erotic sculpture).

Udaipur

Udaipur, southeast of Ranakpur, is called the "City of Dreams"; its ruler, the maharana, the "Sun of the Hindus," a descendant of the highest ranking "Solar" Rajputs. The maharana's island palaces sparkle in post and pinnacles of colored glass, amber, and pale jade. The gray waters of the Pichola Lake—the artificial creation of a fourteenth-century fantasy—reflect the famous eighteenth-century Jag Niwas Lake Palace (now a hotel), which seems to float on the water's surface. Not far from the Lake Palace is the smaller, equally lovely seventeenth-century Jag Mandir.

Udaipur, originally the capital of the state of Mewar, takes its name from Maharana Udai Singh, who founded the city in the middle of the sixteenth century after fleeing the third Moslem attack on the city of Chittaur. Although his act didn't live up to the Rajput code of bravery to the deadly finish, it brought about Udaipur and its gorgeous palaces that everyone now enjoys.

Another legend claims that Udai Singh chose this location for Udaipur after a wandering holy man *(sadhu)* told him that if he built his capital on the edge of the lake, it would never be captured. Given the maharana's predilection for staying alive, he readily took the sadhu's advice. Unfortunately, his son, Maharana Pratap Singh attempted a surprise victory over the Delhi Moslem Empire and succeeded. His success was short-lived. In 1615, his successor, Amar Singh, was forced to sign a conditional submission to the Emperor Jahangir in Delhi. So much for the sadhu's promise.

The maharana's City Palace stands on the crest of a ridge overlooking the lake, an imposing structure, the largest palace in Rajasthan. Built at various periods, it still preserves a harmony of design, enhanced by massive octagonal towers surmounted by cupolas.

In its sumptuous apartments, decorated by multicolor mosaics, mirror work and inlaid tiles abound on all sides, together with some fine paintings and historical relics. Roof gardens afford a wide panorama below. The later island palaces rival the ancient palace on the mainland. Almost in the middle of the lake, Jag Nivas (Lake Palace) consists of apartments, courts, fountains, and gardens. On another island at the southern end, Jag Mandir Palace, started in the seventeenth century, was added to and em-

bellished during the next 50 years. Three stories high, of yellow sandstone
with an inside lining of marble, it is crowned by an imposing dome. Its
interior is decorated with arabesques of colored stones. It was to Jag
Mandir that Sharja, son of Emperor Jahangir, came to hide after leading
an unsuccessful revolt against his father.

Other lakes in the immediate neighborhood, all artificial like Pichola,
are joined to it by canals. Sahelion-Ki-Bari Park, at a two-kilometer (mile-
and-a-half) distance, is a good example of this Hindu art of landscape gardening on a princely scale. It was laid out by Maharana Sangram Singh.
A good road snakes its way along the shores of Fatehsagar Lake. Close
below the embankment is the Sahelion-ki-Bari, the "Garden of the
Maids," designed for the special use of the maharana's ladies, who arrived
in a bunch from Delhi as a peace offering from the emperor. Ornamental
pools, with finely sculptured cenotaphs of soft black stone surrounded by
a profusion of fountains, are the main décor.

Udaipur's Environs

Sixty-five kilometers (40 miles) north is Rajsamand, an artificial lake
of considerable size possessing a masonry embankment, entirely paved
with white marble, constructed by Maharana Raj Singh in 1660. Broad
marble steps lead down to the water, while three delicately carved marble
pavilions jut into the lake. Cut into the stones of the embankment is the
longest Sanskrit inscription known in India, a poem, etched into 25 slabs,
that recounts the history of Mewar.

About 52 kilometers (32 miles) southeast of Udaipur lies Dhebar, or
Jai Samand Lake, one of the largest artificial sheets of water in Asia, created by a dam almost a quarter of a mile across and over 100 feet high—no
small engineering feat considering it was built in the seventeenth century.
A temple of Shiva, flanked by six cenotaphs with a carved elephant in front
of each, stands on the embankment. Bhils tribesmen still inhabit the islands in the lake.

All around Udaipur, you come across lake and shrine, temple and cenotaph—a wealth of white marble overlooking calm waters and interspersed
with trees. Not all are monuments of victory or relics of peace and splendor. Sati stones commemorate the self-sacrifice of women who hurled
themselves into raging fires while their husbands, pledged to death, fought
against the overwhelming odds of invading hordes.

Twenty-two kilometers (14 miles) north of Udaipur is Eklingji, a tiny
temple complex with 108 shrines that are dedicated to Shiva, the diety
of the rulers of the Mewar. The present building, standing on the site of
the original fifteenth-century edifice, is of late eighteenth-century construction. Like most sacred buildings in this region, it's entirely of white
marble. The roof is decorated by hundreds of circular knobs and crowned
by a lofty tower. In the inner shrine is a four-faced black marble image
of Shiva. Outside is the statue of Nandi, his sacred bull. At a short distance, Nagda, now in ruins, bore the brunt of too many Moslem invasions.
One of the most ancient places in Mewar, it has two temples dating from
the eleventh century, both ornamented with interesting carvings.

Continuing north, you arrive at Nathdwara and a famous temple of
Krishna that draws pilgrims in the thousands from all parts of India. The
image, supposedly dating back to the twelfth century, was rescued from
the destructive hands of the Moslems and brought here in 1699. A legend
claims that when it was carted away, the chariot sank suddenly at the site
of the present temple. It couldn't be budged or removed, so here it stayed.

About 66 kilometers (41 miles) from Udaipur is the historic pass of Haldighati. Here the valiant Maharan Pratap defied the might of Akbar, described then as "immeasurably the richest and most powerful monarch on the face of the earth." Outnumbered 100 to one, the Rajputs stood their ground until they all died except Pratap, who managed to escape on his horse, Chetak. From his outpost in the hills, he slowly won back all his strongholds except Chittaur.

Chittorgarh—Cradle of Rajput Courage

Due east of Udaipur is Chittorgarh, a city steeped in heroism. The ancient capital of Mewar State, this city and its ruins represent the origin of Rajput courage. The foundations of the fort of Chittaur are traditionally linked to the seventh century, and it remained the capital until 1567.

The glory of Chittorgarh is the Tower of Victory, set up by Rana Kumbha in the middle of the fifteenth century to commemorate his triumph over the Moslem kings of Gujarat and Malwa. Kumbha, like all the Rajput rulers, was a direct descendant of Bappa Rawal, that great chieftain who reigned in Chittaur in the eighth century. Supposedly, Boppa was "a giant who stood 20 cubits" (the best part of 30 feet!), whose spear no mortal man could lift. Since the start of the dynasty, 59 princes, descendants of this man of mythical dimensions, have assumed the throne of Chittaur.

The front of Chittorgarh presents a battered appearance. Built on the precipitous edge of a hill, the gigantic fort is over 11 kilometers (seven miles) in circumference. Inside are ruins of temples, palaces, and tanks, ranging from the ninth to the seventeenth centuries and the almost-intact Tower of Fame, a Jain structure of the twelfth century.

Chittaur was sacked three times: the first was in 1303, when Allauddin Khilji, a Moslem ruler, attempted to abduct the Rani Padmini, considered the most beautiful woman in the world. The women of Chittaur matched the courage of their men. When the battle on the field went against them, a funeral pyre was lit in a vault. The Rajput women, decked in their bridal robes, plunged into the flames, singing their way to death. When the last warrior had died "for the ashes of his fathers and the temples of his gods," all the conqueror found inside the city was a wisp of smoke rising from the vault.

The second sack was in 1535 by Sultan Bahadur Shah of Gujarat. Once more, the Rajputs, realizing an impending defeat, accepted death. After the queen mother arranged for the safe escape of her infant son, the future Maharana Udai Singh, she led the women into the furnace. Thousands of women died in the flames, while many more men were killed on the field. The third sack took place in 1567, this time at the hands of Akbar, the great Mogul. The two commanders, Jaimal and Patta, who led the defense of the fort, so impressed Akbar that he erected statues of them on elephants and had them set up at the entrance to his palace in Agra.

Kota—Bundi

Kota, Rajasthan's industrial center, is about 184 kilometers (114 miles) northeast of Chittorgarh. Former capital of Kota state, the city is on the right bank of the Chambal River, with an imposing fort standing sentinel over the valley. Inside you can visit the old palace, which now contains the Maharana Madho Singh Museum, with an exquisite collection of Rajput miniatures of the Kota school, sculptures, frescoes, and superb antiques.

North of Kota is Bundi, embedded in a narrow and picturesque gorge, where time moves at a slower pace and history itself seems to have lingered. The old city is enclosed in huge walls, fortified by four gateways. The Chittar Mahal (Palace of Towers), set atop a hill, consists of acres of stone-built structures, one opening out from another. Gardens galore rise up in terraces on the hillside. The palace is covered with spy holes and mysterious foliage-shrouded windows. Even the garden terraces have trapdoors under your feet that presumably served as dungeons in less peaceful times. Shields, swords, and daggers hang on the walls, as well as the martial family portraits of men with inordinately long mustaches brushed up to fall back like cat's whiskers. Those glory days have passed. But within the charming walkable city, you still find hints of those former times, when Rudyard Kipling stayed at Bundi, while tigers lurked in the nearby forests, and crocodiles teemed in the Mej River.

Since those days, a new palace, the Phool Sagar, has been constructed on the lakeside, still in Rajput style with banquet rooms and halls decorated with hunting trophies. And, in the streets of old lovely Bundi, Rajput men with bright turbans and Rajput women, their multicolored skirts flashing in the sun, crowd the dusty roads. With shiny pots on their heads and a child in their arms, they sail by with a smile, accompanied by the jingle of their jewelry.

Before you leave Rajasthan, head back toward Jaipur, by way of Ajmer and Pushkar, northwest of Bundi.

Ajmer and Pushkar

Situated at the foot of a hill, Ajmer is an ancient city (founded in the seventh century) and an important place of pilgrimage for Moslems—a curious anomaly in the land of Hindu Rajputs, an anomaly that also explains its stormy past. The Hindu Chauhans who created Ajmer remained in power until the late twelfth century, when Mohammed Ghori grabbed the city for himself. Then Ajmer changed hands repeatedly. In 1556, it was annexed by Akbar, who made it his royal residence, building the fort that still dominates the city. From here, he could command the main routes from the north. Ajmer also served as his key to the conquest of Rajputana and Gujarat. After the death of the great Moslem saint, Khwaja Muin-ud-Din Chisti, who preached here in the thirteenth century, a tomb, Dargah, was created in his honor. During his reign, Akbar visited once a year and supposedly walked from Agra to the saint's mausoleum, a distance of about 322 kilometers (200 miles). Frequented later by Shah Jahan, it owes its beautiful marble pavilions to his tender care.

All year long, and especially in January during the six-day Urs Mela celebration, this tomb draws Moslems from all over India and Pakistan. Even the Mogul Emperor Akbar made the journey many times. Today, as you walk up the bazaar to the holy site, you feel the emotional intensity as throngs press forward, carrying gifts. Inside the religious complex, Moslems throw money and food into two large caldrons placed on platforms. Each day the money is removed and the food is cooked and served to the people who congregate in the surrounding courtyards.

Close to Ajmer, at the foot of Taragarh Hill, stands a rare specimen of architecture, Adhai-din-Ka-Jhonpra, a mosque supposedly built in 2½ days by Mohammed Ghori on the former site of 30 Hindu temples. James Tod, in his standard work of 100 years back, waxed eloquent about its "gorgeous prodigality of ornament, richness of tracery, delicate sharpness of finish, laborious accuracy of workmanship." Two short minarets with inscriptions were added later.

Ajmer also has a refreshing artificial lake, Anasagar, created in the first half of the twelfth century by the Rajput King Anaji, who raised a vast embankment between two hills. The Mogul emperors were so entranced by this landscape that one after another, they embellished it with gardens, a long parapet, and five elegant pavilions of polished white marble created by Shah Jahan.

Pushkar lies a few kilometers north of Ajmer. Here, during Kartik Poornima (October or November) vast crowds of devout Hindus and tourists assembly at the water's edge where the devout take a ritual dip. This religious festival is also the occasion for a lively camel market, which turns Pushkar into a festive city. According to sacred scripts, Brahma—first of the Hindu trinity—on passing this place let a lotus flower slip from his hand. Water sprang from the spot where the petals fell. The lake was formed and called Pushkar, which means lotus. Many ashrams and temples surround the holy lake—one of them dedicated to Brahma.

PRACTICAL INFORMATION FOR RAJASTHAN

WHEN TO GO. The tourist season runs from September to April when temperatures are in the 80s in daytime and in the 60s at night—ideal weather, thanks to the absence of dampness. But Rajasthan is probably at its best during the monsoon (July–September) when the mountains and hills are covered with greenery and there's plenty of water in the lakes. Rainfall is light—from 12 to 24 inches per year, depending on the region. In the hot season, from the end of March to July, temperatures can rise above 100° F.

HOW TO GET THERE. By Air. Daily *Indian Airlines* flights operate from Delhi, Bombay, and Aurangabad to Jaipur, Jodhpur, and Udaipur. Indian Airlines also has a daily flight from Ahmedabad (Gujarat) to Jaipur and Jodhpur. *Vayudoot* has weekly flights that connect Delhi with Jaipur, Bikaner, Jodhpur, Kota, and Jaisalmer.

By Bus. Daily buses to Jaipur from Delhi are clean, cheap, and fast. In Delhi, call for details; *Rajasthan Roadways* (tel. 2522246). From Jaipur you can get deluxe buses to nearby states. Call Central Bus Station, tel. 75834 or tel. 66579. This is also true in Udaipur; tel. 27191 for details.

By Rented Car with Driver. Good roads connect Jaipur with Delhi and Agra. Car rental with driver costs about Rs. 3 per km, plus night halt charges (Rs. 50 per night).

By Train. From Delhi, the daily *Pink City Express* (five hours, Delhi–Jaipur) enables you to visit the city within a day, which is not enough time and only recommended to those who have no alternative. Other trains are the *Ahmedabad Express* in the morning, the *Chetak Express* later in the morning (each takes 22 hours to Udaipur), and the *Ahmedabad Mail* at night, which gets to Jaipur after dawn and to Abu Road (for Mount Abu) at teatime. The *Jodhpur Mail* covers the distance from Delhi in 17 hours and the *Bikaner Mail* in 12 hours. From Bombay, there are excellent trains that stop at Kota, Sawai Madhopur, and Ahmedabad. In Rajasthan, there are good rail connections throughout the state. For tickets and information in Delhi, contact the *International Tourist Guide,* New Delhi Railway Station, Platform No. 1; open 10 A.M.–5 P.M. (closed Sun.); tel. 3352164. In Jaipur, tel. 72121.

TOURIST INFORMATION. The *Government of India Tourist Office* in Jaipur and the *Rajasthan Tourist Offices* throughout the state have excellent brochures on cities and special interests (wildlife, crafts), with comprehensive information and maps. The Government of India Tourist Office (State Hotel, tel. 72200) is open Monday–Friday, 9 A.M.–6 P.M., and Saturday till 2 P.M. The Rajasthan Tourist Offices are open 10 A.M.–5 P.M., closed Sunday. They are located in the following destinations:

Ajmer. Khadim Tourist Bungalow, Savitri Girls College Rd.; tel. 21626.
Alwar. *Information Center,* Near Purjan Vihar Garden; tel. 3863.
Amber. Near elephant stand; tel. 40764.
Bharatpur. Circuit House, Agra Rd.; tel. 2340.
Bikaner. Junagarh Fort; tel. 5445.
Bundi. Near Collectorate; tel. 301.
Chittorgarh. Janta Avas Grih; tel. 9
Jaipur. Railway Station, tel. 69714 (open 6 A.M.–8 P.M. daily); Central Bus Stand, Sindhi Camp (no phone); 100 Jawaharlal Nehru Marg, tel. 73873.
Jaisalmer. Moomal Tourist Bungalow, tel. 2392.
Jodhpur. Ghoomar Tourist Bungalow, High Court Rd. tel. 25183.
Kota. Chambal Tourist Bungalow, tel. 26527.
Mount Abu. Opposite Bus Stand, tel. 51.
Sawai Modhopur. Project Tiger, Castle Jhoomar Baori; tel. 223.
Udaipur. Kajri Tourist Bungalow, Shastri Circle, tel. 2605; Dabok Airport; Counter at Railway Station.

FOREIGN CURRENCY EXCHANGE. Most Western-style hotels have money-exchange counters. Otherwise, a branch of the *State Bank of India* is open Monday–Friday, 10 A.M.–2 P.M.; Saturday till noon. In Jaipur, the *State Bank of Bikaner and Jaipur* (M.I. Rd., opposite G.P.O.) is open Monday–Friday 2:30–6:30 P.M.

ACCOMMODATIONS. Spending a night in Rajasthan frequently conjures up an interlude in a former raja palace. Sometimes the old castles/hunting lodges are great; sometimes they're a great disappointment, with character exchanged for amenities and a modern decor; and at an awful cost—both in terms of what is lost and what it costs to stay there. Nonetheless, *Rajasthan Tourism Development Corporation* (RTDC), a state-run organization, provides a good range of facilities to meet every budget. Prices are based on double occupancy and don't include taxes: *Deluxe,* over Rs. 1,450; *Expensive,* Rs. 950–Rs. 1,450; *Moderate,* Rs. 500–Rs. 950; *Inexpensive,* under Rs. 500.

AJMER-PUSHKAR

Moderate

Hotel Mansingh Palace. Vaishali Nagar, Ajmer; tel. 30855. 60 rooms with bath. This new hotel, on the edge of Anasagar Lake, is designed to resemble a Rajput fortress, with sandy-brown exterior and parapets. Air-conditioned rooms have marble floors, an attractive contemporary decor, and TV. Room service, multicuisine restaurant, bar, foreign-exchange counter, shops, and cultural entertainment on request. A swimming pool is planned. AE, DC, MC, V.

Inexpensive

Khadim Tourist Bungalow. Savatri Girls College Rd., Ajmer; tel. 20490. This two-story RTDC bungalow, with interior courtyard, offers clean, modestly furnished Western-style rooms. Some rooms are air-conditioned; all have fans. Room service, multicuisine restaurant, bar, tourist office, shop. Rupees only.

Sarovar Tourist Bungalow. Pushkar; tel. 40. 38 rooms with bath. Set on the banks of Sarovar Lake, this lovely older RTDC bungalow has pleasant grounds and simple, clean rooms with an institutional decor. Best rooms are air-conditioned and have balconies overlooking the lake or garden. All rooms have fans. Vegetarian Continental- and Indian-cuisine restaurant and room service. Rupees only.

During the Pushkar Festival, RTDC constructs a memorable tented tourist village in the *mela* (fairground). Accommodations are ordinary and deluxe tents, Rs. 580–Rs. 635, including vegetarian meals. Fair is held around November (see *Seasonal Events*). Book your tent well in advance through Central Reservation Office, Rajasthan Tourism Development Corporation, Ltd.; Chanderlok Building, 36 Jan Path, New Delhi, 110001 or through your travel agent.

ALWAR
(All three facilities listed here are near Siliserh Lake or in or near Sariska Tiger Preserve)

Expensive

Taj Ramgarh Lodge. Jamuva Ramgarh, Alwar; tel. 75141. Nine rooms with bath. This attractive two-story retreat overlooks Ramgarh Lake and is 30 km (19 mi.) from Sariska. Rooms have a modern decor. Indian- and Continental-cuisine restaurant, room service, car-rental service, tennis, billiards. Meals included. AE, DC, MC, V.

Moderate

Sariska Palace Hotel. Sariska District, Alwar; tel. 22. 31 rooms with bath. This former palace and royal hunting lodge on the edge of the Sariska Tiger Preserve has a rustic, old-time ambience. Bedrooms and suites are gigantic and clean. Public rooms still evoke the past—wicker chairs and bits of Victoriana. Some air-conditioned rooms, room service, Indian- and Continental-cuisine restaurant, foreign-exchange counter, doctor, jeep safaris. AE, DC.

Inexpensive

Lake Palace Hotel. Siliserh; tel. 22991. 10 rooms with bath. Set on a hill overlooking Silisar Lake, this former palace, now a RTDC hotel, looks palatial and has stunning views. Rooms, however, are modest with a simple, Western-style decor. Spacious air-cooled rooms are best. Room service, multicuisine restaurant, bar, boating. Rupees only.

BHARATPUR

Inexpensive

Bharatpur Forest Lodge. Bharatpur; tel. 2260. 17 rooms with bath. Set in the bird santcuary, this modest Ashok bungalow offers clean, comfortable rooms, some with decorative interior swings and air-conditioning. All rooms have balconies. Indian- and Continental-cuisine restaurant, room service, foreign-exchange counter, boating, doctor. Off-season discount April–September. AE, DC, MC, V.

BIKANER—GAJNER

Moderate

Gajner Palace Hotel. Gajner Wildlife Sanctuary. Reservations: Lallgarh Palace; tel. 3263. 18 rooms with bath. This quiet hotel, the former hunting lodge of a maharajah, is set on a lovely lake and has a Victorian ambience. Bedrooms are spacious, with simple period decor. Room service, Indian- and Continental-cuisine restaurant, boating. Rupees only.

Lallgarh Palace Hotel. Bikaner; tel. 3263. 34 rooms with bath. This red sandstone turn-of-the-century former palace of the Bikaner Maharajah is right in the city. Palatial-sized rooms have a simple decor with period furnishings. Rooms are either air-conditioned or air-cooled. Indian- and Continental-cuisine restaurant, room service, billiards, swimming pool; Rajasthani cultural programs on request. Rupees only.

CHITTORGARH

Inexpensive

Hotel Padmini. Chanderiya Rd., near Sainik School, Chittorgarh; no phone yet. 16 rooms with bath. This new Western-style hotel, with a spacious marble lobby, is set by a river. Modest bedrooms have a contemporary decor. Some rooms are air-conditioned. Amenities include Continental- and Indian-cuisine restaurant and room service. Rupees only.

JAIPUR

Expensive

Hotel Mansingh. Sansar Chandra Rd., Jaipur; tel. 78771. 100 rooms with bath. This six-story Western-style hotel has an attractive lobby and well-appointed modern bedrooms with air-conditioning and TV. Room service, multicuisine restaurants, bar, travel agency, foreign-exchange counter, doctor, shopping arcade. AE, DC, MC, V.

Taj Jai Mahal Palace. Jacob Rd., Civil Lines, Jaipur; tel. 73215. 102 rooms with bath. A former palace, the Taj Jai has a white-marble exterior and its grounds are Rajasthani regal. Rooms, however, are modern, with a distinct Western touch, with air-conditioning and TV. Room service, multicuisine restaurants, bar, cultural shows, doctor, travel agency, foreign-exchange counter, shopping arcade. AE, DC, MC, V.

Taj Rambagh Palace. Bhawani Singh Rd., Jaipur; tel. 75141. 105 rooms with bath. Jaipur's most famous palace hotel is classy, right down to the peacocks that strut across its perfect lawns. If you want a regal ambience, request a bedroom in the original palace. You'll be surrounded by original furnishings. The new wing is done up in a contemporary decor. Amenities include TV, air-conditioning, room service, multicuisine restaurants, bar, swimming pool, health club, tennis, foreign-exchange counter, travel agency, baby-sitters, cultural entertainment, astrologer, shopping arcade. AE, DC, MC, V.

Moderate

Hotel Clarks Amer. Jawaharlal Nehru Marg, Box 222, Jaipur; tel. 822616. 118 rooms with bath. This seven-story high rise on the outskirts of Jaipur has rooms with an unassuming modern decor. TV, air-conditioning, room service, multicuisine restaurants, bar, swimming pool, cultural shows, mini-coach shuttle to Jaipur, foreign-exchange counter, travel agency, shopping arcade. AE, DC, MC, V.

Hotel Jaipur Ashok. Jai Singh Circle, Bani Park, Jaipur; tel. 75121. 63 rooms with bath. The hotel's exterior is delightful—red sandstone and marble covered with vine. Rooms are clean, but less appealing, with simple modern furnishings, TV, and air-conditioning. Room service, multicuisine restaurants, bar, doctor, swimming pool, travel agency, foreign-exchange counter, shopping arcade. AE, DC, MC, V.

Hotel Meru Palace. Sawai Ram Singh Rd., Jaipur; tel. 61212. 48 rooms with bath. This modern marble high rise has modestly decorated, clean rooms with air-conditioning and small balconies. Some rooms have TV. Multicuisine restaurants, room service, bar, doctor, car-rental service, foreign-exchange counter, shops. AE, DC, MC, V.

Samode Palace. Samode, District Jaipur; tel. 34 or, in Jaipur, 42407. 25 rooms with bath. Set on a bluff at the end of a golden-hued village (45 km [28 mi.] from Jaipur), this summer palace of Jaipur's former maharajah is idyllic. Though the towering structure is lavish, with painted walls and carved marblework, bedrooms are simple and have original Victorian furnishings. Suites are best, with lots of maharajah mementos. Room service, Indian- and Continental-cuisine restaurant, bar, occasional cultural performances. In the area, expect more peacocks, doves, and monkeys than people. Rupees only.

Inexpensive

Atithi Guest House. 1 Park House Scheme (opposite All India Radio), Jaipur; tel. 78679. 9 rooms with bath. This newish Rajasthani home with a tiny garden offers clean, no-frill, fan-cooled rooms, with excellent hospitality. A restaurant is planned. Rupees only.

Gangour Tourist Bungalow. M.I. Rd., Jaipur; tel. 60231. 63 rooms with bath. This two-story RTDC bungalow has clean rooms with an institutional decor; best rooms are air-conditioned and more spacious. Room service, 24-hour multicuisine restaurant, pleasant gardens, foreign-exchange counter, RTDC office for car rentals and tours. Rupees only.

Narain Niwas Palace Hotel. Kanota Bagh, Narain Singh Rd., Jaipur; tel. 65448. 22 rooms with bath. Time stands still in this modest, former palace. Public rooms and higher-priced bedrooms (still inexpensive) are charming, with fabulous objets d'art, mementos, portraits, wall frescoes, and eccentric Victoriana. The less-interesting standard rooms and garden-cottage rooms have simple furnishings. Air-coolers, room service, multicuisine restaurant, attractive lawns, swimming pool, doctor, car-rental service, foreign-exchange counter, shops. AE, DC, MC, V.

JAISALMER

Moderate

Narayan Niwas Palace. Near Malka Prol, Jaisalmer; tel. 2408. 38 rooms with bath. A former caravansary, this appealing hotel offers perfect rooms for a desert city—unassumingly modern, air-cooled, and comfortable. Its interior courtyard has the appeal of a modest oasis. Included are room service, multicuisine restaurant, bar, roof garden, travel agency, foreign-exchange counter, doctor, shops, and camel safari and trekking arrangements. AE, DC, MC, V.

Inexpensive

Moomal Tourist Bungalow. Jaisalmer; tel. 2392. 50 rooms with bath. This RTDC two-story bungalow is modest, but rooms are clean and some are air-conditioned. Multicuisine restaurant, bar, tourist department. Rupees only.

JODHPUR

Expensive–Deluxe

Welcomgroup Umaid Bhawan Palace. Jodhpur; tel. 22316. 66 rooms with bath. This turn-of-the-century pink sandstone palace-hotel, which is still the home of Jodhpur's former Maharajah, is an architectural dream that dominates the landscape. While the exterior, public rooms, and grounds are lavish, many bedrooms are simple and have modest decor. You have to splurge for a deluxe-priced suite to be surrounded by original furnishings and a regal ambience. Also ask for air-conditioning. There are multicuisine restaurants, room service, bar, indoor swimming pool, health club, tennis, billiards, golf, foreign-exchange counter, travel agency, doctor, shops, museum, and village safari and camel rides on request. Hotel guests can also arrange for an overnight train trip to Jaisalmer in the Maharajah's private saloon car. AE, DC, MC, V.

Moderate

Ajit Bhawan Palace. Near Circuit House, Jodhpur, Rajasthan; tel. 20409. 50 rooms with bath. If you want an abundance of charm and less regal display, stay in this enchanting smaller palace and village complex, designed and owned by the Maharajah's younger brother. Each bungalow is decorated in its own Rajasthani motif. The grounds are delightful. Multicuisine restaurant, bar, foreign-exchange counter, travel agency, doctor, shops, cycling, horseback riding, and village jeep tour arrangements. AE, DC, MC, V.

Hotel Ratanda. Residency Rd., Jodhpur; tel. 25910. 50 rooms with bath. This modern Western-style hotel has no regal charm; but it offers good service and decent air-conditioned rooms with a contemporary decor. Multicuisine restaurants, bar, swimming pool, tennis, foreign-exchange counter, shopping arcade. AE, DC, MC, V.

KHIMSAR

Moderate–Expensive

Welcomgroup Royal Palace. Box Khimsar, District Nagaur, Khimsar; tel. 28. 14 rooms with bath. This great escape hotel is set in a fifteenth-century palace. Best rooms have furnishings from the 1920s. Multicuisine restaurant, room service, barbecue, sightseeing, desert tour, camel safari arrangements. AE, DC, MC, V.

KOTA

Moderate

Briraj Bhawan Palace Hotel. Civil Lines, Kota; tel. 23071. 7 rooms with bath. Don't expect a posh palace; but do expect gracious service here. You stay in a sprawling Victorian home filled with mementos of the former maharajah. The drawing room and dining room are especially quaint. Bedrooms are old-fashioned and simple. There is room service from a fixed-menu Indian and Continental restaurant. Rupees only.

MOUNT ABU

Inexpensive–Moderate

Palace Hotel. Bikaner House, Delwara Rd., Mount Abu; tel. 21. 33 rooms with bath. This former summer palace of the Bikaner Maharajah is palatial in size but modest in decor. Photos and simple Victorian furnishings adorn public rooms. Everything is immaculate, with modernization kept to a minimum. The management treats you with care. Suites (moderate) are gigantic; doubles (inexpensive) are large. All bedrooms have unpretentious original furnishings. Room service, fixed-menu Indian and Continental restaurant, billiards, tennis courts, spacious lawns, pony rides arranged on request, foreign-exchange counter. AE, DC, MC, V.

Inexpensive

Hotel Hillock. Opposite Petrol Pump, Mount Abu; tel. 367. 33 rooms with bath. This new multi-story modern hotel has lots of marble in the lobby and bedrooms with contemporary decor. It feels out of place, however, in this little hill station. Multicuisine restaurant, room service, bar, foreign-exchange counter, doctor. AE, DC, MC, V.

Hotel Hilltone. Box 18, Mount Abu; tel. 137. 42 rooms with bath. This Western-style, rambling hotel has a cozy lobby and pleasant gardens. Bedrooms are simply decorated and clean. Cottage suites offer good privacy. Multicuisine restaurant, room service, bar, doctor, swimming pool, health club, shop, foreign-exchange counter. AE, DC, MC, V.

SAWAI MADHOPUR

Moderate

Taj Sawai Madhopur Lodge. Ranthambhor National Park Rd., Sawai Madhopur; tel. 2541. 16 rooms with bath. The former hunting lodge of the Jaipur Maharajah, this pleasant bungalow is set in beautiful gardens about 25 km (16 mi.) from the national park. Attractive rooms have a contemporary decor. Some rooms are air-conditioned. Indian- and Continental-cuisine restaurant, room service, swimming pool, car-rental service. AE, DC, MC, V.

Inexpensive

Castle Jhoomer Baori. Sawai Madhopur; tel. 2495. 12 rooms with bath. This former maharajah's hunting lodge, now an RTDC hotel, is inside Ranthambhor National Park. Don't expect palatial decor; rooms are clean and functional. Room service, multicuisine restaurant, bar, jungle safaris. Rupees only.

SHEKHAVATI AREA

Moderate–Expensive

Castle Mandawa. Mandawa, District Jhunjhunu; tel. 24. 40 rooms with bath. This eighteenth-century castle, now a popular hotel, is still owned by the descendants of the local *thakur* (king). All rooms are different and have period furniture. The suites and some rooms are opulent and spacious. There is an Indian- and Continental-cuisine restaurant; room service; bar; doctor; gift shop; camel, horse, and jeep safari arrangements; cultural shows. AE, DC, MC, V.

Moderate

Dera Dundlod Kila. Dundlod, District Jhunjhunu; tel. 98. Reservations: Dundlod House, Civil Lines, Jaipur; tel. 66276. 15 rooms with bath. This eighteenth-century castle, still owned by the descendants of the former thakur, has a stunning *Diwan-e-Khas* (public room), with original wall frescoes and Louis XIVth furniture. Fastidiously clean bedrooms have painted walls; but they're not opulent. A suite is also available. Under great management, amenities include room service; Continental- and Indian-cuisine restaurant; limited bar; nearby swimming; doctor; palmist; and jeep, horse, and camel safari arrangements. Rupees only.

Desert Camp. c/o Castle Mandawa; tel. 24. 18 cottages with bath. Set on a hill and modeled after a typical Rajasthani village, this terrific camp features clay and brick huts with delightful exterior paintings and thatched roofs. Interiors, with stone floors, are impeccably clean, with an appealing modern-ethnic decor. Indian-and Continental-cuisine restaurant; room service; limited bar; doctor; foreign-exchange counter; swimming pool; cultural shows; and camel, horse, and jeep safari arrangements. AE, DC, MC, V.

Roop Niwas Palace. Nawalgarh, District Jhunjhunu, Shekhavati; tel. 8 or, in Jaipur, 62987. 20 rooms with bath. A mix of Rajput and European architecture, this former palace is on the outskirts of one of the most interesting Shekhavati villages. While the hotel is far from grand, the owners—descendants of the former thakur—aim to please. Rooms are modest but clean, and the grounds are lovely. Room service, Indian- and Continental-cuisine restaurant, limited bar, doctor, billiards, swimming pool, cultural programs, and safaris arrangements. Rupees only.

UDAIPUR

Deluxe

Taj Lake Palace Hotel. Pichola Lake, Udaipur; tel. 23241. 80 rooms with bath. This famous 250-year-old marble palace sits like a vision in Pichola Lake. Interior public rooms are elegant. Spacious bed-sitting-rooms (the most costly) have lake views; less grand "superior" bedrooms, some with balconies, also offer lake views. Some of the "ordinary" rooms (least costly) have views of the lily pond or courtyard. All rooms have a contemporary decor, air-conditioning, and TV. If you want palatial furnishings, splurge on a suite. Multicuisine restaurants, room service, bar, foreign-exchange counter, travel agency, shopping arcade, small swimming pool, cultural programs, and horseback riding and boating arrangements. Reserve well in advance. AE, DC, MC, V.

Moderate–Deluxe

Shivniwas Palace. City Palace, Udaipur; tel. 28239. 31 rooms with bath. This former palace, part of the City Palace complex, is also the current home of the Udaipur Maharajah. It offers great privacy and excellent views of Pichola Lake. Air-conditioned rooms have a contemporary decor, but the sumptuous suites (deluxe price) have a regal appearance. Room service, multicuisine restaurant, swimming pool, tennis, billiards, boating, health club, foreign-exchange counter. AE, DC, MC, V.

Expensive

Laxmi Vilas Palace Hotel. Udaipur; tel. 24411. 54 rooms with bath. An old-time aura is evident at this former palace, on a hill overlooking Fateh Sager Lake. The restaurant and bar recall the British Raj, with Victorian furniture, mounted tiger skins, and old carpets. Rooms are a bit worn, but they're clean and comfortable with air-conditioning and TV. Ask for one with a lake view. Room service, multicuisine restaurant, bar, doctor, foreign-exchange counter, shopping arcade. AE, DC, MC, V.

Hotel Shikarbadi. Goverdhad Vilas, Udaipur; tel. 83200. Just outside the city, this former hunting lodge of the Udaipur royal family is a lovely rustic retreat. Air-conditioned rooms are attractive with tiled ceilings and stone walls. Deer and monkeys come nearly to the door. Multicuisine restaurant, room service, bar, swimming pool, horseback riding. AE, DC, MC, V.

Inexpensive

Lake Pichola Hotel. Outside Chandpole, Udaipur; tel. 29197. 20 rooms with bath. This lovely old palace on the banks of the lake has a pleasant old-time ambience and charming Rajasthani decor in its modest bedrooms. All rooms have marble balconies with a lake view. Room service, multicuisine restaurant, bar, car-rental service, foreign-exchange counter, puppet show, boating. Good value. AE, MC, V.

Circuit Houses. Circuit Houses are often attractive lodges—pleasantly furnished with a turn-of-the-century feel if not decor. They're also usually inexpensive (about Rs. 200 per double). Unfortunately, but perhaps appropriately, Indian government VIPs get first preference. Check on arrival to see if there's a vacancy or write in advance to: *Deputy Secretary, Circuit House Reservations,* General Administration Department, Secretariate, Jaipur, Rajasthan. Some good circuit houses are in Ajmer, Alwar, Bikaner, Bundi, Chittorgarh, Jodhpur, Kota, and Mount Abu.

DINING OUT. In Rajasthan, you can explore Indian vegetarian dining—*thalis, domas, paneer* (cheese), butter *masalas,* and other exotic dishes. You can also find a nonvegetarian, Indian, Continental, or Chinese meal—at least in the bigger cities or at hotels. While we include only the best options, most accommodations listed above also have restaurants. Breakfast is usually 8–10:30; lunch, noon–3; dinner, 7:30–10. Payment is normally in rupees unless the restaurant is connected to a Western-style hotel. The restaurants listed below are informal and, unless noted, are open for all three meals and don't require reservations. Prices, based on one person eating a three-course meal, excluding taxes, tip, or beverage, are: *Deluxe,* over Rs. 120; *Expensive,* Rs. 80–Rs. 120; *Moderate,* Rs. 40–Rs. 80; *Inexpensive,* under Rs. 40.

AJMER-PUSHKAR

Due to Pushkar's religious sanctity, all Pushkar restaurants serve vegetarian cuisine and alcohol is prohibited.

Moderate

Sheesh Mahal. Hotel Mansingh Palace, Vaishali Nagar, Ajmer; tel. 30855. Influenced by Mogul architecture, this handsome restaurant, has delicately mirrored ceilings and white walls with inset arches. The chef serves Continental and especially good Mughlai dishes. Try *murgh tikka masala* (spicy boneless chicken) or *macchhi chutneywali* (marinated pomfret cooked in the tandoor). There are live Indian *ghazels* (musicians) at night. Dinner reservations advised. Open 6:30–10 A.M., 12:30–3 P.M., and 7:30–11 P.M. AE, DC, MC, V.

Inexpensive

R.S. Restaurant. Shri Brahma Temple, Pushkar; no phone. This delightful, open-air restaurant serves good vegetarian Indian and Continental dishes. Open 7 A.M.–10 P.M. Rupees only.

Sobhraj Restaurant. Near the Delhi Gate, Ajmer; tel. 20640. This restaurant, set in Ajmer's oldest hotel, provides a quiet escape from the crowded bazaar. Tables have linen, and ceiling fans whir overhead. Choose from Indian or Continental cuisine. Open 7 A.M.–10:30 P.M. Rupees only.

Sun Set Cafe. Next to the Sarovar Tourist Bungalow, Pushkar; no phone. This open-air restaurant, on a lawn facing the lake, serves good Chinese, Continental, and Indian vegetarian fare. Open 6 A.M.–11 P.M. Rupees only.

JAIPUR

Deluxe

Suvarna Mahal. Rambagh Palace, Bhawani Singh Rd.; tel. 75141. Once the Maharajah's royal banquet hall, this stunning room has handsome drapes, tapestry-covered walls, and high, painted ceilings. Live Indian music is performed at lunch and in the evening. You can choose from Continental and Indian cuisines, including regional dishes such as *safed mans Jaipuri* (rich lamb curry with cashew paste) or *murg mokul* (shredded spicy chicken). Dinner reservations advised. Open 6–9 A.M., 12:30–2:30 P.M.; 7:30–10:30 P.M. AE, DC, MC, V.

Expensive

Shivir. Mansingh Hotel, Sansar Chandra Rd.; tel. 78771. Jaipur's only rooftop restaurant offers a city view, live Indian music at lunch and dinner, and a subdued modern decor. The menu features Continental and Indian cuisine, with the popular choice Mughlai or tandoori specialties. Dinner reservations advised. Open 12:30–2:30 P.M. and 7:30–11:30 P.M. AE, DC, MC, V.

Moderate

Chanakya. M.I. Rd.; tel. 78461. Subdued lighting, table linen, and taped Indian classical music create an appealing ambience in which to enjoy terrific vegetarian meals: Indian, Continental, Chinese. Start with *jal jeera,* an unusual spicy beverage. Follow it with the Chanakya special (a tasty mixture of dried fruits, cottage cheese, vegetables, and spices, topped with edible pure silver) or the Rajasthani special called *gatta* (a spicy dish of gram flour rolled in herbs and spices and cooked in tasty tomato sauce). You can also eat in their new upstairs restaurant, **Kautilya,** directly next door, which has the same menu and hours. Open noon–11 P.M. AE, MC, V.

Golden Sand. 4 Sansar Chandra Rd., opposite Amber Cinema; tel. 70531. This new restaurant, with soft lighting and lattice trim, has a relaxed ambience. The chef serves good Chinese, Continental, and Indian cuisines. Try the tandoori items: good *tangri kebab* (chicken drumsticks) or *seekh kebab* (rolled minced mutton). Dinner reservations advised. Open noon–3:30 P.M. and 6–11 P.M. AE, MC, V.

Niros. M.I. Rd.; tel. 74493. A Jaipur institution, with marble floors and handsome mirrors set into the walls, Niros serves the best non-vegetarian Chinese, Continental, and Indian dishes in town. It also has reliably good vegetarian fare. Specialties include the yummy *rashmi kebab* (skewered boned chicken), *panir tikka* (cottage cheese with skewered tomatoes, onions, and capsicum), or tasty mutton tikka masala. Dinner reservations advised. Open 10 A.M.–11:30 P.M. AE, DC, MC, V.

Inexpensive

Woodlands. Hotel Meru Palace, Sawai Ram Singh Rd.; tel. 61212. This cheery, lavishly marble restaurant is Mogul high-tech. Come here for good South Indian vegetarian dishes: *thalis* (assorted small dishes served on a metal platter), *dosas* (vegetable stuffed Indian crêpe), *idli* (steamed rice dumpling), and *vedas* (fried lentils). Open noon–10:30 P.M. Rupees only.

JODHPUR

Expensive

Marwar Hall. Umaid Bhawan Palace; tel. 22316. A gorgeous palace dining room, Marwar Hall has huge chandeliers hanging from its vaulted ceiling. The chef prepares very good Continental and Indian dishes, including tasty Mughlai and regional Marwari dishes. Dinner reservations advised. Open 8–10 A.M., 12:30–3 P.M., and 7:30–10:30 P.M. AE, DC, MC, V.

Inexpensive

Kalinga. Ardash Niwas Hotel, near Station Rd.; tel. 24066. This popular local restaurant offers good non-vegetarian cuisine, especially tasty Mughlai dishes. Open 8 A.M.–10 P.M. Rupees only.

MOUNT ABU

Moderate

Takshashila Restaurant. Near the taxi stand; tel. 73. This reliable restaurant, with mirrored walls and marble floors, draws a crowd. The chef serves good vegetarian Continental, Indian, and Chinese cuisines. Open 8–11:30 A.M., noon–3 P.M., and 7–10:30 P.M. Rupees only.

Inexpensive

Angan Dining Room. Near the taxi stand; tel. 73. With lots of green marble and a mirrored ceiling, this restaurant looks like an old-fashioned dining hall. It offers an excellent all-you-can-eat Gujarati thali. Come hungry! Open 11 A.M.–2:30 P.M., and 7–9:30 P.M. Rupees only.

Saraswati Hotel Restaurant. Opposite the taxi stand; tel. 7. Another popular all-you-can-eat Gujarati thali restaurant, it's extremely simple, with wooden tables and overhead fans. Food is delicious. Open 11 A.M.–1:30 P.M. and 6:30–8:30 P.M. Rupees only.

UDAIPUR

Deluxe

Neel Kamal. Lake Palace Hotel; tel. 23241. This handsome restaurant was scheduled for renovation in 1990. The menu continues to feature Continental and Indian cuisines, including Rajasthani specialties. Non-hotel guests must call in advance to see if they can be accommodated; the room is small. Open 12:30–2:30 P.M. and 7:30–10:30 P.M. AE, DC, MC, V.

Moderate

Berry's. Chetak Circle; tel. 25132. Udaipur's oldest and most popular restaurant was under renovation at press time. Expect a marble floor, a modern decor, and an extensive menu featuring Chinese, Continental, and Indian cuisines. Open 9 A.M.–11 P.M. AE, MC, V.

Heritage. Hospital Rd.; tel. 23368. This new restaurant, with taped Indian classical music and tapestry-covered and hand-carved chairs, is extremely appealing. The tasty cuisine is "nouvelle" Indian vegetarian, including delicious ice creams with no artificial ingredients. Try *makai masala* (fresh corn simmered in a creamy sauce) and *dum tarkari* (baked vegetables in creamy saffron and cardamom). Open 10:30 A.M.–10:30 P.M. Rupees only.

SWEETS AND TREATS. Jaipur. You can't beat the local ambience and vegetarian snacks and sweets at **LMB Hotel** at Johari Bazaar. Sample their delicious *chaat* (Indian potato salad) with *LMB Bahar* (a combo drink of fresh fruit juices). Also try their sweet Rasmalai special. Open 7 A.M.–11:30 P.M.

Jodhpur. Rawat Mishtan Bhandar on Station Road lives up to what its name means: "treasure trove of sweets." Also try their great beverages. Open 8 A.M.–10 P.M.

HOW TO GET AROUND. From the airports. At Jaipur, a taxi costs about Rs. 80 into the city. At Jodhpur, the taxi fare is about Rs. 100 into the city. At Udaipur, the taxi fare is Rs. 110 into the city.

How you decide to get from city to city within Rajasthan depends on your budget and your time. It's a big state with a lot of territory between major attractions.

By Bus. Good, inexpensive deluxe coach services connect most major cities. In Jaipur, call *Rajasthan Tourism Development Corporation* at Gangaur Tourist Bungalow (tel. 60239), or *India Tourism Development Corporation* at Rajasthan, the State Hotel (tel. 68461).

By Train. Trains are slower than the buses, but they will get you to most cities. In Jaipur, call 72121.

By Rented Car with Driver. Figure about Rs. 2.70 per km for an Ambassador with driver, plus Rs. 50 per night halt charges. With trips around Mount Abu, the cost is Rs. 3.80 per km. Hire a car with driver from a tour operator listed below.

By Taxi. Taxis are unmetered in Rajasthan and are available throughout the state. Rates are about Rs. 2.50 for the first km; Rs. 1.50 per additional km. Set the rate before you start.

By Auto Rickshaw. Rates are about Rs. 1.75 per km for this convenient way to get around any crowded city. Again, set the fare before you depart. You can also hire a rickshaw for four hours for about Rs. 100; bargain.

The following destinations offer additional alternatives.

BIKANER

By Auto Tonga (horse cart). Establish fares in advance. They're the cheapest way to get around and lots of fun.

JAIPUR

By Bike Rickshaw. This should be cheaper than an auto rickshaw; bargain. You can also hire a bike rickshaw for four hours for about Rs. 60.

JAISALMER

This is a walk-around town as far as the old city is concerned.

By Camel and Camel Cart. Lots of fun, but some discomfort. Call the tourist officer for details (tel. 106) or arrange for service through your hotel.

JODHPUR

By Bike Rickshaw and Horse Tonga. Fix the rate in advance. Bargain.

KOTA

By Bike Rickshaw. Cheap, but fix the fare in advance.

MOUNT ABU

By Tonga or Pony. Haggle, and set the fare in advance.

UDAIPUR

By Tonga. Set the fare in advance. Bargain.

TOURS. Contact the New Delhi office of the RTDC (Chandralok Building, 36 Janpath, tel. 3321820) for details on package tours by luxury bus or minibus from Delhi to Jaipur, Mount Abu, Udaipur, Pushkar, Shekhavati area, and some of Rajasthan's national parks. Travelers planning to visit Rajasthan between October and March should also consider taking the luxurious *Palace-on-Wheels* (week-long train excursion); see *Facts at Your Fingertips* (Traveling in India by Train) for details.

Within the state, RTDC offers the following reasonably priced tours, usually by bus. For complete details and reservations, contact the local tourist offices.

Bharatpur. Keoladeo Ghana Bird National Park. Tour operates on demand.

Chittorgarh. Fort, Meera Temple, Victory Tower, Padmini Palace, Rana Kumbha Palace. Time: 8 A.M.–noon; 2–6 P.M.

Jaipur. Five-hour tour (starting at 8 A.M., 11:30 A.M., and 1:30 P.M.) of Hawa Mahal, City Palace, Observatory, Amber Fort, and Palace, Central Museum, Nawab Sahab Ki Haveli.

Full-day tour of Hawa Mahal, City Palace, Museum, Observatory, Amber Fort and Palace, Central Museum, Sisodia Rani Garden, Doll Museum, Galta. Time: 9 A.M.–6 P.M. Car taxi tours are also available, as is a minibus. You can also book through the Tourist Information Bureau, Railway Station Platform No. 1; tel. 69714.

ITDC (tel. 68461) also offers a similar tour at 8 A.M.

Jaisalmer. Fort, Palace, Jain Temple, and Havelis.

Jodhpur. Umaid Bhawan Palace, Mandore Gardens, Mehrangarh Fort, Jaswant Thanda, Government Museum. Time: 9:30 A.M.–1 P.M.; 2–6:30 P.M.

Mount Abu. Nakki Lake, Delwara Temple, Achalgarh, Guru Shikhar. Time: 8 A.M.–1 P.M. Nakki Lake, Delwara Temple, Achalgarh, Guru Shikhar, Sunset Point (Arbuda Devi). Time: 2–7 P.M.

Udaipur. Five-hour tour (starting at 8 A.M.) of Aravali Vatika, Moti Magri, Lok Kala Mandal, City Palace, Jagdish Temple. Five-hour excursion tour (starting at 2 P.M.) to Haldi Ghati, Nathdwara, Eklinji Temple.

Guides are also available at most destinations. Contact the local tourist office. For one to four persons, figure about Rs. 35 for a half-day and Rs. 60 for a full day.

TOUR OPERATORS. For good tours and all your travel needs, including hired car with driver, contact *Rajasthan Tours.* Their head office is at Rambagh Palace Hotel, Jaipur, Rajasthan; tel. 66784. Open 9 A.M.–6 P.M. daily. They also have branches at Jodhpur, Jaisalmer, and Udaipur. You can also arrange for a car with driver through many of the hotels listed above and through RTDC. Also check *Facts at Your Fingertips* for tour operators who offer trips to Rajasthan.

SEASONAL EVENTS. Since the lunar calendar determines most dates, contact the Government of India Tourist Office before setting out for any event.

January. *Urs Mela.* For six days in Ajmer, Moslems flock to the tomb of their revered Saint Khwaja Muin-ud-Din Chisti to honor his death. *Desert Festival.* Jaisalmer's gala event includes traditional Rajasthani music; a display of desert handicrafts, camel caravans, camel races, and turban-tying competitions. Don't miss it if your Rajasthan trip is planned around this time. Book rooms well in advance.

January/February. *Baneshwar Fair.* During this solemn event, Bhil tribals immerse the ashes of their recently departed in a holy confluence of three rivers at Baneshwar (70 km south of Udaipur). Do not take photos. *Naguar Fair.* Nagaur (135 km [84 mi.] from Jodhpur) holds an enormous cattle, camel, and horse fair—a popular event with cultural programs and camel races.

February. *Hadoti Festival.* In Kota, musicians and dancers celebrate the Hadoti culture.

March. *Holi* or *Brij.* On the eve of this festival that heralds the arrival of spring, Rajasthanis have processions with music and dancing. Expect to be doused with colored water. Jaipur also holds an *Elephant Festival,* with richly dressed elephants paraded through the streets. *Gangaur Festival.* This festival in Udaipur and Jaipur honors the goddess Parvati, with festive processions of young girls and this deity, who is the symbol of marital bliss.

June. *Summer Festival.* Mount Abu celebrates the season with folk music and Rajasthani dance performances.

July/August. *Naag Panchami.* This festival in Jodhpur is dedicated to the 1,000-headed mythical serpent, Sesha. Huge cloth *naags* (cobras) are displayed in a festive fair. *Teej Festival.* This festival, dedicated to Parvati, celebrates the beginning of the monsoon. Rajasthani women take to swings hanging from trees and have swinging contests. Procession of the goddess Parvati involving elephants, camels, and dancers. A big event in Jaipur.

October/March. *Shilp Darshan Mela.* At a delightful complex in Udaipur, set up with typical village homes from Rajasthan, Gujarat, Goa, Maharashtra, and Madhya Pradesh, master craftsmen and women from these states show how they create award-winning handicrafts, which are also for sale. Dancers and musicians perform daily. Don't miss this wonderful on-going event.

October/November. *Pushkar Festival.* Rajasthan's amazing festive and religious event has a carnival atmosphere. Gaily festooned cattle and thousands of people gather for a sacred dip at dawn in the holy waters of the lake. Book a tent or room well in advance.

November. *Bikaner Festival.* During this festival in Bikaner, there is folk music and dance, culminating in a fire dance, with men jumping in and out of flames.

December. *Shekhavati Festival.* This festival highlights the old frescoes on Shekhavati's *havelis* (mansions) and celebrates the local arts, traditional music and dance, and cuisine. Another good event!

HISTORIC SITES. Entrance to most places is generally free; where a donation is asked, a few rupees will suffice. Most monuments and historic sites are open daily, sunrise to sunset, unless noted below.

AJMER-PUSHKAR

Adhai-Din-Ka-Jhonpra. In 1193 after Muhammed Ghori destroyed an ancient Sanskrit college and 30 Hindu temples, he construed this mosque of Indo-Islamic style on the temple ruins supposedly in 2½ days. The mosque stands on the pillars, each different, of these temples.

Anasagar. An artificial lake built in the twelfth century by Anaji Chauhan and added to by Jahangir. Shah Jahan built the *Baradari* (pavilions).

Dargah. Tomb of the Sufi saint Khwaja Muin-ud-Din Chisti (1142–1246). Here, Akbar sought the blessings of a son. Open sunrise until 10 A.M. and from 4 until about 7 P.M.

Nasiyan (Red Temple). Jain temple built in the nineteenth century with a two-story hall containing gilt representations of Jain mythology. Open 8 A.M.–4 P.M.

ALWAR

Alwar Fort. A medieval fort, in which Babur hid treasures for his son Humayun. Jahangir stayed here three years. The fort was eventually conquered by Maharajah Pratap Singh in 1775. Gigantic citadel towering on a hill; 15 large and 51 small towers with 446 holes for muskets. Several gates—Jai Pol, Suraj Pol, Laxman Pol, Chand Pol, Hrishan Pol, Andheri Gate. See the remains of Jai Mahal, Nikumbh Mahal, Salim Sagar Pond, Suraj Kund, and numerous temples. Great view of city.

Vinay Vilas Mahal (City Palace). Built in the late eighteenth century in a Rajput and Moghal blend of architecture. Behind the Vinay Vilas, you can see temples and a cenotaph of Maharajah Bakhtawar Singh built by Maharajah Vinay Singh in 1815. Unusual Bengali roof and arches.

BHARATPUR

Jawahar Burj. Old fort built in 1726 by Suraj Mal to commemorate his victories over the Moguls and later the British. Coronation ceremonies of Jat rulers of Bharatpur took place here.

Lohagarh Fort (Iron Fort). Designed in the early eighteenth century by Maharajah Suraj Mal, the founder of Bharatpur, the fort held off numerous British attacks. See Kishori Mahal, Mahal Khas, Kothi Khas. Open 9 A.M.–5 P.M.

Palace. A blend of Rajput and Mogul architecture. Magnificent apartments with beautifully designed floor tiles.

BIKANER AREA

Bhanda Sagar Jain Temple (five km from Bikaner). A sixteenth-century Jain temple, dedicated to the twenty-third Teerthankar Parsvanathji.

Devi Kund (eight km from Bikaner). Royal crematorium with a number of cenotaphs belonging to former rulers of the Bika dynasty. The *chhatri* of Maharajah Surat Singh is white marble with Rajput paintings adorning the ceiling.

Junagarh Fort. Built in the sixteenth century by Raja Raj Singh, an outstanding general of Mogul Emperor Akbar. Encircled by a moat with numerous red sandstone and marble palaces. Suraj Pol (Sun Gate) is the main entrance. Weddings and births were celebrated in Har Mandir (chapel). Numerous palaces are adorned with columns, arches, graceful screens. Open 10 A.M.–5 P.M.

Karni Mata Temple (in Deshnok, 33 km from Bikaner). Dedicated to Karni Mata, an incarnation of Durga. The rats that crawl around here are sacred. Maharajah Ganga Singh donated the massive silver gates.

Lalgarh Palace (Red Fort). Built by Maharaja Ganga Singh in the nineteenth century. Red sandstone with terrific carvings. In the banquet hall, see the collection of old photographs and trophies. Open 10 A.M.–5 P.M. (closed Wednesdays).

BUNDI

Chitter Mahal (Palace of Towers). Massive gates surround an enormous collection of stone buildings built by successive rulers starting in the 1600s. The palace is covered with spy holes and mysterious windows. Visit the Naubat Khana, the Hathi Pol (curious water clock which formerly struck each half hour), the Diwan-i-Am. Also see the Chitra Shala, built by Rao Rajah Shatroo Salji in the 1600s. Terrific Bundi mural paintings which adorn the walls and ceilings were added much later.

Naval Sagar, an artificial lake with a temple of Varuna (Aryan god of water) in the center.

Phool Sagar. A twentieth-century palace and present home of the Durbar (former ruler of Bundi). Also known as the Flower Palace, the magnificent home has banquet rooms, numerous halls, plus an intriguing collection of murals created by Italian prisoners of war. To visit, permission is required; call the secretary, tel. 1, 34.

Taragarh (Star Fort). Built in 1372, the fort with an enormous tank (originally the palace reservoir) provides a commanding view of Bundi.

CHITTORGARH

Chittorgarh Fort. Foundations attributed to the seventh century. Beyond the first gate, Padal Pol, a tablet, marks the spot where Prince Bagh Singh died during the second attack on Chittorgarh. Between the second gate (Bhairon Pol) and the third gate (Hanuman Pol) are two chattris (tombs) where Jaimal of Badnore and Kalla were killed by Akbar in 1567. Near the main gate (Ram Pol), there is another chhatri for Patta of Kelwa, a 15-year-old fighter who died here. The fort is seven miles in circumference and contains some great Rajput architecture. See the *Vijay Stambh* (Victory Tower), nine stories high, and covered with secular sculpture. Built by Maharana Jumbha to celebrate his victory over the Moslem rulers of Malwa and Gujarat in 1440. Kirti Stambh ("Tower of Fame"), built by a Jain merchant in the twelfth century and dedicated to Adinathji (the first of the Jain tirthankaras). The tower is covered with figures from a Jain pantheon. Padmini's Palace, supposedly for Queen Padmini, overlooks a pool. Within the walls, a battle occurred between Allauddin Khilji and Rana Ratan Singh, which ended with the death of Padmini. Meera and Kumbha Shyam Temple, built in the Indo-Aryan style and associated with the mystic poet-wife of Bhojraj, the eldest son of Rana Sanga. Kalika Mata Temple built initially in the eighth century as Surya (Sun Temple) and later converted into Kalika Mata, or a mother goddess temple, in the fourteenth century.

Nagari (14 km north of Chittorgarh). Ancient town that flourished from the Maurya to the Gupta era. Interesting archaeological sites with a distinct connection to Buddhism and Hinduism.

DEEG

Former summer resort of the rulers of Bharatpur (32 km from there). Numerous forts, palaces, and gardens. See *Ghopal Bhavan* and *Suraj Bhavan,* built of marble. Open 8 A.M.–noon; 1–6 P.M. Much of the beauty of these buildings was stolen from Mogul palaces in Agra and Delhi.

JAIPUR

Amber Palace and Fort (11 km from Jaipur). Construction begun by Maharajah Man Singh in early 1700s, completed 100 years later: an excellent blend of Rajput and Mogul influences. See the Hall of Victory, with panels of alabaster and inlay work; *Sheesh Mahal* (Hall of Mirrors)—step inside, close doors, strike a match—the ceiling glows. Rooms are small; typical of Mogul period. Courtyards and narrow passages: typical Rajput. Above the palace is the Jaigash Fort (supposedly still contains hidden treasures of Jaipur). Open: 9 A.M.–4:30 P.M.

City Palace and Museum. Begun by Sawai Jai Singh in the 1700s, with further additions by later maharajahs. Open: 9:30 A.M.–4:45 P.M.

Gaitor (eight km from Jaipur). Royal cenotaphs of kings at the foot of the Nahargarh hills. The cenotaph of Sawa Jai Singh II is of white marble, with intricate carvings over the dome, supported by 20 pillars. Other cenotaphs are for Madho Singh, Ram Singh, and Partap Singh.

Govind Devji Temple. Temple of Lord Krishna facing the City Temple complex. From here, you can get a good view of the City Palace, Chandra Mahal.

Hawa Mahal. (Palace of Winds). Built in 1799 by Maharajah Sawai Pratap Singh. Located on the Johari Bazaar heading north. A five-story building with a pyramidal facade. Overhanging windows with latticed screens, domes, spires. Open: 10 A.M.–5 P.M. Closed Fridays.

Juntar Mantar (Observatory). Built before the city of Jaipur in 1726. Located southeast of Chandra Mahal within the city palace complex. Largest and best preserved of the five astronomical observatories built by Sawai Jai Singh. Open: 9 A.M.–5 P.M.

Nahargarh Fort (15 km from Jaipur). Originally called Sudarshangarh Fort, it was built in 1734 by Sawai Jai Singh. The upper floor was constructed by Sawai Ram Singh II in 1868–69; more apartments were added in 1902–03 by Sawai Madho Singh II. Great view of Jaipur from here. Open: 10 A.M.–5 P.M.

Sisodia Palace and Garden (eight km from Jaipur). Built by Maharajah Sawai Jai Singh in 1770 for his queen, Sisodia. Central room with galleries on three sides surrounded by terraced gardens with fountains, pools, and sculpture.

JAISALMER

Citadel. Constructed by Rawal Jaisal in 1156 on Trikuta hill surrounded by high golden walls. Inside are Jain temples dedicated to Rikhabdevji and Sambhavnathji, constructed from the twelfth to the fifteenth century. Filled with deities and mythological carvings. *Gyan Bhandar* (library), part of the Jain temple complex, contains some of the oldest manuscripts in India.

Havelis: Salim Singh Ki Haveli built by Salim Singh in the seventeenth century. Narrow dimension from ground floor widens at the top, with balconies jutting out. In sad disrepair within; a courteous request (or a few rupees) should get you inside. *Nathmal Ki Haveli* built in the nineteenth century by two architect brothers. The structure is flanked by stone elephants. Look carefully, they are not identical—just harmoniously in tune. Again, a courteous request or a small donation may get you inside. *Patva Havelis*—a string of five havelis built by the Patva brothers. Two of the five are owned by the government and are open to the public (inquire at the tourist department for the times). Handsome carved pillars. Painted murals on some of the interior walls. The other three are accessible, with a small donation, if the owner is in the mood.

JODHPUR

Jaswant Thada. Royal crematorium built in 1899 for Maharajah Jaswant Sinbgh II near the Meherangarh Fort. A white marble structure housing the portraits of past rulers. Plus other cenotaphs, also in marble, to commemorate acts of bravery and generosity of successive rulers. Open: 8 A.M.–6 P.M.; 9 A.M.–5 P.M. (Nov. 1–Apr. 1).

Mahamandir Temple (two km from Jodhpur). Temple with 100 pillars. Richly ornamented with figures in various Yoga postures.

Meherangarh Fort. Overlooking Jodhpur and constructed by Rao Jodha in 1459. Seven gates lead into the fort. Numerous interior palaces and temples and an excellent museum. Open 6 A.M.–6 P.M.; 9 A.M.–5 P.M. (Nov. 1–Apr. 1).

Umaid Bhawan Palace. Built by Maharajah Umaid Singh 1929–42. Also known as *Chhitar Palace* because of the sandstone that was used.

KOTA AREA

Baroli (40 km from Kota). One of the oldest temple complexes in Rajasthan, constructed in the ninth century. Built in the Panchaytan (group of five) style, some still with rich carvings.

Jhalra Patan (60 km from Kota). "City of Bells," with the Jhalra patan, one of the best sun temples in India located within this ancient city. Also see old Jain temples, plus the ruins of Buddhist cave temples recently excavated.

MOUNT ABU

Adhar Devi Temple. Chiseled out of a rock, and dedicated to the goddess Durga.

Dilwara Jain Temples. Constructed from the eleventh to the thirteenth centuries. Open: noon to 6 P.M. for non-Jains.

RANAKPUR

Chanmukha. Jain temple constructed in the fifteenth century and dedicated to Adinathji. Great sculpture throughout interior and on the 1,444 pillars. Open from noon to 5 P.M. for non-Jains.

SHEKHAVATI DISTRICT

The following towns and villages are worth visiting to see the art of frescoes created in the mid-nineteenth century. The frescoes cover the facades and interiors of havelis (mansions of former Marwari merchants). Originally, the themes were religious, then moved to ornamental motifs. In the 1900s, painters called *chitera* began imitating British lithographs and etchings. First, only natural pigments were used; then, around 1890, a gradual switch was made to chemical dyes. The towns are located in this district, which lies between Delhi and Jaipur. Visit Sikar (the old quarter), Mandawa, Fatehpur Sikri, Khetri, and Nawalgarh.

UDAIPUR

City Palace Museum. Begun in the 1600s by Udai Singh and constructed of granite and marble. The main entrance is via the triple gate, Tripolia, with eight carved marble arches. Inside are numerous palaces: Suraj Gokhada (Sun Balcony), Badi Mahal (Garden Palace), Sheesh Mahal, Bhim Vilas, Chini Chitrasala, Mor Chowk (Peacock Courtyard). This is one place where it's worth having a guide. Open: 9:30 A.M.–4:30 P.M.

Eklingji (22 km from Udaipur). The main temple was built in 1734. Ornate pillared hall under a huge pyramidical roof. The important temples are open daily 4–7 A.M., 10 A.M.–1 P.M., and 5–7 P.M.

Jagdish Temple. Built in 1651 by Maharana Jagat Singh I. Largest temple in Udaipur, with good sculptures and carvings. Offers a great view of Udaipur.

MUSEUMS AND GALLERIES. Practically every city and town in Rajasthan—besides being a museum in itself—contains a museum with centuries-old art objects and artifacts. Some of the buildings housing the museums are sights to behold, from palaces to forts. Entrance fees are nominal.

AJMER

Government Museum. Akbar's palace and royal quarters filled with Rajput and Mogul armor and regional sculptures. Open 10 A.M.–5 P.M.

ALWAR

Government Museum (second floor of City Palace). Great collection of Mogul and Rajput paintings from the eighteenth and nineteenth centuries and ancient manuscripts in Urdu, Sanskrit, and Persian. Good collection of armor. Open 10 A.M.–5 P.M.; closed Fridays and official holidays.

BIKANER

Ganga Golden Jubilee Museum. One of Rajasthan's best museums, with a good collection of artifacts from the pre-Harappan civilization and the Gupta and Kushan era, including terra cotta, pottery, paintings, sculpture, armor, and coins. A separate collection of local arts and crafts. Open 10 A.M.–5 P.M.; closed Fridays and holidays.

CHITTORGARH

Government Museum (former Fateh Prakesh Palace). Collection of sculptures from temples and other buildings in the fort. Open 10 A.M.–5 P.M.; closed Fridays and official holidays.

JAIPUR

Albert Hall Museum, in Ram Niwas Garden. Eclectic displays from clay models showing Yogi postures to carpets and displays of folk instruments and Rajasthani culture. Beautiful building. Open 10 A.M.–5 P.M.; closed Fridays and holidays.
City Palace Museum. Collection of royal garments, textiles, carpets, armor, and miniature paintings. Open 9:30 A.M.–4:45 P.M.
Hawa Mahal Museum. Open 10 A.M.–5 P.M.; closed Friday.

JODHPUR

Government Museum, in Umaid Public Garden. Collection of armor, textiles, local arts and crafts, miniatures, portraits, and manuscripts. Open 10 A.M.–4:30 P.M.; closed holidays.
Meherangarh Fort Museum. Within various apartments and palaces of the regal fort are palanquins, howdahs, royal cradles, miniatures, folk instruments, costumes, and furniture. Open 8 A.M.–6 P.M. (April 1–October 30); 9 A.M.–5 P.M. (November 1–March 31).
Umaid Bhawan Palace Museum. Former possessions of the maharajah. Many clocks. Open 10 A.M.–5 P.M.

KOTA

Government Museum. Old coins, Hadoti sculpture. Open 10 A.M.–4:30 P.M.
Maharana Madho Singh Museum. Set in old palace. Rich collection of Rajput miniatures in Kota school, sculptures, frescoes, weapons, and other antiques. Open 11 A.M.–5 P.M.

UDAIPUR

Ahar Museum. Standing in the remains of the old city; royal cenotaphs of the maharanas of Mewar.
Bharatiya Lok Kala Museum. Indian folk art museum. Folk dresses, ornaments, puppets, masks, dolls, instruments, and paintings. Puppet show can be arranged on request. Open 9 A.M.–6 P.M.
City Palace Museum. The only way to see this palace and its museum is with a guide. Open 9:30 A.M.–4:30 P.M.

GARDENS AND ZOOS. Alwar. *Purjan Vihar* (Company Garden), designed in 1868 by Maharajah Shiv Dhan Singh, has a lovely collection of ferns in an area called Simla. This is a great place to get away from the heat.
Bundi. *Kohaksar Bagh,* near Shikar Burj (Royal Hunting Lodge), is an old garden surrounding the cenotaphs of former Bundi kings and queens.
Jaipur. *Ram Niwas Garden and Zoo.* The garden was designed in 1868 by Sawai Ram Singh II. The zoo has a number of birds and animals, plus a crocodile and

python breeding farm. *Sisodia Garden and Palace* was built by Maharajah Sawai Singh in 1770 for his queen, Sisodia. A central room of the palace has galleries on three sides surrounded by terraced gardens with fountains and pools. *Vidyadharji Ka Bagh* was built by Vidyadhar, chief architect of Sawai Jai Singh II, with terraced gardens, fountains, and pools.

Jaisalmer. *Bada Bagh,* 6 km (4 mi.) from Jaisalmer, surrounds the royal cenotaphs, some of which are elaborately carved with sculptures of former rulers on horseback.

Jodhpur. *Mandore Gardens,* 9 km (6 mi.) from Jodhpur, is set at the ancient capital of Marwar, with the "Hall of Heroes"—16 Hindu and folk deities carved out of one rock, plus royal cenotaphs of the Maharajah Jaswant Singh and Maharajah Ajit Singh. Ornate cenotaphs are built atop plinths with exquisite sculpture.

Udaipur. *Gulab Bagh,* a rose garden designed by Maharana Sijjan Singh, contains a lovely building with a library. Children can ride the *Aravalli Express,* a mini-train. *Saheliyon Ki Bari* is the garden of the maid of honor, constructed for the use of the royal ladies. It has ornate pools with delicately carved kiosks and elephants in marble. Fountains surround a lotus pool, marble throne, and sitting room.

SPORTS AND OUTDOOR ADVENTURES. Camel Safaris. Contact the recommended tour operators above, or see those listed under *Facts at Your Fingertips,* for memorable safaris through the desert.

Polo. During Jaipur's polo season (mid-March–March 31 and mid-October–October 31), tournaments are held at the *Rajasthan Polo Club* near the Rambagh Palace. Don't be surprised if you also witness competitions between elephants, camels, and bikes. For details, contact the Rambagh Palace or Jaipur Polo Club, tel. 69235.

WILDLIFE SANCTUARIES. Remember you must arrive at all parks before they close at sunset. Also expect to pay nominal charges for entrance and often camera charges. All fees are paid at the park entrances.

Alwar. *Sariska Tiger Reserve.* The closest sanctuary to Delhi, it's open September–June and is home to tigers, leopards, wild dogs, deer, wild boars, jackals, langurs, and numerous birds, including peacocks.

Bharatpur. *Keolodeo Ghana National Park.* The best time to visit this water-bird sanctuary is October–February. The park, which has recorded over 350 species of birds and some wild animals, was the former hunting preserve of the royal family of Bharatpur.

Jaisalmer. *Desert National Park.* In this vast expanse of sand dunes, you can ride camels and see desert foxes, cats, hares, lizards, sand grouse, the great Indian bustard breeding ground, cranes, eagles, falcons.

Sawai Madhapur, 162 km (100 mi.) from Jaipur. *Ranthambhor National Park.* This famous tiger reserve is also home to deer, wild boars, langurs, leopards, jackals, hyenas, panthers, crocodiles, jungle cats, and numerous birds. There are many lakes, an old fort built in 944, and an eighth-century Ganesh temple. The park is closed July–Sept.

SHOPPING. Rajasthan's craftsmen have been famous for centuries for stonecutting, enameling, setting precious stones, tie-dying textiles, block printing silks and muslins, ivory carving, and lacquer and filigree work. The Rajasthan Government has emporiums in the following cities (called *Rajasthan Government Handicrafts Emporiums*): Ajmer, Bikaner, Chittorgarh, Jaipur, Jodhpur, Kota, and Udaipur. Also just take walks and browse, even buy, in the local bazaars. They're always fun; always interesting. And if you want something, remember to bargain, always! Jaipur and Jodhpur are the two big shopping cities.

JAIPUR

When shopping in Jaipur, beware of guides and drivers who insist that they know the best shops and bargains. They usually get a commission on all purchases, which often increases the price of your "bargain." Also, "government approved" are two meaningless words easily painted over any shop door. The following shops are reliable, provide good service, and sell excellent merchandise:

P. M. Allah Buksh and Son, M.I. Rd., sells the finest hand-engraved, enameled, or embossed brassware. Open 9:30 A.M.–8 P.M.; closed Friday. AE, DC, MC, V.

Gem Palace, M.I. Rd., has the best gems, jewelry, and a small collection of museum-quality curios. Their list of royal clientele also makes Cartier seem third-rate. They guarantee all purchases and will design (quickly) on order. Open daily 10 A.M.–7 P.M. AE, DC, MC, V.

Manglam Arts, Amber Palace Rd., has rooms full of exquisite old and new fine art, including Hindu *pichwies* (cloth temple hangings), Jain temple art, tantric and folk art, plus terra-cotta sculptures, silver furniture, handwoven *dhurries* (rugs), wood carvings, and more. There's also a branch in Udaipur. Both are open daily 10:30 A.M.–7 P.M. AE, DC, MC, V.

Chani Textiles, Amber Palace Rd., and *Anokhi,* 2 Tilik Marg, opposite Udyog Bhawan, sell lovely creations in Rajasthani fabrics (clothes and home furnishings). Open daily 9:30 A.M.–7 P.M. AE, DC, MC, V.

For browsing and bargain-shopping, also stroll through *Johri Bazaar* (for tie-died fabric and brass) and *Ram Ganj Bazaar* (for silver tribal jewelry and perfumes).

JAISALMER

Shopping here can also mean great side trips. Visit the home of *Ishwar Singh Bhatti,* an award-winning master craftsman, who lives at Changani Pada, Ward-4. He creates traditional handwoven camel-hair girths, which make beautiful wall hangings. You can arrive anytime from morning until evening. Rupees only.

Also visit the home of *Lakaram* in Banjota village, 20 km (12 mi.) from Jaisalmer. Another award-winning master craftsman, he creates handwoven camel-hair dhurries that are exquisite and reasonably priced. He's available during the same hours. Rupees only.

JODHPUR

Abani Handicrafts (Anand Bhawan, High Court Rd.) has good handicrafts and curios. Open daily 9 A.M.–8 P.M. Rupees only.

Umaid Arts (383 Third 'C' Rd.) has Rajasthani handicrafts and lovely traditional paintings on wood and on leather boxes. Open daily 9 A.M.–8 P.M. Rupees only.

Bunakar Moti Bhagwan Pargabatri (in nearby Salawas) is an award-winning master craftsman who creates beautiful silk and wool handwoven dhurries. You can visit his home from morning until evening. Rupees only.

MOUNT ABU

Chacha Museum (in the center of town) sells good Rajasthani and Gujarati handicrafts. Open daily 10–10. AE, DC, MC, V.

UDAIPUR

Art Center, Jagdish Rd., near Jagdish Temple; tel. 24939, has good new miniature paintings on silk, marble, and paper created by the award-winning Rajasthani painter, Kanhaiya Soni. Open daily 9 A.M.–8 P.M. V.

Fancy Jewelers, Jagdish Rd., near the Clock Tower, sells good-quality silver jewelry (old and new). Open daily 9:30 A.M.–8 P.M. MC, V.

NIGHTLIFE AND BARS. Most of the better Western-style hotels in Rajasthan provide cultural programs for their guests—dances, singing, and puppet shows.

Hotel bars in Rajasthan are normally open 11 A.M.–2:30 P.M. and 6–10:30 P.M. Three, in particular, offer great ambience:

Jaipur. At the *Polo Bar* in the Rambagh Palace, you're surrounded by exquisite marble and a collection of trophies won by the Maharajah's polo team. An indoor fountain adds to its appeal.

Jodhpur. The *Trophy Bar* at Umaid Bhawan Palace has an unquestionable regal aura.

Udaipur. Hotel guests at the Lake Palace can enjoy the *Amrit Sagar Bar* and gaze out at the dreamy lake. Non-guests should call (tel. 23241) in advance to see if they can be accommodated.

HIMACHAL PRADESH

Mountains, Vales—Unspoiled Serenity

by
KATHLEEN COX

Flanked by the lofty mountains of Jammu and Kashmir in the west, the Garhwal Himalayas of Uttar Pradesh in the east, and the rugged Tibetan mountains in the north, Himachal Pradesh, with its own towering peaks and romantic vales, is an enchanting state too often overlooked by Western tourists traveling in India. Every road in this state seems to bend, climb, and descend with few breaks of a straight stretch. The air, no matter the time of the year, is invigorating—a healthy relief from the plains. And, except for the occasional city, like Shimla or Mandi, the preferred pace of life remains slow and pastoral.

Villages mean a small huddle of shops and stalls supplying necessities and few luxuries, at least for the people who live here. But for foreigners who have the time to linger, Himachal Pradesh offers a hefty dose of outdoor sports at their best—treks, fishing, walks, even rafting and skiing. Its heady vistas change with the terrain, from snow-capped green mountains, to fertile valleys, to barren somber peaks where the monsoon never penetrates. And its people—Sikhs, Hindus and Buddhists—are culturally diverse and wear distinct styles of dress. Himachal Pradesh is also an important haven for Tibetan refugees; it's the present home of the Dalai Lama.

Shimla, the capital of Himachal Pradesh, set atop a six-mile-long winding ridge at an altitude of 2,171 meters (7,238 feet), was originally part of the kingdom of Nepal. In the 1800s, after the Gurkas of Nepal established one-too-many forts in their attempt to usurp new territory, the British East India Company finally intervened and defeated them in the Gurka War of 1819. During the fierce fighting, a British lieutenant just happened to stumble across the thick wooded perch with its stunning vistas and ideal climate, a place already known for its temple dedicated to the goddess Shyamla (another Kali, the goddess of wrath, incarnation). The lieutenant decided this oasis was the ideal place to pitch the tents of the battle-fatigued British.

Three years later, a second British officer, Major Kennedy, constructed the first year-round residence (the house still stands; it serves as the seat of various Himachal Pradesh government offices). But decades still had to pass before Lord Lawrence, the British viceroy, finally adopted the hilltop ridge as his undeclared summer capital in 1864. Only then did Shimla make the grand leap in status, becoming the premiere British hill station, with Lord Curzon adding the piece de resistance when he ordered the construction of the Kalka-Shimla narrow gauge train in 1902 and inaugurated it two years later. This diesel train, still running today, is a great way to begin your exploration of Shimla and Himachal Pradesh.

EXPLORING HIMACHAL PRADESH

Shimla

The old-fashioned train—and don't think posh—chugs its way along a five-hour, 60-mile journey, passing through 103 tunnels, forests of flowering rhododendron, slowly winding into the mountains and only occasionally coming to a halt at a Swiss-chalet-style railway station (a deliberate Lord Curzon touch), one of many that dot the line. This is a nonhurried journey that slows you down, almost too much. For the new Shimla of independent India has changed, stepped up its tempo, making it more city than hill station.

Shimla's old Victorian face is tarnished. Paint is peeling and mortar is crumbling. New buildings have squeezed out lawns, gardens, and the genteel air that came with exclusivity. But democratic Shimla still has the Mall—now crowded with shops, walks, horses, and monkeys—the ridge, all those zig-zag up-and-down streets open only to pedestrians, and those views into the surrounding valleys and distant mountains that are still serene.

Although Shimla is no longer the Shimla of Kipling, who set so many of his stories here, or the former viceroy's idea of a peaceful getaway, give it a chance. Let the new mood grow on you. Besides, a few buildings still try hard to remind you of their time of pomp and glory. See the former Viceroy's Lodge, now the Indian Institute of Advanced Studies. You can't go inside, but the grounds are lovely, the views are terrific, and the exterior of the main lodge is an English Renaissance (Elizabethan) treat. The building was constructed by Lord Dufferin between 1884 and 1888 out of Himalayan gray stone transported to Shimla by mules. At that time, the English thought it was built in too much of a hurry, which was reflected in the constant need for repair. Also, see the Kennedy house, the first house built in Shimla (across the street from the Shimla Railroad Station).

Then, after resting over espresso at the Indian Coffee House, walk up to the Ridge and the Christ Church, supposedly the second oldest church in Northern India, consecrated in 1857. The women who attended this church, which isn't too large, were supposedly lectured in a sermon to cut back on the size of their crinolines, which took up too much room. The women responded by coming to church the next Sunday in their riding habits. From here, head up to the top of Jakhu Hill (two kilometers or 1¼ mile), the highest peak offering the best nearby view of Shimla. On the top is a Hanuman Temple, dedicated to the monkey god, and appropriately guarded by a vigilant band of monkeys. Beware! They're always on the watch for an edible sacrificial offering.

For the true Indian experience, head back down those crooked alleys to the Middle and Lower Bazaar (especially if you're ready to shop, for prices are cheaper here). The mix of people brings you back to the heart of Asia—tall, stately Punjabs; hill tribes in homespun cloth; Tibetans; and an occasional lama with his prayer wheel, tender, and flint.

Shimla is an ideal base for sports and outdoor enthusiasts who are looking for a mountain to climb or a slope to ski down. No matter what direction you go, within minutes all sense of city life is gone. Hills, mountains, peace, and rural simplicity become the pervasive themes.

Take the winding road northeast to Narkanda (65 kilometers). You pass through villages, then scattered dwellings built into the hillsides, and then occasional terraces of wheat and potato fields, usually bordered by pine forests. Snow-capped mountains gleam in the distance. Narkanda is a small village. Not much happens, but it offers great views, walks, and treks into the inner Himalayas.

Naldehra, only 22 kilometers (14 miles) northeast of Shimla, has a nine-hole golf course—India's oldest, which Lord Curzon helped design. The fee for playing is nominal, and the spectacular scenery is enough of a diversion to wreak havoc with your score. This is also another great place for walks and picnics. If you're in the area in June, don't miss Naldehra's Sipi Fair, a gay, colorful festival at which costumed villagers from all over the state sell their handicrafts.

Nirath, Rampur, and Sarahan

Although the district of Kinnaur is off limits to foreigners, other culturally and visually appealing villages exist to the north of Narkanda. Proceed northeast until you reach the small village of Nirath (approximately 121 kilometers [75 miles] from Shimla). Here you can visit an eighth-century *shikara* style Hindu temple, dedicated to the sun god, Surya. The temple is decorated with wooden walls and contains a *mandapa* (entrance hall), recently restored with a typical Himachal Pradesh blue slate roof.

Farther north is the town of Rampur, with tiers of houses that rise against the banks of the Sutlej River. At the lovely monastery, you begin to see the influence of Buddhism in the region. Rampur, the commercial center of the area, is the site of a November Lavi—one of the state's largest trade fairs, which draws thousands of local villagers in colorful traditional dress.

Northeast of Rampur is Sarahan (174 kilometers or 108 miles from Shimla), located high above a valley, with exquisite views of snow-capped mountains and rolling fields. Atop a peak called Srikand (elevation 5,679 meters or 18,626 feet) is a stone image of Shiva, known as Srikand Mahadev. Worshippers offer their blessings by placing a cup of *charas* (a form of hashish) in front of the image. The charas is ignited and reduced to ashes. Other offerings are placed under stones.

In the village of Sarahan, visit the 200-year-old Bhimakali Temple set in a courtyard—an exquisite temple complex that combines Hindu and

Buddhist architecture. Much of the detail of this serenely situated structure is magnificent. Note the elaborate silver doors made by Kinnauri silversmiths at the turn of the century during the reign of Maharajah Sir Padum Singh. Inside the rectangular towers at one end of the courtyard is the Hindu temple, which is served by Brahman priests. The inner sanctum contains Hindu and Buddhist bronzes, numerous masks, and an image of the Bhimakali goddess 80 cm in height.

Chail

Chail (45 km or 28 miles to the southeast of Shimla) is a lovely mountain village and resort developed by Maharajah Bhupinder Singh (the Maharajah of Patiala), who proved to be too dashing and handsome. He charmed the British ladies and enraged their jealous husbands, who made him feel less than welcome in Shimla. The maharajah vowed to stay away from the fusty British and put all his energy and a ton of money into creating his own classy retreat that would put Shimla in its place.

At an altitude of 2,161 meters (7,054 feet), Chail rests on three hills, with the former palace of the maharajah (now the Chail Palace Hotel) a beautiful sprawl atop Rahgarh Hill. The surrounding forests—the palace is situated on over 600 acres—are the home of barking deer, monkeys, occasional leopards, and numerous species of wild birds. You can relax in the quiet of an elegant stretch of lawn, walk for hours along well-marked paths that pass by orchards, gardens, and deep-green woods. Chail also boasts a well-kept cricket field, India's highest, possibly the highest in the world.

Bilaspur

Northwest from Shimla, the road circles through forests, valleys, and mountains at times so rocky that the road seems scooped out of stone. You enter the Arkai Range and Arki, a tiny village with an old yellow stone palace perched on the edge of a hill overlooking a splendid green and yellow valley—the dominant spring colors. Moving on, you reach Bilaspur and a small cafe that overlooks the Gobindsagar Lake, a strange sight that reveals an odd partnership between art and nature. There, in the small lake (not much larger than a pond) are a slew of 200-year-old Hindu temples. This is actually the site of the old city of Palampur, submerged by the construction of the Bhakra Dam. During high season (the monsoon months of July–October), only the spires peek above the water. The rest of the year, as the water recedes, some of the simple stone temples are completely clear of the lake as though built on the water's edge.

Mandi—Gateway to Kullu Valley

On the left bank of the Beas River, Mandi at first glance looks like a New England mill town, with rickety houses packed tight along the river's edge. Mandi is a pleasing city with temple spires poking up everywhere. (There are over 100.) Many of the temples are of recent construction and brightly painted. Others are simple dark granite and date back to the sixteenth and seventeenth centuries, built in an odd blend of Mogul and Hindu styles. The latter have a faintly mausoleum exterior shape, but inside they typify Hindu style, with carved square pillars and an inner sanctum.

Visit in particular the sixteenth-century Panchvaktra on the right side of the riverbank, not far from the bridge leading into the city. Inside the temple, a monolithic and benign granite Nandi faces, not the expected *lingam* (phallic symbol), but an unusual five-faced Shiva sitting in his meditation pose. To the left of the inner sanctum is a stone replica of the deity that sits inside. Also, visit the Bhutnath, set on the river's edge in the heart of the city near a series of colorful new Shiva temples. This time Nandi stands outside the temple facing a small lingam in the inner sanctum. The temple is stark and has few exterior carvings. All the sculptured emphasis is on the double archway entrance, as if drawing our attention to Shiva's symbol. Finally, see the Trilknath Temple, another old temple set back from the river. In February or March, Mandi's Shivratri Fair, which pays homage to Shiva, turns the Bhutnath temple and the city itself into one big party. Devotees carry deities on temple chariots (small gaily dressed palanquins); folk dances and folk music brighten the mood.

All year round, the inner city markets and bazaars are a walker's treat. Take an evening stroll (shops close at 8 P.M.). Every lane is narrow and cobbled and lined with tiny shops or stalls, often with dark rough wood interiors; an occasional temple; a moss covered slope; and even a hearty tree that sneaks its roots into the crowded area. The architecture is stone and bare (or paint faded) wood. Sloping roofs overhang second stories frequently fronted by verandas, balconies, and push-open French-style windows. The overall effect is of an Italian hill town gone Asian. Also, while walking up and down these skinny streets that so often lead ultimately to the river, try to find Ravi Nagar, a pleasant spot, with its spacious rectangular garden and quiet communal courtyard.

Rewalsar Lake

If time permits, visit Rewalsar Lake, 24 kilometers (15 miles) southeast of Mandi. Rewalsar is the resting place of departed saints and the birthplace of the Indian mystic, Padmasambhava (Guru Rimpoche) who spread the Buddhist faith. The drive is beautiful, winding into mountains that overlook terraced fields of wheat and modest square houses of wood or sod with carefully checkered slate roofs that flicker in the sun. Rewalsar Lake is tiny and famous for its floating reed islands. The power of prayer or a minuscule breeze can set them in motion (more often in the eyes of the believer). Three shrines for the three different faiths—Buddhists, Sikhs, and Hindus—dot the edge of the water. The Buddhist complex dominates. Prayer flags rise from courtyards. Prayer wheels encircle the exterior walls of the monastery. Inside sits a golden Buddha surrounded by numerous prayer stalls in which monks read scrolls.

Kullu Valley

From Mandi, the Kullu road proceeds for 40 kilometers (25 miles) through the Mandi-Larji Gorge along the Beas River. The narrow road, blasted through solid rock, has left eerie precipices that tower overhead, while down below, the raging torrent rushes by. At Aut, you turn north along the river and head up the Kullu Valley that hugs the Beas—80 kilometers (50 miles) long and, when the vista opens up, just barely more than two kilometers (1.2 miles) at its broadest. Idyllic, yet wild and dominant. No wonder this valley is known as the Abode of the Gods.

In March, apricot and apple trees burst into pink and white blossoms. On the higher slopes, giant rhododendrons with crimson flowers give the appearance of trees decked out in small lanterns. Early in June, horse chestnuts are in flower, swarms of wild bees humming around them. By July masses of blue and purple irises are splashed over the hillside. Buttercups range in color from the familiar golden yellow to pink-red. The fall brings on an explosion of bright colors. With winter, the vista turns white except for the stately green forests of pine and cedar.

Manikaran

At Bhuntar, about 70 kilometers (43 miles) north of Aut, take the turn east across the bridge for an hour-long memorable trip to Manikaran (Jewel of the Ear). The road, winding along the Parvati River, is hardly wide enough for the public bus that makes the daily journey between Manikaran and Mandi. At intervals along the way, you see homes of mud and stone with straw roofs and fog hugging snow-capped mountains.

Manikaran is a spiritual center. Here Parvati and Shiva, on a journey through the Himalayas, stopped and meditated by the hot and cold streams for 1,000 years. Here, Parvati dropped a jewel from her earring into the river, where it was devoured by the Serpent King, Shesh Nag. Shiva prayed for its return with such power that the world shook and Shesh Nag hissed up Parvati's jewel, creating the bubbling springs. Along with her jewel thousands of others shot out, until 1905, when an earthquake put an end to the bounty.

In the Sri Ramchandra Temple, built in the fifteenth century, Vishnu sits in the inner sanctum below an electric clock. The famous Dussehra festival, now held at Kullu, was once held here. Also see the old Sri Raghunath Temple, dedicated to Vishnu, across from the Tourist Complex. Then head to the river and the little white new Himachal Pradesh temple, dedicated to Shiva and the nearby Gurdwara Sri Guru Nanak Dev Ji Hari Har Ghat, built in the 1940s. You walk through waves of blinding white steam, passing rectangular hot water pits where pots of food are cooking. You enter a hall with chambers here and there, the steam rising up. Inside one, the devout sit in the heat and pray. Inside, other pilgrims purify themselves in bathing tanks. Another room is set up for free tea and meals (although a donation is welcome); there are rooms to spend the night at no charge. Upstairs is the sacred room, gaily decorated, where services are held periodically (evening and early morning). All are welcome.

Every temple has sacred bathing tanks, and all the streets and lanes have gurgling hot pits where clothing is washed and food is cooked. The pace of life nearly stops here: a few tourists, the chatter of crows, the lowing of a cow. It's a place to walk, relax, and enjoy natural beauty in an almost primeval state. Footpaths or friendly villagers gladly show you the way up and up into serene heavenly peaks. And by all means, refresh yourself in a hot spring bath set up in the new tourist complex; it's clean and revitalizing—a rare treat.

Kullu

Just before you enter the bustling little city of Kullu, you pass a large grass square on your right, called the Dhalpur Maidan, and a stadium on your left. This is the site of Himachal Pradesh's famous annual fair, the Kullu Dussehra, which celebrates the victory of good over evil. The October Dussehra is the most important gathering in Himachal Pradesh. To the accompaniment of drums and bells, deities from neighboring villages temples are carried down to Kullu in an evening procession of decorated palanquins that marks the start—the Vijay Dashmi—of the festival. Once the deity arrives at the maidan, it is placed before the supreme deity Raghunathji, the presiding god of Kullu Valley, who sits in his honored position under a festive tent. The maidan is covered with booths, ringed with crowds, and alive with folk dances, music—the full spectrum of Himachal Pradesh village culture. Dussehra ends on an electric, yet squeamish note—the sacrifice of a bull and small creatures as gifts to the gods.

Every year on April 28–30, Kullu also holds a cattle fair on the same popular maidan. People from surrounding villages arrive to buy and sell their livestock. The spirit here is also festive, with folk dances and local cultural events the prime attraction.

While in Kullu, see the Raghunathji Temple, the shrine of the supreme deity, and the Vaishno Devi Temple, involving a delightful walk to a small cave that enshrines an image of the goddess Vaishno. Drive to the foot of Bijli Mahadev Shrine and spend a day climbing 11 km to an altitude of 2,400 meters (8,000 feet). Besides panoramic views of the entire valley, you'll see a remarkable temple, the Bijli Mahadev. The temple is also called the Temple of Lightning because of a curious phenomenon: its 60-foot staff that glistens in the sun supposedly attracts divine blessings in the form of lightning. When lightning strikes, it shoots down the staff and shatters the Shiva lingam. Every year, this supposedly happens and every year the priests restore the image, putting it back together with butter and then awaiting the annual recurrence of the "miracle." And, in the small city of Kullu, spend time wandering through the Akhara Bazaar, a great place to buy Kullu handicrafts—shawls, *pattus* (bolts of cloth), *toppis* (Himachal Pradesh caps), and *pullans* (like bedroom slippers).

Naggar

Two roads lead to Manali. Take the less traveled one, which means turn right at Katrain, 20 kilometers (12 miles) north of Kullu, and cross over to the right side of the Beas River. Before heading north, see Naggar, the former capital of the rajas of Kullu, and a sleepy village, with its door just slightly open to tourism. Perched on a mountainside, the 400-year-old castle, built of weathered wood and stone, is now a newly renovated tourist hotel with minimal amenities but breathtaking views from its veranda. At its feet rests a tiny village with a slew of cozy wooden homes knit together by narrow lanes and paths. Orchards and fields of seasonal crops tumble down the slope to the river.

Naggar is peaceful and friendly. Walk through the narrow lanes to the old stone temple, dedicated to Shiva with Nandi nearby. Here boys play cricket in the temple courtyard and girls play jacks with red clay stones, while a priest, oblivious to all the activity, prays quietly near the idol in the inner sanctum. Stop at a tea stall, where a kettle simmers over a fire. Meander along footpaths that take you into backyards and by wooden huts filled with white rabbits whose angora fur is a precious commodity. Climb to the nearby Tripura Sundari Temple, with its pagodalike appearance and intriguing wood carvings. Walk, relax, and, above all, give in to Naggar's timelessness and that rare chance to discover beauty at every turn.

Manali

From Naggar, stay on the right side of the Beas and continue north 12 kilometers (seven miles) until you reach Jagatsukh, another small village that was a former capital of Kullu and the site of ancient temples: The Shiva temple in Shikhara style and the nearby old Devi Sharvali Temple, dedicated to the Goddess Gayatri (a sister of Durga). Up ahead is Manali, set against the magic of towering snow-capped peaks, many of them unscaled and unnamed. Unfortunately, this mountain town, situated at an altitude of 1,800 meters (6,000 feet), has been overwhelmed by too many new hotels and swarms of tourists. Use Manali only as a base for hikes, treks, mountain climbing, inexpensive winter skiing at nearby Solang, and fishing in the summer.

While in Manali do visit the peaceful 600-year-old Hadimba Devi Temple with a four-tiered pagoda-shaped roof, a somber, wooden shrine set in a cedar grove. The temple is dedicated to a wife in the legendary Pandava family, who figures prominently in the Hindu epic, *Mahabharata*. Legend claims that the artist who created the pretty shrine with its exterior and door covered with handsome carvings received a dubious token of gratitude from the king. He was so enamored with the results, he cut off the artist's hand to prevent him from duplicating another temple that might rival the Hadimba. Undaunted, the artist used his left hand and created a finer temple at Chamba (the Triloknath Temple). Again his work was so admired, no rival was wanted. This time they cut off his head.

Also visit the small village of Vashisht, on the right bank of the Beas. Just off the road in an interior courtyard is another lovely pyramidal stone temple, recently restored. Inside is a granite idol of Vashista with haunting silver eyes. A Shiva lingam sits in the corner and wooden carvings adorn the interior pillars. Vashisht is another source of sulphur springs; near the shrine are two sacred tanks (one for men, the other for women) where devotees purify themselves in hot sulphur water. Just down the road heading back toward Manali, the Himachal Pradesh Tourist Department has set up a delightful complex of hot sulphur baths—clean and refreshing— the perfect way to end any walk. The cost is nominal, and outside the bathing complex is a small outdoor cafe.

The influx of Tibetan refugees in Manali has left its stamp on the town. The new Tibetan Monastery just behind the bus stop in an area called Model Town and adjoining it, the Tibetan Bazaar, are examples. You'll have to look hard to find anything ethnic. The emphasis is decidedly on "West is best," no matter how shoddy.

Farther north from Manali is Kothi, a quiet village at the foot of the Rohtang Pass, offering dramatic views of massive snow-covered peaks. From Kothi, it's three kilometers to the Rahla Falls that shoot water from the Beas into a deep gorge. Solang Valley is Himachal Pradesh's developing ski resort, with good runs at an unbelievably low price that includes all necessary equipment. And here, all year round, the Himalayas will catch hold of you. Finally, continue north another 38 kilometers to the Rohtang Pass, at an altitude of 3,978 meters (13,050 feet), where you see the twin peaks of Geypan and the Sone Pani glaciers. This is the gateway to the next set of valleys—the remote Lahaul and Spiti. Nearly indomitable, the pass is open only from June to September, a little earlier for the intrepid who trek.

Lahaul and Spiti

To the uninitiated, Lahaul and Spiti mean little more than barren rocks, raging torrents, perilous mountain paths, and glaciers unrelieved by ordinary creature comforts. But to anyone who wants a profound confrontation with nature, these valleys on the Indo-Tibetan border represent an unforgettable experience. Here, the Himalayas assume their wildest and most uninhabitable stance. And here, all but the cynical adventurer will feel that dimension of glory that approaches the mystical.

For a trek into the Lahaul valley (unfortunately, Spiti is closed to foreigners), cross the Rohtang Pass. Once you enter the bleak and windswept Khoksar, the first village in the valley, you've also entered that serene realm of Tantric Buddhism, the religion of Tibet. Lahaul reminds us vividly and often of its culture. Prayer wheels, *chortens* (stupas), prayer flags, gompas (monasteries)—they're all here in the valley, as are perpetual repetitions of mantras, which seem to beckon us to continue on.

Summers in Lahaul are cool and pleasant. Like Ladakh, no monsoon unleashes its fury here. The height of the mountains keeps out the rain clouds. Keylong, the capital of Lahaul, is 117 kilometers (73 miles) from Manali—set in a green valley with fields of barley and buckwheat, an oasis surrounded by brown somber hills and massive snowy peaks. The Kardong Gompa, overlooking Keylong from the top of a hill across the river, has exquisite frescoes and murals and an enormous prayer drum with numerous strips of paper, each inscribed with the sacred *mantra: Om Mani Padme Hum* (Hail to the Jewel in the Lotus).

Only those rare, lucky foreigners who are able to procure an Inner-Line Permit from the Ministry of Home Affairs in New Delhi are able to proceed to Spiti, where the valley, in some places, is quite wide. In these flatlands, you find most of the settlements and cultivation bordered by steep rocky mountains that rise several thousand feet. The Spiti River is a fast-moving torrent that, through the years, has cut its way through the bottom of a deep ravine. The valley is less than a mile across, with narrow strips of arable land 300 meters (1,000 feet) above the riverbed. Steep rocky mountains, rise above this land, reaching several thousand feet. The sweeping vista of rugged crags and slopes changes color from pale pink to bright scarlet, tempered by the soft blues and greens of glaciers.

The men of Spiti wear a long double-breasted woolen gown, reinforced by a long woolen rope wrapped around the waist in multiple coils. This belt provides warmth and turns the upper part of the gown into an ample blouse in which all kinds of articles are stored, including a Buddhist prayer wheel; a silver bowl for water, tea, or liquor; a spare garment; or a newly born lamb. The women grease their hair with butter and wear it in numerous thin plaits that are then woven with yak's tailhair to increase the length. Their hairdo resembles a net of black strands that spreads down the back, often hanging to the knees.

Since food is scarce and arable land is limited, the people of Spiti have evolved a scheme to ward off the dangers of overpopulation; the eldest son inherits the land, while the younger sons are sent off to a local lamasery, where they take a vow of celibacy. Women who fail to find husbands often enter convents. Monogamy is the general rule, but both polygamy and polyandry occur occasionally. If the eldest son dies, a younger brother quits the lamasery and takes over the deceased brother's land, his widow, and the children.

Baijnath

Passing through the Kangra Valley, first stop is Baijnath, with its important Hindu temple, constructed in the Shikara style with a low pyramid-shaped roof. This is considered the oldest Shiva shrine in India, built possibly by the legendary Pandavas. Like most stone temples in Himachal Pradesh, the Baijnath is not massive, sitting on the crest of a low mountain above the Binwakund River. Set against the backdrop of the Himalayas and nestled within the relatively tall stone wall of its courtyard, the overall effect accentuates its contained and diminutive size. The Baijnath is quite a contrast to the Dravidian temples of South India, with their soaring towers that humble you before you set foot in the shrine. The four thick pillars supporting the Baijnath have handsome carvings, including an unusual composite image of Vishnu and Lakshmi. Inside, the inner sanctum is a

Shiva lingam (called the Vaidyanath), one of 12 natural lingams worshiped in India.

Dharamsala

Dharamsala is a former British hill station (40 kilometers or 25 miles from Kangra), spilling off a spur of the Dhauladhar range and surrounded on three sides by snow-capped peaks. When the white shrouded mountains first come into view, the rugged slopes appear black and foreboding, but as you draw nearer, the bleak mass softens to green and the white tops shimmer. Even Dharamsala, devastated by an earthquake in 1905, has a gentle aura, befitting the recent influx of Buddhist refugees who, along with their spiritual leader the Dalai Lama, fled Tibet after the Chinese invasion.

Dharamsala is broken into two distinct parts. In Lower Dharamsala, you find the Kotwali Bazaar, schools, businesses, government offices, and a feel that's distinctly Indian and Hindu in character. Upper Dharamsala at Mcleod Ganj (10 kilometers or six miles away), on the far side of an Indian army base and just beyond St. John's Church in the Wilderness, is decidedly Tibetan and Buddhist. Throughout tiny Mcleod, you see European and American students of Buddhism, many with heads shaven, wandering about, discussing their texts.

Visit the Namgyal Monastery, where hundreds of purple-robed monks (men and women) gather inside their new temple and pray, sometimes for hours, reading from scrolls and sitting beneath an enormous golden image of the Buddha that towers over them from the front of the shrine. Non-Buddhists can enter the interior of the shrine from a side entrance, where they can see more large statues. Remove your shoes! Also inquire about Tibetan cultural performances at the Tibetan Institute of Performing Arts, perched on the top of a hill. You may be lucky and see great dancing, hear music, or witness a Tibetan opera.

While in Upper Dharamsala, also visit one special monument that survived the earthquake and remains a stalwart reminder of the days of British rule: St. John's Church in the Wilderness (set not in the wilderness, but in a cozy pine grove), built in 1860. The stained glass windows of this church are treasures; inside is a monument to Lord Elgin, a British viceroy originally from Scotland, who asked to be buried in this church, dedicated to the patron saint of Scotland.

Jwalamukhi Temple

From Dharamsala, take a delightful 53-kilometer (33-mile) trip south to the Jwalamukhi Temple in Kangra Valley. You pass mango, banana, bamboo, and pine groves and charming farming villages with wheat fields that stretch back to the mountains. The Jwalamukhi Temple, a complex of tiny shrines, is the scene of an ongoing festival and one of the most important Hindu pilgrim centers in north India. Here, Hindus celebrate a mysterious, perpetually burning flame that is revered as the manifestation of the goddess Parvati. The Mogul Emperor Akbar tried and failed to smother the flame and left behind a solid gold umbrella, which still remains. The huge brass bell inside the mandapa was a gift of the king of Nepal.

Dalhousie

Dalhousie, the gateway to Chamba Valley (the vale of milk and honey), is set on five different hills rising from the main ridges of the Dhauladhar. Dalhousie is another former British hill station, named after a former British viceroy, Lord Dalhousie, who, weary from one too many battles, sought peace and quiet here. Today, the small village and all the hotels have seen far better days. There's a seedy neglect to many of the old Victorian structures. The effect is dismal and depressing; not even the panorama of spectacular snow-capped peaks justifies much more than the briefest visit. Many of the hoteliers are also gougers, so watch out!

Chamba

After you reach the crest of the mountain, the road begins its slow descent to Chamba, winding continuously while hugging the edge of the mountain that slopes down to the near-dry Ravi River. The closer you get to the valley basin, the more terraced the land becomes. Still, the road seems untraveled; the chosen course appears to be dusty foot paths that race up and down the hills.

Just when you're lost in the peace and quiet, you round a bend, and there's Chamba, sprawling on the mountainside. Even the Ravi comes alive, with the water rushing now. This mountain village/city (with 5,000 people) is the center of the valley and rich in ancient stone temples.

Walk into the center of town and see the Lakshminarain temple complex, with three shrines dedicated to Vishnu and three dedicated to Shiva (the earliest of the six stone temples built in the tenth century and the last constructed in 1828). The temples follow two distinct architectural trends. The Vishnu temples are of the Shikara type, with two overhead "parasol" roofs that are intended to drain off snow; the others are indigenous hill style. Also visit the Bhuri Sing Museum, with its excellent collection of miniature paintings from the Kangra and Basoli schools. As you walk down Museum Street, note the shoe stalls. Chamba is a big sandal town and here is where you buy them.

Take a lazy walk on the Chaugan, grassy public promenade (maidan), above the river and near the center of town. This park often turns into an impromptu trading center for villagers who come in from the surrounding hills. The Chaugan is also the site of the colorful week-long Minjar Fair held annually in August or September at the time of the corn harvest to invoke the rain gods.

Chamba is no great beauty of a city, nor does it require much time to discover. It's very much the local business district. But go in any direction and you're surrounded by serenity and Himalayan magic. And this makes Chamba a good walking and trekking base. See Sahoo, a charming hill village where the Gujjars (seminomadic Moslems) live six months a year. In the winter, they migrate with their families and buffalo to the plains of the Punjab. The people are tall and tend to dress in dark muted clothes; the men wrap thick turbans around their heads, and the women adorn themselves with heavy jewelry. While in Sahoo, also walk to the old Shiva temple with a lingam sitting on a copper base inside the inner sanctum. This walk means an idyllic stroll through green fields into the village proper—into pure village life Himachal Pradesh-style—even if some of the residents live here only half the year.

Bharmour

From Chamba, one beautiful drive should not be missed. Go east from Chamba 65 km to Bharmour. This is Shiva territory, and occasionally you'll pass three-pronged staffs called Trisuls (the three vertical prongs are the symbol of Shiva) stuck into the earth or small lingams set in tiny shrines—tributes to the favored god. This is also Gaddi territory, although you'll still see many Gujjars traveling through. Like the Gujjars, the Gaddi shepherds are seminomads who move their flocks of goats and sheep down from Bharmour in the cold months to warmer Dharamsala and the Kangra valley. Or they used to. Today, many Gaddi families stay put around Bharmour, where they're developing cash crops: wheat, walnuts, almonds, maize, and apples. Gaddi men wear hand-woven beige coats that flair out and end at mid-thigh with rope belts coiled around the waist. The women wear patterned long skirts, heavily gathered at the waist.

For most of your journey, the road stays narrow but essentially level as it hugs the Ravi River flowing along the base of the valley. High rugged peaks crowd in from the other side of the road: thick jagged rock that remains about an arm's-length away. The water of the Ravi is cold and a vivid green. Mountain streams splash down the precipice and across the road. Gorges with small rivulets racing to meet the Ravi slice open the rocky border revealing a quick glimpse of the sky. Footpaths crisscross the difficult slopes and lead to isolated simple houses of wood or stone. Suspension bridges carry animals and villagers back and forth across the river.

You take a sharp turn and leave the Ravi, following the narrower Buddhal. Up ahead are snow-covered mountains, dominated by the not-too-distant Kailash Peak, that extends across the panorama. Minutes later, you arrive in Bharmour, an ancient quiet haven with 84 temples (many of them small structures with simple lingams), nestled in a beautiful court-yard called Churasi (84 in Hindi).

Look at the wooden Laxshna Devi, erected in the seventh century; the stone Narsingh Temple constructed in the tenth or eleventh century, one of the few dedicated to Vishnu with a lionesque idol in the inner sanctum; and the stone Manimahesh, built in the seventh century. Sit in the peaceful courtyard and watch the people—so many of them Gaddis. Take in the views that unfold all around. This is nature and life at its best.

Pangi Valley

From Chamba, you can head north for the rugged Pangi Valley, a dry cold region about 2,400 meters (8,000 feet) above sea level. In the midst of wild hills, the Chenab River (Chandra Bhaga) flows in a deep narrow gorge where it lashes against rugged cliffs. This area is a trekker's paradise; the valley stays dry during the monsoon, and numerous peaks that tower to a level of 6,600 meters (22,000 feet) are still the challenge of mountaineers. Every village and hamlet has its own temple; the most important are Mindhal Vasni about 15 kilometers (nine miles) from Killar and the Purthi about 30 kilometers (19 miles) from Killar.

Killar, 137 kilometers (85 miles) northeast of Chamba (a trekking route), lies in a valley set in a deep narrow gorge of the Chenab River in the high Himalayas. Grand, majestic! From Killar, you can trek northwest to Kishtwar in Jammu and Kashmir, turn east halfway to Kishtwar, and cross the Umasi La Pass into the Zanskar Valley. You can trek southeast to Keylong and Mandi, or trek from Killar to Lahaul, which will land you in Purthi and a convenient rest house on the bank of the Chandra Bhaga.

As is so often true in Himachal Pradesh, the Pangi Valley shows off northern India at its best: unspoiled, less traveled, and with nature clearly in charge. Days spent here are indelible, touching the soul. Time stops. Greater forces have more power.

PRACTICAL INFORMATION FOR

HIMACHAL PRADESH

WHEN TO GO. While Himachal Pradesh—except for Lahaul and remote areas—is accessible year-round, the state is loveliest in spring and fall when flowers are in bloom; nights are crisp and cool, and days are warm. Bring warm woolens. Hotels do their best to supply heat, but you may find that their best is not sufficient.

Chamba and surrounding hill districts: the best seasons are April–mid-July and mid-September–December. The monsoon (July–September) brings rain and mist, but not continuous torrents.

Kangra Valley (Dharamsala area): the best seasons are March–June, September–November. If the monsoon, with its periodic rain doesn't bother you, the summer months are fine.

Kullu Valley and Manali: April–mid-November—the lush months—show off Kullu at its colorful best. Manali is unbearably crowded during May and June. Plan your visit for other months, including the winter when you can ski at nearby Solang Resort.

Lahaul: To get to Lahaul, you're at the mercy of the weather. The road is generally clear of snow mid-June–November. The days can be warm, but the nights are cold.

Mandi: Approachable year-round, but the best time is April–November.

Shimla, Chail, and nearby points: Year-round resort. July–August brings the monsoon, but not constant rain. Winter also turns Shimla into a snowy getaway, with nearby winter sports and white Himalayan views.

HOW TO GET THERE. By Air. For visits to Shimla and southern Himachal Pradesh, *Vayudoot* flies daily from Delhi and Chandigarh into Jubbarhati Airport (23 km or 14 mi. from Shimla). *Indian Airlines* also makes numerous daily flights between Delhi and Chandigarh (117 km or 73 mi. from Shimla). From Chandigarh, regular bus service and fixed-rate taxis (about Rs. 800) fly back and forth between Shimla. For other Himachal destinations, Vayudoot flies from Delhi, Chandigarh, and Shimla into Bhuntar Airport (10 km or 6 mi. from Kullu; 52 km or 32 mi. from Manali). Vayudoot is also starting flights from these same destinations into the new Gaggal Airport in Kangra Valley, 15 km (9 mi.) from Upper Dharamsala. All flights should be booked in advance, and passengers must confirm their tickets 72 hours before departure and arrive at the terminal an hour before the flight.

By Bus. Buses are slow-going, usually crowded, but provide entertaining halts along the way. From Delhi, *Himachal Pradesh Road Transport Corporation* (HPRTC) runs inexpensive deluxe coaches from the Interstate Bus Terminus to Shimla, Dharamsala, Kullu, Manali, and Mandi. The fare to Shimla is about Rs. 125 and the trip takes about nine hours. Tel. in Delhi 3325320 or 2516725, or in Shimla 3556. Within Himachal, HPRTC runs deluxe buses to every important city, many villages, and to the city of Keylong in Lahaul. For routes and schedules, check with the tourist departments (see below under *Tourist Information*).

By Train. Frequent train service is available from Delhi and Chandigarh to Kalka (90 km or 56 mi. from Shimla). The *Himalayan Queen,* which departs late at night from the New Delhi Railway Station, reaches Kalka in time for the morning departure of the British-built *Toy Train,* a narrow-gauge diesel that winds for five hours through the mountains to Shimla. You sit on a wooden bench, but the trip is scenic and fun. Book your ticket in advance: first class (air-conditioned or non–air-conditioned) or second class (air-conditioned). Reserve a sleeper and berth. In Delhi, call *International Tourist Guide*, tel. 352164, 10 A.M.–5 P.M.; in Shimla, tel. 2915. Travelers heading to Dharamsala can go by train from Delhi to Pathankot (90 km or 56 mi. from Dharamsala). There are no other convenient train stations in or near Himachal.

By Rented Car with Driver. From Delhi to Shimla (370 km or 230 mi.), a four-hour ride on a dusty highway through the Indian state of Haryana leads to a scenic climb through the mountains to Shimla. Total trip time is about seven hours. In Delhi, hire a car from a recommended travel agency and figure Rs. 4 per km with a halt charge of Rs. 50–Rs. 100 per night. Within the state, a hired car with driver is a good way to travel. You can stop when you want and take any road that appeals to you. To hire a car in Shimla, contact the *Himachal Pradesh Tourism Development Corporation* (HPTDC), the Mall, tel. 78311 or 77646; or the *Taxi Union Service*, tel. 5123. In other important destinations, use a recommended travel agency. Shimla is about 240 km (149 mi.) from Kullu and 280 km (174 mi.) from Dharamsala. Most roads are fairly well-maintained, but narrow and slow-going.

TOURIST INFORMATION. Himachal Pradesh is an outdoor state, and the tourist department is an excellent source of what to do: where, when, and how. Their offices also have excellent general information on hotels, sightseeing, and travel. Most tourist offices are open Monday–Saturday 10 A.M.–5 P.M., except where noted. In Delhi, you can contact the *Himachal Pradesh Tourist Office*, Chandalok Building, 36 Janpath; tel. 3325320.

In **Shimla**, contact the Himachal Pradesh Tourist Office or HPTDC at the Mall, tel. 78311 or 77646. Open April 1–July 15, 9 A.M.–7 P.M. daily and July 15–March 31, 10 A.M.–5 P.M. daily, except January–March when the office is closed on Sundays. Government tourist offices are also in the following cities:

Dalhousie. Tourism Information Office, tel. 36.

Dharamsala. Tourist Information Center, tel. 3163 and 3107.

Kullu. Tourist Information Office, tel. 2349.

Manali. Tourist Information Assistant, tel. 25. Open April–October, Monday–Saturday, 8 A.M.–midnight; otherwise 9 A.M.–7 P.M.

Most HPTDC tourist bungalows also have free brochures and maps at a nominal cost.

FOREIGN CURRENCY EXCHANGE. Most Western-style hotels have money exchange counters. Otherwise, go to a branch of the *State Bank of India*, open Monday–Friday 10 A.M.–2 P.M.; Saturday till noon.

ACCOMMODATIONS. Himachal Pradesh has some Western-style hotels in the more established tourist areas and some charming old-fashioned guest houses, many of them former private homes. Throughout the state, you'll find dependable adequate facilities—many run by the state government—with clean rooms, decent bathroom facilities, and simple restaurants. The government-run stopovers are moderate to inexpensive, so don't expect more than the minimal extras. But given the mood of Himachal Pradesh—an adventure-oriented, undervisited state for travelers who want to get off the beaten path and be close to the best of nature—the accommodations are appropriate. What follows is a list of hotels, guest houses, and some government bungalows in major scenic areas. This list is supplemented with a second list of rest houses that are suitable for trekkers or travelers going the remote route. Rates are based on double occupancy, and in most cases don't include food; however, some places only offer the American plan and don't include taxes: *Deluxe,* over Rs. 1,450; *Expensive,* Rs. 950–Rs. 1,450; *Moderate,* Rs. 500–Rs. 950; *Inexpensive,* under Rs. 500. Many Western-style hotels accept traveler's checks and credit cards.

BAIJNATH

Expensive

Palace Motel. Taragarh, Kangra Valley; tel. 34. 15 rooms with bath. Built in the 1930s, this former palace of a nawab has been converted into a hotel by its new owner, a member of the Kashmir Hindu royalty. Secluded grounds are lovely. Rooms aren't posh, but they have a homey, old-fashioned ambience. Best rooms are on the ground floor and are spacious, with furniture from the 1940s and 50s and pictures of the current owner's family and the Hindu pantheon. There's a charming family dining room with a fixed, multicuisine menu. Facilities include an old-fashioned TV lounge, swimming pool, tennis court, horseback riding, and trekking and tour arrangements. Meals included. Rupees only.

CHAIL

Inexpensive–Moderate

Chail Palace Hotel. Reservations: Manager, Chail Palace Hotel, Chail; tel. 37 or 43. 19 large rooms with tubs in the hotel; 10 rustic and private cottages with 1–4 bedrooms. While the palace-looking exterior of this HPTDC hotel is decidedly Victorian, rooms are unpalatial and have simple furnishings. Upper-floor rooms, however, are quiet and spacious. Cottages offer privacy and rustic charm, especially the Honeymoon Cottage with its copy of the *Kama Sutra*. Room service, TV in larger rooms, multicuisine restaurant, bar. Rupees only.

CHAMBA

Inexpensive

Hotel Iravati. Reservations: Area Manager, HPTDC, Dalhousie; tel. 94. 12 rooms with bath. This new Western-style HPTDC hotel has spacious rooms with overhead fans. Some rooms have balconies. There is a multicuisine restaurant with room service. Rupees only.

DALHOUSIE

As of this printing, it's difficult to recommend more than one hotel in this hill station. Your best bet is to stay in Khajjiar (see below).

Inexpensive

Aroma 'n Clair's. Court Rd., The Mall, Dalhousie; tel. 99. 20 rooms with bath. The best part of this hotel, which has a lovely location, is its 1930s kitsch. Individual rooms, though large, offer minimal-to-bleak decor. Some amenities are available: TV, multicuisine restaurant, library, bank, shops, tour arrangements. Off-season rates August and November–March 31. AE, V.

DHARAMSALA

Inexpensive

Hotel Bhagsu. Mcleod Ganj, Dharamsala; tel. 3191. 20 rooms with bath. Within walking distance of the prime attractions, this HPTDC bungalow is on a pleasant lawn in Upper Dharamsala. All rooms are clean, with a simple modern decor. "Deluxe" rooms are more spacious and also have TV. Multicuisine restaurant and room service. Traveler's checks accepted.

Hotel Dhauladhar. Dharamsala; tel. 2107. 21 rooms with bath. Rooms in this HPTDC bungalow, which is in Lower Dharamsala and 10 km (6 mi.) from Mcleod Ganj, are clean, with a simple modern decor and private balconies. Best rooms have a valley view. Multicuisine restaurant, room service, terrace, bar. Traveler's checks accepted.

JWALAMUKHI

Inexpensive

Hotel Jwalaji. Jwalamukhi, District Kangra; tel. 81. 25 rooms with bath. Within walking distance of the temple, this two-story HPTDC hotel offers spacious rooms with simple, modern decor. Best rooms are air-conditioned. Room service, good vegetarian restaurant. Rupees only.

JUBBAL

Jubbal Palace Guest House. Reservations: Chapslee Inn, Lakkar Bazaar, Shimla; tel. 77319 or 78242. Set on the grounds of the palace of the Maharajah of Jubbal, this new guest house and inn was slated to open mid-1991. The architecture is grand, with carved-wood ceilings and fine details. The setting is serene, encircled by the Himalayas. Rates were unavailable at press time.

KATRAIN

Expensive

Span Resorts. Kullu-Manali Highway, Katrain, Kullu; tel. 38. 25 rooms with bath. Nestled on the Beas River, these fancy Western-style cottages with modern rooms are 15 km (9 mi.) from the heart of Manali. Multicuisine restaurants, bar, room service, travel counter, doctor on call, gift shop; fishing, croquet, table tennis, and miniature golf facilities. Meals are included. Winter discount. AE.

KEYLONG

Inexpensive

Keylong Tourist Home. Reservations: Tourist Information Office, Manali; tel. 25. 3 rooms with bath; tents available with shared bath. At press time, this simple bungalow was under renovation. By 1991, it should have additional rooms. Currently, simple meals are catered on request. Closed mid-October–mid-June or when the pass is not cleared of snow. Rupees only.

KHAJJIAR

Inexpensive

Khajjiar Hotel Devdar. Reservations: Area Manager, HPTDC, Dalhousie; tel. 36. 11 rooms with bath. This recently renovated HPTDC bungalow has modest, clean rooms that are perfect for its idyllic setting on a hill overlooking a pond. Simple restaurant, room heaters, room service, horseback riding. Open mid-April–November. Rupees only.

KUFRI

Expensive

Kufri Holiday Resort. Shimla Hills; tel. 8300 or 8341. 30 rooms with bath. This new complex, which sits on a bluff, has a Western-style lodge and separate cottages. Cottages offer more privacy, but all rooms have good views and a contemporary decor. Numerous amenities include multicuisine restaurant, room service, pick-up service from Shimla, laundry, car rental, skiing, yak and pony rides, meditation groves. DC.

KULLU

Inexpensive

Hotel Sarvari. Reservations: Tourism Development Officer, Kullu; tel. 2349. 8 rooms with bath. Set on a hill, this one-story HPTDC bungalow has modestly decorated Western-style rooms with overhead fans. Simple restaurant, bar, garden, TV lounge, tourist office. Rupees only.

Hotel Silver Moon. Reservations: Tourism Development Officer, Kullu; tel. 2349. 6 rooms with bath. On a hill on the edge of Kullu, this pretty two-story

HPTDC bungalow has impeccably clean rooms with lots of charm. There are an attractive old-fashioned TV lounge, an intimate restaurant, and a pleasant garden. Rupees only.

MANALI

Expensive

Log Huts. Reservations: Area Manager, Tourist Information Office, Manali; tel. 25. 12 huts with bath. Part of the HPTDC Manali Complex, these two-bedroom cottages overlook a river, with the mountains right outside the door. Facilities include a cafeteria, room service, multicuisine restaurant. Rupees only.

Moderate

John Banon's Guest House. The Manali Orchards, Manali; tel. 35. 10 rooms with bath. Though this isn't Manali's most beautiful lodge, there's a garden and orchard, and the owner is a delightful person who ensures a pleasant stay. Cozy rooms have fireplaces, upstairs rooms open onto a veranda. The mountains and town center are a short walk away. Room service, travel and outdoor adventure assistance. Meals included. Rupees only.

May Flower Guest House. Manali; tel. 104. 22 rooms with bath. Up the road from John Banon's is this charming inn that steals your heart once you step inside. The family-style dining room sets the tone: everything comfortable and orderly. Each room has a fireplace, and you're treated with care. Book well in advance. Room service, restaurant, travel and outdoor adventure assistance. Meals included. Open March–November 15. Rupees only.

Inexpensive

HPTDC Cottages. Reservations: Area Manager, Tourist Information Office, Manali; tel. 25. 12 cottages with bath. The simple cottages in the HPTDC Manali Complex are rustic with minimal decor, but you have pleasant surroundings. Cafeteria, room service, multicuisine restaurant. Rupees only.

Hotel New Hope. Manali; tel. 78. 14 rooms with bath. Owned by John Banon's family, this small lodge is set on a quiet road. It offers plainer rooms, some with fireplaces. Restaurant, room service, trekking and tour arrangements. Meals included. Rupees only.

MANDI

Inexpensive

Hotel Mandav. Mandi; tel. 2123. 7 rooms with bath. On a hill just outside the city, this old two-story HPTDC bungalow has clean, simple rooms that are slightly worn around the edges. The best rooms are upstairs off the veranda. Bar, room service, multicuisine restaurant. Rupees only.

MANIKARAN

Inexpensive

Hotel Parvati. Manikaran; tel. 35. 12 rooms with bath. This two-story HPTDC hotel set on the Parvati River has simple Western-style rooms. Ask for a river view. Multicuisine restaurant, room service, terraces, sulphur baths.

NAGGAR

Inexpensive

Castle Hotel. Reservations: Tourist Office, Manali; tel. 25. 12 rooms, some with attached bath. This newly renovated HPTDC palace-hotel, set on a bluff with a lovely veranda and terrace courtyard overlooking Kullu Valley, has simply furnished, rustic rooms. The older rooms, with fireplaces and attached bathrooms, have more charm; newer rooms have a shared bath. Multicuisine restaurant, outdoor cafeteria, two tiny museums, temple. Rupees only.

NALDEHRA

Inexpensive

Hotel Golf Glade. Reservations: HPTDC, Tourist Information Office, The Mall, Shimla; tel. 78311. 5 rooms and numerous rustic huts, all with bath. This clean, well-run HPTDC facility, near a golf course, has modestly furnished, comfortable rooms, a multicuisine restaurant, and golf course. Rupees only.

PARWANOO

Moderate

Timber Trail Resort and **Timber Trail Heights.** Parwanoo; tel. 497. 14 rooms with bath; 10 tents with shared bath. Across the border from Haryana, this unusual resort is divided into two sections, one on a mountain and the other at the base. You reach the mountain-top site via a ropeway that runs from sunrise to sunset. All rooms are modern and attractive, but the mountain-top retreat offers spectacular views. There are good multicuisine restaurants, attractive gardens, bar, room service, TV, billiards, table tennis. Traveler's checks accepted.

RENUKA LAKE

Inexpensive

Hotel Renuka. Renuka Lake. Reservations: Manager, Hotel Yamuna, Panota Sahib; tel. 41. 4 rooms with bath. This HPTDC facility has modestly furnished Western-style rooms, with a simple restaurant and lakeside cafe. Rupees only.

SARAHAN

Inexpensive

Hotel Shrikhand. Reservations: HPTDC, Tourist Information Office, The Mall, Shimla; tel. 78311. 15 rooms with bath. A new HPTDC bungalow, the Shrikhand offers attractive rooms with a modest contemporary decor, terrific views from private balconies, a restaurant, and lounge. Rupees only.

SHIMLA

Deluxe

Chapslee. Lakkar Bazar, Shimla; tel. 77319 or 78242. 7 rooms with bath. Chapslee is the height of understatement. Its lawn is modest, its exterior far from grand; but step inside this private home of a *kanwar* (prince) and his wife and you're surrounded by sumptuous antiques. Forget about Western amenities; this is Indian class, with a hot-water bottle slipped into your bed at night, afternoon tea, a library with old books. The Pink Suite is gorgeous and has three fireplaces. Gourmet meals included. Reserve well in advance. Closed January–mid-March. Traveler's checks accepted.

Expensive

Oberoi Cecil. The Mall, Shimla; tel. 6041 or 6043. 80 rooms with bath. Under renovation at press time (projected reopening: mid-1991), this fortress-style hotel has a very grand four-story atrium lobby. Rooms are elegant, with Victorian furnishings. Room service, TV, multicuisine restaurant, bar, foreign-exchange counter, travel desk, car-rental service. Meals included. AE, DC, MC, V.

Oberoi Clarkes. The Mall, Shimla; tel. 6091. 33 rooms with bath. Shimla's oldest hotel, Clarkes has a slate-blue and white chalet-look exterior. Rooms are cozy and nicely furnished, but not grand. Ask for a room with fireplace and good views. TV, room service, foreign-exchange desk, travel desk and car-rental service, multicuisine restaurant, bar. Meals included. AE, DC, MC, V.

Woodville Palace Hotel. Himachal Bhawan Rd., Shimla; tel. 6422 or 2763. 12 rooms with bath. This stately 1930s villa, owned by a *kanwar* (prince) and converted into a hotel, offers grand living. The rooms have original Victorian and Art Deco decor. Hollywood stars spent (and spend) time here, no doubt, carousing and playing billiards and croquet. Multicuisine restaurant, gardens, billiard room, car-rental arrangements. Meals included. Reserve well in advance. Rupees only.

Inexpensive–Moderate

Hotel Holiday Home. Cart Rd., Shimla; tel. 6031. 65 rooms with bath. Run by HPTDC, this clean, recently refurbished Western-style hotel, set on a ridge beneath the Mall, offers good value; luxury rooms (moderately priced) are spacious. TV, multicuisine restaurant, room service, bank, car-rental arrangements, bar, shop. DC, V.

Hotel Wildflower Hall. Chharabra, Shimla; tel. 8212. 38 rooms with bath and 12 cottages. This former residence of Lord Kitchener, who also landscaped the gardens, is now an HPTDC hotel. Located 13 km (8 mi.) from Shimla, the Wildflower sports an attractive two-story exterior with an upper story veranda and gables. Appealing cottages are rustic. Interiors of all rooms are simple, yet clean and spacious. Multicuisine restaurant, bar, room service, outdoor café, beautiful grounds, car-rental arrangements, doctor. DC, V.

REST HOUSES AND CIRCUIT HOUSES. Throughout Himachal Pradesh, there are basic yet adequate forest rest houses (sometimes called tourist huts), which are often located in sublime rustic settings, and circuit houses, which are often lovely holdovers from the grand Victorian era. Fees for rest houses—very spartan but clean linen, private rooms and bathroom—are about Rs. 40 per double, and for circuit houses—quality varies but can be the best in town—are Rs. 75 per double. Unfortunately, government officials get first preference at the circuit house. Inquiries should be made via the H.P. Tourist Office (see *Tourist Information*). The rest houses are usually managed by the Public Works Department and the circuit houses by the General Administration Department. Take your chances and book well in advance, or have an alternative booking and check the circuit house on your arrival. Circuit houses are in Chamba, Mandi, Solan, Kasauli, Bilaspur, Dharamsala, Narkanda (near Shimla), Kullu, Manali, and Keylong. Rest houses are numerous, tucked here and there; just write and inquire.

DINING OUT. Except for Shimla and Manali, anticipate only simple—yet good—meals in Himachal Pradesh. Breakfast is usually served 8–10:30; lunch, 12:30–3; and dinner, 7:30–10. Payment is normally in rupees only unless the restaurant is connected to a Western-style hotel. Most of these hotels also accept credit cards. The restaurants listed below are informal and unless noted are open for all three meals and don't require reservations. Prices, based on one person eating a three-course meal, excluding taxes, tip, or beverage, are: *Deluxe,* over Rs. 120; *Expensive,* Rs. 80–Rs. 120; *Moderate,* Rs. 40–Rs. 80; *Inexpensive,* under Rs. 40.

MANALI

Almost all the best meals are served in the private lodges where the dining room is restricted to guests. Here is one exception.

Inexpensive

Mount View Restaurant. The Mall; no phone. This simple restaurant is crowded with booths; music plays unobtrusively; a photo of the Dalai Lama smiles down from the wall. The Buddhists who run this restaurant provide tasty Tibetan, Chinese, Indian, and Japanese meals. Open 8 A.M.–10 P.M. Rupees only.

SHIMLA

Expensive–Deluxe

Chapslee. Lakkar Bazar; tel. 77319 or 87242. This home-turned-inn is filled with antiques and elegance, and the fixed-menu meals match the ambience. There is Indian cuisine at lunch, Continental at dinner. The formal dining room can only accommodate about 12 people. Open 1–2:30 and 8–9:30. Reservations required. Closed January–March 15. Rupees only.

Oberoi Clarkes. The Mall; tel. 6091. Low-key decor and lovely mountain views accompany the good Continental, Chinese, and Indian food served at Clarkes. Try the popular chicken imperial (chicken with mushroom sauce) and *kadai* mutton (mutton pieces in thick masala gravy). There is an evening dance band in May, June, and Christmas week. Open 7–10:30 A.M., 1–3 P.M., and 8–11 P.M. Reservations advised. AE, DC, MC, V.

Woodville Palace. Himachal Bhawan Rd.; tel. 2765. Shimla's other culinary treat, this villa has an interior dining room filled with antiques. The chef offers Chinese, Continental, and Indian dishes, with especially tasty kebabs. Open 1–3 P.M. and 8–10 P.M. Reservations required. Rupees only.

Inexpensive–Moderate

Ashiana. The Ridge; tel. 78464. Shimla's former bandstand is now an informal restaurant. You can choose from Chinese, Continental, and Indian cuisines, including regional Pahari dishes. Specialties include *kamod* (mutton cooked in a spicy curd gravy) and *sepurbadi* (steamed lentils fried in spinach). Meals served 9–11 A.M., 12:30–3:30 P.M., and 7:30–10 P.M. Snacks are served during non-meal hours. Rupees only.

Fascination. The Mall; tel. 6313. This informal upstairs restaurant has two cozy rooms with good views. The chef serves good Indian, Continental, and Chinese meals, including tasty chili chicken. Meals served 9–11 A.M., 12:30–3:30 P.M., and 7:30–11 P.M. Snacks are served during non-meal hours. Rupees only.

SWEETS AND TREATS. Chamba. *Cafe Ravi View.* On the river's edge, this simple café offers good tea and snacks and a pleasant ambience. Open 9 A.M.–9 P.M.

Manali. At *Delhi Chat,* a tiny stall on the Mall, opposite the Tourist Information complex, ask for a plate of *papri chat* (a mess of pastry, potatoes, and yogurt covered in a sweet-and-sour sauce). It's a delicious treat for about Rs. 5.

Mandi. Stop at the *Indian Milk Bar,* 8 km (5 mi.) from Mandi on the road to Sundernagar. Its signboard is in Hindi, so look for a small building with brightly painted stones on the exterior. For about Rs. 3, you can enjoy a great chocolate milk shake.

Shimla. Visit the *India Coffee House* on the Mall, near Evening College. The old eatery looks run-down, but relax over delicious coffee and snacks and let the charm slip through. Open 8:30 A.M.–9 P.M.

HOW TO GET AROUND. All taxi rates are about Rs. 3.50 per km. Bus fares are always inexpensive. **Chamba.** Taxis and HPRTC buses are available. Contact the reception desk at Hotel Iravati (tel. 94), or the HPRTC bus stand (tel. 10).

Dharamsala. Buses and taxis are available at the bus stand (tel. 2243); or the local tourist office (tel. 3163 or 3107).

Manali. From Bhuntar Airport (52 km or 32 mi. from Manali), HPRTC buses go to Kullu and Manali (about Rs. 10). The bus ride to Kullu is about 15 minutes; the trip to Manali takes about 90 minutes. Taxis are plentiful: Kullu (Rs. 40) or Manali (Rs. 180). In Manali, buses and private taxis are available for hire. Manali HPRTC bus stand (tel. 23), or Manali tourist office (tel. 25).

Mandi. Buses and taxis are available in Mandi at the HPRTC bus stand (tel. 2403), or the local tourist office (tel. 2575).

Shimla. From Jubbarhati Airport, you can go by bus or taxi to Shimla. The *Airport Coach Service* (Rs. 20) takes an hour, stops on the Ridge and at the Holiday Home Hotel. For pick-up locations back to the airport, contact HPTDC, Shimla (tel. 78311 or 77646). A taxi (about Rs. 150) will take you to your hotel in about

45 minutes. HPRTC (tel. 3566) provides local bus service in and around Shimla. Taxis and cars for hire are available through the *Taxi Union Service* (tel. 5123). The Mall and the Ridge are strictly prohibited to vehicles; but you can hire a bicycle rickshaw. Set the fare before you start; it should be less than a taxi.

TOURS. HPTDC and the private sector don't sponsor scheduled-departure state-wide tours; but HPTDC does offer day-long tours by bus and private car in and around Dalhousie, Manali, and Shimla. Contact the tourist department in each area for details and reservations.

TOUR OPERATORS. Himachal offers numerous outdoor adventures. Contact the following specialized tour packagers for a memorable experience.

Himalayan Adventurers Pvt. Ltd. (Manali 175131, H.P.; tel. 104) and *Manoo's Mountain Adventures* (Thakur's Hotel, Rahul, Manali, H.P.; tel. 180) sponsor excellent treks, skiing trips, jeep safaris (including the new trip from Manali to Leh), and some white-water rafting.

Himalayan River Runners (188-A, Jor Bagh, New Delhi; tel. 615736) offers excellent rafting runs.

HPTDC (Ritz Annexe, Shimla 171001, H.P.; tel. 3249) organizes good, inexpensive tours, treks, hang gliding, and ski courses. They can also help with all travel needs, including arrangements for a car with driver.

The *Mountaineering Institute of Manali and Allied Sports Complex* (Manali 175131, H.P.; tel. 42) organizes courses in high-altitude trekking, mountaineering, rock climbing, and outward bound–type courses for pre-teens. They also provide porters and guides for treks.

From March to December, you can also experience Himachal's princely past and go on a *Royal Circuit Tour* that features overnight stays in the homes of former maharajahs and *kanwars* (princes), fortress complexes from the 1700s, elegant manor homes from the 1880s, and turn-of-the-century palaces. For complete details, contact Kanwar Ratinjit Singh, Chapslee, Shimla, H.P.; tel. 78242 and 77319.

SEASONAL EVENTS. Himachal puts on some big shows that draw crowds: Hindu festivals, such as Dussehra; Buddhist celebrations, such as Sisu; and gigantic fairs, such as the Lavi Mela. The specific dates for many events are determined by the lunar calendar; consult the Government of India Tourist Bureau for details.

February. Manali and Kufri (near Shimla) hold a week-long *Winter Sports Carnival.*

February/March. The week-long *Shivratri Mela* (religious festival), held in Mandi and at the Baijnath Temple near Palampur, starts with a jubilant procession of temple deities accompanied by chanting and drumming.

March/April. The *Sisu Fair* at Lake Rewalsar honors the Indian mystic, Guru Padmasambhava, who introduced Buddhism to Tibet.

July/August. A pilgrimage to Lake Manimahesh from Bharmour near Chamba takes thousands of Hindus to purify themselves in frigid waters.

July/August. During Chamba's week-long *Minjar Harvest Festival,* hill people appease their rain god with an exuberant procession and offerings.

October/November. The world-famous nine-day *Hindu Dussehra Festival* in Kullu celebrates the victory of good over evil with elaborate parades of deities, dances, music, and animal sacrifices performed around a gigantic bonfire. This is the most famous festival in Himachal.

November. The *Lavi Mela,* on the banks of the Sutlej River in Rampur near Shimla, is one of India's largest fairs. Hill people come to dance and sing.

November. The *Renuka Fair* commemorates the sacrifice of Mother Renuka with the annual immersion of temple deities.

HISTORIC SITES. There is generally no charge for entry, but when donations are requested, a few rupees will suffice. Historic sites are generally open daily, sunrise to sunset, unless otherwise noted.

BHARMOUR

There are 84 temples nestled in a courtyard named after *churasi* (yogis) who came there to meditate centuries ago. *Laxshna Devi* is a wooden temple dedicated to Shiva that was built in the seventh century. *Nargingh Temple* is dedicated to Vishnu from the tenth or eleventh century. *Manimahesh Temple* is dedicated to Shiva and was built in the seventh century.

CHAIL

Chail Palace, former summer capital of the maharajah of Patiala, was built after World War I. Now a state-run hotel, it has great grounds with good walks and pleasant views.

CHAMBA

Lakshminarain is a stone temple complex, with three shrines dedicated to Shiva and three to Vishnu. The earliest was built in the tenth century, the last was constructed in 1828. Vishnu temples are of the Shikara type, with two overhead roofs; the others are in indigenous hill style.

DHARAMSALA

St. John's Church in the Wilderness, built in 1860, contains beautiful stained glass windows and a monument to Lord Elgin, the British viceroy who was originally from Scotland and asked to be buried in this church dedicated to the patron saint of Scotland.

Namgyal Monastery, a new Buddhist monastery with a towering golden image of Buddha, is the current seat of the Dalai Lama, the spiritual leader of Tibet, who fled Tibet after the Chinese invasion. It has daily ceremonies, open to the public, usually at 5 or 6 A.M. and 5 or 6 P.M.

JWALAMUKHI

Jwalamukhi Temple, dedicated to the "Flaming Goddess," is an important northern pilgrimage center, with its flame kept perpetually burning by priests. The golden dome over the temple was a gift of Mogul Emperor Akbar.

KANGRA

Baijnath Temple (A.D. 800), a Shikara-style stone temple with a low pyramid shaped roof, is possibly the oldest Shiva shrine in India, conceivably constructed by Pandavas. Handsome carvings adorn interior pillars, including an unusual composite image of Vishnu and Lakshmi.

KEYLONG

Kharding Gompa is the largest monastery in Lahaul, with colorful frescoes and murals and an enormous prayer drum containing strips of paper with the sacred mantra written a million times. It formerly was the capital of Lahaul.

KULLU

Bijli Mahavev Temple has a 60-foot-high spire that supposedly attracts lightning—divine blessings—which then shatters the Shiva lingam contained inside the temple. The priests reassemble the sacred symbol and wait for the miracle to occur all over again.

Basheshwar Mahadev Temple (in Bajaura, 15 km from Kullu) is a ninth-century pyramidical granite temple dedicated to Shiva and covered with exquisite stone carvings and sculptural detail, some of which was destroyed in the late 1700s.

Raghunathji Temple, built in the seventeenth century, houses the presiding deity of Kullu Valley.

MANALI

Hadimba Devi Temple, 600 years old, is a wooden shrine with a four-tiered pago-da-shaped roof. The temple is dedicated to the goddess Hadimba.

Vashisht Rishi and *Lord Rama* temples (in Vashisht, three km from Manali) are pyramidical stone temples, with sacred sulphur springs and temple baths.

MANDI

Panchvaktra Temple is of the Shikara style, with an unusual five-faced Shiva sit-ting in the meditation pose.

Bhutnath Temple, also of Shikara style, with a small lingam in the inner sanctum, is situated by the river in the old city.

MANIKARAN

Sri Ramchandra Temple was built in the sixteenth century and dedicated to Vish-nu. *Sri Raghunath Temple* is also dedicated to Vishnu. All Manikaran, with its bub-bling sulphur springs and legends connecting it to Shiva and Parvati who supposed-ly meditated in Manikaran for 1,000 years, is imprinted with a sense of spiritual history.

MANIMAHESH

Manimahesh Temple (a 34-km trek from Bharmaur), constructed in the Shikara style, is one of the oldest and most beautiful temples in Himachal Pradesh.

SARAHAN

Bhimakali Temple is sacred to Hindus and Buddhists. Visitors should not turn their back on the inner sanctum's sacred idol, Bhimakali. Cameras are also not al-lowed inside the temple that leads to this sacred chamber.

SHIMLA

Institute of Advanced Studies, former Viceregal Lodge, was constructed in 1884–88 during the time of Lord Dufferin. Sitting atop Summer Hill, the structure was built of Himalayan gray stone in English Renaissance (Elizabethan) style. No en-trance is allowed without prior permission from the secretary of the institute; but enjoy the beautiful grounds and views of Shimla.

Wildflower Hall (13 km from Shimla), former residence of Lord Kitchener built in 1903, is now a state-run hotel. Kitchener landscaped the present gardens, with their lovely grounds and walks.

MUSEUMS AND GALLERIES. *Bhuri Singh Museum,* Chamba, has an excel-lent collection of miniature paintings from the Kangra and Basoli schools, and the rescued murals from nearby Rang Mahal Palace, which suffered a fire years ago. Open 10 A.M.–5 P.M.; closed Mondays and official holidays.

Roerich Art Gallery, Naggar, houses a collection of paintings of the Russian artist Nicholas Roerich. Check with the tourist information office in Kullu (tel. 2349) for the hours.

Himachal State Museum, near Chaura Maidan, Shimla, contains "hill" art and cultural art of Himachal Pradesh, including Pahari (mountain) and other miniature schools, of painting, sculpture, bronzes, costumes, textiles, and jewelry. Open 10 A.M.–1:30 P.M.; 2–5 P.M. Closed Mondays and official holidays.

SPORTS AND OUTDOOR ADVENTURES. Himachal Pradesh does its best to keep the sports enthusiast happy, with new adventures offered each season.

Fishing. Fish for trout in the Pabar River near Rohru, a day-long excursion from Shimla, and in the Beas River near Manali. Try for *mahseer* (Himalayan river fish) on the Beas near Dharamsala. For more details and the required license, contact the District Fisheries Officer for each district. In Manali, contact the Tourist Department.

Golfing. Naldehra, 23 km (14 mi.) from Shimla, has a nine-hole course, with available equipment. The season runs from May to November. For details and reservations, contact the HPTDC in Shimla; tel. 78331 or 77646.

Hang Gliding. HPTDC organizes competitions in hang gliding at Billing, about 50 km (31 mi.) from Palampur. Write in advance to HPTDC, The Mall, Shimla, H.P.

Hot Springs. Manikarin. Hotel Parvati has 14 hot spring baths set up in individual clean cubicles. Contact HPTDC (tel. 35) for details and reservations. Nominal charge. **Tattapani.** Regular bus service from Shimla goes to Tattapani (51 km or 32 mi.) and popular sulphur springs that emerge from the Sutlej River. Private cubicles are available; reservations not necessary. Contact HPTDC for further details; tel. 78331 or 77646. **Vashisht.** HPTDC has eight sulphur baths set up in private cubicles inside a small complex just outside Manali. An adjoining café serves tea and beverages. Open 7 A.M.–10 P.M. daily. Make reservations at the Manali Tourist Office (tel. 25). Nominal charge.

Ice Skating. Shimla's Skating Rink is open from November to February. Nominal charge. Rent reasonable skates from Capital Boot House on The Mall.

Jeep Safari. A new road just opened from Manali to Leh in Ladakh (mid-July–mid-October) that takes you through this remote, "lunar" terrain. Arrangements must be made in advance to cross this sensitive border area. Contact Himalayan Adventurers or HPTDC, addresses above.

Rafting. Himalayan River Runners (188-A, Jor Bagh, New Delhi) sponsors 6-day white-water runs north of Shimla on the Sutlej River (November to mid-December and February to April) and is currently studying a new 3-day run on the Chandra River in Lahaul (mid-August to mid-September). Arrangements must be made in advance. Himalayan Adventurers (Manali, tel. 104) offers a one-day run on the Beas River in Kullu Valley (mid-May to mid-July and mid-August to mid-September).

Skiing. Himachal's skiing facilities aren't sophisticated, but the vistas are lovely, and the price is low, including the cost of good equipment. At **Narkanda** (near Shimla), where the slopes aren't challenging, you can also take ski lessons. Season runs from January to mid-March. Contact HPTDC, Shimla (tel. 78331 or 77646) for details. **Solang Valley,** 13 km (8 mi.) from Manali, is Himachal's premiere resort. The season runs from mid-December to mid-March and lessons are available. Contact the Manali Tourist Office (tel. 25) for details. The Mountaineering Institute and Allied Sports Complex offers comprehensive skiing courses.

TREKKING. No matter where you travel in Himachal Pradesh, there's spectacular trekking. For Manali, Kullu Valley, environs around Shimla, Chamba, and Kangra valleys, the best time to trek is May–June and September–mid-October. The trekking season in Lahaul (June–October) is determined by snow, and treks are strenuous; you're rarely below 3,600 meters (12,000 feet). Trekkers should have a guide and should make arrangements in advance. Contact Himalayan Adventurers (address above), HPTDC (Ritz Annexe, Shimla, H.P.), or a recommended Tour Operator in *Facts at Your Fingertips*. Trekkers can also rent camping equipment or hire porters and guides from Himalayan Adventurers, HPTDC, and the Mountaineering Institute (addresses above). Here are just a few of the best trekking routes, rated by degree of difficulty.

Trek 1. Naggar (south of Manali) to Malana; 28 km (17 mi.) of rugged climbing up to this secluded mountain village, where the malanas have their own language and customs. Three or four days. Moderately difficult.

Trek 2. Bharmour to Lake Manimahesh. This 37-km (23-mi.) trek is best during the Hindu pilgrimage (July or August) to this sacred lake, near a revered peak where Shiva supposedly meditated. Tents surround the water. Thousands of pilgrims take a dip in frigid water. Stalls sell food. Moderate.

Trek 3. Manikaran to Mantali Glacier via Parvati Valley; 100 km (62 mi.) roundtrip; numerous hot springs, villages, and old temples to explore, with Alpine terrain and Himalayan vistas. The massive glacier is the source of the Parvati River, steeped in beauty and mythological importance. Ten days. Moderate.

Trek 4. Lahaul Circular trek via Batal, Chandratal Lake, Baralacha Pass, Phirtsela Pass, Shangse Valley, Shingun La Pass, Darcha; 15 days of high-altitude walking in a Buddhist realm. Himalayan Adventurers offers variations of this trek which require about 12 days. Difficult.

SHOPPING. In Shimla and especially Kullu and Manali, you can buy wonderful handknit or handloomed woolen goods: shawls, sweaters, hats, jackets, gloves. In Manali and Dharamsala, you can also buy beautiful Tibetan handicrafts, clothing, and carpets. In Upper Dharamsala, visit the *Charitable Trust Handicraft Emporium and Bookstore* and the *Showroom of Tibetan Handicraft Production* (both located in the McLeod Ganj bazaar). They're open 9 A.M.–6 P.M., closed Mondays. Chamba is known for its durable and inexpensive leather sandals. In Shimla, look for fine carved walking sticks; and if you're interested in rare books on India and the Himalayas or old etchings, visit *Maria Brothers,* No. 78, The Mall, tel. 5388; open 10:30 A.M.–1 P.M. and 5–8 P.M. Rupees only.

NIGHTLIFE AND BARS. In **Dharamsala,** inquire at the Tibetan Information Office (tel. 2343 or 2457), near the monastery, about Tibetan music and dance performances at the *Tibetan Institute of Performing Arts.* Starting the second Saturday in April, the institute usually puts on a 10-day festive Tibetan opera. In **Shimla,** the old *Gaiety Theater* still has occasional summer productions. The best public bar in Shimla is at Oberoi Clarkes, open 12:30–2:30 P.M. and 7–11 P.M.

KASHMIR, JAMMU, AND LADAKH

A Glimpse of Heaven

by
KATHLEEN COX

Note: Due to increased political unrest in Kashmir and Jammu, the U.S. State Department urges extreme caution in traveling in this part of India. Furthermore, the department at press time (early 1991) advised postponement of travel until further notice to the following areas: Srinigar, Kashmir Valley and surrounding areas (excluding Jammu, Udampur, and Kathwa districts), as well as the Leh District and the Ladakh Region. Check with the department before making final plans.

"Kashmir—only Kashmir!" These were the Emperor Jahangir's final words. To see his summer playground one last time; to die here, surrounded by the mighty Himalayas; to see again the stately Chenars that edged the emerald green lakes; to sit within his treasured gardens, lightheaded with the fragrance of spectacular flowers and mesmerized by the play of his exquisite marble fountains.

But the Mogul's final wish wasn't granted. On his last annual pilgrimage that took him from the heat and dust of the plains to his enchanted vale, Jahangir died. Satraps, nobles, and his imperial court hovered over him on his death bed and begged to know his last request. All he whispered was "Kashmir."

This Oriental super-Switzerland has lost little of the original charm that first attracted the Moguls. Just a breath of the invigorating air and you succumb to the spell of this conspiracy between mountain and nature—India's jewel of the East.

In the third century B.C., Kashmir formed part of Ashoka's far-flung Mauryan Empire. After Akbar grabbed it in 1587, the Mogul emperors never stopped paying lengthy visits, escaping from the unpleasant summer on the plains and taking refuge in this idyllic vale where they laid out, at lavish expense and with impressive technical ingenuity, their elegant "pleasure gardens." It's no surprise that the appeal of this valley survived the fall of the Moguls, also entrapping the British who flocked to Kashmir during the last decades of their rule in India.

In those days, since only the upper echelons could afford the time and expense involved in making the difficult journey, Kashmir never became an official "hill station." A semiautonomous state ruled by the maharajah of Kashmir and Jammu, it also remained a specifically restricted "Kashmiri" homeland, with the maharajah shrewdly passing an edict that prevented foreigners from owning land in his state. This edict gave rise to the houseboat—a Britisher's novel solution to the unfortunate restriction. This boat, aptly called "Victory," offered such an attractive alternative that, in no time, a flotilla of posh floating homes—each one outfitted in Victorian splendor—sat moored in Dal Lake.

Kashmir—slightly smaller than Great Britain, with under six million inhabitants—is in the heart of Asia. Few realize that it's farther north than Tibet. For thousands of years, caravans carrying precious merchandise passed from China and elsewhere through Kashmir on their way to the plains of India. This international flavor continues today. Here, you find a variety of races, national costumes, and traditions. The Kashmiri *pandit* man of letters) forms the Hindu leading minority (Nehru was a Kashmiri pandit, as was his daughter, Indira Gandhi). The Kashmiri Moslems, representing about 90 percent of the population, are extremely devout, industrious, and hardworking. Their daily chanting bears witness to a strong brotherhood—a communal feeling—both joyful and profound.

In late 1989, Moslem factions that periodically called for secession renewed their demand. Some of these secessionists claim Kashmiri Moslems should form their own independent country; others would like to see Kashmir join Pakistan. In the meantime, their demands have led to violence, which, in turn, has led to a firm response from the central government in Delhi, which insists that Kashmir is an integral part of India. At press time, peace in the valley remained illusive; an acceptable solution will be difficult to find.

EXPLORING KASHMIR AND JAMMU

As soon as you enter the Jammu region from Pathankot, you catch sight of the snow-capped peaks of Kashmir, the Pir Panjal range. Jammu splits up naturally into three tracts—the mountainous, the submontane, and the plains. The inhabitants of these three divisions have their own dialects, customs, and dress. The Dogras inhabiting the plains speak Dogri, a mixture of Sanskrit, Punjabi, and Persian. The inhabitants of the "middle-mountains" are called Paharis and occupy themselves in agriculture and

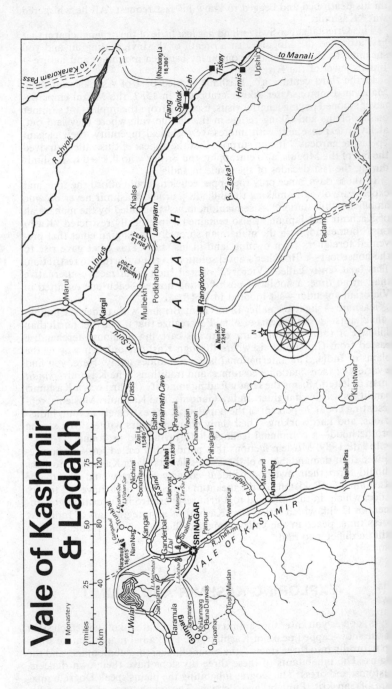

cattle breeding. Like the Kashmiris, they are hearty travelers and cover long distances without fatigue. The Gujjars are seminomadic herdsmen. In summer, they drive their cattle or goats into the high mountains and make temporary flat-topped mud huts for themselves and their livestock; in the winter, they return to the lowlands.

Jammu, known as the "City of Temples," has long been a center of Indian culture in which the arts have flourished. For centuries, the Pahari painters have been well known for their lovely miniatures that show a dexterity of line and a matchless blend of color. Before Independence, Jammu, unlike Kashmir, was a private domain, which the maharajah kept to himself—and the British raj, wisely enough, made no effort to prevent this. No European was allowed to enter without a government permit. Each winter, the maharajah moved down from the snowy heights of Kashmir and retired to his palace in Jammu, which enjoys the winter climate of the plains, standing 1,000 feet above sea level.

Although Jammu is primarily a transit stop to and from Kashmir, try to visit the multitowered Raghunath Temple, the largest temple complex in Northern India. Located in the heart of the city and surrounded by numerous other temples, Raghunath, constructed over a 25-year period beginning in 1835, is dedicated to Lord Rama (a Vishnu incarnation). A good portion of the interior is covered in dazzling gold leaf. Also see the Ranbireswar Temple, built in 1883 and dedicated to Lord Shiva with its 12 large crystal lingams, and the Dogra Art Gallery, which houses a lovely collection of miniatures. You can also visit the sacred cave of the goddess Vaishno Devi, an important Hindu shrine on a hill in Katra, 50 kilometers (31 miles from Jammu), that contains a hilltop cave high above the Jammu plains. The cave is supposedly where Vaishno Devi took shelter after killing a demon.

Srinagar, Capital of Kashmir

About 70 miles beyond the Banihal Pass, the gateway to the Vale of Kashmir, lies Srinagar, the capital of the state, nestled in the mountainous walls of the Himalayas at the center of the famous vale. This is the Venice of the East—a "Venice" ensconced miraculously in the midst of an eastern-style Switzerland (or is it Amsterdam?). Set against the winding Jhelum River with Dal Lake sweeping off to the east and the Himalayas rising up in the distance, Srinagar brings to mind many water-based cities, while retaining a Moslem character completely its own.

Eyes linger on the tall riverside wooden houses, with their intricately carved verandas and balconies jutting precariously over the Jhelum—majestic homes that frequently have their own private *ghats* (front steps) that lead down to the water. Many homes are old and weatherworn, but some still have brightly painted shutters and trim, and always you see that carefully worked Kashmiri gingerbread on the verandas.

Then there's the river, unfortunately muddy and polluted. *Dongas,* large flat-bottom vessels on which entire families live, compete for space on this waterway with lumber-laden barges, houseboats, ducks, swimming children, and *shikaras* (small boats used as water taxis with canopied roofs and fluttering curtains). You could spend days just watching the flow of life that moves back and forth throughout Srinagar.

Take a walk through the old city, giving yourself plenty of time to meander and follow on whim the narrow winding streets that often lead to a dead end or the river, the focus of life. Men in fur caps and women in dark *pherans*—their heads covered in a bright colored scarves or mysteriously veiled in black—walk along the crowded streets. Horsedrawn *tongas* (carts) prance by—the animals robust and jaunty, with the string of bells jangling around their neck adding to the festive air. Old men, frequently smoking their "hubbly-bubbly" (the Kashmiri hookah) sit inside small shops or open-air stalls that display all the artistry of Kashmir: furs and embroidered leather or fabrics, carved woodwork, paper-mâché objects, copper or silver urns and pots, shawls, and magnificent carpets.

Apart from the attractions of the old city and the river still spanned by some original wooden bridges, Srinagar has numerous landmarks. Early one morning, climb the stone steps that lead to the Shankaracharya Temple (built by a Hindu during the tolerant reign of Jahangir) at the top of a 1,000-foot hill on the southeastern edge of Srinagar. You can still see parts of an original temple that existed here (the low enclosing wall and the plinth), believed to have been constructed by the son of Ashoka around 200 B.C. The existing temple provides a striking panorama, well beyond the city to the configurations of the Jhelum River and the adjoining Dal Lake.

There are also great views from the Hari Parbat Fort on top of a hill that is sacred to Hindus—Sharika Hill. Although the fortress dates from the eighteenth century, the wall around Hari Parbat was built by Akbar in the late 1500s. If you want to go inside, get permission from the State Archaeological Department in Srinagar.

Srinagar, a predominantly Moslem city, also has its hefty share of historic mosques. See the Jamia Masjid, the largest in India. First built by Sultan Sikander in the thirteenth century and destroyed three times by fire, the last construction—maintaining the original design—was supervised by the Mogul Emperor Aurangzeb in 1674. An attractive example of Indo-Saracenic architecture, its vast interior contains 400 cedar wood pillars, each made from a single tree trunk. Also, see the Pather Masjid, built entirely of limestone by Jahangir's wife, Nur Jahan, in 1620. And visit the pagodalike Shah Hamdan Mosque, one of the oldest mosques in the city (first constructed in the late fourteenth century) and also destroyed by fires and rebuilt, the last time in 1732—without a single nail or screw. The walls and ceilings are covered with delicate painted woodwork. Unfortunately, only Moslems are allowed inside. Finally, visit the Hazratbal on the western shore of Dal Lake, a new modern shrine that contains a sacred hair of the Prophet Mohammed, which is shown to the public on religious holidays.

Dal and Nagin Lakes

For most, a visit to Srinagar means a vacation, however short, on a legendary houseboat. Although, it's possible to book your boat in advance (in high season this is advised), you can also wait and make a reservation at the Tourist Reception Center in Srinagar. But before you make your choice, it's wise to hire a shikara to see your boat first. The houseboats are moored on Dal and Nagin Lakes, and the Jhelum River. If you want peace and quiet, choose the Nagin or the remote end of Dal. If you're after the hustle and proximity of the city, stay on the southern end of Dal or right on the busy Jhelum—but be ready for noise!

Houseboats come in all sizes and price ranges, but the aura of most of them is genteel elegance. Even the new boats continue the original design—lovely fragrant carved walls and ceilings of cedar, a formal dining room, a handsome sitting room, and bedrooms, a sun deck on the roof plus a cozy veranda from which you can watch the sun rise or set, depending on your location. A word of caution: staying on a houseboat sets you up as easy prey for the small tradesmen—touts—who paddle out in their shikaras transformed into floating stores—wide-eyed hawks casing the joint. Before you unpack, you're besieged with everything available in Kashmir, from a fresh cutting of local flowers (which is quite pleasant) to razor blades and mineral water. Prices can be exorbitant, so bargain for anything you want. And when you've had enough of the handicrafts, salespeople, and tailors, just say "no" with authority and send them away.

Mogul Garden

No trip to Srinagar is complete without a tour of the waterside Mogul gardens—a trip that should be made by shikara. Each small boat for private hire takes up to four passengers, but with two, it constitutes the height of pampered luxury. Once you've stretched out on the comfortable cushions under the shelter of the fringed canopy, you understand why this boat is dubbed the "gondola" of Kashmir. Your boatsman, with his heart-shaped paddle, glides you soundlessly over the calm water. You pass by ingenious floating vegetable gardens; stop, if you're in the right season, and snap off a gorgeous lotus bloom; follow the swooping course of an electric kingfish, and always remind yourself that this heaven is real.

At intervals all around the 12-square-mile surface stand the stately *chenars,* giant plane trees, which turn fire red in the autumn. The chenars, which were favorite trees of the Moguls who first planted them in Kashmir, form the backdrop to the first garden you visit: the Shalimar Bagh (Garden of Love), laid out in the early 1600s by Jahangir for his Queen Nur Jahan—four terraces of lawns and flower beds rising one above the other. A shallow water channel runs down the middle—typical Persian quadrant-style—and on the top terrace, reserved for the royal women, is a black marble pavilion, secluded and elegant. From May to October, you can watch an evening sound and lumiere show here.

A TOUR OF THE LAKES AND VALLEYS

Gulmarg

Gulmarg, the meadow of flowers, 56 kilometers (32 miles), northwest of Srinagar, was a favorite vacation spot of the Moguls and later of the British. At an elevation of 2,460 meters (8,200 feet), this bowl-shaped valley, set high in the mountains and encircled by fir and pine-covered slopes, is not just a convenient base for numerous treks; it is an up-and-coming year-round resort. You can play golf in the warm months on one of the world's highest courses (originally developed by the British). You can sled (called "sledging") or ski in winter on assorted slopes with T-bar, puma, and chair lift, or trek with a *sherpa* up four kilometers (2¼ miles) to Khilanmarg, with its breathtaking view and memorable run (a gondola will soon replace this novel, rigorous uphill climb). Although Gulmarg, with its snug circle of rustic hotels, is more like a frontier town than another Sun Valley or Chamonix, it is one of the best skiing bargains in the world. Lessons, lift tickets, and all equipment (fairly up to date, with outdoor clothes included) cost just a few dollars a day.

Gulmarg is also the place for invigorating walks and spirited pony rides. From its seven-mile-long Circular Path, which takes you through pine forests, you have a magnificent view of the entire valley of Kashmir, including Srinagar. You can also see the distant Nanga Parbat, over 7,800 meters

(26,000 feet). This giant, whose name means naked mountain, dominates the landscape for miles in every direction.

Wular and Manasbal Lakes

From Gulmarg, head northeast to Sangrama and then continue northeast until you reach Wular Lake, the largest freshwater lake in India. Set in magnificent high mountains, the Wular, which is the color of soft jade, is another popular vacation haunt. One legend claims that the Wular was formerly a city of such decadence that the mountains released a deluge that swallowed it up; when the water is low, you can see the remaining ruins, it is said. The Wular has evidently claimed enough lives that the deepest area is known as Mota Khon (Gulf of Corpses).

Just a few miles beyond the Wular is Lake Manasbal, a bird watcher's paradise (30 kilometers or 18 miles from Srinagar). The deepest lake in Kashmir, Manasbal is famous for its lotus blossoms that spread across the water in the summer.

Take the road that branches to the left at Ganderbal and head into the Sindh Valley, one of the most famous in Kashmir. As you travel along the sinuous terrain, the mountains come down precipitously on both sides, covered with that particular Kashmiri pine known as the budle tree. The average specimen stands over 30 meters (100 feet) tall.

Pahalgam and Lidder Valley

Sixty miles southeast of Srinagar is the Lidder Valley, with majestic mountain scenery. As you enter the valley via Baltal, you can take a day-long trek to a height of 3,900 meters (13,000) feet to the sacred cave of Amarnath, believed to be the former abode of Shiva. The pilgrim's rough-hewn treck, steps cut out of rock, leads straight to the object of worship—a stalactite, shaped like a lingam, hanging from the roof of the cave. At the year's most auspicious moment for worship—the night of the full moon between July and August when Shiva supposedly explained the secret of creation to Parvati—pilgrims pour in from every corner of India to offer their prayers to the god.

The Kolahoi Glacier

Lucky the traveler who takes the three-day trek from Pahalgam (equipment, porters, ponies, and guides are available here) up to the Kolahoi Glacier, the Matterhorn of Kashmir. This popular and moderate trek offers some of the most inspiring scenery in Kashmir. Besides seeing great panoramas, you also witness the agility of the nomadic Gujjar who move their herds with sublime grace and speed. The actual journey that leads to the glacier takes you first to Aru, a tiny village situated at the foot of a meadow—a convenient stopping place. On the second day, you come to Lidderwatt, a camping site in a meadow forded by two small streams and surrounded by mountains. Here, the sun pours down from a subtropical sky while the encircling pines hold onto night well beyond daybreak. The third day takes you through a pine forest, then the view bursts wide open at Satlanjan. Here, you cross more narrow streams and finally see the milky green Kolahoi—craggy and daunting.

Snow Bridges

A word of warning for anyone who follows this enchanting village to the watershed: Beware of leaving too late in the year when melting snow can be dangerous. Up to the end of May or the beginning of June, you can rely on the snow bridges; after that, they can be deadly. And in its early phase, what is termed a snow bridge in Kashmir is just barely a bridge. During the winter, the ravines fill in and bridge over with snow, while the mountain torrent continues to force its way through a tunnel underneath. Until the thaw sets in, you can walk up and down these precipitous gorges on top of the snow, with the river crashing its way through beneath, unseen and frequently unheard. But once the snow starts to melt, these bridges become so slender at the middle of their arches they can snap at any moment, which can mean a drop of 4.5 to six meters (15 to 20 feet). Or, the snow bridge may already may have broken up in the middle, leaving a gap of two or three feet, which you then have to jump across. The safest trip is across the giant snowbridge at Chananwari, a six-kilometer (10-mile) pony trek from Pahalgam.

EXPLORING LADAKH

One of the prime adventure opportunities in India is remote and rugged Ladakh, lying between the two highest mountain ranges in the world: the Himalayan and the Karakoram. Ladakh can be approached by road, or you can fly straight to Leh, the capital. However, if you've got the time, the drive is the only way to go. The territory of Ladakh, about twice the size of Switzerland, represents 70 percent of the total area of Jammu and Kashmir and is one of the highest regions on earth—a good portion of it over 2,700 meters (9,000 feet) above sea level. With a total population of only 150,000, Ladakh has one of the lowest population densities in the world (two–three people per square mile). For the most part inhospitable and craggy, the otherworldly terrain is arid beyond belief, with mountain peaks soaring three to four miles high. The joint effects of elevation and isolation amid snowy mountains produce the most unusual climate in the world—a weird combination of desert and arctic. Burning heat by day is followed by piercing cold at night, with everything parched by the extreme dryness of the air. The annual rainfall rarely exceeds three to four inches; few rain clouds get over the prohibitive peaks. As you travel up and down the arid, windswept mountains for miles and miles, you see deserts of granite dust, bare crags, and mountains of different hues. Ladakh is rightly called the "moonland."

In spite of the harsh landscape, Ladakh offers a wealth of environmental intrigue. Pink granite contrasting with a deep blue sky, brisk sunshine, pure air, and green valleys dotted like cases in a vast desert. There are wild yak, the elusive snow leopard, the docile marmot, and blue sheep. But the greatest draw in Ladakh is the chance to witness a rich Buddhist culture firmly rooted in the majority of the people who live here, a culture that's fascinating to ponder. *Gompas* (monasteries) sit perched on high cliffs. *Chortens* (stupas) and *mani walls* (sacred stone walls) keep evil spirits from entering a village; prayer flags flap in the cold, strong wind.

Ladakh is connected with Kashmir Valley by a black-topped road that usually remains open from the end of June to mid-October, depending on the snowfall. The road passes through picturesque villages on the banks of the Sindh River, leaving the valley at Sonamarg. The first pass you cross to reach Ladakh is Zoji La (3,473 meters or 11,578 feet above sea level). On the other side starts the Drass Valley. Each side of the pass provides a startling contrast. You leave behind your last glimpse of forest-clad hills and suddenly stare into a vast mountainous landscape predominately stark, arid, and stony.

Kargil District

Kargil, with a population of about 5,000 predominately orthodox Shiite Moslems, is the second largest town in Ladakh and the headquarters of the Kargil district. Situated in the Suru Valley at the junction of the Drass and Suru rivers, Kargil's elevation of only 2,700 meters (9,000 feet) is low for Ladakh; reduced snowfall and greater warmth have produced fertile fields that are rich in barley, wheat, and vegetables; rows of flourishing poplars and willows, and successful orchards. Kargil is famous for its mulberries and apricots.

Long ago, Kargil, the halfway point to Leh, used to be an important junction on the Asian trade route. Hundreds of caravans from China, Afghanistan, Turkey, and India laid over here, conducting intense bartering in the process—a heavy exchange of silk, jewels, ivory, and carpets. Now tourists who come overland to Leh often opt to stop here. Flanked by Shiite tombs (*Imambaras*) and mosques (over 400 years old), the ancient bazaar is crammed with local handicrafts (traveling hookahs, metalware, jewelry).

After crossing the Suru River, the road follows the Wakha Chu stream. Shergole, a tiny village 10 kilometers (16 miles) from Kargil, is your gateway to Buddhist Ladakh. There, built into a cliff and perched halfway up the mountainside, is a gompa containing some beautifully painted interior walls. Check to see if the lamas are present; it's worth a visit if they're around to let you in. Here, too, you begin to see the traditional prayer flags waving from the roofs of houses and handsome women decked out in their traditional Tibetan costumes.

Mulbekh

From Shergole, it's a few miles to Mulbekh and its gompa with an enormous Buddha carved into rock. Inside the gompa are some beautiful frescoes, statues, and relics.

Indus Valley

Once you leave Mulbekh, the road climbs to the top of the 3,660-meter (12,200-foot)-high pass; the Namika-La. You wind your way back down to a valley and then proceed up and up again until you reach Fota La, the highest point on the Srinagar-Leh road: 4,083 meters (13,609 feet) above sea level. The wind whips around stark, craggy peaks and across barren plateaus, rustling prayer flags mounted atop *chortens* (Tibetan stupas) constructed by Buddhists who have successfully negotiated the treacherous and lonely pass. As you head down to the Indus Valley, you execute one particularly sharp bend in the road. Suddenly, you see the distant whitewashed Lamayuru Gompa—Ladakh's oldest monastery, and the welcome green oasis of an old sleepy village.

Lamayuru Gompa

This was formerly a large monastery with numerous buildings, all constructed in the eleventh century by the Gelug Sect which follows the teachings of the Dalai Lama. In the fifteenth century it was taken over by the Kargyu (Red Hat Sect). Today, Lamayuru has only one remaining intact structure. The biggest prayer hall is filled with statues, *thangkas* (Tibetan cloth paintings), and elaborately painted wood cubbies that hold the Holy Books. Also worth seeing are the mani walls built into the surrounding slopes—each stone carried and put into place by a Buddhist pilgrim. Note the mantra carved into the rocks: *Om Mani Padme Hum* (Hail to the Jewel in the Lotus). More than religiously significant, these walls protect the village from avalanches.

Alchi and Spitok Gompas

Near the village of Saspol, take the turn that leads to the eleventh-century Alchi Gompa, with five important and exquisite structures. You'll see an imposing collection of gigantic painted clay statues of various Buddhas, ornately carved arches and doors, and hundreds of handsome small paintings, 1,000 years old, crammed onto many of the interior walls. Alchi is also unusual in that it is set in the lowlands, rather than on top of a hill.

About five miles from Leh is another important monastery, the Spitok Gompa, built 500 years ago on top of a hillock overlooking the Indus River. This monastery, the seat of the head lama of Ladakh, now contains a new gompa within its walls, plus exquisite *thangkas* (Tibetan cloth paintings) and a separate chamber farther up the hill that pays tribute to Mahakala, "the Black One." The numerous faces on the statue remain veiled except for one day of festive celebration in January. This chamber also contains an exceptional collection of old masks. Unfortunately, some rooms in the Spitok are now off limits to tourists.

Leh—From Buddhist to Military

Your next stop is Leh, seen first from a distance huddling in a narrow valley at the base of snow-covered peaks (part of the Karakoram Mountain Range). By the third century B.C., Leh (at 3,450 meters or 11,500 feet above sea level) was an important Buddhist center; later, it became a major commercial center on the "silk route" in Central Asia. Now the twentieth century has forced Leh to assume an infinitely less glamorous role as an important Indian military base. Even with the army, Leh has remained an isolated, compact town, with its 12,000 inhabitants trying hard to hold on to their original culture.

The most striking buildings in Leh are the sixteenth-century Leh Palace and Temple of the Guardian Deities, both unfortunately in a state of decay and still owned by the Ladaki royal family, perched on a mountain towering over the palace, as if asserting the supremacy of the spiritual realm. Large and rambling, this gompa contains a solid gold statue of the Buddha (weighing just over a ton), painted scrolls, ancient manuscripts, and crumbling wall paintings.

The Leh bazaar may not offer great bargains (prices are better elsewhere), but it has much in the way of local color. Also, within the bazaar, see the Shiite Mosque, a good example of Turkish and Iranian architecture, built in 1594 by a son (Singe Namgyal) for his mother. Finally, just wander into the labyrinth of streets and alleys that take you through the old town on the lower slopes that lead up to the palace. On the plain below is the newer part of town.

Gompas Around Leh

Leh is an excellent base for excursions to several nearby monasteries and other worthwhile points of interest. Most of them are located on the road that heads southeast to the largest Buddhist gompa in Ladakh: the Hemis Gompa, 16 kilometers (25 miles) from Leh. The first stop on your route is the Tibetan Refugee Camp near Choglamsar, where refugees who fled Tibet after the Chinese invasion began the difficult process of establishing a new life in India.

At Shey, visit the fifteenth-century summer palace and monastery that belongs to the royal family of Leh. Here you find a 30-foot-tall, copper-gilt statue of a meditating Sakyamuni, called Shey Thubha (Lord Buddha). The nearby Victory stupa, Ladakh's largest, is crowned in pure gold.

The next attraction is the 800-year-old Thikse Gompa, set atop a hill offering a panoramic view of the fertile Indus Valley. There are numerous chambers, including one hall with a recently constructed enormous painted clay statue of Maitreya in the meditation pose.

Last, but in no way least, is the Hemis Gompa. Built in the 1600s by King Singe Namgyal, this monastery is an imposing architectural tour de force—one that hits you suddenly. Prayer flags fluttering from tall pillars in the courtyard wave you forward. If possible, plan your visit during the Hemis Festival (usually in June or July), which marks the birthday of Guru Padmasambhava. This colorful event features masked dancers gyrating slowly to loud music (the forces of good) to fight off the demons. Hemis also has statues of gold, stupas studded with precious stones, and a great collection of tankas, including one claimed to be the largest in existence, exhibited once every 11 years (the next viewing is 1991 and it won't be shown again until 2000).

Zanskar Valley, the New Frontier

Zanskar Valley, stretching out from a noble height of over 3,900 meters (13,000 feet), is for adventurous, intrepid travelers who are willing to exchange comfort for a journey into a remote area where the ancient Buddhist culture is still largely undisturbed and intact. This district—a collection of isolated hamlets with magnificent gompas lying between the two branches of the Zanskar River—is well guarded by snowcapped peaks.

The climate is severe. A warm day can suddenly turn cold as ice. Winters are harsh, yet not totally unkind. With the cold, the normally endless trip into Leh for the people who live there is dramatically shortened. Once the Zanskar is frozen, they simply walk across, lopping off a good portion of a circuitous trek. "Fair Weather" roads in Zanskar are always difficult, even during fair weather. Still, if you want to see a place that is untouched and remote, go. Zaskar feels cut off from the world and from the rush of time.

To begin your journey through Zanskar, start from Kargil and head south through the Suru Valley, a fertile area with astonishing beauty. Pass the distant Nun (at 7,023 meters or 23,410 feet) and Kun (at 6,966 meters or 23,219), Zanskar's two highest peaks. Continue to follow the river until you reach Rangdum, an isolated hamlet with a seventeenth-century gompa set into the hills. Wind your way up to the Pensa La Pass—4,332 meters (14,440 feet) above sea level—where unexpected hot springs gurgle not far from the summit. A legend claims that these springs gave rise to the ancestor of the famous Zanskar stallion, now declared a protected animal.

Finally you reach Padam, the district headquarters and a tiny village. Be certain to visit the Karsha gompa, the largest and wealthiest monastery in Zanskar, with excellent chambers filled with statues and ancient frescoes. From Padam, the adventurous can also trek to Manali in Himachal Pradesh.

When you return to Kargil, take a dirt road at Tungri and walk up to Dzongkhul, a cave monastery attributed to the tenth-century Indian mystic Naropa, who spent years here in meditation. The monastery contains his supposed footprints, his staff, and numerous small shrines.

PRACTICAL INFORMATION FOR
JAMMU AND KASHMIR

WHEN TO GO. Winter is for skiing and snow-related adventures in Kashmir. Spring and early autumn represent a panorama of beautiful color, with ideal temperatures an extra dividend. In April/May, the snows in the upper reaches usually start to melt and the willows turn green. Almond trees bloom and flowers carpet the landscape. In September, autumn's dahlias and cosmos are in full bloom. The days are pleasant and the nights are cool. Summer is the time to trek, to ride horseback, to go rafting, to bike, to fish—the time to explore the remote magnificence of Ladakh. The passes here remain closed from sometime in October until May or June because of snow. Srinagar is crowded from mid-June until August.

HOW TO GET THERE. By Air. *Indian Airlines* flies to Jammu, Srinagar, or Leh in Ladakh—even in winter, although flights are often delayed or canceled because of inclement weather. From Delhi, Indian Airlines makes a daily flight to Jammu, three daily flights to Srinagar, and two weekly flights to Leh in Ladakh. From Chandigarh, there are five weekly flights to Jammu and Srinagar and two weekly flights to Leh. Within the state, Indian Airlines flies daily between Jammu and Srinagar and five times weekly between Srinagar and Leh. On arrival, foreigners must register at the Foreigners' Regional Registration Office inside each terminal. Flights should be booked well in advance and passengers must confirm their tickets 72 hours in advance and should arrive at the terminal 90 minutes before flight time.

By Bus. *Jammu and Kashmir State Road Transport Corporation* (J&KSRTC) shuttles deluxe buses from Delhi to Jammu. Buses leave Delhi from Ashok Yatri Nivas Hotel, 19 Ashok Rd. Buses also go from Delhi to Srinagar, leaving at 4:30 P.M. and arriving the next day at 5:30 P.M. In Delhi, the firm is at 218 Kanishka Shopping Plaza, 19 Ashok Rd.; tel. 343400, ext. 2243. In Srinagar, call 72698. The fare to Srinagar from Delhi is Rs. 200. A daily bus also runs between Srinagar and Leh, with an overnight halt in Kargil, when the pass is open (summer until early autumn).

By Train. From Delhi, the daily *Shalimar Express* to Jammu Tawi (no railway into Srinagar or Ladakh) takes 22 hours, and the faster *Himsagar Express* runs five times weekly. The *Jammu Tawi Express* runs to Jammu daily from Calcutta and twice-weekly from Bombay. From Jammu to Srinagar, you can take the bus (numerous runs daily) or go by taxi. A fixed-rate taxi costs Rs. 700–Rs. 800 and can be shared by four people.

By Rented Car with Driver. From Jammu or Srinagar, the cost to rent a car with driver should be approximately Rs. 4 per km with a halt charge of Rs. 50–Rs. 100 per night. In Leh, the cost of renting a jeep with a driver is approximately $80 to do one day of local sightseeing. A jeep that carts you around all Ladakh can be costly. Delhi is 587 km to Jammu and 876 km to Srinagar; Srinagar is 434 km to Leh.

By Taxi. A taxi is good for long hauls to popular destinations. Before hiring a taxi, however, get the legal rate from the tourist department. Jammu to Srinagar should be about Rs. 800; from Srinagar to Leh should be about Rs. 2,000. You can share the cost with other travelers.

TOURIST INFORMATION. The *Jammu & Kashmir Tourist Department Corporation (J&KTDC)* is one of the best. They are out to please and have current information covering nearly every conceivable area of interest to the tourist. They also publish *Kashmir A-Z,* an excellent inexpensive directory that contains just about all the nitty-gritty information you need. If you're in Delhi before you head up to Kashmir, you'd be wise to check into the J&K tourist office, 202–203 Kanishka Shopping Plaza, 19 Ashok Rd.; tel. 345373. It's an example of efficiency and gracious service that you can expect in most of the big offices once you head north. The department has offices in major cities in India.

Tourist Reception Centers are in Srinagar (Shervani Rd., tel. 72449 or 77303, open 24 hours), Jammu (Veer Marg, tel. 48172, open 8 A.M.–10 P.M.), and Leh (tel. 97). Following is a list of other offices in the state.

Batote, 113 km from Jammu, tel. 42; *Gulmarg,* tel. 99; *Kargil (Ladakh),* tel. 29; *Katra,* 45 km from Jammu, tel. 3 and 5; *Kud,* 105 km from Jammu, tel. 7; *Pahalgam,* tel. 24; *Ramban,* 148 km from Jammu (no phone).

FOREIGN CURRENCY EXCHANGE. Most of the Western-style hotels have money-exchange counters. Otherwise, head for a branch of the *State Bank of India* or *Jammu and Kashmir Bank,* open Monday-Friday, 10 A.M.–2 P.M.; Saturdays, 10 A.M.–noon. The State Bank of India also has a branch (open weekdays, 4–7 P.M.) in the Srinagar Tourist Reception Center.

ACCOMMODATIONS. You have a wide range of possibilities in the Jammu and Kashmir states—from fancy to rustic minimal. You also have the famous houseboats that run from grand to just barely seaworthy. But, as with the other Himalayan states, a visit should be for the adventure and the ethereal beauty of it all. Some of the most exquisite and remote areas offer few creature comforts (certainly no TV)—but what memories and what breathtaking views! Prices are based on double occupancy: *Deluxe,* over Rs. 1,450; *Expensive,* Rs. 950–Rs. 1,450; *Moderate,* Rs. 500–Rs. 950; *Inexpensive,* under Rs. 500. Most of the Western-style hotels take major credit cards. Kashmir is popular, all of it, so book early. Government-run huts, especially in Gulmarg and Pahlagam, should be reserved two to three months in advance to play it safe.

GULMARG

Expensive

Hotel Highlands Park. Gulmarg; tel. 30. 39 rooms with bath. Old hunting trophies hang in this château-style hotel's lobby. Air-conditioned, pine-paneled rooms are comfortable and have ample heat in the winter. Multicuisine meals are included. Foreign-exchange counter, room service, health club, restaurant, bar. Closed Nov.–Dec. 10. Traveler's checks; no credit cards.

Moderate

Gulmarg Inn. Gulmarg; tel. 57. 6 rooms with bath. This popular small lodge has simple, clean rooms. Multicuisine meals are included. There is a restaurant and room service. Rupees only.

Inexpensive

J&K Tourist Department Huts. J&K Tourist Department, Reception Center, Srinagar; tel. 72499 or, in Gulmarg, tel. 39. 14 huts with bath. These small, very popular wood cottages dot the slopes of the valley. They're not ornate, but with a fireplace in each bedroom, they're just right for Gulmarg. Bring your own sleeping bag, or rent linen at a nominal cost. Reserve two months in advance in the summer. Rupees only.

JAMMU

Moderate

Hotel Asia Jammu Ashok. Jammu Tawi, Jammu; tel. 43127. 49 rooms with bath. Across from the Amar Mahal Palace, this government hotel is modern and has pleasant rooms. There are a swimming pool, bar, multicuisine restaurant, coffee shop, shopping arcade, TV, foreign-exchange and travel counter, doctor on call. AE, DC, MC, V.

Hotel Asia Jammu Tawi. Nehru Market, Jammu; tel. 49430. 44 rooms with bath. A Western-style hotel about 1-½ km (1 mi.) from the center of town, it has reasonably attractive air-conditioned rooms and, best of all, a swimming pool. Included also are a health club, room service, restaurant with live music, bar, foreign-exchange and travel counter, shopping arcade, doctor on call. AE, DC.

KARGIL (LADAKH)

Moderate

Hotel Broadway. Suru View, Kargil; tel. 13. 26 rooms with bath. This excellently managed hotel off the main street has a plain lobby and clean, sparsely decorated rooms. The best rooms overlook the Suru River. Complementing an excellent multicuisine restaurant and room service are transport and trekking arrangements. Rupees only.

Hotel Carvan Sarai. Kargil; tel. 79. 40 rooms with bath. Perched above the center of Kargil, this simple, clean hotel, built in tiers, has a Middle-Eastern ambience. Upper floor rooms have a great river view. There is a multicuisine restaurant. Rupees only.

Hotel Siachen. Kargil; tel. 22. 27 rooms with bath. On the banks of the Suru River and off the main street, this excellently managed, popular hotel has clean, simple rooms with verandas and a garden in its parking lot. Room service, doctor on call, foreign-exchange and travel counter, excellent multicuisine restaurant. DC.

Inexpensive

J&K Government Tourist Bungalows. J&K Government Tourist Information Center, Tourist Office, Kargil; tel. 29. About 12 rooms with bath. The better of these two bungalows is on a hill and has spacious rooms. The other bungalow is near the Suru River. In summer reserve well in advance. Rupees only.

KATRA

Moderate

Asia Vaishnodevi Katra. Katra, Jammu; tel. 627. 37 rooms with bath. This clean, Western-style hotel with simply decorated rooms is a short walk from the bus stand. Included are a vegetarian restaurant, health club with sauna and massage, *puja* (prayer) room, travel counter, barber shop, and room service. DC.

LEH (LADAKH)

Deluxe

Ladakh Sarai. Reservations: Mountain Travel India, Pvt. Ltd. 1/1, Rani Jhansi Rd., New Delhi; tel. 52204, or through any Mountain Travel office. 12 tents. Here, you stay in a *yurt* (tent) in a meadow below the Stok Gompa, 15 km (nine mi.) from Leh. Large, lantern-lit circular tents are attractively furnished. Toilets and solar-heated showers are in separate tents. The lobby, also separate, is Ladakhi-style with comfortable low platforms and a little shrine. Multicuisine meals (for staying guests only) are normally eaten outside. Meals and sightseeing are included. Closed November–March. AE, DC, MC, V.

Moderate

Hotel Kang-lha-chhen. Leh, Ladakh; tel. 144. 25 rooms with bath. Near the center of old Leh, this clean, modest hotel has a distinctly Ladakhi look in its black-trimmed, two-story white-stucco exterior. The best rooms are on the upper floor and overlook the interior courtyard and garden. Multicuisine meals are included. Room service, restaurant (nonguests must call in advance); travel agent, doctor on call. AE.

Hotel Lha-Ri-Mo. Leh, Ladakh; tel. 101. 30 rooms with bath. A short walk from all markets and nestled behind an attractive garden, this is the loveliest hotel in Leh. The restaurant is especially charming with intricately hand-painted beams. The rooms are plain but pleasing. There is an excellent multicuisine restaurant (for hotel guests only) as well as a travel agent and a doctor on call. Closed November–May. AE.

Inexpensive

Jorchung Guest House. Tukcha, Leh, Ladakh; no phone. 5 rooms with shared bath (Indian shower). The traveler looking for the ultimate in peace and quiet should stay in this private Ladakhi home, made of clay and surrounded by a garden and fruit trees in a residential area that's a 10-minute walk from Ladakh. The rooms are plain, but very clean. Gracious hospitality: bed-and-breakfast Ladakhi-style. Reserve in advance. Rupees only.

PADAM (ZANSKAR, LADAKH)

Inexpensive

Padam Tourist Bungalow. J&K Tourist Officer, Kargil; tel. 29. 5 rooms with a bath. If you can get a room in this government bungalow, you'll need a sleeping bag. Linen is clean and there are blankets, but the simple rooms get cold. The restaurant serves good Indian and Continental meals. Some tenting is allowed on the spacious lawn. Reserve well in advance. Rupees only.

PAHALGAM

Moderate

Pahalgam Hotel. Pahalgam; tel. 26. 46 rooms with baths. Set on the main street, this wonderful lodge has been renovated and offers Western-style amenities and attractive, centrally heated rooms. The best rooms have a river view. Multicuisine meals are included. Restaurant, room service, TV, heated swimming pool, health club. Discount December–January. AE, DC.

Plaza Hotel. Pahalgam; tel. 39. 30 rooms with bath. This attractive lodge, enclosed by a pleasant garden, is well managed. It's not fancy, but it's also not expensive and its rooms have a cozy charm. Indian and Continental meals are included. Restaurant, bar. Closed mid-November–mid-March. Rupees only.

Hotel Woodstock. Pahalgam; tel. 27. 95 rooms with bath. This weathered gray lodge was under renovation at press time. Spacious rooms are carpeted, centrally heated, and have a rustic decor. The best rooms have a view of the river. TV, bar, multicuisine restaurant, doctor on call, room service, car rental, health club, shopping mall. Discount November–March. AE, DC.

Inexpensive

J & K Government Tourist Bungalow and Huts. Reservations: J&K Tourism Department, Tourist Reception Center, Srinagar. 7 rooms with bath in the bungalow, 57 huts with bath, and safari-style tents (very inexpensive) with shared bath. These accommodations are a bargain. The stone bungalow is old, with clean, spacious rooms. The huts are charming: little stone dwellings with ample rooms and verandas. Restaurant, bar. In summer reserve well in advance. Rupees only.

SRINAGAR

Expensive

Centaur Lake View Hotel. Chesmeshahi, Srinagar; tel. 75667. This gigantic hotel on Dal Lake has modern rooms and multicuisine restaurants, bar, room service, swimming pool, health club, tennis court, and travel and foreign-exchange counter. AE, DC, MC, V.

Nedous. Reservations: Welcomgroup, tel. 800-325-3535 worldwide. The oldest hotel in Srinagar, Nedous has been purchased by the Welcomgroup chain and was under total renovation at press time—to be completed in late 1990. Set back on a lawn against the river, not far from the heart of the city, this two-story British bungalow with verandas is beautiful from the outside. It could become the hotel of choice. AE, DC, MC, V.

Oberoi Palace. Guptar Rd., Srinagar; tel. 75751. 100 rooms with bath. This was the former home of the maharajah; its beautiful lawns and six-hole golf course overlook Dal Lake. Its spacious rooms need refurbishing, however. Ask for an upper-floor, lakeview room. The hotel is a distance from the road and Srinagar. Excellent multicuisine restaurant, room service, bar, TV, shopping arcade, badminton, travel and foreign-exchange counter. AE, DC, MC, V.

Moderate

Hotel Akbar. Box 95, Srinagar; tel. 74547. 40 rooms with bath. This new, rambling, multi-story structure with lovely gardens is on an island near Dal Gate. Rooms are attractive with carved-wood ceilings and simple furnishings. Good multicuisine restaurant, room service, outdoor adventure arrangements. AE, DC, MC, V.

Lake Isle Resort. Reservations: Naseem Bagh, Srinagar, tel. 78446; or BGA Corporation, 790 Shirley Dr., Tipp City, OH 45371, tel. 513-667-8071. 11 rooms with bath. Set on a secluded island in Nagin Lake, this 50-year-old two-story bungalow with spacious front lawns and great views is a delight. The rooms are in Kashmiri decor. An upstairs library is perfect for reading. Multicuisine meals are included. Restaurant, bar, sightseeing arrangements, badminton, boating and fishing, room service. Closed mid-November–April. AE, MC, V.

Inexpensive

Cheshma Shahi Hutments. J&KTDC, Tourist Reception Center, Srinagar; tel. 73688 or 72644. About 12 huts with bath. On a hill overlooking Dal Lake, near the Cheshma Shahi Mogul garden, these charming new government-run cottages are spacious, economical, and popular, with restaurant, bar, and room service. In summer reserve well in advance. Rupees only.

J&K Government Tourist Hostel. J&K Government Tourism Reservation Center, 2nd Floor, Srinagar; tel. 77305. 25 rooms with bath. This modest hotel is set back on a lawn behind the Tourist Reception Center. Rooms are plain but clean. There is a good, inexpensive restaurant next to the tourist department offices. Rupees only.

HOUSEBOATS. Houseboats moored to the banks of Dal and Nagin Lakes are 80–125 feet long and 10–20 feet wide. An average-sized houseboat has a dining room, living room, one to three bedrooms with attached baths, and, in most cases, hot and cold running water. Most of the houseboats have terraces for sunbathing and lovely verandas. They are electrified and usually nicely furnished. Many kinds of houseboats are available. The approximate costs: *Deluxe Class,* Rs. 500 per double; *A Class,* Rs. 300 per double; *B Class,* Rs. 250 per double. All meals are included. There are lots of houseboats—lots of steal-you-blind houseboats as well as lots of houseboats surrounded by congestion and noise.

The following houseboat operators will give you the houseboat stay you imagine: gracious service and relative peace and quiet. They'll pick you up at the airport and put together all your excursions, from fishing and trekking to traveling around by car. You can rent the entire boat or just a bedroom and share, but given the intimacy of a boat, sharing is an important consideration. To play it safe, stick to the Deluxe, A, or B categories.

Butt's Clermont Houseboats (G. M. Butt & Sons, Clermont Houseboats, Dalgate, Srinagar; tel. 2175–4337) has deluxe-class boats on Dal Lake near the Hazratbal Mosque. The best boats are old and have two bedrooms; you're surrounded by beautiful furnishings and memorabilia. Newer boats with two or three bedrooms are fancy and come with the same classy service. AE, DC, MC, V.

Reshu Boktoo & Sons (Dal Gate, Box 95, Srinagar; tel. 74547) has deluxe and Class A boats on the western side of Nagin Lake. Their classiest boat is the *Golden Lotus.* Nice two-bedroom boats are also available. The owners supervise excellent treks in Kashmir and Ladakh and know the best fishing spots. AE, DC, MC, V.

Abdud Rashid Major & Bros (Nagin Lake, Srinagar, J&K, tel. 74850) has two small, one-bedroom boats, the *H.P. Peony* and *Young Peony,* set on the eastern side of Nagin. When you step aboard, you feel like someone's grandmother supervised the decorating. They're a real bargain. Rupees only.

TOURIST HUTS AND BUNGALOWS. The J&KTDC maintains other inexpensive tourist huts and bungalows in hidden lovely places throughout this part of the state.

Jammu. *Mansar Lake,* 80 km from Jammu, tourist bungalow and huts; and *Surinsar Lake,* 42 km from Jammu, tourist bungalow.

For reservations, contact the Tourist Reception Center, Jammu; tel. 48172.

Kashmir. *Achabal,* former pleasure retreat of Empress Nur Jahan, now a camping ground, 58 km from Srinagar, tourist bungalow and huts; *Aharbal,* 51 km from Srinagar, near a beautiful waterfall, tourist bungalow; *Daksum,* 85 km from Srinagar, a forest retreat surrounded by mountains, tourist bungalow; *Kokarnag,* 70 km from Srinagar, botanical garden and hot springs high up in the mountains, tourist bungalow and huts; *Lake Manasbar,* 32 km from Srinagar, tourist bungalow; *Sonamarg,* 83 km from Srinagar, in a valley way up in the mountains, tourist bungalow and huts; *Verinag,* 80 km from Srinagar, Mogul ruins and hot springs, tourist bungalow; *Yusmarg,* 40 km from Srinagar, lovely valley in the hills of the Pir Pangal range, tourist huts.

For reservations in all of these huts and bungalows, contact the Tourist Reception Center at Srinagar, 190001; tel. 72449.

Ladakh. Simple, sparsely furnished bungalows are located in Drass, Mulbek, and Saspol. Sleeping bags are advised. For reservations, contact the Tourist Department in Leh, Ladakh; tel. 97.

There is also an inexpensive Public Works Department Rest House in **Khalsi.** For reservations: Superintendent Engineer, Public Works Department, Leh, Ladakh.

DINING OUT. In Kashmir, there is a strong hint of Middle Eastern cooking, and *kebabs* (small pieces of chicken, mutton, or balls of minced meat threaded on a skewer and cooked or fried) are great favorites. *Biryanis,* typically Moslem dishes whose pedigree goes back to the Great Moguls, are prepared on all festive occasions. They are made from pigeons, chicken, or mutton with plenty of rice and butter and some spices. Other Kashmiri Mughlai dishes to tickle your palate: *gustava,* a meatball curry cooked in a gravy of yogurt and spices; *rista,* a beaten spicy lamb; *rogan josh,* a mutton cooked on the bone in a spiced curry; and if you're lucky you'll find some chef who can prepare fried spinach cooked in mustard oil, tumeric, and aromatic water in which dried cockscomb flowers have been soaked. After your meal, have sweet Kashmiri tea. Most good restaurants are in the better hotels and are mentioned under *Accommodations,* above. Lunchtime is 12–3; dinnertime is 7:30–10. Dress is casual. Reservations are advised in all hotel restaurants.

Prices, based on one person eating a three-course meal, excluding taxes, tip, or beverage, are: *Deluxe,* over Rs. 120; *Expensive,* Rs. 80–Rs. 120; *Moderate,* Rs. 40–Rs. 80; *Inexpensive,* under Rs. 40.

JAMMU

Moderate

Cosmo Bar and Restaurant. Hotel Cosmopolitan, Veer Marg; tel. 47561. This unpretentious, air-conditioned restaurant has good local ambience and serves tasty Indian, Mughlai, Chinese, and Continental food. Open noon–10 P.M. DC, V.

KARGIL (LADAKH)

Inexpensive–Moderate

Naktul Chinese Restaurant. On the road to the lower tourist bungalow; no phone. This small friendly eatery serves large portions of Chinese food. Open 7 A.M.–10 P.M. Rupees only.

LEH (LADAKH)

Inexpensive

Dreamland Restaurant. Fort Rd.; no phone. Small and informal, Dreamland is often crowded with young Ladakhis chattering with foreigners and eating good Tibetan and Chinese meals. Open 8 A.M.–10 P.M. Rupees only.

Potala Hill Top Restaurant. Lal Chowk; no phone. Don't be put off by the dingy stairwell that leads to this informal and popular restaurant with a quasi-Chinese decor. You'll find good Chinese and Tibetan specialties inside. Open 9 A.M.–10 P.M.

SRINAGAR

Moderate

Adhoo's. Residency Rd.; tel. 72593. This plain restaurant, which is usually crowded, has a terrace out back and offers Kashmiri specialties. Open 9 A.M.–11 P.M. Rupees only.

Lhasa. Boulevard Lane; tel. 71438. If you like Tibetan and Chinese food, eat in Lhasa's super-casual candle-lit garden. Open noon–11 P.M. Rupees only.

Mughal Darbar. Shervani Rd.; no phone. This upstairs restaurant serves big portions of Kashmiri, Indian, and Chinese food in a crowded, dimly lit room. Open 9 A.M.–11 P.M. Rupees only.

SWEETS AND TREATS. Punjabi Vegetarian Roadside Stall. Khalsi (141 km or 87 mi. from Kargil, Ladakh). Look for the sign and two benches by the road and have delicious *chana masala* (tomato curry with potato), *chappati* (unleavened bread), rice, and tea for under a dollar. Open 5:30 A.M. until the electricity shuts off.

Mama Mia's Hotel and Restaurant. On Nagin Lake, Srinagar. This is a houseboat moored to the western bank serving espresso from the super-casual sundeck. Nice ambience; great views. Open all day.

HOW TO GET AROUND. From the Airport. The airport is a short hop to downtown Jammu. A taxi ride should cost about Rs. 20.

By Taxi. Taxis are available, but drivers hate to use their meters. Bargain, using Delhi rates: Rs. 3.30 for the first km, Rs. 2.40 per additional km.

By Auto Rickshaw. The most fun and cheaper than taxis. Just make certain the driver uses the meter.

By Bus. *J & K State Road Transit Corporation (J&KSRTC)* has mini-buses running regularly throughout the city. Contact the Tourist Reception Center (tel. 48172) for routes and fares.

By Rented Car with Driver. Contact the Tourist Reception Center for a list of approved car rental agencies; tel. 43803. Figure the same rate per km at Rs. 4, plus Rs. 100 for night-halt charges.

LEH

From the Airport. Taxis and jeeps are available for about Rs. 30 into Leh. J&KSRTC has buses making local runs to many nearby destinations, but they're crowded and slow. At the taxi stand near the Tourist Bungalow, you can hire an unmetered taxi or jeep for excursions. Get a list of reasonable fares from the tourist department.

SRINAGAR

From the Airport. An airport bus takes you to the Tourist Reception Center in the heart of Srinagar for about Rs. 10. By taxi, figure about Rs. 60 into Srinagar or Rs. 90 for Nagin Lake, the location of the best houseboats.

By Taxi. At about Rs. 3 per km, this is the least-sensible way to travel if you plan to stay in the city, but it's okay for excursions around Dal Lake.

By Auto Rickshaw. Drivers here have the same reluctance to use the meter as elsewhere. Auto rickshaws should be much cheaper than taxis.

By Shikara (lovely Kashmiri gondola). This is the only way to travel here. Although rates are supposedly fixed, no *shikara* owner will agree to them. Negotiate in advance and figure on about Rs. 30 per hour. No more than five passengers are allowed in a shikara. Ideally, they are best for two stretched out in pampered style. They're slow, but who cares? For complete rates for various shikara trips, check at the Tourist Reception Center.

By Tonga. This is another nice alternative. Robust horses with bells around the neck take you around town in two-wheel vehicles. Less expensive than the rickshaw. Haggle, but then enjoy yourself.

By Rented Car with Driver. Good and possibly necessary (if you can afford it) for long excursions. You can rent a car from *J&KSRTC* for about Rs. 3–Rs. 4 per km (overnight halt charges, Rs. 100). Call tel. 76107 for further details. They can also supply a list of reliable private agencies that rent cars with drivers.

By Helicopter. The J&KTD operates *Westland Helicopter*, which offers a 15-minute round-the-city flight at Rs. 250 per person, a round-trip to Gulmarg at Rs. 500 per person, and a round-trip to Pahalgam at Rs. 700 per person. For details and reservations, contact the Tourist Reception Center, tel. 76107.

TOURS. The *Jammu Tourist Reception Center* (Veer Marg, tel. 5421) provides a tour to Amar Mahal Palace Museum, Dogra Art Gallery, Ranbireshwar Temple, Raghunath Mandir, and Bahur Fort (Rs. 120 per person).

The *Srinagar Tourist Reception Center* (Shervani Rd., tel. 72698) runs bus and *shikara* (boat) tours to Shankaracharya Temple, Charchinari, Chashma Shahi, Nishat, Harwan, and Shalimar, with refreshments and lunch (7:30 A.M.–2 P.M., Rs. 75); and to Harwan, Shalimar, Nishat, Charchinari, and Chashma Shahi (2:30–9:30 P.M., Rs. 85); plus day trips to Gulmarg, Pahalgam, Sonamarg, Wular Lake, and Verinag. Each day trip costs about Rs. 50. Times vary with the season.

The *Students' Educational and Cultural Movement of Ladakh* (SECMOL) (Compound Karzoo, tel. 284, ext. 2) has excellent guides for tours to monasteries, palaces, and even private homes. Charges are based on your itinerary and are reasonable.

TOUR OPERATORS. Srinagar is the starting point for a lot of wonderful adventures. Like houseboat *wallahs,* there are good and bad private outfits ready to take you boating and trekking into the wilderness. Many are really just out to take you for a ride. Here is a list of really good packagers, who will give you a memorable *good* time:

Reshu Boktoo & Sons, Travel & Tour Operators, Box 95, Srinagar, India, tel. 74547. Good treks through Kashmir and Ladakh; jeep "treks" (week-long excursions from Srinagar via jeep to Leh and Ladakh); Shikara water treks. Personal attention.

Dragon Tours & Travels (4 Polo View, Srinagar, tel. 77330, and in Leh, tel. 8) is another reliable adventure outfit.

Himalayan River Runners (188-A Jor Bagh, New Delhi, 110003, tel. 615736) runs excellent rafting trips on the Zanskar River in Ladakh.

Mercury Travels (Hotel Oberoi Palace, Srinagar, tel. 78786) provides general travel assistance, outdoor adventures, and tours.

SECMOL (Compound Karzoo, tel. 284, ext. 2) offers inexpensive treks around Leh.

Sita World Travel (Maulana Azad Rd., Srinagar, tel. 78891) provides general travel assistance and tours.

Travel Corporation of India (Maulana Azad Rd., Srinagar, tel. 73525) offers outdoor adventures, including rafting trips on the Lidder and Sindh rivers in Kashmir, and tours.

SEASONAL EVENTS. The three areas of Jammu, Kashmir, and Ladakh are each influenced by three specific religions: Jammu, Hindu; Kashmir, Islam; and Ladakh, Buddhism. Each year, these areas observe the traditional cycle of festivals and religious observances that are celebrated throughout India. The following additional festivals are special to this state:

June. *Hemis Festival.* Ladakh's biggest monastery is the site of a two-day festival commemorating the birthday of Guru Padmasambhava, with masked dancers and eerie music. It's an intensely devout and culturally rich Buddhist festival, heavily attended. Contact the tourist department for details.

July/August. During the full moon, thousands of Hindu devotees trek three–five days to Amar Nath, about 48 km (30 mi.) from Pahalgam and supposedly the abode of Shiva, where they pray before the sacred lingam.

September. *Thikse Festival.* At the Thikse Gompa near Leh, lamas perform ritual *chaams* (dances).

HISTORIC SITES. Entrance to most places is generally free; where a donation is asked, a few rupees will do. Entrance to monasteries is from Rs. 10 to Rs. 20. Important sites are open daily from sunrise to sunset, unless noted below.

JAMMU AREA

Bahu Fort. The oldest building in Jammu, constructed over 3,000 years ago; the interior temple is dedicated to Kali.

Raghunath Temple, dedicated to Lord Rama (Vishnu avatar). Largest temple complex in Northern India, it was started in the nineteenth century and took 25 years to complete. Much of the interior is covered in gold leaf. The surrounding temples are dedicated to other gods and goddesses associated with the *Ramayana.*

Ranbireswar Temple, Jammu, constructed in 1883 by Maharajah Ranbir Singh, dedicated to Shiva. It has 12 crystal Shiva lingams.

Vaishno Devi. A 14-km trek from Katra leads to this important Hindu shrine, a cave dedicated to the goddess Vaishno Devi. The long narrow cave has three rock formations covered with gold canopies, representing the three divine aspects of the goddess Kali, Lakshmi, and Saraswati. An important pilgrimage site for Hindus.

LADAKH AREA

Alchi Gompa, 135 km from Leh, 5 km from Saspol. Six separate structures with a collection of gigantic painted clay statues of the Buddha, carved arches and doors, and hundreds of small paintings (1,000 years old).

Dzongkhul, a cave monastery near Padam, is attributed to the tenth-century Indian mystic who spent years here in meditation. The monastery contains small shrines and sacred idols, and supposedly Naropa's sacred staff and footprints.

Hemis Gompa, 49 km from Leh. Ladakh's biggest monastery built in the 1600s by King Singe Namgyal. Filled with gold statues, stupas studded with precious stones, and a great collection of *tankas,* including one claimed to be the largest in existence, exhibited once every 11 years.

Karsha Gompa, in Padam, Zanskar. The largest and wealthiest monastery in Zanskar, with 500-year-old frescoes.

Lamayuru. Ladakh's oldest monastery, built in the eleventh century. Formerly numerous structures existed; now only one remains. Inside the biggest prayer hall is a cave with a statue of Naropa, an Indian mystic who created the monastery.

Leh Khar Palace and Temple of the Guardian Deities, both in ruins, set above the city. The temple still houses a towering Chamba statue of Buddha carved into the face of an enormous rock,

Mulbekh Gompa and a statue of Avalokitesvara (Buddha of Compassion), with 1,000 eyes and numerous heads. 25 miles from Kargil. Gompa contains beautiful frescoes and statues.

Sankar Gompa, 3 km from Leh, has an excellent collection of miniature gold statues and paintings.

Shey Palace and Gompa. Built in the 1600s on the ruins of another fort, this palace is in decay, but there's a magnificent two-story, copper-gilt statue of a meditating Sakyamuni, called Shey Thubha (Lord Buddha). The gompa contains beautiful frescoes. The Victory Stupa is Ladakh's largest, crowned in pure gold.

Spitok Gompa, 5 km from Leh, was built 500 years ago. The current seat of the head lama of Ladakh, it has exquisite thankas and a separate chamber that pays tribute to Mahakala, "the Black One." Her face is unveiled only one day in January.

Thikse Gompa, 12 km (7 mi.) from Leh, is 800 years old. One chamber contains an enormous statue of Maitreya (Future Buddha) in the meditation pose.

SRINAGAR AREA

Achabal, 58 km from Srinagar. A former Mogul garden, designed by a daughter of the Mogul Emperor Shah Jahan and the favorite retreat of Empress Nur Jahan. Now a grove with water cascades and fountains, a pleasant place to visit.

Amar Nath, 47 km from Pahalgam. A cave that was supposedly the abode of Lord Shiva, with a stalactite in the shape of a lingam created by water dripping through the limestone roof of the cave.

Char Chenar. Shah Jahan's mogul garden is on an island in Dal Lake with a pavilion and three *chenars* (fire trees). There used to be a fourth.

Chasma Shahi (Royal Spring). The smallest Mogul garden, designed by Shah Jahan in the 1630s. Beautiful pavilions, illuminated at night.

Hari Parbat Fort. Built in the eighteenth century by Atta Mohammad Khan, an Afghan governor; the surrounding wall was built by Mogul Emperor Akbar in the late 1500s. Among the numerous ancient structures are a temple dedicated to Parvati, a Moslem shrine and mosque, and a Sikh *gurdwara* built to commemorate the visit of Har Govind Singh to Kashmir. Permission to enter must be obtained from the State Archaeological Department, Lalmandi Square, Srinagar. The fort, however, is poorly maintained; it's the exterior views that make a visit worthwhile.

Harwan, six km from Srinagar. Ruins of a Buddhist monastery dating back to the third century.

Hazratbal. White marble shrine built recently contains a sacred hair of Prophet Mohammed shown to the public on certain days.

Jamai Masjid is the largest mosque in Kashmir. First constructed by Sultan Sikander in the thirteenth century, it was destroyed three times by fire. The last construction was in 1674 by Aurangzeb in Indo-Saracenic architecture and laid out in the style of a Persian court mosque, with 400 cedar wood pillars, each from one tree.

Nasim Bagh (Garden of the Morning Breeze) is a Mogul garden of chenars originally laid out by Akbar in the early 1600s.

Nishat Bagh (Garden of Pleasure) is a Mogul garden designed by Asaf Khan, brother of Nur Jahan, in 1633. Ten beautiful terraces, formal gardens, a water channel with polished marble stepping stones, fountains, and pavilions. Persian in style and magnificence.

Shah Hamdan Mosque. First constructed in fourteenth century, suffered three fires. The last construction was in 1732 with no nails or screws used. Lovely carved windows and entrances. Only Moslems can go inside.

Shalimar Bagh (Garden of Love). Mogul garden constructed by Emperor Jahangir for his Nur Jahan in 1619. Four terraces with a water channel running from level to level. Typical Persian quadrant style. The black marble pavilion on top exclusively used by royal women. Sound and light show.

Shankaracharya Temple. The present temple was built during the reign of Jahangir by an unknown Hindu. It sits on the site of a temple originally constructed around 200 B.C. by a son of Ashoka. The low enclosing wall and plinth belong to the ancient temple.

MUSEUMS AND GALLERIES. *Amar Mahal Palace Museum,* Ram Nagar, Jammu, has an interesting collection of Pahari miniature paintings in a former palace designed like a French château. Open 10 A.M.–noon and 3–5 P.M. in winter; 3–7 P.M. and Sun., 10 A.M.–noon in summer. Closed holidays.

Dogra Art Gallery, Gandhi Bhavan, Jammu, houses nearly 600 miniatures from Basholi and Kangra schools; plus sculptures, terra-cotta pieces, murals. Open 11 A.M.–5 P.M. in winter; 7:30 A.M.–1 P.M. in summer. Closed Monday and holidays.

Shri Partap Singh Museum, Lal Mandi, Srinagar, was started by the maharajah of Jammu and Kashmir. Archaeology, natural history, and products of Kashmiri arts and crafts. Particularly interesting are the finds from Harwan, a Buddhist site of the third century. The collections of coins, carpets, embroideries, and textiles are all from the state. Open 10 A.M.–5 P.M.; closed Wednesdays and holidays.

Stok Palace Museum, Stok, 17 km (11 mi.) from Leh, contains precious stones, thankas, ceremonial dresses, coins, and prayer instruments. Open 7 A.M.–6 P.M.

SPORTS AND OUTDOOR ADVENTURES. Bicycling. The Srinagar Tourist Reception Center (tel. 72449) rents 10-speed bikes.

Fishing. Acclimatized varieties of trout attain greater size and are more plentiful than in their original European or North American habitats. Sturdy equipment is therefore required for fishing in Kashmir's fast waters. The trout fishing season is March–October, and the mahseer fishing season, August–September. Licenses are available from the *Directorate of Fisheries,* Tourist Reception Center, Srinagar (tel. 72449) and at Jammu, Nowabad Canal Road (tel. 47804). Both are open 10 A.M.–2 P.M. Monday-Saturday. Licenses are issued for a maximum of three days at Rs. 75 per rod per day.

This same office periodically publishes maps showing beats and the routes leading to them. It's not necessary to bring your equipment; rods, reels, lines, and lures may be hired locally. Fishing in the Sindh and Liddar rivers is usually poor from mid-May–mid-July owing to the cold water.

Golf. There are excellent golf courses in Srinagar, Gulmarg, and Pahalgam. *Srinagar Golf Club's* links: nine holes and double-flag 18 holes. *Gulmarg Golf Club's* course is good; it was redesigned to fill international standards and is probably the world's highest at 8,700 feet. Spring and autumn tournaments are held both in Srinagar and in Gulmarg (June and September). For details, contact the Tourist Reception Center, Srinagar; tel. 72449. Contact *Kashmir Government Golf Club,* Maulana Azad Rd., Srinagar (tel. 76524) for reservations and temporary membership details; Rs. 20 per day.

Gulmarg Golf Club has temporary membership available; tel. 39 for details. *Pahalgam Golf Club* also has temporary membership available; tel. 51, for details.

Horseback Riding. Contact the Tourist Departments in Gulmarg, Pahalgam, and Sonamarg to arrange rides.

Rafting. In Kashmir, rafters can take a one-day run on the Lidder or a two-day run on the Sindh (May–June and mid-August–September). Contact Travel Corporation of India (see *Tour Operators,* above). In Zanskar, Ladakh, experienced rafters can make a six-day run from Padam to the Indus River (mid-July–mid-September). Arrange in advance through Himalayan River Runners (see *Travel Operators,* above).

Skiing. This is a popular sport in Gulmarg from December to March, when the meadow is covered by a thick blanket of snow 6–10 feet deep. The annual skiing competition is held in three stages during this period. There are now several ski lifts, and all equipment can be hired. Skiing courses are run by the Indian Institute of Skiing and Mountaineering. Information is available from any Government of India Tourist Office or from Commissioner of Tourism, J & K Government, Srinagar. An enjoyable winter holiday with lodge-style hotels, but don't expect European standards for skiing facilities—at least, not yet. Accomplished skiers can also heli-ski in remote Kashmir valleys. Contact Adventure on Skis, 815 North Rd., Rte. 202, Westfield, MA 01085; tel. 413–568–2855 or 800–628–9655.

Trekking. The soaring heights and scenic grandeur of the Inner Himalayas can best be viewed by hiking. Starting points of the seven treks indicated here (and there are many more) can be reached in comfort by bus or taxi. Guides, supplies, ponies, and *mazdurs* (porters) are available at all these points. Since good tents are for hire at several places in Kashmir, we suggest you carry tents even if there are tourist lodges and forest rest houses along the route. In this way, you will be completely independent. Light double-fly tents of medium size are recommended; they can be easily carried by pack ponies or porters and offer adequate resistance to hazardous weather.

For a list of reliable tour operators who'll give you a great personalized trek, see *Tour Operators,* above. The tourist department will be able to help you arrange ponies and porters and will advise you about hiring charges, which should be fixed before you start. The best time to trek in Jammu and Kashmir is April–November; in Ladakh, July–September.

You are well advised to contact the tourist offices in Srinagar, Gulmarg, Pahalgam, Sonamarg, Kargil, Padum, or Leh to get a thorough briefing on the latest conditions of the routes, the location of potentially dangerous streams and snow bridges, and other details before setting out. Carry all the food you need. You'll find little to buy. Also, if you're trekking above 10,000 feet, pay attention to the warning about high-altitude sickness (see *Planning Your Trip*). Here are some of the more popular trek routes, rated by degree of difficulty.

KASHMIR

Trek 1. Pahalgam to Amarnath Cave via Chandanwari-Sheshnag–Panjtarni–(crossing Mahagunas Pass, 14,000 feet); 28 miles, five days. Elevation, 7,200–12,700 feet. *Moderate.*

Trek 2. Pahalgam to Kolahoi Glacier via Aru and Ladderwatt; 22 miles, four-six days. Elevation, 7,200–11,000 ft. *Moderate.*

Trek 3. Kishtwar to Lehinvan or Srinagar, an excellent 9–12-day trek over the Margan Pass through remote valleys with rice paddies, flowering meadows, and a refreshing break at hot springs in Tatowoin village. *Difficult.*

Trek 4. Sonamarg to Gangabal Lake via Nichinai Pass, Vishensar Lake, 16 miles, seven days. Elevation, 8,500 to 12,500 feet. *Moderate* to *Difficult.*

Trek 5. Gulmarg to Alpathar via Khilanmarg, eight miles, two days. Elevation, 8,500–10,100 feet. *Easy.*

Trek 6. Gulmarg to Tosha Maidan via Buna Danwas and Gadala stream, 20 miles, 2½ days. At the end of the trek, visit the lakes near Chinmarg and Tosha Maidan Pass; there is hardly any difference in elevation. The return journey can be made via Riyar and Khag to Tangmarg, 2½ days. *Easy.*

Trek 7. Kangan to Gangabal via Wangat Valley–Nara Tag–Trunkhal, 21 miles, four days. Elevation, 6,800–11,700 feet. *Moderate* to *Difficult.*

LADAKH

Ladakh has extensive posibilities of high and difficult trekking and challenging climbing. There are innumerable towering peaks, most of them unnamed and un-climbed. The Suru and Zanskar valleys are excellent areas for trekking in the shadow of the high peaks of Nun and Kun. The Zanskar valley can be approached from Kargil in about a week's trekking. The 14,000-foot-high pass of Penzi-La has to be crossed to reach the valley. There is a "jeepable" road following the River Suru up to Rangdoom Gompa, about 130 km from Kargil. It is necessary to take all equipment, which can be hired in Srinagar. Here are three of the more popular possibilities:

Trek 1. Lamayuru to Padum. Via Chila–Hanupata–Photaksar–Shanpado Gongma–Linshat–Snertse–Pidmu–Pishu–Padam; eight days. *Difficult.*

Trek 2. Padam to Hemis via Tongde–Zangla–Foot of Sher Sher La–Chup-Cha-Shang Kong Ma–Kurna Sumdo–Nari Narsa–Lang Tang–Hankar Ning Ling-Skakdo–Hemis; two weeks. *Very difficult.*

Trek 3. Padum to Manali via Muney/Raru–Surley–Cha–Phugtal–Purney-Drangze–Karghyak–Gombo–Rangjon–Lartsa–Shingkum La–Gadi Shisa–Darcha-Manali, about 12 days. *Difficult.*

Wildlife Sanctuaries. *Dachigam National Park,* 21 km (13 mi.) from Srinagar. This former royal game preserve belonging to the maharajah is now a protected sanctuary and is home to leopard, Himalayan black bear, brown bear, hangul (Kashmir stag), musk deer, and numerous birds. The best time to visit is June–October. Tourists need a special permit from the Chief Wildlife Warden, J & K Government, Tourist Reception Center, Srinagar; tel. 72449.

Hemis High Altitude National Park, 35 km (22 mi.) from Leh, is the natural habitat of ibex, snow leopard, rare bharal sheep, great Tibetan sheep, and high-altitude birds, including the Himalayan snow cock. Best viewing season is September–May. For passes or permission to camp, contact the Wildlife Warden, Tourist Reception Center, Leh; tel. 97.

Kishtwar High Altitude Park near Jammu has musk deer, Himalayan black and brown bear, and 50 species of birds. Best viewing season is March–May. No pass is required.

SHOPPING. Carpets, woodwork, and shawls take pride of place among the handicrafts of Kashmir. From Ladakh come soft, snug *pashmina* tweeds and shawls made of the belly-wool of the Himalayan goats, and Tibetan-style jewelry of jade and turquoise, set in beaten silver. The Kashmir Valley craftsmen produce decorative articles in papier-mâché in three grades. In the first, pure gold leaf is used; it is rarely exported owing to high customs rates. Here is your chance to buy on the spot at reasonable prices bowls, boxes, and trays of amazing richness of detail and beauty of Oriental design. Other products worthy of attention are *gaba* and *numda* rugs. Gaba are thin and light and can be hung up on the wall like tapestries. Numda are made of thick, light-colored felt with embroidered flower designs. Also good are embroidered wall hangings and fashion fabrics, leather and fur coats, bags, Kashmir silk, and carvings in walnut wood. Time and again you will be accosted by hawkers; first make sure they have a Tourist Department registration card, then start your bargaining session.

NIGHTLIFE AND BARS. Due to the political unrest in Srinagar, bars have been closed. In the rest of the state, the best bars are in the hotels and serve liquor 11 A.M.–3 P.M. and 6–11 P.M.

WESTERN AND CENTRAL REGION

BOMBAY

City on the Move

by
KATHLEEN COX

Razzle-dazzle Indian-style: that's Bombay, the country's most "trendy" city. Its superb harbor provides the city with the country's busiest port. Its airport is also India's most active for international arrivals and departures. And Bombay is not only the financial hub of India, it is one of the largest manufacturing centers in the East.

The capital of Maharashtra rests on the Arabian Sea, an island set off from the rest of India by a winding creek. Perhaps it's this separation that sets Bombay's culture apart from that of the rest of India. Bombay's culture is new, vibrant, and often aggressive, reflecting the affluence and energy of a busy city of nine million people. People often compare this city with New York and insist that, like New York, it's a place you either love or hate. Bombay hits you with that kind of intensity. Its streets are crowded with traffic; Bombay has its share of gridlock. It can also be Manhattan-style expensive.

But in many ways, Bombay is a city unto itself. It's distinctly tropical, with pockets of palm trees and warm, salty breezes that keep you aware of the Arabian Sea. Its weathered Victorian mansions, some still privately owned, and grand public buildings, many beautifully lit at night, stand as a lingering reminder of the days of the British Raj. Then there's the presence of wealthy Arabs in elegant white robes who come to this city—

their favorite playground—especially on weekends. Bombay, or "Bolly-wood" (a sobriquet it achieved when it surpassed Hollywood as the world's largest movie production center), *is* a great playground—a great city to explore and a walker's delight, with miles of shore-front prome-nades.

While emperors, rajahs, and foreign invaders were warring along the river valleys and plains of India, the marshland islands (initially Bombay consisted of seven) remained untouched for many centuries by any but the fishing tribes. Yet the Arabian Sea connected these tribes—along with the inhabitants of the rest of India—to Africa. It was the sea that brought trade to the subcontinent even before the days of the Roman Empire and the sea that brought Europeans who first conquered, then modernized. The sea, in fact, created Bombay.

The first people known to have taken an interest in Bombay's harbor were the Portuguese in the early 1500s. (Vasco da Gama arrived at Cali-cut, farther south, in 1498.) Bom Bahai (Bombay) was ceded to the Portu-guese in 1534 by the sultan of Gujarat in a treaty that was meant to keep them at bay. Some time later, had it not been necessary to add to the desir-ability of a royal princess, Bombay's destiny would have been different: Bombay or Mumbai or Mumbadevi—no one knows the exact derivation— was given as a dowry to Charles II of England in 1661, when he married Catherine of Braganza.

The British occupied the islands, began to join them, and established a fort and trading post. Around this time a young Marathi leader, Shivaji, was amassing power and his own kingdom in the nearby Western Ghats. An astute guerrilla-style fighter, he made some raids on the British and used the booty to fight his wars with the Mogul Emperor Aurangzeb. Al-though British-held Bombay was within his territory, Shivaji was too oc-cupied with the Great Mogul—chasing and being chased—to prevent the British from growing in strength. Eventually, Indians, who saw opportuni-ties for trade and shipping, came to Bombay. The city grew in importance as other towns faded.

After many years of intrigue, betrayals, and mismanagement, the terri-tory Shivaji had governed fell under the British. The *Peshwas,* the minis-ters who took over the rule of Maharashtra from the royal line, lost the Fourth Maratha War in 1818. The pride the British had in Bombay and their power over the western region are symbolized in Bombay's most cele-brated landmark near Shivaji's statue, the Gateway of India, built to com-memorate George V's visit in 1911.

An interplay of favorable circumstances made Bombay into India's in-dustrial metropolis and one of Asia's busiest seaports. When the menace of Maratha sea raiders was finally broken, the East India Company's ships began to call at Bombay. Weavers from Surat settled there and, by 1850, the first cotton mills made their appearance. The outbreak of the American Civil War gave a further boost to this industry, as did a major land recla-mation project in 1862 that joined the seven small islands into one. Soon coastal steamer services were started, followed in 1869 by the opening of the Suez Canal, which revolutionized Bombay's maritime trade with Eu-rope. Since then, this go-ahead city never looked back and today Bombay claims 15 percent of all factories in the country and its textile industry accounts for 40 percent of the country's total.

In the past few decades, there has been a lot of reshuffling. In 1956, the Bombay State created at Independence was enlarged to include other Marathi- and Gujarati-speaking areas. Such a mammoth territory meant there were 48 million people talking in the main two languages, adminis-tered by one roster of government officials. A good deal of energy was

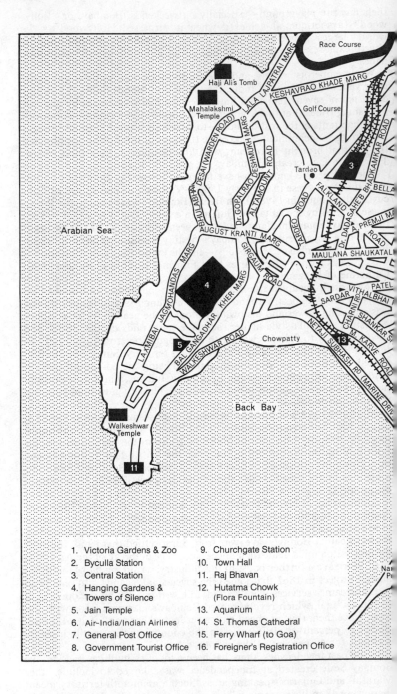

1. Victoria Gardens & Zoo
2. Byculla Station
3. Central Station
4. Hanging Gardens & Towers of Silence
5. Jain Temple
6. Air-India/Indian Airlines
7. General Post Office
8. Government Tourist Office
9. Churchgate Station
10. Town Hall
11. Raj Bhavan
12. Hutatma Chowk (Flora Fountain)
13. Aquarium
14. St. Thomas Cathedral
15. Ferry Wharf (to Goa)
16. Foreigner's Registration Office

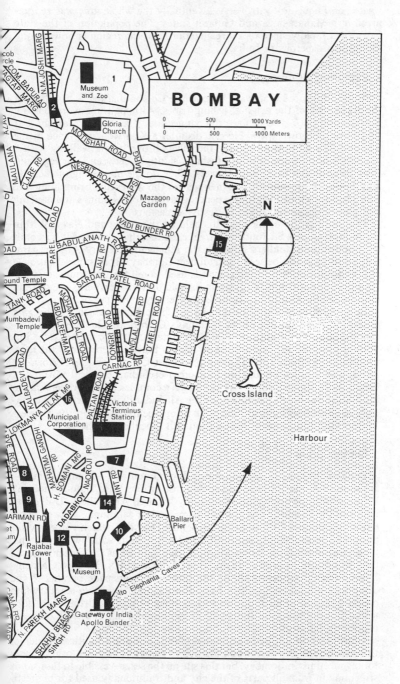

BOMBAY

0   500   1000 Yards
0   500   1000 Meters

N

Museum and Zoo

Gloria Church

Mazagon Garden

Mumbadevi Temple

Cross Island

Harbour

Victoria Terminus Station

Municipal Corporation

Ballard Pier

Rajabai Tower

Museum

to Elephanta Caves

Gateway of India
Apollo Bunder

wasted on linguistic controversy. Eventually the whole area was reorganized into Maharashtra and Gujarat states. The population of the state has grown rapidly since its reorganization, and the region is now among the most prosperous in India.

Exploring Bombay

Not far from the Gateway, beyond the Colaba market, is a village of the Kolis, one of the original fishing tribes. Although one word has a *c* and the other a *k,* you can see the connection. They speak Marathi, but they have their own ways. No one disputes a Koli woman's place in the bus line. The Koli women carry their fish all over town, walking with a fine stride, saris worn, Marathi fashion, skintight between their legs, and their hair, slicked back, with flowers. They do the marketing of the fish, and they keep the money. The men master the waves and bring home the fish. They are a sociable group, spending lavishly on weddings and dancing and playing games all night on festive occasions.

The southern tip of the island is held by the Army and Navy. Within the military area is St. John's Church, called Afghan, because it was built to commemorate soldiers killed in the nineteenth century Afghan campaigns. Its spire can be seen from all over Bombay. Gravestones that once crowded cemeteries near churchyards used to tell the gruesome story behind Britain's attempts to maintain its hold on India: cholera, plague, and malaria hit the families as soon as they entered the harbor.

In contrast to this part of the city is Churchgate, named for the gate in the old fort wall nearest St. Thomas's Cathedral. This area is all reclaimed land. The Mantralaya (State Secretariat), which houses some important government offices, faces an inlet of the sea. Here also is the new, acoustically perfect Tata Theater (National Center for the Performing Arts), which holds regular performances of Indian classical music and dance. At Nariman Point is a rising modern complex of skyscrapers, housing offices, and hotels. Included are the Air India Building, with the country's only rooftop helipad, and a luxurious penthouse atop the Express Towers that Indian press baron Ramnath Goenka calls home.

Marine Drive

Between here and Hutatma Chowk (Flora Fountain)—Bombay's hub—are some of the city's most interesting institutions; the "Indo-Saracenic" Prince of Wales Museum and the nearby Jahangir Art Gallery; University Hall and the Rajabai Tower, which commands a panoramic view of Bombay's "Manhattan." Close to the harbor are the Mint, which you can visit, by special arrangement, and the Town Hall, with its wide sweep of steps.

Skirting along Back Bay is Marine Drive, famous as the Queen's Necklace, which can be seen at night from Malabar Hill's Hanging Gardens. Every evening strollers walk on the extensive promenade parallel to the drive where coconut hawkers from Kerala, wearing ankle-length white cloths wrapped around the waist, sell their refreshing drink and *kulfi-wallahs;* their baskets of Indian ice cream covered in a red cloth offer another popular treat.

Chowpatty Beach, with its statue of Tilak, a great political leader of this century, is Bombay's political nerve center. There are other places for big meetings in Bombay, but this site on the sea, accessible to thousands streaming in from all parts of the city and traditionally used for big festivals, gives a particular significance to any statement or decision made there.

This is where millions teem on big days such as Ganesh Chaturthi, when rich and poor, frail and hearty move to the sea with clay or plaster or even silver or gold representations of Ganesh, the elephant-god. On any evening of the year, Chowpatty is busy; yogis bury themselves in the sand, fishermen haul in their nets, children romp, and hungry working people flock to the stalls for *bhel-puri* (a popular snack) and colored drinks.

Not far from Chowpatty, at 19 Laburnum Rd. (off Pandita Ramabai), is Mani Bhavan, a private home that Mahatma Gandhi visited occasionally. Today, the building is preserved as a national memorial and museum, containing a pictorial exhibit and a library, as well as a glassed-in preserved room where the Mahatma studied and slept.

Farther north, at the end of a causeway that leads out to the Arabian Sea, is the lovely white Haji Ali Shrine, built in honor of this Moslem saint who drowned here years ago. You can only visit the mosque and his tomb at low tide. Nearby is Bombay's oldest Hindu temple, the Mahalakshmi Temple, which is dedicated to Lakshmi, the goddess of wealth. Inside the inner sanctum, the images of three goddesses—Mahalakshmi, Mahakali, and Mahasaraswati—are appropriately adorned with gold jewels and pearls.

Malabar Hill

The east side of Malabar Hill, which you see from Chowpatty, is covered with greenery topped by the Kamala Nehru Park. Up on Malabar Hill and below it on the west side by the sea, are the mansions of wealthy industrialists who made their fortunes mainly in textiles. (Cotton grows in many places just north of Bombay and in what is now the state of Gujarat.)

B. G. Kher Road runs along the top of Malabar Hill. It leads past steep roads winding down to the Arabian Sea; many movies set in Bombay find a place for a car chase on these curving streets. On the hill is "Varsha," the residence of the chief minister of the state. Also on Malabar Hill is the Walkeshwar Temple, dedicated to Shiva. The temple was called the Banganga, now a water tank. Legend claims that this spring emerged after an arrow shot by Laxman, Rama's brother, built around a fresh water spring struck the ground.

Bombay's Parsees

The greenery on the left as you go beyond the gardens is part of the Parsee Towers of Silence, the place where the Parsees dispose of their dead. (There is a model of the towers in the Prince of Wales Museum.) A park surrounded by a high wall nearly conceals these bastions. Even relatives of the deceased are not allowed to go beyond a certain point within the enclosure, but stay in the park where they can sit and meditate. Bearers carry the body to the top of one of these cylindrical towers where it is laid out and devoured by waiting vultures. The skeleton—after a few days' exposure to the elements—is then thrown down the tower's well where it returns to dust.

This strange method of disposal has a twofold explanation. The Zoroastrian religion—of which the Parsees are the last surviving community—respects the earth and the fire too much to pollute them with the bodies of the dead. Another tenet declares that rich and poor must unite in death.

Originally, the Parsees were from the city of Pars in Persia. About 1,300 years ago they fled their homeland to escape Moslem persecution. Today, they represent a small minority of Bombay's population; but their economic and cultural influence is considerable. Largely responsible for building up the city's trade and industry, many of India's leading businessmen and philanthropists are members of this community.

A World of Markets

Bombay, like most cities in India, has numerous shopping haunts waiting to be explored. Visit early one morning the Mahatma Jyotiba Phule Market (formerly Crawford Market), at the junction of Dadabhoy Naoroji Road and L. Tilak Road, and walk through Bombay's fresh produce emporiums. If it's late spring or early summer, treat yourself to a delicious Alphonzo mango, a food worthy of the gods, and, any time of the year, have fresh sherbet or *faluda* (an Indian milk shake) at the famous Badshah Cold Drink Depot and Annexe. From here, wander into nearby Jhaveri and Dagina bazaars, Bombay's crowded jewelry markets, where shops are filled with fabulous gold and silver in every conceivable design.

Chor Bazaar's Mutton Street near the Kutbi Masjid is a narrow thoroughfare lined with stores that are crammed with antiques—clocks, victrolas, brass, and glassware. Allow yourself plenty of time to poke through the shops. Finally, if you want to add to your Western wardrobe, go to Fashion Street (on M.G. Road, opposite the Bombay Gymkhana Club). Here, open-air stalls feature the latest styles at give-away prices.

Environs of Bombay

If you arrive in Bombay by air, Juhu beach is the first strip of land you see as the plane descends. A glimpse is all you get, but you must return to Juhu later. On the way, you cross the Mahim Creek. In this fishing village at low tide you can study the heavy ancient boats designed for the rough seas. Juhu, once a secluded spot, is now crowded on weekends because of its good resorts and beaches. When the tide turns, the undertow can become hazardous for the unwary.

Those who are interested in historical ruins should plan a day trip north of Bombay to the Kanheri Caves, 42 kilometers (26 miles), and Fort Bassein, 76 kilometers (47 miles). The Kanheri Caves, comprising 100 caves cut into the top of a hill, are one of the largest groups of Buddhist underground chambers in Western Indian. The earliest caves were created in the second century, with many of them simple cells that were occupied by Buddhist monks for over 1,000 years. A few of the caves have interesting pillars, sculptures, and interior stupas. The fifteenth-century Bassein Fort was ceded to the Portuguese in 1534 by Gujarat's Sultan Bahadur. This fortified town remained in their hands for 205 years, when it was conquered by the Marathas. British bombardment in 1780 damaged it heavily, but you still can see the civic and ecclestiastic vestiges of this once-prosperous Portuguese city. The *Porta do Mar* (Sea Gate) near the fort commands a splendid view of the sea.

During this excursion, you can also visit the Lion Safari Park, near the Kanheri Caves. Here you can see the Indian lion, roaming free, while you travel around in an enclosed vehicle.

The Elephanta Caves

Elephanta Island, one of Bombay's major tourist attractions, as well as a reminder of India's past glories, is an hour's launch ride from the Gateway of India. Exactly who carved the cave temples on the island, originally called Gharapuri, or when, is not known. It is known, however, that the

Portuguese renamed the island Elephanta after a large stone elephant found near the landing place. (The figure collapsed in 1814 and was subsequently moved to Victoria Gardens and reassembled.)

Shortly before the time of Elephanta's excavation (between the sixth and eighth centuries) Bombay had experienced the Golden Age of the late Guptas, during which the talents of artists had a free scope. Sanskrit had been finely polished, and Kalidasa and other writers—under the Court's liberal patronage—had helped to bring about a revival of Hindu beliefs. It is the worship of Shiva, or Shaivism, that inspired these temples. That Shiva was well loved and the many ramifications of his personality well understood is shown by the polish and refinement of the artwork in the caves.

Crossing Bombay harbor on the way to Elephanta, you see centuries of India's life literally sailing before your eyes. The fishing sailboats in the harbor seem as much a part of the picture as do the modern liners. Tankers come full to Butcher Island, to the left of Elephanta. Their oil goes to Bombay's refineries. Behind them are the Tata electricity plant and the institute connected with atomic energy.

A flashlight and a knowledgeable guide on the island will help you to sort out the figures shown in the sculptures. You would have to be thoroughly familiar with Hindu mythology to understand fully each detail. But you cannot mistake the expressions on Shiva's faces, nor their intent. The powerful representations of strength, love, and spiritual peace at first seem buried in the dark halls. As you stay longer, they appear to grow and the walls to vanish, and you seem them as a world in themselves. Part of the impression conveyed at Elephanta is the unity of dissimilar things, and likewise the differentiation one personage can undergo. Shiva gives good scope for such a portrayal.

The sculptures are great art, not only in the sense that they are beautifully executed, with a secure knowledge of the subject and a superb technique of the chisel. They show things we don't ordinarily think of as being there and combine apparently independent parts into new entities.

The outside of the main cave consists of a columned veranda 30 feet wide and six feet deep, approached by steps flanked by sculptured elephants. At each end of the façade is a pillar projecting from the wall, carved in the shape of a *dwarapala* (doorkeeper). The entire temple is 130 feet square. The main sculptures are on the southern wall at the back. Three square recesses contain giant figures of dwarapalas. The panel to the left shows a manifestation of Shiva combining the male and female forms, while on the right panel you see the figures of Shiva and his consort Parvati. The central recess in the hall contains the most outstanding sculpture, the unusual *Mahesamurti,* the Great Lord Shiva, an 18-foot triple image. The three faces represent three aspects of Shiva as the creator on the right, the preserver in the center, and the destroyer on the left. The multiheaded deity is a composite of the stern, just, loving, father-figure, an expression of the monotheistic tendency of Hinduism. On either side of the recess are pilasters carved with gigantic dwarapalas.

Other sculptures at the doorways and on side panels show Shiva's usefulness. Shiva brought the river Ganga (Ganges) down to earth—the story says—letting it trickle through his matted hair. The facts of the universe are played with in wild delight, represented through this god's acts. Shiva is depicted also as Yogisvara, lord of yogis, seated on a lotus, and as Nataraja, the multiarmed cosmic dancer. The beauty of this sculpture is in the grace, balance, and sense of relaxation conveyed in spite of the multiple action.

The fact that these sculptures were, in many cases, damaged by the Portuguese soldiery does not detract from their beauty. The serenity of facial expressions triumphs over the loss of arms and legs. In the magnificently fierce scene of Shiva destroying the demon Andhaka—he seems to be emerging from clouds in which his legs are hidden—one overlooks the broken rocks, so powerful is the remaining portion.

PRACTICAL INFORMATION FOR BOMBAY

WHEN TO GO. The best time to visit Bombay is November to April. For the next few months, the city turns very hot. In August and September the monsoon brings lots of rain and humidity.

HOW TO GET THERE. By Air. Numerous international carriers fly in and out of Bombay, including *Air India* with flights between London, Frankfurt, and New York. *Indian Airlines* connects Bombay with all major cities, including daily flights from Ahmedabad, Bangalore, Calcutta, Cochin, Coimbatore, Delhi, Goa, Hyderabad, Indore, Jaipur, Jodhpur, Madras, Mangalore, Trivandrum, and Udaipur. There are also occasional flights every week from Vadodara (Baroda), Bhopal, Calicut, Gwalior, and Lucknow. *Vayudoot* has occasional flights every week from Goa and Indore.

By Bus. *Maharashtra State Road Transport Corporation* runs deluxe buses to Bombay from Goa, Bangalore, Mangalore, Indore, Baroda, and Hyderabad. For details and tickets, visit the MSRTC counter at the Central Bus Stand, Bombay Central, or Parel Depot. Kailash Travels (200/202 Triveni House, opposite 13th Khetwadi Lane, Khetwadi Back Road, tel. 365208) has buses going to the same destinations, plus Udaipur and Ahmedabad.

By Train. Regular trains connect Bombay with Agra, Ahmedabad, Bangalore, Bhopal, Bhubaneswar, Calcutta, Cochin, Delhi, Goa, Gwalior, Hyderabad, Indore, Jaipur, Jodhpur, Madras, and Trivandrum. For railway information and reservations in Bombay, contact *Western Railway,* Churchgate, tel. 291952 or 4933535, or *Central Railway,* Victoria Terminus Station, Bori Bunder, tel. 293131 or 446093.

By Ferry. At press time, the overnight ferry service has been resumed between Bombay and Goa. For details and booking, contact the *Maharashtra Tourism Development Corporation* (MTDC), address below.

By Rented Car with Driver. Fairly good roads connect Bombay with the following major cities: Vadodara (Baroda), 432 km (268 mi.); Ahmedabad, 545 km (338 mi.); Panaji, Goa, 597 km (370 mi.), and Hyderabad, 711 km (441 mi.). If you choose to travel by road from Bombay, hire a car with driver from a recommended tour operator listed below. Figure about Rs. 4 per km and a halt charge of Rs. 50–Rs. 100 per night.

TOURIST INFORMATION. You can contact these two good sources of information on Bombay: The *Government of India Tourist Office* (123 Maharshi Karve Rd., Churchgate, tel. 293144) is open 8:30 A.M.–6 P.M., closed Sundays. Every second Saturday of the month, it also closes at 2:30 P.M. You'll also find a counter at both airports. The *Maharashtra Tourism Development Corporation,* or MTDC (C.D.O Hutments, opposite L.I.C. Building, Madam Cama Road, tel. 2026713 or 2027762) is open 9:45 A.M.–5:30 P.M., closed Sundays and the second and fourth Saturdays of every month. Its bus tour and hotel and resort bookings counter (same location is open daily 9:45 A.M.–5:30 P.M.

FOREIGN CURRENCY EXCHANGE. Most Western-style hotels have money exchange counters. Otherwise, try *Grindleys,* 90 Mahatma Gandhi Rd.; *American Express,* (Majithia Chambers, D. Naoroji Rd.; *Thomas Cook,* D. Naoroji Rd.; o a branch of the *State Bank of India.* The banks are open Monday–Friday, 10 A.M.–2 P.M.; Saturday, till noon.

ACCOMMODATIONS. Hotels in Bombay range from compact places with the barest essentials to grand and luxurious structures catering to the visitor's every need. Many new hotels have been built in the main city, but one should book well in advance for these, especially in the winter season, November and December. Prices are based on double occupancy and exclude taxes: *Deluxe,* over Rs. 1,450; *Expensive,* Rs. 950–Rs. 1,450; *Moderate,* Rs. 500–Rs. 950; *Inexpensive,* under Rs. 500. Some Western-style hotels take major credit cards.

Deluxe

Hotel Natraj. 135 Netaji Subhash Rd., Bombay; tel. 2044161. 83 rooms with bath. Facing the Arabian Sea, this Western-style high rise has a comfortable, small lobby and air-conditioned rooms that are adequately furnished, but not fancy. Ask for a room with a balcony that overlooks the water. The Natraj offers TV, room service, multicuisine restaurant, bar, car-rental service, foreign-exchange counter, bookshop. AE, DC, MC, V.

The Oberoi. Nariman Point, Bombay; tel. 2025757. 350 rooms with bath. This elegant skyrise has a marble high-tech atrium lobby where musicians frequently play classical music. Air-conditioned rooms are modern with an understated contemporary decor and TV. Ask for a room with an Arabian Sea view. Besides a floor butler for each floor, the Oberoi has room service, numerous restaurants, health club, swimming pool, travel agency, foreign-exchange counter, shopping arcade, business center, doctor. AE, DC, MC, V.

The Oberoi Towers. Nariman Point, Bombay; tel. 2024440. 650 rooms with bath. Less sumptuous than the Oberoi, but still modern and elegant, this high rise adjoining it is also less pricey. Even-numbered rooms have an Arabian Sea view; odd-numbered rooms have a distant harbor view. All rooms are air-conditioned and furnished in a quiet, modern decor. The same services are available as at the Oberoi (above), except no floor butlers. AE, DC, MC, V.

Taj Mahal Hotel. Apollo Bunder, Bombay; tel. 2023366 or 800–458–8825 in U.S. 347 rooms with bath. This Victorian beauty was constructed at the turn of the century. Its white-trimmed, granite exterior faces Bombay's Harbor and commands great views. Each floor opens onto an interior veranda that draws your eyes to the handsome central dome and skylights. Air-conditioned rooms are spacious, with a contemporary decor. The best rooms have a harbor view. Included are TV, room service, multicuisine restaurants, bar, pool, health club, travel agency, business center, doctor, bank, foreign-exchange counter, and a shopping arcade. AE, DC, MC, V.

Taj Mahal Intercontinental. Same address and phone as above. 303 rooms with bath. This 24-floor high rise adjoins the Taj Mahal Hotel and offers less expensive, but still very deluxe-priced, air-conditioned rooms that are spacious and have contemporary decor. Ask for a harbor view. Amenities include the same services available at the Taj Mahal Hotel. AE, DC, MC, V.

Expensive

The Ambassador. Veer Nariman Rd., Churchgate, Bombay; tel. 2041131. 127 rooms with bath. The old-fashioned lobby to this 1940s high rise is charming, with lots of marble, pretty chandeliers, and antiques. Air-conditioned rooms are simply furnished, but they're spacious. Included are TV, room service, multicuisine restaurants, bar, travel arrangements, foreign-exchange counter, shop, secretarial services. AE, DC, MC, V.

Centaur Hotel. Bombay Airport, Bombay; tel. 6126660. 288 rooms with bath. Close to the airports and 25 km (16 mi.) from the city, this modern hotel offers spacious, contemporary-decor, air-conditioned rooms. TV, room service, multicuisine restaurants, bar, swimming pool, tennis courts, health club, secretarial service, doctor, baby-sitters, shopping arcade, free airport shuttle. AE, DC, MC, V.

Taj Hotel President. Cuffe Parade, Colaba, Bombay; tel. 4950808 or 800–458–8825 in U.S. 319 rooms with bath. This Western-style high rise has a spacious marble lobby. Air-conditioned rooms, done up in a modern decor, offer panoramic views as well as TV and room service. There are multicuisine restaurants, bar, health club, swimming pool, travel agency, foreign-exchange counter, business center, and shopping arcade. AE, DC, MC, V.

Moderate

Fariyas Hotel. 25 Off Arthur Bunder Rd., Colaba, Bombay; tel. 2042911. 80 rooms with bath. This Western-style high rise has a small, pleasant lobby. Air-conditioned rooms are clean, with parquet floors and a vaguely 1970s motel decor. Upper rooms offer the best views. TV, room service, multicuisine restaurant, bar, small swimming pool, tour arrangements, foreign-exchange counter. AE, DC, MC, V.

Garden Hotel. 42 Garden Rd., Colaba, Bombay; tel. 241476. 32 rooms with bath. A pleasant marble lobby distinguishes this intimate Western-style hotel. Air-conditioned rooms are clean, small, with modest furnishings and tiny balconies. TV, room service, multicuisine restaurant. Good value. Rupees only.

Hotel Godwin. 41 Garden Rd., Colaba, Bombay; tel. 2872050. 48 rooms with bath. Another small hotel, the Godwin has an inviting lobby and spacious air-conditioned rooms that are also very moderately priced and clean. TV, room service, roof garden with squawking geese, multicuisine restaurant. Good value. AE, DC, MC, V.

Inexpensive

Chateau Windsor Guest House. 85 Veer Nariman Rd., Churchgate, Bombay; tel. 2043376. 35 rooms with bath. Don't be put off by this hotel's location on an upper floor of an older high rise. The lobby is modest, and the rooms are simply furnished but clean, quiet, and have private balconies. The management also aims to please. Some rooms are air-conditioned. TV, room service, doctor, travel agent. Rupees only.

BOMBAY SUBURBS

Bandra

Deluxe

Welcomgroup Searock Sheraton. Land's End, Bandra, Bombay; tel. 6425454. 400 rooms with bath. Set on a rocky beach, this modern high rise has a spacious white-brick lobby and air-conditioned modern rooms with handsome contemporary furnishings. Best rooms overlook the swimming pool and sea. The beach, however, is too rocky for bathing. TV, room service, multicuisine restaurants, bar, swimming pool, tennis, health club, travel agency, foreign-exchange counter, business center, doctor, shopping arcade. AE, DC, MC, V.

Juhu Beach
About 20 km (12 mi.) from Bombay Center

Expensive–Deluxe

Centaur Hotel. Juhu Tara Rd., Juhu, Bombay; tel. 6143040. 369 rooms with bath. This gigantic Western-style high rise is set on the beach. Air-conditioned rooms are sleek—very white, with a contemporary decor. Best rooms offer a beach view; only deluxe-priced suites face the sea. Numerous multicuisine restaurants, bar, TV, room service, secretarial service, swimming pool, health club, good swimming beach, travel agency, foreign-exchange counter, shopping arcade, free airport shuttle service. AE, DC, MC, V.

Holiday Inn. Bairaj Sahani Marg, Juhu, Bombay; tel. 6206269 or 800 HOLIDAY in U.S. 210 rooms with bath. This Western-style high rise has a modern lobby and air-conditioned rooms with subdued modern decor. Best rooms offer partial beach view; only deluxe-priced suites face the sea. Room service, multicuisine restaurants, bar, TV, health club, swimming pool, good beach with windsurfing, travel agency, foreign-exchange counter, business center, free shuttle to Bombay center. AE, DC, MC, V.

Ramada Inn Palm Grove. Juhu Beach, Bombay; tel. 6149361 (or 800–2 RAMADA in U.S.). 113 rooms with bath. The lobby of this Western-style high rise has a glitzy, plastic appearance. Air-conditioned rooms are modern, with contemporary decor. Best rooms offer a limited view of the beach; only deluxe-priced suites face the sea. Room service, multicuisine restaurants, bar, TV, health club, swimming pool, good beach with windsurfing, business center, foreign-exchange counter. AE, DC, MC, V.

Moderate–Expensive

Horizon Beach Hotel. 37 Juhu Beach, Bombay; tel. 6148217. 161 rooms with bath. This Western-style 1970s hotel has a modest lobby and a more modest price. Clean air-conditioned rooms have simple furnishings and no great decor. Best rooms offer a partial view of the beach; only expensive-priced suites face the sea. Multicuisine restaurants, bar, TV, swimming pool, good beach, travel agency, foreign-exchange counter, secretarial service, doctor, free airport shuttle. AE, DC, MC, V.

Hotel Sea Princess. Juhu Beach, Bombay; tel. 6122661. 72 rooms with bath. This attractive, modern high rise has a pleasant, small lobby. Air-conditioned rooms are cheery and simply decorated in contemporary decor. Best rooms offer a partial beach view; only expensive-priced suites face the sea. Multicuisine restaurants, room service, TV, swimming pool, good beach, foreign-exchange counter. AE, DC, MC, V.

Sun 'n' Sand. 39 Juhu Beach, Bombay; tel. 6201811. 190 rooms with bath. A great tropical ambience is offered at this Western-style hotel, with an intimate lobby that leads out to a garden terrace overlooking the beach. Air-conditioned rooms are pleasant, not lavish, with a modern decor. Best rooms offer a view of the beach; only expensive-priced rooms face the sea. Multicuisine restaurants, room service, bar, TV, swimming pool, good beach, health club. Good value. AE, MC, V.

DINING OUT. In Bombay, you can expect great meals and a wide choice of cuisines: Continental, Chinese, and numerous regional Indian dishes, including Mughlai, Goan, Gujarati, Rajasthani, and Maharashtra's own Mandwani. Many restaurants tend to be pricey, but some tasty bargains will leave you and your wallet quite satisfied. While we include only our selection of the best restaurants, many hotels also have restaurants. Breakfast is usually 8–10:30; lunch, 12:30–3; and dinner, 8–10. The restaurants listed below are informal and, unless noted, are open for all three meals and don't require reservations. Prices, based on one person eating a three-course meal, excluding taxes, tip, or beverage, are *Deluxe,* over Rs. 120; *Expensive,* Rs. 80–Rs. 120; *Moderate,* Rs. 40–Rs. 80; *Inexpensive,* under Rs. 40.

Deluxe

Kandahar. The Oberoi, Nariman Point; tel. 2025757. Featuring tasty, robust North West Frontier cuisine, this elegant restaurant with quiet decor has a view of the sea and a glass-enclosed tandoori kitchen. Try the tandoori *khinga* (king-sized prawns marinated in yogurt and spices, then cooked in a tandoori), *kebab-E-chandni* (deboned chicken drumsticks stuffed with minced chicken, chilis, and cheese), or their special flavored *parathas* (layered flat bread). Reservations advised. Open 12:30–3 P.M. and 8–midnight. AE, DC, MC, V.

Outrigger. Oberoi Towers, Nariman Point; tel. 2024440. A 1990 fire temporarily closed this delightful Polynesian restaurant; but at press time it was scheduled to reopen by 1991. The chef serves an excellent luncheon buffet of Polynesian, Chinese, and Continental cuisine and good à la carte selections at dinner. Polynesian and Chinese dishes are best. Reservations advised. Open 12:30–3 P.M. and 8–midnight. AE, DC, MC, V.

Society. Ambassador Hotel, Veer Nariman Rd., Churchgate; tel. 2041131, ext. 504. If you're in the mood for Continental cuisine and want a good steak, visit this cozy Victorian restaurant, with parquet floors, mirrors, and a red-and-blue decor. Their best steak is named after a former chef—Steak à la Fernandes—and it's cooked at your table. You can also get good prawn dishes. Reservations advised. Open 12:30–3 P.M. and 8:30–11:45 P.M. AE, DC, MC, V.

Tanjore. Taj Mahal International, Apollo Bunder; tel. 2023366. This handsome Indian restaurant, with lots of marble, serves tasty tandooris and north Indian dishes on beautiful silver-plated, banana-leaf–shaped plates. At dinner, you can also enjoy Indian classical dance performances. Specialties include *kathi kebab* (paratha smeared with mint chutney and stuffed with chicken), *aloo moomphali chat* (cold cubed potato and peanuts), and *hariyali jheenga* (grilled prawns marinated in yogurt and fresh mint). Reservations required. Open 12:30–3 P.M. and 7–11:45 P.M. AE, DC, MC, V.

Zodiac Grill. Taj Mahal International, Apollo Bunder; tel. 2023366. This Continental cuisine restaurant is Western-style elegant, with subdued lighting, handsome chandeliers, captains in black jackets, waiters in white (including white gloves), and a pianist playing softly in the background. Specialties include fish basilica or chicken Zodiac; also enjoy a bottle of imported wine. You'll notice a set price list only for the liquor; you pay what you think you should for the sublime service and tasty meal. Reservations required. Open 12:30–3 P.M. and 7:30 P.M.–midnight. AE, DC, MC, V.

Expensive

Chopsticks. 90-A Veer Nariman Rd., Churchgate; tel. 232308. A sleek, modern decor with gray tiled walls, Oriental lanterns, and table linen distinguishes this handsome Chinese restaurant. Chopsticks also has a charming balcony eating area and a sidewalk terrace if you care to dine outside. Try their good sautéed tiger prawn (prawns cooked in a chili and Spanish onion sauce) or their lobster Ming-style (lobster cooked in a black-bean sauce). Reservations advised. Open noon–3 P.M. and 7:30–11:30. DC, MC, V.

Copper Chimney. Dr. Annie Besant Rd., Worli; tel. 4924488. Murals of exotic birds, brass planters hanging from the ceiling, and subdued lighting set an elegant tone at this popular Indian-cuisine restaurant. The tandooris are excellent, especially *reshmi kebab* (mildly spiced and barbecued boneless chicken). Reservations advised. Open 10:30 A.M.–4 P.M. and 7P.M.–12:30 A.M. AE, DC, MC, V.

Gaylord Restaurant. Mayfair, Veer Nariman Rd., Churchgate; tel. 221259. This 40-year-old institution, which serves Continental and Indian cuisines, has an Anglo ambience—upholstered chairs, Victorian mirrors, small crystal lamps, chandeliers, marble floors, and a handsome upstairs balcony. Try the good lobster Newburg or *murg makhani* (boneless chicken cooked in tomato curry with cream). Open 12:30–3:30 P.M. and 7:30–11:30 P.M. AE, DC, MC, V.

Kamling Chinese Restaurant. 82 Veer Nariman Rd., Churchgate; tel. 2042618. This spacious restaurant with traditional Chinese decor—red-enamel pillars and lanterns—serves fine Cantonese cuisine. Specialties include chicken Peking-style (fried with spring onions and soy sauce) or prawns Manchurian-style (fried prawns with garlic, ginger, and chili). Open noon–11:30 P.M. DC.

Khyber Restaurant. 145 Mahatma Gandhi Rd.; tel. 273227. This is one of Bombay's most attractive restaurants, with six delightful rooms done up in a North West Frontier decor—terra-cotta urns, copper trays, handsome murals. The waiters, dressed in Pathan tribal garb, serve delicious Mughlai and North Indian food, including pomfret green masala (fried pomfret stuffed with tangy green chutney and scallions) and *Khyber raan* for two (leg of lamb marinated overnight, then roasted in a clay oven). Very popular. Reservations advised. Open 12:30–4 P.M. and 7:30–midnight. AE, DC, MC, V.

Moderate

Chetana Vegetarian Restaurant and Bar. 34 Rampart Row, Kala Ghoda; tel. 244968. Chetana's Rajasthani decor—handblocked fabrics on the ceiling and traditional *torans* on the walls—provides a cozy ambience in which to enjoy tasty Gujarati *thali* (small portions of assorted regional dishes) at lunch and delicious Rajasthani cuisine at dinner. Sample these Rajasthani dishes: *daal bati* (lentils), *ker sangdi* (cooked cactus), *kadhi* (curd curry), *gatteka saag* (cooked vegetable and gram flour dish), and *mint raita* (curd and mint salad). There is great service, with more waiters than tables. Reservations advised. Open noon–3:30 P.M.; 3:30–6:30 P.M. for snacks, and 7–11 P.M. Rupees only.

Goa Portuguesa. Kataria Rd., opposite Mahim Head Post Office; tel. 454776. Designed like a modern Goan cottage, this charming restaurant serves great Goan dishes. Specialties include spicy *rechiad* fish (pomfret stuffed with red Goan masala) and prawn *balchao with pao* (pickled prawns prepared in a curry with palm vinegar). On Saturday and Sunday nights, you're serenaded with live Goan music. One c

Bombay's new hot spots; reservations are advised. Open noon–3:30 P.M. and 7–midnight. AE, DC, MC, V.

Inexpensive

Hotel Sindhudurg. Sita, R.K., Vaidya Rd., Dadar; tel. 4301610. This simple ethnic eatery has three small rooms filled with booths and patrons. It serves extremely good Maharashtran Mandwani cuisine—tasty non-vegetarian and vegetarian thalis. Another popular place. Open 11:30 A.M.–3 P.M. and 7–11:30 P.M. DC.

Saraswat Restaurant. Gokhle Rd., near Portuguese Church; tel. 4379754. A man in a white *dhoti* (long wrap tied around the waist) will receive you at the door to this very modest and very good Goan restaurant with two small rooms. Try the stuffed pomfret or prawns and rice, and a regional spicy drink called *kokam.* Open 11:30 A.M.–3:30 P.M. and 7–11 P.M. Rupees only.

SWEETS AND TREATS. *Bhel-puri* (a delightful concoction of rice, dahl, and chutneys served with puffed fried bread) is a popular snack available throughout Bombay, especially at the beaches. Follow this hearty, inexpensive meal with mixed *kulfi* (five-flavored Indian ice cream), usually available from the same vendor. One especially good stand is at Chowpatty Beach, next to the Mafatlal Swimming Pool.

For good Bengali sweets, join the crowd at *Brijwasi Sweet Shop* at Churchgate (near Ambassador Hotel). Try *gulab jam* (sweet balls in sugary syrup) or *malai* sandwiches (a milk and sugar-based sweet with heavy-duty calories). Make a special trip to *Badshah Cold Drink Depot and Annexe* (Umrigar Building, opposite Mahatma Phule Market, i.e. Crawford Market) and have some memorable fresh ice cream, sherbet, and *faluda* (milk shake) in yummy original flavors. Open 7:15 A.M.–11 P.M. daily.

HOW TO GET AROUND. From the Airports. The *Airport City Coach Service* will take you to Bombay's Nariman Point on the hour 2–5 A.M. and 7 A.M.–11 P.M. from the international airport (Rs. 25) and every hour on the half hour 2:30–5:30 A.M. and 7:30 A.M.–11 P.M. from the domestic airport (Rs. 20). A taxi from the airports to Nariman Point will cost about Rs. 120. Try to get the driver to use his meter, and once you arrive at your destination ask to see the tariff card, which is used to convert the meter amount into the revised rate; otherwise set the fare before you depart.

By Bus. Buses are cheap, but they're slow going in Bombay's traffic.

By Train. Bombay city is interlinked with an extensive local electric train network. Rates are determined by the distance to the destination. At every station, the train stops for only 15 seconds. To avoid traffic jams and for economic traveling, use local trains, which are the best alternative, although they tend to get overcrowded during rush hours. Trains start for western suburbs from Churchgate and for eastern suburbs from Bombay Victoria Terminus.

By Rented Car with Driver. Rates vary with the make of the car. A non-air-conditioned Ambassador (cheapest) should run about Rs. 4 per km. Use a tour operator listed below.

By Taxi. Taxis should cost about Rs. 4 for the first km, then per tariff card for each additional km.

By Auto Rickshaw. Since Bombay traffic can be slow going, these small three-wheeled vehicles are often the best way to get around. Rates are Rs. 2.75 for the first km, then the meter fare is calculated by the latest tariff card.

TOURS. *India Tourism Development Corporation* (ITDC) and *Maharashtra Tourist Development Corporation* (MTDC) offer city bus tours (9 A.M.–1 P.M. and 2–6 P.M., except Mondays) that include the Gateway of India, Aquarium, Prince of Wales Museum, Hanging Gardens, Jain Temple, and Kamla Nehru Park. ITDC tours depart from Nirmal Building, Nariman Point (tel. 2023343 for details). MTDC also offers a suburban tour (10 A.M.–7 P.M. daily) that includes Juhu Beach; and a boat cruise to Elephanta Caves with guided tour (9–1, 10–2, 11–3, and 2:30–6:30). Contact MTDC for departure points for bus tours (address and phone above). The MTDC launch to Elephanta leaves from India Gate. Many tour operators, listed below, also offer similar tours to these destinations.

Private Guides. The Government of India Tourist Office (address above) can arrange for an excellent guide. For 1–4 persons, figure Rs. 75 (half-day) or Rs. 110 (full-day).

TOUR OPERATORS. The following reliable agencies can take care of your travel needs, including a rented car with driver: *Cox and Kings* (272 D. Naoroji Rd., Bombay, tel. 2043065); *Jetair Tours* (41–42 Maker Chambers III, Nariman Point, Bombay, tel. 223275); *Travel Corporation India* (TCI, Chander Mukhi Bldg., Nariman Point, Bombay, tel. 2021991); *Modern Transport* (opposite R.T.O., Tardeo, Bombay, tel. 4930622); *ITDC* (Nirmal Towers, Nariman Point, Bombay, tel. 2026679 or 2023343).

SEASONAL EVENTS. The specific dates for many events are determined by the lunar calendar; contact the Government of India Tourist Office for details. The following festivals take place throughout Maharashtra, exclusively in Bombay, or in some other particular state destination.

January. *Makar Sankranti.* During this festival, which marks the passing of the sun from Dhanu to Makar, sweets are exchanged.

February. *Elephanta Festival of Music and Dance.* Wonderful cultural shows are performed for three nights in this annual festival held at the famous caves. A beautiful event.

February/March. *Holi.* On this day that marks the start of spring, wear old clothes. Celebrants throw colored water on anything that moves.

February/March. *Shivratri.* This Hindu festival honors Shiva with special celebrations at important Shiva temples.

March. *Jamshed Navroz.* This is the Parsi New Year; gifts are exchanged and prayers are offered at temples.

March/April. *Gudhi Padva.* This is the Maharashtrian New Year; *gudhis* (bamboo staffs), symbolic of victory and achievement, are erected and worshipped to ensure a good year.

April/May. *Shivaji Jayanti.* On the birthday of Shivaji, the great Maharashtrian warrior and leader, parades are held in his honor.

July/August. *Narali Pournima.* This festival celebrates the full moon of Shravana. Fishermen decorate their boats, sing and dance, and offer coconuts to the sea to ensure their safety during the upcoming fishing season.

July/August. *Gokul Ashtami.* On Krishna's birthday, men and boys form human pyramids, then attempt to break money- and curd-filled earthen pots strung across the streets.

July/August. *Pola.* During this harvest festival, the invaluable bullock is bathed, decorated, then paraded through rural villages to the accompaniment of traditional music and dancing.

August/September. *Nag Panchami.* On this day, live cobras, venerated by Hindus, or their images are worshipped. In Battis Shirale, a village near Sangli, devout Hindus show no fear—catching cobras, which they caress and worship, then release. This is also a good time to see Maharashtrian folk dances, especially in the countryside.

August/September. *Ganesh Chaturthi and Festival.* This 10-day festival marks the birthday of the Hindu's elephant-headed god. Elaborately crafted clay images of Ganesh are paraded through streets, installed on platforms and worshipped. On the 10th day, they're carried in enormous processions and immersed in the ocean or the nearest lake. This is an especially big event in Pune and Bombay, where some of the clay images are 9 m (30 ft.) tall. Pune events also include music and dances, bullock cart races, and food fests.

September/October. *Dasara (Dussehra).* During this 10-day Hindu festival that celebrates the victory of good over evil, expect a lot of noise from fireworks and numerous fairs.

October. *Diwali.* On the Hindu New Year, nighttime candles and lamps light up homes to welcome Lakshmi, the Hindu goddess of wealth. There are numerous cultural events.

HISTORIC SITES. Entrance to most sites is generally free or costs a nominal fee; when a donation is asked, a few rupees will suffice. Historic sites are open daily sunrise to sunset, unless noted otherwise below.

Bassein Fort (north of Bombay) was built in the early 1500s by Bahadur Shah Sultan of Gujarat. He ceded it to the Portuguese in the sixteenth century when they ruled over the northern coast.

Elephanta Caves, off the Bombay coast, contain seventh-century temples that are dedicated to Shiva. The most important sculpture is the three-faced Shiva called Maheshmurti. The island is accessable by launch; MTDC offers an excellent tour (see *Tours* above).

Gateway of India, at Chhatrapati Shivaji Marg, is the landmark of Bombay, a 26-meter (85-foot)-high stone archway, designed by Wittett in the sixteenth century in Gujarati style and built to commemorate the visit of King George and Queen Mary to India in 1911. An equestrian statue of Chhtarapati Shivaji and a statue of Swami Vivekanand have been installed here.

Haji Ali Shrine, at the end of a causeway off Lala Laipaitra Marg, honors a Moslem saint who drowned here while on a pilgrimage to Mecca. When a casket containing the mortal remains floated and came to rest on a rocky bed in the sea, devotees constructed the tomb and mosque at this spot. It can be visited only during the low tide.

Jain Temple, B. C. Kher Marg on Malabar Hill, was built in 1904. The marble shrine is dedicated to Adinath, the first *tirthankara* (perfect soul). Interior recesses contain statues of the 24 tirthankaras of the Jain religion. Its walls have dazzling paintings that depict incidents in their lives. The ceiling shows the different planets as personified in the mythology.

High Court, at K. B. Patil Marg, is an attractive building constructed in early Gothic style. The central structure rises 54.2 meters and is surrounded by a statue representing justice and mercy. It was completed in 1878.

Kanheri Caves, 42 km (26 mi.) north of Bombay, has over 100 caves cut into rock, most of them created in the second century by Hinayana Buddhist monks who also lived here. Caves 1, 2, and 3 are especially noteworthy: massive pillars, sculptures, and stupas.

Mahalakshmi Temple, near Lala Laipaitra Marg, is dedicated to Lakshmi, Vishnu's consort and the Hindu goddess of wealth.

Mumbadevi Temple, near Jhaveri Bazaar, is dedicated to the Goddess Mumbai (Mother Earth). The original eighteenth-century Hindu temple was destroyed and replaced, years back, with this structure built by Koli fishermen. Tuesday is a big day of worship.

Municipal Corporation Building, at Mahapatra Marg, is the V-shaped building standing opposite Victoria Terminal. It is designed in early Gothic style, blended with Indian motifs. The dome, its chief architectural feature, is 71.5 meters from the ground.

Prince of Wales Museum, Mahatma Gandhi Marg, was built in 1911 and is named after Britain's King George who laid the cornerstone in 1905. Its Indo-Saracenic architecture, with a magnificent dome copied after the Gol Gumbaz in Bijapur, is one of Bombay's finest Victorian buildings.

Rajabhai Tower, located at K. B. Patil Marg, is 79 meters high. Its university clock tower also houses the university library. Built in nineteenth-century Gothic style, it commands a fine view of the city.

Royal Asiatic Society, Horniman Circle, was once the Town Hall. Now it houses the Asiatic Society Library, one of the oldest and largest in the city, and statues of former British rulers.

St. John's Church, Malabar Hill, was built in 1857 and is dedicated to the British soldiers who fell in the Sind and Afghan campaigns of 1838 and 1843.

Surya Narayan Temple, Surajwadi, Panjiapol Lane, Bhuleshwar, was constructed in 1899 of white stone in honor of the sun god, Surya Narayan. The celestial gatekeepers, Jiy and Vijay, guard its entrance. In the inner sanctum, Surya Narayan sits on a one-wheel chariot drawn by a horse with seven heads and flanked by his two wives.

Towers of Silence, Malabar Hill, is a solemn area with three platforms on which the Parsees leave their dead. It's strictly off-limits.

Victoria Terminal, Dadabahai Noroki Marg, is one of the largest buildings in Bombay. Combining Indian and Gothic architecture, it was completed by the British in 1888. The imposing dome has a life-size statue of Queen Victoria and statues of peacocks, snakes, monkeys, and rats (all auspicious symbols). Its entrance is guarded by two stone lions.

Walkeshwar Temple, Walkeshwar Road, is a Hindu temple dedicated to Shiva, with a lingam supposedly created from *waluk* (sand) in its inner sanctum. Nearby is the Banganga Tank where devotees purify themselves. .

MUSEUMS AND GALLERIES. Entry fees are nominal. *Mani Bhavan,* Laburnum Road, a private home that the great leader Mahatma Gandhi visited, has been converted into a museum with an interesting collection of Gandhi memorabilia. Open 9:30 A.M.–6 P.M.; closed Sundays and Monday afternoons.

Nehru Planetarium and Science Museum, Lala Lajpat Rai Marg, has science exhibits and programs on astronomy (in English 3–6 P.M.). Open noon–7 P.M.; closed Mondays.

Prince of Wales Museum. Bombay's principal museum, located at Mahatma Gandhi Road. It is divided into three sections: art, archaeology, and natural history. The Tata family collection forms part of the archaeology and art sections. The natural history section was started with part of an admirable collection of the Bombay Natural History Society. The picture gallery contains, in addition to ancient Indian paintings, some by European and contemporary Indian artists and copies of Ajanta murals. There is also a large collection of jade, crystal, china, lacquer, and metal objects, both ancient and modern. There are some excellent dioramas in the natural history section. The museum has an interesting collection of exhibits from the Maratha period. Open October–June, 10 A.M.–6:30 P.M.; July–September, till 6; closed Mondays.

Victoria and Albert Museum, situated in Byculla, is the oldest museum in Bombay. The three principal sections are those of natural history, archaeology, and agriculture. There is also a small collection of miscellaneous art objects. Most of the exhibits in the museum relate to Bombay and western India. There are displays of archaeological finds, maps, and photographs of Bombay's history. Open 10:30 A.M.–5 P.M. Mondays, Tuesdays, Fridays, and Saturdays; 10 A.M.–4:45 P.M. Thursdays; 8:30 A.M.–4:45 P.M. Sundays; closed Wednesdays.

Jahangir Art Gallery, near the Prince of Wales Museum at Mahatma Gandhi Road, is Bombay's main art gallery. In the same building is Pundole Art Gallery. Most galleries are open 10 A.M.–7 P.M.

PARKS AND GARDENS. *Ferozshah Mehta Gardens* (Hanging Gardens) at Bal Gangadhar Kher Marg, was laid out in 1881 on top of a reservoir that supplies water to many areas. A special feature of this garden is its topiary hedges that are pruned into animal shapes. A flower clock can also be seen here.

Veermata Jijabai Bhonsle Udyan, Victoria Gardens at Dr. B. Amdeker Rd., has a clock tower, ornamental gates, a varied collection of more than 300 wild plants and trees, and a sun dial, all adding to the beauty of the place, at a bandstand. From time to time, musical programs are performed. Elephant, camel, and pony rides are available for children. Open 8 A.M.–6 P.M.; closed Wednesdays.

Kamala Nehru Park at B. G. Kher Marg, was laid out in 1952. It is mainly an amusement park for children, named after the wife of the first prime minister of India. Civic receptions are also held here. On the slopes of Malabar hills, it offers a panoramic view of Marine Drive and Chowpatty Beach. It is illuminated on the Republic and Independence days.

Lion Safari Park, 38 km (23 mi.) from Bombay, gives visitors an opportunity to watch the Indian lion from special closed vehicles provided by the park. Open 9 A.M.–5 P.M. Closed Mondays and Tuesdays.

Taraporewala Aquarium, Marine Drive, contains interesting specimens of marine life as well as freshwater fish. Open Tuesday–Friday, 11 A.M.–8 P.M.; Saturday–Sunday, 10 A.M.–8 P.M.

SPORTS AND OUTDOOR ADVENTURES. Beaches. Bombay beaches in the main city are no longer clean or maintained properly by the authorities. They are rather crowded and dirty. Suburban beaches are a better alternative.

Chowpatty Beach, at the end of Marine Drive, is a popular beach in the center of the city, where the celebration of festivals such as Ganesh-Chaturthi immersion takes place. It is crowded most of the time, surrounded by kiosks and hawkers selling Bombay special snacks. The beach has become more of a venue for political meetings and gatherings than a place for swimming. The water is too polluted for that, anyway.

Juhu Beach, 21 km (13 mi.) from Bombay center, is a long stretch of beach fringed with palm and coconut trees. A popular beach for all, it has a number of hotels, cottages, and restaurants. Horse, camel, and pony rides are also available. You can swim from October until May.

South of Bombay, MTDC is developing delightful tented beach resorts along its unspoiled and beautiful coast. See the Maharashtra chapter for details.

Boating. Contact MTDC (see *Tourist Information* above) about yacht cruises in the Arabian Sea and Harbor.

Horse Racing. Bombay's race course is one of the finest in the East. The racing season is November to April, Saturday and Sunday.

SHOPPING. Bombay is a great place to shop, with a diversity of options from bargain bazaars and open stalls to trendy boutiques and government-run emporiums. Most shops are closed Sundays. Here are some best bets:

Ensemble, Great Western Bdg., 130/132 Shahid Bhagat Singh Marg, sells exquisite designer *salwar kameez* (loose blouse and pants), antique scarves, handbags, and Western-style clothes for men and women. Very pricey, very beautiful. Open 11 A.M.–8 P.M. AE, V.

Kaysons Sari Shoppe, Stadium House, Churchgate, sells high-quality silk by the meter, salwar kameez, and gorgeous silk scarves and stoles. Open 11 A.M.–8 P.M., closed Sundays. AE, DC, MC, V.

Kala Niketan Silk and Saris, 95 Queens Rd., and neighboring stores also offer a wide range of silk from all over India, scarves, and stoles. Open 9:30 A.M.–7:30 P.M. AE, V.

Ajmal & Sons Perfumers, Shop No. 1, Cecil Court, Lands Downe Rd., behind Regal Cinema, has a wide range of pure essences from flowers, which is poured into small vials and boxed like previous jewelry. It's sold at very reasonable prices. Try morning breeze, lotus, night queen, and the heavenly pure white musk. Rupees only. Open 10 A.M.–7 P.M.

Phillips Antiques, opposite Regal Cinema Museum, has the best old prints, engravings, and maps in Bombay. This store also sells many treasures originally left behind by the British—Staffordshire and East India Company china, old jewelry, crystal, lacquerware, sterling silver. This is a reliable exporter. Open 9 A.M.–7 P.M. AE, V.

Natesan's Antiqarts, Jahangir Art Gallery and Taj Intercontinental Hotel, sells high-quality, guaranteed subcontinental antiquities: wood-carvings, sculptures, and paintings, plus wonderful new artifacts. Can also export. Open 10 A.M.–7 P.M. daily. AE, DC, MC, V.

A. K. Essajee, Suleman Chambers, Side Street, opposite Cottage Industry, sells handsome old and new Indian curios and handicrafts: carved doors and chairs, old perfume bottles, jewelry, Rajasthani chests, Tanjore and Mysore paintings, old silver jewelry, silver, bronze, and Islamic artifacts. Also ships. Open 9 A.M.–7 P.M. AE, V.

Framroz Sorabai Khan & Co., Regal Cinema Bldg., C. Shivaji Marg, sells lovely old and new silver jewelry, curios, and antiques. Open 9 A.M.–6 P.M. Rupees only.

Tribhovandas Bhimji Zaveri, 241-43, Jazeri Bazaar, has fabulous gold jewelry and diamonds, plus other precious and semi-precious stones. It's crowded with merchandise and customers. Open 11:30 A.M.–7:30 P.M. AE, MC, V.

Ramesh Art Emporium and Pukhraj Jawanmal Surana, 47 and 48 Dagina Bazaar, Mumbadevi Rd., near the temple and Jazeri Bazaar, sells top-quality old and new silver jewelry, including good tribal pieces, and silver curios. Bargain. Open 9 A.M.–8 P.M. Rupees only.

MCS (Mehra Carpet Showroom), Crystal, 79 Dr. Annie Besant Rd., Worli, has an excellent selection of Indian carpets and *dhurries* (rugs). Open 10 A.M.–7 P.M. AE, MC, V.

Central Cottage Industries Emporium, 34 Chhatrapati Shivaji Maharaj Marg, by the Gateway, is a great place to pick up good gifts from all over India at fixed prices. Open 10 A.M.–7 P.M. AE, MC, V.

Also visit these good bazaars:

Fashion Street, opposite Gymkhana Club on M. G. Rd., is a row of stalls selling good Western clothes. Open 10 A.M.–8 P.M. daily. Bargain. Rupees only.

Chor Bazaar, Mutton Street near Kutbi Masjid, has numerous shops that sell antiques and curios, especially old phonographs, chandeliers, clocks, nautical instruments, brass and glassware. Open 10 A.M.–7 P.M. Rupees only.

NIGHTLIFE AND BARS. Check the daily newspaper for a listing of ongoing cultural performances. Since this is the world's largest film-producing country, Bombay certainly has its share of movie houses as well as actors and actresses. Indian films generally are extravaganzas, containing a bit of everything from romance and music to drama and suspense. Such films are called *masala,* after the all-purpose word for spices that are added to practically every dish. Few of the Indian-made films are in English, but some have subtitles. There are also some cinemas, like the Foreign Film Theatres, that show films made in the United States or England.

Bombay's hotel bars are usually open from 11:30 A.M.–3 P.M. and 6 P.M.–midnight or later. *Bayview Bar* in the Oberoi Hotel at Nariman Point is one of the prettiest—you sit in art deco surroundings and have a breathtaking view of the Arabian Sea. At night, you can dance to a live band (Sun.–Thurs. until midnight and on Fri. and Sat. until 1:30 A.M.).

MAHARASHTRA

Beaches, Forts, Sacred Caves

by
KATHLEEN COX

After a tour of fast-paced Bombay, you'll find Maharashtra's tempo much slower. Travel just a short distance and you escape the commercial world. You can head south along the coastline where unspoiled beaches, backed by palm groves and dotted with delightful tented resorts, extend to Goa. Travel inland to the Western Ghats, and you can relax in former British hill stations or explore old forts that still reign over their strategic locations. Go north and northwest and wander through cave temples, including the famous Ellora and Ajanta caves, where man's artistry became an epiphany in stone.

The area around Bombay is called the Fort Country of Maharashtra and was a stronghold of the legendary Shivaji, that great warrior. In the seventeenth century, Shivaji gave birth to Maratha power. Drawing inspiration from Hindu religious tales, he was fired by the idea of liberating his country from the grip of the Moslems. The tools were all there: a frugal, sturdy race of men and the hilltops of the Deccan Plateau, which could, with little effort, be made into impregnable small forts, excellent for highly mobile guerrilla warfare. The men under Shivaji were dedicated. They could scale the forts on these hills. They and their ponies could go where the elaborate Moguls could not.

There is the story of a Maharashtrian milkwoman, who, after the gates of one of Shivaji's forts were closed, climbed down a supposedly unscalable wall to return to her baby at home. Shivaji rewarded her and reinforced the defenses. In 1680 he died, leaving behind a new, powerful nation. The Maratha influence spread all over central India and became all-encompassing.

EXPLORING MAHARASHTRA

About 74 kilometers (46 miles) north of out of Bombay, you begin to move toward Kalyan and Ambernath. The eleventh-century Ambernath Temple, covered with beautiful designs, is one of best examples of Deccan temple architecture. A little difficult to find, the temple is in a valley between small hills and has a river running at the compound wall; a grove of trees completes this hidden, contemplative site. Constructed in 1060 to commemorate a king of the Silhara Dynasty and used for the worship of Shiva, this temple of exposed black rock has none of the commercial atmosphere of the paint and plaster city temples. Highly imaginative carvings, playful and spiritual, cover the temple, inside and out. Though the hall is not big, the sculptured dome makes it seem spacious. The *lingam* (phallus) shrine is in a crypt, which you climb down into. For worship, flowers are thrown onto the lingam and a temple priest throws water at intervals that flows out as holy water.

Next stop should be Nasik, 145 kilometers (90 miles) north of Bombay, one of the holy cities of the Hindus who believe that Lord Rama, hero of the epic *Ramayana,* spent the major part of his exile here. Set on the banks of the Godavari, a sacred river, Nasik is also the site of the Kumbh Mela (held every 12 years) when pilgrims by the thousands come for a purifying dip that celebrates an old legend.

Long ago, the gods and demons discovered the existence of a *kumbh* (pitcher) that rested at the bottom of the sea. This kumbh contained a nectar that would make any drinker immortal. During a 12-day battle over its possession, which resulted in Vishnu grabbing the kumbh on behalf of the gods, four drops of nectar fell—one each upon Nasik, Ujjain, Haridwar, and Allahabad. Since a day in heaven, the scene of the battle, equals a year on earth, each of these four cities, in rotation, now has a Kumbh Mela to celebrate this event.

While this city figures prominently in Hindu mythology, its man-made treasures celebrate the Buddhist faith. Eight kilometers (five miles) southeast of Nasik are 23 rock-cut caves that were executed in A.D. first century by members of the Hinayana sect, who were prohibited from creating the Buddha's image. A throne, a footstool, or footsteps symbolized his presence. Called the Pandu Lena caves, many of them were laid out as one-story *viharas* (monasteries) and their setting is unusual and impressive—chiseled out of a conical peak at the end of the Trimbuk Mountain. Caves 3, 8, and 18 are the best. In Cave 3, you find a *stupa* (reliquary mound), and in Cave 18, you can see a *chakra* (wheel)—both are important Buddhist symbols. The images of the Buddha were added later.

Matheran

Matheran, 105 kilometers (65 miles) north of Bombay, is a resort whose name means "woodlands overhead." The hill is an island of trees in an almost treeless plain. The approach to the town is in itself delightful. From Bombay, you can take a train to Neral, two hours out, where you see tiny

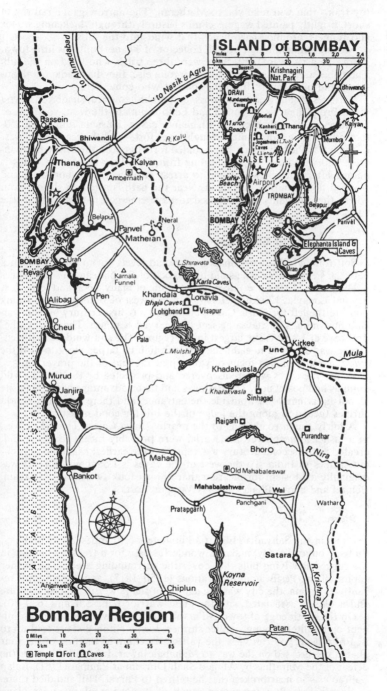

ISLAND of BOMBAY

0 miles · 8 · 12 · 1,6 · 2,0 · 2,4
0 km · 10 · 20 · 30 · 40

Bassein

Krishnagiri Nat. Park

DRAVI
Mandapeshwar Caves

Borivli

Kanheri Caves

Thana

A1 anor Beach

Jogeshwari Caves

L.Tulsi

L.Vehar

SALSETTE I.

Juhu Beach

Airport

Bhiwandi

Kalyan

Mumbra

Juhu Beach

Mahim Creek

TROMBAY

BOMBAY

Belapur

Panvel

Elephanta Island & Caves

Uran

to Nasik & Agra

to Ahmedabad

Bassein

Bhiwandi

R. Kalu

Thana

Kalyan

Ambernath

Belapur

Panvel

Neral

Matheran

BOMBAY

Uran

Revas

Alibag

Pen

Karnala Funnel

L.Shiravata

Karla Caves

Khandala

Lonavla

Bhaja Caves

Lohghand

Visapur

Cheul

Pala

L.Mulshi

Pune

Kirkee

Mula

Khadakvasla

L.Kharakvasla

Sinhagad

Murud

Janjira

Raigarh

Purandhar

Bhor O

R.Nira

Mahad

Bankot

Old Mahabaleswar

Mahabaleshwar

Wai

Pratapgarh

Panchgani

Wathar

Satara

R.Krishna

Koyna Reservoir

Anjanwel

Chiplun

to Kolhapur

Patan

Bombay Region

0 Miles · 10 · 20 · 30 · 40
0 5 km · 15 · 25 · 35 · 45 · 55 · 65

Temple · Fort · Caves

A R A B I A N   S E A

toy trains that will take you to Matheran. The narrow-gauge railway of short, brightly painted wagons climbs leisurely through thickening woods and tunnels, around sharp bends that wind into the hills.

An Englishman, Hugh Mallet, collector of Thane, built this little town. Before he arrived in 1850, there were three tribes who lived on the hill. The tribes are still here, but, like everyone else, they have adapted themselves and now benefit from the tourists who come here.

Varieties of tall trees, some moss- and orchid-covered, shade you as you walk. From the tops of Louisa and Echo Points to the west, you can see Bombay, its oil refineries, the Elephanta caves, Karnala funnel—a 150-foot pillar rising from a much fought-over fort—and the sea. To the west of the hill is Parbal, which has a ruined fort. Between the hills roam panthers and wild boar. A path leading from One-Tree-Hill to the valley is named after Shivaji, who came to arrest an unworthy subordinate and stopped to worship at Matheran. Near the path is a Hindu shrine, from where three lingams are supposed to have emerged naturally, from the rock.

The Karla and Bhaja Caves

Soft rolling hills quickly pass as the road levels out to the open planes between steep ranges. The solid black rock of the plateau, in some places 3,049 meters (10,000 feet) deep, is the home of many caves and forts. Just beyond Lonavla, 120 kilometers (74 miles) west of Bombay, is a turning point to the left for Karla Caves, created in A.D. first century by Hinayan Buddhist monks, of the same sect that carved Kanheri. The main cathedral cave at Karla is the largest in the region. The sun window at the entrance was designed to slant the rays through its lattice work toward the *stupa*, a dome-shaped focus of worship at the end of the prayer hall.

Before the caves were rediscovered and protected by the British, wild animals had possession. The Peshwas had taken advantage of the holy site to put up a temple just outside the entrance, and there are small Hindu shrines tucked in along the ledge of the hill for good measure.

A fairly rough road leads to the nearby Bhaja Caves. These 18 caves, in a lusher atmosphere than Karla, were probably meant for nuns and, created in the second century B.C., represent the earliest examples of rock-cut shrines in India. To the west of the caves is Longhand Fort. It was originally a Moslem fortification that Shivaji took twice, but lost again. Behind and above Bhaja Caves is Visapur Fort.

Pune

Pune, in the Sahyadri Hills 163 kilometers (101 miles) from Bombay, that surround the city. makes a wonderful base for a trekking holiday in the rugged low-lying hills that cover the surrounding areas. The former capital of the Peshwa administrations (1750–1817), and known until recently as Poona, the city was the capital of the powerful Maratha empire and is closely associated with the great warrior King Shivaji (1630–80).

On the south edge of town is Parvati Temple, a white building prominent on a hilltop among smaller shrines. Easily climbed stairs lead up to it. From here, you can view the valley stretching to the first of the four ghats to be crossed on the way to Mahabaleshwar. It is said that after the defeat of the Marathas by Ahmed Shah Durrani at Panipat (1761), Balaji Bajirao was so heartbroken that he retired to Parvati Hill and died there.

Nonetheless, Pune recovered much of its former glory under Nana Peshwa in the latter part of the century. The saying *Jab tak Nana, tab tak Pune* (as long as Nana lives, Pune will live) expressed its faith in him. But the last year of the Empire was filled with strife, and in 1817, Pune finally fell to the British at the Battle of Kirkee. Under them, the city developed into the "monsoon capital" of Bombay Province and became a large military center.

Today, Pune is distinctly divided into the spacious cantonment and the crowded old city, where localities have been named after days of the week. Pune is also the home of the Osho Commune International, whose guru was Bhagwan Shree Rajneesh who once had his ashram in Oregon and who prior to his recent death took to calling himself Osho. Today, visitors who have an obligatory white robe and have test results that prove that they're AIDS-negative and who also leave behind their drugs, cigarettes, and cameras, are welcome to attend a nightly meeting where they can supposedly still feel Osho's presence as they pray before his empty white throne.

Fort Country

Four forts in the vacinity of Pune are worth an excursion. Ahmadnagar, a historical Moslem city 82 kilometers (51 miles) to the north, is named after Ahmed Nizam Shah, founder of the Nizam Shahi dynasty, who built the city in 1490. Sixty years later, its main landmark, the fort, was erected by Hussain Nizam Shah. This battle-scarred citadel lies behind 2½ kilometers (1½ miles) of walls. It gained notoriety when the British used it as a prison for Boer War captives in 1901, and in 1942 for Indian nationalist leaders, including Nehru. The Moslems also left behind other monuments, including Chand Bibi, the tomb of a royal minister, and the Alamgir Dargah, the tomb of Emperor Aurangzeb, who died at Ahmadnagar at age 97 in 1707 (his body was later removed to Aurangabad). Shivneri, farther north, is the birthplace of Shivaji and the site of the impressive Shivneri Fort.

Heading south to Mahabaleshwar, you should visit the Simhagad and Purandhar forts, 25 kilometers (16 miles) and 38 kilometers (24 miles) respectively from Pune. Also connected to this great Maratha warrior, these elaborate forts once had stables for horses (and often for elephants), caches for hiding treasures and men, extensive underground tunnels, outlandishly high and thick walls, semicircular towers, and access that was purposely steep and difficult that usually led to gateways that were hidden from view.

Mahabaleshwar

Winding roads lead through the ghats to Maharashtra's most popular hill station, Mahabaleshwar, 120 kilometers (74 miles) from Pune. As you climb the last ghat, the valley below seems significant. On the right, just before the little city of Panchgani, is a promontory called Harrison's Folly. Farther away is another outreach of land, Sidney Point. From here, you can look up to the top of Krishna Valley, marked by a cone-shaped hill.

Finally, you reach Mahabaleshwar, a tiny village with many hotels. As in so many hill stations, here you find crowds of tourists, horses galore to ride, and numerous good views of the surrounding valleys. You can also find some unexpected treats: fresh strawberries and fresh rose petal and strawberry ice-cream, available in season. You can also use Mahabaleshwar to see two more forts that figure into Shivaji's military exploits: nearby Pratapgarh Fort, which was built in 1656, and Raigarh Fort, 80 kilometers (50 miles) away.

Ellora and Ajanta Caves

Long forgotten and rediscovered by chance in 1819, the cave temples of Ajanta and Ellora rank among the wonders of the ancient world. Here, over a period of 1,400 years—between the second century B.C. and A.D. twelfth century—great armies of monks and craftsmen carved cathedrals, monasteries, and whole cities of frescoed sculpted halls into the solid rock faces. Working with the simplest tools and an ingenious system of reflecting mirrors to provide them with light, they cut away hundreds of thousands of tons of rock to create the cave temples. The precision of their planning, their knowledge of rock formations, and the delicacy and profusion of their art have been called an art form "worthy of the Renaissance," created by a religious fervor as intense as that of medieval Europe.

The cave temples, between them, span three great religions—the Buddhist, the Hindu, and the Jain. First came Ajanta. It is believed that a band of wandering Buddhist monks first came here in the second century B.C. searching for a place to meditate during the monsoons. Ajanta was ideal—peaceful and remote from civilization. The setting was spectacular: a sharp, wide horseshoe-shaped gorge that fell steeply to a wild mountain stream flowing through the jungle below. The monks carved crude caves into this rock face for themselves, and a new temple form was born.

Over nine centuries, the cave temples of Ajanta evolved into a work of splendid art. Today, there are 29 caves in all; some of them were once monasteries, others were *chaityas,* or Buddhist cathedrals. All of them are intricately and profusely decorated with sculptures and murals depicting the many incarnations of Buddha.

Here, as a flickering light shines on the massive murals in the darkness, fables from the Buddhist texts come alive: Princes and princesses go about the splendid ritual of their lives; dancers perform to the sounds of a silent lute; richly caparisoned elephants and horses prance; celestial musicians play their instruments; great scenes of drama are enacted in courts, palaces, and bazaars; and a whole era comes to life again. But everywhere, at all times, spirituality flows deep and quiet below the surface. And the sensuous maidens depicted on the walls, your guide points out, were created to try the will power of the monks.

In the seventh century, for some inexplicable reason, the focus of activity shifted from Ajanta to a site 123 kilometers (76 miles) to the southwest—to a place known today as Ellora. The cave temples of Ellora, unlike those at Ajanta, are not solely Buddhist. Instead, they trace the course of religious development in India—through the decline of Buddhism in the latter half of the eighth century, the Hindu renaissance that followed the return of the Gupta dynasty, and the Jain resurgence between the ninth and eleventh centuries. Of the 34 caves, 12 are Buddhist, 17 are Hindu, and five are Jain.

At Ellora, the cave paintings of Ajanta give way to sculpture, which often covers the walls in an exquisitely ornate mass. In the Buddhist caves, the carvings present a serene reflection of the Buddhist philosophy. But in the subsequent Hindu caves, they acquire a certain exuberance, a throbbing vitality. Gods and demons do fearful battle, Lord Shiva angrily flails his eight arms, elephants rampage, eagles swoop, and lovers intertwine.

The single most incredible edifice at Ellora is the Kailasa Temple—probably the world's largest monolith. Here, 85,000 cubic meters were scooped out of solid rock, laboriously by hand, to reveal a courtyard 45 by 30 meters (147 by 98 feet)—but leaving behind a lavishly carved main temple, and a three-story tower, cupola, and gateway—all linked together

ELLORA CAVE-TEMPLES

(5TH c TO 8TH c AD)

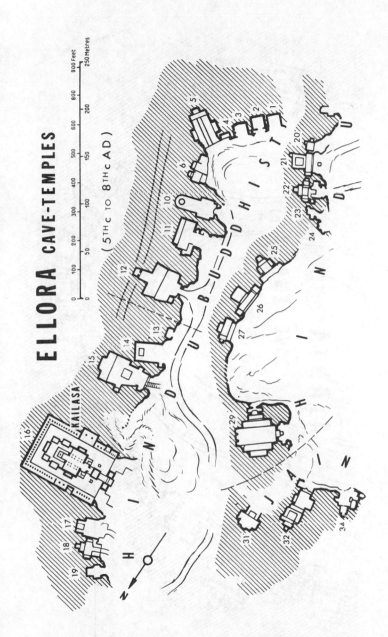

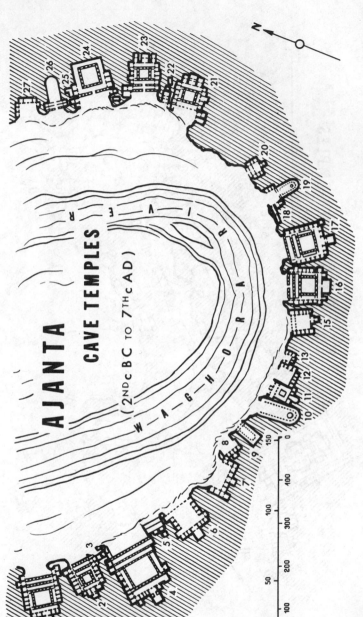

AJANTA

CAVE TEMPLES

(2ND c BC TO 7TH c AD)

W A G H O R A R I V E R

N

by an overhead vestibule. It is a tribute to the infinite genius of the ancient Indian craftsmen and their daring to have even conceived of such an idea. And they worked for hundreds of years. Today these cave temples are one of the wonders of ancient art. Though successive waves of invading Moslem armies badly damaged these artistic treasures, the cave temples that remain are enough to stagger the senses.

Aurangabad

Aurangabad, 375 kilometers (233 miles) northwest of Bombay, takes its name from the Emperor Aurangzeb, the last of the great Moguls, who made it his capital. Here, since time immemorial, the sounds of history have thundered. And in the numerous fine monuments that lie in the region, you can see the influences of various empires, religions, and philosophies. Here lie the seventh-century Aurangabad cave temples—the historic medieval fortress of Daulatabad, with its miles of forbidding ramparts, once, oh so briefly, the capital of Hindustan.

Aurangabad today is a ghost town of legends, with its alleyways steeped in lore. It is the gateway to Ajanta and Ellora and is the most convenient headquarters for a trip there. And as a city in its own right, Aurangabad has many places of interest that will captivate the tourist. It is better to visit the caves here before visiting Ajanta and Ellora, for anything after them might well seem to be an anticlimax.

First there is the Panchakki. This pre-Mogul (seventeenth-century) monument is a mill where water was harnassed to turn large stones to grind flour. It serves as the tomb of a Moslem saint, Baba Shah Musafir, who was buried there in 1624. Baba Shah Musafir lies in a simple grave surrounded by gardens, fountains, basins, and an artificial waterfall.

Just three kilometers (about two miles) from the city center is a far more grandiose affair—the Bibi-ka-Maqbara, the mausoleum built in 1679 by Aurangzeb for his wife, Rabia-ud-Daurani. It is a rather pale imitation of the Taj Mahal, the masterpiece of his father, Shah Jahan, but it's impressive if you haven't seen the Taj. The exterior lacks symmetry and balance, and its interior decoration has nothing comparable with the wonder at Agra. Yet this royal resting place has its own splendor and grace.

Nearby also are Daulatabad and the Aurangabad caves. Daulatabad, a medieval fortress on a pyramid-shaped hill 15 kilometers (nine miles) from the city, was originally known as Devagiri, the "Hill of the Gods." During the fourteenth century, it was renamed Daulatabad, the "City of Fortune," by the sultan of Delhi, Muhammad Tughlaq, who decided to move his capital there, 1,129 kilometers (700 miles) away. He moved the whole population of Delhi, too, a decision so mad that, after thousands died on this forced march, he ordered them to march back to Delhi. But Daulatabad remained, ruling the province from its mountain fort. The fort is surrounded by five kilometers (three miles) of walls, and a visit here means a climb to the top of the rock, 183 meters (600 feet) high. When you get there, you are greeted by a huge cannon, six meters (20 feet) long, which somehow got there in the seventeenth century. One feature of the climb through the citadel is a spiraling tunnel 46 meters (150 feet) long near the top. Its upper entrance is crowned by an iron lid where defenders lighted a fire of hot coals to scorch besiegers in the tunnel. The Chand Minar pillar at the base of the fort was built as a victory column.

And then there are the Aurangabad caves, of which Caves 6 and 7 have the best sculptures. The other caves are separated by hills. At Aurangabad, the caves reproduce two forms of religious structures: the place of worship, or chaitya, and the monastery, or vihara. Carved out during the seventh century, the caves are later forms in Mahayana style. This style can be seen in such temples as Cave 1, with a Buddha on a lotus seat supported by snake-hooded demigods; or Cave 2, where a huge Buddha sits with his feet on a lotus; or Cave 3 with 12 carved pillars and another seated Buddha in front of his shrine. In the second group, which is a mile away, Cave 7 is interesting, with its huge figure of Bodhisattva Padmapani. (A Bodhisattva is a near-Buddha and one of the forms through which Buddha passed before he achieved enlightenment; *padmapani* means lotus-in-hand.) He is praying for deliverance from eight fears that are illustrated dramatically in stone: fire, the enemy's sword, the chains of slavery, shipwreck, attacks by a lion, snakes, a mad elephant, and death portrayed as a demon.

Ellora

Only 30 kilometers (19 miles) from Aurangabad, Ellora represents what is perhaps the finest and most magnificent of Indian sculpture. Unlike Ajanta, where the temples were chopped out of a steep cliff, the caves at Ellora were dug into the slope of a hill in a north-south direction (they face the west and could receive the light of the setting sun). Many of the caves date back to the seventh century when Ajanta was abandoned and its creators moved to Ellora, 66 kilometers (41 miles) away for some unknown reason. It was in this period that Buddhism started its gradual decline; that is why elements of Hinduism and Jainism can be found incorporated in the cave sculptures.

The style is post-Gupta. The 12 caves to the south are Buddhist, the 17 in the center are Hindu, and the five to the north are Jain. A description of the most eye-catching caves should serve as a good introduction to what you can expect when you visit Ellora.

The largest of the Buddhist caves is Cave 5, which is 36 meters by 17 meters (117 feet by 56 feet). It was probably used as a classroom for young monks, and its roof is supported by 24 pillars. Since everything was carved out of the mountain, the word "supported" is more a way of expressing an optical illusion. Working their way down, sculptors first "built" the roof before they "erected" the pillars.

Cave 6 is unusual. It contains a statue of the Hindu goddess of learning, Saraswati, in the company of Buddhist figures. Cave 10 is the "Carpenter's Cave," where Hinduism and Buddhism meet again. Here, the stonecutters reproduced the timbered roofs of their day over a richly decorated façade that imitates masonry work. Light comes into the cave through an elaborate horseshoe window over a porch. Inside this chaitya, the only Buddhist chapel at Ellora, the main work of art is a huge image of Buddha. Despite this image and a number of Buddhist figures on a frieze over the pillars of the temple, this cave is dedicated to Viswakarma, the architect of the Hindu gods and the patron saint of Indian craftsmen.

Cave 11 (two stories) and Cave 12 (three stories) are remarkable for having more than one floor. The two caves comprise a monastery behind an open courtyard that leads to its façade, which looms nearly 15 meters (50 feet) high. Although this façade is simple, the interior is lavish. This block of rock was gouged into a ground-floor hall, a shrine on the story above it, and another hall on the top story with a gallery of Buddhas seated under trees and parasols.

The immediate successors to the Buddhist caves are the Hindu caves, and a step inside them is enough to pull the visitor up short. It's another world—another universe—in which the calm contemplation of the seated Buddhas gives way to the dynamic cosmology of Hinduism in which mythical gods seemingly come alive from stone. These sculptures are estimated to have been created around the seventh and eighth centuries.

Transfixed, the visitor watches the "action" as goddesses battle; Shiva flails the air with his eight arms; elephants big as life groan under their burdens; boars, eagles, peacocks, and monkeys prance around what has suddenly turned into a zoo; and lovers strike poses that leave the imagination somewhere far behind.

Kailasa Temple

The approach to Ellora is dominated by the awe-inspiring mammoth Kailasa temple, or Cave 16—one of the wonders of India. The Kailasa temple, a freestanding shrine, is carved out of solid rock with a small *gopuram* (altar) at the entrance and enormous pillars on either side—of Shiva, Parvati, and Gajalaxmi—with Ravana below shaking Mount Kailasa. The temple is dedicated to Mount Kailasa in the Himalayas, the abode of Lord Shiva, and in some oblique manner this monolith competes with the grandeur of nature's own creations.

The Kailasa is approximately twice the area of the Parthenon in Greece and 1½ times as tall. Exquisitely carved and sculpted with epic themes, no nobler monument exists of India's genius, daring, and skill. The world's biggest monolithic structure, its conception is simply breathtaking. Starting at the top of a cliff, an army of stonecutters removed three million cubic feet of rock to form a vast pit 33 meters deep, 81 meters long, and 47 meters wide (107 feet by 267 feet by 154 feet), leaving a block in the center, which became a temple rising from the foot of what had once been a hill.

This replica of the home of Shiva stands in an open courtyard as three separate structures. The main temple rests on a base 8 meters (25 feet) high that appears to be supported by friezes of elephants. It measures 46 meters by 30 meters (150 feet by 100 feet) under a gabled front and a tower in three tiers beneath a cupola. An overhead bridge links the three buildings of Kailasa and its outer gateway. One gallery has a dozen panels that illustrate the legends of Shiva, while an adjoining panel tells the story of Vishnu as a man-lion, shredding the body of a demon with its claws. This demon was supposed to have been invulnerable to human or animal attackers, but Vishnu, by adopting a form that was neither man nor beast, destroyed the tyrant.

After this panel comes the masterpiece, the tale in stone of "Ravana shaking Kailasa," according to the epic *Ramayana.* Ravana was a demon who decided to show his strength by lifting Kailasa on his head. The mountain trembles in this sculpture, but Shiva remains unperturbed and catches Ravana merely by putting his foot down hard. Parvati is seen clinging to her husband's arm and looking slightly preoccupied.

Ajanta

Nestled on the slopes of a crescent hillside, hewn out of rock, are 30 caves where, two millenia ago, Buddhist monks found sanctuary and left a legend for posterity—Ajanta. The caves contain a series of wall paintings and sculpture, elegantly executed, with an aesthetic appeal that is timeless and craftsmanship that astounds scholars and art lovers even today. The antiquity of these caves ranges between 200 B.C. and A.D. 600, yet the remarkable unity of concept and sense of continuity remains unbroken. Despite their age, some of the paintings have retained their freshness and vivid detail wrought in rich earth colors, lamp black, and lapis lazuli.

The paintings depict the life and teachings of the Buddha. A large segment is devoted to the Buddha's earlier life as a prince surrounded by beautiful women, luxurious settings, and details of court life. Some of the exquisite paintings belong to this section.

The Ajanta caves are like chapters of a splendid epic in visual form. Natural light brightens the caves at different times of the day, and structural engineers are awestruck by the sheer brilliance of those ancient masters who, undaunted by the limitations of seemingly crude implements and tools, material, and labor, created this marvel of art and architectural splendor.

As at Ellora, monumental façades and statues were chipped out of hard rock. But Ajanta was given an added dimension by its unknown creators, a dimension expressed in India's most remarkable examples of cave paintings. The artists lovingly told the story of the Buddha and, at the same time, portrayed the life and civilization they knew. Time has damaged some of these masterpieces, but the vivid colors and the flowing lines that remain continue to astound experts. True, this was religious art, but it was living art as well. When the electric spotlights flicker onto the paintings, the figures seem to awaken and come alive. Life was good then, and love was open. Modern art never succeeded in paying tribute to woman in the way it has been done at Ajanta.

There are 29 caves in all, but they are much smaller than those at Ellora, because the sculptors had to work on a much smaller site. The caves here have no courtyards; instead they were originally carved with steps leading to the river below. Only four caves are chaityas while the rest are viharas. The best paintings are to be found in Caves 1, 2, 16, 17, and 19, and the best sculptures are in Caves 1, 4, 17, 19, and 26.

The paintings at Ajanta are called "frescoes" although they were not executed in the true fresco technique developed in Italy. Here, a rough rock wall was covered with a plaster made from clay and cow dung mixed with chopped rice husks in a layer about a half-inch thick. On top of this layer, a smooth coat of lime was applied, and then the painter began his work. First, the composition was outlined in red and then an undercoating was applied. All the colors used at Ajanta were of local origin: red ocher, burnt brick, copper oxide, lamp black, or dust from green rocks that had been crushed. On this background, the painter then applied his colors. The outline was accentuated and highlights were added before the surface of the mural was polished to a shine.

The life of the Buddha and the illustration of tales from Buddhist fables, or *jatakas,* are the two main themes of the caves at Ajanta. The total effect is that of a magic carpet transporting you back into a drama played by nobles, wise men, and commoners. The caves are numbered from west to east, not in chronological order.

The earliest cave, which dates back to 200 B.C., is Cave 13. However, it is only from A.D. 100 that the exquisite brush and line work begins. Caves 9 and 10 have a chaitya in a hall filled with Buddhas, dominated by an enormous stupa. In breathtaking detail, the *Shaddanta Jataka,* a legend about the Buddha, is depicted in a continuous panel in Cave 10.

Opinions vary as to the most exquisite of the Ajanta paintings. The most popular are those in Cave 1, of the Bodhisattva Avalokitesvara and Bodhisattva Padmapani. Padmapani, or the "one with the lotus in his hand," is credited by the sculptures as being the alter ego of the Lord Buddha and who assumed the duties of the Buddha when he disappeared. The Avalokitesvara is the most esteemed of the Bodhisattvas and is known as the Sangharatna, or "jewel of the order." Padmapani is depicted with his sinuous-hipped wife, one of the most widely reproduced figures of Ajanta.

The painting has been compared in technique to the work of Michelangelo and Correggio.

Cave 2 is remarkable for its ceiling decorations and its murals relating the birth of the Buddha. The Buddha's mother, Queen Maya, dreams that an elephant with six tusks has entered her body. This dream is interpreted to mean that she is to bear a great son. In one panel, you see the birth of the Buddha and the newborn child walking over lotus flowers with the king of gods, Indra, holding an umbrella over his head.

In Cave 4, sculpture is the main interest. It is the largest vihara in Ajanta, and depicts a man and a woman fleeing from a mad elephant, and a man giving up his resistance to a tempting woman. Cave 10 is believed to be the oldest cave at Ajanta, going back to second century B.C.

The mystical heights attained by the artist-monks reach their zenith in Caves 16 and 17, where the viewer is released from the bondage imposed by time and space. Transcending these barriers, one is faced by a continuous narrative that spreads horizontally and vertically, evolving into a panoramic whole—at once logical and stunning. There is an excellent view of the river from Cave 16, which may have been the entrance to the entire series of caves. One painting here is riveting. Known as "The Dying Princess," it is believed to represent Sundari, the wife of the Buddha's half-brother, Nanda, who left her to become a monk. You can almost see the princess' eyes cloud over in death. One agrees with the art critic who said, "For pathos and sentiment and the unmistakable way of telling its story, this picture cannot be surpassed in the history of art."

Cave 17 possesses the greatest number of pictures undamaged by time. Luscious heavenly damsels fly effortlessly overhead, a prince makes love to a princess, and the Buddha tames a raging elephant—all on the portico of the cave.

Another mural tells how Prince Simhala conquered Ceylon (now Sri Lanka), an island of beautiful ogresses who trapped the prince and his 500 companions. The captivity was a merry one, but Simbala sensed the trap and fled on a winged white horse with an ogress in pursuit. This beauteous witch enticed the king of Simhala's country into marriage and ate her husband for their wedding banquet. But Simbala drove out the ogress and conquered her island of Ceylon. Next to this painting is the scene of a woman applying lipstick.

Another favorite is the painting in Cave 18 of a princess performing *sringar* (toilet). For its sheer exuberance and *joie de vivre,* the painting in Cave 2 of women on a swing is adjudged the best.

A number of unfinished caves were abandoned mysteriously, but even these are worth a visit. A steep climb of 100 steps takes you to the caves. You may also take the bridle path that is a gentler ascent with a crescent pathway running alongside the caves. From here, there is a magnificent view of the ravines of the Waghura River. For souvenirs of a memorable experience, you can pick up amethyst-veined rocks strewn generously on the hillside.

PRACTICAL INFORMATION FOR MAHARASHTRA

WHEN TO GO. The best time to visit is October–March. In April the temperature climbs and Maharashtra gets super hot. During the monsoon (usually June–September), the area around Aurangabad becomes lush green and many claim this is an ideal time to visit the Ellora and Ajanta caves. The best viewing time at the wildlife sanctuaries is January–April.

HOW TO GET THERE. By Air. *Indian Airlines* flies daily to Aurangabad from Bombay, Delhi, Jaipur, Jodhpur, and Udaipur. Indian Airlines connects Pune with a few flights a week from Delhi and Bangalore and a daily flight from Bombay. To get to Nagpur, the gateway to Melghat Tiger Reserve and Nawegaon National Park, Indian Airlines flies daily from Bombay and a few times a week from Pune and Delhi. From Bombay, *Vayudoot* has daily flights to Aurangabad; six flights a week to Ratnagiri, near Ganpatipule Beach; and a few flights a week to Nagpur. From Goa and Indore, Vayudoot also has occasional flights to Pune.

By Bus. *Maharashtra State Road Transport Corporation* (MSRTC) runs deluxe buses from Bombay to major destinations in the state. For details and tickets in Bombay, visit the MSRTC counter at the Central Bus Stand, Bombay Central, or Parel Depot. *Maharashtra Tourism Development Corporation* (MTDC, address below under *Tourist Information*) also runs buses to Aurangabad (daily), Mahabaleshwar (no service in the monsoon season), Gantatipule (no service in the monsoon season), and Nasik (daily). *Kailash Travels* (200/202 Triveni House, opposite 13th Khetwadi Lane, Khetwadi Back Rd., Bombay, tel. 365208) has buses going to many of these same destinations. ITDC (address below under *Tours*) also has bus service between Bombay and Aurangabad.

By Train. No major trains go directly to Aurangabad; it's only connected by meter gauge. Broad-gauge trains will take you as far as Manmad, 113 km (70 mi.) from Aurangabad, where you switch to a meter-gauge train to Aurangabad. There's excellent train service from Bombay to Pune, including express trains that make better time than going by car. For train information in Bombay, see the Bombay chapter. For train information in Pune, call 667333 and 667340. In Aurangabad, call 24815.

By Rented Car with Driver. Fairly good roads connect major destinations in Maharashtra with these out-of-state cities: Ahmedabad, Vadodara (Baroda); Panaji (in Goa); and Hyderabad. If you choose to travel by road from Bombay, hire a car with driver from a tour operator recommended in that chapter. Rates are about Rs. 4 per km and a half charge of Rs. 50–Rs. 100 per night.

TOURIST INFORMATION. *MTDC* is extremely helpful, with good brochures on major destinations. The head office is in Bombay, C.D.O. Hutments, opposite L.I.C. Bldg., Madam Cama Rd.; tel. 2026713 or 2027762. It also has offices in these locations:

Aurangabad. MTDC Holiday Resort, Station Rd.; tel. 23298. Open 7 A.M.–8 P.M. daily. There's also an airport counter.

Nagpur. 96 Booty Rd., Deshmukh House, opposite Patwardhan High School, Siabuldi; tel. 33325. Open 10 A.M.–5:45 P.M.; closed Sundays and second and fourth Saturdays.

Pune. I Block, Central Bldg.; tel. 668867. Open 10 A.M.–5:45 P.M.; closed Sundays and second and fourth Saturdays. Counters at the airport and railway station are open 8 A.M.–8 P.M., daily.

For good information in Aurangabad, also visit the *Government of India Tourist Office,* Krishna Vilas, Station Rd.; tel. 4817. Open 10 A.M.–5:30 P.M.; closed Sundays and second and fourth Saturdays. It also has a counter at the airport.

FOREIGN CURRENCY EXCHANGE. Most Western-style hotels have money-exchange counters. Otherwise, go to a branch of the *State Bank of India;* open Monday–Friday, 10 A.M.–2 P.M., Saturdays till noon. In Aurangabad, the Ashok Hotel bank is open Monday–Saturday, 5 P.M.–8 P.M. MTDC Holiday Resort may also have a bank in 1991 that will exchange foreign currency 8 A.M.–10 A.M. and 5–8 P.M. Monday–Saturday.

ACCOMMODATIONS. Aurangabad, Pune, and Mahabaleshwar offer a range of hotels to fit all budgets. Other places, such as the beautiful coastline and sanctuaries, have limited options. Some coastal areas now have MTDC tented beach resorts with walk-in two-bed and four-bed tents. These attractive tents have windows, front and back entrances, and plenty of space to walk around. They come with comfortable cots, clean linen, electricity, fans, and filtered drinking water. Each tented resort also has separate bathrooms and shower facilities, a delightful thatch-covered restaurant usually serving Indian and limited Continental cuisines, and an unspoiled beach. The tented resorts are closed June 15–Oct. 1. For advance booking at a tented resort or any MTDC facility (unless noted otherwise below), contact MTDC, Tours Division and Reservation Office, opposite L.I.C. Bldg., Madam Cama Rd., Bombay, Maharashtra; tel. 2026713. For tented resorts, include a full deposit (Rs. 250 per night per double occupancy); meals are included. Tents are restricted to couples or families. The deposit amount for other MTDC facilities is listed below. Prices for all accommodations are based on double occupancy and exclude taxes: *Expensive,* Rs. 950–Rs. 1,450; *Moderate,* Rs. 500–Rs. 950; *Inexpensive,* under Rs. 500. Some Western-style hotels take major credit cards.

AURANGABAD

Expensive

Ajanta Ambassador Hotel. Chikalthana, Aurangabad; tel. 82211. 125 rooms with bath. Sweeping lawns and a circular drive lead up to this marble hotel. Its lobby is filled with lovely Indian antiques; spacious, air-conditioned bedrooms have a Western decor with TV. Best rooms overlook the pool. Multicuisine restaurant, room service, Gujarati-decor bar, swimming pool, gardens, tennis, foreign-exchange counter, doctor, shopping arcade. AE, DC, MC, V.

Welcomgroup Rama International. R-3 Chikalthana, Aurangabad; tel. 82241. 100 rooms with bath. This attractive two-story hotel has a white exterior with red bands of elephants chiseled on its facade. The modern lobby is lavish. Air-conditioned bedrooms are modern and have TV. Multicuisine restaurant, room service, swimming pool, health club, tennis, mini-golf, travel agency, foreign-exchange counter, doctor, astrologer, shopping arcade. AE, DC, MC, V.

Moderate

Hotel Aurangabad Ashok. Dr. Rajendra Prasad Marg, Aurangabad; tel. 24520. 66 rooms with bath. This yellow two-story bungalow has a spacious lobby. Air-conditioned rooms are simply decorated and have TV. Ask for a room with a tub. Room service, multicuisine restaurant, bar, swimming pool, travel agency, foreign-exchange counter, bank, shopping arcade. AE, DC, MC, V.

Inexpensive

MTDC Holiday Resort. Reservations: Manager, Station Rd., Aurangabad; tel. 23298. 62 rooms (28 with attached bath; the rest have shared bath). This complex of two-story bungalows offers clean, functional rooms with a plain decor. Some rooms are air-conditioned; all rooms have fans and mosquito netting. There is a simple but decent multicuisine restaurant; also room service, bar, tourist office, handicraft shop, small garden. For advanced booking, include a full deposit of Rs. 250 per night per double room. Rupees only.

Hotel Nandanvan. Opposite Fire Station, Railway Station Rd., Aurangabad; tel. 23311. 29 rooms with bath. This simple Western-style hotel offers clean rooms with basic furnishings and small balconies. Some rooms are air-conditioned, others have fans. Room service, TV, south Indian cuisine (vegetarian) restaurant, bar. V.

CHIPLUN

Inexpensive

Taj Gateway Riverview Lodge. Village Dhamandivi, Taluka Khed, District Ratnagiri; tel. 57. 37 rooms with bath. This new three-story bungalow, with tiered gardens and a sweeping view of the Vishista River and valley, is six hours from Bombay en route to Goa. It's peaceful, with spacious Western-decor rooms that have balconies. Limited room service, Indian- and Continental-cuisine restaurant, bar, doctor, and arrangements for trekking and river excursions in typical wooden fishing boats. Rupees only.

DIVE AGAR BEACH
230 km (143 mi.) from Bombay

Inexpensive

MTDC Tented Resort. Dive Agar Beach; tel. 2026713. This new tented beach resort was scheduled to be in operation in 1991. Tents, possibly superfancy with attached bathrooms, are set in groves of coconut and cashew nut trees on a four-km (2½-mi.) beach.

GANPATIPULE BEACH

Because this is also an important Hindu pilgrimage site, 375 km (233 mi.) from Bombay, no liquor is available in either facility listed below.

Inexpensive

Courtesy Hotel. Reservations: Courtesy Hotels, 5 Dhanashri Nanda Patkar Rd., Vile Parle (East), Bombay; tel. 6123094. 24 rooms with bath. Under construction at press time, this Western-style hotel on a hill above a beautiful beach was scheduled to open in early 1991. Rooms have a stream-lined modern decor and sea views; fans or air-conditioning, room service, multicuisine restaurant, foreign-exchange counter. Rupees only.

MTDC Tented Resort. Reservations: MTDC, tel. 2026713. 45 tents. Nestled in a coconut grove on the edge of a cove, this complex also offers exceptionally good Chinese, Indian, and limited Continental dishes in its thatch-covered restaurant.

HARIHARESHWAR BEACH
200 km (124 mi.) from Bombay

Inexpensive

MTDC Tented Resort. Reservations: MTDC, tel. 2026713. 30 tents. In this delightful complex, set in an inlet and backed by hills, tents are located near two beaches. The more secluded beach is preferable.

KARLA CAVES

Moderate

Fariyas Holiday Resort. Frichley Hill, Lonavla; tel. 2701. 92 rooms with bath. 10 km (6 mi.) from the caves. Lovely terraced gardens, a sleek modern lobby, and gigantic indoor swimming pool are highlights at this hilltop Western-style hotel. Air-conditioned rooms have a lackluster contemporary decor, but they're spacious and have private balconies. Included are TV, room service, multicuisine restaurants, bar, health club, sightseeing arrangements, foreign-exchange counter, shops. AE, DC, MC, V.

Inexpensive

MTDC Karla Holiday Resort. Karla; tel. 30. 64 rooms with bath. Very near the caves. In a secluded area back from the road, this complex offers two good bargain-priced options: air-conditioned suites with two bedrooms and sitting room; and recently renovated "A-type" old-fashioned bungalows with one bedroom, pitched tile roofs, and verandas. Limited room service, Indian- and Chinese-cuisine restaurant, bar, boating, nice grounds. For advanced booking, include a full deposit of Rs. 300 per night for suites and Rs. 100 for bungalows. Rupees only.

KIHIM BEACH
136 km (84 mi.) from Bombay

Inexpensive

MTDC Tented Resort. Reservations: MTDC, tel. 2026713. 35 tents. In a coconut grove on the edge of a beach, the best located tents in this five-acre complex have an unobscured beach view and are positioned away from the bathroom facility. Also avoid the weekends for optimum privacy.

MAHABALESHWAR

Moderate

Hotel Anarkali. Mahabaleshwar; tel. 336. 37 rooms with bath. The best modern Western-style hotel in this hill station, Anarkali offers a good location and spacious, contemporary-decor rooms, with TV and room service. Indian- and Chinese-cuisine restaurant, bar, car-rental service, horse rides. 50 percent discount during off season (usually October–March). Traveler's checks accepted.

Inexpensive

Fredrick Hotel. Mahabaleshwar; tel. 240. 32 rooms with bath. The bedrooms in this modest bungalow are simple, but they still evoke some old-fashioned hill station charm. Included are TV, room service, multicuisine restaurant, car-rental arrangements. Discount October–March. Traveler's checks accepted.

MALVAN BEACH
514 km (319 mi.) from Bombay

Inexpensive

MTDC Tented Resort. Reservations: MTDC, tel. 2026713. This new facility was scheduled to open in late 1990. Expect a good beach and tents nestled in a palm grove, and a thatched-covered restaurant with local Malwani cuisine and fresh mangos in season. Rupees only.

MELGHAT TIGER PROJECT

Inexpensive

MTDC Semadoh Forest Lodge. Chikhaldara, District Amravati; tel. 11. 20 rooms with bath and some tents with shared bath. Here, concrete cottages with basic but clean furnishings are set on a hill in the forest; tents are deeper in the forest. Included are simple catering, elephant safaris, and regional folk dances on request. For advanced bookings, include full deposit of Rs. 100 per night per room; Rs. 75 for tent. Rupees only.

NAWEGAON NATIONAL PARK

Inexpensive

MTDC Nawegaon Forest Lodge and Tents. Reservations: MTDC, tel. 2026713. About 15 units and 15 tents. Set on stilts in a forested area on the edge of a lake, "Sanjay Kutir A-Type" rooms have slatted wood exteriors and rustic, but very clean, interiors with attached baths. There's no electricity; lanterns light your way. You can also stay in safari-style tents (shared bathrooms) that are deeper in the forest. There are also simple, catered meals on request, elephant safaris, rowboats, fishing (bring your own equipment). For advance bookings, include a full deposit of Rs. 100 per night for a room; Rs. 75 for tents. Rupees only.

PUNE

Moderate–Expensive

Blue Diamond. 11 Koregaon Rd., Pune; tel. 663775. 111 rooms with bath. A Western-style high rise, with an attractive lobby, Blue Diamond offers expensive-priced "deluxe" rooms that are very spacious and elegant, and moderate-priced "executive" and "economy" rooms (least expensive and a good bargain) that are slightly smaller but well-appointed. Best rooms face the pool. Air-conditioning, TV, room service, multicuisine restaurants, bar, business center, swimming pool, health club, travel agency, foreign-exchange counter, bank, sightseeing, golf, yoga, and bird-watching arrangements. AE, DC, MC, V.

Moderate

Hotel Executive Ashok. 5 University Rd., Shivajinagar, Pune; tel. 57391. 71 rooms with bath. This Western-style hotel has a modern lobby and rooms with a modern decor. The best rooms overlook the pool. Air-conditioning, TV, room service, multicuisine restaurants, bar, doctor, business center, travel agency, foreign-exchange counter, swimming pool, health club, shops. AE, DC, MC, V.

Kohinoor Executive. Apte Rd., Deccan Gymkhana, Pune; tel. 58938. 70 rooms with bath. This new Western-style hotel is in a quiet yet centrally located neighborhood. Its modern lobby is intimate, with a small fountain. Air-conditioned rooms have pretty contemporary furnishings and TV. Room service, multicuisine restaurants, bar, foreign-exchange counter. Good value. DC, MC, V.

Hotel Sagar Plaza. 1 Bund Garden Rd., Pune; tel. 661880. 80 rooms with bath. Another new deluxe hotel, Sagar Plaza has an atrium lobby with a glass elevator. Modern, air-conditioned rooms are done up in pretty pastels and have TV. Multicuisine restaurants, room service, bar, business center, foreign-exchange counter, travel agency, small swimming pool, book shop. AE, DC, MC, V.

Inexpensive

Hotel Amir. 15 Connaught Rd., Pune, Maharashtra, tel. 661840. 108 rooms with bath. Amir, a Western-style hotel, has a friendly ambience and provides good service. "Deluxe" rooms (also inexpensive) are the best option—spacious and clean, with a modern decor and a painted mural of a Pune scene on one wall. Excellent multicuisine restaurants, air-conditioning, TV, room service, bar, shops, health club, foreign-exchange counter, Indian Airlines office. DC, MC, V.

DINING OUT. Except for Aurangabad and Pune, you're eating options in Maharashtra are limited. Breakfast is usually served 8–10; lunch, noon–3; dinner, 7:30–10. The restaurants listed below are informal and, unless noted, are open for all three meals and don't require reservations. Prices, based on one person eating a three-course meal, excluding taxes, tip, or beverage, are *Deluxe,* over Rs. 120; *Expensive,* Rs. 80–Rs. 120; *Moderate,* Rs. 40–Rs. 80; *Inexpensive,* under Rs. 40.

AURANGABAD

Deluxe

Madhuban. Welcomgroup Rama, R 3, Chikalthana; tel. 82241. This elegant restaurant has a marble fountain and live Indian instrumental music at night. The chef serves Continental, Chinese, or Indian dishes, with especially good tandoori items. You can sample all three at a luncheon or dinner buffet, or eat à la carte. Dinner reservations advised. Open 6:30–10 A.M., 12:30–2:45 P.M., 7:30–10:30 P.M. AE, DC, MC, V.

Expensive

Tandoor Restaurant and Bar. Shyam Chambers, Bansilal Nagar, Station Rd.; tel. 8482. At this popular restaurant with brown tiled walls, plants, and subdued lighting that highlights an understated Egyptian motif, very good Chinese and Indian cuisines are served. Tandoori items are delicious. Dinner reservations advised. Open 11:30 A.M.–11:30 P.M. Rupees only.

Moderate

Angeethi. Mehar Chember, 6 Vidya Nagar, Jalna Rd.; tel. 27966. Cozy Angeethi has brick-and-tile walls and upholstered chairs. The chef serves Indian, Continental, and especially popular Chinese dishes. Try the chicken Manchurian or fried fish with lemon sauce. Open for buffet lunch noon–3 P.M., and à la carte dinner 7–11 P.M. Rupees only.

Minglinghs. Hotel Rajdoot, Jalna Rd.; tel. 25991. When you enter this large old-fashioned restaurant, you walk past "waterfalls" into a sea green room with a fountain centerpiece. The menu offers Indian, Continental, and Chinese dishes. Go for the Chinese. Try Minglingh special prawns or the ginger chicken. Open 11 A.M.–3 P.M. and 7–11 P.M. Rupees only.

Shaolin Chinese Restaurant. Pawandeep, Jalna Rd.; tel. 27291. By the name of this Oriental decor restaurant you may expect only Chinese cuisine; but the menu also features good Indian dishes as well. Specialties include chicken *tangri kebab* (drumsticks cooked in a tandoori) or chicken a la Canton. Open 6 A.M.–11:30 P.M. Rupees only.

Inexpensive

Bhoj Restaurant. Printravel Hotel, Dr. Ambedkar Rd.; tel. 28481. This cheery restaurant with bright-yellow walls and a Rajasthani mural serves very good Indian vegetarian fare (South Indian and Punjabi cuisines). Sample the *thalis* (numerous small portions served on a platter). Open 6 A.M.–11 P.M. Rupees only.

PUNE

Expensive

Ashvamedh. Hotel Blue Diamond, 11 Koregaon Rd.; tel. 663775. A rustic decor—handsome wooden pillars and trim—and live Indian instrumental music at night add up to an attractive ambience here. The chef serves Indian dishes; the tandooris are especially good. Dinner reservations advised. Open 12:30–2:30 P.M. and 7:30–11:30 P.M. AE, DC, MC, V.

Moderate

Golden Arch. Hotel Executive Ashok, 5 University Rd.; tel. 57391. Scheduled for renovation, Golden Arch continues to serve Continental, Chinese, and Indian cuisines. Indian and Continental are best. The good tandoori mixed grill and *macchi amritsari* (marinated pomfret in garlic and ginger paste served in a spicy red gravy) are recommended. Dinner reservations advised. Open 12:30–2:30 P.M. and 7:30–11 P.M. AE, DC, MC, V.

Haveli Bar and Restaurant. 7 Dr. Coyaji Rd. (East St.); no phone. While you can eat indoors, this delightful restaurant with Haveli palace decor has an enchanting courtyard with a *shamiana* (canvas roll-up roof) overhead and a narrow canal with fountain in the center. The chef serves good Indian cuisine, including tasty tandoori items. Among the specialties are *jal tarang* (stuffed pomfret marinated with mint chutney, then cooked in a tandoori) and *begum bahar* (chicken pieces cooked in gravy with bran). Open 11 A.M.–3 P.M. and 7–11 P.M. Rupees only.

Kapila Garden Restaurant. Dhole Patil Rd.; tel. 666902. In this open-air garden, you eat at informal tables under small thatch-covered huts, seated on plastic chairs. No beef and pork are served, but you'll find good chicken, fish, and vegetables prepared in Indian and Continental dishes. Their butter chicken (curried chicken) is extremely popular. Reservations advised. Open 7–11 P.M. Rupees only.

Kebab Korner. Amir Hotel, 15 Connaught Rd.; tel. 661840. This outdoor restaurant has an Indian village decor: thatched huts, a small waterfall, red lights set into a brick wall, and a "bangle-wallah" creating pretty bangles (for sale) in a corner. Live Indian *ghazals* are performed Wednesday nights. The excellent Indian cuisine matches the charming ambience. Try the delicious butter chicken and tandoori items, such as the pomfret or rolled minced mutton, with Kashmiri *pillau* (vegetable and dried-fruit rice dish). Reservations advised November to March. Open 7:30–11:30 P.M. DC, MC, V.

Portico. J.M. Road, Deccan Gymkhana; tel. 55503. An antique car (Austin) stands guard at the entrance to this handsome modern restaurant done up in black and white. You can choose from Continental and Indian cuisines. There's also a salad bar. A specialty is chicken Portico (minced chicken and mutton prepared in a gravy with dried fruit, boiled eggs, and cream). Reservations advised. Open noon–3 P.M. and 7–12 A.M. AE, DC.

Suzie Wong. Amir Hotel, 15 Connaught Rd.; tel. 661840. This open-air restaurant, with simple Oriental touches—pavilion and red-cane chairs and tables—serves Chinese cuisine. Popular choices are the mildly spicy fried Mandarin pomfret, *sun tung mein* noodles (minced chicken and peas cooked in soy sauce and served with soft noodles), or Chinese sizzlers (spicy-hot dishes). Reservations advised November to March. Open noon–3 P.M. and 7–12 P.M. DC, MC, V.

Inexpensive

Shabree Restaurant. Hotel Parichay, 1199/2 A.F.C. Rd.; tel. 59901. Extremely informal and popular, this restaurant, scheduled to undergo renovation, serves one meal: a Maharashtrian vegetarian *thali.* Come with a big appetite and be prepared to eat Indian-style with your right hand. Waiters will offer an unending series of dishes. Say "ho," and you'll be served; "noko" means no thanks. Lots of fun and very inexpensive. Open 11 A.M.–3 P.M. and 7–11 P.M. Rupees only.

SWEETS AND TREATS. Aurangabad. For good Indian and Continental snacks and tasty sweets, including ice cream and milk shakes, drop in at *Food Wala's Fast Food Centre* (Denshaws Ice-Cream Parlour, Nirala Bazaar). You can also get fresh fruit juices. Open 9 A.M.–10 P.M.

Mahabaleshwar. Just outside Mahabaleshwar on the road to Pune, stop at a roadside stall—some are vine-covered with tables and chairs set underneath—and have freshly made strawberry or rose ice cream (complete with crushed rose petals), shakes, and juices. Available March to June.

Pune. Don't miss a visit to *Badshah Cold Drink Annexe and Snack Bar,* 7 Dr. Coyaji Rd.—also called East St. Arrive hungry, and try the vegetarian South Indian snacks or pizzas and the exquisite fresh fruit juices, fruity milk shakes (rose, raspberry, and "chikoo" are sublime), and then make room for the excellent *kulfi* (Indian ice cream). The pretty outdoor terrace, covered with woven bamboo, and the downstairs interior room, with mirrored walls and fresh fruit display, are both open 7:30 A.M.–12:30 P.M.; the air-conditioned upstairs family room is open 4 P.M.–midnight. At *Karachi Sweet Mart,* 562 Sachapir St., you'll find the best north Indian sweets, created by a family in this business for over 100 years. Order the *badam pak* (a little square of milk, Kasmiri saffron, cashews, almonds, and pistachios), *kaju roll* (sugar and crushed cashews rolled in edible silver), or *rosmalai* (a fried milk, refined wheat, and sugar ball served in sugary syrup). Open 8 A.M.–8 P.M. daily. At *Chitale Bandhu Mitaiwale* on Bajirao Rd., join the crowd and try Maharashtrian sweets, such as *ba sundi* (ice milk), *mango barfi* (a curd-and-sugar, mango-flavored sweet), or *shrikand* (pudding of curd, sugar, saffron, and nutmeg). Open Tuesday–Sunday, 8 A.M.–1 P.M. and 3:30–8:30 P.M.; Monday, till noon.

HOW TO GET AROUND. From the Airports. Most airports are within 10 km (6 mi.) of the city. Taxis should cost about Rs. 35; auto rickshaws, when available, should cost about Rs. 15–Rs. 20.

By Plane. *Vayudoot* flies three times a week between Pune, Nagpur, and Aurangabad.

By Hired Car with Driver. This is the best way to see the Maharashtra coastline and for getting from Aurangabad to the Ellora and Ajanta caves. If you plan to fly into Nagpur to visit the sanctuaries, a car with driver is also recommended. Hire a car from a tour operator listed in the Bombay chapter. For trips in areas outside Bombay, rates are about Rs. 4 per km, with a halt charge of Rs. 50 per night.

By Taxi. Throughout Maharashtra, a taxi for local trips should cost about Rs. 3.75 per km; Rs. 2 per additional km. In Aurangabad, a taxi to and from Ellora should cost about Rs. 250; and to and from Ajanta should cost about Rs. 500.

By Auto Rickshaw. Good for short trips, especially in congested areas, these three-wheel vehicles charge about Rs. 2.25 for the first km and Rs. 1.20 for each additional km.

TOURS. *MTDC* conducts package bus tours from Bombay to places within the state. For details and bookings, contact Tours Division and Reservation Office (MTDC, address above). Here are some of the best tours:

Aurangabad Tour via Nasik to Ellora and Ajanta. Four days and three nights; daily departures. Stay in MTDC Holiday Resort or in a choice of hotels.

Ganpatipule Holiday at MTDC Tented Beach Resort. Three days and two nights; departures Oct. 15–June.

Harihareshwar Holiday at MTDC Tented Beach Resort. Same trip length and departures as the Ganpatipule tour, above, but to MTDC tented resort in Harihareshwar.

Kihim Holiday at MTDC Tented Beach Resort. Three days and two nights; departs Monday, Wednesday, Friday. This trip involves a pleasant journey by boat.

Malvan Holiday at MTDC Tented Beach Resort. This is a new package trip that was slated to begin in late 1990. Details were not available at press time.

Melghat Tiger Safari. Five days and four nights. Weekly departures.

Vidarbha (Darshan and Jungle Safari). Highlights include visits to Vidarbha Temple and Nawegaon National Park. Six days and five nights. Weekly departures.

Indian Tourism Development Corporation also offers deluxe bus tours from Bombay to Aurangabad. In Bombay, contact ITDC, Nirmal Towers, Nariman Point, Bombay; tel. 2026679 or 2023343. In Aurangabad, ITDC is at Hotel Aurangabad Ashok, Dr. Rajendra Prasad Marg; tel. 24520.

Ellora and Ajanta Conducted Tour From Aurangabad. Daily bus tour to Ellora, 9:30 A.M.–5:30 P.M., and Ajanta, 8 A.M.–5:30 P.M. Reservations are required, contact MTDC, Holiday Resort, Station Rd.; tel. 23298.

ITDC also has similar tours. Reservations required; contact ITDC in Aurangabad (address above).

Pune. MTDC offers a four-hour bus tour of local sights, including Shaniwar Wada (old palace ruins), Kelkar Museum, Agha Khan Palace (Gandhi National Memorial), and Shinde's Chhatri. Departs at 8 A.M. and 2 P.M. For details and reservations, contact MTDC in Pune (address above).

Private Guides. The *Government of India Tourist Office* has good private guides available for visits to the Ellora and Ajanta caves. You can hire them at an office near the ticket windows at the sites or make arrangements in advance through MTDC or the Government of India tourist offices in Aurangabad (addresses above). For one–four people, a guide should cost about Rs. 50 for a half day and Rs. 90 for a full day.

TOUR OPERATORS. For all travel needs, including a hired car with driver, use a reliable agency listed under this category in the Bombay chapter. Also see *Special-Interest Tours* in *Facts at Your Fingertips* for the names of India-based agencies that can create a special trip in Maharashtra.

SEASONAL EVENTS. See the Bombay chapter for a list of important seasonal events in Maharashtra.

HISTORIC SITES. Entrance to most places is generally free or nominal; where a donation is asked, a few rupees will suffice. Historic sites are open daily sunrise to sunset, unless noted otherwise below.

CAVES

Ajanta Caves (approached from Aurangabad). These caves are famous for their exquisite murals and rock-cut carvings of Buddhist origin. Five of the caves, nos. 9, 10, 19, 26, and 29 are *chaityas* (halls) for group worship; the others are *viharas* (monasteries).

Bedsa Caves (near Lonavala). The most interesting second-century B.C. rock-cut cave has a main cathedral hall that is similar to the cathedral hall at Karla. Inside are pillars with good carvings.

Bhaja Caves (near Lonavala). Built in the second century B.C., Cave No. 12 has a handsome vault; the last cave to the south has good sculptures, including a prince on an elephant, a prince on a horse, and a dancing couple.

Ellora Caves (approached from Aurangabad). These renowned rock-cut caves are more than ten centuries old. Of the 34 caves, 12 are of Buddhist origin, 17 are Hindu, and five are Jain. Among the Buddhist caves, nos. 5, 10, 11, and 12 are outstanding. Of the Hindu caves, nos. 16, 21, and 29 stand out. No. 16, Kailash Temple, is an intricately hewn monument that is perhaps the world's largest monolith. Of the Jain group, nos. 32 and 34 should be seen.

Karla Caves (near Lonavala). The Buddhist rock-cut temples date back to the second century B.C. The main cathedral, one of the finest Buddhist caves in India, has beautiful pillars with *mithuna* (copulating) couples and capitals with delicately wrought elephants.

Pandu Lena Caves (Nasik). These 23 caves, built in A.D. first century, were predominently built as one-story monasteries. The best caves are nos. 3, 8, and 18.

FORTS

Ahmedanagar Fort (north of Pune). This fort was built in the 1500s by Hussain Nizam Shah and was used as a prison by the British.

Daulatabad Fort (near Aurangabad). An imposing structure, with novel architectural tricks to confuse and thwart an attacking force, this fort was captured in the fourteenth century by the Sultan of Delhi who turned it into his second capital.

Purandhar Fort (south of Pune). Once the capital of the Maratha Kingdom, Purandhar is one of the most imposing forts in Maharashtra.

Raigad Fort (south of Pune). This fort was Shivaji's capital from 1664 to 1680.

Simhagad Fort (south of Pune). Called the "Lion Fort," this edifice on top of a sheer-sided hill was captured in the 1600s by one of Shivaji's most trusted warriors, Tanaji Malasure, whom he called "the lion"; the battle also claimed the lion's life.

Shivneri Fort (north of Pune). This fort is set above the old city where Shivaji was born.

MUSEUMS AND GALLERIES. Entrance to the following places is free or a nominal fee is charged.

Pune. *Raja Dinkar Kelkar Museum* ("Kamal Kunj", Raja Kelkar Museum St., Natu Baug) contains the excellent collection of this raja—instruments, cloth paintings, terra-cottas, saris, wooden carvings and doors, brasswork, plus the palace of his favorite Moslem dancing girl. Open daily 8:30 A.M.–12:30 P.M. and 3–6 P.M.

SPORTS AND OUTDOOR ADVENTURES. Beaches. Backed by coconut groves and palm trees, great beaches extend from Bombay to Goa. You won't find resort hotels yet, but this is expected to change soon. Already, many idyllic coves and harbors have tented beach resorts run by MTDC (see above under *Accommodations*). Here are some of the best stretches with good surf and sand: *Kihim,* 136 km (84 mi.) from Bombay; Harihareshwar, 200 km (120 mi.) from Bombay; Dive Agar, 230 km (143 mi.) from Bombay; Ganpatipule, 375 km (233 mi.) from Bombay; Malvan, 514 km (319 mi.) from Bombay.

Camping. MTDC rents tents and sleeping bags that you can pitch in Maharashtra. Nominal fees. Contact any MTDC office.

Fishing. Bring your own equipment and plan to fish at Chiplun or Nawegaon National Park.

Rock climbing. From November to February, MTDC runs a rock and fort climbing course that teaches rock climbing and includes some trekking around Karla. Contact MTDC in Bombay.

Wildlife Sanctuaries. *Melghat Tiger Reserve* covers 1,571 sq. km (607 sq. mi.) of forest area and is home to tigers, bison, panthers, sambar, and flying squirrels. You can also visit the historic Gawilgarh Fort. *Nawegaon National Park* (near Melghat) has a lovely lake with good fishing. The best time to visit both parks is December–May. The best approach is from Nagpur, 260 km (161 mi.) from the sanctuaries. See the MTDC tours, listed above, that take you on trips to discover these sanctuaries.

Yoga. *Romani Iyengar Memorial Yoga Institute* (1701-B/1, Shivaji Nagar, Pune; tel. 58134) has courses available to individuals who are already familiar with his technique.

SHOPPING. Aurangabad is famous for its *bidriwork* (gun metal inlaid with intricate bits of silver) and *himroo* shawls made of silk and cotton. Visit these two excellent shops: *Aurangabad Himroo Factory's Handicrafts Emporium* (Shahganj, opposite Gandhi Statue), which has authentic handwoven himroo and beautiful pure silk shawls. Open daily 8 A.M.–8 P.M. Rupees only. *Ajanta Agate Handicrafts* (Ajanta Rd., Harsul) has excellent quality bidriwork and a selection of semi-precious stones set in jewelry or worked into statues and other small items. Open daily 10 A.M.–8 P.M. Rupees only.

In Pune, you can bargain for inexpensive Western-style clothes at open-air stalls on M. G. Road. Along Mal Dhakka Mangalwarpeth, stalls sell old curios, including brass and glassware, every Wednesday and Sunday; bargain! Rupees only.

NIGHTLIFE AND BARS. Your best bet is to have your nightcap in your hotel. Bars are generally open 11 A.M.–2:30 P.M. and 6:30–11 P.M.

GUJARAT

Salt Marshes, Lush Lands, and Lions

by
KATHLEEN COX

In Gujarat, India's westernmost state, salt flats of the Indian subcontinent meet with the monsoon lands of peninsular India. Here you find India's largest marshland and its only sanctuary of Asiatic lions.

Gujarat's lakes are mostly man-made for irrigation. Its forests give shelter to thousands of birds. In spring, fragrant flowers bloom across the landscape. In winter, mist rises from rivers that empty into the Arabian Sea. India's 5,000-kilometer (1,524-mile) coastline begins in Gujarat, and runs 1,650 kilometers (503 miles)—the longest coastline of any state in India. The hills, low and forested, rise gently to 1,000 meters (305 feet). In upland hamlets are bred India's finest cattle, making Gujarat the home of India's dairy industry.

Women, in swirling skirts and blouses of black and red heavy fabric embellished with mirrors and rich embroidery, reflect Gujarat's passion for the bright and colorful: bounteous greens, earthy reds, deep maroons, light saffrons, and sapphire blues suffuse Gujarat's handicrafts and textiles, its folk dances, and its festivals. Even the Hindu temples, Jain shrines, Moslem mosques, and secular palaces are adorned with Gujarati ornamentation that sets them apart from monuments in the rest of India.

The northwestern border of Gujarat forms part of India's international frontier with Pakistan, while Rajasthan adjoins Gujarat on the northeast

278

Madhya Pradesh on the far east, and Maharashtra on the south. The large state has a population of 34 million. Of the original inhabitants, only the Bhil and about a dozen subtribes have survived. After the fall of the Ashoka empire, various local dynasties ruled in different parts of Gujarat until the Moslem conquest of the entire area. When the British came in 1856, Gujarat and Maharashtra formed one huge bilingual state; in 1960, the two were divided.

With a large Jain population, the people of this state are largely vegetarians. Masters of vegetarian cooking, Gujaratis make a variety of mouth-watering dishes out of the simplest lentils and vegetables. The Gujarati *thali* (vegetarian) meal is an endless procession of savory vegetables cooked in aromatic spices, supported with a variety of crisply fried snacks and delicious confections made from sweetened, thickened milk or thick cold curd mixed with nuts. The farmhouse dinner is a Gujarati innovation. It consists of crisp hot *rotis* (flat unleavened bread) made from *jawar* or millet flour, huge dollops of butter, a pungent garlic chutney, and fresh vegetables steamed in an earthen oven. It is washed down with thick, sweetened milk flavored with sliced nuts and saffron.

The Gujaratis are, however, better known for their sharp business acumen exemplified by the citizens of Ahmedabad, the former state capital of Gujarat. The new capital, Gandhinagar, is 30 kilometers (19 miles) away on the banks of the Sabarmati river.

Some festivals of Gujarat are unique; others are slightly different from those in other states. (See "Fairs and Festivals" in *Practical Information*, below.)

Gujarat offers a scintillating range of fabrics. Textile weaving, vegetable-dye painting, tie-and-dye work, gold and silver thread work *(zari)*, intricate silk embroidery, and patola- and tanchoi-type saris have been Gujarat's pride for centuries. The lacquered furniture of Sankheda, the mirror works of Kutch, bead-encrusted artifacts from Rajkot, and fine wood carvings from the vicinity of Ahmedabad have become popular with tourists, as have experimental paintings and murals at roadside art shows, the main markets, and the emporiums at Ahmedabad, Jamnagar, Surat, and Vadodara (Baroda).

Exploring Gujarat

Just over the state line, going from Bombay to Ahmedabad is Sanjan, where a masonry flame-topped pillar marks the landing place of the Parsis in A.D. 745 after they had spent 19 years in Diu, and island south of Saurashtra. Why they left Diu is not known, but they set off in the same ships that had brought them from Persia. They had to keep moving the sacred fire for protection, and it was only after 700 years that they set it up permanently at Udvada, a little north of Sanjan. Now there are Parsi groups in almost every Gujarati town, and many of their last names are derived from the names of these towns.

Along the palm-fringed coast sliced by frequent banyan-lined rivers running into the Gulf of Cambay are many ancient ports, including Surat, at the mouth of the Tapti River. By the fourteenth century, Surat, which was founded by a Hindu Brahman, was the most important port on India's west coast. This city became a flourishing international trade center; and over the years, the Moguls, Portuguese, Dutch, French, and English envied its prosperity.

Surat's fortress-castle was built in 1546 and it changed hands repeatedly, indicative of the port's value. After the sixteenth century Mogul Emperor Akbar captured it from the Portuguese, it became a gateway for

Mecca. About a 100 years later, the Maratha-ruler Shivaji raided Surat four times; the size and elaborateness of the Dutch and English tombs indicate the amount of wealth the Europeans were anxious to defend.

Today, Surat manufactures 70 percent of India's synthetic textiles. And most of its population is still engaged in three of its oldest enterprises: diamond cutting and polishing, the creation of zari (gold and silver thread work), and textile production.

Due south of Surat is Saputara, or the "abode of serpents," a hill resort set on the second-highest plateau of the Sahyadri Range. From here, you can visit the Mahal Bardipara Forest Wildlife Sanctuary and Gira waterfalls.

Vadodara (Baroda)

About 113 kilometers (70 miles) south of Ahmedabad lies the "garden city" of Vadodara, which has boulevards lined with flaming gulmohur trees. Once a princely capital, it acquired its original name, Vadodara ("In the Heart of the Banyan Trees") because of the profusion of banyans.

The reign of the family that governed Vadodara until independence started in the early eighteenth century. Damaji Gaikwar was the son of a Maratha general in the Peshwa's army. He was allowed to levy one-fourth of the income of certain areas conquered by the army. Damaji II, along with the Peshwa, took Ahmedabad in 1753, ending Moslem rule in the region. The victors then divided the country. After Damaji II returned from the Battle of Panipat (against the Afghans), which destroyed much of the Peshwa's power, he chose Anhilwad Patan as his capital. His area dwindled in the course of controversies. By 1802, for receiving British help, he had to cede further land to the British, retaining small segments throughout Gujarat and Saurashtra.

Lakshmi Vilas Palace, an architectural blend of the occidental and Oriental and a conglomeration of domes, towers, and spires set in a beautifully landscaped garden, is still the personal residence of the former royal family and not open to the public. Though the museum of armor and sculpture on this estate is supposedly accessible, it's hours are extremely erratic. You can visit the Oriental Institute with its rich collection of ancient Sanskrit manuscripts, including a historic copy of India's great epic, *Ramayana*. You can also enjoy two good museums. The Baroda Museum and Art Gallery, set in a lovely park, contains good Mogul miniatures and European paintings. Nearby is the Maharajah Fateh Singh Museum, with more paintings by European masters and numerous Oriental and Indian exhibits.

Some of the royal family's treasures, including the famous jewel "Star of the South," are at the Nazarbagh Palace, one of the spacious old dwellings of former times. In the collection is an embroidered cloth laid with stones, intended originally for the Prophet's Tomb. Two other palaces with well-kept gardens are the Pratap Vilas and Markarpura, which is south of the town. Also inquire about performances at Baroda Gharana, an important school of Indian classical music.

At the Dabhoi Fort ruins, 27 kilometers (17 miles) southeast of Vadodara, you can see the remains of walls, temples, and especially gates that are fine examples of the Gujarat style of Hindu military architecture. The Malika Mata (Kali) Temple, built in the shape of a Greek cross, is covered inside with fine carvings.

Nearby, farmers, dressed all in white, and women in flared red skirts can be seen tending the fertile fields. Abutting these fields is the busy town of Anand. Much of India's milk and butter comes from this cooperative dairy organization, which is helped by Danish experts and equipment supplied by UNICEF.

Modhera

The sun temple of Modhera, 97 kilometers (60 miles) northwest of Ahmedabad, claims its place among India's most significant monuments. Built in A.D. 1026–27 on an exceptionally high plinth, it is designed to let the sun's rays penetrate the shrine. Full of grandeur and balance, its lines are enhanced by a wide bank of steps descending to a tank. A pillared dancing hall leads to the Assembly Hall and shrine. Such is the design of the shrine that the Surya (Sun God) image—now missing—would be highlighted by the rising sun and the equinoxes.

On the road to Saurashtra is Sarkhej, once a deserted country retreat of sultans. Here are the tomb and mosque of Mahmud Begara, whose name, Begara, came from his enormous mustache shaped like the curved horns of a bullock. Among this group of buildings is the tomb of Ganj Bakash, a saint and spiritual guide of Begara. Sarkhej's monuments, although Moslem, are almost purely Hindu inspired.

About 30 kilometers (18 miles) northeast of Modhera is Patan, famous for its Patola silk saris, made from an intricately dyed yarn that, when woven, reveals exquisite geometric patterns. Above all, Patan is noted for the Rani Vav step-well. Found almost exclusively in Gujarat, these architectual marvels were gigantic, elaborately carved stone staircases with various levels of subterranean wrap-around corridors and at the bottom, a well—all of which offered water and shade from the sun.

Named after the Mahatma, Gandhinagar, on the west bank of Sabarmati, is the new capital of Gujarat. Government buildings, children's gardens, a thermal power house, legislative assembly, and Sarita Garden are some of the places worth a visit in this new capital.

Echoes of Ancient Egypt

Travel 76 kilometers (47 miles) south of Ahmedabad to a place called Lothal, where archaeologists have recently uncovered the earliest known urban civilization of the subcontinent. This site is, in fact, an extension of the Harappan civilization that is found at Mohenjo-Daro and Harappa (now in Pakistan). Here, archaeologists have excavated part of an ancient port, complete with dockyard, streets, houses, underground drains, and a wall. Lothal was probably one of ancient India's important ports having maritime connections with Mesopotamia and Egypt.

Among the interesting discoveries at this site is a terra-cotta that represents a joint burial of a man and a woman. It is probable that when Mohenjo-Daro and Harappa fell into decadence, Gujarat continued to preserve the same civilization for several centuries until it merged into the all-assimilating culture of the Aryans.

Literally meaning a hundred kingdoms, Saurashtra is a region draped in romance and valor. In every city of Saurashtra, its rulers have left behind palaces, temples, mosques and museums, gardens, and sunsparkling fountains. Parrots, which form the favorite motif of interior decoration and paintings of the region, flock by thousands and feed on the wild berries in the nearby bushes. Peacocks spread out their tails in the well-kept gardens.

From the centrally located university city of Rajkot, where Mahatma Gandhi spent his childhood, Saurashtra's many tourist destinations can be covered in day trips. The 50-year-old Watson Museum in Rajkot has numerous antiques—furniture, crystalware, carpets, bronzes, hunters' trophies, and jewels.

About 48 kilometers (30 miles) north of Rajkot is the former kingdom of Wankanar, with its ornate palace, built early in this century by the then maharajah. Farther north is the Rann of Kutch, a vast salt flat that also happens to be the last remaining outpost of the Asiatic wild ass and the world's largest flamingo breeding ground. Within this strange expanse, you can visit old walled cities, such as Bhuj, and an area called Banni, with its mud-hut villages. Throughout Kutch, you can also find some of India's best handicrafts: locally embroidered and mirror-worked fabrics, bandanna tie-dye fabrics, and exquisite silverwork. This is a rarely traveled, yet fascinating, part of Gujarat.

The city of Junagadh, at the foot of the sacred Girnar Mountain, is a few hours' drive south from Rajkot. Junagadh has many venerated Hindu and Jain temples; an Ashoka edict inscribed on a rock; an important Moslem mausoleum, Maqbara, which contains the remains of illustrious nawabs; and the Darbar Museum, an alabaster-white palace with a collection of Continental crystalware, chandeliers, and furniture upholstered with silver and gold-encrusted brocades.

Atop Girnal Hill, you can see the beautifully carved Neminath Temple, one of five marble Jain shrines that overlook the city. This is also the site of a Hindu temple, dedicated to Shiva, and a tomb of a Moslem saint. Also visit Upar Kot, a historic fort on the eastern side of the city, which has impressive gates, some walls 228 meters (70 feet) high, and an interior mosque. "Junagadh" means old fort and owes its name to this massive structure. Near Upar Kot are some interesting Buddhist caves with good carvings.

Sasan Gir, a forest preserve 54 kilometers (33 miles) from Junagadh, is the only remaining home of the majestic Asian lion. Here, in forest clearings or at its vast Kamleshwar Lake, you have a good chance of sighting the royal beast in its natural habitat. Within the park, also visit villages that are home to the Sidis, a tribal group that came back from Africa more than 200 years ago.

Southward from Junagadh lie the port town of Veraval and the sacred temple of Somnath at Prabbas Patan. Sacked and pillaged seven times and each time built anew to greater glory, the Shiva temple at Somnath, looking west to the Arabian Sea, is a magnificent edifice eulogized by the great historian-astronomer-mathematician Abu Raithan Al-Beruni. The museum reassembles the saga of the temple's destruction and rededication. Nearby is Bhalka Tirth, believed to be the place where Lord Krishna breathed his last. Coastal ships are built at Veraval.

Gujarat's Coastline

Northwest of Somnath is Porbandar, a small port town and the birthplace of Mahatma Gandhi. Its narrow lanes are flanked by residential quarters with antique charm. Kirti Mandir, Gandhi's ancestral home, is open to the public. The exterior is attractive and the procession of pilgrims coming to honor him is touching; but the interior is spartan. A swastika (Sanskrit for "doing good for all") marks the spot where he was born. In another room, you can see a photo exhibit of the important events in his life. Gandhi's wife was born next door.

As the Saurashtra peninsula narrows northward into a small strip at Dwarka, you approach one of the most sacred Hindu shrines, the Krishna Temple, with its spire supported by 60 pillars. Dwarka is believed to have been the kingdom of Lord Krishna. Over 2,000 generations have chanted hymns in this shrine. Among the other temples at Dwarka, the most beautiful is dedicated to Rukmani, Krishna's consort. Close to the port city of Okha on the Bet Dwarka islands are the Pat Rani temples. Lord Krishna supposedly lived on Bet Dwarka.

Just inland from Dwarka is Jamnagar, founded in 1540 by Jam Raval. An industrial town, it is also a good place to pick up tie-dye fabrics. Places of interest include the city lake with its historic Lakota Fort that is now a museum.

On the other end of the Saurashtra Peninsula is Palitana, 217 kilometers (134 miles) from Ahmedabad. On the hills of Shatrunjaya that rise over the little city are 863 Jain shrines that have been called the "Abode of the Gods." Their construction began in the eleventh century and continued over a period of 900 years. Their finely carved spires and towers glisten in the sunlight. Their exteriors are covered with friezes and sculptures; interiors are filled with statues of their *tirthankars* (perfect souls) who are the apostles of their faith. The entire hilltop seems a prayer in stone, a feeling emphasized by the presence of devout Jain *Sadhus* (holy men) and *Sadhivs* (holy women) dressed in crisp white.

Ahmedabad

Ahmedabad is a city that quietly blends the glorious past and a vibrant present, with an eye on a promising future. Ahmedabad means different things to different people. For architects, it is a remarkable repository of distinctive architectural styles—from the early Indo-Saracenic of the fifteenth century Moslem sultans to the experimental modern form of the legendary Le Corbusier. Rich detail, delicate tracery, and ornamental minarets impart a very Indian character to what had originally been foreign concepts. Continuity was the essence.

Founded in A.D. 1411 by the Moslem Sultan Ahmed Shah, Ahmedabad flourished under the Gujarat dynasty and subsequently became the seat of the Mogul governors of Gujarat—Jahangir, Shah Jahan, and Aurangzeb, all of whom later became emperors.

Industrially, the city has seen many ups and downs over the centuries. It is said that Ahmedabad used to hang on three threads: gold, silk, and cotton. Today, Ahmedabad is a thriving city that is once again the Manchester of the East, with about 70 mills that employ thousands and produce about one-third of India's total textiles.

In Ahmedabad, more than anywhere else in India, you can see the strong Hindu and Jain influences on Moslem forms. Communal tolerance was the rule in the city. While Ahmedabad was a center of Moslem power and splendor and the home of a rich Islamic military official elite and of skilled Moslem weavers, its wealth came from trade and industry, which were largely controlled by Hindu and Jain merchants and bankers. When the city was a major center on the important trade routes, they controlled Ahmedabad's export trade in textiles and the import trade in luxuries for the courts, collected revenue for the state, and financed princes and armies.

From the second quarter of the seventeenth century, the city fell into a century-long decline. From 1630 to 1632, a terrible famine struck. By the time the British took over the city, it was a desolate sight. Empty buildings were filled with rubbish and weeds. Wild animals roamed around broken-down city walls.

Amidst all its color, its historical splendor, and its present-day business activity, there is a quiet corner in Ahmedabad that marks the city as the home of Mahatma Gandhi, the apostle of peace and nonviolence. On a peaceful stretch of the Sabarmati river, north of the city, Mahatma Gandhi set up a simple retreat in 1915. This was his Satyagraha Ashram, which means "Insistence for Truth," and for many years the nerve center of India's freedom movement. From here, he also started the famous Dandi March to the sea in protest over the British-imposed salt tax, an event that launched the "Quit India" movement that brought about the end of British rule. Hridaya Kunj, his simple cottage, is now a national monument, preserved as it was during the Mahatma's lifetime. A Gandhi Memorial Center and Library and a sound-and-light show offer an interesting display of his life and work.

Those looking for fine ancient architecture must not miss the following: The Jumma Masjid (1423), which has been described as the most beautiful mosque in the East; the Sidi Saiyad Mosque (1430), celebrated the world over for its exquisite window of pierced stone tracery; the Rani Rupmati Mosque (1435), the Queen's mosque with its perforated stone screens; the Sarkhaj Rauza (1445–51), an elegant architectural complex of mosque, palace, tomb, and pavilions grouped around a great stepped tank; the Shining Minarets of Sidi Bashir's Mosque, an amazing phenomenon (when one minaret is shaken, the other vibrates too).

The Calico Museum of Textiles in Ahmedabad is one of the most famous textile museums in the world. It was privately founded in the 1940s by members of the textile family of the Sarabhai and today possesses an extremely rich and varied collection of Indian textiles from five centuries. In a building whose fascinating architecture combines Gujarat's traditional wood structures with modern functional forms that are well adapted to the presentation of textiles, the visitor can admire folk art embroidery, colorful applique hangings, rich brocades from the Mogul period, temple pictures painted on fabric, costumes, and carpets. Indian and international textile experts also engage in a wide range of research work here that has produced many valuable books on the history and techniques of textiles.

PRACTICAL INFORMATION FOR GUJARAT

WHEN TO GO. The best time to visit Gujarat is October to March, when the temperature ranges between 55° and 85° F. During the monsoon (July to September), northern Gujarat experiences a light rain that cools the air; it's a pretty time to visit. During the summer months, however, southern Gujarat is extremely hot and uncomfortable.

HOW TO GET THERE. By Air. Gujarat has numerous airports; the two largest serve Ahmedabad and Vadodara (Baroda). *Indian Airlines* has daily flights to Ahmedabad from Bombay, Delhi, Jaipur, and Jodhpur, and a few flights each week from Madras and Bangalore. Indian Airlines has daily flights to Vadodara from Bombay and a few flights a week from Delhi. Indian Airlines also has a few flights a week from Bombay to Bhuj, Jamnagar, and Rajkot. From Bombay, *Vayudoot* flies daily to Porbandar and a few times a week to Bhavnagar, near Palitana.

By Bus. Deluxe buses from Bombay make frequent runs to Ahmedabad and Vadodara. There's also frequent bus service to Ahmedabad from Pune in Maharashtra and Ajmer, Udaipur, and Mount Abu in Rajasthan.

By Train. Ahmedabad and Vadodara are well connected with Bombay and Delhi by train. Among many good trains are the *Sarvodaya Express, Delhi-Ahmedabad Express,* and the *Gujarat Express.* You can also reach Ahmedabad by meter gauge lines from Rajasthan and Agra. Remember, if you travel overnight, you must reserve a sleeping berth or you can be booted from the train. For reservations and information in Bombay or Delhi, see those chapters. In Ahmedabad, call tel. 344657 or tel. 343535; in Vadodara, call tel. 557575 or tel. 327979.

By Hired Car with Driver. Ahmedabad and Vadodara are on National Highway 8, which connects Bombay and Delhi. From Ahmedabad, Bombay is 510 km (316 mi.); Delhi, 886 km (549 mi.); Jaipur, 625 km (388 mi.); Ajmer, 561 km (348 mi.); Udaipur, 287 km (180 mi.); Mount Abu, 222 km (138 mi.); Bhopal, 571 km (354 mi.). From Vadodara, Bombay is 425 km (264 mi.); Delhi, 995 km (617 mi.); Jaipur, 725 km (450 mi.); Udaipur, 370 km (229 mi.); Bhopal, 515 km (319 mi.); Indore, 348 km (216 mi.). In Gujarat, hire a car from a tour operator listed below. Figure Rs. 4 per km, with a halt charge of Rs. 50–Rs. 100 per night.

TOURIST INFORMATION. For information on Gujarat, contact the *Tourist Corporation of Gujarat* (TCG). Offices are open 10:30 A.M.–6 P.M., closed Sundays and second and fourth Saturdays. The head office is at H.K. House, off Ashram Rd. (behind Jivabhai Chambers), Ahmedabad; tel. 449683 and 449172. Other offices are in the following cities:

Rajkot. Bhavnagar House, Jawahar Rd. (behind State Bank of Saurashtra); tel. 31616.

Surat. 1/847 Athugar St., Nanpura; tel. 26586.

Vadodara. Narmada Bhavan, C-Block, Indira Avenue; tel. 540797 or 65088.

FOREIGN CURRENCY EXCHANGE. Most Western-style hotels have money-exchange counters, as do branches of the *State Bank of India,* open Monday–Friday, 10 A.M.–2 P.M.; Saturdays till noon.

ACCOMMODATIONS. While good Western-style hotels exist in Ahmedabad, Vadodara, and Surat, and some lovely palace-hotels provide comfortable stays in a few remote destinations, much of Gujarat offers only simple accommodations. Arrive with the proper expectations, because Gujarat is also a dry state. Liquor permits must be obtained from your hotel or from the Government of India Tourist Office in your home country before you depart. This permit allows you to purchase liquor from hotel permit rooms for consumption in your room. Prices, none of which can be termed expensive, are based on double occupancy and exclude taxes: *Moderate,* Rs. 500–Rs. 950; *Inexpensive,* under Rs. 500. Some Western-style hotels take major credit cards.

AHMEDABAD

Moderate

Cama Hotel. Khanpur, Ahmedabad; tel. 25281. 55 rooms with bath. Currently Ahmedabad's poshest Western-style hotel, Cama has a quiet back lawn and cheery air-conditioned rooms with attractive contemporary furnishings and TV. Higher-priced doubles (still moderate) have balconies. Ask for a pool view. Room service, permit room, multicuisine restaurants, doctor, car-rental service, swimming pool, attractive lawn. AE, DC, MC, V.

Hotel Karnavati. Ashram Rd., Ahmedabad; tel. 402161. 48 rooms with bath. This four-story Western-style hotel has a spacious lobby and large air-conditioned rooms with simple, modern decor and TV. Corner rooms, called "deluxe," but moderately priced, are best. Room service, multicuisine restaurants, permit room, doctor. AE, DC, MC, V.

Hotel Klassic Gold. 42 Sardar Patel Nagar, near Navrangpura Telephone Exchange, Ahmedabad; tel. 447344. 25 rooms with bath. This new marble hotel offers modest rooms with pleasant Western-style furnishings, air-conditioning, and TV. Room service, multicuisine restaurant, car-rental service, doctor. Rupees only.

Hotel Nataraj. Ashram Rd., Ahmedabad; tel. 448747. 25 rooms with bath, an additional 12 rooms under construction. This five-story Western-style hotel has a cozy lobby and a pleasant ambience. Spacious rooms have attractive Gujarati-touches. Good value, with air-conditioning, TV, room service, multicuisine restaurant, doctor. AE, DC, MC, V.

Hotel Riviera. Khanpur, Ahmedabad; tel. 24201. 69 rooms with bath. This Western-style hotel has good rooms with modern decor, air-conditioning, and TV. Multicuisine restaurant, room service, permit room, doctor, car-rental service. AE, DC, MC, V.

AHMEDPUR MANDVI

Moderate

Samudri Beach Resort. Ahmedpur Mandvi via Una; tel. 116. 15 cottages with bath. You enter this delightful government-run resort, converted from a former royal retreat, through a *Haveli* (palace) gate and stay in attractive clay-covered cottages. Verandas have traditional Gujarati swings; interiors are tastefully decorated in Gujarati decor. There are overhead fans, room service, multicuisine restaurant, 6-km (4-mi.) swimming beach, water sports. Rupees only.

BHAVNAGAR

Moderate

Welcomgroup Nilambag Palace. Bhavnagar, Gujarat; tel. 24340. 14 rooms with bath. 55 km (34 mi.) from Palitana. This lovely, yet not grand, turn-of-the-century palace is now an excellent hotel. Belongings of its former maharajah still adorn interior rooms. Bedrooms are gigantic, with handsome furnishings. There's a pretty garden and a pool. Room service, Indian- and Continental-cuisine restaurant, library, tennis, swimming pool. AE, DC, MC, V.

CHORWAD

Inexpensive

Chorwad Beach Palace Resort. Via Gadu, Chorwad; tel. 96. 12 rooms with bath in palace; 18 rooms with bath in palace annex. This twentieth-century palace of a former nawab, now a government-run hotel, is in an idyllic setting facing the sea. Unfortunately, while rooms are palatial in size, furnishings are clean but worn in the palace and very modest in the annex. At the abutting beach, the current is too swift for swimming, but you can swim a few kilometers away. Overhead fans, room service, multicuisine restaurant. AE, DC.

JAMNAGAR

Inexpensive

New Aram Hotel. Nand Niwas, Pandit Nehru Marg, Jamnagar; tel. 78521. 30 rooms with bath. This bungalow's weathered exterior and enormous lobby barely evoke what must have been a great past. The best rooms are air-conditioned and called "deluxe"; they're spacious and have a simple Western decor and TV. There's a garden restaurant serving Gujarati thali and vegetarian cuisines. Rupees only.

Hotel President. Teen Batti, Jamnagar; tel. 70516. 26 rooms with bath. This small Western-style hotel has clean, modest rooms. Those called "super deluxe" and "deluxe" (all inexpensive) are best—with air-conditioning, carpets, and TV. All rooms have overhead fans and room service, and there is a multicuisine restaurant. DC, MC, V.

PORBANDAR

Inexpensive

New Oceanic Hotel. Chowpatty, Villa No. 8, Porbandar; tel. 20717. 4 rooms with bath. Facing the ocean, this small Western-style hotel has air-conditioned rooms with plain furnishings; but they're very clean. Vegetarian Indian- and Continental-cuisine restaurant, TV lounge. Rupees only.

Toran Tourist Bungalow. Chowpatty, Porbandar; tel. 22745. 20 rooms with bath. This government-run "no-frills" bungalow faces the sea. Western-style rooms, with individual terraces, are clean. Best rooms are air-conditioned. Overhead fans, room service, vegetarian multicuisine restaurant, TV lounge. Rupees only.

RAJKOT

Inexpensive

Hotel Jayson. S.V.P. (Canal) Rd., Rajkot; tel. 26404. 18 rooms with bath. Currently Rajkot's only decent hotel, Jayson has a comfortable, pleasant lobby. Some rooms are air-conditioned. All rooms are clean, with Western-style decor. Overhead fans, TV, room service, multicuisine restaurant, permit room, foreign-exchange counter, free airport pick-up. Rupees only.

SASAN GIR

Inexpensive

Lion Safari Lodge. Sasan Gir; tel. 21. 24 rooms with bath. This government-run Western-style bungalow is set on the edge of the Gir Sanctuary. Rooms are clean, with plain modern decor and balconies that overlook a river. Some rooms are air-conditioned; all rooms have fans. Included are room service and a simple restaurant. Rupees only.

SURAT

Inexpensive

Hotel Oasis. Near Vaishali Cinema, Varachha Rd., Surat; tel. 41124. 25 rooms with bath. This Western-style hotel offers decent rooms with a pleasant decor. Some rooms are air-conditioned. Room service, multicuisine restaurant, permit room, swimming pool, health club, doctor. AE, DC.

VADODARA

Moderate

Express Hotel. R.C. Dutt Rd., Vadodara; tel. 323131. 64 rooms with bath. This Western-style high rise has a small, modest lobby and pleasant, modern rooms with air-conditioning and TV. Room service, multicuisine restaurants, permit room, travel agency, foreign-exchange counter, secretarial services, free airport shuttle. AE, DC, MC, V.

Welcomgroup Vadodara. R.C. Dutt Rd., Vadodara; tel. 323232. 102 rooms with bath. A three-story luxury hotel, this place offers attractive rooms with a contemporary decor, air-conditioning, and TV. Ask for a room with a pool view. Multicuisine restaurants, room service, permit room, swimming pool, health club, travel agency, foreign-exchange counter, secretarial services, shopping arcade. AE, DC, MC, V.

Inexpensive

Surya Palace Hotel. Opposite Parsi Agyari, Sayajigunj, Vadodara; tel. 329999. 80 rooms with bath. This new multistory high rise has a modern lobby and spacious contemporary-decor rooms with air-conditioning and TV. Room service, multicuisine restaurants, permit room, swimming pool, health club, doctor, secretarial service, travel agency, foreign-exchange counter, free airport shuttle, shopping arcade. AE, DC, MC, V.

Hotel Utsav. Prof. Manekrao Rd., Navrang Cinema Compound, Vadodara; tel. 557045. 28 rooms with bath. This small hotel offers comfortable Western-style rooms with air-conditioning and TV. Multicuisine restaurant, room service, foreign-exchange counter, secretarial services, car-rental service. AE, DC, V.

WANKANER

Moderate

The Palace. Wankaner, 38 km (24 mi.) from Rajkot; tel. 324. 21 rooms with bath. Still maintained by the former maharajah of Wankaner, this estate on a quiet hillside has rooms in a guest house that adjoins the sumptuous main palace (built in 1901) and rooms in nearby Oasis Palace (set in an orchard by a river). The Oasis has an indoor swimming pool, an exquisite old step-well, and four rooms with Art Deco furnishings. Other rooms in both facilities have older furnishings that aren't particularly ornate; but rooms are always comfortable and pleasant. All meals are in the main palace dining room. There are overhead fans, room service, fixed-menu Indian- and Continental-cuisine meals, horseback riding, land-boat arrangements in nearby salt flats, jeep excursions to wildlife sanctuaries. Folk dance performances may also be provided on by request. Meals included. Rupees only.

DINING OUT. Gujaratis, predominately vegetarians, have created a wonderful regional cuisine with delicate flavoring. The best way to sample Gujarati dishes is to order a *thali*—a variety of dishes (dry-cooked vegetables, cooked vegetables in gravy, lentils, yogurt) served in small metal bowls on a metal platter. Many restaurants offer a limited thali or an unlimited thali. Unlimited means come hungry and let them keep refilling your plate. Breakfast is usually served 7:30–10; lunch, 12:30–3; and dinner, 7:30–11. Most restaurants take only rupees unless they are connected to a Western-style hotel. The restaurants listed below are informal and, unless noted, are open for all three meals and don't require reservations. Prices, based on one person eating a three-course meal, excluding taxes, tip, or beverage, are: *Expensive,* Rs. 80–Rs. 120; *Moderate,* Rs. 40–Rs. 80; *Inexpensive,* under Rs. 40.

AHMEDABAD

Expensive

Aab-o-Daana. Cama Hotel, Khanpur; tel. 25281. This attractive Mogul-influenced restaurant has lots of marble and lattice screens. A sitar player entertains at night. The chef serves Indian, Continental, and especially good Chinese meals. Try the chili fried chicken. Open 7:30–10 A.M., 12:30–3 P.M., 7:30–11 P.M. AE, DC, MC, V.

Patang. Ashram Rd.; tel. 77708. Ahmedabad's loveliest restaurant revolves atop a modern building. The decor is stylish Gujarati—brass ceiling, rough-stone interior walls. Live Indian classical music is played nightly. The chef prepares good Indian, Continental, and Chinese cuisines. Specialties include assorted kebab platter, chicken *kadai* (chicken in a spicy brown gravy cooked and served in a special kadai dish), or vegetarian *paneer pasand kadai* (cottage cheese in a spicy tomato gravy garnished with cashews). There's a buffet at lunch. Reservations advised. Open 12:30–3:30 P.M. and 7–11 P.M. DC, MC, V.

Moderate

Aatithya. Hotel Nataraj, Ashram Rd.; tel. 448747. This spacious restaurant was under renovation at press time. The menu offers good Gujarati thali at lunch and Punjabi, Chinese, and Continental selections at lunch and dinner. Live Indian music is played nightly. Open noon–3 P.M. and 7–11 P.M. AE, DC, MC, V.

Angeethi Restaurant. Trade Center, near Stadium Ahmedabad; tel. 464794. This delightful eatery has a café ambience—tile floor, red-and-white checkered placemats—and an upstairs balcony with a hideaway dining nook for couples. Punjabi, Continental, and Chinese meals are served; ask about the daily specials. Open 12:30–3 P.M. and 7–11 P.M. Rupees only.

Dine High. Hotel Klassic Gold, 42 Sardar Patel Nagar, near Navrangpura Telephone Exchange; tel. 447344. Dine High's dark wall mirrors, cool marble floors, and subdued lighting create an inviting ambience. You can choose from Continental, Indian, and especially good Chinese cuisines. Try the delicious sliced lamb with garlic sauce or any of the daily specials. Open noon–2:30 P.M. and 7–10:30 P.M. Rupees only.

Garden Cafe. Ashram Rd.; tel. 77708. On the second-story terrace of a modern complex, this outdoor café, with plants surrounding fountains and small pools, plays piped-in Western music. It serves good multicuisine meals—tandooris, fresh *chats* (cold mixed vegetables), pizzas, and sandwiches. Open 6 P.M.–midnight. AE, DC, MC, V.

Riwaaz. Riviera Hotel, Khanpur; tel. 24201. At press time, this restaurant was under renovation, with plans calling for a terrace extension. Come here for good tandoori and butter chicken (curried chicken). You can also order Chinese and Continental dishes. Open 7–11 A.M., noon–3 P.M., and 7–11 P.M. AE, DC, MC, V.

Vishalla. Opposite Vasana Tol Naka; tel. 403357. A few kilometers outside the city center, this excellent outdoor restaurant serves a delicious Gujarati thali in purely ethnic surroundings. You eat with your right hand off a banana leaf under charming thatched huts. While you wait for your meal, you can visit its Gujarati handicrafts museum or watch an evening performance of traditional entertainment. The manager will help you decipher the menu board. Open 11 A.M.–1 P.M. and 7–11 P.M. Rupees only.

Inexpensive

Gopi Dining Hall. Behind V.S. Hospital, Ashram Rd., Ellisbridge; tel. 76388. This popular dining hall serves an excellent thali in a fast-food ambience. If you order "limited" thali (cheaper) and you're still hungry, you can switch over to the unlimited. The place gets crowded. Open 10 A.M.–2:30 P.M. and 7–11 P.M. Rupees only.

PORBANDAR

Inexpensive

Swagat Dining Hall. M. G. Rd.; tel. 20246. This upstairs restaurant, with booths and formica tables, serves tasty vegetarian dishes—Indian, Continental, and Chinese. Try the popular *dosas* (vegetable-stuffed crêpe). There is taped music and courteous service. Open 9 A.M.–3 P.M. and 5–10 P.M. Rupees only.

RAJKOT

Inexpensive

Bhabha Dining Hall. Panchnath Rd., near Alfred High School; no phone. Too bad you can't make reservations; this tiny, popular restaurant draws a crowd. It serves one dish: Gujarati thali. Here, the unlimited thali is called the "special." Arrive good and hungry. Open 10:30 A.M.–3 P.M. and 7–10 P.M. Rupees only.

SURAT

Inexpensive

Dhawalgiri Restaurant. Dhawalgiri Guest House, Dhawalgiri Apartment, opposite Collector's Bungalow, Athwalines; tel. 40040. This very good restaurant serves excellent multicuisine vegetarian dishes, which are supposed to promote good health. Open 10 A.M.–10 P.M. Rupees only.

VADODARA

Expensive

Ruchika Restaurant. Welcomgroup Vadodara, R.C. Dutt Rd.; tel. 323232. In an elegant contemporary decor, tasty Mughlai cuisine and especially good tandoori items are offered. Dinner reservations advised. Open 12:30–3 P.M. and 7:30–11 P.M. AE, DC, MC, V.

Moderate

Mandap. Express Hotel, R.C. Dutt Rd.; tel. 323131. If you're in the mood for a good Gujarati thali, this informal restaurant will satisfy your craving. Open 11 A.M.–3 P.M. and 7–10 P.M. AE, DC, MC, V.

SWEETS AND TREATS. Ahmedabad. For good ice cream, Western snacks, and good coffee, drop in at *Hasty Tasty,* Anand, near Municipal Market, Navrangpura; open 11:30 A.M.–11 P.M. For delicious Western pastries and cakes, visit the *Bakery Cafe,* near Stadium Crossroads, Trade Center, Navrangpura; open 8 A.M.–

11 P.M. For good Indian sweets and snacks, go to the nearest *Mehta Bengali Sweet Shop.* One branch is at the Municipal Market, Navrangpura; open 6 A.M.–11:30 P.M.

HOW TO GET AROUND. From the Airports. Ahmedabad. The airport is 10 km (six mi.) from the city. *Ahmedabad Municipal Transport Service* (AMTS) runs buses from the airport to the city for Rs. 2. You can also go by taxi for about Rs. 90. **Vadodara.** The airport is 6 km (four mi.) from the city. You can take a taxi (about Rs. 30) or an auto rickshaw (about Rs. 15). From the other airports, your choice is also taxi or auto rickshaw.

By Plane. *Indian Airlines* has four flights a week between Rajkot and Bhavnagar and three flights a week between Bhuj and Jamnagar. *Vayudoot* has six flights a week between Surat and Bhavnagar and a daily flight between Keshod (near Chorwad) and Porbandar.

By Bus. *Gujarat State Road Transport Corporation* buses tend to be crowded and slow going; but they do go to every place in the state. In Ahmedabad, for schedules and reservations, contact the Central Bus Station, Geeta Mandir; tel. 344764. In Vadodara, contact the Central Bus Station, near Railway Station; tel. 327000.

By Train. From Ahmedabad, you can go by train to Bhavnagar, Vadodara, Surat, Junagadh, Veraval (near Somnath), Jamnagar, Porbandar, Rajkot, and Bhuj. For information and reservations in Ahmedabad, contact *Ahmedabad Junction Railway Station;* tel. 343535, 333535, or 344657. In Vadodara, contact *Railway Station, Sayajigunj;* tel. 557575, 63535, or 327979. If you travel at night, remember to reserve a sleeping berth.

By Rented Car with Driver. From Ahmedabad, Vadodara is 113 km (70 mi.); Surat, 120 km (74 mi.); Lothal, 84 km (52 mi.); Rajkot, 216 km (134 mi.); Porbandar, 394 km (244 mi.); Palitana, 217 km (134 mi.); and Bhuj (in Kutch), 310 km (192 mi.). With reasonably good roads throughout Gujarat, this is a good way to explore the state. The cost of a car is about Rs. 4 per km, with a halt charge of Rs. 50–Rs. 100 per night. Hire a car from a recommended tour operator listed below.

By Taxi. Tourist taxis are usually available at city railroad stations and airports. They charge by the hour, with a minimum tariff. For short hops, it's cheaper to use an auto rickshaw.

By Auto Rickshaw. Auto rickshaws should cost about Rs. 1.75 per km. Make sure the driver uses his meter; or negotiate before you start up.

TOURS. Tourist Corporation of Gujarat (TCG) offers two economical five-day bus tours that depart from Ahmedabad. For details and booking, contact TCG at H.K. House, off Ashram Rd., Ahmedabad; tel. 449683.

Saurashtra Darshan Tour includes Rajkot, Jamnagar, Dwarka, Porbandar, Somnath, Sasan Gir, Junagadh, Veraval, Palitana, Velavadar, Lothal. It departs each Friday.

North Gujarat and Rajasthan Tour includes Udaipur, Chittorgarh, Mount Abu, Ambaji, Khumbharia, Modhera, Bahucharaji. It departs first and third Saturdays.

Ahmedabad Municipal Corporation (AMC) conducts two local bus tours of Ahmedabad. For details and booking, contact AMC, tel. 365610.

Morning Tour: Sidi Saiyad, Hutheesing Jain Temple, Sardar Patel Museum, Calico Museum, Dadahari step-well, Lake Kankaria, Geeta Mandir, Shah Alam Mosque.

Afternoon Tour: Gandhi Ashram, Vechaar Utensils Museum, Snake Farm, Municipal Museum.

Vadodara Municipal Corporation (VMC) conducts three afternoon bus tours of sites around Vadodara. For details and booking, contact VMC, tel. 329656.

Tour 1: EME Temple, Sayaji Garden, Kirti Mandir, Geeta Mandir, Baroda Dairy, Fatehsinh Museum, Aurobindo Society. Offered on Tuesday, Wednesday, and Friday.

Tour 2: Nimeta (picnic spot), Ajwan (Brindavan pattern garden). Offered July–September on Saturday, Sunday, and Monday.

Tour 3: Both above tours combined. Offered October–June on Saturday, Sunday, Monday (tour lasts until 9 P.M.).

A five-day *South Gujarat, Ajanta, and Ellora Tour* leaves on the second and fourth Saturday of each month and returns the following Wednesday.

TOUR OPERATORS. For all travel needs, including rented car with driver, contact the following dependable agencies:

Voyagers, Urja House, Swastik Char Rasta, Navrangpura, Ahmedabad; tel. 449503.

TCI, near Natraj Theatre, behind Handloom House, Ashram Rd., Ahmedabad; tel. 407061.

TCG also has cars available for hire. Contact their office in Ahmedabad (address above).

Exotic Journey (26 Sector 2 Market, R.K. Puram, New Delhi; tel. 670221) sponsors good safaris into the Rann of Kutch desert. Also see Special-Interest Tours in *Facts at Your Fingertips* for names of other India-based agencies that can create a special trip in Gujarat.

A five-day *South Gujarat, Ajanta, and Ellora Tour* leaves on the second and fourth Saturday of each month and returns the following Wednesday.

SEASONAL EVENTS. Since most of the events are determined by the lunar calendar, contact the tourist offices for the exact dates. Fairs, which may be rooted in religion to commemorate events in honor of gods or goddesses, are truly secular social events in which all are invited to participate.

January. *Makar Sankranti.* During this festival, which marks the passing of the sun from Dhanu to Makar, sweets are exchanged and kite-flying contests fill the skies.

January/February. *Bhavnath Fair.* This five-day event is held during Mahashivatri at the foot of Mount Girnar. After a holy dip in the Mrigi Kund, pilgrims offer prayers at the temple. An awe-inspiring midnight ritual is a *Mahapuja,* in which holy men from all over the country ride about the fair on caparisoned elephants to the reverberating accompaniment of musical instruments. Great folk dancing!

February/March. *Holi.* On this day, marking the start of spring, wear old clothes. Celebrants throw colored water on anything that moves.

March/April. *Rathyatra.* This is by far the biggest festival in Ahmedabad, with a day-long procession of thousands of devotees walking behind temple chariots accompanied by adorned elephants, camels, and trucks carrying mythological tableaux. The procession commemorates the visit of Krishna and Balram to Mathura.

August. *Gokulashtami.* Krishna's birthday is celebrated as a joyous festival, with feasting and merrymaking. Large fairs are held in Dwarka. Gujaratis perform the Ras, a folk dance supposedly introduced by Krishna.

August/September. *Tarnetar Fair.* This three-day tribal fair takes place at the Trineshwara (three-eyed) Temple. One ongoing event involves the "hunt for a husband," with marriageable young girls eyeing eligible young boys and sometimes finding a match. Colorful costumes, good folk dances and music.

September/October. *Navratri.* The most famous of all festivals, this consists of nine nights of music and dancing devoted to the nine forms of the mother goddess Durga. During the festival, there is a competition of traditional Gujarati *garba* dancing.

November. *Diwali.* Candles adorn practically every house at night; firecrackers go off in every village and city. The day preceding Diwali is celebrated as the new year, believed to be an auspicious day to enter any business transaction.

HISTORIC SITES. Entrance is usually free; where a donation is asked, a few rupees will suffice. Monuments are open sunrise to sunset, unless noted otherwise below.

AHMEDABAD ENVIRONS

Ahmed Shah Mosque, southwest section of Bhadra, was built for the founder of Ahmedabad. Originally a Hindu temple, it was ransacked and rebuilt as a mosque.

Hutheesing Jain Temple, outside Delhi Gate, was built in 1850 and is dedicated to Dharmanath, the 15th Jain Tirthankar. The white-marble structure is surrounded by 52 small shrines.

Jama Masjid, one of the largest Indian mosques, was built in 1423. It has 300 pillars that divide the huge prayer hall into 15 large squares, each one surmounted with a dome.

Sidi Sayyid Masjid, Relief Rd., near the river, is a 500-year-old mosque that is famous for its latticed windows carved in single-stone panels. The pattern of one window is an exquisite rendering of the Tree of Life.

Siddi Bashir Mosque, the architectural marvel of Gujarat, rises above the Sarang-pur Gate. The mosque has two delicately carved, three-story minarets, with balanced stone balconies wrapped around each story. Gently push one minaret and both shake in unison. Across the railway line, Raj Bibi Mosque also had a pair of shaking minarets before the British demolished one to unravel its mystery.

Rani Vav in Patan, 30 km (19 mi.) from Ahmedabad, is one of the finest stone step-wells in Gujarat, with subterranean sculptured corridors and steps leading to a well.

OTHER GUJARAT SITES

Ambaji, Arasur Hill near Mount Abu, 194 km (120 mi.) from Ahmedabad, is dedicated to the worship of Shakti and is one of the most important Hindu pilgrimage centers in Gujarat. Gujarat Bhavai, a folk drama, is often staged in the temple complex.

Dwarka, where Lord Krishna supposedly established his kingdom, is one of the four most sacred Hindu pilgrimage centers in India. Archaeological excavations show that present-day Dwarka is the sixth city on this site; the others were reclaimed by the sea. The five-story Dwarkadhish Temple, said to be over 2,500 years old, is supported by 60 columns and is crowned by a soaring, elaborately carved spire. Also see the nearby Rukmani Temple, dedicated to one of Krishna's consorts, and Nageshwar Mahadev and Gopu Talav Teerth, two other important shrines near Dwarka. Krishna's actual residence is said to be on nearby Bet Dwarka Island, approached by public boat launch. Here the Hindu god Vishnu supposedly killed the demon Shankhasura.

Modhera Sun Temple is one of the finest examples of Indian architecture of its period. Built in 1026 during the reign of King Bhimdev I of the Solanki dynasty, the temple is dedicated to the sun god Surya and stands high on a plinth overlooking a deep stone-stepped tank. Every inch of the edifice, both inside and outside, is magnificently carved with gods and goddesses, birds, beasts, and flowers. The inner sanctum, which housed the presiding deity, was so designed that the first rays of the rising sun lit up the image of Surya.

Palitana, a picturesque temple city atop the holy Shatrunjaya Mountain, is dedicated to Shri Adhishwara, the first Jain trithanker. Every Jain dreams of walking up the hill to build a temple, adding to the 900-plus shrines already at the bejeweled crest. The fantastic collection of temple jewels can be seen by special permission of the Hill Inspector or Manager of Anandji Kalyanji Trust in Palitana or during deity-adorning ceremonies at Shri Adishwara Temple. Photos are not permitted.

Somnath, one of India's 12 most sacred Shiva temples and called a Jyotorlinga, is a majestic seashore monument. It was ransacked and destroyed repeatedly by Moslem invaders, then rebuilt. It is believed that the temple was first built of gold, then silver, wood, and finally stone. The present temple is a twentieth-century reconstruction. The shrine's gates were carried away by Mahmud of Ghazni in 1026. Suraj Mandir, near the shrine, is also a sun temple. A museum housed in the temple contains relics of the old Somnath shrine. Also see Bhalka Teerth, near Somnath, where Lord Krishna, mistaken for a deer, was wounded by an arrow; and Dehotsarga at Triveni Ghat, also nearby, where Krishna was cremated.

MUSEUMS AND GALLERIES. Gujarat has several museums worth visiting, notably in Ahmedabad and Vadodara. Collections range from ancient artifacts and treasures to displays of present-day technology. Entrance is usually free or costs a nominal fee.

AHMEDABAD

Calico Museum of Textiles (Sarabhai House in Shah Bagh) is considered one of the finest textile museums in the Far East. Its rare collection of fabrics dates to the seventeenth century. Included are Patola fabrics from Patan and south India, temple cloths, textiles from the Mogul period, handwoven cloths, brocades, and wooden blocks showing the Portuguese influence. A museum shop sells reproductions of some of the pieces on display, as well as cards and books. Open 10:30 A.M.–12:30 P.M. and 2:30–5:30 P.M.; closed Wednesdays.

N. C. Mehta Museum of Miniatures (Sanskar Kandra) was designed by the noted architect Le Corbusier. It houses rare Indian miniatures, a collection amassed by a philanthropist who donated them to the museum. Other paintings are also on display. Open 9–11 A.M. and 4–7 P.M.; closed Mondays.

Sabarmati Ashram (Sabarmati River), was Mahatma Gandhi's headquarters for 15 years. Many of Gandhi's historical events, such as the Dandi March, commenced here. The ashram was founded in 1915 and today houses many of Gandhi's personal effects. It still makes handicrafts, handmade paper, and spinning wheels. Open 8:30 A.M.–6:30 P.M. daily. On Sundays, Tuesdays, Thursdays, and Fridays, at 8:30 P.M., there is a *son et lumiere* show in English with a small admission fee.

Shreyas Folk Museum is in the sloping green woodland that makes up the Shreyas Foundation. The museum has a fine collection of folk art and objects that illustrate the culture of Gujarat. On display are exquisite embroideries; unusual pots, pans, and other utensils; handicrafts; weapons; and bullock and camel carts. The museum also has a children's section that displays costumes, folk art, puppets, coins, and legends of various Indian states. Open afternoons only; call tel. 78295 for details.

VADODARA

Baroda Museum and Art Gallery, in Sayaji Bagh, was founded in 1894 and has sections on art, archaeology, ethnology, geology, and natural history. The art gallery, in an adjoining building, contains Indian and European paintings. Open daily 9:30 A.M.–4:30 P.M.

Maharaja Fateh Singh Museum, Nehru Road, has a unique collection of art treasures of the former rulers of Baroda. Also on display are the works by Murillo, Raphael, and Titian, as well as modern European and Indian paintings and sculptures and a fine collection of Chinese and Japanese art. Open daily except Mondays 9 A.M.–noon and 3–6 P.M. July–March, 4–7 P.M. April–June.

PARKS AND GARDENS. Ahmedabad. *Deer Park,* next to Sarita Udyan in Indrada village, is a sprawling reserve for deer.

Satira Udyan, in Gandhinagar, 23 km (14 mi.) from Ahmedabad, is an ideal spot along the river for picnics.

Sundervan Snake Garden, off M. Dayanand Road, has snakes from all over India. There is also a daily show that includes demonstrations with live snakes. For the less queasy, the garden is inhabited by freely roaming tame ducks and rabbits. And there's even a puppet show in the evenings!

SPORTS AND OUTDOOR ADVENTURES. Beaches. Gujarat's relatively unexploited coastline is gradually being developed into resorts, each with its own features, unique identity, and attraction.

Ahmedpur-Mandvi is an untouched beach located in Saurashtra and near the Union Territory of Diu. The beach has palm trees of a unique variety not found generally in India. The government-run Tourist Village resort is an attractive place to stay.

Camel Safaris. You can arrange a camel safari in the Rann of Kutch; see Special-Interest Tours in *Facts at Your Fingertips.*

Land Yachts. You can arrange to skim across the Kutch salt flats on these novel land-based crafts. Contact Wankaner Palace (see *Accommodations,* above).

WILDLIFE SANCTUARIES. *Sasan Gir Forests.* Asiatic lions, those increasingly rare beauties, can be spotted at close range in this sanctuary, the last major stronghold of the beasts. Also in the 500-square-mile forest are leopards, antelope, sambars, varieties of deer, and wild boar.

The best time to visit is March–May, when you have a chance to see the animals lazing near water holes. The forest is closed during the monsoon season.

Little Rann of Kutch Sanctuary. The only home of the rare wild ass and the world's largest flamingo breeding ground, this wide salt-flat area is just a few feet above sea level and is completely dry November–June, when you can drive through by jeep. The best time to visit is December–May.

Valvadar Sanctuary. This grassland preserve is home to the exquisite black buck, one of the swiftest animals. The best time to visit is October–June.

SHOPPING. Gujarat offers a scintillating range of fabrics, including woven textiles, tie-dye work, gold and silver thread work *(zari),* silk embroidery, and various styles of saris. Also popular and lovely are mirror work on cloth, bead-encrusted artifacts from Rajkot, lacquered furniture from Sankheda, textiles and silverwork from Kutch, and wood carvings from Ahmedabad.

In Ahmedabad, visit the following reliable fixed-price shops:

Banjara, 2 and 3 Ground Floor, Jasmine, Khanpur, sells custom-designed leather goods from caps to footwear. Open 9 A.M.–8 P.M., closed Sunday. Rupees only.

Handloom House, Ashram Rd., has beautiful Gujarati textiles, plus a good sampling of Indian handicrafts. Open 10 A.M.–7 P.M., closed Sunday. AE, DC.

Gurjari, Ashram Rd., a government-run emporium, has delightful Gujarati handicrafts and textiles (hand-embroidery, mirrorwork, patchwork, rabira embroidery, tanka stitchery, blockprinting). Also visit *Garvi,* the companion store in the back of the same building. Here, you find more beautiful Gujarati fabrics and excellent ready-made clothes, wall hangings, bedspreads, cushion covers, and *dhurries* (rugs). Both shops are open 10:30 A.M.–2 P.M. and 3–7 P.M., closed Sunday. AE, DC.

Mintissa, Ratnam Bungalow, Stadium Rd., sells beautiful silk and cotton *salwar kameez* (long blouse and loose pants)—ready-made and on order. Open 10 A.M.–12 P.M. and 4–6 P.M.; closed Sunday. Rupees only.

Avni Boutique, near H.L. Commerce College, Navrangpura, and *Bandhej,* opposite L.D. Commerce, University Area, also sell exquisite *salwar kameez*—ready-made and on order. Open 10 A.M.–7 P.M.; closed Sunday. Rupees only.

If you're prepared to bargain, or just like to browse, also visit these two fascinating bazaars. *Manek Chowk* in the old city. Here, you can find beautiful Gujarati textiles by the meter. One must-stop is *Gamthiwala* (Rani's Hajira Naka, 1st Shop) Open 10 A.M.–7 P.M., closed Sunday. Rupees only.

Law Garden Bazaar is a delightful nighttime bazaar set up on the sidewalk that sells Gujarati products. Examine items carefully. Some fabrics are hand-embroidered, but many items are embroidered by machine. Bargain! Rupees only.

In Vadodara, the best shopping area is *Leheripura Mandir Bazaar,* with its many shops dealing in fabrics, jewelry, and curios. In the *Fine Arts Faculty Building* of Baroda University can be found a wide selection of pottery, from antique to newly made pieces.

NIGHTLIFE AND BARS. Gujarat is a dry state; all alcohol must be consumed in your room. In Ahmedabad, enjoy good cultural performances at Vishalla under the stars. See *Dining Out,* above.

MADHYA PRADESH

India's Heartland

by
KATHLEEN COX

A journey into the heart of India carries you back to historic moments of valor, glory, passion, and divinity. Madhya Pradesh's life is etched in stone—arrested by the chisels of master craftsmen. This lovely state is also studded with meandering rivers, extensive lush forests, hills and ravines, and some of the rarest species of birds and beasts, including the exquisite and elusive tiger. Conservationists have rated the Kanha and Bandhavgrah National parks, with their undulating meadows and abundant wildlife, as the finest in the country. Indeed, Madhya Pradesh is the original Kipling country, the hunting grounds of Akela the wolf, Kaa the python, and Sher Khan the tiger.

Long before the written word, the magic of this central state was inscribed in colors that defied time, remaining as permanent reminders inside nearly 500 labyrinthine caves of Bhimbetka. On the caves' walls, a series of prehistoric paintings in vivid and panoramic detail sweep you back to at least 8000 B.C. In fact, you can call this entire state a museum without walls—one that contains over 1,800 man-made monuments, including some of the world's finest. Here, you can visit the *stupa* (shrine) at Sanchi, purportedly the best example of Buddhist architecture in India; the Bhimbetka rock shelter paintings that date back to the Mesolithic Period (approximately 8000 B.C.); and the Gwalior Fort, which Babur called "the pearl in the necklace of Indian forts." You can also see the beautifully preserved medieval town of Orchra; Mandu, a city built for joy by the Moslems in the fifteenth and sixteenth centuries about which the Emperor Jahangir wrote, "Of all places in Hindustan none is more beautiful than Mandu after the rains"; and, of course, the unforgettable temples at Khajuraho, where the ecstasy of passion has been immortalized in stone.

The Historic Record

When the great Ashoka ruled over the Maurya Empire in the third century B.C., he laid the foundation of the great stupa at Sanchi. Shortly after his death, his empire collapsed and the Sungas took over, followed by the Guptas (A.D. 300–500), whose reign is referred to as the Golden Age. Repeated invasions of the Huns from Central Asia finally led to triumph over the splendor of the Guptas' Malwa Empire. The Huns, in turn, were defeated early in the seventh century by the famous Hindu emperor Harsha, who supposedly put 60,000 war elephants and 100,000 horses on the battlefields to achieve his conquest. Despite the fear this man inspired on the battlefield, Harsha did have a benevolent streak. Every five years he distributed to the poor all his accumulated riches until finally he was reduced to begging.

The close of the tenth century witnessed a period of confusion from which emerged the Paramara dynasty with the great king Bhoja, a renowned Sanskrit scholar. The succeeding Chandellas created the magnificent temples at Khajuraho. The first Moslem invasions in the eleventh century ushered in a 400-year period of constant skirmishing between Moslems and Hindus—the latter reasserting themselves each time the Delhi sultanate showed any weakness; then, the stake in the battle was usually the fabled city of Mandu. The last of the great Mogul emperors, the fanatic Aurangzeb, managed to extend his rule through this part of India, but at such tremendous financial cost, his empire collapsed with his death. Next came the Marathas, who started life as peasants skilled in guerrilla warfare. They reigned over Malwa until the advent of the British at the close of the eighteenth century.

EXPLORING MADHYA PRADESH

Bhopal and the Narmada River

Unfortunately, Bhopal is known primarily for the catastrophic Union Carbide gas-leak tragedy in 1984, which killed thousands who lived under the shadow of the plant. But Bhopal is much more than this now-closed industrial complex; it's a lovely city in India's heartland. Nestled in rich foliage, it's half hidden among mountains. A myriad of lights from houses are reflected in the placid waters of a pretty lake. Tall minarets and mosques stand majestically against the backdrop of shimmering city lights.

It was in the eleventh century that the legendary Raja Bhoj (1010–53), fond of lakeside views, created a lake around which grew a sprawling city, Bhopal, named after him. Soon more lakes and gardens, parks and ponds were constructed, but succeeding battalions of invaders seemed determined to erase it from the face of the earth, and Bhopal went into oblivion.

For a long while, Bhopal remained silent. But with the coming of the extravagant Moguls in the fourteenth century, the city was reborn.

The Afghan general of the Moguls, Dost Muhammed Khan, came here and was taken by its natural beauty. He set out a plan, and the new city of Bhopal began to take life on the ruins of the old city. Soon, the city, with its lakes, parks, gardens, and broad avenues, became a popular retreat. The Moguls made it a refuge for artists and musicians and a city of monuments and mausoleums. Their influence still lingers. Amuse yourself by watching a man, late in the night, with a *paan* in his mouth, an exquisitely carved silver purse in his hand, humming the lines of a poem. He has just come out of a *mushaira,* a symposium of poets.

Khan started the trend of creating picturesque lakes and raising beautiful monuments, with each ruler being more ambitious than his predecessor. Centuries have passed, rulers have come and gone, but the monuments are still under construction. The sprawling Taj-ul-Masajid, started by Begum Shah Jahan in the 1500s, still incomplete, consists of an impressive main hall with an interarched roof, a broad facade, and a wide courtyard. Other monuments include the Jama Masjid, built by Kudsia Begum, which has tall dark minarets crowned with glittering golden spikes. The famous Moti Masjid is patterned on Delhi's Jama Masjid.

An outstanding feature of Bhopal, of course, is its two picturesque lakes. An overbridge divides one lake into two—Upper Lake and Lower Lake. The Upper Lake is over two square kilometers in size. From Idgah and Shamla Hills you get a fabulous view of the sunset and the twinkling city lights on the lakes.

Bhojpur is also renowned for the remains of its magnificent Shiva temple and of two huge dams. The temple, known as the Bhojeshwar Temple, was constructed in a simple square plan, with each wall measuring 66 feet—an unusual design for such buildings. Its richly carved dome, though incomplete, has a magnificent soaring strength of line and is supported by four pillars. These pillars, like the dome, have been conceived on a massive scale, yet retain a remarkable elegance because of their tapered form.

Richly carved above, the plain doorway is a sharp relief from the two exquisitely sculpted figures that stand on either side. On the temple's other sides are balconies, each supported by massive brackets and four intricately carved pillars. The lingam in the sanctum rises to an awe-inspiring height of $7\frac{1}{2}$ feet with a circumference of 18 feet. Set on a massive platform $21\frac{1}{2}$ feet square and composed of three superimposed limestone blocks, the architectural harmony of the lingam and platform creates a superb synthesis of solidity and lightness. The temple was never completed, and an earthen ramp used to raise stones to dome-level still stands.

A vast lake once lay west of Bhojpur, but nothing remains today except the ruins of two huge dams that contained the lake's waters. The lake was destroyed by Hoshang Shah of Malwa (1405–34), who cut through the lesser dam, either intentionally or in a fit of destructive rage, and added an enormous fertile area to his possessions. According to a Gond legend, it took an army three months to cut through the dam and three years to empty it; then its bed was not habitable for 30 years. The climate of Malwa was considerably altered by the removal of this vast sheet of water.

Surrounded by the northern fringe of the Vindhyan ranges, Bhimbetka lies 40 kilometers (25 miles) south of Bhopal. In this rocky terrain of dense forest and craggy cliffs, over 700 rock shelters were recently discovered, extending back to the Neolithic Age. Hundreds of paintings in the caves depict the life of the prehistoric cave dwellers, making the Bhimbetka group an archaeological treasure, an invaluable chronicle of the history of humanity.

Executed mainly in red and white with occasional greens and yellows and with themes taken from the everyday events of eons ago, most scenes depict hunting, dancing, music, horse and elephant riders, animal fights, honey collection, decoration of bodies, disguises, and household scenes. Animals, such as bisons, tigers, lions, wild boar, elephants, deer, antelopes, dogs, monkeys, lizards, and crocodiles, are also shown in abundance. In some caves, popular religious and ritual symbols occur frequently. The superimposition of paintings indicates that the same canvas was used by different people at different times.

Sanchi

Sanchi, 46 kilometers (29 miles) from Bhopal, sits on a hill crowned by a group of stupas and pillars that represent the peak of perfection in Buddhist art and architecture. This holy site occupies a unique position in the history of Buddhism. Originally consecrated by the Kushan rulers in A.D. first century, Emperor Ashoka sought to give permanence to this site by replacing the original wooden structures and railings with perfectly wrought stone embellished in forms and symbols that expressed Buddhist teachings. After he constructed eight stupas at Sanchi, he built a nunnery for his queen, who came from Vidisha, espoused Buddhism, and entered the holy order of nuns. Meanwhile, his son, Mahendra, went to Sri Lanka spreading the faith to that island.

The glory that was Sanchi, seat of Buddhist learning and place of pilgrimage during the third century B.C., can still be experienced in the site's serene complex of structures. Every form of Buddhist architecture found expression here: stupas, temples, pillars, monasteries, and four magnificent *toranas,* or gateways. The master builders and carvers of these stupendous portals made of buff sandstone taken from the mines in Raisen drew inspiration from the *Jataka* tales (stories about the previous lives of the Buddha). The carvers, by trade silversmiths from Vidisha, brought to fruition on stone all the intricate, detailed skill of design and pattern consistent with their jeweler's art. The profuse carvings on the gateways depict the Buddha's incarnations and all the great moments in his life, which, in dramatic sequence, reveal the intense faith and supreme artistry of the creators of Sanchi.

After the decline of Buddhism in India, Sanchi went into oblivion. In 1818, Sir John Marshall, the director general of the Archaeological Survey of India, rediscovered the numerous remains. The architectural pieces and sculptures displayed here include the Ashoka pillar and images of the Buddha and Kushan.

At Sanchi, be certain to see the following:

Great Stupa No. 1. 36.5 meters (120 feet) in diameter and 16.4 meters (54 feet) high, this magnificent commemorative structure is a landmark in Buddhist architecture. Its construction was started during the reign of Emperor Ashoka but was completed by his successors in the second and first centuries B.C. The present stupa is a superstructure with a hemispherical dome that contains Buddhist relics built over the original earthen mound. It surmounts a high circular dome with a railing around its base. The railing encompassing the dome has four elaborately carved toranas that are among the finest examples of Buddhist art.

Gateways. Bas-reliefs on the toranas depict tales of the Buddha's previous incarnations and main events in his life in symbolic form—footprints, the Bodhi tree, the Wheel of Law, and the stupa motifs. The eastern gateway depicts the departure of Gautama (who eventually became the Buddha) from his father's place, his mother's dreams before his birth, and the miracles of Gautama as the Buddha. The western gateway shows the seven incarnations of the Buddha. The middle architrave exhibits the preachings

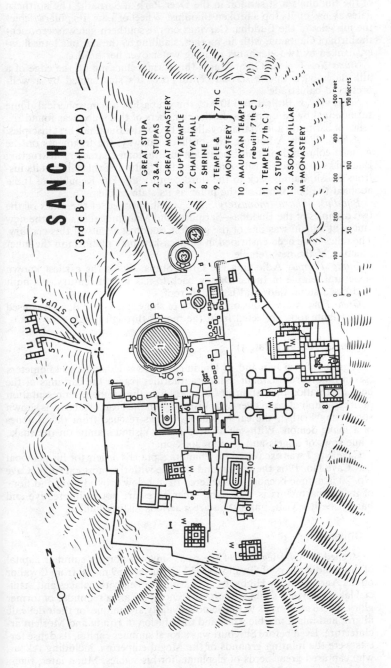

SANCHI

(3rd c BC – 10th c AD)

1. GREAT STUPA
2. 3 & 4. STUPAS
3. GREAT MONASTERY
4. GUPTA TEMPLE
5. CHAITYA HALL ⎫
6. SHRINE ⎬ 7th C
7. TEMPLE & ⎭ MONASTERY
8. MAURYAN TEMPLE (rebuilt 7th C)
9. TEMPLE (7th C)
10. STUPA
11. ASOKAN PILLAR

M = MONASTERY

TO STUPA 2

500 Feet
150 Metres

N

of the Buddha's first sermon in the Deer Park at Sarnath. The northern gateway has on its top a broken Buddhist Wheel of Law. Its pillars depict the miracles of the Buddha. Carvings on the southern gateway represent the birth of Gautama, with his mother, standing by the side of a lotus flower, flanked by two elephants pouring water over her head.

Stupa No. 2. Near Great Stupa, this shrine, standing on the edge of a hill, dates back to the second century B.C. It's surrounded by a well-preserved balustrade.

Stupa No. 3. Built 150–140 B.C., this stupa has a hemispherical dome surmounted by an umbrella. In the chambers of this stupa was found the relics of Sariputta and Mahamogallena, two of the Buddha's first disciples.

Ashoka Pillar. Adjoining the southern gateway, the fragments on the Ashoka column depict an inscription in Brahman characters instructing Buddhists to avoid schism. An outstanding feature of this pillar is its lustrous polish, dating back to the third century B.C. The Republic of India adopted the lion motif on the pillar as its state emblem.

Buddhist Vihara (monastery). The reenshrinement of the relics of the two disciples of the Buddha—Sariputta and Mahamogallena—in the new vihara at Sanchi was one of the greatest Buddhist events of this century. The relics have been enshrined in glass caskets on a platform in the inner sanctum of the new temple.

Gupta Temple. Adjoining the Great Stupa, this is the earliest known structural temple in India. Dating back to A.D. fourth century, it's built of dressed stone slabs and has a flat roof.

Great Bowl. Carved out of one piece of stone, the Great Bowl was used to distribute food collected from the monks through begging.

The Caves at Udaigiri

A group of two Jain and 18 Hindu caves are at Udaigiri, 13 kilometers (seven miles) from Sanchi. Hindu authorities regard the carvings of the boar incarnation of Vishnu in Cave No. 5 as the ultimate representation of the triumph of good over evil. Vishnu, with the head of a boar, is shown supporting Prithvi, the earth goddess he has rescued from the clutches of a snake demon. With self-assured poise, Vishnu stamps on the snake while rows of angels and demons look on.

Cave No. 7 was excavated on Chandragupta II's orders for his personal use. Cave No. 19 is the largest and the one with the most carvings. Cave No. 20 is unique because it is entered from below ground level and none of its compartments is high. The other caves are not as impressive and hardly merit a visit, unless you are a serious history buff.

Shivpuri

Steeped in royal legacies of the past, Shivpuri, former summer capital of the Scindia rulers of Gwalior, is 112 kilometers (69 miles) from Gwalior on the Agra-Bombay Highway. A charming town, with palaces and artificial lakes, Shivpuri's fabled *chattries* (cenotaphs) are a reminder of former glory. These memorials to the Scindia dynasty are unique for their delicate filigree and inlaid marble work and their fusion of Hindu and Moslem architecture. Even before Shivpuri was a royal summer capital, its dense forests were the hunting grounds of the Mogul emperors, including Akbar, who captured great herds of elephants for his stables. Much later, tigers roamed the wooded hills, and royal *shikaris* (hunters) bagged many a magnificent beast. Shivpuri was also a natural choice for the summer resort capital. Shivpuri's royal ambience lives on in the exquisite palaces and hunting lodges and the graceful, intricately embellished marble chattries erected by the Scindia princes.

A sanctuary for rare wildlife and avifauna, Shivpuri is best known for its Madhav National Park. Driving through its 156 square kilometers (61 square miles) of jungle may offer a glimpse of deer, black buck, wild boar, and a variety of rare birds. The park, open throughout the year, is equally rich in waterfowl. An artificial lake, Chandpata, is the winter home of migratory geese, pochard, pintail, teal, mallard, and gadwall. The point where the forest track crosses the wide rocky stream that flows from the Waste Weir provides a good site for bird-watching. Species that frequent this spot are redwattled lapwing, large-pied wagtail, pond heron, white-breasted kingfisher, cormorant, painted stork, white ibis, lagger falcon, purple sunbird, paradise flycatcher, and golden oracle.

The cenotaphs of the Scindias are set in a Mogul garden, with quiet nooks under flowering trees intersected by pathways with ornamental balustrades, illuminated by Victorian lamps. The chattries of Madho Rao Scindia and Maharani Sakhya Raje Scindia, the dowager queen, face each other across a water tank. With their shikhara-type spires and Rajput and Mogul pavilions, they synthesize the architectural idioms of the Hindu and Islamic styles. The white marble surface of Madho Rao Scindia's cenotaph follows the pietradura style, with lapis lazuli and onyx creating a spectacularly rich effect that is heightened by the delicacy of the trellis work on the sides. The dowager queen's cenotaph has a noble dignity of line and superb structural harmony. Both memorials contain life-size images of the Scindias, which ceremonially dressed retainers bless with flowers and incense each day. Each evening, classical ragas break the stillness that envelops the statues.

Rising from a natural eminence is Madhav Vilas Palace, the elongated rose-pink summer palace of the Scindias that was built on truly royal proportions. A fine example of colonial architecture, the "Mahal," as it is called, has remarkable marble floors, iron columns, graceful terraces, and a Ganapati *mandapa* (pavilion). From the turrets, the view of Shivpuri and the park beyond is spectacular.

At the highest point, deep within the forests of the park, is the turreted George Castle, built by Jiyaji Rao Scindia, that offers a lovely view of the lake. The best time to visit the castle is at sunset when the lake mirrors the changing hues of the day. Edging the forests of the Madhav National Park is the Sakhya Sagar lake, habitat of a variety of reptiles, including marsh crocodile or mugger, Indian python, and the monitor lizard. Bhadaiya Kund nearby is a scenic picnic spot at a natural spring, whose water is rich in minerals, with supposedly curative powers.

Gwalior Fort

About 112 kilometers (69 miles) from Shivpuri is Gwalior—and yet another chapter in Indian history, where the Moguls only played a minor part near the end of a long drama.

Gwalior is practically synonymous with its fort, one of the oldest in India (it is mentioned in an inscription dated A.D. 525). According to a legend, Suraj Sena, a local leader suffering from leprosy, met a Hindu saint, Gwalipa, on the rocky hill where the fort now stands. Gwalipa offered him a drink of water from Suraj Kund, a sacred pool. The drink cured the leper. Gwalipa then told Suraj Sena to build a fort on the hill (the derivation of the name Gwalior) and to use the name of Pal if he wanted his dynasty to survive. Suraj Pal's family flourished until one cynic refused to obey the tradition. Naturally, that was the end of the kingdom.

The grandeur of Gwalior dates back to another dynasty, the Tomars, who established their rule in the fourteenth century. A Tomar king, Mansingh (1486–1516), built the Man Mandir, a six-towered palace that forms the eastern wall of the fort and one of the sights of India. About 104 meters long and 24 meters deep (300 feet by 80 feet), it is decorated with perforated screens, mosaics, floral designs, and moldings in Hindu profusion. Beneath it, two underground floors were burrowed into the 300-foot-high hill of the fort, serving as air-conditioned summer quarters for Mansingh—and dungeons for the prisoners of the Moguls who, under the rule of Akbar, seized the fort.

Captured by the Marathas in 1784, Gwalior Fort became the scene of fierce fighting again in 1857, when it was the base for 18,000 Indians who rose up against the British in the Sepoy Revolt (Indian Mutiny), the beginning of India's struggle for independence. Under Tantia Topi and a woman hero, Rani Lakshmi Bai of Jhansi, the Indians made a valiant last stand. The rani's cenotaph is in Gwalior.

Mansingh also built the Gujari Mahal, a turreted palace of stone—now the home of an archaeological museum. This palace was also built for love. The king met a Gujar maiden, Mrignayani (the "Fawn Eyed"), famed for her skill as a slayer of wild animals. She agreed to marry him only if he brought the waters of the Rai River, the secret source of her strength, into the fort. For the sake of his bride, Mansingh built the Gujari Mahal and an aqueduct linking it to the Rai.

A visit to the Gwalior Fort requires an arduous climb up to the gates (elephants, bearing royalty, once used the road, which is too steep for cars). The fort contains a mosque on the site of the shrine of Saint Gwalipa; Chaturbhuj Mandir temple housing a four-armed idol of Vishnu; and five groups of gigantic Jain sculptures carved out of rock walls. The biggest, the image of the first Jain pontiff, Adinath, is 17 meters (57 feet) high with a foot measuring about three meters (nine feet). It was constructed in 1440.

Vishnu also reigns in eleventh-century temples known as Sas Bahu (the mother-in-law and daughter-in-law temples). Another temple, the ninth-century Teli Ka Mandir with its 30-meter (100-foot) tower, is the highest building in the fort. This temple is an interesting blend of Dravidian architecture from south India, typified by the spire, with Indo-Aryan decoration on its walls. Finally, visit the Suraj Kund, the oldest Gwalior shrine, the pond that cured Suraj (Sena) Pal.

Outside the fort, Gwalior offers the tomb of Muhammad Ghaus, a Moslem saint worshiped by the Moguls, and the tomb of Tansen, one of Akbar's court musicians, which is still venerated by musicians. Lashkar, a mile from the fort, is a "modern" city built in 1809 on the site of an encampment. There you can visit two palaces, the Jai Vilas and the Moti Mahal, and a picturesque bazaar, the Inderganj Chowk. Gwalior is an ideal departure point for many other destinations within the state.

Other Sites Out of Gwalior

The medieval township of Orchha has hardly been touched by the hand of time. Lying 120 kilometers (74 miles) from Gwalior on the road to Khajuraho, Orchha is famous for its palaces and temples, built in the seventeenth century. Orchha was once the capital of the Bundela Rajputs, later under Mogul rule, and some of its palaces contain murals of the Bundela school. Particularly worth seeing is the Jahangir Mahal, a rectangular palace with eight minarets, which the Bundela raja, Bir Singh Ju Deo, built to commemorate the Emperor Jahangir's visit in the seventeenth century. See three important temples: the Chaturbhuj, Ram Raja, and Laxminarayan mandirs. The Laxminarayan Mandir has exquisite paintings that adorn the ceilings and walls of three corridors. Vibrant in color and stylization, the paintings are in an excellent state of preservation and express religious themes and historical events. The exterior of this temple is an interesting combination of temple and fort architecture.

The Madhya Pradesh State Tourism Development Corporation has converted the Sheesh Mahal into a hotel unit, giving visitors to Orchha the unique opportunity of experiencing the bygone splendor of this ancient city.

Datia, 69 kilometers (43 miles) from Gwalior, is a town whose antiquity can be traced back to the *Mahabharata*. A town of great historic significance, highlighted by a seven-storied palace built entirely of stone and brick by Raja Bir Singh Ju Deo in 1614. The palace is considered one of the finest examples of Bundela architecture in the country. Within it are some fine wall paintings of the Bundela school. The Mogul frescoes in Datia's other attraction, the imposing Gopeshwar Temple, also reveal an interesting blend of cultures.

Surrounded by forested hills and lakes, Chanderi is a craft center famous for its saris and brocades. This city, 239 kilometers (148 miles) from Gwalior, has been influenced in its architecture by the Bundela Rajputs and the sultans of Malwa. The Koshak Mahal, built on the orders of Mohammed Khilji of Malwa in 1445, has an architectural style similar to the Jahaz Mahal in Mandu. The Jama Masjid and Shahzadi Ka Rouza were also built by the Malwa sultans, as was the Battisi Bandi built in 1485 by Sultan Ghyasuddin Shah. Northwest of Chanderi is the picturesque tank and temple complex of Parameshwar Tal, built by the Bundela kings. The old city of Chanderi, which has Jain temples of the ninth and tenth centuries, remains an important center of pilgrimage.

Narwar was once the capital of Raja Nal, whose love for Damyanti has been the theme of many legends and folksongs. Narwar lies 122 kilometers (76 miles) from Gwalior. Like Gwalior, it is dominated by a magnificent fort, standing on a hill overlooking the town. The fort and Narwar's palaces are typically Rajput in style, with flat ceilings, fluted columns, and multifoil arches. Glass beads are an interesting interior embellishment.

Known as Padmavati in ancient times, Pawaya is a fascinating complex of ruins, 68 kilometers (42 miles) from Narwar on the Gwalior-Jhansi road. Pawaya's ruins still bear testimony to the days when it was the capital of the Nag Kings in A.D. 3. Particularly noteworthy is the life-size statue of Chaksha Manibhadra of A.D. 1. The ruins of the medieval fort built by the Paramars and the nearby Dhoomeshwar Mahadeo Temple are Pawaya's other attractions.

Indore

Indore, India's fourth-largest textile center, with a population of over one million, is a newcomer among cities in India. The area was given to Malhar Rao Holkar in 1733 by the Marathas Peshwas for whom he fought. While Holkar was away fighting, he left the affairs of state to his widowed daughter-in-law, Ahalyabai, whom he had saved from being a *sati*. Since her son, who was insane, died young, she became the ruler. At a time when all other states were floundering, her reign was a model of good administration.

Indore's outstanding temple is the Jain Kanch Mandir, or Glass Temple. Here every available surface is inlaid with mother-of-pearl, glass, and colored beads. Huge crystal chandeliers and carved silver tables add glitter, but paintings illustrating the dreadful punishments visited on sinners form a bizarre contrast with the scintillating interior. The ex-maharani's residence is the Manik Bagh. Guests were asked to stay in Lal Bagh, which was set in lovely grounds outside the city. The dignified old palace, with its graceful Audience Hall, is half hidden behind rows of bangle sellers on the main square of the city. The new palace is across the square. Around it the daily life of the small city carries on.

Ujjain

Ujjain, with a population of over 350,000, was described by Chandra-gupta II's court poet, Kalidasa, as "the town fallen from heaven to bring heaven to earth." Kalidasa also found "its palaces like mountains and its houses like palaces." Though the Gupta capital was Patiliputra, this was the city from where the emperor ruled for long periods. When Buddha was born, Ujjain was already a thriving city and the capital of a kingdom called Avanti. Legend goes that Shiva lived here after destroying a demon and thus Ujjain was born.

One of the four drops of heavenly nectar from the kumbh seized by Vishnu also supposedly dropped on Ujjain. Once every 12 years, millions of Hindu devotees congregate to celebrate the Kumbh Mela, the most sacred festival in the Hindu calendar. The next Kumbh Mela is January 1992.

Ujjain's literary, scientific, and religious life continued for centuries, and it was hundreds of years later that another poet was captivated enough to see it as "the very home of the golden age; paved with jewels, full of romance, with dancing girls in the temples and love in everyone's hearts." Politically, Ujjain went through swift transitions, from the hands of the Rajputs and the Moslems, to the Marath Scindias of Gwalior.

The Scindias rebuilt the Mahakaleshar, the main temple, and dedicated it to Shiva, on the ruins of an earlier one destroyed by the Moslems. To the south is Bade Ganeshki Ka Mandir, a temple dedicated to the elephant-headed god. Set in lovely seclusion is Navagraha Mandir (Temple of Nine Planets), on the road to Indore at the confluence of the Shipra and two other rivers.

According to Hindu geography, the first meridian passes through Ujjain. A legend claims that the moon and Mars were born here. Ujjain's scientific work was done in an observatory built in the eighteenth century by Sawai Jai Singh of Jaipur. It was called the Jantar Mantar. Also see Kaliadeh Palace, surrounded by the Shipra River and built in 1458, with its Persian-style central dome; and the nineteenth-century Gopal Mandir, a temple dedicated to Krishna, with a beautiful silver image of this god in its inner sanctum.

Mandu

Mandu is a celebration in stone, of life and joy, of the love of the poet-prince Baz Bahadur for his beautiful consort, Rani Roopmati. Balladeers of Malwa still sing of the romance of these royal lovers. High up on the crest of a hill, Roopmati's pavilion continues to look down on Baz Bahadur's palace—a magnificent expression of Afghan architecture.

Perched along the Vindhyan ranges, at an altitude of 610 meters (2,000 feet), Mandu, with its natural defenses, was originally the fort-capital of the Paramar rulers of Malwa. Later, toward the end of the thirteenth century, it came under the sway of the sultans of Malwa, the first of whom renamed it Shadibad, "the city of joy." And indeed, this was the pervading spirit of Mandu, with its rulers building exquisite palaces like the Jahaz and Hindola Mahals, ornamental canals, and graceful baths and pavilions. Each of Mandu's structures is an architectural gem; some are outstanding, like the massive Jami Masjid and Houshang Shah's Tomb, which inspired the builders of the Taj Mahal centuries later. Under Mogul rule, Mandu was a pleasure resort, its lakes and palaces the scenes of splendid and extravagant festivities. The glory of Mandu lives on, in its palaces, mosques, legends, and songs chronicled for posterity.

Twelve gateways punctuate the 45-kilometer (28-mile) parapet of walls that encircle Mandu. Most notable of these is the Delhi Darwaza, the main entrance to the fortress city, approached through a series of well-fortified gateways with walled enclosures and strengthened by bastions, such as the Alamgir, Kamani, Bhangi Barwaza, and Gadi gates, through which the present road passes.

Those with an appetite for royal architecture can feast on the following:

Jahaz Mahal. This 120-meter (394-foot)-long "ship palace," built between the two artificial lakes, Munj Talao and Kapur Talao, is an elegant two-story palace. It was probably built by Sultan Ghyas-ud-din Khalji for his large harem. With its open pavilions, balconies overhanging the water, and open terrace, the Jahaz Mahal is an imaginative re-creation in stone of a royal pleasure craft. Viewed on moonlit nights from the adjoining Taveli Mahal, the silhouette of the building, with the tiny domes and turrets of the pavilion gracefully perched on the terrace, is an unforgettable spectacle.

Hindola Mahal. An audience hall also from Ghiyas-ud-din's reign, this structure derives the name of "Swinging Palace" from its sloping sidewalls. Superb and innovative techniques are also evident in its ornamental façade: delicate trellis work in beautifully moulded sandstone columns. To the west of Hindola Mahal stand several unidentified buildings that still bear traces of past grandeur. Note the elaborately constructed wall called Champa Baoli that is connected to underground vaulted rooms in which cold and hot water were once available. Other places of interest in this enclave are Dilawar Khan's mosque, the Nahar Jharokha (tiger balcony), Taveli Mahal, and two large wells called the Ujali (bright) and Andheri (dark).

Ashrafi Mahal. This "palace of gold coins," which faces the Jama Masjid, was built by Hoshang Shah's successor, Mahmud Shah Khilji. Conceived as an academic institution (*madrassa*) for young boys, the study cells still remain in a fair state of preservation. In the same complex, Khilji built a seven-story tower to celebrate his victory over Rana Khumba of Mewar; only one story survives. The tomb, intended to be the largest structure in Mandu, is also in ruins.

Baz Bahadur's Palace. Built in the sixteenth century, the palace's unique features include a spacious courtyard surrounded by halls and high terraces that afford a superb view of the surrounding countryside.

Nilkanth Mahal. This palace, which belongs to the Mogul Era, was constructed as a pleasure resort for Akbar's Hindu wife. On the walls are inscriptions, written during Akbar's time, that refer to the futility of earthly pomp and glory.

Hoshang Shah's Tomb. India's first marble edifice is a refined example of Afghan architecture. Examine the magnificently proportioned dome, marble latticework of remarkable delicacy, and porticoed courts and towers that mark each corner of the rectangle. Shah Jahan sent four of his greatest architects to study the tomb's design. Among them was Ustad Hamid, who has been linked to the construction of Shah Jahan's Taj Mahal.

MANDU FORT
(NOT TO SCALE)

HILL
RIVER
ROAD
RAMPART
WATER TANK

N

GATE

TOURIST BUNGALOW

RAMPOL GATE

CHISTI KHANS PALACE

DELHI GATE

ALAMGIR GATE

BHANGI GATE

UJALA BAOLI

JAHAZ MAHAL

TAWELI MAHAL

RAM MANDAR

LALKOT

SURAJ TALAO

HINDOLA MAHAL

MUNJA TALAO

ASHRAFI MAHAL

JAMI MASJID

HOSHANG'S TOMB

LOHANI GATE

JAIN MANDAR

EK THAMBA

CHOR KOTO

CHHAPPAN MAHAL

DARYA KHAN'S TOMB

HATHI MAHAL

LAL BUNGALOW

LAL SARAI

MALIK MUGHITH'S MOSQUE

BAIHAN KAMAHAL

DAI KA MAHAL

ECHO POINT

SAGAR TALAO

NILKANTH

JALI MAHAL

REWA KUND

BAZ BAHADUR'S PALACE

BHAGWANIYA GATE

RUPMATIS PAVILION

SONGARH

TARAPUR GATE

Jami Masjid. The great mosque of Damascus inspired the Jami Masjid, conceived on a grand scale with a high plinth and a huge domed porch projecting into the center. Similar imposing domes with seemingly innumerable domes filling the intervening space dominate the background. Most visitors are immediately struck by the vastness of the building and the simplicity of its construction. The great court of the mosque is enclosed by huge colonnades with a rich and pleasing variety of arches, pillars, number of bays, and domes above.

Roopmati's Pavilion. This graceful pavilion was originally built as an army observation post and later served as a retreat for the queen. From its hilltop perch, the queen could see Baz Bahadur's palace and the Narmada flowing through the Nimar plains far below.

Hathi Mahal, Darya Khan's Tomb, Dai ka Maha, Malik Mughith's Mosque, and Jali Mahal are some of Mandu's other fascinating monuments. Also visit Echo Point, the "Delphic Oracle" of Mandu, where a shout reverberates some distance and is clearly heard back.

The Lohani caves and temple ruins, not far from the royal enclave, also merit a visit. While you are there, pause at Sunset Point, in front of the caves. From here, you'll have a panoramic view of the surrounding countryside.

Omkareshwar

Omkareshwar, the sacred island, is shaped like the holiest of all Hindu symbols, *Om,* and has drawn a hundred generations of pilgrims. Here, at the confluence of the rivers Narmada and Kaveri, the devout have gathered to kneel at the temple of Shri Omkar Mandhata. And here, as in so many of Madhya Pradesh's sacred shrines, the works of nature complement those of man to provide an awe-inspiring setting.

Shri Omkar Mandhata Temple stands on a small island that has been formed by the fork of the Narmada. Constructed of pliant soft-stone, the temple is exquisitely carved. Note especially the friezes on the upper portion of the roof. Encircling the shrine are verandas with columns that are carved in circles, polygons, and squares.

The Siddhnath Temple is a fine example of early medieval Brahmanic architecture. Its unique feature is a frieze of elephants, carved on a stone slab, at its outer perimeter. Twenty-four Avators, a cluster of Hindu and Jain temples, are remarkable for their skillful use of varied architectural modes.

Maheshwar

Called Mahishmati when it was the capital of King Kartvirarjun, Maheshwar, 91 kilometers (56 miles) from Indore, was a glorious city in the dawn of Indian civilization. This temple town on the banks of the Narmada was mentioned in the *Ramayana* and *Mahabharata.* Revived to its ancient position by the Holkar queen Rani Ahilyabai of Indore, Maheshwar's temples and mighty fort-complex stand in quiet beauty, mirrored in the river below.

A life-size statue of Rani Ahilyabai sits on a throne in the Rajgaddi within the fort complex. This is the right place to begin a tour of Maheshwar, for this pious and wise queen was the architect of its revived importance. Other fascinating relics and heirlooms of the Holkar dynasty can be seen in rooms that are open to the public. Within the complex is an exquisite small shrine that is the starting point of the ancient Dussehra ceremony still enacted today.

Peshwa Ghat, Fanase Ghat, and Ahilya Ghat line the river Narmada. Their steps lead down from the sandy banks to the river. Throughout the day, you can see a kaleidoscope of rural India in the pilgrims and holy men who sit at the ghats in silent meditation, in the rows of graceful women who carry gleaming brass pots down to the holy (life-giving) river, and in the ferry loads of villagers who cross and recross these surging waters. Lining the banks, too, are poignant stone memorials to the *satis* of Maheshwar, who perished on the funeral pyres of their husbands.

Crowned by soaring spires, the many-tiered temples of Maheshwar are distinguished by their carved overhanging balconies and their intricately worked doorways.

Maheshwari saris are renowned throughout India for their unique weave, introduced 250 years ago by Rani Ahilyabai. Woven mostly in cotton, the typical Maheshwari sari has a plain body and sometimes stripes or checks in several variations. The mat border designs have a wide range in leaf and floral patterns.

Jabalpur

A pleasure resort and the capital of the Gond Kings during the twelfth century, Jabalpur, in the center of the state, was later the seat of the Kalchuri dynasty. The Marathas held sway over Jabalpur until 1817, when the British wrested it from them and left their impression on the spacious cantonment with its colonial residences and barracks. Today, Jabalpur is an important administrative center bustling with commercial activity. The places of interest in Jabalpur are Madan Mahal Fort, Sangram Sagar and Bajnamath, the Rani Durgavati Memorial and Museum, and the Tilwara Ghat from where Mahatma Gandhi ashes were immersed in the Narmada. Also of interest are the twelfth-century Mala Devi Mandir, Pisan Hari Jain Temples, and Roopnath. Jabalpur is the most convenient base for visits to the famous Kanha (173 kilometers) and Bandhavgarh (194 kilometers) national parks.

Marble Rocks

Marble Rocks, soaring in glittering splendor, rise to 30 meters (100 feet) on either side of the Narmada River, creating a scene of cool serenity. In his *Highlands of Central India,* Captain J. Forsyth speaks eloquently about the infinitely varied beauty of the rocks:

The eye never wearies of the effect produced by the broken and reflected sunlight, now glancing from a pinnacle of snow-white marble reared against the deep blue of the sky as from a point of silver; touching here and there with bright lights the prominences of the middle heights; and again losing itself in the soft bluish greys of their recesses.

Boating facilities are available from November to May, and the recent installation of floodlights adds a new dimension to their splendor at night. The Narmada, making its way through the rocks, narrows down and then plunges in a waterfall known as Dhuandhar, or the smoke cascade. The falls and the breaking of the water at the crest present an awesome spectacle.

Situated atop a hillock and approached by a long flight of steps, the Chausath Yogini Temple commands a singularly beautiful sight of the Narmada flowing through the Marble Rocks. Dedicated to goddess Durga, this tenth-century temple has exquisitely carved stone figures of deities belonging to the Kalchuri period. According to a local legend, this ancient temple is connected to the Gond Queen Durgavati's palace through an underground passage.

Satpura Mountain Range Retreat

Pachmarhi, 210 kilometers (130 miles) from Bhopal and set in the Satpura Mountains, is Madhya Pradesh's premiere Hill Station. Don't expect big crowds or an abundance of hotels; this little village is still a quiet getaway, with enjoyable walks that lead to good views as well as some interesting historic caves. You can explore the Pandav Caves, where the five Pandava brothers of the *Mahabharata* epic supposedly spent some time, and numerous cave shelters filled with old paintings.

PRACTICAL INFORMATION FOR
MADHYA PRADESH

WHEN TO GO. The temperature and weather are ideal for visits from mid-October to mid-March. The monsoon brings heavy rain from mid-June to September. The best viewing time in the national parks is February–June; they're closed from July to Oct. 31.

HOW TO GET THERE. By Air. From Bhubaneshwar, *Indian Airlines* flies daily to Bhopal and Raipur. From Delhi, Indian Airlines flies daily to Bhopal, Indore, and Gwalior. From Bombay, Indian Airlines flies daily to Indore and three times a week to Bhopal and Gwalior. *Vayudoot* flies three times a week to Bhopal from Jaipur. To Indore, it flies six times a week from Bombay and three times a week from Kota, Jaipur, and Nagpur.

By Bus. For information on deluxe buses from Bombay to Indore, see the Bombay chapter. To reach Gwalior by deluxe bus from Delhi, Agra, and Jaipur, see those chapters. A bus trip from any other Indian state to Bhopal, which is in the center of this large state, involves a long journey; it's not recommended. For bus information in Bhopal, contact Bhopal Bus Stand, tel. 54081; in Indore or Gwalior, contact MPSTDC.

By Train. Bhopal and Gwalior are on the Bombay–Delhi and Madras–Delhi line of the Central Railway. They're easily accessible from Bombay and Delhi. *Shatabdi Express* is your best bet from Delhi. *Punjab Mail, Dadar Express,* and *Jhellum Express* are the best options from Bombay; they're also good for Delhi. The best trains to Indore from Bombay and Delhi are the *Malway Express* and *Punjab Mail.* For train information and reservations in Bombay or Delhi, see those chapters. In Bhopal, contact Bhopal Railway Station, tel. 540170 and 550001–3; in Gwalior, contact Gwalior Railway Station, tel. 25306 or 22544; in Indore, contact Indore Railway Station, tel. 36185 or 23284–86. If you travel overnight, remember to reserve a sleeping berth.

By Rented Car with Driver. Bhopal is on National Highway 12. Here are some important distances from Bhopal: Delhi, 741 km (459 mi.); Bombay, 789 km (489 mi.); Hyderabad, 813 km (504 mi.); Ahmedabad, 571 km (354 mi.). Gwalior is on National Highway 3 and is 119 km (74 mi.) from Agra, 321 km (199 mi.) from Delhi, and 338 km (210 mi.) from Jaipur. Indore is on National Highways 12 and 3 and is 602 km (373 mi.) from Bombay, 806 km (500 mi.) from Delhi, and 803 km (498 mi.) from Hyderabad. Hire a car from a tour operator recommended below. If you're coming from outside Madhya Pradesh, refer to this same listing in that state chapter. In M.P., a rented car with driver should cost about Rs. 4 per km, with a halt charge of Rs. 50–Rs. 100 per night.

TOURIST INFORMATION. *The Madhya Pradesh State Tourism Development Corporation* (MPSTDC) is extremely helpful and has excellent brochures and maps.

The head office is in Bhopal 4th Floor, Gangotri, T.T. Nagar; tel. 66383 and 64388; open 10:30 A.M.–5:30 P.M., closed Sundays. MPSTDC also has offices in the following destinations (same hours):

Gwalior. Motel Tansen, 6 Gandhi Rd.; tel. 21568

Indore. Tourist Bungalow, behind Ravindra Natya Griha; tel. 3888

Jabalpur. Railway Station; tel. 23163.

Jhansi (in nearby Uttar Pradesh). Railway Station; no phone.

Pachmarhi. Amaltas, near Tehsil; tel. 100.

Raipur. Railway Station; tel. 23163.

Satna. Railway Station; tel. 3241.

Ujjain. Shipra Motel; tel. 4862.

FOREIGN CURRENCY EXCHANGE. Most Western-style hotels have money-exchange counters. Otherwise, go to a branch of the *State Bank of India,* open Monday–Friday, 10 A.M.–2 P.M.; Saturday, till noon. In Bhopal, the State Bank of India in New Market is also open Monday–Saturday, 3:30–8 P.M.

ACCOMMODATIONS. While only the big cities and a few smaller destinations in M.P. have private hotels, MPSTDC does have a network of extremely nice accommodations that are also good value, with breakfast included in the room price. To reserve a room more than five days in advance, contact Central Reservations, MPSTDC in Bhopal (address above). Less than five days in advance, contact the manager of each unit. Include a 50 percent deposit (about Rs. 175 per double per night). Prices are based on double occupancy and exclude taxes: *Expensive,* Rs. 950–Rs. 1,450; *Moderate,* Rs. 500–Rs. 950; *Inexpensive,* under Rs. 500. Some Western-style hotels take major credit cards.

BANDHAVGARH

Inexpensive

White Tiger Forest Lodge. Bandhavgarh National Park. Reservations: MPSTDC; tel. 66383 in Bhopal. 11 cottages; each has 2 units with attached bath. This cluster of thatch-roofed cottages set on pillars is adjacent to the park. Ethnic-style interiors have clay walls, tile floors, and modern furnishings. All rooms are extremely clean and offer fans. Some rooms are air-conditioned. Room service, Indian- and Continental-cuisine restaurant, bar, jeep and elephant safaris. Closed July 1–Oct. 31. Rupees only.

GWALIOR

Expensive

Welcomgroup Usha Kiran Palace. Jyendraganj, Lashkar, Gwalior; tel. 23453. 27 rooms with bath. The former guest house of the Gwalior Maharajah is now an appealing hotel, with his stylish furnishings still adorning the rooms. Don't think grand, but do expect good comfort. Some rooms are air-conditioned; all rooms have fans. Room service, multicuisine restaurant, bar, billiards, buggy rides, elephant rides and golfing on request, travel agency, foreign-exchange counter. AE, DC, MC, V.

Inexpensive

Motel Tansen. 6 Gandhi Rd., Gwalior; tel. 21568. 36 rooms with bath. A modern two-story MPSTDC hotel, the rooms are spacious and clean, with Western-style decor. All rooms have fans; some are air-conditioned. Room service, Indian- and limited Continental-cuisine restaurant, bar, car-rental service, MPSTDC office. Rupees only.

BHOPAL

Moderate

Hotel Lake View Ashok. Shamla Hills, Bhopal; tel. 541600. 45 rooms with bath. This "deluxe" Western-style hotel, jointly run by Ashok and MPSTDC, sits on a hill overlooking the lake. Air-conditioned spacious rooms have a modern decor and small balconies that offer good views. TV, room service, multicuisine restaurant, bar, baby-sitters, doctor, secretarial service, shopping arcade, foreign-exchange counter, travel agency. Good value. AE, DC, MC, V.

Jehan Numa Palace Hotel. Shamla Hills, Bhopal; tel. 540100. 61 rooms with bath. Once the secretariat of a Moslem nawab, this lovely two-story palace, with a new wing that architecturally fits in, is now a hotel. The marble lobby (with a stuffed tiger) opens into an inviting interior courtyard. The two upper-floor rooms are best, with spacious private verandas and period furnishings. In the other rooms, which have modernish furnishings, you lose all sense of the palace once you close your door. TV, air-conditioning, room service, multicuisine restaurant, travel counter, foreign-exchange counter, gift shop. AE, DC, MC, V.

Inexpensive

Hotel Palash. Bhopal; tel. 553006. 33 rooms with bath. This new MPSTDC Western-style hotel has a spacious lobby and decent rooms with modern decor and balconies. Best rooms are air-conditioned; all rooms have overhead fans. TV, room service, multicuisine restaurant, bar, car-rental service. MC, V.

Hotel Panchanan. New Market, Bhopal; tel. 551647. 5 rooms with bath. On the upper floor of a nondescript high rise, this MPSTDC hotel has clean, air-conditioned rooms with modern decor and good views of Bhopal. TV, room service, Indian- and Continental-cuisine restaurant, bar, car-rental service. Rupees only.

INDORE

Inexpensive

Indotels Manor House. A.B. Rd., Indore; tel. 32121. 66 rooms with bath. Indore's fanciest hotel has a pretty lobby, with lots of marble. Executive rooms are more spacious than the ordinary doubles; both offer an attractive contemporary decor. Included are air-conditioning, TV, room service, multicuisine restaurant, bar, secretarial service, foreign-exchange counter. AE, DC, MC, V.

Hotel Surya. 5/5 Nath Mandir Rd., Indore; tel. 38465. 28 rooms with bath. This small high rise has an intimate lobby and offers air-conditioned VIP rooms in various decors that range from garish, with lots of chrome and leather, to quietly modern. Other air-conditioned rooms have a subdued contemporary decor and balconies with street views. Both options provide TV. Ordinary rooms are not air-conditioned. Room service, multicuisine restaurant, bar. Good service. Rupees only.

JABALPUR

Inexpensive

Hotel Kalchuri. Near Circuit House No. 2, Jabalpur; tel. 27411. 30 rooms with bath. This new MPSTDC Western-style hotel has clean, spacious rooms with a modern decor. Some rooms are air-conditioned; all rooms have fans. Room service, Indian- and limited Continental-cuisine restaurant, bar, car-rental service. Rupees only.

KANHA NATIONAL PARK

Inexpensive

Baghira Log Huts. Kisli, Kanha National Park; no phone. 16 rooms with bath. Surrounded by dense forest and near the Kisli Entry Gate, this cluster of rustic

MPSTDC log huts, with thatched-roofs, is perfect for its location. Room interiors have lots of wood trim; modern, clean furnishings; and offer good privacy. There are overhead fans, room service, Indian- and limited Continental-cuisine restaurant, car-rental service, jeep and elephant safaris. Closed July 1–Oct. 31. Rupees only.

Kanha Safari Lodge. Mukki, Kanha National Park; no phone. 30 rooms with bath. Set on the Banzar River, near the Mukki Entrance Gate, this three-story facility is less remote; rooms have an appealing modern decor. Some rooms are air-conditioned; all rooms have overhead fans. Room service, Indian- and limited Continental-cuisine restaurant, bar, jeep and elephant safaris, car-rental service, river swimming and fishing (bring your own equipment). Closed July 1–Oct. 31. Rupees only.

MANDU

Inexpensive

Tourist Cottages. Roopmati Rd., Mandu; tel. 35. 10 cottages; each has 2 units with attached bath. These MPSTDC cottages, set on nice grounds, offer privacy and clean, large rooms with a Western-style decor. Some rooms are air-conditioned; all rooms have fans. There is also a pleasant and informal open-air restaurant with Indian and limited Continental cuisines, room service, and a bar. Rupees only.

Traveller's Lodge. Mandu; tel. 21. 8 rooms with bath. Consider this older two-story MPSTDC bungalow the second option in Mandu. Air-cooled rooms are clean, with Western-style decor. An Indian- and limited Continental-cuisine restaurant provides room service. Rupees only.

ORCHHA

Inexpensive

Sheesh Mahal. Orchha; tel. 24. 8 rooms with bath. This MPSTDC hotel is part of an impressive medieval palace complex set on a bluff. While the furnishings are very simple, verging on rustic, the rooms are clean and spacious, with delightful Mogul touches in the architecture. Upper-floor rooms, including the suite, have spectacular views of the quiet, monument-strewn village. Room service, Indian- and limited Continental-cuisine restaurant. Rupees only.

PACHMARHI

Inexpensive

Satpura Retreat. Pachmarhi; tel. 97. 6 rooms with bath. This former British bungalow, now an MPSTDC hotel, has a tile roof and sweeping verandas that offer good mountain views. Air-cooled rooms are spacious, with simple period furnishings. The sitting room and dining room are also old-timey and delightful. Room service, Indian- and limited Continental-cuisine restaurant, car-rental service. Rupees only.

SAGAR

Inexpensive

Tourist Bungalow. Near Rest House, Cantonment, Sagar; tel. 3402. 5 rooms with bath. This MPSTDC hotel is a good stopover between Bhopal and Khajuraho or Shivpuri. Air-cooled rooms are spacious and clean, with Western-style decor. Room service is provided by an Indian- and limited Continental-cuisine restaurant. Rupees only.

SANCHI

Inexpensive

Tourist Cafeteria. Sanchi; tel. 43. 2 rooms with bath. This new MPSTDC set-up, near the monuments, has clean, air-cooled rooms, with simple modern decor. Room service, Indian- and limited Continental-cuisine restaurant. Rupees only.

Traveller's Lodge. Sanchi; tel. 23. 8 rooms with bath. Also run by MPSTDC, this older bungalow has clean, spacious rooms with Western-style decor that open onto a courtyard. Some rooms are air-conditioned; all rooms have overhead fans. Room service, Indian- and limited Continental-cuisine restaurant. Rupees only.

SHIVPURI

Inexpensive

Tourist Village. Near Bhadaiya Kund, Shivpuri; tel. 2600. 20 cottages with bath. This delightful MPSTDC complex has an attractive reception and dining hall, and pleasant grounds next to the Madhav National Park and a small lake. You stay in immaculate cottages with red-tile roofs and a modern ethnic decor: simple *dhurris* (rugs) and bamboo rugs, jute and bamboo chairs, electric lanterns. All cottages have overhead fans, good views, and privacy; some cottages have air-conditioning. Room service, multicuisine restaurant, bar, TV lounge; a handicrafts shop is planned. Rupees only.

UJJAIN

Inexpensive

Shipra Motel. Ujjain; tel. 4862. 30 rooms with bath. This new MPSTDC Western-style motel, scheduled to open in late 1990, offers modern-decor rooms. Some rooms are air-conditioned; all rooms have overhead fans. Room service, Indian- and limited Continental-cuisine restaurant, bar, car-rental service. Rupees only.

DINING OUT. Good private restaurants are rare in Madhya Pradesh; the best places to eat are in the hotels. While we include only the best options, most of the accommodations listed above have restaurants. Breakfast is usually served 7:30–10; lunch, noon–3; and dinner, 7–10. The restaurants listed below are informal and, unless noted, are open for all three meals and don't require reservations. Prices, based on one person eating a three-course meal, excluding taxes, tip, or beverage, are: *Expensive,* Rs. 80–Rs. 120; *Moderate,* Rs. 40–Rs. 80; *Inexpensive,* under Rs. 40. Most Western-style hotels accept credit cards.

BHOPAL

Expensive

Garden Barbecue. Jehan Numa Palace Hotel, Shamla Hills; tel. 540100. With a non-working but beautiful marble fountain, towering mango tree, and flowers, this courtyard restaurant is enchanting. You can choose from Continental, Chinese, or Indian cuisines. Try the chicken Bhopal *rizali* (chicken cooked in melon seeds and garnished with coriander) or delicious barbecue items. Open October–February, 1–3 P.M. and 7:30–10:30 P.M.; it's open just for dinner during other months. Dinner reservations advised. AE, DC, MC, V.

Moderate

Kinara. Hotel Lake View Ashok, Shamla Hills; tel. 541600. In this modern-decor restaurant, with a bank of windows overlooking the lake, you can enjoy extremely good Continental and Indian cuisines, including princely dishes from Madyha Pradesh. Try the *mans ka soola* (beaten and marinated mutton cooked in a tandoori) or the *kebab-e-murgh* (whole chicken with the breast stuffed with coriander, fruit, and chilis, then cooked in the tandoori). Dinner reservations advised. Open 7–10 A.M., 1–3 P.M., and 7:30–10:30 P.M. AE, DC, MC, V.

Inexpensive

Gagan Restaurant. Hotel Panchanan, New Market; tel. 551647. Its name means sky, and that explains the blue-and-white decor in this cozy, very informal restaurant on the sixth floor of a high rise. The chef serves Indian and Continental dishes, especially good fish and chips, and the night view of Bhopal is the best you'll find in the city. Open 7–10 A.M., 1–3:30 P.M., and 7:30–10:30 P.M. AE, DC, MC, V.

INDORE

Expensive

Three Seasons. Indotels Manor House, A.B. Rd.; tel. 32121. The decor at Three Seasons is elegant, with candlelight by night. The chef serves Continental, Chinese, and Indian dishes. Try the Chinese smoked chicken with red peppers, the good tandoori items, or *navratan* curry (nine vegetables cooked in a coconut-flavored curry). Scheduled for renovation. Dinner reservations advised. Open 7–10 A.M., 12–3 P.M., and 7–11 P.M. AE, DC, MC, V.

Moderate

Surya Restaurant. 5/5 Nath Mandir Rd., behind the hotel; tel. 38465. The decor of this upstairs restaurant features lots of chrome and mirrors, but subdued lighting cuts the glare and the food is good. Choose from Chinese, Continental, and Indian cuisines. Try the *murgh musalman* for two (roasted chicken stuffed with dried fruits and spices) or the Surya special vegetables (mixed vegetables cooked in a dry curry). Dinner reservations advised. Open 8–11 A.M., 1–4 P.M., and 7–11 P.M. Rupees only.

SWEETS AND TREATS. Bhopal. For good Western-style snacks served in a pretty environment, stop at the *Garden Barbecue,* Jehan Numa Palace, Shamla Hills, between 3:30 and 7:30 P.M. **Indore.** For good Indian-style snacks, go to *Surya Restaurant,* 5/5 Nath Mandir Rd., between 4 and 7 P.M.

HOW TO GET AROUND. From the Airports. The Bhopal and Gwalior airports are 11 km (7 mi.) from the city. The Indore airport is 9 km (6 mi.) from the city. You can take a taxi (Rs. 3.30 per km) or auto rickshaw (Rs. 2 per km).

By Plane. From Bhopal, *Indian Airlines* flies three times a week to Gwalior and Indore and daily to Raipur. From Gwalior, Indian Airlines flies three times a week to Bhopal and Indore. From Indore, Indian Airlines flies three times a week to Bhopal and Gwalior. *Vayudoot* flies a few times each week between Bhopal and Raipur, Bhopal and Jabalpur, Bhopal and Indore, and Jabalpur and Raipur.

By Bus. Buses are crowded and slow-going, but they do travel throughout the state. For bus information in Bhopal, contact Bhopal Bus Stand, tel. 54081; in Indore and Gwalior, contact MPSTDC, tel. 3888 in Indore and 21568 in Gwalior.

By Rented Car and Driver. Fairly good roads run through M.P. Here are some important distances from Bhopal: Sanchi, 60 km (37 mi.); Indore, 186 km (115 mi.); Ujjain, 189 km (117 mi.); Mandu, 290 km (180 mi.); Khajuraho, 387 km (240 mi.); Gwalior, 422 km (262 mi.); Kanha, 540 km (335 mi.). In M.P., a rented car with driver should cost about Rs. 4 per km, with a halt charge of Rs. 50–Rs. 100 per night. Hire a car from a tour operator listed below.

By Taxi. Taxis should cost about Rs. 3.30 per km. If the driver won't use his meter, set the fare beforehand.

By Auto Rickshaw. Figure about Rs. 2 per km. Again, if the meter is "broken" or absent, set the fare in advance.

TOURS. MPSTDC offers comprehensive bus tours of Madhya Pradesh that start in Calcutta, Bombay, and Delhi, with arrival in M.P. by train. Contact MPSTDC in Bhopal (tel. 66383) for details. MPSTDC does not offer any tours once you arrive in M.P.

TOUR OPERATORS. For all your travel needs, contact *Radiant Travels,* Maharana Pratap Nagar, Bhopal, M.P.; tel. 554773 or 540817. Also see Special-Interest

Tours in *Facts at Your Fingertips* for the names of India-based agencies that can create a special trip in M.P.

SEASONAL EVENTS. Since the lunar calendar determines most events, contact the Government of India Tourist Office for exact dates.

January–February. *Vasant Panchami.* This festival honors Saraswati, the Hindu goddess of learning, with lots of kites flying in the air. It's also a popular time to marry.

February. *Shivratri.* Hindu devotees worship Shiva and sing sacred songs in important Shiva temples.

February–March. *Holi.* During this boisterous festival that celebrates the start of spring, people throw red colored water on everyone. Wear old clothes.

September–October. *Dussehra.* This 10-day event celebrates the victory of good over evil and honors Durga, the Hindu goddess. On the 10th day, effigies of Ravana, the demon and embodiment of evil, are ignited.

October–November. *Diwali.* This festival marks the start of the Hindu New Year. Candles, welcoming the Goddess Lakshmi (Goddess of Wealth), light up most homes. Lots of firecrackers.

December. *Thansen Music Festival.* Gwalior honors Akbar's great musician, Miya Thansen, with days of wonderful music performances by India's top talents. A great treat!

HISTORIC SITES. Entrance to monuments is generally free or nominal in cost; where a donation is asked, a few rupees will suffice. Historic sites are open daily sunrise to sunset. For more details about Mandi and Sanchi, refer to the introductory essay above.

BHOJPUR

Bhojeshwar Temple, an exquisite eleventh-century shrine dedicated to Shiva, contains numerous Shiva images and temples built into its walls. The Shiva linga in the inner sanctum is carved from one stone.

BHOPAL

Taj-ul-Masajid was started in the 1600s and is one of the largest mosques in India, with an impressive main hall, broad facade, and courtyard.

Jama Masjid, with lovely gold spires, was built in 1837 by Kudsia Begum, supposedly on the site of a former twelfth-century temple.

Shaukat Mahal, at the Chowk entrance, is the palatial whimsy of a Frenchman, who incorporated numerous architectural styles: Occidental, post-Renaissance, and Gothic.

Sadar Manzil, also at the Chowk entrance, was the Hall of Public Audience of the former Bhopal rulers.

GWALIOR

Gwalior Fort, one of the largest Indian forts, was built in the fifteenth century by Raja Mansingh Tomar and contains numerous monuments:

Gujari Mahal was built for his queen, Mrignayani. Its beautiful interior now houses the architectural museum.

Sas Bahu Ka Mandir is an eleventh-century temple dedicated to Shiva.

Teli Ka Mandir is a ninth-century temple dedicated to Vishnu, with a Dravidian roof and an Indo-Aryan, northern India decorative exterior.

Suraj Kund is the site of the pond where Suraj Sena was cured by Saint Gwalipa, who set in motion Gwalior's illustrious history.

JABALPUR

Madan Mahal Fort, overlooking the city, was built by Raja Madan Shah in 1116.

MANDU

This historic pleasure resort of Hindu and Moslem rulers, with 12 gateways, is strewn with monuments. Here are the best.

The Tomb of Hoshang Shah (1405–1435), India's first marble edifice, is a superb example of Afghan architecture, with an exquisite dome, marble latticework, and delicate courtyards and towers. The Mogul Emperor Shah Jahan sent his builders to analyze its construction before he built the Taj Mahal.

Jami Masjid, inspired by the great mosque at Damascus, was started by Hoshang Shah and completed by Mahmud Khiki in 1454. It's considered Mandu's most impressive structure, with a huge domed porch, beautifully decorated entrances, and a roof with 61 domes.

Asharfi Mahal, facing the Jami Masjid, was called the "palace of gold coins." Now in ruins, it was once a college for young Moslem boys.

Rewa Kund, built by Moslems, is a holy lake for Hindus.

Baz Bahadur's Palace, built in the 1500s, was a pleasure retreat, with rooms on four sides of a courtyard with a beautiful cistern.

Roopmati's Pavilion was originally an army observation post before it became a retreat for Queen Roopmati.

Nilkanth Mahal, built on the site of a Hindu shrine dedicated to Shiva, was a palace built for Akbar's Hindu wife. It offers one of the best views of Mandu.

Hindola Mahal, also known as the "Swinging Palace" because of sloping walls that create the illusion of a swaying building, was probably constructed in the fifteenth century.

Jahaz Mahal, called the "ship palace," is set between two artificial lakes. The Mogul Emperor Jahangir and his wife, Nur Jehan, used to stay in this two-story architectural marvel, which was probably built in the late 1400s.

OMKARESHWAR

Shri Omkar Mandhata Temple, set on an island and dedicated to Shiva, is a unique example of early medieval Brahmanic architecture.

Twenty-Four Avatars is a complex of Hindu and Jain temples in various architectural styles.

ORCHHA

Jahangir Mahal, a rectangular palace with eight minarets, was built in the seventeenth century to commemorate a visit by this Mogul emperor.

Ram Raja Temple, a palace-turned-temple, has soaring spires and grand architectural detail. It's the only temple in India where Rama (Vishnu) is worshipped as a king.

Laxminarayan Temple. This fort-style temple has exquisite Bundela paintings covering the walls and ceiling of three halls.

Chaturbhuj Temple. Set on a massive platform, this shrine is dedicated to Vishnu.

SANCHI

Great Stupa No. 1 was started during Ashoka's reign, but was completed in the second and third centuries B.C. It contains Buddhist holy relics.

Stupa No. 2 dates back to the second century B.C. and has a well-preserved balustrade.

Stupa No. 3, a hemispheric dome surmounted by an umbrella, was built 150–140 B.C.

Ashoka Pillar dates back to the third century. Only a fragment remains.

Buddhist Vihara contains the re-enshrinement of the holy relics of two disciples of the Buddha.

MUSEUMS AND GALLERIES. Entrance is free or nominal in cost.

Bhopal. *Modern Art Center* has paintings, sculpture, and tribal artifacts. Open February–November, 2–8 P.M. and November–February, 1–7 P.M.; closed Mondays throughout the year.

Roopanker Museum of Fine Arts (Bharat Bhawan) houses works of art with special emphasis on folk and tribal art. Roopanker arranges special exhibitions, seminars, artist camps, lectures, and orientation courses in art. Open 3–9 P.M., closed Mondays.

Gwalior. *Archaeological Museum* (Gujari Mahal) has good collections of sculpture, inscriptions, metal images, terra-cotta objects and archaeological pieces, including those recovered at the ancient sites of Besnagar, Pawaya, and Ujjain. It also contains an interesting collection of coins, paintings, among them copies of frescoes from the Bagh Caves (Buddhist caves from the sixth and seventh centuries). Open 10 A.M.–5 P.M., closed Mondays. Nominal fee.

Indore. *Kendriya Sangrahalaya* contains sculpture, painting, and natural history exhibits. Open 10 A.M.–5 P.M., closed Mondays.

Sanchi. *Archaeological Museum* has antiquities recovered from the ongoing excavation. Open 9 A.M.–5 P.M.

SPORTS AND OUTDOOR ADVENTURES. Wildlife Sanctuaries. *Bandhavargh National Park* lies in the Sal Forest in the heart of the Vindhyan Mountain Range. It has a variety of wildlife, including tigers, panthers, spotted deer, sambar, barking deer, wild boar, and bison. There are also the archaeological remains of the Kalchuri period; adjacent to the remains are a large number of prehistoric caves. Vehicles and elephants are available at the Forest Lodge for touring the park. The park is closed Fridays and during the monsoon season (July–October).

Kahna National Park can be reached by a regular bus service from Jabalpur. Considered one of India's best parks, Kahna is the natural habitat of a large variety of wild animals, including tigers, panthers, sambar, cheetahs, black bucks, and barking deer. Vehicles and elephants are available at the tourist lodge for touring the park. The park is closed Mondays and during the monsoon season (July–October).

SHOPPING. There are lots of good handicrafts in Madhya Pradesh, where craftsmen have kept alive skills and traditions that go back hundreds of years. Small shops in bazaars and government-operated stores are located in practically each city and town, displaying handwoven brocades of Chanderi and Naheswar and *kosa* silks of Raigarh, along with leather toys and exquisitely wrought metal bells. Other specialties include silver jewelery, lacquer bangles, golden-thread embroidery, marble ashtrays, and boxes, and beaded tapestries of gods and goddesses.

Bhophal has a fascinating old *Chowk* (bazaar), where you can look for interesting silver tribal jewelry and lovely handlooms. Rupees only. Bargain! Bazaars are open 9:30 A.M.–7:30 P.M., closed Sundays. Also visit *Mrignayani,* near Sangam Cinema, Hamidia Road, the government-run emporium, which has all of the state's handicrafts under its roof. Open 10 A.M.–7 P.M., closed Sundays.

If you're in Mandu on a Tuesday, be sure to stroll through the weekly village market, about 8 km (5 mi.) from the historic city. It's a must stop for taking photos. Open 8 A.M.–6 P.M.

NIGHTLIFE AND BARS. The best place to have a nightcap is in your hotel. Bars are generally open 11 A.M.–10 P.M.

THE TEMPLES
OF KHAJURAHO

by
KATHLEEN COX

> Above, half seen, in the lofty gloom,
> Strange works of a long dead people loom,
> What did they mean to those who now are dust,
> These rioting figures of love and lust?
> *The Garden of Kama*

America wouldn't be discovered for 500 years; the groundwork for Chartres Cathedral wouldn't be laid for a hundred years, but in the year 1000, Central India was in its grand ascendancy, especially the region of Khajuraho, under the rule of the Chandella Rajputs. The Chandellas, like so many other Rajputs, traced their lineage back to the lunar god Chandra.

Chandra noticed Hemavati, the beautiful daughter of a Brahman priest, while she bathed in a moonlit pool. Hemavati's indiscretion led to her seduction, with the child of this unexpected alliance none other than Chandravarman, founder of the Chandella dynasty. Many years later, when Chandravarman came to power, his mother supposedly visited him in a dream. Build temples, she said—and build them he did, as did subsequent rulers.

During this time (A.D. 950–1050), India was the Asian Eldorado. People were rich, the land was fertile, life brimmed with pleasure. *Purdah* (the

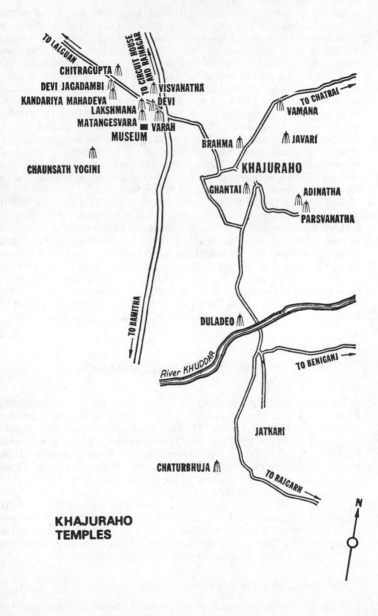

TO LALGUAN

TO CIRCUIT HOUSE AND RAJNAGAR

CHITRAGUPTA

DEVI JAGADAMBI

KANDARIYA MAHADEVA

LAKSHMANA

MATANGESVARA

MUSEUM

VARAH

CHAUNSATH YOGINI

VISVANATHA

DEVI

BRAHMA

TO CHATRAI

VAMANA

JAVARÍ

KHAJURAHO

GHANTAI

ADINATHA

PARSVANATHA

TO BAMITHA

DULADEO

River KHUDDAR

TO BENIGANJ

JATKARI

CHATURBHUJA

TO RAJGARH

N

KHAJURAHO
TEMPLES

seclusion of women) hadn't yet cast its inhibiting pall on all the joy. Everyone lived the tenth-century-style good time: trooping off to fairs, feasts, hunts, dramas, music, and dancing.

All this untroubled abundance provided the perfect climate for creativity, with temple building emerging as the major form of expression. No strict boundaries existed between the sacred and the profane. The temple was the house of god, meeting hall, neighborhood social club, and gossip center. Offerings of the faithful filled the Rajput's coffers, and he, in turn, provided for his people, overseeing the construction of more temples—a happy, nonvicious cycle that led to the creation of 85 temples in a hundred years. And everyone of them was built at a time when architects and sculptors had passed through the classic and mannerist stages into the flamboyant baroque, the zenith of artistic power under the Chandellas.

What did these sculptors choose to represent on the temples that clustered around the now-tranquil village called Khajuraho? God, as the Hindu understands Him—Shiva, Vishnu, Brahma—and the Jainist saints that are all lavishly honored. But, despite the interest in heaven, the real focus was more earthbound, rooted in the facts of life.

And not just the hunt and war, feasting, music, and dancing, but the side of life that many Westerners discuss only in whispers. Here, portrayed with no false modesty and even less prudery, virile men and voluptuous women, immortalized in stone, cavort in the most intimate and extraordinarily erotic postures. To call these sculptures "pornography" is irrelevant. Although some of the decorative sculpture might be too revealing for the excessively innocent or too titillating for the sexually adventurous, most adults will be fascinated by what they see. Here is the best of Hindu sculpture: sinuous, twisting forms; human and divine, throbbing with life, tension, and conflict. Here, every carving exudes consummate skill.

EXPLORING KHAJURAHO

The small village of Khajuraho is in the Chattarpur district of Madhya Pradesh in North-Central India. It's hard to imagine that this rural area was ever politically important. The only significant river is some distance away, and the village itself seems far removed from any kind of substantial economic activity. Yet in this remote area, the Chandellas placed their temples—some monumental, some small. Over their small corner of rich civilization, in which people adored the gods and the gods showered their blessings on people, this dynasty reigned for five centuries until history, which rarely shows any regard for human happiness, intervened. The Chandella kingdom, which gave all its energies to enjoying life, succumbed to invaders of a stronger moral fiber. In the year 1100, Mahmud the Turk began the Holy War against the "idolaters" of India. By 1200, the sultans of Delhi ruled over the once-glorious Chandella domain.

The Khajuraho Temples

When you face the entrance of any of the 22 remaining Khajuraho temples, the row of ascending and separate finials looms upward, like a series of mountain peaks. The analogy is deliberate; these temples represent a highly imaginative rendering of the Himalayas, the legendary abode of the sacred gods who are worshiped within. The obvious upward movement also represents the Hindu path toward heavenly Nirvana: one first fulfills material obligations (the lowest peak), then social obligations, and then religious ones until one finally reaches the highest station and total peace, or nirvana. Also notice the placement of exterior carvings. That, too, is intentional. Human forms dominate the lower half, with abstract design— god's play—relegated to the celestial top.

The Khajuraho temples are of the Indo-Aryan type and are generally classified as *Nagara* or North Indian. But they have definite features that set them apart; indeed, no others like them exist in any part of India. Though dedicated to different deities (Shiva, Vishnu, or the Jain Tirthankaras—"perfect souls"), the general outline remains the same.

Each temple stands on a high platform and without the customary enclosure. The larger shrines (at least one in each group) have a central sanctuary for the honored god and one more at each corner for the lesser deities. The floor plan is divided into five distinct sections (three in the smaller temples). The appearance resembles a cross with two sets of arms. The visitor enters through the portico (*ardhamandapa*) into the assembly hall (*mandapa*), which leads to the sanctum where the idol is enshrined. There is a vestibule (*antarala*) to cross and then finally the *garbhagriha,* or cell-shaped sanctum. Around this shrine is the ambulatory or processional passage (*pradakshinapatha*). The smaller temples omit this last feature and the assembly hall. But the most noteworthy aspect of the Khajuraho temple is the *shikhara* (spire) surrounded and flanked by countless sister towers that push each other heavenward.

Although the floor plan and the silhouette of the temples are unique and noteworthy, the eye rightfully focuses on the soaring vertical lines that are beautifully balanced by two or three horizontal bands that are covered with hundreds and hundreds of sculptured figures—gods and goddesses, celestial nymphs and handmaidens (*apsaras* and *surasundaris*), bold serpents and leonine beasts, and the array of human females (*nayikas*), usually made more sexy and alluring than their heavenly counterparts. And, of course, the major theme, which has given Khajuraho its reputation: the *mithuna* couples, "these rioting figures of love and lust," which, oddly enough, only account for 3–4 percent of the carvings.

How to interpret the preoccupation with the erotic? One explanation is rooted in religion, specifically the Tantric doctrine that was popular in the Chandella period. This cult, the antithesis of asceticism, emphasised the female as the dominant force of creation and taught that the senses are the equal of the spirit. The gratification of earthly desires is a step toward the attainment of nirvana. Another explanation is that the sculptors wanted to exhibit the full range of human life, which they certainly did. However, while many of the mithuna groups are explicitly carnal, others portray a wide spectrum of human emotion: jealousy, fear, modesty, and the tenderness and tranquility of love fulfilled.

Tour of the Temples

The three groups of temples cover an area of about eight square kilometers (three square miles). The Western Group is the largest and most important (the Khajuraho Archaeological Museum is located here, too). It includes the oldest (Chausath Yogini); the largest (Kandariya Mahadeo); plus the Devi Jagdambe, particularly "mithunaised." The Eastern Group, which is close to Khajuraho village, contains the Brahman and Jain shrines. The Southern Group is about two kilometers (one mile) south of the village and has only two temples, but they should be seen.

Western Group

Begin your tour with the Chausath Yogini Temple on the west side of the Shivsager Tank. The oldest temple at Khajuraho (some date it as early as A.D. 820 but 900 seems closer), it is dedicated to Kali, the goddess of wrath. Chausath means 64, which equals the number of female nymphs serving the fierce goddess. This temple is also built of granite (all the others are a pale, warm-toned sandstone), the only one oriented northeast-southwest instead of the usual north-south, and was once surrounded by 64 roofed cells for the figures of Kali's attendants, of which only 35 remain. Different in material and design, it is one of two temples at Khajuraho that does not follow the typical style.

Lalguan Mahadeva stands about a half kilometer (a third of a mile) from Chausath Yogini. This Shiva temple is in ruins and the original portico is missing, but it is of historical interest, since it is built of both granite and sandstone and represents the transition from Chausath Yogini to the later temples.

Kandariya Mahadeo is to the north of Chausath Yogini. This is the biggest and, by common consent, the best temple at Khajuraho and one of the best in India, representing the Indian "Golden Age" of temple art. Built in the typical Hindu five-shrine design, this temple is dedicated to Shiva; the inner sanctum houses a marble lingam with a four-foot circumference. The entrance archway is decorated with statues of musicians, lovers in fond embrace, crocodiles, and flying gods and goddesses. The ceilings, circles set in a square, are carved with scrolls and scallops; the pillars are ornamented with beasts and grotesque dwarfs; and flowers and pennants decorate the lintels and doorjambs of the sanctum. Outside, the three bands of sculpture around the sanctum and transept bring to life the whole galaxy of Hindu gods and goddesses, mithuna couples letting loose with every fantasy, celestial handmaidens, and lions. One art historian counted 872 statues—226 inside and 646 outside. This temple, with its imposing size, fine proportions, and inexhaustibly rich sculpture, is a high point of the Khajuraho tour.

Mahadeva Temple, also dedicated to Shiva, shares its masonry terrace with the Kandariya and the Devi Jagdambe. Although mostly in ruins, the temple still boasts a remarkable freestanding statue in the portico of a man caressing a lion.

Devi Jagdambe Temple was dedicated successively to Vishnu, Lakshmi, and then, because the scared image of the goddess is black, Kali (the goddess of wrath). It is of the three-shrine design and, from the inside, seems shaped like a cross. The third band of sculpture has a series of mithuna themes of uncensored erotica. The ceilings are similar to those of the Kandariya, and the three-headed, eight-armed statue of Shiva is one of the best cult images at Khajuraho. Over the entrance to the sanctum is a carving of Vishnu.

Chitragupta Temple lies slightly north of the Devi Jagdambe and resembles it in construction. Facing east toward the rising sun, the presiding diety is Surya, the sun god, who finds his most grandiose tribute at Konarak. The temple cell contains his five-foot-high image with his chariot and seven horses that carry him away at dusk. He is also depicted above the doorway. In the central niche to the south of the sanctum is an image of Vishnu shown with 11 heads. The central head is his own, while the others represent his numerous incarnations. A profusion of sculpture—scenes of animal combats, royal processions, masons at work, and joyous dances—depict the lavish country life of the Chandellas.

The Vishwanath and Nandi temples face each other on a common terrace to the east of Chitragupta and Devi Jagdambe. There are two staircases; the northern flanked by a pair of lions and the southern, by a pair of elephants. Since it is an important Shiva temple, the Vishwanath has a simpler extra shrine to house the god's mount, the massive and richly harnessed statue of the sacred bull Nandi. It also supposedly had two original lingams (stylized phallic symbols)—one of pure emerald, the other of simpler stone. Only one, unfortunately the less valuable, remains. The Vishwanath is similar in dedication and floor plan to its larger sister, the Kandariya, but, unlike the latter, two of the original corner shrines remain. On the outer wall of the corridor surrounding the cells is an impressive image of Brahma, the three-headed Lord of Creation, and his consort, Saraswati. On all the walls, the form of the woman dominates, portrayed in all her daily tenth-century occupations: writing a letter, holding her baby, studying her reflection in a mirror, applying makeup, or playing music. The nymphs of paradise are voluptuous and provocative; the sexy scenes, robust. An inscription states that the temple was built by Chandella King Dhanga in 1002.

Parvati Temple, near Vishwanath, is a small and relatively unimportant shrine originally dedicated to Vishnu. But the original idol was supposedly replaced by the goddess Ganga standing on a crocodile. The name Parvati (wife of Shiva) is a misnomer.

The Lakshmana Temple, though dedicated to Vishnu, is almost in all respects similar to the Vishwanath. It is also a perfect example of the fully developed five-shrine Khajuraho style, since all four shelters for the minor gods are undamaged. The ceiling of the hall is charmingly carved in shell and floral motifs. The highly decorated lintel over the entrance to the main shrine shows Lakshmi, goddess of wealth and consort of Vishnu, with Brahma, Lord of Creation (on her left) and Shiva, Lord of Destruction (on her right). The planets are depicted on a frieze above the lintel. The relief on the doorway illustrates the scene of the gods and demons churning the ocean in order to obtain a pitcher of miraculous nectar from the bottom. The gods won the ensuing 12-day battle over the pitcher, drank the nectar, and gained immortality. Another doorway relief shows Vishnu in his nine incarnations. The idol in the sanctum with two pairs of arms and three heads represents the same god in his lion and boar incarnations. Outside, two (not the usual three), sculptured bands display boar hunting, elephants, horses, soldiers, and—on the upper one—celestial maidens and some of those famous mithunas absorbed in their erotic pleasure.

Matangesvara Temple, south of Lakshmana, is the only "living temple," with worship taking place in the morning and afternoon. Its square construction and simpler floor plan is exceptional for Khajuraho. The temple has oriel windows, a projecting portico, and a ceiling of overlapping concentric circles. An enormous lingam, nearly 8½ feet tall, is enshrined in the sanctum.

Varah Temple, in front of the preceding shrine, is dedicated to Vishnu's Varaha-Avatar, or Boar Incarnation. The huge boar, snouty and stolid, is swathed and ringed with more than 600 carvings of gods and demons.

The Archaeological Museum is across the street from the Matangeswara Temple. Three separate galleries contain interesting sculptures and stone panels salvaged from ruined temples.

Eastern Group

This group lies close to the village and includes three Hindu temples (Brahma, Vamana, and Javari) and three Jain shrines (Ghantai, Adinath, and Parsvanath). This proximity of the cults attests to the religious tolerance of the times in general and of the Chandella rulers in particular. About halfway between the western group of temples and the village is a modern building housing a tenth-century idol of Hanuman, the monkey god.

Vamana Temple is northernmost and is dedicated to Vishnu's dwarf incarnation. The idol in the sanctum, however, looks more like a tall, sly child than a dwarf. The hall, a squat, heavily adorned pile of masonry and sculpture, contrasts strongly with the relatively plain-ribbed shikhara. The sanctum walls show total tolerance—almost all the major gods appear with their consorts in attendance. Vishnu appears in many of his forms, with even a Buddha thrown in. Outside, two tiers of sculpture are mainly concerned with the nymphs of paradise, who strike charming poses under their private awnings. The sculptors obviously enjoyed lavishing their energy on so many full-blown female bodies, so many ornaments, and so many handsome coiffures. Here, too, you see the unexpurgated mind at work.

Javari Temple is just to the south. It is small and of the simplified three-shrine design, but well proportioned and lovely. The two main exterior bands again boast hosts of heavenly maidens.

Brahma Temple is slightly to the south and opposite the Javari. Made of both granite and sandstone, it is considered one of the earliest temples. Its general outline, particularly that of the spire, suggests some other style of Indian temple. It was originally dedicated to Shiva, but the idol in the shrine was miscalled Brahma, and the name stuck.

The Jain Temples are to the south of this group, beginning with a little gem, the Ghantai. This open-colonnaded structure is only the shell of what was once a complete temple, but it is still one of the most attractive monuments at Khajuraho. Note the classicism and detail of the pillars. These slender columns seem decorated with French *passementerie*—bugles, braid, and bell-like tassels hang in graceful patterns. Adorning the entrance are an eight-armed Jain goddess riding the mythical bird, Garuda, and a relief illustrating the 16 dreams of the mother of Mahavira, the greatest religious figure in Jainism and a contemporary of the Buddha.

Adinath Temple is east of Ghantai. A minor shrine, the porch is a modern addition, as is the statue of Tirthankara (perfect soul) Adinatha. The shikhara and its base are richly carved.

Parsvanath Temple, to the south, is the largest and finest of the Jain temples and probably the best construction, technically speaking, in all Khajuraho. Although Kandariya may have the best design, Parsvanath makes up for its lack of size and architectural perfection with marvelous sculpture. Its unrelievedly chiseled facades, turrets, and spires demand close inspection. The sanctum has a carved bull (Adinatha's emblem) standing on a pedestal. In 1860, another image was installed, that of Parsvanath. The outer walls have excellent statues of sloe-eyed beauties in naturalistic poses, occupied in feminine pursuits with children, cosmetics, and flowers. A statue of Shiva and Parvati is almost the epitome of love: her breast cupped in his hand, they regard each other with tenderness and desire. Almost all the exterior offers some of the best Hindu art in India. There is another temple in this group, the Shantinath, which is modern but does contain some ancient Jain sculpture.

Southern Group

There are only two temples in this group; the first, one of the major attractions of Khajuraho, the second, smaller and at a hiking distance or via car along a road.

Duladeo Temple, south of Ghantai Jain Temple, though built in the customary five-shrine style, looks flatter and more massive than do the typical Khajuraho shrines. It lacks the usual ambulatory passage and has no crowning lotus-shaped finials that are of a later period than the actual high point of Khajuraho statuary. The decoration is still graceful and well executed, particularly the multiple-figure bracket capitals inside and the flying wizards on the highest carved band outside. Here, too, in this temple dedicated to Shiva, eroticism works its way in.

Chaturbhuj Temple is nearly two kilometers (one mile) farther south of Duladeo. Small, but with an attractive colonnaded entrance and a nice feeling of verticality, it enshrines an impressive large, four-handed image of Vishnu. The exterior sculpture, with a few exceptions, falls short of the Khajuraho mark.

Intermission

Although the temples are Khajuraho's major attraction and the compelling reason for any visit, lovely nearby respites from the intense concentration of sculpture do exist. See the Eastern Temples at sunset. Sit on the steps of the Vamana and watch the villagers come home from working the fields or fill their brass vessels at the nearby well. Walk into the adjacent Khajuraho village and meander around the streets crowded with boar, goats, buffalo.

One afternoon, take a five-kilometer (three-mile) ride by rickshaw to the tiny village of Rajnagar, with the maharajah's former fortress now a school set on the crest of a hill. Roam the narrow winding streets lined with charming whitewashed houses and shops. This easy excursion is a must if you are lucky to be in Khajuraho on a Tuesday, the day villagers from all around trek into Rajnagar for a daylong colorful bazaar.

PRACTICAL INFORMATION FOR KHAJURAHO

WHEN TO GO. Avoid May through August, when the thermometer climbs over 100°. Rainfall in July and August is also heavy. Best time to visit is from October to the end of March; the rainy season has ended then; and the temperature is delightful most of the time.

HOW TO GET THERE. By Air. The best way is the morning *Indian Airlines* flight, daily throughout the year, from Delhi (1½ hours) and Agra (40 minutes). The same flight continues to Varanasi and Kathmandu (Nepal). *Vayudoot* also flies to Khajuraho six times a week from Delhi and three times a week from Agra, Bhopal, and Varanasi. If you're in a rush, you could cover Khajuraho in a day, leaving Delhi or Agra in the morning and flying back early the same afternoon. But that's the speed demon's pace, which gives about five hours in Khajuraho, barely enough time to fly through the important temples. The best plan is to stay overnight. Take in the temples in the gentler light of late afternoon or early morning. Khajuraho can get hot by midday.

By Train. Trains are impractical; the nearest station is 70 km (43 mi.) away.

By Bus. Buses from Agra, Bhopal, Jhansi, and Indore make the run to Khajuraho. For bus information in Khajuraho, contact the tourist offices (addresses below).

By Rented Car with Driver. Good roads lead to Khajuraho. Here are some important distances: Agra, 395 km (245 mi.); Allahabad, 285 km (177 mi.); Bhopal, 372 km (231 mi.); Varanasi, 415 km (257 mi.); Lucknow, 287 km (178 mi.); Delhi, 598 km (371 mi.). Hire a car from a tour operator listed below.

TOURIST INFORMATION. Two separate tourist departments offer different information on Khajuraho. Both are helpful and worth a visit or telephone call.

Government of India Tourist Office, opposite the Western Temple Complex; tel. 2047; open Monday–Friday, 10 A.M.–5 P.M. *Madhya Pradesh State Tourism Development Corporation* (MPSTDC), Khajuraho Airport; no phone; open daily 8 A.M.–7 P.M. It also has an office at the MPSTDC Tourist Bungalow, tel. 2051; open 10:30 A.M.–5:30 P.M., closed Sundays.

FOREIGN CURRENCY EXCHANGE. Most Western-style hotels have money-exchange counters. Otherwise, go to the *Canara Bank* in Hotel Khajuraho Ashok; open Monday–Tuesday and Thursday–Friday, 10 A.M.–2 P.M., Saturday till noon.

ACCOMMODATIONS. Khajuraho has a limited number of hotels in all price ranges. Prices are based on double occupancy and exclude taxes: *Expensive,* Rs. 950–Rs. 1,450; *Moderate,* Rs. 500–Rs. 950; *Inexpensive,* under Rs. 500. Some Western-style hotels take major credit cards. Peak season (October–end of March) can be busy, so book in advance.

Expensive

Jass Oberoi. By-Pass Rd., Khajuraho; tel. 2066. 54 rooms with bath; 50 under construction. Khajuraho's most elegant hotel, its marble lobby has lovely Indian curios and a circular staircase covered by a dome. Best rooms overlook the pool. All rooms have balconies and handsome furnishings and are air-conditioned. TV on request, room service, multicuisine restaurants, bar, swimming pool, tennis courts, health club, travel agency, foreign-exchange counter, cultural entertainment, shopping arcade. AE, DC, MC, V.

Taj Hotel Chandela. Khajuraho; tel. 2054. 102 rooms with bath. A two-story deluxe hotel, the Taj Chandela has lovely lawns and a marble lobby with a small fountain. Best rooms open onto a courtyard and pretty pool. All rooms are air-conditioned and spacious with a modern decor. Multicuisine restaurants, room service, bar, swimming pool, health club, mini-golf course, tennis court, foreign-exchange counter, car-rental service, shopping arcade, cultural entertainment. AE, DC, MC, V.

Moderate

Hotel Khajuraho Ashok. Khajuraho; tel. 2024. 40 rooms with bath. The lobby is gloomy in this two-story Western hotel, and there's a strong smell of pesticide. Some rooms, however, do offer a view of the temples. The decor is Western modern. Air-conditioning, room service, multicuisine restaurant, bar, swimming pool, foreign-exchange counter and bank, travel counter, shopping arcade. AE, DC, MC, V.

Inexpensive

Hotel Payal. Khajuraho; tel. 2076. 14 rooms with bath. This MPSTDC hotel is attractive and modern. Air-conditioned rooms are spacious and clean, with Western decor and balconies. Room service, multicuisine restaurant, bar, car-rental service. Good value. Rupees only.

Tourist Village. Khajuraho; no phone. 7 cottages with 13 rooms and attached baths. This complex, with a pleasant garden, is designed after a local Bundelkhandi village, with white stucco interiors trimmed in dark rough wood, mosquito netting, ethnic touches to the decor, and a bamboo-and-tile ceiling. Poor lighting at night, however, can create a dungeonlike atmosphere. Rooms are also hot May–September. Fans, room service, multicuisine restaurant, car-rental service. Rupees only.

DINING OUT. The restaurants listed below are informal and, unless noted, don't require reservations. Prices, based on one person eating a three-course meal, excluding taxes, tip, or beverage, are: *Expensive,* Rs. 80–Rs. 120; *Moderate,* Rs. 40–Rs. 80; *Inexpensive,* under Rs. 40. Most Western-style hotels accept credit cards.

Expensive

Apsara. Jass Oberoi, By-Pass Rd.; tel. 2066. In this attractive restaurant, with teak lattice screens and silk bird paintings, the chef prepares good Continental and Indian dishes. Try the chicken *korma* (boneless chicken cooked in an onion and tomato curry) with Kashmiri pilaf (rice prepared with dried fruits and cashews). From 7:30 to 8:30 P.M., you're entertained by a sitarist. Dinner reservations advised. Open 7–10:30 A.M., noon–3 P.M., and 7:30–10:30 P.M. AE, DC, MC, V.

Rasana. Taj Hotel Chandela; tel. 2054. One wall of this intimate restaurant has Rajasthani jewelry sewn into bright textile hangings. At night, candles add a romantic touch. Choose from Continental, Chinese, or Indian cuisines. The chef creates especially good tandoori dishes. Dinner reservations advised. Open 11 A.M.–2 P.M. and 7:30–10:30 P.M. AE, DC, MC, V.

Inexpensive

Raja Cafe. Opposite the Western Temple group; no phone. At this popular, informal eatery, you can eat inside, on the terrace, or on the roof. While the chef also prepares Chinese and Indian dishes, repeat customers go for Continental favorites, especially the southern fried chicken and macaroni. Open March–November, 7 A.M.–10:30 P.M.; otherwise, 8:30 A.M.–9 P.M. Rupees only.

Tourist Village Restaurant. No phone. Set in the MPSTDC ethnic village complex, this open-air restaurant in the style of a *dhaba* (diner) has a bamboo and Indian-tile roof, brick floor, and hanging lanterns. You can choose from Indian and limited Continental dishes. Open for meals 6–10 A.M., noon–2 P.M., 7–10 P.M.; snacks available during non-meal hours. Rupees only.

SWEETS AND TREATS. For a fun experience, visit the *Jungle River Deck* in the nearby Vindhya Hills and next to the Panna National Park (25 minutes by car from Khajuraho). After swimming in the river, enjoy a cool drink in India's only tree deck, a cleverly designed oasis built into the branches.

HOW TO GET AROUND. From the Airport. The airport is six km (four mi.) from the temples. A taxi should cost about Rs. 30.

By Taxi. Private taxis are good for excursions beyond Khajuraho. Rates are about Rs. 3.30 per km. You can also engage a taxi for about Rs. 80 for four hours of local sightseeing. Set the fare before you depart.

By Bicycle Rickshaw. Once you're in the small village, this is the best way to get around. Drivers are supposed to follow fixed rates, but they like to keep this fact a secret. Negotiate hard or check with the Government of India Tourist Office (across from the Western Temple complex); an outside board lists the rates. Once you've seen the Western Temple complex, the other temples are spread around Khajuraho. Hire a rickshaw for a few hours (Rs. 40 per hour hours) and have the driver take you from temple to temple, the old village and your hotel.

SEASONAL EVENTS. March. The *Khajuraho Dance Festival* gives you a week-long opportunity to see numerous forms of classical Indian dance performed by India's best dancers in culturally compatible outdoor surroundings. Contact tourist offices for specific details. Nominal fee. Buy tickets in advance.

TOURS. There are no longer any government-run tours of the temples; but you can hire an excellent guide from the *Government Tourist Office* or at Raja Cafe (two–four hours; about Rs. 50). Many of the guides are fluent in German, Japanese, Italian, English, and French. Don't get taken in by those who pose as guides inside the temple complex. They'll talk your head off, but the facts they tell are their own.

TOUR OPERATORS. For all travel needs, including a car with driver, contact Orient Express (Hotel Taj Chandela, tel. 2049).

HISTORIC SITES. See all the 20 remaining tenth- and eleventh-century temples and their fabulous carvings. The best times of day to view the temples are early morning and late afternoon, when the light is soft and shadows highlight the delicate carvings. They are in three main groups, those of the west being generally acknowledged to be the best. Close to Khajuraho village is the eastern group, while three miles from there stand the southern groups. Out of these 20 temples, five are easily accessible—Kandariya Mahadeva Temple is by far the largest and the finest, the others being Lakshmana, Visvanatha, Chitragupta, and Devi Jagdambe. These temples are found in a group close to each other and make an imposing picture with their elegant spires against the sky. Temples are open from early morning to sunset. Western Complex, Rs. 2; others, free.

MUSEUMS. The *Archaeological Museum* near the Western Group of Temples has three galleries: Jain, Buddhist, and miscellaneous, essentially sculptures collected on the temple sites. Tickets for the Western Group also include entry to the museum. Open 10 A.M.–5 P.M.; closed Fridays. Nominal entry charge.

The *Jain Museum,* near the Jain temples, has artifacts from the Eastern group of temples. Open daily 9 A.M.–5 P.M. Nominal entry charge.

SHOPPING. Opposite the Western Group of Temples is a square with numerous carts of so-called curios—most of which are new. Buy what you like and bargain hard. Also visit these two good shops:

Mrignayni Emporium, opposite the Archaeological Museum and run by the Handicraft Board of Madhya Pradesh, sells tribal art, textiles, and local handicrafts. Open 10 A.M.–6 P.M.; closed Tuesdays. Rupees only.

Karan Jewelers, in the bazaar opposite the Western Group of Temples, has good bronzes, paintings, and jewelry; and semi-precious and precious stones, especially diamonds that are mined nearby. AE, MC, V.

NIGHTLIFE AND BARS. Bars are open 10 A.M.–10 P.M. The best bar is the *Temple Bar* at Jass Oberoi, which quietly reflects Khajuraho's historic legacy and offers an elegant ambience.

SOUTHERN REGION

MADRAS AND TAMIL NADU

Glories of Dravidian India

by
KATHLEEN COX

In almost any country, the south has a personality of its own, and India is no exception. The pace of living in this sun-drenched state is more leisurely and more traditional than the rest of the country.

The region covers the State of Tamil Nadu and some of its environs, along the coast of the Bay of Bengal on the east and the Western Ghats on the west. It was formerly a number of separate princely states that were amalgamated, for linguistic reasons, after Independence.

The land of Tamil, founded by Dravidians over 5,000 years ago, is primarily agrarian. It has frequent lush green vistas, charming narrow waterways, vast groves of coconuts, bananas, and sugarcane, and innumerable tiny villages with huts of thatch, wood, mud, or brick—well-tended homes that are pleasingly neat and tidy. Throughout the region, you'll see colorful drawings on the ground or pavement in front of each dwelling. Each morning the woman of the house, using her imagination, and white or colored powder, creates *kolams* (or *rangolis*) in intricate geometric or flower designs. Traditionally, the powder was made from rice and the design was then eaten by insects or birds. In this way the woman pleased the gods by starting her day with an act of charity. Even Madras, the capital, offers glimpses of the traditional way of life that has all but vanished in many other cities of India. And when Madras becomes too hot, the southern hill stations and the beaches offer a great escape.

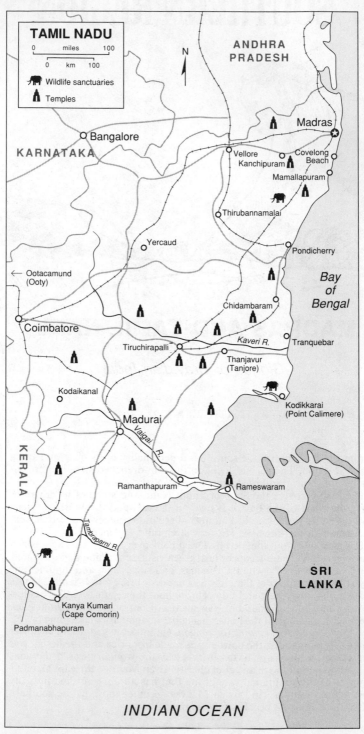

The difference between South India and the rest of the country is much greater than a few degrees on a thermometer. The south has been relatively unaffected by the waves of invasion that shaped India for centuries, even though it was the starting point of the last invasion of all—that of the Europeans. Alien empire builders either never reached the south during the long centuries of Indian history or their fury and zeal were spent by the time they got here.

The result is a fascinating survival of ancient India in its purest form. Nowhere else is classical dancing performed on the scale of the Bharata Natyam dances of Madras and other, smaller cities. Nowhere else can you experience the exuberance of medieval India as you can in old Madurai or Tiruchirapalli. The temples of South India can't be classified according to the dictates of Western architecture and esthetics. Their *gopura* (towers) are massive, and some—especially the more recent ones—have colors in combinations that no Westerner sees outside Miami Beach. But, as expressions of traditional India, the ancient temples are the heart and soul of any trip.

EXPLORING TAMIL NADU

MADRAS

Madras is the fourth largest city in India—outranked by Delhi, Bombay and Calcutta for the dubious distinction of cramming as many people as possible into one place. Fortunately, you don't feel the density in Madras. The sprawling city, which is divided in two by the Cooum River, has few tall buildings to mar the impression of an easygoing market town. The welcome sense of spaciousness is enhanced by Madras's waterfront on the Bay of Bengal, one of the world's largest and most attractive beaches set in the heart of a city.

In spite of its large population, currently over four million, this city has a gentle pace and is made for people watching. The southerners are different from their northern counterparts, having the poise and self-assurance that comes from carrying the civilization of thousands of years. Saris aren't worn in the same manner as in northern India and though some men dress in the elegant white *dhotis* of the north, they often wear brightly colored *lungis* (cloth draped around the waist and worn long or pulled up between the knees).

That gracefulness is present in Madras in such liberal quantities is appropriate. In the Government Museum, you can see the famous bronze of the Chola period (tenth century) of Nataraja-Shiva in the cosmic dance pose. Although it's only two feet high, this beautifully executed statue seems to be constantly moving. It has rightfully become the symbol of Indian art that is recognized all around the world.

No visitor should leave Madras without seeing a performance of the Bharata Natyam. Many of these dance recitals are about Krishna, the most popular of Vishnu's nine incarnations, symbol of the ideal man. As they dance, the women appear to express their infatuation with the god, described in one prayer as "Lord Krishna, with eyes like lustrous pearls, head bedecked with peacocks' feathers and body of the hue of Heaven." The dancers exhibit perfect control over each muscle in their bodies, while executing intricate movements with clockwork precision. Once you've seen a Bharata Natyam dancer move her neck while keeping her head still, you'll respect the artistry and skill behind this classical Indian dance form.

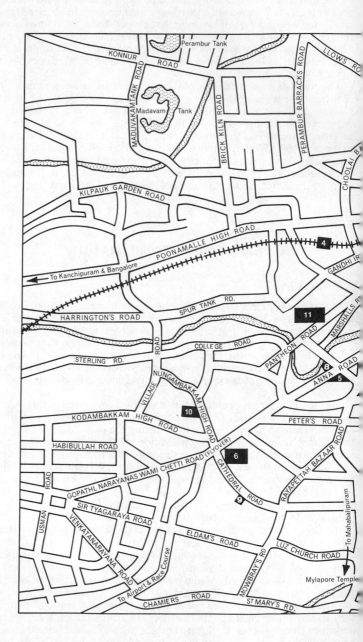

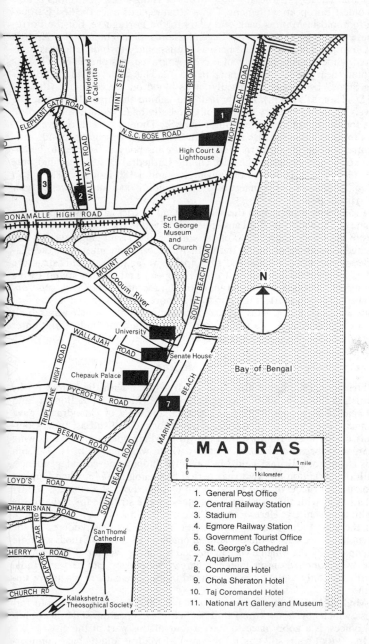

MADRAS

0 _____ 1 mile
0 _____ 1 kilometer

1. General Post Office
2. Central Railway Station
3. Stadium
4. Egmore Railway Station
5. Government Tourist Office
6. St. George's Cathedral
7. Aquarium
8. Connemara Hotel
9. Chola Sheraton Hotel
10. Taj Coromandel Hotel
11. National Art Gallery and Museum

Paradoxically, this least Westernized of India's Big Four cities is also its oldest European settlement. The written records trace the first European foothold in Madras back 500 years to the Portuguese, but the Portuguese were only latecomers. Legend claims that Thomas the Apostle ("Doubting Thomas") came here as a missionary to India and was martyred while praying in front of a cross engraved in stone on St. Thomas Mount (near the Madras Airport) in A.D. 72. This stone, called the "Bleeding Stone" because it supposedly sheds blood on December 18 (the day of St. Thomas's death), is now installed behind the high altar inside the lovely sixteenth-century Church of Our Lady of Expectation, erected on the foundation of an earlier church that St. Thomas is said to have built. His revered name has also survived in St. Thomé, a pleasant seaside residential section of southern Madras, while his body is believed to be entombed in the center of the San Thomé Cathedral Basilica, a handsome neo-Gothic structure with elegant arches and a 180-foot steeple, built in 1896. Inside, notice the image of Christ standing on a lotus flower (a typical Hindu pose).

From here, wander into the nearby inland district called Mylapore, the home of Tiruvalluvar, the Tamil poet who lived in the second century and wrote the *Kural,* the greatest of all works in the Tamil language. It's still recited reverently in South India. In Mylapore, you must visit the Kapaleeswarar Temple dedicated to Kapaleeswarar (Shiva). This structure offers an impressive contrast to the European architecture found in the cathedral. The sawed-off pyramid of its recently renovated *gopuram* (tower entrance) shatters the horizon far more violently than does the slim spire of San Thomé. This typical Dravidian temple, which was rebuilt about 300 years ago, is a riot of color. Although non-Hindus can't enter the sanctum sanctorum (inner shrine), they can enter the outer courtyard.

Fort St. George, the Original Madras

Strickly speaking, the history of Madras began with the history of the British in India. In 1639, 25 years before the British reached Bombay and 50 years before they arrived in Calcutta, the Raja of Chandragiri gave Francis Day a lease to open a trading post for the British East India Company on the site of Madras, then known as Madraspatram. The following year, work began on Fort St. George, which was finished in 1653. From this stronghold, Britain held Madras until India achieved independence, with the exception of a two-year period beginning in 1746, when Dupleix took it for France, only to lose it again in 1748. Fort St. George is tightly interwoven with the swashbuckling story of the struggle for India in the eighteenth century. Here, Robert Clive arrived in 1743 as a modest clerk for the East India Company. When Fort St. George surrendered to the French, Clive escaped and became an officer in the army of the East India Company. By the time he was 30, he had become governor of Madras and was well launched on his meteoric career, which saw him preserve India for Britain only to die by his own hand in disgrace back in his native England.

Modern Madras has grown around Fort St. George, and the old fortress, which now houses the Tamil Nadu State Legislature and other political offices, is a good place to start a tour of this part of the city.

Its 20-foot walls still guard the center of Madras and its busy commercial artery, Anna Salai (Mount Road). Inside the walls, you can stroll through the pages of history. Clive's house is still here, and Colonel Wellesley, who later became the Duke of Wellington, lived in another old home, which can also be seen within the fort.

Inside Fort St. George, visit the oldest Anglican church in India, St. Mary's Church, consecrated in 1680. The records show that one of its most generous benefactors was Elihu Yale, the Boston-born English merchant who also showed his generosity to the university that now bears his name. Yale, too, was a governor of Madras, although his term in office is not as memorable as that of Clive. The roof and walls of St. Mary's are five feet thick and bombproof, which probably explains why the French ransacked the sacred interior and committed the profane: turning the building into a military fortification. Finally, look at the Fort St. George Museum, once used as an exchange by the merchants of the East India Company, and now containing many interesting relics from that era.

George Town, the original Madras, lies north of the fort. Its streets still bear such names as China Bazaar Road, Evening Bazaar, Portuguese Church Street, and Armenian Street, all reminiscent of the four-century history of Madras as a center of international trade. On Armenia Street, notice the fine old Armenian Church, built originally in 1620. It subsequently became the cornerstone of the influential Armenian community. And don't miss the great Evening Bazaar (also called Parrys—pronounced Paris—after the former British confectionary factory that made Parrys Sweets, those candies you get on Indian Airlines). Evening Bazaar (which is in high gear all *day*) is located near Broadway and Nataji Subhash Chandra Bose Road (known as NSC Bose Road to taxi drivers). Produce in profusion fills the narrow streets and the senses. The odors change from street to street in this photographer's haven—a wholesale emporium of countless open stalls, selling fruit, vegetables, pastries, flowers, colorful paper ornaments, bangles—a thoroughly fascinating bustle of bartering and noise.

Marina Beach and Other Sights

South of Fort St. George along the Bay of Bengal, Madras puts on its elegant face. South Beach Road runs past Madras University, the Senate House, the Chepauk Palace (the nawabs of the Carnatic once held court in this Moorish-style structure, now a government building). This is the Marina, the shore drive that every Madras citizen proudly tells you is the second-longest beach in the world. The Marina has an elegant promenade with flowerbeds along its lane and a glistening sand beach that is never crowded—at least not with swimmers. The waters off the Marina are infested with sharks. As a consolation, there's a swimming pool on the Marina, next to the dreary Madras Aquarium.

Near this aquarium is another memento of East India Company days, an old building known as the "Ice House." The Ice House was used to store ice brought all the way from New England by Yankee seafarers for the benefit of sunbaked businessmen in the pre-air-conditioned age. Also visit the Anna Samadhi, burial place of and shrine for Dr. C. N. Annadurai, the great orator and revered leader of Tamil Nadu, who died in 1969. The true "sight" here are the ordinary people who pay homage to one of the great heroes of their culture. It is said that when Dr. Annadurai died, a number of devoted followers committed suicide. Come in the evening when families visit the beach to relax in the cooling breeze that floats off the Bay of Bengal.

Madras has two good museums: the Government Museum and the National Art Gallery (both on Pantheon Road). The Government Museum has a vast collection of the best South Indian bronzes (see the famous Cosmic Dancer) all made by the lost-wax method, plus wonderful archaeological remains from excavations at the Amravati Buddhist stupa, part of which was constructed in the first and second centuries. The National Art Gallery has a good collection of ancient and modern Indian art.

At the headquarters of the Theosophical Society, which was started at the turn of the century to encourage the comparative study of religion, philosophy, and science while promoting a universal brotherhood without regard to race, creed, or sex, you'll find an excellent library with old palm-leaf manuscripts and rare books. The grounds of the society, just over Elphinstone Bridge on the Adyar River, also have one of India's oldest banyan trees. This tree is mammoth—500 people can stand under its branches, which offer 40,000 square feet of shade.

Also in Adyar, visit the Kalakshetra School, where classical dance, as well as other important South Indian art forms, is taught. You can also see the ancient designs of Indian textiles reproduced anew.

The Madras Snake Park and Conservation Center, situated in beautiful Guindy Deer Park in Madras, was founded by Romulus Whitaker, an American who settled in India. The park gives the public a chance to see, photograph, and touch the common snakes of India (over 500 species), most of which are housed in an open "pit." Other reptiles—crocodiles, alligators, monitor lizards, and chameleons—also call the park home. Over a half million people visit the park each year. The entrance fees, apart from covering the cost of maintaining the park, are used for various wildlife projects and relevant surveys. The Snake Park has received numerous grants and the continued support of the World Wildlife Fund. While you're here, ask how the snake's skin is removed to make those articles that are hawked in abundance. You may decide to do without them.

The borders of Madras extend 37 miles south and 57 miles southwest to Mahabalipuram and Kanchipuram, respectively. No visit to the capital of South India should overlook these two monuments to the glory of the Pallava emperors.

MAHABALIPURAM

There's a good road between Madras and Mahabalipuram, on the Bay of Bengal. This city was once the main harbor and naval base of the great Pallava empire, the capital of which was in Kanchipuram. Although the reign of the Pallavas waned some 1,200 years ago, its gifts still stand on and near the shore of this "city of the seven pagodas," its European designation. Tiny Mahabalipuram, with its 4,000-plus population, offers a breathtaking display of masterful sculpture carved out of solid rock. In fact, the Pallavas developed four distinct kinds of sculpture: *rathas* (temple chariots), bas-relief sculptural panels, rock-cut caves, and freestanding temples. Here, humans worked nature into sublime art, although nature is now taking its revenge. The salt spray of the bay is carving the rock temples all over again.

The Five Rathas

The so-called pagodas of Mahabalipuram are actually seventh-century rathas, although, to a Western eye, they resemble small pyramid-shaped temples cut off by flat roofs. The walls of these freestanding, monolithic temples—each chiseled from a single rock—are a picture book of Hindu mythology. The five rathas, also known as the Pancha Pandava Rathas after the heroes of the *Mahabharata,* a Hindu epic, are dedicated to Durga, Shiva, Vishnu, and Indra. Near these delicate temples, life-size stone statues of an elephant, a lion, and a bull mount guard. These rathas, which

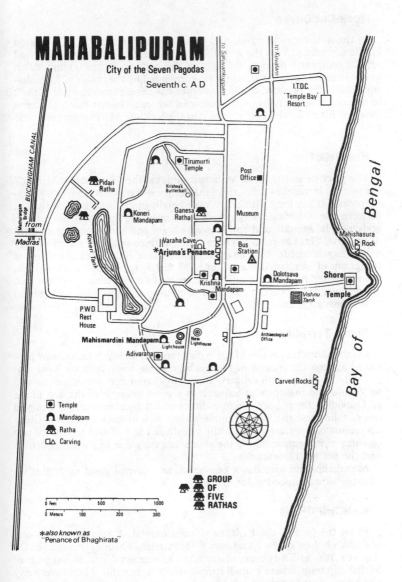

MAHABALIPURAM
City of the Seven Pagodas
Seventh c. A D

BUCKINGHAM CANAL

to Saluvankuppam

to Kovalam

I.T.D.C.
'Temple Bay'
Resort

Bay of Bengal

Mathurapam Bridge

from Madras

Pidari Ratha

Koneri Tank

Koneri Mandapam

Tirumurti Temple

Krishna's Butterball

Ganesa Ratha

Post Office

Museum

Mahishasura Rock

Varaha Cave

*Arjuna's Penance

Bus Station

Krishna Mandapam

Dolotsava Mandapam

Shore Temple

Vishnu Tank

P.W.D. Rest House

Archaeological Office

Mahismardini Mandapam

Old Lighthouse

New Lighthouse

Adivaraha

Carved Rocks

N

Temple
Mandapam
Ratha
Carving

0 Feet   500   1000
0 Meters   100   200   300

GROUP
OF
FIVE
RATHAS

*also known as
"Penance of Bhaghirata"

are not overpowering in size, are well proportioned even though they are all unfinished. The finials are not in place.

Rock-Cut Caves

In the nine rock-cut caves, you'll find some of India's most animated Hindu sculptures. Visit the seventh-century Mahishasura Mandapam and see the sculptural relief of the fight of the goddess Durga, riding a lion in her struggle against evil, which is represented by the image of Mahishasura, the buffalo-headed demon. Another bas-relief shows the god Vishnu in his cosmic sleep, lying on the coils of a serpent. Quieter pastoral scenes from the life of Krishna are carved into the Krishna Mandapam cave temple.

Bas-Relief

The pièce de résistance at Mahabalipuram is the "Penance of Arjuna," the world's largest bas-relief and a masterpiece of composition: two gigantic rocks (80 feet long with an average height of 20 feet); a crack runs in between. On either side of the crack are nearly 100 figures of gods, demigods, people, animals, and birds—nearly every real and mythological form of creation. This bas-relief has been called a fresco in stone, and its vitality makes its figures lifelike. The most prominent of its myriad characters is the group of elephants, one of them 17 feet long. Then there's Arjuna, the emaciated figure standing on one leg and doing penance—praying to Lord Shiva for a powerful weapon to destroy his enemies. All creation is witnessing his act.

Shore Temple

On the shore stands one of the oldest temples in South India, now protected against the erosion of the sea by a stone wall. Built by King Rajashimha in the seventh century, the temple comprises two shrines—one to Vishnu and the other to Shiva. It is a good example of the first phase of Dravidian temple architecture. Surrounded by a row of bulls carved out of solid rock, the Shore Temple stands with its back to the sea, rising up against blue waters with a white wreath of foam. There were once two or three more temples along the shore, but only one has withstood time and the sea for 12 centuries.

Mahabalipuram also has a fine beach and several good resorts; it's a relaxing slow-tempoed place to stay.

KANCHIPURAM

From the port of the Pallavas to their capital at Kanchipuram—one of India's holiest cities—is an easy 64-kilometer (40-mile) trip inland. On the way, stop at Thirukkalikundram, 13 kilometers (eight miles) west of Mahabalipuram, where a small temple stands atop a hill. There, every day just before noon, a priest feeds two white kites—birds that the faithful believe are the spirits of two saints. In the village at the foot of the hill, there is also a Pallaya rock temple dedicated to Shiva. And, along the route, notice more of those kolam (or rangoli) drawings on the ground in front of each Tamil Nadu dwelling.

The Golden City of Temples, Kanchipuram, is currently a charming, bustling village with numerous whitewashed homes featuring open porches stretched across the front with all the trim brightly painted. Kanchipuram contains no less than 124 shrines and is sacred both to Shiva and to Vishnu, which makes it an important stopping place for Hindus making their rounds of the seven holy cities of India (the other six are Haridwar, Ujjain, Varanasi, Mathura, Ayodhya, and Dwarka). Kanchipuram is the "Varanasi of the South," and its religious architecture is a treat.

Kanchipuram's Pallava temples were built by its kings, who also founded Mahabalipuram. The kings patronized not only architecture and sculpture but all the arts, transforming their capital into one of India's greatest centers of learning. Hindu and Buddhist philosophies flourished here side by side. Since you would need a lifetime to visit and examine all the temples, here are a few of the best:

Kailasanatha Temple

The first temple built in Kanchipuram was the Kailasanatha Temple constructed in the early eighth century by King Rajashimha. A smaller temple built by his son, Mahendra, stands in the east end of the courtyard. Dedicated to Shiva, these sandstone temples are considered the finest examples of Pallava architecture. They are adorned with excellent sculptures—a big *nandi* (bull-headed god) on a raised platform, other nandis everywhere, and images of Shiva galore—as well as many lovely paintings on the walls. Note, too, the unusual tiny shrines built around the courtyard, each with its own shrine and pillared pavilion—58 exquisite monuments of fastidious labor.

Vaikunthaperumal Temple

Built a few years after the Kailasanatha Temple, the Vaikunthaperumal, with its three-story *vimana* (tower over the central temple), was built by King Nandivarman and is dedicated to Lord Vishnu, who is shown repeatedly: sitting, standing, and reclining—the figures often appearing one on top of another. Notice the sculptured panels of the *mandapa* (pavilion in front of the central temple); they recount the history of the Pallavas, including their battles with the Chalyukas. At that time, such nonreligious subject matter in a temple was unusual, possibly a first. In many ways, this temple, with its colonnade of lion pillars, marks the next stage in the development of Dravidian architecture. On its walls, you can also see more surviving Hindu murals.

Ekambareswara Temple

Although originally constructed by the Pallavas, this temple's most significant feature—its 196-foot *goporum* (tower entrance) with more than ten stories of intricate sculpture—was the result of a sixteenth-century addition by the Vijayanagar kings. This temple is also dedicated to Shiva; inside the courtyard is an important mango tree that is supposedly 3,500 years old. It is said that each leaf is different, the fruit of each branch offers a different taste, and when women wishing to become pregnant come here to pray, their wish is granted. Of the original 1,000 pillars that once stood in the mandapa only about 600 remain.

Sri Varadaraja Temple

Smaller, but probably more pleasing to the eye, is the 100-foot goporum of the Varadaraja Temple, originally built in the eleventh century but overhauled by the Vijayanagar kings 500 years later. Also known as the Devarajaswamy Temple, this edifice is dedicated to Vishnu, and its 1,000-pillared mandapa—all of it exquisitely carved—is one of the best. Be certain to see the massive chain carved from one stone, as well as the handsome pillars standing in the courtyard.

Sri Kamakshi Temple

In the heart of the old town, the Sri Kamakshi, with its fancy gold-plated goporum, is dedicated to the goddess Kamakshi (Parvati). This temple is the site of an annual winter car festival, when numerous small deities from nearby temples are pulled by wooden temple cars in a procession, led by an elephant. The colorful event draws huge crowds.

Although Kanchipuram is most famous for its temples, it's also well known as a silk-weaving center. "Connjeevaram sari" (what the English formerly called Kanchipuram) is still synonymous with the best in Indian silk saris as well as silk by the meter.

Vellore

About 56 kilometers (35 miles) to the west of Kanchipuram is Vellore, on the banks of the Palar River. The heart of Vellore is its fort, built in the thirteenth century and still an excellent example of military architecture, despite a long and bloody history of battles. The last siege of Vellore occurred in 1806 during a sepoy mutiny caused by military grievances, antedating the great upheaval of the Indian Mutiny of 1857 by 51 years.

Across a moat, impressive gates lead into the fort. Inside, there's an exquisite temple of Shiva, probably built in the fourteenth century, which was not in use until a *lingam* (phallic symbol) was installed in 1981. Attractive sculpture adorns the temple's ceiling and pillars.

Thiruvannamalai

From Vellore, head south to Thiruvannamalai and one of South India's largest temples. Sprawling over 25 acres, the Arunachala Temple is dedicated to Tejo Lingam (Lord Shiva in his fire incarnation—one of the five elements he represents). Here, a goporum rises 200 feet with 11 sculpture stories. Behind it in the temple grounds is a magnificent pavilion of a 1,000 pillars.

The Arunachala Temple lies at the foot of a hill that bursts with celebration during the Karthikai Deepam festival during the full moon around the end of November. A huge bonfire, ignited on top of the hill and visible for miles, guides pilgrims to the shrine of a Hindu saint, Sri Ramana Maharisha, who spent much of his time here.

Pondicherry

Head east to Tindivanam, then south to Pondicherry. The atmosphere of a sleepy French provincial town is struggling to survive since this former tiny enclave was returned to Indian administration in 1954 after 250 years of French rule. Near its handsome Government House by the sea is a statue of Dupleix, the unsuccessful rival of Clive, who governed Pondicherry for 40 years in the eighteenth century. The French touch is completed with a statue of Joan of Arc.

Another influence that has begun to change Pondicherry was started by Sri Aurobindo, philosopher, poet, and patriot who withdrew to Pondicherry in 1910, after a political trial that lasted two years. With the help of a French woman, called "Mother," he founded the ashram that bears his name. His ideal, a superman who surpasses his fellowmen in the things of the spirit, is the antithesis of Nietzsche's; and his humanism is distinctly different from the philosophy of modern Western thinkers. The residents of the ashram, which can be visited, are supposed to be living according to the Master's (and Mother's) teachings—he died in 1950, she died in 1973—in a rarefied atmosphere of *sachidananda* (pure spirit). But the ashram and nearby Auroville, "the City of Dawn," an international commune of sorts, launched in 1968 by Mother, are embroiled in nonspiritual bickering. Much of Pondicherry's economy is Aurobindo-oriented. At Auroville, you see stabs at futuristic architecture in settlements called Aspiration and Revelation, in 17 different types of windmills, and in the Matri Mandir, a humongous sphere (an intended meditation hall) that has been under construction since 1971.

Chidambaram

Continuing south, you enter the South Arcot district—the southern India rice bowl—vibrant green with paddies where men lead water buffalo back and forth through lush, fertile fields. After about 64 kilometers (40 miles) you reach Chidambaram. Chidambaram is the site of the oldest temple in South India, the Nataraja Temple, conceivably (no one knows for sure) built in the fifth century by a Chola king. Suffering from leprosy, according to legend, the king took the advice of a resident saint, bathed in a sacred tank, and recovered. Supposedly, he showed his gratitude by building the earliest stages of this temple (the sacred tank is inside) erected over a span of centuries. The Nataraja is dedicated to Shiva in various aspects, including the cosmic dancer prancing on the remains of evil and ignorance.

In the Chit Sabha (the inner sanctum) covered with gold plate, the presiding deity is identified by one of the five elements (all of which Shiva represents): air, known as the Akasa Lingam. What you see is a black curtain, standing for ignorance, that is raised three times daily. There are four other halls: the Nritta Sabha, Deva Sabha, Kanaka Sabha, and Raja Sabha. The Kanaka, also covered in gold plate, houses the famous Nataraja image of Shiva, the cosmic dancer cast in an alloy of five metals. The Nritta Sabha, the Hall of Dance, has over 50 pillars depicting dancing figures. Representing a heavenly chariot carved in stone, it contains an image of Shiva engaged in a dance contest with the goddess Kali. Shiva won. Deva Sabha is the Hall of Festivals, where all the processional deities are kept. Then, there's the Raja Sabha, some call it the most spectacular, 340 by 190 feet, with 1,000 pillars. Here the Pandyas and Cholas celebrated their victories. Two of the temple's four goporums of granite (no one knows how the granite reached Chidambaram; there's none within a 80-kilometer or 50-mile radius) are covered with sculptures illustrating the 108 dance positions of Bharata Natyam.

Vishnu is also worshiped at Chidambaram, although his Govindaraja temple is overshadowed by the shrine of Shiva. This temple is a more recent work, but it has an excellent statue of Lord Vishnu lying on a bed of snakes. The shrine closes at 11:30 A.M.

If you are lucky enough to be at Chidambaram in the early evening, visit the Siva-Sakthi Music and Dance School at 123 East Car Street. Inside this elegant old building with massive stone pillars, you might see a class of poised, talented girls learning the Bharata Natyam. Their instructress is a former dancer, regal, with perfect grace. As she provides the beat with a slap of her hands against a pillar, and the girls move with stunning grace, the effect is magic, memorable. A small donation would be an appropriate gift in return, although it's not required.

An interesting side trip from Chidambaram, is the old Danish trading port and town of Tranquebar, with its well-preserved fort and sleepy old colonial air. This town was Denmark's major Asian holding from 1620 until 1840, when the whole settlement was sold to the British. Still well preserved are the fort, Dansborg Castle, two churches, and the houses of colonial administrators and merchants.

Thanjavur: Showplace of Chola Architecture

Not far from Kumbakonam is Thanjavur (Tanjore), lying at the foot of what has been called India's greatest temple, the Brahadeeswarar Temple, dedicated to Shiva. Thanjavur was the capital of the Chola Empire from the tenth to the fourteenth centuries. A Chola king, Rajah Chola, who held the throne from 985 to 1016, built the greatest of the empire's 74 temples: the Brahadeeswarar, with its soaring tower (vimana) over the inner sanctum—a tower that rises more than 200 feet. On its dome rests a single block of granite weighing 80 tons. The enormous hulk was inched up to the top along an inclined plane that began in a village six kilometers (four miles) away, a technique used by the Egyptians to build the Pyramids. This is also the first of four Chola temples in Tamil Nadu to have a vimana soaring over the goporum.

The main shrine of the temple lies at the end of a paved courtyard and houses a huge lingam. This courtyard is guarded by another goporum tower. As you near the inner shrine of Brahadeeswarar, you will encounter India's second largest statue of Nandi the bull (the biggest is at Lepakshi near Anantapur). Sixteen feet long in black granite, Nandi is the mount of the god Shiva. Other sculptures inside the temple draw upon Vishnu and Buddhism as well as Shiva for their subjects. The walls of the inner courtyard of the temple are covered with excellent frescoes of the Chola and the Nayak periods. For a long time, the earlier and more interesting Chola frescoes lay hidden under the upper layer of the Nayak paintings. Only when the modern archaeologist was able to expose the bottom layer did art historians realize the existence of an excellent school of painting in the Chola period, comparable to the famous frescoes in the Ajanta cave shrines.

Near the temple is a vast palace built by the Nayak and Maratha dynasties. Although much of the palace is in ruins, it does contain the celebrated Saraswathi Mahal Library with 30,000 volumes (8,000 of these are manuscripts written on palm leaves). In Tamil, Sanskrit, Marathi, Telugu, and a number of European languages, the manuscripts cover subjects from dancing to astronomy. The palace also has a superb collection of bronzes, poorly displayed in an old audience hall.

At Thanjavur also see the Schwartz Church built by a raja in 1779 to express his friendship for a Danish missionary, Rev. C. V. Schwartz, and the nearby Shiva Ganga Tank, known for its sweet water. Close to Thanjavur lies Thiruvaiyar, the nineteenth-century home of Sri Thyagaraja, saint and composer. He wrote more than a thousand songs in Carnatic (Southern Indian) music. In his honor, a major music festival is held here every January.

Tiruchirapalli

West of Thanjavur and 56 kilometers (35 miles) by road, you leave the "rice bowl" and enter the ancient Cauvery delta town of Tiruchirapalli

(Tiruchi), built up by the Nayaks of Madurai. Tiruchi has always been a seat of power in South India and it bears the scars of wars fought to control it, particularly by the French and English.

The military and architectural heart of Tiruchi is its famous Rock Fort, rising 300 feet over the city on the banks of the Cauvery River. A staircase with 434 steps out into the rock, some of them tunneled, leads up to the summit and a temple dedicated to Lord Vinayaka (closed to non-Hindus). Along the way are various landings and shrines: an ancient temple dedicated to Ganesh (the elephant-headed god), a Shiva temple (called Thayumana Swamy Temple) with its hundred-pillared hall (also off-limits to non-Hindus), and cave temples cut into the rock—the two biggest were executed by Pallava sculptors who placed seven pillars across the facade and a square shrine at one end of a hollowed-out wall. Finally at the top, you are rewarded with a breathtaking view of the city and the countryside below.

Below the rock at the base of the fort, a "must" walk is through China Bazaar, the Big Bazaar, and down the interesting narrow side streets—all of which make up the heart of the Old City. You'll share the streets with crowds of people and the typical Indian array of animals, including donkeys. Have a "yard of coffee," so named for the way it is poured, at any of the *bhavans,* "French cafes"—Tamil-Nadu style.

Tiruchi has several other points of interest, including St. Joseph's Church, with its lovely Our Lady of Lourdes Parish, all done up in warm tropical colors and a gorgeous sandlewood altar. Also see the eighteenth-century Christ Church built by the Danish missionary, Reverend Schwartz; and the Teppakulam, a large tank, surrounded by a flower market and open-air stalls. Tiruchi is a busy place, industriously turning out hand-loomed cloth, cigars, mats, textiles, and several kinds of artificial diamonds.

Five kilometers (three miles) to the north, though, the glory of religious India explodes again on Srirangam, an island in the Cauvery linked to the mainland by a bridge with 32 arches. Here, worshipers of Vishnu come to one of India's largest temples dedicated to their god—the Ranganatha Swamy Temple built between the fourteenth and seventeenth centuries. The people of Srirangam and the town itself exists primarily inside this 156-acre temple, which has seven sets of walls. It's a fascinating bustling complex. The temple itself really begins when you reach the mandapa behind the fourth wall. This is another of those 1,000-pillared halls (although only 940 remain). There are 22 towers around the temple, with the intended tallest nearing completion. This is very much a "living temple." Pilgrims from all over India come here every year in January for the Vaikunta Ekadasi festival. It is then that Heaven's Gate is opened and the idol of Ranganatha is brought into the mandapa from the inner shrine under a golden dome. This temple also houses a beautiful collection of jewelry.

Another temple, smaller but of more pleasing design, is about two kilometers (one mile) to the east: a shrine of Shiva. Here, in the Mambukeswaram pagoda, is a lingam, the symbol of Shiva, submerged in water. This temple is also called Thiruvanaikkaval after the legendary elephant that once worshiped the lingam.

The water surrounding Srirangam island is not only holy but useful. In the eleventh century, a Chola ruler built a stone dam below the island to harness the Cauvery River. He built it so well that you can still see it today, a sturdy, long wall serving the same purpose today as before.

Madurai

In Madurai, 155 kilometers (96 miles) from Tiruchi, you throw out all your points of reference and bases of comparison. Here, architecture and sculpture are not passive monuments but living backdrops for scenes that must have been enacted in the cathedral cities of the Middle Ages. Although Madurai is not a pretty city, it's the beating heart of the land of the Tamils and the high point of a journey south from Madras.

Madurai was thriving when Augustus took the throne of Rome (coins found here point to the existence of trade with Rome). Until the fourteenth century, it was the capital of the Pandya rulers of South India, who made it the mother city of Tamil literature with their generous patronage of poets and academics. Then the Nayaks ruled Madurai from the middle of the sixteenth century to 1743 and their majestic imprint is still fresh. The 10 tall goporums of the Meenakshi Temple raised during their dynasty are your first glimpse of Madurai, whether you arrive by car, train, bus, or airplane.

From the air, though, you can also see the two hills of rock marking boundaries between the "sweet place" (the meaning of "Madurai") and its surrounding green paddy fields. They are known as Yanai Malai and Naga Malai (the elephant hill and the snake hill). Three kilometers (two miles) long, the Yanai Malai of gray and pink granite does seem to resemble a recumbent elephant. The sweetness of Madurai comes from the nectar that fell from the hair of the god Shiva on the city.

It is Shiva and his wife, Meenakshi, who are honored in Madurai's greatest landmark, the Meenakshi Temple. This, incidentally, is the first big Indian temple whose towers are being restored to their original polychrome colors. Concrete moldings and bright fresh paint have replaced the gentle pastels and crumbling stones of weathered Hindu sculpture. The result is fascinating. A few hundred leering incarnations of deities from the Hindu pantheon are not something you'll forget in a hurry. The goporums are lavishly covered with brilliant carvings of gods, goddesses, animals and mythical figures.

Rich Pandemonium

The temples are a city within a city that includes a fascinating bazaar, bustling from dawn to nightfall. As you set out to visit the Meenakshi Temple, you will find yourself in a human tide on which the Southern women float gracefully, flowers in their jet-black hair and bright saris draped around their straight bodies.

Although there are four entrances to the Meenakshi Temple, enter through the eastern entrance and stop, for a moment, to notice the mural on the upper-right in the entrance mandapa. In 1923, when paintings were added, the Indian artist included an image of Mahatma Gandhi. When the British insisted on its removal, the artist simply turned Gandhi into a holy man with long hair. He cleverly used watercolor that eventually disappeared, revealing Gandhi, as a young man—hands held together in the traditional *namaste* greeting.

The swirling life of the Meenakshi Temple never seems to stop. However, the temple is closed to devotees from 12:30 to 4 P.M.—a time when visitors are allowed to take photographs. Too bad, for then the temple seems dead. Madurai is known as the "city of festivals" and there seems to be one just about every day. Trumpets, drums, and religious chanting constantly fill the air but do not seem to disturb pilgrims taking a quick snooze under shady arcades.

Although nonbelievers are denied access to the two sanctuaries where Meenakshi and Shiva, in his incarnation as Sundereswarar, are enshrined, they can visit the rest of the temple quite freely. Hindus have no corporate worship and perform the *puja* (worship of the gods) either themselves or through the intermediary of a priest. It used to be possible to climb to the top of one of the goporums from where the panorama over the city of temples is extraordinary, but bomb threats have entered the arena and the goporums were temporarily closed at this writing.

A legend says that this temple was founded by Indra, the Hindu god of thunder, who found a lingam in the jungle and ordered his builders to house Shiva's symbol in a temple. When Indra set foot in the temple, he found that its tank was filled by some miracle with golden lilies. You can see this tank, surrounded by a colonnade (from which you get an excellent view of the goporums, as well). Worshipers bathe in the tank of the Golden Lily, where women perform some marvelous sleights-of-hand that enable them to change saris without ever appearing to be undressed. In the past, a bath in the lily tank served another purpose: tradition has it that a Tamil author's works were judged here by the simple expedient of placing his manuscript on the water. If it stank, it sank.

The high point of the Meenakshi Temple, however, is its Hall of a Thousand Pillars. Here, again, the figure is an approximate one; the exact number of pillars is 997. This hall was built around 1560 and is as great a work of structural engineering as it is of art. The pillars are a picture book in stone that run the gamut of human expression from stateliness and grace to lusty humor and ribaldry. It has been said that visitors can wander through these pillars—which represent a grove of a thousand palm trees where a god was once found—and see something new no matter how often they return. Baroque is about the only European style approaching the exuberance of this Dravidian temple.

Outside the Hall of a Thousand Pillars are more pillars. But these are the famous "musical pillars" of the Meenakshi Temple, and they play musical notes when they are struck. The temple also contains a hall known as the Kambatti Mandapam, where Shiva in all of his various manifestations is represented on sculptured pillars.

At any time, this temple of Shiva and his wife is filled with worshipers pouring oil on minor gods, depositing flower offerings, and going through pujas in front of their deities. But its greatest day comes around the end of April during a festival celebrating the marriage of the sacred couple. The wedding is reenacted in the temple and then the images are paraded through the streets of Madurai. In all, the festive proceedings last three days. During the celebrations of the Tamil New Year (mid-April), the evening processions have a particular charm.

Once outside the majestic entrance goporums of the temple, see another example of the architectural mastery of the Nayaks. This is the palace or *mahal* of Tirumala Nayak, a blend of Hindu and Saracen architecture. Its curved dome, which soars without any visible support, is quite an accomplishment. In the evening, it is the location for an impressive *son et lumiere* presentation.

The modern city of Madurai lives side by side with its traditions. Spinning and weaving mills turn out some of the best cloth of all South India, and the city is an educational center as well. One of its two colleges was founded by an American Protestant mission (Madurai was the headquarters for missionaries as early as the seventeenth century when an Italian Jesuit came here and learned Tamil). Also, plan time to visit the Gandhi

Museum, a display of many of his possessions that is touching in its simplicity and understatement.

Five kilometers (three miles) outside Madurai is the famous Teppakulam (tank) with an island temple. It's a peaceful place, away from the hubbub and bustle. Eighteen kilometers (11 miles) away is Azhagarkoil, with some excellent sculpture in the hall of a temple, dedicated to Lord Azhagar (Vishnu). Azhagar is the brother of Meenakshi in Hindu mythology.

Rameswaram

This side trip from Madurai can be the jumping point from South India to Sri Lanka. The sacred island of Rameswaram, said to be in the shape of Lord Vishnu's conch, is about 160 kilometers (100 miles) south from Madurai, with Sri Landa only 74 kilometers (46 miles) away on the other side of Palk Strait. This sliver of land, separating the Bay of Bengal in the north from the Indian Ocean, is one of the main goals of Hindu pilgrims who come here to pay tribute to Rama, the hero of the epic *Ramayana*. Rama came here in search of his wife, Sita, who had been kidnapped. Rama is one of the ten incarnations of Vishnu, and to many pilgrims, Rameswaram is as holy as Varanasi. It is built on the site where Rama worshiped Shiva to do penance for killing Ravana, the 10-headed demon king of Lanka. Rama wanted to set up a lingam to honor Shiva, so he told the monkey god, Hanuman, to find one by a certain hour, which he was unable to do. Sita, Rama's wife, made one of sand; that explains the lingam in the principal sanctum. When Hanuman returned with a second lingam, Rama saw the monkey god's disappointment and installed this lingam too. That in turn, explains the lingam in the northern sanctum. Rameswaram is so intimately linked with Rama that, to the Hindus, every grain of sand is considered sacred.

The temple of Rameswaram, rising above a lake as a vast rectangle about 1,000 feet long and 650 feet wide, is one of the most beautifully sculptured in India. It dates back to the twelfth century, although the process of building it took 3½ centuries, with the inspiration for its construction coming from one of the princes of Sri Lanka.

Here, you find a nine-story goporum, typical of Dravidian temples. But the corridors of the Rameswaram Temple are unique. They surround the rectangle, stretching out over a distance of 4,000 feet. Through occasional apertures, light filters into these corridors and flits over the carved pillars lining every foot on both sides. Each pillar is an individual composition carved out of solid granite—one of an army—and the total effect of the two ranks standing watch on the sides of the corridors is stunning. Leading authorities call this the most evolved of all Dravidian temples.

Also try to visit the Kothandaramasamy Temple near the southernmost tip of the island. This temple marks the location where Vibishana, the kidnapper of Sita and brother of Ravana, surrendered to Rama. It is the only structure on Dhanushkodi (the tip) that survived a devastating cyclone in 1964.

Cape Comorin (Kanya Kumari)

At Dhanushkodi, two seas meet; at Cape Comorin (Kanya Kumari) at the southernmost part of India, the Bay of Bengal, the Arabian Sea, and the Indian Ocean all flow together. It was known to the ancients, too. Ptolemy called it *comaria akron* on his maps and Marco Polo knew it as Comori.

If time is a premium, this southern tip of India is overrated—crowded with too many tourists and hustling hawkers selling junk. The distance from Madurai to the cape is a good 193 kilometers (120 miles) or more, depending on the number of side trips. One possible stop is Courtallam, which lies in the Western Ghat mountain range. Its main claims to fame are the 300-foot waterfalls of the Chittar River and a small temple dedicated to Shiva. The falls have a local reputation as a spa—bathing in them is supposed to invigorate a worn-out body. From here, it's a four-hour drive to Kanya Kumari.

To the southeast, also on the sea, is Tiruchendur, with a temple dedicated to Subrahmanya, built on the seashore. After driving through the Tirunelveli district, considered one of the oldest centers of civilizations in India (prehistoric burial urns have been discovered here), you reach Kanya Kumari. Here, the Western Ghats, which begin in Mysore, run into the sea, creating an obstacle course of jagged rocks that make the cape dangerous for ships. According to legend, this is where Shiva married the goddess Parvati, daughter of King Himalaya. The seven varieties of rice thrown at the wedding were transformed for eternity into the seven-colored sands of Kanya Kumari: red, brown, yellow, silver, orange, dark blue, and purple, as they have been preserved by Varuna, god of the sea.

The Kanya Kumari Temple, erected on a promontory of the cape, is revered by Hindus. Offshore lie the two rocks where Swami Vivekanda sat overnight in meditation before dedicating himself to improving the prestige of Hinduism by visiting America to expose Westerners to his faith. Also visit the Mahatma Ghandhi Memorial, constructed on the spot where the urn containing Gandhi's ashes was relinquished to the sea. The building was specifically designed so that on his birthday—October 2—at noon, the sun's rays fall through openings in the roof and shine directly on the center of his memorial. Then, for a quiet walk, meander through the fishing village near the Catholic church. The tiny community has an appealing quasi-Portuguese feel.

Not far from Kanya Kumari is the Suchindram Temple, with its seven-story goporum and exquisite oversized water tank. This is one of the few temples that worships the trinity of Shiva, Vishnu, and Brahma. Non-Hindus can't enter the inner sanctum; the lingam inside is of three parts: the top represents Shiva, the middle represents Vishnu, and the bottom represents Brahma. The rest of the temple area (not off limits) is colorfully decorated and has musical pillars and an enormous statue of Hanuman.

Padmanabhapuram

Continue north to Padmanabhapuram, the ancient seat of the rulers of Travancore, who trace their ancestry back to A.D. 849. The Padmanabhapuram Palace, with its steep tiled roofs, white walls, woodcarvings, glossy black floors made from a crazy concoction including ash and eggwhite, and small courtyards, has an elegant pagodalike beauty that is reminiscent of Japanese domestic architecture. The palace also contains a museum with excellent old murals. In the adjoining Ramaswamy Temple, beautiful carved panels portray scenes from the *Ramayana*. From here, you can head back to Madurai or continue up the Malabar Coast into Kerala. (See *Kerala* chapter).

Kodaikanal and the Nilgiri Hill Stations

Tamil Nadu also has gentle, wooded hills framing a lake or two, which offer cool nights and a rest from temple-city intensity. Within the borders of this state are three of India's hill stations: Kodaikanal, only a short distance from Madurai; Ooctacamund (Ooty) and other delightful resorts in the Nilgiri Hills farther north; and Yercaud (east of Ooty) in the Salem district.

Kodaikanal is 121 kilometers (75 miles) from Madurai via a scenic road that runs through coffee plantations and forests as it climbs up through the Western Ghats to Kodai, at an altitude of over 2,134 meters (7,000 feet). Europeans first discovered this spot in the Palni Hills in 1821. Fifteen years later, the collector of Madurai (the equivalent of a district governor) built a house that was soon followed by a rush of imitations. The descendants of these nineteenth-century Europeans still flock to Kodaikanal for the holiday seasons (April-June and September-October), when vacationers can count on the cooperation of the climate and sun.

It's not just the weather that brings people to Kodaikanal; the ride *is* gorgeous. A wise man, Sir Vere Levenge, put a finishing touch on the hill resort landscape by damming a stream to form a lake, with a three-mile walkway and riding trail around it. Boating on the lake is one of the popular pastimes in Kodaikanal. There are also tennis and golf clubs and numerous walks you can take, but no elegant old-fashioned hotels.

The Queen of Hill Stations—Ooty

The Queen of South India's hill stations is Ootacamund, "Snooty Ooty," the capital of a chain of resorts in the Nilgiris or the Blue Hills (*nila* means blue and *giri* means hill) on the northern edge of Tamil Nadu.

With its green downs, gentle rains, and temperatures ranging between 50 and 60 degrees Fahrenheit most of the time, Ootacamund was adopted as a summer home away from home at an early date by British officials and planters in South India. After a few tentative attempts to penetrate the Nilgiris, whose scenic beauties were previously enjoyed only by the aboriginals, a collector of Coimbatore named John Sullivan went up to Ootacamund in 1819. Sullivan liked it so much that he became the first European to build a house there. By 1824, other English people were settling in the hills, and they were followed by Indian maharajahs. Then, the British governors of Madras made Ooty their summer resort and built the Government House there. One of them, the duke of Buckingham, brought his English penchant for gardening with him, making life hell for the workers laying out the gardens of Government House. One morning, informally unshaven and dressed in old clothes, he started to give advice to one of the gardeners who didn't recognize him. The gardener finally had enough. He turned to him in disgust and said, "The way you go on, man, it would seem you was the duke himself."

The Todas and other hill people encountered by Sullivan in 1819 would never recognize their Ootacamund today. Thousands of summer houses are scattered over the hills, with the owners busy playing golf and tennis or shopping on Charing Cross, the heart of Ooty. The town boasts botanical gardens, an annual flower show, a number of hotels, and a select circle of clubs where "snooty" of Ooty fulfills its name.

The downs of Ootacamund might well be in Devon or Yorkshire. There are 80 kilometers (50 miles) of them, fortunately served by excellent roads, and they offer golf, hunting, or just walking. Closer by are the 110-year-old Government Botanical Gardens with more than 650 varieties of plants. An artificial lake, conceived by Sullivan in 1823, gilds the lily of Ooty's natural beauty. It's small, but it offers pleasant boating and good fishing. Near the shore of the lake is Hobart Park where weekly horse races are run in season.

Ooty is also a good jumping-off point for short and medium-length side trips into the hills. The biggest of these is Doddabetta, 2,634 meters (8,640 feet) high (most of it is done by car). Snowdon and Elk Hill (with its rock temple) are the two runners-up in size, though heavily wooded Cairn Hill is certainly the most beautiful.

Mukurthi Peak, a drive of 26 kilometers (16 miles) down the picturesque Mysore Road, is the Todas' gateway to heaven. In days when female infanticide still prevailed among them, the condemned babies used to be taken to this hill to be done away with. Unlike the other Nilgiri tribes, these handsome people did not turn to agriculture or handicrafts; they still preserve their ancient way of life as herdsmen of the hills. Barely a thousand of them, they are recognizable by their flowing beards and long toga-like robes.

About 64 kilometers (40 miles) from Ooty is the Mudumalai Game Sanctuary, with a full roll call of Indian wildlife.

Besides Ooty, there are two other hill stations in the Nilgiris. Kotagiri is 1,981 meters (6,500 feet) above sea level and 19 kilometers (12 miles) from Ooty, while Coonoor is 29 kilometers (18 miles) down the mountain railway line at an altitude of only 1,707 meters (5,600 feet). The climate here is somewhat warmer than at Ooty. Coonoor is surrounded by tea plantations and has a shady park (Sim's Park) and some pleasant walks for hikers. Kotagiri is an island of green fields (including a golf course) surrounded by thick forests. It's one of the quietest spots in the Nilgiris and in all of South India.

Yercaud—the Jewel of the South

Northeast of Ooty is Yercaud, a quiet resort in the Servaroyan Hills (Sheraroy Range), about an hour's drive beyond Salem. At an elevation of 3,048 meters (5,000 feet), the climate is inviting all year round. Yercaud has appealing vistas, gardens, waterfalls, and a lake. You can also arrange a trip to the Servaroyan Temple stop, the third highest peak in the Sheraroy Range. During the annual festival in May, hundreds of tribal people from the Yercaud area arrive at the temple area, a festive and colorful event. Yercaud is also the least expensive hill station in Tamil Nadu, and the least "discovered."

PRACTICAL INFORMATION FOR TAMIL NADU

WHEN TO GO. This is a place to visit during winter. Here the thermometer never falls below 70° F but often rises to 90° F between November and February, and humidity can be high. When it's overcoat weather in Delhi (December-February), you can lie on the beach in Tamil Nadu. Summer (April-June) is forbidding, except in hill resorts like Ootacamund or Yercaud. The beach resorts of the South, like Mahabalipuram, are fun all year long, since you've got the water to cool off from the heat. Festivals, especially the spectacular "car" processions in major temple towns, are found year round, but most frequently in March-April. The best months for the hill stations are April-June and September-October.

HOW TO GET THERE. By Air. The following cities in India have direct daily *Indian Airlines* flights into Madras: Bangalore, Bombay, Calcutta, Cochin, Delhi, Hyderabad, and Trivandrum. Madras is also an international airport connecting the city to Colombo in Sri Lanka (*Air India* and *Air Lanka*), to Penang and Kuala Lumpur in Malaysia (*Malaysian Airline System*), and to Singapore (*Singapore Air-*

lines and Air India). *Vayudoot* has occasional flights to Madras from Bangalore, Cochin, Calicut, Rajahmundry, Tirupathi, Trivandrum, and Vijayawada.

By Bus. *The Thiruvalluvar Transport Corporation* (TTC) operates daily express deluxe coaches from Madras, to Bangalore, Ernakulam (Cochin), Mysore, Pondicherry, Trivandrum, and other important southern Indian cities. As with most deluxe buses running throughout India, these buses are usually rolling television sets: Hindi movies blaring from the first kilometer to the last. So be prepared. Otherwise, the buses are more efficient, cleaner, cheaper, and faster than any train. For details, fares, and reservations, call *Express Bus Stand,* Esplanade, tel. 561835/36 in Madras.

By Train. There are some daily fast train services from India's principal cities to Madras (central). Some of the crack trains are the air-conditioned *Tamil Nadu Express* (reclining seats and so forth) four times weekly (journey time, 30 hours), and the *Grand Trunk Express,* with air-conditioned coaches, operating daily, both from Delhi. From Calcutta, the best train is the *Coromandel Express,* with air-conditioned coaches. From Madras (Egmore), you can reach Colombo by rail and ferry, which links Rameswaram with Talaimanar in Sri Lanka. The best train is the *Rameswaram Express,* which reaches Rameswaram in approximately 17 hours. Usually, you have to spend the night in Rameswaram to catch the ferry, which operates three times a week. The steamer from Rameswaram to Talaimanar Pier (Sri Lanka) takes 3½ hours. It does not run in December and January. Remember that with every train that involves an overnight ride, you must pay for a sleeper and *reserve* a berth. Otherwise, you might find yourself off the train. Also travel at night via first class, first class air-conditioned, or second class air-conditioned. And always check to see if your class sleeper supplies bedding (it usually only comes with first class air-conditioned). Sometimes you can rent bedding for the night.

By Rented Car with Driver. You can reasonably drive to Madras from the following cities: Bangalore, 334 km (207 mi.); Pondicherry, 162 km (100 mi.); Mysore, 465 km (288 mi.); and the Periyar Wildlife Sanctuary, 554 km (343 mi.). Hire a car from a tour operator listed below or listed in the state chapter from which you depart. Rates are about Rs. 3–Rs. 4 per km, with a Rs. 50–Rs. 100 halt charge per night.

TOURIST INFORMATION. When you get to Madras, visit the *Tamil Nadu Government Tourist Office* at 143 Anna Salai (Mount Road), Madras (tel. 840752, open 9:45 A.M.–5:45 P.M., closed Sundays). There's also a Tamil Nadu Information Center at the airport (8 A.M.–8 P.M.) and another branch at the Central Railway Station Counter (7:15 A.M.–7:15 P.M.). Also contact *Tamil Nadu Tourism Development Corporation* (TTDC), at the same address (tel. 849803 and 849115), to arrange for low-budget tours or to book government-run accommodations and a car with driver. Open daily, 24 hours. You can also contact the *Government of India Tourist Office* at 154 Anna Salai (Mount Road), Madras (tel. 869685; open 9 A.M.–5:30 P.M.; closed Sundays). It also has a counter at the airport, open around the clock.

These two bureaus have excellent information and maps on Madras and the rest of Tamil Nadu. They also offer excellent guides and can give you information about Tamil Nadu sightseeing tours. The staffs are extremely helpful. In the rest of the state, you'll find Tamil Nadu Tourist offices or counters in the following cities and areas. Most of them are open 9:45 A.M.–5:45 P.M., Monday–Friday.

Chidambaram. Railway Feeder Road, tel. 2739.

Coimbatore. Railway station, no phone.

Kanya Kumari (Cape Comorin). Beach Road, tel. 276.

Kodaikanal. Township Bus Stand.

Madurai. Hotel Tamil Nadu Complex, West Veli Street (near Central Bus Stand), tel. 22957; at the Railway Junction, tel. 24535; and at the Madurai Airport.

Mahabalipuram. Tel: 232.

Ootacamund. Super Market Building, Charing Cross, tel. 3977.

Pondicherry. Old Secretariate Building, Campagnie Street, tel: 4398 or 4406.

Rameswaram. 14 E. Car Street, tel. 371.

Salem. (near Yercaud) Tel: 66449.

Thanjavur. Hotel Tamil Nadu Complex, Gandhiji Road.

Tiruchirapalli. No. 1 Williams Road, tel. 40136. Information also at airport and railroad station.

FOREIGN CURRENCY EXCHANGE. Most Western-style hotels have exchange counters. Otherwise, go to a branch of the *State Bank of India,* open Monday–Friday, 10 A.M.–2 P.M.; Saturdays, till noon.

ACCOMMODATIONS. Hotel and guest house accommodations in Tamil Nadu run the gamut from expensive (by Indian standards) to cheap. Madras, in particular, has numerous hotels, but many are substandard and offer shoddy service, especially the hotels in the inexpensive range. The hotels we list may not have the most luxurious appearances, but looks can deceive. Our choices offer courteous service and clean rooms. Prices are based on double occupancy and exclude taxes: *Deluxe,* over Rs. 1,450; *Expensive,* Rs. 950–Rs. 1,450; *Moderate,* Rs. 500–Rs. 950; *Inexpensive,* under Rs. 500. Some Western-style hotels take major credit cards.

CHIDAMBARAM

Inexpensive

Hotel Tamilnadu. Station Rd., Chidambaram; tel. 2323. 23 rooms with bath. This modest, government-run hotel offers clean, simple rooms with fans. Some rooms are air-conditioned. There is a multicuisine restaurant and a bar. Rupees only.

COIMBATORE

Inexpensive

Hotel Surya International. 105 Race Course Rd., Coimbatore; tel. 37751. 44 rooms with bath. A Western-style hotel, its rooms have simple decor and TVs. Request air-conditioning, if that's your preference. Multicuisine restaurant, bar, room service, foreign-exchange counter. AE, DC, MC, V.

Hotel Tamilnadu. Dr. Nanjappa Rd., Coimbatore; tel. 36311. 49 rooms with bath. This government-run facility offers clean simple rooms with fans; some rooms are air-conditioned. Multicuisine restaurant and bar. Rupees only.

COVELONG BEACH
32 km (20 mi.) from Madras

Expensive

Taj Fisherman's Cove. Chingleput District; tel. Chingleput 6268. 100 rooms with bath. This resort, set in a cove, offers modern air-conditioned rooms in a high rise or in cottages nestled in a grove. Cottages offer more privacy. All rooms overlook the sea and have TV. Multicuisine restaurants, bar, room service, foreign-exchange counter, travel agency, swimming pool, tennis, water sports, baby-sitters, doctor, shops. AE, DC, MC, V.

KANCHIPURAM

Inexpensive

Hotel Tamilnadu. Kamatchi Sannathi St., near Railway Station, Kanchipuram; tel. 2561. 18 rooms with bath. This new government-run hotel has clean, modestly furnished, air-conditioned rooms. Multicuisine restaurant, room service. Rupees only.

KODAIKANAL

Expensive

Carlton Hotel. Lake Rd., Kodaikanal; tel. 252. 93 rooms with bath. On a lovely lawn overlooking a lake, this Western-style hotel has spacious modern rooms with TV. Multicuisine restaurant, bar, room service, golf and tennis arrangements, boat-

352 INDIA

ing, shopping arcade, health club, travel agency, foreign-exchange counter. Meals included. AE, DC, MC, V.

MADRAS

Expensive

Oberoi Trident Hotel. 1/24 G.S.T. Rd., Madras; tel. 434747. 162 rooms with bath. Located near the airport and 10 km (six mi.) from the city, this new Western-style hotel has an attractive lobby with an enclosed interior garden and water cascade. Spacious, air-conditioned rooms are elegant, with a decor that incorporates Indian fabrics. Best rooms overlook the pool. TV, room service, multicuisine restaurants, bar, swimming pool, health club, foreign-exchange counter, travel agency, business center, courtesy airport shuttle, shopping arcade, 12-hour room rate (half-price) for transit travelers. AE, DC, MC, V.

Taj Coromandel Hotel. 17 Nungambakkam High Rd., Madras; tel. 810441. 225 rooms with bath. Centrally located, this high rise has an elegant lobby with teak pillars and teak set into the ceiling. The air-conditioned rooms are scheduled for renovation. TV, room service, multicuisine restaurants, bar, swimming pool, health club, doctor, foreign-exchange counter, travel agency, business center, shopping arcade. AE, DC, MC, V.

Taj Hotel Connemara. Binnys Rd., Madras; tel. 860123. 149 rooms with bath. The city's prettiest Western-style hotel, it's also centrally located and has a lovely lobby and numerous quiet lounges and garden areas. The old wing has "deluxe" rooms that have contemporary furnishings. Best rooms in this class have private terraces leading to the pool. Standard doubles (in the new wing) are also attractive. Ask for a river view. Air-conditioning, TV, multicuisine restaurants, bar, room service, swimming pool, baby-sitters, doctor, travel agency, foreign-exchange counter, shopping arcade, business center. AE, DC, MC, V.

Welcomgroup Adayar Park. 132 TTK Rd., Box 1453, Madras; tel. 452525. 160 rooms with bath. A centrally-located, modern monolith, the Adayar Park has a marble lobby that is lavish and spacious. The air-conditioned rooms are done up in soft hues, including satin print curtains and bedspreads, and have TV. Multicuisine restaurants, bar, room service, swimming pool, health club, foreign-exchange counter, travel agency, shopping arcade, business center. AE, DC, MC, V.

Welcomgroup Chola Sheraton. 10 Cathedral Rd., Madras; tel. 473347. 133 rooms with bath. This hotel is also centrally located. Rooms are air-conditioned and spacious, with a contemporary decor. Best rooms overlook the pool. TV, room service, multicuisine restaurants, bar, foreign-exchange counter, travel agency, health club, swimming pool, golfing arrangements, bank, business center, shopping arcade. AE, DC, MC, V.

Moderate

Ambassador Pallava. 53 Montieth Rd., Madras; tel. 868584. 120 rooms with bath. This centrally located, Western-style hotel offers spacious rooms with a reasonably modern decor. Best rooms have balconies that overlook the pool. Air-conditioning, TV, room service, multicuisine restaurants, bar, swimming pool, health club, business center, foreign-exchange counter, travel agency, shopping arcade. AE, DC, MC, V.

Savera Hotel. 69 Dr. Radhakrishnan Rd., Madras; tel. 474700. 125 rooms with bath. This Western-style high rise is centrally located, has a pleasant lobby, and offers modern air-conditioned rooms with uninspired decor. Best rooms overlook the pool. TV, room service, multicuisine restaurants, bar, swimming pool, foreign-exchange and travel counter, shopping arcade. AE, DC, MC, V.

Sindoori Hotel. 24 Greams Lane, off Greams Rd., Madras; tel. 471164. 79 rooms with bath. This new Western-style hotel is centrally located and has a pretty marble lobby. Spacious "deluxe" doubles have attractive contemporary furnishings and TV. All rooms are modern and air-conditioned. Room service, multicuisine restaurants, bar, foreign-exchange and travel counter, business center, doctor, shopping arcade. Excellent value. AE, DC, MC, V.

Inexpensive

Hotel Blue Diamond. 934 E.V.R. Periyar Salai, Madras; tel. 665981. 33 rooms with bath. This small Western-style hotel, which is centrally located, isn't fancy, but its simple rooms are clean and have TV. Best rooms are air-conditioned. Multicuisine restaurant, room service, foreign-exchange and travel counter. AE, DC, MC, V.

Madras International Hotel. 693 Mount Rd., Madras; tel. 861811. 63 rooms with bath. This centrally located hotel offers good service and rooms with simple modern furnishings, air-conditioning, and TV. Just insist on a quiet room, with a view, on an upper floor. Multicuisine restaurant, room service, bar, foreign-exchange and travel counter. AE, DC, MC, V.

Hotel Maris. 9 Cathedral Rd., Madras; tel. 470541. 70 rooms with bath. This centrally located high rise has large, clean rooms with balconies and simple, modern decor. Best rooms are air-conditioned and have TV. Vegetarian Indian-cuisine restaurant, bar, room service, foreign-exchange and travel counter, doctor. Rupees only.

Transit House. 26 Venkataraman St., T. Nagar, Madras; tel. 441346. 4 rooms with bath. Set in a middle-class neighborhood, this house has very simple air-conditioned rooms; but they're clean and the service is excellent. Breakfast on request. Very inexpensive. Rupees only.

MADURAI

Moderate

Hotel Madurai Ashok. Alagarkoil Rd., Madurai; tel. 42531. 43 rooms with bath. A Western-style, two-story bungalow, the Madurai Ashok has modern rooms that are spacious, clean, and air-conditioned. There's also a lovely lawn. TV, room service, multicuisine restaurant, bar, foreign-exchange counter, doctor. AE, DC, MC, V.

Pandyan Hotel. Racc Course, Madurai; tel. 42470. 57 rooms with bath. Madurai's best hotel, the Pandyan has reasonably attractive, air-conditioned rooms and an inviting lawn. TV, room service, multicuisine restaurant, bar, travel agency, foreign-exchange counter, shopping arcade. AE, DC, MC, V.

Inexpensive

Hotel Tamilnadu. Alagarkoil Rd., Madurai; tel. 42461. 51 rooms with bath. This Western-style, government-run hotel has clean rooms with fans. Best rooms are air-conditioned. Amenities include room service, restaurant, bar, shops. Good value. Rupees only.

MAHABALIPURAM

Inexpensive–Deluxe

Silver Sands. Mahabalipuram; tel. 228. Reservations also available through Silver Sands, Safire Theatre, Mount Rd., Madras; tel. 477444. 75 rooms with bath. A secluded beach resort, Silver Sands has a whimsical ethnic decor that creates a charming rustic ambience. Villas (deluxe price) have beach views, TV, and music systems. One villa has its own interior swimming pool; another has a private sundeck. Beach front rooms (moderately priced) have a sitting room with swings and verandas overlooking the ocean. "Deluxe" rooms (also moderate) lack an ocean view, but have a sitting room with swing and delightful decor. Standard rooms (inexpensive) have interior swings, but no sea view. All rooms are air-conditioned. There are open-air, multicuisine restaurants, bars, room service, excellent beach, swimming pool, mini-golf, fishing and cultural program arrangements, disco, yoga, free shuttle into Mahabalipuram, foreign-exchange counter, travel arrangements, bikes for rent, shops. Off-season discount May–October. AE, DC, MC, V.

Moderate

Temple Bay Ashok Beach Resort. Mahabalipuram; tel. 251. 23 rooms with bath. Overlooking the ocean, this complex offers rooms in the main building and in cottages (two doubles per unit). Air-conditioned cottages are best, with beach views and modern furnishings. TV, room service, multicuisine restaurant, bar, swimming pool, good beach, foreign-exchange and travel counter. AE, DC, MC, V.

Inexpensive

Ideal Beach Resort. Mahabalipuram; tel. 240. 25 rooms with bath. A personalized beach resort, Ideal Resort features a Sri Lankan touch with lush green gardens decorated with sculptures. Best rooms are upstairs in two-story, air-conditioned cottages, with modest decor and a veranda offering an ocean view. Room service, multicuisine restaurant, swimming pool, good beach, foreign-exchange and travel counter. AE, DC, MC, V.

MUDUMALLAI WILDLIFE SANCTUARY

Inexpensive

Bamboo Banks Farm Guest House. Masinigudi, Nilgiris, Tamil Nadu; tel. 22 via Ooty. 6 rooms with bath. Located in the sanctuary, this place has comfortable double rooms in the guest house and pleasantly furnished cottages. There is a multicuisine restaurant as well as facilities for horseback riding, swimming, birdwatching, and wildlife safaris by jeep or elephant. Charges for activities can be steep; set the cost in advance. AE, DC.

Jungle Hut. Masinigudi, Nilgiris; tel. 40 via Ooty. 8 rooms with bath. Also in the sanctuary, this charming resort offers rooms featuring exposed-brick and stone walls and Indian "country-style" furnishings—lots of bamboo and handlooms. Excellent multicuisine buffet meals, room service, jeep and elephant safaris, swimming; trekking arrangements and fishing available on advance notice. Traveler's checks or rupees.

OOTACAMUND

Moderate

Quality Inn Southern Star. 32 Havelock Rd., Ootacamund; tel. 3601. 67 rooms with bath. A new Western-style hotel overlooking Ooty, Southern Star has spacious rooms with modern furnishings and TV. Multicuisine restaurant, bar, room service, health club, billiards, travel and foreign-exchange counter, shopping arcade. AE, DC, MC, V.

Taj Savoy Hotel. Club Rd., Ootacamund; tel. 4142. 60 rooms with bath. Ooty's finest hotel is set on a lawn with lovely gardens. The pink-stucco bungalow is well-appointed with reminders of the Raj; separate cottages are attractively furnished. TV, room service, multicuisine restaurant, bar, doctor, car-rental service, foreign-exchange counter, tennis, billiards, golfing, trekking, horseback riding, and fishing arrangements. AE, DC, MC, V.

PONDICHERRY

Moderate

Grand Hotel d'Europe. 12 Rue Suffren, Pondicherry; tel. 404. 6 rooms with bath. Set on a quiet street, this older hotel, established in 1891, is run by a fastidious Frenchman. The ambience is wonderful and the food is delicious. The rooms are simply furnished, but immaculate, and have fans and mosquito netting. Room service and restaurant. Meals included. Rupees only.

Hotel Pondicherry Ashok. Chinahalapet, Pondicherry; tel. 440. 20 rooms with bath. Set on a beautiful beach, this new two-story hotel has spacious, air-conditioned rooms done up in a modern decor. Best rooms are facing the sea. TV, room service, Indian- and Continental-cuisine restaurant, bar, doctor, foreign-exchange counter, shopping arcade. AE, DC, MC, V.

Inexpensive

Park Guest House. Goubert Salai, Pondicherry; tel. 4412. 80 rooms with bath. This Western-style hotel, set on the beach and run by the Auroville Ashram, is a bargain as long as you don't mind pictures of "Mother" and other important ashram figures on the walls. Clean rooms have fans and mosquito netting. Ask for a room overlooking the beach. Indian and Continental restaurant, room service, bike rentals. Rupees only.

RAMESWARAM

Inexpensive

Hotel Tamilnadu. Rameswaram; tel. 277. 26 rooms with bath. This beach-front government-run hotel offers clean, simple rooms with fans and balconies that overlook the ocean. Some rooms are air-conditioned; restaurant, room service. Rupees only.

THANJAVUR

Inexpensive

Hotel Parisutham. 55 G. A. Canal Rd., Thanjavur; tel. 21466. 42 rooms with bath. This new Western-style hotel, set on a pleasant lawn, has attractive modern rooms with fans or air-conditioning and TV. Multicuisine restaurants, bar, room service, foreign-exchange counter, travel agency, secretarial services. AE, DC, MC, V.

Hotel Tamilnadu. Gandhi Rd., Thanjavur; tel. 57. 31 rooms with bath. This government-run hotel has a simple Western-style decor, but fan-cooled rooms are clean. Best rooms open onto an upstairs veranda overlooking an interior courtyard. Multicuisine restaurant, bar, room service. Rupees only.

TIRUCHIRAPALLI

Moderate

Hotel Sangam. Collectors Office Rd., Tiruchirapalli; tel. 41514. 58 rooms with bath. A Western-style hotel, set on a lawn, Sangam offers reasonable rooms with a modern decor, air-conditioning, TV, and room service. Multicuisine restaurant, bar, foreign-exchange counter, travel agency, doctor, shopping arcade. AE, DC.

Inexpensive

Hotel Aristo. 2 Dindigul Rd., Tiruchirapalli; tel. 41818. 31 rooms with bath. Though this Western-style hotel has spacious rooms in the main complex, the best rooms are in "theme" cottages done up in eclectic decors, such as Tamil Nadu and vintage California kitsch. Service is excellent; the price is just right. Some rooms are air-conditioned. Indian- and Continental-cuisine restaurant, room service, travel agency, foreign-exchange counter, doctor, shopping arcade. AE, DC.

Rajali Hotel. 3/14 MacDonalds Rd., Tiruchirapalli; tel. 41301. 78 rooms with bath. Rooms in this Western-style hotel have a modern decor with TV. The management is extremely helpful. Excellent multicuisine restaurants, bar, room service, swimming pool, health club, shopping arcade, doctor, travel agency, foreign-exchange counter, secretarial services. AE, DC, MC, V.

YERCAUD (SALEM)

Inexpensive

National Hotel. Omalur Rd., Salem; tel. 54100. 90 rooms with bath. This Western-style complex offers modern rooms in the main building and rooms in pleasant cottages. Best rooms in both facilities are air-conditioned. Multicuisine restaurant, room service, travel counter. Rupees only.

DINING OUT. South India's curries, mixed with coconut milk, are hotter than in the north but not as rich; instead of fat, only a light oil is used in most dishes. Since many South Indians are vegetarians, you find a wide variety of tasty vegetable dishes. Some of the best—and least expensive—meals are found in simply decorated *bhavans* (Indian-style coffee shops) that serve delicious coffee and *thali* (named after the metal plate on which the meal is served). Thali is an epicurean's delight: generous servings of numerous tasty items (curried vegetables, rice, *dhal*, curd, *poori*). Sometimes the meal is served on a clean banana leaf. Bhavans also serve traditional *dosas, pakora, idli,* and vegetable cutlets. We list some excellent bhavans, but if you see a crowded restaurant, its popularity is a good indication that the food is good.

Also keep in mind that many accommodations listed above also have restaurants. Breakfast is usually 8–10; lunch, noon–2:30; dinner, 7:30–10. Payment is normally in rupees unless the restaurant is connected to a Western-style hotel. The restaurants listed below are informal and, unless noted, are open for all three meals and don't require reservations. Prices, based on one person eating a three-course meal, excluding taxes, tip, or beverage, are *Deluxe,* over Rs. 120; *Expensive,* Rs. 80–Rs. 120; *Moderate,* Rs. 40–Rs. 80; *Inexpensive,* under Rs. 40.

CHIDAMBARAM

Inexpensive

This small town has numerous good bhavans that serve excellent vegetarian meals in ethnic surroundings. All are open 7 A.M.–9 P.M.; no phones; rupees only:

Sri Mahalakshmi Vilas. East Gate.

Star Restaurant. South Car St.

Udipi Sri Krishna. South Car St.

KODAIKANAL

Expensive

Silver Oaks and **Terrace.** Carlton Hotel; tel. 252. Overlooking the back lawn and lake, Silver Oaks serves good Indian and Continental dishes. Dinner reservations advised. Open 7:30–10 A.M., 12:30–2:30 P.M., 7:30–10:30 P.M. The Terrace, in the back lawn, serves tandoori specialties and grilled barbecue dishes. Open 11:30 A.M.–2:30 P.M. and 6–8:30 P.M. AE, DC, MC, V.

MADRAS

Deluxe

Dakshin. Welcomgroup Adayar Park, 132 TTK Rd.; tel. 452525. A handsome restaurant, with Tanjore paintings, South Indian statues, and brass lanterns shaped like temple bells, Dakshin features the cuisines of India's southern states. Meals are served on a banana leaf set in a silver thali dish. At night, there's an Indian flutist. The non-vegetarian or vegetarian thali gives a taste of all the cuisines. Dinner reservations advised. Open 12:30–3 P.M. and 7:30–midnight. AE, DC, MC, V.

Golden Dragon. Taj Coromandel Hotel, 17 Nungambakkam High Rd.; tel. 810441. Oriental elegance sets the tone of this intimate Chinese restaurant: brass lanterns hang from the ceiling, dragon murals adorn the walls. Specialties include fish in hot tomato sauce, stir-fried lobster with garlic and scallions, and Cantonese stir-fried shredded lamb. Reservations advised. Open 12:30–3 P.M. and 7:30–11:45 P.M. AE, DC, MC, V.

The Other Room. Ambassador Pallava, 53 Montieth Rd.; tel. 868584. Thousands of seashells hang from this restaurant's ceiling, mirrors decorate its walls. Nightly, except Wednesdays, a Western rock band entertains and you can dance. At lunch, enjoy a good buffet or order à la carte from the Continental and Indian-cuisine menu. Try the lobster thermidor, chateaubriand, or the *sikandri raan* (spicy leg of lamb cooked in a tandoori). Dinner reservations advised. Open 12:30–3 P.M. and 8–midnight. AE, DC, MC, V.

Peshawri. Welcomgroup Chola Sheraton, 10 Cathedral Rd.; tel. 473347. Peshawri's Pathan decor—rough stone walls, copper plates, and soft lighting—is handsome. The Indian Northwest Frontier cuisine, with an emphasis on tandooris, is good. Among the specialties are tasty *murgh malai kebab* (boneless chicken marinated in cheese, cream, and lime juice) and *kadak seekh reshni* (crispy rolled chicken cooked over a grill). Dinner reservations advised. Open 12:30–3 P.M. and 7:30–midnight. AE, DC, MC, V.

The Rain Tree. Taj Hotel Connemara, Binnys Rd.; tel. 861023. This outdoor restaurant is in a delightful garden with delicate lights strung in the trees. It offers a Bharata Natyam dance recital and an Indian flute performance, and tasty Tamil Nadu *chettinad* cuisine served on a banana leaf set in a copper plate. Specialties include *vathal kozhambu* (sun-ripened berries cooked in a spicy chettinad gravy) and *yera varuwal* (prawns marinated in chettinad masala, then deep fried). Dinner reservations advised. Open 7:30–midnight. AE, DC, MC, V.

The Residency. Welcomgroup Adayar Park, 132 TTK Rd.; tel. 452525. Wrought-iron gates lead into The Residency; inside are a mirrored ceiling, lace curtains bordered by heavy drapes, and a rich red-and-green decor. The food is good, whether you choose tasty Chinese, Indian, or Continental dishes. At lunch, there's a buffet; at night, expect a Western dance band and à la carte menu. Order the good butter chicken, spicy chili chicken, or the pepper steak. Dinner reservations advised. Open 12:30–3 P.M. and 7:30–midnight. AE, DC, MC, V.

Shanghai. Oberoi Trident Hotel, 1/24 GST Rd., near the airport; tel. 434747. Pretty upholstered chairs, lacquered black lattices, paintings of emperors, and a good view of an enclosed interior garden and water cascade add up to an appealing ambience for Chinese fare. Try the spicy king prawns sautéed in *sambal* sauce (a chili paste mixed with fruit jam) or the mildly spicy chicken served in lotus leaves. Dinner reservations advised. Open 12:30–2:45 P.M. and 7:30–11:45 P.M. AE, DC, MC, V.

Expensive

Chinatown. 74 Cathedral Rd.; tel. 476221. An upstairs restaurant, Chinatown has subdued lighting and a bright red and black Oriental decor in its three adjoining rooms. The Chinese food is tasty, including fried crab in green pepper or chicken in oyster sauce. Dinner reservations advised. Open 11 A.M.–3 P.M. and 7–midnight. AE, DC, MC, V.

Moderate

Cascade. Kakani Towers, K.N.K. Rd., near Taj Cormandel Hotel; tel. 472514. This pleasant restaurant, run by a professor, has some mirrored walls, a chipped marble fountain, and a white- and silver-blue decor. Quiet Chinese taped-music creates the right mood for tasty Chinese, Malayasian, Japanese, and Thai cuisine. Specialties include *phukut* fish (fried sailfish fillet with garlic and chili paste), chili crab, and Szechuan *sapo* (prawns, chicken, fish, or lamb marinated in five-spice powder, then cooked and served in a sapo dish). Don't over order; portions are large. Dinner reservations advised. Open noon–3 P.M. and 7–11 P.M. AE, DC, MC, V.

Inexpensive–Moderate

Dasa. 806 Mount Rd., no phone. This spacious informal restaurant, with a high ceiling, attractive cedar gazebo, lattice screens, and Tiffany-style lamps is cosmopolitan chic. The food is tasty vegetarian—Indian and Continental. There's also a salad bar, delicious ice creams, and fresh fruit drinks. At lunch, a pianist plays Western standards. Open noon–3 P.M. and 7–midnight. DC, V.

Inexpensive

Amaravathi Hotel. 1 Cathedral Rd., opposite Music Academy; tel. 476416. An older restaurant, this place has four small rooms with booths and tables and usually a crowd that comes for the excellent Andhra Pradesh–style cuisine. House favorites are spicy chicken Amaravathi or the "vegetable meal" served on a banana leaf. Open 11 A.M.–3 P.M. and 7–11 P.M. Rupees only.

Hotel Hari Nivas. 168 Thambu Chetty St., near High Court Building; tel. 582121. This 52-year-old Madras institution is in an old hotel in a crowded bazaar. Have fun while you eat vegetarian Indian food served on a banana leaf if it's the set meal, on a metal plate if it's a snack. For snacks, you can eat in a fan-cooled lunch hall or in an air-conditioned side room with an illuminated shrine to Krishna. For a set meal, you can eat in an air-conditioned room with a shrine to its owner.

Lunch rooms are open 8 A.M.–7 P.M. Set meal rooms are open 10 A.M.–3 P.M. and 6–9 P.M. Rupees only.

Navaratna. Safire Theatre Basement, 614 Mount Rd.; tel. 477444. An intimate downstairs restaurant, with Gujarati and Rajasthani decor and soft lighting, Navaratna serves an authentic Gujarati and Rajasthani vegetarian thali (small portions of assorted dishes served on a metal platter). Come hungry; portions are unlimited. Open 12:30–3:30 P.M. and 7:30–10:30 P.M. Rupees only.

MADURAI

Inexpensive

New Arya Bhavan. 242 West Masi St.; tel. 34577. This popular, air-conditioned eatery is simple and clean. Its vegetarian fare is delicious. You can also eat in the garden. Open 6:30 A.M.–10:30 P.M. Rupees only.

MAHABALIPURAM

Moderate–Expensive

Seafront Restaurant. Silver Sands; tel. 228. This open-air restaurant and bar, set under a thatched roof on the beach, offers excellent Chinese, Continental, and Indian dishes, including fresh seafood. Open 24 hours. AE, DC, MC, V.

Whispering Woods. Silver Sands; tel. 228. Eat at tables set in a pine grove out of sight but not sound of the beach. While waiting for your food, relax in a hammock and swing. The cuisine is similar to Seafront. It also has occasional nighttime concerts. Open 10 A.M.–11 P.M. AE, DC, MC, V.

Moderate

Fiesta Bar-B-Q Restaurant. Shore Temple Rd.; no phone. This charming, super-informal restaurant is in a thatched hut with an interior courtyard that has palm trees and plants. Sand is beneath your feet and at night seashell lights and candles create a romantic touch. The chef prepares good multicuisine dishes. Try the *tava* fried prawns grilled with masala or the fish *shaslic* (batter-dipped pieces of fillet fried and served with a tangy sauce). Open 7 A.M.–11 P.M. Rupees only.

Ideal Beach Resort. Beach Rd.; tel. 240. Eat in a pretty garden or in a simple interior restaurant with Sri Lankan murals and sculptures. The chef serves Indian, Continental, and especially good Sri Lankan items, such as Sri Lankan rice and curry or Sri Lankan fish curry. Follow your meal with *vatil appam* (custard). Open 7 A.M.–10 P.M. AE, DC, MC, V.

Sunrise Restaurant. Beach Rd.; no phone. Set in a cozy thatched hut (no ocean view but cool tropical breezes), this restaurant serves Indian, Continental, and Chinese cuisines. Order the fish steak steamed with tomato, garlic, and butter, or the grilled lobster or jumbo prawns. Open 7:30 A.M.–11 P.M. Rupees only.

PONDICHERRY

Moderate–Expensive

Grand Hotel d'Europe. 12 Rue Suffren; tel. 404. The chef in this hotel dining room prepares excellent French food. There is a fixed-menu. You must call in advance for lunch or dinner, noon–3 and 7–midnight. The dining room is extremely small. Rupees only.

Moderate

Hotel Aristo. 30 E. Nehru St.; tel. 4524. This informal rooftop restaurant serves reliably good Chinese, Indian, and Continental cuisines. It's popular, so don't expect a fast meal. Open 7 A.M.–10 P.M. Rupees only.

Inexpensive

Indian Coffee House. Nehru St.; no phone. You can get good vegetarian dishes and coffee at this popular and informal restaurant. Open 7 A.M.–10 P.M. Rupees only.

THANJAVUR

Inexpensive

Hotel Karthik. 73 South Rampart St.; tel. 21116. This wonderful local restaurant, with an extremely simple decor, serves excellent coffee and vegetarian meals on a banana leaf. Lots of fun. Open 7 A.M.–10 P.M. Rupees only.

Sathars Restaurant. Near the Bus Station; no phone. Another plain restaurant, Sathars offers good tandooris and spicy non-vegetarian and vegetarian Indian meals. Open 7 A.M.–10 P.M. Rupees only.

TIRUCHIRAPALLI

Moderate–Expensive

Chogori Restaurant and **Silent Spring.** Rajali Hotel, 3/14 MacDonald's Rd.; tel. 41301. These two restaurants serve the best meals in "Tiruchi." Silent Spring offers delicious vegetarian dishes, including especially good *poriyal* (carrot curry). Chogori has tasty Mughlai fish and chicken tangri kebab, plus good Chinese and Continental dishes. Chogori is open 12:15–2:30 P.M. and 7:15–11:30. Silent Spring is open 8 A.M.–9 P.M.

SWEETS AND TREATS. Madras. After visiting the National Gallery, walk to nearby Alsa Mall and its downstairs *Hot Bread Bakers and Confectioners* and adjoining coffee shop. You'll find Danish pastries, pizzas, donuts, cookies, ice cream, and even curry in a bun. Open 5:30 A.M.–10 P.M. *Nala Sweets,* 1 Cathedral Rd., has a quiet, old-time ambience and good Indian snacks and sweets, including ice cream. Open 8 A.M.–11 P.M. Another good choice is the popular *Woodland's Drive-In Restaurant,* 29/30 Cathedral Rd. Its name is a misnomer. You don't drive in and place an order. Instead choose from numerous eating halls surrounded by gardens; then choose from a large selection of Indian sweets and snacks. Open 6 A.M.–9 P.M.

Madurai. *New Arya Bhavan,* 242 West Masi St., has tasty snacks and excellent coffee; open 6:30 A.M.–10:30 P.M.

Tiruchirapalli. On China Bazaar, relax at *Sree Renga Bhavan* or *Vasantha Bhavan*—two enjoyable sidewalk bhavans—and have delicious coffee and memorable snacks; open early morning until late at night.

HOW TO GET AROUND. From the Airport. Madras. The Meenambakkam (Madras) Airport is about 15 km (nine mi.) from the center of Madras. The PTC (public bus system) offers an airport minicoach service to most hotels and to the Egmore Railway Station. (Rs. 20; tickets issued on the coach). Service runs at frequent intervals. You can also get into Madras by taxi, but insist that the driver turn on the meter. Rates are about Rs. 75, plus a Rs. 5 flat charge for luggage. You can also take a pre-paid taxi (about Rs. 40). Or take an auto rickshaw, but again insist on the meter. The auto rickshaw should be cheaper; it won't be faster. **Madurai.** A taxi (about Rs. 40) will take you the 10 km (six mi.) into the city. **Tiruchirapalli.** A taxi is also your best bet (about Rs. 40).

By Plane. *Indian Airlines* flies daily between Madras and Madurai, Madras and Tiruchirapalli, and Madras and Coimbatore. *Vayudoot* flies daily, except Sunday, between Madras and Pondicherry, Madras and Madurai, Madras and Tiruchirapalli. It flies daily between Madras and Coimbatore.

By Train. Good trains connect Madras with most important Tamil Nadu cities. For train information in Madras, contact the *Egmore Railway Station* (inquiries and reservations: tel. 566565 for 1st class; tel. 566555 for 2nd class). In Madurai, contact the *Madurai Junction Railway Station,* West Pell St. (inquiries: tel. 37597; reservations 1st class, tel. 23535; 2nd class, tel. 33535. Reservations are open 7 A.M.–1 P.M. and 1:30–8 P.M.).

By Bus. *Thiruvalluvar Transport Corporation* has state-run buses that travel throughout the state; but they're always crowded. For bus information in Madras, contact *Parry's Bus Stand,* Esplanade; tel. 561835.

By Rented Car with Driver. This is the best way to see Tamil Nadu. Here are some important distances from Madras: Coimbatore, 486 km (301 mi.); Madurai, 461 km (286 mi.); Mahabalipuram, 64 km (40 mi.); Pondicherry, 162 km (100 mi.); Rameswaram, 613 km (380 mi.); Salem, 326 km (202 mi.); Tiruchirapalli, 143 km (89 mi.). Hire a car from a recommended agency listed under "Tour Operators." Figure about Rs. 3–Rs. 4 per km and a halt charge of Rs. 50–Rs. 100 per night.

By Taxi. A good way to see sights around major cities, a taxi should cost about Rs. 3.50 for the first km, Rs. 2 per additional km. Make sure the driver uses his meter or set the fare in advance.

By Auto Rickshaw. In congested cities and small towns, this is an economical and fast alternative. Rates are about Rs. 2.50 for the first km, Rs. 1.75 per additional km.

By Bike Rickshaw. In temple cities and villages, this is a leisurely, pleasant way to travel and it's cheaper than an auto rickshaw. But remember, pedaling in the heat is rough. Set the fare in advance.

TOURS. *The Tamil Nadu Tourism Development Corp. Ltd.,* (TTDC) at 143 Annasalai, VST Motors Building, Madras, 600002 (tel. 849803), sponsors a series of inexpensive Tamil Nadu deluxe bus tours with guides. Departures are from the Central Railway Station parking area and the TTDC office (address above).

Madras City Sightseeing Tour. Daily 7:30 A.M.–1:30 P.M. and 1:30–6:30 P.M. Full day tour: 8:10 A.M.–7 P.M.

Sakthi Temple Tour to Tiruverkadu, Melmaruvatur, and Mangadu. Tuesdays, Fridays, and Sundays. 7 A.M.–5 P.M.

Mahabalipuram Tour (Kanchipuram-Thirukkalikundram-Mahabalipuram). Daily, 6:20 A.M.–7 P.M.

Tirupati Tour (Andhra Pradesh Temple). Tirupati-Tirumala-Tiruchanur. Daily 6 A.M.–9 P.M.

Tamil Nadu Weekend Package Tour (Thanjavur, Velankanni, Nagore, Tirunallar, Poompuhar, Vaitheeswaran Koil, Chidambaram, Pitchavaram, Pondicherry). Late Friday-Sunday.

Tamil Nadu Eight-Day Package Tour (Highlights: Chidambaram, Pondicherry, Tiruchirapalli, Kodaikanal, Madurai, Kanyakumari, Suchindram, Tiruchendur, Rameswaram, Thanjavur). Leaves Saturday and returns the next Saturday.

TTDC also offers a seven-day *East–West Coast Tour* covering major destinations in Kerala and Tamil Nadu and a 14-day *Sunny South Tour* covering Tamil Nadu, Kerala, Pondicherry, and Bangalore in Karnataka. Contact TTDC for details. *India Tourism Development Corporation* (29 Victoria Crescent, near Ethiraj College), Commander-in-Chief Road, Madras; (tel. 47888) offers similar tours. Tickets are also available at the ITDC counter in the Government of India Tourist Office at 154 Anna Salai Rd.; tel. 474216.

If you wish to hire a guide, the best trained and most knowledgeable are available through the Tamil Nadu Tourist Office throughout the state. General rates: four hours for four people, about Rs. 45; eight hours for four people, about Rs. 70 plus a Rs. 15 lunch allowance.

TOUR OPERATORS. The following agencies can take care of all travel needs, including car with driver (also see the listings under Special-Interest Tours in *Facts at Your Fingertips* for adventures offered in this state):

India Tourism Development Corporation (ITDC), 29 Victoria Crescent, Commander-in-Chief Rd., Madras; tel. 478884.

Tamil Nadu Tourism Development Corporation (TTDC), 143 Mount Rd., Madras; tel. 849803.

Travel Corporation India (TCI), 734 Mount Rd., Madras; tel. 868813.

Trade Wings, 752 Mount Rd., Madras; tel. 864961.

Ganesh Travels, 36 PCO Rd., Egmore, Madras; tel. 8250066.

SEASONAL EVENTS. The specific dates for many events each year are determined by the lunar calendar; consult the India Tourist Office for details.

January. *Pongal.* This colorful three-day festival that gives thanks to the sun, the earth, and the cow is held at the close of the harvest season. This is Tamil Nadu's best festival, with bonfires, bulls and cows fancied up with beads and garlands, games, and dancing.

January/**February.** *Madurai Float Festival.* During the Vandiyur Mariamman Teppakulam (temple) annual festival, decorated floats carry the sacred deities around the temple tank. This is a beautiful and interesting event.

February/**March.** *Natyanjali Festival.* This five-day event in Chidambaram is dedicated to classical dance and Shiva, "The Cosmic Dancer."

March. *Arupathumoovar.* This 11-day religious festival is held at the Kapaleeswarar Temple in Mylapore, Madras. The 11th day is the grand moment with over 60 sacred deities taken out in an elaborate procession.

March/**April.** *Pondicheery Carnival.* The former French colony celebrates its heritage during a carnival and parade with costumed participants and bands.

April/**May.** *Chitra Festival.* This spectacular 10-day festival at Madurai's Meenakshi Temple celebrates the marriage of goddess Meenakshi to Lord Shiva. Numerous deities are carried around in a chariot procession that also includes lots of traditional devotional music. A fascinating fair; heavily attended.

May. *Kanchipuram Temple Festival.* During this 10-day festival in Kanchipuram, deities from the nearby temples are carried through the city. The procession occurs on the third day and is declared an official city holiday, so every local resident gets to attend, along with all the people who come to see the event.

May. *Servaroyan Temple Festival.* In Yercaud, nearby tribal people celebrate their heritage with a festival.

August/September. *Ganesh Chaturthi.* Celebrated throughout Tamil Nadu, this festival involves Ganesh, the elephant-headed god, with processions and ritual baths of the deity in rivers.

September/**October.** *Navarathri.* This nine-day festival is observed throughout Tamil Nadu honoring the Hindu goddesses, Durga, Lakshmi, and Saraswati.

October/**November.** *Deepavali.* A two-day festival throughout Tamil Nadu and the rest of India, it marks the start of the Hindu New Year. Fireworks and lots of raucous celebrating.

December/January. *Madras Music and Dance Festival.* A three-week festival of music and dance in Madras is presented by the Indian Fine Arts Society, with great dance and music performed by India's best. At about the same time, in Tiruchirapalli, the *Vaikunta Ekadesa* festival is another procession and deity celebration, held at the Srirangam Temple.

HISTORIC SITES. Entrance to most places is generally free; where a donation is asked, a few rupees will suffice. Historic sites are open sunrise to sunset unless noted otherwise below.

Madras. *Church of Our Lady of Expectations,* was built in the sixteenth century on the foundation of a church built by St. Thomas in the second century. The "Bleeding Stone" on which a cross is engraved is supposed to shed blood on the day that marks St. Thomas' death, December 18.

San Thomé Cathedral Basilica, Madras, is a neogothic structure with a 180-foot steeple erected in 1896. The interior has an interesting image of Christ standing on a lotus flower (Hindu pose).

Kapaleeswar Temple in Mylapore is typically Dravidian. Dedicated to Shiva, it was built in the 1600s. Painted in terrific bright colors. Non-Hindus can enter the courtyard, but only Hindus can enter the inner sanctum. Open 5 A.M.-noon; 4–8:30 P.M.

Parthasarathy Temple in Triplicane, eighth century, dedicated to Vishnu, was originally constructed by Pallavas and rebuilt by the Vijayanagar kings in the seventeenth century. Open 6:30 A.M.-noon; 4 P.M.–8 P.M. Non-Hindus can enter the courtyard but not the inner sanctum.

Fort St. George, Madras, was built in 1640 by Francis Day for the East India Company. It now houses the Tamil Nadu State Legislature, offices of the ministry and secretaries to the government. See St. Mary's Church, consecrated in 1680, the oldest Anglican church in India.

Chidambaram. *Nataraja Temple,* dedicated to Shiva, is the oldest temple in South India. It was built in the fifth century by a Chola king and covers 40 acres. The roof of the sanctum sanctorum is covered with gold plate.

Kanchipuram. *Kailasanatha Temple* was built in the early eighth century by Pallava King Rajasimha. The smaller temple at the east end of the courtyard was built by his son. Dedicated to Shiva, sandstone temples are excellent examples of Pallava architecture.

Vaikunthaperumal Temple, Kanchipuram, was built in the eighth century by the Pallava King Nandivarman and dedicated to Vishnu. Unusual three-story vimina (tower over the central temple).

Ekambareswara Temple, Kanchipuram, was originally constructed by the Pallavas in the seventh and eighth centuries. The sixteenth-century Vijayanagar kings added the 10-story, intricately carved goporum (tower entrance). Dedicated to Shiva. the nearby mango tree is supposedly 3,500 years old.

Kanya Kumari Temple, Kanya Kumari, is dedicated to the virgin goddess Kanniyakumari, who protects the country. The eastern gate facing the Bay of Bengal is opened only five times a year, and a ritual bath at the Kumari ghat is considered sacred. Temple open 4:30–11 A.M.; 5:30–9 P.M.

Gandhi Memorial, Kanya Kumari, was constructed on the spot where the urn with Gandhi's ashes was kept on public view until relinquished to the sea. The building was designed so that on Gandhi's birthday, October 2, a ray of sun falls on the spot where the urn was kept.

Vivekananda Rock Memorial, Kanya Kumari, was built in 1970 to commemorate where Swami Vivekananda meditated before dedicating his life to spreading the ideals of Hinduism. A blend of all temple architectural styles in India. Ferry services to the memorial, 7–11 A.M.; 2–5 P.M. Nominal fee.

Suchindram Temple (13 km north of Kanya Kumari) has inscriptions dating to the ninth century. One of the few temples to worship the trinity of Shiva, Vishnu, and Brahma. Exquisitely carved seven-story goporum, lovely musical pillars, and a huge Hanuman (monkey god) statue, plus an enormous bathing tank. Very pretty. Non-Hindus can enter the courtyard but not the inner sanctum.

Padmanabhapuram Palace (45 km north of Kanya Kumari) was the ancient palace of the rulers of Travancore until A.D. 1333. Palace (open 9 A.M.–5 P.M., closed Mondays and holidays; Rs. 0.50) contains excellent murals and stone sculptures.

Madurai. *Meenakshi Temple* is dedicated to Shiva and is one of the biggest temple complexes in India. Most of the current structure was erected between the twelfth and the eighteenth century, but references to the temple date back to seventh century. Open between 4:30 A.M.–12:30 P.M.; 4 P.M.–9:30 P.M. Photography, however, is permitted only after a Rs. 5 payment and during the hours the temple is closed: 12:30–4 P.M.

Tirumalai Nayak Palace, Madurai, was built in Indo-Saracenic style in the seventeenth century by Thirumalai Nayak. Beautiful courtyard surrounded by an arcade supported by vast pillars. All that's left of the once-enormous complex are two royal residences. Used to have quarters for the harem, relatives, a theater, a pond, and a garden. Open 8 A.M.–noon; 1–5 P.M. Rs. 0.40. Sound and light show every evening on the life of this Nayak king: 6:45 P.M., Rs. 1–3.

Rock-cut Caves, Mahabalipuram, are of seventh-century Pallava construction. The Mahashasuramardhini mandapam has a sculptural relief of the fight between the goddess Durga and Mahishasura, the buffalo-headed demon and the bas-relief of Vishnu in his cosmic sleep. In the Krishna mandapam are excellent scenes depicting the life of Krishna. The bas relief—the world's largest, (80 feet long with an average height of 20 feet—is also a Pallava construction.

Shore Temple, at Mahabalipuram has two shrines, one dedicated to Shiva and the other dedicated to Vishnu. Built by Pallava king Rajashima in the seventh century, it is an excellent example of Dravidian architecture.

Pondicherry. *Auroville* is an international commune started by a French woman, now deceased, called "Mother," who was involved with Sri Aurobindo. Futuristic architecture can be seen here, especially the *Matri Mandir* meditation hall, a gigantic sphere under construction since 1971.

Rameswaram. *Ramanathaswamy Temple* was built over a 300-year period starting in the twelfth century. An excellent example of Dravidian architecture, with the longest pillared temple corridor in all India.

Srirangam. *Rangagantha Swamy Temple* was built between the fourteenth and the seventeenth centuries. A temple town with seven sets of walls leading to the most sacred areas. There are 21 towers. A fascinating complex teeming with life.

Thanjavur. Brahadeeswarar Temple, dedicated to Shiva, was constructed between 985 and 1016 by Raja Chola. The first of four Chola temples in Tamil Nadu to have a vimana soaring over the gopora. The vimana is constructed from one single granite block.

Thiruvannamalai. *Arunachala Temple* sprawls over 25 acres. It is one of South India's largest. Dedicated to Shiva in his fire incarnation, the goporum is 11 stories high. The exact date of its construction is unknown; parts existed as early as the seventh century.

MUSEUMS AND GALLERIES. Most museums are free or have a nominal entrance fee; some accept a small donation. Listed here are some of the more important museums in the state.

The Fort Saint George Museum. South Beach Rd. Featured here are costumes, prints, and paintings of the British in India. Open 9 A.M.–5 P.M.; closed Fridays.

The Government Museum and National Art Gallery. Pantheon Rd., Egmore. Established in 1857, it has one of India's best all-around art collections, including Hindu, Buddhist, and Jain sculptures from Tamil Nadu, Andhra Pradesh, and Mysore, with sculptures from the Buddhist site of Amaravati (first century B.C.), the earliest surviving sculptures from the south. In the galleries devoted to metal work are South Indian lamps; objects connected with household and temple worship; and images in bronze, including the famous Nataraja. Also see the collection of woodcarvings from processional temple cars. The contents of the Arms Gallery are mostly from the palace at Thanjavur and Fort St. George, and those of the prehistoric gallery include antiquities from the Iron Age sites of Adichannallar and Perumbiar. The Bronze Gallery contains some of the best of India's ancient icons and some excellent modern bronzes. Open 8 A.M.–5 P.M., closed Fridays.

The National Art Gallery. Pantheon Rd., Egmore. Set in a beautiful Indo-Saracenic building, the gallery houses an excellent collection of old and new art, including rare Rajput and Mogul miniatures, exquisite tenth- through thirteenth-century bronzes, and twelfth-century Indian handicrafts. Open 8 A.M.–5 P.M., closed Fridays.

MADURAI

The **Gandhi Museum** has a picture gallery and some of Gandhi's personal possessions. Open 9 A.M.–1 P.M.; 2–5:30 P.M.; closed Wednesdays.

The **Meenakshi Temple Art Museum** in the 1,000-pillared hall contains temple art and architecture. Open 6 A.M.–8 P.M., daily.

PONDICHERRY

The Government Museum is a celebration of Pondicherry history, starting with Chola bronzes and sculptures, moving to French cultural artifacts, and ending with traditional Indian handicrafts. Open 10 A.M.–5 P.M.; closed Mondays.

THANJAVUR

The **Tanjore Art Gallery,** Palace Buildings, contains ancient Chola statues in bronze and granite. Open 9 A.M.–1 P.M. and 3–6 P.M.; closed Fridays.

GARDENS. Madras. *The Gardens of the Horticultural Society,* established in 1835 next to Saint George Cathedral on Cathedral Rd., is open 8 A.M.–12 P.M. and 1:30–5:30 P.M.; closed Thursday. *Children's Park and Deer Sanctuary,* eight km (five mi.) from the heart of Madras in Guindy, has a large number of Indian antelope and numerous other animals, including monkeys and reptiles. The best time to visit is early morning or early evening. Open 8:30 A.M.–5:30 P.M.; closed Thursdays. *Snake Park,* in Guindy, is home to numerous reptiles. Good demonstrations on the hour start at 10 A.M. daily. Open 9 A.M.–6 P.M.

Ootacamund. The *Botanical Gardens,* established in 1847 by the Marquis of Tweedale, contains exotic and ornamental plants. Children's *Lake Garden* has flowers and musical lights. Both open sunrise to sunset.

Pondicherry. The *Botanical Gardens,* planted in 1826, contains exotic plants from all over the world, and an aquarium. Open sunrise to sunset.

Thanjavur. *The Children's Park* has a small diesel train to take the children around. Open sunrise to sunset.

SPORTS AND OUTDOOR ADVENTURES. Beaches. You can swim at these good beaches: *Elliots Beach,* 11 km (seven mi.) south of Madras; *Covelong,* 38 km (24 mi.) south of Madras—a lovely fishing village with a resort; *Pondicherry;* and *Mahabalipuram,* which boasts beautiful stretches of sand with temples on the shore. *Rameswaram* has many good beaches, but watch the current. At *Kanya Kumari* beaches, also watch the current; they're rugged!

Boating. You can do backwater boating in Chidambaram. and Pondicherry. Inquire at the local tourist departments. You can rent boats on the lakes in Kodaikanal, Ootacamund, and Yercaud.

Fishing. To fish in Kodaikanal, get a license and details from the local Sub-Inspector of Fisheries; in Ootacamund, contact the local Assistant Director of Fisheries.

Golfing. You can golf in Kodaikanal and Ootacamund. Equipment is available at each.

Trekking. For information about treks around Kodaikanal and Ootacamund, contact the Tamil Nadu Tourist office (see address under Tourist Information above).

Wildlife Sanctuaries. Anamalai Wildlife Sanctuary. Coimbatore District. Open all year, the best time to view the elephants, bison, tigers, wild boar, and crocodiles is October–April. You can go through the sanctuary on an elephant or in a van. Lodging is available.

Mudumalai Wildlife Sanctuary. Nilgeris (60 km or 37 mi. from Ootacamund). Open all year, the best season is February–May. This park is home to deer, bison, elephants, gaur, monkeys, and reptiles including pythons and crocodiles. Elephant rides for viewing animals are available, as is lodging.

Point Calimere Wildlife Sanctuary. Thanjavur District. Open all year, the peak season is November–January when the migratory birds are in the park. April–June many birds have moved on. You can also see deer and wild boar.

Mundanthurai Tiger Sanctuary. Tirunelveli District. The peak season in this park is January–September. The forest department provides tours, and lodging is available in simple rest houses.

Vedanthangal Water Birds Sanctuary (70 km or 43 mi. from Madras). One of India's major bird sanctuaries, most birds congregate here from October–November to March. Peak time is usually December–January; but the bird population always depends on the monsoons. Check with the tourist office before you visit. Species include cormorants, egrets, storks, and herons. Rudimentary accommodations are available.

For more details and lodging reservations at these sanctuaries, contact the State Wildlife Warden, Forest Department, Administrative Office Building, Teynampet, Madras, Tamil Nadu.

SHOPPING. Madras. The three best markets are *Jam Bazaar,* junction of Pycroft's and Triplicane roads (bustling fruit and vegetable market); *Evening Bazaar* (also called Parrys) near Broadway and N.S.C. Bose Road (wholesale markets); and *Burma Bazaar* at the eastern end of N.S.C. Bose Road along the harbor (best visited at night). You may not want to buy anything, but they're fun for browsing. If something strikes your fancy, haggle. Also visit these good shops:

Aparna Art Gallery (5 Bawa Rd.) sells excellent old and new curios in wood and bronze, Tanjore and Mysore paintings, and miniatures. Open 9 A.M.–6:30 P.M., closed Sundays. It also has a branch at Welcomgroup Chola Sheraton Hotel. AE, DC, MC, V.

Bapalal & Co. Jewellers (24/1 Cathedral Rd.) sells excellent gold and diamonds. Open 9:30 A.M.–1:30 P.M. and 2:30–6:30 P.M., closed Sundays. AE, MC, V.

Nalli Chinnasami Chetty (opposite Panagal Park, T. Nagar) has two floors filled with silks (including the beautiful Kanchipuram silk), handlooms, and patrons. Also visit Kumaran Silks (a few shops down to the right), another enormous emporium. They're open 9 A.M.–9 P.M., closed Sundays. MC, V.

Sharanya (72 Mowbray's Rd., Alwarpet) and *Shilpi* (Shop No. 1, Gee Gee Minar Building, 23 College Rd.) sell exquisite handlooms by the meter and handloom products, lovely salwar kameez (loose blouse and trousers), skirts and blouses, shawls, handbags, linen. These two shops are terrific. Open 10 A.M.–8 P.M., closed Sunday. Shilpi takes V; Sharanya, rupees only.

Poompuhar Sales and Show Room (818 Mount Rd.) has a good selection of Tamil Nadu handicrafts: brass, wood, papier-mâché sculptures, handlooms. Open 10 A.M.–7:30 P.M., closed Sunday. AE, DC, MC, V.

S.M.C.S. (14A College Rd.) also has a good assortment of Tamil Nadu products. Open 9 A.M.–8 P.M., closed Sundays. AE, DC, MC, V.

Madurai. In Madurai, just wander around the temple complex. The markets are fascinating; you'll find rows and rows of men sitting behind sewing machines sewing up ready-mades in minutes flat and stalls with all kinds of merchandise. It's fun just to wander and watch.

Thanjavur. For good curios visit *V.R. Govindarajan,* 31 Kuthiraikatti St., tel. 20282. Great stuff clutters up numerous rooms.

Subhashini Arts (1680 Krishnan Koil 2nd St., M. Chavady) sells exquisite Tanjore glass painting by an award-winning Indian artist. Open 10 A.M.–1 P.M. and 2–6 P.M. Rupees only.

Tiruchirapalli. Visit *China Bazaar* and *Big Bazaar* near the base of the fort.

NIGHTLIFE AND BARS. Don't leave Tamil Nadu without seeing a performance of the *Bharata Natyam*—the purest and in some ways the most beautiful classical dance form in India. In Madras, check the newspaper, *Hindu,* or call the Government of India Tourist Office (tel. 869685), which keeps a list of current cultural events. The following theaters and halls also have cultural events with some frequency:

Kalaivanar Arangam, Government Estate, Wallaja Rd., tel. 565669; *Raja Annamalai Hall,* Esplanade, tel. 561425; *Rani Seethai Hall,* 603 Mount Rd., tel. 474863; *Museum Theatre,* Pantheon Road, Egmore, no phone; *Music Academy,* 115 East Mowbray's Rd., tel. 475619.

In the last week of December, the Siva-Sakthi Music and Dance School, 123 East Car Street, Chidambaram, holds a formal Bharata Natyam program with its students. The students are young and talented. The building is old with pillars, perfect for this classic dance form.

In Madras, the best bars are in the luxury hotels; they're generally open noon–3 P.M. and 6:30–11:45 P.M.

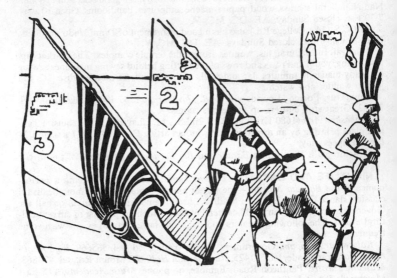

KERALA

Palm-Fringed Paradise

by
KATHLEEN COX

Just around the corner of Cape Comorin, the southernmost tip of India, begins a strange land of paradox. Kerala is one of India's most progressive regions, but it has all the ingredients of a tropical paradise, right to the palm trees waving over sandy beaches. A thin strip along the southwest coast, isolated by the wall of the Western Ghats, Kerala is unbelievably cosmopolitan, with a heritage of 3,000 years of relations involving the rest of the world. Phoenicians, Arabs, Jews, Chinese, and Europeans came by boat to do heavy trading in this rich land that still raises its valuable cash crops: tea, rubber, cashews, teak, and a wide assortment of spices, including "black gold" (pepper). Yet Kerala moves at a leisurely pace, like the slow moving boats that float through its network of canals and backwaters.

Kerala isn't for the hurried tourist, eager to chalk up a city a day. Forget the airline ticket to Cochin, with a quick hop to Trivandrum and the beach. Plan to travel into the Western Ghats—winding roads that take you by tea plantations and palm and rubber trees. Arrange for a languid cruise through the stunning backwaters. The state is small, but there's a lot to do.

Kerala didn't exist on the map until 1956, when it became one of India's smallest states, created out of Travancore-Cochin and the Malabar Coast district of Madras State. The result of this redrawing of the map of India is a slender but picturesque wedge along the Malabar Coast, which faces the Arabian Sea, with forest-clad mountains that rise as high as 5,000 feet at its back. Twenty-four million people live within this state that is slightly smaller than Switzerland. Though there isn't much room for newcomers, the population of Kerala has increased 20 percent over the past decade.

Despite Kerala's brief existence, it soon made a name for itself, becoming the first place in the world to adopt a communist regime in a free election: a political event that caused tremendous discussion and speculation, since Kerala also happens to be the most educated state in India. With a near-70 percent literacy rate (against a national rate of 36 percent), nine out of 10 children attend school, a startling figure anywhere in Asia. Although the communists lost control a few years back, they still carry some influence.

The scenery of Kerala is shaped by a partnership of geography and history. At least a quarter of its area is covered by forests that contain 600 varieties of trees, which makes timber an important industry—one in which woodsmen still use elephants as bulldozers. Up in the mountains are vast plantations of tea and cardamom (its name came from the Cardamom Hills of Kerala). Down below, pepper, coffee, rubber, cocoa, ginger, and turmeric—an essential spice in curry—grow in wild profusion. The mountains lord over a contrasting landscape of coconut trees and gray farmhouses built under palm-thatched roofs.

At times, when you travel through Kerala, it's hard to realize where you are. Towns and villages are heavily sprinkled with well-built churches, and one-quarter of the state's population is Christian. But nestling next to a church might be a house under a Chinese roof, gracefully bowed in the center with carved woodwork below the pointed ends. Or, at Cochin, you can even wander into a Jewish synagogue.

This human kaleidoscope developed over thousands of years. Behind the ramparts of the Western Ghats—there are only 16 passes through these mountains and none of them is easy—the Malabar Coast escaped domination by successive waves of empire builders who conquered ancient India by land. Long before Vasco da Gama, the Phoenicians came here to trade for spices, ivory, and sandalwood. Around 1000 B.C., King Solomon's ships visited Biblical Ophir, supposedly the village of Poovar, south of Trivandrum, the present capital of Kerala.

The spice treasure of Kerala, especially pepper, lured fortune seekers from a good many European countries. The Dutch preceded the Portuguese, although their stay was short. In 1516, the Portuguese signed a treaty with the rani of Quilon (wife of the raja) and clung to it even though Arab traders, jealous of competition, talked the rani into harrassing the encroachers. The Portuguese did some harassing themselves. When they discovered that the Christians, who were sharing this part of India with them, had never heard of the Pope, these pious Catholics persecuted the "heretics."

In 1602, the Dutch, under the banner of the Dutch East Indian Company, reappeared and succeeded in forcing out the Portuguese in 1663 through skillful public relations with local chieftains. Still, the European procession was far from over. The British East India Company (on the Malabar Coast since 1684) opened its first settlement at Anjengo, south of Quilon. In the eighteenth century, the British won over the raja of Travancore. By 1795, the Dutch were down and out. (Travancore was originally known as Thiruvazhum Kode, an alluring name that meant the abode of prosperity, but the British had difficulty with the pronunciation and solved the problem by substituting their corrupted phonetic version: Travancore.)

Kerala's Diverse People

The people of Kerala who speak Malayalam seem unaffected by the Europeans' unending game of monopoly. One of the most important Hindu castes of Kerala, the Nairs (or Nayars), were traditionally governed by the matriarchal system under which property was inherited through the female side of a family. Though the matriarchal system is on the wane, Nair women maintain a proud position in Kerala society. In the past, though, the Nair male was quite a warrior—Nairs only gave up dueling under British pressure. The Nair family is a huge unit. Their ancestral home is known as the *tarawad,* and some Nair tarawads are handsome structures with rich carvings on their heavy wooden doors and door frames.

Kerala's Brahmans, the Namboodiris, have another unique family system. Until recently, only the eldest son was allowed to take a wife from his own caste (the others had to marry Nairs who are Kshatriyas, and their children had no right to the family's heritage).

Because there weren't enough Brahman eldest sons to go around, many Namboodiri women went through life unmarried. Now most Namboodiris marry within their own community, and the old system has died out. Another Hindu community, the Ezhavas, produced a great religious teacher, Narayan Guru Swami, who preached the revolutionary notion of one caste, one god.

Hindus, Christians, Jews, and Moslems, all form part of the human flow of Kerala. Most of the men dress in impeccable *dhotis* (white wraps around the waist) or *lungis* (colorful wraps), and the women wear multicolored saris. Soon, you even get used to the rather incongruous sight of the ever present black umbrella held over the head to ward off the equally ever present sun or the occasional shower that strikes unexpectedly.

The people of Kerala are worth watching when they relax, too. The Kathakali dance drama is one of India's most electric dance forms, and it originated here in this tropical state. Festivals crop up at regular intervals—with the most picturesque Onam, a four-day harvest celebration (August or September) that ends with races of exotic giant snake boats manned by 100 oarsmen.

EXPLORING KERALA

There's no fixed itinerary for visiting Kerala, but for convenience, we've arranged the main points of interest south to north.

Trivandrum and Environs

Trivandrum, built on seven hills, offers proud buildings that overlook quiet valleys. The main architectural landmark of Trivandrum is the Padmanabhaswami Temple, dedicated to Vishnu, a handsome example of South Indian temple architecture with a seven-story *goporum* (tower). No one knows the date of construction. One legend traces it back to 3000 B.C., but everyone knows how it was built. Four thousand masons, 6,000 laborers, and 100 elephants did the job in six months. In the main courtyard, the Kulasekhar Mandapam, there is some intricate granite sculpture; more sculpture can be appreciated on nearly 400 pillars supporting the temple corridor. Only Hindus may penetrate the sanctuary itself.

If you're an Indian art buff, visit Trivandrum's Museum and the Sri Chitra Gallery. The latter has a good collection of paintings as eclectic as Kerala itself. On its walls hang examples of the Rajput, Mogul, and Tanjore schools; copies of the Ajanta and Sigirya frescoes; and works from China, Japan, Tibet, and Bali, along with canvases by modern Indian painters. At a more earthy level, see the wonderful display of local arts and crafts in the museum, housed in a rambling palace with a Cubist pattern of gables. For travelers who wants their nature in easily digested form, there's a zoo and an excellent aquarium (also used by marine biologists and fishery experts). To see what life was like here before modern India, visit the Kaudiyar Palace, the residence of the maharajah of former Travancore-Cochin.

Trivandrum, the state capital and once a sedate city, now boasts an international airport that has brought an influx of tourists. Many of these recent arrivals spend languorous days on Kovalam beach, 16 kilometers (10 miles) south of Trivandrum. Here, you can take long walks on beautiful sandy beaches lined with palm-fringed lagoons and rocky coves. Or, just laze around and watch lungi-clad fishermen as they drag in nets filled with the day's catch, then push their slender wooden fishing boats out again with a Malayalam "heave-ho" chant.

Trivandrum to Quilon

Once you've experienced Kovalam, head north 52 kilometers (32 miles) to Varkala, a seaside town set against a backdrop of red cliffs with mineral water springs spurting down to the beach. Varkala is the goal of Hindu pilgrims bound for its Janardhana Temple, reputed to be 2,000 years old.

Varkala is also where Narayana Guru Swami, one of modern India's greatest Hindu religious reformers and saints, entered into *samadhi* (contemplative retirement) in 1928. Instead of the bewildering pantheon of Hindu gods, he preached a simple faith; "One Caste, One Religion, and One God." It's appropriate that this movement should have sprung up in tolerant and progressive Kerala. Now it's carried on by a brotherhood of his disciples. Their message is that of their leader: "Man must improve, whatever his religion."

Not far from Varkala lies a more mundane historical spot, Anjengo, where the British East India Company opened its first trading post on the Malabar Coast. You can visit the remains of an old fort built by these seventeenth-century merchants.

Nineteen kilometers (12 miles) north, you reach Quilon, one of the oldest ports along the Malabar Coast. The ancients reached it long before, though: Phoenician, Persian, Greek, Roman, and Arab vessels all traded here. The most industrious were the Chinese. During the T'ang Dynasty (seventh to tenth centuries), China established trading posts in Quilon and, under the reign of Kubla Khan (thirteenth century), it exchanged envoys with this prosperous Indian city state (it became part of Travancore only in 1742).

To the visitor, Quilon offers its vista on Ashtamudi Lake, indented by red capes jutting from a shoreline of palms. Along the shore stand the Thevally Palace and Government House. Three kilometers (two miles) from Quilon, you can wander through Thangassery, with its lighthouse, ruined forts, and slumbering Portuguese, English, and Dutch cemeteries.

Quilon is also the starting point of a beautiful stretch of inland waterways—83 kilometers (53 miles) of backwaters, called *kayals,* that snake through canals frequently shaded by the leaves of coconut palms. It's a lazy calm voyage that takes you all the way to Alleppey. You can go by public boat, very cheap, but it takes about a day. Or you can hire a launch for around $100 and make the journey in half the time. In either case, you'll travel by hidden villages and lush vegetation—a panorama of rural/waterside life Kerala style.

Alleppey

When you arrive in Alleppey, a water-borne city (a miniature Cochin), you will find its canals teeming with numerous straw-roofed country boats introduced by the Chinese. Alleppey is a busy place. From coconut husks, it makes coir rope (the leading industry) and carpets (mats). It also thrives on the production of black pepper.

Also in Alleppey, as in Cochin, you can see Chinese "fishing machines," immense contraptions consisting of a huge net lowered into the water on the end of a pole poised on a fulcrum. Once a catch has been lured into its meshes by a lantern on top of the "machine," it takes a half-dozen men on the other end of the pole to lift the haul out of the water. The boats, *wallams,* which serve as water trucks for the Kerala countryside, are Chinese in design. Flat-bottomed and built of planks stitched together with cords, they are about 40 feet long and carry nearly 20 tons. Like ferries, they are double ended, some with beautiful scrollwork on their bows. Cargo is carried under a roof of woven coconut fronds aboard these wallams. Although motor launches ply the backwaters of Kerala for tourists and travelers in a hurry, the wallam is still man powered. Its two-man crew drives it by punting, planting their long poles in the bottom at the bow and then walking a bit to propel their boat, just as bargemen (not gondoliers) still do on the canals of Venice. If you visit in August, you may just get to witness the Nehru Trophy Boat Race—a competition with those exotic snake boats.

Kottayam to Lake Periyar

From Alleppey, head for Kottayam. This small city has always been a busy base for Christian missionaries, and it boasts a number of old churches, including its Syrian Church: the Cheria Palli with colorful murals and numerous carved altars. From Kottayam, turn inland toward the east—the start of a beautiful side trip that takes you into swift change of scenery and ultimately to the Periyar Lake Wildlife Sanctuary (115 km). At first, you run through lush vegetation and palm-thatched villages dominated incongruously by churches built in an exuberant Portuguese colonial style.

After passing through low-lying palms and paddies, the road begins to wind up the Ghats, lined with prosperous tea plantations where plants are carefully pruned to a four-foot height (any higher, their leaves are no longer tender). These tea plantations, established early in the century by the British and now mainly under Indian management, are a flourishing industry. The picking of the tea by nimble-fingered women goes on for most of the year; then the baskets of young leaves go to factories for drying, rolling, fermenting, and sifting the leaves. About 80 kilometers (50 miles) from Kottayam, the road passes through Peermade, a hill station, and then it reaches Thekkady, close to Periyar Lake.

Periyar Game Sanctuary

The lake is a human-made touch added to the natural beauty of the Western Ghats: a reservoir created by a dam on the Periyar River. This lake, with its many fingers that wind around capes and hills, some rising 914 meters (3,000 feet) above its surface, is the heart of the 777-square-kilometer (300-square-mile) wildlife sanctuary.

Periyar offers one of the most sybaritic ways of seeing big game. Here, forget exhausting treks or long safaris. You lounge in a motor launch as it drifts around a bend and comes into sight of elephants or deer or bison stopping at the shores of the lake for a drink. During the dry season, when waterholes in the forest are empty, leopards and tigers also pad up to the water. One word of advice: either bribe all the Indian kids to be quiet—they love to scream and shout at a sighting—or hire a private launch.

Shooting, of course, is prohibited, but the hunter's loss is the photographer's gain. Elephant herds are so accustomed to *quiet* visitors drifting next door in launches that they hardly notice the intrusion. This is no place to be caught short of film, and specially built tree perches provide good observation posts. Elephants with their young graze beside deer, gaue (wild oxen) and sambar (large Asiatic deer); you may even glimpse tigers and bears. Of course, all the jungle's smaller creatures are photo material.

Cochin

Although Cochin is not a pretty city, it is one of those rare places where the twentieth century and ancient civilizations exist side by side. Cochin's past is so rich that it has a valid claim as a museum city. Cochin is also one of the three biggest ports on the west coast of India and the biggest in Kerala, handling over five million tons of cargo in a year, and a prosperous center of the coir industry. Stroll through the streets behind the docks lined with old merchant houses, *godowns* (warehouses), and open courtyards heaped with betel nuts, ginger, peppercorns, and hanks of coir. The air is filled with the smell of spices and the shouts of men pushing heavy carts. This Eastern scene has changed little over the centuries.

Cochin manages to pursue its various lucrative trades in its setting of wooden islands and canals winding past houses on stilts. Both in the past and in the present, Cochin has displayed a lively blend of people and architecture that is worth seeing. It's one of the few places in the world where you can visit a Jewish synagogue, Portuguese churches, Dutch buildings, and a couple of mosques and Hindu temples and see Chinese fishing nets all in the same day.

We use "Cochin" as a handy name for a cluster of islands and towns. Over on the mainland, three miles from the harbor but linked by bridges and ferries, lies Ernakulam, once the capital of the former state of Cochin. If you arrive by air, your terminal will be on Willingdon Island, a human-made island (it consists of material dredged in an ambitious harbor-deepening operation). On Vypeen Island, facing the sea, fishermen still use their Chinese cantilever contraptions. The coir makers work on Gundu Island in a cooperative where excellent samples of their products are on display, although businessmen dealing in coir make their homes in the residential quarter of Fort Cochin, where, in tropical India, you stumble onto an English village green, pseudo-Tudor houses, lawns, a club, and a perfect replica of a prosperous London suburb—except that palms betray where you are. Bolghatty Island is the most beautiful of the lot, and its colonial mansion, formerly used by the Dutch governor and later by the British

Resident, is now a hotel. Finally, there is Mattancheri, southwest of the harbor: the home of a dwindling Jewish community. History at Cochin is found in the most abundant quantities here and at Fort Cochin.

Fort Cochin is believed to be the oldest European settlement in India. It first saw the Portuguese flag in 1500; three years later, Alfonso de Albuquerque came with half a dozen ships bearing settlers and built Fort Cochin. He also brought five friars who built the first European church in India in 1510, still standing in Fort Cochin as St. Francis Church. Vasco da Gama first arrived in Cochin in 1502. He returned again in 1524 as Portuguese viceroy of the Indies. He died here and was buried in St. Francis Church. You can still visit his gravestone, but his remains were shipped back to Portugal in 1538 (he's buried in Lisbon). St. Francis Church, the oldest European church in India, reflects the colonial struggle for India. It was a Dutch Reformed church from 1664 to 1804, an Anglican church from 1804 to 1947, and now it's part of the Church of South India. The giant fans in the nave are operated from outside. The church contains Dutch gravestones and has the *Doop Book,* a register of baptisms and marriages from 1751 to 1894. You can look at a photographic reproduction of the vital statistics (the original is too fragile).

St. Francis is a sedate church in the Spanish style, but not nearly as flamboyant as the Santa Cruz Cathedral in Fort Cochin, which verges on the gaudy. The Santa Cruz was completed in 1904.

The White Jews of Cochin

Fort Cochin may be old but, compared to Mattancheri, it's an upstart. The first emigration of Jews to Kerala supposedly took place in the sixth century B.C., followed by a much bigger wave in the first century A.D., when Jews fleeing Roman persecution in Jerusalem came to Cranganore and settled there. One of the most impressive sights in the synagogue of Mattancheri are the copper plates presented to the Jewish community by King Bhaskara Ravi Varma in the fourth century A.D., who awarded them the village of Anjuvannam, a name meaning "five castes" (the Jews were considered the lords of five castes of artisans). Incidentally, both Jews and Christians have always been considered of high caste in Kerala. The plates state that Anjuvannam shall be the hereditary possession of Joseph Rabban and his descendants "so long as the world and moon exist."

The king's word was good, and the Jewish colony flourished, serving as a haven to Jews from the Middle East and, in later centuries, Europe. The Portuguese put an end to this state of affairs. When Albuquerque discovered the Jews near Cochin, he requested permission from his king to "exterminate them one by one" and destroyed their city at Cranganore. Moslem anti-Semitism flared up, too. It was with the arrival of the Dutch that the Jews of Cochin were able to live without fear once more—as they always had in India.

The synagogue in Mattancheri's Jewish colony was built in 1568 after the expulsion of the Jews from Cranganore. It was considerably embellished in the mid-eighteenth century by Ezekiel Rahabi, who build a clock tower and paved the floor of the synagogue with hand-painted tiles of willow pattern (each one different), brought all the way from Canton in China. Indeed, the entire synagogue is beautiful, and the elder loves to show his visitors around.

Sadly though, the congregation has almost vanished; and, as an active synagogue, its days are probably numbered. Few of the pale, blond White Jews of Cochin are left (unlike the "Black Jews" from the mainland of India who are a mixture of Jewish and Hindu stock). Many of the White

Jews emigrated to Holland and to England in the past two centuries, and others have gone to Israel.

Mattancheri also offers Cochin's other most interesting building—the "Dutch Palace"—built by the Portuguese (hence the quotation marks) in the middle of the sixteenth century. The Dutch Palace was taken over by the Dutch, who added some improvements before presenting it to the rajahs of Cochin, who used it as a palace. The rajas, in turn, made more improvements, notably some excellent mythological murals. In one room, you can see the entire story of the *Ramayana* on the walls. The palace also contains a rare example of traditional Keralan flooring, which looks like polished black marble but is actually a subtle mix of burned coconut shells, charcoal, lime, plant juices, and egg whites. Both the synagogue and the palace are within easy walking distance of the boat jetty at Mattancheri.

While in Cochin, you must see a Kathakali dance-drama. There are many dance companies, and you can also attend a "short" two-hour performance at the Gurukalam Kathakali Yogam in Ernakulam, a tiny theater (bring mosquito repellent) that is weirdly magical. The dancers wear fantastic makeup and spectacular costumes. When the show begins, the stylized movements are larger than life—eerie, and wondrous—and an unequivocal delight. No surprise, since the performers begin rigorous training to master control of the eyeballs, neck, toes, fingers, and cheek muscles at age five.

From Cochin to Trichur

After Cochin, the pace slows down again. Sixteen kilometers (10 miles) north is industrial Alwaye, the "Ruhr of Kerala." Here Travancore made a successful stand against Tipu Sultan, an invader from neighboring Mysore who came storming into Alwaye in 1790. Actually, Travancore was helped by a flood on the Periyar River, which forced Tipu to cancel his plans. Alwaye is also the home of the Union Christian College, one of the few started in India by Indians, not foreign missionaries. But the main reason to visit is that Alwaye is on the route to Kaladi, birthplace of Sankaracharya. Sankaracharya was an eighth-century saint and philosopher, the father of the *Advaita* doctrine of Hindu philosophy and one of the first of the monotheists who seem to flourish in Kerala—whether as Hindus, Christians, Jews, or Moslems.

Along the shore north of Alwaye, you reach old Cranganore, now known as Kodungalloor. The Cheraman Perumals, the early rulers of this part of the Malabar Coast, had their capital here, and an old building known as Cheraman Parambu is said to have been their palace. Kodungalloor was not always a drowsy seaside town. It was the first of Kerala's international harbors, and the heritage of its history includes a Portuguese fort, a number of Hindu temples (the best known are the Thiruvanchikulam and the Bhagavathi), and India's first mosque. Nearby Kottappuram adds a Christian touch: here St. Thomas the Apostle is said to have landed in India, and a church is dedicated to him.

Back inland once more, the main road and rail line run from Alwaye to Trichur, which has a zoo (quite a collection of snakes), an art exhibition in its town hall, an old palace, and a fort. Trichur is a must-see if you happen to be in Kerala during its Pooram festival, an annual affair occurring in April or May. This is one of South India's biggest shows, complete with processions, huge fireworks displays, and elephants decked out regally.

Kozhikode (Calicut)

The landscape reverts once more to coconut palms, tea, rubber plantations, and groves of tropical fruit trees as you head toward the sea from Trichur north to Kozhikode (Calicut). Kozhikode is rather remote from the rest of Kerala and, prior to 1956, it was not in the same state.

Long ago, it was a center of power of the Malabar Coast under its rulers, the Zamorins, a name meaning lords of the sea. The lovely city is noted for its block-printed cotton cloth and is the origin of the word *calico.*

The city, which has a large Moslem population, has always been a major port of the Malibar Coast, with its glory days as a trading center beginning when Vasco da Gama landed here on May 20, 1498, after rounding the Cape of Good Hope. The English first appeared in Kozhikode in 1615, and the British East India Company gained control of the city in 1792 following a treaty with Tipu Sultan.

Lakshadweep Islands

India's smallest Union Territory lies off the coast of Cochin in the Arabian Sea: the Lakshadweep Islands, a chain of 36 coral atolls, some of which have been inhabited for centuries by devout Sunni Moslems. The government understands the appeal of such a destination; but to protect the people and the fragile island ecology from the impact of tourism, it has judiciously opened up just Bangaram, an uninhabited island, to foreigners. Already a lovely resort sits on a pearly white beach surrounded by lagoons, with calm waters and extensive coral reefs that offer superb snorkeling. If you visit Bangaram, admire the marine life and coral; but don't try to leave with any coral souvenirs. Taking the coral is a serious offense. Foreigners need an entry permit to visit; it's easily arranged when you book into the one resort.

PRACTICAL INFORMATION FOR KERALA

WHEN TO GO. The peak season in Kerala is October–March when the weather is warm and pleasant. From March to September, it's hot and steamy, with heavy rain beginning in June. From September until December sporadic light showers turn Kerala a lush green. The best season for Lakshadweep is October–May.

HOW TO GET THERE. By Air. Trivandrum has international flights to and from Columbo and the Maldive Islands. *Indian Airlines* has daily flights to Cochin from Bangalore, Bombay, and Madras. It has daily flights to Trivandrum from Bangalore, Bombay, Madras, and a few flights each week from Delhi and Goa. *Vayudoot* also connects Cochin with Madras and has a few weekly flights from Trivandrum to Bangalore and also Madras.

By Bus. Various luxury coaches connect Kerala with important South Indian cities: Bangalore, Kanya Kumari (Cape Comorin), Madras, Madurai, Mangalore, Pondicherry, and so on. If you don't mind the near-constant blare and glare of video, buses are usually clean, and cheap, and much faster than the train. For details, contact: *Kerala State Road Transport Corporation* (KSRTC) in Ernakulam (Cochin), Bus Terminus, tel. 352033. In Trivandrum, call KSRTC, Central Bus Station, Thampanoor, tel. 63886.

By Train. Good rail connections link Cochin and Trivandrum with Bangalore, Bombay, Cannanore, Delhi, Madras, and Mangalore. For details, call Ernakulam

(Cochin) Rail Station, 353100; from Trivandrum, call 62966 (days); 63066 (evenings).

By Rented Car with Driver. To Cochin from Bangalore, 575 km (357 mi.); Ootacamund, 300 km (186 mi.); Madurai, 340 km (211 mi.); Madras, 675 km (419 mi.); Mysore, 450 km (279 mi.). To Trivandrum from Bangalore, 720 km (446 mi.); Madras, 784 km (486 mi.); and Madurai, 307 km (190 mi.). Kerala has some of the best and most scenic roads in India.

TOURIST INFORMATION. The Government of India and the state of Kerala have pretty good basic tourist information on Kerala, including some maps and some brochures. Before your visit, or when you arrive, contact the following offices:

Government of India Tourist Office, Willingdon Island, Cochin, Kerala; tel. 6045. Open 9 A.M.–5 P.M., closed Saturdays and Sundays.

Kerala State Tourist Information Center, Old Collectorate, Park Ave., Ernakulam, Cochin; no phone. Open 10 A.M.–5 P.M., closed Sundays and second Saturdays.

Kerala Tourism Development Corporation (KTDC), Tourist Reception Center, Shanmughom Rd., Ernakulum, Cochin; tel. 353234. This office handles bookings for government-run tours and accommodations. Open 8 A.M.–6 P.M.

Kerala Tourist Information Center, Department of Tourism, Park View, Trivandrum, Kerala; tel. 61132. Open 10 A.M.–5 P.M. Monday–Saturday.

Kerala Tourist Information Counter, Central Bus Station, Thampanoor, Trivandrum; tel. 67224. Open 24 hours.

Kerala Tourist Information Counter, Railway Station, Thampanoor, Trivandrum; no phone. Open 24 hours.

Kerala Tourist Information Counter, Trivandrum Airport; tel. 71035. Open during flight times.

FOREIGN CURRENCY EXCHANGE. Most Western-style hotels have money-exchange counters. Otherwise, go to a branch of the *State Bank of India,* open Monday–Friday, 10 A.M.–2 P.M.; Saturdays, till noon.

ACCOMMODATIONS. In Cochin and Trivandrum, you can find a good range of hotels to suit all budgets. The rest of the state has limited, but adequate, options. In the peak season (October–March), book your room early. Prices are based on double occupancy and exclude taxes: *Deluxe,* over Rs. 1,450; *Expensive,* Rs. 950–Rs. 1,450; *Moderate,* Rs. 500–Rs. 950; *Inexpensive,* under Rs. 500. Some Western-style hotels take major credit cards.

ALLEPPEY

Inexpensive–Moderate

Alleppey Prince Hotel. A.S. Rd., N.H. 47, Alleppey; tel. 3752. 30 rooms with bath. This pleasant Western-style hotel has modern air-conditioned rooms, plus two great suites (moderately priced) that are done up in Kerala decor—bamboo walls and curios—and are so inviting you feel like you're in a modest, private home. Best rooms overlook the pool. Multicuisine restaurant, bar, TV, room service, swimming pool, backwater cruise arrangements, foreign-exchange counter. DC, MC, V.

COCHIN

Expensive

Taj Malabar Hotel. Willingdon Island, Cochin; tel. 6811. 91 rooms with bath. This resort, with good privacy and sea views, has a pleasing lobby with lots of carved dark wood and two choices of air-conditioned rooms. If you want antiquity and handsome, older furnishings, ask for a room with wooden floors in the old wing. Rooms in the new wing have a modern decor. In the entire hotel, best rooms have a seaside view; the next best have garden views. Multicuisine restaurants, bar, TV, room service, swimming pool, car-rental service, doctor, foreign-exchange counter. AE, DC, MC, V.

Moderate

Casino Hotel. Willingdon Island, Cochin; tel. 6821. 69 rooms with bath. This very moderately priced Western-style hotel offers excellent value and privacy. Its lobby is cozy, with cane furnishings. Air-conditioned rooms are spacious with a contemporary decor. Best rooms overlook the lawn and swimming pool. TV, room service, multicuisine restaurants, bar, foreign-exchange counter, local tours, car-rental service, backwater trip arrangements, swimming pool, doctor, shop. AE, DC, MC, V.

Inexpensive

Hotel Abad Plaza. M.G. Rd., Ernakulam, Cochin; tel. 361636. 41 rooms with bath. Set in the city, this Western-style hotel provides good service and modern air-conditioned rooms with a pleasant decor. Best rooms are in the back, away from any street noise. TV, room service, multicuisine restaurant, travel agent, shopping arcade, foreign-exchange counter. AE, DC, MC, V.

KOTTAYAM

Inexpensive

Anjali Hotel. Kottayam; tel. 3661. 30 rooms with bath. A modest Western-style hotel, Anjali has a small lobby and clean rooms with a simple modern decor. Some rooms are air-conditioned. Restaurants, bar, room service, car-rental service, backwater cruise arrangements, doctor, foreign-exchange counter, shops. AE, DC, MC, V.

KOVALAM

Expensive

Kovalam Ashok Beach Resort. Kovalam Beach, Trivandrum; tel. 68010. 125 rooms with bath. Built in tiers into a bluff overlooking the Arabian sea, this luxury resort lacks great character and warmth; but it is located on a beautiful beach. Rooms in the main block have modern furnishings and private verandas. Ask for an unobstructed sea view. Cottages, with tiled floors and a cozier feel, offer sea views and privacy. Air-conditioning, TV, room service, multicuisine restaurants, bar, swimming pool, health club, tennis court, foreign-exchange counter, travel agency, shopping arcade. AE, DC, MC, V.

Inexpensive

Hotel Rockholm. Light House Rd., Vizhinjam (Kovalam), Trivandrum; tel. Vizhinjam 306. 16 rooms with bath. The Rockholm's exterior is modest, but its superb location on a bluff overlooking the sea and its good service make this hotel popular. The small lobby is filled with reading material. Rooms are extremely clean, with modest contemporary furnishings and verandas. Upper-floor rooms are best. Fans, room service, multicuisine restaurant, good beach nearby, car-rental and backwater cruise arrangements, foreign-exchange counter. AE, DC, MC, V.

Hotel Samudra. Samudra Beach, Kovalam, Trivandrum; tel. 62089. 50 rooms with bath. This government-run complex offers good value and a secluded location on a quiet beach. Best rooms are air-conditioned, have a TV, and are set in cottages with views of the beach. All rooms have plain, clean furnishings and private verandas overlooking the ocean. Room service, multicuisine restaurant, bar, car-rental service, bank, foreign-exchange counter. AE, DC, MC, V.

KOZHIKODE (CALICUT)

Inexpensive

Alakpuri Guest House. Maulana Mohammed Ali Rd., Calicut; tel. 73361. 41 rooms with bath. The best rooms in this modest, Western-style hotel are air-conditioned. There's also a nice lawn. Room service, multicuisine restaurant, bar. DC, V.

Sea Queen Hotel. Beach Rd., Calicut; tel. 60201. 27 rooms with bath. Another Western-style hotel, Sea Queen has rooms that are simply furnished but clean. Some rooms are air-conditioned. Room service, multicuisine restaurant, bar. DC, MC, V.

LAKE PERIYAR

Moderate

Aranya Nivas. Thekkady, Idukki District; tel. Kumily 23. 23 rooms with bath. This Western-style hotel is near the lake and public boat launch. Don't expect much privacy or sense of the sanctuary. Rooms have a contemporary decor; spacious "deluxe" rooms are best. Room service, multicuisine restaurant, bar, car-rental service, foreign-exchange counter, boating. AE, DC.

Hotel Lake Palace. Thekkady, Idukki District; tel. Kumily 24. 6 rooms with bath. This wonderful former hunting lodge is set on an island inside the sanctuary. Lovely rooms open onto a sweeping porch with good views. The ambience is idyllic; the food is reasonably good. Fixed multicuisine menu, boating, trekking. Meals included. AE, DC.

LAKSHADWEEP ISLANDS

Delxue

Bangaram Island Resort. Lakshadweep. Reservations: Casino Hotel, Willingdon Island, Cochin; tel. 6821. 30 double rooms with bath. Set on an island dotted with lagoons, coconut groves, and beautiful beaches, this new resort seems like a real oasis. You stay in thatched cottages (two or four rooms to a unit), with bamboo walls, terra-cotta floors, and pleasant modern furnishings. The resort will help you procure the obligatory permit and book your 90-minute Vayudoot flight and 90-minute boatride. Excellent multicuisine restaurant, room service, bar, wind-surfing, kayaking, snorkeling, glass-bottom boats, fishing trips. Meals included. Off-season discount Apr. 1–Oct. 1. AE, DC, MC, V.

TRIVANDRUM

Moderate

Hotel Luciya Continental. East Fort, Trivandrum; tel. 73443. 52 rooms with bath. This five-story Western-style hotel has spacious air-conditioned rooms with a contemporary decor. For maximum quiet, ask for a room away from the street. Multicuisine restaurant, TV, room service, bar, doctor, foreign-exchange and travel counter. AE, DC, MC, V.

Inexpensive

Hotel Horizon. Trivandrum; tel. 66888. 46 rooms with bath. A modest Western-style hotel, Horizon has an attractive rooftop garden and pleasant rooms with a simple modern decor. Best rooms have TV, air-conditioning, and are back from the street. Room service, multicuisine restaurant, bar, doctor, car-rental service, foreign-exchange counter. AE, DC, MC, V.

Mascot Hotel. Trivandrum; tel. 68990. 40 rooms with bath. The Mascot, a government-run hotel, was once a grand British bungalow. Its entrance is imposing. Rooms are gigantic and clean, and the humble furnishings are adequate. But the interior decor is the handiwork of a mad painter: one room has blue and purple walls. Best rooms are air-conditioned and overlook a great swimming pool. Service can be erratic, but a polite complaint brings results. Room service, multicuisine restaurant, bar, foreign-exchange counter, swimming pool, health club. AE, DC, MC, V.

Hotel Pankaj. Opposite Secretariat, M.G. Rd., Trivandrum; tel. 76667. 52 rooms with bath. This small modern hotel has a comfortable lobby and contemporary-decor rooms. Best rooms are air-conditioned and have TV. Multicuisine restaurants, room service, bar, foreign-exchange counter, travel agency. Good value. AE, DC, MC, V.

DINING OUT. For all you beef lovers, Kerala has the real thing. It also has great seafood and Southern Indian vegetarian cuisine. In fact, this is a state—like Goa—that offers good good eating; both Indian and non-Indian. Besides some of the best options listed here, many accommodations listed above also have restaurants. Breakfast is usually 8–10:30; lunch, noon–3; dinner, 7:30–10. Payment is normally in rupees unless the restaurant is connected to a Western-style hotel. The restaurants listed below are informal and, unless noted, are open for three meals and don't require reservations. Prices, based on one person eating a three-course meal, excluding taxes, tip, or beverage, are *Deluxe,* over Rs. 120; *Expensive,* Rs. 80–Rs. 120; *Moderate,* Rs. 40–Rs. 80; *Inexpensive,* under Rs. 40.

ALLEPPEY

Moderate

Vembanad Restaurant. Alleppey Prince Hotel, A.S. Rd.; tel. 3752. Vembanad's decor is simple—a few oars tacked on one wall, fresh flowers, crisp linen. The accent is on good food: Continental, Chinese, and Indian cuisines, including Kerala dishes. Try *kozni olath* (diced chicken cooked with coconut chips) or, if you can order in advance, fish *vevichathu* (deep-fried sailfish coated in hot spices). At lunch, sample the good Kerala *thali* (assorted regional dishes served on a platter). Portions are large. Open 7–11 A.M., noon–2:30 P.M., and 7–9:30 P.M. DC, MC, V.

COCHIN

Deluxe

Jade Pavilion. Taj Malabar Hotel, Willingdon Island; tel. 6811. Elegance is the keynote at the Jade, with an interior Oriental pavilion, exotic wall mural, and brass lanterns that create a romantic touch. The extensive Chinese menu includes lobster *sing-tu* style (spicy lobster cooked in chili and oyster sauce), tiger prawns in garlic sauce, and tasty steamed fish. Reservations advised. Open noon–3 P.M. and 7:30–11 P.M. AE, DC, MC, V.

Expensive

Fort Cochin. Casino Hotel, Willingdon Island; tel. 6821. Enjoy the day's catch in an attractive Kerala-style cottage with subdued lighting. The chef is terrific and can cook up your choice to your specifications, from simple to grand, with delectable sauces. Reservations advised. Open 7 P.M.–midnight. AE, DC, MC, V.

Moderate

Pandhal. M.G. Rd., opposite Grand Hotel; tel. 367759. This modern multicuisine restaurant with rough white stucco walls, pine ceiling, and small waterfall serves an excellent Kerala thali and a variety of seafood. Its Chinese cuisine is especially popular. The place is usually crowded. Dinner reservations advised. Open 11:30 A.M.–3 P.M. and 7:30–11 P.M. AE, DC, MC, V.

Regency. Hotel Abad Plaza, M.G. Rd.; tel. 361636. This handsome restaurant with dark-wood pillars inlaid with mirrors offers Continental, Indian, and Chinese dishes. Specialties are spicy Szechuan deep-fried prawns and island chicken curry served in a pineapple. You can also enjoy great seafood. No liquor is served, but at night you're entertained by Indian or Western musicians. Dinner reservations advised. Open 11:30 A.M.–3 P.M. and 7:30–11 P.M. AE, DC, MC, V.

Inexpensive

Frys Village Restaurant. Chittoor Rd., next to Mymoon Cinema; tel. 353983. Somehow this city restaurant—four pavilions with bamboo curtains—screens out the surrounding bustle. It also serves the typical Kerala set meals (thalis): fish *molly* (fillet in a sweet green curry with coconut), fish curry (spicy hot), or the very inexpensive *kadala* (Kerala plain curry) with *puttu* (steamed rice and coconut cake) for under Rs. 5. Open 12:30–3 P.M. and 6–11:30 P.M. Rupees only.

KOVALAM BEACH

Moderate

Rockholm Hotel Restaurant. Light House Rd.; tel. 306. While you can eat indoors, the best ambience here is on the delightful terrace set on the bluff with the ocean pounding below. Kovalam's best chef prepares excellent multicuisine dishes, including the day's catch. Try the excellent grilled pomfret, fried mussels, or prawns served Kerala-style. Dinner reservations suggested. Open 7 A.M.–9:30 P.M. AE, DC, MC, V.

TRIVANDRUM

Moderate

Marthanda. Hotel Pankaj, opposite Secretariat, M.G. Rd.; tel. 76667. This cozy all-white restaurant, with soft lighting, offers Chinese, Continental, and Indian dishes, including regional specialties. Try the fish *malabari* (fish curry cooked with coconut) or the diced chicken Szechuan. Sandhya, an upstairs restaurant, has the same menu and offers a lunch buffet and a good view of Trivandrum. Open 7–10 A.M., noon–3 P.M., and 7–11 P.M. AE, DC, MC, V.

Mira. Hotel Horizon, Trivandrum; tel. 66888. An upstairs restaurant, Mira's decor is green, green, green! A country-western band plays nightly, except Tuesday. The cook prepares Indian, Continental, and Chinese dishes. Specialties include chicken *chettinad* (boneless deep-fried chicken served in a spicy red gravy), which isn't on the menu, and *malai kofta* (mashed vegetables cooked with saffron, cashews, and almonds). Open 6 A.M.–11 P.M. AE, DC, MC, V.

Nalukettu. Opposite Trivandrum Club, Vellayambalam; tel. 69287. This 70-year-old traditional Nair family house with a pitched tile roof is delightful. Among the numerous dining rooms, the air-conditioned one is best, but walk around and see the interior *nalukettu* (courtyard). You can also eat outside at night. The chef prepares multicuisine dishes, including Kerala items. Best bet is the mutton or chicken *nalukettu* (curry dish prepared with chopped coconut, coconut milk, and masala spices). Reservations advised. Open 11 A.M.–11 P.M. MC, V.

SWEETS AND TREATS. Cochin. You can escape the crowds and have good vegetarian Indian snacks and sweets (*barfi* and *pedas* made from a sugary milk paste) in the tiny air-conditioned *Mezbaan,* 38/1278 M.G. Rd., Padma Junction; open daily 9 A.M.–8 P.M. For Western or Indian snacks and sweets, including good ice cream, go to *Pandhal,* M.G. Rd. Snacks are served daily 3 P.M.–7 P.M.

HOW TO GET AROUND. From the Airport. Cochin. City buses run regularly between the airport and Cochin (Rs. 1). A taxi to your hotel should cost about Rs. 40; bargain! A taxi into Trivandrum is your best bet and should cost about Rs. 50–Rs. 60; to Kovalam Beach, Rs. 100–Rs. 130.

By Plane. *Indian Airlines* flies three times a week between Cochin and Trivandrum. *Vayudoot* flies three times weekly from Calicut to Cochin and Trivandrum. It also flies three times a week to the Lakshadweep Islands from Calicut and Cochin.

By Bus. Buses ply the streets, but they're crowded. For bus information in Cochin, call 352033; in Trivandrum, call 63886.

By Train. You can travel Cochin–Kottayam–Quilon–Trivandrum–Kozhikode (Calicut) via train. In Cochin, for train information and reservations, call 353100; in Trivandrum, call 62966 (days) and 63066 (evenings).

By Tourist Taxi. These comfortable white Ambassadors are the best way to get around Kerala's good, scenic roads. They're available for hire at most good Western-style hotels and through travel agencies listed below under *Tour Operators.* Rates are about Rs. 3–Rs. 3.50 per km, with a halt charge of Rs. 50 per night. Minimum change is Rs. 25.

By Taxi. Yellow-topped taxis are available in most cities. Rate is about Rs. 3 per km; minimum charge is Rs. 20.

By Boat. In **Kerala,** ferries cruise along a network of backwater canals that provide a lazy way to get from city to city.

Alleppey. You can take a public ferry backwater day-long trip to Quilon for less than Rs. 25. For details, inquire at the boat jetty or at the Tourist Department in Cochin or Trivandrum before you arrive. In addition, you can hire a lovely old wooden boat with a captain and do the trip in grand leisurely style, but for a far grander price (Rs. 100 per hour). Arrangements can be made through travel agents, tourist departments, and hotels, or through *Vembanad Tourist Service,* Akkarakalam Building, near Bus Stand, Jetty Road, Alleppey, Kerala; tel. 3395.

Cochin. Frequent ferry service runs from early morning until about 10 P.M. There are ferries from Fort Cochin, Ernakulam, Mattancherry, Willington Island, plus numerous other runs. Ask at your hotel for specifics, or contact the local tourist office.

Kottayam. This is a convenient starting and ending point for a backwater trip to Alleppey. Inquire at the boat jetty.

Quillon. From here, you can take the day-long public ferry that weaves through the backwaters to Alleppey. Go to the boat jetty for information. You can also do shorter trips and you can rent a boat for the day.

By Auto Rickshaw. This is the cheapest and most convenient way to travel in Trivandrum and Cochin. Rates are about Rs. 2 per km.

TOURS. Alleppey to Quillon. You can join a fixed-departure, day-long boat tour for each direction, which includes a guide and makes interesting stops along the way. For these tours, contact *Alleppey Tourism Development Co-operative Society,* Karthika Tourist Home, Alleppey; tel. 2554. Boats depart from Alleppey on Monday, Wednesday, Friday; from Quinlon on Tuesday, Thursday, Saturday; Rs. 70 each way. Bring your own lunch.

Cochin (Ernakulam). KTDC (Tourist Reception Center, Shanmughom Rd., Ernakulam, tel. 353234) conducts the following inexpensive deluxe bus and boat tours (bus tours depart from the Tourist Reception Center): *Boat Sightseeing Tour of Cochin.* Two daily 3-½-hour tours; departs 9 A.M. and 2 P.M. from the Boat Jetty in front of Sealord Hotel. *Cochin–Thekkady.* Two-day weekend bus tour to Periyar Wildlife Sanctuary; departs 7 A.M. Saturday and returns Sunday night. *Cochin–Velankanni.* Three-day bus tour, including Periyar Wildlife Sanctuary and Tamil Nadu temple cities of Madurai, Tiruchi, and Thanjavur; departs every 2nd Friday and returns Monday morning.

Trivandrum. KTDC (Tourist Reception Center, Thampanoor, near Central Bus Station, tel. 75031) conducts a series of bus tours: *Trivandrum Tour,* full-day tour departs at 8 A.M., except Mondays. *Kanyakumari Tour* (Cape Comorin) is a full-day trip, starting at 7:30 A.M. daily. *Ponmudi Tour* (Hill station) departs daily at 8:30 A.M. *Lake Periyar Wildlife Sanctuary* (two-day tour) departs Saturdays 6:30 A.M. *Kodaikanal Tour* (Tamil Nadu hill station) is a three-day trip starting 6:30 A.M. on the last Saturday of each month.

Private Guides. The *Government of India Tourist Office* in Cochin (see address above) can supply good guides. For one–four people for four hours, Rs. 45; for eight hours, Rs. 65.

TOUR OPERATORS. The following full-service agencies can handle all your travel needs, including car with driver:

Sita Travels, Tharakan Building, M.G. Rd., Ravipuram, Cochin; tel. 361101.

Travel Corporation of India, Telstar Building, M.G. Rd., Ernakulam, Cochin; tel. 351646.

The following two reputable agencies also offer special outdoor adventures in Kerala (also see the listings under Special-Interest Tours in *Facts at Your Fingertips*):

Markar Travel Corporation (Marikar Building, M. G. Rd., Trivandrum; tel. 78211) sponsors good treks in wildlife sanctuaries.

EMPL Tours (108 Vishal Phawan, 95 Nehru Pl., New Delhi; tel. 6828310) offers good bike trips.

SEASONAL EVENTS. Since the lunar calendar determines most events, contact the Government of India Tourist Office for details.

April–May. *Pooram.* Kerala's most spectacular temple festival takes place in Trichur. Elephants, sporting gorgeous gold-plated mail, carry Brahmans with ceremonial umbrellas and the temple deity, Vadakkunathan, in a procession accompanied by the beat of temple drums. Great festivities and fireworks.

August. *Nehru Trophy Boat Race.* On the second Saturday of August, snake boats compete at Alleppey for the Nehru Trophy. Big tourist draw.

August–September. *Onam,* Kerala's biggest festival, celebrates the harvest season. Lasting three days, it features dancing, singing, and exotic snake boat races at Alleppey, Aranmula, and Kottayam. Boats of all descriptions—beak shaped, kite-tailed, curly-headed—and lots of hoopla!

November–December. *Makaravilakka Festival.* This important Hindu pilgrimage to the Ayyappa Temple at Sabarimala (180 km northeast of Trivandrum) is held November–January. The procession involves only men and prepubescent and post-menopausal women. The arrival of the devotees who come from all over India is supposed to coincide with the conclusion of a 60-day fast. Many just make a five-km trek from the sacred Pampa River.

HISTORIC SITES. Entrance to most places is generally free; where a donation is asked, a few rupees will suffice. Monuments are open sunrise to sunset unless noted otherwise below.

Dutch Palace in Mattancherry (eight km from Ernakulam) was built by the Portuguese and given to the maharajah in 1568. It's called Dutch because the Dutch later renovated it. The center of the building contains a large coronation hall, and seventeenth-century murals tell the entire story of the *Ramayana.* Three temples are dedicated to Vishnu, Shiva, and Pazhavayannoor Bhagavathi. Open 9 A.M.–5 P.M., closed Fridays.

Cochin Synagogue, Mattancherry, was originally constructed in 1568 and rebuilt in the late 1600s and 1700s after partial destruction. Beautiful Chinese floor tiles—no two alike—were added in 1762 by Ezekiel Rahabi, who also built the clock tower. The Cochin maharajah gave the synagogue the great scrolls of the Old Testament and copper plates. The entire building is a treasure vault. Open 10 A.M.–noon and 2:30–5 P.M. Closed Saturdays.

St. Francis Church, Fort Cochin, was the first European church built in India, constructed in 1510. Vasco da Gama was buried here. You can see his gravestone, but his remains were shipped back to Portgual. Sedate, stark architecture.

Vallia Palli, Kottayam, is a Syrian church that supposedly contains a cross brought from a church in Kodungalloor (Cranganore) that was established by St. Thomas.

Janardhana Temple, Varkala, 54 km north of Trivandrum, is claimed to be 2,000 years old. A famous pilgrimage center for Hindus, the temple is dedicated to Vishnu.

MUSEUMS AND GALLERIES. Entrance is usually free or there is a nominal fee. **Trivandrum.** *Chitra Art Gallery* has an eclectic collection of paintings, including Rajput, Mogul, and Far Eastern art. Open 8 A.M.–5 P.M.; closed Mondays.

Cochin. *Parishath Thanburam Museum,* Darbar Hall Road, Ernakulam. Emphasis here is on archaeology, models of temples, sculptures, and old photography, old paintings, and antiques from the nineteenth century. Open 9:30 A.M.–noon and 3–5:30 P.M.; closed Mondays and holidays.

Hill Palace Museum, Tripanithura (13 km or eight mi. south of Cochin), which belonged to the former Cochin maharajah, has royal costumes, coaches, old weapons, and coins, sculptures, and paintings. Open 9 A.M.–5 P.M., closed Mondays.

Calicut. *Pazhassiraja Museum,* East Hill, five km from Calicut, has copies of ancient mural paintings, antique bronzes, old coins, archaeological findings. Open 10 A.M.–5 P.M.; closed Mondays.

SPORTS AND OUTDOOR ADVENTURES. **Beaches.** Kerala is aware of its prize beaches—palm-fringed with towering cliffs and coves; but bad zoning policies could destroy their beauty.

Kovalam Beach. 18 km (11 mi.) from Trivandrum. Lovely beaches backed by cliffs; but the "hippies" and their drugs have also made this beach their home.

Lakshadweep. The one island open to foreigners in this gorgeous archipelago with lagoons and coral reefs requires a permit and an expensive yet delightful stay at the one resort (see above under Accommodations). It's an ideal place for swimming, boating, snorkeling.

Golf. You can golf at the Trivandrum Golf Club. Inquire at the tourist office for details.

Yoga. Cochin. Ramaswamy Yogadham (Woman's Club, North End, near Embarkation Jetty, Willingdon Island; no phone) runs hour-long classes for men and women 7 A.M.–11 A.M., closed Saturday and Sunday.

WILDLIFE SANCTUARIES. *Lake Periyar Wildlife Sanctuary* surrounds a large artificial lake. Inexpensive boat trips are available, but fellow passengers tend to squeal at the slightest sign of distant movement. Splurge and get a boat for yourself (Rs. 200). You can see elephants, maybe leopards, tigers, langur, wild boar, deer, and numerous birds. You can also hire a guide and hike; there are lookouts to climb. Best time to visit is October–May. Contact Manager, Aranya Niwas, Thekkady, or the Field Director, Project Tiger, Kanjikuzhi, Kottayam (tel. 8049) for more details.

Neyyar Wildlife Sanctuary, 32 km (20 mi.) from Trivandrum, is a large reservoir with boats available for hire. You may see elephants, sloth bears, wild boar, langur, tigers, leopards, and birds. The sanctuary is also a crocodile breeding center and deer park. Best time to visit is October–May. For more details, contact Wildlife Warden, Forest Headquarters, Trivandrum; tel. 60674.

Parambikulam Wildlife Sanctuary is set around three dams, 48 km (30 mi.) from Pollachi northeast of Trichur. Elephants, tigers, deer, gaur, otters, bears, and crocodiles abound. Facilities for boating and forest rest house accommodations are available in an area called Top Slips. For details and room reservations, contact the Tamil Nadu Government, Indira Gandhi Wildlife Sanctuary, Mahalingapuram, Pollachi, Kerala; tel. 4345. Bring a sleeping bag or linen.

SHOPPING. In Kerala, you can buy wonderful handicrafts in natural fibers (palm, screw pine, banana leaf, bamboo) as well as sandlewood and rosewood products, great papier-mâché masks, brass bell-metal work, and, in Cochin and Trivandrum, old curios.

Cochin. *Kairali* (M.G. Road, Ernakulam), a government-run shop, has a good collection of Kerala handicrafts and curios. Open 9 A.M.–8 P.M., closed Sundays. AE, DC, MC, V.

Surabhi (M.G. Road, Ernakulam), run by the state's Handicrafts Cooperative Society, also has a good selection of locally made products. Open 9:30 A.M.–1:30 P.M. and 3:30–7:30 P.M., closed Sundays. Rupees only.

Indian Arts and Curios (Jew Town) is the oldest and most reliable shop on this curio and antiques-laden street. The shop has two outlets, each filled with brass and wood items and Tanjore glass paintings. Open 8:30 A.M.–5:30 P.M. AE, MC, V. Bargain. In all the shops in this area, buy what you like, but not for investment. Often "old" means no more than 24 hours old.

Trivandrum. *Natesan's Antiquarts* (M.G. Road and Kovalam Ashok Beach Resort) sells lovely old and new curios, including statues and paintings from South India. Extremely reliable. Open 10 A.M.–8 P.M., closed Sundays. AE, DC, MC, V.

Lawrence Handicrafts (M.G. Road and Kovalam Ashok Beach Resort) sells a similar range of curios. Open 9:30 A.M.–8:30 P.M., closed Sundays. AE, V.

Gifts Corner (M.G. Road) is a great place to poke around for old and new curios. They also have two warehouses that they'll take you to visit. Open 10 A.M.–8 P.M., closed Sundays. AE, MC, V.

S.M.S.M. Institute (Central Handicrafts Emporium, Puthenchanthai, behind the Secretariat) sells good Kerala curios. Open 9 A.M.–8 P.M., closed Sundays. AE, DC, MC, V.

Kottayam. Make a 40 km (25 mi.) excursion to Aranmula, via Chenannur, and visit the *Viswatharathy Handicrafts Center*. This is one of the only family-operated places still creating metal mirror products, an unfortunately dying artform, which turns bronze into mirror. You can buy exquisite compacts, hand-mirrors, and other items at reasonable prices. The best selection is available November–January. Open daily 10 A.M.–8:30 P.M. Rupees only.

ENTERTAINMENT. A trip to Kerala must include seeing a performance of the Kathakali dance form. *Katha* means story; *kali* means play, and that's what you see: a story/dance form over 400 years old—Indian pantomime performed in painted face and with great costumes. The performers start training at a very young age, learning how to control every muscle in their bodies and toes. Traditional performances can run for hours; but you can see an abridged version and a demonstration of the intricate application of the make-up. These shows are wonderful, even for the young. Call for reservations and details.

Cochin. *Art Kerala,* 35/346 Kannathodath Lane, Valanjambalam, Ernakulam, tel. 366238. Daily performance is 7–8:30 P.M. *Cochin Cultural Center,* Durbar Hall Ground, Ernakulam; tel. 367866 and 353732. Daily 6:30–8 P.M. *Gurnkulam Kathakali Yogam,* Kalathiparambil Lane, Ernakulam; tel. 369471. This delightful theater has daily shows from 6:30–8:30 P.M.

Trivandrum. At *Trivandrum Kathakali Club, Drysyavedi,* and *Margi,* regular Kathakali programs are organized. Inquire at the Tourist Information Center for details.

Bars. The best bars are in the better hotels. They're generally open noon–2:30 P.M. and 6:30–10:30 P.M.

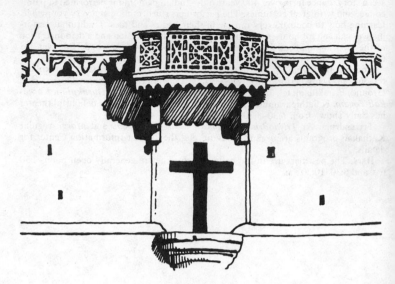

GOA

Tropical Gold Coast

by
KATHLEEN COX

If you think every paradise in the world is first discovered then ruined by the discoverers, go to Goa. No bigger than a thumbprint on the Malabar Coast map, this former Portuguese territory—the home of about one million easygoing, hospitable people, both Hindu and Christians—is in India, but not entirely of it.

The climate and scenery are resort perfect. Outside the monsoon season (June to September), which affects most of India, the temperature and weather stay high and dry. Most who visit Goa dream of becoming marooned in a charming village where the silvery sands of some of the world's most beautiful beaches are never more than a few steps away. The palm-bordered rivers move wide and lazily down to the Arabian Sea, while the towns are a pleasing blend of Portuguese and Indian. Houses gleam with a light wash of color set off by brightly painted pillared front porches and trim. Goa appears to be the epitome of well-cared-for tropical suburbia.

In the not-too-distant past, Goa was like an Asian Tangiers, with connections to Europe as well as the East. A constant flow of European products (legal and illegal) were uncrated in Goa's ports. Yet, after four centuries of heavy-handed Portuguese Catholicism, somehow only about 30 percent of the people became Christian. It also seems that the somewhat puritan atmosphere of India proper had trouble penetrating the borders.

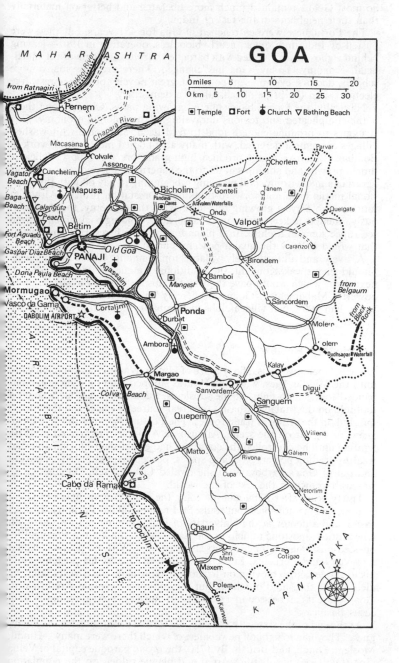

GOA

0 miles	5	10	15	20
0 km	5	10	15	20	25	30

⊡ Temple ▢ Fort ✚ Church ▽ Bathing Beach

So most Goans remained much more liberated and better off materially than their neighbors in the rest of India.

The Portuguese were entrenched in Goa for 451 years, but they were ousted by India in a quick, nearly bloodless, operation in 1961—leaving behind a ghost town studded with baroque churches and a plentiful, if artificial, economy. Today, Goa has changed. There are now many more schools, doctors, ever-present cows, the great novelty of a free press, free elections, and the pride of self-rule in a democracy.

Naturally, the Goans have suffered growing pains. Chief among them is the complicated and tedious unraveling of the colonial economy. Goa struggles to produce enough food to feed itself, and some whitewashed villages are almost deserted, with many able-bodied men seeking work in Bombay. But iron mines produce high-grade ore for export; delicious tinned prawns and shrimp sail off to the supermarkets; and conscientious agrarian and environmental planning is beginning to pay off with the occasional model farm and forward-thinking reforestation project. Although tourism also plays a growing role in reviving the economy, the state seriously attempts to keep an eye on Goa's beauty, holding back hoteliers who see rupee signs in architectural plans for mammoth resort monstrosities that would destroy the quaint peaceful charm.

A lively and unfortunately volatile topic among Goans is language: Should they speak Konkani, the traditional tongue, or Marathi, spoken next door, which would pave the way for absorption by the larger, more powerful Maharashtra? Goans are fiercely loyal to their state (there are more than 300 Goan village clubs in Bombay), India takes second place in their heart.

A Historic Review

Early Goan history is a hazy maze of Hindu dynasties and subdynasties until the Middle Ages, when the Hindus stopped fighting each other and banded together to fight off the Moslems. Suddenly, everyone wanted a foothold on the Malabar Coast—the great source of spices and the important link in the Arabian trade routes. The Portuguese were the first Europeans to appear on the scene. Alfonso de Albuquerque arrived in 1510, fighting until he controlled the coast and had established a formidable and wealthy trading power. Silks and spices, porcelains and pearls, passed in and out of Goa's harbors until she rivaled Lisbon itself. "Golden Goa" was well known to the rest of the world.

Thirty years after Albuquerque came the most famous figure in Goan history, seeking not spices but souls: St. Francis Xavier. Born in a Spanish castle, and a doctor at the University of Paris, Francis left for Goa with a new title—apostolic nuncio to the East—when the king of Portugal requested missionaries for his overseas territories. With no possessions but a breviary and a crucifix, Francis transformed Goa by his preaching and his example before moving on to more distant lands. Ten years later, he died on the threshold of China, but his body was eventually returned to Goa, where it can be seen in a state of eerie quasi-preservation in the Bom Jesus Basilica.

At the end of the sixteenth century, life turned precarious for the Portuguese. They had to fight off newcomers of which there were many—Hindu, Moslem, Dutch, and British. By 1750, the proud baroque capital of Velha Goa (Old Goa) was battle scarred and plague ridden, so the population moved down river to Panaji. The Portuguese methods of rule degenerated as badly as did the buildings, with Goans suffering from the Inquisition, set up after Francis Xavier's death. This horrendous tool of injustice finally gave up the ghost in 1812. And the viceroyship, which was a political plus that enriched its possessor, did little for the Goans. Throughout the nineteenth and early twentieth centuries abortive revolts sprang up— fragile sparks of rebellion that were ruthlessly quelled by the Portuguese. In December, 1961, India put a stop to what was, from her point of view, an intolerable situation. Operation Vijaya brought Goa back to India after a 451-year absence.

Daman and Diu, two other Portuguese vest-pocket enclaves, fell to India at the same time. Daman (56 square kilometers or 22 square miles), north of Bombay, and Diu (38 square kilometers or 15 square miles), across the Gulf of Cambay, share Goa's character, religions, and rural pursuits.

EXPLORING GOA

Let's face it—if you're in Goa, it's partially for the sun, sand, and surf! Goa has 132 kilometers (82 miles) of coastline plus deep river estuaries, so you have quite a choice of public beaches. Closest to Panaji, the capital, are Miramar and Dona Paula beaches. At Miramar, closer of the two, the swimming is marred by a strong undertow and the view is marred by an unfortunate stretch of architectural eyesores erected before Goa wised up. The Dona Paula Beach is palm fringed and commands a fine view of the Mormugao Harbor. Across the Mandovi River from Panaji is gorgeous Calangute Beach. This "queen of Goan beaches" is 16 kilometers (18 miles) in length, with Baga, Anjuna, then Vagator cloistered in dramatic rocks and cliffs—a spectacular place to watch the sun disappear over the water. Another good public beach is the Colva, on the south coast near Margao. Here, the nomadic Lambanis, who travel the western states of India, set up shop on portable blankets cluttered with great handicrafts, jewelry, embroideries, and quilts.

Panaji, a pleasant whitewashed city, was only a sleepy village before the Portuguese transferred their capital closer to shore. The most important monument dating from the precapital days is the Secretariat Building— once a Moslem palace, then a Portuguese fort. Near the building stands the statue of the Abbé Faria, priest and hypnotist, portrayed in the act of mesmerizing a female patient. The best view of Panaji is from the Church of Our Lady of the Immaculate Conception or, if you're lucky, from the Portuguese-style villa of a Goan host who happens to live on the hillside. You can also get a good sense of Panaji from the banks of the wide Mandovi, where slow-sailing craft journey up and down the gray water.

The scenery around the capital is lush, with rice paddies, palms, groves of mango, and jackfruit. But plan for a leisurely pace, because of the number of linking ferries, usually crowded but still offering an easygoing, enjoyable ride. One easy excursion is to Velha Goa. The sixteenth-century Portuguese capital is a study in splendor and decay. Go by boat, if you can, so that, after you disembark, you can drive or walk through the Vice-regal Arch, as each viceroy had to do before taking possession of his office. This arch, where Vasco da Gama gazes out from his niche in full regalia, was the symbolic entry to the city, as well as the gateway from the harbor.

The tiny city was once the greatest commercial center east of Suez, rivaling Lisbon in grandeur. "Whoever has seen Goa, need not see Lisbon" was no careless boast. Now the great square, the site of the trials of the Inquisition, is little better than a neglected field.

The following is a convenient order for a tour of Velha Goa:

St. Cajetan, an Italian and contemporary of St. Francis Xavier, lent his name to this handsome church and convent of the Theatin Order. Constructed in the seventeenth century, the church was modeled after St. Peter's Basilica in Rome. The facade is neoclassic, with twin towers flanking the great dome, but the interior decoration is pure unrestrained baroque. The main altar soars nearly to the top of the edifice, the patron saint's altar is adorned with twisted columns, and the pulpit is an exercise in delicate carving. A large arched window, whose tiny panes are made of seashells, is interesting. In the crypt are the tombs of generations of Portuguese rulers.

Another curious feature, located beneath the raised platform, the present site of the altar, is a tank, or a well, which has led many to believe that this was the site of a temple tank, meaning that this church replaced a former Hindu shrine. Many of the paintings that adorn the walls were brought from Europe in the fifteenth century; others were done locally.

The Se Cathedral, the largest church in Velha Goa, is an imposing white structure constructed between 1562 and 1652. Unfortunately, its facade is lopsided after the collapse of the north tower in 1776. The Cathedral's tiny congregation seems out of proportion to its 230-foot length and the magnificence of its decoration. The bell in the existing tower is referred to as the "Golden Bell" because of its rich tone, immortalized in a Portuguese poem. Notice also the Chapel of the Blessed Sacrament, the third chapel on your left as you face the altar. The closed blue doors combine three schools of art: the bottom panel is characteristically Hindu, the middle panel is Moslem, and the top panel below the arch is Greek. The main altar, dedicated to St. Catherine, is simple in shape with classical arches and Corinthian columns; richly gilded scenes in deep relief portray episodes in the saint's martyrdom. In the left nave are the chapels of St. Joseph, ornamented on every possible surface, of St. George, and of Our Lady of Necessity.

On the right is the chapel of the Holy Spirit, with its lovely altarpiece showing Mary surrounded by the black-bearded apostles on the day of Pentecost. Other chapels on this side are dedicated to St. Bernard, St. Anthony, and the Holy Cross. Almost hidden in this last chapel in the Mauresque style is a cross on which a vision of Christ is said to have appeared in 1919.

St. Francis of Assisi Church and Convent (built in 1661) is easily the best example of Portuguese religious art in Old Goa. The Franciscan Order was the first to arrive in Goa, even though nearly everyone thinks of Francis Xavier and the more spectacular results of the Jesuits in connection with Goa. True to the humility of their founder, the Franciscans went straight to the poor and downtrodden, whereas the Jesuits allied themselves with the resident Brahmans. The Franciscan church is simple and handsome, spacious and harmonious. The portal is pure Manueline style; inside, this theme is developed in rich stucco ceilings and a profusion of carvings. High above the main altar, Christ crucified is shown with his right arm detached from the cross in order to embrace St. Francis. In the convent next door, visit the museum and gallery with portraits of 16 Franciscan martyrs.

The Chapel of St. Catherine is an endearing little Renaissance church, one of the first erected by Albuquerque in 1510 to celebrate his arrival in Velha Goa on St. Catherine's Day.

The Bom Jesus Basilica took 10 years to build and is a striking example of Jesuit architecture. The interior is perhaps the richest of the churches in Old Goa, highly and heavily decorated, yet admirably proportioned. Built in the sixteenth century, the basilica is sacred to the Infant Jesus, but the Babe's statue is dwarfed by that of Ignatius of Loyala, founder of the order of Jesuits, which stands above the gilded high altar.

Most will visit Bom Jesus not for its size or its style but for the relic on display. Here, in a splendor he constantly refused during his lifetime, lies the body of St. Francis Xavier. The body traveled after death almost as much as the saint had done in life, but in spite of each transfer (at least four) to this final resting place, the body resisted damage. Indeed, the deceased Francis suffered more from piety than anything else—both big toes were bitten off by female fanatics and an arm was severed at the request of a pope and carried off to Rome.

St. Francis owes his opulent casket to the generosity of the duke of Tuscany, who received the saint's pillow as a relic and sent the Florentine tomb in exchange. The entire chapel is covered with marble, inlaid with semiprecious stones, and decorated with paintings portraying the life of the saint. In recent years, the casket was cut open. Now, the curious or the worshiping can have a grisly glimpse of the head and shoulders of Francis.

Walk up the road from Bom Jesus to the Monte Santo or Holy Hill. Here you can see a number of other remnants of Portuguese glory. The most interesting is the Convent and Church of Santa Monica, which once housed more than 100 nuns, then slowly dwindled in importance until the last nun died in 1885. The church is refreshingly simple, in the Doric style, and contains a supposedly miraculous cross in one chapel. Its building is massive, more like a fortress than a nunnery.

Also on the Monte Santo are other churches, most of them ruined; and, on a less saintly level, a black stone whipping post where prisoners were given the Portuguese third degree. The best preserved of the group of churches is the little chapel of St. Anthony. Because St. Anthony is the patron saint of soldiers, the saint's image used to receive an annual salary from the commander of the army. One ill-advised general, who considered this a wasteful expense, cut off the payment. He died from a fall on the saint's feast day. The next general restored Anthony's stipend.

Despite the number of Christian churches, Goa is 68 percent Hindu and just 30 percent Christian. If there are few temples in proportion to the Hindu population, it's partially because the first wave of Portuguese destroyed them. The temples were rebuilt, but inland, at a safe distance from the foreign colonizers. In and around Ponda, there are seven temples within a five-kilometer (three-mile) radius. The most interesting is the small but lovely Shri Manguesh, set on a lush green hill. Dedicated to Shiva, the temple has an air of tropical elegance, with its blue pillars, tiles on the wall, old locally made crystal chandeliers, and large silver idols. The special Shri Mahadeva at Tambdi Surla, 66 kilometers (41 miles) from Panaji, in the foot of the ghats is the only example of Kadamba temple architecture (the Kadambas ruled from the eleventh to the thirteenth century) remaining in Goa. Built of basalt stone, the temple is in a tranquil setting on a river bank and site on a simple plinth with intricately carved pillars in the *mandapa* (pavilion). There is no use of mortar anywhere in the structure—stone is hammered into stone.

Once, dozens of mosques dotted the countryside, but the Portuguese, who showed no favoritism, pursued their policy of destruction and quickly demolished them. The only remaining mosque of any historic importance dates back to 1560 and is known as the Safa Shahouri Masjid, built by

Ibrahim Adilshah of Bijapur. Unfortunately, an extensive garden with fountains that surrounded the mosque succumbed to the wrath of the marauding Portuguese.

Today, Old Goan homes are splendid sites, both inside and out. Some of them are open to the public. Contact the Tourist Department when you arrive.

PRACTICAL INFORMATION FOR GOA

WHEN TO GO. Goa can be lovely during the monsoon from June to September. There will be periodic downpours, but Goa will be tropically lush. Otherwise, temperatures vary little, averaging 79°F. December, January, and February are great (a light wool sweater might be good to have in the evening). Because of various festivals, Goa is very crowded from December to February. Book accommodations well ahead.

HOW TO GET THERE. By Air. *Indian Airlines* has daily flights into Dabolim Airport, Goa, from the following major cities: Bombay, Delhi, Cochin, Trivandrum, and Bangalore. *Vayudoot* also has occasional flights from Pune, Hyderabad, and Bombay to Goa.

By Bus. Buses can get you to Goa, but they're usually crowded. Nevertheless, a bus is usually reliable, clean, and fast. And best of all, it's easy to make reservations and get a ticket—easy by Indian standards.

The *Kadamba Transport Corporation Ltd.* (KTC, a government of Goa, Daman, and Diu undertaking), the *Karnataka State Road Transport Corporation* (KSRTC), *Maharashtra State Road Transport Corporation* (MSRTC), *Maharashtra Tourism Development Corporation,* and numerous private buses, can take you to and from the major destinations. Consult the appropriate chapter for details. In Panaji, Goa, contact KTC Bus Terminus, tel. 3334; KSRTC Bus Terminus, tel. 5126; and MSRTC Bus Complex, tel. 4363.

By Hired Car with Driver. Most drives from the major cities—Bangalore, Bombay, Mangalore, and Mysore—are long trips. Although the roads are good, by Indian standards, they are unlit and narrow. Rates are about Rs. 3.30 per km with a halt charge of Rs. 50–Rs. 100 per night. Make arrangements before you depart with an agency listed below under *Tour Operators.*

By Train. The train is more complicated to take than the bus and goes slower. However, long-distance trains do provide an alternative to planes, and by traveling on the ground, you see more. From Bangalore, you can take the *Vasco Mail* (a direct train), the *Kittun Express* or *Mandovi Express,* all of which involve a change of trains. From Delhi, you can take the *Jhelum Express, Sahyadra Express,* or *Mandovi Express.* From Bombay, take the *Miraj Express, Gomantak Express, Sahyadra Express,* or *Mandovi Express.*

By Boat. An overnight ferry service operates between Bombay and Panaji. The trip takes about 22 hours and runs fairly regularly except during the monsoon (mid-May–mid-September). The boat is by no means glamorous, but it can be fun. We recommend the top accommodations: owner's cabin (Rs. 300), attached toilet and bath with two berths; or first-class deluxe A (Rs. 260), attached toilet and shower with two berths. The cheapest rate is the lower deck (lower class) at Rs. 48, with many other possibilities in between. Contact the Goa Tourist Office (address below) or the Maharasthra State Tourism Development Corporation, C.D.O. Hutments, Madam Cama Road; tel. 2026713.

TOURIST INFORMATION. Goa is a well-organized state when it comes to tourism. The *Tourist Department* is efficient, courteous, and responsive. If you want a list of hotels, contact the Tourism Department. Current information is available on almost every topic of interest to the traveler. *Goa Tourist Directory,* a free brochure published by the department, is especially helpful, supplying basic information about what to do and how to do it. It also contains minimal information on "sights" to see in Goa. Here's a list of department offices:

Main office. Department of Tourism, Government of Goa, Daman, and Diu, Tourist Home, Patto, Panaji, Goa; tel. 5583. Open 9:30 A.M.–5:45 P.M., closed Saturdays and Sundays.

Dabolim Airport. Tourist Information Office; tel. 2644. Open during plane arrivals.

Interstate Bus Terminus. Tourist Information Center, No. 5; tel. 5620. Open 9:30 A.M.–5:30 P.M., closed Sundays.

Margao. Tourist Information Center, Tourist Hostel; tel. 22513. Open 10 A.M.–5:30 P.M., closed Sundays.

Vasco da Gama. Tourist Information Center, Tourist Hostel; tel. 2673. Open 9:30 A.M.–5 P.M., closed Sundays.

FOREIGN CURRENCY EXCHANGE. Most Western-style hotels have money-exchange counters. There's a *State Bank of India* opposite Hotel Mandou, Panaji, and a branch in Margao, Papusa, and Vasco-da-Gama. Hours are Monday–Friday, 10 A.M.–2 P.M., and Saturday till noon.

ACCOMMODATIONS. Goa has a great assortment of beach resorts to fit all budgets. Some of the best accommodations in terms of seclusion and ambience, are extremely low priced. Most hotels also offer discounts after the peak season (December–January). Inquire when you book. During the peak season, you must book your room months in advance. Prices are based on double occupancy and exclude taxes: *Deluxe,* over Rs. 1,450; *Expensive,* Rs. 950–Rs. 1,450; *Moderate,* Rs. 500–Rs. 950; *Inexpensive,* under Rs. 500. Some Western-style hotels take major credit cards.

Deluxe

Taj Aguada Hermitage. Sinquerim, Bardez; tel. 7501. 40 rooms with bath. This secluded resort, a cluster of Goan-style, air-conditioned villas, is set on a hill overlooking Sinquerim Beach. Each unit offers individual veranda and garden and a modernized Goan interior in the living room, adjoining dining area, and bedroom. A regular car service shuttles you to their nearby Taj Fort Aguada Beach Resort, which offers numerous amenities (see below). AE, DC, MC, V.

Expensive

Cidade de Goa. Vainguinim Beach, Dona Paula; tel. 3301. 101 rooms with bath. Built into a hillside and modeled after a Portuguese hill town, this resort offers two distinct room decors. Damao rooms have a Gujarati ambience with terra cotta, mirror-work, and a sleeping platform. Casa rooms are faintly Iberian with white walls and wicker furniture. Service can be erratic, but complaints bring results. Air-conditioning, TV, room service, multicuisine restaurants, bars, swimming pool, water sports, health club, tennis courts, travel and foreign-exchange coutner, shopping arcade, doctor, airport shuttle service. AE, DC, MC, V.

Majorda Beach Resort. Majorda, Salcette; tel. 20751. 122 rooms with bath. Facing Majorda Beach, this resort with a modern Portuguese influence offers air-conditioned rooms in its main redstone building that are spacious, with cane furnishings and seaside verandas. Best rooms are upstairs with garden and ocean views. You can also stay in a villa (up to four units per villa), which have a similar decor, plus a veranda or porch. Best rooms face a well-landscaped garden. TV, room service, multicuisine restaurants, bar, baby-sitters, two swimming pools, tennis, windsurfing, water scooter, health club, travel and foreign-exchange counter, doctor, shopping arcade, airport shuttle service. AE, DC.

Oberoi Bogmalo Beach. Bogmalo; tel. 2191. 121 rooms with bath. This high rise looks more like Miami Beach than Goa, but it does have an air of elegance. Air-conditioned rooms have rough stucco white walls, handsome furnishings, and individual sea-facing verandas with cane swings. Multicuisine restaurants, TV, room service, bar, health club, swimming pool, speedboats, water scooters, windsurfing, water-skiing, para-sailing, tennis, tour arrangements, travel and foreign-exchange counter, shopping arcade, airport shuttle service. AE, DC, MC, V.

Taj Fort Aguada Beach Resort. Sinquerim, Bardez; tel. 7501. 120 rooms with bath. You can stay in the posh main building in a contempory-style room with views of the nearby ocean, or in an intimate, tile-roofed cottage (two units per cottage), which offers more privacy. Air-conditioning, TV, room service, multicuisine restaurants, bar, foreign-exchange and travel counter, doctor, baby-sitters, shopping arcade, swimming pool, health club, tennis, sailing, water-skiing, windsurfing, boating, para-sailing, airport shuttle service. AE, DC, MC, V.

Taj Holiday Village. Sinquerim, Bardez; tel. 7514. 100 rooms with bath. Designed like a ritzy Goan village, this delightful tropical resort features tile-roofed cottages scattered around gardens and extensive lawns that face Sinquerim Beach. Air-conditioned rooms have a modern decor. Multicuisine restaurants, TV, room service, bar (with some seats right in a swimming pool), baby-sitters, travel and foreign-exchange counter, tennis, squash, volleyball, water-skiing, para-sailing, windsurfing, boating, health club, airport shuttle service. AE, DC, MC, V.

Moderate

Prainha Cottages by the Sea. Dona Paula Beach. Reservations: Palmar Beach Resorts, "Glendela," 3rd Floor, Rua de Ormuz, Box 98, Panjim, Goa; tel. 4004. 27 rooms with bath. While not secluded, this complex, set in a palm-backed harbor facing the beach, nevertheless offers a peaceful ambience. Stay in the main building or in a room in a row of attached two-story cottages. Immaculately clean, air-conditioned rooms have tiled floors, a streamlined modern decor, and a veranda. Best rooms are on the upper floors. Multicuisine restaurant, room service, bar, baby-sitters, doctor, foreign-exchange counter, tour arrangements; car, motorcycle, and bike rentals. Rupees only.

Vagator Beach Resort. Vagator, Bardez; tel. Siolim 41. 83 rooms with bath. Secluded and very moderately priced, this Goan-style complex offers two options. Nestled in a palm grove facing the beach, brick and tile-roofed cottages (two units per cottage) have a private veranda and simple, clean furnishings. Chapora Fort cottages, set on a hill and a short walk to the beach, offer similar furnishings, private porches or veranda, and sweeping views. Multicuisine restaurants, bars, room service, swimming pool at Chapora Fort, lovely gardens, foreign-exchange counter, taxi service, boutique, surfboards. Good value. Rupees only.

Inexpensive

Bambolim Beach Resort. Vodgali, Bambolim; tel. 6499. 52 rooms with bath. A narrow road through a charming Goan village leads to this new resort at Bambolim Beach. Air-conditioned rooms, set in cottages, have tiled floors and modern furnishings. Best rooms have verandas overlooking the ocean. Open-air multicuisine restaurant, bar, TV, room service, windsurfing, boating, swimming pool, foreign-exchange and travel counter. AE, DC, MC, V.

Coqueral Holiday Home. Kamotim-Waddo, Candolim Beach; tel. 2469. 16 rooms with bath. This yellow bungalow/guest house offers good service and a homey ambience. Clean, fan-cooled rooms are plainly furnished and have pleasant verandas or porches. Upstairs rooms have great ocean views. The beach is just beyond its secluded back lawn. A small porch restaurant provides Goan- or Continental-style meals with a two-hour notice. Motorbike and bike rentals, taxi arrangements. Rupees only.

Estrela Do Mar Beach Resort. Cobrawado, Calangute, Baga; tel. 14. 10 rooms with bath. If you want seclusion and beautiful gardens within walking distance of a beach, stay here. The main bungalow is especially charming, with a brick and yellow exterior. Best rooms offer ocean views. All rooms are simply decorated and have ceiling fans and private verandas. Open-air multicuisine restaurant, room service, bar. Rupees only.

Tourist Cottages. Colva, Magao; tel. 22287. 41 rooms with bath. This government-run complex on Colva Beach offers rooms in clean cottages with verandas. Hot water is provided by the bucket. Rooms in the front complex face the beach; but the best rooms for privacy and sea views are upstairs in the rear block. Fans, room service, multicuisine restaurant, bar, government-run sightseeing tour departure point. Rupees only.

Tourist Resort. Calangute; tel. 24. 76 rooms with bath. This government-run complex on a beach offers clean rooms with an institutional decor and suites that are a bargain. Upstairs rooms have good ocean views. Fans, room service, multicuisine restaurant, bar, government-run sightseeing tour departure point. Rupees only.

DINING OUT. Goan food is a taste feast. Portuguese dishes have been adapted with Indian Goan zest: a healthy pinch of red chili tempered with coconut milk. Sample Goa's excellent seafood—like pomfret *recheiado* in a red or green sauce or tiger prawns *baffad* (spicy-Goan style). Try squid, sardines, and stuffed fried oysters. The catch will be fresh if it's offered, and these dishes are not the same prepared anywhere else. Also, try *Feni,* the local brew, but watch out! It packs a punch. Prices depend on what you choose to eat. Shrimp is expensive; other fish dishes are not.

While we include only the best options, many accommodations listed above also have restaurants. Breakfast is usually 7:30–10; lunch, noon–3; dinner, 7:30–10. Payment is normally in rupees only unless the restaurant is connected to a Western-style hotel. The restaurants listed below are informal and, unless noted, are open for all three meals and don't require reservations. Prices, based on one person eating a three-course meal, excluding taxes, tip, or beverage, are *Deluxe,* over Rs. 120; *Expensive,* Rs. 80–Rs. 120; *Moderate,* Rs. 40–Rs. 80; *Inexpensive,* under Rs. 40.

Deluxe

Banyan Tree. Taj Holiday Village, Calangute Beach; tel. 7514. You walk over a small footbridge to enter this Thai-style restaurant, where you can eat on the thatch-covered veranda or inside an air-conditioned, sleek, Thai-decor central room. Subdued lighting and taped Thai music accompany the Thai and Chinese cuisines. Specialties include *gari goong* (prawns cooked in green curry) and *padd Thai* (noodles tossed with bean sprouts and garnished with peanuts). Open 12:30–2:30 P.M. and 7:30–10:30 P.M. Dinner reservations advised. AE, DC, MC, V.

Expensive

Casa Portuguesa Restaurant and Bar. Baga, Bardez; no phone. This lovely old Portuguese-Goan home with whitewashed walls, vaulted ceilings, elegant darkwood trim, and hand-carved wooden chairs serves tasty Goan and Portuguese dishes. The ambience is romantic with softly lit wall sconces and a guitarist who serenades at night. Try *peixe em alhos* (catch-of-the-day fish grilled in garlic), *postas de salmao* (fried salmon), or the daily special. You can also eat on the veranda or in the garden. Open 6:30–11:30 P.M., closed second day of each month. Rupees only.

Haystack. Arpora, Bardez; Set in a simple stucco building with a thatched roof, this restaurant serves a great Goan buffet, or you can order à la carte selections. Expect a crowd and a great ambience, with Goan dances and music. Open only Friday nights 7–midnight. Rupees only.

Moderate

Coconut Inn. Candolim, next to Shanta Durga Temple; no phone. This Goan house, now a restaurant, is nestled in palm trees and lush green gardens. Eat on a softly lit veranda surrounded by antiques or in a garden with lovely Indian statues. The chef serves Goan- and Continental-style dishes, including fresh seafood. Open 8 A.M.–12 P.M. and 6–11 P.M. Rupees only.

O Pescador Restaurant. Dona Paula; tel. 4255. Overlooking Dona Paula Bay, this restaurant serves good Polynesian food. The interior room has a simple decor, with the emphasis on the views. You can also eat outside. Try their popular creamed prawns curry or *bandu lagoon* prawns (prawns in the shell cooked in a spicy sauce). Open noon–3 P.M. and 7–11 P.M. Rupees only.

Inexpensive

Martin's Beach Corner. Caranzalem Beach; tel. 4357. Don't leave Goa without enjoying at least one meal at this place. You won't find better seafood or prices. The owner, Martin, is the chef and his restaurant is Goan simple—three thatched huts overlooking the beach. You name the dish, he'll prepare it. His fried mussels are exquisite, as are the crab chili fry and the tiger prawns. If your hotel tells you that Martin's is closed, don't believe it. Hotels are jealous of his popularity and prices. Dinner reservations advised. Open 11 A.M.–3 P.M. and 7–11 P.M. Rupees only.

Silver Star Deluxe Bar N Restaurant. Tourist Complex, Colva Beach; no phone. This plain restaurant, with tables set outside at night, serves remarkably good food—Indian, Goan, Continental, and Chinese. Try the excellent fried fish, prawns masala (prawns cooked in spicy curry), or fish curry and rice. Open 8 A.M.–4 P.M. and 5–11 P.M. Rupees only.

SWEETS AND TREATS. For delicious sweets, go to *A Pastelaria*, Mandovi Apartments, Dr. Dada Vaidya Rd., Panaji. Sample the cashew nut slices, chocolate walnut roll, or Goan *bebinca* (cake made with coconut juice and eggs). Open 9–9. At *Chit Chat*, in the Tourist Hotel, Panjim, you can relax on the second-floor terrace restaurant and enjoy good snacks with soda or beer. Open 7 A.M.–10:30 P.M.

HOW TO GET AROUND. From the Airport. Many hotels offer free-shuttle service. The airport coach to Panjim costs Rs. 15 and runs frequently. Taxis cost Rs. 150 to Panjim. Once you're in Goa, take advantage of the state's greatest natural resource: water.

By Ferry. Free ferries cross the Zuari River and the Mandovi River between Panaji and Betim while the new bridge is under repair. They're usually crowded and slow paced, but picturesque and relaxing. Most of these ferries also carry cars for a nominal charge.

By Bus. KTC buses run between the main towns. In Panjim, call tel. 3334.

By Taxi. Yellow-topped, metered taxis are available in most central areas and from most hotels. Fare: Rs. 3.85 for the first km; Rs. 3.30 per additional km.

By Tourist Taxi. Luxury cars can be hired from most hotels or from tour operators listed below.

By Auto Rickshaw. Goa also has the standard auto rickshaw. Fare: about Rs. 2.20 for the first km; Rs. 2 per additional km.

By Motorcycle Taxi. Unique to Goa, this transportation is perfect for the solo traveler. Rate: Rs. 5 for 3 km in the cities. To go to distant villages, you must negotiate, especially if the driver has to return without a fare.

TOURS. The *Goa Tourism Development Corporation* (GTDC) conducts inexpensive deluxe bus sightseeing tours. For reservations, contact the head office, Trionara Apartments, Panaji, tel. 6515, or its counters at the tourist hostels in Panaji, Margao, Vasco, Mapusa, Calangute, Colva, and Farmagudi.

North Goa Tour. Daily 9 A.M.–6 P.M. from Panaji.

South Goa Tour. Daily 9:30 A.M.–6 P.M. from Panaji. Also departs daily from Tourist Hostels in Mapusa and Calangute at 8:30 A.M.

Pilgrim Special. Old churches and important temples. Daily 9:30 A.M.–12:30 P.M. from Panaji.

Beach Special. Calangute, Anjuna, and Vagator beaches. Daily 3 P.M.–7 P.M. from Panaji.

Goa Darshan Tour. Religious sites. Daily 9:30 A.M.–6 P.M. from Panaji.

GTDC also conducts wonderful hour-long **boat cruises** with cultural programs on Mandovi River. All cruises start from the Steamer Jetty: *Sunset Cruise* at 6; *Sundown Cruise* at 7:15; *Full Moon Cruise* at 8:30–10:30. Dinner is optional.

Private Guides. GTDC also has guides for hire. For one–four people, Rs. 50 half-day; full-day, Rs. 80.

TOUR OPERATORS. The following agencies can take care of all travel needs, including hired car with driver:

Manish Tours and Travels, opposite Mascarenhas Building, Panaji; tel. 4138.

West Coast Tours and Travels, Panaji; tel. 5723.

You can also hire a car and driver from these additional companies:

Goa Tourism Development Corporation (address above under *Tours*).

Goa Tours, 2 May Fair Apartments, Dr. Dada Vaidya Rd., Panaji; tel. 3277.

Alcon International, Hotel Delmon, Caetano Albuquerque Rd., Panaji; tel. 5197.

SEASONAL EVENTS. A religious feast is usually a great excuse to sing, dance, and hold a village fair. Goans love music; you ought to hear a *mando*—not quite a waltz and not quite a Portuguese *fado,* but with strains of both. Since the lunar calendar determines many events, contact the Government of India Tourist Office for details. What follows is a list of Goa's unusual festivals:

January—*Feast of the Three Kings* at Reis Magos, Cuelim and Chandor.

February/March—*Carnival,* held three days before Lent, is Goa's best party, with costumes, floats, music, and dancing.

March—*Shigmotsav.* Goa celebrates its annual spring festival.

March/April—*Procession of All Saints of the Franciscan Third Order,* held the fifth Monday in Lent, is another colorful procession of 40 statues of saints paraded through Goa Velha, on the way to the airport—the only such procession held outside Rome.

August—*Festival of Novidades,* an offering of the first sheaves of the rice crop to the head of state.

August/September—Ganesh Chaturthi, a festive celebration of the birthday of Ganesh, the elephant-headed god.

October/November—*Deepavali,* the fireworks-and-all start of the Hindu New Year.

December—*Feast of St. Francis Xavier,* Patron saint of Goa at Old Goa.

December—*Feast of Our Lady of Immaculate Conception* at Panaji and Margao. December 25—Christmas all over Goa.

HISTORIC SITES. The Director of Tourism has a list of old Goan houses with antique furniture and *objets d'art* that are privately owned but available for viewing on request. Contact the main office when you arrive (see address under *Tourist Information*). If the cultural mood takes over suddenly, you can see the following churches and temples, at almost any time, sunrise to sunset.

Old Goan Churches. *Basilica of Bom Jesus* (sixteenth century), with the remains of St. Francis Xavier. *Se Cathedral* (1562–1652), dedicated to St. Catherine and the largest of the old churches. Richly embellished interior. *Church of St. Francis of Assisi* (1661), simple harmonious structure. Exquisite carvings and paintings. *Chapel of St. Catherine* (1510), constructed by Albuquerque to commemorate his arrival in Old Goa. *St. Cajetan Church* (seventeenth century), modeled on the design of St. Peter's Basilica in Rome.

Temples. *Shri Manguesh* (22 km from Panaji) in Ponda. Dedicated to Shiva; colorful interior. *Shri Mahalsa* (one km from Manguesh) The deity worshiped is Mohini, a reincarnation of Vishnu. *Shri Mahadeva* at Tambdi Surla (66 km from Panaji) in the foot of the Ghats. Only thirteenth-century temple remaining in Goa.

Mosque. *Safa Shahouri Masjid,* at Ponda, built in 1560.

MUSEUMS. Goa is not a museum-rich state, unless you define the term loosely and include the old churches and temples. But while seeing the churches, visit the *Archaeological Museum and Portrait Gallery* in Old Goa. The museum contains numerous sculptures of the early and late medieval periods collected around Goa, including friezes depicting self-immolation. The Portrait Gallery displays the portraits of the Portuguese rulers. There are also religious paintings on canvas and wood. Open 10 A.M.–noon; 1–5 P.M.; closed Fridays. Free.

SPORTS AND OUTDOOR ADVENTURES. Beaches. At *Miramar* (Gaspar Dias), close to Panaji, watch the stiff undertow and avoid looking at the "modern" backdrop of concrete high rises. *Dona Paula,* also near Panaji, is palm-fringed with fine views of Mormugao Harbor. *Calangute Beach,* across the Mandovi River in the Bardez district, is the "Queen of Goa (public) Beaches," with 16 km of sand. It includes the Baga, Anjuna, and Vagator beaches (each progressively farther north). The northern end of Goa is backed by dramatic cliffs for great sunset viewing. *Colva Beach,* south of Panaji and directly west of Margao, has long stretches of beautiful sand.

Watersports. *Trochus* (The Beach Club, Bogmalo Beach, Goa; tel. 2489) offers a full range of water activities: surfing, waterskiing, snorkeling, para-sailing, dingy sailing. You can rent equipment and take lessons. They also arrange for fishing trips (equipment provided). Office is open daily 8:30 A.M.–7 P.M.

WILDLIFE SANCTUARIES. There are three sanctuaries in Goa, all providing a day away from too much sand and surf. The *Bhagwan Mahavir Sanctuary* is the biggest (240 sq. km or 149 sq. mi.) in Molem about 35 km (22 mi.) due east of Margao. Thick forests with bison, cobra, python, deer, langurs (monkeys), and the elusive panther (don't expect to see one). It's also well populated by a rich variety of birds (crested serpent eagle, brown fish owl, green pigeon, shrike).

The Bondla Sanctuary is also a jungle resort (20 km northeast of Molem). A great sanctuary for kids or the "kid" in all of us, with minizoos, a deer park, wilderness trail, and elephant ride. Closed Thursday.

The Cotigao Wildlife Sanctuary is on the southeastern edge of Goa. Set in a hilly, forested terrain, it protects the same animals as does the Bhagwan Mahaver Sanctuary.

Yoga. *Kalpana* (Hotel Silver Sands, Colva Beach) offers good yoga classes and great massages. Make an appointment through the hotel, tel. 21645.

SHOPPING. While Goa isn't a great state for shopping, some stores do offer a good selection of handicrafts.

Enrico's and *Khazana* (opposite Taj Holiday Village, Sinquerim, Bardez) have good selections of Rajasthani, South Indian, and Goan handicrafts and jewelry. Open 9 A.M.–9 P.M. AE, DC, MC, V.

Also visit *Goa Handicrafts* (Tourist Hotel, Panjim), a government-run shop that sells Goan products: wooden curios, crochet lacework, terra-cotta. Open 10 A.M.– 1 P.M. and 2–7 P.M., closed Sundays. Rupees only. *Terra-cotta Pottery Center* (Bicholim, Shed No. D-7, Industrial Estate) is another state-run company that sells excellent wares. Open 9 A.M.–6 P.M., closed Sundays. Rupees only.

Near Colva Beach and next to the Colva Beach Resort, wander through the *Lamani Bazaar,* operated by Karnataka tribals from September to May. They sell lovely mirror-work and cowrie shell-covered hats, belts, bags of all sizes, wallhangings, bedspreads—created from their traditional fabrics, plus tribal jewelry. Bargain. Rupees only.

NIGHTLIFE AND BARS. The bar at *Casa Portuguesa Restaurant* (Baga, Bardez, no phone) is cozy—one table and five chairs at the bar. The house is charming. Open 6 P.M.–midnight, closed second day of each month. Any other good bar is at *Martin's Beach Corner* (Caranzalem Beach, tel. 4357). There is no music, just the sound of pounding surf. Open 11 A.M.–3 P.M. and 7–11 P.M.

BANGALORE AND KARNATAKA

Oriental Splendor and Hindu Rococo

by
KATHLEEN COX

Within the borders of Karnataka (formerly Mysore), you can find the most colorful and most fascinating aspects of India, plus an occasional high level of comfort that can be Orientally sumptuous and Occidentally efficient. Although the lowlands can be hot in the summer, the plateau of Karnataka is situated at an angle where two mountain ranges converge into the beautiful Nilgiri Hills. One visit to this part of the state explains why Karnataka is called "the emerald land." It's green and gorgeous, with lush rice paddies and gentle sloping hills. The hill climate is pleasant and warm—in some places bracing—and even the rains that start in May are not the nonstop torrents experienced elsewhere, but quick showers are immediately followed by blue skies. There are rivers and waterfalls; forests filled with wild game and precious woods like teak, ebony, and sandalwood; and flowers everywhere. Much of the northern areas of Karnataka, at a superficial glance, seem right out of the American West—scrubby, near-barren land, studded with enormous boulders and dramatic craggy hills. However, your first sighting of a historic temple, tomb, or ancient fort reminds you that this is the exotic Indian subcontinent.

Karnataka, the size of New England, probably has been inhabited as long as anywhere else on earth. Thousand-year-old Hindu temples, decorated with carvings of amazing virtuosity; grandiose Moslem monuments; remains of lost civilizations; and some excellent modern city planning are just a few of the reasons to visit.

The scenes of village life are bound to linger. The 40 million people of Karnataka, called Kannadigas after their language known as Kannada, are sinewy and robust. Colorfully dressed women wait patiently to fill their jugs with water at the village well, which is also the social center.

The men, often scantily dressed in *lungi* (colorful wraps) and *dhotis* (white wraps), work in the fields walking slowly behind buffalo dragging plows that have not changed much in 3,000 years. In Karnataka, the climate makes it possible to live perpetually outdoors—the huts in the villages are often of rudimentary construction, and people think nothing of setting up their beds outside. Throughout much of the central and northern part of this exotic state, you encounter the delightful tribal nomads, the Lambanis—the women strutting their hips and wearing gay layered, mirror-covered, bejewelled skirts and blouses, and heavy silver jewelry on their ears, necks, fingers, arms, feet, and ankles.

The simplicity of the country is one extreme balanced by another: the grand palaces and formal gardens; the splendor of such festivals like Dussehra; and the relics of centuries of royal living—Hindu and Moslem. Scattered throughout the state in places like Belur, Halebid, Hampi, Aihole, Pattadakal, and Badami, you find some of the best religious monuments in India.

Parts of Karnataka are geologically among the oldest formations in the world. People have lived here at least 10,000 years, probably longer. And, because they have had little geographic possibility or incentive to move beyond their frontiers, they've remained faithful to the traditions of their forefathers. The state's history is intimately entwined in the great epic, the *Ramayana*. After India's first great emperor, Chandragupta Maurya, embraced Jainism, he retired to Shravarabelacola, renouncing all worldly possessions, including his empire. Many of the great names of India's early history, like the Cholas and the Gangas, ruled parts of Karnataka. Saints and philosophers followed each other on this auspicious soil. The Hoysala Dynasty (A.D. 1000–1300) was the first to control all of what is now modern Karnataka. They were great builders, creating the magnificent temples at Somnathpur, Belur, and Halebid. The Moslem hordes swept in here, too, with the Hoysala capital at Dwarasumudra (the modern Halebid) sacked by Malik Kapul in 1310 and again by Mohammed-bin-Tughlaq in 1327.

Power continued to swing back and forth between the Hindus and the Moslems. Vijayanagar, whose ruins are at Hampi, was Hindu; other places like Bijapur remained resolutely Moslem. Taking advantage of the general chaos, Hyder Ali, an adventurous commander-in-chief of the army, engineered a successful *coup d'etat* in 1761 and grabbed control. Then he and his son, Tipu Sultan, humbled the British who had their own expansionary plans. The two men added to the province (with the help of the French) and ruled it from Sriangapatna. In 1799, the British bounced back with a vengeance. Taking control, they eventually returned sovereignty to the old Hindu Dynasty in the person of Sri Krishnaraja Wadiyar III, ancestor of the last maharajah, who set up his capital in Mysore City. This family provided an unbroken line of enlightened rulers who made modern Karnataka a model state. The last maharajah was so popular that the new Republic of India retained him as the state's governor.

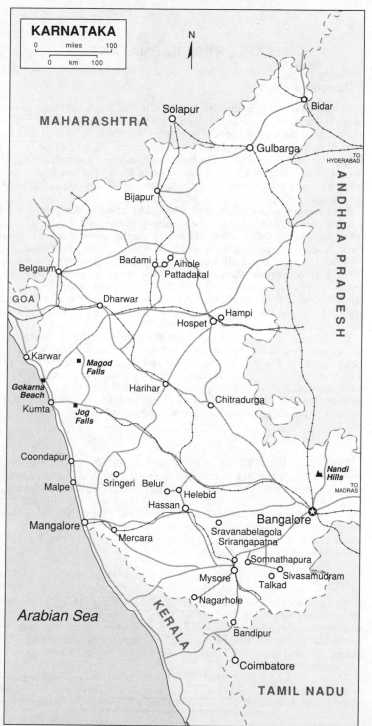

EXPLORING KARNATAKA

Bangalore

Bangalore is a flourishing city of over three million inhabitants, capital of the state, an industrial center, and a garden spot. So little of Bangalore is old that at the end of the 1500s, nothing was there but a mud fort and a small bull temple, both built by a chieftain and founder of Bangalore, Kempe Gowda, in the 1500s. The bull temple is reminiscent of the Dravidian style and contains a gigantic monolith of Nandi (15 feet high and 20 feet long). The mud fort was rebuilt in stone by Hyder Ali in the 1700s. It's in ruins today.

With the city and suburbs well planned in advance, Bangalore is not a sprawling, confused place. It feels orderly, serene, and regal, especially when you see the Vidhana Soudha, on the northern boundary of Cubbon Park. A sprawling white granite structure built in the neo-Dravidian style in 1956, it houses the State Legislature and the Secretariat. Permission is required to go inside. Bangalore is also the site of the prestigious Indian Institute of Science, established with the philanthropy of the Tata family (India's Rockefellers). In short, Bangalore is a snazzy city where Western-style luxuries such as a drive-in movie, 15 flavors of ice cream, and video game arcades exist, but with an Eastern flair.

Bangalore's charm peeks through tree-shaded gardens, manicured lawns, and ever-blooming fragrant flowers. The beautiful botanical Lal Bagh Gardens, designed by Hyder Ali and Tipu Sultan, are landscaped with a variety of centuries-old trees, fountains, lotus pools, terraces, a Japanese garden, and an assortment of tropical and subtropical herbs and plants spread out over several acres. The huge Glass House at Lal Bagh is also the delightful arena for special exhibits.

Nandi Hills

The Nandi Hills, 59 kilometers (37 miles) from Bangalore, witnessed numerous savage battles for centuries. Now it's a much-appreciated health and pleasure resort. Two 1,000-year-old Shiva temples grace the charming landscape: one at the foot and the other at the top of the hill, and four rivers have their source here. Back in the 1700s, Tipu Sultan made these hills the site of his summer palace. Take a walk to Tipu's Drop, a 609-meter (2,000-foot) sheer cliff. Here, condemned criminals met a grisly fate—they were pushed over the edge.

Mysore

An excellent 137-kilometer (85-mile) road leads from Bangalore to Mysore, the city of palaces. On the way, you pass through country strewn with strange-shaped boulders and pass near Ramnagar, the site of an experimental center for rural health, and Channapatna, which produces lacquered toys and spun silk. Finally, you reach the city of palaces, gardens, and Oriental splendor.

Mysore, no longer the official capital, still survives as the principal residence of the former royal family, which makes it every inch a princely city. Mysore, beautifully planned and executed, gives little evidence of the crushing poverty so often associated with India. When you see what the maharajas accomplished in the way of public service, you will understand why his highness was appointed the first governor of Karnataka.

Maharajah's Palace

By far the most impressive Mysore building is the Maharajah's Palace, a massive edifice that took 15 years to build (started in 1857 on the site of the former wooden palace destroyed by fire). Here the Oriental decorative imagination runs wild. The palace, one of the biggest of its kind in India, is in the Indo-Saracenic style—a gigantic synthesis of Hindu and Islamic architecture. Entrance gateways, domes, arches, turrets, colonnades, lovely Hoysola-like carvings, glittering chandeliers, and etched window panes—are all in magnificent profusion. On Sundays and holidays, the palace is illuminated with thousands of tiny lights that turn the palace into a glittering statement of wealth.

Inside the palace, you can see a few of the royal family's private rooms, plus the impressive Durbar Hall (*Durbar* is a feudal term for receiving the nobility). This hall is an elegant preservation of history, with its ornate ceilings and huge "grandstand" awning that overlooks the great court. The Kalyana Mandap (Marriage Hall), where the women sat behind screened balconies, has lifelike paintings of the Dussehra procession, and in the museum is the solid gold *howdah* (elephant throne) that the maharajah used during the festivals and other ceremonial occasions.

Public Buildings

Everything seems palatial in Mysore, even if the building in question turns out to be the Maternity Hospital, the Technical Institute, or even the Railway Office. The city's central square—Statue Square—just across from the palace, houses the marble effigy of the last maharajah's grandfather and predecessor, standing beneath a golden domed canopy.

Mysore also has an enjoyable wholesale bazaar (Devraja Market) near Krishnaraja Circle—a covered market of manageable size, with rows of hanging bananas, displays of other fruit, vegetables, and flowers galore, plus all the other foodstuffs India offers. It's bustling, noisy, and lots of fun.

Lalitha Mahal

As you head out of the center of Mysore toward Chamundi Hill, you see a dignified white edifice called the Lalitha Mahal, built in 1921 by the Wadiyars to house distinguished foreign guests. The palace has now joined the legion of those royal residences that have been converted into hotels, a second life that allows the mere ordinary, Indian, and foreign to taste some of that grandeur earlier reserved for royalty. These palaces are usually in superb locations, and the Lalitha Mahal is no exception. The interior is equally becoming a magnificent lofty dining hall with stained-glass dome, and an Italian marble staircase that is sublime.

Chamundi Hill

Continue to Chamundi Hill, named after the royal family's patron goddess, Chamundi. A good road leads to the top, but if you're spry and eager for exercise, climb the thousand steps (three centuries old). About two-thirds of the way up is a 16-foot Nandi (Shiva's holy bull), constructed in the 1600s from a single piece of granite, including the garlands and bell around his neck.

The view from the top of the hill is superb: a beautiful panorama of all Mysore and the surrounding hills, lakes, and turrets of temples and churches. The Sri Chamundeswari Temple is dedicated to the royal Wadiyar family's titular deity. The base of the temple, dating back to the twelfth century, was supposedly built by the founders of Mysore; the ornately sculptured pyramidal tower was constructed in the 1800s. Next to the temple is the giant statue of Monster Mahishasura (Mysore is named after him), who was killed by goddess Chamundi, bringing peace to the country. Here he stands, built in mortar about 35 years ago, with sword and snake held aloft in each hand.

If possible, time your visit to Mysore to coincide with the 10-day Dussehra festival (September/October). The city is at its best, clothed in color, light, and joy. This is the same major Hindu celebration feted under different names all over India, but here it is a royal as well as a popular festival. The pomp, grandeur, and ceremony are not to be missed. Until a few years ago, the late maharajah sat on his jeweled throne every night of Duesehra; on the tenth day, he left the palace in a royal procession seated in his golden howdah atop a magnificently caparisoned elephant. The maharajah's son does not take part in the parade, but the infantry, cavalry, and camel corps still do. The torchlight and daylight parades are unique. *Theppotsava,* the worship of deities on decorated barges afloat in a flood-lit lake, is magical.

Brindavan Gardens

Only 19 kilometers (12 miles) northwest of Mysore are the Brindavan Gardens that extend in terraces beneath the Krishnarajasagar Dam, which anyone except possibly Louis XIV would compare favorably with Versailles. The place started life functionally—as an irrigation dam at the confluence of three rivers. The dam is two kilometers (1¼ miles) long and forms an enormous lake. It is constructed entirely in stone and crushed bricks and is ornamented with parapets and a niche for the river goddess. Even though the dam is one of the biggest in India, it commands only slight attention next to the gardens, exquisitely designed and alive with bright flowers and silvery fountains. An excellent time to go is at night, when the gardens are illuminated and hundreds of fountains and pools of all colors, sizes, and shapes bring out the best. (But beware of traffic jams.)

Srirangapatna

Srirangapatna is an island fortress between two branches of the Cauvery River and the former capital of the Mysore rajahs from 1610 to 1799. Hyder Ali and Tipu Sultan were its most famous residents. For 180 years, all this area of India was in a constant battle for control. The first to succeed were the British, on the fourth try in 1799, when Tipu Sultan lost his life in the skirmish.

Visit the fort and its imposing surroundings. The Moslems lived cheek to jowl with two Hindu temples, one of which, the Sri Ranganatha, is about 1,000 years old. Here, you can see the dungeons where captured British officers were imprisoned. The "Breach" marks the place where the British finally smashed through the fortifications and entered the town; the Water Gate was Tipu's last stand. See the ruins of Tipu's fortified palaces near the old parade grounds and the sultan's favorite mosque, the

Juma Masjid, with its twin minarets. The top of the minarets offer a good view of the fort and another glimpse of Mysore.

Without doubt, the best monuments are outside the fort: Tipu's summer pleasure palaces (he indulged himself) and his mausoleum, the Gumbaz.

Daria Daulat Bagh

The Daria Daulat Bagh Palace, set in a charming garden, doesn't look so impressive from the outside. Once inside, you'll think otherwise; there are carved ornate arches, liberally gilded wall panels, eighteenth-century colored frescoes. On the right of the entrance, you see Hyder Ali and Tipu riding at the head of their troops. On the left, there's a vain reminder of the victorious first battle against the British. All along the walls, in tiered bands, are scenes from the happy lives of the ruling Moslem nabobs obviously enjoying the comfort of their palaces, holding court, or simply looking important. These warmly colored frescoes are good sized, easier to admire than the Persian miniatures they closely resemble.

Gumbaz

Two kilometers (one mile) from the palace is the Gumbaz, a beautiful monument to the preference of the Moslem rulers for taking their eternal rest in lavish style, too. In the center of a garden stands the cream-colored Gumbaz on its black marble pillars. The pillars support the lowest tier of the monument: a balconylike wall, delicately and minutely carved, surmounted at the four corners by miniature minerals. Above the veranda formed by the columns and this balcony is another tier, ornamented with arches and a carved plinth that, in turn, supports a third tier repeating the theme of the first on a larger scale—the whole crowned by a bulbous dome.

The interior of the mausoleum is lacquered with Tipu Sultan's tiger-stripe emblem, and the doors are of ebony inlaid with ivory. Next to the elegant Gumbaz is a prayer hall in the same style.

Karapur Forest and Nagarhole National Park

An infamous event occurred in Karnataka in years past called *Khedda,* or "Operation Wild Elephant." The big pachyderms of Karnataka, considered the handsomest and strongest of the breed, were in great demand by maharajahs and princes who could afford them, circuses, zoos, and people wanting efficient working animals for construction projects. The arena for these roundups was in the Karapur forest, 79 kilometers (49 miles) south of Mysore, with the opponents—swarms of skilled tribesmen—against a herd of trumpeting mammoths.

Much of this area has now been flooded by a new dam, and kheddas are in decline. But in their time, they provided one of the most overwhelming spectacles of India. Hundreds of forest tribesmen would stalk the elephants. To the frenzied commotion of villagers beating bamboo poles against empty tins, drums, or gongs and with clouds of thick smoke billowing around them, the elephants would become dazed and frightened, moving unknowingly toward the trap set for them in the Kabini River. Once captured, they were trained.

Today, instead of the sight of animals in terror, you can watch wild elephants—untrapped and untamed—moving in peaceful security around the same forests. Kabini River Lodge, operated by Jungle Lodges and Resorts of India and the government of Karnataka, is a terrific resort at

Karapur. Visitors stay in the renovated Victorian hunting bungalows of the maharajah of Mysore and the British viceroy. Excellent game-viewing tours by jeep take you through the Nagarhole National Park, with Colonel Wakefield and his staff skillful at stalking the wild beasts. Here, you're likely to spot the rare Indian gaur (bison), wild boar, sambar, barking deer, families of elephants (mothers, calves, "aunt" elephants, and tuskers), and maybe a leopard or tiger. You also have the unusual chance to paddle along the waterways in a *coracle,* a round, basket-shaped boat lined with buffalo hide. Coracles are so slow and quiet that you can approach very close to the families of wild animals and the abundance of birdlife (over 225 different species).

Sravanabelgola

About 84 kilometers (52 miles) north of Mysore is Sravanabelgola, presided over and dominated by the colossal statue of the Jain saint Gomateshwara. His monolithic image, 57 feet tall, watched over pilgrims for 1,000 years, ever since the time of the Ganga kings under whose patronage Jainism flourished. The religion has declined now in numeric importance, but the statue reminds us of its principles: Gomateshwara's nakedness suggests renunciation of all worldly things, and the still posture indicates perfect self-control. The gigantic image rises atop one of Sravanabelgola's two hills, Indragiri, where many smaller statues and a beautiful temple also stand. A rock-hewn stairway of 614 steps leads to the summit and the monolith, which is 26 feet across the shoulders and sports a 10-foot waistline, and 9-foot-long feet. As one critic said: "There is nothing grander or more imposing anywhere out of Egypt, and even there, no known statue surpasses it in height." Every 12 years, Jains from all over India gather here for the spectacular bathing festival where priests clamber up specially built scaffolding to pour hundreds of pots of 16 substances over Gomateshwara's head, including milk curds, honey, rice, fruit, and even gold and silver coins and precious jewels. The last festival was celebrated in February 1981.

Belur

Between Sravanabelgola and Hassan, 56 kilometers (35 miles), there is grassland and woodland that will make any New Englander or Englander feel right at home. From Hassan, it is only 35 kilometers (22 miles) through lush tropical landscapes to Belur, a flourishing city under the Hoysala kings during the twelfth century. The frontier-style town boasts only one reminder of that splendid time—but what a reminder! The Belur Temple of Lord Channakeshava, still a functioning temple dedicated to this Vishnu incarnate, stands almost as perfectly preserved as the day it was completed. (Started in 1116 by the Hoysala King Vishnuvardhana, it was completed 103 years later.) Legend claims that when Moslem conquerers came to Belur to destroy the temple, they left it alone, overawed by its magnificence.

Carved of soapstone, the Belur temple is like Somnathpur in design: star shaped, with the squat temple set on a platform. It is also flat on top, without Somnathpur's suggestion of a spire. Superbaroque Belur is a contemporary of Chartres, with more in common than meets the eye. In both cases, the patience of the anonymous medieval artisans seems infinite. Although each monument serves a different religion, they both share the desire to instruct the faithful through the only means open to them at the time: the image. At Belur we find gods and goddesses in all their varied aspects and incarnations and scenes from the great Indian religion epics. But, perhaps because the Indian's natural state is more religious, without the Westerner's tendency to separate religion from the realities of life, we also find hunters, dancers, musicians, and beautiful women dressing and adorning themselves.

Except at the bottom of the temple, the friezes are not as long and continuous as those of Somnathpur, and a series of semi-detached pillars and ornamented porches lend greater variety to the facade. The plan of the temple is the traditional porch-vestibule-shrine. The shrine has three doorways on the east, south, and north, with the eastern the loveliest of all. A railed parapet sculpted with eight exquisite friezes runs along the side of this doorway. On the rail to the right of the door are epic scenes and tiny musicians seated here and there. Above these ornamental rails are about 20 pierced stone windows showing a variety of scenes or geometric designs. The jambs of the northern doorways are carved with female bearers, and to the northeast is a chain of destruction: a double-headed eagle attacking a mythical beast that is going for a lion that is clawing an elephant that is seizing a snake that is swallowing a rat—followed by a sage pondering the entire spectacle. The southern doorway is crowded with gods, demons, and animals. Beyond the railed parapet are about 80 fine-chiseled separate images of goddesses. Each entrance is flanked by two pavilions with carved figures and at the sides, the crest of the Hoysalas: Sala, their ancestor, stabbing a stylized tiger.

Back in the center of the temple, notice the domed ceiling supported by four pillars—a majestic lotus bud with depictions of scenes from the *Ramayana*. Notice, too, the sculptures of the women at the top of the four pillars. Some of the jewelry they wear can be moved: the bracelets on an arm and a head ornament. The women are beautiful, voluptuous, full breasted, and full hipped, taking any number of graceful poses beneath the intricately pierced, scrolled, and scalloped stone canopies.

The nineteenth-century architect and critic, James Fergusson, summed up Belur this way: "These friezes . . . carved with a minute elaboration of detail . . . are one of the most marvelous exhibitions of human labor to be found even in the patient East. Here the artistic combination of horizontal with vertical and the play of outline and of light and shade far surpass anything in Gothic art." South of the main temple, a smaller shrine built over a period of 250 years, the Channigaraya Temple, is worth a good look. The other remaining Hoysala temple (Viranarayana) has rows of very fine images on its outer walls.

Halebid

Near Belur is its sister temple at Halebid. The Hoysaleswara Temple was constructed a decade after Belur by the same king but left uncompleted after 180 years of labor. It, too, is a star-shaped plan but a double-shrine temple. At Halebid the sculptor's virtuosity reaches its peak—one can't "explain" this carving, but it is possible to say that these artists were able to treat stone like wood or ivory. One reason, apart from patience and talent, was that they worked in soft soapstone, which hardens with time. The friezes are breathtaking; first comes a row of elephants for stability, then one of lordly lions, then convoluting scrolls of swift horses. Above more scroll work are scenes from the religious epics that not only present philosophical ideas but mirror the living conditions of the time. Mythical beasts and swans follow. The largest frieze is also the most exuberant; based on a heavenly theme, it gives heavenly results. Here are the *apsarasis* or celestial maidens, clothed in jewels, with bracelets on each arm—

sometimes they have as many as six arms. Sitting or standing in graceful postures under pierced canopies, the maidens are eight centuries old, yet eternally young. The walls are also graced by small turrets, beadwork cornices, columns and by what many consider Halebid's *pièce de résistance:* the entire Hindu pantheon brought to life in stone. Many of these carvings are on the west facade and include not only the gods and goddesses but many of their incarnations and such curious deities as Ganesh, the elephant god, with his papal-like tiara. There are 280 figures, mostly feminine, that rival the best in Gothic art.

Also take a look at the smaller Kedareswara Temple whose friezes are similar to the other's and executed with equal finesse. There is, in addition, a relatively unadorned early Jain temple, dedicated to Parsvanatha, whose finally polished pillars serve as fancy mirrors.

Sringeri

From Halebid, either head straight for the ancient temple city of Hampi, or, if time permits and your soul wants a break for reflection, meander there via Sringeri, Jog Falls (if they're running), and the district of Coorg. The road passes through majestic forest scenery. Then you arrive at Sringeri, situated on the bank of the Tunga River and scenically beautiful. Sringeri is also an important center of pilgrimage. Here St. Sankaracharya established a monastery to protect Hinduism (from the advance of Islam) and to help establish the Vijayanagar empire. In the lovely fourteenth-century Vidya Shankara Temple, 12 zodiac pillars are so arranged that the sun's rays fall on the pillar that corresponds to that month. And the statuesque stone lions have stone balls inside their mouths. You can rotate them but cannot pull them out.

After passing through Sringeri, continue toward Jog Falls. You cross the river Sharavati, which leaps over a 274-meter (900-foot) precipice in four separate waterfalls—the "four R's." The "Rajah" is the grandest; halfway down, the violent "Roarer" meets it; close to them are the "Rocket," which is a multistaged one, and the "Rani," or Queen, which glides gracefully over the cliff. The columns of foam and spray created by all four of them make Jog Falls a myriad of prisms by day and hauntingly beautiful by moonlight.

One point: the falls are part of a hydroelectric scheme, so check that they will be "switched on" at the time of your visit.

Mangalore and Karnataka's Beaches

Mangalore, on Karnataka's coast, is the world's principal cashew nut port and a thriving city. Near Mangalore, you find important Hindu pilgrimage centers, such as Dharmasthala, Udipi, and Kollur. Mudbidri and Karkala, an hour's drive northeast of Mangalore, are important Jain destinations, with remarkable Jain carvings and giant stone images.

Swimming enthusiasts should also visit the beaches around Mangalore. Nearby Ullal Beach, which has a strong undertow, is to the south. Panambur and Surathkal beaches are to the north of Mangalore. Karnataka's best beach is at Malpe, 62 kilometers (38 miles) north of Mangalore. Here you can hire a small fishing craft from local villagers, who will take you five kilometers (three miles) to St. Mary's Island, a beautiful hideaway with great rock foundations.

Vijayanagar—Hampi

Across the center of Karnataka, northeast toward Hampi, is a different kind of tranquility—the tranquility of departed spirits. If you like ruins—not the battered fort or the tottering temple or even the Pompeii-like state of suspended animation—but real desolation that brings to mind Shelley:

> My name is Ozymandias, King of Kings
> Look on my works, ye Mighty, and despair!
> Nothing beside remains, round the decay
> Of that colossal wreck, boundless and bare
> The lone and level sands stretch far away. . . .

Then see Hampi (Vijayanagar).

In this once-proud city of Vijayanagar, the vista is extensive plains interrupted by red hills with craggy boulders, precariously balanced. But in all other respects the story is the same: Hampi is the shell of a colossal empire. The brilliance of Vijayanagar from the fourteenth to the midsixteenth century accentuates the debacle. Travelers then found it "as large as Rome" and "the best provided city in the world." And so well protected—surrounded by the turbulent Tungabhadra River and rocky ridges. Most notable of its rulers was Krishnadeva Raya (1509–29) whose military prowess, lavish hospitality, and love for the arts made him known beyond the confines of India.

Unfortunately, the reigning rajahs were continually at war with the Moslem sultanates of the Deccan, who eventually combined against the Hindu kingdom. Enormous armies clashed in 1565 north of the capital. A few hours of fighting was enough to destroy the place. Ramaraja, the last of a great dynasty, was decapitated. The city lost its life, too.

Plan at least a day to wander through Hampi. The vast ruins include temples, palaces, baths, and pavilions. All of Hampi's architecture is in perfect harmony with its natural surroundings, blending into the hills, rocks, caves, and rivers. The most sacred buildings are on either side of the Tungabhadra River or on the peaks of the surrounding hills.

The Virupaksha Temple

The Virupaksha Temple, dedicated to Shiva and now considered the most sacred structure in Hampi, is still active—active with monkeys, too. When the bells are rung early morning and evening, the critters race into the interior courtyard for food. The temple, completed in the sixteenth century, has a nine-story goporum at one end of the formerly world-famous Hampi Bazaar that once sold heaps of precious jewels and diamonds. At the opposite end of the bazaar is a pavilion containing a destroyed Nandi.

On the surrounding hills are more temple complexes, including the Matanga Hill Temple, dedicated to a ferocious aspect of Shiva. This hill gives a good view of the original Hampi layout. Just below the hill and on the river bank is the Kodandarama Temple, which contains an image of Rama and is considered to be the most sacred bathing ghat on the Tungabhadra.

Vitthala Temple Complex

The most famous and imposing single complex, to be saved for a lingering visit at sunset, is the Vitthala Temple complex, the highest glory of

Vijayanagar architecture. Constructed in the sixteenth century and dedicated to Vishnu, the walled rectangular courtyard contains the renowned chariot with lotus-shaped wheels: the entire vehicle intricately carved from a single granite stone.

Notice, too, the Vitthala Temple, with the elephant balustrades, and horses on the entrance columns, and its exquisite hall of imaginatively carved musical pillars, each hewn from a single stone. With the tap of the hand, each pillar duplicates the sound of a specific instrument. Music used to fill the temple—singing and dancing at sunrise and sunset. The sacred dancing was performed in the other detached hall in the southern part of the courtyard, its numerous columns all intricately carved.

Hazara Rama Complex

The other interesting temple complex takes you away from the sacred center of Hampi to the royal center, farther away from the river. This temple, in a rectangular compound, is called the Hazara Rama and is also dedicated to Vishnu. The Hazara Rama was for the private worship of the king. Surrounding this temple are the ruins of numerous civic buildings, royal residences, wells, aqueducts, and gigantic tanks. Of these, don't miss the Lotus Pavilion, the Queen's Bath, and the Elephant's Stables still in a reasonable state of repair.

As you leave Hampi and head for the bustling little city of Hospet, keep in mind as you enter the level plains that you have also entered the suburban area of the former empire. Little remains of this area—most of the dwellings for the common folk were built of wood, mud, or other perishable materials. Only a few temples have survived.

Badami, Aihole, and Pattadakal

A group of three enchanting villages—Badami, Aihole, and Pattadakal, glories of post-Gupta architecture (sixth to eighth centuries)—lie northwest of Hampi on the road to Bijapur. These three tiny temple hamlets are off the beaten path, but what a peaceful trip they provide through simple yet exquisite villages that are the epitome of pastorale. The only intense or noisy gatherings crop up at the occasional "shandy" (market), usually held once a week on the outskirts of a tiny town. Villagers come from miles around to sell livestock, fruits, vegetables, clay pots, dried fish, colorful powders and spices, soaps, and incense. If you happen upon a shandy, stop and wander through; they're lots of fun.

Badami, a charming village and the former second capital of the Chalukyas, is nestled between red sandstone hills. The cave temples may not surprise anyone who has seen Ajanta-Ellora, but they should astound everyone else. All these temples were hewn out of solid rock, some as early as A.D. 550. And their setting is magical: carved into hills above a lovely reservoir with quaint, tiny temples dotting the edge. The four most important caves follow a set plan: a veranda with pillars, a hall with columns, and a small cell to enshrine the deity. Though the exteriors appear simple, with borders of grotesque dwarfs, the interiors are remarkable.

The first cave, possibly the earliest, is dedicated to Shiva and burrows deep into the rock. Dwarfs decorate the front of the veranda. Inside you see a Nandi bull (with a human body) on the left, and on the right, a unique carving of Nataraja (Shiva) as the Cosmic Dancer with 18 hands (the only one of its kind in India). The hands are so well placed that any right hand matches up with any left hand. In the panel near the Nataraja, look for Shanmukha riding a peacock. Below this image is a carving of two boys that, on close inspection, creates the illusion of four. The columns and the ceiling are so artfully turned and executed that it is hard to believe that the rock was removed from around them; this cave looks like all the others—looks constructed, not dug out.

The second cave is the smallest and is dedicated to Vishnu, with its sanctuary depicting the god's various incarnations. You see Varatha, (the boar), who rescued earth from a flood; Vishnu riding Garuda (an eagle); Vishnu as Trivikrama with one leg on the ground and the other kicked up in the air; plus Vishnu as Krishna depicted in scenes at the top of the wall.

Between the second and third caves is a path that leads to a rough excavation in which a Buddhist figure has been carved into the wall.

The third cave, also dedicated to Vishnu, is considered the finest excavation, with the same dwarfs waiting to greet you. Just inside the veranda on the left wall is an enormous image of Vishnu as Trivikrama, similar to the one in the second cave, yet the tallest of its kind in India. On the opposite wall is another huge image of Vishnu with eight hands. If you stand just inside the cave with your back to the shrine, you see, on the panel above the entrance, an image of Garuda with the beak and wings of a bird but a human face. Stand up close, it looks serious; step back, it grins. Examine all the columns covered with couples, (some of them are definitely sexy). Look for the traces of faded frescoes, the huge reliefs of Narasimha (the half-lion Vishnu incarnation) and Harihara (half-Shiva and half-Vishnu), and the image of Vishnu seated on a serpent. This is also the biggest cave, with a double row of pillars.

The final major cave is Jain and was probably built, or rather hewn, a hundred years after the others. Enshrined here are huge figures of Parasnatha (the Jain saint) and Mahavira (the founder of Jainism).

Six kilometers (four miles) from Badami is the Banashankari Temple, originally built in the eighth century by the Chalukyas. Dedicated to a manifestation of Parvati, the current temple, constructed in the seventeenth century, has a black stone image of this goddess seated on a lion and trampling a demon to death. Out front is a large sacred pond, Harida Tirtha.

Aihole

The temples in Aihole are the oldest and most numerous: 150 shrines dating from A.D. 400 to 750, presenting the panorama of the genesis of Hindu medieval art. In an enclosure surrounding a tank, you'll find the U-shaped Durga, the largest and most elaborately carved temple. Named for a fort, not the goddess, the Durga is dedicated to Vishnu and was probably built in the seventh century.

The oldest temple is the Lad Khan where an eye accustomed to Hindu architecture will see much of the medieval temple form in an embryonic stage. The Suraya Naryana Temple, dedicated to the sun god, was built in the fifth or sixth centuries and contains an intriguing statue of the presiding deity surrounded by eight planets. Hit the stone in various places and it makes music. A short ride from these temples takes you to the Ravanaphadi (or Brahmanical) Cave. A carved Nandi guards the approach. Stone steps lead into the rock-cut cave with the dancing form of Shiva and other lovely statues.

Pattadakal

The temples of Pattadakal pick up where Aihole leaves off, with the evolution toward the high-towered, much-sculptured structure that is familiar in India. The sculpture, however, is not so much representative as decorative: pilasters, pillars, balconies, pierced work, and high relief of the faces of the towers. These temples are Chalyukan or Dravidian, and the best examples in each group are the Pampanath and the Virupaksha.

Bijapur

Bijapur, "The City of Victory," is a walled, medieval Moslem city, due north of Badami, that boasts over 50 mosques, 20 tombs, and at least as many *mahals* (palaces). The architecture here is not the florid, overdecorated Oriental type often associated with Moslems, but Turkish—restrained and severe though grandiose in proportion.

The dominant building is the Gol Gumbaz, the vast mausoleum of Mohammed Adil Shah who ruled his kingdom from Bijapur in the seventeenth century. His mausoleum was built in the mid-1600s around the same time as the Taj Mahal. The dome of the tomb is the second largest in the world: 124 feet in diameter, with St. Peter's in Rome outdoing it by merely 15 feet. The square monument has arched entranceways on each facade and an octagonal tiered turret at each angle. The inside is severely bare except for four tall pointed arches supporting the dome. The acoustics of the enclosed space make it a remarkable whispering gallery, where any sonic message, from the flicking of a match to a shout, is repeated 12 times over.

Other monuments in Bijapur include the ornate tomb of Adil Shah's father; the Ibrahim Rauza, with its richly decorated walls and perforated stone windows; and the unfinished tomb of Ali Adil Shah. There are plenty of palaces: the Asar-I-Sharif, supposed to contain a hair of the Prophet Mohammed's beard; the Anand Mahal, where the harem lived; the Gagan Mahal, with its three magnificent arches; the Sat Manzil, a seven-story pleasure palace overlooking the city; and the Chini Mahal.

The Jama Masjid, built in 1565, is one of the finest mosques in India, remarkable for its harmonious proportions, its graceful minarets, the construction of the bulbous domes and the execution of the ornamental detail. Others are the Old Mosque, a converted Jain temple; the Andu Masjid, two-stories with a fluted dome; the miniature Makka; and the Mehtar Mahal, with its finely wrought gateway. Some of these buildings were sadly mutilated by Emperor Aurangzeb, but in spite of the ravages of time and men, Bijapur remains a splendid sight. The town is also notable for its many fine gardens.

If you're in Bijapur on Sunday, visit the Gandhi Market, where the nearby Lambanis set up shop in a center square selling colorful material and jewels. It's a photographer's paradise.

Bidar

Our last stop in Karnataka is Bidar, northeast of Bijapur. Bidar is a deceptive city. The modern area is uninteresting, but head straight to the area containing the old inner fort and the inner city, the former capital of the fifteenth-century Bahmani kings. Its remarkable ruins are a monument to the time of its glory.

Spend a morning wandering through the remains of the inner fort. See the beautiful Rangin Mahal (the Colorful Palace), with its small rooms and tile work; the Zanani Masjid, the oldest Moslem building in Bidar; the Gagan Mahal (Heavenly Palace), where you can meander down old stone steps into half-destroyed chambers and halls; the Royal Pavilion with more underground rooms; and the numerous other ancient constructions.

After seeing the fort, visit the nearby Bahamani Tombs of departed kings. Although not well maintained, they provide a sense of timeless grandeur. Wear good walking shoes and bring a flashlight.

PRACTICAL INFORMATION FOR KARNATAKA

WHEN TO GO. Karnataka, which is near-tropical, is at its best from mid-August to mid-April, when days are warm and nights are balmy. The monsoon arrives in June, with heavy downpours that turn to light rains by mid-August, when Karnataka is lush green.

HOW TO GET THERE. By Air. *Indian Airlines* connects Bangalore with Ahmedabad, Bombay, Calcutta, Cochin, Delhi, Goa, Hyderabad, Madras, Madurai, and Trivandrum. From Bombay, daily flights go to Mangalore. *Vayudoot* has occasional flights: Bangalore to Tirupati, Calicut, and Trivandrum. From Bombay, daily flights go to Belgaum.

By Train. Trains can be fun; but they're not the fastest or most comfortable way to travel. A night on a train means making reservations early for the berth as well as for the sleeper. Make sure you have both reservations or you may be kicked off the train at bedtime. Travel second class air-conditioned or first class to get a reasonable night's rest. Daily trains from Bombay to Bangalore: *Udyan Express, Mahalakshmi Express, Sahyadhri Express* (24 hours). From Delhi to Bangalore: *Karnataka Express* (40 hours). Daily trains from Madras: *Bangalore Mail, Bangalore Express, Brindavan Express* (six hours). In Bangalore, contact the Railway Station for information and reservations; tel. 74172 (first class) and tel. 76351 (second class).

By Bus. Buses are crowded and slow-going. They are not recommended.

By Hired Car with Driver. The cost of car with driver is about Rs. 3.50 per km, plus a halt charge of Rs. 50 per night. Hire a car with driver from a recommended tour operator listed below or one in the state from which you depart. Here are some important distances from Bangalore: Bombay, 1,100 km (682 mi.); Cochin, 578 km (358 mi.); Hyderabad, 566 km (351 mi.); Madras, 334 km (207 mi.); Ooty, 297 km (184 mi.); Panaji, 570 km (353 mi.); Trivandrum, 761 km (472 mi.).

TOURIST INFORMATION. The Tourist Department throughout Karnataka tries to be helpful. Some departments have excellent brochures (most of which are available in Bangalore) on destinations and monuments. The pamphlet on Bidar is especially good, as are the maps of the state and various cities. Most offices are open 10 A.M.–5:30 P.M., closed Sundays.

Bangalore. *Karnataka Tourism,* Directorate of Tourism, Cauvery Bhawan, 1st Floor, F Block, K.G. Rd., Bangalore, Karnataka, tel. 215489. *Tourist Information Center,* 52 Shrungar Shopping Centre, Mahatma Gandhi Rd., tel. 572377. *Tourist Information Center,* Airport, HAL; tel. 571467. City Railway Station; tel. 70068. *Tourist Information Center,* St. Marks. Rd., tel. 213139.

Bijapur. *Hotel Adil Shahi,* Anand Mahal Rd.; tel. 20934.

Hassan. *Tourist Officer,* Department of Tourism, B.M. Rd.; tel. 8862.

Hospet (Hampi). *Tourist Information Office,* Station Rd., tel. 8537; or Manager, Hotely Mayura Vijayanagar, T. B. Dam, tel. 8270.

Mangalore. *Tourist Information Office;* no phone.

Mysore. *Regional Tourist Office,* Old Exhibition Bldg.; tel. 22096.

The Government of India also has a tourist office in Bangalore at KFC Building, 48 Church St.; tel. 579517. Open 10 A.M.–5:30 P.M., closed Saturday and Sunday.

FOREIGN CURRENCY EXCHANGE. Most Western-style hotels have money-exchange counters. Otherwise, ask your hotel to recommend a local bank. In Bangalore, the *State Bank of India* is at Almas Center, Mahatma Gandhi Rd., and *Thomas Cook* is at 55 Mahatma Gandhi Rd. Banks are open Monday–Friday, 10 A.M.–2 P.M.; Saturdays, till noon.

ACCOMMODATIONS. In many large cities and popular tourist areas in Karnataka, excellent facilities exist—some Western-style posh; some Eastern-style posh. Other undervisited areas have few options, but what's there is adequate. And remember that the benefit of the visit far outweighs the lack of carpeting in a room—or ought to. For reservations at Karnataka Tourist Department (KTD) facilities, contact in advance the Directorate of Tourism (address above under *Tourist Information*). For reservations in Karnataka State Tourism Development Corporation (KSTDC) facilities, contact in advance: KSTDC, 10/4 Kasturba Rd., Queen's Circle, Bangalore, Karnataka; tel. 212901. Prices are based on double occupancy and exclude taxes: *Expensive,* Rs. 950–Rs. 1,450; *Moderate,* Rs. 500–Rs. 950; *Inexpensive,* under Rs. 500. Some Western-style hotels take major credit cards.

AIHOLE

Inexpensive

Tourist Home. Aihole; tel. 41. Reservations: KTD, tel. 572377. 14 rooms—10 with Western-style toilets, 4 with Indian-style. This newly renovated facility offers clean rooms with fans and a modest decor. Its modesty is in keeping with its setting next to ancient temples. Room service and Indian or Continental cuisine meals provided on request. Rupees only.

BADAMI

Inexpensive

Hotel Mayura Chalukya. Badami; tel. 46. 10 rooms with bath. This bungalow, with an interior courtyard, was slated to be renovated by 1991. Clean rooms are modestly furnished. Fans, room service, Indian-cuisine restaurant, bar. Rupees only.

Hotel Mukambika. Opposite Bus Stand, Badami; tel 67. 7 rooms with bath. This simple two-story, Western-style hotel has clean rooms with overhead fans and good management. Multicuisine restaurant, bar, room service, car rental-arrangements. Rupees only.

BANGALORE

Expensive

Holiday Inn Bangalore. 28 Sankey Rd., Bangalore; tel. 77931. 190 rooms with bath. This modern high rise has a reasonably attractive marble lobby with a glass atrium. Air-conditioned rooms are spacious, but have an uninspired modern decor. For ultimate quiet, ask for an interior room above the pool; for the best view, ask for a room overlooking the golf course. TV, room service, multicuisine restaurants, bar, swimming pool, health club, foreign-exchange and travel counter. AE, DC, MC, V.

Welcomgroup Windsor Manor. 25 Sankey Rd., Bangalore; tel. 79431 or 258030. 140 rooms with bath. Bangalore's prettiest hotel was recently built, but adheres impeccably to Indo-Gothic architecture. The exterior is strikingly white, with arched windows and wrought-iron touches. The magnificent lobby has a marble fountain beneath a domed skylight and massive teak pillars. Handsome air-conditioned rooms have modern furnishings with Victorian touches. TV, room service, multicuisine restaurants, bar, health club, swimming pool, golfing arrangements, business center, foreign-exchange counter, travel agency, doctor, shopping arcade. AE, DC, MC, V.

Moderate

Hotel Ashok. High Grounds, Bangalore; tel. 269462. 181 rooms with bath. A high rise with an inviting marble lobby, the Ashok offers spacious air-conditioned rooms with a contemporary decor. Best rooms overlook the pool. Multicuisine restaurants, bar, TV, room service, swimming pool, golfing arrangements, tennis court, health club, bank, foreign-exchange counter, travel agency, doctor, shopping arcade. AE, DC, MC, V.

Taj Gateway Hotel on Residency Road. 66 Residency Rd., Bangalore; tel. 573265. 98 rooms with bath. This Western-style high rise, a recent addition to the Taj chain, offers pleasant rooms with contemporary furnishings at a very moderate price. Air-conditioning, TV, room service, multicuisine restaurants, bar, swimming pool, health club, foreign-exchange and travel counter, secretarial services, doctor, shops. MC, V.

Taj Residency. 41/3 Mahatma Gandhi Rd., Bangalore; tel. 568888. 170 rooms with bath. A 10-story high rise, the Taj Residency has a spacious lobby and pretty modern-decor, air-conditioned rooms with balconies. Best rooms are on the upper floors with a lake view. TV, room service, multicuisine restaurants, bar, swimming pool, health club, baby-sitters, business center, foreign-exchange counter, travel agency, doctor, book shop. AE, DC, MC, V.

Taj West End Hotel. Race Course Rd., Bangalore; tel. 29281 or 74191. 140 rooms with bath. A former 1920s British bungalow, this place has an exterior and public rooms that are decidedly Victorian. Air-conditioned rooms are done up in a contemporary decor. Best rooms are on the second floor opening onto a veranda overlooking the pool. TV, room service, multicuisine restaurants, swimming pool, tennis courts, horseback riding and golfing arrangements, doctor, baby-sitters, foreign-exchange counter, travel agency, shopping arcade. AE, DC, MC, V.

Inexpensive

Ashraya International Hotel. 149 Infantry Rd., Bangalore; tel. 75569 or 258146. 72 rooms with bath. This five-story, Western-style hotel offers spacious, clean rooms with plain furnishings. Best rooms are air-conditioned. TV, room service, multicuisine restaurant, bar, travel desk. Good value. AE, DC, MC, V.

Harsha Hotel. 11 Venkataswamy Naidu Rd., Bangalore; tel. 565566. 80 rooms with bath. You'll find a small swimming pool at this Western-style hotel and simply decorated, clean rooms. Best rooms are air-conditioned and located on an upper floor away from the road. TV, room service, multicuisine restaurants, bar, travel and foreign-exchange counter, pool, book shop. AE, DC, MC, V.

BHIMESWARI

Inexpensive

Cauvery Fishing Camp. Bhimeswari; no phone. Reservations: Jungle Lodge and Resorts Ltd., 2nd Floor, Shrungar Shopping Center, Mahatma Gandhi Marg, Bangalore, Karnataka; tel. 575195. Six tents with separate bathroom facilities. This excellent fishing resort has well-appointed safari-style tents set near the Cauvery River, on which you can enjoy great fishing from coracle boats (round animal-hide crafts). Meals included; multicuisine restaurant, bar, fishing equipment. Open January–April. AE, DC, V.

BIJAPUR

Inexpensive

Hotel Mayura Adil Shahi. Anand Mahal Rd., Bijapur; tel. 934. Reservations: KSTDC, 10/4 Kasturba Rd., Queens Circle, Bangalore; tel. 212901. 19 rooms with bath. This bungalow, with an interior courtyard, has clean, modestly furnished rooms. Overhead fans and mosquito nets, room service, multicuisine restaurant, bar, nearby tourist department office. Rupees only.

Hotel Sanman. Opposite Gol Gumbaz, Bijapur; no phone at press time. 40 rooms with Western-style and Indian-style bathrooms. A new modest high rise, Sanman offers clean, simply decorated modern rooms. Best rooms overlook the Gol Gumbaz. Fans, room service, Indian cuisine restaurant, bar. Rupees only.

BRINDAVAN GARDENS

Inexpensive

Hotel Krishnarajasagar. Mandya District, Karnataka; tel. 22, Belagola. 22 rooms with bath. This delightful British bungalow, with pleasant grounds and views, has charming rooms with cozy, Victorian-style furnishings. Fans, room service, multicuisine restaurant, bar, foreign-exchange counter, car rental, doctor, shop. AE, DC, MC, V.

GOKARNA BEACH

Inexpensive

Tourist Cottages. Gokarna Beach; no phone. Reservations through KTD, tel. 572377. 4 cottages with bath. These cottages offer a valley view and are near a good swimming beach. Rooms are clean, with a modest modern decor and have small front porches. Fan, room service, Indian vegetarian-cuisine restaurant. Rupees only.

GULBARGA

Inexpensive

Hotel Mayura Bahamani. Public Gardens, Gulbarga; tel. 20644. Reservations: KSTDC, tel. 212901. 15 rooms with bath. In this simple two-story bungalow, rooms are plain and clean. Fans, room service, multicuisine restaurant, bar. Rupees only.

Hotel Pariwar. Station Rd., Gulbarga; tel. 21522. 45 rooms with Western-style and Indian-style bathrooms. A modest hotel, Paliwar offers simple rooms with Western-style furnishings. Fans, room service, Indian and Continental vegetarian-cuisine restaurant. Rupees only.

HASSAN

Moderate

Hotel Hassan Ashok. Bangalore-Mangalore Rd., Hassan; tel. 8731. 46 rooms with bath. This three-story hotel offers excellent value and pleasant rooms with a modern decor. Some rooms are air-conditioned. Room service, Indian and Continental cuisine restaurant, bar, health club, foreign-exchange counter, doctor, shopping arcade. AE, DC, MC, V.

HOSPET

Inexpensive

Malligai Tourist Home. 6/143 Jambunatha Rd., Hospet; tel. 8101. 40 rooms with bath. A new two-story hotel, this place has Western-style, air-conditioned rooms. Room service, multicuisine restaurant, bar, foreign-exchange counter, tour arrangements, doctor, shops. AE, DC, MC, V.

Hotel Priyadarshni. Station Rd., Hospet; no phone yet. 60 rooms with bath. Also new, this Western-style hotel has a simple lobby and clean, modestly decorated rooms. Some rooms are air-conditioned. Room service, multicuisine restaurant, bar. Rupees only.

MANGALORE

Moderate

Welcomgroup Manjarun. Bunder Rd., Mangalore; tel. 31791. 101 rooms with bath. An attractive lobby and appealing contemporary-decor rooms are highlights at this high rise. Room service, TV, multicuisine restaurants, bar, travel agency, foreign-exchange counter, swimming pool, doctor, shopping arcade. AE, DC, MC, V.

Inexpensive

Summer Sands Beach Resort. Chotamangalore, Ullal, Mangalore; tel. 6400. 64 rooms with bath. Cottages in this beach resort, 10 km (six mi.) from Mangalore, offer clean rooms done up in whimsical theme decors. Some rooms are air-conditioned. Room service, multicuisine restaurant, bar, swimming pool, massages, travel and foreign-exchange counter. AE, DC, MC.

MYSORE

Expensive

Ashok Lalitha Mahal Palace Hotel. Mysore; tel. 27650. 54 rooms with bath. Situated just outside the city center, this 1920s palace, now a hotel, is sumptuous—one of India's best treats. Its air-conditioned interior is Italian baroque, with painted walls that are lavishly trimmed with ornate plaster moldings, huge pillars, gorgeous domes. Best rooms are in the original structure and have appealing, but not necessarily grand, Victorian furnishings. Rooms in the new wing have a contemporary decor. TV, room service, multicuisine restaurant, bar, billiards room, health club, swimming pool, tennis courts, travel agency, foreign-exchange counter, doctor, shopping arcade, helipad. AE, DC, MC, V.

Moderate

Southern Star Mysore. 13–14 Vinobha Rd., Mysore; tel. 27217. 108 rooms with bath. This new Western-style high rise has a spacious marble lobby and air-conditioned rooms with a modern decor. Best rooms overlook the pool. TV, room service, multicuisine restaurant, bar, swimming pool, health club, foreign-exchange counter, car rental-service, doctor, shopping arcade. AE, DC, MC, V.

Inexpensive

Dasaprakash Paradise. 104 Vivekananda Rd., Uadavagiri, Mysore; tel. 26666. 90 rooms with bath. Rooms in this Western-style hotel are clean and have modest, modern furnishings. Best rooms are on the upper floors with views of Mysore. Some rooms are air-conditioned. TV, room service, Indian-vegetarian restaurant, bar, travel and foreign-exchange counter. Good value. AE, DC, MC, V.

Hotel Metropole. 5 Jhansi Lakshmi Bai Rd., Mysore; tel. 20681. 20 rooms with bath. This lovely old British bungalow is faultlessly maintained. Best rooms are on the upper floor off a sweeping veranda. Victorian furnishings are charming and evoke the 1940s. Fans, room service, multicuisine restaurant, bar, foreign-exchange and travel counter, shop. Good value. AE, DC, MC, V.

NAGARHOLE

Moderate

Kabini River Lodge. Karapui, Nagarhole Wildlife Sanctuary. Reservations: Jungle Lodge and Resorts, 2nd Floor, Shrungar Shopping Center, Mahatma Gandhi Rd., Bangalore; tel. 575195. 14 rooms with bath. Once the former vice-regal and maharajah's hunting lodge, this resort set in the sanctuary is wonderful. It is run by Colonel Wakefield and his staff, who are gracious and knowledgeable. Chances are you will see wildlife nearby. The ambience is peaceful; modern rooms have a rustic decor. Open-air multicuisine restaurant, room service, bar, jeep and elephant safaris, coracle rides on the nearby lake. Meals are included. AE, DC, V.

SRIRANGAPATNA

Inexpensive

Hotel Mayura River View. Srirangapatna; tel. 114. Reservations: KSTDC, tel. 21291. 8 rooms with bath. Four cottages, each with two units, make up this riverside complex. Cottages have clean rooms with a modern decor and a pleasant porch. There is a multicuisine restaurant and room service. Rupees only.

DINING OUT. Except for Bangalore, Mangalore, and Mysore, don't expect a lot of dining options. Bangalore is about as Western as you can get, with almost too many American-style fast-food reminders. Throughout Karnataka, you *will* find reasonable food, but limited menus. Besides the restaurants listed here, hotels also have restaurants. Breakfast is usually 8–10:30; lunch, noon–2:30; dinner, 7:30–10. Payment is normally in rupees unless the restaurant is connected to a Western-style hotel. The restaurants listed below are informal and, unless noted, are open for all three meals and don't require reservations. Prices, based on one person eating a three-course meal, excluding taxes, tip, or beverage, are *Deluxe,* over Rs. 120; *Expensive,* Rs. 80–Rs. 120; *Moderate,* Rs. 40–Rs. 80; *Inexpensive,* under Rs. 40.

BANGALORE

Deluxe

Memories of China. Taj Residency, 41/3 Mahatma Gandhi Rd.; tel. 568888. This elegant restaurant has exquisite rice paper murals, smoked-glass lanterns, and taped Chinese music. The chef prepares Hunan and Szechuan dishes, which you can sample during a lunch and dinner buffet. If you order à la carte, try spicy Szechuan king prawns in hot garlic sauce or nonspicy Hunan crispy lamb in black bean sauce. Reservations advised. Open 12:30–3 P.M. and 7 P.M.–midnight. AE, DC, MC, V.

Paradise Island. Taj West End Hotel, Race Course Rd., tel. 29281. An open-air restaurant in a British gazebo surrounded by water and lush plantings, Paradise Island has an extensive multicuisine menu. At lunch, it also offers one of Bangalore's best buffets; at night, order à la carte. Indian and Continental dishes are best. Dinner reservations advised. Open 12:30–3:30 P.M. and 7:30–11 P.M. AE, DC, MC, V.

Royal Afghan. Welcomgroup Windsor Manor, 25 Sankey Rd.; tel. 79431 or 258030. This intimate outdoor restaurant by a pool serves Northwest Frontier Indian specialties cooked on the grill or in the tandoori. Small lights strung in trees add a romantic touch. Reservations advised. Open 12:30–3 P.M. and 7:30–11:30 P.M. AE, DC, MC, V.

Wellington Room, Welcomgroup Windsor Manor, 25 Sankey Rd.; tel. 79431 or 258030. You're surrounded by Victorian elegance here: antique-look furnishings, upholstered chairs, old paintings on the wall. The Continental menu matches the ambience. Specialties include lobster thermidor and petit veal escallops sautéed in butter and flambéed in vodka. Reservations advised. Open 12:30–3 P.M. and 7:30–11:30 P.M. AE, DC, MC, V.

Expensive

Chaupal. Harsha Hotel, 11 Venkataswamy Naidu Rd.; tel. 565566. This intimate restaurant with subdued lighting and a slight Mogul decor—white-brick arches and low ceilings—offers multicuisine dishes, but the Muglai items are best. Try the *shahjahani kebab* (marinated spicy boned chicken cooked in a tandoori) or, if you can order in advance, *raan-e-sikandari* (marinated leg of lamb cooked in a tandoori). Open 7:30–10 A.M., 12:30–3 P.M., and 7 P.M.–midnight. AE, DC, MC, V.

Mandarin Room. Ashok Hotel, High Grounds; tel. 269462. A rooftop restaurant with a good view of Bangalore, Mandarin Room can also boast Bangalore's best Chinese food. Especially good are the delicious non-spicy chicken with bean curd, crisp lamb Peking-style, and the spicy shredded lamb in chili sauce. You can also dance to a good Western band. Reservations advised. Open 8 P.M.–midnight. AE, DC, MC, V.

Tandoor. 28 Mahatma Gandhi Rd.; tel. 563330. The Tandoor's exposed tandoori ovens are part of the decor. Its lighting is subdued, and taped Hindi music plays discretely. The cuisine is Indian, with especially good tandoori items. Try chicken *lovabdar* (spicy roasted boneless chicken barbecued in red curry) or mutton *sagwala* (non-spicy lamb cooked in a spinach curry). Open noon–3:30 P.M. and 7 P.M.–midnight. AE, DC, MC, V.

Moderate

Nanking Restaurant. 3 Grant Rd.; tel. 214301. In this Chinese restaurant, delicate glass paintings line one wall, lanterns hang from a cool white ceiling, and the lighting is subdued at night. The sweet and sour dishes and noodle preparations are popular choices. If you call a day in advance, you can also have dim sum. Open noon–3:30 P.M. and 7:30–11:30 P.M. Rupees only.

Inexpensive

Chit Chat. EGK Complex, 100 Mahatma Gandhi Rd.; tel 572293. This popular two-story restaurant has a British Regency decor, with a downstairs marble fountain that plays at night and an enormous chandelier hanging from the ceiling. It serves good multicuisine vegetarian fast-food fare. Specialties include the *paneer butter masala* (cottage cheese cooked in tomato gravy) and the assorted *dosas* (Indian-style stuffed crêpes), topped off with fresh ice cream. Open 9 A.M.–noon. Rupees only.

Mavalli Tiffin Rooms. Lalbagh Rd.; tel. 220022. For a wonderful time and Indian vegetarian food, visit this Bangalore institution, established in 1924. Front rooms, with ceiling fans, are crowded with marble tables. The small backroom is air-conditioned. You won't find better *dosas* (Indian-style stuffed crêpes); and you can't beat the price (Rs. 5). You can also enjoy great sweets and superb coffee. You may have to wait for a table; but once the dhoti-clad bearer takes your order, it's fast food all the way. Open 6:30–11 A.M. and 3:30–7:30 P.M.

R.R. Plaintain Leaf. Church St.; tel. 578229. A small footbridge over a pool fed by a waterfall leads into this popular eatery that serves dishes from Andhra Pradesh on banana leaves. The downstairs room has ceiling fans and booths. Upstairs is air-conditioned with soft lighting. Menus are the same, but lower-priced downstairs. Try the spicy vegetarian meal (portions of assorted dishes) or the famous chicken *biryani* (rice dish). Open 11:30 A.M.–3 P.M. and 6:30–11:30 P.M. Rupees only.

HOSPET

Moderate

Garden Restaurant and Bar. Malligai Tourist Home, 6/143 Jambunatha Rd.; tel. 8101. This attractive open-air restaurant has linen on its tables and soft lighting at night along with classical Indian music. The chef serves Chinese, Continental, and especially good Indian cuisines. Open noon–3 P.M. and 7–10:30 P.M. AE, DC, MC, V.

MANGALORE

Expensive

The Galley. Welcomgroup Manjarun, Bunder Rd.; tel. 31791. This British-decor restaurant serves Chinese, Continental, and Indian cuisine. The Indian and Chinese, especially the seafood dishes, are preferred. Dinner reservations advised. Open 7:30–10 A.M., noon–3 P.M., and 7:30–11 P.M. AE, DC, MC, V.

MYSORE

Expensive

Lalitha Mahal Palace Hotel Restaurant. Mysore; tel. 27650. Here, you eat in the maharajah's former ballroom—a tour de force of Italian baroque-regal with stained-glass domes and sky-blue walls enhanced by ornate plaster moldings. The food is delicious, especially the Indian cuisine. You can also choose Continental or Chinese dishes. There's Indian classical music at lunch and dinner to punctuate the elegant ambience. Dinner reservations advised. Open 6–11 A.M., 12:30–3 P.M., and 8–11 P.M. AE, DC, MC, V.

Moderate

Jyothi. Southern Star Hotel, 13–14 Vinobha Rd.; tel. 27217. This restaurant was recently renovated, with an Indian decor, subdued lighting, and Indian classical music at lunch and at night. Best bets on the multicuisine menu are the good tandoori items. Open noon–2:45 P.M. and 7:30–11:30 P.M. AE, DC, MC, V.

Inexpensive

R. R. Plaintain Leaf. Chandragupta Rd., next to Sangam Cinema; tel. 23377. Two fan-cooled rooms with subdued lighting comprise this modest place. The cuisine from Andhra Pradesh, which you eat off a banana leaf, is tasty. Open 11 A.M.–3:30 P.M. and 7–10:30 P.M. Rupees only.

SWEETS AND TREATS. Bangalore. After a visit to the Lalbagh Gardens, drop in at the *Mavalli Tiffin Rooms* on Lalbagh Rd. for a great time and tasty snack and coffee. While shopping on Mahatma Gandhi Rd., relax at *Chit Chat* and enjoy an ice-cream treat, fresh pastries, or a vegetarian snack. For a truly ethnic experience, go to *Arya Bhawan* at K.G. Circle, a stand-up place that prepares fresh Indian sweets each morning that sell out by the time it closes at 10 P.M. Try the *kesari peda* or *dudh peda* (Rs. 2 each)—sweets made from sugary milk paste.
Bangalore-Mysore Road. In Maddur, about 85 km (53 mi.) from Bangalore, look for a white roadside stand with a signboard that says *Maddur Vadai.* Stop and enjoy its *vadai,* a deliciously crispy and spicy treat served with chutney.

HOW TO GET AROUND. From the Airport. Bangalore. An airport bus makes frequent runs to most Western-style hotels and central Bangalore (Rs. 5). A taxi will take you to your hotel for about Rs. 150. **Belgaum.** A taxi into town will cost about Rs. 50. **Mangalore.** A taxi should cost about Rs. 75.
By Plane. *Indian Airlines* flies three times weekly between Bangalore and Mangalore and Bangalore and Belgaum.
By Train. Numerous express trains run from Bangalore to Mysore. Other good trains connect Bangalore with Bijapur, Mangalore, and other important cities. In Bangalore, contact the Bangalore City Railway Station, tel. 258465 for inquiries; call tel. 76351 for first-class reservations, or tel. 74172 for second-class reservations. In Mysore, contact the Mysore Railway Station, tel. 20100.
By Bus. While most buses are crowded and not recommended, there is good bus service between Mysore and Bangalore. Consult the tourist departments for details.
By Hired Car with Driver. This is the best way to see Karnataka. Rates are about Rs. 3.50 per km with a halt charge of Rs. 50 per night. Hire a car from an agency listed below under *Tour Operators.*
By Taxi. This is a good option for travel outside a city. Rates are about Rs. 3 for the first km; Rs. 2.75 per additional km. In Bangalore you can hire a taxi for Rs. 85 for four hours.
By Auto Rickshaw. In congested cities, this is a convenient, quick way to travel. Rates: Rs. 2.50 for the first km; Rs. 1 per additional km. Set the fare in advance.
By Bike Rickshaw. An enjoyable way to travel, this should be cheaper than an auto rickshaw.

TOURS. *KSTDC* 10/4 Kasturba Road, Bangalore (tel. 212901), conducts numerous tours from Bangalore, Hubli and Mysore to various regions of the state.

Buses are usually deluxe and very comfortable, providing an inexpensive way to see much of the state if you don't have a rented car and driver. You can also book a tour at any of the Tourist Information centers (addresses above). In Mysore, KSTDC is located at the Transport Wing, Old Exhibition Building, Irwin, Rd. (tel. 23652).

BANGALORE

Bangalore City Tour. Half-day tours departing at 7:30 A.M. and 2 P.M. Tippu's palace, Bull Temple, Lalbagh, Cauvery Handicrafts Emporium, Vidhana Soudha, Museum, and Ulsoor Lake.

Tirupati, Mangapura, and Kalahasthi Tour (three days). Departures Wednesday through Saturday.

Ooty Tour (three days). Daily departures from October to January.

Tour to Sravanabelgola-Belur-Halebid (one day). Daily departures.

Mysore Tour (one day). Daily departures.

Tour to Hampi via Mantralaya and Tungabhadra Dam (three days). Every Friday.

MYSORE

Mysore local sightseeing (one day). Includes Somnathpura and Srirangapatna. Daily.

Belur, Halebid, and Sravanabelgola (one day). Every Tuesday, Wednesday, Friday, and Saturday.

Ooty Tour (one day). Every Monday, Thursday, and Saturday.

TOUR OPERATORS. The following agencies can take care of all your travel needs, including car with driver:

Trade Wings, 48 Lavelle Rd., Bangalore; tel. 574595.

Travel Corporation of India, 9 Residency Rd., Bangalore; tel. 574595.

The following agencies specialize in special tours and adventures (also see *Special-Interest Tours* in *Facts at Your Fingertips*):

Victoria Tours and Travels ("Padmashree," No. 326 6th Main Rd., Vijayanagar, Bangalore; tel. 357712) offers theme-oriented trips that concentrate on yoga, classical dance and music, temples, and village life.

EMPL Tours (108 Vishal Phawan, 95 Nehru Pl., New Delhi; tel. 6428310) offers good adventures: hang gliding, trekking, and biking.

SEASONAL EVENTS. The specific dates for many events each year are determined by the lunar calendar; consult the India Tourist Office for details. **March.** In Nanjangud, the *Car Festival* is a procession of deities from the temple in small chariots. Festive Hindu occasion.

April/May. Melcote (52 km from Mysore) observes *Vairamudi Festival.* Vishnu deity is adorned with a diamond-studded crown witnessed by thousands of devotees. Much festivity. *Karaga* is Bangalore's most popular festival, which symbolizes strength of mind represented by balancing contests (who can hold the most pots on the top of their heads). Very interesting.

In North Coorg, *Suggi* is associated with the harvest, involving colorful local dances unique to this area.

August/September. *Ganesha Chaturthi,* throughout Karnataka, is a three-day festival celebrating Ganesha with songs and dances in the hopes that paying tribute to this god will return blessings and especially good fortune.

September/October. Mysore and the rest of Karnataka observe *Dasara,* a 10-day festival that takes on tremendous pomp and pageantry. The festival celebrates the victory of goddess Chamundi over the demon Mahishasura. While the maharajah no looker takes part, the rest of the city does. The palace is lit up and glows. On the 10th day there is a fantastic procession including the camel corps, infantry, and cavalry.

Hampi Festival. Hampi has a three-day festival of cultural shows, with Karnataka music and folk dances performed at the ruins. A beautiful event.

November/December. *Kadalekaye Parishe* (Groundnut fair) held on the premises of the Bull Temple, Bangalore. Main event: who can consume the largest amount of groundnut. The temple bull is bedecked with a garland of groundnut to prevent him from ruining the local crops of this valuable product.

HISTORIC SITES. Karnataka is rich in historical sites. Indeed, some places are temple villages in themselves. A few of these are in close proximity to each other and can be visited in a half day. Such is the case of Aihole, Badami, and Pattadakal, as well as Belur and Halebid. We've grouped these villages together so that you can better organize your visits. Historic sites are generally free or have nominal entrance fees. They are open from sunrise to sunset unless noted otherwise.

AIHOLE-BADAMI-PATTADAKAL

Aihole alone has 150 temples dedicated to Hindu gods and goddesses. This temple village represents the cradle of Dravidian architecture. Aihole was founded by the first Chalukyan king around A.D. 450, and most of these temples are from 400 to 750. The simple towers of Aihole are precursors of the massive goporums in the south. See especially the temple of *Lad Khan,* possibly the oldest, the U-shaped *Durgan,* the *Suraya Naryana Temple,* the *Ravanaphadi* (Brahmanical cave).

Badami. This second capital of the Chalukyas was founded by Pulakesin I around A.D. 550. A beautiful, serene village with stunning cave temples dating back to the sixth century.

Pattadakal (22 km or 14 mi. from Badami). City founded by King Vikramaditya II in the eighth century and the site of the Chalukyan coronation ceremonies. The next stage in temple evolution after Aihole, with 10 temples constructed from the 600s to the 700s. The *Papanath Temple* (A.D. 680) is the earliest example of pure Chalukyan style—a simple structure with plain pillars. The facades are decorated with themes from the *Ramayana.* The *Mallikarjuna Temple,* with Nandi standing out front, is decorated with scenes from the *Bhagvadgita.* The temple was constructed by a queen (Trilokya Mahadevi) of Vikramaditya II. The *Virupaksha Temple,* built in A.D. 740 by Lokamaha Devi, depicts scenes from the *Ramayana* and *Mahabharata.* See if you can find the carving that looks like an elephant from one side and a buffalo from the other.

BANGALORE

Bull Temple (five km or three mi. from Bangalore) is a monolithic bull built in the 1500s in the Dravidian style (15 feet high by 20 feet long) by Kempe Gowda, founder of Bangalore. Supposedly the iron plate on its head keeps the bull from growing.

Nandi Hills (59 km or 37 mi.) has 2,000-year-old Shiva temples, and is the former site of Tipu Sultan's summer palace. Walk up to Tipu's Drop, a 2,000-foot sheer cliff, where the condemned were pushed over the edge.

Tipu's Palace and Fort, just northwest of Lal Bagh, were originally built of mud in 1537 by Kempe Gowda; rebuilt in stone in the 1700s by Hyder Ali and embellished by his son Tipu Sultan. Palace was the summer residence of Tipu Sultan. Open 8 A.M.–6 P.M.

Vidhana Soudha, on the northern boundary of Cubbon Park, is an enormous white granite structure built in the neo-Dravidian style in 1956. On top sit three lions—India's national symbol. Permission is needed to go inside.

BELUR-HALEBID

Belur, (39 km or 24 mi. from Hassan) is a former twelfth-century city under the Hoysala kings. *Belur Temple of Lord Channakeshava* (a Vishnu avatar and still a place of active worship) was begun in 1116 by Hoysala King Vishnuvardhana and completed 103 years later. Star-shaped and sitting on a platform, the squat temple is of soapstone. The guides are very informative, and Rs. 20 will make them very happy.

Halebid (16 km or 10 mi. from Belur) was started by the same king 10 years after the construction of Belur began. It took 180 years of work. Has the same star-shaped pattern with a double shrine, again of soapstone, and a marvel of sculpture. Again, an informative guide (Rs. 20) will bring the gorgeous temple to life.

BIDAR

Bidar Fort, the former capital of the fifteenth-century Bahmani kings, is a creation that mixes Hindu and Moslem influences. There's a small museum as you enter, with an archaeological department. The hours are "iffy"—sort of 8 A.M.–4 P.M. Try to get a guide to show you around. The Karnataka Tourism Department has a good pamphlet on all the monuments within the fort and around Bidar. The pamphlet contains excellent information and is intelligently written, but it has no map. Bring a flashlight and good walking shoes and plan for plenty of time (two-three hours).

Bahamani Tombs are not far from the fort. Visit early in the day to see the interior paintings (best in the morning light). Again, a flashlight is a must. Buried here are eight former kings of Bidar. The tomb of Ahmed Shah-al-Wali Bahamani is 107 feet high and built on a square plane, with a dome that is three-quarters of an orb. No external decorations, but the interior was once quite colorful. You still see remnants of intricate floral designs and calligraphy. Also, set into the dome are supposedly nine diamonds—but you need a powerful flashlight to see them. Also visit the tomb of Sultan Allauddin Shah II. It originally glittered with the exterior covered with tilework, some of which still remains. Finally, visit the Chaukhandi of Hazrat Khalil-Ullah, on the way to the Ashtur tombs. Steps lead up to the entrance of an octagonal structure that encloses another tomb. This building was also formerly covered with tilework. Notice the beautifully carved granite pillars and the entrance decorated with floral motifs. The *Baridi Tombs* are situated to the west of Bidar on Nanded Road. Usually Moslem tombs are closed on the western side where a *mihrab* is built for saying prayers. Not so at the Tomb of Ali Barid (1542–1580). Legend claims that Ali Barid wanted his grave kept clean by the wind and sun, and kept it open.

BIJAPUR

Bijapur has 50 mosques and 20 tombs. This Moslem-dominated city is best appreciated with a government-approved guide. The *Gol Gumbaz,* built in the mid-1600s, encloses the second-largest domed space in the world, with a wonderful whispering gallery that can only be appreciated early in the morning when children have not arrived. The inscription on the entrance arch states that this tomb houses the mortal remains of Mohammed Adil Shah, who, on his death, became "an inhabitant of Paradise and also a Particle of the Firmament."

The *Jama Masjid,* built in 1565, has lovely proportions, graceful minarets, and lovely bulbous domes and is covered with ornamental detail. You can enter the courtyard, but only Moslems may enter the shrine itself. This is the largest mosque in the Deccan; 2,250 people can pray here, one to each painted block.

The *Ibrahim Rauza* has richly decorated walls and perforated stone windows. Built by Mohammed Adil Shah, it contains the tomb of his father, Ibrahim Adil Shah. Special acoustics enable the voice of the muezzin calling devotees to prayer to be heard from a mosque 200 feet away, while that same voice can't be heard outside the tomb. Try it.

HAMPI

Hampi, the ruins of the Vijayanagar empire, is also a place best appreciated with a government-approved guide, which can be arranged at the Hospet Tourist Bureau. A reasonable visit of the considerable ruins, spanning 15 miles, requires a day. The grand flourish of this empire lasted from the fourteenth to the mid-sixteenth century. Do not miss seeing the *Virupaksha Temple* (visit early in the morning when the temple bells are rung and the monkeys come running to eat); the *Vitthala Temple Complex,* with its renowned stone chariot; and the *Hazara Rama Complex.*

MYSORE

Chamundi Hill is named after the royal family's patron goddess, Chamundi. See the 16-foot *Nandi,* constructed in the seventeenth century from a single granite boulder; the *Sri Chamundeswari Temple* dating back to the twelfth century, with a richly carved tower constructed in the eighteenth century; and the *statue of Mahishasura,* built of mortar about 35 years ago (the goddess Chamundi killed this demon to bring peace to the country).

Lalitha Mahal Palace, now a hotel, was built in 1921 by the maharajah for his foreign guests. Beautiful interior and exterior. Have tea, at least.

Maharajah's Mysore Palace, built in 1857 on the former site of a former wooden palace that burned down, is one of the biggest palaces in India. The architecture is Indo-Saracenic, a synthesis of Hindu and Islamic design. On Sundays and holidays, the palace is illuminated with thousands of tiny lights. See the impressive Durbar Hall, with its ornate ceiling and huge "grandstand" awning. Also, the Kalyana Mandap (Marriage Hall), where women sat behind screened balconies; on the wall are lifelike paintings of the Dussehra procession. Plan at least an hour. Open 10:30 A.M.–5:30 P.M.

SRAVANABELGOLA

Here, you'll find a colossal statue of the Jain saint, *Gomateswara.* The monolithic statue is 57 feet high and over a 1,000 years old. The statue's nakedness is symbolic of the renunciation of worldly possessions.

SRINANGAPATNA

This is an island fortress and former capital of the Mysore rajah from 1610 to 1799. Its most famous residents were Hyder Ali and Tipu Sultan. Visit the fortress with the mosque inside; the summer palace called *Daria Daulat;* and Tipu Sultan's mausoleum, the *Gumbaz* (both are outside the fort).

SRINGERI

Sringeri is an important Hindu center of pilgrimage. See St. Sankaracharya's monastery, created just at the start of the Vijayanagar empire, and the fourteenth-century *Vidya Shankara Temple,* with its 12 zodiac pillars arranged so that the sun's rays fall on the pillar that corresponds to that month.

TALKAD

Talkad's 30 temples lie beneath a strange stretch of sand dunes on the banks of the Cauvery River. Two main temples are the *Vaidyesvara,* a Dravidian temple of granite perhaps built in the fourteenth century, with later additions; and the beautiful *Kirtinarayana,* possibly erected in 1117 (an example of the Hoysalan style temple). The sand is a result of deforestation, the construction of a reservoir in the fourteenth century, and the yearly monsoon.

MUSEUMS AND GALLERIES. Entrance to these places is free or nominal cost. **Bangalore.** *Government Museum,* set in Cubbon Park and established in 1887, is one of the oldest museums in India. It has exhibits in archaeology, ethnology, geology, art, and sculpture, and excavations from the Mohenjo-Daro ruins that date back to 5000 B.C. Open 10 A.M.–5 P.M., closed Wednesday.

Venkatappa Art Gallery, Cubbon Park, exhibits the work of the court painter, S.K. Venkatappa, who painted in the late 1800s. You can also see musical instruments that he designed. Open 10 A.M.–5 P.M., closed Wednesday.

Mysore. *Sri Jayachamarajendra Art Gallery,* in the Jaganmohan Palace, has various schools of Indian art, beautiful antique furniture, and decorated musical instruments. No picture-taking. Open daily 7:30 A.M.–5:30 P.M.

GARDENS AND ZOOS. Bangalore. *Cubbon Park,* laid out in 1864, has imposing Greco-Colonial-style buildings, including the Public Library, High Court, and Government Museum; plus an aquarium and a delightful toy train for children.

Lal Bagh. The name means red roses, which grow in abundance here. Designed by Hyder Ali in 1760 and added to by his son, Tipu Sultan, the garden has over 100 varieties of trees, thousands of flowers and plants. At the garden center is a stunning glass house reminiscent of the Crystal Palace in London. Its foundation stone was placed by Prince Albert of Wales in 1889. You'll also find a three-billion-year-old rock called Peninsula Gneiss. Annual flower shows are held in January and August. Open 8 A.M.–6 P.M.

Mysore. The *Zoological Garden* has a large and varied collection of animals and birds in a large park. Open 7:30 A.M.–5:30 P.M.

Brindavan Gardens, 19 km (12 mi.) from Mysore, stretch out in terraces below the Krishnarajasagar Dam. At night, garden lights twinkle, fountains play, and, yes, there's music. The lights actually respond rhythmically to the beat. Gardens are lit up for one hour weekday nights and two hours on Sundays and holidays. Nominal entrance fee.

SPORTS AND OUTDOOR ADVENTURES. Beaches. You'll find good beaches near Mangalore. Surathakal, Ullal, Someswaria, and Panambur are okay for swimming, but watch out for the undertow. Just 66 km (41 mi.) north of Mangalore is Malpe, Karnataka's best beach, with great sand and surf. In Udipi, near Malpe, you can enjoy simple, clean accommodations, and lots of tasty seafood. You can also hire a boat to go to St. Mary's Island, a beautiful hideaway with strange rock formations. North of Malpe are Marvanthe, Bilikerem, and Karwar beaches, which are also good for swimming.

Golfing. The *Bangalore Golf Club,* designed by the British in 1876, has temporary memberships and equipment for hire. Call tel. 27121 for details.

Horse Racing. The *Bangalore Turf Club* goes into high gear September–December and March–June. Call tel. 72391 for details.

Wildlife Sanctuaries. *Bandipur Wildlife Sanctuary,* 80 km south of Mysore, covers 689 sq km adjoining the Mudumalai forest. Once the private preserve of the maharajas of Mysore, it offers good opportunities to see herds of bison, elephants, spotted deer, elephants, and, if you're lucky, a tiger or a leopard. There are observation platforms for viewing, and jeep rides are available. For more details, contact the Mysore Tourist Office. The best time to visit is July–February.

Bannerghatta National Park, 22 km from Bangalore, is a new park covering 104 km, with a variety of wildlife, a crocodile farm, and a snake park. It also has a "Lion Safari," where lions roam freely as visitors are transported through in vehicles. Open 9 A.M.–noon and 2–5 P.M., closed Tuesdays.

Nagarahole National Park, 96 km south of Mysore, comprises 572 sq km of forests and swamps that were once part of the exclusive preserve of the maharajahs. It has at least 250 species of birds and numerous animals, including antelopes, bears, jungle cats, barking deer, wild dogs, elephants, langur, mongooses, panthers, porcupines, sambar, tigers, and lots of reptiles. Vehicle and guides are available. Numerous tribesmen also live here (the Jenu Kurubas and Betta Kurubas). You can also trek, with permission from the Chief Wildlife Warden, Aranya Bhavan, 18th Cross, Malleswaram, Bangalore, tel. 31993. Van, jeep, or mini-bus are available for game viewing drives. You can stay at the delightful Kabini River Lodge. The best season is October–March.

Ranganathittu Bird Sanctuary, 18 km from Mysore, is made up of six islets in the Cauvery River. A large variety of birds (night herons, little cormorants, snakebirds, spoon bills), flying foxes, and reptiles. Boating is available. Accommodations are available; contact: KSTDC (address above). The best time to visit is from June to September.

Yoga. *Kalpana* (Lalitha Mahal Palace Hotel, Mysore; tel. 27650) has yoga classes and gives ayurvedic, acupressure, Japanese shiatsu, or Thai massages. Open daily 9 A.M.–10 P.M. Rupees only. They also have a branch at Hotel Hassan Ashok; tel. 8731 for details.

SHOPPING. The skill of the old Karnataka craftsmen is still flourishing; inlaid furniture and ivory and sandalwood carvings are made in a variety of designs that delight the connoisseur. For hundreds of years, Karnataka has been the home of sandalwood. Statuettes and panels, beads, and pendants are executed in this delicately scented wood. Carved tables, screens, and dinner gongs are made in lovely designs. Its silks are also highly rated in India.

Bangalore. Visit these excellent fixed-price shops: *Natesan's Antiqarts* (64 Mahatma Gandhi Rd.) sells an unusual collection of high-quality stone, bronze, and wood antiquities; old paintings; and exquisite new artifacts, plus silver jewelry and precious stones. Merchandise is guaranteed and authorized for export. Open 10 A.M.–8 P.M., closed Sundays. AE, DC, MC, V.

Ashok Silks (Shrungar Shopping Center, Mahatma Gandhi Rd.) sells beautiful silk from Karnataka and all of India by the meter. It also has silk salwar kameez, scarves, men's silk shirts, ties, *kurtas* (pajamas), and can make items quickly on order. Open 10 A.M.–8 P.M., closed Sundays. AE, DC, MC, V.

Roopkala Silks and Sarees (No.1, DJC Complex, Hudson Circle) also sells good silks and a similar range of silk ready-mades. They can design on order. Open daily 10 A.M.–9 P.M. AE, DC, MC, V.

Cauvery (49 Mahatma Gandhi Rd.), a state-run store, sells all of Karnataka's products: sandalwood handicrafts, terra-cotta, carved rosewood furniture, silk, leatherwork, jute products, lacquered toys, bidriwork, embossed bronze, soaps, perfumes, incense, and sachets. Open 10 A.M.–1:30 P.M. and 3–7:30 P.M., closed Sundays. AE, DC.

Mysore. For good sandalwood and rosewood inlaid products, visit *Ganesh Industrial and Fine Art Works*, 532 Dhanavantri Rd. Open daily 9 A.M.–9 P.M. AE, DC, MC, V.

For silks by the meter, visit *K.S.I.C.* (Government Silk Factory Complex, Manandavai Rd.). The silks are excellent and the prices are good. Open 9 A.M.–3 P.M., closed Sundays. Rupees only.

Karnataka Cottage Emporium (Mysore Hotel Complex, opposite Lido Theater, 2729 Bangalore Nilgiri Rd.) also has a good selection of silk. Open daily 9 A.M.–9 P.M. AE, MC, V.

Handicrafts Sales Emporium and Kaveri Silk Emporium (Hotel Dasharath Complex, opposite Mysore Zoo) has a wide range of Karnataka handicrafts and products. Open daily 9 A.M.–6 P.M. AE, DC, MC, V.

NIGHTLIFE AND BARS. Bangalore's prettiest bar is the *Jockey Club*, Taj Residency, 41/3 Mahatma Gandhi Rd. Belgian mirrors are set into carved teak walls; you're surrounded by paintings of Bangalore's derby winners. An exquisite centerpiece of palm trees adds a tropical touch. The lighting is always subdued; and at night, a pianist adds to the mood. Open noon–midnight.

Mysore's best bar is at the *Lalitha Mahal Palace Hotel*. While not palatial, the Victorian furnishings are comfy. The casual ambience feels right. Open 11 A.M.–11 P.M.

HYDERABAD AND ANDHRA PRADESH

India's "Melting Pot"

by
KATHLEEN COX

Andhra Pradesh is not on the itinerary of most Western visitors to India. It should be. The ancient Andhra culture reaches back into the great Indian epics: *Ramayana* and *Mahabharata*. Beautiful temples still stand from the earliest days of Hindu, Jain, and Buddhist worship, as do impressive Moslem forts, mosques, and palaces. A fine stretch of beach along the Bay of Bengal tempts you. Then there's Hyderabad, a fascinating city, with what many travelers regard as the liveliest market in all India.

If you're visiting Goa, Kerala, Madras, or any of southern India's many fascinating places, you'll find Andhra Pradesh on your route. Planes, trains, and buses from the north pass through Hyderabad on their way south. Spend four or five days in Hyderabad and its environs and enjoy the rich and varied culture, shopping, and delicious food.

Geographically, Andhra Pradesh includes fertile river systems in the north, the arid vastness of the Deccan plain, an extensive coastline along the Bay of Bengal, and the hilly Chitaur district of the south. Situated in central India, Andhra Pradesh has always been a "melting pot." Here many great forces in Indian history clashed, mixed, and created the unique character of this region. Hindu, Jain, and Buddhist sites are within a few kilometers of one another. Moslem buildings are fashioned from the stones of Hindu structures, and mosques and Moslem palaces are decorated with Hindu motifs.

Andhra's history reaches back to the time of Emperor Ashoka (c. 230 B.C.), when this state marked the southern boundary of his great empire. At Ashoka's death, Satavahana, a local chieftain, established a dynasty that would endure for four centuries. The Ikshavaku rulers who succeeded the Satavahanas lasted only 57 years, yet it was during their reign that Buddhist culture flowered. The Buddhist monastery in Nagarjunakonda Valley was built at this time—a major center of learning for all southeast Asia. The Pallavas of Tamil Nadu held sway over much of Andhra Pradesh for 3½ centuries until the Chalukyas supplanted them. Under successive Chalukyan kings, Andhra's Telegu culture came into its own. Each of India's major regions is fiercely proud of its language; yet all over India, Telegu is known for its gracefulness and intrinsic musical qualities.

In the thirteenth century, the Kakatiyas undertook bold projects to control the great river systems of northern Andhra. Then, in the fourteenth century, Moslem armies of the Delhi Sultanate swept through the Deccan plateau and captured two Hindu princes in Warangal. The princes were brought to Delhi, converted to Islam, and sent south to establish a Moslem stronghold in Andhra and Karnataka. But the new religion had less hold than the wish for power.

In 1336, one of the two "converts" established the Vijayanagar kingdom, and for close to two centuries Vijayanagar rulers struggled for power with their Moslem counterparts—the Bahmanis, whose kingdom across the Krishna River included the fabled diamond mines of Golconda. Tension between ambitious Hindu and Moslem forces placed much of Andhra in a state of constant strife. But, in years to come, these clashing elements would be reconciled and give rise to the region's vigorous mixed culture.

In 1518, Qutb Shahi broke away from the Bahmani kingdom and founded a dynasty responsible for the creation of Hyderabad and its memorable architecture. The dynasty ruled for 100 years until Aurangzeb's armies of the north conquered the area in 1687. Intrigue and treachery marked the next 40 years as the Mogul administration in Delhi tried in vain to maintain control over its new conquests in the Deccan. When Aurangzeb died in 1717, only seven years passed before Nizam-ul-Mulk took power and founded the Asafia Dynasty, known for its fabulously rich rulers (Nizams), who controlled the region—India's largest and most important princely state—until Independence in 1947.

EXPLORING ANDHRA PRADESH

When you visit Andhra Pradesh, expect variety in the scenery. The Eastern Ghats wind their hilly way along the eastern and northern borders; dense forests stretch along the east near the Bay of Bengal and farther west near Warangal. To the south is the Deccan plateau, which lies across all India at this longitude, and two important rivers that flow toward the sea: the northern Godavari and the southern Krishna. Sleepy canals serve as inland waterways. The weather remains humid year round, with relatively little variation in temperature. The environment is ideal for coconut palms, mango trees, and lush flowers. The world's third-largest artificial lake spills around the Nagarjunasagar Dam, a recently constructed gigantic hydroelectric project. Around Hyderabad City, huge granite boulders are strewn naturally on the bare plain as if by giants playing a game.

HYDERABAD

Today, Andhra Pradesh preserves vivid monuments from its complex past. There's no better place to begin than in Hyderabad. With upwards of 1½ million inhabitants, Hyderabad is India's fifth-largest city. Unlike so many of this nation's cultural attractions, Hyderabad doesn't have its origins in antiquity. The city derives its name from the romantic liaison of the Moslem ruler, Quli Qutb Shahi—the fourth king of the Qutb Shahi Dynasty that ruled from the forbidding fortress of Golconda. This king had a Hindu mistress named Bhagyamati (*bhagya* = lady luck; *mati* = harbinger). Early in his reign, he started building a new city because the Golconda stronghold had grown crowded and unhealthy. Six kilometers (3.6 miles) to the south by the river Musi he found a site, which he named Bhagyanagar—city of good luck—after his mistress. Here he erected a palace for her and named it Hydermahal. Later, in 1589, Bhagyanagar was renamed after this palace—and Hyderabad was born.

The diamond mines of Golconda gave the Nizams unlimited resources. Hyderabad is filled with magnificent structures—palaces that have been converted to public buildings, hotels, hospitals, universities, and museums.

The Heart of Hyderabad

The center of Hyderabad is defined by four great arches facing the cardinal points. Charkaman (*char* = four; *karman* = gate) was constructed by Quli Qutb Shahi in 1592 when Hyderabad was still coming into being. Within the area defined by these arches, you'll find Charminar and Mecca Masjid, the city's two most striking structures, as well as a teeming market filled with Hyderabad's well-known pearl and bangle shops.

Charminar (four towers or minarets) is a rectangular granite edifice built in 1591. The building has elegant, tall arches and four minarets and is designed in Indo-Saracenic style—which, like so much of Andhra culture, means it combines elements of both Moslem and Hindu art. The arches, domes, and minarets show Persian-Islamic influence, while various decorative motifs of leaves, petals, and flowers are done in Hindu style. At one time, an underground tunnel connected Charminar with Golconda Fort, some six kilometers (3.6 miles) away.

Walk through the Charminar Market and you'll understand why Hyderabad is a shopper's paradise. Here you can buy all kinds of fabrics, especially cotton prints and lightweight shirts and drawstring pants made from *khadi* cloth. Hyderabad is also famous for *nirmal* toys: wooden figurines of people and animals painted in bright lacquer. There's also *bidriware:* trays, vases, boxes, and other objects made from an alloy of zinc and copper that turns gun-metal black—in vivid contrast to the silver patterns traced across its surface. For Rs. 250–600 you can buy a terrific example of this ancient craft. Ask someone to point you to *laad* (lacquer) bazaar, a bustling side street where bangles, pottery, nirmal toys, and bidriware are displayed in many stalls.

Best of all, Hyderabad is the unlikely world center for the pearl trade. Here in Charminar, in the heart of landlocked Andhra Pradesh, there are hundreds of shops dealing in pearl jewelry of all qualities and description. The pearls come from China and Japan: India's skilled jewelers and inexpensive labor make it a profitable enterprise. If you come looking for perfectly shaped natural pearls, you'll find them—but at no particular bargain. Instead, let the shopkeeper show you rice pearls, wheat pearls, flower pearls, seed pearls, Chinese bean pearls in various shapes and sizes. For less than Rs. 600, you can buy an attractive triple-strand necklace of rice pearls. You can try to bargain, but prices are set according to weight, so unless you're making a fairly substantial purchase, don't expect the shopkeeper to knock more than 10 percent off the asking price. The two most respected shops are Mangatrai and Omprakash & Sons, both in the Charminar area. Just ask—everyone knows where they are. Mangatrai has a new air-conditioned shop outside the Charminar Market on Bashir Bagh, opposite Hotel Naragjuna, where you can see the jewelry being made. Prices are the same; you'll be more comfortable, but you'll miss the fun of buying pearls in the picturesque Moslem market.

Mecca Masjid is the second-largest mosque in India (after Jama Masjid in Old Delhi) and the seventh-largest mosque in the world. Its enormous colonnades are carved from single slabs of granite. Ten thousand people can gather under its double dome and in its vast courtyard for prayer. (Non-Moslems are welcome except during prayer services.)

Mecca Masjid is so named because soil was brought from the holy city of Mecca and mixed with Indian soil when construction was started in 1618. According to legend, completion of the mosque would herald the end of the Qutb Shahi Dynasty. Aurangzeb's forces defeated the Qutb Shahi armies, bringing central India under the sway of the Delhi moguls in 1687—the very year that construction of Mecca Masjid was finally completed.

Salar Jung Museum

The Salar Jung family served the Nizams of Hyderabad for five generations as prime ministers. In 1911, the last of the Nizams, Mir Osman Ali Khan, appointed the youthful Mir Yousuf Ali Khan to serve him as Salar Jung III. But this new prime minister was more devoted to art and literature than to his administrative duties. Within three years, he resigned his post and spent the rest of his life amassing an eclectic collection of some 45,000 objects, ranging from ivory furniture and jewel-crusted weapons to children's toys. When he died in 1949, he left his collection to the government of India. The museum is worth a visit.

The first room you enter is the Portrait Gallery. Here canvases depict the Nizam Dynasty. If you have a guide, he or she will tell you with the utmost conviction that Mahboob Ali Khan, the sixth Nizam, was so blessed that the mere mention of his name cured someone of the disastrous consequences of a poisonous snakebite.

At the far end of the room is a display case in which Salar Jung kept two dozen clay figurines, each modeled after one of his personal attendants. Possibly people of such great wealth and power too easily confused human lives with clay figures.

In other rooms, there are displays of magnificent silver and crystal pieces presented to Salar Jung by the British royal family, including a collection of stone sculptures from all over India: Chola, Pallava, Jain, and Buddhist art. In the gallery for wood carving you'll see elaborately carved furniture, plus a formidable representation of Garuda, the bird-like creature who is Lord Vishnu's mount (and the symbol of Indonesian Airlines.)

Two works of Western art draw the attention of curiosity seekers. *The Veiled Rebecca* by Benzoni, done in 1876, is a marble statue of a woman draped in a veil. It's more like a trick-or-treater done up as a ghost or a "wrapping" by the conceptual artist Christo. The second bizarre piece is *Mephistopheles and Margaretta,* a German work of the nineteenth century.

From the front, you'll stand face to face with Goethe's satanic tempter. From the other side, all you see is the virtuous Margaretta. Good and evil back to back.

Don't miss the eighteenth century clock that presides over a covered courtyard. Children gather on benches to watch a mechanical blacksmith pound out the seconds on his anvil. On the hour, 10 soldiers file out of a sentry station to ring a brass bell the appropriate number of times. It's as much fun to watch the children as it is to watch the clock.

Golconda Fort

Eight kilometers (five miles) from the center of Hyderabad the ruins of Golconda Fort sprawled for many acres over the top of a granite hill. The fort's origins go back to the thirteenth century, but it was rebuilt by the Qutb Shahi Dynasty in 1525 where it remained their seat of power for 162 years until Aurangzeb seized the fort after a ten-year seige.

At one time Golconda was the center of one of the world's great diamond markets, making it the object of curiosity from Marco Polo and the first European visitors of the thirteenth and fourteenth centuries. Golconda's riches provided extra incentive to the northern moguls' dreams of expanding south. The Hope Diamond, the Orloff Diamond of Catherine the Great, and the British Crown's Kohinoor diamond all came from mines near the fort.

Climb the steep stone steps to a panoramic view of the city and surrounding countryside. Move on to Qutb Shahi Tombs where the seven rulers of the dynasty were laid to rest. Here, as at Charminar, you'll see Moslem architectural design joined with Hindu motifs in a style that's typical of Hyderabad. The dome and square base of the tombs are Moslem, as is the gallery of pointed arches. Hindu motifs include lotus leaves and buds, a chain and pendant design, projecting leaves, and cruciform capitals.

EXPLORING OUT OF HYDERABAD

Once you've seen Hyderabad, take in sights in the surrounding regions. Bidar Fort (see *Karnataka* chapter) is 132 kilometers (82 miles) northwest of the city and can be visited in a day's excursion. For those with two or three free days, an interesting tour can take in Warangal, Ramappa Temple, Nagarjunakonda, and Srisailam—a loop that will give you a vivid sampling of Hindu, Jain, Moslem, and Buddhist culture.

Yadagirigutta and Mahaveer Jain Temple

Warangal, your destination, is 140 kilometers (85 miles) north of Hyderabad on the Hanamkonda Road. There are two worthwhile stops along the way. When you are 69 kilometers (41 miles) out of Hyderabad, you'll pass through the town of Bhongir. A few kilometers more and you'll spot Yadagirigutta (in Telegu, *yada* means shepherd; *giri* and *Cutta* both mean hill), a small village perched at the foot of a rocky hill. Legend has it that Lord Vishnu revealed himself to the local saint, Yadava, by appearing in three forms of *narasimha* (*nara* = human; *simha* = lion). It is said that Lord Vishnu made this spot his abode, residing in a cave that, in time, became covered by thick forest. Many years later, Vishnu appeared to a local villager in a dream and guided him to the holy spot where the villager discovered a natural cave containing the three narasimha images. A temple was built to mark the sacred shrine for Hindu pilgrims.

It's worth a 30-minute detour to see *Lakshmi Narasimha Swami Temple,* an unprepossessing structure built around the legendary cave that serves as sanctus sanctorum. Even if there weren't a temple, the trip would be worthwhile if only to climb the hill at Yadagirigutta for a view of the Deccan Plateau spreading majestically in every direction. In some respects it's evocative of sections of the American plains; yet the view remains distinctly Indian, with palm trees, simple huts, oxen, and busy villages dotting the great expanse.

Enter the temple and pass on to the inner sanctum, flanked by silver portals. Inside the holy cave, you'll see Lord Vishnu in his half-lion, half-human incarnation slaying the demon Kiranyakasipa. Give yourself time to stand back and watch the pilgrims file in. They have come hundreds of miles to pray in this sacred cave.

Most temples sell *prassadum* (god's gift)—food that pilgrims buy to take home to relatives and friends as a way of sharing their blessings. Here, for only one rupee, you can buy a delicious *pulihara,* a tasty mixture of rice, tamarind, and spices served on a coconut leaf. It is clean, nourishing food—a fine snack for less than a dime.

From here on to Warangal, look for toddy tapsters clambering up the palm trees with pots and tools slung over their shoulders and tied around their waist. Just 15 kilometers (nine miles) north of Yadagirigutta and 10 minutes off the main highway, you will come to Kolanapaka and the Mahaveer Jain Temple, a pleasant cluster of small buildings that houses magnificent sculptures of Jain *tirthankaras* (perfect souls). The temple is flanked by two elephant heads carved in bas-relief at the foot of the entrance. These are *dwarapalaka* (door guards) placed there to drive away visitors with evil intentions. Nevertheless, their spirit is far more one of *swagatham* (welcome) than of forbidding authority.

A few minutes inside this temple will reveal the power of Jain art. Sculptures of various Jain tirthankaras reside in closet-sized niches, seated in the Buddha-like lotus posture. Yet these Jain figures appear more muscular and energetic than the serene Buddha. Whereas the Buddha usually seems content to keep his position through all eternity, those broad-shouldered, barrel-chested deities look ready to jump up at any moment and do something unexpected.

In the far left corner of the main hall is a charming sculpture of the subdeity Sri Bumiya Ji and his son Sri Manibadr Ji that looks like an amiable pumpkin and child. To the right is Mahaveer himself—the twenty-fourth and last Jain god—five feet high and solid jade! Mahaveer's lips curl in a wide, radiant smile. You will see few works of art of any religion that are so generously concerned with the joy of existence.

In Jain temples, there are often several sculptural representations of deities, all of them virtually identical. But here, the sculptures are sharply individual. To Mahaveer's right is Adeshwar, first of the Jain gods. The jewels in his forehead are valued at close to half a million dollars. And nearby is Shankeshwar, the second of the 24 gods—equally expressive, though less lavishly endowed.

All these gods have eerie, piercing eyes that, literally, bulge from their heads. Actually, each sculpture has a less startling set of eyes carved into the stone itself. What we see are called *chakshu* (spectacles) that have been added on to the deities to give them a startling, formidable presence. It makes us stop and take notice.

Warangal

Warangal, which includes the old town of Hanamkonda, was once the capital of the Kakatiya kingdom that controlled two-thirds of present Andhra Pradesh for most of the twelfth and thirteenth centuries. Warangal is best known for its mighty fort that now lies in ruins. Even so, enough remains to suggest the scope and ambition of the Kakatiya rulers.

Constructed between 1199 and 1261, Warangal Fort was surrounded by three walls. Driving through the Warangal area, you can still see traces of the outlying wall that once covered 127 kilometers (76 miles) to encircle this stronghold. The middle wall is still visible in most parts; a sloped earthen mound facing out on a broad moat. These two walls served to impede large invading forces. The inner wall, an imposing stone fortification, turns a daunting vertical face to the outside; on the inside, the wall is built in steps so the Kakatiya defenders could rapidly mount the parapets to repel an attacking army. Marco Polo once passed through the triple-turning entrance and made his way to the dazzling royal court within.

When you arrive at the site of the Kakatiya court, you'll see a rugged hill nearby. Actually, it's one enormous boulder. This was an ancient religious site, named, appropriately, *orunallu* (one stone). Centuries later, Moslem rulers inadvertently transformed the ancient Telegu to Warangal.

Though the Kakatiya were ambitious builders, they were not completely practical. Their great buildings were erected on sand rather than stone foundations. In time, the great walls of Warangal Fort sank under their own weight; pillars tilted and fell, and the roof caved in. The awesome hall that Marco Polo visited is now a large field of broken columns and fractured statues. Goats graze among the solemn ruins. Still, it's a stirring sight.

Only the four grand entrance gates *(thorana)* remain standing. Each thorana is supported by four monolith pillars rising nine meters (30 feet). Perched on the crossbars atop these pillars are pairs of *hamsa,* the emblematic bird of India's ancient kings. Somewhere between a swan and a fat duck, the hamsa's blue blood is made clear in a legend not unlike *The Princess and the Pea.* It is said that if equal parts of milk and water were mixed together in a bowl, the hamsa would sup at it and remove only the water, skillfully leaving the milk untouched. Apparently, milk was too thick for the hamsa's delicate blood. Today, these remarkable birds are as extinct as dodos.

In 1323, the Kakatiyas submitted to the overwhelming might of Tughlaq Moslem invaders from Delhi. Sitab Khan was a military commander who was appointed district governor of the Warangal Fort area in the early fourteenth century. To celebrate his good fortune, he began to build Kush Mahal, which you can look at while you're exploring the fort.

The story of Kush Mahal is like a moral fable. Kush Mahal means happy home, and for Sitab Khan, happiness came from pillaging Hindu religious sites to gather construction materials for his Moslem dream house. If you look carefully, high up on arches that once supported the ceiling, you can see stones carved with the Hindu lotus, Sitab Khan's way of boasting of the temples he dismantled. On other stones, you can make out the Moslem crescent moon. Lotus and cresent moon—united by conquest. But Sitab Khan never had the chance to enjoy the happy home that looting built. He died before its completion.

The 1,000 Pillar Temple in Warangal will introduce you to Chalukyan temple design. Instead of the soaring grandeur of Tamil Nadu temple construction, here we have low star-shaped buildings—intimate and cloistered—built on a series of platforms. This is a Shiva temple (the Kakatiyas were great devotees of Shiva. Like virtually all Shiva temples of the south, there are three main architectural elements:

• The *mandipam* is a formal entrance hall used for festivals, marriages, and celebrations. The mandipam here is dilapidated because of an inadequate foundation. The ceiling has fallen, and pillars tilt at crazy angles.

• Passing through the mandipam, you come to a small central courtyard presided over by a monolith statue of *Nandi*. Nandi, the bull, is Shiva's vehicle—as much a part of the god's life and legend as Silver is to the Lone Ranger.

• Worshipers touch Nandi's flanks before entering the *temple* to pray at the Shiva *lingam* (phallic symbol). Hindu gods are each called by dozens of different names according to regional legends and language differences. Here Shiva is known as Rudresvara.

Many centuries ago, an underground passage connected this temple to Warangal Fort, some 11 kilometers (6.6 miles) away. It's exhausting just imagining the effort that went into tunneling through all that stone and rocky earth.

The well beside the temple is still working after over 800 years. Both the well and the temple were completed in 1163.

Only a few minutes from the 1,000 Pillar Temple is Bhadrakali Temple. It overlooks a broad, shallow lake where fishermen stand waist-deep in the silty water to cast their nets. The temple and its stone image of Kali (or Durga, as she is called elsewhere)—with her eight hands all brandishing weapons—require only a brief visit. Most interesting, perhaps, is the opportunity you'll have to get a vivid glimpse of Indian life, for this is a popular pilgrimage spot.

Indian villagers in the Warangal area pay from their minuscule savings to go on packaged bus tours that bring them to several such temples and holy shrines in a few days. The buses bring their own cooks, utensils, and food. It's likely that you'll encounter one of these groups resting or eating on the covered stone terrace just outside the inner temple.

Palampet

In Palampet, 64 kilometers (38 miles) from Warangal, Rudresvara Temple (popularly called Ramappa Temple) has some of the finest sculpture in India. The temple stands less than a kilometer away from Ramappa Dam, a mammoth wall of earth formed to link two chains of hills and thus create an artificial lake. Built by the Kakatiyas in 1213, the dam clearly indicates the Kakatiyas' strong belief that the gods meant for them to rule and control the land.

Like all Hindu temples, Rudresvara faces east, though now visitors approach it from its western porch where the goporum is currently under restoration. Before entering the temple, examine the basalt obelisk in the courtyard. The Telegu inscription proudly proclaims the creation of Ramappa Lake and of the Shiva temple. The top of the obelisk is adorned with different images on each of its four faces: (1) the shiva lingam, (2) Ganesha, Shiva's beloved son, (3) Nandi, and (4) a double image of the sun (representing the Hindu faith) and crescent moon (symbol of Moslem faith). The implication is that there's room on this planet for many religions, but the great god Shiva includes all faiths.

At one time, a canal diverted water from the nearby lake to form a shallow basin around the temple's outer wall—the architect's way of acknowledging that Hindu worshipers must bathe their feet before entering a temple.

Much of the pleasure this temple offers comes from the sculptural elements along the outer walls. The base of the temple has four layers of sculptured bands that wrap around the entire building. At the bottom is a procession of hundreds of elephants that represent the earthly power of the Kakatiya Dynasty. Only along the southwest wall is the procession interrupted to include a menagerie of snakes, birds, and other indigenous wildlife. Above the elephants is a row of open lotus blossoms, a sign of faith and, presumably, the divine favor shown to the Kakatiyas. The third strip of sculpture depicts various aspects of social life. Each of the hundreds of panels is unique. There are images of dance, music, wrestling, social customs, worship, and sexual intercourse. Above these lively images of twelfth-century life is a second strip of lotus flowers to remind believers that transient life is surrounded by the eternal kingdom of god.

Charming as these representations are, probably more striking are the black basalt human figures that peer down as brackets above the outer platform. Most other Hindu temples contain the repeated figures of Narasimha, the "human lion," perched triumphantly on an elephant's head. Here, an interesting feature has been added. Standing between the elephant's head and the squatting lion is a human form, further reminder that the Kakatiyas saw themselves as wielding the combined qualities of these creatures—the elephant's brute strength and the lion's warriorlike ferocity.

Flanking the three entrances to the temple are the most notable sculptures to be found at Palampet: pairs of lively female figures, almost life-size, carved from highly polished basalt. No matter what these women are doing, they seem to be dancing. Their simplicity, energy, and lithesome form reminds one of Matisse's dance panels, done near the end of his career. Beside the north porch, one of these women is caught in a crisis: a monkey has yanked her sari loose; with one hand she shoos away the mischievous creature, with the other, she tries to cover her private parts. Along the east porch, a woman hunter balances on one leg while an attendant removes a thorn from her foot. Also on the east porch is a dancing woman wearing the twelfth-century's version of platform shoes.

Inside the temple are more fine sculptures, though nothing is quite as impressive as the 12 figure brackets that stand outside. The four basalt pillars and the ceiling are crowded with scenes from the great religious epics. Particularly charming is a panel carved on the pillar to the right of the inner sanctum. Krishna, the playboy of the Hindu deities, has stolen all the clothing of a group of shepherd girls he saw bathing. The panel shows Krishna sitting merrily in a tree while the naked girls implore him to restore their clothes.

Even the most knowledgeable guide won't be able to account for all the legends and epics represented in this temple. Nevertheless, you'll be dazzled by the gaiety and sheer abundance of sculpture that makes Rudresvara Temple such an important site.

After you see the temple, you may want to stop at the Vanavihar Tourist Rest House for a snack or a cup of tea.

Less than one kilometer away and overlooking the lake, it is a lovely spot to relax before your return to Warangal.

Nagarjunakonda

A day's drive from Warangal (240 kilometers or 144 miles) or a shorter excursion from Hyderabad (144 kilometers or 86 miles) will bring you to the town of Nagarjunasagar, where one of the world's largest dams blocks the Krishna River. In 1926, excavations in the Nagarjunakonda Valley uncovered relics from the early and middle stone age, as well as evidence of a great Buddhist civilization that flourished here during the third and fourth centuries. After Prime Minister Nehru set in motion the Nagarjunasaga Dam project in 1954, Indian archaeological teams devoted six hurried years to saving as many of the Buddhist treasures as they could. In 1960, the historic valley disappeared beneath the vast artificial lake created by the dam, but treasures from the Buddhist temples and learning center have been relocated and beautifully exhibited in the government museum set on Nagarjunakonda Island, 10 kilometers (six miles) from the dam.

At Anupa, five kilometers (three miles) from the dam, a *vihara* (Buddhist monastery) has been partially reconstructed from stones and pillars unearthed during excavations of the valley. This vihara was created by the Buddhist scholar, Acharya (teacher) Nagarjuna, founder of the Madhyamika school of Mahayana Buddhism, as his instrument for teaching: a study center that attracted Buddhist scholars from as far away as Kashmir, Uttar Pradesh, Sri Lanka, and Southeast Asia. Here, Nagarjuna taught medicine, engineering, surgery, and astronomy, as well as pursued alchemical experiments in search of *amrit,* the heavenly herbal medicine said to produce immortality. (Legend has it that he succeeded and took a deep draught himself, a poetic way of saying that the spirit of the man lives on.) It's from Nagarjuna's teaching that Buddhism developed the doctrine of *Shunyata* (the void), the belief that we are surrounded by delusory forms and notions—that the truly enlightened reject illusion and experience all as a great, unchanging void.

The first thing you'll encounter as you approach the vihara site is a circular brick structure. This was once a *stupa,* an integral element in Buddhist worship that symbolizes the Buddha himself and his spiritual progress to nirvana, beyond all concepts and forms. The stupa's parasol-like crown was divided into eight sections representing eight great precepts of the Buddha's teachings: (1) *Devatha:* devotion to God, to the Lord Buddha; (2) *Ghourva:* respect for one's guru or teacher; (3) *Ahimsa:* refusal to cause pain, injury, or physical punishment to one's fellow beings, which became an essential part of Gandhi's philosophy of nonviolence; (4) *Dharma:* obedience to sacred law; (5) *Moxa:* faith in salvation, striving for enlightenment; (6) *Araha:* renunciation of wealth and material needs; (7) *Kama:* renunciation of carnal desire; and (8) *Sanga:* commitment to the society of fellow Buddhists.

Turn from the remains of the eight-spoked stupa and you face a low brick wall that was once the main residential hall of the monastery. *Mahayana,* the form of Buddhism practiced by Nagarjuna, regards the Buddha as both a teacher and a god, whereas *Hinayana,* the older and more orthodox sect, regards the Buddha as supreme teacher but not as God. Both branches of Buddhist thought were given separate meditation chambers at Nagarjuna's monastery. To the left is a meditation room, or *chaitya griha* (*chaitya* = idol; *griha* = house), where Mahayanas could meditate before an idol in the Buddha's image. To the right is an identical building, but it is a *stupa griha* (house with stupa), where Hinayanas could meditate on the Buddha's teachings without having to worship before a carved representation of the Buddha himself.

Just outside the door to the chaitya griha is a semicircular step ringed with a frieze of carved animal figures. This step, called "moonstone," symbolizes the Buddha's concept that life is a fragile bubble (the curved stone suggests the bubble shape), a reminder that our task in life is to seek enlightenment before the bubble bursts. A second function of the moonstone was to divert one's attention before entering the sacred space. When one's eyes were drawn down to the curved step and the animal figures, one was supposed to empty one's mind of evil thoughts. Otherwise, the intense act of meditating might accidentally concentrate the "evil eye" with such force that the entire shrine might shatter.

Nagarjunakonda Museum

A pleasant 20-minute boat ride leads to Nagarjunakonda Island and a gem of a museum. In the entrance gallery of the museum, on the wall to the right, are photographs of the excavations that unearthed the collection that is housed here. One series of photos shows several jars—terra-cotta, copper, silver, and gold—fashioned to fit inside each other in decreasing size. Inside the small gold jar, archaeologists found human bones, along with an inscription attesting that these were from the Buddha himself. The bones are not exhibited; they are kept in a secure vault on the island. But their very presence makes Nagarjunakonda a place of great importance to the Buddhist faithful.

At the entrance to the main exhibition hall, the visitor is greeted by a pair of chubby troll-like creatures. These are *Yaksha Padmanidhi* (*yaksha* = god of wealth; *padma* = lotus). Their heads are decorated with hanging lotus petals. A geyser of gold coins springs from the crown of each head, falling in a giant braid into each creature's left hand. It's an auspicious greeting: may you, too, be blessed with prosperity.

There are many appealing sculptures in this bright, spacious room. But if you want to learn a bit more about the Buddha's life, you can begin by studying the fourth display on the left wall, which is divided into five sections, each depicting a crucial stage in the story of the Buddha. Beginning on the far right of the panel you see the Buddha's birth (in 563 B.C.); his Renunciation, when the Buddha left behind his wife, family, and earthly riches to seek enlightenment; Mara's attack, the temptation of sexuality and various negative emotional forces; the Buddha's first preaching at Sarnath; and the Buddha's death.

As with so many artists, the sculptor who created this five-part narrative appears to have lavished particular attention on the forces of temptation. Mara's attack is depicted in the middle section: the Buddha sits in the center of the scene while, to the right, sexual demons plot against him. To the left of the Buddha, Kama (sex) tries to tempt him, and just below Kama, wicked cherubs representing pride and miserliness await their chance to besiege him. On the far left of this group, pride (in woman's form) glowers harshly; beneath her, a little demon, anger, joins the band of tempters. The Buddha, of course, remains divinely unperturbed.

It's impossible to spend more than a few moments in the exhibition hall without being drawn to the 10-foot statue of the Buddha that dominates the room. No need for description—it communicates without words.

The renunciation episode in the Buddha's life is narrated with economy and understated emotion in display No. 48, which hangs in the exhibition room connected to the main hall from the right. The story is told in three sections proceeding from the bottom to the top. As a young prince, Siddhartha Gautama (the Historic Buddha) led a cloistered life that was calculated to shield him from the harshness of the external world. The bottom bas-relief depicts the day Siddhartha explored the marketplace. The scenes of human misery and mortality—an old man, a diseased man, a corpse, and an ascetic who had renounced the world—disturbed him, and he understands the shallowness of his youthful vision of life. The middle section shows Siddhartha spending the night reflecting on what he has seen and vowing to pursue the ascetic's path. In the top section, he leaves his father's palace in search of enlightenment.

Though the museum is small, it's easy to enjoy several hours here and outside in the pleasant gardens. But make sure you arrange in town for a government guide to accompany you before you go. The Andhra Pradesh Tourist Department provides guides at no charge, and they'll bring these storytelling friezes to life. (The booking counter for the boat shuttle is near the dam. It costs 10 rupees round trip. Try to book in advance at the government tourist department office.)

Amaravati

Another ancient Buddhist center, Amaravati, lies east of Nagarjunasagar on the right bank of the Krishna, a river inseparably linked with the history and culture of this region. Formerly an ancient Buddhist capital known as Dhyanakataka, Amaravati was a flourishing center of Buddhism in the first century B.C.—one of the four most important places of Buddhist worship in the country. Monasteries and a university brought devotees from as far away as China.

The ruins of the 2,000-year-old settlement are highly poetic, and much of the Buddhist culture is extremely elegant and remarkably well preserved. The stupa was originally the largest in the country. Although its size has been diminished (ravaged by the less spiritual), the richly carved panels and remaining friezes showing scenes of the life of the Buddha are beautiful and worth your careful scrutiny.

Srisailam

Srisailam offers few of the conveniences that many Western travelers seek, but visitors who are willing to make a long day's excursion (from Hyderabad or Nagarjunasagar) or stay in a shabby government tourist house, will be rewarded by a firsthand look at the powerful emotion generated by Hindu worship.

Bhramaramba is the regional name for the goddess Durga (or Kali). Mallikarjunaswamy is the regional name for Shiva. Here Shiva and Durga exist in perpetual honeymoon—married anew every evening in a ceremony performed for thousands of pilgrims who flock here from all over India. This temple is particularly revered, for it holds one of the 12 *Jyotorlingas* in India. (Jyoto means light—in this case, spiritual light.) These 12 Jyotorlingas are said to have been formed by the divine force of nature itself.

In the central courtyard, a large map of India shows the location of the other 11 Jyotorlingas. These sacred places are scattered in every corner of the subcontinent.

This temple has no outstanding architectural or sculptural features, but its importance and popularity make it a memorable place to experience a Hindu prayer service. As you approach the temple, you'll see worshipers buying small baskets filled with coconut, fruits, and fragrant jasmine to offer the deity. Inside the low-ceilinged worship hall, devotees crowd along a metal railing, while a priest passes down the central aisle, chanting as he makes his way from the small Nandi statue toward the sanctus sanctorum, the small room that houses the sacred lingam. These quiet moments are merely a prelude to the actual ceremony. The priest enters the sanctus sanctorum and draws back a curtain to reveal the Jyotorlingam beneath a brass canopy covered with lotus blossoms. Instantly, an incredible clamor breaks forth—imagine a railroad train crashing through an orchestra that is playing *The Rites of Spring*. Drums, bells, curved horns, and brass gongs join in a deafening riot of sound. Numerous devotional candles are lit and passed over the lingam, as the Hindu faithful clasp their hands in prayer: wonder, reverence, and delight reflected in their faces.

This ceremony lasts for 10 minutes, after which the priest files past the worshipers once again, distributing jasmine flowers and collecting offerings. Worshipers are then invited into the sanctus sanctorum (non-Hindus can join them), where they kneel to kiss the lingam.

Note: It's best to attend the first prayer service at 5:45 A.M. to avoid the long lines that form by mid-morning.

There are several other temples here and numerous other shrines in the Srisailam area, but nothing else leaves the lasting impression of this joyful ceremony.

The Bay of Bengal

Unless you're journeying between Calcutta or Bhubaneswar and Madras, this area is off the beaten path. Nevertheless, it offers several interesting attractions. Visakhapatnam, or Vizag, as it is commonly known, is a thriving seaport flanked by long stretches of excellent beach. Rama Krishna Mission Beach is one of the cleanest beaches on India's east coast. Mount Kailas, six kilometers (3.6 miles) away, overlooks another good beach.

From Vizag it's only a short trip (16 kilometers or 9.6 miles), to Simhachalam (hill of the lion), famous for its eleventh-century Narasimha Temple. Devotees flock to this dramatic hillside setting to celebrate Lord Vishnu's heroic defense of Prahlada, his follower. They smear the Vishnu image with sandal paste until it's unrecognizable. Once a year, on the third day of Vaisakha (April–May), the idol is cleansed in a ritual called Chandana Visarjana, during which Lord Vishnu is revealed. The temple is known for its many elegant sculptures.

Bheemunipatnam is 35 kilometers (21 miles) from Vizag by a road that runs along the beach. It is the site of a former Dutch trading settlement of the seventeenth century. A ruined fort remains, as well as Hollanders Green, the original Dutch cemetery. There's a good beach here. The spot hasn't been developed for super-tourism, but if you're willing to live in a modest guest house, consider Bheemunipatnam as the place to retreat and relax a few days.

Southeast Andhra Pradesh

The best approach to Tirupati in the hilly Chitaur district of southeast Andhra Pradesh is from Madras, in Tamil Nadu. Tirupati, with its temple of Lord Venkateswara in nearby Tirumala, is visited by millions of pilgrims every year. It's a popular temple, in large part because a visit here is said to bring good fortune.

Fortune is very much a part of the temple's history. In the days of the Pallava and Chola Dynasties, several rulers presented vast treasures at the hill temple. When Krishnadeva, the Raya king, visited the temple for the first time in 1513, he presented the deity with a jewel-studded crown, a necklace of pearls and precious stones, and 25 silver plates. Later that year, he returned to deliver a sword embedded with diamonds, rubies, and sapphires. The following year, glowing after a series of military victories, he buried the Lord's image in a pile of 30,000 gold coins.

This tradition of lavish offerings has made Tirumala the wealthiest temple in India. When you consider that India is a land of thousands of temples, this is no small distinction. Buses arrive from pre-dawn until evening, conveying thousands of pilgrims who wait patiently for their chance to pray in the temple and make offerings to the treasury. (Those who administer the temple treasury have distributed the money to fund a university, research institutions, health care, and social welfare organizations.)

On arriving in Tirupati, many pilgrims choose to walk to Tirumala by rock steps that have been traveled for centuries. There is also a winding road that cuts into the hills, providing magnificent views as you make your way by bus or taxi to Tirumala. Non-Hindus are barred from witnessing some parts of the worship, but if you want that blessing of wealth and want to experience India in all its spiritual intensity, the pilgrims' path from Tirupati to Tirumala offers a wealth of that sort, too.

PRACTICAL INFORMATION FOR

ANDHRA PRADESH

WHEN TO GO. From mid-October to late March is best. Temperature ranges from 60° F to 90° F with cooler evenings. Summer begins at the end of March, when temperatures climb above 100. Monsoon rains from June to August are welcome to farmers but not to tourists.

HOW TO GET THERE. By Air. *Indian Airlines* flies daily to Hyderabad from Bangalore, Bombay, Delhi, and Madras. It makes three flights a week to Hyderabad from Calcutta. Indian Airlines also flies four times a week to Visakhapatam from Calcutta and Madras. *Vayudoot* flies into Hyderabad two times a week from Madras and Goa. It also flies to Rajahmundry, three times a week from Madras; to Tirupati, three times a week from Bangalore and Hubli; and to Vijaywada, five times a week from Madras.

By Bus. *Andhra Pradesh State Road Transport Corporation* (APSRTC) runs luxury coaches (many with loud unceasing video sets blaring) to most important southern Indian cities: Bangalore, Madras, and Bombay, plus numerous tourist spots in the state. For details and fares, contact in Hyderabad: APSRTC, RTC Cross Roads, Musheerabad; tel. 64571. *Indian Tourism Development Corporation* (ITDC) also runs deluxe interstate buses in and out of Andhra Pradesh. For details, contact ITDC 3–6–150/4 Lidcap Building Himayatanagar, Hyderabad; tel. 220730. *Tiruvalluvar Transport Corporation* from Tamil Nadu runs deluxe coaches to and from Tirupati, as does APSRTC. In Madras, contact either at the Express Bus Stand; tel. 561835.

By Train. To Hyderabad (the station is actually at Secundrabad), daily trains from Bombay are *Hyderabad–Bombay Express* and *Minar Express;* from Delhi, *Hyderabad Niz Express;* from Madras, *Navjivan Express;* from Bangalore, *Bangalore–Hyderabad Express.* To Waltair, there are numerous daily trains from Calcutta (Howrah Station). To Tirupati, two daily trains from Madras. Day trains are not hard to arrange. Sleepers with reserved berths (a must—don't just buy a sleeper ticket) require early reservations. For details and fares, contact Railway Inquiry at Hyderabad; tel. 221352.

By Rented Car with Driver. Hyderabad is 566 km (351 mi.) from Bangalore, 735 km (458 mi.) from Bombay, and 704 km (436 mi.) from Madras. Hire a car from an agency recommended below under Tour Operators. Rate is about Rs. 4 per km with a halt charge of Rs. 50–Rs. 100 per night.

TOURIST INFORMATION. The main office for the *Andhra Pradesh Travel and Tourism Department* is in Hyderabad at Gagan Vihar, Fifth Floor, M.J. Road; tel. 557531. Open 10 A.M.–5 P.M., Monday–Saturday. The department can help arrange excursions and will give you brochures and suggest hotels. Other tourist offices: **Hyderabad Airport,** tel. 77192; open 10 A.M.–5 P.M.; Monday–Saturday.

Nagarjunasagar. Tourist Information Officer, Hill Colony; tel. 3625. Open 10 A.M.–5 P.M., Monday–Saturday.

Tirupati/Tirumala. Tourist Information Officer, T.P. Area, Tirupati; tel. 4698. Open 10 A.M.–5 P.M., Monday–Saturday.

Visakhapatnam (Vizag). Tourist Information Officer, Hotel Apsara Arcade, Visakhapatnam; tel. 63106. Open 10 A.M.–5 P.M., Monday–Saturday.

Warangal. Tourist Information Officer, Tourist Rest House, Kazipet, Warangal; tel. 6201. Open 10 A.M.–5 P.M., Monday–Saturday. The Government of India also has a tourist office in Hyderabad at Sandozi Building Himayatnagar, Hyderabad 500029; tel. 66877. Open 9 A.M.–5 P.M., Monday–Saturday.

FOREIGN CURRENCY EXCHANGE. Most Western-style hotels have money-exchange counters. Otherwise, go to a branch of the *State Bank of India,* open Monday–Friday, 10 A.M.–2 P.M.; Saturdays, till noon.

ACCOMMODATIONS. Hyderabad has a good range of hotels in all price ranges. Throughout the rest of Andhra Pradesh, facilities exist, but not at the level or variety as in Hyderabad. Prices are based on double occupancy and exclude taxes: *Expensive,* Rs. 950–Rs. 1,450; *Moderate,* Rs. 500–Rs. 950; *Inexpensive,* under Rs. 500. Some Western-style hotels take major credit cards.

AMARAVATI

Inexpensive

Inspection Bungalow. Amaravati. Reservations: District Collector, Guntar, Andhra Pradesh; no phone. About 5 rooms with bath. For this price, clean is what you get. Very minimal. Catered simple meals are available at nominal cost. Rupees only.

HYDERABAD-SECUNDERABAD

Expensive

The Krishna Oberoi. Banjara Hills, Rd. No. 1, Hyderabad; tel. 222121. 270 rooms with bath. Set on nine acres overlooking Lake Hussain Sagar, the Krishna Oberoi is a striking blend of modern architecture tempered by strong Mogul influences. Beautiful fountains and formal gardens grace its front lawn. Rooms are elegant, with pastel decor. Air-conditioning, room service, TV, multicuisine restaurants, bar, swimming pool, health club, business center, travel agency, foreign-exchange counter, book shop. AE, DC, MC, V.

Moderate

Hotel Ritz. Hill Fort Palace, Hyderabad; tel. 233571. 40 rooms with bath. Set on a hill, this small, older hotel was once the palace of a Hyderabadi *nizam* (Prince) and has a lovely courtyard, attractive lawns, and roof-top garden. Air-conditioned rooms aren't palatial or grand, but they do have a comfortable old-fashioned ambience. Room service, TV, multicuisine restaurant, bar, tennis, swimming pool, doctor, travel agency, foreign-exchange counter, bank, secretarial services. AE, DC, MC, V.

Taj Gateway Hotel on Banjara Hill. Banjara Hill, Hyderabad; tel. 222222. 124 rooms with bath. This modern highrise overlooking a lake offers attractive contemporary-style rooms. Air-conditioning, room service, TV, multicuisine restaurants, bar, swimming pool, secretarial services, travel and foreign-exchange counters, shops, doctor. Good value. DC, MC, V.

Inexpensive

Hotel Asrani International. M.G. Rd., Secunderabad; tel. 822267. 65 rooms with bath. This modern hotel offers pleasant contemporary-style rooms and good service. Air-conditioning, TV, room service, multicuisine restaurant, bar, travel agency, foreign-exchange counter, doctor, secretarial services, courtesy airport shuttle. AE, DC, MC, V.

Hotel Deccan Continental. Sir Ronald Ross Rd., Secunderabad; tel. 840981. 70 rooms with bath. A good value Western-style hotel, The Deccan Continental offers a great view of Lake Hussain Sagar and the city. Air-conditioned rooms are modern; best rooms have a balcony. Room service, multicuisine restaurant, bar, swimming pool, shops. AE, DC, MC, V.

Hotel Sampurna International. Mukramjahi Rd., Hyderabad; tel. 40165. 120 rooms with bath. This Western-style hotel, with a large Indian mural in its lobby, offers modern clean rooms. The price is good, but don't expect great character. Air-conditioning, room service, TV, multicuisine restaurant, bar, travel agency, foreign-exchange counter, shopping arcade. AE, DC, MC, V.

NAGARJUNASAGAR

Inexpensive

Vijay Vihar Complex. Reservations: Asst. Manager, Tourist Guest House, V.V. Complex Nagarjunasagar; tel. 3625. 8 rooms with bath and 5 cottages. This government-run complex offers plain, minimal-decor rooms. Some rooms are air-conditioned. Room service, simple Indian and Continental restaurant. Rupees only.

VIJAYAWADA

Inexpensive

Hotel Kandhari International. M.G. Rd., Vijayawada; tel. 61311. 73 rooms with bath. The city's best hotel, this place is modern, with clean air-conditioned rooms. Room service, TV, multicuisine restaurant, bar, doctor, travel agency, shopping arcade. AE, DC.

Hotel Mamata. Eluru Rd., opposite bus stand, Vijayawada; tel. 61251. 59 rooms with bath. Right in town, this hotel has some air-conditioned rooms, which are best. The decor is modest modern. Room service, TV, Indian and Continental restaurant, bar. Rupees only.

VISAKHAPATNAM (VIZAG)

Moderate

Park Hotel. Beach Rd., Visakhapatnam; tel. 63081. 64 rooms with bath. On the beach, this fancy modern hotel offers attractive rooms and a good quiet location. Air-conditioning, room service, TV, multicuisine restaurant, travel and foreign-exchange counters, swimming pool, secretarial services, doctor. AE, DC, MC, V.

Inexpensive–Moderate

Dolphin Hotels Ltd., Dabagardens, Visakhapatnam; tel. 64811. 147 rooms with bath. This large hotel, also on the beach, has clean Western-style rooms. Best rooms are "superior" or "executive" and are very moderately priced. Standard rooms, which have a simpler decor, are inexpensive. Room service, TV, multicuisine restaurants, bar, travel and foreign-exchange counters, secretarial services, baby sitters, doctor, shopping arcade. AE, DC, MC, V.

Inexpensive

Ocean View Inn. Kirlampudi, Visakhaptnam; tel. 54828. 30 rooms with bath. This small beach hotel offers good service and pleasant simple rooms. Best rooms are air-conditioned. Room service, TV, multicuisine restaurant. Rupees only.

Taj Hotel Sea Pearl. Beach Rd., Visakhapatnam; tel. 64371. 42 rooms with bath. Just acquired by the Taj hotel chain, this Western-style hotel is on the beach and has nice lawns. At press time, air-conditioned rooms were modern but had simple, adequate furnishings; however, an upgrading was planned. Multicuisine restaurant, room service, TV, foreign-exchange counter, car rental service, secretarial services. AE, DC, MC, V.

WARANGAL

Inexpensive

Hotel Ashoka. Main Rd., Hanamkonda, Warangal; tel. 85491. 31 rooms with bath. This pleasant Western-style hotel is modest; but rooms are clean and comfortable. Amenities include air-conditioning, room service, multicuisine restaurant, bar. Rupees only.

DINING OUT. Andhra Pradesh cooking, especially in Hyderabad, reflects the same historical and cultural influences mentioned earlier in the chapter. Moslem and Hindu, north and south all come together to produce a wide selection of tasty dishes. Generally speaking, you're likely to eat better in Hyderabad than anywhere else in India, with the exception of Goa. Once you leave Hyderabad, options are extremely limited. On day excursions to popular destinations, be adventurous and just pick a crowded restaurant. Most likely, it'll be extremely informal; but a crowd is a safe indication that the food is good. Many accommodations, listed above, also have restaurants. Breakfast is usually 8–10:30; lunch, noon–3; dinner, 7:30–10. Payment is normally in rupees unless the restaurant is connected to a Western-style hotel. The restaurants listed below are informal and, unless noted, are open for all three meals and don't require reservations. Prices, based on one person eating a three-course meal, excluding taxes, tip, or beverage, are: *Deluxe,* over Rs. 120; *Expensive,* Rs. 80–Rs. 120; *Moderate,* Rs. 40–Rs. 80; *Inexpensive,* under Rs. 40.

HYDERABAD

Deluxe

Firdaus. The Krishna Oberoi, Banjara Hills, Rd. No. 1; tel. 222121. Done up in pink and gold, this restaurant evokes the elegance of the nizams. It also serves their authentic Hyderabadi cuisine. Specialties include *achar gosht* (lamb cooked in pickled tomato masala paste) and *bagare baingan* (eggplant in a spicy poppy seed and sesame sauce). Dinner reservations advised. Open 12:30–3 P.M. and 7:30–11:30 P.M. AE, DC, MC, V.

Kebab-E-Bahar. Taj Gateway Hotel on Banjara Hill, Banjara Hills; tel. 222222. This outdoor restaurant is set on a lovely lawn and serves an excellent Hyderabadi-cuisine buffet or à la carte. Try the very good kebabs and barbecue items. Reservations advised. Open from 8 A.M.–11:30 P.M. DC, MC, V.

Lambadi. Taj Gateway Hotel on Banjara Hill, Banjara Hills; tel. 222222. Walls are white, with handsome paintings and dark wood pillars. Upholstered chairs and settees are intimately placed around the room. The chef serves tasty Andhra Pradesh and Deccan region specialties. This is a good place to order *haleem* (pounded wheat blended with spicy mutton and gravy). Reservations advised. Open 1–3 P.M. and 7:30–11:30. DC, MC, V.

Szechuan Garden. The Krishna Oberoi, Banjara Hills, Rd. No. 1; tel. 222121. Overlooking beautiful waterfalls and surrounded by a Chinese rock garden, the Szechuan Garden offers delicious Szechuan cuisine. Try the honey spare ribs, chicken in lotus leaves, or prawns in oyster sauce. Dinner reservations advised. Open 12:30–3 P.M. and 7:30 –11:30 P.M. DC, MC, V.

Expensive

Golden Deer. Abid Rd.; tel. 236081. This popular eatery, on the second floor, has subdued lighting and mirrored pillars. Besides the excellent Chinese fare or the Indian specialties, the chef also prepares Continental dishes. Portions are large. Dinner reservations advised. Open 11 A.M.–11 P.M. Rupees only.

Palace Heights. Triveni Complex, Abid Rd.; tel. 232898. This upperfloor restaurant in a modern high rise offers a great city view and elegant surroundings. Pictures of former Niwams grace the walls. Antiques add a refined touch. Ask for a table by a window and choose from Continental, Chinese, and Indian cuisines, including excellent Hyderabadi specialties. Dinner reservations advised. Open 11 A.M.–11 P.M. Rupees only.

Moderate

Golden Gate. Three Aces Compound, Abid Rd.; tel. 232485. Here, you will find a modern decor, lots of wooden paneling, and a large menu that features Indian, Chinese, and Continental specialties. The tandoori and Mughlai items are best. Dinner reservations advised. Open 11 A.M.–11 P.M. AE, DC, V.

Gulmohar Restaurant. Hotel Nagarjuna, Bashirbagh; tel. 237201. The decor here could be more inspired—lots of brass lamps on the walls and hanging from the ceiling, simple drapes drawn shut, white pillars. But the Gulmohar is air-conditioned and the Mughlai cuisine is delicious, especially the kebabs. Open 12:30–3 P.M. and 7:30–11 P.M. AE, MC, V.

Inexpensive

Annapurna Hotel. Nampally Station Rd.; tel. 557931. The decor is "budget" no-frills; but this popular vegetarian restaurant is air-conditioned and the prices can't be beat. Try the *thalis* (assorted dishes). The "Annapurna special" is especially good and the servings are huge. Open 6:30–10 A.M., 11–2:30 P.M., 7:30–10 P.M. Rupees only.

Kamat Hotel Restaurant. Secretariat Rd., Saifaibad; tel. 232225. This plain restaurant, with a modest decor and an extremely informal ambience, is also known for its excellent South Indian vegetarian cuisine. Again, the thalis are delicious; so are the *dosa* (Indian-style stuffed crêpe). The place is usually crowded. Open 7–10 A.M., 11–2:30 P.M., and 7:30–10. Rupees only.

VIJAYAWADA

Moderate

Hotel Greenlands Restaurant. Bhavani Gardens; tel. 73081. This delightful restaurant, with simple huts set on a lawn, serves Indian and Continental cuisines. Try the good curries or kebabs. Open 11 A.M.–2 P.M. and 6:30–11 P.M. Rupees only.

WARANGAL

Inexpensive

Classic Bar and Restaurant. Hotel Ashoka; tel. 85491. The restaurant is simple, with a slightly upscale Indian-style coffee shop decor; but the food is the best in town. The Indian dishes are memorable, but the chef also prepares Continental and Chinese meals. Try the tasty mutton *do piaza* (mutton curry with onions) and chicken *masala* (chicken cooked in a spicy gravy). Just hope that this talented chef isn't snapped up by a big hotel chain. Open 12:30–3 P.M. and 7:30–10:30 P.M. Rupees only.

SWEETS AND TREATS. In Hyderabad, stop in at the popular fast-food place, Mughal Durbar on Basherbagh Rd., and enjoy great Indian snacks and good ice cream. Open 9 A.M.–10 P.M. *Chandrala Restaurant* in the Hotel Kakatiya, Nampally Station Rd., is famous for its tasty *idlis* (steamed rice cakes) served with a spicy sauce. Open 8 A.M.–8 P.M. *Montgomery's Cafe,* near Park Lane Hotel, Secunderabad, is a Hyderabad institution. An English tearoom, it has survived from the days of the Raj. Expect simple snacks and plenty of atmosphere. Open 11 A.M.–9 P.M. Best in the late afternoon.

HOW TO GET AROUND. By Plane. *Indian Airlines* flies daily between Hyderabad and Visakhapatnam. *Vaydudoot* has six weekly flights connecting Hyderabad with Tirupati, and two weekly flights between Hyderabad and Vijayawada. It has five weekly flights between Tirupati and Vijayawada, and three weekly flights between Tirupati and Rajamundey. It connects Vijayawada and Rajamundey three times a week.

From the Airport. Taxis into Hyderabad, Vizag, or Tirupati cost Rs. 50–Rs. 75. Regular bus service from the airport is much less, but it is also much less convenient.

By Rented Car with Driver. This is a good way to travel through the state. Here are some important distances from Hyderabad: Amaravati, 334 km (207 mi.); Nagarjunasagar, 150 km (93 mi.); Srisailam, 219 km (136 mi.); Tirupati, 580 km (360 mi.); Visakhapatnam, 667 km (414 mi.); Vijayawada, 271 km (168 mi.). Hire a car from an agency recommended below under Tour Operators. Rates are about Rs. 4 per km with a halt charge of Rs. 50–100 per night.

By Taxi. Taxis are good for excursions on the outskirts of major cities. Rates are about Rs. 3.60 for the first km; Rs. 3 per additional km.

By Auto Rickshaw. In crowded cities, this is the easiest way to maneuver in congested streets. Rates are about Rs. 2.60 for the first km; Rs. 2 per additional km. If the driver claims a "broken" meter, set the fare in advance.

By Bus. There are local buses, too, throughout most of Andhra Pradesh, but they're a bit much to handle. Especially in Hyderabad, where you have to be a wild leaper to jump aboard.

By Boat. Another attractive option—at least for one leg of your journey—is the motor launch connecting Nagarjunasagar with Srisailam. It's simple, fast, cheap, and far more pleasant to travel the 100 km between these two towns by boat (three hours) than over rough country roads (4½ hours). Launch leaves Nagarjunasagar for Srisailam at 6 A.M.; from Srisailam, the launch returns at 3 P.M., allowing you to do a loop of Hyderabad-Nagarajunasagar–Srisailam–Hyderabad in either direction. The one-way fare is Rs. 100. From April–June, the worst months to be traveling in this area, the water level of the Krishna River may make this excursion impossible. From July–March boat service is usually in operation.

TOURS. *APTTDC* is eager to help tourists visit the state. It has inexpensive government tours, in deluxe coaches, that will take you on the following excursions accompanied by a guide. For details and reservations, contact the head office of APTTDC (Gagan Vihar, 1st floor, M.J. Rd., Hyderabad, Andhra Pradesh; tel. 556493), or their counters at the airport or railway station.

Hyderabad City Sight Seeing. Daily 8 A.M.–6 P.M.

Nagarjunasagar. Daily tours 6 A.M.–9:30 P.M., one-way trips in either direction, and overnight package tours.

Yadagirigutta. Two daily tours to the Laxminarasimha Swamy Temple. 8 A.M.– 1 P.M. and 2–7 P.M.

Mantralayam. Every Saturday at 10 A.M., returning on Sunday at 9 P.M. Tour to Raghavendra Swamy Temple, Alampur Temple, Pillalamarri.

Srisailam. Every Saturday at 12 noon, returning on Saturday at 9 P.M.

Vijayawada. Local sightseeing. Daily 8 A.M.–7 P.M.

Tirupati-Tirumala. Every Friday at 7:30 P.M. and returning Monday at 5 A.M.

Visakhaptnam. City Sightseeing. Daily from 8 A.M.–7 P.M.

Warangal. Every Saturday and Sunday, departing at 7 A.M. and returning the same night at 9:30.

State-wide Tours. *Pilgrim's Tour.* Seven-day tour of Bhadrachalam, Simhachalam, Annavaram, Vijayawada, Tirupati, Kanchi, and Srisailam. The fifth of each month.

Andhra Panorama Tour. Comprehensive seven-day tour of major destinations. The 15th of each month.

Heritage Tour. Six-day tour of Nagarjunasagar, Tirupatai, Horsley Hills, Lepakshi, Puttaparthi, Mantralayam. The 25th of every month.

TOUR OPERATORS. For all your travel needs, including a car with driver, contact any of these reputable agencies:

Thomas Cook, Saifabad, Hyderabad; tel. 222689.

Mercury Travels, Public Gardens Rd., Hyderabad; tel. 2344411.

Sita World Travels, Hyderguda and Chapel Rd., Hyderabad; tel. 233638.

You can also rent a car with driver from APTTDC (address above).

SEASONAL EVENTS. Since most events are determined by the lunar calendar, contact the Government of India Tourist Office for details.

January. Throughout Andhra Pradesh, *Pongal* is a three-day harvest festival. The sun is worshiped on the first day, then cows and bullocks (painted and decorated) are fed *pongal,* a rice concoction, as part of a ceremony of thanksgiving. Processions and lots of happy celebration ensues.

April/May. Simhachalam observes the *Vaisakha Festival.* The sandpaste-covered image of Vishnu is cleansed in a ritual called *Chandana Visarjana,* revealing before crowds of devotees, the actual image of Lord Vishnu.

June/July. A Moslem holy day, *Id-ul-Fitr* marks the end of Ramadan, a time of month-long fasting. Lot's of feasting and celebrating.

September/October. *Dussehra,* a 10-day festival, celebrates the victory of good over evil. There are numerous events and noisy firecrackers.

October. *Muharram.* Muslims honor the martyrdom of Hussain, the grandson of the Prophet Mohammed. Processions of *tazias* (bamboo and paper replicas of the martyr's tomb at Karbala) are paraded through the streets.

October/November. *Diwali,* marks the start of the Hindu New Year. Candles are lit on every house to welcome Lakshmi, the goddess of wealth.

HISTORIC SITES. Entrance to most places is free; where a donation is requested, a few rupees will suffice. Monuments are open sunrise to sunset, unless noted otherwise below.

AMARAVATI

Amaravati is a former Buddhist center that flourished in the first century B.C.—one of the four most important places of worship for Buddhists in India. Its stupa, which was originally the largest in India, is made of brick and covered with marble. Now mainly in ruins, it's still a peaceful site.

HYDERABAD

Charminar, a beautiful granite structure with a slender minaret rising from each corner, was built in 1592 by Quli Qutb Shahi, the founder of Hyderabad. The arches face the cardinal points: north, south, east, and west. The rooms above the arches may have been used as a college. The structure was possibly built as an offering to drive away an epidemic that was destroying the population of the then new city.

Golconda Fort, six km (3.6 mi) from Charminar, is a thirteenth-century fort rebuilt by the Qutb Shahi kings in the sixteenth century and made their capital. It has great acoustics. A loud noise made under the dome of the front gate can be heard at the highest point in the fort. An ingenious water supply system—clay pipes and Persian wheels—carried water to roof gardens and palaces.

Mecca Masjid is the biggest mosque in South India. Ten thousand devotees can pray inside. Construction was started in 1614 by the sixth Qutb Shahi king, Abdullah Qutb Shahi, and completed by the Mogul Emperor Aurangzeb. Colonades and door arches were made from single slabs of granite.

Qutb Shahi Tombs are memorials for seven of the Qutb Shahi kings. Structures have a strange infusion of Hindu influence. Note the lotus leaves and buds.

Venkateswara Temple is a marble structure, dedicated to Lord Venkateswara, completed in 1976 by the Birla Foundation. An excellent fusion of north and south temple architecture. Workmen from all over India were involved, including some craftsmen who were supposedly descended from the artists who worked on the Taj Mahal. The idols were made by south Indian sculptors. Open to all, regardless of faith, 8 A.M.–noon; 4–8 P.M.

KOLANAPAKA

Mahaveer Jain Temple is claimed to be 2,000 years old. Inside is a five-foot-high sculpture of Mahaveer, the last of the Jain *tirthankaras* (gods), built of solid jade. Another deity, Adeshwar (the first of the Jain tirthankaras) has jewels in his forehead valued at half a million dollars.

NAGARJUNAKONDA

Anupa, five km (three mi.) from Nagarjunakonda, is a Buddhist monastery reconstructed from excavated ruins of a lost city and an important Buddhist settlement dating back to the third century. The original city was flooded by the Nagarjunasagar Dam, which created the world's third-largest artificial lake.

PALAMPET

Rudresvara Temple (also called Ramappa Temple), dedicated to Shiva, was constructed by the Kakatiyas around A.D. 1234. This is a must-see if you're in the area. You'll find some of the best temple sculpture in India.

SRISAILAM

Bhramaramka Mallikarjunaswamy Temple contains a *Jyotorlinga,* which means natural lingam created by a god (one of 12 in India). The temple is enclosed in huge walls and gateways with bas-reliefs illustrating legends and avatars connected to Shiva. Parts of the temple complex extend back to the second century A.D. The daily *puja* (prayer service) is spectacular.

TIRUMALA/TIRUPATI

At Tirumala, *Sri Venkateswara Temple* is the abode of the "Lord of the Seven Hills" and home of one of the richest temples in southern India. The shrine is an essential pilgrimage, a great example of early Dravidian art. Non-Hindus are allowed inside. The temple sits on a peak, with its several *goporums* (towers) visible during the ascent. The main door, Vimana, over the sanctum sanctorum (inner shrine) and the temple flagpost are covered in gold plate.

Chandragiri Fort, 11 km (6.6 mi.) from Tirupati, was important during the last days of the Vijayanagar empire. Built in A.D. 1000, it features interesting remains of palaces and temples. Nearby, two palaces are used by members of the royal family.

Kalahahasti, east of Tirupati, is another important pilgrimage center and old temple with inscriptions that connect it to the Cholas in the 900s right through to the Vijayanagar Empire in the 1500s. The huge goporum was built in 1516. According to legend, the lingam inside the temple was worshiped by a spider *(sri),* a snake *(kala),* and an elephant *(hasti),* which obviously explains its name. The temple is dedicated to Vayu, the god of the winds.

At Simhachalam, 16 km (9.6 mi.) from Vizag, the 11th century *Narashima Temple* is dedicated to Lord Vishnu in his incarnation as Narasimha in the form of a boar. The pillars in the mandapas have beautiful carvings.

WARANGAL

One Thousand Pillar Temple in Warangal, capital of Kakatiya Dynasty between the eleventh and twelfth centuries, was constructed in 1163 by Rudra Deva in the Chalukyan style, with each pillar richly carved. A six-foot Nandi stands out front. This temple is dedicated to Shiva.

Warangal Fort covers an enormous area; constructed between 1199 and 1261 by the Kakatiya rulers.

YADAGIRIGUTTA

Lakshmi Narasimha Swami Temple is situated on top of a lovely hill offering a good view of the Deccan Plateau. The temple is built around a cave where Lord Vishnu supposedly lived. In the inner sanctum, flanked by silver doors, Lord Vishnu lies in his half lion-half human incarnation slaying the demon Kiranyakasipa.

MUSEUMS AND GALLERIES. Entrance is free or there is a nominal cost. **Amaravati.** *Archaeological Museum* holds Buddhist antiquities from third century B.C. to A.D. twelfth century. Open 10 A.M.–5 P.M.; closed Monday.

Hyderabad. *Andhra Pradesh State Museum* in the Public Gardens was established in 1930. It features collections of weapons, bidriware, bronzes, miniatures, manuscripts, and sculpture and a prehistoric section complete with a mummy. Open daily except Mondays and official holidays, 10:30 A.M.–5 P.M.

Birla Museum in the Asmangadh Palace at Malakpet, near the TV tower, houses bronzes, sculptures, paintings, armor. Excellent miniatures from the Deccani,

Mogul, and Rajasthani art schools. In fact, you'll find art from all over the world here. Very eclectic displays. For hours, contact Director, Birla Archaeological and Cultural Institute, tel. 558347.

Salar Jung Museum has 38 galleries of priceless art treasures amassed in the early 1900s by Yousuf Ali Khan, aka Nawab Salar Jung. A lonely man, he surrounded himself with every conceivable notion of art: South Indian bronzes, miniatures from Shah Jahan's personal album, Nur Jahan's emerald and ruby dagger, and ivory furniture as well as Western Chippendale and Louis XIV furnishings, Persian carpets, even ordinary garden tools. A must-see, including the clock in the courtyard. Open daily except Fridays and official holidays, 10 A.M.–5 P.M.

Nagarjunasagar. *Nagarjunakonda Island Museum* is designed in the model of a Buddhist *vihara* (monastery) and set on a hill. Here you can see the reconstructed relics of a third- and fourth-century Buddhist civilization: Buddhist stupas, actual relics of the Buddha, viharas, sacrificial altars, statues, even a peaceful garden. A boat takes you to the museum. Booking counter is near the dam. Rs. 10 per person. Departures 9 A.M. and 1:30 P.M.; return trips 1 and 5 P.M. Buy tickets *early!*—boats fill up fast. Museum is open 9 A.M.–4 P.M.; closed on Fridays. Admission free. For further details, call tel. 3625 in Nagarjunasagar.

GARDENS AND ZOOS. *Lion Safari Park* and *Nehru Zoological Park* comprise 300 acres with almost 2,000 animals. Train ride and animal rides for kids. Also, see life-size fiberglass models of dinosaurs. Open 9 A.M.–5 P.M., closed Mondays. Rs. 1 per person for minibus ride through the lion safari. *Osmansagar* and *Himayatsagar* are two nearby lakes with gardens. Lovely for walks and picnics. Open sunrise to sunset. *Bagh-i-Am* is a beautiful public garden in the middle of Hyderabad containing plants from all over, a cypress garden, lotus pools, and a rose garden. Open sunrise to sunset.

BEACHES. You'll find lovely beaches around Vishakapatnam that are just opening up for tourism. Beaches extend north and south along the Bay of Bengal and include *Mount Kailasa, Rama Krishna Beach, Waltair,* and *Bheemunipatnam Beach.* Lovely coves and long stretches of sand grace each of these.

SHOPPING. Bidriware work, made from a special alloy with its vivid contrast of dull black and lustrous white, is a distinctive craft of Hyderabad. Attractive novelties inlaid with pure silver wire in intricate designs are manufactured from this alloy, which resembles gun metal in composition. Bangles, buttons, cigarette cases, trays, cuff links, fruit bowls, and so forth, are also made of this material. Nirmal toys are made of very light wood. Amusing specimens of animals painted with brilliant, metallike lacquer are manufactured for the delight of the children. Gold filigree work is another popular craft in this area. Ikat textiles (a process of tie-dye weaving) are also available.

Ivory and horn carving is also a cottage industry in Andhra Pradesh. Intricate designs in ivory combined with excellent workmanship go to produce exquisite articles like brooches, powder boxes, earrings, combs, and necklaces. Among other handicrafts are carpet weaving and rugmaking. Carpets of Warangal are famous and have won prizes in various international exhibitions. These carpets are of three kinds: silk, cotton, and woolen. Their designs conform to Persian patterns.

The principal shopping centers are Abid Road and Pathergatty in Hyderabad, Rashtrapathi Road and Gandhi Road in Secunderabad, Chowrastra in Warangal and Hanamkonda. Best addresses: Government Cottage Industries Emporium, Gunfoundry, Hyderabad; Nirmal Industries, Khairatabad, Hyderabad; Weavers Cooperative Society in Warangal.

Hyderabad is the center of India's pearl trade. Near Hyderabad's famous Charminar area, there is a row of small shops whose display cases gleam with treasures from the sea. Pearls of every shape and hue are polished and sorted before being shipped throughout India.

Indeed, *Charminar Market* itself is one of the best in India. It's fun, interesting, and teeming with tempting items to buy—fabrics, bangles, bidriware—all the crafts and handiwork for which Hyderabad is famous. It's a place to bargain, a place to browse, and a place to get a good look at India.

NIGHTLIFE AND BARS. Most of the better hotels in Hyderabad have bars, generally open during lunch and from the early evening until 11 P.M. The *Golconda Bar* in the Krishna Oberoi is elegant and offers good views of Husain Sagar Lake.

EASTERN REGION

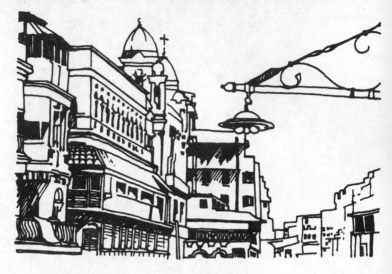

CALCUTTA

City of Astonishments

by
LISA SAMSON and AMIT SHAH

Lisa Samson is a free-lance writer and photographer whose photographs have been published in India and the United States. She has lived in Southeast Asia and has traveled extensively there and in India.

Amit Shah is a free-lance writer whose work has been published in more than a dozen publications in the United States and in India.

You are always unprepared for Calcutta. You have readied yourself for the grime, the filth, and the statistics of poverty that numb the most rational minds. You were right. They exist. A tourist brochure of a decade ago announced that "Calcutta assaults the senses like few other cities"; the burly, grimy, sweaty city is toiling, calculating, blind to suffering, and yet indispensable to the fabric of India.

You cannot remain objective about Calcutta. It is an intensely personal city, like New York, and you will not leave it without feeling a sense of bewilderment or coming under its bewitching spell. Revulsion is only for the ignorant. In Calcutta, you cannot hide from one of the largest cities in the world, a world of developing economies, of urban planning gone awry. For those who know its historic rise from obscurity in the 1700s to the beginning of its decline in the mid-1900s, Calcutta is a reminder of why and how the British Empire was created in India and what happened when the empire was dismantled.

448

Calcutta is a city of astonishments. Hundreds of refugees pour in across the Bangladesh border every day and make their way to the commercial nerve center, while migrants from across India come to the fabled city and revolutions threaten to disembowel the political structure altogether. Calcutta persists and surmounts.

You did not prepare yourself for Calcutta's inhabitants—the Bengalis—animated, laconic, intellectual, spirited, argumentative, anarchic, imaginative, and creative. They have dominated the city and have made it, for over 1½ centuries, the soul of India. They were among the first to react to the intellectual and political stimuli of the West and have produced, despite their sometimes desperate state, many of the most renowned filmmakers, writers, scientists, musicians, dancers, and philosophers in twentieth-century India. Blending the European humanism of the nineteenth century with the indigenous culture that was revived by Rabindranath Tagore, among others, Bengalis made the first organized efforts to oust the British in the early twentieth century, ultimately breaking away from Gandhian politics and choosing terrorism (a reason why the British moved their capital from Calcutta to Delhi in 1911).

Leisurely Visit Advised

The city is a dynamo—exhausting and exhaustive. It is not an "easy" travel destination but an essential one if you want to claim that you have visited India. Many Western travelers hurry through their visit to Calcutta and return home to spread misconceptions about India and this city on the flimsy basis of their short stay. A few years ago, a graffiti-splattered wall (in English) in Calcutta summed up the feelings of Indians about such tourists: "Calcutta Needs Development, Not Insults." Calcutta is the essence of India in many ways—its economic and developmental pitfalls coupled with its imagination and tenacity.

The Calcutta metropolitan district covers 426 square kilometers (883 square miles) and has a population of nearly 11 million. It comprises two municipal corporation areas (Calcutta and Howrah), 32 municipalities, 62 nonmunicipal urban centers, and over 500 villages. By any count a huge cosmopolitan city, it sprang from three small fishing villages under the direction of the British East India Company.

A Bit of History

On November 9, 1698, Job Charnock, an agent for the East India Company, bought for a settlement three sleepy villages—Sutanati, Gobindpur, and Kali Kutta—for Rs. 1,200 from Sabarna Roy Choudhury, a local landowner. Charnock arrived in India in 1690 and started a "factory" at Sutanati. He negotiated the purchase of the first factory site with the Mogul Emperor Aurangzeb's emissary in 1690. An undistinguished man by all historical accounts, Charnock won the hearts of Bengalis by a personal deed: he rescued a young Bengali widow about to be burned at the funeral pyre of her dead husband, as was the custom of *seti,* married her, and lived and died in Calcutta. His grave is at St. John's Church, off Dalhousie Square. Through Charnock's real estate acquisition, the British gained a foothold in what had been the Sultanate of Delhi under the Moguls. Thus began the great drama known as the British Raj in India.

The English built Fort William—near what is now Benoy-Badal-Dinesh Bagh (BBD Bagh)—and consolidated their position till 1756, when Siraj-ud-Daula, the nawab of Murshidabad, attacked the garrison. Many of the British residents fled. Robert Clive, fighting in Madras at the time, raced

1. National Library
2. Zoological Garden
3. St. Paul's Cathedral
   and Planetarium
4. Museum
5. W. Bengal Tourist Office
6. General Post Office
7. Writer's Building
8. Howrah Station
9. Ashutosh Museum
   and University
10. Sealdah Station
11. Ferry Landing Stage
12. Victoria Memorial
13. Raj Bhavan
14. Govt. of India Tourist Office

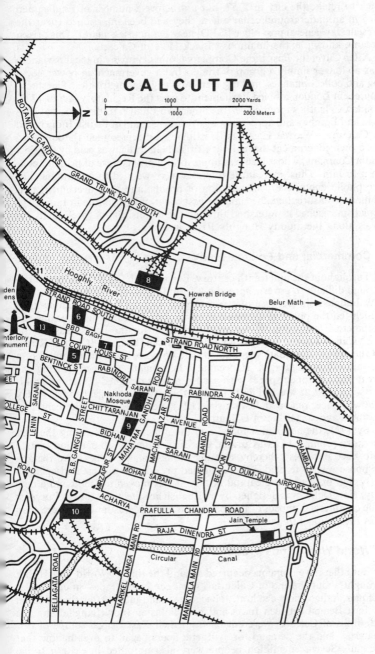

back to retake the city in 1757, but not before a number of Englishmen died in an underground cellar where they had been imprisoned (near the present-day general post office [GPO] near Dalhousie Square). This prison became known as the infamous "Black Hole of Calcutta."

After Clive, the East India Company (John Company in local parlance) was no longer simply a group of traders but a government in power, levying and collecting taxes, making wars, and negotiating treaties. The stockholders in London lobbied Parliament to pass the Regulatory Act of 1773, making Calcutta supreme over the other two English trading posts at Madras and Bombay and appointing a governor-general of British India based in Calcutta—Warren Hastings. Hastings, who represented the king and the crown government throughout British-held India, was paid by the East India Company, whose business interests and profits were of primary concern to him. Thus, mercantile interests were wedded to government for the public good. The accumulation of profits, and the government machinery to ensure them, became the first order of British rule in India. Colonialism reached a watershed through the acquisition of three small villages along the muddy Hooghly River in India.

Commercial and Political Hub

Throughout the nineteenth century, Bengal, with Calcutta as its capital, though difficult to govern, spread out from the eastern reaches of present-day Bangladesh. Because of the resurgent Bengali cultural nationalism, which fed the political nationalism of the late 1800s, Bengal became the commercial and political center of India and for the British east of the Suez Canal. The old pilgrim road that ran from the north (Chitpur Road) to the south (Kalighat) was named Chowringhee after the disciples of a hermit, Chowringheegiri. It became a fashionable boulevard facing the great *Maidan* (open space) with garden houses designed by Italian architects. In 1859, it was the first street in the city to have gas lamps. Today Chowringhee, renamed Jawaharlal (J.L.) Nehru Road, is the center of business and social life in Calcutta.

By 1905, the nationalist mood and the difficulty in governing the vast territory prompted Lord Curzon, the British viceroy, to partition Bengal into East and West, thereby splitting the nationalist forces. The Bengali response was so ferocious that a unified presidency was created again in 1912, but only after the capital of the raj was moved to Delhi and a new city, New Delhi, was designed by an English architect, Sir Edwin Lutyens. The commercial impact of this change in capitals was far less severe than was the political impact.

World War II Ends Trade

But other developments occurred around the time of World War II that brought about the end of Calcutta's great economic trade—in cloth, silk, lacquer, indigo, rice, betelnut, tobacco, tea, and jutes. After the partition of East Bengal between India and East Pakistan (now Bangladesh), the jute mills of Calcutta were cut off from their East Bengal source of raw material, and the demand for synthetic fibers began to overshadow that for jute. Seventeen million people were also uprooted in eastern India; fewer than 30 years later, during the 1972 Bangladesh War, another large migration began that has continued in a steady stream. Decay had begun to set in. After a period of post-independence reconstruction under the Congress Party, the late 1960s brought Calcutta to a cathartic battle between the forces of change and the established, somewhat moribund, political forces.

One of the richest cities between Rome and Tokyo, in accumulated wealth and representations, Calcutta was once a leader of Indian exports, controlling 15 percent of the manufacturing industry, collecting over 30 percent of the national tax revenues, and surpassing the rest of India in the manufacture of light machinery. In the late 1960s-early 1970s, Calcutta went into a depression of monumental proportions. Manufacturing plants closed because of labor disputes, schools and colleges couldn't offer examinations because of student strikes, transportation creaked, basic services were overtaxed, and political violence wrenched the city in a frightening rage that peaked in 1970.

Left Front in Control

In May 1977, the Congress Party lost its grip on the political wheel of Bengal, and the Marxists (Communist Party of West Bengal), with a coalition group, the Left Front, were elected by an overwhelming majority. Much is heard about the Left Front in Calcutta—their work was probably invented by a Biblical Job. In power, they are pragmatists more than ideologues, and their balance sheet for the past decade has been mixed. The pressures from New Delhi (Congress), which controls the funds that could repair Calcutta's collapsing infrastructure and promote large-scale development, are enormous.

The Left Front's strategy of first consolidating its rural base in Bengal has worked, but in Calcutta, the politicization has practically crippled the legitimate functioning of public hospitals, government offices, and even the police. Some of the Left Front's gains are no mean achievements: doubling the rice production to the second state in India, increasing literacy in rural areas, providing health and legal benefits for sharecroppers, and decreasing the percentage of people below the poverty line. Living in a city with over 11 million people, 150,000 "pavement dwellers," power shortages, and huge population increases, Calcuttans hope for long-term investment projects and less short-term lectures by politicians and urban development "experts." A recent poster, in English, summed up the feelings of many Calcuttans: Many say that Calcutta is a dead city. Yet, hundreds throng to Calcutta each day from neighboring states. Are they scavengers feeding on the mortal remains? No. They come in the hope for opportunities for a livelihood and survival. They do get them and settle down. They are not scavengers and Calcutta is very much alive.

EXPLORING CALCUTTA

Calcutta, unlike other metropolitan cities in India, is a relative newcomer, having sprouted from three sleepy fishing villages in the late seventeenth century. The course of British imperial history on the subcontinent is mirrored in Calcutta's own history and development.

If you come in by train, you're in for the experience of a lifetime. Howrah Station, situated on the west bank of the Hooghly River, is the major railway station in eastern India. A "permanent" population seems to reside on the platforms among the ferocious intensity of thousands on the move. This atmosphere extends to Howrah Bridge, a Calcutta landmark, built in 1941, a web of girders stretching 1,500 feet over the Hooghly. Passing over eight lanes of chaotic traffic, which includes all manner of trans-portation—rickshaws, cars, scooters, bicycles, pushcarts, and animal-drawn carts—two million people cross this single-span cantilevered bridge each day. Howrah, already a congested suburb of Calcutta, is becoming the fastest-growing population center in the metropolitan area.

A second Howrah Bridge at Hastings has been under construction for a number of years, and its completion is not expected for many more. Once over the bridge, you're near the Botanical Gardens. Spread over 270 acres and containing over 30,000 varieties of plants and trees, it is India's oldest (built in 1787). A 200-year-old banyan tree with over 600 branches taking root around the central tree creates a veritable forest—an awesome sight. Its circumference is 1,367 feet. Tour buses race through these gardens, which, with the view of the Hooghly, are an ideal spot for picnicking. If you can, hire a car and go there early in the day to avoid the crush of humanity that clogs the narrow street in Shibour that leads to the gardens. The road is lined with jute mills, once Bengal's main export industry.

About 10 kilometers (6½ miles) north of the gardens is Belur Math, the headquarters of the Ramakrishna Mission, a reform movement that has an impact far beyond Bengal. Ramakrishna Paramahansa, who died in 1886, forsook his Brahman status and preached the unity of religious faiths and an adherence to the altruistic values for all people. His disciple, Swami Vivekananda, established the mission in 1898. The Belur Math Temple resembles a church, a temple, or a mosque, depending on which angle you see it from.

A short distance north is Dakshineshwar Kali Temple (1847), a major pilgrimage site to which devotees continue to flock to see the temples of Shiva, Kali, Radha, and Krishna. It was here that Ramakrishna received his spiritual vision; his room is a museum. Open till 10 P.M.

Either on the way north of the city or returning south from Belur, a stop at Parasnath, one of Calcutta's most interesting Jain temples, is rec-ommended. Built in 1867 on Budree Das Temple Street and dedicated to Sitalnathji, the tenth of the 24 *tirthankas* (perfect souls), it is a flamboyant structure filled with mirror-inlay pillars, stained-glass windows, marble floors in a floral design, a gilded dome, and chandeliers from nineteenth-century Paris and Brussels. In the garden, there are blocks of glass mosaics with European figures and statues that have been covered with silver paint. It is an unusual place of honor for the ascetic Jains. If you've been lucky and beaten the midday traffic back to the center of town, take a break to freshen up (without a doubt you will sweat in any season in Calcutta), have lunch (you might want to try one of the many brands of Indian beer—Bengal brews many of them), and when the midday heat abates a little, resume your sightseeing.

The Indian Museum (see *Museum* section), the Nehru Children's Muse-um, Victoria Memorial, and Birla Planetarium, are all within a few kilo-meters.

The British came to Calcutta to trade, and they needed political stability and an infrastructure to manage the indigenous population. Toward this end, they brought in soldiers, priests, and clerks. Their legacies remain in Fort William, on the east bank of the Hooghly near Strand Road; the fort is an irregular octagon surrounded by a moat almost 50 feet wide. Built in 1773, and named after William III, it was said to be impregnable, a boast that has never been put to the test.

St. John's Church, built in 1784, is where Job Charnock, founder of Cal-cutta, is buried. In the garden, there is a monument to the victims of the "Black Hole" tragedy.

Nearby, St. Paul's Cathedral, with its soaring Gothic steeple, was built in 1847. Two earthquakes destroyed the previous steeples; the present one is a model of the one at Canterbury Cathedral. Florentine frescoes, the stained-glass western window, and a gold communion plate presented by Queen Victoria are of special interest. The hours of services are posted near the entrance gate.

Writers Building, on one side of Dalhousie Square (BBD Bagh), built in 1780, housed the "writers" or clerks of the East India Company. It was synonymous with mind-numbing bureaucracy from its inception and is, today, the dreaded bottomless pit of the present government's paper mill. The Gothic structure, with rows of Ionic pillars and groups of statues, is evocative of a Victorian architecture that is a photographer's delight.

Another sight of interest in this city that blends Victorian order and the anarchic bustle of a developing country is the Ochterlony Monument (Shahid Minar) at the northern tip of the Maidan near the Park Street Metro entrance on J. L. Nehru Road. This 158-foot pillar, erected to commemorate Sir David Ochterlony's victories in nineteenth-century Nepal, is designed with a curious blend of Middle Eastern architecture. Its base is Egyptian, its pillar is Syrian, and its cupola is Turkish! It was the focal point for political rallies (much like Nelson's at London's Trafalgar Square). The Raj Bhawan (Government House), the residence of the governor and more or less a copy of Keddleston Hall in Derbyshire, is another such sight. Completed in 1802, it contains the throne of Tipu Sultan, the nemesis of the British, and a polished teak ballroom floor. Without an official invitation, however, tourists are not permitted. While in this area, stroll through the green expanse of Eden Gardens, which has lakes for boating and a wooden pagoda from Burma.

Leaving the center of the city, go south past the Calcutta Racecourse and the Maidan, where English officers once hunted wild game but which is now the "green lung" of the city, with almost two square miles of open parkland. The original forests were cut down to provide a clear field of fire for Fort William. Near the racecourse are the Zoological Gardens, opened in 1876, with some of the best collections of reptiles and white tigers in India. The zoo also has a children's zoo and an aquarium; its easy to walk around and attractive. The air-conditioned snack bar, located near the entrance, is mobbed during the summer.

The Kali Temple at Kalighat is near a canal called Adiganga (the "real Ganga" because it is believed to be the original bed of the Hooghly). Built in 1809, the Kali is one of Hinduism's renowned pilgrimage sites, containing temples to Radha, Shiva, Krishna, and Kali. Human sacrifices were reputed to be common in the last century, but only goats are slaughtered now and offered to Kali with Ganges water and *bhang,* an uncultivated hemp.

Coming back north, there is a Nakhoda Mosque, built in 1926, the largest Moslem mosque in Calcutta, modeled after Akbar's tomb at Sikandra (Agra). The mosque can accommodate 10,000 people.

The Agro-Horticultural Society's gardens are behind the National Library at Belvedere on Alipore Road. Founded in 1820, the gardens are in full bloom during December and January, and some flowers are out as late as early March. This is a soothing side trip.

At Muktaram Babu Street in Chorebagan (thieves' garden) is another site of historic interest, the famed Marble Palace, built in 1835 by Raja Rajendra Mullick. A member of Bengal's landed gentry, with lands in what is now Bangladesh (then East Bengal), Raja Mullick chose to spend his money in the "second city of the Empire"—Calcutta. Lavishly built of Italian marble, the palace's dark walls are covered with paintings, clocks, statues, crystal, and china. The palace is said to contain paintings by Houdon, Gainsborough, Reynolds, and Reubens and a statue by Michelangelo. The grounds have aviaries and a family temple, as well as Roman fountains.

Calcutta's historical sights can keep you busy for days. Less well-known sights include Jorasanko Thakurbari at 5 Dwarkanath Tagore Lane, the house where Rabindranath Tagore lived and worked. Now a university, Rabindra Bharati, it actively fosters cultural activities. With its cupolas and balconies, Thakurbari (House of Tagores) was once known as a nerve center of intellectual life in Bengal. Today, part of it is a museum housing a splendid collection of Tagore memorabilia. Tagore and stalwarts, such as Michael Madhusudan Dutt, Bankim Chandra Chatterjee, Ishwar Chandra Vidyasagar, Raja Ram Monun Roy, Sarat Chandra Chatterjee, Sri Ramkrishna, and Swami Vivekananda, brought about a renaissance in Bengali cultural, social, and political life in the nineteenth and early twentieth centuries. To walk the Thakubari's lanes, made for pedestrians and palanquin bearers rather than cars and buses, is to "feel" the old city.

South Park Street Cemetery is a treasure trove of British imperial history buried in Calcutta. Opened in 1767, the funereal obelisks are a testament to those participants in the British raj who made Calcutta their home. Among those whose graves are here are William Thackeray's father, Richmond; the linguist William Jones, founder of the Royal Asiatic Society; Colonel Charles Deare, who fought Tipu Sultan; and Anglo-Indian poet Louis Vivian Derozio. Bhowanipor Military Cemetery is the burial place of Charles Dickens's second son, Walter Landor Dickens, who died in Calcutta as a lieutenant.

PRACTICAL INFORMATION FOR CALCUTTA

WHEN TO GO. Calcutta is best visited between October and March, when temperatures are between 98° F and 45° F. From April to June and during the July and August monsoon, humidity can reach 100 percent. During the monsoon, rains invariably flood city thoroughfares and Calcutta's antiquated, late nineteenth-century sewage and drainage system.

HOW TO GET THERE. By Air. Daily *Indian Airlines* flights connect Calcutta with all major cities in India. Calcutta is an international airport served by *Aeroflot, Air India, Bangladesh Biman, Druk Air, Royal Nepal Airlines, Singapore Airlines,* and *Thai International,* among others. India's feeder airline, *Vayudoot,* also has a number of flights to Calcutta. The state government is trying to upgrade and revitalize airport services to attract other international carriers to serve this city, which used to be a regular stopover for flights to and from Southeast Asia and the Pacific, including Australia.

After being lulled by the brisk efficiency of airports at Bombay, Delhi, and Madras, you should be prepared for long slow-moving lines in Calcutta's International Arrivals area. Airport personnel are less helpful here than at India's other international airports, and patience will be needed to surmount the aggravation caused by the airport authorities' lack of organization. If possible, use another international airport to enter India from abroad. The domestic section is reasonably well managed and should present no hazards.

By Train. Calcutta is well connected by rail to all major cities. Howrah Station, the focal point of rail travel in the eastern region, is an extraordinary place, teeming with thousands of people, and the terminal for such folkloric trains as the Delhi-Howrah Mail (26 hours); Air-conditioned Express (same distance in 24 hours); the Rajdhani Express (fastest, in 22 hours); the Calcutta Mail (36 hours from Bombay);

the Gitanjali Express (30 hours from Bombay); the Coromandel Express (25 hours from Madras).

With computerization now available, you can purchase tickets at any of the following *Eastern Railway* booking offices: 14A Strand Rd., Calcutta 700 001 (near the GPO); 6 Fairlie Pl., Calcutta 700 001 (close to the Reserve Bank of India, a few blocks from the GPO). Tickets are also available at the railway stations (Howrah and Sealdah—the latter being the local commuter station in Southern Calcutta) although the lines and the waiting periods can be daunting. *Southeastern Railway* tickets are available for all classes from Esplanade Mansions, Esplanade East (near Raj Bhavan or Governor's House). If you're traveling overnight, remember to reserve a sleeping berth.

By Rented Car with Driver. India's oldest and most famous highway, the Grand Trunk Road, connects Delhi, Bombay, and Madras; but the closest major city, Madras, is a long journey—about 1,200 km (744 mi.). The *Automobile Association of Eastern India,* 13 Promothesh Barua Sarani (tel. 475131), can provide road maps and vital information on gas stations, lodging, detours, and the like enroute.

By Bus. *North Bengal State Transport Corporation* operates buses from Calcutta to North Bengal, various other parts of the state, Bihar, and Orissa. Booking offices are at Esplanade Bus Terminus, diagonally opposite the Central Cottage Industries Emporium at the hub of Calcutta's Chowringhee Road (J. L. Nehru Road).

TOURIST INFORMATION. The *Government of India Tourist Office* at Shakespeare Sarani (tel. 4443521) and the *West Bengal Tourist Information Center,* 3/2 BBD Bagh (East) (tel. 288271) can provide you with all the information you require. The Government of India Tourist Office is open Monday–Friday, 9 A.M.–6 P.M.; Saturday, till 1 P.M. The West Bengal Tourist Information Center is open Monday–Friday, 7 A.M.–5:30 P.M.; and the first and third Saturdays, till noon. The West Bengal Tourist Information Center has a free booklet, *Calcutta,* which lists the addresses and telephone numbers of airlines, trains, buses, ferries, travel agents, shipping companies, hotels, restaurants, medical services, banks, consulates, and tourist information counters for all other Indian states. The other guide to pick up, *Calcutta Briefs,* is sold at local bookstores (try Cambridge or Oxford on Park Street) for Rs. 15 (a little over a dollar) and includes information on shopping, local performances and art exhibits, and notes on Bengali cuisine. It is simple, informative, and amusing.

FOREIGN CURRENCY EXCHANGE. Most Western-style hotels have money-exchange counters. Otherwise, go to the American Express office, 21 Old Court House St.; *Bank of America,* 8 India Exchange Pl.; *Citibank,* Tata Center, 43 J.L. Nehru Rd.; Grindlays Bank, 19 N.S. Rd.; the *State Bank of India,* 33 J.L. Nehru Rd. Banks are open Monday–Friday, 10–2; Saturday, 10–noon.

ACCOMMODATIONS. Prices are based on double occupancy and don't include taxes: *Deluxe,* over Rs. 1,450; *Expensive,* Rs. 950–Rs. 1,450; *Moderate,* Rs. 500–Rs. 950; *Inexpensive,* under Rs. 500. Most Western-style hotels accept major credit cards.

Deluxe

Oberoi Grand. 15 Jawaharlal Nehru Rd., Calcutta; tel. 292323. 250 rooms with bath. Super posh and newly refurbished, this Victorian landmark has spacious modern rooms; the best ones overlook the courtyard and pool. TV, air-conditioning, room service, restaurants, bar, pool, health club, shops, foreign-exchange and travel counter. AE, DC, MC, V.

Taj Bengal. 34 B, Belvedere Rd., Alipore, Calcutta; tel. 283939. 250 rooms with bath. Calcutta's newest hotel is elegant, with a handsome atrium lobby filled with palm trees, water channels, and Indian art and antiques. Air-conditioned rooms are done up in a contemporary decor with pretty floral bedspreads and drapes. Best rooms overlook the pool and offer a view of Victoria Memorial Hall. TV, room service, multicuisine restaurants, bar, swimming pool, health club, business center, foreign-exchange counter, travel agency, shopping arcade. AE, DC, MC, V.

Expensive

Hotel Airport Ashok. Calcutta Airport, Calcutta; tel. 575111. 156 rooms with bath. This modern hotel with pleasant rooms is primarily for the traveler with just an overnight stop. TV, air-conditioning, room service, restaurants, bar, pool, shopping arcade, foreign-exchange and travel counter. AE, DC, MC, V.

New Kenilworth. 1 & 2 Little Russell St., Calcutta; tel. 448394. 100 rooms with bath. Popular with repeat visitors to Calcutta, this hotel has two attractive wings—one new and the other refurbished—surrounded by gardens. The rooms are comfortable and spacious. TV, air-conditioning, room service, restaurants, travel counter, book shop. AE, DC, MC, V.

Park Hotel. 17 Park St., Calcutta; tel. 297336. 155 rooms with bath. This Western-style hotel has small rooms with narrow beds. Best feature is its good central location. TV, air-conditioning, room service, restaurants, pool, foreign-exchange and travel counter. AE, DC, MC, V.

Moderate

Fairlawn Hotel. 13/A Sudder St., Calcutta; tel. 244460. 20 rooms with bath. If you want old-fashioned charm, consider staying here. A Calcutta landmark, Fairlawn was built in 1801 on a side street. The rooms are furnished with chintz and memorabilia. In the hot months, ask for air-conditioning. Amenities include TV in a lovely upstairs sitting room, multicuisine restaurant. Meals included. AE, MC, V.

Great Eastern. 1 Old Court House St., Calcutta; tel. 282331. 200 rooms with bath. Once Kipling's favorite hotel, Great Eastern is now run by the government. Though the management is wonderful, the hotel has lost its grandeur. The air-conditioned rooms are spacious and clean, however, and the location is ideal for Calcutta sightseeing. TV, room service, restaurants, bar, foreign-exchange and travel counter. AE, DC, MC, V.

Lytton Hotel. 14 Sudder St., Calcutta; tel. 291872. 59 rooms with bath. This unpretentious Western-style hotel has plain carpeted rooms with TV and air-conditioning. Restaurants, room service, bar. AE, DC, MC, V.

Inexpensive

International Guest House. Ramakrishna Mission Institute of Culture, Golpark, Ballygunge, Calcutta; tel. 463431. Available here are decent, simple rooms, far from the city center in southern Calcutta. Rupees only.

YMCA. Chowringhee. J.L. Nehru Rd., Calcutta; tel. 233504. The "deluxe" section of this hostel, between Metro Cinema and the Grand Hotel, has air-conditioned rooms. Rupees only.

YWCA International Guest House. 1 Middleton Row, Calcutta, West Bengal; tel. 240260. Couples are permitted to stay in this simple, clean hostel. Rupees only.

DINING OUT. The passions of Calcuttans can be listed as politics, argument, *adda* (a spirited blend of gossip and intellectual discourse), cricket, and food. Bengali cuisine, with its accent on fish and prawn dishes, is fabulous. If you have the opportunity try these delicacies: freshwater fish (*macher jhol*); sweets, especially *sandesh* and *rossogolla; chingri* (prawns) in coconut sauce; fish in rich yogurt sauce (*doi maach*); smoked *hilsa*. Other cuisines that provide Calcutta with a pleasant flavor are Cantonese Chinese, Burmese, all manner of North Indian and South Indian food, and Continental Western food, as well as the movable feasts of roadside stalls at the southern end of the Maidan. *Daab* water, fresh coconut juice, fresh fruit juices, and *lassis* (yogurt and fruit drinks) are available during the summer near the Lighthouse Cinema, off Chowringhee (J. L. Nehru Road) on Humayun Place.

Most accommodations listed above also have restaurants. Breakfast is usually served from 8–10:30; lunch is usually noon–3; and dinner, 7:30–11. The restaurants listed below are informal and unless noted don't require reservations. Dry days (no liquor) and meatless days (no red meat is served) are Thursdays. Prices, based on one person eating a three-course meal, excluding taxes, tip, or beverage, are *Deluxe,* over Rs. 120; *Expensive,* Rs. 80–Rs. 120; *Moderate,* Rs. 40–Rs. 80; *Inexpensive,* under Rs. 40.

Deluxe

Chinoiserie. Taj Bengal, 34 B, Belvedere Rd.; tel. 283939. This elegant restaurant with an interior pavilion and handsome Chinese murals serves delicious Szechuan fare. Among its specialities are king prawns in pepper salt (fried prawns tossed in a mildly spicy sauce) and *tau su* chicken (fried chicken prepared in a wok with spices). Open noon–3 P.M. and 7–midnight. AE, DC, MC, V.

Ming Court. Oberoi Grand, 15 Jawaharlal Nehru Rd.; tel. 292323. This elegant restaurant, with subtle Chinese touches, serves excellent Szechuan and Polynesian dishes. Dinner reservations advised. Open 12:30–2:30 P.M. and 8–11:30 P.M. AE, DC, MC, V.

Moghul Room. Oberoi Grand, 15 Jawaharlal Nehru Rd.; tel. 292323. A sleek modern decor with lots of marble and Indian *ghazals* (musicians) nightly highlights the Moghul Room. The Indian cuisine, with the emphasis on Mughlai dishes, is superb. Dinner reservations advised. Open 12:30–2:30 P.M. and 8–11:30 P.M.

Expensive

Blue Fox. 55 Park St.; tel. 297948. This Calcutta landmark, popular with the smart set, is spacious and has high ceilings. It has a quiet decor in which to enjoy excellent Indian and Continental cuisines. The sizzlers and crab or lobster thermidor are excellent. Open 11 A.M.–10:30 P.M. Dinner reservations advised. Rupees only.

Sky Room. 57 Park St.; tel. 294362. Extremely pretty, with upholstered chairs, crisp table linen, a ceiling with twinkling stars, and handsome murals, the Sky Room serves Indian and Continental dishes, with most people raving over the Western fare. Dinner reservations advised. Open 10:30 A.M.–midnight. Closed Tuesdays. Rupees only.

Moderate

Amber. 11 Waterloo St.; tel. 283018. An upstairs restaurant with subdued lighting, this popular eatery serves Continental and Indian cuisines, including especially tasty tandoori items. Open noon–4 P.M. and 7–11 P M Dinner reservations advised. Rupees only.

Bar-B-Q. 43 Park St.; tel. 249348. This upstairs restaurant, with a bank of windows looking out at trees, copper vessels on shelves, and wagon wheels with lanterns hanging from its ceiling, serves great Cantonese and Szechuan dishes. Try the crispy fried chicken served with a mild "surprise" sauce or the boneless chili chicken. Open 11A.M.–3 P.M. and 7–10:30 P.M. Weekend reservations advised. AE, DC, MC, V.

Peter Cat. 18 Park St.; tel. 298841. In this intimate restaurant, with white stucco walls, Tiffany-style lamps, and soft lighting, you can enjoy good Continental and Indian dishes, especially tandoori. Open 10 A.M.–midnight. Dinner reservations advised. DC, V.

Suruchi. 89 Elliot Rd.; tel. 293292. In this popular restaurant with an understated, pleasant decor, the accent is on excellent Bengali dishes, possibly the best in Calcutta. Try the delicious *hilsa* (river fish) or the day's catch from the sea. Open 11 A.M.–10 P.M. Rupees only.

Inexpensive

Aminia. 6 A, S.N. Banerjee Rd.; tel. 241318. This restaurant has a gigantic front room with overhead fans and taped Hindi music echoing off the walls; family rooms in the back have curtained booths. Waiters bustle around serving delicious tandoori chicken, biryani dishes, kebab, and great snacks. Open 10 A.M.–10 P.M. Rupees only.

Chung Wah. 13 A & B, Chittaranjan Ave.; tel. 277003. Popular and extremely informal, Chung Wah has been serving excellent Chinese dishes for 60 years. Popular choices are the delicious Szechuan prawns and the *yai chai* pork (steamed pork stuffed in cabbage leaves then garnished with a tangy sauce). Open 11 A.M.–11 P.M. Closed Thursdays. Rupees only.

Sabir's. 71 Biplabi Anukul Chunder St.; no phone. A large, plain room with about 50 tables and chairs and whirring overhead fans, Sabir's serves excellent North Indian fare. Try the good mutton biryani. Open 10 A.M.–10 P.M. Rupees only.

Vineet. 1 Shakespeare Sarani; tel. 440788. This popular restaurant serves excellent vegetarian food (Continental, Chinese, and Indian) and has live Indian music at night. Open noon–3 P.M. and 7–11 P.M. Rupees only.

SWEETS AND TREATS. Bengali sweets—*rosogollah, sandesh, rosomallai, gulab jamun, sitabhog, shorbhaja,* and *barfi,* to name a few—are available at a variety of places. Cool your feet and relax at *K. C. Das,* 11 Esplanade Rd. East; *Ganguram's* Chowringhee, near the Birla Planetarium; *Kathleen's Bakery,* 12 Free School St., which is unfortunately closed Thursdays; *Tulika's,* 41 J.L. Nehru Rd., which has great pizzas and sundaes; and *Flury's Swiss Confectionery,* 18 Park St.

After savoring some of the city's gastronomic delights, one last taste treat awaits you, *paan*—a concoction of betel nut and other items wrapped in a paan leaf that has been spread with lime paste. This after-dinner digestive is an acquired taste, but one worth trying, especially after a huge Indian meal.

Paan is prepared in many different ways. Ask for *mitha paan* (sweet paan), which has sweet condiments (no *masala* or spices) and mint. It will be given to you folded into a trianglar shape that you pop whole into the back of your mouth. Next: chew! (Make your first bite a tentative one—sometimes the betel nut is so hard that you can do damage to fillings if you bite down too vigorously.)

Varieties of paan include one that contains *zarda,* a legal, mild narcotic. Restaurants will get it for you for a small tip. Paan shops are abundant in Calcutta, often selling cigarettes and soft drinks as well. We recommend the shop near Kwality's on Park Street, the one opposite the Waldorf restaurant on Park Street, and the one next door to the Amber restaurant.

HOW TO GET AROUND. From the Airport. The airport is 15 km (nine mi.) from the the center of Calcutta. Only the Hotel Airport Ashok offers free pickup service. The airport coach (Rs. 15) goes to most of the better hotels and the city center; their counter is near the baggage claim area. To go by taxi, the fare is about Rs. 70.

By Bus. Calcutta still operates over 225 separate public bus routes, over 25 "special" tram routes with carriages for women only, and over 50 minibus routes (buses that travel an express route). Fares, extremely inexpensive, are based on the distance traveled.

By Ferry Boat. There are ferries on the Hooghly River (as the Ganges is called in this area). As of mid-1987, there were eight ferry landings around metropolitan Calcutta, shuttling workers between Calcutta and Howrah.

By Metro. Calcutta has a "first" in India in terms of mass transit. It is the *Metro,* the first subway on the subcontinent, built over a period of 15 years amid great controversy, long delays, and huge cost overruns. The butt of many a Bengali joke, it shuttles about 10,000 commuters each day over a 10-km (six-mi.) route from the eastern Tollygunge section to the business district of Park Street. Trains arrive promptly every 15 minutes at spotless platforms, with announcements being made in three languages (Hindi, Bengali, and English). The doors open without a fuss, and air-conditioned cars disgorge their occupants, who cannot believe that such an efficient, clean system will remain so for long. In mid-1990, a 16-km (10-mi.) system was opened between Tollygunge and Dum Dum (near the airport). Many Calcuttans use the Metro as a tourist attraction, much like the beginning years of Washington, D.C.'s system. Ride it for pleasure and for a fast ride down Chowringhee (J. L. Nehru Road). The fare depends on the distance traveled; the minimum is Rs. 1.50.

By Taxi. Taxis have meters, but drivers won't use them. Ask your hotel for the appropriate fare, then negotiate.

By Auto Rickshaw. Again don't expect meters to work. Fares should be cheaper than taxis.

By Bicycle Rickshaw. This is the cheapest way to get around. Negotiate the fare before you start; but have sympathy for the driver, who works hard for his rupees.

By Rented Car and Driver. For excursions around Calcutta, hire a car with driver from a recommended travel agency (see *Tour Operators* below). Rates are about Rs. 3.50 per km with a halt charge of Rs. 50 per night.

For a complete and authoritative guide to all bus and tram routes in the city, we recommend the *Calcutta and Howrah Guide,* sold for less than $1 at, among other places, the Oxford Booksellers on Park Street, next door to Kwality restaurant.

TOURS. The *West Bengal Government Tourist Office* at 3/2 BBD Bagh East, near Great Eastern Hotel (tel. 288271) offers numerous conducted and package tours. If you don't see printed information sheets at the office, ask; the tourist officers are helpful and informed. The ITDC at 4 Shakespeare Sarani (tel. 440901) also operates similar services. Tourist taxis are available from both locations. A full-day guided tour that takes in over 12 sights costs Rs. 30 (non-air-conditioned); Rs. 45 (air-conditioned).

From October to March, the West Bengal Tourist Office has a number of package tours (including meals and accommodations) via train, bus, and boat to North Bengal and the Sunderbans (the swampy delta region of the Bay of Bengal that has the largest population of Indian tigers). The prices for these tours, which run from two days to a week, are reasonable. The tours are worth investigating if you are short of time and have a limited budget.

During the festival of Durga Puja, this office also conducts excellent tours to traditional prayer services performed in some of Calcutta's older private homes. At night, they also offer a tour of the fabulous Durga Puja displays erected around the city. From April to August, they sponsor evening cruises on the Hooghly River.

TOUR OPERATORS. For all travel needs, contact *American Express,* 21 Old Court House St., tel. 286281; *Mercury Travels,* 46-C J. L. Nehru Rd., tel. 443555; or *Travel Corporation of India,* 46-C J.L. Nehru Rd., tel. 445469. *ITDC* (c/o Government of India Tourist Office, 4 Shakespeare Sarani, tel. 440901) also provides hired cars with driver. Most of these offices are open Monday–Saturday, 10 A.M.–5 P.M.

SEASONAL EVENTS. Calcutta embodies Hindu India's "museum of festivals" and secular India's joy in celebrating its diverse cultures. There is a festival of some kind almost every week. Since the specific dates for most festivals each year are determined by the lunar calendar, consult the Government of India Tourist Office for details.

January/February. *Ganga Sagar Mela.* During this Festival of the River Ganges, pilgrims from all over India celebrate the most important natural element in their mythology—the river, source of life, purifier, destroyer, and nurturer.

January/February. *Vasant Panchami.* This festival honors Saraswati, the goddess of learning and the arts, with immersion of her image into nearby rivers.

March. *Holi* or *Dol Jatra.* The festival of colors heralds the arrival of spring. Celebrants splatter each other with colored water. Wear old clothes.

April/May. *Baisak.* This festival celebrates the Bengali New Year.

June/July. Another interesting festival that occurs in the Calcutta area is the *Baul Festival* of song and prayer. The Bauls are wandering minstrels who worship Krishna and who, through their haunting songs, search for the divine in all of us. They carry on impromptu conversations with Krishna through their music as they travel from village to village through the winter and spring months. Baul music is being revived by individual groups in and around Calcutta in an effort to preserve it. Inquire at the tourist office for more information.

September/October. *Durga Puja.* This fabulous event, which is celebrated for three weeks, honors Kali, one of Durga's incarnations. Each neighborhood has its own separate shrine with elaborate clay figures, some over a full story high, on bamboo and straw skeletons, that are uniquely constructed by a group of artisans in north Calcutta at Kumartulli, near Chitpur Road. At the close of the festivities, these statues are taken by open flatbed trucks, with surging crowds guiding them through the streets, to the Hooghly (*Ma Ganga*—Mother Ganges) and floated away. If you take a tour of neighborhoods at night to see the different forms that this colorful and imaginative folk art takes, along with the panoply of neon lights, jatras, and music, you won't be disappointed.

October/November. *Diwali.* This Festival of Lights celebrates the return of Rama from his exile and his victory over Ravana, the demon, in the epic myth of the *Ramayana.* Almost all houses are lit with small terra-cotta oil lamps that ring the balconies and rooftop edges. Prayers are offered to Lakshmi, the goddess of wealth and prosperity, who is welcomed into households with crescendos of firecrackers. At least for another year, good has triumphed over evil.

December. *Boro Deen.* This is the Bengali version of Christmas. The weeks before the holiday offer an opportunity to hear some of the city's excellent amateur choirs at churches such as St. Paul's Cathedral, to shop in the well-stocked stores, and to visit the traveling exhibits at fairs that are set up in the Maidan during this season.

HISTORIC SITES. Entrance to most places is generally free; where a donation is asked, a few rupees will suffice. Most sites are open daily from sunrise to sunset unless noted otherwise below.

Belur Math. Established in 1898, this is the center of the Ramakrishna Mission. Open daily 6:30 A.M.–noon and 3:30–7:30 P.M.

Botanical Gardens. This enormous garden, constructed in 1787, has over 30,000 varieties of plants and trees.

Dakshineshwar Temples. Built from 1847 to 1855, this complex with 13 temples, near the Vivekananda Bridge, is an important pilgrimage site.

Jorsanko House. Located at 5 Dwarkanath, this rambling house, the home of Rabindranath Tagore, recently suffered serious damage from heavy rain and was under renovation at press time. You can, however, visit the nearby museum with wonderful family memorabilia. Open 10 A.M.–5 P.M; Saturdays till 1:30 P.M.

Kalighat Kali Temple. This intriguing Hindu temple complex, built in 1809, is near Kalighat Road.

Marble Palace. Filled with outlandish whimsy and paintings, the Marble Palace, built in 1835, is set on a small estate with live birds and a melange of sculptures on Muktaram Babu Street. Closed Monday and Thursday; on other days it's open 10 A.M.–4 P.M. You supposedly need a pass to enter, but no one ever asks for it. Make a small donation to the obligatory guide.

Mother Theresa Homes. The headquarters of the Missionaries of Charity is at 54A, Lower Circular Road.

Nakhoda Mosque. The largest mosque in Calcutta, the Nakhoda, near Mahatma Gandhi Road, was built in 1926.

Ochterlony Monument. This pillar, erected in 1828, is at the northern end of the Maidan. To climb the spiral staircase you need prior permission from the Police Commissioner; consult the West Bengal Tourist Office.

Parasnath Temple. Constructed in 1867 on Budree Das Street, this magnificent structure has exquisite details and statues. Open daily 6 A.M.–noon and 3–7 P.M.

St. Andrew's Church. Built in 1847, this church is easy to spot. Soaring spires jut above Jawaharlal Nehru Road.

St. John's Church. Erected in 1784, this beautiful church is on Kiron Sankar Roy Road.

Writers Building. This expansive Victorian structure, built in 1780, is on Dalhousie Square.

MUSEUMS AND GALLERIES. Calcutta's cultural energy is ever present in the diversity and range of its museums, galleries, and constantly changing exhibits. From November to March, fairs and exhibitions dot the central Maidan. Most of the museums and galleries listed here are free. When donations are accepted, Rs. 5 will suffice.

Ashutosh Museum of Indian Art, College Street, is a small museum, located in the Senate House of Calcutta University. It has an excellent and noteworthy collection of Bengal folk art, textiles, and terra-cotta clay models. The museum is open daily 10:30 A.M.–4:30 P.M. (Saturdays till 3 P.M.). It is closed Sundays and university holidays.

The Asiatic Society, 1 Park St., founded in 1784, is a research center for Indology. The library contains 20,000 volumes of rare Sanskrit, Arabic, Persian, and Hindi manuscripts. The society was reorganizing its collection at press time; consult the tourist department for details.

Birla Academy of Art and Culture, 109 Southern Ave., houses contemporary paintings, graphic arts, and photographs. Open daily except Mondays 3–8 P.M.

Birla Planetarium, J. L. Nehru Road, near Victoria Memorial, is modeled after a Buddhist *stupa* (shrine) at Sanchi. Built in 1962, it was India's first planetarium and is one of the largest in the world. Daily programs are in English, Hindi, and Bengali. Open daily 11:30 A.M.–8 P.M.

Bungiya Sahitya Parishad, 243/1 Upper Circular Rd., has collections of paintings of the Bengal School, sculptures, coins, and rare books in Sanskrit and Bengali. Check with the tourist department for hours.

Gurusaday Museum, Bratacharigram, Thakurpukur, off Diamond Harbor Rd., about 19 km (12 mi.) from the city center, has exhibits including Bengali folk art, especially Kalighat *pat* (scrolls), similar to the murallike Orissan palm leaf paintings. Open 11:30 A.M.–4:30 P.M.; closed Thursdays.

The Indian Museum on Chowringhee (J. L. Nehru Road) is the oldest in India and one of the largest and most comprehensive collections in Asia. It opened in 1878, after being in construction for three years. Known locally as *Jadu Ghar,* the "House of Magic," the museum has 36 galleries, including one of the best natural history collections in the world. The archaeology section has a representative collection of antiquities from prehistoric times to the Mogul period, including relics from Mohenjo-Daro and Harappa, the oldest excavated Indus valley civilizations. The southern wing includes the Bharhut and Gandhara rooms (Indian art from second century B.C. to A.D. fifth century), the Gupta and Medieval galleries, and the Mogul gallery.

The coin collection, which you require special permission to see, contains the largest collection of Indian coins in the world. Gems and jewelry are also on display. The art section is on the first floor and has a good collection of Indian textiles, carpets, wood, papier-mâché, and terra-cotta pottery. A gallery on the third floor contains exquisitely drawn Persian miniatures, Indian paintings, and Tibetan monastery banners. The anthropology section on the first floor is devoted to cultural anthropology. The museum is planning a major change in the near future to establish India's first comprehensive physical anthropology exhibit in a major museum. The geological section is the largest in Asia. Some interesting specimens on display are an Egyptian mummy donated in 1880 by an English seaman, a fossilized 200-million-year-old tree trunk, the lower jaw of an 84-foot whale, and meteorites dating 50,000 years. Open daily 10 A.M.–5 P.M. (March–October) and 10 A.M.–4 P.M. (November–February). Closed Mondays and public holidays.

Nehru Children's Museum, 94/1 J. L. Nehru Rd., adjoining St. Paul's Cathedral, has excellent exhibits for young and old that enliven mythology and history through the use of models and dolls. Open Tuesday–Sunday, noon–8 P.M. Closed Mondays.

Victoria Memorial, J. L. Nehru Road, was conceived in 1901 by Lord Curzon and constructed over a 20-year period. This "poor man's Taj Mahal" is designed in a mixture of Italian Renaissance and Saracenic architectural styles. Surrounded by spaciously laid-out gardens and Calcutta's great Maidan, Victoria Memorial houses an interesting collection of artifacts illustrating British roots in India. It includes Queen Victoria's writing desk and piano, pistols used by Warren Hastings, a governor-general, notebooks of Tipu Sultan, and prints, Indian miniature paintings, water colors, and Persian books. Open daily 10 A.M.–4:30 P.M. except Mondays. Cameras are not allowed; you must leave your cameras in the checkroom near the ticket booth.

Other museums and galleries of interest are *Academy of Fine Arts,* Cathedral Road, next to St. Paul's Cathedral. Besides extensive galleries, plays are staged here daily. *Philatelic and Postal History Museum,* next to the GPO at BBD Bagh; closed Sundays. *Ramakrishna Mission Institute of Culture,* Golpark, Ballygunge. *Birla Industrial and Technological Museum* at 19A Gurusaday Rd. *Netaji Bhawan,* 38/2 Elgin Rd., originally the house where the nationalist, Subhas Bose, Bengal's favorite son, lived and worked. Historical exhibits are on display. Other art centers include *Art and Prints Gallery,* 31 Park Mansion; *Calcutta Painters,* 37C College Rd; *Society of Contemporary Artists,* 68/4 Purnadas Rd; *Rabindra Bharati Museum,* 6/4 Dwarkanath Tagore La.; and *Indian Society of Oriental Art,* 15 Park St.

For updated and current information on gallery offerings and museum exhibits, we recommend the Sunday edition of the *Telegraph* newspaper and *Calcutta: This Fortnight,* a free booklet available from the Government of India Tourist Office or the West Bengal Tourist Information Center.

PUBLIC LIBRARIES AND READING ROOMS. Calcutta has over 150 libraries (listed in *Calcutta and Howrah Guide,* Rs. 15, available at bookstores and newsstands). The *National Library* is at Belvedere, across from the Calcutta zoo, in the former viceregal residence. The biggest library in India, it contains over eight million manuscripts in various languages. The reading rooms are quiet and restful. Open 8 A.M.–8 P.M. Here are a few other libraries with the best locations and facilities: *American Library (USIA),* 7 J. L. Nehru Rd.; *Asiatic Society,* 1 Park St.; *British Council,* 5 Shakespeare Sarani; and *Ramakrishna Mission Institute of Culture,* Golpark.

Recommended Reading. Two books are informative supplements to your visit: *Calcutta,* published by the West Bengal Tourist Office in conjunction with IBH

Publishing, is available at Oxford Booksellers on Park Street. Its quirky, often amusing, writing exhibits a loving feel for this chaotic yet mesmerizing city. Also available at Oxford is Geoffrey Moorhouse's *Calcutta* (New York: Holt, Rinehart, and Winston, 1985), which is essential reading for anyone who visits this astonishing city.

GARDENS AND ZOOS. The *Botanical Gardens,* nine km (six mi.) from Calcutta, is the largest and oldest of its kind in India, with over 30,000 varieties of trees and plants. Take a ferry from Metiaburuz and picnic on the grounds. The garden is open 7 A.M.–5 P.M. *Eden Gardens,* located on the Maidan, was laid out in 1835 and has a pagoda hauled in from Burma. *Zoological Gardens* in Alipore, three km (two mi.) from Calcutta, was established in 1876 and is the largest zoo in India. Open daily.

SPORTS AND OUTDOOR ADVENTURES. Calcuttans love sports, especially cricket. From November to February, the cricket season rules the day when work comes to a standstill and Eden Gardens overflows. With television the motto has become, "If you can't play, watch." Matches of people with various levels of skills— from international test matches to backyard alley games—are fielded every day. Bengal's obsession with sports also includes **soccer,** which was, until recently, the best-loved sport. You always know when a divisional soccer match is in progress near the Maidan; the roar of the crowd is like a "cathartic release of emotion," according to one local observer.

Clubs were formed during British times to set off the rulers from the ruled, and clubs continue to be an arena for much of Calcutta's passion for sports. A new hierarchy has been established through membership dues, and **sports clubs** continue to flourish. You have to be a guest of a member to attend, or you can apply for temporary membership. There are over 100 such clubs in Calcutta. The *Calcutta Cricket Club,* at 19/1 Gurusaday Rd., was founded in 1792 and is the oldest sports club outside England. The *Royal Calcutta Golf Club,* Golf Club Road and Tollygunge Road, is the oldest golf club in India.

Winter is also the time for **horse racing** and **polo.** The *Royal Calcutta Turf Club,* 11 Russell St., and the *Calcutta Polo Club,* 51 J. L. Nehru Rd., provide the organizational services for these two sports. The *Calcutta Racecourse,* built in 1819, is the scene of frenetic activity every Saturday, not just by the rich in box seats, but by ordinary racing enthusiasts perched atop the tallest tree branches on the outside of the track. Polo is played in sections of the Maidan.

Other sports include **rowing** at the *Lake* and *Bengal Rowing* clubs, both near Dhakuria Lake in Ballygunge; **horseback** riding at the *Tollygunge Club;* **swimming** at the *Saturday Club,* 7 Wood St., and the *Calcutta Swimming Club,* 1 Strand Rd.; **tennis** at the *Calcutta Cricket Club;* and **squash** at the *Calcutta Racket Club,* near St. Paul's Cathedral.

SHOPPING. Calcutta's *Central Cottage Industries Emporium,* next to the USIA on J. L. Nehru Road, and the many state emporiums around the city offer India's art, crafts, and fabrics. During the winter, craft and textile exhibitions are often held on the Maidan. Don't go when they first open (it sometimes takes a few days for all exhibitors to get set up) or too late, when goods have been picked over. Though the selection from other states is generally better in Bombay and Delhi, Bengal's crafts and fabrics are best bought in Calcutta.

Terra-cotta crafts from the Bankura, Birbhum, and Midnapore, districts of West Bengal, especially brightly painted figurines of animals and dancers and bas-relief plaques of deities such as Krishna and Radha, make unusual gifts, but one must pack these fragile items carefully. From Krishnanagar come clay figurines in both realistic and stylized shapes. Pottery bowls, mugs, plates, and serving bowls, glazed a rich aqua blue, are beautiful. Perhaps the most delightful of the crafts from Bengal are the frequently whimsical *dokra* figures made of a mixture of clay and metal, usually cast in the lost-wax method. The most popular forms of these Bengali folk bronzes and Hindu deities or animals. Shells are fashioned by shonkhari craftsmen into bangles, toe and finger rings, and exquisitely shaped demitasse spoons. Bell-metal work, bidri work, soapstone boxes and plates, and leather goods are some other indigenous crafts.

Textile buys are abundant in Calcutta. *Jamdani* weaving, a cotton fabric that is brocaded with cotton and *zari* (silver) threads is one of the more unusual weaves. Made on looms similar to the jamdani is the exquisite Baluchar brocaded silk from Murshidabad, with its deep purple or mauve background and ornately printed end pieces. For those who sew or have tailors back home, elegant Tussore silks are available by the meter.

In Calcutta's bazaars, more than in village bazaars, these items are plentiful. You can purchase men's *kurtas* (loose thigh-length shirts) that are popular with both men and women for the quality and coolness of their handwoven cotton fabric (*khadi*) and the freedom of their design. Women find *salwar kameez* sets (loose dress-length tops worn with baggy pants that fit tightly at the ankle) especially comfortable, although they are not always as available ready-made as are kurtas.

Kantha embroidery is a Bengali needlework specialty in which a quilted surface is embroidered with all manner of shapes, from the more usual birds, animals, and trees to abstract designs. Some of Calcutta's destitute women have been organized to make embroidered bedspreads and pillow covers that have plain or multihued floral designs on heavy cotton. Though the embroidery work in them is not as fine as that in Kashmiri woolen shawls, it is vigorous, cheerful, and appealing.

Shopping in bazaars around Calcutta can be either an exhilarating—if exhausting—experience or a lengthy test of wills. Parts of the famous *Sir Stuart Hogg Market,* better known as *New Market,* 19 Lindsay St., burned down a few years back, and many vendors have been relocated to J. L. Nehru Road, across from the Grand Hotel. The 110-year-old New Market houses about 2,500 stores under one roof, selling cotton *tangail* saris, Bankura clay horses, Malda brassware, leather from Santiniketan, silk from Murshidabad, Khadi cloth, poultry, cheeses, nuts, and other foods. It is one of Calcutta's most extensive bazaars. The new location lacks the bustling charm of the original New Market, and most visitors will find the undamaged part of the old area a more intriguing place to poke around. The bearers/touts at the old New Market are often difficult to discourage. (No matter how insistent they are, do not change foreign currency with them, and if they show you around the shops, you should be aware that they usually get a percentage of whatever you spend.) Another good market is *Treasure Island,* just opposite globe Cinema, near Hogg Market.

Other bazaar areas where Calcuttans go are *Gariahat,* 212, 214, and 216 Rash Behari Ave., *Barabazar,* in North Calcutta, and *Shyambazar,* 1A R. G. Kar Rd. On Sundays, traditionally the market day for Calcuttans, large wholesale markets spill from sidewalks into the streets in the North Calcutta area. At *Hathibagan,* 80, 81, and 82 Bidhan Sarani, even if one isn't interested in buying the goods being offered here—racing pigeons, parakeets, bright cotton children's clothes, inexpensive men's shirts and trousers, and plants—the energy and color are infectious. *Ulta-danga Market,* 22 Ultadanga Rd., caters primarily to small retail businesses; both vendors and buyers are men, and few women are seen on the streets. Taxis waiting to transport businessmen's large purchases line the side streets.

Bargaining is essential at all markets. Transactions are cash only; credit cards are not accepted.

Some specialty markets are on or near Chitpur Road, where there are shops that make musical instruments—sarods, sitars, harmoniums, *dholaks* (drums), and costumes for the traveling theatrical ensembles (*jatras*). At *Bowbazar,* the home of the jewelers' trade, one finds artisans who work in gold. Bentinck Street is known for its shoes and leather goods, and College Street, near the Ashutosh Museum, is the center for second-hand English and Bengali books. This street is packed tight with stalls overflowing with textbooks on every possible subject. Careful rummaging might turn up a first edition for a small price.

State-run emporiums lack the stimulating entrepreneurial energy of bazaar areas, but the quality of goods is usually better, and goods sell at fixed prices. Credit cards, usually American Express and Visa, are accepted in emporiums, such as *Central Cottage.*

Industries Emporium, which is at 7 J. L. Nehru Rd. (Chowringhee), next to the USIA Library. As the name implies, it has goods from all over India. Among other items, one can find colorful, intricate Mithila paintings from Bihar, beautiful hand-printed writing paper and envelopes, and wooden toys. Bengal Home Industries is at No. 57, where you'll find a wide selection of Bengali handicrafts and items made in Bengal's cottage industries.

Also on this road are *Cauvery Karnataka Upahar,* at No. 17; *Kashmir Government Art Emporium,* at No. 12, which sells this lovely northwestern state's renowned crafts, such as papier-mâché objects covered with intricate brushwork designs in silver and gold, finely woven textiles, richly embroidered woolen shawls, and silk and woolen carpets in traditional patterns; *Rajasthan Handicrafts,* at No. 30E), offers silver jewelery and miniature paintings; and *Tripura Administration Sales Emporium,* at No. 58B, has leather and bamboo crafts.

Four shops on Lindsay Street make convenient stops: *Handloom House,* at No. 3, where textiles by the yard and by the piece are available; *Manjusha,* at No. 7/1D; *Uttar Pradesh Government Emporium* at No. 12B; and *Manipur,* at No. 15L.

The *Punjab Government Emporium* is at 26B Camac St. *Refugee Handicrafts* is now located at 2A and 3A Gariahat Rd. and sells, among other things, textiles by weavers who relocated from East Pakistan. Textiles are also available at *Khadi Gromodyog Bhavan,* 24 Chittaranjan Ave. At the *Assam Emporium,* 8 Russell St., one can get unusual baskets and honey from other northeast states. In south Calcutta, a new shopping center of emporiums has opened recently, the *CIT Market* on Dakshinapan near Dhakuria. Batik fabric, appliqued silk salwars and pillow covers, and woolen shawls highlight the Gujarat emporium located here, and the *West Bengal Emporium* has a good selection of dokra figurines on the second floor. Most emporiums are open 9:30 A.M.–7 P.M., often take a lunch break 1 P.M.–3 P.M, and are closed on Sunday. Bazaars are generally open daily 9 A.M.–7 P.M.

Since Calcutta is cosmopolitan, it has some very special shops worth exploring. For lovely ready-mades for men or women or fabric by the meter, visit these stores:

Ananda, 13 Russel St.; open Monday–Friday, 10 A.M.–6:30 P.M. and Saturday till 2 P.M.

Take 'n Talk, 2 Russel St.; open Monday–Friday, 10 A.M.–7 P.M. and Saturday till 5 P.M.

Indian Silk House, College Street Market and 129 A Behari Ave.; open Monday, 2–7 P.M. and Tuesday–Saturday, 10 A.M.–7 P.M.

Kanishka, 2/1 Hindustan Rd., Gariahat; open Monday, 2–7 P.M. and Tuesday–Saturday, 10 A.M.–7P.M.

For good jewelry, visit these reliable stores:

Ram Lakshman, 7 A Lindsey St.; open Monday–Friday, 10:30 A.M.–6:30 P.M. and Saturday till 2.

Satramdas, 12J Park St.; open Monday–Friday, 10 A.M.–7 P.M. and Saturday till 1 P.M.

P.C. Chandra, 127/ 1A B.B. Banguly St. and 49C Gariahat Rd.; open Monday 3–7 P.M., and Tuesday–Saturday 10:30 A.M.–7 P.M.

Calcutta is also the center of the tea trade in India. Tea auction houses flourish, as they have for almost 150 years. Packaged tea, loose or in teabags, is readily available at stores.

ENTERTAINMENT. Calcutta takes its sustenance from the fervent creativity of its artists. Throughout the years of political strife and population and economic disasters, and browbeaten by the irritations and fatigue of daily life, Calcuttans have taken solace that their city has produced and keeps on producing some of India's most imaginative cultural representatives. It was here that Rabindranath Tagore wrote, becoming the first Asian to be selected for the Nobel Prize for literature. Tagore created a school of music, Rabindra Sangeet, whose two most famous expositions are the national anthems of India and Bangladesh. It is in Calcutta that filmmaker Satyajit Ray works and has brought a distinctively Bengali point of view of middle-class India to millions of viewers in the West. Here, too, Uday Shankar worked and brought Indian classical dance to the attention of the rest of the world, and Ravi Shankar, his younger brother, played sitar, to the joy of thousands the world over. It is here also that Bengali journals and broadsheets are sold for pennies on the street, poets hawk their poems on street corners, and where theater, both traditional and modern, flourishes. Calcutta's entertainment possibilities are manifold.

To start out, look up *Calcutta: This Fortnight* (a free pamphlet from the West Bengal Tourist Office) and the Sunday edition of the *Telegraph* newspaper for daily listings of cultural and other entertainment news.

Dance. Besides the Bharat Natyam and Kathak, there are performances of the Manipuri and Odissi (Orissa) styles at the *Academy of Dance and Music,* 5 Dwarkanath Tagore La.; *Academy of Fine Arts,* near the Birla Planetarium; and at *Kala Mandir.* A smorgasbord of Indian dances at the *Oberoi Grand* is held nightly but is only for those who are not adventurous enough to experience the local culture in its authentic settings.

Two splendid versions of dance-dramas or performance arts that are unique to Bengal are the *jatras* and *Kavi gan.* Jatra (folk theater) is enacted outside the traditional dramatic set. The audience sits in the open air and the actors and actresses sing or act their roles, while a small orchestra sits to one side of the performance space and accompanies the action. Taken traditionally from mythology or from old Bengali novels, jatras also address historical and political issues these days. The action here is broad and the scope of emotions is great. Although once considered an unsophisticated form of entertainment by urban Bengalis, the jatra has been enjoying a revival that has brought some of Bengal's most popular film actors and actresses to the stage. *Rabindra Bharati University,* 6/4 Dwarkanath Tagore La., once part of Tagore's residence, offers courses in jatra, and the university's performances are worth seeing. Watch the newspaper listings during the winter months for the performance times.

Kavi gan is a stylized duet of poets who sing their responses in verse, *ex tempore,* on selected themes. Once immensely popular, it is a rare phenomenon now, though there are occasions that are advertised during the winter season.

Music. *Rabindra Sadan,* A. J. Bose Road, near St. Paul's Cathedral; *Kala Mandir* and *Ramakrishna Mission Institute of Culture,* Golpark; and *Mahajati Sadan,* 166 Chittaranjan Ave. are some of the major venues for the world-renowned maestros of Indian music. These include Niser Hussain Khan, Latafat Hussain Khan, and Girija Devi, who follow in the tradition of Bade Gulam Ali, and Allaudin Khan, whose disciple was Ravi Shankar. There is also a developed folk music school in Bengal, known at Puratani (of old times). The subgroups are Panchali, Ramprasadi, Kirtan, and Toppa.

Theater. Bengali theater is the fulcrum of much of the city's cultural activities. Watch for performances at *Kala Mandir,* 48 Shakespeare Sarani; *Rabindra Sadan,* A. J. Bose Road, near St. Paul's Cathedral; *Star,* 79/3/4 Bidhan Sarani (tel. 55–1839); *Rungmahal,* 76/1B Bidhan Sarani (tel. 55–1619); Biswaroopa, 2A Raja Kissen St. (tel. 55–3220); and *Rangana,* 153/2 Acharya Prafulla Chandra Rd. (tel. 55–6846). The groups to watch for are Bahuroopi, People's Little Theatre, and Drama Libraries-Museums.

Bars. Calcutta's independent bars are not sprightly places. The most attractive places to enjoy a nightcap are the Oberoi Grand and the Taj Bengal. Bars stay open until 11 P.M. or midnight and are closed on Thursday.

WEST BENGAL AND BIHAR

Calcutta's "Suburbia" and Rural Neighbor

by
LISA SAMSON and AMIT SHAH

Calcutta's lack of "real" antiquities is sufficiently made up in the region surrounding it. After the British had merged Bengal with Bihar under the Bengal presidency in 1765, the modern-day states of West Bengal, Bihar, and Orissa were one—the land of the bounty of the Ganges.

Like all great river deltas, Bengal was unquestionably a cradle of civilization. Ptolemy's geography mentions it as a seafaring nation. The Pala kings who ruled from the eighth to the twelfth centuries were patrons of the arts and learning; their artists traveled far south, even to Indonesia, and their religious scholars carried the Buddhist gospels to Tibet. During the Mogul period, Akbar conquered Bengal, but Bengal became virtually a separate kingdom under the independent nawab, Siraj-ud-Daula, who was routed in 1757 at Plassey, north of Calcutta, by Robert Clive through a series of treacherous conspiracies. The British thus won control over Bengal after the Dutch, the French, and the Portuguese had all made some efforts. The subsequent history of Bengal is synonymous with Calcutta and is outlined in that chapter of this guide.

Today, bounded by Sikkim and Bhutan in the north, by Assam and Bangladesh in the east, by the Bay of Bengal and Orissa in the south, and by Bihar and Neap in the west and northwest, West Bengal covers 87,617 square kilometers (54,446 square miles) and has a population of over 54 million, an increase of nearly 24 percent since 1971.

Many travelers to West Bengal go north into the Himalayas to Darjeeling or Kalimpong, two hill stations established by the British during the days of the Raj. Once you leave Bagdogra, the northern gateway, the mountains dominate the landscape, towering above the waterfalls that thunder down ravines, the deep gorges sliced by fast-flowing rivers, and the terraced slopes of tea plantations. On clear days, Mount Kanchenjunga, the world's third-tallest peak, draws all eyes to its snow-clad pinnacles. No one may climb this mountain, the abode of Indra, the Hindu god of rain.

Darjeeling—Queen of the Himalayas

After the British acquired Darjeeling in 1835, crude huts of the original inhabitants gave way to manor houses, bungalows, and cottages with gingerbread trim. English-style gardens flowered everywhere. Tea gardens thrived in the perfect climate. By 1881, when a narrow-gauge Toy Train began to zigzag up the mountains, the hill station was completely anglicized. The British lived on the town's top ridge, and their workers lived on the hills below—a social and geographic stratification that exists today, with the Indian upper classes taking the place of the British.

From Chowrasta (The Mall), walk to Observatory Hill and the Mahakali Temple, a cave sacred to Shiva. Shiva's faithful bull, Nandi, guards the shrine along with two stone temple lions, your clue that this is also a solemn site for Buddhists—the location of a former monastery called Dorje Ling, which was destroyed in the nineteenth century by Nepalese Gurkhas. You see Buddhist prayer wheels, *chortens* (small shrines containing sacred relics), prayer flags alongside bells for Hindus to clang to announce their arrival to Shiva. Pilgrims to the shrine first get a blessing from a Hindu priest who sits in the inner sanctum, then they receive a blessing from a Sikkimese Buddhist Lama. Then devotees of both religions circle the structure three times, spinning the prayer wheels, ringing the bells, and burning incense in the chortens.

From Chowrasta, walk down C.R. Das Road and visit the Bhutia Busty Monastery, which belongs to a Buddhist Red Hat Sect and was built in 1934 by a former *chogyal* (king) of Sikkim. On the way to the monastery you pass Step Aside, a modest museum commemorating the Indian Nationalist leader, Chittaranjan Das.

Head south to Lloyds Botanical Garden, which is set on Darjeeling's lowest ridge. Over 125 years old, this garden has over 2,000 species of orchids in its Orchid House. The terraced gardens have Sikkim spruce, geraniums, arum lilies, alpine plants, azaleas, rhododendrons, magnolias, and a variety of Himalayan conifers.

Another garden, The Shubbery, planted by a former British governor of West Bengal, is at Jawahar Parbat (formerly Birch Hill) behind Raj Bhawan (Governor's House), northwest of the town square. From here, you get a magnificent view of Mount Kanchenjunga and the Singla Valley.

The Himalayan Mountaineering Institute, on Jawahar Road West, is a unique contribution to mountaineering that India established after the first successful climb of Mount Everest in 1953. Tenzing Norgay, who made the climb with Sir Edmund Hillary, was the institute's first principal. The institute trains hundreds of mountaineers of all ages and nationalities. Its excellent museum has photographs and displays of equipment and notebooks from all the legendary climbs, successful and tragic, including memorabilia from Mallory's ill-fated attempt.

Ghoom

The Yiga-Choling Buddhist Monastery in Ghoom, eight kilometers (five miles) from Darjeeling, is the oldest *gompa* (shrine) in the area, established in 1850 by a famous Tibetan astrologer, Lama Sherap Gyansto. Currently, 25 Gelug (Yellow Hat) sect lamas are in residence. The small prayer hall, with crumbling but lovely wall frescoes, has an enormous gilded statue of Maitreya (Future Buddha) behind the front altar. You also see statues of Gyansto, Avolokitesvara (Buddha of Compassion), and Padmasambhava, the Indian mystic.

Tiger Hill, 11 kilometers (seven miles) from Darjeeling, is the place for a sunrise view of Mount Kanchenjunga. The golden glow of the rising sun changes the color of the snowcapped peaks to crimson, pink, and shining gold as you watch from the observation deck.

Kalimpong

Kalimpong, 52 kilometers (32 miles) from Darjeeling, is a tiny hill station with a central street lined by buildings built in the 1920s. Walks offer views of the Deola Hills to the north; the Durbindara Hills to the south; and, on a clear day, the plains of Nepal's Terai and the lofty summits of Kanchenjunga.

At Tripai Hills, three kilometers (two miles) from the center of town, visit the Tharpa Choling Monastery, built in 1922 and belonging to the Gelug sect that follows the Dalai Lama. A pavilion with a gigantic prayer wheel and walls covered with old frescoes leads to a prayer hall filled with more old frescoes and statues. On the left side of the front wall is a statue of Guru Padmasambhava, the Indian mystic. To the right is a statue of Nowang Kegang, the founder of the monastery. Behind the altar is a statue of Sakyamuni (Historic Buddha) surrounded by photos of the gurus of the Dalai Lama. To his right is a polished bronze statue of the Avolokitesvara (Buddha of Compassion). Exquisite *thang-kas* (religious paintings) brought from Tibet hang in the center of the hall along with prayer drums.

The new Zangdogpalrifodang Monastery, on Durpin Dara Hill at the other end of Kalimpong, also belongs to the Gelug. Stairs to the side of the monastery lead to the *Cherisi* (prayer chamber) covered with brightly painted frescoes. Here a replica of a celestial chorten that was destroyed by the Chinese in Lhasa dominates the room. It took the lamas two years to construct at a cost of Rs. 50,000. The statue of the Buddha to its right was originally in Lhasa. On the top floor is a tiny chamber containing 1,000 small statues of the Buddha. The walls of the main hall on the ground floor, where the daily prayer services are held, are covered with frescoes, and the front altar enshrines a large statue of the Buddha.

Exploring Southern West Bengal

In the district of Malda, 338 kilometers (210 miles) north of Calcutta, you find the ancient cities of Gour and Pandua. Former capitals of Bengal and important cities during the Mogul era, these cities have exquisite historic monuments, including Adina Masjid—one on the largest mosques in India.

Murshidabad, the capital of Bengal in the 1700s, is 209 kilometers (130 miles) north of Calcutta. Here you find more historic monuments including the Katra Mosque and Hazarduari Palace, built in 1837 and known for its 1,000 doors. The palace contains firearms, china, and plates that are reputed to crack if poison is placed on them.

The seventeenth- and eighteenth-century capital of the Malla dynasties, Vishnupur is also the "terra-cotta capital" of West Bengal. Numerous historic building facades are covered with terra-cotta embellishments and depictions of legendary events.

Santiniketan, 136 kilometers (84 miles) northwest of Calcutta, is Rabindranath Tagore's "Abode of Peace," an open-air institution created in 1901 by the famous writer, painter, and philosopher. Here, in accordance with Tagore's philosophy, students learn the traditional arts of India's heritage in a setting that also reinforces man's relation with nature. In nearby Bakreswar, you can enjoy hot springs.

Diamond Harbour, a former Portuguese pirate stronghold 48 kilometers (30 miles) south of Calcutta, has a natural harbor and is an ideal picnic area. To the south, you find the Sunderbans, a jungle delta—approachable by boat—and the legendary home of the Bengal tiger. Bakkhali and Digha, 131 (81 miles) and 185 kilometers (115 miles) south of Calcutta, are West Bengal's most popular beach resorts.

Bihar

Bihar, bounded in the north by Nepal, east by West Bengal, south by Orissa, and west and southwest by Uttar Pradesh and Madhya Pradesh, was part of the great Magadh empire from 500 B.C. to A.D. 500. Pataliputra (present-day Patna) was designated by Chandragupta Maurya as the empire's capital city. Maurya's grandson, Ashoka, later became the evangelist of Buddhism. During A.D. fourth and fifth centuries, Pataliputra formed part of the great Gupta Empire, which saw the revival of Hinduism. Factional and fractious battles denied Bihar a stable rule until the eighth century, when the Palas of Bengal won paramountcy. In 1193, Bihar was overrun by Moslem invaders and remained part of the sultanate in Delhi till the second half of the fourteenth century. In 1529, Babur, the first of the Moguls, wrested it from the Lodhi rulers and was eventually ousted by the English in 1765, more because of weak-kneed, indolent nawabs than any British supremacy. In 1912, the British separated Bihar and Orissa from Bengal and divided the three into separate provinces in 1936.

Though rich in minerals, producing about 40 percent of the nation's mica, coal, copper, and iron ore, Bihar is still one of India's poorest states. Only 26 percent of its cultivatable lands are irrigated. Bihar, however, is amply endowed with important pilgrimage sites: Buddhist Bodhgaya, where Siddhartha Gautama (the Historic Buddha) attained enlightenment; and Gaya, a Hindu city second in importance to Varanasi. Bihar also has one of India's largest tribal populations, many of whom live in charming remote villages.

Exploring Southern Bihar

From West Bengal, the first stop in Bihar is Parasnath Hill. The site of numerous temples, this is the eastern center of Jain worship, and Parasnath, the 23rd Tirthankara (perfect soul) is said to have gained nirvana on this hill.

Southwest of Parasnath is Ranchi, a busy industrial city and the summer capital of Bihar. From here, travlers can discover southern Bihar's beautiful countryside. Travel 45 kilometers (30 miles) northeast to Hundra Falls, one of the highest falls in Asia. Here, when the Subarnarekha River is at its postmonsoon highmark, the falls are spectacular. Ninety-five kilometers (60 miles) to the south is the quiet town of Hazirabagh and its near-by National Park. About 154 kilometers (95 miles) to the west is the small hill station of Netarhat, surrounded by forests and the Chotanagpur Plateau. This last journey takes you into the heart of a tribal area, where infrequent hamlets are marked by just a few roadside stalls. For miles, you pass a procession of fields and see the tribals as they turn up the soil with wooden plows pulled by bullocks or gather about their huddled homes of clay covered with dung and subtle decorations.

At Bodhgaya, 208 kilometers (129 miles) north of Ranchi, stands the peepal tree (the Bodhi tree) underneath which, 2,500 years ago, Siddhartha Gautama, attained enlightenment and became the Buddha. The original Bodhi tree died, and saplings from it form the present tree. The Emperor Ashoka erected a shrine near the Bodhi tree that was replaced in the second century by the Mahabodhi Temple. The temple has been renovated many times, adding contours through the centuries. It shows the influence of various Buddhist countries, especially the curvilinear Burmese style. The surrounding railings are richly carved, and ornamented votive *stupas* (shrines) surround the main temple. The carvings are from the *Jataka* tales ("birth stories") and depict the Buddha's previous incarnations. The north side is flanked by the "jewel walk" or Chankramana—a raised platform with carved lotus flowers, where the Buddha is said to have paced back and forth, meditating and deliberating about whether he should reveal his wisdom and knowledge to the world. Bodhgaya is a pilgrimage spot for both Hindus and Buddhists. The Hindus consider the Buddha to be an incarnation of Vishnu. On the banks of the Niranjana River, where Siddhartha, a worldly young prince came to seek the ultimate truth, modern-day visitors stand in awe, looking at and touching the relics and objects of veneration of one of the world's oldest religions. Near the Chankramana is the *Tibetan Monastery,* built in 1938. A six-foot-high metal drum painted in golds and reds, the Dharma Chakra, or wheel of law, is the main object on view. For forgiveness of all past sins, turn the wheel three times, from left to right. There are also Chinese, Japanese, and Thai Buddhist temples here.

About 15 kilometers (nine miles) north of Bodhgaya is Gaya, a dusty little town at a major rail junction. Second only to Varanasi in sanctity for Hindus, Gaya attracts pilgrims from all over India, who come here after the deaths of their parents to offer *pindas* (funeral cakes) to the souls of the departed. This offering symbolically releases the dead from earthly bondage and is essential in Hindu ritual.

The center of the pilgrimage is the *Vishnupada Temple,* said to have been built over the footprints of Vishnu. Renovated in 1787, the structure is 97 feet high and has eight rows of sculpted pillars supporting the *mandapa* (hall). Non-Hindus are not allowed in the inner sanctum, but the exterior is well worth the visit. There's a banyan tree nearby under which the Buddha is said to have meditated for six years. One kilometer (half mile) away is *Bramanjuni Hill,* with 1,000 stone steps. Climb to the top and you'll see Gaya's rooftops and Bodhgaya's spires. On the Sone River at Baragaon, two kilometers (one mile) from Gaya, is the *Surya Temple,* dedicated to the Sun God, where pilgrims come to celebrate the Chhatha Vrata festival (see *Seasonal Events* section).

About 50 kilometers (31 miles) from Gaya are the *Barabar Caves,* on which E. M. Forster based his Marabar Caves in *Passage to India.* These are the earliest specimens of Buddhist rock-cut shrines, dating back to 200 B.C.; two of them bear inscriptions of Emperor Ashoka. One hundred kilometers (62 miles) west of Gaya is *Sasaram* and one of the finest Moslem mausoleums. Sher Shah, the builder of the Grand Trunk Road, the oldest highway in India, is entombed here under a five-tiered hexagon with arches, latticework cupolas, and a 150-foot dome. It stands in the middle of a lake with fountains. Two other excursions from Gaya, to Rajgir (64 kilometers or 40 miles) and Nalanda (66 kilometers or 41 miles) complete this tour.

Rajgir is one of the ancient towns associated with Buddhism. It was here that the first Buddhist Council met after the Buddha attained enlightenment and where his teachings were written down. Lord Buddha spent 12 years here, as did Mahavira, the founder of the Jain religion. Today, it is a health spot known mainly for its hot springs. Besides the hot springs, you can see ruins from an aerial chairlift. The Japanese have built a new monastery, *Vishwa Shanti Stupa* (World Peace Stupa), whose four Buddha statues depict birth, death, enlightenment, and teaching. There are Burmese and Thai monasteries; *Venuvena,* the bamboo park where the Buddha and his disciples lived; and Jain and Hindu temples, among others. The *Cyclopean Wall,* originally (48 kilometers or 30 miles) of perfectly joined stones that girdled the city, is now in ruins. Also, there is the *Ajatshatru Fort,* built in the fifth century B.C. by a king whom the Buddha had cured of a plague of boils.

The most famous center of ancient Buddhist scholarship is Nalanda, the "place that confers the lotus" (*nalam*)—a symbol of spiritual learning. Between the fourth and twelfth centuries, Nalanda was one of the most celebrated university towns. The Chinese traveler-scholar Hiuen T'sang spent 12 years here in the early seventh century and recorded that there were 10,000 monks and students and 2,000 teachers. He also left detailed descriptions of the vigorous university life, where nine million volumes of manuscripts were available for students from as far as Japan, Sumatra, Java, and Korea. In 1199, an Afghan marauder, Bhaktiar Khilji, torched the university and massacred its residents. Buddhism in India suffered a severe blow, and monks fled to caves or out of the country. Painstaking excavations have uncovered large areas of the university complex, including six temples and 11 monasteries. The most imposing is the *Sasiputa Stupa* (the Great Stupa), built by Ashoka to honor Ananda, the Buddha's first disciple. Also excavated is *Sarai Mound,* with frescoes of horses and elephants. Thai Buddhists have recently constructed a temple, *Wat Thai Nalanda,* here.

Exploring Northern Bihar

Traveling from the tranquility of the Buddhist excavated sites to the ancient capital, Pataliputra (present-day Patna), is not an altogether pleasant experience. Patna, an overcrowded city of over two million on the banks of the Ganges, stretches for over 13 kilometers (eight miles). It is the logical jumping-off point for your travels in Bihar, since it is linked to all major Indian cities. While you are here, you should take a quick tour of the city. *Golghar,* a beehive-shaped building, previously a gravnary built in 1787 to store grain following a famine in 1770, is a squat, impressive structure, 88 feet high and 410 feet wide, with 13-foot walls. Two staircases lead to the top, from where you can see the Ganges and Patna over the rooftops. *Harmandirji* is a shrine consecrating the birthplace of Guru Gobind Singh, the tenth and last Sikh guru. One of the holiest of Sikh shrines, it contains some personal belongings of the guru and Sikh scriptures.

Gulzaribagh is the site of a former opium factory used by the British East India Company, which made hefty profits with this lucrative trade from China. It is now a printing office for the government. You can visit the opium storage areas if you are a history buff. About five kilometers (three miles) from the Patna Railway Station is Kumhrar, where excavations have unearthed relics of four continuous periods 600 B.C.–A.D. 600.

Moslem mosques in Patna are *Patherki Masjid* and *Shershahi Masjid,* the oldest in Patna, built in 1545. Other places of interest are the Bihar Institute of Handicrafts and Designs and Birla Mandir. Daily tours are operated by the Bihar State Tourism and ITDC. From Patna, trips can also be arranged for Nalanda, Rajgir, Gaya, Bodhgaya, and Vaishali.

PRACTICAL INFORMATION FOR

WEST BENGAL AND BIHAR

WHEN TO GO. Northern West Bengal. The most popular times to visit Darjeeling and Kalimpong are April–mid-June and mid-September–November. The monsoon rages in the summer; and winter is cold, but you'll find no crowds in these snowy hill stations. **Southern West Bengal and Bihar.** These areas are ideal between October and March. The weather is dry and sunny and the mornings are crisp and pleasant. The average temperature ranges from 50° F to 85° F. The Chotanagpur Plateau and the Hararibagh region are slightly cooler because of their altitude and forestation.

HOW TO GET THERE. Restricted Area Permits. Foreign nationals planning to visit Darjeeling in northern West Bengal who fly to Bagdogra (the nearest airport), then take the Toy Train, taxi, or bus to Darjeeling for a stay of fewer than 15 days don't need a Restricted Area Permit. They must, however, register at the Foreigner's Registration Office at the Bagdogra Airport on arrival and departure.

A Restricted Area Permit is necessary for a visit to Kalimpong that exceeds 48 hours. (See *Travel Documents* in *Facts at Your Fingertips* and allow 12 weeks for clearance.) If you plan just a two-day visit, you can obtain a permit in Darjeeling at the Foreigner's Registration Office.

If you go by train, car, or bus between Calcutta and Darjeeling you also need a Restricted Area Permit, which is also necessary to visit the Jaldapara Wildlife Sanctuary.

By Air. *Indian Airlines* has daily flights into Bagdogra from Calcutta, Delhi, and Guwahati in Assam. To get to Patna, Indian Airlines has daily flights from Calcutta, Delhi, Lucknow, and Ranchi; five weekly flights from Guwahati; and three weekly flights from Bombay. Indian Airlines also has daily flights to Ranchi from Delhi, Calcutta, Lucknow, and Patna.

By Bus. Many buses connect Calcutta to destinations in Bihar and West Bengal. Buses leave from the Esplanade Terminus on Jawaharlal (J.L.) Nehru Road (Chowringhee) in Calcutta, diagonally opposite the Metro cinema hall. Go there in person; phones are unreliable in Calcutta. From Sikkim, the *Sikkim National Transport Service* runs frequent coaches (about Rs. 35 per person) between Gangtok and Darjeeling; a Restricted Area Permit is required. For departure times in Gangtok, contact *Sikkim Tourist Information Office* (tel. 2064). From Darjeeling, contact the *West Bengal Tourist Office* (tel. 2050).

Numerous buses also make the two-day run between Kathmandu in Nepal and Patna in Bihar. In Nepal, contact the *Kathmandu Tourist Office* for details. In Patna, *Himalayan Tours and Travels* (New Market) offers an excellent one-way package to Kathmandu or round-trip (with an open date return) that includes lodging and breakfast on the road. (Rs. 250 each way.)

By Train. If you have a Restricted Area Permit, you can take a 12-hour train from Calcutta's Howrah Station to New Jalpaiguri, which is about 81 km (50 mi.) from Darjeeling. From New Jalpaiguri, a taxi to Darjeeling is about Rs. 400 and takes about four hours. Bihar's capital, Patna, 10 hours from Calcutta, and Gaya are on the main lines of the railways between Delhi and Calcutta. From Calcutta, you can also go by train to Ranchi (about eight hours). Trains also connect Jamshedpur and north Bihar. Complete train information is available in Calcutta through *Eastern Railway Offices* at 14A Strand Rd., near the General Post Office (GPO); 6 Fairlie Pl., near Benoy-Bidal-Dinesh Bagh (BBD Bagh); and Southeastern Railway at Esplanade Mansion, near the Great Eastern Hotel. If you travel at night, remember to reserve a sleeping berth.

By Rented Car with Driver. From Calcutta, Ranchi is 456 km (283 mi.); Patna, 597 km (370 mi.); Gaya, 491 km (304 mi.); Bodhgaya, 540 km (335 mi.). Calcutta is 730 km (453 mi.) from Darjeeling; but to make this trip you must have a Restricted Area Permit. Travelers, who have a Restricted Area Permit, can also drive between Gangtok and Darjeeling, a six-hour excursion. Hire a car with driver from a travel agency recommended in Calcutta, Sikkim, and below under *Tour Operators.*

TOURIST INFORMATION. West Bengal. Contact the *Government of India Tourist Office* ("Embassy," 4 Shakespeare Sarani, Calcutta, West Bengal) or the *Regional Tourist Office of West Bengal* (Government of West Bengal, 3/2 B.B.D. Bagh, Calcutta, West Bengal). Offices are also located at the Calcutta Airport and Howrah Railway Station; at the Bagdogra Airport; at the New Jalpaiguri Railway Station; and in Darjeeling (1 Nehru Rd., Chowrasta, tel. 2050). Tourist offices are generally open Monday–Saturday, 10 A.M.–5 P.M.

Bihar. Contact the *Bihar Tourist Information Center,* Fraser Rd., Patna, Bihar, tel. 225295; open daily 10 A.M.–5 P.M. For government tours, accommodations, or car rentals, contact *Bihar State Tourism Development Corporation,* BSTDC, Beer Chand Patel Path, Patna, Bihar, tel. 225320; open daily 8 A.M.–8 P.M. Tourist Information Centers are also located at the Patna Airport, Patna Junction Railway Station, and Hotel Pataliputra Ashok in Patna. The Government of India Tourist Office is at the Kautilya Vihar in Patna and is open Monday–Friday, 10 A.M.–5 P.M. Bihar Tourist Offices are also located in the following destinations (open 8 A.M.–8 P.M.): Bodhgaya, tel. 26; Hazaribagh, tel. 236; Nalanda, tel. 29; Pawapuri, no phone; Rajgir, Kund Market, tel. 26; Ranchi, Court Compound, Circular Rd., tel. 20426.

FOREIGN CURRENCY EXCHANGE. Most Western-style hotels have money-exchange counters. Otherwise, go to a branch of the *State Bank of India,* open Monday–Friday, 10 A.M.–2 P.M.; Saturdays, till noon.

ACCOMMODATIONS. Prices are based on double occupancy and exclude taxes: *Deluxe,* over Rs. 1,450; *Expensive,* Rs. 950–Rs. 1,450; *Moderate,* Rs. 500–Rs. 950; *Inexpensive,* under Rs. 500. Most Western-style hotels take major credit cards.

WEST BENGAL

West Bengal Tourist Development Corporation (WBTDC) tourist lodges and bungalows can be booked three months in advance through WBTDC, Reservation Counter, 3/2 Benoy-Badal Dinesh Bagh (East), 1st Floor, Calcutta, West Bengal, or through the Tourist Offices in Calcutta or Darjeeling (see addresses above). Reservations cannot be made on arrival at most lodges. For peace of mind, confirm bookings through Calcutta. Inquire about off-season discounts. WBTDC in Calcutta has a free booklet with detailed listings of over 40 lodges, which is updated regularly.

Bakkhali

Inexpensive

Bakkhali Tourist Lodge. Lakshmipur Prabartak, West Bengal; tel. KAKDWIP 76. Reserve through WBTDC (address above). About 10 rooms with bath and 8 dormitories with shared bath. Simply furnished rooms are available in this lodge, shaded by casuarina groves; rooms open onto a deck that faces the beach. There is a restaurant. Breakfast and lunch included. Rupees only.

Darjeeling

Moderate

Hotel New Elgin. Darjeeling, West Bengal; tel. 2182. 25 rooms with bath. This rambling 100-year-old bungalow is set on a ridge near the Mall. New rooms have been added through the years; but the older rooms are still the most pleasing and comfortable. There is a small garden. Multicuisine restaurant, bar, room service, travel counter, car rental, doctor on call, baby-sitters, library, cultural programs on request. Meals included. Discount mid-November–mid-March. AE, DC.

Windamere Hotel. Darjeeling, West Bengal; tel. 2841. 27 rooms with bath. Situated near the uppermost ridge, this charming bungalow with cottages is surrounded by gardens. It's owned by an elegant Tibetan woman in her 80s. In its cozy drawing room warmed by a fireplace, Hook Cook met her future husband, the king of Sikkim. Cottages and upper-floor rooms are spacious, with lots of chintz. A fireplace will be blazing by the time you slip into bed, and your feet will be warmed by a hot-water bottle. Fixed-menu restaurant, bar, travel counter, gardens, foreign-exchange counter. Reserve well in advance. Meals included. Rupees or traveler's checks.

Inexpensive

Hotel Alice Villa. Darjeeling, West Bengal; tel. 2381. 10 rooms with bath (hot water by bucket). Each room in this small bungalow opens onto an enclosed veranda. The decor is plain, with clean furnishings and working fireplace. There are a restaurant and bar. Discount mid-June–mid-September and mid-November–April. Rupees only.

•

Diamond Harbor

Inexpensive

Diamond Harbor Tourist Center. Diamond Harbor, West Bengal; tel. 46. Reserve through WBTDC (address above). About 20 rooms with bath and 3 dormitories with shared bath. From this lodge, with modestly decorated, clean rooms, you can take excursions to nearby fishing harbors. There is a good restaurant. Lunch and dinner included. Rupees only.

Digha

Inexpensive

Digha Tourist Lodge. Digha, West Bengal; tel. 55 & 56. Reserve through WBTDC (address above). About 15 rooms with bath, a dormitory with shared bath, and rustic cottages with bath. On the coast, near Orissa and overlooking the Bay of Bengal, this government-run resort offers modest rooms that add up to a bargain beach vacation. The lodge has a simple multicuisine restaurant. Rupees only.

Jaldapara Wildlife Sanctuary

Inexpensive

Hollong Forest Lodge. Madarihat, West Bengal; no phone. Reserve through WBTDC (address above). 7 rooms with bath. Inside the Jaldapara Sanctuary, this rustic lodge has modest rooms with an institutional decor. A caretaker can prepare plain meals. Rupees only.

Madarihat Tourist Lodge. Madarihat, West Bengal; tel. 30. Reserve through WBTDC (address above). 8 rooms with bath. One km (half mi.) from the Jaldapara Wildlife Sanctuary, this two-story lodge offers unadorned, clean rooms. Included are a restaurant and transportation to the park. Rupees only.

Kalimpong

Moderate

Himalayan Hotel. Kalimpong, West Bengal; tel. 248. 9 rooms with bath (hot water by bucket). A short walk from the center of town, this secluded hotel is a former British residence built in the 1920s. The hotel features a mix of the East and the West—*thang-kas* share the walls with family memorabilia. Ask for an upstairs room with mountain views. The dining room has an appealing attached sitting room. Meals included, beer available. Reserve well in advance. Rupees only.

Hotel Silver Oaks. Kalimpong, West Bengal; tel. 296. 25 rooms with bath. This modern hotel, close to the main market, has an attractive lobby, beautiful gardens, and rooms with a subdued decor. Ask for a room with a view of the Kanchenjunga range. Multicuisine restaurant, bar, room service, foreign-exchange and travel counter, car rental, baby-sitters, doctor on call. Meals included. AE, DC.

Inexpensive

Kalimpong Tourist Lodge. Kalimpong, West Bengal; tel. 384. Reserve through WBTDC (address above). 7 rooms with bath. This handsome granite lodge, located about 3 km (2 mi.) from the heart of Kalimpong, was built in the 1930s and is set on seven acres of lawns and gardens. The upper-floor rooms offer the best views. The rooms are spacious, with mosquito netting and working fireplaces. There are a restaurant and bar. Rupees only.

Malda

Inexpensive

Malda Tourist Lodge. Malda, West Bengal; tel. 2213. Reserve through WBTDC (address above). About 10 rooms with bath and a dormitory with shared bath. The decor here is institutional, but the rooms are clean. Some rooms are air-conditioned. Multicuisine restaurant. Dinner is included. Rupees only.

Murshidabad

Inexpensive

Berhampore Tourist Lodge. Berhampore, West Bengal; tel. 439. Reserve through WBTDC (address above). About 8 rooms with bath and a dormitory with shared bath. This lodge has some air-conditioned rooms and a restaurant. Rupees only.

Santiniketan

Inexpensive

Santiniketan Tourist Lodge. Bolpur, West Bengal; tel. 399. Reserve through WBTDC (address above). This comfortable lodge, which offers some air-conditioned rooms, is modestly furnished, yet perfect for this small but frequently visited area. The lodge has an excellent restaurant. Two meals included. Rupees only.

Siliguri

Moderate

Hotel Sinclairs. Pradhan Nagar, Siliguri, West Bengal; tel. 22674. 54 rooms with bath. This modern Western-style hotel has pleasantly decorated rooms. Multicuisine restaurants, bar, room service, swimming pool, TV, foreign-exchange and travel counter. DC.

Inexpensive

Mainak Tourist Lodge. Pradhan Nagar, Siliguri, West Bengal; tel. 20986. Reserve through WBTDC (address above). About 15 rooms with bath. This Western-style lodge offers clean, reasonably decorated rooms; some are air-conditioned. Multicuisine restaurant, bar, TV in lounge, travel counter, doctor on call. Rupees only.

Sunderbans

Inexpensive

Sajnekhali Tourist Lodge. Sunderbans, West Bengal; no phone. Reserve through WBTDC (address above). 30 rooms with bath. Set in the Sunderbans, this rustic lodge, approachable by boat, has modestly furnished, clean rooms that are perfect for the location. There is also a restaurant. Rupees only.

Vishnupur

Inexpensive

Vishnupur Tourist Lodge. Vishnupur, West Bengal; tel. 13. Reserve through WBTDC (address above). About 8 rooms with bath and a dormitory with shared bath. There is a reasonable restaurant here; breakfast is included. Rupees only.

BIHAR

Bodhgaya

Moderate

Hotel Bodhgaya Ashok. Bodhgaya, Bihar; tel. 22708. 30 rooms with bath. This small Western-style hotel has a cozy lobby and air-conditioned rooms in a new wing and air-cooled rooms that open onto a lovely interior courtyard. All rooms are attractive, with modern decor. Multicuisine restaurant, room service, TV, bar, doctor on call, shopping arcade. AE, DC, MC, V.

Patna

Moderate–Expensive

Welcomgroup Maurya Patna. South Gandhi Maidan, Patna, Bihar; tel. 222061. 80 rooms with bath. This luxury high rise is modern, and offers three room options. In expensive-priced rooms, you're paying only for more personalized service. All rooms are air-conditioned and have a contemporary decor. TV, room service, multicuisine restaurant, bar, swimming pool, travel agency, foreign-exchange counter, secretarial services, shopping arcade, golfing. AE, DC, MC, V.

Moderate

Hotel Pataliputra Ashok. Beer Chand Patel Path, Patna, Bihar; tel. 223467. 46 rooms with bath. While not as classy as the Maurya, this newly renovated hotel has an attractive lobby with a statue of the Buddha. Air-conditioned rooms are modern, with a cheery decor and TV. Multicuisine restaurant, room service, bar, foreign-exchange counter, travel agency, tourist office, shopping arcade, swimming pool. AE, DC, MC, V.

Rajgir

Deluxe

Centaur Hokke Hotel. Rajgir, Bihar; tel. 31. 46 rooms with bath. Built by the Japanese, this luxury hotel has a red-brick exterior, stupa-shaped lobby, Buddhist prayer hall, and air-conditioned rooms (Western-style modern or sleek Japanese with sleeping mats on the floor). Indian- and Japanese-cuisine restaurant, bar, room service, doctor on call, Japanese hot baths, foreign-exchange counter, car rental, shops, table tennis. Rupees only.

Ranchi

Moderate

Hotel Ranchi Ashok. Doranda, Hinoo, Ranchi, Bihar; tel. 300037. 30 rooms with bath. This Western-style hotel has an attractive lobby and nice grounds. The spacious air-conditioned rooms have a pleasant modern decor and TV. Multicuisine restaurant, bar, room service, foreign-exchange counter, doctor on call. DC, MC, V.

Inexpensive–Moderate

Hotel Yuvraj Palace. Doranda, Ranchi, Bihar; tel. 300805. 25 rooms with bath. This Western-style hotel has a spacious marble lobby and large "deluxe" rooms (moderately priced), with a separate sitting area, and smaller ordinary doubles (inexpensive). All rooms are pleasantly furnished with a contemporary decor, airconditioning, and TV. Indian- and Chinese-cuisine restaurant, bar, foreignexchange counter, travel agency, doctor on call, courtesy airport shuttle service. DC, MC, V.

TOURIST BUNGALOWS. *Bihar State Tourism Development Corporation* has very inexpensive tourist bungalows, called *vihars,* scattered around the state. Rooms are clean, with unpretentious furnishings that include mosquito netting over the beds. To reserve in advance, contact Bihar State Tourism Development Corporation, Paryatan Bhawan, Beer Chand Patel Path, Patna, Bihar; tel. 225320. You can also reserve a room through the individual manager at each vihar. Rupees only.
Siddharth Vihar. Bodhgaya, Bihar; no phone. 6 rooms with bath. Best rooms are air-conditioned. Meals can be supplied.
Prabhat Vihar, Netarhat, Bihar; no phone. 8 rooms with bath. Simple meals available.
Kautilya Vihar, Patna, Bihar; tel. 225411. 42 rooms with bath. Best rooms are air-conditioned. Indian- and Chinese-cuisine restaurant, bar.
Tourist Bungalow. Rajgir, Bihar. Reserve through central office in Patna or Gautam Vihar, Rajgir; tel. 39. 32 rooms with bath. Best rooms in this new place are air-conditioned. Indian- and Chinese-cuisine restaurant.
Birsa Vihar. Ranchi, Bihar; no phone. 20 rooms with bath. Indian- and Chinesecuisine restaurant, bar, car-rental service, Bihar tour arrangements.

TREKKER'S HUTS. Rustic trekker's huts are available on trails in Manaybhanjang, Sandakphu, and Phalut, West Bengal. Bring a sleeping bag. For reservations, contact Deputy Director of Tourism, 1 Nehru Rd., Darjeeling, West Bengal; tel. 2050. (Rs. 10 per bed.) Rupees only. There's also a rustic bungalow in Nilpara. Reserve through WBTDC, Reservation Counter, 3/2 Benoy-Badal-Dinesh Bagh (East), 1st Floor, Calcutta, West Bengal.

DINING OUT. Many accommodations, listed above, have restaurants. Breakfast is usually served 7:30–10:30; lunch is usually noon–3; and dinner, 7:30–10. Payment is normally in rupees unless the restaurant is connected to a Western-style hotel. The restaurants listed below are informal and unless noted are open for all three meals and don't require reservations. Prices, based on one person eating a threecourse meal, excluding taxes, tip, or beverage, are *Expensive,* Rs. 80–Rs. 120; *Moderate,* Rs. 40–Rs. 80; *Inexpensive,* under Rs. 40.

WEST BENGAL

Darjeeling

Expensive

Glenary's. Nehru Rd.; tel. 2055. Darjeeling's most famous restaurant—dating back to British rule—was under renovation at press time. A large upstairs establishment with banks of windows, Glenary's was refurbishing its tin ceiling and fireplaces, replacing lace curtains, and sprucing up the bar. It offers good multicuisine choices. Open 8 A.M.–9 P.M. daily. AE, DC.

Kanchan. Hotel New Elgin; tel. 2182. This cheery hotel restaurant is in an old Raj-style bungalow. Fixed meals are Continental, Indian, Tibetan, or Nepalese. Reservations advised. Open 7–9:30 A.M., 1–2 P.M., 7–9 P.M. AE, DC.

Shangrila Restaurant. Nehru Rd.; tel. 2026. This attractive restaurant, with tile floor, fireplaces, and sleek decor, serves tasty Szechuan dishes. Open mid-March–mid-November, daily 7:30 A.M.–10 P.M.; otherwise till 7:30. Rupees only.

Windamere Hotel. Tel. 2841. A lovely old restaurant with wonderful views, this dining room offers gracious service that matches its ambience—tablecloths, fresh flowers. The mixed menu includes mildly spiced Indian and Continental cuisines. Reservations required. Open 8–9 A.M., 1–2 P.M., 7–8:30 P.M. Rupees only.

Moderate

Hotel Alice Villa. Tel. 2381. This dining room is cozy, with crockery set up on sideboards and a few small, wooden tables. The fixed menu offers Indian and some Continental dishes. Reservations advised. Open 7–9:30 A.M., 1–2 P.M., 7–9 P.M. Rupees only.

Kalimpong

Moderate

Gompo's Restaurant and Bar. Just off Main Rd.; no phone. Set in the back of Gompo's Hotel, this casual restaurant offers views of the valley and good Chinese, Tibetan, and Indian meals. Open 9 A.M.–9 P.M. Rupees only.

Kalimpong Park Hotel Restaurant. Tel. 304. This simple restaurant, with Buddhist symbols painted on the walls, serves excellent Chinese food and good Indian or Tibetan meals. Open 7 A.M.–9 P.M. Rupees only.

Mandarin Restaurant. Taxi Stand; no phone. Lace curtains, family booths, a slightly Chinese look, and subdued lighting add up to a pleasant ambience here. The menu is multicuisine. Open 7 A.M.–7 P.M. Rupees only.

BIHAR

Patna

Expensive

Vaishali. Welcomgroup Maurya Patna, South Gandhi Maidan; tel. 222061. Handsome Vaishali paintings adorn the pillars and walls of this appealing restaurant, with a bank of windows overlooking the hotel swimming pool. You can enjoy good Continental, Chinese, and Indian cuisines. Try the *murgh mumtaz* (mildly spicy, boneless chicken cooked in a tandoori) or chicken stroganoff. Open 7:30–10:30 A.M., noon–2:45 P.M., and 8–11 P.M. AE, DC, MC, V.

Moderate

Amrapali. Kautilya Vihar; tel. 225411. The lighting at Amrapali is so subdued that you can barely see the Madhubani and Vaishali paintings that cover the walls. Hindi taped music sets an ethnic tone. The chef prepares Chinese, Indian, and Continental dishes. Specialties include chicken leg kebab and tasty paneer butter masala (cheese cooked in a spicy curry). Open 7–11 A.M., noon–3 P.M., and 8–11 P.M. Rupees only.

Mumta Restaurant. Fraser Rd.; tel. 225888. This informal restaurant, with a bar in front and a family dining room in back, has very low lighting that offers an escape from Patna's intense heat and sun. You can order either Chinese or Indian cuisine. Especially good is the chicken butter masala (chicken pieces cooked in a spicy curry). Open noon–4 P.M. and 7–11 P.M. Rupees only.

Hotel Patliputra Ashok Restaurant. Beer Chand Patel Path; tel. 223467. Newly renovated with handsome chandeliers, mirrors on the ceiling and walls, and cedar pillars, this attractive restaurant serves Indian, Continental, and Chinese cuisines. Chinese is best, particularly the spicy garlic chicken or chicken capsicum and vegetables. Open 12:30–2:30 P.M. and 7:30–10:30 P.M. AE, DC, MC, V.

Inexpensive

Rajasthan Restaurant. Fraser Rd.; tel. 22268. This popular eatery, with subdued lighting and booths and tables, serves delicious vegetarian fare—Chinese and Indian. Best bets are the fresh cheese marshal cutlet (fried patty of cheese, potato, peas, and cashew nuts) and vegetable *malai kofta* (potato stuffed with cashew nuts and spices). Open noon–3:30 P.M. and 7–10:30 P.M.

Ranchi

Moderate

Mithala. Hotel Ranchi Ashok, Doranda, Hinoo; tel. 300037. This pretty restaurant designed like a modern Bihari village home, with red tiles on the walls and thatched overhangs set above a bank of windows and a large Madhubani painting, serves Indian and Chinese cuisines. Specialties include *kebab-E-banu* (boneless chicken marinated in gram flour and masala spices and cooked in the tandoori) and *gosht saagwala* (spicy lamb pieces cooked with spinach in a rich gravy). Open 6–10 A.M., 12:30–2:45 P.M., and 7:30–10:30 P.M. DC, MC, V.

Shafali. Hotel Yuvraj, Doranda; tel. 300805. This cozy restaurant, with light blue walls and white ceiling, has light Mogul touches such as arches set into the walls. There are live *ghazals* (romantic songs) Saturday nights. You can order Indian or Chinese cuisine. Try the *reshmi kebab* (boneless chicken cooked in a tandoori) or the Yuvraj special chicken (roasted chicken with spices). Open 10:30 A.M.–3:30 P.M. and 7:30–11 P.M. DC, MC, V.

Inexpensive

Kaveri Restaurant. Church Shopping Complex, Main Rd.; tel. 25193. In this popular restaurant, with subdued lighting and modern decor, you can have tasty Indian or Chinese vegetarian dishes. Their *paneer pasanda* (fried bread stuffed with cheese, vegetables, and fruit) is good, as is their *dosas* (stuffed crêpes). For dessert, enjoy their special *Kaveri* sweet (a cold milk-and-fruit pudding) or fresh *kulfi* (Indian ice cream). Open 10 A.M.–10 P.M. Rupees only.

SWEETS AND TREATS. West Bengal. *Penang Restaurant* on Laden La Rd., north of the Dhirdham Temple, in Darjeeling is a hole-in-the-wall, with curtained booths, that serves the best Tibetan *momo* (dumplings) in Darjeeling. (Order beef; pork can be risky if it's undercooked.) Open daily 11 A.M.–7 P.M. *Glenary's Pastry Shop* on Nehru Rd. has good lemon tarts, cookies, cakes, and even fresh cheese. Open daily 7 A.M.–6 P.M. An unnamed bar above Sonny Video Parlour on Rishi Rd., Kalimpong, serves great *chang* (fermented millet) and momo. Sit in the tiny dark room crowded with tables. Let your chang brew 10 minutes after hot water is added, then sip it through the straw. Open from 9 A.M. to late at night.

Bihar. Visit the *Rajasthan Restaurant,* Fraser Rd., Patna, from 3:30 P.M. to 8 P.M. and have great vegetarian *samosa* (Indian fried dumplings) or tasty mixed *chat* (a yummy sweet-and-sour vegetable concoction). You can also get good ice cream and coffee. At *Maner,* 13 km (eight mi.) from Patna toward Sasaram, stop at a roadside stall and try the famous *ladu* sweets (little balls of butter, sugar, and ghee). On National Highway 31, 50 km (31 mi.) from Patna toward Rajgir, stop at *Mamta*

Hotel. Sit outside or in the large interior hall and try *kheer* (a warm milk, rice, and sugar custard) or *kulfi* (Indian ice cream). Open 24 hours. At *Silao,* on the road six km (four mi.) from Nalanda toward Rajgir, stop for tasty *mita* (sweet) or *nam-kine* (salty) *khaja* (flaky pastry). It's delicious and freshly made in every stall.

HOW TO GET AROUND. West Bengal. From the Airport. To get from Bagdo-gra to Darjeeling, you can take the delightful narrow-gauge *Toy Train* from the nearby New Jalpaiguri Railroad Station. The train departs at 9:30 A.M. and arrives at 5 P.M. Tickets cost about Rs. 100. You can also take the *West Bengal Tourist Department's Tourist Coach,* which has departures and arrivals coinciding with all flights (Rs. 30 for the four-hour drive), arrange for a hired car with driver, or take a taxi. The taxi or hired car with driver will cost about Rs. 300 and takes about three hours.

By Rented Car with Driver. For excursions from Darjeeling, travel by hired car with driver so you can be sure to meet the 48-hour visiting limit for Kalimpong and its surrounding area. Hire a car through your hotel or a recommended travel agency in Darjeeling (see *Tour Operators* below). Fares are usually determined by destination. For southern West Bengal, hire a car in Calcutta. Rates are about Rs. 3 per km, with a halt charge of Rs. 50 per night.

By Bus. The *North Bengal State Transport Corporation* runs buses throughout the state. For schedules and fares, contact the Booking Office: Calcutta, Esplanade Bus Terminus; Darjeeling, tel. 3133; Kalimpong, tel. 525.

By Taxi. Taxi fares should be about Rs. 2.50 per km.

By Bicycle Rickshaw and Auto Rickshaw. Both these modes of transport should be cheaper than a taxi, with a bicycle rickshaw the most economical.

Bihar. From the Airports. A taxi is your best bet at the Patna and Ranchi airports. Neither airport is far from town; fare should be about Rs. 20.

By Plane. *Indian Airlines* flies daily between Patna and Ranchi.

By Rented Car with Driver. Reasonably good roads connect Patna and Bodhgaya, a distance of 181 km (112 mi.), and Patna and Raxaul (on Nepal border), a distance of 290 km (180 mi.). Figure the cost of a rented car with driver at Rs. 3 per km, with Rs. 50 halt charge per night. Hire a car from an agency listed below under *Tour Operators.*

By Bus. Avoid buses in this state; they're extremely slow and extremely crowded.

By Taxi. Taxis cost about Rs. 2.50 per km.

By Bicycle Rickshaw. Rates are about Rs. 1 per km—a delightful way to travel in Bodhgaya.

TOURS. West Bengal. The *West Bengal Tourist Bureau* runs a number of long-distance tours in air-conditioned coaches from Calcutta between September and March. Fares are reasonable. Inquire at 3/2 BBD Bagh (East) for complete information. The *Darjeeling Tourist Bureau* offers three tours by jeep or bus in northern West Bengal. By jeep you can take half-day sightseeing trips around Darjeeling (Rs. 20), a day excursion to Kalimpong (Rs. 68), or a two-day excursion to Gangtok via Kalimpong (Rs. 135). For details, contact the Darjeeling Tourist Bureau, 1 Nehru Rd.; tel. 2050.

Bihar. *BSTDC* (Paryatan Bhawan, Beer Chand Patel Path, tel. 225320) offers the following tours by bus: Patna sightseeing, Rs. 25; Patna–Ranchi, Rs. 45; Ranchi–Patna, Rs. 45; Patna–Rajgir–Nalanda–Pawapuri–Patna, Rs. 35; Patna–Hazaribagh, Rs. 35; and Hazaribagh–Patna, Rs. 35.

TOUR OPERATORS. West Bengal. For hired car with driver and general travel needs, contact *ITDC,* c/o Government of India Tourist Office, 4 Shakespeare Sarani, Calcutta, tel. 440901; *American Express,* 21 Old Court House St., Calcutta, tel. 286281; *Mercury Travels,* 46-C J.L. Nehru Rd., Calcutta; tel. 443555, or *Travel Corporation of India,* 46-C J.L. Nehru Rd., Calcutta; tel. 445469. Travel Corporation of India also has a branch in Darjeeling, Bellavista Apartments, Room No. 5, Gandhi Rd., tel. 2694. *Nawang Gombu Sherpa* (Himalayan Mountaineering Institute, Jawahar Parbat, Darjeeling) sponsors the best treks in northern West Bengal.

Bihar. *Travel Corporation of India* (Maurya Center, South Gandhi Maidan, Patna, Bihar; tel. 31016) can arrange tours in Bihar and provide all travel assistance, including rented car with driver. You can also rent a car with driver from BSTDC (see address above under *Tourist Information*).

SEASONAL EVENTS. The specific dates for many events each year are determined by the lunar calendar; contact the Government of India Tourist Office for details.

WEST BENGAL

January. *Makar Sankranti.* This week-long Lepcha and Bhutia fair, which is held on the banks of the Teesta River near Kalimpong, celebrates their new year.

Mid-January. *Ganga Sagar Mela.* During this gigantic fair on Sagar Island, a 10-hour cruise south of Calcutta, throngs of Hindu devotees from all over India take a holy dip at the confluence of the Hooghly River and Bay of Bengal. Big event!

January/February. *Vasant Panchami.* This festival that honors Saraswati, the goddess of learning, is an important festival at Santniketan, Tagore's university.

Mid-February. *Losar.* Around the time of Losar, the Tibetan New Year, ritual *chaams* (dances) are performed in all the important Buddhist monasteries.

March. *Holi* or *Dol.* During this festival that marks spring's arrival, youngsters splash everyone with colored water. Wear washable clothes.

April. *Poyla Baisakh.* Bengalis celebrate their New Year.

June/July. *Id-ul-Fitr.* This Moslem holy day marks the end of Ramadan, a period of month-long fasting, with a big feast.

August/September. *Indrapuja.* In Vishnupur, Hindus celebrate this festival that pays tribute to Indra, the god of thunder.

September/October. *Durga Puja.* This Hindu festival, called Dussehra in most of India, is a 10-day celebration of Rama's victory over evil. It's visually breathtaking and deafening, with music and fireworks.

October/November. *Diwali.* Also called the Festival of Lights, this Hindu occasion honors Lakshmi, goddess of prosperity, and Kali, signifying strength and depicting the horrors that mortals have brought on themselves. Images of bamboo and clay, profusely and intricately adorned, are created throughout West Bengal.

December. *Paus Mela.* At Santiniketan and rural Bengal, Hindus energetically celebrate a fair that honors the Bengali month of Paus.

BIHAR

March/April. *Mahavira Jayanti.* This Jain festival is dedicated to Mahavira, the 24th tirthankara (perfect soul). It's a big event at Parasnath Hill.

May. *Buddha Jayanti.* Celebrated at Buddhist pilgrimage sites in Bihar, this festival commemorates the Buddha's birth, enlightenment, and death.

July. *Rath Yatra.* This is an especially important Hindu chariot festival at Jagannathour near Ranchi.

August. *Ganesh Chaturthi.* This harvest festival honors Ganesh, the plump and docile elephant-headed god. His image is brought into houses and stored for good luck.

November. *Cattle Fair.* One of the largest of its kind in the world, this month-long fair has herdsmen from all over India walking their cattle into Sonepar to the fairgrounds on the banks of the Ganges. Decorated with colorful ribbons, horns festooned with garlands, and ankles circled with bells, cattle wade the river onto the shore, accompanied by the blowing of conch shells. This fair is at the heart of a rural tradition and shows that India is imaginative, vigorous, and alive.

November. *Chhatha Vrata.* About a week after Diwali, Bihar holds its most important annual event: a sun festival. The harvest season begins and the first crop is offered to the sun, the lord of the crops. The banks of the Ganges, at Patna, is the best place to witness this event.

HISTORIC SITES. Entrance to most places is generally free; where a donation is asked, a few rupees will suffice. Historic sites are open daily sunrise to sunset unless noted otherwise below.

WEST BENGAL

Darjeeling

Dhirdham Temple. Styled along the lines of the famous Pashupatinath Temple in Kathmandu, Nepal, and dedicated to Shiva, this temple (near the railway station) allows visits by non-Hindus, unlike the temple in Kathmandu.

Observatory Hill. Visit old shrines sacred to Buddhists and Hindus.

Tibetan Refugee Self-Help Center. Established after China took over Tibet, this center is home to over 600 refugees. Visit the handicraft and carpet factories, shops, training centers, gompa. The center also performs occasional cultural shows for the public. Consult the tourist department for a schedule of activities. Shops and factories are closed Sundays.

Yiga-Choling Monastery. This monastery in Ghoom, eight km (five mi.) from Darjeeling and built in 1850, has lovely frescoes and statues. But it's unlit, so bring a flashlight.

Kalimpong

Tharpa Choling Monastery. Built in 1922, this monastery has exquisite frescoes, thank-gas, and statues. A flashlight will help you view them. Prayer ceremonies are held about 5 A.M. and 2 P.M.

Zangdogpalrifodang Monastery. This new monastery has great frescoes, statues, and a stunning replica of a celestial chorten. The original was destroyed by the Chinese in Lhasa.

Other Destinations

Malda. Adina Mosque. This fourteenth-century shrine is partially in ruins, but remaining details are worth a visit.

Murshidabad. Katra Mosque. Styled along the lines of the great Islamic mosque at Mecca, Katra contains the tomb of its builder, Murshid Kuli Khan.

Hazarduari Palace. Built by the Nawab Hymayun Jah in 1837, this palace contains interesting exhibits of old firearms, crockery, and paintings. Open 9 A.M.–5 P.M.

Tagore. Santiniketan. Tagore's unusual and delightful open-air university accepts visitors from 3–5 P.M. in summer and 2–4 P.M. in winter. Throughout the year Tuesday visiting hours are from 10 A.M.–noon.

BIHAR

Bodhgaya. This ancient seat of Buddhist learning where Siddhartha Gautama attained enlightenment has numerous important sites connected to the Historic Buddha. Be sure to see the *bodhi* (fig) tree, which is said to have grown from the original tree under which the Buddha meditated; the Mahabodhi temple, the most sacred Buddhist temple dedicated to Lord Buddha; the Animeshlochan Chaitya, where the Buddha stood after attaining enlightenment; Ratnagar (water tank), where he spent a week in contemplation; and Chankramana (Jewel Walk) where he strolled in meditation.

Gaya. Vishnupada Temple. Supposedly built over Vishnu's footprints, this temple, which was renovated in 1787, has beautifully sculpted pillars. An important pilgrimage site for Hindus, who believe that if they perform the last rituals for the deceased at Gaya, the dead will be absolved of all sins.

Parsanath Hill. On this hill, an extremely important Jain pilgrimage site, the 23rd tirthankara (perfect soul) gained enlightenment.

Patna. Golghar. This granary, built in 1770 after a great famine, offers excellent views of Patna. Open 10 A.M.–6 P.M.

Harmandirji. This *gurdwara* (Sikhs' temple) is dedicated to Guru Gobind Singh, the tenth guru of the Sikhs who was born in Patna in 1766.

Shershahi Masjid. Patna's oldest mosque and an excellent example of Afghan architecture, it dominates the city's skyline.

Rajgir. Griddhakuta (Vulture's Peak). On this bluff, the Buddha set in motion his second Wheel of Law and preached here to his disciples during the rainy season. To commemorate these events, the Japanese have built the Shanti (Peace) Stupa. You can take a chairlift to the top 9:15 A.M.–1 P.M. and 2–5 P.M., except Thursdays.

Nalanda. Founded in the fifth century, this ancient international Buddhist university is still under excavation. The Buddha and Mahavira (founder of the Jain religion) visited this school. Numerous kings built monasteries and temples, including Emperor Ashoka and Kumaragupta of the Gupta dynasty. Today, it's still a great pilgrimage center.

Sasaram. Sher Shah Mausoleum. Set in a garden in the middle of a lake, this tomb—Bihar's finest—honors the sixteenth-century Moslem ruler who founded Patna. Nearby are the tombs of Sher Shah's father and son.

MUSEUMS AND GALLERIES. West Bengal. Ava Art Gallery. Hill Cart Road, on the way to Ghoom (near Darjeeling), has a fine collection of embroidery and art. Open 8 A.M.–noon and 12:30–6:30 P.M. daily.

Himalayan Mountaineering Institute, on Jawahar Road West, Darjeeling, has excellent retrospective displays of equipment, photographs, and other memorabilia of Mount Everest and other twentieth-century Himalayan expeditions. Open daily 9 A.M.–5 P.M. in summer; 9 A.M.–4 P.M. in winter; closed 1–2 P.M. and all day Tuesdays. Fee.

Natural History Museum. Meadowbank Road, Darjeeling, has 4,300 exhibits of the fauna of Darjeeling, Sikkim, Tibet, Bhutan, Nepal, and the Eastern Himalayan region. Very well presented. Open 10 A.M.–4 P.M. (Wednesdays from 1 P.M.); closed Thursdays.

Tenzing's House, on D. B. Giri, Darjeeling, was the home of the Sherpa who scaled Mount Everest with Edmund Hillary in 1953 and became the first to do so. Now a museum. Check with the tourist department for hours.

Bihar. Bodhgaya Site Museum, Bodhgaya, has a collection of archaeological exhibits excavated from the local area. Entrance is free to the museum, which has a fine collection of gold, bronze, and stone statues of Buddha. Open 10 A.M.–5 P.M., closed Fridays.

Nalanda Museum, Nalanda, has an excellent collection of Buddhist and Hindu relics that date back to the seventh century. Also on display are the great seal of the twelfth-century university, panels depicting the avatars of Vishnu, stone and copper-plate inscriptions, and pottery. Open 10 A.M.–5 P.M., closed Fridays.

Jalan's Quila, Patna, has a rich collection of jade, Chinese paintings, and silver filigree work of the Mogul period. Prior permission is needed, since this is a private collection. Open 10:30 A.M.–4:30 P.M., closed Mondays.

Khuda Baksh Oriental Library, Patna, contains excellent Arabic and Persian manuscripts, Rajput and Mogul paintings, a tiny Quran that measures only one inch in width, and books rescued from the plunder of a university in Cordoba, Spain. Open 9 A.M.–5 P.M.

Patna Museum, Patna, has a good collection of metal and stone sculptures from the Maurya and Gupta periods, terra-cotta figurines and a 52½-foot fossilized tree that dates back 2,000 years. It also has a Tibetan section. Open 10:30 A.M.–4:30 P.M., closed Mondays.

GARDENS. In Darjeeling, *Lloyds Botanical Garden,* with plants from around the world and 2,000 species of orchids, is open 6 A.M.–5 P.M. Also visit the *Shrubbery,* an old garden with excellent views of the Himalayas. Same hours.

SPORTS AND OUTDOOR ADVENTURES. West Bengal. Fishing. In the area around Darjeeling, fishing is currently banned to increase the stocks.

Hot Springs. Bakreswar has numerous hot springs to enjoy.

Rafting. You can make a one- or two-day run on the Teesta and Rangit Rivers September–May. Make all arrangements in advance. Contact Travel Corporation of India (see *Tour Operators* above).

Swimming. Enjoy the beach resorts of Digha and Bakkhali in southern West Bengal.

Trekking. Treks in northern West Bengal may not exceed 15 days starting from arrival at Bagdogra or the railway station in Siliguri. Trekkers must also register with the Foreigner's Registration Office in Darjeeling before setting off to hike more than two days and they must also report their arrival at the Check Post at any destination. Except for the monsoon season, you can make an easy two-day roundtrip trek from Darjeeling to Tiger's Hill to catch the sunrise view of Mount Kanchenjunga. An excellent four- or five-day trek starts from Manaybhanjang, 26 km (16 mi.) from Darjeeling, and heads to Sandakphu village on the border of Nepal, with views of Kanchenjunga and Everest. You walk through rhododendron forests and tropical valleys, and visit a hamlet with a lovely monastery. You can extend this trek to six days and walk to Phalut on the border of West Bengal, Sikkim, and Nepal. This trek is best April–May and October–mid-December.

Wildlife Sanctuaries. At *Jalpaiguri,* 145 km (90 mi.) from Siliguri, is a sanctuary for bison, deer, elephants, tigers, leopards, barking deer, and Indian one-horned rhinoceroses. Lying below Bhutan and covering 93 sq. km (58 sq. mi.) of *terai* (sub-Himalayan forests), the sanctuary also has rich bird life that includes the lesser florican, great stone plover, and jungle fowl. The best viewing time is November–April. Elephant rides are available. For further information, contact the Tourist Bureau, Government of West Bengal, Hill Cart Road, Siliguri, West Bengal.

Sunderbans. These dense mangrove swamps in the delta region require a delightful three-hour trip by car through beautiful Bengali villages, then a four-hour boat cruise to the park area. Sunderbans, the "beautiful forest," has the largest population of tigers (200) in India. This extensive estuarine land has tigers swimming in its channels (only the lucky spot them), along with crocodiles, deer, and wild boar. The best time to visit is November–March. Contact the West Bengal Regional Tourist Office in Calcutta (see address above under *Tourist Information*) for weekend excursions by coach and boat, details for permission to visit this sanctuary, and accommodation information.

Bihar. Wildlife Sanctuaries. *Palamau Tiger Reserve* (Betla Sanctuary) is the largest tiger reserve in Bihar and also home to elephants, panthers, wild boar, sambar (antlered Indian deer), pythons, and numerous birds. Palamau is 173 km (107 mi.) west of Ranchi. For accommodation on the edge of the sanctuary, you can reserve a room in a new BSTDC bungalow or in a forest lodge. Contact the Field Director, Project Tiger, Palamau Tiger Reserve, Daltonganj, Palamau District, Bihar. This park is most enjoyable September–March.

Hazaribagh Sanctuary. In the undulating forests of the Damodar Valley and once the private land of a local maharajah, this 182 sq. km (113 sq. mi.) reserve is home to tigers, sambar, leopards, wild boar, panthers, hyenas, and spotted deer. The sanctuary is 115 km (71 mi.) north of Ranchi. For further information, contact the Divisional Forest Officer, Hazaribagh, West Division, Hazaribagh, Bihar. The best time to visit is February–May.

SHOPPING. West Bengal. *Baluchar,* "figured muslin," as it is known in Bengal, is woven in the Murshidabad region of north Bengal and is one of the finest materials to emerge from Indian looms. Cotton fabrics are brocaded with *zari* (silver threads), and colors of deep purples and maroons highlight the weaving. Borders are ornamented with floral motifs and figurative works. Baluchar is a Moslem weaver's craft. In Murshidabad, the renowned Moslem center of pre-British Bengal, weavers under royal patronage made the town of Murshidabad synonymous with silk and cotton weaving. Murshidabad is also known for its gold and silver inlay work on wood, primarily as bases for hookahs (water pipes). Carved, painted, and stained ivory has long been an art form in Murshidabad, but it is illegal to import ivory into the United States.

· Bengal's potters at Bankura, Birphum, and Midnapore make painted dolls, animal figures, and smooth, blue-glazed earthenware. Metalwork, *dokra* figures of metal and clay, soapstone carvings, bamboo crafts, and quilts are all found in bazaars. Little known to most tourists are *sholapith* toys. Sholapith is the core of a plant that grows wild in marshy areas, and delicate images of deities and flowers are fashioned from it. It is also commonly made into traditional headgear for weddings. Another Bengali craft is *shonkari* (shell craft), most often seen as bangles and toe rings.

If you visit Santiniketan or Vishnupur, you may come across the rural tradition of narrating stories with the aid of painted scrolls. As in Orissa, these *pats* are common in rural Bengal, with separate pieces depicting scenes of the story. In Calcutta, you can see them in a museum.

Vishnupur and Santiniketan also produce leather goods, bell metal wares, fine Tussar silks and terra-cotta figurines that are common in most Bengali households.

Darjeeling's crafts are different from those in the rest of Bengal. Nepalese and Tibetan brasswork and jewelry, gems, woodwork, carpets, and wool weavings are the mainstays. And, of course, you can buy the renowned Darjeeling tea directly from some of the tea estates after having taken a tour to see their production methods.

In Darjeeling, visit the following shops for, Tibetan curios: *Habib Mullick and Son,* The Mall, and *Nepal Curio House,* 16 Nehru Rd. For handmade Tibetan carpets, woolen sweaters, socks, and handicrafts, stop in at the *Tibetan Refugee Self Help Center,* Lebong, and *N.P.A.A. Functional Literacy Shoppe* in Hayden Hall, Market Rd.

In Kalimpong, visit the *Kalimpong Arts and Crafts Cooperative Society,* off Main Rd., for good Bhutanese, Lepcha, and Sikkimese handicrafts: appliqués, embroidered bags and purses, hankies, and placemats; *Book Depot Shop,* Main Rd., which sells handicrafts and handmade sweaters, caps, socks, baby clothes, and Nepali caps; and *Kazi Ratna Sakya & Bros.,* Main Rd., which has a good selection of Tibetan and Bhutanese curios, jewelry, and thang-kas. All shops are open 10 A.M.–6 P.M., closed Sundays.

Bihar. Patna is well known for its wooden inlay work on metal, ivory, and stag horn. Artisans also use wood chips of unusual grain and color to decorate table tops, wall hangings, and trays.

Bihar has recently "discovered" a cottage industry that has become a lucrative and widely known art form—Madhubani paintings. The women painters of Mithila (for it is primarily the women who paint) in north Bihar create highly original paintings, previously done on mud walls but now done on paper and canvas. Growing out of myth and ritual, the forms are striking in their simplicity of execution and in the complexity of their images.

In Patna, you can find all these products and the Madhubani paintings at the *Bihar State Handloom and Handicraft Emporium,* Apna Bazaar, near East Gandhi Maidan. Open 10 A.M.–5 P.M., closed Sundays. Rupees only.

NIGHTLIFE AND BARS. West Bengal. For intimacy, you can't beat the bar at the Windamere Hotel, Darjeeling, where 10 people means a crowd. The ambience creates good conversation. Glenary's, on Nehru Rd., has an open bar attached to its restaurant, which is popular with the year-round population in Darjeeling.

Bihar. Your best bet for a nightcap is in a Western-style hotel.

ORISSA

Natural and Spiritual Beauty

by
LISA SAMSON and AMIT SHAH

"Every standing tree is an ovation to life" is not an inscription on an ancient temple wall but a painted roadside sign put up by the Department of Forestry in the state of Orissa. The sign's ambiguous language testifies to one of Orissa's claims to fame: its abundant natural beauty. It also suggests the spiritual underpinnings, Buddhist and Hindu, that were the motivational factors for much of the man-made wonders to be seen here. Once a center of Buddhist learning and propagation, Orissa is one of Hinduism's most active pilgrimage sites. Some say that to see Orissa is to see India, and certainly, visitors to Orissa have much to choose from. In the temple cities of Bhubaneswar, Puri, and Konarak, you can see the unusual Orissan temple architecture, with its strange shapes and fabulous and frequently erotic sculptures. On the coast and in the north, west, and south, you can indulge yourself, as ancient Orissans must have, in the pleasures of nature.

For many years, Orissa has attracted tourists primarily to its three temple cities of Puri, Konarak, and Bhubaneswar. It is here that Hinduism's distinctive Orissan temple architecture reached its peak in the tenth century A.D. The state also has a large number of important Buddhist and Jain sites, such as the beautifully preserved rock edicts of Emperor Ashoka at Dhauli, which date from about 260 B.C.; the first-century B.C. caves at

Khandagiri, cut out and used by monks as meditation cells; and the ruins of the seventh-century Buddhist university at Ratnagiri-Lalitagiri. In these architectural monuments, you can trace the history of Orissa from its early Buddhist and Jain roots through the flourishing Orissan civilization between the fourth and thirteenth centuries, when the great Hindu temples were built. But there is much more to explore in Orissa.

In the past few years, Orissa has begun to develop other rich offerings for travelers: its fertile countryside, idyllic coastal towns, forested mountains, deep-cut gorges, varied waterways, and wildlife preserves. Orissa's unpopulated beaches, which stretch from Chandipur near the West Bengal border to Gopalpur-on-Sea; its hot springs at Atri and Taptapani; its wildlife preserves of Chilka Lake, Simlipal, and Ushakothi; and its Biological Park and Botanical Garden at Nandankanan (near Bhubaneswar) are just a few of the natural sights that are now popular with tourists.

Bounded by Bihar on the north, by West Bengal on the northeast, and by Andhra Pradesh and Madhya Pradesh on the south, Orissa consists of an extensive plateau in the interior that drops to a rich alluvial coastal plain crisscrossed by large rivers, including the great Mahanadi. The plateaus and hills in the north and south of the state have peaks that rise up to 1,676 meters (5,500 feet), at times creating spectacular waterfalls. Through the central part of the state, five rivers descend from higher reaches, cutting rocky gorges and creating fertile green valleys as they flow to the Bay of Bengal. Along the coast, which has beautiful isolated beaches, one also finds fertile land as one leaves the hills to the west and approaches the sandy stretches that adjoin the Bay. Rice paddies; cashew and mango groves; sugarcane fields; and jute, casuarina, and sal forests dot this primarily agricultural state of 29 million people. Though over 80 percent of the population cultivates rice, forests of sal, teak, sandal, and bamboo occupy 43 percent of the state's area. Historically slow to industrialize, Orissa now boasts a growing number of medium-sized industries based on minerals, sugar, glass, textiles, and handloom weaving that have begun to provide a secure economic base for this predominantly agricultural state. Steel plants at Rourkela, the Hirakud Dam Project on the Mahanadi River (one of the largest earth dams in the world), Asia's largest aluminum plant, and the profusion of high-tech companies around Bhubaneswar assure this state of steady growth into the twenty-first century.

Looking Backward

Orissa, known in earlier times as Kalinga, is noted in some of the most ancient Indian epics. Legend has it that Kalinga, one of the five sons of a sage, traveled as far as the hills of the Eastern Ghat and, looking down on the lovely countryside below him, decided to settle his people here, "where Nature abounds in wanton profusion." An early Kalinga king is believed to have sided with the Kauravas in the Mahabharata war, recorded in the great Indian epic of the same name. Part of the state is still called Kalinga by local people. Orissa was also known as Utkala ("land of arts and crafts"), a title that holds true today.

The recorded history of Orissa began in 260 B.C., with the edicts of the Mauryan Emperor Ashoka carved in rock at Dhauli, near Bhubaneswar. Ashoka, once known as Ashoka the Terrible, is said to have looked down from the hill at Dhauli to survey the plains of Kalinga strewn with the carnage of the Kalinga Wars that he had begun as conflicts of conquest. Horrified at what he saw, Ashoka repented for his deeds and converted to Buddhism, then the religion of Orissa. He actively propagated the Buddhist philosophy of nonviolence far beyond the borders of India. Soon after

Ashoka's death, Orissa reasserted its independence. In the first century B.C., Kharavela, the third Chedi king and perhaps the greatest king to rule Kalinga, extended his empire from near Agra in the north to Kanya Kumari in the south, bringing Jainism to Orissa.

It was during his reign that the Khandagiri and Udayagiri caves (near Bhubaneswar) were carved for Jain monks out of the rock faces of these hills, to be used as meditation cells. Many of these tiny cells are covered with friezes; the Hathi Gumpha (the Elephant Cave) at Udayagiri bears a Pali inscription carved in the rock that records Kharavela's reign. Some say that relics of Ashoka and Kharavela were preserved in Dhauli and Udayagiri and, therefore, that the hills that flank Bhubaneswar became sacred spots. After Kharavela, the Chedi dynasty of Kalinga declined, and Jainism was again replaced by Buddhism in about A.D. 100.

The zenith of Orissan civilization and architecture was reached between the fourth and thirteenth centuries, when the Kesari and Ganga kings brought Hinduism to this Buddhist land. The Lingaraj temple at Bhubaneswar and the Jagganath Temple at Puri were constructed during the brilliant Kesari period. The Ganga kings ruled from the twelfth to the fifteenth century, during which time the magnificently engineered Sun Temple at Konarak was built on what were then coastal dunes. Moslem incursions into the state, prompted partly by a need to keep the Moslem armies equipped with war elephants that could be found in the Orissan wilds, culminated in the occupation of Orissa in 1568. The Afghans controlled Orissa until Akbar's Hindu general, Man Singh, annexed it for the Moguls in 1592. During their control, the Moslems destroyed many temples of the "idol worshipers." Of Bhubaneswar's 7,000 temples that once lined the banks of the sacred Bindusagar Lake, only about 500 are in some sort of preservation today.

The Dutch came to Pipli, now a village of craftsmen near the coast, and the British East India Company came to Balasore near the West Bengal border in the seventeenth century. In 1751, the Moguls ceded Orissa to the Marathas, who held it until the British took it over in 1803. They did little to improve the economic condition of the country or of the people. After Indian independence, the modern state of Orissa was shaped by encompassing some 26 small kingdoms. Its move toward industrialization has involved some impressive strides in irrigation and energy production, and the capital, Bhubaneswar, is developing steadily in light industry and high-tech companies.

Tribes

Descendants of the people who lived in Orissa before the Aryan invasions over 3,000 years ago, the Adivasi tribals of Orissa are numerous. Over 60 tribes, each marked with its own culture, are concentrated in the forest and hill regions of the state, and many still live in much the same way that they have for thousands of years. Once forced back from their hereditary land into less fertile places, they are now protected by the Indian government under the Protection of Aboriginal Tribes regulations.

Many of the tribes, especially those in the northwestern industrialized area, are beginning to leave their traditional hunting and agricultural lifestyles to seek jobs in places like the iron fields. It is difficult to say how much longer these people, who have held onto their traditions through thousands of years of dynastic changes, will be able to continue passing them on to future generations.

EXPLORING ORISSA

The Temples

Bhubaneswar, Puri, and Konarak are famous for their stunning examples of Orissan temple architecture and for their spectacular religious celebrations. Many of the temples were constructed during the golden age of Orissan temple building, the eighth to the thirteenth centuries. Taken together, the Orissan shrines, especially those at Bhubaneswar, represent a coherent development of the Nagara style of Indo-Aryan architecture.

The Orissan temple consists almost entirely of a vaulting spire that thrusts upward in a pinnacle among much lower replica turrets that seem like mere surface wall decorations. The temple contains the *jagamohan,* or porch, which is usually square with a pyramidal roof. Immediately following the jagamohan is the *deul,* the cubicle inner apartment that enshrines the deity and that is surmounted by the soaring tower. Sometimes one or two more halls—*natmandir* (the dancing hall) and *bhogmandir* (the hall of offerings)—are set in front of the porch.

The architecture of Orissan temples may seem strange and heavy, but the sculpture on these temples is graceful, often unashamedly erotic, and steeped in mythology. There is a musical, dancelike, animated quality to many of these sculptures. Beautifully detailed, the statues range from voluptuous, amorous couples to musicians; to fierce beasts; to historical scenes; to birds, flowers, and foliage, all of which alternately tease and soothe the viewer.

Bhubaneswar and Its Environs

The capital of Orissa since 1952, Bhubaneswar is known as the "Cathedral City of India" and has over 500 temples in various stages of preservation. In Bhubaneswar and its immediate environs are presented a nearly 2,000-year panorama of Orissan art and history. From the third century B.C. to A.D. 1500 one can witness in the rock edicts of Dhauli, the caves at Khandagiri, the fort ruins at Sisulpalgarh, and the temples of Bhubaneswar a rarely preserved architectural record of the many dynasties that flourished and died out.

In Bhubaneswar, the greatest of the temples, the Lingaraj, is off-limits to non-Hindus. Its huge tower is visible from miles away, but the closest foreigners will get to it is a viewing stand erected during the period of the raj when Lord Curzon, the British viceroy, visited the temple. Other temples to visit are the ornate Parsurameswara, said to be the oldest surviving temple in the city; the Mukteswar, with the unmatched intricacy of its carved detail; the Rajrani, with its embracing couples; and the Brahmeswar.

Using Bhubaneswar as a base, you can travel easily into the surrounding countryside to explore the important Buddhist sites of Dhauli and Khandagiri or go farther afield to Konarak and Puri. The roads between the three major cities pass through Orissan villages with monochrome mud huts decorated, by women, in complex rice-paste designs dedicated to Lakshmi—the goddess of wealth and beauty—along paddy fields green in the hot sun, past irrigation canals and ponds thick with water hyacinth, and—between Puri and Konarak on Marine Drive—past groves of casuarina, cashew, and mango, alongside the sea. Within minutes of leaving the fast-growing metropolitan area, you see images of the rural Indian landscape that appear timeless. As wooden bullock carts creak under their loads of hay, and as farmers stand in watery ditches separating young rice shoots for replanting, and as children play among themselves with handmade toys, you catch the continuation of the cycles of life, which thousands of years ago inspired the artisans who sculpted the temples of Orissa.

Ten kilometers (six miles) west of Bhubaneswar, the twin hills of Khandagiri and Udayagiri are worth a visit, especially for a short drive at dusk. You can see the mount at Dhauli and Bhubaneswar's rooftops from here. The caves and inscriptions are worth visiting more for their historical significance than for their artistic merit.

Dhauli, about six kilometers (four miles) southeast of Bhubaneswar, overlooks the Kalinga Plains. The irrigation canals, neatly lined palm trees, and the sculpted paddy fields offer a serene view of what was once the scene of tremendous bloodshed that finally persuaded Emperor Ashoka to convert to Buddhism in the third century B.C. This view, with its historical associations, is moving, and the rock edicts, in which Ashoka calls all men his children, are well preserved.

Konarak

The sleepy town of Konarak is home to one of India's most fabulous temples—the Sun Temple of "Black Pagoda," so named because of the dark patina that covered it over the centuries. Legend shrouds the Sun Temple. Constructed in the thirteenth century by King Narasimha, probably as much as a monument to himself as to honor Surya, the sun god, it is an architectural and engineering wonder. Built in the shape of Surya's chariot, with 24 huge chariot wheels and pulled by seven straining horses, this is a breathtaking temple. To see the temple lit at night and almost deserted in the early morning, stay overnight in one of the two simple government tourist lodges.

Puri

Puri, on the coast, is a seaside town that contains one of the holiest sites of Hinduism. In the ninth century, the seer Sankaracharya designated Puri as one of the four pilgrimage sites (*dhams*) for Hindus. Pious Hindus believe that a pilgrimage to Puri is an obligation and that if one stays here for three days and nights, one will gain freedom from the cycle of births and rebirths.

As you enter the tropical town with its pastel-colored ashrams and *dharmasalas* (rest houses), a religious aura intensifies, nearly leading you to its famous temple and its busy square. Here, in the old quarter of Puri, open-air stalls sell religious souvenirs and trinkets. Pilgrims buy *prasads* (gifts) for the sacred diety. Devotional songs blare out of speakers.

Jagannath is also the starting point for one of the most spectacular of India's temple fairs, Ratha Yatra, the Car Festival. Held in mid-summer and attracting crushing hordes throughout the weeks of the celebration, the festival swells the already huge number of pilgrims to the Jagannath Temple to unbelievable proportions. Non-Hindus are not allowed to enter the Jagannath Temple, but you can see into the compound from nearby rooftops.

Buddhist Excavations

In addition to the rock edicts at Dhauli, there are other Buddhist sights of interest in Orissa. About 100 kilometers (62 miles) north of Bhubaneswar is the finest, the Ratnagiri-Lalitagiri complex, where Buddhists built Puspagiri, a university, in the seventh century. In A.D. 639, the Chinese pilgrim, Hiuen-T'sang, described Puspagiri in detail, stating that it was one of two Buddhist universities in Orissa. The ruins of sculptured portals and pagodas have been excavated and are in good condition.

Natural Beauties

Orissa's natural beauties are many, although few have the kind of Western accommodations that are available in Bhubaneswar and Puri. However, some of them are near areas with such accommodations and so can be visited in one day.

Near the West Bengal border is Chandipur, which has one of the best beaches in India. Here, the sea recedes five kilometers (three miles) each day at low tide. See it before it is unavailable for such casual visits. It's located in Balasore district and is in the middle of a raging controversy with the central government in New Delhi, which would like to set up a National Test Range for missiles, rockets, and pilotless target aircraft. The residents of Balasore have resisted the government's promises of relocation and compensation. This might not be an attractive locale for very long.

Simlipal Tiger Reserve in the center of Mayurbhanj, the northern-most district of Orissa, is breathtakingly beautiful. Aside from the wild animals (tigers, leopards, elephants, bison, and sambars) there are vast tracts of sal forest, cascading waterfalls, and lush grasslands. Popular with Bengalis and Biharis because it is near their borders, one needs to book a stay here long in advance.

Ushakothi is another of Orissa's many wildlife sanctuaries. Located in the northwest corner of the state, it can be reached on National Highway 6 not too far from the huge Hirakud Dam.

Toshali Sands, between Puri and Konarak on Marine Drive, bills itself as Orissa's ethnic village resort. Its guests can enjoy the tranquil beauty of an almost deserted beach without having to be at the far reaches of civilization.

Chilka Lake, a huge lake on the coast south of Puri, is favored by many migratory birds and is a renowned sanctuary. However, check with local tourist officers about visiting the sanctuary. The practice shelling at the nearby military gunnery range drives birds away for weeks.

South of Chilka Lake is Gopalpur-on-Sea, a quiet seaside resort with good surf and sailing and a prewar quaintness. Like Toshali Sands, it offers a lovely beach without requiring that you forgo the creature comforts.

If your time is limited, Nandankanan Biological Park, near Bhubaneswar, is a lovely spot in which to see some of what the wilds of India have to offer. Wild animals found throughout India are kept here in their natural habitat. The park also boasts a botanical garden and a lake for boating.

Hot springs are located in various places throughout the state, but two can be visited in day trips. Taptapani, 64 kilometers (40 miles) from Gopalpur-on-Sea, is in a forest, and water from the spring is channeled into a nearby pond. Atri, a little over 40 kilometers (25 miles) from Bhubaneswar, has the additional attraction of the Temple of Lord Hatakeswar.

PRACTICAL INFORMATION FOR ORISSA

WHEN TO GO. From October to mid-March is the best season for visiting Orissa, when the monsoons are over and temperatures are at their most temperate. Near the sea and in the western hills, this period can be extended until mid-April. In the higher reaches of the Simlipal Range, where the Simlipal Tiger Reserve is located, the temperatures are cool and enjoyable even in May and June. These cooler times are also drier periods, and unpaved roads—or roads under repair—and unplanted fields create extremely dusty conditions. In the higher elevations, cooler evening mists can be quite penetrating, so be prepared to be damp after evening outings.

Note: When you prepare for your journey to Orissa, we recommend that you read Alistair Shearer's *The Traveler's Key to Northern India* (New York: Alfred A. Knopf, 1989), which contains two well-researched and illuminating chapters that will benefit those who are interested in architectural history.

HOW TO GET THERE. By Air. *Indian Airlines* has daily flights to Bhubaneswar from Bombay, Calcutta, Delhi, Hyderabad, Nagpur, Raipur, and Varanasi. *Vayudoot* has three weekly flights from Hyderabad to Bhubaneswar and Jeypore.

By Train. The *Howrah-Puri Express, Jagannath Express,* and *Dhaulli Express* are first-class express trains that connect Bhubaneswar and Puri with Calcutta. The *Utkal Express* and *Nilachal Express,* also first-class trains, connect Bhubaneswar and Puri with Delhi. In Bhubaneswar, contact the Bhubaneswar Railway Station, tel. 52233.

By Bus. A bus can get you to Orissa; but buses are normally crowded and provide non-stop video movies. Take the train.

By Rented Car with Driver. Good roads link Bhubaneswar with Calcutta, 480 km (298 mi.); and Visakhapatnam in Andhra Pradesh, 426 km (264 mi.). Hire a car from a tour operator listed below. Rates are about Rs. 3.30 per km and a halt charge of Rs. 50 per night.

TOURIST INFORMATION. For good brochures on Orissa, information on accommodations, tours, and travel assistance, contact these agencies:

Orissa Tourist Office, Jayadev Marg, near Panthanivas, Bhubaneswar; tel. 50099. Open 10 A.M.–5 P.M., closed Sundays and the second Saturday of each month. It also has a counter at the Bhubaneswar airport (tel. 54715) and at the railroad station (tel. 54715).

Government of India Tourist Office, B-21 Kalpana Area, Bhubaneswar; tel. 54203. Open 10 A.M.–5 P.M., Monday–Friday. It also has a counter at the Bhubaneswar airport.

Orissa Tourist Offices are also located in the following places:

Puri, Station Rd., tel. 2131. *Konarak,* Tourist Bungalow, tel. 21. *Cuttack,* Arunodaya Market Building, Link Rd., Cuttack; tel. 23525. *Berhampur,* Old Christian St., Berhampur, tel. 3226. *Rourkela,* U.G.I.E. Square, Rourkela, tel. 3923.

FOREIGN CURRENCY EXCHANGE. Most Western-style hotels have money-exchange counters. Otherwise, go to a branch of the *State Bank of India,* open Monday–Friday, 10 A.M.–2 P.M.; Saturdays, till noon.

ACCOMMODATIONS. There are good Western-style hotels in Puri, Gopalpur-on-Sea, and Bhubaneswar, which offer excellent value and numerous amenities. In other areas, your best bet is to stay in an OTDC facility listed below under *Tourist Huts and Bungalows.* Prices are based on double occupancy and exclude taxes: *Expensive,* Rs. 950–Rs. 1,450; *Moderate,* Rs. 500–Rs. 950; *Inexpensive,* under Rs. 500. Some Western-style hotels take major credit cards.

BHUBANESWAR

Expensive

The Oberoi. Nyapalli, Bhubaneswar; tel. 56116. 70 rooms with bath. Bhubaneswar's majestic Lingaraj Temple was the model for this elegant luxury hotel. The lobby's lights are tucked inside huge brass temple bells. A balcony, guarded by carved temple lions, is mounted atop exquisite sandstone pillars. Air-conditioned rooms, overlooking either the pool or extensive landscaped gardens, have an attractive modern decor that includes lovely Orissan fabrics and TV. Multicuisine restaurants, bar, room service, swimming pool, tennis court, health club, business center, foreign-exchange counter, travel agency, baby-sitters, shops. AE, DC, MC, V.

Moderate

Hotel Kalinga Ashok. Gautam Nagar, Bhubaneswar; tel. 53318. 64 rooms with bath. This handsome modern hotel has spacious grounds and an inviting lobby with appealing Orissan touches, including a colorful copy of the temple chariot at Puri. Air-conditioned rooms are cheery, with a modern decor and TV. Multicuisine restaurants, bar, room service, bank, foreign-exchange counter, travel agency, business center, shops. AE, DC, MC, V.

Inexpensive

Hotel Natraj. A/19 Cuttack Rd., Bhubaneswar; tel. 57648. 30 rooms with bath. A very inexpensive Western-style hotel, the Natraj has a lobby that is unadorned and clean. Air-conditioned rooms are best, with a modest modern decor, TV, and spacious balconies. Multicuisine restaurant, bar, room service, bank, foreign-exchange counter, travel agency, doctor, shops. AE, DC, MC, V.

Hotel New Kenilworth Bhubaneswar. 86/ A-1 Gautam Nagar, Bhubaneswar; tel. 54330. 72 rooms with bath. This Western-style high rise has an attractive lobby dominated by a brightly painted Orissan "lac" painting. Air-conditioned rooms are spacious, with a modern decor and TV. Best rooms overlook the pool. Room service, multicuisine restaurants, bar, small swimming pool, health club, foreign-exchange counter, travel agency, doctor, shops. AE, DC, MC, V.

Hotel Prachi Bhubaneswar. 6 Janpath, Bhubaneswar; tel. 52689. 48 rooms with bath. Its cheery lobby has a small shrine to Ganesh, the elephant-headed god, and lots of Orissan touches. Air-conditioned rooms are best, with a modern decor and TV. Ask for a room overlooking the pool. Multicuisine restaurants, bar, room service, swimming pool, gardens, health club, travel agency, foreign-exchange counter, doctor, shops. AE, DC, MC, V.

Hotel Safari International. 721 Rasul Garh, Bhubaneswar; tel. 53443. 60 rooms with bath. This new hotel complex with spacious grounds was almost ready for opening at press time. Spacious modern cottages (two units per dwelling), which have an interior thatched ceiling, are set around a garden and a projected swimming pool. TV, room service, multicuisine restaurants, bar, pool, health club, tennis court, doctor, foreign-exchange counter, travel agency, baby-sitters, courtesy airport shuttle. AE, DC, MC, V.

Hotel Swosti. 103 Janpath, Bhubaneswar; tel. 54178. 48 rooms with bath. A well-run Western-style hotel, the Swosti has a cozy lobby with lovely Orissan *patta-chitra* (silk paintings). For maximum quiet, ask for a room in the back. All rooms are spacious and very clean, with a contemporary decor, TV, and air-conditioning. Multicuisine restaurants, room service, travel agency, foreign-exchange counter, doctor. Good value. AE, MC, V.

CUTTACK

Inexpensive

Hotel Akbari Continental. Dolmundai, Cuttack; tel. 25242. 60 rooms with bath. This new Western-style high rise is Cuttack's best hotel. Its lobby has lots of marble, a water fountain, and sandstone pillars. Spacious, air-conditioned rooms are very clean, with a modest contemporary decor and TV. Best rooms overlook the back lawn. The service is excellent. Indian- and Chinese-cuisine restaurant, room service, bar, foreign-exchange counter, sercretarial services, doctor. AE, DC, MC, V.

GOPALPUR-ON-SEA

Expensive

Oberoi Palm Beach. Gopalpur-on-Sea, District Ganjam; tel. 21. 19 rooms with bath. This one-story luxury 1920s bungalow has such an air of exclusivity that once you arrive, you don't want to leave. A sweeping veranda looks out at the beach and ocean. Tiered lawns lead down to the sand. Spacious rooms have a modern decor. Ask for a room with a good sea view. Indian and Continental restaurant, bar, room service, tennis court, yoga, foreign-exchange counter. AE, DC, MC, V.

PURI

Moderate

Hotel Nilachal Ashok. Adjoining Raj Bhavan, VIP Rd., Puri; tel. 2968. 36 rooms with bath. Lovely exterior grounds and a handsome lobby, with interior wraparound verandas and a fountain surrounded by greens, are highlights at this Western-style hotel on a good beach. But air-conditioned rooms, though spacious and clean, have an uninspired decor. Ask for an unobstructed beach view. TV, room service, Indian- and Continental-cuisine restaurant, bar, car-rental service, foreign-exchange counter, doctor. DC.

Toshali Sands. Konarak Marine Dr., Baliguali, Puri; tel. 28888 (or, in Bhubaneswar, tel. 50074). 42 rooms with bath. One of India's finest getaways, this secluded resort is set on 12 beautifully landscaped acres and has an upscale Orissan village decor and ambience. Villas (also moderate in price) are best, with two spacious rooms. All rooms have cozy porches with terra-cotta sculptures. Modern interiors include Orissan handlooms and "patta chitra" paintings. Air-conditioning, TV, room service, multicuisine restaurant, bar, doctor, foreign-exchange counter, travel agency, swimming pool, tennis court, health club, free transport to excellent beach, boating, bullock-cart rides, trekking, bicycling and fishing arrangements, cultural programs on request, shopping arcade. AE, DC, MC, V.

Inexpensive

Hotel Prachi. Swargadwar, Gourbarsahi, Puri; tel. 2638. 37 rooms with bath. This two-story hotel is on the beach at the edge of the city. Its attractive lobby has an Orissan decor. Air-conditioned rooms, with balconies overlooking the sea, are spacious and clean, with a plain, modern decor. Room service, multicuisine restaurant, bar, foreign-exchange counter, car-rental service, doctor, shopping arcade. Good value. AE, DC.

South Eastern Railway Hotels. Puri; tel. 2063. 35 rooms with bath. This former British bungalow, on the edge of Puri, overlooks the ocean. If you want an old-time ambience, stay here—preferably in the newer wing in a spacious, clean room. Sweeping verandas are ideal for relaxing. There's even a sign board reminding guests that quiet hours are from 10 P.M.–6 A.M. and 2–4 P.M. A fixed-menu restaurant serves Indian dishes at lunch and Continental dishes at dinner. There are also a bar, billiards, library, beautiful grounds, beach, and travel agency. Meals included. Rupees only.

TOURIST HUTS AND BUNGALOWS.

Throughout Orissa, OTDC has numerous bungalows, small hotels, and cottages that offer clean rooms, with decent furnishings, for under Rs. 200 per double (rupees only). To reserve a room, contact the manager at the specific facility or contact in advance the Divisional Manager (A & C), OTDC Ltd., Old Panthaniwas Building, Lewis Rd., Bhubaneswar, Orissa; tel. 54727. One day's room rent should be included with request.

Mahodadhinivas Puri-on-Sea. Puri; tel. 2507. 9 rooms with bath. In this home of a former maharajah, upstairs rooms are best, with fine ocean views. Fans, room service, restaurant, beach, garden, conducted tours departure point.

Panthanivas Barkul-on-Chilika Lake. Balugaon, District Puri; tel. Balugaon 60. 18 rooms with bath. Best rooms are air-conditioned. Restaurant, room service, bar, boating.

Panthanivas Chandipur-on-Sea. Chandipur, District Ganjam; tel. 46. 10 rooms with bath. Best rooms are air-conditioned. Restaurant, room service, bar, conducted tours departure point.

Panthanivas Cuttack. Buxi Bazar, Cuttack; tel. 23867. 34 rooms with bath. Best rooms are air-conditioned. Restaurant, room service, bar, conducted tours departure point.

Panthanivas Konark. Konark, District Puri; tel. 31. 7 rooms with bath and fans. Close to the temple. Nearby restaurant.

Panthanivas Tatapani. Tatapani, District Ganjam; tel. Digapahandi 21. 5 rooms with bath. Best rooms are air-conditioned and have their own private sulphur baths. Restaurant, room service.

DINING OUT. In the major cities and resort areas, you will find good eating, including fresh seafood. Also try Orissan specialties, especially curries prepared with coconut milk and delicious eggplant and lady-finger vegetable dishes. Breakfast is usually 7:30–10:30; lunch, noon–3; dinner, 7–10. Payment is normally in rupees unless the restaurant is connected to a Western-style hotel. The restaurants listed below are informal and, unless noted, are open for all three meals and don't require reservations. Prices, based on one person eating a three-course meal, excluding taxes, tip, or beverage, are *Expensive,* Rs. 80–Rs. 120; *Moderate,* Rs. 40–Rs. 80; *Inexpensive,* under Rs. 40.

BHUBANESWAR

Expensive

Chandini. Oberoi Bhubaneswar, Nayapalli; tel. 56116. Its name means canopy, and in this elegant restaurant an antique chandini is suspended from the center of the ceiling, and paintings of Rajput heroes adorn the walls along with old daggers and mounted *gharokahs* (carved Indian bay windows). The cuisine is Indian and delicious, especially the *dahi machli* (fish cooked in creamy yogurt gravy) and *hari-machli* (fish marinated in spices and coriander, then fried). Reservations recommended. Open 7:30–11:30 P.M. AE, DC, MC, V.

Moderate

Executive-Swosti. Hotel Swosti. 103 Janpath; tel. 54178. This cozy restaurant has a Japanese mural, mirrored pillars, upholstered chairs, and crisp table linen. The Indian cuisine is best, although the chef also prepares Continental and Chinese dishes. Try the delicious chicken butter masala (chicken cooked in spicy red gravy) or the exquisite tandoori prawns. For dessert, don't miss the fresh *kulfi* (Indian ice cream). Dinner reservations advised. Open 11 A.M.–3 P.M. and 7–11 P.M. AE, MC, V.

Inexpensive

East & West Restaurant Complex. 76 Buddha Nagar, tel. 57390. Here, you can choose from three distinct ambiences. Touch 'n Go is a plain room with a brick partition and plants. Sheba has low lighting, overhead fans, and a mural that sparkles at night. Olive Garden is on the roof, with lots of plants and soft lights draped in thatched pillars. All three are extremely informal and serve Chinese, Indian, Continental, and even Arabic and Mexican cuisines. Specialties include sizzlers, Orissan *navratan* curry (curry of mixed vegetables and pineapple), and fish *kesa* (deboned whole fish cooked in a spicy tomato gravy). Open 9 A.M.–10 P.M. Rupees only.

Hare Krishna Restaurant. Lalchand Market Complex, Master Canteen; tel. 57186. This delightful upstairs restaurant has subdued lighting; mirrored walls and ceiling; unobtrusive Hindi and Orissan taped music; and, best of all, a charming fountain in which Shiva is on top of Mount Kalash with the River Ganga flowing out of his hair. The cuisine is Indian or Chinese vegetarian, and includes tasty "Keshaba's favorite" (vegetables sautéed in spicy tomato gravy), and "Makhan *chor* delight" (grated cheese and carrots simmered in a mild tomato gravy). Finish with *kheer* (sweet rice and milk pudding). Open 11 A.M.–3 P.M. and 7:30–11 P.M. Snacks served in between meal times. Rupees only.

CUTTACK

Moderate

Darvat. Hotel Akbari Continental, Dolmundai; tel. 25242. A visit to Cuttack should include a meal in this excellent Indian and Chinese restaurant, one of Orissa's best. The decor is vaguely Mogul—with arches built into one wall—and Western, with lace curtains and chandeliers. At night, there's a good *ghazal* singer. Favorite choices are the chicken 69 (marsala-coated chicken pieces cooked in a tandoori), chili chicken, and delicious Orissan specialties: navratan curry *korma* (mild curry made with cheese, vegetables, and cream), and *kalara* (unusual crispy-fried gourd with potatoes). Open 7–10 A.M., noon–3 P.M. and 7:30–11 P.M. AE, DC, MC, V.

PURI

Moderate–Expensive

Phulpatna. Toshali Sands, Konarak Marine Dr.; tel. 2888. Phulpatna's walls and pillars are decorated with Orissan village designs. Tablecloths are created from Orissan handlooms. The chef serves Chinese, Continental, and Indian cuisines, and, with a few hours notice, Orissan specialties. Try the tandoori prawns, the Orissan *maccha* or *chingudi pattara poda* (fish or prawns wrapped in a banana leaf and roasted over charcoal), and ask for the special regional eggplant dishes or *dahl* (lentils). Open 11:30 A.M.–3:30 P.M. and 7–11 P.M. AE, DC, MC, V.

Moderate

Udichi Restaurant. Hotel Prachi, Swargadwar, Gourbarsahi; tel. 2638. Here, you'll find a good ocean view and Orissan decor—*patta chitra* paintings and a colorfully decorated ceiling. You can choose from Chinese, Continental, and Indian dishes, including delicious regional favorites such as tasty fish curry or grilled fish along with fried *baigan* (eggplant) and exquisite *bhendi* (lady fingers). Open 7–10 A.M., noon–3 P.M., and 7–11 P.M. AE, DC.

SWEETS AND TREATS. For good snacks and sweets, go to Venus Inn (217 Bapuji Nagar, Bhubaneswar), a popular upstairs dining hall. The menu is an endless variety of *dosas* (Indian-style stuffed crêpes) and *uttappams* (Indian-style pizzas). Sample the *rawa masala sada dosa* (slightly salty and sweet) or butter coconut uttappam, an Orissan speciality. For sweets, come early and have fresh *kassatta* (multi-flavored ice cream mixed with cashew nuts). It's sold out by early afternoon. Open 6:30–11 A.M. and 3–9 P.M. for snacks.

HOW TO GET AROUND. From the Airport. Tourist taxis (white Ambassador cars) will take you to Bhubaneswar hotels for about Rs. 40. The transfer from Bhubaneswar to Puri costs about Rs. 300.

By Bus. Private buses travel to all parts of the state. They're inexpensive and relatively comfortable, but they do take time. For information, go the Central Bus Stand on Rajpath.

By Rented Car with Driver. This is the best way to see Orissa. Here are some important distances from Bhubaneswar: Chilaka Lake, 130 km (81 mi.); Cuttack, 32 km (30 mi.); Konarak, 65 km (40 mi.); Puri, 62 km (38 mi.). Rates are about Rs. 3 per km, with a halt charge of Rs. 50 per night. Hire a car from an agency listed below under *Tour Operators.*

By Auto Rickshaw. Some auto rickshaws are available in the bigger cities; they should be cheaper than a tourist taxi. Rates are about Rs. 2 for the first km and Rs. 1.75 per additional km. Set the fare in advance.

By Bicycle Rickshaw. The most leisurely way to travel, rickshaws are also the most expensive. Rates are about Rs. 4 per km, but you're expected to bargain.

TOURS. OTDC (address above) conducts excellent, inexpensive tours by luxury bus.

Bhubaneswar Day Tour. 9 A.M.–5:30 P.M., Tuesday–Sunday. Departs from Panthanivas Tourist Bungalow.

Bhubaneswar–Puri–Konarak Tour. 7:45 A.M.–7 P.M., daily. Departs from Panthanivas Tourist Bungalow.

Sights Around Chandipur Seaside Resort. 7 A.M.–2 P.M., daily. Departs from Chandipur Panthanivas.

Cuttack–Bhubaneswar Tour. 8 A.M.–6 P.M., Tuesday–Sunday. Departs from Cuttack Panthanivas.

Cuttack–Puri–Konarak Tour. 7:45 A.M.–7 P.M., daily. Departs from Cuttack Panthanivas.

Puri–Konarak–Bhubaneswar Tour. 7A.M.–7 P.M., Tuesday–Sunday. Departs from Puri-on-the-Sea Panthabhavan.

Private Guides. The Government of India Tourist Office in Bhubaneswar (address above) provides good guides. For one–four people rates are about Rs. 60 for four hours; Rs. 120 for eight hours.

TOUR OPERATORS. The following agencies can take care of all your travel needs, including a hired car with driver:

Travel Wings, Oriental Travel Wings Pvt. Ltd., Bapuji Nagar, Bhubaneswar, Orissa; tel. 52689.

Sita Travels, Hotel Kenilworth, Bhubaneswar, Orissa; tel. 53330.

Mercury Travels, Hotel Oberoi, Bhubaneswar; tel 54216.

You can also rent a car with driver from OTDC, Transport Unit; tel. 53356.

SEASONAL EVENTS. Festivals in Orissa offer a good glimpse of this state's unique culture and religious rituals. The specific dates for many events each year are determined by the lunar calendar; consult the Government of India Tourist Office for details.

February. *Konarak Dance Festival.* For five days, you can watch *Odissi* (classical Orissan dances) performed at the Sun Temple during this wonderful event.

February/March. *Mahasivaratri.* Throughout Orissa, pilgrims flock to Shiva temples, especially the Lingara Temple in Bhubaneswar and Lord Loknath Temple in Puri, to honor Shiva. It's a joyous occasion, with intriguing rituals.

February/March. *Magha Saptami.* Held at the Konarak Sun Temple, this event is Orissa's second-largest festival. Pilgrims from all over India take a sunrise ritual dip at the mouth of the Chandrabhaga River

March/April. *Ashokastami.* During this car festival at Bhubaneswar, the image of Lord Lingaraj is taken from its inner sanctum in a mammoth charriot to the nearby Rameswar Shrine, then returns after four days. A big event.

Mid-April. *Chandan Yatra.* Honoring Lord Jagannath, this 21-day event features processions with devotees who carry images of deities to sacred tanks where they're rowed around in decorated boats. Especially colorful, with music and dances in Puri and Bhubaneswar.

May. *Snan Yatra.* In Puri, the images of Jagannath, Balabhadra, Subhadra, and Sudarsan are placed on a festive platform and given their annual ceremonial bath before they're put in seclusion for 15 days.

June. *Sitalsasthi.* This festival honors the marriage of Shiva and Parvati. A colorful wedding ceremony includes lavish processions with chariots carrying idols of the sacred couple. In Sambalpur, you can also see Odissi folk dances.

June/July. *Rath Yatra.* During Orissa's most sacred festival, Puri is crowded for seven days with celebrants. Lord Jagannath, Balabhadra (his brother), and Subhadra (his sister) are carried on spectacular chariots from their holy temple to Gundicha Mandira, another nearby shrine, to the Jagannath Temple in a similarly spectacular procession. At the end of these festivities the huge chariots are dismantled and their parts are sold to pilgrims. Because it is such a magnet for Hindu pilgrims, this festival is recommended if you want to experience the intensity of a particularly exhilirating, exhausting religious celebration.

HISTORIC SITES. Entrance to most places is generally free; where a donation is asked, a few rupees will suffice. Although some of the Orissan temples, such as the Lingaraj Temple in Bhubaneswar and the Jagannath Temple in Puri, are closed to non-Hindus, others are accessible except for their inner sanctums. Signs are posted indicating the restrictions. Most sights are open sunrise to sunset.

BHUBANESWAR

The eleventh-century *Lingaraj Temple,* is considered to be the ultimate in Orissan temple architecture. Closed to non-Hindus, its exterior carvings can be viewed from a raised platform on its periphery (bring binoculars and a few rupees as an "offering"). It is set in a huge walled-in compound that holds at least 70 smaller votive shrines. Like the great Jagannath Temple in Puri, the Lingaraj compound is a world in itself. Dating from about A.D. 1000, the Lingaraj Temple originally consisted only of the porch and shrine; the dancing hall and the hall of offering were added about a hundred years later. The curvilinear tower (*vimana*), built without mortar, rises to a height of 45 meters (147 feet). The tower is divided into vertical sections; at the top, just below the lineal spire, are figures of a lion crushing an elephant. The tower is hollow, and the top is reached by an interior staircase hewn out of walls that are seven feet thick. The inner walls of the shrine, which have no adornment, house the *lingam* (phallic symbol) of Shiva. Outside, the sculpture is profuse, representing a high point of Hindu decorative art.

Near the Lingaraj Temple is one of Bhubaneswar's many sacred tanks (man-made ponds). The biggest of these tanks, *Bindusagar,* is surrounded by a stone embankment. Pilgrims believe that it is filled with water from every sacred stream and tank in India and can therefore wash away sins. It is said that 7,000 temples once stood on the shores of Bindusagar.

The *Vaital Deul Temple* (mid-700s–early 800s), near Bindusagar, is one of the earlier temples. Unlike other temples in Bhubaneswar, its double-storied and barrel-shaped roof shows the influence of Buddhist rock architecture.

About one km (½ mi.) to the east of the northeast corner of the Lingaraj is "The Grove of the Perfect Being." In this mango grove are more than 20 temples including the oldest surviving temple in the city, the *Parasurameswar;* the diminutive *Mukteswar,* considered the gem of Orissan architecture; the *Siddheswar;* and the *Kedareswar.* The Parasurameswar was built in A.D. mid-600s and is decorated with sculpture that is executed with great vigor.

The *Mukteswar* (A.D. 10th century), called a "dream realized in sandstone" and the smallest temple in Bhubaneswar, bears very fine sculpture. An emaciated hermit teaching, a lady riding a rearing elephant, cobras darting their heads, and lions fighting are some of the themes represented. The most distinctive feature of the temple, its *torana* (arch gateway), shows the influence of Buddhist architecture and is intricately carved with peacocks and feminine figures in languorous positions.

Adjoining the Mukteswar is another of Bhubaneswar's many sacred tanks. Beyond it stands the *Kedareswar Temple,* with its eight-foot statue of Hanuman, the monkey god, and another of the goddess Durga standing on a lion. Northwest of the Mukteswar is the Siddheswar.

About one km (½ mi.) from the Lingaraj is the *Brahmeswar Temple* (A.D. 11th century), built around the same time and sumptuously carved.

Standing by itself in green rice fields is the *Rajrani* (A.D. 11th century), perhaps the most harmoniously proportioned temple in the city. So enchanting are its erotic sculptures that it has been suggested that it was built by some early Orissan king as a pleasure dome rather than as a temple.

AROUND BHUBANESWAR

Five km (three mi.) to the west of Bhubaneswar are the hills of Udayagiri and Khandagiri, with caves dating back to the second century B.C. Used by Jain monks for meditation, many of the caves feature rough sculpture. In front of the *Hatigumpha Cave* is a Palli inscription of Kharavela, one of Orissa's early princes, which describes the events of his 13-year rule. The *Ranigumpha Cave* (Queen's Cave) and the *Ganesh Gumpha* are the most interesting. These three caves are located on Udayagiri, the hill to the right of the road. To the left is Khandagiri hill and the *Ananta Cave,* with its veranda and decorated pilasters. From the top of this hill, you can look across the plains to Bhubaneswar and Dhauli.

DHAULI

In Dahauli, eight km (5 mi.), southeast of Bhubaneswar, Emperor Ashoka supposedly witnessed the carnage of the Kalinga Wars and resolved to put an end to such killing. His conversion to Buddhism, which began here, had profound effects on the propagation of Buddhism outside India. A huge elephant carved out of a large rock, representing the Buddha, Emperor Ashoka's "Rock Edicts" stating that all men are his children, a Hindu temple to Shiva, and the Buddhist Peace Pagoda, built in the early 1970s by Japanese Buddhists, are nearby.

KONARAK

Long ago, the Sun Temple, built in the shape of the sun god's chariot and Orissa's most impressive temple, was even more spectacular. Today, only half the main temple and the audience hall approximate its original shape. The original compound consisted of a dancing hall, an audience hall, and a tremendous tower that must have been 69 meters (227 feet) high if it conformed to traditional proportions of Indian temples. Part of the tower still existed as late as 1837, but it fell to ruin by 1869. Then the Audience Hall had to be filled with stone slabs and sealed off to prevent its collapse. The temple's location on sand, near the sea, which has since receded three kilometers (two miles) from the site, is majestic; but the salty air and the softness of the sand dunes have taken their toll.

The original architect, Sibai Santra, directed 1,200 workmen to lay the foundation of this temple, but the sand dunes on which it was being built did not provide him with much hope of success. Legend claims that when he failed in his attempts to raise the structure, he fell asleep on the nearby beach, crestfallen and dejected. When he awoke, an old woman offered him a plate of hot food. Seizing the plate, he dipped his fingers into the center of the steaming porridge and burned them. The woman chided him, saying, "My son, your manner of eating is like Sibai Santra's manner of building the temple. You must start from the edges and not in the center, as he throws stones into the middle." A wiser man, Sibai Santra started the construction afresh, and finally created his vision in stone.

The Sun Temple is constructed in the form of a huge chariot with 24 huge wheels pulled by seven straining horses. Every area of the temple is intricately carved with some of the most fantastic sculpture to be seen in India. Platforms, horses, colossal-sized elephants, pillars, and boundary walls of the main plinth are covered with mythical animals, whimsical depictions of daily life, war, trade, erotic sculptures of amorous dalliances—the panoply of a culture's finest instincts: its imagination, mythology, history, and knowledge of the life cycle. Each structural feature of the temple has a hidden meaning. The seven horses of the chariot represent the seven days of the week, the 24 wheels are the 24 fortnights of the Indian year, and the eight spokes of each wheel are the eight *pahars* into which the ancients divided day and night.

As was usual with temples of this period, both the spire, which was supported by the half-ruined structure (near the pagoda), and the audience hall, which remains, stood on a high plinth. Now that the hall has been blocked off, the entrance to the shrine is inaccessible. Three flights of steps lead up to it from the east, north, and south, and the main door on the west leads to the principal temple. The three-tiered roof, with space between each tier for closer inspection, is covered with elaborate carvings. The walls rise to about 14 meters (45 feet) before they begin to contract inward toward the flat ceiling.

To get a leisurely close-up look at the Sun Temple and its fabulous, intricate carvings, arrive between 7 and 8 A.M., before busloads of pilgrims and other tourists.

The Archaeological Survey of India provides a guide service, but be sure to ask the guide for an identification badge, since many less-informed free-lance guides are eager to take you around. At the entrance to the compound, vendors sell well-researched guidebooks to the Sun Temple and other Orissan monuments for a few rupees.

PURI

The Jagannath Temple, abode of Jagannath, lord of the universe, is a majestic, tiered structure layered with carvings. Like the Lingaraj in Bhubaneswar, entry to the temple is prohibited to non-Hindus (so strictly is this rule enforced that former Prime Minister Indira Gandhi was refused admittance because she had married a Parsi and was thus outside the faith). You can view this imposing structure from the roof of the Raghunandan Library opposite the eastern gate of the temple. A few rupees donation is expected. If the library is closed, the nearby Jaya Balia Lodge will let visitors climb to its roof. Binoculars are recommended. The temple, set in a compound surrounded by a wall, has the traditional porch and shrine, surmounted by a conical tower. The hall of offerings and the pillared hall of dance were added several centuries after the original temple was built in about 1030. Just as in Bhubaneswar, the compound is filled with smaller votive shrines.

Lord Jagannath's abode is a land of superlatives. Devotees lavish this holy city of Hinduism with their offerings:—the temple kitchen, reportedly the largest kitchen in the world, feeds Mahaprasad, its unique steamed cuisine, to over 10,000 people daily and, during festival times, to 25,000.

RATNAGIRI-LALITAGIRI

At Ratnagiri-Lalitagiri, the seat of Puspagiri, the A.D. seventh-century Buddhist University, excavations are gradually revealing a magnificent sight. Stupas, monasteries, and stone sculptures are in excellent condition.

MUSEUMS AND GALLERIES. Bhubaneswar. The *Orissa State Museum* has palm-leaf manuscripts and a few sculptures from temple ruins. Open 10 A.M.–4 P.M., closed Mondays. *Tribal Museum of Man* (Harijan & Tribal Research Institute) has ornaments, weapons, and dresses of Orissa's many tribes. Open 10 A.M.–5 P.M., closed Sundays. *Handicraft Museum* (Joint Director of Industries) has Orissan handicrafts. Open 10 A.M.–5 P.M., closed Sundays.

Konarak. The *Archaeological Museum* (near the temple) features sculptures from the temple. Open 10 A.M.–5 P.M., closed Sundays.

SPORTS AND OUTDOOR ADVENTURES. Beaches. *Gopalpur-on-Sea,* an enchanting seaside resort nestled at the foot of cliffs, is located 13 km (eight mi.) from Berhampur. Berhampur is on bus lines from Bhubaneswar, Puri, and Rourkela. Gopalpur-on-Sea can be reached by regular bus service from town. If you want seclusion, this is a quiet spot to spend a beach vacation.

Toshali Sands, located on Marine Drive between Konarak and Puri, is a beautifully designed "ethnic village resort" surrounded by a thick coconut grove and well-maintained gardens. Although not on the beach, its guests have access to a nearly deserted beach a short distance away through groves of casuarina that seem to sigh with the slightest breeze. Hotel shuttles provide transportation between the hotel and the beach.

Puri Beaches. The long stretch of beach in Puri doesn't offer seclusion, but you'll find good sand and surf.

Hot Springs. Atri. A holy place 42 km (26 mi.) from Bhubaneswar, this lovely hot spring is also the sight of the Temple of Hatakeswar.

Taptapani. 50 km (31 mi.) from Berhampur, and thus a convenient outing from Gopalpur-on-Sea, this hot sulphur spring is in a forest. The nearby panthanivas (travelers' lodge) has hot sulphur baths in two rooms.

Wildlife Sanctuaries. Nandankanan. This lovely zoological park, situated in the Chandaka Forest 12 miles from Bhubaneswar, is highly recommended for those who are interested in seeing some of India's wildlife but are on a tight schedule. Here tigers, including the rare white tiger; lions; panthers; leopards; pelicans; peafowl; pythons; and gharial crocodiles are on exhibit in their natural habitat. Across the lake from the zoological park is a botanical garden. OTDC has a tour from Bhubaneswar that includes a visit to Nandankanan.

Simlipal. In the hilly Mayurbhanj district in northern Orissa is the less accessible Simlipal Forest. Here, you find the Simlipal National Park, also designated a Tiger

Reserve, covering 2,750 sq. km (1,700 sq. mi.). Scenery in this park, with its valleys, gorges, waterfalls, vast grasslands, rivers and streams edged with ferns and mosses, and thickly wooded slopes, with their abundance of sal trees and orchids, is ample reason for at least a short visit. Tigers, elephants, Indian wolves, leopards, sambar and deer, hill mynas, peafowl, parakeets, and a variety of snakes all make their home here. Jeeps are necessary within the park and should be arranged for through the field director. You need permission to visit this park. Contact the Field Director, Simlipal Tiger Project, Baripada, District Mayurbhanji, Orissa, or the District Forest Office (also at Baripada). These offices can also arrange for a jeep and accommodations in forest rest houses.

Chilka Lake. On the coast between Bhubaneswar and Gopalpur-on-Sea, Chilka Lake spreads over 1,100 sq. km (680 sq. mi.), making it the largest inland lake in India. Its brackish water, dotted with islands bearing such whimsical names as Honeymoon and Breakfast islands, is rich with marine life, and from November to March it is the temporary home of migrating birds—ducks, pelicans, golden plovers, cormorants, flamingoes, ospreys, and other birds from as far away as Siberia. Water transport facilities are available through the OTDC at Barkul.

SHOPPING. Shopping can mean great sidetrips into the beautiful hidden Orissan villages that are home to master craftsmen. A particularly interesting one of these is Raghurajpur, about 12 km (7 mi.) from Puri on the way to Bhubaneswar. It's an idyllic village set back from the main road, with every dwelling owned by an artisan. The art you will discover—stone and wood carvings, *patta chitra* (finely wrought temple paintings), *talapatra* (palm leaf art)—is worthy of a visit. Ask to visit the studios of Jagannath Mahapatra (patta chitra master craftsman); Kalucharan Barik (patta chitra and talapatra master craftsman); and Bhagaban Subudhi (master woodcarver). Other good artisans will also invite you inside. Prices are lower than you'll pay anywhere else, but bargain and expect to pay in rupees.

Pipli. This village, 16 km (10 mi.) southeast of Bhubaneswar, has stalls lining the street that are filled with gaily colored appliqué-work. You name it, they make it—even great beach umbrellas. Rupees only.

Bhubaneswar. Sri Satya Badi Moharana, a renowned artisan, creates lovely stone carvings at reasonable prices (rupees only). His home is in old Bhubaneswar (Bibhisena Colony, Lingaraj Rd.). To see other craftsmen in Bhubaneswar who do patta chitra paintings or stone carvings, contact the Orissa Tourist Office.

Utkalika (Orissa State Handicrafts Emporium, Eastern Tower Market Building) sells great handicrafts. Open 9:30 A.M.–1 P.M. and 4–8:30 P.M., closed Sundays. V.

Orissan State Handloom W. C. S. Ltd. (Western Tower Market Building) has good fabrics. Open 9 A.M.–12:30 P.M. and 4–8:30 P.M., closed Sundays.

Puri. *Utkalika* (Mahodadhi Market) is open 9 A.M.–1 P.M. and 5–9 P.M., closed Sundays. *Arts and Crafts Complex* (same market) is open 9 A.M.–12:30 P.M. and 4–8:30 P.M., closed Sundays. Government-run, fixed-price shops, they sell Orissan handicrafts and fabrics.

Sudarshan Crafts Museum (Station Rd.) sells beautiful stone carvings. Open daily 6:30 A.M.–noon and 2–8 P.M. MC, V.

Cuttack. This city is famous for its filigree jewelry. *Parekh Bros.* (Naya Sarak) has good designs in silver. Open 9:30 A.M.–8:30 P.M., closed Sundays. Rupees only. *Madhavji Jewellers* (Naya Sarak) has good designs in gold. Open 10 A.M.–1 P.M. and 3–8 P.M., closed Sundays. Rupees only.

ENTERTAINMENT AND NIGHTLIFE. *Odissi,* the classical dance form of Orissa, is perhaps the most lyrical style of Indian dance, with graceful gestures and postures. When you see a performance, it's as if the lovely sculpted dancers on the Sun Temple at Konarak had suddenly come to life. In addition to classical Odissi dance, folk dances and tribal dances are still performed during festival times throughout Orissa. To find out about on-going dance performances in Bhubaneswar, contact the Orissa Tourist Office or the College of Dance, Drama, and Music, near Rabindra Mandap.

For a nightcap in Orissa, the best bar is at the Oberoi Hotel. Bars are generally open 11 A.M.–3 P.M. and 6:30–11 P.M.

ASSAM, MEGHALAYA, AND THE NORTHEAST STATES

Foothills of the Himalayas

by
LISA SAMSON and AMIT SHAH

Note: Due to continuing tensions and disturbances in Assam, the U.S. State Department advises deferring travel to this state.

The northeast states of Arunachal Pradesh, Assam, Manipur, Meghalaya, Mizoram, Nagaland, and Tripura are beautiful and culturally fascinating areas of this diverse country. However, they have been troubled areas of India for many years, an Achilles heel of sorts to the central government. Connected to the rest of the subcontinent by a narrow corridor of land, encompassing foothills of the Himalayas, marshy grasslands, and wild mountainous areas, these seven states are home to many of India's tribal peoples and site of one of its ancient Hindu states.

Almost engulfed by Burma, Bangladesh, and China, the seven states have been all but inaccessible to foreign travelers for years. Political strife in the northeast, fueled by long-simmering internal disagreements or resulting from pressures brought about by conflicts in Bangladesh that overflow into India, erupt periodically into open conflict between disputing internal factions or against the central government.

As a result, regulations for access to these areas change frequently, making travel in this area somewhat of a gamble. At press time, only Assam

504

and Meghalaya were open to foreign travel and all foreigners must obtain a Restricted Area Permit (see *Facts at Your Fingertips* and the *Practical Information* section of this chapter). Before planning any trip to Assam, travelers should also check with the proper government agency in their home country (the State Department in the United States) to see if travel to this state is advised.

EXPLORING ASSAM

Through Assam winds the magnificent Brahmaputra River, its name meaning "son of Brahma," lord of the universe. And an apt name it is, providing life-nourishing water to irrigate the rich alluvial plain through which it runs or meting out devastation during the monsoons, when rains have risen its crest to over 40 feet above its natural level. The river traverses east to west and makes Assam one of the most fertile areas of India. Rice grows in abundance here, but it is for tea that Assam is better known. Tea plantations abound in Assam, their low-lying green foliage dwarfed by the tall shade trees above them. At harvest time, women with woven baskets strapped to their heads move slowly through the tea plants, picking the tender leaves, all the while seeming to swim through a waist-high sea of green. Tea grew wild in this area for centuries; the first organized tea estates were established by the British in the 1800s. Almost 800 such estates now blanket the hillsides of Assam, producing about 50 percent of India's tea.

Assam is not just a picture postcard state continuing traditions of the raj, however. Rich oil fields were discovered in the area surrounding Digboi, where the first oil refinery in Asia was built and where 50 percent of India's crude oil is now produced.

A Bit of History

Assam's ancient history, which is not well documented, is largely discussed in terms of the plains people, not the numerous tribes who populated the surrounding hills. In the thirteenth century, the Ahoms of Burma gained power in Upper Assam, gradually conquering the lands once ruled by the Kacharis. Moslem invaders in the 1500s were defeated by the Ahoms, but, in the 1600s, Lower Assam was ceded to Aurangzeb, the great Mogul emperor. A constant location of conflict, Assam came under the control of the East India Company in 1826 and remained under British control in one administrative guise or another until 1947. Since Independence, conflict has continued. What was once Assam and the North East Frontier Agency (NEFA of Assam) has been restructured, creating the states of Nagaland (in 1963), Meghalaya (in 1972), and Mizoram (in 1987) from parts of Assam and Arunachal Pradesh (in 1987) from the NEFA.

Guwahati

Guwahati, the traditional capital of Assam (Dispur, part of Guwahati, is now the temporary capital), was called "Light of the East" and "City of Astrology." It sits on the southern bank of the Brahmaputra and is one of the few locations that is accessible to foreign travelers. Various religious and scholarly centers are found nearby. Hajo, 24 kilometers (15 miles) away, attracts Buddhists and Hindus, who come to worship the remains of the Buddha at the Hayagriba Madhab Temple, and Moslems who come to worship at the Pir Giyasuddin Aulia, believed to be one-quarter as holy as the great mosque in Mecca. Within Guwahati, the Nabagraha Shrine, with its inner sanctum a reflection of the solar system, was once a center of astrology and astronomy.

Guwahati's most famous shrine, however, is the tantric Kamakhya Temple, dedicated to the Hindu goddess Sati (also known as Kali or Shakti). Legend claims that after Sati's father insulted Shiva, her consort, Sati was so humiliated that she threw herself on a funeral pyre. Shiva took her body and circled the world, causing so much destruction that Vishnu, the Hindu god of creation, trailed after him and slowly hacked Sati's body into 51 pieces, which fell all over the Indian subcontinent. Her *yoni* (vagina), considered the source of all creation, fell on Nalachal Hill, which is said to represent Shiva's lingam. Kamakhya Temple commemorates their union. In time, Sati reappeared in a new manifestation, Parvati, who became Shiva's new consort.

The temple complex you see today—an assortment of beehive-shaped shrines commemorating the various manifestations of the Mother Goddess—represents renovations and remaining bits of temples first constructed in the thirteenth century by the Ahom dynasty. After it was destroyed by Moslems, a king of neighboring Cooch-Bihar restored the complex.

Long ago, kings sacrificed humans at this tantric temple. When this practice was banned, Kali, another manifestation of the Mother Goddess, had to make do with a goat, representing lust, or buffalo—bestial passion. Tantrics believe that the act of sacrifice destroys their own base instincts and also gives the sacrificed animal an opportunity for rebirth at a higher station.

Though non-Hindus are not permitted into the main shrine with its revered yoni, they can witness the purifications and sacrifices performed in the extensive complex. A door to the left of an old pavilion leads into the temple; a set of stairs descends to the sacred cave. The hallowed stone yoni, which is always dressed (covered with a cloth), is under a gold canopy inside the cave. Not even the special class of people allowed to clean the temple and purify the yoni set their eyes on the stone, but perform their tasks blindfolded.

Once you've circled the main complex, drive to the Bhubaneswari Devi Temple on a nearby foothill. Here, the Goddess Bhubaneswari, yet another manifestation of the Mother Goddess, is represented by a red slab of rock located under a canopy in a sunken dark chamber. Hindus say that the rock represents the abdomen of the goddess and, to protect her modesty, it's purposely difficult to see.

Manas and Kaziranga Wildlife Sanctuaries

What most attracts people to Assam, however, are the two great wildlife sanctuaries near Guwahati—Kaziranga and Manas. Swaying on top of an elephant, you traverse the grasslands of these two splendid parks in the hopes of seeing some of its rare wildlife. Kaziranga, bounded by the Brahmaputra River and the Mikir Hills, is best known as the home of the largest population of Indian one-horned rhinoceroses. These massive beasts were mistaken for the legendary unicorns by Marco Polo, who proclaimed them "hideous." On the verge of extinction in the early 1900s, the rhinoceros population has increased steadily since 1908 when this sanctuary was set aside for them as a forest reserve. Not known for being sweet tempered, the powerful rhinoceros creates vibrations in its wanderings that are an ample warning that it is not to be taken lightly. The elephants you ride through the parks, well acquainted with the moody rhinoceros, keep a respectful distance. Kaziranga also has wild elephants and water buffaloes—another impressive animal—sambar, swamp deer, bears, and a great variety of birds.

Manas Wildlife Sanctuary, a beautiful spot, watered by many rivers and streams, is an excellent place for those who are interested in fishing. Considered to be among the loveliest of India's wildlife sanctuaries, it was set up in 1928 as an original tiger reserve and is part of "Project Tiger." Sharing the riverine sanctuary with the tiger are one-horned rhinoceroses, wild buffaloes, sambar, and the unusual pygmy hogs and hispid hares. Manas has a great variety of birds; spectacular daily flights of great pied hornbill wing across the Manas River into neighboring Bhutan.

EXPLORING MEGHALAYA

India's decision at independence to keep foreigners out of Meghalaya was rooted in a bit of unfortunate history. To subdue headhunting tribals who lived within the hills, the British, during their rule, had divvied up this area among missionaries of various Christian faiths. While their choice of weapon—the Bible—did lead to pacification and, no doubt, saved a few heads, it also contributed to the destruction of the indigenous cultures.

Today, the Western missionaries are gone, but native itinerant preachers continue to spread the Word to non-Christian Meghalayans; and Meghalaya—India's "Bible Belt"—remains at a precarious crossroads, with traditional culture still facing extinction. In no other Indian state currently open to foreigners do travelers cross such cultural extremes. There's the capital, Shillong, very Western, with Western music, Western clothes, and Western problems like drugs and divorce. Travel one day to the east and you're in remote hill country, where many of the people have never seen foreigners, where *borangs* (tree houses) jut above the fields, where women are apt to be bare breasted. The only statewide common symbol is the Christian cross. The British chose a powerful weapon.

Meghalaya has three racially distinct hill tribes, all of them matrilineal societies: the Khasis, who live primarily in the central Khasi Hills and trace their ancestry back to the Khymer of Cambodia; the Jaintias of Indo-Chinese descent, who live in the western Jaintia Hills; and the Garos, who migrated from Tibet to the Garo Hills. All three show greater physical affinity with their original ancestry than with the rest of India.

Throughout the state, educated tribal women hold important positions in the government and business community. Bara Bazaar, the popular tribal market in Shillong, is run by women. Though many marriages are still arranged, dowries don't exist; and the husband, not the wife, moves in with his spouse's family—which sets Meghalaya apart from Hindu and Moslem India.

Shillong

Set on a series of rolling hills, Shillong, the capital, is unlike any other Indian hill station. You won't find the traditional pedestrian mall on an upper ridge; you won't see billboards promoting the ideal honeymoon retreat. You will see evidence of Christianity: More pictures of Jesus than of Shiva are placed in homes and shops; church spires are everywhere.

Walk through Bara Bazaar, a produce market run by tribal women. Then get away from the bustle and explore the quiet, well-kept grounds of the Botanical Garden, or go boating on the adjacent Wards Lake.

Cherrapunjee

Cherrapunjee, 55 kilometers (34 miles) south of Shillong, is the wettest place on earth. Every year almost 450 inches of rain are dumped on this region. It is also an area studded with caves and beautiful waterfalls. The Nohkalikai Falls, the fourth-highest in the world, are near the village of Serrarim, about five kilometers (three miles) from Cherrapunjee. The falls, which plummet into an aquamarine pool, are named after Ka Likai, whose husband, a jealous stepfather, cooked her child and served it to her as an unnamed delicacy. Ka Likai soon discover the child's fingers, which her husband had hidden in a basket of betel nut. She then leaped over the falls that now bear her name.

Garo Hills

Any visit to Meghalaya should include a trip east to the Garo tribal villages set in the Garo Hills. One perfect place to visit is the William Nagar Forest Reserve, about 220 kilometers (136 miles) from Shillong. This is the stomping ground of wild elephants and, with the Simsang River meandering through its borders, an angler's treat. Here you can also arrange to visit a typical Garo village—a work of art made of bamboo.

Usually the entrance to a Garo village is through a grove of jackfruit trees, which produce an important food staple. In the compound, even chickens have their own miniature bamboo homes—coops complete with ladders for easy access. Pigs are kept in tidy bamboo pens. The *nokpante* (thatch-covered pavilion), crowded with men who live here from age 12 until they marry, is in the central courtyard; and, in a nearby field, stands the village *borang* (bamboo watchtower) from which villagers watch for animals, wild or domesticated, that may wander into precious crops.

From the William Nagar Forest Reserve, you can also continue on to Tura, the district headquarters of the West Garo Hills, about 70 kilometers (43 miles) away. If it's Monday, plan to stop at Chinabat village, at about 14 kilometers (eight miles) from the forest reserve, and walk through the festive weekly market. If it's Friday, stop in Rongrem, closer to Tura. In these temporary bazaars you'll see Rajastanis, Punjabis, and northeastern tribal peoples selling everything from locally grown tobacco to exotic medicinal potions. You'll also get a good introduction to the Garo's fascinating culture.

Balpakram National Park

The Balpakram National Park, straddling the Bangladesh border, features prominently in Garo mythology as the land of their dead. Inaugurated in 1987, the park sits on a high plateau of thick jungle and forest—threaded with rivers feeding into small lakes—and is surrounded by a vast canyon. Here, you may see wild buffalo, bears, leopards, tigers, wild elephants, plus a large number of migrating birds: hornbills, peacocks, and Siberian ducks.

One last attraction is the nearby Siju Cave, on the bank of the Simsang River. This is one of the biggest caves in Meghalaya; and its interior, filled with stalactites, stalagmites, and bats, awaits thorough exploration.

PRACTICAL INFORMATION FOR
ASSAM AND MEGAHALAYA

WHEN TO GO. Assam. The best time to visit is September–June. The monsoon rages in the summer months. The best time to see animals in Manas Tiger Reserve is January–April; in Kaziranga National Sanctuary, from November–March. You can also plan a vacation around the Rongali Festival in April and Durga Puja in October.

Meghalaya. October–April is the best time to visit. There are torrential rains the rest of the year. In November, the Garo tribals put on two of India's best festivals: Ka Pamblang Nongkrem and Wangala (for more information, see *Seasonal Events,* below).

RESTRICTED AREA PERMIT. To visit Assam and Meghalaya, you must have a Restricted Area Permit (see *Travel Documents* in *Facts at Your Fingertips*).

Assam. When you fill out the permit for Assam, list Guwahati and the two game parks (Manas and Kaziranga). As of this writing, the tourist department was trying to open up the cities of Sibsagar and Tezpur. Trip length is currently limited to a week; this is also under review. Ask the Government of India Tourist Bureau for the latest information. Travelers can also visit Assam as part of a tour group. Two good tour operators who sponsor trips are *Travel Corporation Pvt. Ltd.* (Chander Mukhi, Nariman Point, Bombay, tel. 2021881 and Hotel Metro, First Floor, N-49 Connaught Place, New Delhi, tel. 3315181) and *Sheba Travels,* listed below. Also check the listings in *Facts at Your Fingertips.*

Meghalaya. Seven-day trip permits are easy to obtain for groups of four or more to Meghalaya. Individuals, however, should contact the Government of India Tourist Office in their home country to see if restrictions for individuals have been relaxed. If there's been no change, follow the procedure outlined in *Facts at Your Fingertips.* Three good agencies in Meghalaya also sponsor group tours: *Travel Corporation Pvt. Ltd.* (listed above); *Sheba Travels* (Crowborough Building, Police Bazaar, Shillong, Meghalaya, tel. 23015 or 26222); and *A.S. Sen* (Shillong Club, Shillong, Meghalaya, tel. 23354 or 2545). Also refer to the recommended listings in *Facts at Your Fingertips.* If your trip plans are flexible or geared to a major festival, chances are you'll get in. Your tour operator will help you procure the obligatory Restricted Area Permit. On this permit, list the following specific destinations: Shillong, Tura in Garo Hills, Jowai in Jaintia Hills, and Nongstoin in West Khasi Hills.

HOW TO GET THERE. Since the distances to Assam and Meghalaya are great, only air travel is recommended. To travel between the two states, you have many options. The distance from Guwahati to Shillong is about 103 km (64 mi.).

ASSAM

By Air. *Indian Airlines* has daily flights connecting New Delhi, Calcutta, Bagdogra, and Patna with Guwahati in Assam. Jorhat, the town nearest to the Kaziranga Wildlife Sanctuary, is connected by Indian Airlines to Calcutta and Guwahati. Guwahati is also connected to various cities in the northeast that are currently off-limits to foreign travelers: Agartala, Dibrugarh, Dimapur, Imphal, and Tezpur. *Vayudoot* has a daily flight from Calcutta to Guwahati.

Meghalaya Tourist Development Corporation (MTDC) has a helicopter service that flies daily except Sunday between Guwahati and Shillong in Meghalaya. For all flights, all foreigners must show their permit to airport police on arrival and departure.

By Bus. Private and state-run deluxe buses make the trip to Shillong in about four hours. In Guwahati, contact *Assam State Transport Corporation* (ASTC) through the Assam Tourist Department, tel. 27102; *Meghalaya Transport Road*

Service (MTRC), Guwahati Airport; *Blue Hill Travels,* Ashok Hotel and Paltan Bazaar, tel. 31427; *Assam Valley Tours and Travels,* Paltan Bazaar, tel. 26133.

By Rented Car with Driver. You can hire a car from the Assam Tourist Department in Guwahati, Station Rd., tel. 27102. Rates are about Rs. 3.75 per km and Rs. 50 per night halt charge. *Blue Hill Travels* in the Ashok Hotel also rents cars for about Rs. 400 per day, plus a halt charge of Rs. 100 per night.

MEGHALAYA

By Air. *Vayudoot* has a daily flight between Shillong and Calcutta. Otherwise, the closest airport is in Guwahati, Assam (see above). Within Meghalaya, MTDC (Shillong Tourist Hotel, Polo Rd., tel. 22129) has a **helicopter service** from Shillong to Tura that currently runs three times a week.

By Bus. For trips from Shillong to Guwahati, contact *MRTC,* Jail Rd., Police Bazar, tel. 23206; or *Blue Hill Travels,* tel. 31427. MRTC can also make reservations for ASTC, Blue Hill Travels, and Assam Valley Tours and Travels.

By Taxi or Rented Car with Driver. Hire a car with driver from *Sheba Travels,* Crowborough Building, Police Bazaar, Shillong, Meghalaya, tel. 23015 or 26222; or *A.S. Sen,* Shillong Club, Shillong, Meghalaya, tel. 23354 or 2545. The cost to Guwahati is about Rs. 400.

TOURIST INFORMATION. Assam. Contact the *Assam Directorate of Tourism,* Station Rd., Guwahati, Assam, tel. 27102; open 10 A.M.–5 P.M., closed Sunday. It also has counters at the airport and railroad station, plus branch offices in important destinations.

Meghalaya. Contact the *Tourist Information Center,* Police Bazaar, Shillong, tel. 6220; *Meghalaya Tourism Development Corporation Ltd.,* Shillong Tourist Hotel, Polo Rd., Shillong, tel. 22129; or the *Government of India Tourist Office* G.S. Rd., Police Bazaar, Shillong, tel. 25632. Each is open 10 A.M.–5 P.M., closed Sunday. The Meghalaya Tourist Department also has an office in Tura, Garo Hills.

FOREIGN CURRENCY EXCHANGE. Most Western-style hotels have money-exchange counters. Otherwise, go to a branch of the *State Bank of India,* open Monday–Friday 10 A.M.–2 P.M.; Saturdays till noon.

Assam. In Guwahati, the State Bank of India is on M.G. Rd. and *Grindlays Bank* is in Fancy Bazaar.

Meghalaya. In Shillong, the State Bank of India is on G.S. Rd.

ACCOMMODATIONS. Once you leave Guwahati and Shillong, you'll find limited accommodations and simple rooms. Prices are based on double occupancy and exclude taxes: *Moderate,* Rs. 500–Rs. 950; *Inexpensive,* under Rs. 500. Some Western-style hotels take traveler's checks and major credit cards.

ASSAM

Guwahati

Moderate

Hotel Belle Vue. M.G. Rd., Box. 75, Guwahati; tel. 28291. 45 rooms with bath. Guwahati's oldest hotel is away from the bustle on a hill overlooking the Brahmaputra River. The interior is whimsical and lovely—an elevator painted with a blue sky and clouds. Carpeted rooms are spacious, with air-conditioning and TV. Corner rooms offer the best river views. Multicuisine restaurant, room service, house doctor, car rental, bar, foreign-exchange counter. AE, DC, MC, V.

Hotel Brahmaputra Ashok. M.G. Rd., Guwahati; tel. 32632. 50 rooms with bath. Guwahati's stylish new hotel is on the Brahmaputra River near the center of town. Rooms are centrally air-conditioned and spacious, with contemporary Assamese decor and TV. The best rooms have a river view. Multicuisine restaurant, room service, bar, foreign-exchange and travel counter, house doctor, and projected shopping arcade and swimming pool. AE, DC, MC, V.

Inexpensive

Hotel Chilarai Regency. H.P. Brahmachari Rd., Guwahati; tel. 26877. 44 rooms with bath. At this reasonably modern hotel near Pan Bazaar, rooms are carpeted and clean and have a subdued decor. Some rooms are air-conditioned. Multicuisine restaurant, room service, house doctor, car-rental and travel counter. Rupees only.

Hotel Kuber International. Hem Barua Rd., Guwahati; tel. 32601. 75 rooms with bath. This multistory hotel inside a shopping arcade in the middle of Fancy Bazaar has a Mogul-kitsch ambience with Hindu statues. Rooms are clean and carpeted and have simple decor. Multicuisine restaurants, room service, bar, car rental, travel and foreign-exchange counter, house doctor, shopping arcade. AE, DC, MC, V.

Kaziranga

For reservations, contact Deputy Director Tourism, Kaziranga National Park, P.O. Kaziranga Sanctuary, District Jorhat, Assam, 785109; tel. 23 or 29. Apply at least two months in advance. Rupees only.

Inexpensive

Kaziranga Forest Lodge. 24 rooms with bath. The rooms in this nondescript new hotel are clean, adequately furnished, comfortable, and have balconies. Multicuisine restaurant, bar, shop. Discount rates when park is closed.

Tourist Lodge No. 1. 5 rooms with bath. This attractive Assamese-style bungalow has cozy, simply furnished rooms with mosquito netting and fans. Upstairs rooms open onto a veranda. There is a dining room serving Indian and Continental food.

Tourist Lodge No. 2. 8 rooms with bath and a dormitory with shared bath. The rooms in this Assamese bungalow with a front veranda are plainly furnished. The beds are clean and have mosquito netting and fans.

Manas

For reservations, contact Reservation Authority, Deputy Field Director, Project Tiger, Barpeta Rd., Assam 781315; tel. 153 or 19. Reserve your room at least two months in advance. The caretaker at each lodge will prepare meals for a small fee; but you must bring your own provisions. Rupees only.

Inexpensive

Upper Bungalow. 7 rooms with baths. This lodge, on a hill overlooking the river, is typically Assamese and offers the best location. The rooms are spacious and have simple furnishings and overhead fans. The upper rooms open onto a veranda with great views.

Lower Bungalow. 2 rooms with bath. From this bungalow of Assamese design, you can hear the river. The rooms are spacious and comfortable, but have minimal furnishings and no overhead fan. There's a private front porch.

Cottages. 3 cottages with nearby shared bath. The cottages are near the lower bungalow. The rooms are small and sparse, but the linen is clean.

MEGHALAYA

Shillong

Moderate

Crowborough Hotel. This new MTDC multistory hotel was scheduled to open in late 1990. It is a modern structure with 117 rooms and numerous amenities. Rooms could not be inspected at press time. For details, contact MTDC, Shillong Tourist Hotel, Polo Rd., Shillong, Meghalaya; tel. 22129.

Hotel Pinewood Ashok. Shillong; tel. 23116. 70 rooms with bath. On a hill above the center of Shillong, this is a charming 100-year-old bamboo-and-wood bungalow with cottages. The rooms are carpeted and comfortable and have fireplaces. The best ones open onto a veranda. Cottages, divided into suites, are less well appointed, yet nicely located on the extensive grounds. TV, house doctor, room service, bar, coffee shop, multicuisine restaurant. AE, DC, MC, V.

Thadlaskein Lake

Inexpensive

Thadlaskein Lake. Reservations: MTDC, Shillong Tourist Hotel, Shillong, Meghalaya; tel. 24933. 6 rooms with bath. Newly renovated by the MTDC, this lakeside bungalow offers pleasant, simply furnished rooms. There is a multicuisine restaurant. Rupees only.

Tura

Inexpensive

Orchid Lodge. MTDC, Tura, West Garo; no phone. 9 rooms with bath. This new bungalow, managed by MTDC, has clean rooms with overhead fans, multicuisine restaurant, room service, tourist office. Rupees only.

TOURIST HUTS AND BUNGALOWS. These simple accommodations are very inexpensive and accept only rupees. A caretaker will also prepare meals for a small fee.

Assam. Reservations: Assam Tourist Department, Guwahati, tel. 27102. Patacharuchi has a two-room Assamese-style *Inspection Bungalow* with an inviting veranda. Each bedroom has a double bed with mosquito net and an attached bath and fastidiously clean dining room.

Meghalaya. Reservations: Deputy Commissioner, East Garo Hills, William Nagar, Meghalaya. The new *Baghmara Circuit House* has about 5 furnished rooms with attached baths. Reservations: Sub-Divisional Officer (Civil), Baghmara, East Garo Hills, Meghalaya. The *William Nagar Circuit House* has about 10 furnished rooms with attached baths.

DINING OUT. Breakfast is usually served from 7–10; lunch is usually noon–3; and dinner, 7:30–9 or 10. Payment is normally in rupees unless the restaurant is connected to a Western-style hotel, in which case it may also accept credit cards. The restaurants listed below are informal and unless noted are open for all three meals and don't require reservations. Prices, based on one person eating a three-course meal, excluding taxes, tip, or beverage, are *Expensive,* Rs. 80–Rs. 120; *Moderate,* Rs. 40–Rs. 80; *Inexpensive,* under Rs. 40.

ASSAM

A specialty in Assam is the Assamese *thali*—assorted small portions of moderately spicy regional dishes, such as *pabha* (river fish simmered in mustard paste), *moricha* (a spinachlike green cooked in mustard oil), *roho* (fish in lemon or tomato sauce), *dahi* (lentils), and *omita* (fried papaya simmered with baking soda).

Guwahati

Expensive

Parag. Hotel Kuber International, Hem Barua Rd., Fancy Bazaar; tel. 32601. An enormous restaurant on an upper floor of a hotel, Parag offers views of Guwahati and a decor that's a blend of coffee-shop and Indian-ornate. Food is equally eclectic and excellent. Open 11 A.M.–3 P.M., 7–11 P.M. AE, DC, MC, V.

Ushaban. Hotel Brahmaputra Ashok, M.G. Rd.; tel. 32632. This cozy restaurant is modern Assamese, with white ceilings and lots of lacquered lattice. The chef cooks excellent multicuisine dishes. Reservations advised. Open 12:30–2:30 P.M., 7:30–10 P.M. AE, DC, MC, V.

Moderate

Paradise. G.N.B. Rd.; no phone. Guwahati's most popular restaurant, with upscale chain-restaurant decor, serves the best Assamese cuisine in town. Try the delicious thali. Open 10 A.M.–3:30 P.M., 6:30–10 P.M. Serves beer until 7:30. Rupees only.

MEGHALAYA

Shillong

Moderate

Pinecone Restaurant. Hotel Pinewood Ashok; tel. 23116. This restaurant, with a handsome rustic ambience, serves the best food in Shillong: Chinese, Indian, Continental. Open 1–2:30 P.M., 8–10 P.M. AE, DC, MC, V.

Inexpensive

Jadoh Stall. Police Bazaar; no phone. Kasai food is offered at the Jadoh Stall: *jadoh* (Khasi rice), *turembah* (fermented soy), or chicken dishes. Open 8 A.M.–9 P.M. Rupees only.

Orchid Restaurant. Shillong Tourist Hotel; no phone. Overlooking a bazaar, this informal restaurant pipes in hit tunes from the West and serves decent multicuisine meals. Open 6:30 A.M.–9:30 P.M. Rupees only.

SWEETS AND TREATS. *The Orbit,* a tiny circular restaurant, revolves on the top of Hotel Kuber International, Hem Barua Rd., Fancy Bazaar in Guwahati, Assam, and serves tasty snacks and flavorful ice cream. Open 7 A.M.–11 P.M. In Shillong, Meghalaya, *Wards Lake Cafe* serves good snacks, coffee, and cold drinks. Open 9 A.M.–5:30 P.M.

HOW TO GET AROUND. Assam. From the Airport. The airport is 21 km (13 mi.) from Guwahati. A bus meets the Indian Airlines airbus from Calcutta, currently the afternoon flight, and goes to Guwahati for Rs. 10. A taxi costs about Rs. 60.

By Bus. *ASTC* (reservations through the Assam Tourist Department, tel. 27102), *Blue Hill Travels* (Ashok Hotel and Paltan Bazaar, tel. 31427), and *Assam Valley Tours and Travels* (Paltan Bazaar, tel. 26133) run daily trips to Manas Tiger Reserve and Kaziranga National Sanctuary.

By Taxi and Rented Car with Driver. For short excursions, hire a non-metered taxi (about Rs. 3 per km). For longer excursions arrange for a car with driver from the *Assam Tourist Department* in Guwahati (Station Rd., tel. 27102) or *Blue Hill Travels* (Ashok Hotel).

By Rickshaw. For trips within Guwahati, take an auto rickshaw (about Rs. 2 per km) or use a bicycle rickshaw (Rs. 1.50 per km).

Meghalaya. From the Airport. The airport is 127 km (79 mi.) from Shillong. A taxi (Rs. 400) takes about three hours. You can also take a MRTC bus which runs every hour from the airport (Rs. 45). The trip takes four hours.

By Bus. *MRTC* runs daily deluxe buses to Jowai, Cherrapunjee, Nongstoin, and Tura from the Bus Station, Jail Rd., Police Bazaar; tel. 23206. Most trips cost under Rs. 100. MRTC can also make reservations for similar trips offered by ASTC, Blue Hill Travels, and Assam Valley Tours and Travels.

By Taxi or Rented Car and Driver. If you hire a car with driver, the cost is determined by destination. From Shillong, a roundtrip fare to Jowai is Rs. 400; to Nongstoin, Rs. 600; to Tura, Rs. 1,500. For overnights, add Rs. 100 per halt. Hire a car from *Sheba Travels* (Crowborough Building, Police Bazaar, Shillong; tel. 23015 or 26222) or *A.S. Sen* (Shillong Club, Shillong, tel. 23354 or 2545). For short excursions by taxi, rates are Rs. 5 per km.

TOURS. Assam. The *Directorate of Tourism* (Station Rd., tel. 27102) offers overnight tours by minibus from Guwahati to Kaziranga and Manas (Rs. 200). It also has a day trip to Shillong (about Rs. 70) and a Sunday river cruise on the Brahmaputra (Rs. 20).

Meghalaya. *MTDC* sponsors daily tours by non-air-conditioned deluxe bus that cover local sightseeing around Shillong as well as trips to Cherrapunjee and Jaintia Hills. Tours depart from the Shillong Tourist Hotel and Bus Station on Jail Rd. For reservations, contact MTDC, Shillong Tourist Hotel, tel. 22129.

TOUR OPERATORS. There are two reliable tour operators who sponsor trips in Assam and Meghalaya. Each has two locations. *Travel Corporation Pvt. Ltd.:* Chander Mukhi, Nariman Point, Bombay, tel. 2021881; and Hotel Metro, First Floor, N-49 Connaught Pl., New Delhi, tel. 3315181. *Sheba Travels:* G.N. Bordoloi Rd., Ambari, Guwahati, 781001, Assam, tel. 23280; and Crowborough Building, Police Bazaar, Shillong, Meghalaya, tel. 23015 or 26222).

SEASONAL EVENTS. Assam and Meghalaya celebrate numerous unique and splendid events. Since the lunar calendar determines the specific dates for many events, contact the Government of India Tourist Office for details.

ASSAM

Mid-April. *Rongali.* This week-long festival celebrates spring and the Assamese New Year. Women perform beautiful dances while men play traditional drums, horns, and flutes.

June. *Ambubashi Mela.* The Hindu Kamakhya Temple in Guwahati is closed for three days—a symbolic menstruation of the enshrined goddess Kali. On the fourth day, the temple is reopened, and the goddess is given a sacred bath and re-draped in her cloth.

October. *Durga Puja.* This important Hindu festival is a big event at the Kamakhya Shrine in Guwahati.

MEGHALAYA

April. *Khasi Spring Festival.* Khasi tribals perform the Shad Suk Mynsiem (Dance of Joyful Hearts) in Weiking on the outskirts of Shillong.

November. *Ka Pamblang Nongkrem* is a a five-day knock-out Khasi ceremony with bejeweled Khasi virgins dancing and young men waging mock sword combats. On the final day, animals are sacrificed.

November/December. *Wangala* or the *Hundred Drums Festival.* During this terrific harvest celebration, Garo tribals in elaborate feathered headpieces dance for four days to traditional accompaniment.

HISTORIC SITES. Entrance to most places is generally free; where a donation is asked, a few rupees will suffice. Important monuments are open daily sunrise to sunset unless noted otherwise below.

ASSAM AND ENVIRONS

Guwahati

Kamakhya Temple. This temple, with its swelling beehive-shape that dominates Nilachal Hill, was first constructed in the thirteenth century and has been renovated numerous times. Dedicated to Kali, this is one of the most important tantric temples in India.

Umanada Shiva Temple. During the Shivratri festival, thousands of Hindus visit this temple on Peacock Island in the Brahmaputra River, dedicated to Shiva.

Nabagraha Shrine. Nabagraha, meaning nine planets, sits on Chitrashala Hill and was once the center of astronomical and astrological study.

Hayagriba Madhab Temple. In Hajo, on a hill 24 km (15 mi.) from Guwahati, this temple is sacred to Buddhists who believe that it contains relics of the Buddha and to Hindus who come to honor Vishnu.

Pao Mecca. This mosque of Pir Giyasuddin Aulin, also in Haja, is believed by Moslems to have one-quarter of the sanctity of the holiest Moslem shrine in Mecca.

MEGHALAYA

Khasi Sacred Grove. In Mawplang, 25 km (16 mi.) from Shillong, a path leads to one of the few remaining Khasi sacred groves where Khasi tribals still evoke the blessings of spirits. Everything is considered sacred; don't remove anything, not even a leaf.

Nartiang Village, Jantia Hills, has a hilltop filled with historic monoliths erected by Jantia tribals from 1500 to 1835.

MUSEUMS AND GALLERIES. Assam. The *Assam State Museum's* collection includes costumes of Ahom kings, sculpture, pottery, coins, art, and archaeological artifacts. It is open 9:30 A.M.–3:30 P.M. Tuesday–Saturday, 9:30 A.M.–12:30 P.M. Sundays; closed Mondays. Guwahati also has many small museums. The following are open 10 A.M.–4 P.M. Monday–Friday, 10 A.M.–1 P.M. Saturdays, and are closed Sundays: *Assam Forest Museum, Assam Government Cottage Industries Museum,* which displays traditional crafts, and the *Anthropological Museum* (Department of Anthropology, Guwahati University, tel. 88248). The *Department of Historical and Antiquarian Research,* which has a collection of old manuscripts, and the *Museum of Animal Husbandry* at the Assam Veterinary College are open 10 A.M.–4 P.M. Monday–Saturday; closed Sundays.

Meghalaya. *Meghalaya's State Museum* in Shillong includes anthropological, cultural, botanical, and wildlife exhibits. Open 10 A.M.–4:30 P.M. in summer and till 4 P.M. in winter. Closed Sundays and holidays.

GARDENS. Meghalaya. Shillong's Botanical Garden is a delightful, quiet place for a stroll. Open 9 A.M.–5 P.M.

SPORTS AND OUTDOOR ADVENTURES. Assam. Fishing. There's good fishing at Manas Tiger Reserve (permit costs Rs. 10 per day) from February to March. Bring your own rod and reel.

Wildlife Sanctuaries. *Kaziranga National Sanctuary,* open mid-October–mid-April, covers 430 sq. km (267 sq. mi.) of forests and grasslands and is the most famous home of the Indian one-horned rhinoceros. In 1908, when hardly a dozen of these powerful, armored animals lived in the area, Kaziranga was declared a forest reserve. Today, the rhinoceros, numbering close to 1,000, coexist with wild elephants, tigers, wild buffalos, sloth bear, jungle cats, leopards, langur, and barking deer. Gliding and darting over its *jheels* (swampy flats surrounded by shallow pools of water) are a rich variety of water birds, including ibis, purple herons, black-necked storks, egrets, ring-tailed fishing eagles, river terns, and pelicans. On arrival, visitors must stop at the Mihimukh Forest Range Office to pay nominal entrance fees and to make arrangements for jeep and elephant rides or excursions to a Karbi tribal village or a tea plantation.

Manas Tiger Reserve, open from October to May, covers 2,837 sq. km (1,759 sq. mi.) in the Himalayan foothills, bordering Bhutan. Manas is laced with many streams and rivers, which contribute to its reputation as one of India's most beautiful sanctuaries. The birds are exceptional. The early morning sight of large flocks of great pied hornbills crossing the river to feed in Bhutan is memorable. Manas has an abundance of waterbirds, such as the white-capped redstart, the merganser, egret, ruddy shelduck, cormorant, and a variety of ducks. Wildlife in the sanctuary includes tigers, Indian rhinoceros, golden langur, wild buffalos, elephants, swamp deer, rare pygmy hogs, and hispid hares. On arrival, visitors must show their permits at the Foreigner's Check Gate and stop at the Field Office to pay nominal park fees and to make arrangements for elephant rides, boat rentals, or fishing permits.

Meghalaya. Archery Contests. Daily, except Sunday, you can watch archery contests in Shillong's Polo Ground: a popular sport with Khasi tribals.

Caving. Meghalaya has a vast network of limestone caves open for exploration: Syndia in the Jaintia Hills, Siju in the Garo Hills, and Mawsmai near Cherrapunjee.

Fishing. At present, no license is required, and you must bring your own rod and reel. Best fishing is from February to November. You can fish at *Umiam Lake,* about 16 km (10 mi.) north of Shillong; in and near *William Nagar Forest Reserve* and in *Balpakram National Park,* which are located in Garo Hills.

Golfing. Play golf at the *Shillong Golf Club* (tel. 3071), which is one of India's prettiest golf courses. Green fees are Rs. 30 per day; equipment is available at a nominal cost.

Wildlife Sanctuaries. *Balpakram National Park and Biosphere* is a new park on a vast plateau in Garo Hills, bordering Bangladesh. You can walk to lakes and see peacocks, pheasants, and hornbills, and you can count on seeing wild elephants. Park fees weren't established at press time. Best time to visit is from November to February.

SHOPPING. Assam. Be sure to see this state's beautiful handwoven cottons and rare silks: *endi* (raw silk), *pat* (soft hand-dyed silk); *muga* (naturally golden, heavy silk). In Guwahati, you can also buy good tea and honey and products of bamboo, cane, jute, and brass. The following shops are open Monday–Saturday and take rupees only.

Government of Assam Emporium (G.N.B. Rd.), open April–September 10 A.M.– 7 P.M., otherwise till 6, for excellent handicrafts and handlooms at reasonable fixed prices. *Jagaran Artfed Handloom House* (G.N.B. Rd.), open 10 A.M.–7 P.M., also government-run, offers a similar selection. *Purbashree Northeastern Handicrafts* and *Handlooms Development Corporation* (G.N.B. Rd.), open April–September 10 A.M.– 2 P.M. and 3 P.M.–7 P.M., otherwise 10 A.M.–6 P.M., has handicrafts and handlooms from the northeastern states. For Assamese tea, try *Kamrupa* (G.S. Rd., Paltan Bazar) or *Kalpataru* (H.B. Rd., Pan Bazaar), both open 10 A.M.–7 P.M. Traditional heavy hand-tooled brass products are at the *Assam Cooperative Bell Metal Manufacturing Society* (S.R.C.B. Rd., Fancy Bazaar), open 8 A.M.–7 P.M. This is one of few shops that sell good "bell metal" tea cups, curry bowls, platters, and tumblers.

In Swalkuchi, the village of weavers not far from Guwahati, you can see the creation of *muga* and *pat* silks. Ask to visit the home of *Bogaram Baishya;* he'll show you his cottage industry and take you to others. Muga or pat is 30 percent cheaper here than in retail shops. Baishya can also make on order and ship.

Meghalaya. In Shillong, visit the *Meghalaya Handloom and Handicraft Development Corporation* (Jail Rd.), open 9 A.M.–7 P.M., closed Sundays, for woolblend shawls, *jainsem* (traditional dresses), cotton fabric, carpets, bamboo products. It takes rupees only. Shillong's *Pubashree Northeastern Handicrafts and Handlooms Development Corporation* (Jail Rd.), open weekdays 10 A.M.–1 P.M. and 3 P.M.–7 P.M., and Saturdays 10 A.M.–2 P.M., sells handicrafts from all the northeastern states at only a few rupees.

NIGHTLIFE AND BARS. Assam. With rare exception, you can drink only beer and only in hotel bars, open 11–11. Thursday and the first and last day of the month are "dry" days, when no beer is sold.

Meghalaya. The best bar is in Shillong's Hotel Pinewood, with a quiet ambience and rustic decor. It's open from 10 A.M.–2 P.M., 6–10 P.M.

SIKKIM

Tiny State with Giant Vistas

by
KATHLEEN COX

There is a Sikkimese legend that goes something like this: Stars are the laughter of the Sikkimese that, having risen far into the sky, have frozen into the myriad stars.

Something in this tiny state, one of India's newest, snuggled into the eastern Himalayas, makes you believe—or want to believe—in this legend. Perhaps it is the high altitude or the disconcerting lay of the land, which seems continually to rise or fall, never leveling out for any distance. Or perhaps it is the strange effect of witnessing ancient Buddhist religious rituals that are so bound up in the Sikkimese's daily life. The Sikkimese, despite the constant incursions into their country by aggressive neighbors, continue to exhibit a gaiety that gives credence to the legend.

Sikkim has always been vulnerable because it contains the best natural passes through the Himalayas and therefore the routes of choice for trade between India to the south and Lhasa, Tibet, to the north. For centuries, this tiny kingdom has been caught in a series of disputes over who should rule it. Since 1975, however, Sikkim has been the twenty-second state of India. Inside its tiny borders is an odd combination of forces; masses of Indian military troops remain perpetually on alert on the Tibetan border and a basically peaceful people go about their daily lives following the non-aggressive tenets of Mahayana Buddhism.

517

Sikkim is a magnificent state dominated by Kanchenjunga, the third-highest mountain in the world, which is revered by the Sikkimese as the presiding deity, the home of gods. And, indeed, from many a monastery vantage point, one can feel the greatness of this majestic mountain. In its shadow are other great beauties—forests thick with over 500 species of orchids, beautiful birds and butterflies, red pandas, blue sheep, rhododendrons, and blue poppies. In this visually lovely land, the people have been nurtured by Buddhism, which finds its expression in simple yet beautifully ornamented monasteries and shrines and festivals that are filled with colorful dances.

Distinct ethnic groups share Sikkim. The Lepchas, or Rongkup (Children of Rong), originally lived in seclusion in North Sikkim. Although many have converted to Buddhism, most still worship many aspects of their physical surroundings—rainbows, clouds, rivers, and trees. Village priests preside over elaborate rituals, including animal sacrifices, to appease animist deities.

Tibetan Bhutias came into Sikkim in the seventeenth century with the first *chogyal* (king) and were members of a three-tiered hierarchy: the aristocracy; the landholding Kazi; and the commoners. Every Bhutia village has its prayer flags and *chortens* (small shrines containing relics); most families have a relative who has joined a monastery or nunnery. Every home has an altar room.

The Bhutias' culture dominates Sikkim. The national dress for women is the traditional *kho* or *bhoku,* a slim-fitting sleeveless robe—the epitome of elegance.

Nepalese immigrants are responsible for the introduction of terrace farming to Sikkim. Although most Nepalese are Hindu, you see few Hindu temples in Sikkim; often their faith incorporates Buddhist beliefs and practices as it does in Nepal.

EXPLORING SIKKIM

Gangtok

Travelers interested in Buddhism should visit the Research Institute of Tibetology, founded by the Dalai Lama in 1957 and the most important Buddhist study center in India. It has a vast collection of rare Lepcha, Tibetan, and Sanskrit manuscripts, many donated by the Dalai Lama; numerous priceless statues, including one seven feet tall of Mahjushri and a small copper image of Avalokitesvara; and rare *thang-kas* (paintings with a Buddhist theme), some created on tapestry.

From here, a short walk leads to the Orchid Sanctuary, with numerous species in bloom during the winter months. In nearby Deorali Bazaar is the Do-Drul Chorten, built in 1945 by the Venerable Trulsi Rimpoche, head of the Nyingmapa (Red) Sect. Surrounded by 108 prayer wheels, this chorten commemorates the Buddha's victory over evil. Nearby are two statues of Guru Padmasambhava.

You have to time your visit with a festival to get into Tsuklakhang, the royal gompa of the former chogyal of Sikkim. On a ridge above Gangtok, it's constructed in typical pagoda style. It was the most important monastery in Sikkim. The main hall has exquisitely carved and painted woodwork, frescoes, and precious Buddhist icons. Here kings were crowned and royal marriages were consecrated. Across the meadow sits the Royal Palace, also closed to the public.

Around Gangtok

Set on a mountain spur north of Gangtok, Enchey Monastery, built in 1840, is called the Palace of Solitude. This active monastery with 200 Nyingmapa monks has an interior which is an artistic celebration of the Buddhist faith. Old frescoes line the walls. Your eyes are drawn to the front altar and a gilded Lord Buddha, flanked by Avalokitesvara (Buddha of Compassion) and Guru Padmasambhava with his two consorts.

Phodang, north of Enchey, is a recently built monastery, not far from the still standing original *gompa* (shrine) which also contains old frescoes. Phodang belongs to the Kagyupa sect. If the sky is clear, you can get splendid views from this monastery.

A lovely drive 24 kilometers (15 miles) southwest of Gangtok takes you through rice fields and bamboo groves to Rumtek Monastery. When the Chinese occupied Tibet, His Holiness Gyalwa Karmapa, the 16th incarnation of the founder of the Karmapa sect of Tibet, took refuge in Sikkim. The chogyal of Sikkim gave him 75 acres to set up this monastery—a replica of the gompa at Chhofuk in Tibet.

Following the custom, before Gyalwa Karmapa died in 1982, he wrote and hid a lengthy prophesy that described the 17th incarnation. In May 1988, the four head *rimpoches* (religious reincarnations) of the monastery discovered the document. At an auspicious time, they will locate the child it describes and bring him to Rumtek for his enthronement.

Rumtek contains numerous chambers (some not open to non-Buddhists). A courtyard leads to the entrance of the ornate main prayer hall. The throne, facing the assembly hall, is for His Holiness and has a photo of the 16th incarnation on its right. Steps behind the right of the exterior lead to the prestigious Nalanda Institute for Higher Studies and the Great Golden Reliquary, which contains the relics (bones and remnants of the cremated body) of the 16th Gyalwa Karmapa and a gold-plated chorten surrounded by statues of former Gyalwa Karmapas.

West Sikkim

The town of Rabangla, 65 kilometers (40 miles) from Gangtok, is the Gateway to West Sikkim. You traverse dark tropical forests with moss hanging from trees. The road winds, then descends, taking you past a small monastery (Yung Drum) studded with flags. Moments later, you round a sharp bend, and on a distant peak you see the Tashidang Monastery, its golden pinnacle catching the sun. Behind it looms the spectacular Mount Kanchenjunga, with clouds swirling around its crest.

Tashidang sits on a hill between the Rangit and Ratong rivers. It's an active monastery with about 60 monks from the Nyingmapa order. According to legend, Guru Padmasambhava shot an arrow in the air and where it fell—which was here—he vowed to pray. In 1642, one of the three lamas who consecrated the first chogyal built a *lhakhang* (shrine) venerating this sacred spot. In 1716, the main monastery was constructed.

Tashidang's exterior remains a lovely example of Sikkimese temple architecture; but its interior, including the old frescoes, needs repair. See the Thongwa Rangdol, reputed to contain the holy relics of Manjushri (Buddha of Transcendent Wisdom). Just the sight of it is said to cleanse the devotee of sin. Guru Padmasambhava is also credited with the creation of the *bumchu* (pot of holy water), which you can see during the Bumchu Celebration in February, when the sacred bumchu, which has a perpetual sweet aroma and has not been refilled since its discovery, is emptied of its holy contents. The amount of water determines Sikkim's prosperity in the new year.

At Geysing, farther west, a shortcut by jeep leads to Pemayangtse, Sikkim's most important monastery, with 200 Nyingmapa lamas. The original lhakhang, constructed in the mid-1600s by Lhatsun Chenpo, is the second-oldest monastery in Sikkim. Since then, the monastery has been renovated several times.

A gaily decorated entrance leads into the main assembly hall. Old frescoes cover the walls. Behind the front altar stands a large gold-covered clay statue of Guru Padmasambhava flanked by his two consorts—all of them protected by a wooden arch of Nagas (sacred serpents). To the right is a statue of Avalokitesvara with his disciples; a statue of the Buddha is to the left.

Steps on the right lead to upper floors. The first chamber, Guru Lhakhang, has frescoes and statues depicting Guru Padmasambhava. On the right wall near the statues, a fresco portrays the consecration of the first chogyal of Sikkim (he's on the left).

Interior walls of the other chamber on this floor are covered with 1,000 images of the Buddha; the room contains the holy scriptures and the main statue of Lord Buddha. A 20 × 30-foot thang-ka depicting the Buddha is kept in this room and unfurled only during the annual festival (usually in February).

On the third floor is the "must-see" chamber with its astonishing chorten. Three decades ago, Dungzin Rimpoche, now deceased, spent five years reconstructing a description of a vision of Sangthokpalri, the celestial palace of Guru Padmasambhava. The miniature palace takes into account the tiniest details: a combination of the whimsical and the serene.

PRACTICAL INFORMATION FOR SIKKIM

WHEN TO GO. The most popular time to visit is from mid-February to June and October to mid-December. Summer temperatures range from 68°F–76°F and winter temperatures fluctuate between 26°F and 50°F. As in other mountainous areas, it is recommended that you wear layered clothing that can ensure your comfort at a variety of altitudes, with their accompanying variation in temperature.

RESTRICTED AREA PERMIT. Because of Sikkim's sensitive border location, foreigners need a Restricted Area Permit to visit (see *Travel Documents* in *Facts at Your Fingertips*). A general permit is good for 15 days, but does not allow for trekking. For a general permit, list Gangtok, Phodang, and the Rumtek and Pemayangtse monasteries. If you want to trek, you must apply for a trekking permit, which is also good for 15 days. For a trekking permit, list the above destinations, plus Dzongri. Once you have filled out your permit follow the guidelines in *Facts at Your Fingertips*. If you apply to a consular office or a mission in your home country, allow a few days for clearance. In India, the permit *should* be issued on the spot.

Travelers can also visit Sikkim with a tour group. See the listings under *Tour Operators* below and in *Facts at Your Fingertips*.

HOW TO GET THERE. By Air. Flying to Bagdogra Airport in northern West Bengal, 124 km (77 mi.) from Gangtok, the capital, is the best approach to Sikkim. Going by train to New Jalpaiguri, near Bagdogra, or in a bus or car takes a long time and requires a Restricted Area Permit for northern West Bengal. *Indian Airlines* makes daily flights to Bagdogra from Calcutta, Assam, and Delhi. Book well in advance and reconfirm your ticket 72 hours before flight time. At Bagdogra, foreigners must register their permit with the police.

By Bus. *Sikkim National Transport Service* (SNTS) runs luxury coaches between Darjeeling and Gangtok. Trip time is about six hours and costs about Rs. 35. In Gangtok, contact the *Sikkim Tourist Information Office,* tel. 2064. In Darjeeling, contact the *West Bengal Tourist Office,* tel. 2050.

By Taxi or Rented Car with Driver. The journey to Gangtok from Bagdogra, Kalimpong, or Darjeeling takes about five hours and costs about Rs. 600 per vehicle. In Darjeeling, hire a car from *Travel Corporation of India,* Bellavista Apartments, Room No. 5, Gandhi Rd.; tel. 2694. In Gangtok, hire a car from the *Sikkim Tourist Information Office,* Mahatma Gandhi Marg, Gangtok, Sikkim, tel. 2064.

TOURIST INFORMATION. Contact the Sikkim Tourist Information Office, Mahatma Gandhi Marg, Gangtok, Sikkim; tel. 2064. Open daily from mid-September to mid-November, 9 A.M.–5:30 P.M.; otherwise Monday–Saturday 10 A.M.–4 P.M., closed Sunday and second Saturday of the month. There's also a counter at the Bagdogra Airport.

FOREIGN CURRENCY EXCHANGE. Most Western-style hotels have money-exchange counters. Otherwise, go to a branch of the *State Bank of India,* open Monday–Friday, 10 A.M.–2 P.M.; Saturday, till noon. In Gangtok, the State Bank of India is on Mahatma Gandhi Marg.

ACCOMMODATIONS. Many hotels in Sikkim have appealing Buddhist touches. Prices are based on double occupancy and don't include taxes: *Moderate,* Rs. 500–Rs. 950; *Inexpensive,* under Rs. 500. Some Western-style hotels take major credit cards and traveler's checks.

GANGTOK

Moderate

Hotel Norkhill. Gangtok; tel. 2386. 25 rooms with bath. Gangtok's oldest hotel, once owned by the king, is on a quiet ridge below the city. It has a lovely garden and lawn and excellent views. Its exterior and public rooms are in a sedate Sikkimese style. The rooms are clean, but they lack elegance. Ask for a room with a view and a tub. Fixed-menu restaurant (non-hotel guests must have reservations), bar, room service, baby-sitters, gift shop, library, house doctor, travel and foreign-exchange service, Sikkimese dances on request. Meals included. AE, DC, MC.

Inexpensive

Hotel Mayur. Paljor Namgyal Stadium Rd., Gangtok; tel. 2752 or 2825. 25 rooms with bath. Centrally located, this spiffy hotel has nicely furnished rooms and pine ceilings and trim. Some rooms have modern bathrooms with tubs or showers. Standard rooms are smaller and have simple decor. Ask for a room with mountain view. Multicuisine restaurant, bar, room service, house doctor, car rental, TV. Rupees only.

Hotel Tashi Delek. Mahatma Gandhi Marg, Gangtok; tel. 2038 or 2991. 45 rooms with bath. Also centrally located, this hotel's public rooms feature Sikkimese decor in colors bright enough for sunglasses. The bedrooms are small and simple with partial views of the mountains. Multicuisine restaurant, bar, rooftop garden, baby-sitters, travel and foreign-exchange counter, small shopping arcade. AE, DC, MC, V.

Hotel Tibet. Paljor Namgyal Stadium Rd., Gangtok; tel. 2523 or 21568. 28 rooms with bath. Run by the Dalai Lama Charitable Trust, this hotel is centrally located and has wonderful Tibetan ambience. The best views are from rooms with tubs or showers. Multicuisine restaurant, room service, bar, car rental, foreign exchange. DC, MC.

PEMAYANGTSE

Inexpensive

Hotel Mount Pandim. Pemayangtse, Pelling, West Sikkim; tel. 56. 25 rooms with bath. This lovely government-run bungalow is set on a hill with great views and an attractive garden. The modestly furnished rooms are large; ask for one with a view. Multicuisine restaurant, room service, bar, laundry, tour guide and car rental, doctor on call, library, gift shop. Meals included. Rupees only.

TOURIST HUTS AND BUNGALOWS. In West Sikkim, the government has put up simple trekkers' huts with rustic rooms or dormitories in delightful locations. Bring a sleeping bag and bug repellent. A caretaker will prepare plain meals for a modest fee. At present, trekkers' huts are at Pemayangtse, Barshey, Yoksum, Tsokha, and Dzongri. For reservations, contact the Assistant Manager, Hotel Mount Pandim, Pemayangtse, P.O. Pelling, West Sikkim; tel. 56.

DINING OUT. Expect good eating and a diversified cuisine in Gangtok: Tibetan, Indian, Chinese, Continental, and Sikkimese cuisines. Try Sikkimese sautéed ferns (in season), sautéed bamboo shoots, nettle soup, and roast pork. If you like *momo* (Tibetan dumplings), order the beef or vegetable variety—pork is risky if under-cooked. Sikkim also makes good local brews: cherry or musk brandy, wine, Teesta River white rum, juniper gin, *pan* (mixed nuts and leaves) liquor, and *chang* (fermented wine). Keep in mind that many accommodations listed above have restaurants. Breakfast is usually served from 8–10:30; lunch is usually noon–3; and dinner, 7–9. Payment is normally is rupees unless the restaurant is connected to a Western-style hotel. The restaurants listed below are informal and, unless noted, are open for all three meals and don't require reservations. Prices, based on one person eating a three-course meal, excluding taxes, tip, or beverage, are *Expensive,* Rs. 80–Rs. 120; *Moderate,* Rs. 40–Rs. 80; *Inexpensive,* under Rs. 40.

GANGTOK

Expensive

Blue Poppy. Hotel Tashi Delek, Mahatma Gandhi Marg; tel. 2038. This delight-ful Sikkimese-style restaurant, with star cutouts on its blue ceiling, pastiche every-where, and views of the mountains, serves good steaks, as well as Chinese, Indian, Sikkimese, and Continental fare. Reservations advised. Open 8 A.M.–10 P.M. AE, DC, MC, V.

Shapi Restaurant. Hotel Mayur, Paljor Namgyal Stadium Rd.; tel. 2752. A mod-ern hotel dining room with a bank of windows that provides great views. The food is extremely good, whether Chinese, Indian, or Continental. There's an attached bar. Open 7 A.M.–9 P.M. Rupees only.

Moderate

Blue Sheep. Next to Tourist Information Center on Mahatma Gandhi Marg; no phone. This informal upstairs restaurant is done up in modern Sikkimese style. You can choose Continental, Tibetan, or Indian food. There's an attached bar. Open 9–9, closed Sundays. Rupees only.

Snow Lion. Hotel Tibet, Paljor Namgyal Stadium Rd.; tel. 2523. This peaceful restaurant is run by the Dalai Lama's staff. Snow Lion has soft lighting, Tibetan decor, and good views of Mount Kanchenjunga. Popular and informal, it serves excellent Tibetan, Japanese, Chinese, and Indian food. Open 7 A.M.–9:30 P.M. DC, MC.

Inexpensive

House of Bamboo. Mahatma Gandhi Marg; no phone. Another upstairs restau-rant, it's very informal, very Tibetan, and very cheap. You can also choose Chinese dishes. There's an attached bar. Open 8–8; closed on full moon, half moon, and the Tibetan New Year. Rupees only.

SWEETS AND TREATS. *Risur Hotel & Bakery,* Deorali Bazaar, Gangtok, serves great *momo* (Tibetan dumplings) in its popular restaurant. Open 8–8, closed Tibetan holidays.

HOW TO GET AROUND. From the Airport. Taxis are always plentiful. Rates are about Rs. 600 for the five-hour journey. You can also go by SNTS bus for about Rs. 35; inquire at the airport Tourist Information Office.

By Bus. *SNTS* runs buses to most places in Sikkim that are open to foreigners. For schedules and fares, contact its booking office just below the Tourist Information Center in Gangtok.

By Taxi. Taxis are unmetered and frequently pick up extra passengers. Rates are always cheap—Rs. 3 per km.

By Rented Car with Driver. In Gangtok, hire a car with driver from the *Manager of Transport,* Sikkim Tourist Information Office (address above), for about Rs. 400 per day (petrol not included); also there's a Rs. 200 per night halt charge. This office plans to rent jeeps with drivers. Contact them for details. Some hotels also arrange car rentals.

TOURS. From Gangtok, the *Sikkim Tourist Information Office* runs a 35-minute helicopter flight around Kanchenjunga from mid-September to mid-November, weather permitting. They also offer two daily local sightseeing tours to the Government of Cottage Industries, Deer Park, Do-Drul Chorten, Research Institute of Tibetology, Orchid Sanctuary, Enchey Monastery (10 A.M.–12:30 P.M.; by bus: Rs. 25); and around Gangtok to the Orchidarium, Rumtek Monastery, Tashi View Point, Phodang Monastery (1:15–4 P.M. by bus: Rs. 35). These same tours by car cost Rs. 160. No private guides are available in Gangtok.

TOUR OPERATORS. The *Sikkim Tourist Information Office* (address above) arranges some treks and tours, yak safaris, fishing, rafting, and car or jeep rentals. For good privately run treks, contact *Nawang Gombu Sherpa,* c/o Himalayan Mountaineering Institute, Jawahar Pargat, Darjeeling 734101, West Bengal. *Travel Corporation Pvt. Ltd.* (Chander Mukhi, Nariman Point, Bombay, tel. 2021881 and Hotel Metro, First Floor, N-49 Connaught Place, New Delhi, tel. 3315181) sponsors general tours and outdoor adventures. Also check the listings under *Tour Operators* and *Facts at Your Fingertips.* In Gangtok, many of the hotels also have travel counters that arrange car rentals or excursions.

SEASONAL EVENTS. Most of Sikkim's festivals are Buddhist celebrations with lamas, adorned in elaborate masks and ornate costumes, performing *chaams* (dances). Each chaam re-enacts a legend connected to Buddhism that reaffirms the triumph of good over evil. Since the lunar calendar determines the specific dates for most events, contact the Sikkim Tourist Information Office or the Government of India Tourist Bureau for details.

February. *Losar.* The Tibetan New Year is celebrated with much pageantry at Pemayangste and Rumtek monasteries.

February. *Bumchu Ceremony.* During the Bumchu Ceremony at Tashidang Monastery, the sacred bumchu is shown to the public, and its contents are poured into 21 cups. The amount of water determines Sikkim's well-being for the next year.

May/June. *Saga Dawa.* During Saga Dawa, lamas, playing musical instruments and carrying holy books, lead huge processions at all the monasteries.

June. *Tse-Chu Chaams.* At Rumtek Monastery, lamas, dressed as the eight manifestations of Guru Padmasambhava, reenact his various triumphs.

August. *Drupka Tseshi.* Buddhists commemorate Lord Buddha's first teaching with ceremonial prayers at the Do-Drul Chorten in Gangtok.

August/September. *Pang Lhabsol.* At Tsuklakhang Monastery, costumed lamas perform ritual warrior dances.

October. *Autumn Festival.* The Sikkim Tourist Department sponsors a month-long festival in Gangtok that highlights Sikkim's culture.

November/December. *Kagyat Chaams.* Lamas at Tsuklakhang Monastery dance, then burn effigies—the triumph of good over evil. This colorful event ushers in Losar and celebrates the harvest.

December/January. *Drag-dMar Chaam.* At Enchey Monastery, lamas perform dances in honor of Guru Padmasambhava.

HISTORIC SITES. Entrance to many places is free; where a donation is asked, a few rupees will suffice. Most important sites are open daily from sunrise to sunset unless noted otherwise below.

GANGTOK AREA

Do-Drul Chorten. Near two statues of Guru Padmasambhava, this stupa was built in 1945 and is surrounded by prayer wheels.

Enchey Monastery. Just north of Gangtok, this gompa belongs to the Nyingmapa Sect. Check with Tourist Office for the timing of daily ceremonies.

Phodang Monastery. Located several km north of Gangtok, Phodang is one of Sikkim's five principal monasteries and one of the most beautiful.

Research Institute of Tibetology. This exquisite building and important Buddhist study center has precious religious icons and thang-kas. Remove your shoes before entering. Open Monday–Saturday, 10 A.M.–4 P.M.

Rumtek Monastery. Rumtek, southwest of Gangtok, is the state's largest monastery and belongs to the Karmapa Sect. Also visit the adjoining Nalanda Institute for Higher Studies and Great Golden Reliquary, with holy relics, statues, and gold-plated chorten. Prayer services are around 4 A.M. and 6 P.M.; check with the tourist department.

Tsuklakhang. The royal monastery of the former chogyal of Sikkim is only open to the public on certain festival days (see above).

WESTERN SIKKIM

Dhubdi Monastery. An hour's climb from Yoksum, Dhubdi, also called the Hermit's Cell, is Sikkim's oldest monastery—a simple wooden altar with exalted views.

Pemayangtse Monastery. This is Sikkim's most important monastery and belongs to the Nyingmapa Sect. Be sure to visit the exquisite upper floor chambers. No photographs allowed.

Tashidang Monastery. This monastery also belongs to the Nyingmapa sect. Be sure to see the Thongwa Rangdol which supposedly contains the holy relics of Manjushri (Buddha of Transcendent Wisdom).

GARDENS. *Orchid Sanctuary,* near the Institute of Tibetology in Gangtok, displays over 500 varieties of orchids. The best time to visit is April–May and December–January, when the orchids are in full bloom.

SPORTS AND OUTDOOR ADVENTURES. Fishing. Contact the tourist department in Gangtok for information regarding permits and locations. The season runs from mid-October until March. Bring your own equipment.

Hot Springs. Good hot springs await the trekker to Dzongri in western Sikkim.

Rafting. One- or two-day rafting trips from September to May on the Teesta River were under review at press time. Contact the Sikkim Tourist Information Office for details.

Trekking. The best treks are in western Sikkim, with the most popular season from mid-September to June. A good four-day trek heads from Makha to Rabangla via Maenam. You pass through rhododendron forests and villages. *Moderate.*

An excellent seven-to-10-day trek heads from Yoksum to Zimathang, via Bakhim, Dzongri, and Thangsing. You climb through villages, can relax at hot springs, and always have great views of Kanchenjunga. *Moderately difficult.*

Trekkers should also get in touch with the *Sikkim Tourist Information Office* for details about projected theme-oriented treks that will highlight Sikkim's unique culture. Some treks will concentrate on villages and village life; others will be organized around flora and avifauna taking you through mountainous stretches of rhododendron, orchids, and wildflowers and into a world populated by incredible butterflies. Some of the treks may be available in 1991, but details weren't ready at press time. The tourist department also rents sleeping bags and good tents.

SHOPPING. In Gangtok, the *Government Institute of Cottage Industry* sells excellent wool carpets; new thang-kas; traditional clothes; handlooms in wool, silk, and cotton; jewelry; handbags; shawls; hand-knit sweaters; masks; wood carvings; and furniture. Open Monday–Saturday 9:30 A.M.–12:30 P.M. and 1–3:30 P.M. Fixed-price; rupees only. The *Tourist Department Gift Shop* (Mahatma Gandhi Marg) also sells good fixed-price handicrafts. Open mid-September–mid-November, daily 8:30

A.M.–6:30 P.M.; otherwise open 10 A.M.–5 P.M., closed Tuesday and government holidays. Rupees only. *Babu Kazi Sakya* (Mahatma Gandhi Marg) sells new and old traditional jewelry, curios, and handicrafts at fixed prices. Open 8 A.M.–7 P.M., closed Hindu holidays. Rupees only. Two good tailors make handsome traditional costumes: *Pema Seyden, Tibetan Tailor* (Lall Market Rd.) is open 7 A.M.–8 P.M., closed Tuesday. Pema will help you pick fabric in a nearby shop. *Lhasa Tailors* (Wangdi Children Park near Market Taxi Stand) is open 7 A.M.–8 P.M. Both are reliable, inexpensive, and will complete your order in two days. Rupees only. On Sunday, walk through *Lal Bazaar*. Bhutias and Lepchas in traditional clothes come from nearby villages to sell vegetables, spices, chickens, clothing, and trinkets. Begins around 8 A.M.

NIGHTLIFE AND BARS. Gangtok shuts down early unless there's a festival or *chaam* (dance) underway. Hotels and most restaurants have bars. Try the local brandies or chang—just remember that they're potent. *Snow Lion Bar* in the Hotel Tibet is cozy, with good views; open 10–10. *Yak Bar* in the Hotel Tashi Delek is jazzy Sikkimese with red brocade-draped booths and good views; open 10–9.

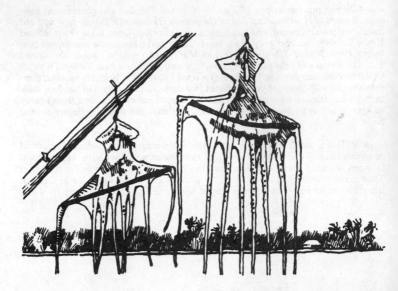

ANDAMAN AND NICOBAR

ISLANDS

Vacation Retreats in the Making

by
LISA SAMSON and AMIT SHAH

One descends from the heavens to Port Blair, Andaman Islands, like the monkey god, Hanuman, is believed to have done in his valiant quest to rescue Sita, the lovely wife of Rama. The *Ramayana's* most mischievous character, Hanuman is said to have used these exquisitely beautiful tropical islands as his bridge to Lanka, and his name has been lent to the Andaman Islands (from *Handuman*), the larger island group of this Union Territory. Only his pressing task of rescuing Sita can explain why this fun-loving, self-indulgent god didn't linger here, enjoying the invigorating sea breezes, the vast tracts of dense forests, and the stunning marine life found in coral beds that surround many of these islands. The modern-day traveler to India, having no such epic responsibilities, would do well to stay here for a time to explore the natural beauty and historical sights of these islands.

The Andaman and Nicobar Islands (the territorial name of the two groups of islands) form the peaks of a submarine mountain range that stretches for hundreds of miles into the Bay of Bengal, some 1,370 kilometers (850 miles) east of Madras, separating it from the Andaman Sea. Rising out of shimmering turquoise waters speckled a darker blue, where coral beds spread out from white sandy beaches, these islands hold the promise of evolving into one of India's most beautiful, relaxing vacation spots in the next decade. The islands, inaccessible to all but the indigenous aboriginal tribes for thousands of years and then used primarily as a penal colony by the British, are developing slowly. At present the changing policies that govern accessibility to the islands by foreign nationals place much of the islands' natural beauty off-limits, but not so much that one shouldn't go now, before aspects of the fragile loveliness are altered.

Ptolemy, the Roman geographer, recorded the Andaman and Nicobar Islands in his first map of the world in the second century. I'Tsing, the Buddhist scholar, referred to the Nicobar Islands in the seventh century as the "land of naked people." And the adventurer, Marco Polo, inaccurately stated that the Andaman Islands were one large island. Though their existence has long been recorded, the reputed ferocity of some of the various aboriginal populations, the inhospitable environment, and the lack of "sweet" water on many of the islands long ensured their isolation from the rest of the world. Even today, only 38 islands of the 293 are inhabited and of these, many support only a diminishing number of tribes.

Inhabited by Aborigines

Until the 1600s, the various aboriginal tribes, which date back to the Paleolithic age, lived alone on the islands. Then the Mahrattas annexed the islands in the late seventeenth century and used them as a base to harass the British, Dutch, and Portuguese who used this route for trade. The British attempted to establish a settlement in the Andamans in the late 1700s, but were successful only after the Indian Mutiny in 1857, when they built a permanent penal colony at Port Blair. In the Nicobar Islands, France, Denmark, Austria, and Great Britain all had some vague rights at various periods from the seventeenth century onward.

The Danes in particular were tenacious in their attempts to occupy the islands until they relinquished them to the British in 1869. The Japanese were in control of the Andaman and Nicobar Islands from 1942 till 1945. They allowed Subhas Chandra Bose, the Indian nationalist who formed the Indian National Army (INA), to fly the Indian tricolor for the first time. Bose had aligned with the Japanese to fight for Indian independence, but his group fell afoul of Japanese territorial ambitions, and the INA had a short-lived tenure at Port Blair. From the time the islands were liberated by the Allies until Indian independence in 1947, they were again controlled by the British.

Once a Penal Colony

Arriving today in Port Blair, the capital, one finds it difficult to comprehend the sense of dread felt by the political activists and criminals who were deported here when the British used it as a penal colony. Known by them as Kala Pani or "Black Waters," there is little now to indicate the brutalizing punishment that was meted out to these prisoners except what can be seen at the Cellular Jail, now a national museum, whose stark simplicity testifies to those bleak times.

Today Port Blair, a relatively modern town for India, is the only metropolitan locale on this island chain that is accessible to foreign tourists. Its population consists primarily of Tamils, Assamese, Bengalis, Burmese, and Malays, many of whom count as their ancestors those prisoners who were once deported here.

India's history since independence is also uniquely etched into the demographics of the Andamans because displaced persons from East Bengal, evacuees from Burma, Indian emigrants from the former British Guiana, and, more recently, refugees from Bangladesh (formerly East Pakistan) have been relocated here. What growth has occurred in population over the past decades has done so largely through emigration, not from an increase in the aboriginal population.

Tribal Reserve Areas

The inaccessibility of the tribal population, preserved for thousands of years by their unwillingness to have contact with others, is now preserved by the Indian government under the Protection of Aboriginal Tribes regulations. Of the islands' six tribes, five are confined to their traditional habitation areas, which have been set aside by the government as "Special Primitive Tribal Reserve Areas." Contact with any of the tribes is completely restricted by the government, even to ethnologists.

In February 1987, a more remote tribal group with whom a government-sponsored party of local officials, sociologists, and anthropologists were trying to make contact, rebuffed the attempt by firing arrows with poison tips at the boat bearing the party. The existence of these ancient peoples, some of whom exist exactly as they did in the Stone Age, is an intriguing and provocative fact, but, in general, the closest you can come to their culture is a visit to the small but informative Anthropology Museum in Port Blair. Here you can learn of the Andamanese, Onges, Jarawas, and Sentinelese, who are the five Negrito tribes of the Andamans, and the Mongoloid tribes of the Nicobars, the Nicobarese and the Shompens.

As is true of much of what is accessible to tourists in these islands, you can get only a glimpse of the treasures that are here, but that glimpse alone is fascinating and haunting.

Few Islands Accessible

If you come to the Andaman and Nicobar Islands expecting to see the spectacular natural beauty particular to such isolated, undeveloped tropical islands, you will not be disappointed as long as you get out of Port Blair. In Port Blair, you don't expect to find the unusual, curious collection of museums and tourist sights that are there. Although few of the hundreds of islands are accessible to foreign tourists, those that are offer some of the world's most spectacular coral reefs, guaranteed to dazzle and enchant even experienced divers. Here are the colors you dream of, spread out in warm, clear waters. The rich variety of marine life, from the vibrantly colored parrot fish to the shy seahorse, is mesmerizing. As schools of fish dart and glide through a background of intensely colored coral, you will understand the stories of divers who, becoming enraptured with such beauties, fail to remember their limited oxygen supply.

To experience the marine beauties of the islands, you must put up with some frustration at the limits placed on travel here. However, measured against the possibility of upsetting the fragile ecology of these islands in a rush to develop them too quickly, these are frustrations that you must take in your stride. Currently, only trips are permitted to the coral-encircled islands of Jolly Buoy, Redskin, North and South Cinque, Neil, and Havelock. But with the vivid colors and intriguing shapes and the sometimes amusing, sometimes compelling, activity of the myriad marine animals you see, the few hours spent here will yield a surplus of memorable images on which you will reflect long after you return to the mainland.

Other water sports, such as windsurfing and sailing, can be enjoyed in the Andamans. They are all arranged through the larger hotels, since there is little evidence of a tourist industry here other than these hotels.

Cellular Jail

Sightseeing in the Andamans, though limited, offers some interesting finds. The primary attraction is the Cellular Jail, where thousands of men and women who fought for independence were interred, some of them for years, in tiny, spartan, isolated cells. Built by the British, it was completed in 1906 and part of it is still in use until the new local jail is completed.

Looking down from the central guard tower into the current prisoners' garden or walking through the grounds alongside some of the elderly Freedom Fighters who occasionally come back to visit, one senses how contemporary is this part of India's history, compared to what one sees on the mainland. Of the original seven wings of the jail, only three remain, the others having been destroyed in 1943 by an earthquake. A number of small museums are worth visiting for the information on the islands that they provide. In addition to the Anthropological Museum, there are the Marine and Forest Museums.

Rare Beauties Protected

The Andaman Islands are not the bustling, glamorous "resort" vacation spot that Thailand's Phuket is fast becoming. Rather, they are a peaceful vacation spot that offers outdoor activities associated with beach resorts but with restrictions to protect their rare beauty. At times, one wonders if the tourist is really here to stay or if, like the early Danes and British who came to colonize the islands, tourists will ultimately give up and leave the local population to enjoy this bit of paradise without further outside influence.

The fact that these islands aren't yet a developed tourist haven adds a great deal to their charm but is also the source of some irritation. The government has plans to expand the tourist facilities and is considering a variety of recommendations to take greater advantage of the islands' richness of botanical and marine life. Right now, however, tourists are set down in an environment that is uncluttered with the amenities of other island resorts. Although the hotel staffs are solicitous of your needs, you have a refreshing if frustrating feeling that to the rest of the islanders you just don't matter much. The sleepy, soothing atmosphere makes it a reviving spot to come to after the more boisterous encounters you have had on the mainland.

PRACTICAL INFORMATION FOR
ANDAMAN AND NICOBAR ISLANDS

WHEN TO GO. The climate in the Andaman and Nicobar Islands is tropical and temperate with temperatures varying between 62°F and 86°F throughout the year. Constant sea breezes bring relief even during hot spells. The relative humidity is 75 percent, and the annual rainfall, which is about 120 inches, is spread evenly over eight months, from mid-May to mid-September during the South-Western monsoons, and from early November to mid-December during the North-Eastern monsoons. The ideal time for vacationing here is mid-October–mid-May, when conditions are optimum for enjoying water sports and the islands' natural beauty.

PERMITS. Foreign nationals need a permit to visit the Andamans; the Nicobar Islands are off-limits. While you can obtain a permit from the Indian Mission or Consular offices in your home country, permits are also available on landing at Port Blair. This permit is restricted to Port Blair municipal area, and the islands of Jolly Buoy, Redskin, Cinque, Neil, and Havelock. Night halts are only permitted in Port Blair and Havelock.

HOW TO GET THERE. By Air. *Indian Airlines* flies three times a week to Port Blair from Madras, Delhi, and Bhubaneswar. It flies four times a week from Calcutta.

How to Get From the Airport. When you arrive in Port Blair, airline **vans** transport you from the plane to the edge of the runway, where there is a shed, a parking lot, and not much more. After claiming your luggage and getting your permit to visit the islands (if you haven't already done so), either take the **taxi** sent by individual hotels or hire one of the private taxis in the parking lot next to the arrival shed. Depending on where you are staying, the fare to hotels should be Rs. 25–35. You'll have to do some bargaining, since taxis often do not run their meters.

By Ship. You can go by ship from Calcutta and Madras, and occasionally from Vishakhapatnam in Andhra Pradesh. The trip takes about three days. For information and reservations, contact the *Shipping Corporation of India* (SCI), 13 Strand Rd., Calcutta, West Bengal; SCI, Madras Port Trust, Old Warehouse Building, near Customs House, Rajaji Salai, Madras, Tamil Nadu; SCI, Aberdeen Bazaar, Port Blair, Andaman Islands; and Bhanojiraw & Garuda, Pattabiramayva and Company, Box 17, Vishakhapatnam, Andhra Pradesh.

TOURIST INFORMATION. For information on the islands, contact these government offices:

Deputy Director, Information, Publicity & Tourism, Andaman & Nicobar Administration, Port Blair, Andaman Islands; tel. 20694.

Tourist Information Center, Tourist Home, Port Blair, Andaman Islands; tel. 2300.

Government of India Tourist Office, VIP Rd., Port Blair, Andaman Islands; tel. 21006. Open Monday–Friday, 8:30 A.M.–5 P.M.; Saturday, till 1:30 P.M.

FOREIGN CURRENCY EXCHANGE. Most Western-style hotels have money-exchange counters. Otherwise, go to a branch of the *State Bank of India,* open Monday–Friday, 10 A.M.–2 P.M.; Saturdays, till noon.

ACCOMMODATIONS. Since traveling to the Nicobar Islands is restricted, your stay must be prearranged when you apply for a permit. The Andaman Islands, however, have some lovely places to stay—most with modern Western amenities and accoutrements. Even Indian-style hotels have a charming, relaxed atmosphere. None of the places can be considered expensive. Prices are based on double occupancy and exclude taxes: *Moderate,* Rs. 500–Rs. 950; *Inexpensive,* under Rs. 500.

Moderate

Andaman Beach Resort. Corbyn's Cove, Port Blair, Andaman Islands; tel. 3381 or 2599. 52 rooms with bath. Operated by Travel Corporation of America, this resort, with lovely gardens, is seven km (four mi.) from the downtown area and overlooks a perfect beach. The lobby is cozy and tropical. Rooms have delightful bamboo furnishings and are whistle-clean. Some rooms are air-conditioned. There is a good restaurant serving Indian, Chinese, and Continental cuisines, plus a bar, diving equipment, scuba diving, snorkeling, windsurfing, tennis, foreign-exchange counter, and travel arrangements. AE, DC, MC, V.

Hotel Assiana. South Point, Port Blair, Andaman Islands; tel. 21159 or 21165. 23 rooms with bath. This new five-story resort, still under construction, sits high over the sea, halfway between Corbyn's Cove and Marine Hill. Air-conditioned rooms have a modern-decor, with balconies that face the water. Some rooms have TV. Restaurant serving Indian, Chinese, and Continental cuisines, bar, room service, car-rental arrangements, doctor. Rupees only.

Welcomgroup Bay Island. Marine Hill, Port Blair, Andaman and Nicobar Islands; tel. 2881. 48 rooms with bath. This charming resort, built on a steep hill overlooking Ross Island and one km from the downtown area, was designed by Charles Correa, one of India's best architects. It is modeled after a cluster of tribal huts. Open breezeways connect the handsome lobby with each group of rooms, where furnishings are upscale-ethnic and comfy. Best rooms have a sea or bay view. Some rooms are air-conditioned. Good restaurant serving Burmese, Indian, and Continental cuisines; room service; bar; doctor; swimming pool; fishing, snorkeling, and scuba diving equipment and arrangements; foreign-exchange counter; travel agency. AE, DC, MC, V.

Inexpensive

Megapode Nest. Reservations: Deputy Director, Information, Publicity & Tourism, Port Blair, Andaman Islands; tel. 20694. 10 rooms with bath. In this government-run facility, you'll find clean rooms with simple decor; some are air-conditioned. There is a restaurant serving simple meals. Rupees only.

DINING OUT. All restaurants in Port Blair are part of the hotels, and they combine Indian, Chinese, Continental, and Burmese cuisines. Buffets are common for lunch and dinner. Because most food and drink are flown in from Calcutta and Madras, the prices are higher and fresh fruits are not always available. The price of a meal, based on one person eating a three-course meal, excluding taxes, tip, or beverage, is *Expensive* (Rs. 80–Rs. 120)–*Deluxe* (over Rs. 120) at Andaman Beach Resort and Welcomgroup Bay Island; and *Moderate* (Rs. 40–Rs. 80)–*Expensive* at Assiana.

HOW TO GET AROUND. From the Airport. After you arrive in Port Blair, obtain your permit if you have not already done so; then take a taxi to your hotel. Fare is about Rs. 50.

By Boat. From the Fisheries Jetty, Port Blair, a ferry service runs three times a day around South Andaman Island. If you want to hire your own private launch, contact the *Marine Department or Oceanic Company,* M.G. Rd., Middle Point.

By Taxi. Taxis are available at all hotels for sightseeing around Port Blair. Rates are about Rs. 3.70 per km.

By Rented Car with Driver. Another alternative for local sightseeing; make arrangements through your hotel. Figure about Rs. 50 per hour.

By Bike. This is a delightful and inexpensive way (about Rs. 20 per day) to move around Port Blair. Ask your hotel to recommend a rental shop in town.

TOURS. The Directorate of Information, Publicity, and Tourism conducts a daily bus tour around Port Blair and boat cruises in the harbor. Contact the Tourist Information Center or Directorate (addresses above).

TOUR OPERATORS. *Island Travels* (Aberdeen Bazaar, Port Blair, Andaman Islands, tel. 3034) and the better hotels can take care of all your island travel needs, including boat cruise arrangements and a hired car with driver.

HISTORIC SITES. Monuments are either free or have a nominal fee.

Cellular Jail, just north of the Aberdeen Jetty, is now a national memorial to the Indian Freedom Fighters who were interred here by the British before independence. Built by the British between 1886 and 1906, its original design was a seven-winged building radiating out from a central guard tower. It contained 698 small cells in which prisoners were kept in solitary confinement. Today, to the right and left of the compound entrance, galleries hold photographs of many of these Freedom Fighters, grouped according to the incident for which they were imprisoned. Various prison artifacts, such as a device for holding prisoners when they were flogged, and information regarding food rations and work responsibilities, testify to the harsh treatment these "criminals" received. Within the compound, you can visit the gallows and the narrow whitewashed cells on the upper floors of the unoccupied wing on your right as you enter. Names of the Freedom Fighters are inscribed in stone at the top of the central guard tower. Open 9 A.M.–noon and 2–5 P.M., Monday–Saturday.

Chatham Saw Mill, Asia's oldest and one of its largest sawmills, gives informal tours to tourists. You get to follow the process that turns huge logs into finished planks of wood. Timber, brought in from the islands, is unloaded from boats, sawed into planks on large pre-World War II band saws, trimmed and planed, and then cured in huge temperature-controlled kilns. Once seasoned, the planks are sorted by grade and stored for shipment. You are also allowed to watch artisans in workshops turning premium-grade wood into furniture. Photographs not permitted.

MUSEUMS. The *Anthropological Museum* has extensive information on the islands' tribal peoples. You can see models of tribal villages, everyday tribal artifacts, and photographs of the various expeditions that have made contact, or, in some cases, failed to make contact, with the islands' six tribal groups. Powerful reminders of their cultural fragility are two photographs of a tribal couple, the first taken in their tribal dress, the second taken in Western attire. Publications on sale provide anthropological information on the tribes. A small research library on the second floor has an extensive collection of books on the islands. The museum is open 9 A.M.–noon and 1–4 P.M., closed Saturdays.

Forest Museum, near Chatham Saw Mill, displays the variety of local woods and illustrates how each is put to use by the lumber industry. Dominating the two-room collection is a large tree fashioned out of pieces of all the tree varieties, from the velvety red padauk to the unusual marblewood. Open 8:30 A.M.–4 P.M. daily.

Marine Museum, near Marine Park, provides information on life under the sea. Any novice diver will appreciate the display of the coral that is found in the offshore waters. There are also preserved fish specimens. Open 8:30 A.M.–4 P.M., closed Sundays.

GARDENS AND ZOOS. *Marine Park,* a pleasant strip of land that runs along the sea, has modest, well-maintained topiary gardens.

Mini Zoo is home to some of the islands' unusual animal life and has a saltwater crocodile-rearing farm. Open 7 A.M.–noon and 1–5 P.M., closed Mondays.

SPORTS AND OUTDOOR ADVENTURES. The **coral beds** throughout the islands support some of the most spectacular underwater marine life in the world, and the multihued waters in which they are found are astonishingly clear and bath-water warm. From close to shore you can snorkel out to where the sea floor is covered with coral. Water temperatures range from 78° F on the surface to about 60°F at a depth of 130 feet. There is good visibility to 50 feet below the surface; at a depth of 80 feet, there is a visibility to about 15 feet. Whether you snorkel from the surface or skin dive, the anemones, angelfish, sweetlips, parrot and squirrel fish, brain coral, and sea fan are vividly displayed in languid waters.

Coral beds are easily accessible at *Jolly Boy* and *Cinque* islands, both of which are uninhabited islands of great beauty. Convenient day trips can be arranged through the better hotels or the tour operator listed above. Since these islands are so isolated, have the hotel prepare a picnic lunch or take along food from shops in Port Blair. Drinking water and other beverages should also be taken.

The management of the *Andaman Beach Resort* is especially knowledgeable about the Islands' underwater attractions and is active in organizing **scuba-diving** and **snorkeling** expeditions. If this is your reason for coming to the Andamans, contact them. The information and arrangements they provide will prove invaluable.

Although some snorkeling equipment is available through hotels and Island Travels, we recommend you bring at least a well-fitting mask and snorkel. The much-advertised "glass-bottom" boat is no more than a motorized dinghy with a small plexiglass section through which passengers sitting in the middle of the boat can peer.

If **sunbathing** and **swimming** are of interest, the best spot near Port Blair is *Corbyn's Cove,* a peaceful spot at the southern end of Port Blair. The beach, like that of the other islands to which day trips are permitted, has clean white sand, gentle surf, and clear, warm waters. Ringing the crescent-shaped beach are tall palms that cast long shadows across the sands in the late afternoon.

SHOPPING. In Port Blair, the *Cottage Industries Emporium* (open 9 A.M.–1 P.M.; 1:30–5 P.M., closed Mondays and Fridays) has a sparse display of wood and shell items for sale in its sleepy showroom. Although shops near the *Aberdeen Bazaar* seem to carry only cheap "shell art" at first glance, you can find some beautiful shells in their natural state, such as mango shell, chambered nautilus, nancowry, spiney murex, and king shell if you poke around. Since tourism is only now becoming important to the islands' economy, local raw materials, such as the unusual varieties of woods, are rarely used in native crafts. When available, items of marble-wood and padauk are beautiful and, in the case of the latter, a pleasure to touch. Hard bargaining and comparison shopping are suggested at these shops.

NIGHTLIFE AND BARS. The best places to watch the sunset, while sipping a drink, are the Welcomgroup Bay Island and the Andaman Beach Resort. Bars are generally open noon–2:30 P.M. and 6–10:30 P.M.

NEPAL

NEPAL

Reaching the Ultimate Heights

by
KARL SAMSON

Karl Samson is a free-lance travel writer and photographer whose work has been published in newspapers and magazines in the United States and in Asia. He has traveled extensively in Southeast Asia, Nepal, India, Ladakh, and in Europe.

Nepal, a country where myths endure and mysteries persist, is a land of striking contrasts. Bananas and papayas ripen in the warm subtropical sun not 40 kilometers (25 miles) from the snowcapped peaks of the world's highest mountains. Cows, unperturbed by blaring car horns, steal vegetables from produce vendors who line the crowded, narrow streets of Kathmandu. Buddhist monks circle a *stupa* (shrine) under the all-seeing eyes of Lord Buddha, while pious Hindus line up beside an ornate temple to the goddess of smallpox, which stands only a few feet away. Throughout the country, the Middle Ages coexist with the twentieth century. It is just these contrasts that have attracted tourists since the country first opened its doors to the West in 1951.

Nepal stretches for 806 kilometers (500 miles) along the northeast border of India and is only 160 to 240 kilometers (100 to 150 miles) wide. It is bounded in the east by Sikkim and West Bengal, in the south and west by Bihar and Uttar Pradesh, and in the north by the Chinese Autonomous Region of Tibet.

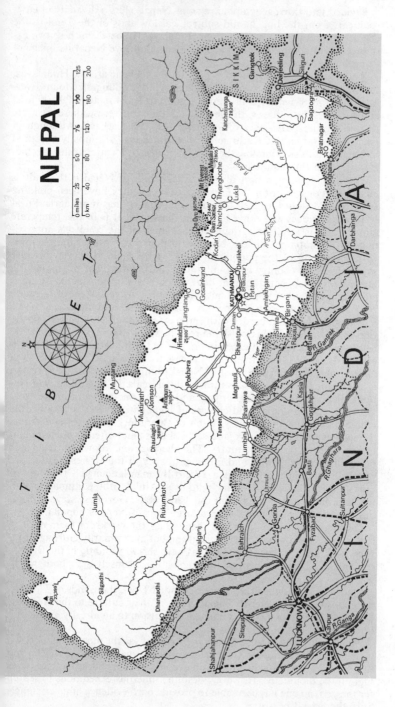

NEPAL

0 miles	25	50	75	100	125
0 km	40	80	120	160	200

Divided into three geographic regions, Nepal offers a diversity of environments from the hot, humid subtropical lowlands of the Terai to the frigid, snowbound peaks of the high Himalayas. In between these two extremes lie the rolling hills and green valleys that give Nepal its image of being a true Shangri-la.

Running the entire length of Nepal like a backbone are the Himalayas, the tallest mountains in the world and some of the youngest. Mount Everest, known as Sagermatha in Nepal, towers to 8,874 meters (29,106 feet) and straddles the border with Tibet. In addition to Everest, there are more than 100 other peaks over 6,098 meters (20,000 feet) tall. Although in Nepal's capital city of Kathmandu, the Himalayas are mostly obscured by the high hills surrounding the city, many nearby locations offer spectacular views of the mountains.

The most striking aspect of the midland hills of Nepal is the endless terracing. For centuries, the farmers of this country have been building terraced fields into the steep hillsides. The country has more agricultural terraces than does any other nation in the world. It is in this temperate climate that is ideal for agriculture that most of the country's approximately 18 million people live. Nepal is primarily an agricultural country, with 93 percent of the population working the land. However, because so much of the country is mountainous, only 26 percent of the land is under cultivation. Much of that land would never be considered for agriculture in any other country, but with the extensive system of terraces, Nepal's farmers have made the most of their land and climate.

Along the southern border with India extends the Terai, Nepal's fertile rice-growing region. This low-lying region, which averages only about 250 feet above sea level, is an extension of the Indo-Gangetic plains of northeastern India. With relatively easy access to India and the best roads in Nepal, the Terai supports most of Nepal's limited industries. This region is also home to some of Asia's rarest wild animals. In Royal Chitwan National Park, live royal Bengal tigers and Indian one-horned rhinoceroses.

Just as the geography and climate of Nepal are diverse, so, too, is the ethnic makeup of the country. Each of the numerous castes and ethnic groups has its own language and style of dress and often is predominant in a specific region of the country. The Sherpas, well known for their help on mountain expeditions and found primarily in the Everest region, are primarily Buddhists and speak a Tibeto-Burman language. Other important groups include the Newars, who live mainly in the Kathmandu Valley, and the Tharus, who live in the Terai. Rais, Gurungs, Magars, Limbus, and Tamangs also make up a large part of Nepal's population.

Gurkhas, known and admired throughout the world for their valor in battle, are not of one specific ethnic group but are primarily Gurungs, Magars, Rais, and Limbus. The Gurkhas have served valiantly in the British, Indian, and Nepalese armies, distinguishing themselves in both world wars.

Since the 1950s when the Chinese invaded Tibet, thousands of Tibetans have taken refuge in Nepal. The addition of their culture to the Nepalese lifestyle has added a new and unusual dimension to an already exotic cultural melting pot.

Many myths and legends persist in Nepal; by far the most widely known is that of the Abominable Snowman, known as the *yeti* in Nepal. The yeti has been known for centuries from records kept in Sherpa monasteries high in the mountains. However, despite numerous expeditions to search for the yeti, no one has been able to provide hard evidence of its existence. Still, the legend persists.

Nepal is also the home of living gods. The king of Nepal is considered an incarnation of the Hindu god Vishnu. It was this sacred position that prevented the king from being dethroned when the Rana prime ministers took control of the country in the mid-nineteenth century. Nepal's other living god is a young girl known as the Kumari, the virgin goddess who lives a life of isolation in a beautiful old home on Kathmandu's Durbar Square. Whenever the Kumari first bleeds, a sign that she is human after all, she is replaced by another specially chosen young girl.

With its medieval cities, colorful religions, high mountains, and sweltering lowland jungles, Nepal is a compact country of amazing diversity. Over the centuries, its mountainous geography has played an integral role in its economic, cultural, religious, and military development. Today, these many unusual contrasts are making Nepal one of the world's most interesting destinations.

A Bit of History

Although Nepal is an ancient country, its early history is inextricably bound up in the region's myth and folklore. Few historical records are available to document the legends that often refer to historical figures as well as gods and goddesses. It is known that more than 2,000 years ago, advanced cultures were living throughout the region now occupied by modern Nepal.

According to legend, the Kathmandu Valley was formed when a powerful god from China emptied the waters of the lake that once filled the valley. Modern geological exploration has determined that the Kathmandu Valley was indeed a vast lake at one time. However, the lake had drained long before humans appeared in the area. The rich soil of this ancient lake bed has accounted for the development of the valley as the cultural center of Nepal.

The earliest known inhabitants of the valley were the Ahirs, or shepherd kings, who occupied the area as long ago as the eighth century B.C. The primitive people are believed to have migrated into Nepal from northern India. The Indian epics *Ramayana* and *Mahabharata* both refer to the Kirats, who occupied the eastern foothills of the Himalayas. Records show that the Kirats probably moved into the valley about 700 B.C., but little is known about them.

In the Terai region west of the Kathmandu Valley, the Shakyas, a Rajput clan from northern India, had founded the city of Kapilvastu by the sixth century B.C. The beauty of this city was renowned and its culture flourished. It was here, in the city's Lumbini Gardens, that Prince Siddhartha Gautama was born in 563 B.C. The prince would later become enlightened while sitting beneath a bo tree and become known as the Buddha.

Ashoka, the emperor of India who embraced Buddhism and helped spread this religion throughout the subcontinent, visited Lumbini in 250 B.C. and erected a stone pillar. Legends contend that Ashoka continued on to the Kathmandu Valley to erect the four stupas surrounding Patan. However, there are no records to support this belief.

About A.D. 200, another powerful north Indian tribal group, the Lichhavis, began moving into Nepal. With their center of power in the Kathmandu Valley, the Lichhavis ruled until about the ninth century. Under the Lichhavis, Nepal saw its first flowering of art and architecture and became a powerful and prosperous country. The pagoda style of temple architecture developed at this time, and many temples and palaces were constructed. Unfortunately, few of these buildings have survived. However, some excellent stone carvings from this period can still be seen at Changu Narayan and other places.

Nepal's medieval period then began with the rise of the Malla dynasty, which lasted until the eighteenth century. The Malla kings were great patrons of the arts and culture. Trade, industry, architecture, and religion all flourished during this period. Most of the beautiful temples and palaces of the Kathmandu Valley were built by the Mallas.

By the middle of the fifteenth century, the powerful king Yaksha Malla had extended his domain to include parts of Tibet and India, as well as the Kathmandu Valley and much land to the east and west. However, with the death of Yaksha Malla, the power of the Mallas slowly began to wane. Having divided the valley's cities among his sons, Yaksha Malla had unknowingly set in motion the decline of the Malla dynasty. The sons and their descendants fought among themselves and slowly weakened the city-states that they had created. By the middle of the eighteenth century, these individual kingdoms were unable to unite against the advancing army of Ghorka ruler Prithvi Narayan Shah, who stormed across Nepal from the west.

Prithvi Narayan Shah, fearing an invasion by the British who had taken control of India, set out to unify the many tiny kingdoms of Nepal so that country could better defend itself against the British threat. Between 1744 and 1768, he succeeded in conquering all of Nepal's many kingdoms and, for the first time in history, Nepal was a unified country.

British India was not the only threat to Nepal. Because of trading disputes, relations with Tibet had deteriorated. When Nepal annexed part of Sikkim (then a part of Tibet) and looted several Tibetan monasteries, Tibet turned to China for help. In 1792, war broke out between Nepal and China. Nepal's small army was no match for the 70,000 Chinese troops sent to Tibet, and a treaty requiring a ransom to be paid to China every five years was eventually signed.

In 1814, border disputes along its southern border brought about a war with British India. The treaty that ended the war in 1816 gave much of the disputed land to the British, but, in 1860, most of it was returned to Nepal. Today's borders are those established in 1860.

In 1846, a bloody massacre in Kathmandu allowed the prime minister, Jung Bahadur Rana, to usurp power from the king. The king and queen fled to India, and Jung Bahadur installed the crown prince as king. Because the Nepalese believed their king to be an incarnation of the god Vishnu, Jung Bahadur maintained the monarchy but removed all its power.

The title of prime minister was made hereditary, and the Ranas ruled Nepal for the next 104 years. The period of Rana autocracy was a time of almost uninterrupted peace for Nepal. For many years, the Ranas enjoyed popularity both at home and abroad. Although Nepal was officially isolated from the rest of the world during this period, the Ranas made several trips to Europe. Jung Bahadur Rana, after visiting England, instituted many civil and military reforms. However, to maintain power, the Ranas withheld education from the people. By ignoring the public welfare of Nepal, these despotic rulers amassed substantial fortunes and reduced the country to an impoverished condition.

Eventually, infighting among Rana family members and pressure from a newly independent India began to take its toll on the prime ministers. Public support in Nepal waned as unemployment and food prices rose. The inefficient government of the Ranas had brought itself to the brink of revolution.

In November 1950, King Tribhuvan took refuge in the Indian Embassy and was later flown to Delhi. Mohan Shumsher, ruling prime minister at the time, installed the king's grandson as the new king. Despite the support that Ranas had received from other nations, no country was willing to fight against the wishes of India in this situation, and India refused to recognize the new king.

Nepalese in India and at home began an open revolt against the Rana government. Protests in Kathmandu and attacks along the border by insurgents based in India quickly undermined the government. In February 1951, King Tribhuvan returned to Nepal, and more than a century of Rana rule officially came to an end.

Nepal Today

During the more than a century when the Ranas exploited Nepal and its people for their personal gains, little thought was given to developing the country. Political isolationism had left Nepal with few international relations. When King Tribhuvan regained power, he was faced with the immense task of creating a new system of government, solving the country's many economic problems, and opening relations with the rest of the world. Even now, 40 years later, the country is still struggling with many of the same dilemmas.

King Tribhuvan died in 1955, the year Nepal joined the United Nations, and his son, Mahendra, ascended to the throne. In 1975, King Mahendra's son, who had been educated in England, the United States, and Japan, became King Birendra Bir Bikram Shah Dev. As the current ruling monarch of this independent kingdom, he wields nearly absolute power in matters of state. He is supported by a partyless political system based on the Panchayat, or village council, that is ostensibly a democratic form of government. However, dissatisfaction and frustration with the ineffective Panchayat system has led the people to demand a more representative and democratic form of government.

Dissatisfaction finally led to organized protest in 1990. Workers, students, housewives, and even young children took to the streets to demand a multi-party system and democracy. Days of protest led to violence and the loss of lives; but King Birendra and his followers recognized that they were hopelessly outnumbered. Birendra gave in to the pro-democracy movement and heeded the call of powerful world leaders who championed the democratic cause. He dissolved the government and removed the ban on political parties.

As of press time, Nepal is now ruled by a much-weakened king and a government with representatives from all factions, including the formerly banned parties. Now the people await their promised new constitution that will officially restore the multi-party system and allow this small kingdom to add its name to the growing list of democratic countries.

A landlocked country, Nepal has for years acted as a buffer between its two large and powerful neighbors, India and China, both of which have sought to influence Nepal's government for their own benefit. However, Nepal has managed to maintain good relations with both countries for some time. With the hope of preserving peace in the region and continuing good relations with both neighbors, King Birendra, on his coronation, proposed that Nepal be declared a zone of peace. In his address calling for the zone of peace, King Birendra stated, "We need peace for security, we need peace for independence and we need peace for development. . . . We believe that only under a condition of peace will we be able to create a politically stable Nepal with a sound economy." This proposal, which adheres to a policy of nonalignment, has been supported by more than 73 countries.

It was not until 1951 that Nepal began to take serious notice of the outside world. Before then, it had diplomatic relations with only four countries. After Nepal opened its doors to the Western world, it was still quite a few years before many people other than mountain climbers visited the country. It took the construction of Kathmandu's international airport and the beginning of flights from Bangkok in 1968 to open the eyes of tourists to this unique Himalayan kingdom. Since 1968, tourism has become the country's single largest source of foreign exchange. This relatively rapid escalation of tourism in a country that had been shut off from the rest of the world has had a huge impact on the culture of Nepal. However, the effects are still confined mainly to Kathmandu and the country's few other tourist destinations. Outside these areas, life goes on much as it has for hundreds of years.

It is this unchanging lifestyle that presents Nepal with many of its economic problems. The same rugged mountains that allowed many small independent kingdoms to develop over the years have inhibited economic development. The lack of communication within the country is one of the greatest problems facing Nepal today.

There are only 2,170 kilometers (3,500 miles) of roads in Nepal, and these are not always passable. About 40 small airstrips have now been opened throughout the country to provide many isolated regions with a direct link to Kathmandu. Still, much of the country remains remote and inaccessible.

Many other nations have taken a keen interest in assisting Nepal with the numerous problems facing the developing nation. Agricultural, medical, educational, and industrial programs have been implemented throughout Nepal by numerous foreign aid agencies. Farmers are being assisted in land management and crop production. Reforestation programs are being implemented with foreign aid. Nepalese doctors are being trained abroad, and foreign doctors and nurses are volunteering their services to help bring adequate health facilities to remote regions of the country. Laborers are being trained in new skills to help them set up alternative industries to produce in Nepal some of the products that are currently being imported.

In addition to the foreign aid, the Nepalese government continues to implement programs of its own aimed at bolstering the nation's economy by improving communication, developing employment opportunities, educating the people, raising agricultural production, providing medical facilities, controlling population and conserving natural resources.

EXPLORING NEPAL

Most explorations of this country begin with the Kathmandu Valley, the country's cultural, commercial, and administrative capital. At an elevation of 1,372 meters (4,500 feet), Kathmandu has a pleasant climate year round. Even in the middle of winter, it rarely freezes in the valley. However, because Kathmandu is in a low valley, the beautiful Himalayas are only partially visible. For an unobstructed view, it is necessary to venture into the surrounding hills. Several small towns perched on the high ridges offer spectacular views of the mountains, with sunrise and sunset excursions particularly popular.

For one of the most extraordinary and closest views of the Himalayas, a trip to Pokhara, a 30-minute flight west of Kathmandu, is a necessity.

This quiet rural valley on the edge of a picturesque lake is Nepal's answer to Kashmir. Bananas, papayas, banyans, and poinsettias grow throughout the valley, giving it a lush tropical feel the year round.

Down in the tropical lowlands of the Terai region, Chitwan National Park offers a chance to view some of Asia's rarest animals in the wild— Bengal tigers, one-horned rhinoceroses, crocodiles, sloth bears, and other rare creatures make their home in this nature preserve. Also in the Terai region is Lumbini, the birthplace of the Buddha, which is a popular pilgrimage site for Buddhists and an interesting excursion for anyone interested in Buddhism or the ancient culture of Nepal.

For the adventurous, Nepal has some of the most exciting attractions in the world. The Himalayas, which are the highest mountains in the world, offer almost unlimited opportunities for trekking, white-water rafting, and mountain biking. However, because of the inaccessibility of the snows in Nepal, there is little in the way of winter sports.

Kathmandu

Originally known as Kantipur, Kathmandu is believed to have been founded in A.D. 723 by King Gunakama Deva. With few historical records from so long ago, however, there is some dissent over the founding date of the city. Some scholars say the city was founded as late as the twelfth century. Nevertheless, there is a great deal of evidence to show that there were developed communities in the valley 2,000 years ago.

Kathmandu probably derived its name from the Kasthamandap, a wooden temple erected in the early seventeenth century by King Laxmi Narsingha Malla. The Kasthamandap stands at the southwest corner of Kathmandu's Durbar Square. According to legend, the large open structure was constructed from a single tree. The name means wooden pavilion.

In the early morning, produce vendors surround the ancient Kasthamandap, and devout Hindus stop to leave offerings at the small Maru Ganesh shrine beside the building. Ganesh is the elephant-headed god of good luck. Ganesh shrines are found on nearly every street in Kathmandu, but this beautiful little temple, with its shining gilded roof, is one of the finest. Whenever a new king is crowned in Nepal, one of his first acts is to visit this temple with offerings.

Behind and to the right of this pagoda-style temple is an old building with intricately carved windows and doorways. Through the low doorway is a small courtyard filled with more beautifully carved windows.

This is the Kumari Bahal, the home of the living goddess, Kumari. Born a Buddhist in 1980, this child is believed to be an incarnation of Kali, the wrathful consort of Shiva. The goddess, who is not allowed to smile, is sometimes seen waving to visitors from an upstairs window. It is forbidden to photograph her within her home.

The child is chosen from among the goldsmith caste of Buddhists and lives an isolated life in this building. She leaves her home only on a few special occasions, the most important being the festival of Indra Jatra, when the king, considered an incarnation of the god Vishnu, receives her blessings. When the Kumari first shows signs of blood, indicating that she is actually human, she is replaced by a new Kumari.

Palace Not in Harmony

Across the busy square from the Kumari Bahal is a large white building that looks out of place with its Grecian pillars and painted facade. This is the Gaddi Baithak, which was built in 1908 by one of the Rana prime ministers who ran the country for more than 100 years after usurping power from the royal family. This is just one of the many European-style palaces built by the Ranas during their years of rule. Many of their other extravagant palaces have now been converted into government office buildings and hotels.

Directly in front of the Gaddi Baithak is Maju Deval, a three-tiered Shiva temple perched atop a platform. Steps lead up to the temple, which offers a splendid panorama of Durbar Square and the surrounding neighborhoods. This temple is an excellent vantage point for observing the bustle of activity in the square. Rickshaws, motorcycles, taxis, and cars haphazardly negotiate their way through the square, managing to avoid hitting the pedestrians and vendors who thread their way back and forth across the flagstone pavement. Vendors selling a wide assortment of curios arrange their wares on the platforms of the square's many temples, while children amuse themselves with imaginative games.

From an upper window of the two-story Shiva Parvati temple that resembles an old house on the north side of the square, colorfully painted statues of the god Shiva and his consort Parvati peer down on the chaos in the square. This temple is built in the domestic style, meaning that it resembles a house. There are only a few of these domestic-style temples scattered around Kathmandu. Most of the important temples in Nepal are pagodas, and it is believed that the pagoda style of architecture made its way to China and Japan after developing in Nepal.

Near the tall Maju Deval temple, you can see a small, white, plastered shikhara-style temple. This type of temple architecture originated in north India. Shikharas are most often constructed of plastered bricks or stones.

Heart of Old Kathmandu

Behind the Shiva and Parvati temple is Hanuman Dhoka square, the heart of old Kathmandu. Bordering Hanuman Dhoka, which means the gate of Hanuman, is the old Royal Palace. Near the palace's Golden Door, which is guarded by two large painted stone lions, is a curious red figure atop a short pedestal. This is the image of the monkey god Hanuman from which the square derives its name. The statue of the monkey god Hanuman has been the object of the people's devotion ever since it was installed in 1672 by King Jaya Pratap Malla and, over the years, it has become covered with oils and red powder. It is no longer possible to distinguish any of the features of this statue, which is protected by an umbrella and usually wrapped in a scarlet cloak.

Just inside the beautiful golden door is another striking statue. This one is of the black-skinned half-man, half-lion god Narsingha (an avatar of Vishnu), who is depicted slaying the demon Haranyakashipu, who tortured his son for worshiping this god.

The royal palace is built around 14 large courtyards. Nasal Chowk, the largest and the one into which the golden door leads, is able to hold as many as 10,000 people. It is here that the coronation of the king is held. Although parts of the royal palace date back to the 1500s, most of it was built about 300 years ago. Much of the palace now houses the Tribhuvan Memorial Museum, which is dedicated to the king who led the revolt against the Ranas in 1951.

At the south end of the courtyard is the nine-story Basantapur Tower. With beautifully carved windows on each floor, this building commands a spectacular view across the roof of the palace and of all Kathmandu beyond. From here, you can easily see the unusual round-roofed pagoda temple to Hanuman at the opposite end of the courtyard.

Temple Erotic Art and the Swastika

Just outside the golden door is the large Jagannath Temple, with its carved wooden roof struts depicting erotic scenes. On many temples in Kathmandu, you see images of the male and female sexually united. This is an artistic rendering of the tantric concept that salvation comes from the union of the male and female force. Tantrics believe that through meditation, through a series of mysterious rituals, and, above all, through the mystical power of sexual union, you can realize Nirvana. In this regard, they compare human existence to the lotus. The root comes from mud; the flower represents perfect beauty. You can't achieve Nirvana without emerging through the dark.

The erotic art also depicts the tantric division of the human body into seven *chakras* (centers of energy). One must master the sexual urge before one obtains enlightenment. Erotic temple art is always outside. In the shrine you usually find a carved lotus. Erotic art also serves a second function. Each female stands for a vowel; each male represents a consonant. If you line up the figures on a temple, they spell out a prayer to the deity in the inner sanctum.

The swastika, a symbol so corrupted by Adolf Hitler and his Nazism, confuses the Westerner who sees it on wood carvings, bronze castings, and *thang-kas* (Paintings with a Buddhist theme). "Swastika" is Sanskrit for "well-being" or "doing good for all." Its four arms stand for pure love, compassion, happiness, and indifference—the qualities that lead Buddhists and Hindus to salvation.

Along the palace wall opposite Jagannath Temple is a stone inscription in 15 languages, placed here in 1664 by King Pratap Malla. Among the languages used in the inscription are English and French.

If you walk straight out from the golden door, you will find on your left at the end of the wall a huge golden mask hidden behind a lattice work of intricately carved wood. This is the Seto Bhairav. Each year on the festival of Indra Jatra, the screen is opened and a big pot of local rice beer is placed behind it. During the day's celebrations, people drink the beer through a long straw that passes through the mouth of the mask.

On the far side of the square from the Seto Bhairav is a small building that houses a terrifying bas-relief of the Kalo Bhairav. With its ferocious fangs and necklace of human skulls, this is the most frightening incarnation of the god Shiva—an appropriate visage for the god of destruction and terror. In the past, the Kalo Bhairav was used as a lie detector. It was believed that anyone telling a lie in front of this statue would immediately bleed to death.

Atop a pillar between the images of the Kalo Bhairav and the Seto Bhairav is a bronze statue of King Pratap Malla surrounded by his four sons. The statue was placed atop its square stone pillar in 1670.

Temple Entrance Forbidden

Just to the north of the palace complex is another large, ornate temple. This is the Taleju Temple, which only the royal family and certain priests can enter, except one day during Durga Puja when it is open to the Hindu public. Housed within its walls is an image of the goddess Taleju Bhawani that was brought here from India in the 1500s. Taleju Bhawani was the family deity of the Malla kings, and it is believed that human sacrifices once took place here.

The three gilded roofs of the temple are topped by a gilded pinnacle and a gold umbrella. Large bronze faces of the goddess gaze from the windows of the building's upper floors. From each of the temple's three roofs hang small bells. Within the walled compound surrounding the temple are many small pagodas.

Just outside the colorfully painted gateway to the Taleju Temple is the small, unusual Krishna Mandir Temple. Originally constructed in 1681 and renovated after the 1934 earthquake, this temple has a typical Nepalese-style first floor with a white-plaster Indian-style shikhara second floor.

A flagstone road, Makhan Tole, leading past the Taleju Temple will take you into the bazaar section of old Kathmandu. Here vendors, shoppers, and an occasional stray cow crowd the dark streets. Shops selling Tibetan carpets, thang-kas, masks, and other unusual items open directly onto the street. Flute sellers carrying what appear to be upside-down Christmas trees made of bamboo and wooden flutes stand in the sun playing beautiful melodies on their instruments. Devout Hindus on their way to a temple stop to buy garlands of marigolds and poinsettias as offerings to the gods. Small brass images of Nepal's many gods stare out of shop windows on a street scene little changed by the passage of time.

Makhan Tole, which leads diagonally away from Hanuman Dhoka Square, also contains a few more temples of interest—an excellent place to combine some shopping with sightseeing.

Three Small Squares

Indra Chowk is the first of three small squares along the length of this street. A domestic-style temple with a facade of red, green, and white tiles faces the busy square. Inside the temple is a silver image of Akash Bhairav. Four statues of ferocious-looking beasts gaze down from their second-floor perches. Non-Hindus are permitted inside but are not allowed to visit the inner sanctum.

In the second square, Kel Tole is one of Nepal's holiest and most ornate temples—the temple of the Seto Machendranath, who is worshiped by Buddhists and Hindus alike. Buddhists revere this idol as Avalokitesvara (Buddha of Compassion); Hindus revere it as a manifestation of Shiva.

The temple is well hidden within a small courtyard. A small Buddha on a stone pillar and two metal lions mark the entrance. In front of the small pagoda-style temple stand two bronze statues of the goddess Tara and an incongruous Greek statue of a woman. An ornately embossed and gilded facade surrounds the doorway of the temple, where people congregate with offerings for the small image of Machendranath. Several metal banners hang from the pinnacle of the gilded roof to just below the lowest tier. Known as *dhvajas,* these banners provide a pathway for the gods to come down to earth. Many of Nepal's temples are equipped with these gilded banners.

In Asan Tole, the third and busiest of the three squares, there are four small temples. The three-story Annapurna Temple enshrines a holy silver pitcher. Other temples in Asan Tole are dedicated to Ganesh, Narayan (Vishnu), and Uma Maheshwara.

A short distance beyond Asan Tole, the road ends at a small lake. This is the Rani Pokhari, the queen's pond. In the middle, connected to the bank by a causeway, stands a Mogul-style Shiva temple constructed by Rana Prime Minister Jung Bahadur. Many frightening ghost stories are told about this quiet pond, and on winter mornings, when a thick fog hangs over Kathmandu, it is easy to imagine spirits rising from the mists over the water.

Temples "On Parade"

Stretching south from the Rani Pokhari is the Tundikhel, one of the largest parade grounds in the world. Along its length there are temples, the Martyr's Memorial, statues of Rana rulers, a marketplace, a park, a grandstand, and a pasture for the city's many goats and cows.

A block west of the Tundikhel's southern end is what appears to be a minaret. This tower, known as Bhimsen's Tower, or *Dharahara,* was built by Prime Minister Bhimsen Thapa in 1832 as a memorial to a dead queen. During the earthquake of 1934, the tower collapsed but was later rebuilt.

Kalmochan Temple, near the Patan bridge, is another Mogul-style building erected by Jung Bahadur Rana, who built the temple in Rani Pokhari. With its four ferocious gilded beasts standing on the roof, Kalmochan is an imposing structure. Two statues, one of Jung Bahadur Rana and another of Garuda, stand in the courtyard, which is usually empty. The Nepalese believe that the temple is built above a mass grave containing the remains of people killed in a massacre ordered by Jung Bahadur Rana. Consequently, they avoid the site, and it is in need of repair.

Nearby is a large, though plain, temple that also sees few worshipers. This is the Tripureshwar Mahadev Temple, constructed in the nineteenth century by the wife of Jung Bahadur Rana to honor her husband.

The Rana prime ministers were admirers of both Mogul architecture, as can be seen at the Rani Pokhari and Kalmochan Temple, and European architecture. Another of their extravagant Victorian palaces can be seen just east of the Tundikhel. Singha Durbar, an immense white structure fronted by a reflecting pool, had more than 1,000 rooms when it was built in 1901. Unfortunately, much of the palace was destroyed by fire in 1973. Now used as a government office building, Singha Durbar has been greatly restored, and work continues to return it to some of its former grandeur.

The current residence of the king of Nepal is the Narayanhiti Royal Palace at the north end of Durbar Marg, a popular shopping street. Little can be seen of the king's residence but the unremarkable annex that was built in 1970.

PATAN

Just across the Bagmati River to the south of Kathmandu is the ancient city of Patan (also known as Lalitpur). From its position above the valley floor, Patan offers some of the valley's best views of the Himalayas. Patan is more widely known, however, as a city of exquisite temples and talented artists and craftsmen.

According to legend, Patan was founded by the Indian emperor Ashoka, a Buddhist, who is said to have visited the Kathmandu Valley in 250 B.C. Standing at the four corners of old Patan are four Buddhist stupas, simple hemispherical mounds of brick and earth, said to have been erected by Ashoka.

There is still a strong Buddhist influence in Patan, and many of Nepal's most outstanding Buddhist temples can be found here, along with outstanding Hindu temples and old palaces. The old buildings date mostly from the fourteenth to the eighteenth century. At that time, Patan was an independent kingdom ruled by the Mallas. Quite a few of the city's buildings have been restored, some more than once. The earthquake that struck the Kathmandu Valley in 1934 razed many of Patan's temples, almost all of which have been reconstructed.

As in Kathmandu, Durbar Square is the heart of the city, and it is here that a tour should begin. The most striking building on Durbar Square is the Krishna Mandir, a four-story stone temple that is considered one of the finest examples of Nepalese art and architecture. Graceful finials top the numerous peaked roofs of the temple, and excellent carvings depicting scenes from India's ancient epics, *Ramayana* and *Mahabharata,* are depicted on the temple's friezes. Atop a pillar in front of the Krishna Mandir is a large bronze statue of Garuda, the vehicle of Vishnu, which was placed here by one of the Mallas when the temple was completed.

Palace Complex

Across the street from the Krishna Mandir is an extensive palace complex built in the seventeenth century. Divided into three main courtyards known as *chowks,* the palace, which is the oldest one in the Kathmandu Valley, is a stunning example of Nepalese craftsmanship.

The entrance to the northern chowk is notable for its beautiful "golden" gate, an excellent example of the fine metalwork characteristic of this period. Mul Chowk, the central courtyard, houses the entrance to the Taleju Bhawanti temple. The main doorway to this temple is flanked by life-sized bronze figures of the Hindu deities Ganga (standing on a crocodile) and Yamuna (standing on a tortoise). In the Sundari Chowk is the royal bath, a large sunken pool surrounded by intricate stone carvings and a miniature version of the Krishna Mandir, which stands across the street. The water spout of the bath is another fine example of Newari metalwork.

Directly across the street from the entrance to the royal bath is an unusual octagonal stone Krishna temple built in 1723 in the shikara style. Beside this temple is a huge bronze bell erected in 1736. In the past, the bell was used to signal alarms during worship at the main Krishna Mandir.

Several typical Nepalese pagoda-style Hindu temples are also to be seen on Durbar Square. The three-story Hari Shankar Temple, to the north of the bell, is dedicated to Vishnu and Shankar. Two prostrate stone elephants guard the entrance to this temple. To the right stands the Char Narayan Temple, believed to have been built in 1566, the oldest temple on the square. Two stone lions and two guardians of Narayan, Ajaya and Vijaya, flank the steps leading to the entrance of this two-tiered pagoda.

Cobra-Coiffed King

Between the Hari Shankar Temple and the Char Narayan Temple is a bronze statue of King Yoganarendra Malla perched atop a tall stone pillar. The king sits beneath a cobra with a flared hood, and on the cobra's head rests a small bird. Although this king lived during the early eighteenth century, popular belief holds that the king will not die until the bird flies away and that some day he will return to the royal palace, which always has a window and door left open for his return.

Several other interesting temples are to be found within a few minutes' walk of Durbar Square. Two large maps have been erected on the square to help visitors orient themselves and locate these other temples. Not far from the square is the five-tiered temple of Khumbeshwar. Hindus believe that the god Shiva resides in this temple during the six months of winter before returning to his summer home on Mount Kailash in Tibet. The only other five-tiered pagoda in the Kathmandu Valley is Nyatapola Temple in Bhaktapur.

The temple of Rato (red) Machendranath was first built in 1408. Once a year, the dark red wooden image of Machhendranath is taken out of the temple and paraded through the city on a huge chariot. Both Hindus and Buddhists worship Machhendranath. Nearby is the Minanath Temple, with its Buddhist image of Avalokitesvara.

Another noteworthy Buddhist temple is Mahabouddha (Temple of 1,000 Buddhas), named for the images of the Buddha featured on the golden-colored bricks of which the temple is constructed. The structure is in the shikhara style. Another such smaller shikhara can be seen in the same compound. The small building was constructed from bricks left over after the main temple, destroyed in the 1934 earthquake, was rebuilt.

Golden Temple

Hiranya Varna Mahavihara, known as the Golden Temple, is a Buddhist monastery near Durbar Square. It contains one of the most beautiful and ornate examples of Buddhist art in the Kathmandu Valley. Two large painted lions guard the temple's nondescript entrance, which gives no hint of the treasures that are hidden within. In a tiny courtyard stands a small shrine with ornate silver doors and a gilded roof. Behind this temple is the main building, protected behind an iron gate. The intricately embossed, gilded walls, from which the temple derives its popular name, shine in the sun. A three-tiered roof, also gilded, crowns this spectacular building.

Although Patan is full of beautiful and unusual temples, it is not known only for its historical offerings. It is also a city of artists and craftspeople. A large percentage of the city's population is employed in the home manufacture of handicrafts. Brass and bronze statues, copper pots, wood carvings, and wool carpets are all manufactured in Patan.

BHAKTAPUR

With few vehicles crowding its narrow ancient streets, Bhaktapur retains more of a medieval feel than does either Kathmandu or Patan. Also known as Bhadgaon and the city of devotees, Bhaktapur has been extensively renovated with aid from West Germany. The city's temples, royal palace, and ancient homes look now much as they did in the seventeenth and eighteenth centuries. Bhaktapur is a quiet city in which people go about life much as they have for hundreds of years. Located about 15 kilometers (nine miles) east of Kathmandu, the city was founded in A.D. 889 with streets laid out in the design of a conch shell.

At the heart of the city is Durbar Square, (yes, that's the square's name here, too), entered through a large gate on its western side. Statues of Bhairav and Hanuman flank the gate, and many other images decorate the colorful archway. There are several other gateways of special interest within Durbar Square. Immediately to your left, behind two ornate stone lions, are seventeenth-century statues of the god Bhairav and goddess Ugrachandi Durga.

To your right as you face these statues is another pair of stone lions guarding the entrance to the National Art Gallery. Behind these lions are statues of Hanuman Bhairav and Narsingha Narayan. Within the art gallery are excellent examples of Nepalese paintings and stone carvings from the thirteenth to the nineteenth centuries. Most of the pieces displayed here depict Hindu and Buddhist Tantric deities. The gallery is housed in the old royal palace, which extends for much of the length of Durbar Square.

Nepalese Art at Its Best

The main entrance to the royal palace is the stunning Golden Gate. This magnificent gilded gateway is considered the finest example of Nepalese art in the country. Constructed in the mid-1700s by King Ranjit Malla, the Golden Gate features intricately wrought gods, demons, and mythical animals. Facing the gate is a bronze statue of King Bhupatindra Malla seated with his hands together in a gesture of devotion to the goddess Taleju Bhawani, whose temple is behind the Golden Gate.

The shining gateway also leads to the oldest section of the royal palace—the palace of 55 windows. Constructed in 1427 and renovated in the seventeenth century, the palace is known for its third-floor balcony; which consists of 55 ornately carved windows positioned side by side.

In front of the palace is the shikhara-style stone temple of Batsala, which is covered with detailed carvings. On either side of the temple are two large bells. The smaller of the two bells is known as the bell of the barking dogs. Whenever the bell is rung, the dogs in the neighborhood begin barking.

Behind the Batsala Temple is the oldest temple in Bhaktapur, the Pashupatinath Temple, which is a replica of the famous Pashupatinath Temple in Kathmandu. Erotic carvings decorate the roof struts of this temple.

Pagoda-Style Temple

Down a short street behind the Pashupatinath Temple is Taumadhi Square, which is dominated by the tallest temple in Nepal. The Nyatapola Temple is one of the finest examples of Nepal's pagoda-style temples. With its five-tiered roof and five-stage platform, it is beautifully symmetrical. On each of the five platforms of the temple stand a pair of stone statues, each of which is said to be 10 times stronger than the pair below. At the bottom are the wrestlers, Jaya and Patta, who were said to be 10 times stronger than ordinary men. Above them are two elephants, then two lions, two griffins, and finally, at the top, two demigoddesses, Baghini and Singhini. Because the temple was never officially inaugurated, its doors have remained closed since its construction in the early eighteenth century.

Also in Taumadhi Square is a large temple dedicated to the god Bhairav. A third pagoda-style structure on the square has been converted into a cafe, which offers excellent opportunities for unobstrusively observing the life of this square.

Ten minutes' walk from Taumadhi Square is Dattatreya Square, where some of the most intricately carved windows in Bhaktapur can be found. The peacock windows that grace the Pujari Math Hindu monastery are renowned as the finest examples of the Nepalese woodcarvers' art. Pujari Math stands beside the unusual three-story Dattatreya Temple, which is said to have been built from the trunk of a single tree. What makes this building unique is a small room, on the second story of the temple, that abuts the main section of the temple.

On the opposite side from Pujari Math is the Brass and Bronze Museum, which houses a collection of examples of Nepal's fine brass and bronze work dating from the eighteenth century. Oil lamps, water pots, cooking pots, ritual vessels, and other metal objects are on display in this restored building. In the vicinity of Dattatreya Square are many old houses that have been restored as part of the West German project.

Potters, Weavers at Work

Bhaktapur has traditionally been known for its pottery and handwoven fabrics, and it is still possible to observe the city's potters and weavers at work. The center of pottery manufacturing is only a short distance from Taumadhi Square. Potters spin their heavy wooden wheels by hand and quickly shape their pots, bowls, and vases, which are then lined up to dry in the sunny streets.

Within the dark houses of Bhaktapur can often be heard the rhythmic clacking of hand looms. Here the women stay busy weaving the black and red saris that are characteristic of this area.

On Dattatreya Square, you can also watch woodcarvers carry on the ancient art that has produced the intricate windows of Nepal's many old buildings. At Taumadhi Square, thang-ka painters can be seen creating highly detailed Buddhist images on canvas.

KATHMANDU VALLEY

According to legend, the Kathmandu Valley was formed when Manjushri (Buddha of Transcendent Wisdom) used his sword to cut through one of the hills surrounding the lake that filled the Kathmandu Valley at that time. In the southern part of the valley beyond Patan is Chobar Gorge, through which the waters of the valley drain. This narrow gorge is believed to be the gash made by Manjushri in ancient times. At the lower opening of the gorge is a small temple. People can often be seen bathing at this sacred spot. In recent years, the natural beauty of this setting has been ruined by a large cement factory that constantly spews smoke into the air and has covered the vicinity with a fine layer of cement dust.

Manjushri drained the ancient lake, the legend goes, so that he could better worship a flaming lotus flower that floated on it. This burning flower was the Adi Buddha, or primordial Buddha. When the waters had receded, the lotus rested on a high hill in the middle of the valley. On that hill was later built the huge Buddhist stupa of Swayambunath.

The hill on which this beautiful stupa sits is now a pleasant forested park. Swarms of small monkeys live here and scavenge the food offerings left by devoted Buddhist and Hindu pilgrims who daily visit the hill's many shrines. The top can be reached either by walking up the steep steps on the east side of the hill or by taking a roundabout road that leads up from the southwest. Those who choose to climb the steps will be rewarded with the site of the stupa's large eyes peering down at them as they make the steep ascent. Along the way are several brightly painted stone Buddhas, many small *chaityas* (miniature stupas) and stone statues of various animals that are vehicles of deities. At the entrance to the hill is a large colorful gate, behind which is a small building containing a large prayer wheel. To the right of the gate is a long wall of smaller prayer wheels. Tibetan people can often by seen here spinning the prayer wheels before making the climb to the top. Along the steps, other Tibetans, refugees, and pilgrims, may be seen carving prayers stones or weaving colorful belts, which they sell to passing tourists.

With its all-seeing eyes of the Buddha gazing out in four directions, Swayambunath is an extraordinary sight. Multicolored Tibetan prayer flags flutter in the breezes as pilgrims circle the stupa. Originally built more than 2,000 years ago, Swayambunath is a large white hemisphere of brick and earth crowned by a gilded copper spire consisting of 13 concentric circles and an intricate metal umbrella. Remember to circle the stupa only in a clockwise direction. To walk counterclockwise is considered sacrilegious.

Prayer Wheels and Shrines

All around the base of the stupa are prayer wheels and small shrines containing images of the different Buddhas and their consorts. Over the years, many other shrines have been built around Swayambunath. One of these is an ornate temple to Hariti, the Hindu goddess responsible for averting smallpox and ensuring fertility. On Saturdays, the shrine is packed with worshipers who have come with offerings to ask special favors of the goddess.

Also on this hill are several Buddhist monasteries that contain beautiful wall murals and large statues of the various Buddhas. Another Hindu temple on the hill is dedicated to Saraswati, the goddess of learning.

You have an excellent view of the entire Kathmandu Valley from Swayambunath. In the distant eastern side of the city, it is possible to discern the valley's other large stupa, Boudanath, which is the holiest site in the country for Tibetan Buddhists. Boudanath, though not as old as Swayambunath, is much larger—one of the largest stupas in the world. Once again, the all-seeing eyes of the Buddha peer out from their tower atop the white hemisphere of brick and earth. Within the stupa is an unknown relic placed there when the shrine was constructed. Some people believe that it actually contains a piece of bone from the body of the Buddha.

Nepal's Most Sacred Temple

Not far from Boudanath is Pashupatinath, the most sacred Hindu temple in Nepal. Dedicated to the god Shiva, the temple complex stands on the banks of the sacred Bagmati River, which is a tributary of the Ganges. Hindus regularly come to Pashupatinath to bathe in the waters of the river. It is here that many cremations are performed. The ashes are then sprinkled on the river so they can eventually join the holy Ganges. Each year in late February or early March, thousands of pilgrims visit Pashupatinath on the holy day of Shivaratri. From all over India and Nepal, thousands of Hindus, including many *saddhus* (wandering holy men), come to worship Shiva and bathe in the waters of the Bagmati.

Although the main temple is open only to Hindus, it is possible to catch glimpses of this ornate structure from across the river. Intricate silver doors and walls surround the lower level of the two-tiered temple, which is crowned with gilded roofs. Within the building is a huge Shiva lingam, and outside stands an equally large gilded bull, Shiva's mount, Nandi.

Numerous small white shrines on the bank opposite the temple contain small stone lingams. A paved path leads up a wooded hillside behind these stupas to several other shrines dedicated to various gods and goddesses.

When you arrive at Pashupatinath, you are likely to be approached by a young Nepali man speaking excellent English. He will want to give you a guided tour of the grounds. If you do not want his assistance, you must be insistent. Otherwise he will follow you, diligently explaining the temples and expect payment for his services at the end of the tour. If you accept his tour, Rs. 30–Rs. 40 is sufficient payment.

Just over the wooded hill from Pashupatinath is Guheshwari Temple, dedicated to Shiva's consort, Parvati. However, this temple is also open only to Hindus, and little of the building is visible from beyond the high walls of the courtyard.

North of Kathmandu is another sacred and unusual pilgrimage site dedicated to the god Vishnu. In the middle of a small pond is a 15-foot-long stone statue of Vishnu sleeping on a bed of huge snakes. Carved in the seventh century, it is believed that the statue was later rediscovered by a farmer plowing his fields. A Nepalese legend holds that the reigning king will soon die if he visits Budhanilkantha.

Animals Offered for Sacrifice

Farther along the picturesque road that leads past Shesh Narayan is the temple of Dakshin Kali, which is dedicated to Kali, the goddess of terror. Every Tuesday and Saturday, Hindus visit this small temple to offer animal sacrifices to Kali. After being sacrificed, the animals are taken home and prepared for dinner, thus serving a dual purpose. Hindus believe that animals sacrificed in this manner will have a much better life in their next incarnation. A trip to Dakshin Kali is definitely not for the squeamish. The gruesome nature of the shrine is in striking contrast to the tranquil atmosphere of the surrounding forested hills.

Kirtipur, a small medieval town of historical significance, makes a pleasant stop on the way back to Kathmandu from Dakshin Kali. Perched atop a high hill, this fifteenth-century town was once a fortress guarding the valley below. In his campaign to unify Nepal during the eighteenth century, King Prithvi Narayan Shah was forced to make three attempts before he was able to capture Kirtipur. Among the town's ancient temples and houses, old lifestyles persist.

Dating back to the fourth century, the Changu Narayan temple complex, 13 kilometers (eight miles) east of Kathmandu, is a shining example of the art and architecture of the Lichhavi period. Several of the stone statues here were carved in the fifth and sixth centuries, making this one of Nepal's most extensive repositories of art from this early period in Nepalese history. Although it is difficult to reach this hilltop shrine, which requires a 45-minute walk through beautiful countryside, it is well worth a visit.

Elephant Rides and Picnics

Close to Changu Narayan is Gokarna Safari Park, which has pleasant natural surroundings for hiking and picnicking and offers elephant rides and horseback riding. Here in the park's forested hills can be seen several species of deer, as well as monkeys. For anyone who does not have enough time to visit Chitwan National Park in the Terai region of the country, this small park offers visitors the experience of exploring the forest from high atop an elephant. Gokarna is also home to one of the two golf courses in the Kathmandu Valley.

Two other parks offer pleasant hikes and quiet surroundings for picnicking and escaping the hectic activities of Kathmandu. Nagarjun Royal Forest encompasses the forested mountain just to the northwest of Kathmandu. At the top of the park's Jammacho Peak stands a small white Buddhist stupa, which can be seen from the valley floor. It is a two-hour walk from the park entrance to the stupa at the top. A lookout tower beside the stupa provides excellent views across the valley and over the snowy Himalayas to the north. Along the trail may be seen many species of birds and an occasional deer.

Nine kilometers (six miles) south of Patan is the Royal Botanical Garden in Godawari. Although the gardens are not impressive, it is a quiet place for a picnic. Several paths wind through the shady grounds and past a small stream.

The National Museum, which is located near Swayambunath stupa, houses exhibits of the culture and arts of Nepal. Nearly 1,500 years of the country's art are on display here, including wood, stone, brass, and bronze sculptures. Many fine paintings and old books are also shown. In a separate building, there are natural history exhibits as well as displays of the arms and armor of past kings and their armies. Another wing of the museum is dedicated to the late King Mahendra.

HIMALAYAN HORIZONS

It comes as a disappointment to many people, but there are only limited views of the Himalayas from Kathmandu. To view the full grandeur of these spectacular peaks, it is necessary to make an excursion from the Kathmandu Valley. Tour Companies in Kathmandu offer several alternatives for sunrise and sunset excursions into the hills that surround the Kathmandu Valley. From these heights, it is possible to see for hundreds of miles in every direction. Nagarkot, which is known especially for its colorful sunrise vistas, is at an altitude of 2,286 meters (7,500 feet) and is 35 kilometers (22 miles) east of Kathmandu. From Mount Everest in the east to Dhaulagiri in the west, nearly 20 mountain peaks over 6,097 meters (20,000 feet) tall are visible from this beautiful natural setting of pine forests and pastures. The Tara Gaon Resort Hotel, run by the government of Nepal, provides simple overnight accommodations here. There are also numerous small lodges offering the most basic accommodations (no showers and shared toilets).

Although not as high as Nagarkot, the old town of Dhulikhel, 29 kilometers (18 miles) east of Kathmandu on the road to the Chinese border, offers spectacular sunsets as well as sunrises. However, because Dhulikhel is only at 1,829 meters (6,000 feet), it is not possible to see Mount Everest or the Annapurnas and Dhaulagiri. Thus, only about 15 peaks over 6,097 meters (20,000 feet) are visible here. Dhulikhel has two small resorts offering comfortable accommodations and food—the Dhulikel Mountain Resort and the Himalayan Sun-and-Snow.

If the view from your plane as you flew into Kathmandu seemed more exciting than any of the vantage points on the ground, you can take Royal Nepal Airlines' "Mountain Flight" for an hour of extraordinary vistas. This flight leaves several times each morning, weather permitting, from October to March, at times extending to April or even May. During the flight, which covers the eastern Himalayas, 18 peaks over 6,097 meters (20,000 feet) feet tall can be seen, including Mount Everest.

THE TERAI

Contrary to what many people believe, Nepal is not an entirely mountainous country. Running the length of its border with India is the Terai—an extension of the low-lying Indo-Gangetic plains.

The Terai, with its groves of bamboo and banana trees jutting above rice paddies, is home to the Tharu, former nomads who migrated from the Thar desert in India during the twelfth century to escape conversion to the Moslem religion. First the women came, accompanied by male servants who served as helpmates and later became the women's lovers. Today women still rule the roost. Even the man designated the village chieftain must bow to their power. When his wife serves him his meal, she kicks it to him across the floor.

Their dark complexions make the Tharu easy to recognize. Many of the men wear a loincloth—ancient garb that contrasts with the modern black umbrellas that shield their exposed bodies from the sun. The women usually wear white saris and heavy silver ornaments on the ankles, wrists, and necks; gold adorns the ears and nose. Women also tattoo their legs. In the past, these markings kept away Moslems, offended by the practice. Now it's primarily an artistic embellishment.

In the Terai, you can visit the Royal Chitwan National Park, southwest of Kathmandu, and the Royal Bardia Wildlife Reserve in the extreme west. The town of Lumbini is midway between the two parks, a destination with minimal lodging but important cultural significance—the birthplace of Sakyamuni, the Historic Buddha.

Royal Chitwan National Park

Bordering the Rapti River, the Royal Chitwan National Park was once the private playground and hunting preserve of Nepal's rana prime ministers. In 1962, King Mahendra turned the area into a wildlife sanctuary. Only 22 tigers and 100 rhinoceroses had survived the hunter's gun. Eleven years later, Chitwan was declared a national park. Today, it's closely guarded by armed forces who keep out poachers. Even the Tharu are restricted to one annual two-week harvesting of elephant grass they use for thatching.

By 1987, 100 tigers and over 400 rhinoceroses were spotted in the park. The sanctuary is also home to leopards and other jungle cats, elephants, buffalo, sloth bear, gaur (wild oxen), wild boars, langur and rhesus monkeys, freshwater dolphins, freshwater crocodiles, pythons, and king cobras, plus over 350 species of birds, including giant hornbills, peacocks, and eagles. Chitwan has been called the best sanctuary in Asia, and its excellent accommodations, beautiful vistas, and the splendid wildlife justify the claim.

The best way to explore the park is from a Land-Rover, on the back an elephant, in a dugout canoe cruising quietly down the Rapti River, or from the cover of a *machan* (watchtower) built deep in the forest. Unlike Africa, where animals roam in herds, most of Chitwan's protected species rarely move in large groups. The elusive tiger is a nocturnal hunter; your best chance of a sighting is early morning or early evening, when numerous lodges arrange excursions. Also remember to wear neutral-colored clothes.

Royal Bardia Reserve

In the western Terai, the Royal Bardia Reserve is a vast stretch of sal (hardwood) forest bordered by the Karnali River. You can see black buck, swamp deer, wild boar, otters, monkeys, and many species of birds. The lucky will see wild elephants, the solitary tiger, freshwater crocodiles, and freshwater dolphins.

Lumbini: the Buddha's Birthplace

At this isolated spot, 136 kilometers (84 miles) from Chitwan and near the Indian border, Lord Buddha was born around 563 B.C. In 1895 a German archaeologist discovered an inscribed pillar honoring Lumbini as the birthplace of Sakyamuni (Enlightened One), which was left behind by north India's Emperor Ashoka in 250 B.C. The discovery triggered other archaeological excavations, currently assisted by the United Nations. Since then, Lumbini has become one of the holiest places for Buddhists.

Today, Ashoka's pillar marks the formal Royal Garden at Lumbini as the Buddha's birthplace. Behind this pillar is the A.D. third century brick shrine, which honors the Buddha's mother, Maya Devi. Inside, ancient stone carvings depict the Buddha's birth. A small pond nearby is said to be the pool where Maya Devi bathed before giving birth. Not far from these remains, foreign Buddhist sects have built monasteries and shrines, including the Dharma Swami Maharaj Buddhavihar, a Tibetan monastery with a golden statue of the Buddha.

POKHARA

In Pokhara, the Himalayas seem close enough to reach out and touch. With spectacular mountain views, a picturesque lake, green fields, and giant pipal trees everywhere, Pokhara offers a refreshing, relaxing atmosphere that is perfect for recuperating after a hectic schedule. People often just sit here for days, gazing up at the dozen or so magnificent snowcapped peaks at the north end of the valley. Its natural setting is definitely Pokhara's main attraction. Nowhere else in Nepal is it so easy to get so close to the majestic Himalayas that attract people from all over the world.

Dominating the valley is the pyramid-shaped peak of Machhapuchhare, the Fishtail Peak, which rises up directly from the valley floor. Machhapuchhare derives its name from the fish-tail shape of its summit. Unfortunately, that shape cannot be seen from Pokhara. It is necessary to trek two days into the hills outside the valley before the "fish tail" can be properly viewed.

Machhapuchhare is a sacred peak and consequently has never been climbed, although one expedition ascended to within a few yards of the peak. Arrayed behind Machhapuchhare are the glittering peak of Dhaulagiri, the world's fifth-highest mountain, and the Annapurnas. Annapurna I is the sixth-highest peak in the world. Other peaks that are visible from Pokhara include Hiunchuli, Gangapurna, and Lamjung Himal.

Pokhara is a small city located on the edge of picturesque Phewa Lake, which stretches for nearly three kilometers (1 ½ miles) through the valley. On one side of the lake are forested hills, and on the other side, green terraces cling to the foothills that rise up toward the peaks of the Himalayas. Boats can be rented here with or without an oarsman. Few experiences can match the serenity of floating on this beautiful lake with the reflection of the snowy Himalayas reflected in the calm waters. On a small island in Phewa Lake stands a pagoda-style temple surrounded by trees that makes a pleasant excursion by boat. Two other smaller lakes, Begnas and Rupa, are also nearby.

Unusual natural phenomena abound in the Pokhara area. Just to the south of Phewa Lake are David's Falls. These mysterious waterfalls cut their way through a steep, narrow ravine before suddenly disappearing into a large dark hole in the ground. The Seti Gorge, a similar ravine, cuts through the river valley just to the east of town. From the middle of the Mahendra Bridge, it is possible to look down into the gorge, which is barely six feet wide. Far below, the river courses through its narrow chute. North of town is one of Nepal's only known limestone caves, the Mahendra Cave, which is full of stalactites and stalagmites.

MOUNT EVEREST AND NORTHEAST NEPAL

Seeing Mount Everest fills you with awe. Jagged pinnacles jut up like daggers and glaciers mirror the heavens. Black rock contrasts with icy slopes and crowded snow mastifs. The Nepalese call the mountain Sagarmatha (Mother Goddess of the Universe); the Tibetans call it Chomolungma (Mother Goddess of the Winds). When Sir Edmund Hillary and Tenzing Norgay made their successful ascent in 1953, they, too, paid their respects. Norgay, a Buddhist, buried a small parcel of sweets. Hillary added a crucifix.

Today's climbers and trekkers have left behind less touching gifts. In 1987, just 11 years after the Everest region was declared the Sagarmatha National Park, Sir Edmund announced, "Everest is a junkpile." Fully 75% of the forest cover at the base of the mountain is gone. Many local Sherpas, who once revered the trees, now prefer the money they make selling bundled firewood to trekkers. By the year 2000, if the current rate of deforestation persists, visitors to Sagarmatha will see not the peak's forest mantle, but barren slopes.

Visitors to this region are requested to bring in all their own firewood and take out all their trash. If you want to trek in relative peace and quiet, you should consider the "walk-in" trek from Jeri, north of Kathmandu. Trekkers should also consider a new destination. In 1989, the Nepalese government removed the restrictions against trekking around Mount Kanchenjunga, the third-highest peak in the world and a peak sacred to the Sikkimese, who call this mountain their guardian deity. To visit this area to the east of Everest, you must trek with an authorized trekking outfit (see the list below under *Tour Operators* and this same category in *Facts at Your Fingertips*).

JUMLA AND NORTHWEST NEPAL

Since this area was long closed to foreigners, not many have heard of Jumla or Nepal's largest body of water, Lake Rara, tucked in the northwest. This lake, at an elevation of 2,980 meters (9,774 feet), is the showpiece of Lake Rara National Park, considered by many the prettiest park in Nepal. In the northwest, the distant Himalayas form a ridge—a natural barrier that guards this ancient kingdom, the summer capital of the Mallas, who ruled Nepal in the fourteenth century. The land is reminiscent of the American west—wide rough valleys filled with scrub and occasional huddled settlements of houses with flat, stone roofs. This area, compared to the rest of Nepal, is sparsely populated. Its people are unaccustomed to foreigners.

LANGTANG VALLEY

Glaciers, high-altitude lakes, imposing mountains, and proximity to Kathmandu and the Tibetan plateau make Langtang and its valley a popular trekking alternative to Everest or Annapurna, especially for the visitor who is short on time. In this area, 75 kilometers (47 miles) north of Kathmandu, you're surrounded by gigantic peaks, including Langtang Lirung, 7,246 meters (23,773 feet), the highest in the region. Huge glaciers spill down mountain slopes, spread across high valley floors, and empty into the sacred Gosainkund Lake. As in neighboring Everest, the people who inhabit Langtang are Sherpas. Their handsome villages and monasteries add a peaceful touch to the formidable landscape.

In 1976, to save the beauty of Langtang Valley and Gosainkund, Nepal turned the area into its second-largest national park, a protected area for the endangered musk deer, Himalayan thar (wild goat), pandas, and elusive snow leopards.

PRACTICAL INFORMATION FOR NEPAL

WHAT IT WILL COST. Nepal is still a bargain. You can buy a cup of tea for under 30¢ or have a meal for $1. Except for Kathmandu and the wildlife sanctuaries, where fancy accommodations mean fancy prices, lodging is never more than $50 per double and usually inexpensive, under $25 for a double. However, the cost of a car or jeep with driver, which is determined by destination, is more expensive than in India. A car costs about $60 (Rs. 1,380) per day, a jeep about $85 (Rs. 1,955). Also plan on a halt charge of about $6 (Rs. 150) per night. Often a flight to your destination is cheaper.

CURRENCY. The units of Nepalese currency are the rupee and paisa (a hundred paisas equal one rupee). Paper money appears in denominations of 1, 2, 5, 10, 50, 100, 500, and 1,000 rupees; coins are in 5, 10, 25, 50, and 100 denominations. At press time the rate of exchange was U.S. $1=Rs. 23; £1=Rs. 37. Carry lots of small denominations. Few taxi, rickshaw, and scooter drivers have change.

You can bring any amount of hard currency, including traveler's checks, into Nepal; but you must fill out a Currency Declaration Form on arrival. Stay away from the illegal black market in foreign currency exchange. Convert your currency at Foreign Exchange Counters authorized by the *Nepal Rastra Bank* (State Bank of Nepal). A passport is required. Non-Indians entering from India can't exchange Indian rupees for Nepalese currency.

American Express and Thomas Cook, which are the traveler's checks of choice in Nepal, are at *Yeti Travels Pvt. Ltd.,* Hotel Mayalu, Jamal Tole, Durbar Marg; tel. 13596. These offices are only useful to report a loss or theft; they don't cash checks. *Nepal Bank Ltd.,* at the intersection of New Road and Dharma Path, and offices of Rastriya Banijya Bank will cash your checks as will your hotel if you are staying in a Western-style hotel with a foreign-exchange counter. When you travel outside Kathmandu, take sufficient rupees. Credit cards don't work in small villages, and traveler's checks can also pose problems. In Pokhara you can change money at the Rastriya Bank Exchange Counter at Ratnapuri. With trips to the Terai, flights often land after banking hours. Banks are also out of the way if you are going to a game park.

CREDIT CARDS. Western-style hotels, tour operators, and fancier shops usually accept the following credit cards: American Express, Diners Club, MasterCard, and Visa. Throughout the book we use the following abbreviations: AE, DC, MC, V.

TRAVEL DOCUMENTS. All foreigners need a valid passport and a tourist visa from the Nepalese Consulate or Embassy in their home country. You can obtain a 30-day tourist visa that's good for Kathmandu Valley, Pokhara, and other areas linked by highways. To get the visa, you need two passport photos and a valid passport. Cost is $10. If you apply in person, the visa is ready in three working days. If you apply by mail, allow for a month. You can also wait and get a 15-day visa at any valid international entry point, but there's usually a long line at the Kathmandu Airport. You can extend this visa at the Central Immigration Office in Kathmandu or at any Police Office in Nepal. You can also extend your 30-day visa at the Kathmandu office. To extend it a second and maximum third month, you must fill out a visa application form, present your passport, a passport-size photo, and a foreign exchange receipt proving you've exchanged $5 per day of extension. Extended visa fee: $15–$20 per month.

Americans should contact the Permanent Mission of the Kingdom of Nepal to the United Nations, 820 Second Ave., Suite 1200, New York, NY 10017, tel. 212–

370–4188; or Royal Nepalese Embassy, 2131 Leroy Pl. N.W., Washington DC 20008, tel. 202–667–4550. Canadians should contact the Royal Nepalese Consulate, 310 Dupont St., Toronto, Ont., tel. 416–968–7252. Britons should contact the Royal Nepalese Embassy, 12A Kensington Palace Gardens, London, W8 4QU, tel. 071–229–1594.

TOUR OPERATORS. No government tourist office exists outside Nepal. the Nepalese embassies and consulates have some free brochures on Nepal (see above).

General Interest Tours. To arrange for a car or jeep with driver or a general tour, contact the following reliable agencies:

Adventure Travel Nepal, a division of Tiger Tops, Box 3989, Durbar Marg, Kathmandu; tel. 223328.

Marco Polo Travels, Box 2769, White House, Kamal Pokhari, Kathmandu; tel. 413632.

Natraj Tours and Travels, Box 495, Ghantaghar, Durbar Marg, Kathmandu; tel. 222014.

Nepal Travel Agency, Ram Shah Path, Kathmandu; tel. 213106.

Yeti Travels, Box 76, Durbar Marg, Kathmandu; tel. 211234.

Special-Interest Tours. The following companies offer great outdoor adventures. Their guides are excellent; service is tops. All of them sponsor treks in the Annapurna, Everest, and Khumbu regions; some travel into the remote northeast and northwest. You can join a fixed-departure trip or let them custom design a vacation. Also see the list of special-interest tour operators in *Facts at Your Fingertips.* Make all arrangements before you depart.

Amadablam Trekking (Box 3035, Lazimpat, Kathmandu, tel. 410219) offers the standard routes, plus treks to Arun Valley in the east, and around Jumla and Rara Lake in the northwest. They also sponsor rafting runs on Tisuli, Sunkosi, Arun, and Karnali rivers, wildlife safaris in Royal Chitwan National Park, mountain climbing, and long distance mountain biking in the Terai.

Himalayan Horizons (Box 35, Pokhara [Airport], tel. 253) is the only trekking company that focuses exclusively on Pokhara Valley. It sponsors year-round nature treks, fishing treks, nature and culture treks for children, and treks for the disabled.

Himalayan Journeys (Box 989, Kantipath, Kathmandu, tel. 226138) is one of the best companies in Nepal. It does all the standard treks, including the long walk to Tibet, and is planning treks into eastern Nepal around Mount Kanchenjunga and to Dolpo in the northwest. If the Mustang Region in northern Nepal opens up to foreigners, the company is set to go.

Himalayan Mountain Bikes (Box 2769, Kamal Pokhari, Kathmandu, tel. 413632) offers three bike trips around Kathmandu Valley; trips connected with trekking in Pokhara Valley and Annapurna, Langtang National Park, and Everest; and trips into the Terai combined with jungle sararis and rafting or kyaking.

Himalayan River Exploration and Mountain Travel Nepal, part of Tiger Tops Nepal (Box 170, Kathmandu, tel. 414508), is the pioneer in Nepal rafting, trekking, mountaineering, and wildlife safaris. It sponsors all the standard treks and many theme-oriented or family treks. It arranges white-water runs on numerous rivers and safaris in its classy resorts at Royal Chitwan National Park and Royal Bardia Wildlife Reserve. It also offers a combination of biking, trekking, and rafting around Kathmandu Valley.

Pokhara Pony Trek (Box 35, Pokhara, tel. 253) is the only horseback riding outfit in Nepal. Its trips are exclusively in Pokhara Valley and range from a half-day excursion to a 50-day extensive valley tour.

Rapid Adventures Nepal (Box 3863, Thamel, Kathmandu, tel. 412480) offers excellent no-frills rafting excursions (great food and equipment—just no classy extras).

Treks and Expeditions Services (Box 3057, Corner House, Kamal Pokhari, Kathmandu, tel. 412231) offers all the standard treks and mountaineering, plus crafts, cultural, or participatory religious walks and tours around Kathmandu and Annapurna. It also offers high-quality "tea house" treks (all you need is a backpack) that patronize inns that respect the environment.

The *Nepal Mountaineering School,* run by Nepal Mountaineering Association (Ram Shah Path, Kathmandu, tel. 411525) has two excellent courses in mountaineering. Apply months in advance.

CLIMATE. The climate of Nepal varies according to season and elevation. October–April, the visibility is likely to be good for mountain viewing and the daytime climate in the valleys is mild, but nights can be cold November–March. Neither area receives snow, and the temperature rarely goes down to freezing. In the mountains, it can get extremely cold at night, but during the day it is usually comfortable in the sun.

From March onward, visibility gradually deteriorates until the monsoon, which usually lasts from early June to early October. Cloud cover is generally constant during this time, and rains can be torrential. Landslides and blocked roads frequently occur. In Kathmandu, winter temperatures can reach 68°F and summer temperatures, 86°F. The Terai region along the Indian border is warmer and more humid throughout the year. By March, temperatures in the Terai can reach 100°F.

WHEN TO GO. Nepal's peak season is September–December. Make all travel arrangements in advance. This season also coincides with two of the most popular festivals, Durga Puja and Indra Jatra. It's also high season for trekking. Unless you go to a remote area, you see many hikers. The best time to raft is September–June. The best time to visit Royal Chitwan National Park and Royal Bardia Wildlife Reserve is October–June.

HEALTH INFORMATION. Follow the same guidelines under this category in *Facts at Your Fingertips.* A valid international certificate of vaccination against yellow fever is required if you're arriving from certain countries in Africa and Central and South America.

HOW TO GET THERE. By Air. The best way to reach Kathmandu, the point of entry into Nepal, is by plane. Only *Royal Nepal Airline* (RNAC) and *Lufthansa* fly in to Tribhuvan International Airport from Europe (Frankfurt). Other flights originate in Asia: *Thai Airways* from Bangkok; *Singapore Airlines* from Singapore; *PIA* from Karachi in Pakistan; *Biman Bangladesh Airlines* from Dhaka; *Air India* and *Indian Airlines* from Calcutta and Delhi; *CAAC* (China) from Lhasa (April–November); *Dragon Air* from Hong Kong; *Druk Air* from Paro; *RNAC* from Bangkok, Delhi, Calcutta, Colombo in Sri Lanka, Dhaka, Dubai via Karachi, Hongkong, Rangoon in Burma, and Singapore. Reconfirm your ticket 72 hours before flight time. Arrive at the airport at least two hours before flight time. Planes are frequently overbooked.

By Overland. The **train** service from Calcutta to the border post of Raxaul requires several changes and stamina. **Bus** service is also available through India to the Nepalese border, including direct express links between Delhi or Patna and Kathmandu. The Indian-built mountain highway, from the Nepalese border town of Birganj (a Rs. 30 rickshaw ride from the Indian border at Raxaul) to Kathmandu is called the Tribhuvan Rajpath. Opened in 1956 and not carefully maintained since then, the Rajpath offers 258 km (160 mi.) of mountain driving hardly equaled anywhere else in the world. Taking eight hours by bus or taxi, the serpentine route hairpins up to a pass of 2,439 meters (8,000 ft.) before descending into the Kathmandu Valley. Most buses now take a longer, but much less hair-raising, route.

CUSTOMS ON ARRIVAL. On arrival foreigners must fill out a disembarkation card and declare all baggage. Visitors can bring in personal effects, 200 cigarettes or 20 cigars, bottle of distilled liquor or two bottles of beer, pair of binoculars, camera with 15 rolls of film, movie camera, video camera, Walkman, tape recorder, pocket calculator, portable typewriter, tent, sleeping bag, and backpack.

CUSTOMS ON DEPARTURE. Nepal will only reconvert 10% of the total amount of foreign currency cashed on presentation of an exchange receipt. Foreigners must fill out an embarkation card and pay Rs. 200 airport tax. Don't export antiques (over 100 years old), animal skins, loose precious stones, drugs, or weapons. Get a certificate or stamp from the Department of Archaeology (National Archives Building, Ram Shah Path, Kathmandu) for any reasonably old item and be prepared to show it on departure.

For information about customs on arrival in the United States, Canada, or Britain, follow the guidelines under this category in *Facts at Your Fingertips.*

AIRPORT-TO-TOWN TRANSPORTATION. The airport is eight km (five mi.) from Kathmandu. A couple of hotels provide courtesy airport service (see *Accommodations* below). An airport bus (tel. 521064 or 522144) shuttles between the airport, Sheraton Hotel, Blue Star Hotel, Yellow Pagoda Hotel, Hotel Woodland, New Road Gate, Thamel, Durbar Marg, and Singha Durbar. It runs daily 8 A.M.–10 P.M. and costs Rs. 15. A taxi to Kathmandu should cost Rs. 40.

TOURIST INFORMATION. The *Tourist Information Center* has a counter at the International Airport and an office on New Road, near Basantpur and Old Kathmandu, that is open Sunday–Thursday, 9 A.M.–5 P.M. and Friday till 4. Ask for a free copy of "Nepal Traveler," which has useful information and maps. In Pokhara, the tourist office, across from the airport, is open Sunday–Friday, 10 A.M.–5 P.M. Also visit Check List Service at the airport, same hours.

BEHAVIOR. Photography is generally allowed outside Buddhist and Hindu temples and at religious festivals; but ask before you photograph any artifacts inside. Many villagers are afraid of the camera, so ask before you take their pictures. In Nepal shoes are considered unclean. Remove them before you enter a Nepali house or temple. Also, it's discourteous to point your finger at a person or statue, to stand with your feet pointed at people or religious objects, or to sit in a situation that forces someone to step over you. In Kathmandu, beware of pickpockets. Watch your handbag, backpack, and camera, especially in crowded places.

BEGGING. Beggars are becoming much more common in tourist-visited areas of Nepal. Follow the guidelines under this category in *Facts at Your Fingertips.*

ACCOMMODATIONS. Though Kathmandu, Pokhara, and Royal Chitwan National Park offer a range of options, from Western-style hotels to budget lodges, there are few choices in other areas. In most Western-style hotels, rupees are accepted only on presentation of a foreign exchange receipt; otherwise, foreign nationals must pay their hotel bills with foreign currency, traveler's checks, or credit cards.

Prices are based on double occupancy: *Deluxe,* over Rs. 2,300 ($100); *Expensive,* Rs. 1,380–Rs. 2,300 ($60–$100); *Moderate,* Rs. 595–Rs. 1,380 ($25–$60); *Inexpensive,* under Rs. 595 ($25). These prices are based on an exchange rate of Rs. 23 to $1.

KATHMANDU

In the high season, reserve well in advance. For Hotel de L'Annapurna, book your room through the Taj Group of Hotels: in the United States, tel. 800–458–8825; in Britain, tel. 800–282669; or in Canada, tel. 212–972–6830 collect. For Yak & Yeti, contact Utell International in New York, tel. 800–448–8355, or in London, tel. 081–995–8211. For Soaltee Oberoi, call Oberoi in New York, tel. 212–223–3110, or 800–223–6800; in Canada, tel. 514–286–4056, 416–281–3491, or 800–341–8585; in London, tel. 071–583–3050.

Deluxe

Hotel de L'Annapurna. Durbar Marg, Kathmandu; tel. 221711. 159 air-conditioned rooms with bath. This old three-story hotel, newly acquired by the Taj chain, has a lovely lobby and offers excellent service. The rooms are spacious, but have no inspired decorative touches. The best rooms front the garden and a gorgeous pool. Amenities include restaurants, bar, room service, health club, pool, tennis and billiards, shopping arcade, foreign-exchange and travel counter, car-rental service. AE, DC, MC, V.

Soaltee Oberoi. Tahachal, Kathmandu; tel. 211211. 300 air-conditioned rooms with bath. On a ridge 15 minutes from Durbar Square, this Western-style hotel is decorated in attractive Newari style with lots of brick and wood trim. Rooms in the Himalayan Wing are large and lavish; rooms in the older Garden Wing are quieter but less spacious. Restaurants, bar, room service, baby-sitters, swimming pool, tennis court, health club, foreign-exchange and travel counter, car rental, shopping arcade, casino, courtesy bus to airport and Kathmandu. AE, DC, MC, V.

Yak & Yeti. Durbar Marg, Kathmandu; tel. 413999. 120 air-conditioned rooms with bath. This eighteenth century palace, with an additional new wing, is quiet and elegant. Rooms are attractively decorated with Newari carvings and brick and white stucco walls. Best rooms face the garden and pool. Restaurants, bar, room service, swimming pool, tennis court, health club, baby-sitters, shopping arcade, foreign-exchange and travel counter. AE, MC, V.

Expensive

Hotel Himalaya. Box 2141, Sahid Sukra Marg, Lalitpur (Patan), Kathmandu; tel. 523900. 94 air-conditioned rooms with bath. On a hill 10 minutes from Durbar Square, the Himalaya is modern and streamlined, with a marble interior that highlights an enclosed Japanese rock garden and sleek, understated decor in the rooms. Room service, restaurants, bar, free center-city shuttle service, foreign-exchange and travel counter, shopping arcade, swimming pool, tennis court. AE, MC, V.

Hotel Shangrila. Box 655, Lazimpat, Kathmandu; tel. 412999. 57 rooms with bath and air-conditioning. A handsome Newari hotel in the diplomatic enclave, the decor here has lots of brick, stucco, and wood trim. The best rooms overlook a lovely garden. Room service, air-conditioning, restaurants, bar, free airport and center-city shuttle service, foreign-exchange and travel counter, shopping arcade. AE, MC, V.

Hotel Shanker. Box 350, Lazimpat, Kathmandu; tel. 410151. 94 air-conditioned rooms with bath. The nineteenth-century former palace and birthplace of the present queen, the Shanker is opulent, with numerous attractive sitting rooms—some evoke Versailles, others are traditional Nepalese with brick-and-wood trim. A few bedrooms have painted ceilings and other rococo touches. The garden and enormous front lawn are ideal for relaxing. The downside: In peak season, service can be indifferent; don't hesitate to complain. Room service, restaurants, bar, travel and foreign-exchange counter, shopping arcade, swimming pool. AE, DC, MC, V.

Moderate

Dwarika's Kathmandu Village Hotel. Box 659, Battisputali, Kathmandu; tel. 414770. 12 rooms with bath. The only hotel in Nepal to have received the coveted Pacific Area Travel Association Heritage Award for cultural conservation efforts, this hotel is in a shady compound with brick terraces; each room has carved antique windows and traditional furnishings. One drawback: The heating is not great. Dining room, library, bar, foreign-exchange and travel counter. Traveler's checks.

Summit Hotel. Box 1406, Kupondole Height, Kathmandu; tel. 521894. 37 rooms with bath. About three km (two mi.) from Durbar Square, this popular two-story hotel is quiet and charming with lovely gardens and lawns and excellent views of the mountains and valley. The cheery rooms have traditional touches—the best ones are upstairs overlooking the lawn and swimming pool. The management is very competent. Room service, air-conditioning, swimming pool, restaurant, bike rentals, bar, foreign-exchange and travel counter. AE, V.

Inexpensive

Hotel Ambassador. Box 2769, Lazimpat, Kathmandu; tel. 410432. 34 rooms with bath. Recently renovated, this old hotel is in a quiet location near Thamel. The air-conditioned rooms have a minimal decor but are clean. Restaurants, bar, room service, foreign-exchange and travel counter, gift shop, bike rentals. AE.

Kathmandu Guest Hotel and Maya Apartments. Thamel, Kathmandu; tel. 413632. 104 rooms with bath. This 25-year-old Kathmandu institution caters to the traveler on a tight budget. The best rooms in the newer Maya Apartments are upstairs with a veranda that overlooks a spacious lawn and garden. Lower-price rooms in the older wing are simpler, without air-conditioning or room service. Reserve well in advance. No smoking is allowed. Air-conditioning in some rooms, kitchen facilities, restaurant, roof-top garden, foreign-exchange and travel counter, car-rental service. AE.

Tibet Guest House. Box 1132, Chhetrapati, Thamel; tel. 214383. 37 rooms with bath. This three-story hotel has a Tibetan ambience and helpful management. The rooms are plain with adequate, clean furnishings; tubs available. Room service; fans; roof garden; bike, motorbike, and car rental; travel counter. Rupees only.

POKHARA

Deluxe

Pokhara Mountain Lodge. Tiger Tops, Box 242, Durbar Marg, Kathmandu; tel. 222706, or through their offices based abroad (see *Tour Operators* in *Facts at Your Fingertips*). At press time, Tiger Tops was constructing a Gurung-style village on a ridge east of Pokhara. Projected opening was late 1990. The resort will offer the amenities of other excellent Tiger Tops facilities.

Moderate

Dragon Hotel. Box 15, Pardi, Lake Side, Pokhara; tel. 20391. 22 rooms with bath. In a quiet neighborhood away from the lake and center of town, modest Dragon Hotel is impeccable; the service is excellent and rooms are very clean. There are great views of the mountains from the roof terrace. Restaurant, bar, room service, cultural performances in season, car rental, foreign-exchange and travel counter. Rupees only.

Fishtail Lodge. Box 10, Pokhara; tel. 20071, or reserve through Hotel de L'Annapurna in Kathmandu or Utell International (addresses above). 50 rooms with bath. Space-age–style Fishtail Lodge is secluded in landscaped gardens on Phewa Lake island. The rooms are in modular units; the best ones have mountain views. Air-conditioning or fans, restaurant, bar, cultural programs in season, travel and foreign-exchange counter. AE, DC, MC, V.

Pokhara View Point. Reserve through Dragon Hotel (see above). About 4 cottages with bath. On a mountain spur about 15 minutes from the airport, this complex under construction at press time (projected opening late 1990), will offer privacy and stunning views, plus a chance to stay in a clay-and-wood Gorkha-style cottage. Meals will include home-grown vegetables from the surrounding garden, other amenities. Rupees only.

Inexpensive

Gurka Lodge. Lakeside, Pokhara; no phone. 3 rooms with bath. Hidden on an interior lane, this charming lodge in a lush garden takes a bit of searching for. You're likely to be greeted by a water buffalo outside the gate. Clean, sparsely furnished rooms are in idyllic thatched cottages. Restaurant serves simple but good meals. Rupees only.

ROYAL CHITWAN NATIONAL PARK

Rates include full board, with a fixed, multicuisine menu; elephant safaris; nature walks; bird-watching; canoeing; and jeep rides. All lodges have bars, but drinks are extra. Exceptions or additions are noted.

Deluxe

Chitwan Jungle Lodge. Box 1281, Durbar Marg, Kathmandu; tel. 410918. 22 huts. Nine km (six mi.) inside the park and four km (2½ mi.) from the Rapti River, this lodge offers a popular two-night package to road travelers from Kathmandu or Pokhara for about $225 per person. You can also raft a day for an additional $50 per person. You stay in a thatched clay hut with attractive furnishings and an attached bathroom. You can swim in the nearby river. At night, you eat in a round house and can attend lectures by naturalists or watch cultural programs. Open September–May. AE.

Hotel Elephant Camp. Box 78, Durbar Marg, Kathmandu; tel. 213976. About 12 cottages. At the edge of the park by the Rapti River, this modest resort has great service and a pleasant ambience. Individual thatched cottages with attached bathroom are nicely decorated. The National Park Museum and its park elephants are nearby. You're also close to Thrau villages. Elephant Camp offers two three-day packages: by road from Kathmandu or with a day of rafting. Summer discount. Rupees only.

Gaida Wildlife Camp. Box 2056, Durbar Marg, Kathmandu; tel. 220940. 20 rooms; 10 tents. Also in the park, Gaida has cottages and tents. Each thatched cottage has two double rooms (each with an attached bathroom) and a veranda overlooking the Dungla River. The nearby lodge serves good food; the bar is well stocked. At night, you can attend cultural programs and wildlife lectures. Safari-style tents (cheaper), with shared bathrooms, are farther in the jungle. Gaida offers a three-day package or a four-day package that includes one day of rafting. Open year-round. AE, DC.

Machan Wildlife Resort. Box 3140, Durbar Marg, Kathmandu; tel. 222823. 15 rooms, 10 tents. You can stay in a shady grove in a mud-and-timber cottage (attached bathroom) near an attractive lodge and small swimming pool or go deeper into the park and stay in a safari-style tent (cheaper), with shared bathroom, and eat your meals around a campfire. Machan offers the three-day package by road, with an extra day of rafting. Open year-round. Summer discount. AE.

Tiger Tops Royal Chitwan. Box 242, Durbar Marg, Kathmandu; tel. 222706 or through their offices based abroad (see *Tour Operators* under *Facts at Your Fingertips*). 20 rooms in the lodge, 10 tents, 12 rooms at Tharu. Set deep within the park, Tiger Tops is the class act in Chitwan. You can stay in attractive rooms with attached bathrooms at the Jungle Lodge. (The best views are on the upper floor.) Or stay in an island-based fancy safari-style tent with shared bathrooms. Also available is a typical mud hut in Tharu Village, just outside the park, where you can see Tharu cultural programs, observe the Tharu lifestyle, and enjoy a new swimming pool. You can also design a package that includes all three. Tiger Tops offers two special packages: a three-day deluxe rafting trip down to Chitwan (October–May); a five-day excursion with two days of rafting, two days at Tharu, and a trip to Lumbini (May–September). It also offers a three-day package from Kathmandu (by car or plane) and will make pick-ups from Pokhara. Reserve well in advance. Camp and lodge are closed mid-June–mid-September. AE.

ROYAL BARDIA WILDLIFE RESERVE

Rates include full board, park activities, and taxes, but not alcoholic drinks or service charges.

Deluxe

Tiger Tops Karnali Lodge and Tented Camp. Box 242, Durbar Marg, Kathmandu; tel. 222706 or reserve through the Tiger Tops offices abroad. 10 rooms in the lodge, 14 tents. The lodge is on a grassy plain outside the jungle. The rooms have an attractive ethnic-style decor; and the attached bathrooms are modern. Tucked in the forest and overlooking the Karnali River, the tented camp (cheaper) has secluded safari-style tents with shared bathrooms. In either facility, you can go on nature walks, ride a jeep or an elephant, embark on a river cruise, visit Tharu villages, and go fishing. AE.

OTHER DESTINATIONS

Expensive

Dhulikhel Mountain Resort. Box 3203, Durbar Marg, Kathmandu; tel. 220031. 26 rooms with attached bathrooms. Extremely appealing thatched cottages (two double rooms in each) are perched on a Himalayan foothill and have mountain views or overlook lovely gardens and lawns. Rooms are attractive, but there's no electricity—only candlelight, a romantic touch. Amenities include multicuisine restaurant; bar; cultural programs on request; and trekking, camping, and rafting arrangements. Meals are included. AE.

DINING OUT. The standard fare is Nepali (not quite as spicy as Indian cuisine) and Tibetan (with lots of noodle and dumpling dishes). Dinner is usually served early, even in Kathmandu. Many restaurants shut down by 10 P.M. Breakfast is usually served from 8–10:30; lunch is usually noon–3; and dinner, 7:30–10. Payment is normally in rupees unless the restaurant is connected to a Western-style hotel. The restaurants listed below are informal and unless noted are open for all three meals and don't require reservations. Prices, based on one person eating a three-course meal, excluding taxes, tip, or beverage, are *Expensive,* over Rs. 230; *Moderate,* Rs. 115–Rs. 230; *Inexpensive,* under Rs. 115.

KATHMANDU

Kathmandu's restaurants offer a wide range of international cuisines and ambiences. Local and imported liquors are available.

Indian and Nepalese

Expensive

Himalchuli. Soaltee Oberoi, Tahachal; tel. 211211. Himalchuli is dark and intimate, with Nepalese cultural performances every night except Tuesday and delicious Kathmandu specialties. Dinner reservations advised. Open 12:30–2:30 P.M., 7–11. AE, DC, MC, V.

Naachghar. Yak & Yeti Hotel, Durbar Marg; tel. 413999. A formal restaurant set in a neo-Grecian palace, Naachghar has Italian marble floors, pink walls with ornate plaster moldings, Belgian chandeliers, and a painted ceiling. Nepalese classical music and Indian *ghazals* are performed evenings except Sunday and accompany traditional specialties, including *banel tareko* (fried wild boar), *charako achhar* (shredded marinated chicken), *hansko sekua* (grilled marinated duck), and *dhukur tareko* (grilled marinated dove). Dinner reservations advised. Open 12:30–2:30 P.M., 7–10:30. AE, MC, V.

Moderate

Ghar-E-Kabob. Hotel de L'Annapurna, Durbar Marg; tel. 221711. Above a coffee shop, Ghar-E-Kabob has a Mogul decor with miniatures on the wall and ghazels performed nightly except Thursday. The accent is on the food, which many claim is the best north Indian and Nepalese in Kathmandu. Dinner reservations advised. Open noon–3 P.M., 7–11. AE, DC, MC, V.

Inexpensive

Greenlands Vegetarian Restaurant. Woodland's Hotel, Durbar Marg; tel. 220123. Don't be put off by the coffee-shop look, the food is great—north and south Indian vegetarian, with especially good *dosa* (vegetable-filled crêpe) and *thalis* (small portions of various dishes). Open 8 A.M.–10 P.M. Rupees only.

Nepalese and Tibetan

Moderate

Sunkosi. Durbar Marg; tel. 215299 or 220299. Very popular, Sunkosi is cozy, with brick walls and wood trim, and serves excellent dishes. Try *cherako sekwa* (grilled chicken), *kalejo sandeko* (mildly spicy liver), or *golbheda bari* (lamb meatballs). The chef also prepares an excellent Tibetan *gyakok* for two (pork, prawns, fish, bean curd, egg, meatballs, and vegetables), which you must order in advance. Don't miss the famous dessert—*sikarni* (spicy whipped yogurt). Dinner reservations advised. Open 11 A.M.–10 P.M. AE.

Chinese and Tibetan

Moderate

Arniko Room. Hotel de L'Annapurna, Durbar Marg; tel. 221711. Done up in understated Chinese decor, Arniko has excellent spring rolls, fried prawns, and fried spicy bean curd. Dinner reservations advised. Open noon–3 P.M., 7–11. AE, DC, MC, V.

Golden Gate Restaurant. Durbar Marg, opposite Indonesian Bank; tel. 223705. In this upstairs restaurant with flamboyant Chinese decor, enjoy nonspicy Beijing and Cantonese and spicy Szechuan specialties. Dinner reservations advised. Open 12:30–2:30 P.M., 6:30–10:30. AE, DC.

Inexpensive

Ras Rang. Across from Hotel Ambassador, Lazimpat, Kathmandu; tel. 410432. Eat in its cozy Newari interior with a large brass fireplace or outside on the lawn. Choose from good Hakka, Cantonese, and Szechuan specialties. Dinner reservations advised. Open 12:30–3 P.M., 5–10:30. AE.

Utse Restaurant and Bar. 16/101 Thamel; tel. 412747. Laid-back Utse serves excellent Chinese and Tibetan food. Sit for hours; no one minds. Open 10–10. Rupees only.

Japanese

Inexpensive–Moderate

Fuji Restaurant. Kantipath, across from the American Embassy; tel. 225272. Set back from the road, this restaurant, in an old brick palace, is approached via a wood foot bridge over a pond. Eat inside at a table, on cushions, on the veranda, in the garden, or at the counter. Try a *teppan* dish (grilled beef or chicken with vegetables) or *sanma* (grilled fish) or *aji* (roast mackerel). Dinner reservations advised. Open 10–10. Rupees only.

Continental

Expensive

Chimney. Yak & Yeti Hotel, Durbar Marg; tel. 413999. Inside a former palace, Chimney has an après-ski lodge decor with an enormous copper fireplace. Its multicuisine menu emphasizes Russian dishes. Dinner reservations advised. Open 6:30–11 P.M. AE, MC, V.

Moderate

Coppers. Kaisermahal, Thamel; no phone. Under construction at press time, this fancy restaurant will feature imported Western specialties—eggs Benedict, steak-and-kidney pie, patés—and have a separate deli providing Western-style sandwiches to go. Open 7 A.M.–10:30 P.M.

Kokonor. Hotel Shangrila, Lazimpat; tel. 412999. Decorated in traditional Newari decor, Kokonor serves the best fish dishes in Kathmandu and good mixed grills. Indian and Nepalese classical music is performed nightly except Wednesday. Dinner reservations advised. Open noon–2:30 P.M., 7–10. AE, MC, V.

Rumdoodle. Thamel, not far from Kathmandu Guest House; no phone. This famous place, with the best bar in town and good food, has a super casual "mountaineering" motif. Tents hang from the ceiling. Walls have yeti "footprints" autographed by the Himalayan greats—Sir Edmund Hillary and Reinhold Messner. It's usually crowded in season. Open 8–10 A.M., 1–3 P.M., 5–10; closed Tuesday. AE, V.

POKHARA

All restaurants are casual and serve multicuisine, unless noted. From October to March, make dinner reservations.

Moderate

Fishtail Restaurant. Fishtail Lodge; tel. 20071. Fishtail is cozy, with a fireplace in the middle of a circular room. The bar is nearby. Though waiters push the fixed menu, you can also eat à la carte. Open 7–9:30 A.M., noon–2 P.M., 7–9:30. AE, DC, MC, V.

Flying Dragon Restaurant. Hotel Mount Annapurna; tel. 20027. Bright and cheery, Flying Dragon has Tibetan frescoes on the wall. Open 6–10 A.M., 11 A.M.–1 P.M., 6–9:30. AE.

New Crystal Restaurant. Nagdhunga; tel. 211932. On the second floor of the hotel, this handsome restaurant serves good mixed grill, chicken butter marsala (chicken in a spicy tomato sauce), and mixed vegetable curry. Open 7–9:30 A.M., noon–2:30 P.M., 7–9:30. AE, DC, MC, V.

Solo. Dragon Hotel, Pardi; tel. 20391. Solo is unpretentious, with a few antique Buddhist urns, thang-kas (paintings with a Buddhist theme), and good views of the mountains. Try the tasty soups and curries. Open 7–10 A.M., noon–3 P.M., 6–10. Rupees only.

Inexpensive

Himalchuli Restaurant. Pardi Damside, Phewa Lake; tel. 20189. In a spacious *khar ko jhupadi* (thatched hut), Himalchuli is informal and its menu is hearty international fare, including pizza and Mexican cuisine. Open September–June, 5:30 A.M.–11 P.M.; otherwise 7 A.M.–10 P.M. AE, V.

New Om Restaurant and Bar. Chhetrapati; tel. 212224. A spacious restaurant with an understated Tibetan decor, New Om serves excellent Chinese and Tibetan dishes, especially good *momo* (fried dumplings). Open 8 A.M.–10 P.M. Rupees only.

SWEETS AND TREATS. In Kathmandu, stop at *Helena's* (Thamel) for apple pie, brownies, or cappuccino, open daily 8 A.M.–10 P.M.; or *Pizzeria La Cimbali* (Thahity Kwabahal, Thamel), open daily 9 A.M.–10 P.M. For ice cream, go to *Nirula's* (Durbar Marg), open daily 10 A.M.–10:30 P.M.

At *Cafe de Patan* (Block No. 14/83, Mahapa Tole, Patan) open daily 8 A.M.–9 P.M., enjoy multicuisine snacks in a quiet garden.

Relax at *Cafe Nyatapola* (in the middle of Taumadhi Tole, Bhaktapur) and have a light snack. Open daily 9–9.

HOW TO GET AROUND. Roads are subject to landslides and washouts in much of Nepal. If you plan to trek in remote northern areas, fly to the nearest airport or airstrip. If you plan to visit Pokhara Valley or the Royal Chitwan National Park and Lumbini, you can fly or go by road, even in the monsoon when landslides occur, but it can be slow going. For the Royal Bardia Wildlife Reserve in the western Terai, you should fly to Nepalgunj, then plan for a five-hour trip by road.

By Air. From the domestic terminal near Tribhuvan International Airport, *RNAC* (Kantipath, tel. 220757 or 214491) flies to Pokhara (two flights daily); Nepalgunj—approach to Royal Bardia Wildlife Reserve (over 10 weekly flights); Bhairawa—approach to Lumbini (daily flight); Maghauli—approach to Royal Chitwan National Park (daily); Tumlingtar—approach to Arun River (five weekly flights); Jumla (two weekly winter flights); Jomsom, north of Annapurna (one weekly winter flight); Lukla, near Everest and Khumbu (three daily winter flights; year-round flights under consideration); Taplejung—approach to Mount Kanchenjunga (two weekly winter flights). RNAC also arranges numerous charters, including one to Langtang, north of Kathmandu. Book all flights early. Reconfirm at least 72 hours before departure and arrive at the airport 90 minutes in advance.

RNAC offers a 25% discount to students with a valid International Student Identity Card. Some fares are lower during the monsoon. Check with your tour operator. For domestic flights you must also pay Rs. 25 airport tax.

By Train. No trains exist in Nepal.

By Bus. The most expensive luxury buses (leather seats) are cheap and they go virtually to any spot accessible by road; but they tend to be slow, crowded, and uncomfortable. Definitely for the hardened traveler only.

By Rented Car with Driver. Major road routes include the Tribhuvan Rajpath, 258 km (160 mi.) from Kathmandu to Birganj on the Indian border; the Prithvi Rajpath, 257 km (159 mi.) from Kathmandu to Pokhara; the Arniko Highway, 104 km (64 mi.) from Kathmandu north to Kodari on the Tibetan border; the Mugling Narayanghat Highway, 161 km (100 mi.) from Kathmandu to Chitwan National Park. Distances along these roads can be deceptive; the 257-km journey from Kathmandu to Pokhara can take six hours.

The cost of a car with driver is determined by the destination and length of stay. For excursions around Kathmandu figure about Rs. 600 ($26) for three hours or 60 km (37 mi.) round-trip. A two-night excursion from Kathmandu to Pokhara costs about Rs. 4,025 ($175); an overnight excursion from Kathmandu to Lumbini costs about Rs. 3,680 ($160); a day excursion to the Tibetan border costs about Rs. 1,840 ($80). Only hire a car or jeep with driver from a recommended tour operator and make all arrangements before you depart during the high season.

By Taxi. Taxis, with black-and-white license plates, are inconvenient in Old Kathmandu. At night, the fare is doubled. For longer excursions, insist the driver use the meter or fix the fare beforehand. A taxi should cost about Rs. 1,035 ($45) per day.

By Rickshaw. A better option for the old city, *tempo* (auto rickshaw) rides should be cheaper than taxi rides. Bicycle rickshaw is a wonderful way to travel through Kathmandu and other cities; it should be cheaper than a tempo.

By Bicycle. Bicycling is the nicest way to get around Kathmandu and Pokhara. Many recommended hotels rent bicycles. Shops in Kathmandu (Freak Street and Thamel) and in Pokhara rent bikes. Rates are about Rs. 10 per day.

TOUR-GUIDE SERVICES. The recommended tour operators conduct half-day tours by car, mini-bus, or bus to Bhaktapur (Bhadgaon), Pashupatinath and Boud-hanath, Kathmandu City, Patan (Lalitpur), and Swayambunath; morning tours to Dakshin Kali; and overnight trips to Dhulikhel for a good view of the sunrise and sunset over the Himalayas. During the peak season, book your tour as soon as you arrive. These same operators can supply excellent guides.

Royal Nepal Airlines offers a morning "Mountain Flight" that provides a close-up view of Mount Everest and other peaks. The one-hour flight runs twice daily September–May; every other day, weather permitting, the rest of the year. The cost is Rs. 1,725 ($75) plus Rs. 30 ($1.30) airport tax. Arrange your flight through a tour operator or directly through RNAC on Kantipath.

TOURING ITINERARIES. Because it is a small country, Nepal can easily be seen in one to two weeks. During the busy tourist season of October and November, it is wise to have confirmed hotel reservations. At other times, it is easy to make arrangements once you have arrived in the country.

One-Week Tour

Day 1. Sightseeing in Kathmandu; evening cultural program.

Day 2. Mountain flight or sunrise excursion to see the Himalayas; see Patan's Durbar Square, Tibetan Refugee Center, handicrafts center, and Swayambunath Stupa in the afternoon.

Day 3. Visit Dakshinkali, Shesh Narayan, Chobar Gorge and Kirtipur in the morning; the restored city of Bhaktapur, Boudhanath Stupa, and Pashupatinath in the afternoon.

Day 4. Travel to Chitwan National Park for a jungle safari.

Day 5. Elephant rides, dugout canoe trip, nature walks, bird-watching in the park.

Day 6. Travel to Pokhara; take an afternoon boat ride on Phewa Lake.

Day 7. Get up early to see the sunrise over the Himalayas, tour Pokhara, and return to Kathmandu in the afternoon.

Two-Week Tour

Day 1. Sightseeing in Kathmandu; evening cultural program.

Day 2. Morning mountain flight to view the Himalayas; see Patan's Durbar Square, Tibetan Refugee Camp, handicrafts center, and Swayambunath Stupa in the afternoon.

Day 3. Trip by car to the Chinese road on the spectacular Kodari Highway.

Day 4. Visit the restored city of Bhaktapur in the morning; travel to Dhulikel or Nagarkot for sunset over the Himalayas and spend the night.

Day 5. Sunrise over the Himalayas; visit Changu Narayan Temple on the way back to Kathmandu; see Boudhanath Stupa and Pashupatinath in the afternoon.

Day 6. Visit Dakshinkali, Shesh Narayan, Chobar Gorge and Kirtipur in the morning; in the afternoon, visit Budhanilkantha Temple.

Day 7. Raft trip down the Trisuli River; spend the night camping beside the river.

Day 8. Go to the Royal Chitwan National Park for a jungle safari and take an elephant ride through the jungle.

Day 9. Elephant rides, canoes rides, nature walks, bird-watching.

Day 10. Travel to Pokhara, take an afternoon boat ride on Phewa Lake, and see the sunset over the Himalayas.

Day 11. See the sunrise over the mountains and the sights in Pokhara in the morning; relax by the lake in the afternoon.

Day 12. Take a day hike or pony trip through the foothills outside Pokhara; visit old villages.

Day 13. Travel to Lumbini, birthplace of the Buddha.
Day 14. Return to Kathmandu.
Three-Week Tour
Same as the two-week tour but spend one week trekking.

TIPPING. Major hotels usually add a 10 percent service charge to the bill, so tipping the many employees who have been seeing to your needs is not necessary. However, if you wish to tip bellhops, Rs. 5–Rs. 10 is usually sufficient. In first-class restaurants, if the service and food were particularly good, a 5–10 percent tip is acceptable. It is not necessary to tip taxi drivers.

TIME. Nepalese time is 5 hours 45 minutes ahead of Greenwich Mean Time, noon in London being 5:45 P.M. in Nepal. Nepal is 15 minutes ahead of Indian Standard Time.

MAIL AND TELECOMMUNICATIONS. The General Post Office on Kantipath in Kathmandu is open in winter, 10 A.M.–4 P.M.; summer, till 5 P.M., closed Saturday and government holidays. Nearby is the Central Telegraph Office, open the same hours as the post office, with international telephone, cable, and telex facilities. Leading hotels and travel agents also have telex facilities. You can also place international calls from many Western-style hotels. Just expect to pay a service charge.

An airmail postcard costs Rs. 4 to America or Europe. A 20-gram airmail letter to America costs Rs. 8 and to Europe, Rs. 7. All aerograms and postcards cost Rs. 5. It is easiest to buy stamps at your hotel desk and place your cards and letters in the post box provided. Cards and letters, although they take a while to reach their destination, usually do go through. However, it is a better idea to carry souvenirs home rather than have them mailed. Mailing packages yourself from the special foreign post office can be a tedious, time-consuming, and aggravating experience and is best avoided. There are shipping companies that can package and forward any large items for you. *Sharmasons* is one of the most reliable shipping agencies.

BUSINESS HOURS. Most commercial shops (not necessarily including bazaars) and government offices are closed Saturday, the national day off, and government holidays. Government offices and museums are open 10 A.M.–5 P.M., February–November, and till 4 P.M. the rest of the year. Banks are open Sunday–Thursday, 10 A.M.–3 P.M.; Friday, till noon. Nepal Bank on Kantipath is also open Saturday, 9 A.M.–1 P.M., but is closed on Sunday.

All major hotels have money exchange counters that are open every day. In addition, two exchange bank counters in Kathmandu are open every day of the year: *Rastriya Banijya Supermarket Branch,* New Road, 10 A.M.–5 P.M. and *Rastriya Banijya Thamel Branch,* Thamel, 7:30 A.M.–7 P.M.

ELECTRICITY. Electric voltage is 220, 50 cycles. If you have appliances that adapt to this voltage, bring converters with two-pin round-headed plugs.

USEFUL ADDRESSES AND PHONE NUMBERS. The police telephone number (emergencies) is 226998 in Kathmandu. But when you need help, it is best to contact the management of your hotel first because few of Nepal's police officers speak English.

Tourist Information Center, Gangapath, tel. 220818.
Central Immigration, Maiti Devi, tel. 412337.
American Embassy, Pani Pokhari, tel. 411179, 412718.
British Embassy, Lainchaur, tel. 414588, 411789.
Indian Embassy, Lainchaur, tel. 410900, ext 230.
Air India, Kantipath, tel. 212335.
Biman Bangladesh Airlines, Durbar Marg, tel. 222544.
British Airways, Durbar Marg, tel. 222266.
Burma Airways, Durbar Marg, tel. 224839.
Royal Nepal Airlines, New Road, tel. 220757.
Thai International Airways, Durbar Marg, tel. 223565.

HISTORIC SITES. Entrance to most places is generally free; where a donation is asked, a few rupees will suffice.

KATHMANDU VALLEY

Bhaktapur. The following architectural sites are open daily sunrise–sunset: Royal Palace with its Golden Gate and famous carved windows, Taleju Bhawani Temple, Batsala Temple, Pashupatinath Temple, Nyatapola Temple, Bhairav Temple, Pujari Math Monastery with its beautiful Peacock Windows, and Dattatreya Temple.

Boudanath Stupa. Built in the seventh century, this is the most important Tibetan Buddhist center outside Tibet. Open daily sunrise–sunset.

Changu Narayan. This beautiful Hindu temple complex contains the oldest architecture in the valley.

Dashin Kali. At this Hindu temple, dedicated to Kali (goddess of wrath), spiritually intense sacrifices take place on Tuesday and Saturday mornings.

Kathmandu. The following architectural sites, on or near Durbar Square, are open daily sunrise–sunset unless noted: Kasthamandap Temple, Maru Ganesh Temple, Kumari Bahal (home of the Living Goddess), Gaddi Baithak (closed to the public), Maju Deval Temple, Shiva Parvati Temple, Royal Palace with its Golden Door, numerous interior squares (some closed to foreigners), and Basantapur Tower; Jagannath Temple, Seto Bhairav mask, Kalo Bhairav bas-relief, Taleju Temple (closed to foreigners), and Krishna Mandir Temple. On Indra Chowk are the Akash Bhairav Temple and Seto Macchendranath Temple. On Asan Tole are the Annapurna Temple, Ganesh Temple, Narayan Temple, and Uma Maheshwara Temple. Near the Tundikhel parade grounds are Kalmochan Temple, Tripureshwar Mahadev Temple, and Singha Durbar (closed to the public).

Pashupatinath. The most sacred Hindu temple in Nepal, it's closed to non-Hindus, but you can get an excellent view of it from across the river.

Patan. The following architectural sites are open daily sunrise–sunset: Krishna Mandir, Royal Palace with its Golden Gate, Taleju Bhawani Temple, Royal Bath, and Krishna Temple; Hari Shankar Temple, Char Narayan Temple, Khumbeshwar Temple, Rato Macchendranath, Minanath Temple, Mahabouddha Temple, and Hiranya Varna Mahavihara Monastery.

Swayambunath Stupa. At this complex, open daily sunrise–sunset, try to see a Buddhist ceremony. Inquire at the tourist office for hours.

LUMBINI

Lumbini, the birthplace of Siddhartha Gautama (the Historic Buddha), has numerous excavated ruins and contemporary monasteries attached to this important Buddhist pilgrimage site. Open daily sunrise–sunset.

FESTIVALS AND SEASONAL EVENTS. Nepal is a land of festivals. Hardly a day passes without the celebration of a festival somewhere in the kingdom. The Nepalese are devoutly religious, and their numerous Hindu and Buddhist deities are the focus of most of their events. Since the lunar calendar determines the dates for many events, check with the embassy or your travel agent for details.

February. *Shivaratri* is one of Nepal's most important festivals and, as the name implies, it is dedicated to the god Shiva. Hundreds of thousands of Hindus from Nepal and India make the pilgrimage to worship at Pashupatinath Temple in Kathmandu. There is much feasting and ritual bathing in the holy Bagmati River.

February. *Sri Panchami* is the first day of spring, according to the Nepalese calendar, and it is also a day for honoring Saraswati, the Hindu goddess of learning. Students all over the Kathmandu Valley visit shrines dedicated to Saraswati. In the morning, the Saraswati Temple at Swayambunath is a particularly good place to observe students worshiping.

February/March. *Losar* (Tibetan New Year) is a big event at Boudanath Stupa in Kathmandu. Tibetans who have spent the winter here hold festivities before making the long trip back to Tibet. Tibetans and Sherpas perform folk songs and dances.

February/March. During *Holi Purnima,* people throw colored water on each other. There is much laughter and fun, but it can get messy. Watch your camera and clothes.

April. *Chaitra Dasain,* for the goddess Durga, is celebrated with animal sacrifices. Dasain is held again in October with many more festivities.

April. *Bisket Jatra* is the biggest festival in Bhaktapur and falls on the Nepalese New Year. A week of celebration includes chariot processions, feasting, and the ceremonial raising of a huge wooden pole.

April 13. *Nava Barsha (Nepalese New Year)* a national holiday, is celebrated with much music and dancing.

April. During *Seth Macchendranath Rath Jatra,* a tall spire of green foliage is mounted on a huge chariot bearing the image of the White Machhendranath and pulled through the old sections of Kathmandu for four days. This festival is celebrated by Hindus and Buddhists alike.

April. *Red Machhendranath Jatra,* is Patan's biggest festival and is similar to the celebration of the White Machhendranath in Kathmandu. A large chariot is pulled through the city for several days.

May. *Buddha Jayanti,* which falls on the full moon, honors the Buddha's birth, enlightenment, and death are celebrated at Buddhist shrines throughout Nepal. In Lumbini, the birthplace of Buddha, there is a special fair. In the Kathmandu Valley, Swayambunath Stupa is the best place to observe the festivities.

August. *Gai Jatra,* a carnival-type festival, lasts for eight days, during which time cows and teenagers dressed as cows parade through the streets. Gaijatra is meant to help family members who have died during the year complete a smooth trip to heaven. Cows are believed to be helpful in this journey. Dancing, singing, and humorous performances satirizing current sociopolitical situations are all part of this festival.

September. *Krishna Jayanti* honors the birthday of Krishna, an incarnation of the god Vishnu. Celebrations are held at the Krishna Mandir in Patan and at Changu Narayan Temple east of Kathmandu. There is a procession through the streets of Patan, as well as singing and dancing. It is also a day of fasting.

September. *Teej* is a women's festival during which Hindu women in Kathmandu visit Pashupatinath Temple to worship Shiva and Parvati. Ritual bathing in the sacred Bagmati River is meant to wash away all the sins of the past year.

September. *Indra Jatra,* which lasts for eight days, is dedicated to Indra, the Hindu god of rain. Masked dancers perform nightly in Kathmandu's Hanuman Dhoka Square, and the huge mask of the White Bhairav is displayed for the only time during the year. The king visits the Kumari, Nepal's living goddess, before she is paraded through the old city in an ornate chariot. Several other chariots are also pulled through the streets of old Kathmandu.

October. *Bada Dasain (Durga Puja),* Nepal's most important festival, lasts 10–15 days. Celebrated at the end of the monsoon season, Bada Dasain is dedicated to the goddess Durga and the triumph of good over evil. In Hanuman Dhoka Square, there are many bloody animal sacrifices to Durga. In rural villages, giant swings are set up for the children.

November. *Tihar (Lakshmi Puja)* is a five-day festival marked by the worship of different animals, including crows, dogs, and cows. Lakshmi, the goddess of wealth, is also worshiped, and, on one day of the festival, thousands of tiny butter lamps line the streets as each household welcomes the goddess.

November. *Mani Rimdu.* Celebrated most enthusiastically in Namche Bazaar, this Sherpa festival features masked lamas performing traditional dances in the courtyards of monasteries throughout the region near Mount Everest.

December 28. *Shri Panch Ko Janma Divas* honors the birthday of the present king with a huge parade, fireworks, and many other festivities. At the main rally on the Tundikhel parade grounds in Kathmandu, groups of people from all over the country dress in their traditional costumes and perform songs and dances.

MUSEUMS, GALLERIES, AND LIBRARIES. The *National Museum* (tel. 211504), just west of Kathmandu near Swayambunath Stupa, has an interesting collection of artwork dating back to the fifth century. Stone statues of gods and goddesses display the skill of the early Lichhavis. Bronzes, wood carvings, religious paintings, and beautifully illustrated old books are among the displays in the art gallery. Another wing of the museum contains natural science displays and an arms and armor display. There is also a memorial museum dedicated to the late King Mahendra. The museum is open every day except Tuesday, 10 A.M.–4 P.M. in winter and 10 A.M.–5 P.M. the rest of the year. The entrance fee is Rs. 3 and Rs. 8 if you carry a camera.

The *Tribhuvan Museum* (tel. 212294), devoted to the life of former King Tribhuvan, and a numismatic collection are housed in part of the old Royal Palace in Hanuman Dhoka Square, Kathmandu. Although the museum is of little interest to tourists, it is necessary to buy a ticket to see the inside of the old palace. In addition to the beautiful window carvings that line the palace's courtyards, there is Basantapur Tower, which rises nine stories above the ground and affords spectacular views of the city. The museum is open 10:15 A.M.–4:15 P.M. daily except Tuesdays. The entrance fee is Rs. 5 and Rs. 8 if you carry a camera.

The *National Art Gallery* (no phone), Durbar Square, Bhaktapur, has an excellent collection of traditional and religious art, which is partially housed in the old Palace of 55 Windows. Open 10 A.M.–5 P.M. daily except Tuesdays. The entrance fee is Rs. 5 and Rs. 8 with camera.

The *Brass and Bronze Museum* (no phone), Dattatreya Square, Bhaktapur, houses many fine examples of Nepalese metal crafting of the past two centuries. Open 10 A.M.–5 P.M. daily except Tuesdays. The entrance fee is Rs. 5 and Rs. 8 with a camera.

Swayambunath Museum (no phone), beside Swayambunath Stupa, is a small collection of old stone statues. Open daily. Free.

The *Natural History Museum* (tel. 212889), located near the foot of Swayambunath Hill, has an extensive collection of stuffed and preserved birds, mammals, reptiles, insects, and plants from all over Nepal. Open 10 A.M.–5 P.M. daily except Saturdays. Free.

Several art galleries in Kathmandu specialize in the contemporary art of Nepal. *Shrijana Art Gallery, October Gallery* and *NAFA Art Gallery* are some that regularly have exhibits and sales.

There are two English language libraries in Kathmandu. The *American Library* (tel. 221250) on Juddha Sadak (corner of New Road) has an excellent selection of current periodicals and newspapers from the United States; there is also a small collection of books. The *British Council Library* (tel. 213796) on Kantipath requires a local sponsor for membership. The *Kaiser Library* (tel. 213562), housed in an old Rana palace just off Kantipath, includes old books in many languages. This was once a private collection.

In Pokhara, there is a cultural museum that features life-size dioramas and photographs of several of that region's different ethnic groups. Open daily except Tuesday. *Craft of Pokhara,* a small craft shop and gallery near the airport, has displays with information about many of the local handicrafts.

SPORTS AND OUTDOOR ADVENTURES. Bicycling. This sport has become popular in Nepal. Bikes are available for hire throughout Kathmandu and Pokhara. Some tour operators listed under *Special-Interest Tours* also arrange mountain-biking excursions around Kathmandu Valley, Pokhara, the Terai, and Everest. Make arrangements before you depart.

Fishing. You can fish along the Sun Kosi River October–March, in the game parks in the Terai, and in Pokhara Valley. Bring your own equipment. No license is required.

Golfing. Nepal has two nine-hole courses in the Kathmandu area. The Golf Club (tel. 412836) is located near the airport, and the second course is located at Gokarna Safari Park (tel. 211063). The greens fee for nonmembers at each course is Rs. 75. Clubs are available.

Horseback Riding. In Pokhara, you can arrange to ride for a half-day to 50 days. Contact Pokhara Pony Treks, (see *Special-Interest Tours* above for details).

Physical Fitness and Yoga. The *Kathmandu Physical Fitness Center* (across from the Ambassador Hotel; tel. 412473) offers aerobic dance classes, massages, weight training, sauna, Jacuzzi, and courses in yoga. The facilities are modern and clean; costs are nominal. Hours vary according to season.

Rafting. Though rafting is possible year-round on the Sun Kosi River (east of Kathmandu) and the crowded Trisuli River (west of Kathmandu), the best white-water period is September–November. Short trips (under four days) can be arranged on arrival. Longer trips should be arranged in advance. See special-interest tour operators listed above and in *Facts at Your Fingertips.* You can also raft on the rivers to the game parks in the Terai and on the Arun River in the southwest. The best rafting time for these rivers is September–June. Make arrangements in advance.

TREKKING. Thousands of miles of trails lace the Himalayas and their foothills, and many of these paths are open to adventurous foreign travelers who come in search of mountain vistas and the Nepal of past centuries. More than half of Nepal's population lives in the hills and mountains on small farms carved out of the steep hillsides. These people, far from roads and electricity, live a lifestyle that has not changed in centuries. Different ethnic groups inhabit different parts of the country. It is this cultural diversity, along with the spectacular Himalayas, that is attracting more and more trekkers each year.

Trekking in Nepal can be as easy or as difficult as you want it to be, and trips can last from a few days to three months. To arrange a trek, contact a recommended tour operator in *Special-Interest Tours* above and in *Facts at Your Fingertips*. Make arrangements before you depart.

On treks arranged through an agency, porters will carry everything except what you want to carry yourself such as a camera, canteen, and snacks. Each night, tents will be set up for you and dinner prepared. In the morning, after breakfast, you will start out on the trail while the porters break camp. Even with their heavy loads, the porters will easily catch up with you. A long lunch break provides ample opportunity for slow walkers to catch up and even get in a bit of rest before continuing to that day's destination. Usually no more than six hours a day are spent walking, and this is at a leisurely pace.

The best months for trekking are October and November. After the monsoon ends, the forests and fields are green, the skies are clear, and temperatures, even at high elevations, are moderate. During March and April, also popular months for trekking, the wildflowers are in bloom in the middle elevations. Particularly beautiful are the white, pink, and red flowers of the huge rhododendron trees that grow in thick forests throughout Nepal. During the winter months, the skies are clear and the snowy peaks sparkle in the bright sun. By day, the temperature is ideal for walking, but at night, it can drop below freezing. Above 2,740 meters (9,000 ft.), snow can be a problem. May and June are a good time to visit the higher altitudes of the Himalayas. The snows have melted and the monsoon has not yet started. During the monsoon months from June to September, many trails are washed away by the heavy rains. Landslides and swollen rivers also make travel nearly impossible. Land leeches are quite common at this time.

Before beginning a trek, you must obtain a trekking permit. These permits are easily obtained from the *Central Immigration Office* in Kathmandu or the *Immigration Office* in Pokhara. If you plan to trek into two different areas, you need separate permits. The charge for individual trekkers is Rs. 90 per week for the first month, Rs. 112.50 per additional week. The trekking permit also substitutes for a visa extension. If you trek with a recommended tour operator listed below, the company will obtain the permit for you. To obtain your own permit, you must submit two passport-size photographs and your passport with the application. Special permits, obtainable from the *Nepal Mountaineering Association,* are necessary for mountaineering expeditions. The more well-known peaks are often booked for years in advance, but many lesser peaks are readily available.

If you trek in the Annapurna Sanctuary, Sagarmatha National Park (Everest area), and the Langtang National Park, you must also pay Rs. 250 entrance fee.

TREKKING ROUTES

There are three main trekking areas in Nepal. Within each region, many different treks are possible, depending on your abilities, interests, and available time. Where you begin your trek is up to you. You can begin trekking just outside Kathmandu, but new roads now make it possible to start much farther into the mountains. This is also true in the Pokhara region. Several small airstrips are scattered throughout these main trekking areas and can be used if your time is limited. However, because of weather conditions, these airstrips are often shut down for several days at a time. Be sure to leave plenty of room in your schedule if you plan to use one of them.

The most popular trek in Nepal is the **Pokhara-to-Jomosom Trek.** This route climbs up from the valley floor past terraced hillsides and small villages. As the trail climbs higher into the foothills of the Himalayas, it passes through dense rain forests, rhododendron forests inhabited by large langur monkeys, evergreen forests, and small terraced valleys and eventually reaches the barren, high desertlike regions along the Kali Gandaki River. This is the edge of the Tibetan Plateau; beyond this, there are no forests visible.

Because different ethnic groups inhabit the numerous small villages along this trek, each settlement has a different character. Building styles change from town to town, crops vary, and people look and dress differently, depending on their cultural heritage. For centuries, this trail has been a major trading route between the highlands of Tibet and the lowlands of Nepal and northern India. Many of the towns, especially those beyond Jomosom, look as if they have been around for thousands of years. For more than 2,000 years, the tiny village of Muktinath, beyond Jomosom, has been a pilgrimage site for Buddhists and Hindus. Several small temples have been built here, and one of them houses the mysterious water and stone that burn. These eerie blue flames, caused by natural gas seepage, are considered holy, and thousands of pilgrims make the journey to see them every August. Nearby are the ancient towns of Jarakot and Kagbeni, both occupied by Tibetan people. This trek can be made in 16–20 days.

Another possible trek in this region is the classic **Around Annapurna Trek,** which takes about 25 days and includes much spectacular scenery before crossing the 5,396-meter (17,700-ft.) Thorong Pass. Below this pass is Muktinath, where the trail joins the Jomosom-to-Pokhara trek.

For many people, nothing will do but to make the trek to Everest Base Camp. This high-altitude camp sits at the base of Mount Everest, with several other peaks rising up around it. This is the land of the Sherpas, the sturdy mountain people who have assisted so many mountaineering expeditions and treks. The Sherpas, being of Tibetan origin, are Buddhists; consequently, this region is full of Buddhist monasteries, which are one of the main attractions for trekkers. To reach the high elevations of Khumbu near Everest Base Camp, it is necessary to cross nearly 242 km (150 mi.) of rugged foothills known as the Solu region. Although there are many picturesque villages, forests, and terraced valleys throughout the Solu, there are few glimpses of the mountains. To save themselves the long, grueling hike into the Khumbu region, with its spectacular scenery, many people choose to fly into the airstrip at Lukla. This places you within two days' walk of Namche Bazaar, the gateway to the Khumbu region and Sagarmatha National Park. However, because Lukla is at 2,827 meters (9,275 ft.), a day's rest is necessary for acclimatization. At this elevation, altitude sickness is a real problem, and precautions must be taken to prevent becoming ill.

The third popular trekking area is the **Helambu-Gosainkund-Langtang** region just north of Kathmandu. These three distinctive regions offer a variety of trekking experiences. Each area is ideal for a one-week trek, or the areas can be combined for two- or three-week treks.

Helambu, which follows the northeast rim of the Kathmandu Valley, is a hilly region of moderate elevation, with many forests and terraced hillsides. Because it is south of the main Himalayas, with high mountains in between, there aren't many views of the snow-clad peaks from here. In the spring, when the rhododendrons are in bloom, Helambu is particularly stunning.

Nepal recently opened up two new areas for trekking—the mysterious Dolpo kingdom in the northeast and the Mount Kanchenjunga area in the northwest. To visit these areas you must go with a government approved agency, which includes the tour operators under *Special-Interest Tours* above and in *Facts at Your Fingertips.*

PHOTOGRAPHY. Film is readily available in Kathmandu. You will also find a few computerized one-hour film processing centers for color print film. These centers usually provide acceptable service, but it is best to carry your undeveloped film home with you. Most airports will hand check film and cameras, so it is not necessary to expose them to the possible damaging effects of X rays. Lead-foil film-storage bags to protect film from X rays are also available at camera shops.

Overexposure of photographs can be a problem in Nepal because of the intense light at high altitudes. A UV or skylight filter is a necessary accessory if your camera is equipped to accept filters. A polarizing filter, which will cut high altitude glare even more than a UV filter, can come in handy.

MEDICAL NOTES AND FACILITIES. Medical facilities in Nepal are extremely limited, and those that are available often are far below Western standards.

Gastrointestinal illnesses are the most common problem for tourists. Frequently encountered disorders vary from upset stomachs and abdominal cramps to diarrhea and vomiting accompanied by fever. These symptoms may be brief (24 hours) or more long-term and are attributable to a variety of organisms. Most common, however, is the sort of illness that comes on quickly and disappears with equal speed. Rest and plenty of fluids are the best treatments for such an illness, which is commonly caused by a change in diet and different bacteria in the environment. To minimize your risk of getting ill, avoid street stalls, eat only fruits that have been peeled, and avoid uncooked vegetables unless you know that they have been treated to kill bacteria (this is a common practice at better restaurants, which usually post a notice in the menu that their salads have been treated).

Rabies is also common in Nepal. Dogs and monkeys are the two most commonly encountered carriers of this serious disease. It is advisable to give both of these animals a wide berth, if possible. Most important, do not harass or otherwise disturb baby monkeys or puppies; the mothers are much more likely to attack you to protect their young. If you are bitten by an animal, immediately wash the wound for 20 minutes with running water to remove all saliva. The postexposure rabies vaccine should be taken as soon as possible. In Kathmandu, the vaccine is available at the *Kalimati Clinic* (tel. 214743) and the *CIWEC Clinic* (tel. 410983).

Trekkers who hike to elevations above 9,000 feet may develop altitude sickness. Symptoms of altitude sickness include shortness of breath, headache, nausea, vomiting, weakness, and insomnia. More serious cases can develop into pulmonary and cerebral edema, which can cause death. The only cure for altitude sickness is to descend to lower elevations. A slow ascent is the best way to avoid the illness. The *Himalayan Rescue Association* (tel. 215855) by Kathmandu Guest House has an informative pamphlet on this subject.

If you need a doctor while in Nepal, first ask at your hotel. English-speaking doctors are on call with all the major hotels. For more serious illnesses or hospitalization, the *Patan Missionary Hospital,* Lagankhel, Patan (tel. 521034, 521048, 522266), is staffed by English-speaking doctors.

The Kalimati Clinic, Kalimati, Kathmandu, offers postexposure rabies vaccine and gamma globulin injections for the prevention of hepatitis. It is supervised and staffed by American volunteers.

The CIWEC Clinic, Baluwatar, Kathmandu, is staffed by American doctors and Western nurses.

For a more extensive list of English-speaking doctors in Nepal, contact the U.S. Embassy.

DRINKING WATER. Do not drink tap or stream water in Nepal unless you are certain that it has been boiled, filtered, or treated. Hotels usually provide each room with a bottle of water that is safe for drinking and brushing teeth. In restaurants, it is best to stick to hot tea, coffee, or bottled drinks. Soda water and mineral water are also widely available. When trekking, take extra precautions, such as boiling *and* treating water, if possible. Iodine is the best water treatment and is available in Kathmandu.

LANGUAGE. The national language, Nepali, is rooted in Sanskrit and is of the Indo-Aryan family of languages. Distinct dialects are spoken in many districts. Among the most important of these are Newari, Sherpa, Gurung, Magar, Limbu, and Tamang. Since the influx of Tibetan refugees, Tibetan is being spoken more widely. English is widely understood in cities and towns where great importance is placed on an English education for children. Along popular trekking routes, innkeepers usually speak English, but other people you encounter along the trail likely will not.

SHOPPING. Look for lovely *thang-kas* (paintings with a Buddhist theme); statues; brass work; masks; wood carvings; jewelry; and beautiful wool sweaters, gloves, hats, and carpets. Antiques are illegal purchases. With rare exception, bargain. All shops are closed on Saturday and public holidays.

Kathmandu. The *Kashmiri Bead Bazaar,* open daily 9 A.M.–6 P.M., is behind Indra Chowk. It's run by Kashmiri Moslems who sell fine glass beads from Belgium,

Czechoslovakia, and Japan. Sit on a platform and pick out strands, which the shopkeeper will quickly make into a necklace. One of the best shops is No. 388, where you can bargain. Rupees only. For good thang-kas, visit *Mannies Art* (Sakya Arcade, Durbar Marg, tel. 223931), open 9:30 A.M.–7:30 P.M. No bargaining here. AE, MC, V.

For old artwork and curios, visit these shops on Durbar Marg and bargain: *Karma Lama Ritual Art Gallery* (tel. 223410), open 10 A.M.–6 P.M. rupees only; *Oriental Handicraft Curio Centre* (Basantpur), open 10 A.M.–7 P.M., AE; *Treasure Art Concern* (Annapurna Arcade, Shop No. 5), open 11 A.M.–7:30 P.M., AE; *Curio Concern* (D2–478 tel. 22487), open 10:30 A.M.–7:30 P.M., AE. In Thamel, don't miss *Yeshi Phuntsok's Zambala* (12/902 Thamel), open 9 A.M.–1 P.M. and 3–8 P.M., AE. This shop sells excellent Tibetan and Bhutanese handicrafts and gorgeous textiles, especially nice traditional raw silk scarves, shawls, blankets, and vests.

For stylish clothing made from handblocked cotton, stop at *Durga Design* in Thamel, open 10 A.M.–7 P.M.; rupees only. *Roof of the World—D. D. Tibetan Boutique* (Kantipath, tel. 220349) is open 9:30 A.M.–7 P.M., and sells classy handknit sweaters and contemporary Western- and Tibetan-style dresses; AE. You can also find good woolen handknits in Thamel and on Freak Street.

The following shops sell handknits and handicrafts, with all proceeds helping destitute women or Tibetan refugees: *Women's Skill Development Project* in Lazimpat near the French Embassy, open 8 A.M.–8 P.M., and in Pulchowk, Lalitpur (Patan), open 10 A.M.–5 P.M. *Mahaguthi Shop* (Durbar Marg, near the Annapurna Coffee Shop), open daily 10 A.M.–6:30 P.M.; *Tibetan Refugee Center* (Tibetan Camp, Jawalakhel, tel. 522414), open 8:30 A.M.–noon and 1–5 P.M. All these cooperatives sell at fixed prices and take rupees only.

NIGHTLIFE AND BARS. The *New Himalchuli Cultural Group* (tel. 410151) performs traditional Nepalese dances daily in their auditorium in the Hotel Shanker compound, October–March 6:30–7:30 P.M., April–September 7–8 P.M. Admission Rs. 80.

The *Everest Cultural Society* (tel. 220676) performs classical and folk dances daily at Hotel de L'Annapurna, 7–8 P.M. Admission Rs. 80.

Casino Nepal (next door to Soaltee Oberoi). Foreigners flying into Kathmandu get Rs. 100 worth of free coupons upon presentation of a passport and used airline ticket. (The offer expires seven days from arrival.) The entrance looks like a dive, but downstairs it's a mini Las Vegas. Open 24 hours.

Bars. The best bars are at Rumdoodle (happy hour with complimentary snacks, 5:30–7 P.M., closed Tuesday), at Hotel Shanker, and the bar at the Yak and Yeti Hotel. Most bars close around 11.

HINDI-ENGLISH VOCABULARY

Although English is the *lingua franca* of India, and is spoken by almost everyone who has received a high-school education, you may find yourself in a position where no one understands your English (although this is highly unlikely unless you stray by car far from the usual tourist paths). There being more than a dozen major languages and hundreds of dialects, we are quoting below only a few expressions of courtesy in Hindi, understood in most parts of India, together with the more current terms in art and architecture, religion, etc., you will come across in this volume. They are mostly of Sanskrit origin, the sacred language of the Indo-Aryans. Some are from Arabic and Persian.

You know more words of Indian origin than you think: they entered the English vocabulary during the presence of the East India Company and during subsequent British rule, spread everywhere English is spoken and were eventually absorbed into other languages.

Various

atcha	(ach-*cha*)	O.K.
bagh	(b*ag*)	a garden
baksheesh	(baksh*eesh*)	a tip, a reward
dhoti	(dhoetee)	skirtlike garment worn by Indians
ha (nasal)	(h*a*)	yes
howdah	(how-d*a* h)	the seat fixed on an elephant's back. It usually accommodates two in front and two behind.
ji	(j*ee*)	a respectful suffix (Gandhi*ji*); also used as an address (ha-ji—yes sir).
mahout	(*ma* hoot)	elephant driver
maidan	(*ma*-eh-*dan*)	plain
mehrbani se	(may-her-banee-say)	please
nahin	(na*heen*)	no
namastey	(na-ma-stay)	word for all greetings
nawab	(*na* wab)	title given to important Moslem landowners
ram-ram	(*ram-ram*)	equivalent of "hello"
sahib	(sa*heeb*)	master
Shri (or Sri); Shrimatee	(Shr*ee* /Shr*ee*-m*a*-*tee*)	Mr; Mrs
shukriya	(sh*oo* kr*ee* ya)	thank you
wallah	(wal-*lah*)	a fellow (rickshaw wallah)

Art-Architecture

chaitya	(*cha*-eet-ya)	a Buddhist prayer hall
dravida	(dra-*vee-da*)	Southern or Dravidian style of architecture
dvarapala	(Varapala)	door guardian statue
ghazal	(*gha*-zal)	poetry set to music, originating from Persia and now usually sung in Urdu
geet	(geet)	light popular song
ghats	(*gha* ts)	terraces on a sacred river bank (also mountains)

gopurum	(go-poo-ram)	monumental gates of South Indian temple enclosures
gurudwara	(goo-rood-wara	Sikh temple
jagamohan	(jag-mohan)	in Orissan architecture an enclosed porch preceding the sanctuary
Kathakali	(katha-kalee)	classic dance form of Kerala
mandir	(mandeer)	Hindu temple
mandapa	(mandapa)	porch
Manipuri	(maneepooree)	classical dance form of Manipur (Assam)
mithuna	(meethoonaa)	statues of amorous couples
Nagara style	(Nagaara)	the Northern or Indo-Aryan type of temple characterized by the tower
stupa	(stewpaa)	Buddhist sacred mound
sitar	(seetaar)	stringed instrument with movable frets, played by plucking the strings
torana	(towrana)	gate of a temple enclosure
vihara	(*vee* har)	a Buddhist monastery

Religion

ahimsa	(a-heem-saa)	non-violence, harmlessness
apsara	(aapsaaraa)	a damsel of Indra's heaven
ashram	(*aash* raam)	a hermitage
avatar	(ahvatar)	one of the various incarnations of Vishnu
Bodhisattva	(Bodheesatt*va*)	potential Buddha who before final enlightenment ministers to humanity
Brahma	(Bramma)	the creator of all things in Hindu Trinity
Brahman	(Bra m-ma n; nasal "n" pronounced)	the first, or priestly class in Hinduism
Buddha	(B*oo* dh*a*)	Prince Siddhartha, born on the Nepalese border about 563 B.C. Buddha means "the Enlightened One"
Devi	(Day*vee*)	Parvati, consort to Siva in her benevolent form
dharma	(Dh*a* rm*aa*)	path of conduct
dharmachakra	(dhar*ma* chakra)	the Buddhist Wheel of the Law, an ancient solar symbol
Durga	(Doorg*a*)	Parvati, consort of Siva in her form as a destroyer of evil
guru	(gooroo)	spiritual teacher
hatha yoga	(haatha yog)	the mystic path of physical exercise
hinayana	(heenayana)	"small vehicle": early Buddhism with emphasis on the doctrine, rather than on worship
Jainism	(Ja-ay-nee-sum)	a religion founded by Mahavira in the 6th century B.C. preaching solicitude for all life
jatakas	(Ja-ta-kas)	tales about the Buddha in his previous incarnations
Kali	(Kalee)	the goddess Parvati in her terrible form
kirtan	(*keer* tan)	religious songs
Krishna	(Kreesh-*na*)	hero of the epic Mahabharata. One of Vishnu's incarnations
Kshatriya	(sh*a* t-ree-y*a*)	the second, or warrior, caste in Hinduism
Lakshmi	(laksh-mee)	Goddess of wealth and beauty, the consort of Vishnu

lingam	(leengum)	sacred symbol of Siva
mahayana	(maha-yeah-na)	"great vehicle". Later from Buddhism, with emphasis on Buddha's divinity
mantra	(*man* tra)	a word or sentence used as an invocation
maya	(ma-yeah)	escape from material reality, an illusion
moksha	(mawksh*a*)	release from all material desires
mudra	(moodr*a*)	ritual gestures denoting mystic powers
Nandi	(Nandee)	the sacred bull, Siva's mount
Nirvana	(Neervana)	eternal bliss
Pariahs	(paree-ahs)	the untouchables or outcasts of Hinduism (this practice is now banned in India)
Parvati	(Parvatee)	wife of Siva
prana	(pran; nasal "n" pronounced)	Breath of Life, sustaining the body
puja	(pooja)	wishful prayer performed before a god's image
Puranas	(pooranas)	Hindu mythology. There are eighteen Puranas and a number of epics which include the *Ramayana* and the *Mahabharata*
Rama	(Raam)	hero of the Ramayana
rishi	(reeshee)	Hindu sage
sadhu	(sadhoo)	a celibate holy man
samadhi	(samad*hee*)	the deepest form of yoga meditation
samsara	(saamsaaraa)	the cycle of life and rebirth
Saraswati	(Sa-ras-wa-tee)	Goddess of wisdom
Siva or Shiva	(Seeva or Sheeva)	God of the Hindu Trinity. The destructive and creative aspect
Sudra	(soodra)	the fourth main caste in Hinduism (farmers and artisans mostly)
sutra	(sootra)	a sacred text
swami	(swam-ee)	a teacher of certain branches of Hinduism
tandava	(tan-da-va)	Siva's cosmic dance, symbolic of his function of creation and destruction
Tirthankara	(Teerthankara)	one of the twenty-four Jain patriarchs who attained perfection
Trimurti	(Tree-moor-tee)	physical shape of the Hindu Trinity (Brahma, Vishnu, Siva)
twice-born		a term used to denote high-caste Hindus who are said to have a second birth when invested with the sacred thread of their caste
Vedanta	(Vay-dan-ta)	an inquiry into the aim of all knowledge; a metaphysic of intuition
Vedas	(Vay-das)	the four most ancient Hindu scriptures
Vishnu	(Veesh-noo)	the Preserver of Mankind in the Hindu Trinity
yoga	(yog*a*)	a discipline of meditation by which the powers of man over himself are developed
yogi	(yog*ee*)	a follower of yoga

INDEX

INDIA

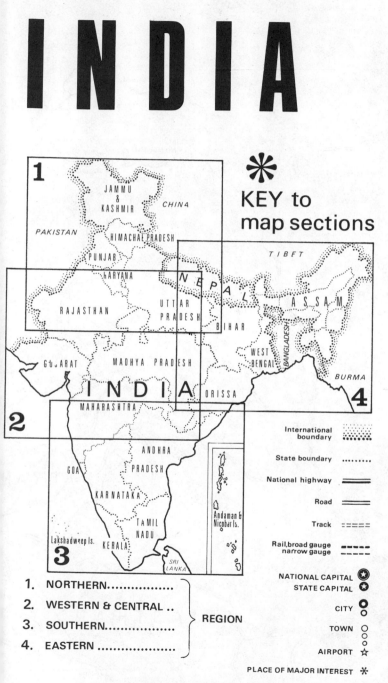

✳ KEY to map sections

Legend

- International boundary ∵∵∵∵
- State boundary ········
- National highway ═══
- Road ══
- Track ═════
- Rail, broad gauge / narrow gauge ━━━━
- NATIONAL CAPITAL ◉
- STATE CAPITAL ★
- CITY ⊙
- TOWN ○
- AIRPORT ☆
- PLACE OF MAJOR INTEREST ✳

Map sections

1. NORTHERN..................
2. WESTERN & CENTRAL ..
3. SOUTHERN...................
4. EASTERN .... } REGION

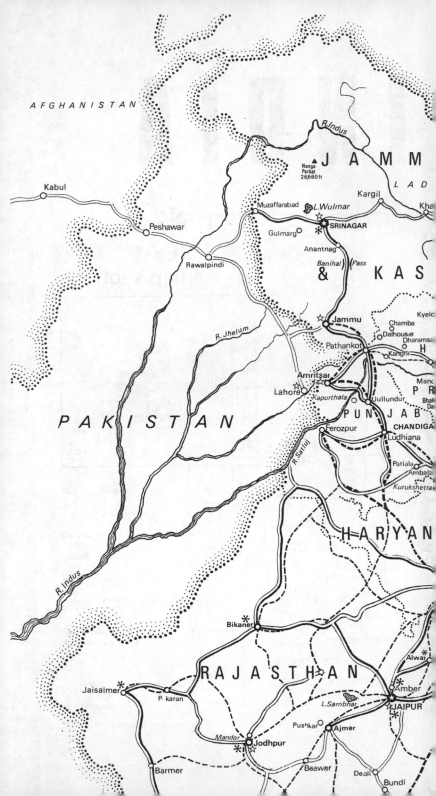

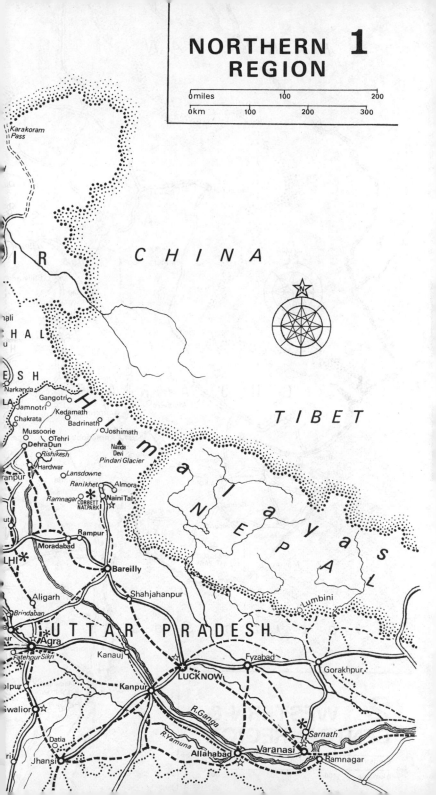

NORTHERN REGION 1

0 miles — 100 — 200
0 km — 100 — 200 — 300

CHINA

TIBET

Karakoram Pass

H i m a l a y a s

N E P A L

Narkanda
Gangotri
Jamnotri
Chakrata
Kedarnath
Badrinath
Mussoorie
Tehri
Joshimath
Dehra Dun
Rishikesh
Hardwar
Nanda Devi
Pindari Glacier
Lansdowne
Ranikhet
Almora
Ramnagar
CORBETT NAT. PARK
Naini Tal
Rampur
Moradabad
Bareilly
Aligarh
Shahjahanpur
Lumbini
Brindaban
UTTAR PRADESH
DELHI
Agra
Kanauj
Fyzabad
Gorakhpur
Fatehpur Sikri
LUCKNOW
Kanpur
R. Ganga
Datia
R. Yamuna
Sarnath
Gwalior
Jhansi
Allahabad
Varanasi
Ramnagar

IR

HAL

ESH

LA

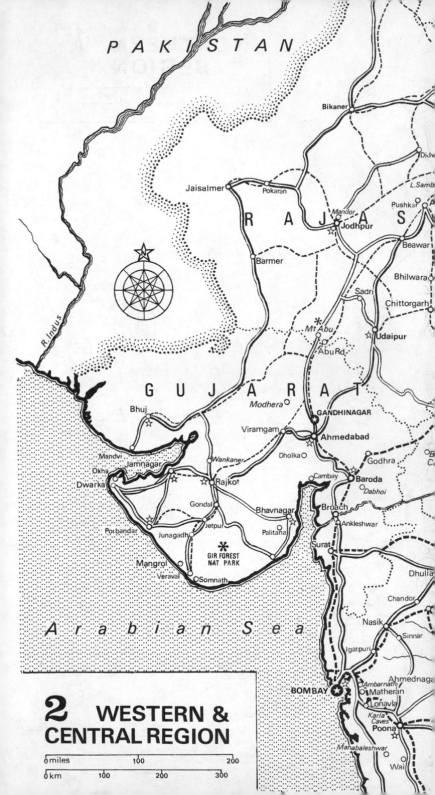

2 WESTERN & CENTRAL REGION

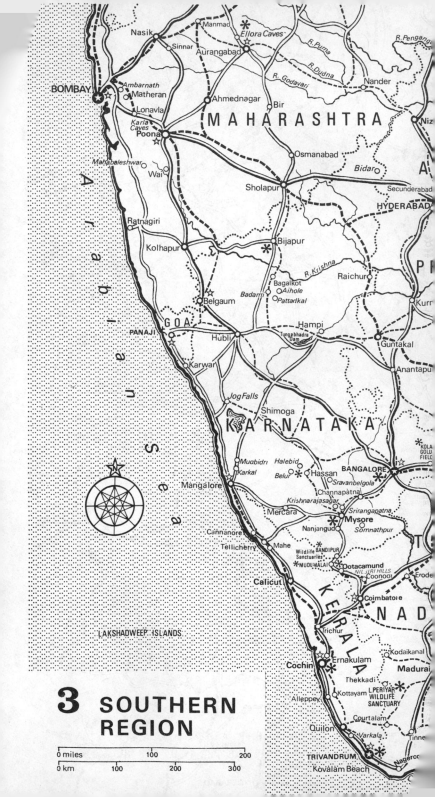

3 SOUTHERN REGION

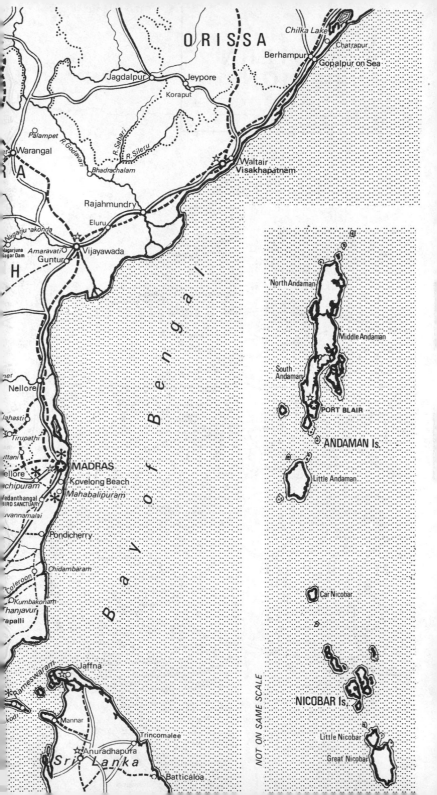

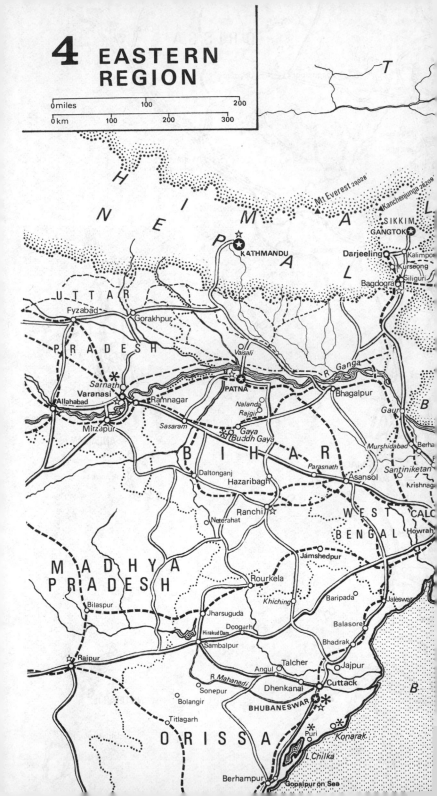

4 EASTERN REGION

0 miles   100   200
0 km   100   200   300

T

H I M A L
N E P A L
Mt Everest 29028
Kanchenjunga 28209
SIKKIM
GANGTOK
KATHMANDU
Darjeeling
Kalimpo
Kurseong
Siliguri
Bagdogra
B

UTTAR
Fyzabad
Gorakhpur

PRADESH
Vaisali
R Ganga
Sarnath
Varanasi
PATNA
Bhagalpur
Allahabad
Ramnagar
Nalanda
Rajgir
Gaur
Mirzapur
Sasaram
Gaya
Buddh Gaya
Murshidabad
Berha

B I H A R
Daltonganj
Parasnath
Santiniketan
Hazaribagh
Asansol
Krishnag
Ranchi
WEST
Neterahat
BENGAL
CALC

Howrah

M A D H Y A
PRADESH
Jamshedpur
Bilaspur
Rourkela
Baripada
Jaleswar
Khiching
Jharsuguda
Deogarh
Balasore
Hirakud Dam
Sambalpur
Bhadrak
Raipur
Angul
Talcher
Jajpur
R Mahanadi
Dhenkanal
Cuttack
B
Sonepur
BHUBANESWAR
Bolangir
Titlagarh
Puri
Konarak
O R I S S A
L Chilka
Berhampur
Gopalpur on Sea

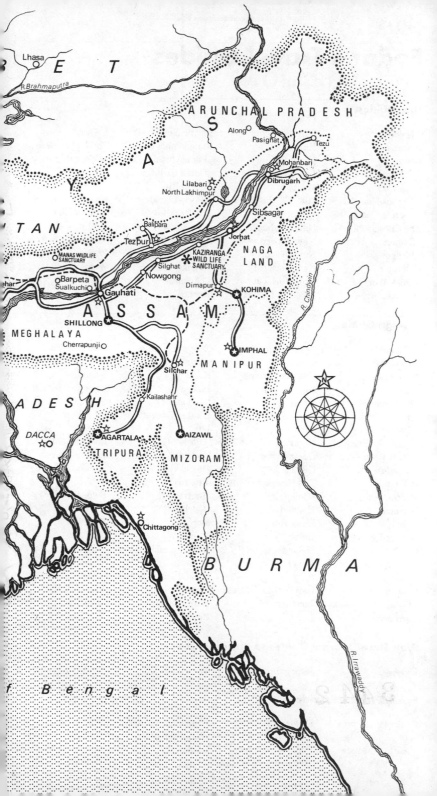

Fodor's Travel Guides

U.S. Guides

Alaska
Arizona
Boston
California
Cape Cod
The Carolinas & the
 Georgia Coast
The Chesapeake
 Region
Chicago
Colorado
Disney World & the
 Orlando Area

Florida
Hawaii
Las Vegas
Los Angeles
Maui
Miami & the
 Keys
New England
New Mexico
New Orleans
New York City
New York City
 (Pocket Guide)

Pacific North Coast
Philadelphia & the
 Pennsylvania
 Dutch Country
Puerto Rico
 (Pocket Guide)
The Rockies
San Diego
San Francisco
San Francisco
 (Pocket Guide)
The South
Texas

USA
The Upper Great
 Lakes Region
Vacations in
 New York State
Vacations on the
 Jersey Shore
Virgin Islands
Virginia & Maryland
Waikiki
Washington, D.C.

Foreign Guides

Acapulco
Amsterdam
Australia
Austria
The Bahamas
The Bahamas
 (Pocket Guide)
Baja & the Pacific
 Coast Resorts
Barbados
Belgium &
 Luxembourg
Bermuda
Brazil
Budget Europe
Canada
Canada's Atlantic
 Provinces
Cancun, Cozumel,
 Yucatan Peninsula
Caribbean

Central America
China
Eastern Europe
Egypt
Europe
Europe's Great Cities
France
Germany
Great Britain
Greece
The Himalayan
 Countries
Holland
Hong Kong
India
Ireland
Israel
Italy
Italy 's Great Cities
Jamaica
Japan

Kenya, Tanzania,
 Seychelles
Korea
Lisbon
London
London Companion
London
 (Pocket Guide)
Madrid & Barcelona
Mexico
Mexico City
Montreal &
 Quebec City
Morocco
Munich
New Zealand
Paris
Paris (Pocket Guide)
Portugal
Rio de Janeiro
Rome

Saint Martin/
 Sint Maarten
Scandinavia
Scandinavian Cities
Scotland
Singapore
South America
South Pacific
Southeast Asia
Soviet Union
Spain
Sweden
Switzerland
Sydney
Thailand
Tokyo
Toronto
Turkey
Vienna & the
 Danube Valley
Yugoslavia

Wall Street Journal Guides to Business Travel

Europe

International Cities

The Pacific Rim

USA & Canada

Special-Interest Guides

Cruises and Ports
 of Call
Healthy Escapes

Fodor's Flashmaps
 New York
Fodor's Flashmaps
 Washington, D.C.

Shopping in Europe
Skiing in North
 America

Smart Shopper's
 Guide to London
Sunday in New York
Touring Europe